GW00420044

STREET ATLAS
Birmingham
and West Midlands

Contents

III Key to map symbols

IV-V Key to map pages

VI-VII Route planning

VIII Administrative and post code boundaries

1 Street maps

163 Extra-large-scale maps of town centres

    163 Wolverhampton
    164 Birmingham
    165 Coventry

166 Index of hospitals, railway stations, schools, shopping centres, street names and universities

PHILIP'S

First published 1998 by

George Philip Ltd, a division of
Octopus Publishing Group Ltd
2-4 Heron Quays, London E14 4JP

First colour edition 1998
Fourth impression 2001

ISBN 0-540-07603-1 (hardback)
ISBN 0-540-07604-X (spiral)

Digital Data

The exceptionally high-quality mapping
found in this book is available as digital
data in TIFF format, which is easily
convertible to other bit-mapped (raster)
image formats.

The index is also available in digital form
as a standard database table. It contains
all the details found in the printed index
together with the National Grid reference
for the map square in which each entry
is named and feature codes for places
of interest in eight categories such as
education and health.

For further information and to discuss
your requirements, please contact
Philip's on 020 7531 8440 or
george.philip@philips-maps.co.uk

Motorway with junction number	
Primary route – dual/single carriageway	
A road – dual/single carriageway	
B road – dual/single carriageway	
Minor road – dual/single carriageway	
Other minor road – dual/single carriageway	
Road under construction	
Pedestrianised area	
DY7 **Postcode boundaries**	
County and unitary authority boundaries	
Railway	
Tramway, miniature railway	
Rural track, private road or narrow road in urban area	
Gate or obstruction to traffic (restrictions may not apply at all times or to all vehicles)	
Path, bridleway, byway open to all traffic, road used as a public path	
The representation in this atlas of a road, track or path is no evidence of the existence right of way	
126 **94** **Adjoining page indicators**	
164 **The map area within the pink band is shown at a larger scale on the page indicated by the red block and arrow**	

■ The dark grey border on the inside edge of some pages indicates that the mapping does not continue onto the adjacent page
■ The small numbers around the edges of the maps identify the 1 kilometre National Grid lines

Railway station *Walsall*	
Midland Metro	
Private railway station	
Bus, coach station	
Ambulance station	
Coastguard station	
Fire station	
Police station	
Accident and Emergency entrance to hospital	
H **Hospital**	
Places of worship	
i **Information Centre** (open all year)	
P **Parking**	
P&R **Park and Ride**	
PO **Post Office**	
Important buildings, schools, colleges, universities and hospitals *Prim Sch*	
River Medway **Water name**	
Stream	
River or canal (minor and major)	
Water	
Tidal water	
Woods	
Houses	
House **Non-Roman antiquity**	
VILLA **Roman antiquity**	

Allot Gdns	**Allotments**	Ent	**Enterprise**	Liby	**Library**	PH	**Public House**
Acad	**Academy**	Ex H	**Exhibition Hall**	Mkt	**Market**	Recn Gd	**Recreation Ground**
Cemy	**Cemetery**	Ind Est	**Industrial Estate**	Meml	**Memorial**	Resr	**Reservior**
C Ctr	**Civic Centre**	Inst	**Institute**	Mon	**Monument**	Ret Pk	**Retail Park**
CH	**Club House**	Ct	**Law Court**	Mus	**Museum**	Sch	**School**
Coll	**College**	L Ctr	**Leisure Centre**	Obsy	**Observatory**	Sh Ctr	**Shopping Centre**
Crem	**Crematorium**	LC	**Level Crossing**	Pal	**Royal Palace**	TH	**Town Hall/House**

						Trad Est	**Trading Estate**
						Univ	**University**
						Wks	**Works**
						YH	**Youth Hostel**

The scale of the maps is 5.52 cm to 1 km
3½ inches to 1 mile 1: 18103

0	¼		½		¾		1 mile
0	250m	500m	750m	1 kilometre			

The scale of the maps on pages numbered in red
is 11.04 cm to 1 km 7 inches to 1 mile 1: 9051.4

0	220 yards		440 yards		660 yards		½ mile
0	125m	250m	375m	½ kilometre			

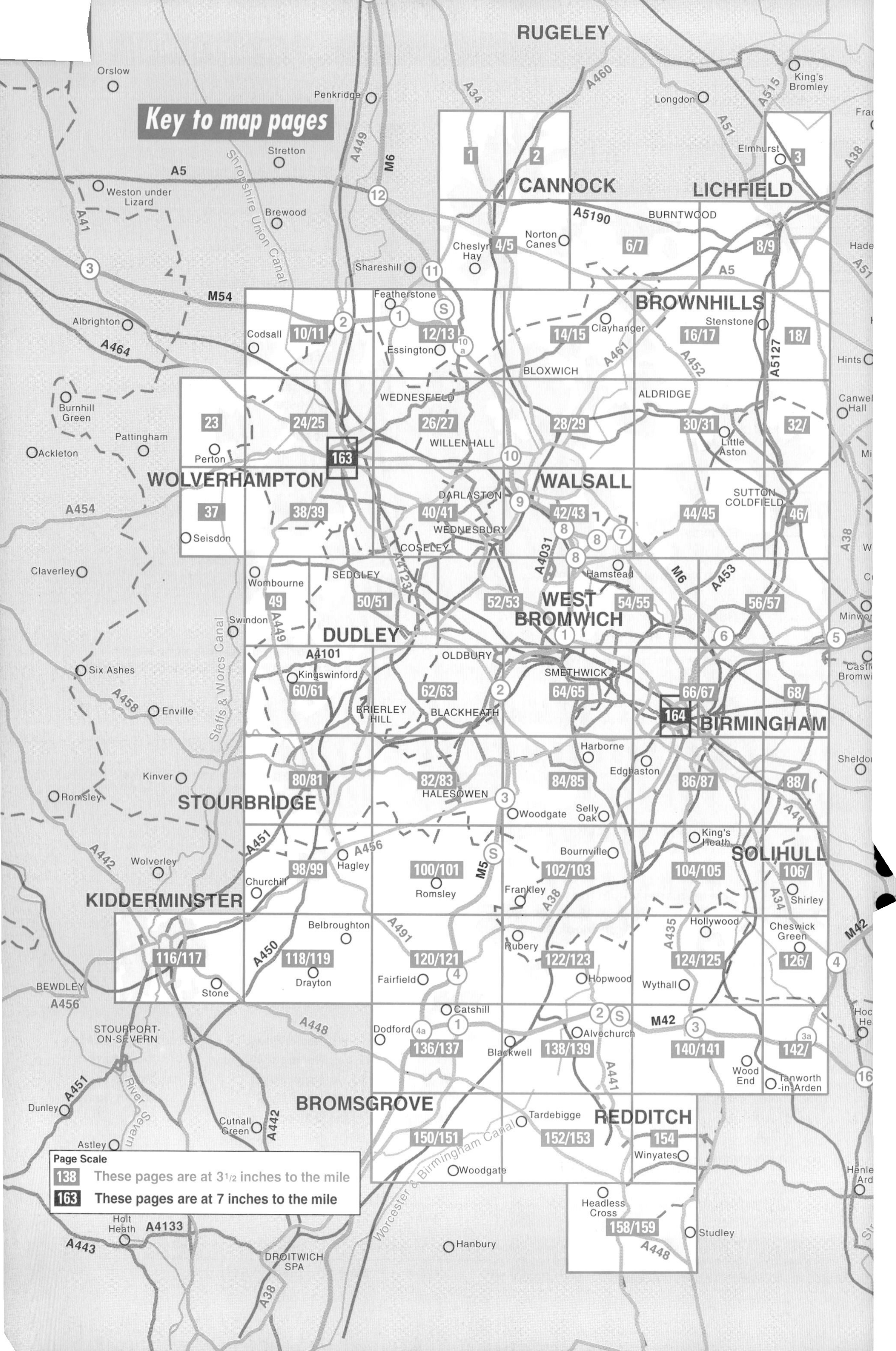

Key to map pages

RUGELEY

Orslow
Penkridge
King's
Bromley
Longdon
Elmhurst

Weston under
Lizard
Stretton

A5

1   **2**

Brewood

CANNOCK

3

LICHFIELD

A5190   BURNTWOOD

Shareshill

Cheslyn
Hay   **4/5**   Norton
Canes   **6/7**   **8/9**

A5

Featherstone   **11**   **S**

BROWNHILLS

Albrighton   M54

Codsall   **10/11**   **2**   **1**   **12/13**   10
a

14/15   Clayhanger

Stenstone   **16/17**   **18/**

A464

Essington

Hints

BLOXWICH

Burnhill
Green   Pattingham   WEDNESFIELD   ALDRIDGE

Ackleton   **23**   **24/25**   **26/27**   **28/29**   **30/31**   **32/**

Perton   **163**   WILLENHALL   Little
Aston

Canwell
Hall

WOLVERHAMPTON   **10**   **WALSALL**

A454   **37**   **38/39**   DARLASTON   **9**   **40/41**   **42/43**   **44/45**   SUTTON
COLDFIELD   **46/**

Seisdon   WEDNESBURY   **8**   **7**
8

COSELEY   **8**

Claverley   Wombourne   SEDGLEY   Hamstead

49   **50/51**   **52/53**   **WEST**   **54/55**   **56/57**
BROMWICH

Swindon   **1**   **6**

Six Ashes   **DUDLEY**   **5**

A4101   OLDBURY   SMETHWICK   Casti
Bromwi

Enville   Kingswinford   **60/61**   **62/63**   **2**   **64/65**   **66/67**   **68/**

Romsley   BRIERLEY
HILL   BLACKHEATH   **164**   **BIRMINGHAM**

Kinver   Harborne

80/81   **82/83**   **84/85**   Edgbaston   **86/87**   **88/**

STOURBRIDGE   HALESOWEN   **3**

Woodgate   Selly
Oak

King's
Heath   **SOLIHULL**

Wolverley   Hagley   **S**   Bournville   **104/105**   **106/**

KIDDERMINSTER   **98/99**   **100/101**   **102/103**   Shirley

Churchill   Romsley   Frankley   Hollywood   Cheswick
Green

Belbroughton   **124/125**   **126/**   **4**

116/117   **118/119**   **120/121**   Rubery   **122/123**   Hopwood   Wythall

BEWDLEY   Fairfield   **4**   Wood
End   **3a**   **16**

A456   Drayton   Stone   M42   **2**   **S**

STOURPORT-
ON-SEVERN   Catshill   Alvechurch   **140/141**   **3**

Dodford   4a   **1**   **138/139**   **142/**
136/137   Blackwell   Tanworth
-in-Arden

Dunley   **BROMSGROVE**   **REDDITCH**

Astley   Tardebigge   Winyates

Cutnall
Green   **150/151**   **152/153**   **154**

Holt
Heath   A4133

Woodgate

Headless
Cross

158/159   Studley

Hanbury

DROITWICH
SPA

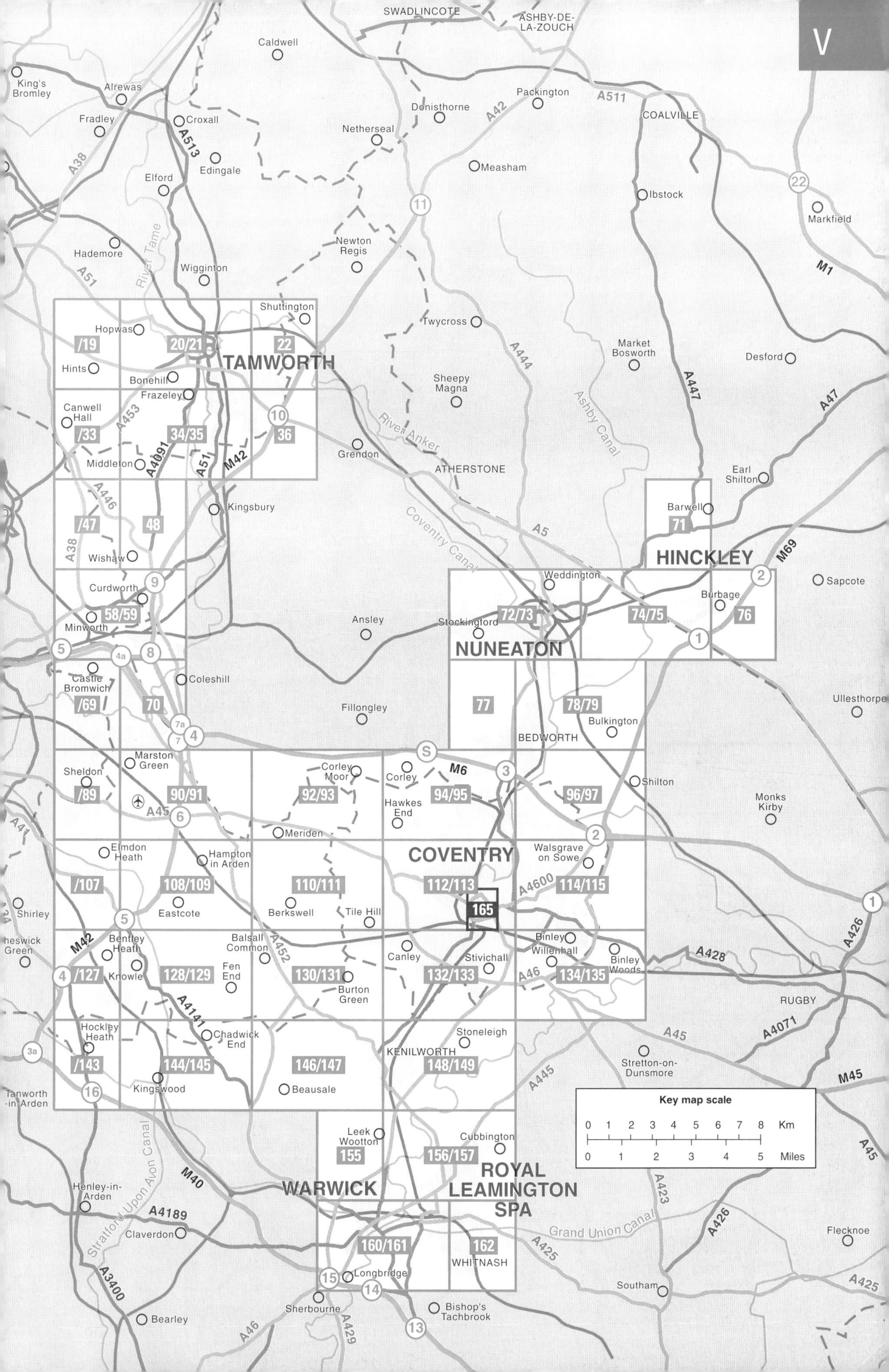
SWADLINCOTE
ASHBY-DE-LA-ZOUCH
Caldwell
King's Bromley
Alrewas
Fradley
Croxall
A513
A38
Edingale
Elford
Donisthorne
Netherseal
A42
Packington
A511
COALVILLE
Measham
11
22
Ibstock
Markfield
Hademore
River Tame
A51
Wigginton
Newton Regis
M1
Shuttington
Twycross
A444
Hopwas
/19
20/21
22
TAMWORTH
Hints
Bonehill
Market Bosworth
Desford
Sheepy Magna
A447
Ashby Canal
A47
Canwell Hall
Frazeley
A453
/33
34/35
10
36
River Anker
Grendon
Middleton
A4091
A51
M42
ATHERSTONE
Earl Shilton
A446
Coventry Canal
Kingsbury
Barwell
71
/47
48
A5
A38
Wishaw
HINCKLEY
M69
Curdworth
9
Weddington
2
Sapcote
58/59
Burbage
72/73
74/75
76
Minworth
Ansley
Stockingford
5
4a
8
NUNEATON
1
Castle Bromwich
Coleshill
/69
70
77
78/79
Ullesthorpe
Fillongley
Bulkington
7a
7
4
BEDWORTH
Marston Green
Corley Moor
S
Sheldon
Corley
M6
3
Shilton
/89
90/91
92/93
94/95
96/97
Monks Kirby
A45
6
Hawkes End
A41
Meriden
2
Elmdon Heath
Hampton in Arden
COVENTRY
Walsgrave on Sowe
/107
108/109
110/111
112/113
A4600
114/115
1
Shirley
Eastcote
Berkswell
Tile Hill
165
5
A426
Bentley Heath
Balsall Common
A452
Binley
Willenhall
M42
Canley
Stivichall
A428
Binley Woods
4
/127
Knowle
128/129
Fen End
130/131
132/133
A46
134/135
Burton Green
A4141
RUGBY
Hockley Heath
Chadwick End
Stoneleigh
A45
A4071
3a
KENILWORTH
Stretton-on-Dunsmore
/143
144/145
146/147
148/149
16
A445
Tanworth-in-Arden
Kingswood
Beausale
M45
Key map scale
0 1 2 3 4 5 6 7 8 Km
0 1 2 3 4 5 Miles
Leek Wootton
Cubbington
155
156/157
A45
Stratford Upon Avon Canal
M40
ROYAL LEAMINGTON SPA
WARWICK
A423
Henley-in-Arden
A4189
A426
Grand Union Canal
Claverdon
160/161
162
A425
Flecknoe
WHITNASH
A3400
15
Longbridge
14
Southam
A425
Sherbourne
Bishop's Tachbrook
Bearley
A46
A429
13

VI
Route planning
Mitton
Marston
Penkridge
Whiston
Wheaton Aston
Lapley
Blymhill
Belvide Resr
Stretton
Weston-under-Lizard
Bishop's Wood
Horsebrook
Gailey
Hatherton
Four Crosses
Calf Heath
Huntington
Brindley Heath
Upper Longdon
Armitage
Longdon
Rileyhill
Alrewas
Fradley
Hazelslade
Castle Ring
Cannock Wood
Hednesford
Littleworth
Heath Hayes
Gentleshaw
Farewell
Chorley
Elmhurst
Hilliard's Cross
Streethay
CANNOCK
Burntwood
LICHFIELD
Whittington
Norton Canes
Norton East
Chasetown
Chasewater
Hammerwich
Wall
Tong
Chillington Hall
Coven
Standeford
Bridgtown
Cheslyn Hay
Great Wyrle
Shareshill
Landywood
Featherstone
Little Wyrley
BROWNHILLS
Chesterfield
Hopwas
Cosford Sta
Codsall Wood
Codsall
Bilbrook
Clayhanger
Pelsall
Shire Oak
Weeford
Shenstone
Albrighton
Oaken
Lane Green
Essington
Ashmore Park
Walsall Wood
Stonnall
Little Hay
Hints
Boningale
Wergs
Bushbury
BLOXWICH
Shelfield
Burnhill Green
Patshull Hall
Oxley
Tettenhall
WEDNESFIELD
Rushall
ALDRIDGE
Canwell Hall
WOLVERHAMPTON
Little Aston
Mere Green
Perton
Pattingham
Streetly
Four Oaks
Roughley
WILLENHALL
WALSALL
The Walls
Trescott
Blakenhall
BILSTON
SUTTON COLDFIELD
Shipley
Lower Penn
DARLASTON
Great Barr
Sutton Park
Seisdon
WEDNESBURY
SEDGLEY
Kingstanding
Wylde Green
Trysull
COSELEY
Walmley
Claverley
Wombourne
Hamstead
Short Heath
TIPTON
Heathton
Halfpenny Green
Himley
WEST BROMWICH
Perry Barr
Erdington
Tyburn
Swindon
DUDLEY
Gravelly Hill
The Village
Handsworth
Aston
Castle Bromwich
Bobbington
OLDBURY
Six Ashes
Kingswinford
BRIERLEY HILL
Rowley Regis
SMETHWICK
Enville
Wordsley
Quarry Bank
Amblecote
BLACKHEATH
Chad Valley
Stourton
Yardley
Kinver
Lye
Harborne
Acock's Green
Sheldon
Birmingham International Airport
STOURBRIDGE
HALESOWEN
Edgbaston
Moseley
Pedmore
Woodgate
Selly Oak
Springfield
Whittington
Olton
Kingsford
Shatterford
Blakeshall
BIRMINGHAM
West Hagley
Illey
Hall Green
King's Heath
Caunsall
Cookley
Hagley
Bournville
Wolverley
Clent
Clent Hills
Frankley
Romsley
King's Norton
Fairfield
Trimpley
Churchill
Holy Cross
Northfield
Shirley
SOLIHULL
Franche
Longbridge
Habberley
Blakedown
Broome
Rubery
Blakebrook
KIDDERMINSTER
Hollywood
Whitlock's End
Wribbenhall
Belbroughton
Stone
Drayton
Lickey
Cofton Hackett
Hopwood
Wythall
Bentley Heath
Cheswick Green
Fairfield
Mustow Green
Barnt Green
Ribbesford
Chaddesley Corbett
Bournheath
Catshill
Earlswood
STOURPORT-ON-SEVERN
Shenstone
Dodford
Lickey End
Blackwell
Alvechurch
Rowney Green
Portway
Wilden
Wood End
Areley Kings
Rushock
BROMSGROVE
Hockley Heath
Hartlebury
Tutnall
Beoley
Holt End
Tanworth-in-Arden
Astley Cross
Elmley Lovett
Lincomb
Norchard
Cutnall Green
Elmbridge
Aston Fields
REDDITCH
Crossway Green
Stoke Heath
Winyates
Ullenhall
Astley
Dunhampton
Upton Warren
Woodgate
Webheath
Noutard's Green
Wychbold
Mappleborough Green
Henley in Arden
Sytchampton
Doverdale
Hampton Lovett
Headless Cross
Upper Bentley
Crabbs Cross
Oldberrow
Oldfield
Shrawley
DROITWICH SPA
Hunt End
Studley
Morton Bagot
Hanbury
Ham Green
Holt Heath
Ombersley
Salwarpe
Holt
Hadzor
Feckenham
Astwood Bank
Sambourne
Wootton Wawen
Grimley
Hawford
Bradley Green
Little Alne
Sinton Green
Great Alne
Martin Hussingtree
Coughton
New End
Aston Cantlow
Moseley
Oddingley
Holberrow
Worcester and Birmingham Canal
Staffs & Worcs Canal
M6
M54
M5
M42
A5
A34
A38
A41
A449
A454
A460
A461
A452
A4041
A453
A4123
A457
A459
A4101
A491
A458
A456
A450
A448
A442
A451
A4025
A4133
A443
A441
A435
A4023
A4189
A3400
A5127
A5190
A51
A515
A47
A45
A4031
A4124
B4128
B4101
B4096
B4090
B4091
B4176
B4188
B4551
B4102
B4151
B4196
B4092
B5012

VII
Route map scale
0 1 2 3 4 5 6 7 8 Km
0 1 2 3 4 5 Miles
Alrewas
Fradley
Hilliard's Cross
Streethay
LICHFIELD
Whittington
Whittington Barracks
Elford
Hademore
Catton Hall
Croxall
Edingale
Coton in the Elms
Lullington
Overseal
Netherseal
Haunton
Harlaston
Clifton Campville
Thorpe Constantine
Seckington
No Man's Heath
Chilcote
Donisthorpe
Short Heath
Moira
Oakthorpe
Stretton en le Field
Measham
Appleby Magna
Snarestone
Appleby Parva
Norton-Juxta-Twycross
Packington
Ravenstone
Normanton le Heath
Heather
Swepstone
Newton Burgoland
Odstone
Shackerstone
Congerstone
Whitwick
COALVILLE
Ibstock
Ellistown
Stanton under Bardon
Markfield
Copt Oak
Bagworth
Thornton
Thornton Resr
Nailstone
Barton in the Beans
Barlestone
Botcheston
Osbaston
Desford
Carlton
Market Bosworth
Newbold Verdon
Bilstone
Twycross
Orton-on-the-Hill
Warton
Austrey
Newton Regis
Shuttington
Alvecote
Amington
Glascote
Kettlebrook
TAMWORTH
Hopwas
Weeford
Hints
Bonehill
Fazeley
Two Gates
Wilnecote
Polesworth
Wigginton
Little Hay
Canwell Hall
Drayton Bassett
Dosthill
Dordon
Grendon
Grendon Common
Baddesley Ensor
Wood End
Middleton
Roughley
Sheepy Magna
Sheepy Parva
Ratcliffe Culey
ATHERSTONE
Witherley
Mancetter
Wellsborough
Sibson
Upton
Shenton
Sutton Cheney
Cadeby
Peckleton
Kirkby Mallory
Stoke Golding
Dadlington
Fenny Drayton
Higham on the Hill
Stapleton
Barwell
Earl Shilton
Elmesthorpe
Stoney Stanton
Sapcote
HINCKLEY
Burbage
Aston Flamville
Sharnford
Kingsbury
Baxterley
Hurley
Bentley
Ridge Lane
Oldbury
Hartshill
Marston
Lea Marston
Wishaw
Walmley
Wylde Green
Curdworth
Minworth
Water Orton
Nether Whitacre
Church End
Galley Common
Weddington
NUNEATON
Stockingford
Attleborough
Burton Hastings
Over Whitacre
Ansley
Arley
Astley
Shustoke
Castle Bromwich
Coleshill
Maxstoke
Fillongley
Corley Ash
Griff
BEDWORTH
Bramcote
Wolvey
Claybrooke Magna
Wibtoft
Bulkington
Withybrook
Shilton
Goodyers End
Exhall
Corley
Neal's Green
Keresley
Longford
Barnacle
Ansty
Foleshill
Monks Kirby
Tile Cross
Marston Green
National Exhibition Centre
Birmingham International Airport
Elmdon
Bickenhill
Elmdon Heath
Sheldon
Acock's Green
Yardley
Corley Moor
Hawkes End
Allesley
Meriden
Hampton in Arden
Four Oaks
Eastern Green
Walsgrave on Sowe
Combe Abbey
COVENTRY
Stretton under Fosse
Easenhall
Pailton
Brinklow
Harborough Magna
Newbold on Avon
SOLIHULL
Eastcote
Barston
Berkswell
Tile Hill
Earlsdon
Binley
Binley Woods
Bretford
Church Lawford
Long Lawford
Copt Heath
Knowle
Balsall Common
Canley
Stivichall
Willenhall
Brandon
Bentley Heath
Cheswick Green
Dorridge
Fen End
Burton Green
Baginton
Ryton-on-Dunsmore
Wolston
Chadwick End
Mee End
Coventry Airport
Stoneleigh
KENILWORTH
Bilton
Hockley Heath
Honiley
Kingswood
Wroxall
Beausale
Lapworth
Bubbenhall
Princethorpe
Stretton-on-Dunsmore
Bourton on Dunsmore
Dunchurch
Thurlaston
Ashow
Weston under Wetherley
Wappenbury
Frankton
Marton
Draycote
Draycote Water
Birdingbury
Eathorpe
Rowington
Shrewley
Lowsonford
Haseley
Hatton
Leek Wootton
Old Milverton
ROYAL LEAMINGTON SPA
WARWICK
Cubbington
Ullenhall
Henley in Arden
Preston Bagot
Pinley Green
Oldberrow
Claverdon
Budbrooke
Hampton on the Hill
Offchurch
Grand Union Canal
Stockton
Radford Semele
WHITNASH
Bascote
Bascote Heath
Lower Shuckburgh
Langley
Norton Lindsey
Longbridge
Wootton Wawen
Edstone
Wolverton
Sherbourne
Ufton
Southam
Little Alne
Bearley
Bishop's Tachbrook
Barford
Harbury
Napton on the Hill
Aston Cantlow
Snitterfield
Stratford Upon Avon Canal
Coventry Canal
R Anker
R Tame
R Mease
R Sence
R Blythe
R Cole
R Sowe
R Leam
R Itchen
M1
M6
M42
M40
M45
M69
A38
A51
A5
A453
A4091
A446
A4097
A452
A45
A41
A42
A444
A447
A47
A511
A4600
A4082
A46
A428
A423
A445
A4071
A4177
A4189
A3400
A429
A425
A452
B5493
B5000
B4116
B4114
B4098
B4102
B4112
B4109
B4065
B4029
B4027
B4455
B4669
B581
B582
B585
B4113
B4453
B4452
B4451
B4439
B4101
B4106
B4102
B4115
B5006
B4116
B4428

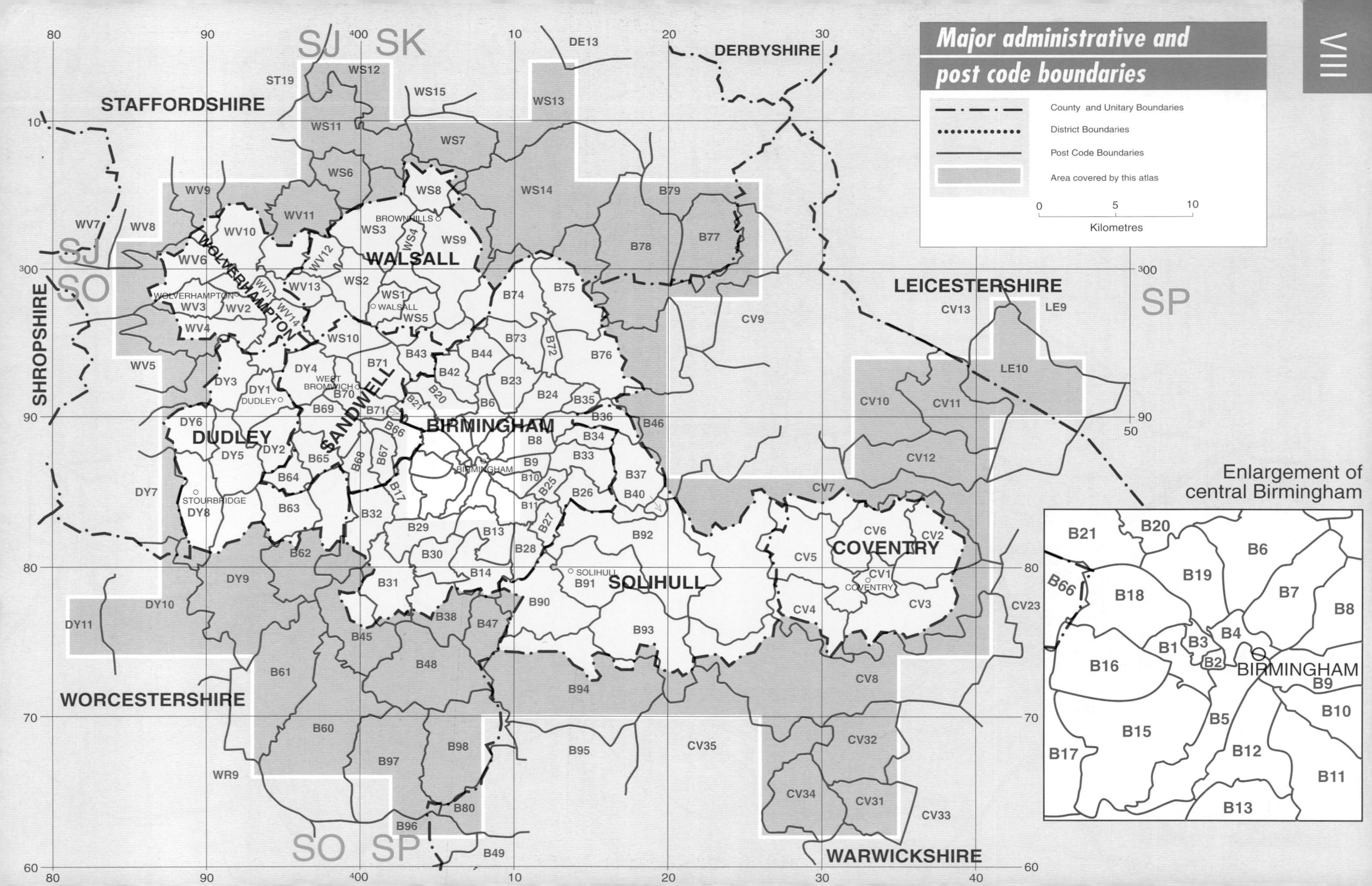

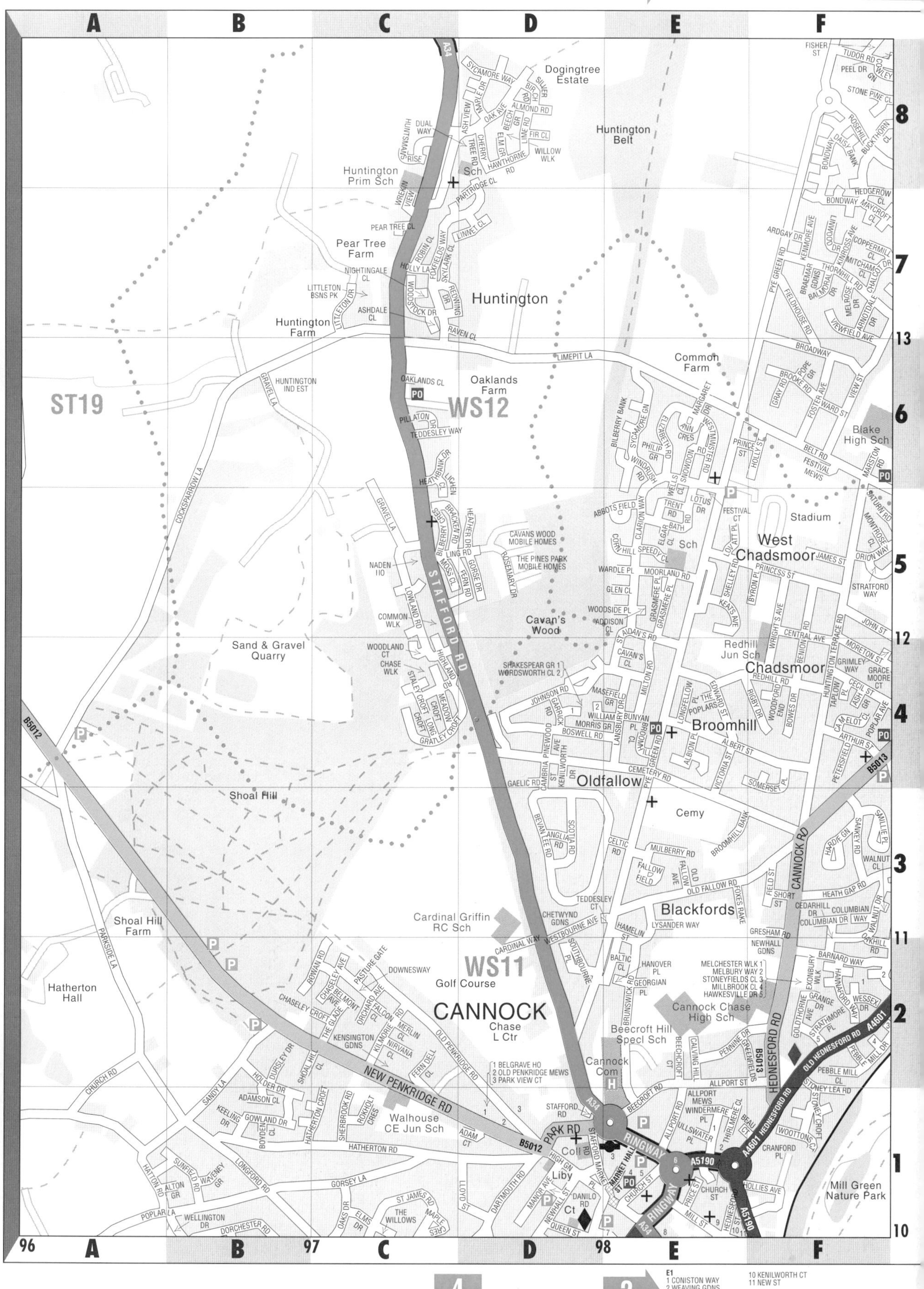

E1
1 CONISTON WAY
2 WEAVING GDNS
3 CANNOCK SH CTR
4 PEEL CT
5 PRINCE OF WALES CTR
6 QUEENS SQ
7 BACKCROFTS
8 KINGSTON ARC
9 WESLEY CT
10 KENILWORTH CT
11 NEW ST

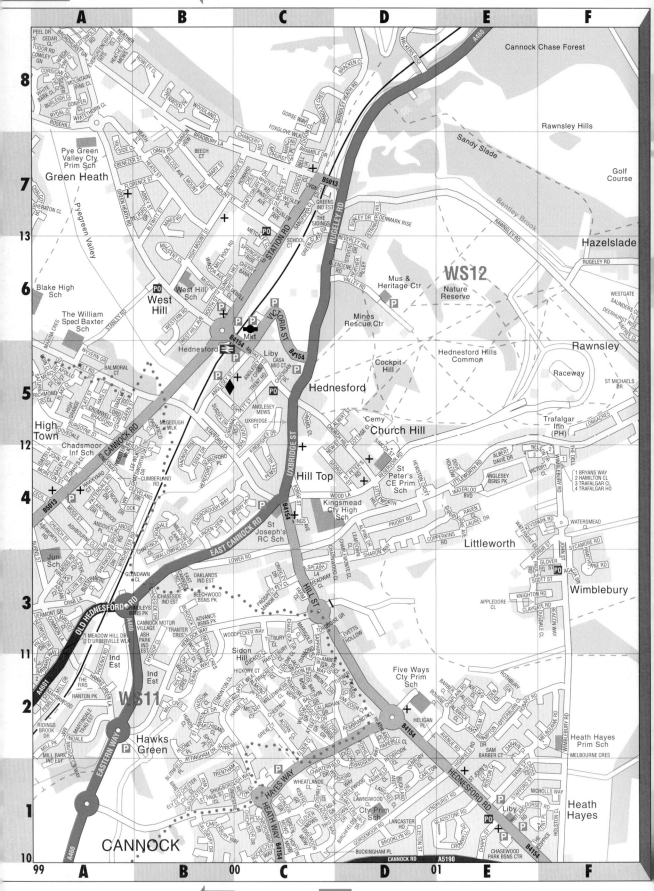

A B C D E F

8 7 13 6 5 12 4 3 11 2 1 10

Cannock Chase Forest
Rawnsley Hills
Sandy Slade
Golf Course
Bentley Brook
Hazelslade
WS12
Mus & Heritage Ctr
Nature Reserve
Mines Rescue Ctr
Hednesford Hills Common
Cockpit Hill
Rawnsley
Raceway
Hednesford
Cemy
Church Hill
Trafalgar Inn (PH)
St Peter's CE Prim Sch
Hill Top
Kingsmead Cty High Sch
St Joseph's RC Sch
Littleworth
Wimblebury
Five Ways Cty Prim Sch
Heath Hayes Prim Sch
Heath Hayes
Cty Prim Sch
Liby
Pye Green Valley Cty Prim Sch
Green Heath
Pyegreen Valley
Blake High Sch
West Hill Sch
West Hill
The William Specl Baxter Sch
Hednesford
Mkt
High Town
Chadsmoor Inf Sch
Jun Sch
Sidon Hill
Ind Est
WS11
Hawks Green
CANNOCK
Oaklands Ind Est
Chaseside Ind Est
Beechwood Bsns Pk
Brindleys Bsns Pk
Advance Bsns Pk
Cannock Motor Village
Ash Park Ind Est
Ranton Pk
Martindale Trad Est
Mill Park Ind Est
Anglesey Bsns Pk
Chasewood Park Bsns Ctr
Greens Ind Est
The Sidings

CANNOCK RD A5190 A460 A4601 B5013 B4154
RUGELEY RD
STATION RD
UXBRIDGE ST
EAST CANNOCK RD
OLD HEDNESFORD RD
EASTERN WAY
HILL ST
HAYES WAY
HEATH WAY
HEDNESFORD RD
VICTORIA ST
MARKET ST
WOOD LA
LOWER RD
PRIORY RD
WIMBLEBURY RD
RAWNSLEY RD
LONGACRES
JOHN ST
STANLEY RD
STAFFORD LA

1 BRYANS WAY
2 HAMILTON CL
3 TRAFALGAR CL
4 TRAFALGAR HO

1 MEADOW HILL DR
2 D'URBERVILLE WLK

99 A B 00 C D 01 E F

1
5

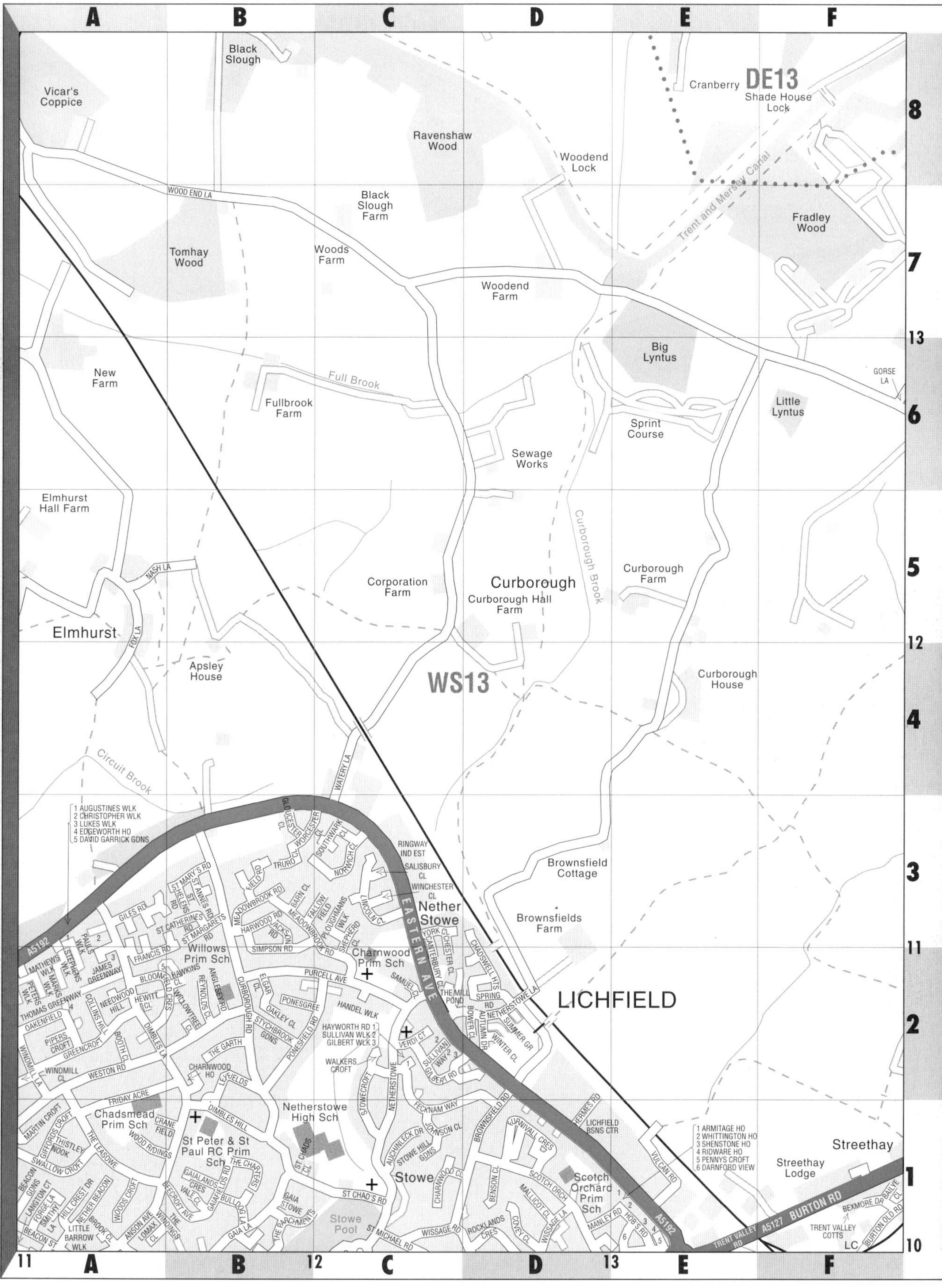
A
B
C
D
E
F
8
7
13
6
5
12
4
3
11
2
1
10
Black Slough
Vicar's Coppice
Ravenshaw Wood
Cranberry
DE13
Shade House Lock
Woodend Lock
Trent and Mersey Canal
WOOD END LA
Black Slough Farm
Fradley Wood
Tomhay Wood
Woods Farm
Woodend Farm
Big Lyntus
GORSE LA
New Farm
Full Brook
Fullbrook Farm
Little Lyntus
Sprint Course
Sewage Works
Elmhurst Hall Farm
Curborough Brook
NASH LA
Corporation Farm
Curborough
Curborough Farm
Curborough Hall Farm
Elmhurst
FOX LA
Apsley House
WS13
Curborough House
Circuit Brook
WATERY LA
1 AUGUSTINES WLK
2 CHRISTOPHER WLK
3 LUKES WLK
4 EDGEWORTH HO
5 DAVID GARRICK GDNS
RINGWAY IND EST
SALISBURY CL
WINCHESTER CL
Brownsfield Cottage
Nether Stowe
EASTERN AVE
Brownsfields Farm
A5192
Willows Prim Sch
Charnwood Prim Sch
LICHFIELD
PURCELL AVE
HANDEL WLK
HAYWORTH RD 1
SULLIVAN WLK 2
GILBERT WLK 3
WALKERS CROFT
FRIDAY ACRE
Chadsmead Prim Sch
Netherstowe High Sch
LICHFIELD BSNS CTR
1 ARMITAGE HO
2 WHITTINGTON HO
3 SHENSTONE HO
4 RIDWARE HO
5 PENNYS CROFT
6 DARNFORD VIEW
Streethay
Streethay Lodge
St Peter & St Paul RC Prim Sch
Stowe
Scotch Orchard Prim Sch
ST CHAD'S RD
Stowe Pool
BURTON RD
A5127
TRENT VALLEY RD
BEXMORE DR
TRENT VALLEY COTTS
BURTON OLD RD
LC
11
A
B
12
C
D
13
E
F

9

1

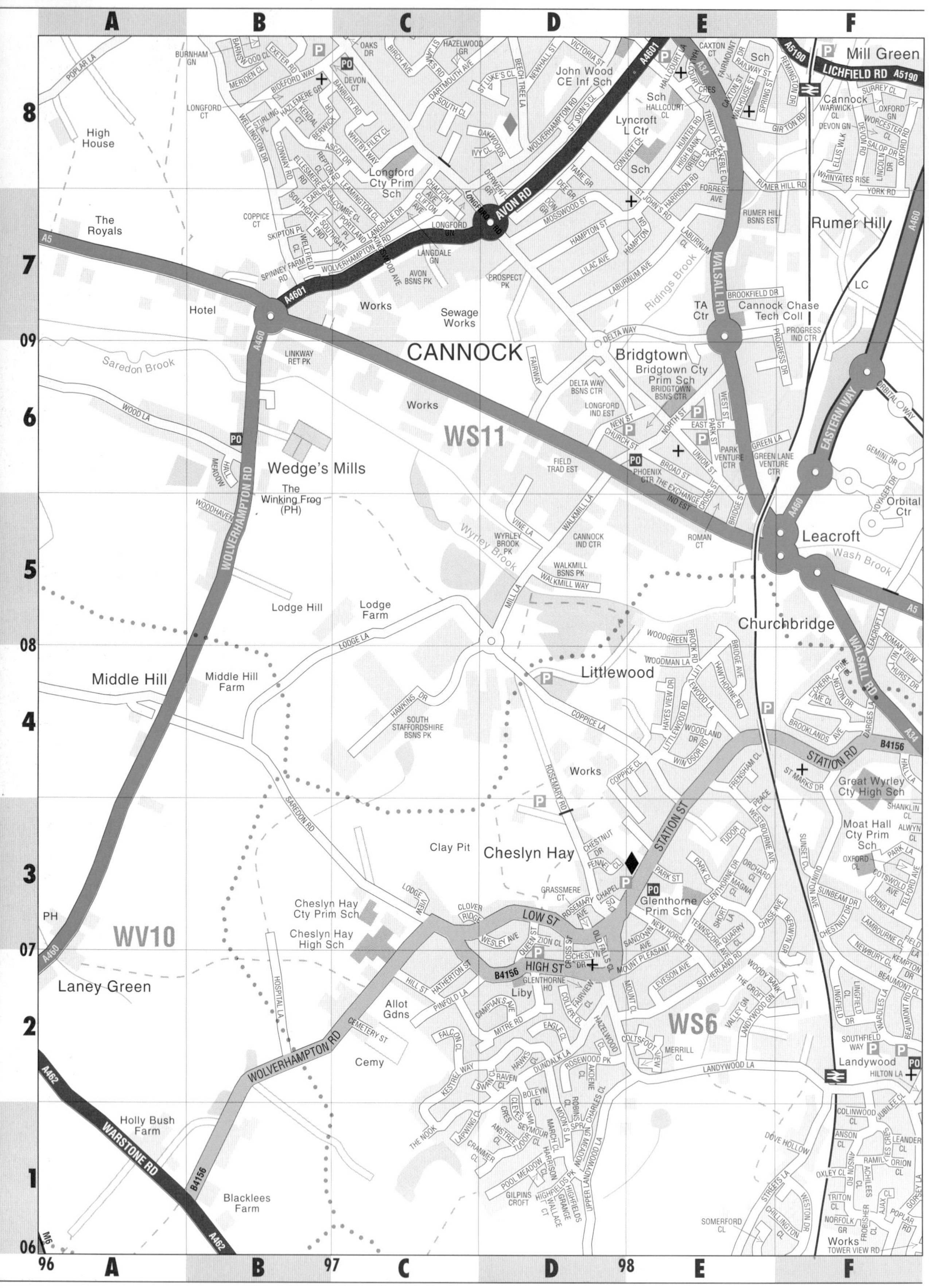
A
B
C
D
E
F
8
7
09
6
5
08
4
3
07
2
1
06
96
97
98
CANNOCK
WS11
WS6
WV10
Mill Green
LICHFIELD RD A5190
A5190
Cannock
High House
The Royals
Hotel
Saredon Brook
WOOD LA
PO
Wedge's Mills
The Winking Frog (PH)
WOODHAVEN
WOLVERHAMPTON RD
A460
A5
A4601
AVON RD
Works
Sewage Works
LINKWAY RET PK
Longford Cty Prim Sch
John Wood CE Inf Sch
Lyncroft L Ctr
Sch
Bridgtown
Bridgtown Cty Prim Sch
DELTA WAY
FAIRWAY
Ridings Brook
WALSALL RD
A34
TA Ctr
Cannock Chase Tech Coll
PROGRESS IND CTR
Rumer Hill
RUMER HILL RD
RUMER HILL BSNS EST
LC
EASTERN WAY
ORBITAL WAY
Orbital Ctr
Leacroft
Wash Brook
Churchbridge
FIELD TRAD EST
PHOENIX CTR
THE EXCHANGE
CANNOCK IND CTR
WALKMILL LA
WALKMILL BSNS PK
WALKMILL WAY
Wyrley Brook
WYRLEY BROOK PK
ROMAN CT
Lodge Hill
Lodge Farm
LODGE LA
Middle Hill
Middle Hill Farm
HAWKINS DR
SOUTH STAFFORDSHIRE BSNS PK
Littlewood
COPPICE LA
ROSEMARY RD
Works
STATION RD
STATION ST
B4156
Great Wyrley Cty High Sch
Moat Hall Cty Prim Sch
Clay Pit
Cheslyn Hay
SAREDON RD
Cheslyn Hay Cty Prim Sch
Cheslyn Hay High Sch
LOW ST
HIGH ST
Glenthorne Prim Sch
Liby
PH
Laney Green
HOSPITAL LA
WOLVERHAMPTON RD
CEMETERY ST
Allot Gdns
Cemy
LANDYWOOD LA
Landywood
A462
WARSTONE RD
Holly Bush Farm
Blacklees Farm
M6
Works
TOWER VIEW RD

13

A B C D E F

8
7
09
6
5
08
4
3
07
2
1
06

LICHFIELD RD
A5190
CANNOCK RD
EASTERN WAY
A460
SALISBURY DR
ROCHESTER WAY
TRURO
KENSINGTON PL
GORSEMOOR RD
HEATH VIEW
NEWLANDS CT
B4154 NORTON RD
WS12
NEWLANDS LA
OLD HALL LA
STOKE'S LA
Tip
COAL HAULAGE RD
NORTON LA
WOODFIELD CL
WOODFIELD DR
HEDNESFORD RD
HILL ST
Newlands Brook
RICHARDS CT
NORTON TERR
Stoke's La
Long La
BROADOAKS CL
Norton Canes
NORTON SPRINGS
EWATER WAY
GAINSBROOK CRES
LEIGHSWOOD CL
HANBURY'S FARM
SPINNEY CL
KINGSWOOD DR
HUSSEY RD
GROVE CL
WS11
The Jerome Prim Sch
PO
JEROME RD
CHAPEL ST
CASTLECROFT
Streetway Farm
Wash Brook
WASHBROOK LA
THE HAMLET
BRIDGES RD
BRIDGES CRES
WALLACE CL
BELLSIZE CL
APEX BSNS PK
St Thomas More RC Prim Sch
BELMONT
POOL VIEW
KINGSWOOD DR
HUT HILL LA
CHURCH VALE
PINFOLD LA
CHARTER CL
PENNY CRES
NORTON GRANGE CRES
NORTON GRANGE
GN
NORTON GREEN LA
Works
CHURCH RD
JACKSON CL
BUTTS WAY
BUTTS CL
WALSALL RD
NORTON LA
BETTY'S LA
SHANKLIN CL
FERN DR
MANOR AVE
Norton Hall Farm
Swan Farm
NORTON HALL LA
Works
HALL LA
ALWYN CL
TREVOR AVE
JULIAN CL
LOVE LA
BUTTS LA
Norton Green
FOLLAND AVE
BARN CROFT
PO
PARK LA
PADDOCK LA
BROOK LA
ASH LA
HARTWELL LA
APPLEDORE CL
PH
PH
Liby
JOHNS LA
LEA LA
WALSALL RD
WS6
Great Wyrley
GAINS LA
PH
A5
KEMPTON DR
HILTON LA
MOAT LA
THE CRESCENT
BROAD MEADOW LA
HAZEL LA
Mine (dis)
Gains Brook
SCHOOL LA
WALSALL RD
ESTRIDGE LA
MEADOW GR
LIME LA
SAXON CL
SHAW'S LA
NEW ST
FOREST WAY
WS3
JONES LA
BENTON'S LA
GORSEY LA
B4154
OAK HO
OAK AVE
ACORN CL
Home Farm
WYRLEY LA
Gorsey Lane Farm
Pelsall Road Bridge
HAWTHORN AVE
WHARWELL LA
CROMWELL CT
WELL LA
FAIR OAKS DR
DARK LA
POPLAR RD
JACOB'S HALL LA
Jacob's Hall
Cadman's La
Hall Farm
GROVE LA
BLUEBELL LA
A34

99 A B 00 C D 01 E F

14
6

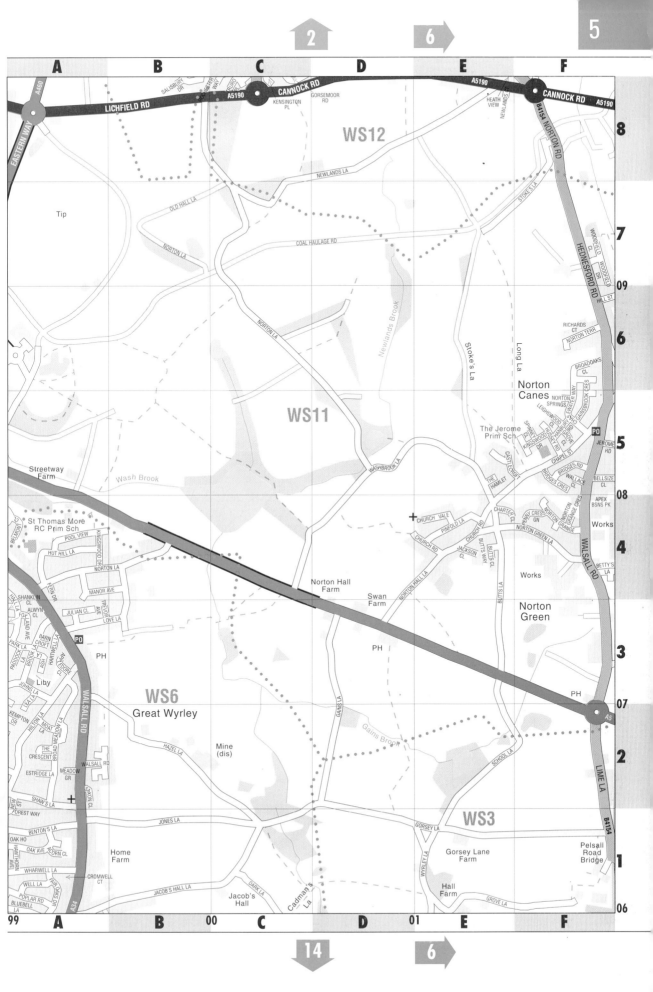

5

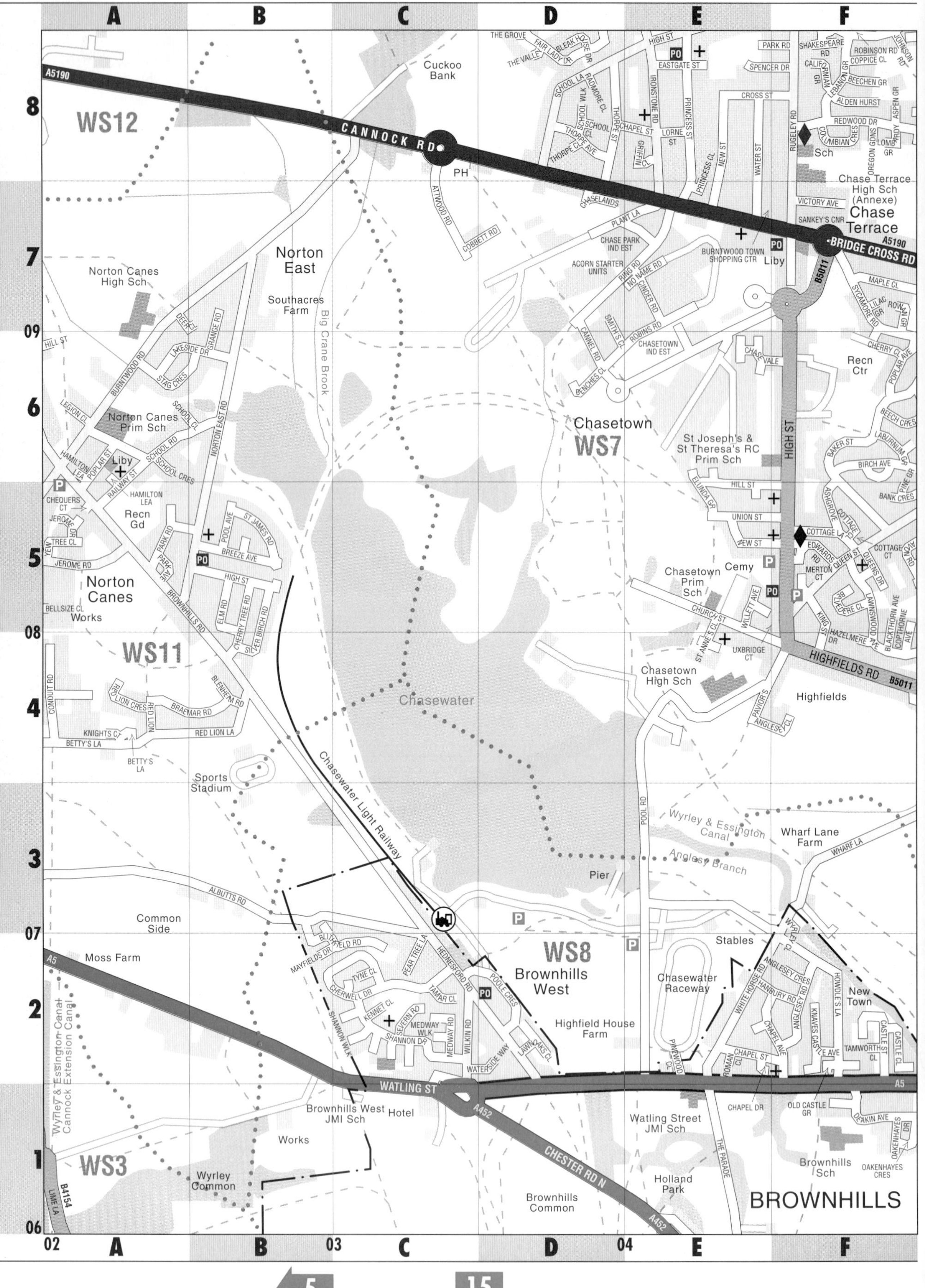
A
B
C
D
E
F
8
7
09
6
5
08
4
3
07
2
1
06
02
03
04
A5190
WS12
CANNOCK RD
Cuckoo Bank
PH
ATTWOOD RD
COBBETT RD
THE GROVE
THE VALLEY
FAIR LADY DR
BLEAK HOUSE DR
SCHOOL LA
SCHOOL WLK
RADMORE CL
SCHOOL CL
THORPE AVE
THORPE CL
THORPE ST
CHAPEL ST
IRONSTONE RD
GRIFFIN CL
LORNE ST
PRINCESS ST
PRINCESS CL
NEW ST
WATER ST
HIGH ST
EASTGATE ST
PO
CROSS ST
PARK RD
SPENCER DR
SHAKESPEARE RD
CALIFORNIAN GR
LEBANON GR
BEECHEN GR
ROBINSON RD
COPPICE CL
JOHNSON RD
ALDEN HURST
ASPEN GR
REDWOOD DR
COLUMBIAN CRES
OREGON GDNS
LOMBARDY GR
RUGELEY RD
Sch
Chase Terrace High Sch (Annexe)
Chase Terrace
VICTORY AVE
SANKEY'S CNR
BRIDGE CROSS RD
B5011
MAPLE CL
SYCAMORE RD
LILAC GR
ROWAN GR
CHERRY CL
POPLAR AVE
Recn Ctr
CHASELANDS
PLANT LA
CHASE PARK IND EST
ACORN STARTER UNITS
RING RD
NO NAME RD
CINDER RD
ROBINS RD
SMITH'S CL
CANNEL RD
CHASETOWN IND EST
BENCHES CL
BURNTWOOD TOWN SHOPPING CTR
Liby
CHASE VALE
Norton Canes High Sch
Norton East
Southacres Farm
Big Crane Brook
HILL ST
DEER CL
GRANGE RD
LAKESIDE DR
STAG CRES
BURNTWOOD RD
LEGION CL
Norton Canes Prim Sch
SCHOOL CL
NORTON EAST RD
SCHOOL RD
SCHOOL CRES
HAMILTON LEA
POPLAR ST
RAILWAY ST
CHEQUERS CT
JEROME DR
YEW TREE CL
JEROME RD
Recn Gd
POOL AVE
ST JAMES RD
PARK RD
PARK AVE
BREEZE AVE
HIGH ST
ELM RD
CHERRY TREE RD
SILVER BIRCH RD
BROWNHILLS RD
Norton Canes
BELLSIZE CL
Works
WS11
CONDUIT RD
RED LION CRES
RED LION LA
BRAEMAR RD
BLENHEIM RD
KNIGHTS CT
BETTY'S LA
Chasetown
WS7
St Joseph's & St Theresa's RC Prim Sch
ELUNDA GR
HILL ST
UNION ST
NEW ST
COTTAGE LA
ASHGROVE
COTTAGE ST
EDWARDS RD
QUEEN ST
QUEENS DR
MERTON CT
BAKER ST
BEECH GR
LABURNUM GR
BIRCH AVE
PINE GR
BANK CRES
COTTAGE CT
Chasetown Prim Sch
Cemy
CHURCH ST
WILLETT AVE
ST ANNE'S CL
UXBRIDGE CT
KING ST
HAZELMERE DR
LAWNSWOOD AVE
BLACKTHORN AVE
COPTHORNE AVE
HIGHFIELDS RD
Chasetown High Sch
PAVIOR'S RD
ANGLESEY CL
Highfields
Chasewater
Sports Stadium
Chasewater Light Railway
POOL RD
Wyrley & Essington Canal
Anglesey Branch
Wharf Lane Farm
WHARF LA
Pier
ALBUTTS RD
Common Side
Moss Farm
A5
WS8
Brownhills West
BLITHFIELD RD
MAYFIELDS DR
PEAR TREE LA
TYNE CL
CHERWELL DR
HEDNESFORD RD
TAMAR CL
POOLE CRES
KENNET CL
SEVERN RD
MEDWAY WLK
MEDWAY RD
SHANNON DR
SHANNON WLK
WILKIN RD
WATERSIDE WAY
LAWNOAKS CL
Highfield House Farm
Stables
Chasewater Raceway
PINEWOOD CL
WHITE HORSE RD
ANGLESEY CRES
HANBURY RD
ANGLESEY RD
WYRLEY CL
CHAPEL AVE
CHAPEL ST
ROMAN CL
KNAVES CASTLE AVE
HOWDLE'S LA
New Town
CASTLE CL
TAMWORTH CL
WATLING ST
Wyrley & Essington Canal
Cannock Extension Canal
Brownhills West JMI Sch
Hotel
A452
CHESTER RD N
CHAPEL DR
OLD CASTLE GR
DEAKIN AVE
OAKENHAYES DR
Works
WS3
Wyrley Common
Watling Street JMI Sch
THE PARADE
Holland Park
Brownhills Common
Brownhills Sch
OAKENHAYES CRES
BROWNHILLS
B4154
LIME LA

5

15

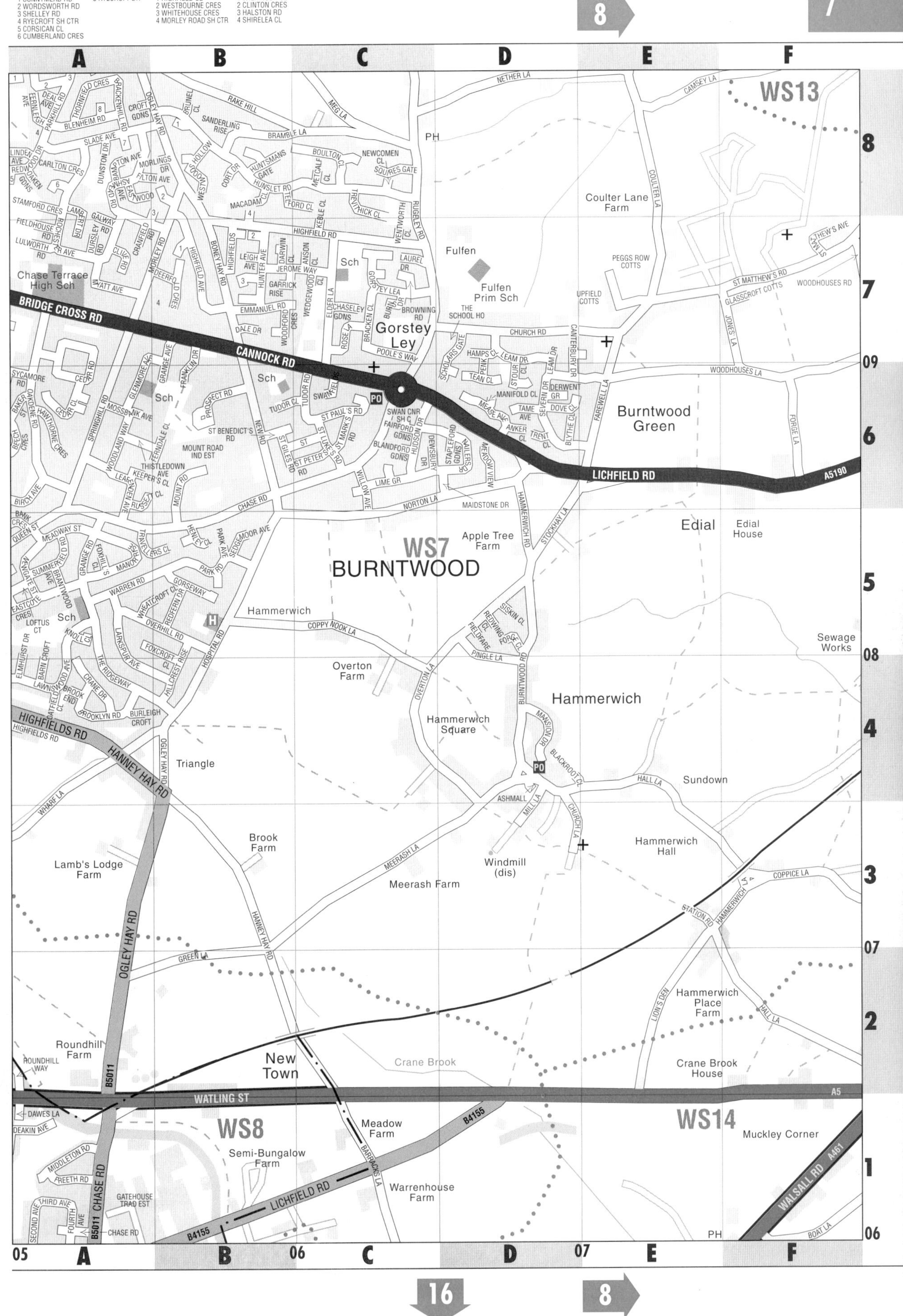
A8
1 SUNNYMEAD RD
2 WORDSWORTH RD
3 SHELLEY RD
4 RYECROFT SH CTR
5 CORSICAN CL
6 CUMBERLAND CRES
7 MARTON AVE
8 RYECROFT DR
B7
1 HIGHFIELD CL
2 WESTBOURNE CRES
3 WHITEHOUSE CRES
4 MORLEY ROAD SH CTR
B8
1 WILKINSON CL
2 CLINTON CRES
3 HALSTON RD
4 SHIRELEA CL
8
A
B
C
D
E
F
WS13
8
7
09
6
5
08
4
3
07
2
1
06
05
06
07
NETHER LA
CAMSEY LA
RAKE HILL
MEG LA
SANDERLING RISE
BRAMBLE LA
BLENHEIM RD
SLADE AVE
CARLTON CRES
STAMFORD CRES
FIELDHOUSE RD
LULWORTH RD
Chase Terrace High Sch
MORLINGS DR
FILTON AVE
HIGHFIELD RD
BOULTON CL
NEWCOMEN CL
SQUIRES GATE
HUNTSMANS GATE
HUNSLET RD
MACADAM CL
KEBLE CL
RUGELEY RD
WENTWORTH CL
Coulter Lane Farm
COULTER LA
Fulfen
Fulfen Prim Sch
PEGGS ROW COTTS
UPFIELD COTTS
THE SCHOOL HO
ST MATTHEW'S RD
ST MATTHEW'S AVE
GLASSCROFT COTTS
WOODHOUSES RD
JONES LA
BRIDGE CROSS RD
CANNOCK RD
Gorstey Ley
JEROME WAY
GARRICK RISE
EMMANUEL RD
DALE DR
CHASELEY GDNS
BROWNING RD
POOLE'S WAY
CHURCH RD
CANTERBURY DR
WOODHOUSES LA
Sch
SWAN CNR SH C
ST PAUL'S RD
TUDOR RD
PROSPECT RD
ST BENEDICT'S RD
MOUNT ROAD IND EST
THISTLEDOWN AVE
MANIFOLD CL
DERWENT GR
DOVE CL
FAREWELL LA
Burntwood Green
FORGE LA
LICHFIELD RD
A5190
CHASE RD
NORTON LA
MAIDSTONE DR
LIME GR
MEADOW VIEW
HAMMERWICH RD
STOCKHAY LA
Edial
Edial House
Apple Tree Farm
WS7
BURNTWOOD
WARREN RD
GORSEWAY
OVERHILL RD
Hammerwich
COPPY NOOK LA
SISKIN CL
REDWING CL
FIELDFARE
PINGLE LA
Sewage Works
Overton Farm
OVERTON LA
BURNTWOOD RD
Hammerwich
Hammerwich Square
MANSION DR
BLACKROOT CL
HALL LA
Sundown
HIGHFIELDS RD
HANNEY HAY RD
OGLEY HAY RD
Triangle
WHARF LA
ASHMALL
MILL LA
CHURCH LA
Brook Farm
Lamb's Lodge Farm
MEERASH LA
Windmill (dis)
Meerash Farm
Hammerwich Hall
COPPICE LA
STATION RD
HAMMERWICH LA
GREEN LA
Hammerwich Place Farm
LION'S DEN
Roundhill Farm
ROUNDHILL WAY
New Town
Crane Brook
Crane Brook House
B5011
WATLING ST
A5
DAWES LA
DEAKIN AVE
WS8
Meadow Farm
B4155
WS14
Muckley Corner
MIDDLETON RD
REETH RD
Semi-Bungalow Farm
BARRACKS LA
Warrenhouse Farm
WALSALL RD
A461
CHASE RD
GATEHOUSE TRAD EST
LICHFIELD RD
B4155
PH
BOAT LA

16
8

7

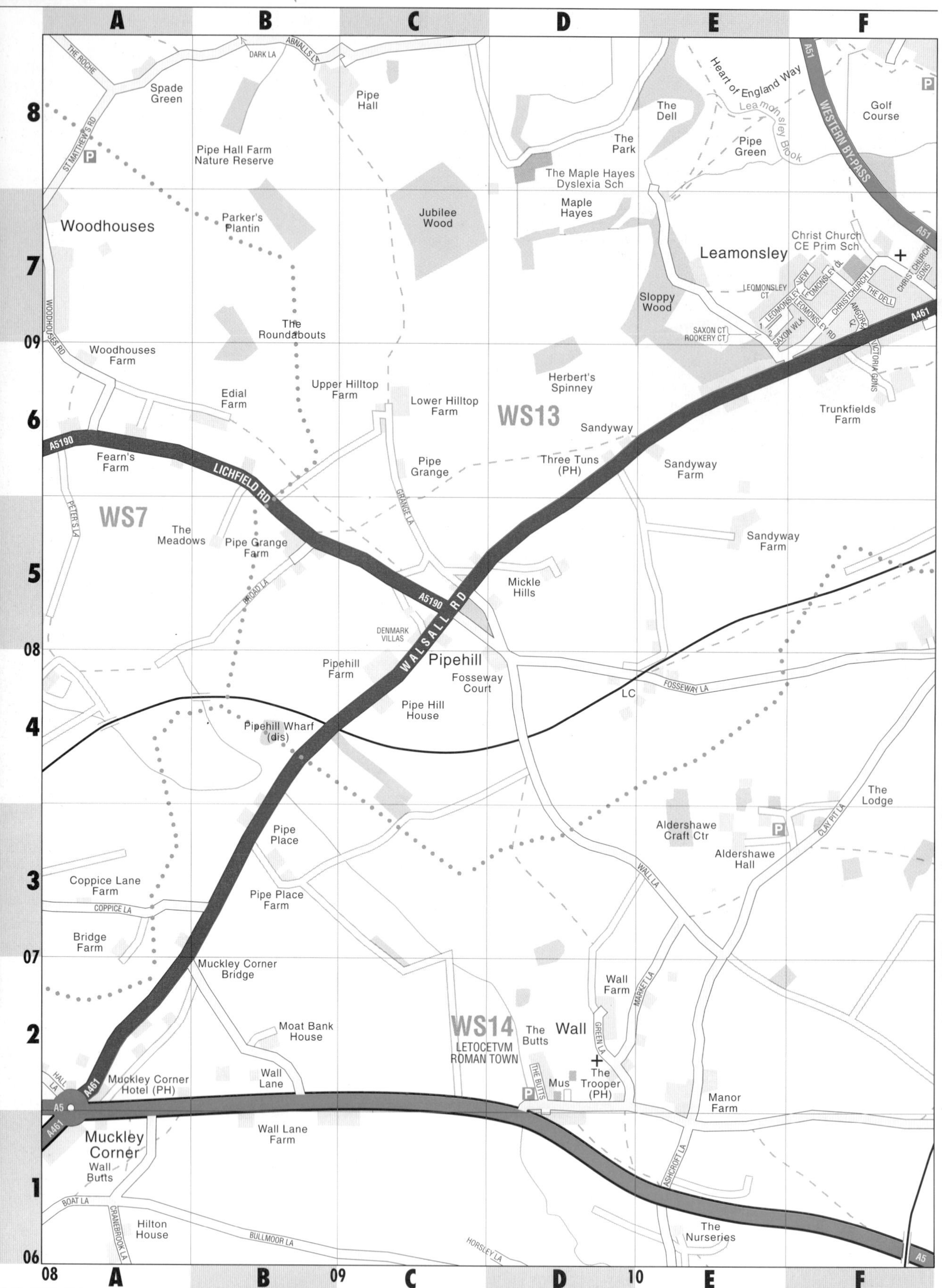

A
B
C
D
E
F
8
7
09
6
5
08
4
3
07
2
1
06
08
09
10
THE ROCHE
DARK LA
ABNALLS LA
Spade Green
Pipe Hall
Heart of England Way
Leamonsley Brook
The Dell
The Park
Pipe Green
A51
WESTERN BY-PASS
Golf Course
ST MATTHEW'S RD
Pipe Hall Farm Nature Reserve
The Maple Hayes Dyslexia Sch
Maple Hayes
Jubilee Wood
Woodhouses
Parker's Plantin
Christ Church CE Prim Sch
Leamonsley
Sloppy Wood
The Roundabouts
WOODHOUSES RD
SAXON CT
ROOKERY CT
LEOMONSLEY CT
A461
Woodhouses Farm
Herbert's Spinney
Upper Hilltop Farm
Lower Hilltop Farm
Edial Farm
WS13
Trunkfields Farm
Sandyway
A5190
Fearn's Farm
LICHFIELD RD
Pipe Grange
Three Tuns (PH)
Sandyway Farm
GRANGE LA
PETER'S LA
WS7
The Meadows
Pipe Grange Farm
Sandyway Farm
Mickle Hills
BROAD LA
A5190
WALSALL RD
DENMARK VILLAS
Pipehill
Pipehill Farm
Fosseway Court
FOSSEWAY LA
LC
Pipe Hill House
Pipehill Wharf (dis)
The Lodge
Pipe Place
Aldershawe Craft Ctr
CLAY PIT LA
Aldershawe Hall
WALL LA
Coppice Lane Farm
Pipe Place Farm
COPPICE LA
Bridge Farm
Muckley Corner Bridge
Wall Farm
MARKET LA
Moat Bank House
WS14
LETOCETVM ROMAN TOWN
The Butts
Wall
GREEN LA
HALL LA
Muckley Corner Hotel (PH)
Wall Lane
THE BUTTS
Mus
The Trooper (PH)
Manor Farm
A5
A461
Muckley Corner
Wall Butts
Wall Lane Farm
ASHCROFT LA
BOAT LA
CRANEBROOK LA
Hilton House
BULLMOOR LA
HORSLEY LA
The Nurseries
A5

7
17

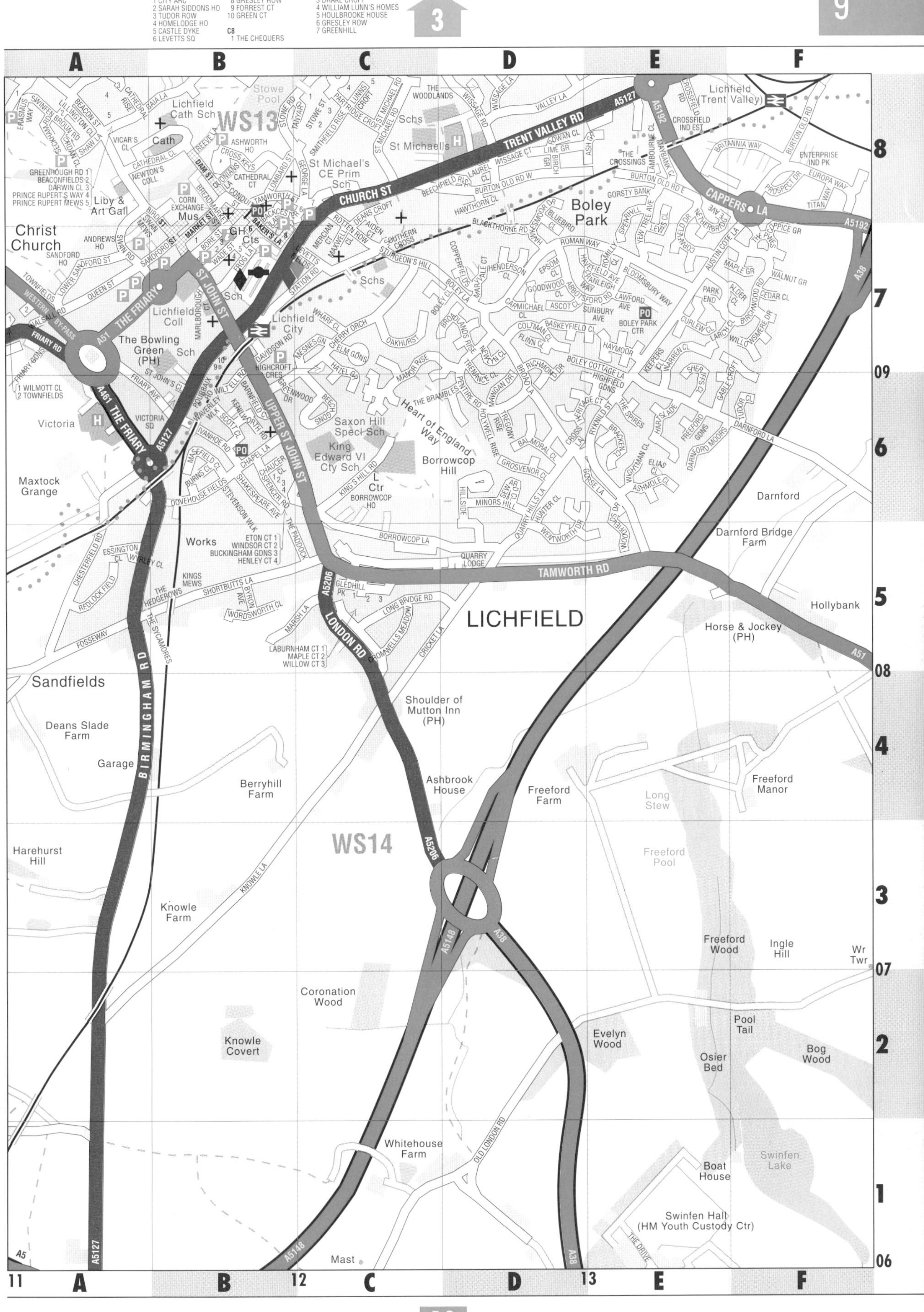

B7
1 CITY ARC
2 SARAH SIDDONS HO
3 TUDOR ROW
4 HOMELODGE HO
5 CASTLE DYKE
6 LEVETTS SQ
7 THREE SPIRES SH CTR
8 GRESLEY ROW
9 FORREST CT
10 GREEN CT
C8
1 THE CHEQUERS
2 MALLARD CROFT
3 DRAKE CROFT
4 WILLIAM LUNN'S HOMES
5 HOULBROOKE HOUSE
6 GRESLEY ROW
7 GREENHILL
3
9
A
B
C
D
E
F
8
7
09
6
5
08
4
3
07
2
1
06
11
12
13
WS13
WS14
LICHFIELD
Lichfield Cath Sch
Stowe Pool
Cath
Liby & Art Gal
Mus
GH
Cts
Christ Church
Sch
Lichfield Coll
The Bowling Green (PH)
Lichfield City
Schs
St Michael's
St Michael's CE Prim Sch
Lichfield (Trent Valley)
CROSSFIELD IND EST
ENTERPRISE IND PK
Boley Park
BOLEY PARK CTR
Heart of England Way
Saxon Hill Specl Sch
King Edward VI Cty Sch
L Ctr
BORROWCOP HO
Borrowcop Hill
Victoria
Maxtock Grange
Works
Sandfields
Deans Slade Farm
Garage
Berryhill Farm
Shoulder of Mutton Inn (PH)
Ashbrook House
Freeford Farm
Long Stew
Freeford Manor
Freeford Pool
Harehurst Hill
Knowle Farm
Freeford Wood
Ingle Hill
Wr Twr
Coronation Wood
Knowle Covert
Evelyn Wood
Pool Tail
Osier Bed
Bog Wood
Whitehouse Farm
Swinfen Lake
Boat House
Swinfen Hall (HM Youth Custody Ctr)
Mast
Darnford
Darnford Bridge Farm
Hollybank
Horse & Jockey (PH)
TRENT VALLEY RD
CHURCH ST
CAPPERS LA
TAMWORTH RD
LONDON RD
BIRMINGHAM RD
THE FRIARY
FRIARY RD
UPPER ST JOHN ST
ST JOHN ST
BURTON OLD RD E
DARNFORD LA
BORROWCOP LA
KNOWLE LA
OLD LONDON RD
CRICKET LA
A5127
A5192
A51
A38
A5206
A5148
A461
A5
THE DRIVE
18

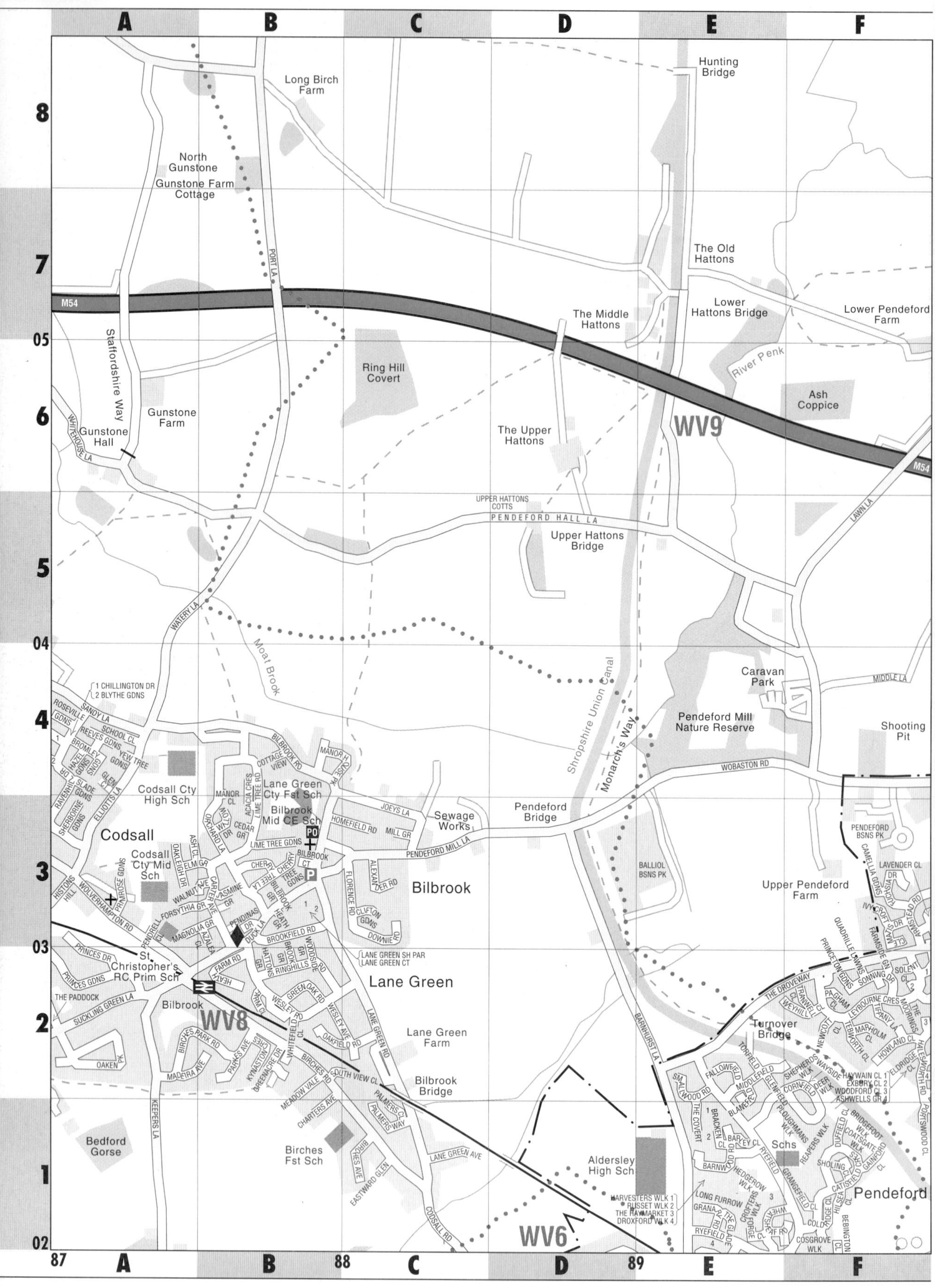

M54
Long Birch Farm
North Gunstone
Gunstone Farm Cottage
Hunting Bridge
The Old Hattons
Lower Hattons Bridge
Lower Pendeford Farm
The Middle Hattons
Ring Hill Covert
River Penk
Ash Coppice
Staffordshire Way
Gunstone Farm
Gunstone Hall
The Upper Hattons
WV9
Upper Hattons Cotts
Pendeford Hall La
Upper Hattons Bridge
Port La
Watery La
Moat Brook
Shropshire Union Canal
Monarch's Way
Caravan Park
Pendeford Mill Nature Reserve
Shooting Pit
Middle La
Lawn La
Wobaston Rd
Codsall Cty High Sch
Lane Green Cty Fst Sch
Bilbrook Mid CE Sch
Sewage Works
Pendeford Bridge
Codsall
Codsall Cty Mid Sch
Bilbrook
Balliol Bsns Pk
Pendeford Bsns Pk
Upper Pendeford Farm
St. Christopher's RC Prim Sch
Lane Green
Lane Green Farm
Turnover Bridge
WV8
Bilbrook Bridge
Bedford Gorse
Birches Fst Sch
Aldersley High Sch
Schs
Pendeford
WV6
Codsall Rd
Lane Green Rd
Barnhurst La
Keepers La
Wolverhampton Rd
Pendeford Mill La
The Droveway

12

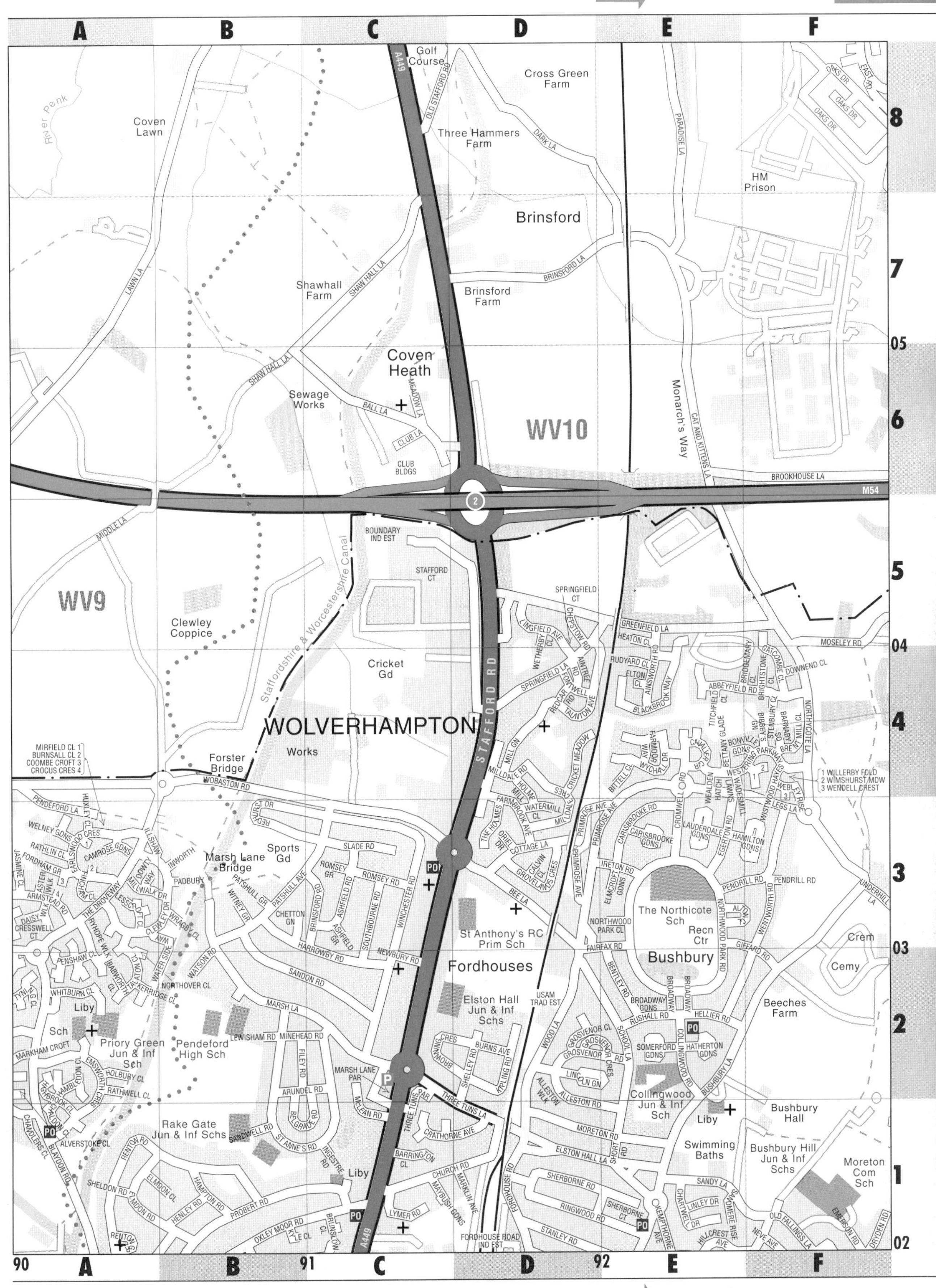

A
B
C
D
E
F
8
7
05
6
5
04
4
3
03
2
1
02
90
91
92
River Penk
Coven Lawn
Golf Course
A449
OLD STAFFORD RD
Cross Green Farm
Three Hammers Farm
DARK LA
PARADISE LA
OAKS DR
EAST RD
HM Prison
Brinsford
BRINSFORD LA
Brinsford Farm
Shawhall Farm
SHAW HALL LA
LAWN LA
Coven Heath
MEADOW LA
Sewage Works
BALL LA
CLUB LA
CLUB BLDGS
WV10
Monarch's Way
CAT AND KITTENS LA
BROOKHOUSE LA
M54
2
MIDDLE LA
BOUNDARY IND EST
STAFFORD CT
Staffordshire & Worcestershire Canal
WV9
Clewley Coppice
SPRINGFIELD CT
GREENFIELD LA
HEATON CL
MOSELEY RD
Cricket Gd
STAFFORD RD
WOLVERHAMPTON
Works
Forster Bridge
WOBASTON RD
MIRFIELD CL 1
BURNSALL CL 2
COOMBE CROFT 3
CROCUS CRES 4
1 WILLERBY FOLD
2 WIMSHURST MDW
3 WENDELL CREST
PENDEFORD LA
Marsh Lane Bridge
Sports Gd
SLADE RD
ROMSEY RD
PO
St Anthony's RC Prim Sch
The Northicote Sch
Recn Ctr
Bushbury
PENDRILL RD
UNDERHILL LA
Crem
Cemy
Fordhouses
Elston Hall Jun & Inf Schs
USAM TRAD EST
Beeches Farm
Liby
Sch
Priory Green Jun & Inf Sch
Pendeford High Sch
MARSH LA
MARSH LANE PAR
THREE TUNS LA
Collingwood Jun & Inf Sch
Bushbury Hall
Rake Gate Jun & Inf Schs
Swimming Baths
Bushbury Hill Jun & Inf Schs
Moreton Com Sch
OXLEY MOOR RD
FORDHOUSE ROAD IND EST
OLD FALLINGS LA

25
12

11

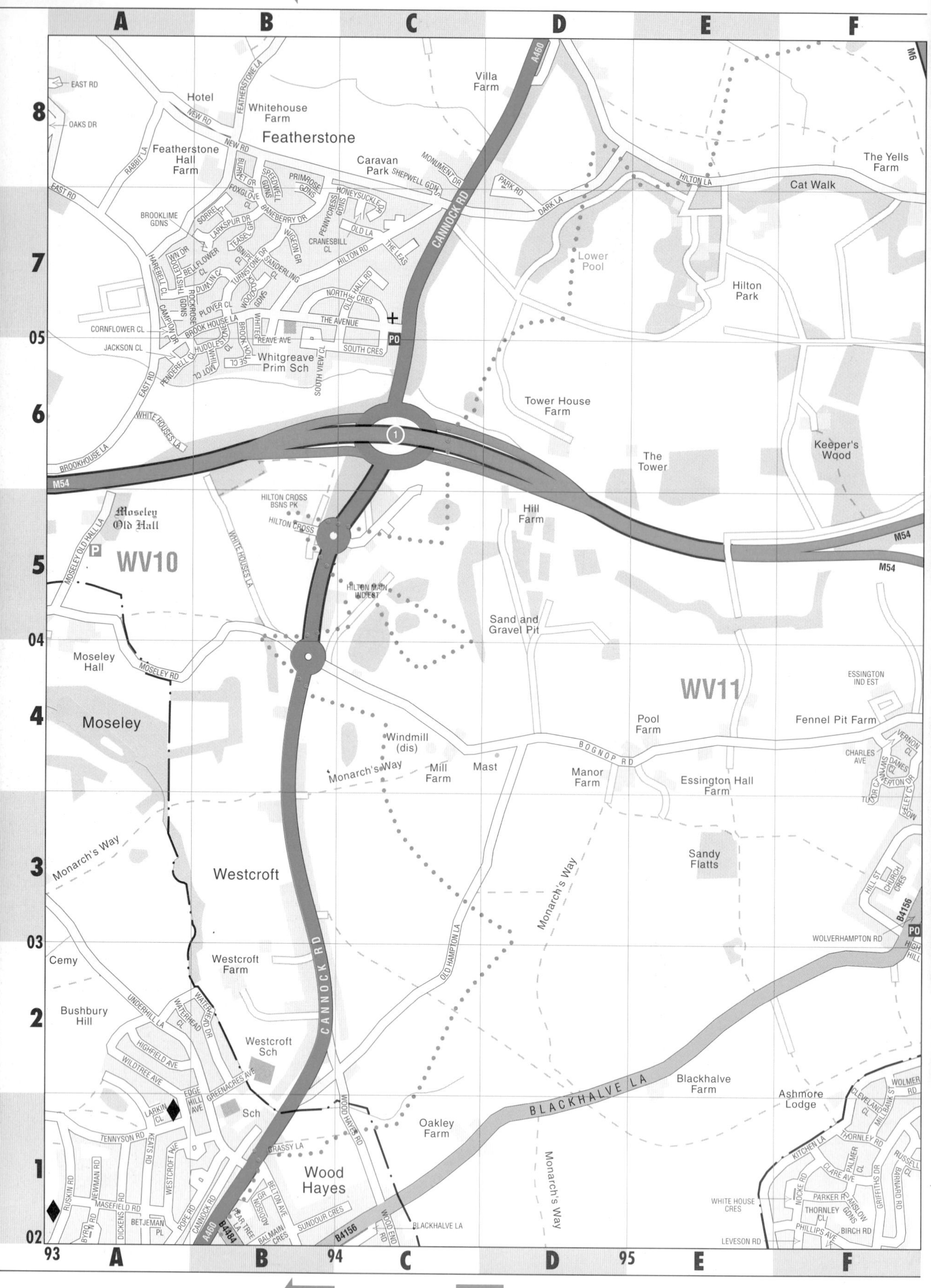

Featherstone
Whitehouse Farm
Hotel
Featherstone Hall Farm
Caravan Park
Villa Farm
The Yells Farm
Cat Walk
Lower Pool
Hilton Park
Whitgreave Prim Sch
Tower House Farm
Keeper's Wood
The Tower
Hill Farm
Moseley Old Hall
WV10
WV11
Sand and Gravel Pit
Moseley Hall
Moseley
Windmill (dis)
Mill Farm
Mast
Pool Farm
Manor Farm
Fennel Pit Farm
Essington Hall Farm
Sandy Flatts
Westcroft
Monarch's Way
Westcroft Farm
Cemy
Bushbury Hill
Westcroft Sch
Sch
Wood Hayes
Oakley Farm
Blackhalve Farm
Ashmore Lodge
CANNOCK RD
BLACKHALVE LA
BOGNOP RD
HILTON LA
M54
M6
A460
B4156
B4484

11
26

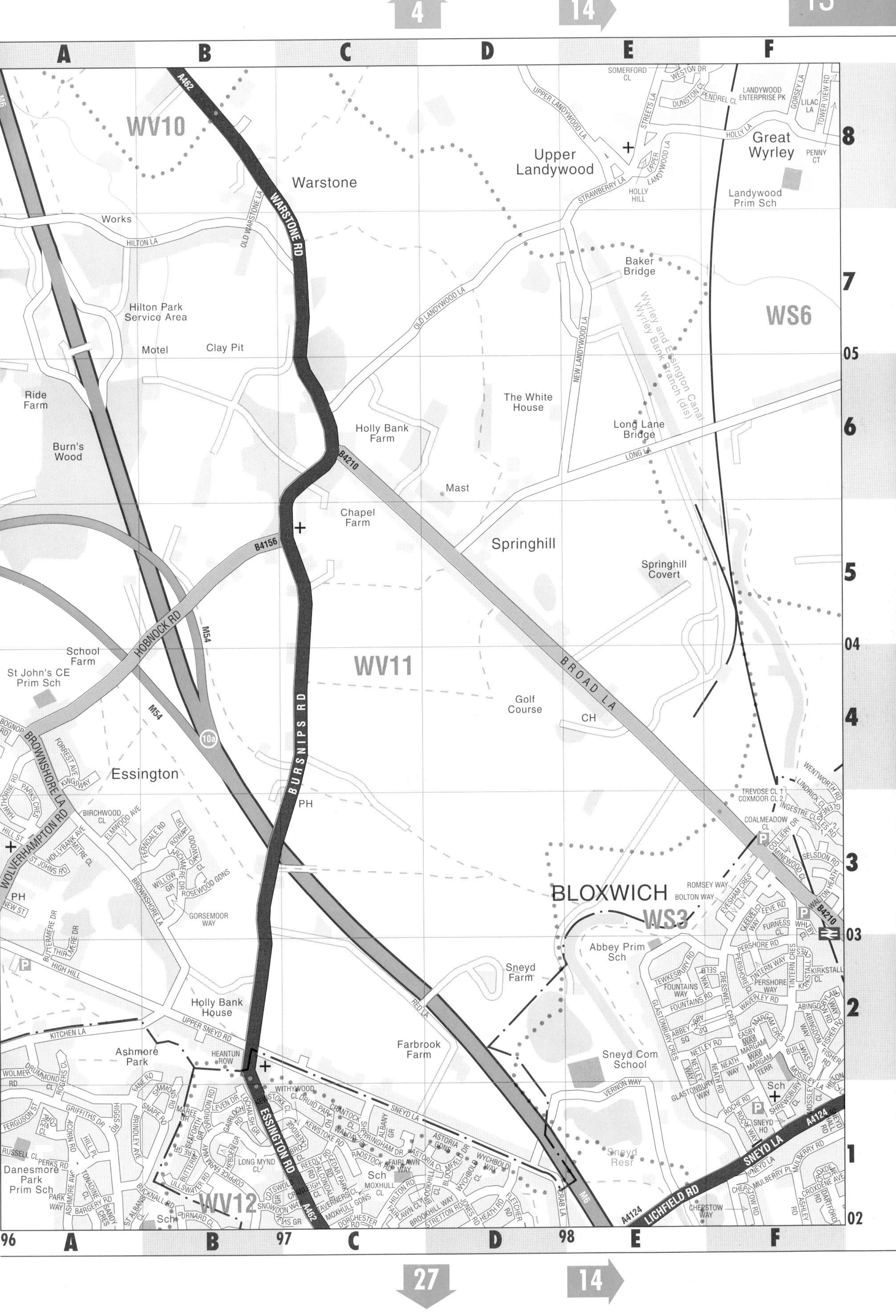
A
B
C
D
E
F
WV10
Warstone
Upper Landywood
Great Wyrley
Landywood Prim Sch
Works
HILTON LA
WARSTONE RD
Baker Bridge
WS6
Hilton Park Service Area
Motel
Clay Pit
Ride Farm
Burn's Wood
The White House
Holly Bank Farm
Long Lane Bridge
LONG LA
Wyrley and Essington Canal Wyrley Bank Branch (dis)
B4210
Mast
Chapel Farm
Springhill
Springhill Covert
B4156
HOBNOCK RD
M54
School Farm
St John's CE Prim Sch
WV11
BROAD LA
Golf Course
CH
BURSNIPS RD
Essington
PH
BLOXWICH
WS3
Abbey Prim Sch
Sneyd Farm
Holly Bank House
Farbrook Farm
Sneyd Com School
Ashmore Park
ESSINGTON RD
Danesmore Park Prim Sch
WV12
Sch
Sneyd Resr
LICHFIELD RD
SNEYD LA
A4124
M6
8
7
05
6
5
04
4
3
03
2
1
02
96
97
98

13 5

A B C D E F
8 7 6 5 4 3 2 1
WS6
WS3
WALSALL
BLOXWICH
Little Wyrley
Little Wyrley Hall
Hobble End
Newtown
Fishley
Little Bloxwich
Wallington Heath
Pelsall Wood
The Hills
Oakenhayes Farm
Newtack Farm
Lower Farm
Home Farm
Hobble End Farm
Wyrley Common Bridge
Wyrley Grove Bridge
Green Bridge
Pelsall Common Bridge
Pelsall Junction
Golf Range
Pear Tree Farm
Wood Common
Fishley Bridge No 1
Freemasons Arms (PH)
Ivy House (PH)
Newtown Farm
Golf Course
Yieldfields Hall
Lower Farm Cty Prim Sch
Little Bloxwich CE Prim Sch
Pelsall Jun Mixed & Inf Schs
T P Riley Com Sch
St Peter's RC Sch
Goscote House Farm
Field House Farm
Goscote Hall Bridge
Wyrley & Essington Canal
Cannock Extension Canal
Beacon Way
Wash Brook
WALSALL RD
STAFFORD RD
LICHFIELD RD
WOLVERHAMPTON RD
BELL LA
HIGH ST
BROAD LA
HOBBLE END LA
LONG LA
FISHLEY LA
WYRLEY LA
CADMAN'S LA
1 HOLLINWELL CL
2 THE BERKSHIRE
3 ALDEBURGH CL
4 MAXSTOKE CL
5 MUXLOE CL
6 KEDLESTON CL
1 THOMAS HO
2 SMITH HO
1 LAMBOURN CL
2 WALLINGTON CL
B1
1 DAVIES HO
2 CARTWRIGHT HO
3 CLARKE HO
4 WIGHTWICK CL
5 ROCKINGHAM CL
6 QUEENS PAR
7 THE EXCHANGE
99 00 01
05 04 03 02

13 28

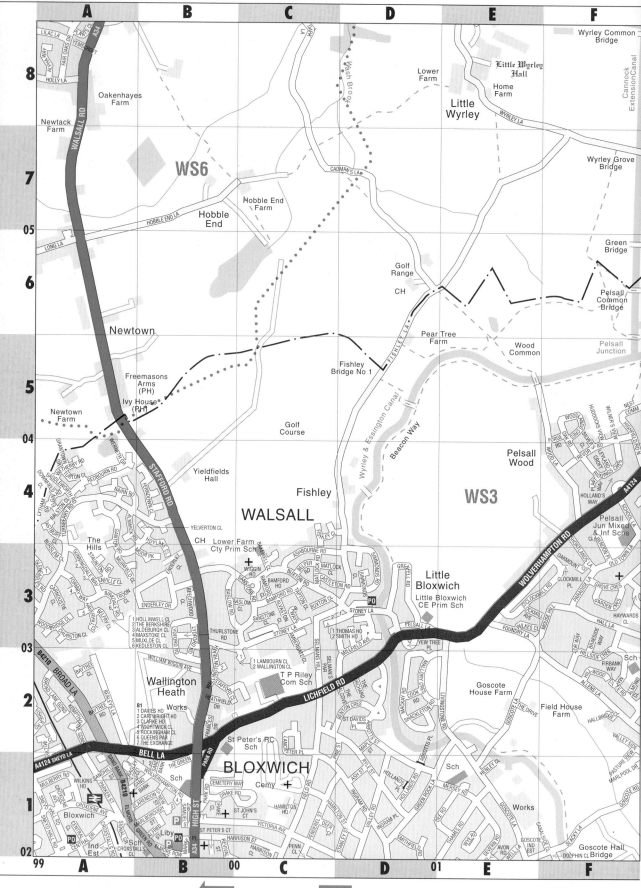

6
16

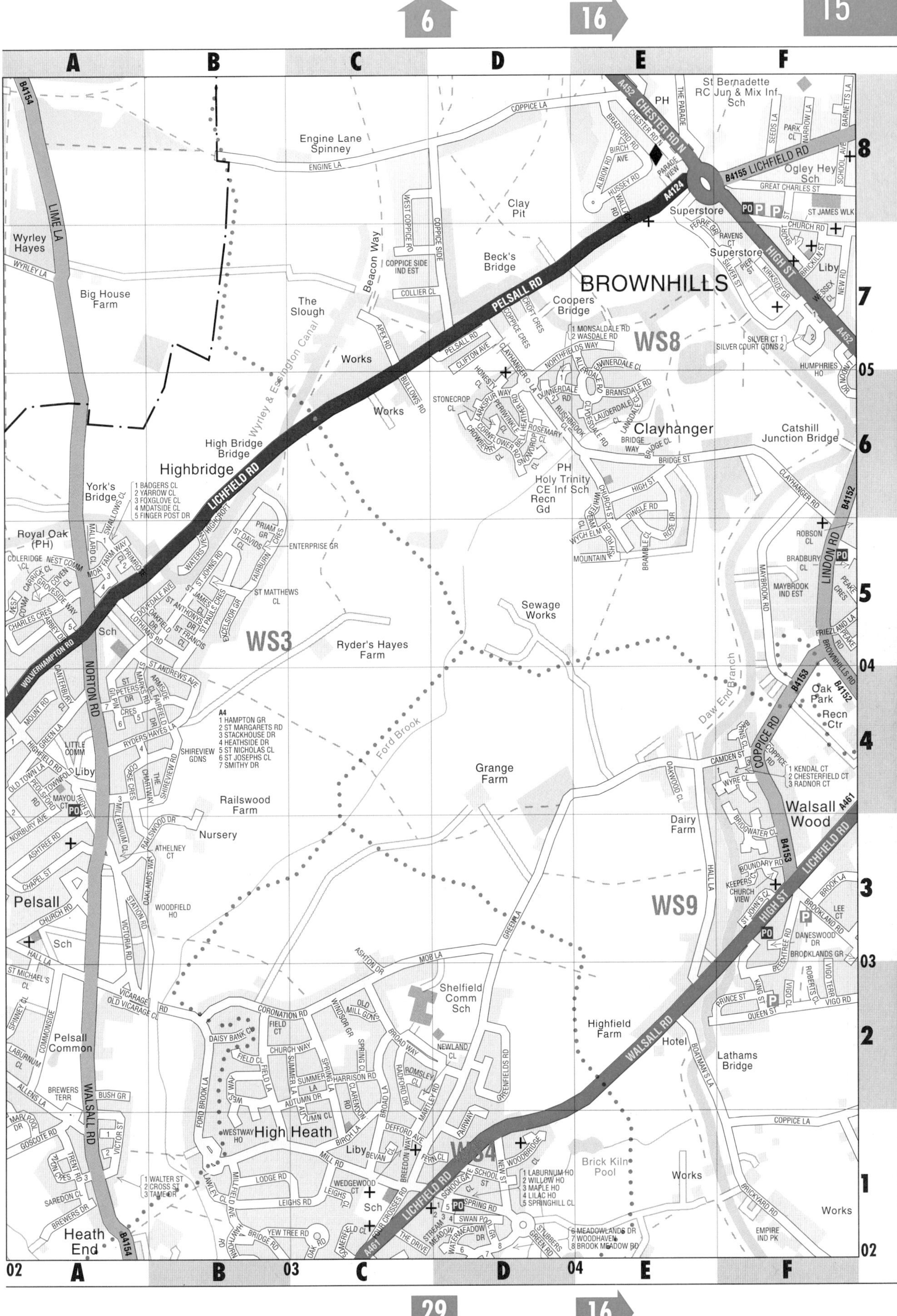
A
B
C
D
E
F
8
7
05
6
04
4
3
03
2
1
02
02
03
04
BROWNHILLS
WS8
WS3
WS9
WS4
Clayhanger
Highbridge
Pelsall
High Heath
Walsall Wood
Heath End
Wyrley Hayes
Big House Farm
Engine Lane Spinney
The Slough
Clay Pit
Beck's Bridge
Coopers Bridge
Works
High Bridge Bridge
York's Bridge
Royal Oak (PH)
Sewage Works
Ryder's Hayes Farm
Grange Farm
Railswood Farm
Nursery
Dairy Farm
Highfield Farm
Hotel
Lathams Bridge
Brick Kiln Pool
Shelfield Comm Sch
Pelsall Common
Catshill Junction Bridge
Holy Trinity CE Inf Sch
Recn Gd
Oak Park
Recn Ctr
St Bernadette RC Jun & Mix Inf Sch
Ogley Hey Sch
Superstore
Liby
Sch
PH
Wyrley & Essington Canal
Ford Brook
Daw End Branch
LIME LA
NORTON RD
WALSALL RD
LICHFIELD RD
PELSALL RD
WOLVERHAMPTON RD
CHESTER RD N
HIGH ST
COPPICE RD
LINDON RD
B4154
B4155
B4152
B4153
A452
A4124
A461
COPPICE LA
ENGINE LA
WYRLEY LA
BRIDGE ST
MOB LA
GREEN LA
HALL LA
CORONATION RD
COPPICE LA
EMPIRE IND PK
MAYBROOK IND EST
COPPICE SIDE IND EST
1 BADGERS CL
2 YARROW CL
3 FOXGLOVE CL
4 MOATSIDE CL
5 FINGER POST DR
A4
1 HAMPTON GR
2 ST MARGARETS RD
3 STACKHOUSE DR
4 HEATHSIDE DR
5 ST NICHOLAS CL
6 ST JOSEPHS CL
7 SMITHY DR
1 MONSALDALE RD
2 WASDALE RD
1 KENDAL CT
2 CHESTERFIELD CT
3 RADNOR CT
1 WALTER ST
2 CROSS ST
3 TAME GR
1 LABURNUM HO
2 WILLOW HO
3 MAPLE HO
4 LILAC HO
5 SPRINGHILL CL
6 MEADOWLANDS DR
7 WOODHAVEN
8 BROOK MEADOW RD
SILVER CT 1
SILVER COURT GDNS 2

29
16

15
7

A
B
C
D
E
F
8
7
6
5
4
3
2
1
05
04
03
02
05
06
07
LICHFIELD RD
B4155
FOURTH AVE
SECOND AVE
FIRST AVE
B5011
Works
POPLAR AVE
POPLAR RD
GREAT CHARLES ST
VERNON AVE
VICARAGE CL
FIRST ST
CEDAR AVE
SADLER RD
VICARAGE RD
OGLEY CRES
OGLEY RD
MILL RD
SADLERS MILL
SPRINGHILL RD
Wyrley & Essington Canal
VALLEY VIEW
MILLFIELD
CATSHILL RD
WARREN PL
Millfield JMI Sch
A452
HIGH ST
FULLELOVE RD
HODGKINS CL
LINDON DR
LINDON CL
1 BAYLEY HO
2 WAINE HO
3 CHANDLERS KEEP
Catshill
BROWNHILLS
B4152
LINDON RD
HARLEY CL
WS8
Shire Oak
HILLSIDE
COMMON SIDE
CAPE CL
SIMMONDS WAY
HILLSIDE CL
FRIEZLAND WAY
PATERSON PL
WREKIN VIEW
ST JOHNS RD
COLLINS RD
ADAMS RD
PAULS COPPICE
FRIEZLAND LA
ST MARKS RD
MARKLEW CL
LINDON VIEW
PEAKE CRES
PROFFITT CL
COMMON SIDE
PEAKE RD
Shire Oak Com Sch
PARKWOOD CL
OCCUPATION RD
LITTLE LAWNS CL
Walsall Wood JMI Sch
BROWNHILLS RD
B4152
LICHFIELD RD
WEATHEROAKS
ANDREWS RD
SHIRE RIDGE
NAOMI WAY
GAIL CL
HILL PK
SWALLOWDALE
ARBOR GATE
STREETS CORNER GDNS
BLACKBERRY LA
PRIORY CT
WOLVERSON RD
GWENDOLINE WAY
A461
Liby
BROOK LA
BROOK CL
STACKHOUSE CL
SALLY WARD DR
HOLLY LA
FEREDAY RD
SIMPKINS CL
OAK RD
POXON RD
Sch
BEACON WAY
Sch
HIGHLAND RD
FOX WLK
BROOK LA
LABURNUM RD
DRUIDS WLK
BLAKEMORE RD
Sch
BLUEBELL RD
CORONATION RD
NEW WOOD GR
SALTER'S RD
DIANA CL
STEWART RD
FORT CRES
CASTLEFORT RD
LINK RD
CASTLEHILL RD
LAWNSWOOD DR
BROOKLAND RD
CASTLE RD
Holly Bank
VIGO RD
SUNNYSIDE
Works
Vigo
GREENWOOD RD
GREEN WAY
FAR VIEW
BANKSIDE WAY
CHURCHSIDE WAY
HIGHFIELD WAY
HIGH CROFT
HILL VIEW
COPPICE LA
NORTHGATE
GRANGE AVE
ST THOMAS CL
JORDAN WAY
GREENWOOD PK
LONGLEAT RD
HEADBOROUGH WLK
KINGSHAYES RD
HEYGATE WAY
WOOD END WAY
HILL TOP WLK
1 STAMFORD WAY
2 MARCH WAY
WALTON RD
CLIVEDEN AVE
BRANCHAL RD
BAR WLK
WALSALL WOOD RD
GLENDOWER RD
WIDNEY AVE
GREENHILL WAY
LAZY HILL RD
LEIGHSWOOD IND PK
BROOKFIELD CL
HERBERT RD
JESSIE RD
LEACROFT CL
SANDRINGHAM DR
COTSWOLD CL
BROOKFIELD RD
CORNWALL CL
RUTLAND CRES
COPPY HALL GR
KINVER CRES
MALVERN DR
WARWICK WAY 1
SURREY WLK 2
B4152
DORSET DR
KENT CL
DRUIDS AVE
KNOLL CROFT
CLIFTON AVE
LEDBURY CL
BARRACKS LA
Summerhill
A461
Little Oaks Farm
Ivy House Farm
Crane Brook
WALSALL RD
The Springhill Farm
Springhill
POUK LA
Poplars Farm
Hope Cottage Farm
WS14
Sandhills Farm
WHITACRE LA
Whiteacre Farm
CRANEBROOK LA
Home Farm
Fighting Cocks' Farm
CARTERSFIELD LA
LYNN LA
Shepherds Farm
Sand & Gravel Pit
HEATH CL
WALLHEATH CRES
WALL HEATH LA
BERRYFIELDS
LOWER FARM
St Peter's CE Prim Sch
GARNET CL
WESTWICK CL
THORNES CROFT
WS9
MILL LA
MAIN ST
CHURCH LA
PH
ST PETER'S CL
Stonnall
Thornes House
PO
GLENWOOD RISE
Castlebank Plantation
CHESTER RD
CHURCH RD
Thornes Hall Farm
Grove Hill
GRAVELLY LA
LAZY HILL
Gainsborough Hill Farm
BIRCH LA
Birch Farm
STONNALL RD
BACK LA
A452
WOOD LA

15
30

8
18

A
B
C
D
E
F
8
7
05
6
5
04
4
3
03
2
1
02
08
09
10
Barn Farm
Hilton
Hilton Farm
CRANEBROOK LA
Cranebrook Farm
THORNYHURST LA
Bullmoor Lane Covert
BULLMOOR LA
HORSLEY LA
Crane Brook
Chesterfield Lodge
Chesterfield Farm
Chesterfield
Lawton Grange
ASHCROFT LA
Ashcroft Farm
Poultry Houses
RAIKES LA
Gayley Cottage
Keeper's Cottage
Malkin's Coppice
FODEN CL
GROSVENOR CT
MILLBROOK DR
PINFOLD HILL
CROFT
LINCOLN
HOLM VIEW CL
STATION RD
PO
ASTON CL
TRINITY CL
MAIN ST
Lynn Lane House
LYNN LA
BIRCH BROOK LA
BIRCHBROOK IND PK
Shenstone
Dairy Farm
NEW RD
ADMIRAL PARKER DR
RICHARD COOPER RD
CHURCH RD
Shenstone
The Bungalow
Owlett Hall Farm
WS14
FOOTHERLEY RD
ST JOHN'S HILL
Lynn
The Nurseries
HOLLY HILL RD
CHESTNUT DR
Footherley Rough
HOLLYHILL LA
ST JOHN'S DR
Laurels Farm
MILL LA
Lower Stonnall
Keeper's Cottage
COURT DR
Swan Farm
Spinney Farm
FOOTHERLEY LA
Footherley Hall
Shenstone Court
NEW BARNS LA
HOOK LA
GRAVELLY LA
Home Farm
Footherley
New Barns Farm
Griffin's Covert
Footherley Brook
WS9
Cockheath Coppice
Croft Farm
Footherley Farm
Bagot's Barn
MOOR LA
Whites Farm
WOOD LA
Biddle's Field Wood
Bosses
BACK LA
FORGE LA

31
18

17
9

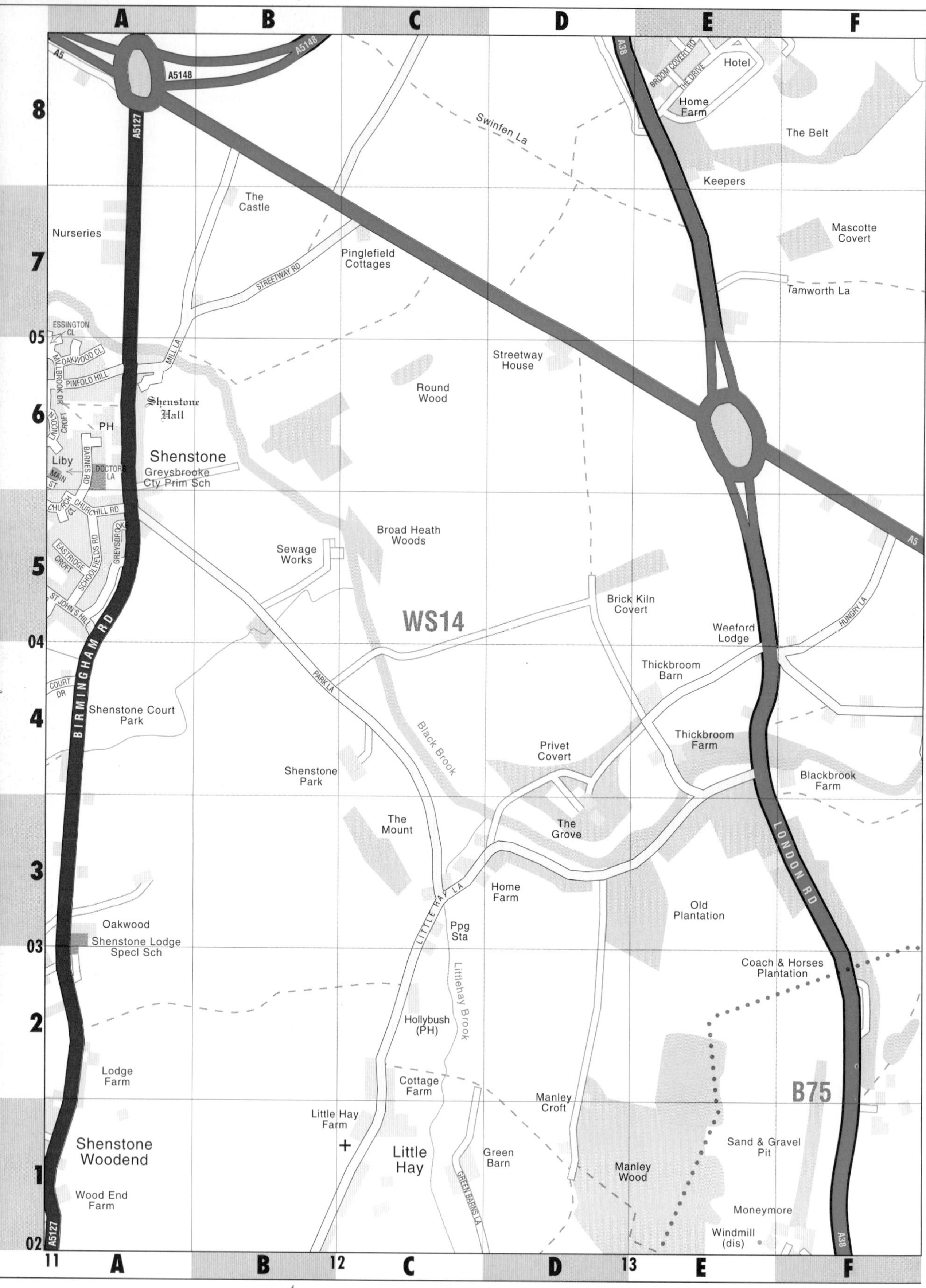
A
B
C
D
E
F
8
7
05
6
5
04
4
3
03
2
1
02
11
12
13
A5
A5148
A5127
A38
Hotel
BROOM COVERT RD
THE DRIVE
Home Farm
The Belt
Keepers
Swinfen La
The Castle
Nurseries
Pinglefield Cottages
STREETWAY RD
Mascotte Covert
Tamworth La
ESSINGTON CL
OAKWOOD CL
MILLBROOK DR
PINFOLD HILL
MILL LA
LINCROFT
Shenstone Hall
PH
Shenstone
Liby
BARNES RD
DOCTORS LA
MAIN ST
Greysbrooke Cty Prim Sch
Streetway House
Round Wood
CHURCH CL
CHURCH RD
HILL RD
EASTRIDGE CROFT
SCHOOLFIELDS RD
GREYSBROOKE
ST JOHN'S HILL
Broad Heath Woods
Sewage Works
WS14
Brick Kiln Covert
BIRMINGHAM RD
Weeford Lodge
HUNGRY LA
COURT DR
PARK LA
Thickbroom Barn
Shenstone Court Park
Black Brook
Privet Covert
Thickbroom Farm
Shenstone Park
Blackbrook Farm
The Mount
The Grove
LONDON RD
LITTLE HAY LA
Home Farm
Old Plantation
Oakwood
Ppg Sta
Shenstone Lodge Specl Sch
Coach & Horses Plantation
Littlehay Brook
Hollybush (PH)
Lodge Farm
Cottage Farm
B75
Manley Croft
Little Hay Farm
Shenstone Woodend
Little Hay
Green Barn
Sand & Gravel Pit
GREEN BARNS LA
Manley Wood
Wood End Farm
Moneymore
Windmill (dis)

17
32

20

A
B
C
D
E
F
8
7
05
6
5
04
4
3
03
2
1
02
14
15
16
Broadfields
Packington Moor
JERRY'S LA
A51
Hopwas Hays Wood
Moor Covert
Common Barn
Heart of England Way
Tamworth La
KNOX'S GRAVE LA
Riding School
HOPWAS HILL
Sand & Gravel Pit
Packington Farm
WS14
Buck's Head Cottages
Hare Park Wood
FLATS LA
PACKINGTON LA
Mast
Transmitting Sta
Rodbaston Coll
The Devil's Dressing Room
Weeford
Buck's Head Farm
B78
Hanging Wood
Church Wood
Sand & Gravel Pit
Long Island
Common Plantation
DOG LA
The Lodge
Black Brook
ROCK HILL
HINTS LA
Hints Lane Farm
Bourne House
Snake's Hill
Gold's Clump
Hints
Hints Hill
Manor Farm
Job's Hill
Rough Leasow
Home Farm
SCHOOL LA
A5
Bangley Lodge
ROOKERY LA
Ford
HINTS CT
Gorsey Hill
Botley House
Rookery
Sewage Works
Crow's Castle
Bourne Brook
B75
Rookery Farm
New Plantation
White Owl Farm
Roundhill Wood
BROCKHURST LA

33
20

19

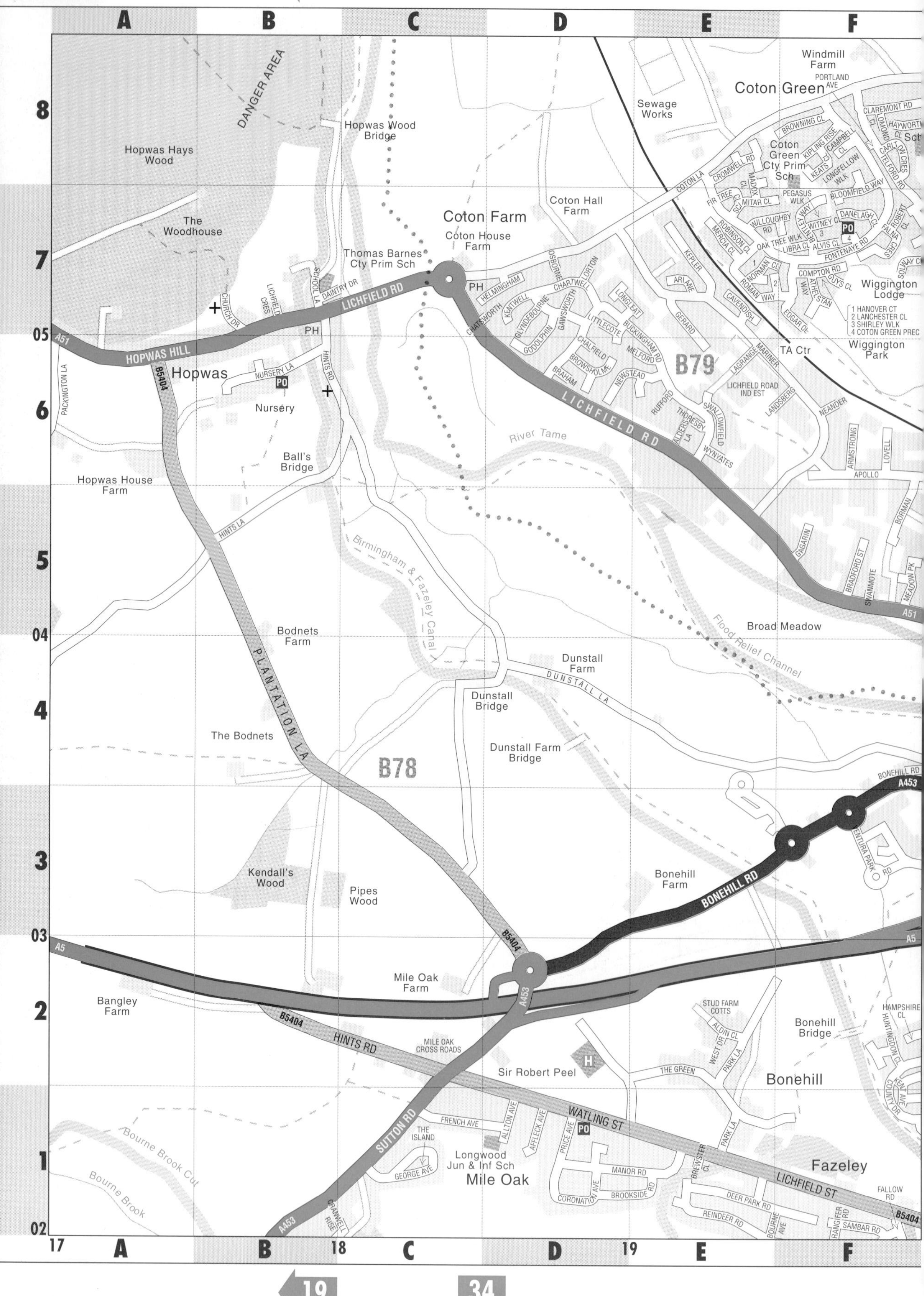
A B C D E F
8
7
05
6
5
04
4
3
03
2
1
02
17 18 19
Hopwas Hays Wood
DANGER AREA
Hopwas Wood Bridge
The Woodhouse
Coton Farm
Coton House Farm
Coton Hall Farm
Thomas Barnes Cty Prim Sch
Sewage Works
Windmill Farm
Coton Green
Coton Green Cty Prim Sch
Wiggington Lodge
Wiggington Park
1 HANOVER CT
2 LANCHESTER CL
3 SHIRLEY WLK
4 COTON GREEN PREC
TA Ctr
LICHFIELD ROAD IND EST
B79
LICHFIELD RD
HOPWAS HILL
A51
B5404
Hopwas
Nursery
Ball's Bridge
River Tame
Hopwas House Farm
HINTS LA
HINTS RD
PACKINGTON LA
Birmingham & Fazeley Canal
Bodnets Farm
PLANTATION LA
Dunstall Farm
DUNSTALL LA
Dunstall Bridge
Dunstall Farm Bridge
The Bodnets
B78
Broad Meadow
Flood Relief Channel
Kendall's Wood
Pipes Wood
Bonehill Farm
BONEHILL RD
A453
A5
Mile Oak Farm
Bangley Farm
MILE OAK CROSS ROADS
Sir Robert Peel
WATLING ST
SUTTON RD
Longwood Jun & Inf Sch
Mile Oak
Bonehill
Bonehill Bridge
Fazeley
LICHFIELD ST
Bourne Brook Cut
Bourne Brook
STUD FARM COTTS
THE GREEN
THE ISLAND
FRENCH AVE
GEORGE AVE
MANOR RD
BROOKSIDE RD
CORONATION AVE
DEER PARK RD
REINDEER RD
SAMBAR RD
FALLOW RD
CRANWELL RISE
BREWSTER CL
PARK LA
ALDIN CL
WEST DR
HAMPSHIRE CL
HUNTINGDON CL
KENT AVE
COUNTY DR
VENTURA PARK RD
BONEHILL RD
PH
PO
H

19
34

22

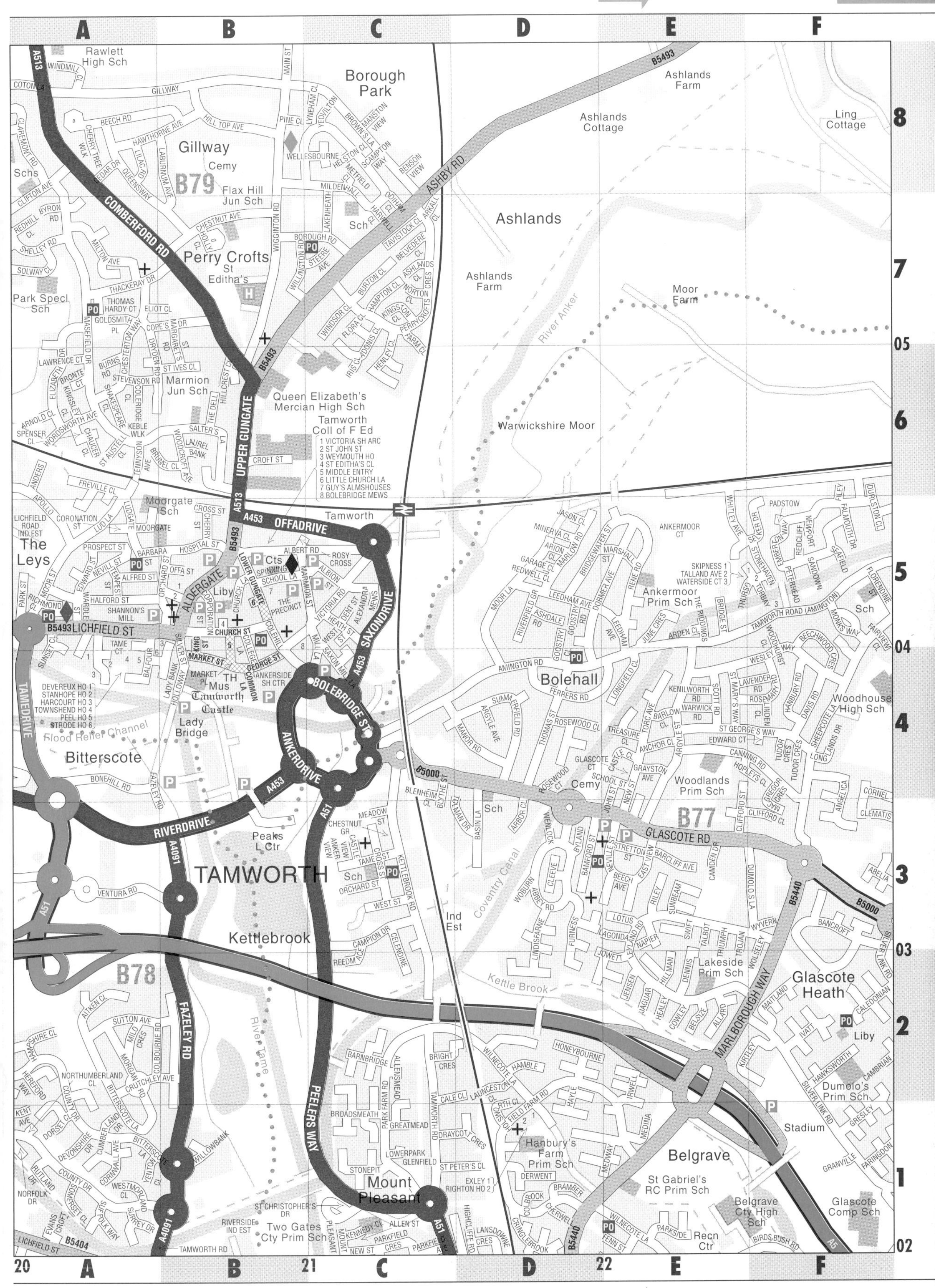
A
B
C
D
E
F
8
7
05
6
5
04
4
3
03
2
1
02
20
21
22
Rawlett High Sch
Borough Park
Ashlands Farm
Ashlands Cottage
Ling Cottage
Gillway
Cemy
B79
Flax Hill Jun Sch
Schs
Ashlands
Perry Crofts
St Editha's
Ashlands Farm
Moor Farm
Park Specl Sch
COMBERFORD RD
ASHBY RD
B5493
A513
GILLWAY
UPPER GUNGATE
Marmion Jun Sch
Queen Elizabeth's Mercian High Sch
Tamworth Coll of F Ed
1 VICTORIA SH ARC
2 ST JOHN ST
3 WEYMOUTH HO
4 ST EDITHA'S CL
5 MIDDLE ENTRY
6 LITTLE CHURCH LA
7 GUY'S ALMSHOUSES
8 BOLEBRIDGE MEWS
Warwickshire Moor
River Anker
Moorgate Sch
The Leys
Tamworth
A453 OFFADRIVE
SAXONDRIVE
ALDERGATE
LICHFIELD ST
Ankermoor Prim Sch
Sch
Bolehall
TAMWORTH ROAD (AMINGTON)
AMINGTON RD
Woodhouse High Sch
DEVEREUX HO 1
STANHOPE HO 2
HARCOURT HO 3
TOWNSHEND HO 4
PEEL HO 5
STRODE HO 6
SKIPNESS 1
TALLAND AVE 2
WATERSIDE CT 3
Mus
TH
Tamworth Castle
Lady Bridge
Flood Relief Channel
Bitterscote
BOLEBRIDGE ST
ANKERDRIVE
TAMEDRIVE
RIVERDRIVE
B5000
Cemy
Woodlands Prim Sch
B77
GLASCOTE RD
Peaks L Ctr
TAMWORTH
Coventry Canal
Ind Est
Kettlebrook
B78
Lakeside Prim Sch
Glascote Heath
Kettle Brook
River Tame
FAZELEY RD
PEELERS WAY
MARLBOROUGH WAY
Liby
Dumolo's Prim Sch
Stadium
Hanbury's Farm Prim Sch
Belgrave
St Gabriel's RC Prim Sch
Belgrave Cty High Sch
Glascote Comp Sch
Mount Pleasant
Two Gates Cty Prim Sch
Recn Ctr
RIVERSIDE IND EST
LICHFIELD ST
B5404
TAMWORTH RD
A4091
A51
A5
B5440

35
22

21

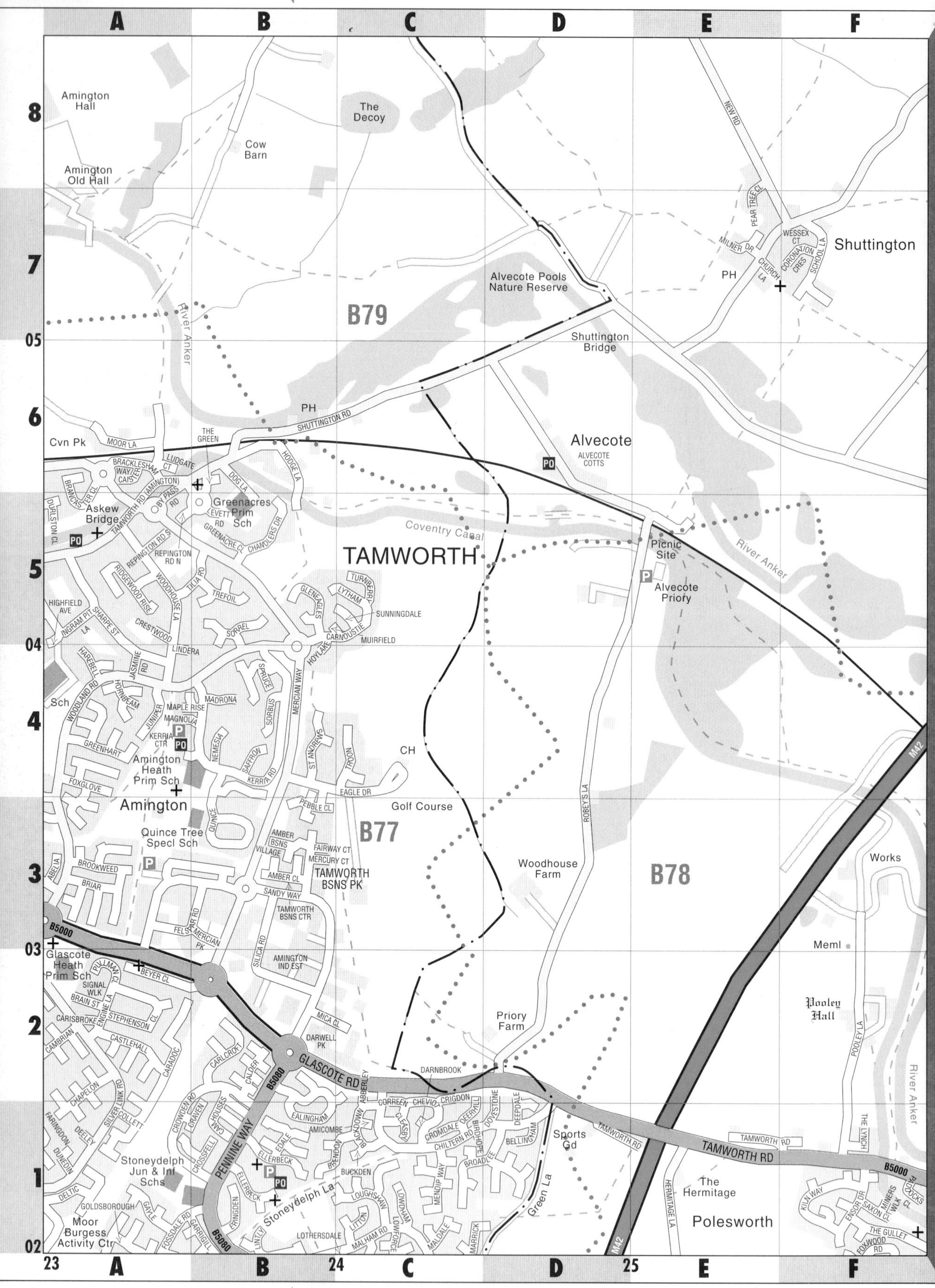

Amington Hall
The Decoy
Cow Barn
Amington Old Hall
Shuttington
Alvecote Pools Nature Reserve
B79
River Anker
Shuttington Bridge
SHUTTINGTON RD
Alvecote
Coventry Canal
TAMWORTH
Picnic Site
Alvecote Priory
Askew Bridge
Greenacres Prim Sch
Amington Heath Prim Sch
Amington
Quince Tree Specl Sch
Golf Course
B77
Woodhouse Farm
B78
TAMWORTH BSNS PK
ROBEY'S LA
Works
Meml
Pooley Hall
Glascote Heath Prim Sch
Priory Farm
GLASCOTE RD
PENNINE WAY
Stoneydelph Jun & Inf Schs
Stoneydelph La
Green La
Sports Gd
TAMWORTH RD
The Hermitage
Polesworth
Moor Burgess Activity Ctr
M42
B5000
B5080

21
36

24

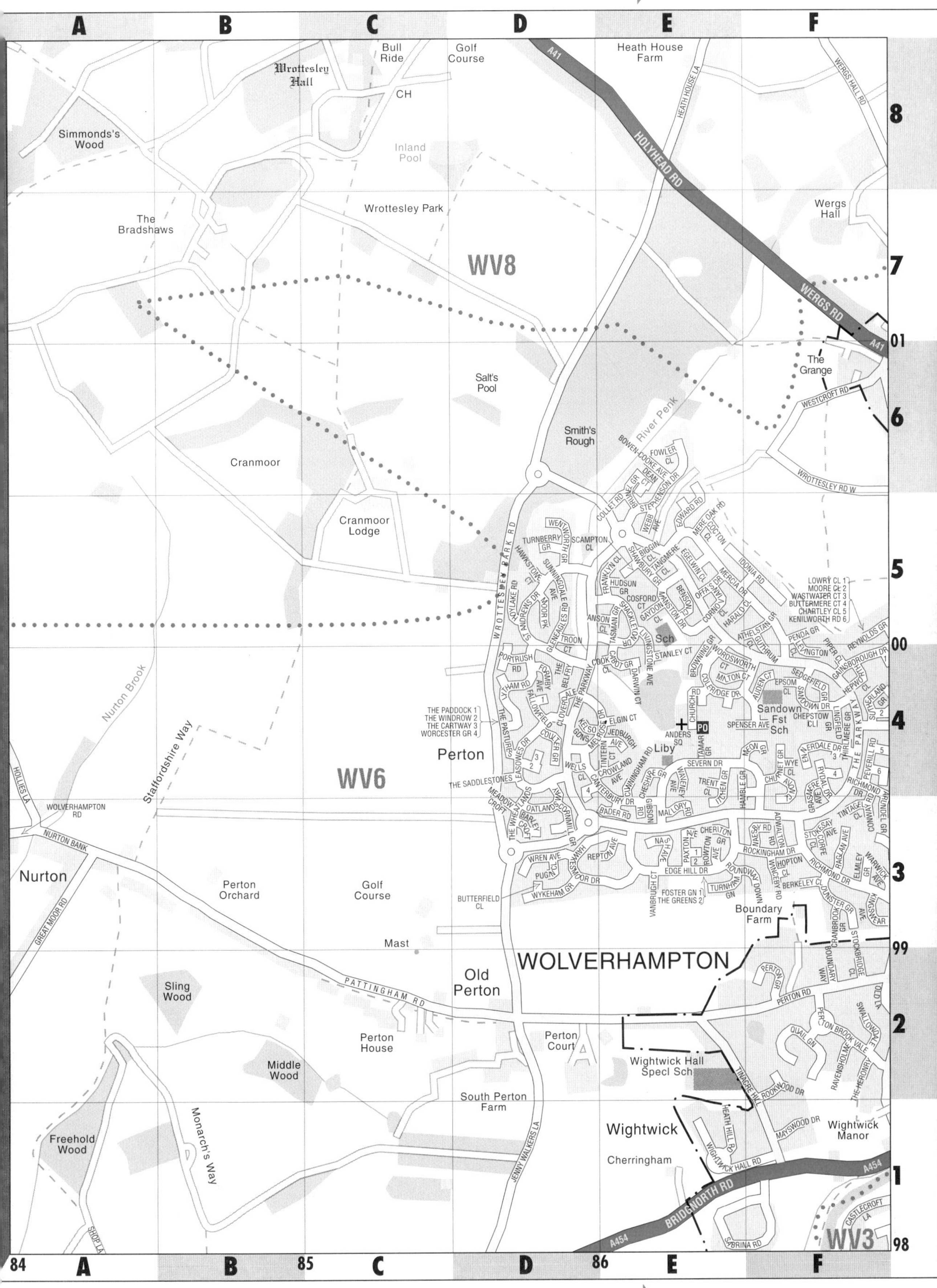
A
B
C
D
E
F
Bull Ride
Golf Course
Heath House Farm
Wrottesley Hall
CH
Simmonds's Wood
Inland Pool
HEATH HOUSE LA
HOLYHEAD RD
WERGS HALL RD
The Bradshaws
Wrottesley Park
Wergs Hall
WV8
WERGS RD
A41
The Grange
WESTCROFT RD
Salt's Pool
River Penk
Smith's Rough
Cranmoor
Cranmoor Lodge
WROTTESLEY RD W
WROTTESLEY PARK RD
LOWRY CL 1
MOORE CL 2
WASTWATER CT 3
BUTTERMERE CT 4
CHARTLEY CL 5
KENILWORTH RD 6
Sch
Sandown Fst Sch
THE PADDOCK 1
THE WINDROW 2
THE CARTWAY 3
WORCESTER GR 4
Perton
Liby
ANDERS SQ
PO
Nurton Brook
Staffordshire Way
HOLLIES LA
WV6
THE SADDLESTONES
WOLVERHAMPTON RD
NURTON BANK
Nurton
GREAT MOOR RD
Perton Orchard
Golf Course
BUTTERFIELD CL
FOSTER GN 1
THE GREENS 2
Boundary Farm
Mast
WOLVERHAMPTON
Sling Wood
PATTINGHAM RD
Old Perton
PERTON RD
Perton House
Perton Court
Middle Wood
Wightwick Hall Specl Sch
South Perton Farm
Monarch's Way
Freehold Wood
JENNY WALKERS LA
Wightwick
Cherringham
Wightwick Manor
BRIDGNORTH RD
A454
SHOP LA
SABRINA RD
CASTLECROFT LA
WV3
8
7
01
6
5
00
4
3
99
2
1
98
84
85
86

37

24

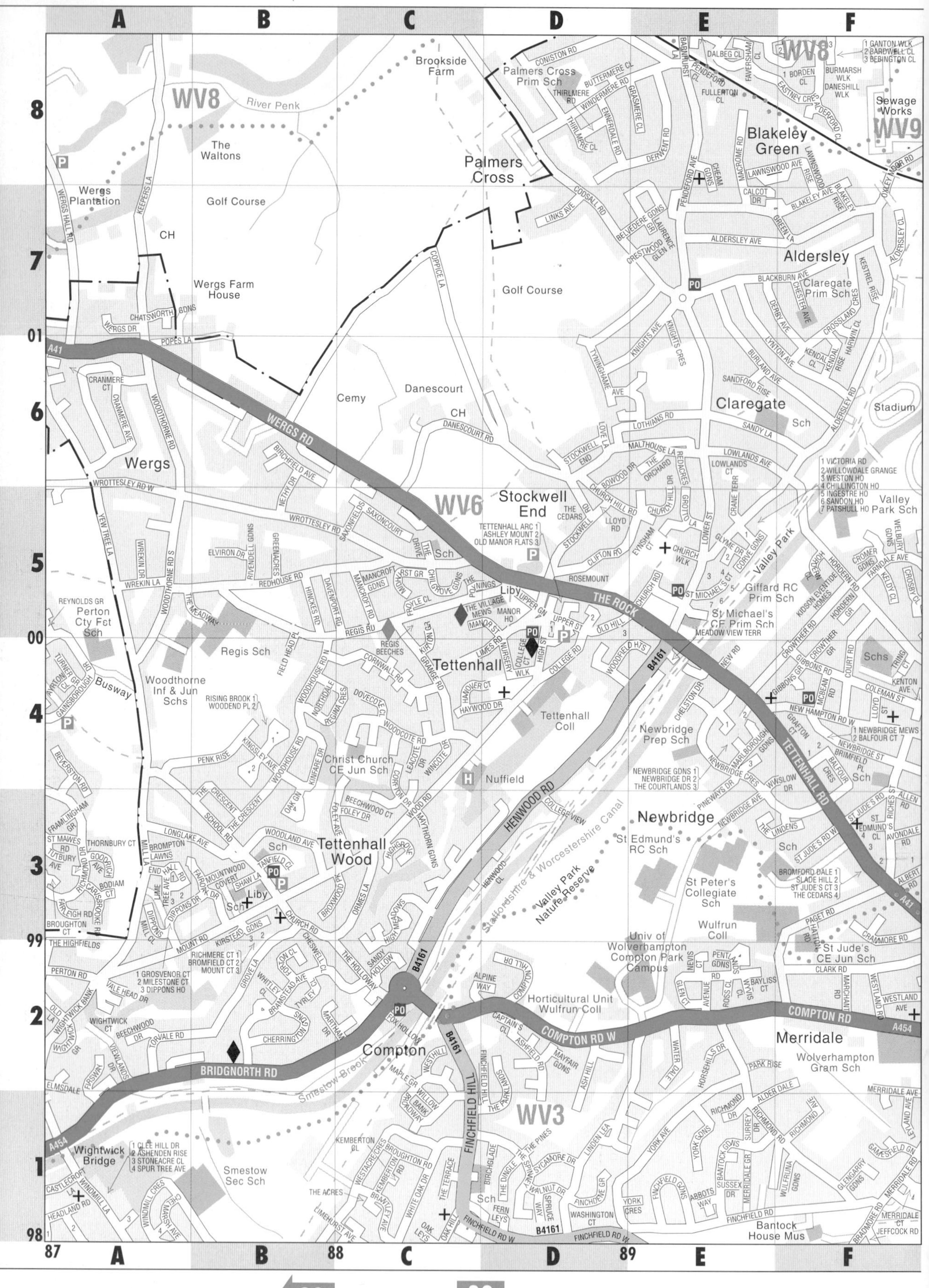
A B C D E F
8 7 01 6 5 00 4 3 99 2 1 98
87 88 89
WV8
River Penk
The Waltons
Brookside Farm
Palmers Cross Prim Sch
Palmers Cross
Wergs Plantation
Golf Course
CH
Wergs Farm House
WERGS HALL RD
KEEPERS LA
CHATSWORTH GDNS
WERGS DR
POPES LA
A41
COPPICE LA
CONISTON RD
BUTTERMERE CL
WINDERMERE RD
THIRLMERE RD
GRASMERE CL
ENNERDALE RD
THIRLMERE CL
DERWENT RD
CODSALL RD
LINKS AVE
BARNHURST LA
PENDEFORD AVE
FULLERTON CL
DALBEG CL
FAVERSHAM CL
BORDEN CL
EASTNEY CRES
BURMARSH WLK
DANESHILL WLK
1 GANTON WLK
2 BARDWELL CL
3 BEBINGTON CL
Sewage Works
WV9
Blakeley Green
CHEAM GDNS
MACROME RD
LAWNSWOOD AVE
LAWNSWOOD RISE
CALCOT DR
BLAKELEY AVE
BLAKELEY RISE
GREEN LA
OXLEY MOOR RD
ALDERSLEY AVE
Aldersley
ALDERSLEY CL
BELVEDERE GDNS
LAURENCE GR
CRESTWOOD GLEN
BLACKBURN AVE
Claregate Prim Sch
CHESTER AVE
DERBY AVE
CROSSLAND CRES
KESTREL RISE
KNIGHTS AVE
KNIGHTS CRES
TYNINGHAME AVE
LYNTON AVE
KENDAL CL
KENDAL RISE
HARWIN CL
BURLAND AVE
SANDFORD RISE
Claregate
Sch
ALDERSLEY RD
Stadium
Golf Course
Cemy
Danescourt
CH
DANESCOURT RD
CRANMERE CT
CRANMERE AVE
WOODTHORNE RD
Wergs
WERGS RD
BIRCHFIELD AVE
NETHY DR
WROTTESLEY RD W
WROTTESLEY RD
YEW TREE LA
SAXONFIELDS
SAXONCOURT
THE DRIVE
Sch
WV6
Stockwell End
LOVE LA
LOTHIANS RD
SANDY LA
STOCKWELL END
MALTHOUSE LA
THE ORCHARD
REDACRES
LOWLANDS CT
LOWLANDS AVE
CRANE TERR
BOWOOD DR
CHURCH HILL RD
CHURCH HILL DR
GROTTO LA
LOWER ST
THE CEDARS
LLOYD RD
STOCKWELL RD
TETTENHALL ARC 1
ASHLEY MOUNT 2
OLD MANOR FLATS 3
EYNSHAM CT
CHURCH WLK
GLYME DR
CORVE GDNS
Valley Park
1 VICTORIA RD
2 WILLOWDALE GRANGE
3 WESTON HO
4 CHILLINGTON HO
5 INGESTRE HO
6 SANDON HO
7 PATSHULL HO
Valley Park Sch
WREKIN DR
WOODTHORNE RD S
ELVIRON DR
RIVENDELL GDNS
GREENACRES
WREKIN LA
REDHOUSE RD
HINCKES RD
DAVENPORT RD
MANCROFT GDNS
MANCROFT RD
FOYLE CL
CHILGROVE GDNS
THE POYNINGS
Liby
UPPER GN
THE VILLAGE MEWS
MANOR HO
MANOR ST
ROSEMOUNT
CLIFTON RD
THE ROCK
CHURCH RD
ST MICHAEL'S CT
Giffard RC Prim Sch
St Michael's CE Prim Sch
MEADOW VIEW TERR
CROMER GDNS
FARNDALE AVE
WELBURY GDNS
KELDY CL
CROSBY CL
HORDERN RD
HORDERN GR
KIDSON EVENTIDE HOMES
REYNOLDS GR
Perton Cty Fct Sch
THE MEADWAY
Regis Sch
FIELD HEAD PL
REGIS RD
REGIS BEECHES
KINGS CT
GRANGE RD
Tettenhall
LIMES RD
NURSERY WLK
COLLEGE CT
HIGH ST
UPPER ST
OLD HILL
COLLEGE RD
WOODFIELD HTS
B4161
NEW RD
CROWTHER RD
CROWTHER GR
GIBBONS GR
GIBBONS RD
COURT RD
Schs
TRING CT
KENTON AVE
COLEMAN ST
TURNER GR
AYNTON CL
GAINSBOROUGH DR
Busway
Woodthorne Inf & Jun Schs
RISING BROOK 1
WOODEND PL 2
WOODHOUSE RD N
NORTHDALE
REGINA CRES
CORNWALL RD
DOVECOTE CL
HANOVER CT
HAYWOOD DR
Tettenhall Coll
CHELSTON DR
Newbridge Prep Sch
MCBEAN RD
NEW HAMPTON RD W
LLOYD ST
GRAFTON CT
TETTENHALL RD
1 NEWBRIDGE MEWS
2 BALFOUR CT
NEWBRIDGE ST
BRIMFIELD PL
BALFOUR CRES
Sch
BEVERSTON RD
PENK RISE
KINGSLEY AVE
WOODHOUSE RD
KINFARE DR
Christ Church CE Jun Sch
WOODCOTE RD
LEACOTE DR
WINCOTE DR
Nuffield
NEWBRIDGE GDNS 1
NEWBRIDGE DR 2
THE COURTLANDS 3
MARLBOROUGH GDNS
NEWBRIDGE CRES
WINSLOW DR
PINEWAYS DR
FRAMLINGHAM GR
ST MAWES RD
TUTBURY AVE
THORNBURY CT
RICHMOND DR
GOODRICH AVE
CAINSBROOKE RD
BODIAM CT
THE CRESCENT
SCHOOL RD
OAK GN
BEECHWOOD CT
FOLEY DR
FOLEY AVE
CORNDON DR
WOOD RD
MAYTHORN GDNS
HENWOOD RD
COLLEGE VIEW
Newbridge
NEWBRIDGE AVE
THE LINDENS
ST JUDE'S RD
RICHES ST
ALLEN RD
ST EDMUND'S CL
AVONDALE RD
LONGLAKE AVE
BROMPTON LAWNS
MILL LA
END HALL RD
TREE AVE
LIME TREE
MOUNTWOOD COVERT
FAIRWAY
SHAW LA
WOODLAND AVE
TANFIELD CL
Sch
Tettenhall Wood
HIGHGROVE
Staffordshire & Worcestershire Canal
St Edmund's RC Sch
St Peter's Collegiate Sch
Valley Park Nature Reserve
HENWOOD CL
BROMFORD DALE 1
SLADE HILL 2
ST JUDE'S CT 3
THE CEDARS 4
ALBERT RD
Liby
Sch
DIPPONS LA
DIPPONS DR
FARLEIGH RD
BROUGHTON CT
THE HIGHFIELDS
BROXWOOD PK
ORMES LA
Wulfrun Coll
PAGET RD
HATTON RD
CRAMMORE RD
St Jude's CE Jun Sch
CLARK RD
MOUNT RD
KIRSTEAD GDNS
CHURCH RD
CHESWELL CL
THE HOLLOWAY
SANDY HOLLOW
HIGH MEADOWS
Univ of Wolverhampton Compton Park Campus
COMPTON HILL DR
PENTLAND GDNS
NEWIS CT
GLEN CT
AVENUE RD
ROSS CL
SYLVIS CL
BAYLISS CT
MARCHANT RD
WESTLAND RD
WESTLAND AVE
PERTON RD
RICHMERE CT 1
BROMFIELD CT 2
MOUNT CT 3
1 GROSVENOR CT
2 MILESTONE CT
3 DIPPONS HO
VALE HEAD DR
GROVE LA
WHITLEY CL
BRANSTEAD AVE
TYRLEY CL
TYNDALE CL
ALPINE WAY
Horticultural Unit Wulfrun Coll
COMPTON RD
COMPTON RD W
A454
Merridale
OLD LA
WIGHTWICK BANK
WIGHTWICK CT
WIGHTWICK GR
BEECHWOOD DR
TORVALE RD
VIEWLANDS DR
ORMISTON DR
BRIDGNORTH RD
CHERRINGTON GDNS
MARTHAM DR
FOX HOLLOW
Compton
CAPTAIN'S CL
ASHFIELD RD
MAYFAIR GDNS
ASH HILL
WATER DALE
HORSEHILLS DR
Wolverhampton Gram Sch
ELMSDALE
Smestow Brook
MAPLE GR
WESTHILL
WILLOW BANK
BROADWAY
FINCHFIELD HILL
SOMMERFORD
THE PARKLANDS
WV3
PARK RISE
ALDER DALE
RICHMOND DR
RICHMOND RD
SURREY DR
MERRIDALE AVE
LEYLAND AVE
Wightwick Bridge
1 CLEE HILL DR
2 ASHENDEN RISE
3 STONEACRE CL
4 SPUR TREE AVE
Smestow Sec Sch
KEMBERTON CL
WESTACRE CRES
BROUGHTON RD
KEMBERTON RD
THE TERRACE
BIRCHGLADE
THE DINGLE
THE PINES
THE SPINNEY
SYCAMORE DR
WALNUT DR
LINDEN LEA
YORK AVE
YORK GDNS
BANTOCK GDNS
SUSSEX DR
MERRIDALE GR
WULFRUNA GDNS
GLENGARRY GDNS
GAMESFIELD GN
MERRIDALE RD
CASTLECROFT LA
WINDMILL LA
HEADLAND RD
WINDMILL CRES
MARSH AVE
THE ACRES
LIMEHURST AVE
BRANTLEY AVE
WHITE OAK DR
OAK LEYS
OAK HILL
Sch
FERN LEYS
SPRUCE WAY
FINCHDENE GR
WASHINGTON CT
YORK CRES
FINCHFIELD GDNS
ABBOTS WAY
FINCHFIELD RD
FINCHFIELD RD W
Bantock House Mus
BRADMORE RD
MERRIDALE CT
JEFFCOCK RD

11
26

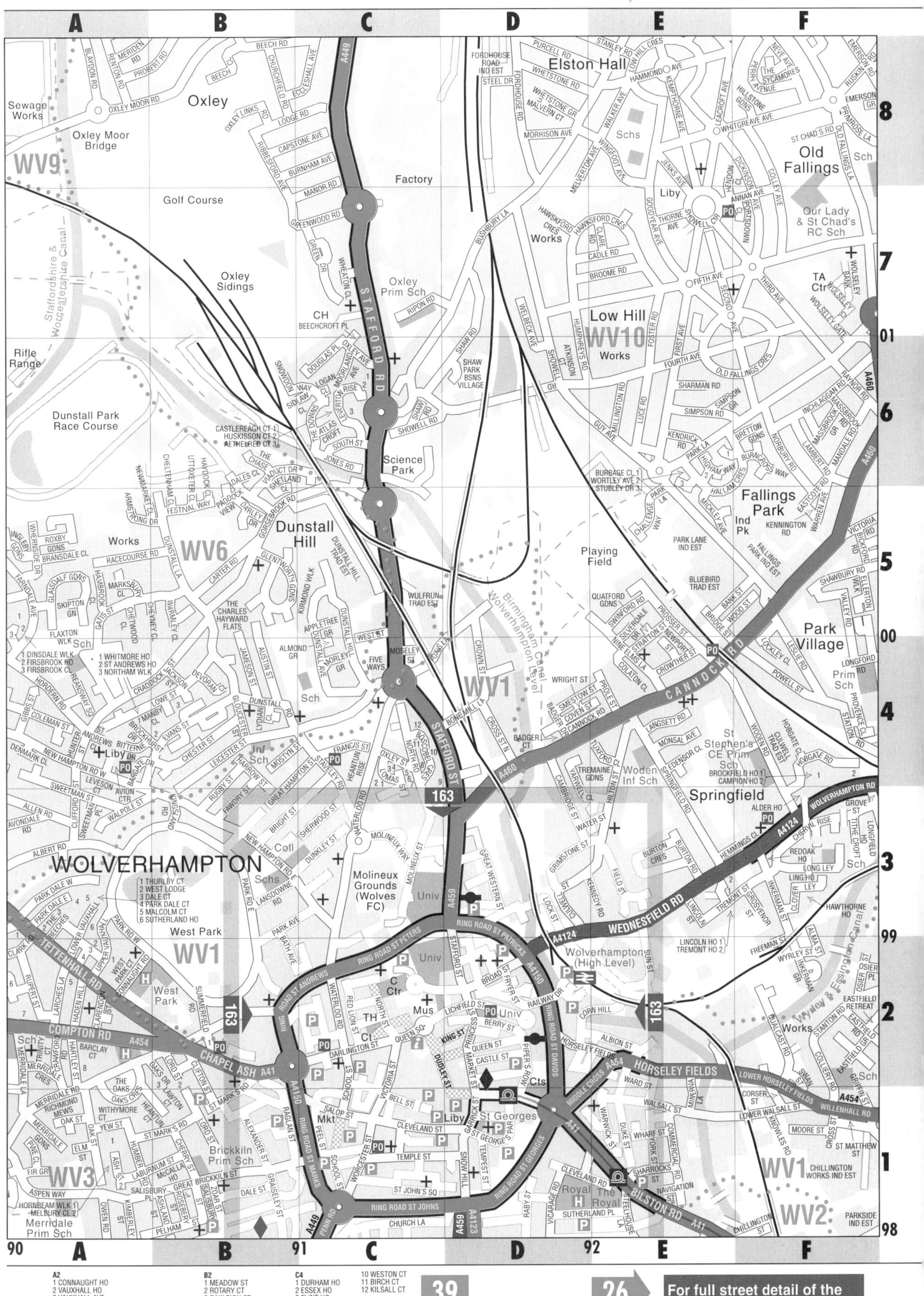

A2
1 CONNAUGHT HO
2 VAUXHALL HO
3 VAUXHALL AVE
4 MIDDLE VAUXHALL
5 HADEN CT
6 WESTLAND GDNS
7 COMPTON CT
8 BRIGHTON MEWS

B2
1 MEADOW ST
2 ROTARY CT
3 OAKLEIGH CT

C4
1 DURHAM HO
2 ESSEX HO
3 FLINT HO
4 GLOUCESTER HO
5 ARGYLL HO
6 BEDFORD HO
7 CUMBERLAND HO
8 LANC CT
9 TONG CT
10 WESTON CT
11 BIRCH CT
12 KILSALL CT

39
26
For full street detail of the highlighted area see page 163.

25
12

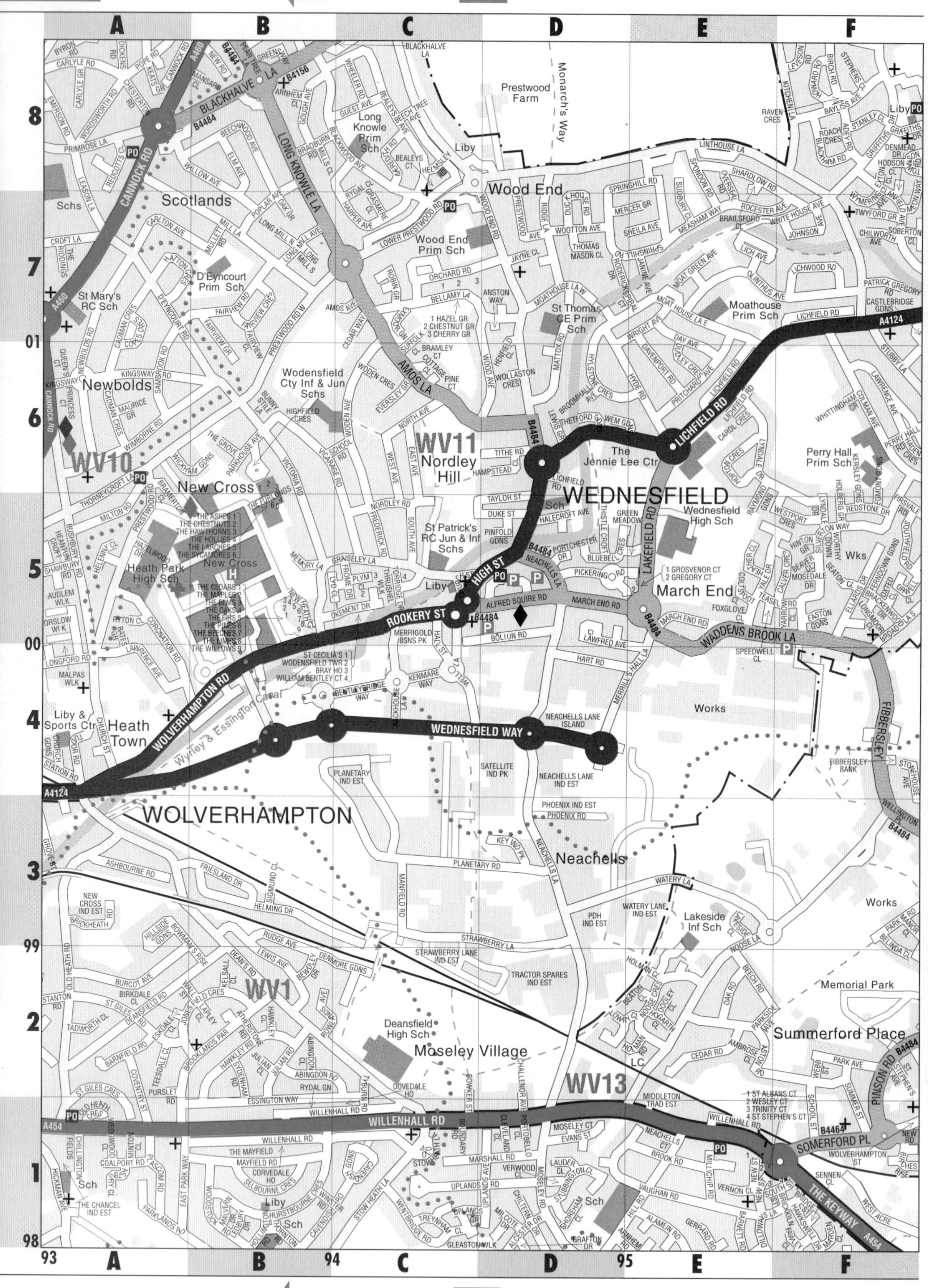
A
B
C
D
E
F
8
7
01
6
5
00
4
3
99
2
1
98
93
94
95
Prestwood Farm
Monarch's Way
Long Knowle Prim Sch
Liby
Wood End
Wood End Prim Sch
Scotlands
Schs
D'Eyncourt Prim Sch
St Mary's RC Sch
Newbolds
Wodensfield Cty Inf & Jun Schs
St Thomas CE Prim Sch
Moathouse Prim Sch
WV11
Nordley Hill
The Jennie Lee Ctr
WEDNESFIELD
Wednesfield High Sch
Perry Hall Prim Sch
WV10
New Cross
Heath Park High Sch
St Patrick's RC Jun & Inf Schs
March End
Wks
Works
Liby & Sports Ctr
Heath Town
WOLVERHAMPTON
Wyrley & Essington Canal
Neachells
Lakeside Inf Sch
Memorial Park
WV1
Deansfield High Sch
Moseley Village
Summerford Place
WV13
Sch
CANNOCK RD
BLACKHALVE LA
LONG KNOWLE LA
AMOS LA
LICHFIELD RD
HIGH ST
ROOKERY ST
WOLVERHAMPTON RD
WEDNESFIELD WAY
LAKEFIELD RD
WADDENS BROOK LA
FIBBERSLEY
WILLENHALL RD
THE KEYWAY
SOMERFORD PL
PINSON RD
A460
A4124
A454
B4484
B4156
B4464

25
40

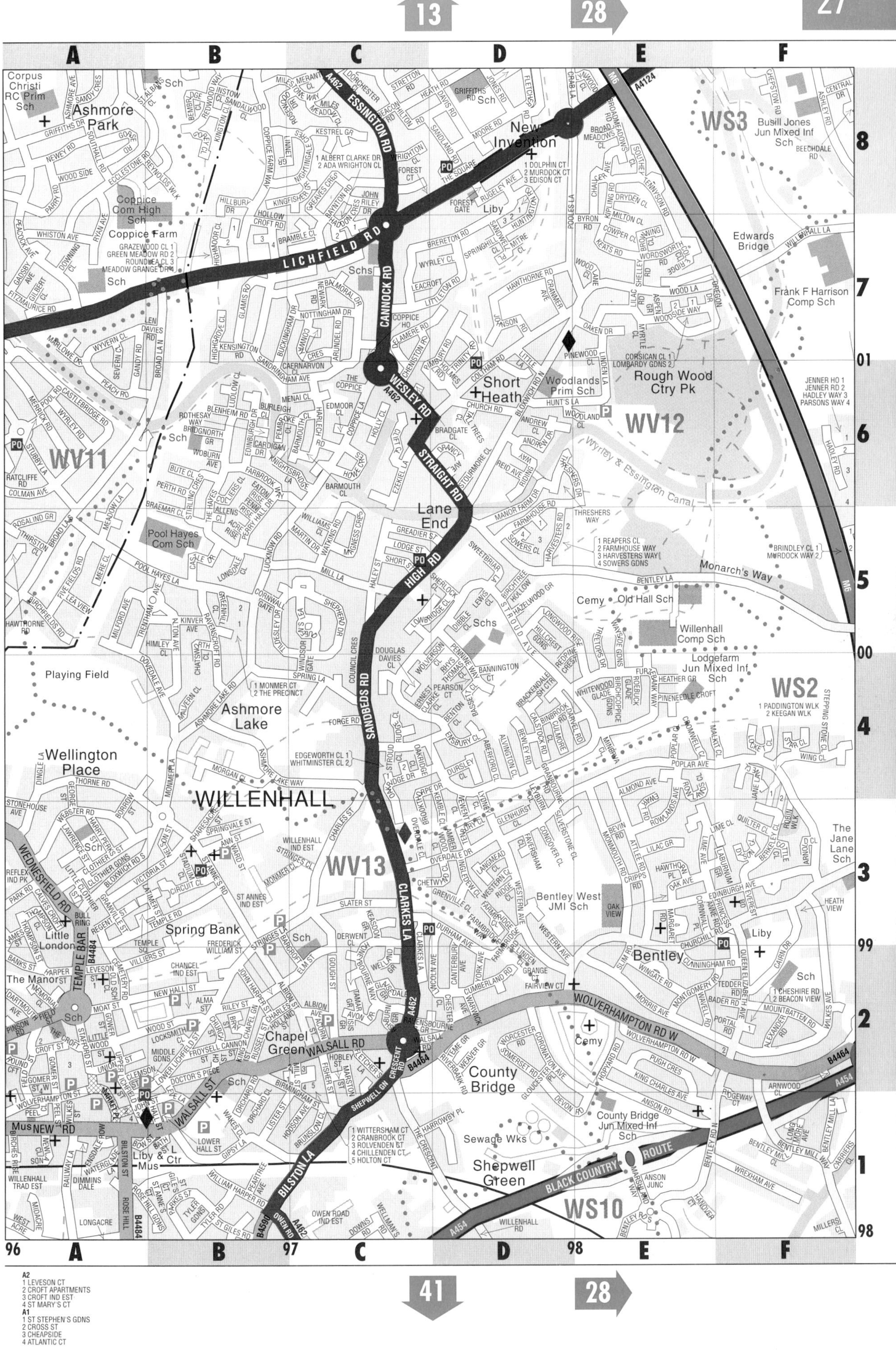

13
28
A
B
C
D
E
F
8
7
01
6
5
00
4
3
99
2
1
98
96
97
98
Corpus Christi RC Prim Sch
Ashmore Park
Coppice Com High Sch
Coppice Farm
Sch
New Invention
WS3
Busill Jones Jun Mixed Inf Sch
Edwards Bridge
Frank F Harrison Comp Sch
ESSINGTON RD
LICHFIELD RD
CANNOCK RD
WESLEY RD
STRAIGHT RD
HIGH RD
SANDBEDS RD
CLARKES LA
WALSALL RD
BILSTON LA
WOLVERHAMPTON RD W
BLACK COUNTRY ROUTE
A462
A4124
M6
A454
B4464
B4484
Short Heath
Woodlands Prim Sch
Rough Wood Ctry Pk
WV12
WV11
Wyrley & Essington Canal
Lane End
Pool Hayes Com Sch
Monarch's Way
Cemy
Old Hall Sch
Willenhall Comp Sch
Lodgefarm Jun Mixed Inf Sch
WS2
Playing Field
Ashmore Lake
Wellington Place
WILLENHALL
WV13
Spring Bank
Little London
The Manor
Chapel Green
County Bridge
Bentley West JMI Sch
Bentley
The Jane Lane Sch
County Bridge Jun Mixed Inf Sch
Sewage Wks
Shepwell Green
WS10
Liby & L Ctr
Mus
41
28
A2
1 LEVESON CT
2 CROFT APARTMENTS
3 CROFT IND EST
4 ST MARY'S CT
A1
1 ST STEPHEN'S GDNS
2 CROSS ST
3 CHEAPSIDE
4 ATLANTIC CT

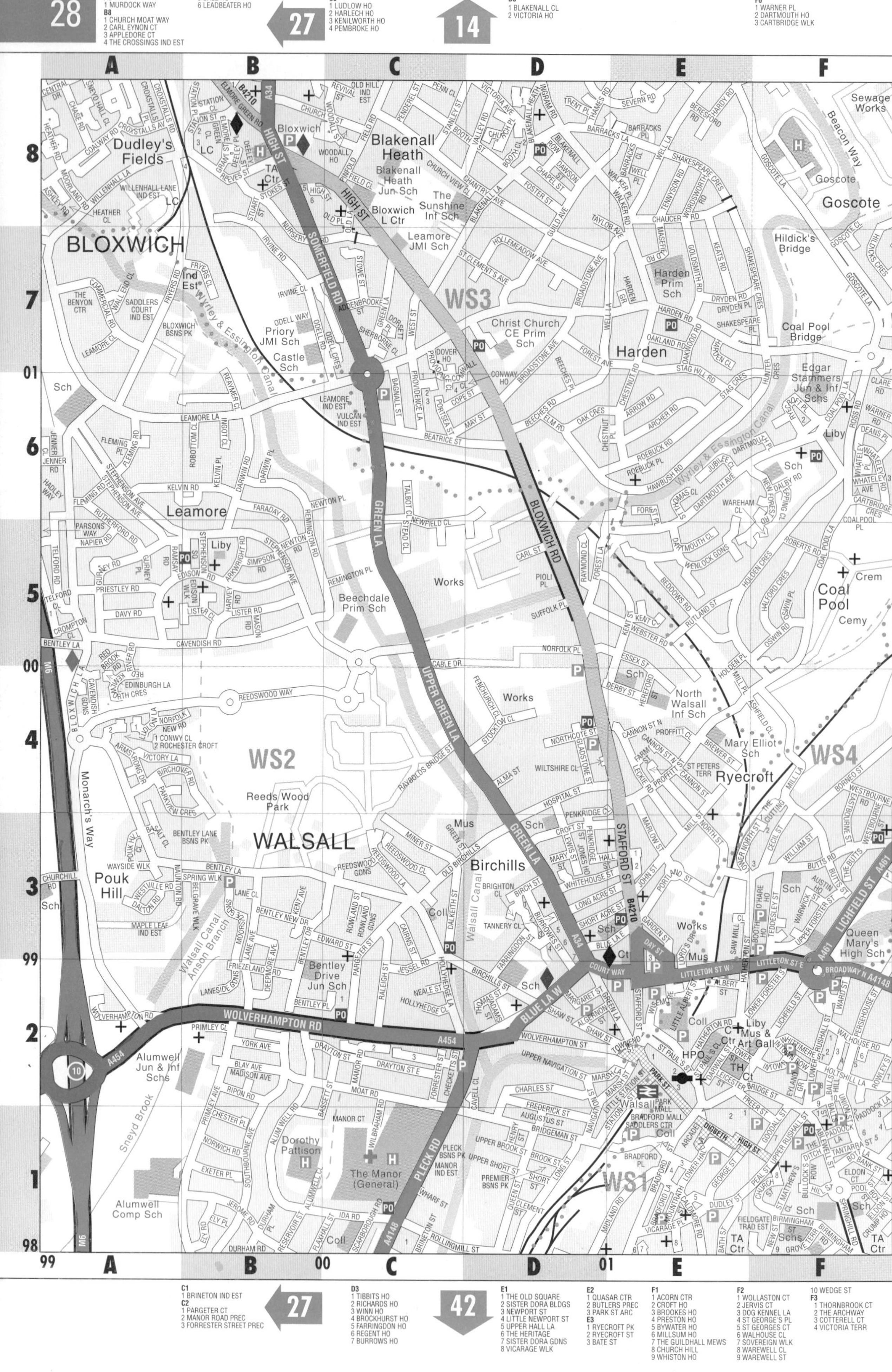

28

A5
1 MURDOCK WAY
B8
1 CHURCH MOAT WAY
2 CARL EYNON CT
3 APPLEDORE CT
4 THE CROSSINGS IND EST

5 BALL HO
6 LEADBEATER HO

27

C6
1 LUDLOW HO
2 HARLECH HO
3 KENILWORTH HO
4 PEMBROKE HO

14

D8
1 BLAKENALL CL
2 VICTORIA HO

F6
1 WARNER PL
2 DARTMOUTH HO
3 CARTBRIDGE WLK

C1
1 BRINETON IND EST
C2
1 PARGETER CT
2 MANOR ROAD PREC
3 FORRESTER STREET PREC

27

D3
1 TIBBITS HO
2 RICHARDS HO
3 WINN HO
4 BROCKHURST HO
5 FARRINGDON HO
6 REGENT HO
7 BURROWS HO

42

E1
1 THE OLD SQUARE
2 SISTER DORA BLDGS
3 NEWPORT ST
4 LITTLE NEWPORT ST
5 UPPER HALL LA
6 THE HERITAGE
7 SISTER DORA GDNS
8 VICARAGE WLK

E2
1 QUASAR CTR
2 BUTLERS PREC
3 PARK ST ARC
E3
1 RYECROFT PK
2 RYECROFT ST
3 BATE ST

F1
1 ACORN CTR
2 CROFT HO
3 BROOKES HO
4 PRESTON HO
5 BYWATER HO
6 MILLSUM HO
7 THE GUILDHALL MEWS
8 CHURCH HILL
9 WHISTON HO

F2
1 WOLLASTON CT
2 JERVIS CT
3 DOG KENNEL LA
4 ST GEORGE'S PL
5 ST GEORGES CT
6 WALHOUSE CL
7 SOVEREIGN WLK
8 WAREWELL CL
9 WAREWELL ST

10 WEDGE ST

F3
1 THORNBROOK CT
2 THE ARCHWAY
3 COTTERELL CT
4 VICTORIA TERR

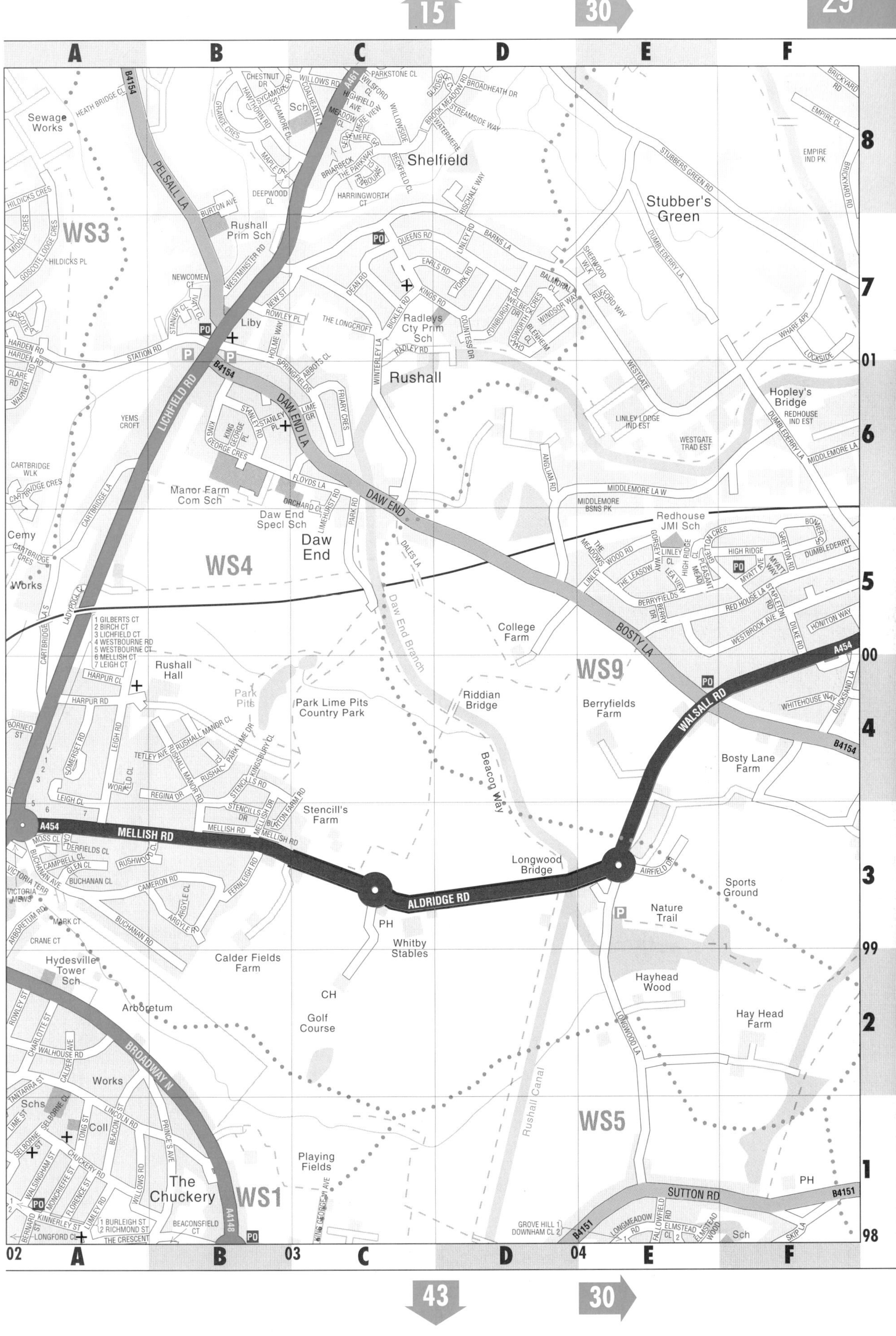
15
30
A
B
C
D
E
F
8
7
01
6
5
00
4
3
99
2
1
98
02
03
04
Sewage Works
HEATH BRIDGE CL
B4154
PELSALL LA
CHESTNUT DR
SYCAMORE RD
WILLOWS RD
COALHEATH LA
A461
HIGHFIELD AVE
MEADOW CL
WILSFORD CL
PARKSTONE CL
WILLOWSIDE
GLADES
BROOK MEADOW RD
BROADHEATH DR
STREAMSIDE WAY
WATERMERE
HAWTHORN RD
GRANGE CRES
MAPLE GR
MERE VIEW
THE PARKWAY
BRIARBECK
BECKFIELD CL
Shelfield
RISCHALE WAY
STUBBERS GREEN RD
BRICKYARD RD
EMPIRE CL
EMPIRE IND PK
Sch
DEEPWOOD CL
HARRINGWORTH CT
BURTON AVE
Rushall Prim Sch
HILDICKS CRES
MIDDLE CRES
GOSCOTE LODGE CRES
HILDICKS PL
WS3
WESTMINSTER RD
PO
QUEENS RD
BARNS LA
LINLEY RD
Stubber's Green
DUMBLEDERRY LA
SHERWOOD WLK
RUFFORD WAY
BALMORAL CL
WINDSOR WAY
EARLS RD
YORK RD
KINGS RD
DEAN RD
BICKLEY RD
NEWCOMEN CT
NEW ST
ROWLEY PL
STANIER CL
WATT CL
Liby
THE LONGCROFT
HOLME WAY
Radleys Cty Prim Sch
RADLEY RD
COUNTESS DR
EDINBURGH DR
WELBECK DR
CHATSWORTH CL
BLENHEIM
WHARF APP
LOCKSIDE
HARDEN RD
CLARE RD
WARNER RD
STATION RD
P
LICHFIELD RD
B4154
SPRINGFIELDS
ABBOTS CL
WINTERLEY LA
Rushall
WESTGATE
Hopley's Bridge
REDHOUSE IND EST
YEMS CROFT
DAW END LA
LIME GR
FRIARY CRES
STANLEY RD
STANLEY PL
KING GEORGE PL
KING GEORGE CRES
LINLEY LODGE IND EST
WESTGATE TRAD EST
DUMBLEDERRY LA
MIDDLEMORE LA
CARTBRIDGE WLK
CARTBRIDGE CRES
CARTBRIDGE LA
Manor Farm Com Sch
FLOYDS LA
ORCHARD CL
LIMEHURST RD
PARK RD
DAW END
ANGLIAN RD
MIDDLEMORE LA W
MIDDLEMORE BSNS PK
Daw End Specl Sch
Redhouse JMI Sch
Cemy
CARTBRIDGE CRES
WS4
Daw End
DALES LA
THE MEADOWS
LINLEY WOOD RD
GORSEY WAY
LINLEY CL
HIGH RIDGE CL
GRETTON CRES
HIGH RIDGE
GRETTON RD
BOWER CL
DUMBLEDERRY CT
THE LEASOW
LEA VIEW
MEAD
PLEASANT
MYATT AVE
MYATT WAY
Works
LADYPOOL CL
Daw End Branch
BERRYFIELDS
BERRY DR
RED HOUSE LA
STAPLETON RD
WESTBROOK AVE
DILKE RD
HONITON WAY
CARTBRIDGE LA S
1 GILBERTS CT
2 BIRCH CT
3 LICHFIELD CT
4 WESTBOURNE RD
5 WESTBOURNE CT
6 MELLISH CT
7 LEIGH CT
Rushall Hall
College Farm
BOSTY LA
WS9
A454
HARPUR CL
HARPUR RD
Park Pits
Park Lime Pits Country Park
Riddian Bridge
Berryfields Farm
WALSALL RD
WHITEHOUSE WAY
QUICKSAND LA
BORNEO ST
SOMERSET RD
LEIGH RD
TETLEY AVE
RUSHALL MANOR CL
RUSHALL MANOR RD
PARK LIME DR
KINGSBURY CL
Beacon Way
Bosty Lane Farm
B4154
STENCILLS RD
LEIGH CL
REGINA DR
STENCILLS DR
BURTON FARM RD
Stencill's Farm
A454
MELLISH RD
MELLISH DR
MOSS CL
DERFIELDS CL
CAMPBELL CL
GLEN CL
RUSHWOOD CL
BUCHANAN AVE
BUCHANAN CL
FERNLEIGH RD
CAMERON RD
ARGYLE CL
ARGYLE RD
Longwood Bridge
AIRFIELD DR
Sports Ground
VICTORIA TERR
VICTORIA MEWS
ARBORETUM RD
MARK CT
CRANE CT
BUCHANAN RD
ALDRIDGE RD
PH
Whitby Stables
Nature Trail
Calder Fields Farm
Hydesville Tower Sch
Hayhead Wood
Arboretum
CH
Golf Course
LONGWOOD LA
Hay Head Farm
ROWLEY ST
CHARLOTTE ST
WALHOUSE RD
CALDER AVE
BROADWAY N
Works
TANTARRA ST
Schs
LIME ST
SELBORNE CL
SELBORNE ST
Coll
TONG ST
LINCOLN RD
BEACON ST
PRINCE'S AVE
Rushall Canal
WS5
WALSINGHAM ST
MONCRIEFFE ST
CHUCKERY RD
FLORENCE ST
LUMLEY RD
WILLOWS RD
The Chuckery
Playing Fields
KING GEORGE V AVE
WS1
SUTTON RD
B4151
PH
BERNARD ST
KINNERLEY ST
LONGFORD CL
1 BURLEIGH ST
2 RICHMOND ST
THE CRESCENT
BEACONSFIELD CT
A4148
GROVE HILL 1
DOWNHAM CL 2
B4151
LONGMEADOW RD
FALLOWFIELD RD
ELMSTEAD CL
ELMSTEAD WOOD
Sch
SKIP LA

43
30

29
16

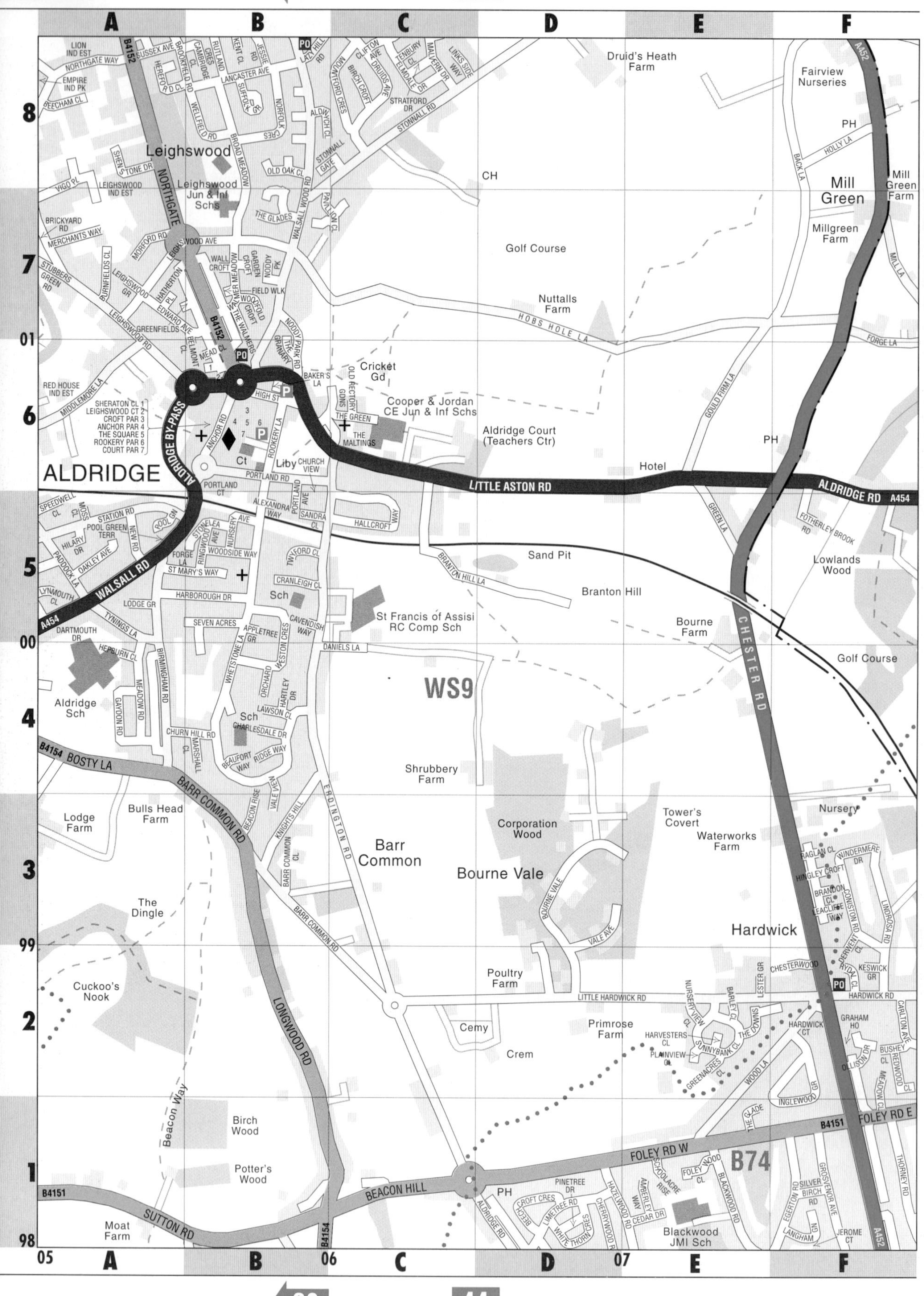
A
B
C
D
E
F
8
7
01
6
5
00
4
3
99
2
1
98
05
06
07
ALDRIDGE
Leighswood
Leighswood Jun & Inf Schs
NORTHGATE
B4152
LION IND EST
NORTHGATE WAY
EMPIRE IND PK
BEECHAM CL
SUSSEX AVE
LANCASTER AVE
SUFFOLK GR
NORFOLK CRES
WELLFIELD RD
BROAD MEADOW
OLD OAK CL
THE GLADES
WALSALL WOOD RD
STONNALL GATE
STONNALL RD
STRATFORD DR
CLIFTON AVE
BIRCH CROFT
DRUIDS AVE
TENBURY CL
FELMDALE DR
MALVERN DR
LINKS SIDE WAY
ALDRIDGE CRES
VIGO PL
LEIGHSWOOD IND EST
BRICKYARD RD
MERCHANTS WAY
MORFORD RD
LEIGHSWOOD AVE
STUBBERS GREEN RD
BURNFIELDS CL
LEIGHSWOOD GR
HATHERTON PL
EDWARD AVE
GREENFIELDS
LEIGHSWOOD RD
BELMONT CL
MEAD CL
WALL CROFT
GARDEN CROFT
NODDY PK
FIELD WLK
WOODFOLD CROFT
THE WALMERS
NODDY PARK RD
THE GRANARY
BAKER'S LA
HIGH ST
RED HOUSE IND EST
MIDDLEMORE LA
SHERATON CL 1
LEIGHSWOOD CT 2
CROFT PAR 3
ANCHOR PAR 4
THE SQUARE 5
ROOKERY PAR 6
COURT PAR 7
ALDRIDGE BY-PASS
ANCHOR RD
ROOKERY LA
Ct
Liby
CHURCH VIEW
PORTLAND RD
PORTLAND CT
OLD RECTORY GDNS
THE GREEN
THE MALTINGS
Cricket Gd
Cooper & Jordan CE Jun & Inf Schs
Aldridge Court (Teachers Ctr)
CH
Golf Course
Nuttalls Farm
HOBS HOLE LA
Druid's Heath Farm
Fairview Nurseries
PH
HOLLY LA
BACK LA
Mill Green
Mill Green Farm
Millgreen Farm
MILL LA
FORGE LA
GOULD FIRM LA
Hotel
LITTLE ASTON RD
ALDRIDGE RD
A454
A452
SPEEDWELL CL
MOSS CL
STATION RD
POOL GREEN TERR
HILARY DR
PADDOCK LA
OAKLEY AVE
NEW RD
POOL GN
STONELEA
NURSERY AVE
RINGWOOD AVE
FORGE LA
WOODSIDE WAY
ST MARY'S WAY
ALEXANDRA WAY
PORTLAND AVE
SANDRA CL
HALLCROFT WAY
TWYFORD CL
CRANLEIGH CL
Sch
HARBOROUGH DR
LYNMOUTH CL
WALSALL RD
LODGE GR
TYNINGS LA
SEVEN ACRES
APPLETREE GR
CAVENDISH WAY
St Francis of Assisi RC Comp Sch
DANIELS LA
BRANTON HILL LA
Sand Pit
Branton Hill
GREEN LA
FOTHERLEY BROOK RD
Lowlands Wood
Bourne Farm
CHESTER RD
Golf Course
DARTMOUTH DR
HEPBURN CL
Aldridge Sch
GAYDON RD
MEADOW RD
BIRMINGHAM RD
WHETSTONE LA
ORCHARD
WESTON CRES
HARTLEY DR
LAWSON CL
CHARLESDALE DR
CHURN HILL RD
MARSHALL CL
BEAUFORT WAY
RIDGE WAY
WS9
B4154
BOSTY LA
BARR COMMON RD
BEACON RISE
VALE VIEW
KNIGHTS HILL
BARR COMMON CL
ERDINGTON RD
Shrubbery Farm
Lodge Farm
Bulls Head Farm
Barr Common
Corporation Wood
Bourne Vale
Tower's Covert
Waterworks Farm
Nursery
RAGLAN CL
WINDERMERE DR
HINGLEY CROFT
BRANDON CL
LEACLIFFE WAY
CONISTON RD
LINDROSA RD
DERWENT CL
RYDAL CL
KESWICK GR
Hardwick
The Dingle
BOURNE VALE
VALE AVE
Poultry Farm
Cuckoo's Nook
LITTLE HARDWICK RD
CHESTERWOOD
LESTER GR
NURSERY VIEW CL
BARLEY CL
THE DOWNS
HARVESTERS CL
PLAINVIEW CL
SUNNYBANK CL
GREENACRES CL
WOOD LA
HARDWICK CT
GRAHAM HO
HARDWICK RD
CARLTON AVE
BUSHEY CL
OLLISON DR
REDWOOD CL
MEADOW CL
Cemy
Primrose Farm
Crem
LONGWOOD RD
INGLEWOOD GR
THE GLADE
B4151
FOLEY RD E
FOLEY RD W
FOLEY WOOD CL
SCHOOLACRE RISE
BLACKWOOD RD
B74
Beacon Way
Birch Wood
Potter's Wood
BEACON HILL
PH
PINETREE DR
CROFT CRES
LIMETREE RD
WHITE THORN CRES
CHERRYWOOD RD
HAZELWOOD RD
AMBERLEY WAY
CEDAR DR
ALDRIDGE RD
BEECH
Blackwood JMI Sch
EGERTON RD
SILVER BIRCH RD
GROSVENOR AVE
LANGHAM GN
JEROME CT
THORNEY RD
SUTTON RD
Moat Farm

29
44

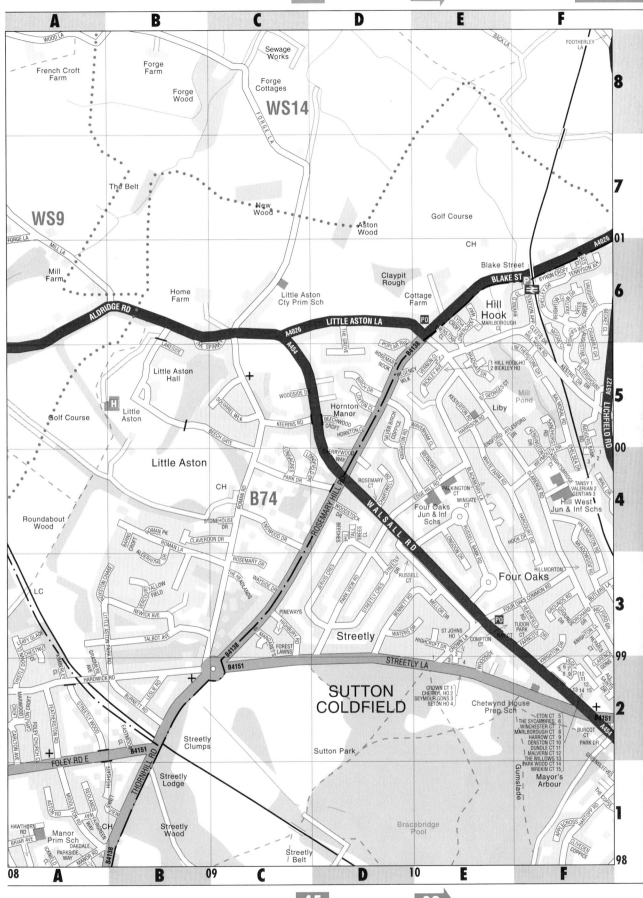

A B C D E F

WOOD LA
French Croft Farm
Forge Farm
Forge Wood
Sewage Works
Forge Cottages
FORGE LA
WS14
BACK LA
FOOTHERLEY LA
The Belt
WS9
New Wood
Aston Wood
Golf Course
CH
FORGE LA
MILL LA
Mill Farm
Home Farm
Little Aston Cty Prim Sch
Claypit Rough
Cottage Farm
Blake Street
BLAKE ST
A4026
ALDRIDGE RD
LITTLE ASTON LA
A4026
PO
Hill Hook
LAKESIDE
THE SPINNEY
THE GROVE
A454
B4138
POPLAR RISE
ROSEMARY NOOK
REGENCY WLK
VERNON CL
BICKLEY AVE
SHENSTONE CL
LYDIA CROFT
LOWCROFT
RYKNILD CL
STATION APP
MARLBOROUGH CL
CLEEVE DR
HILL HOOK RD
BYRON CROFT
KEATS CL
TENNYSON AV
SHELLEY DR
SAXTON DR
YATES CROFT
VAUGHAN CL
BECKET CL
BEIGHTON CL
BISHOPS WAY
CRANMER GR
AUGUSTINE GR
MOORE CL
KESTREL DR
PETERSHOUSE DR
NETHERSTONE GR
BRADGATE DR
1 HILL HOOK HO
2 BICKLEY HO
ST GEORGES CT
Mill Pond
Liby
Little Aston Hall
Golf Course
H
Little Aston
SQUIRREL WLK
WOODSIDE DR
BIRCH DR
LOXTON CL
Hornton Manor
BEECHWOOD CROFT
HORNTON CL
KEEPERS RD
BEECH GATE
SILVER BIRCH COPPICE
KNIGHTON RD
WAVENHAM CL
KESTERTON RD
HARRISON RD
ENSFORD CL
AYLESFORD DR
KENSINGTON DR
SANDHURST RD
BALMORAL RD
CHELSEA DR
BADGERS BANK RD
A5127
LICHFIELD RD
Little Aston
CHERRYWOOD WAY
LONGACRES
LONGFIELD DR
PARK DR
ROSEMARY CT
CHARTWELL DR
BERKSWELL CL
EDGE HILL RD
PACKINGTON CT
WINGATE CT
BLACKBERRY LA
WHITE FARM RD
WEYMOUTH DR
KNIGHTSBRIDGE
CLARENCE RD
TANSY 1
VALERIAN 2
GENTIAN 3
WALL DR
CH
B74
ROMAN RD
Four Oaks Jun & Inf Schs
Hill West Jun & Inf Schs
Roundabout Wood
STONEHOUSE DR
ROSEMARY HILL RD
WOODSTOCK DR
WALSALL RD
ROMAN PK
BARNS CROFT
ROMAN LA
CLAVERDON DR
ENDWOOD DR
BEECHES
THE TALL TREES CL
LONGDON DR
RUSSELL BANK RD
HARCOURT DR
HOOK DR
HILLMORTON RD
MEADOWSIDE RD
ALDERHITHE GR
ROSEMARY DR
THE HEADLANDS
WAYSIDE DR
JERVIS CRES
PARK VIEW RD
STREETLY CRES
STREETLY DR
RUSSELL CT
HILLMORTON
Four Oaks
LC
ROYSTON CHASE
VERCOURT
TALLOW FIELD
BENNETT RD
MELLOR DR
FOUR OAKS COMMON RD
BUTLERS LA
NEWICK AVE
LITTLE ASTON PARK RD
PINEWAYS
HIGHBURY RD
ST MARGARETS
Streetly
WATERS DR
ST JOHNS HO
HEATHFIELD RD
TUDOR PARK CT
RAY CT
FARNCOTE DR
GROUNDS RD
GROUNDS DR
ORCHARD GR
WELFORD GR
KNIGHTON CL
HERMES CT
LEAFY GLADE
CHESTNUT CL
TALBOT AVE
FOREST LAWNS
HIGHCROFT DR
CROWN LA
COMPTON CT
KNIGHTON RD
THISTLE DOWN
KIMBERLEY CL
GRASMERE AVE
B4138
B4151
STREETLY LA
WOODSIDE
VESEY CL
CLARENCE GDNS
ALL SAINTS DR
HARDWICK RD
LESLIE RD
+
SUTTON COLDFIELD
CROWN CT 1
CHERRYL HO 2
SEYMOUR GDNS 3
SETON HO 4
Chetwynd House Prep Sch
MARWOOD CROFT
CARHOLTON CROFT
FEATHERSTON RD
STREETLY WOOD
BURNETT RD
EASTMOOR CL
B4151
A454
FOLEY CHURCH CL
CARLTON AVE
ETON CT 5
THE SYCAMORES 6
WINCHESTER CT 7
MARLBOROUGH CT 8
HARROW CT 9
DENSTON CT 10
DUNDLE CT 11
MALVERN CT 12
THE WILLOWS 13
PARK WOOD CT 14
WREKIN CT 15
BURCOT CT
PARK DR
FOLEY RD E
B4151
THORNHILL RD
Streetly Clumps
Sutton Park
GREENSLEEVES
Streetly Lodge
HIGHGATE
TWIN VIEW
Gumslade
Mayor's Arbour
ASTOR RD
MIDDLETON RD
REDLANDS WAY
FAIRGREEN WAY
THE COPSE
CH
HARTOPP RD
HAWTHORN RD
Manor Prim Sch
Streetly Wood
Bracebridge Pool
APPLECROSS
BRIAR AVE
OAKDALE
PARKSIDE WAY
MANOR RD
ICKNIELD CL
B4138
Streetly Belt
CLIVEDEN COPPICE

8 7 01 6 5 00 4 3 99 2 1 98

08 A B 09 C D 10 E F

31
18

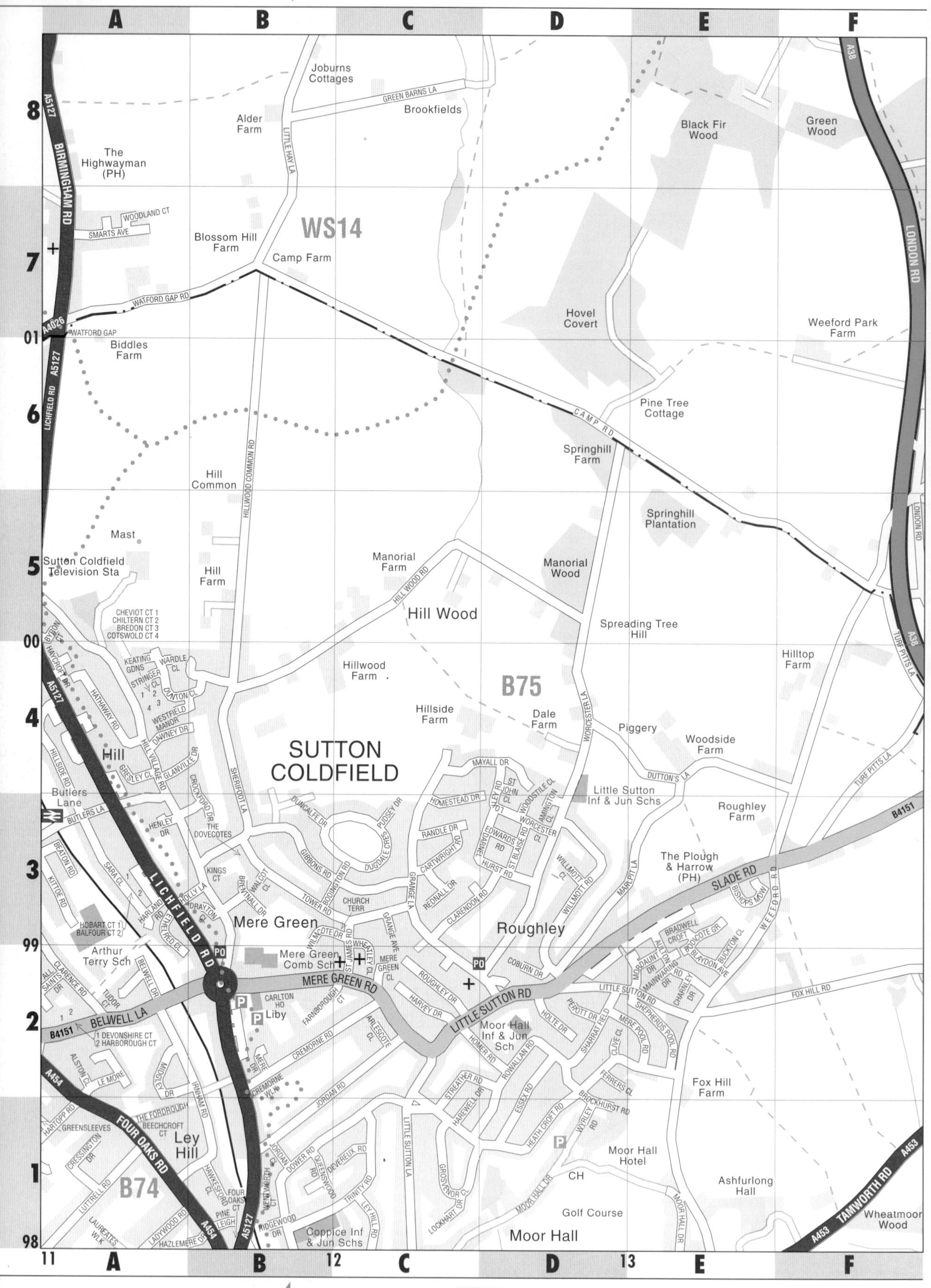
A
B
C
D
E
F
8
7
01
6
5
00
4
3
99
2
1
98
11
12
13
Joburns Cottages
GREEN BARNS LA
Brookfields
Alder Farm
LITTLE HAY LA
Black Fir Wood
Green Wood
A38
The Highwayman (PH)
BIRMINGHAM RD
A5127
WOODLAND CT
SMARTS AVE
WS14
Blossom Hill Farm
Camp Farm
LONDON RD
WATFORD GAP RD
A4026
WATFORD GAP
Biddles Farm
Hovel Covert
Weeford Park Farm
LICHFIELD RD
Pine Tree Cottage
CAMP RD
Springhill Farm
Hill Common
HILLWOOD COMMON RD
Springhill Plantation
Mast
Sutton Coldfield Television Sta
Hill Farm
Manorial Farm
HILL WOOD RD
Manorial Wood
Hill Wood
Spreading Tree Hill
CHEVIOT CT 1
CHILTERN CT 2
BREDON CT 3
COTSWOLD CT 4
Hillwood Farm
B75
Hilltop Farm
TURF PITTS LA
Hillside Farm
Dale Farm
WORCESTER LA
Piggery
Woodside Farm
SUTTON COLDFIELD
Hill
MAYALL DR
DUTTON'S LA
Little Sutton Inf & Jun Schs
Roughley Farm
B4151
Butlers Lane
BUTLERS LA
The Plough & Harrow (PH)
SLADE RD
WEEFORD RD
Mere Green
Roughley
HOBART CT 1
BALFOUR CT 2
Arthur Terry Sch
Mere Green Comb Sch
MERE GREEN RD
PO
BELWELL LA
LICHFIELD RD
LITTLE SUTTON RD
Liby
Moor Hall Inf & Jun Sch
FOX HILL RD
1 DEVONSHIRE CT
2 HARBOROUGH CT
A454
Fox Hill Farm
FOUR OAKS RD
Ley Hill
B74
Moor Hall Hotel
CH
Ashfurlong Hall
TAMWORTH RD
A453
Golf Course
Wheatmoor Wood
Coppice Inf & Jun Schs
Moor Hall

31
46

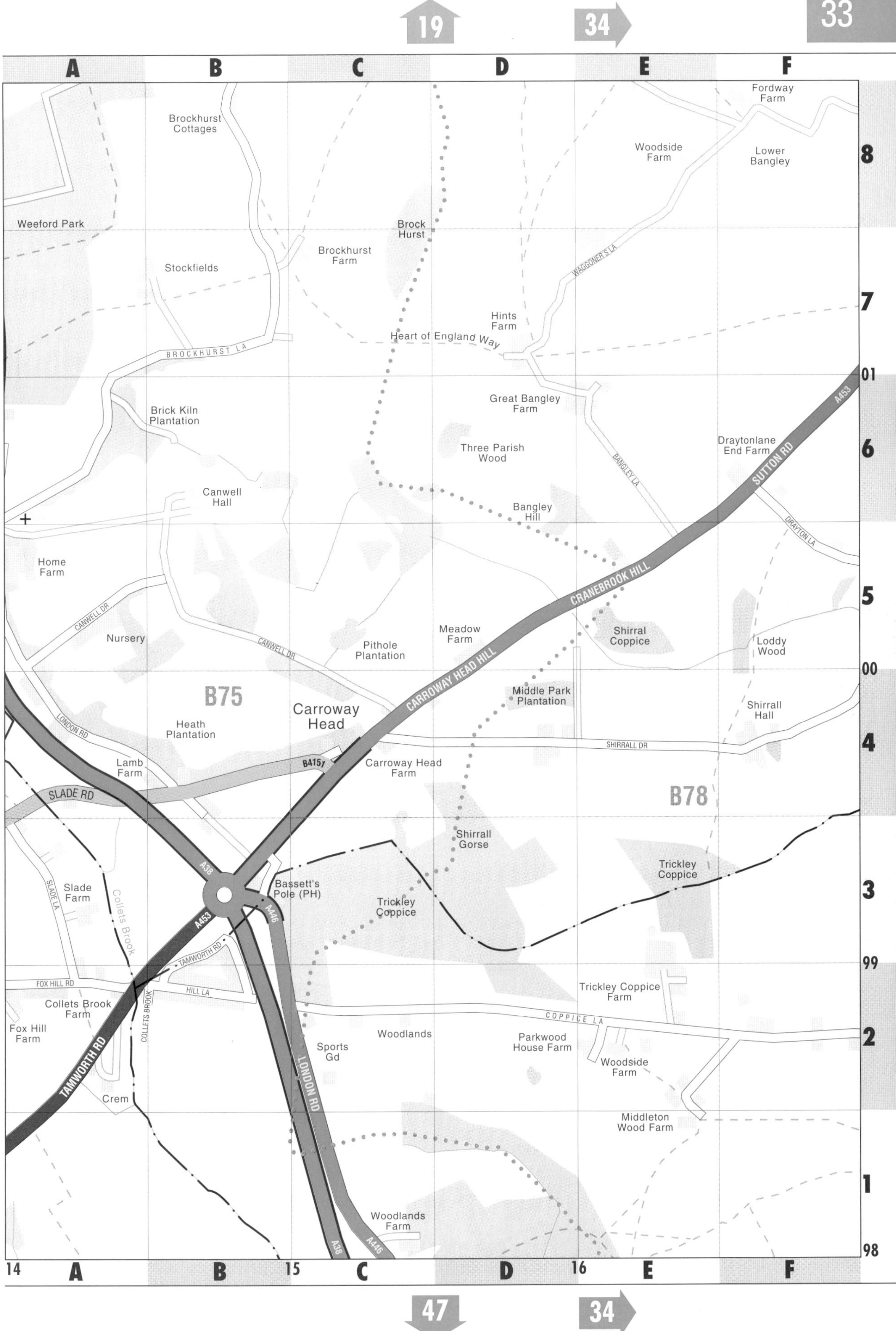

A B C D E F

8

Fordway Farm
Woodside Farm
Lower Bangley

Weeford Park
Brockhurst Cottages
Brock Hurst
Brockhurst Farm
WAGGONER'S LA

Stockfields
Hints Farm

7

BROCKHURST LA
Heart of England Way

01

Brick Kiln Plantation
Great Bangley Farm
Three Parish Wood
Draytonlane End Farm
SUTTON RD
A453

6

Canwell Hall
Bangley Hill
BANGLEY LA
DRAYTON LA

Home Farm
CANWELL DR
CRANEBROOK HILL
Shirral Coppice
Loddy Wood

5

Nursery
CANWELL DR
Pithole Plantation
Meadow Farm
CARROWAY HEAD HILL
Middle Park Plantation
Shirrall Hall

00

B75
Carroway Head
Heath Plantation
SHIRRALL DR

4

LONDON RD
Lamb Farm
B4151
Carroway Head Farm
B78

SLADE RD
Shirrall Gorse
Trickley Coppice

3

Slade Farm
SLADE LA
A38
Bassett's Pole (PH)
Trickley Coppice
A453
A446
Collets Brook

99

FOX HILL RD
HILL LA
Trickley Coppice Farm
COPPICE LA

Collets Brook Farm
COLLETS BROOK
Woodlands
Parkwood House Farm
Woodside Farm

2

Fox Hill Farm
TAMWORTH RD
LONDON RD
Sports Gd

Crem
Middleton Wood Farm

1

Woodlands Farm
A38
A446

98

14 A B 15 C D 16 E F

33
20

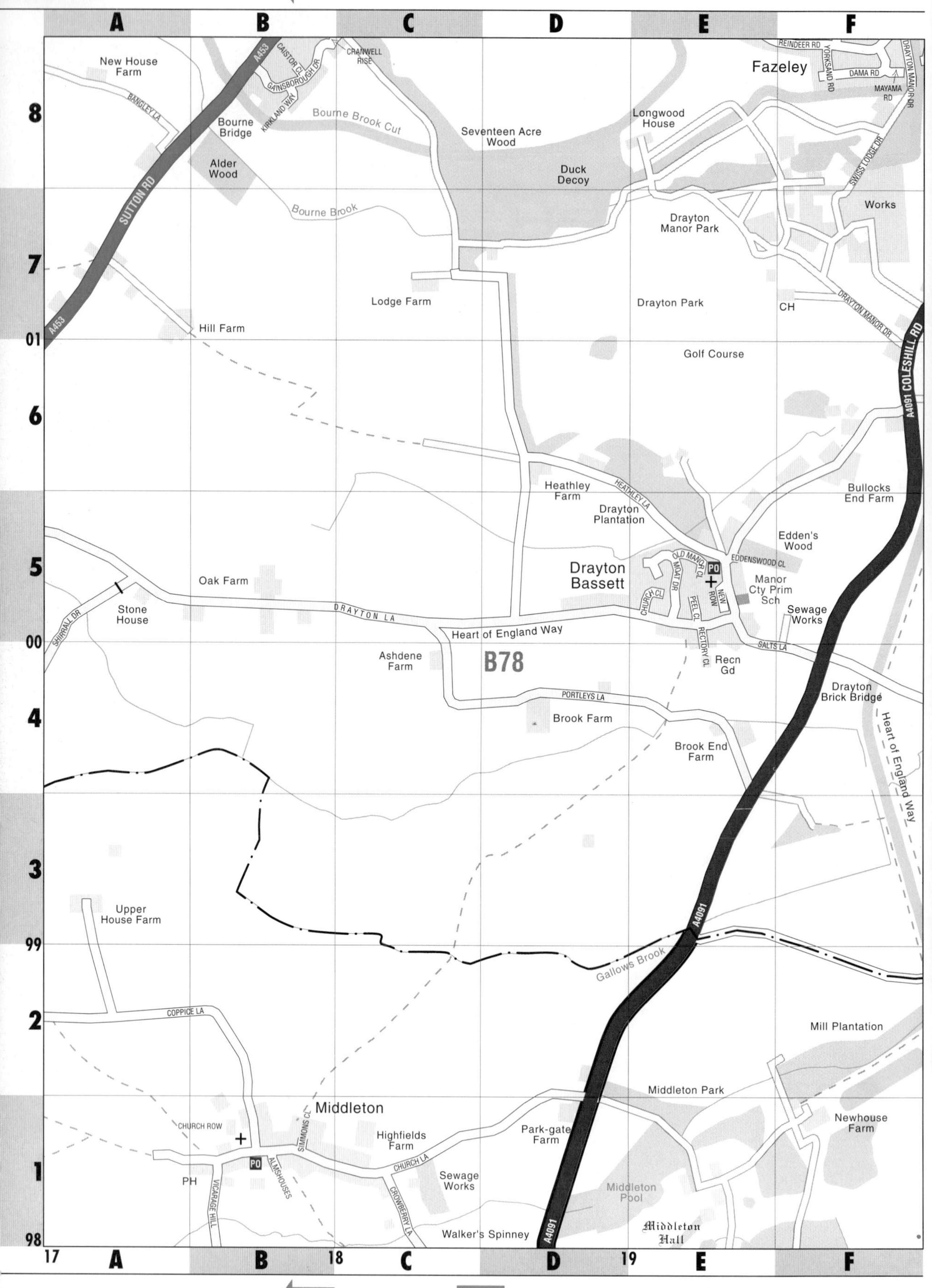
A
B
C
D
E
F
New House Farm
BANGLEY LA
A453
CAISTOR CL
GAINSBOROUGH DR
KIRKLAND WAY
CRANWELL RISE
Bourne Bridge
Bourne Brook Cut
Alder Wood
Seventeen Acre Wood
Duck Decoy
Longwood House
Fazeley
REINDEER RD
YORKSAND RD
DAMA RD
MAYAMA RD
DRAYTON MANOR DR
SWISS LODGE DR
Works
SUTTON RD
Bourne Brook
Drayton Manor Park
Lodge Farm
Drayton Park
CH
DRAYTON MANOR DR
Hill Farm
Golf Course
A4091 COLESHILL RD
Heathley Farm
HEATHLEY LA
Drayton Plantation
Bullocks End Farm
Edden's Wood
EDDENSWOOD CL
OLD MANOR CL
MOAT DR
PO
Drayton Bassett
CHURCH CL
PEEL CL
NEW ROW
Manor Cty Prim Sch
Oak Farm
Stone House
SHIRRALL DR
DRAYTON LA
Heart of England Way
Sewage Works
SALTS LA
RECTORY CL
Ashdene Farm
B78
Recn Gd
Drayton Brick Bridge
PORTLEYS LA
Brook Farm
Heart of England Way
Brook End Farm
Upper House Farm
A4091
Gallows Brook
COPPICE LA
Mill Plantation
Middleton Park
Middleton
SIMMONS CL
CHURCH ROW
Highfields Farm
Park-gate Farm
Newhouse Farm
PO
ALMSHOUSES
CHURCH LA
PH
VICARAGE HILL
CROWBERRY LA
Sewage Works
Middleton Pool
Walker's Spinney
A4091
Middleton Hall
8
7
01
6
5
00
4
3
99
2
1
98
17
18
19

33
48

B8
1 BURLINGTON CT
2 PEEL CT
3 ANSON CT
4 VICTORY TERR
5 TAME CT

21
36

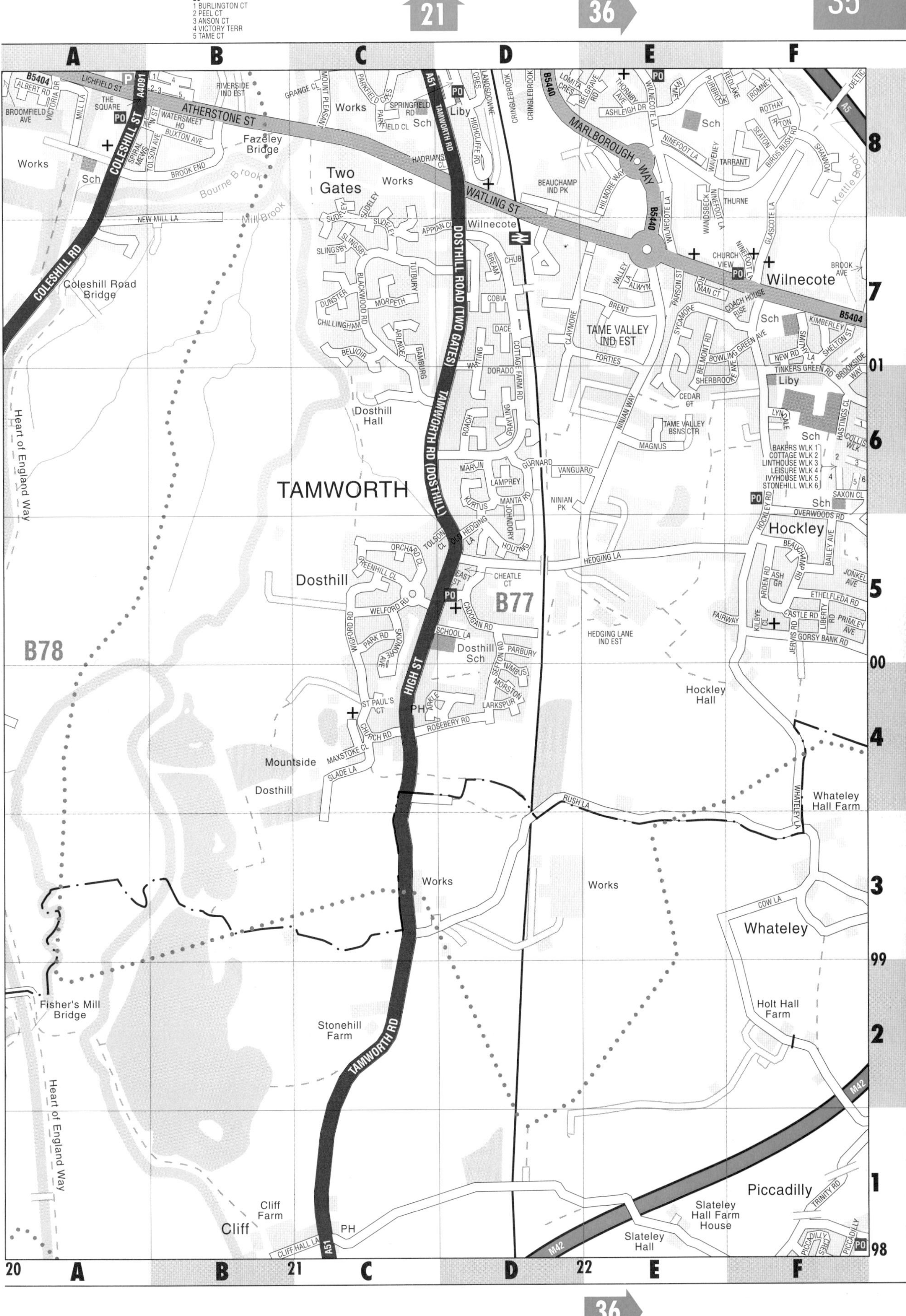

36

35
22

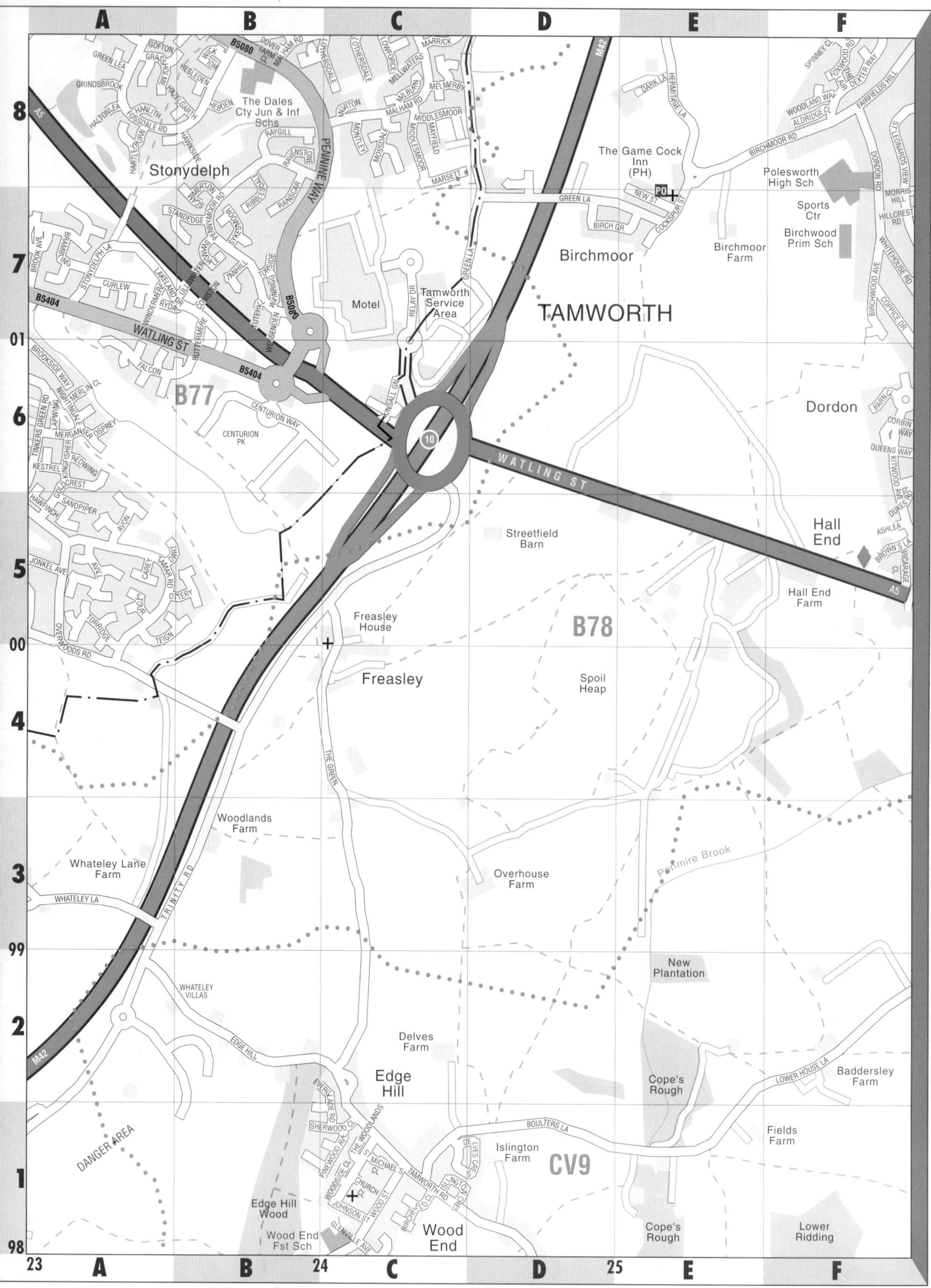
Stonydelph
The Dales Cty Jun & Inf Schs
PENNINE WAY
B5080
A5
B5404
WATLING ST
B77
CENTURION PK
CENTURION WAY
Motel
Tamworth Service Area
TAMWORTH
Birchmoor
The Game Cock Inn (PH)
Polesworth High Sch
Sports Ctr
Birchwood Prim Sch
Birchmoor Farm
Dordon
Hall End
Hall End Farm
Streetfield Barn
Freasley House
Freasley
B78
Spoil Heap
M42
Woodlands Farm
Whateley Lane Farm
WHATELEY LA
TRINITY RD
WHATELEY VILLAS
Overhouse Farm
Penmire Brook
New Plantation
Delves Farm
Edge Hill
EDGE HILL
Cope's Rough
Baddersley Farm
LOWER HOUSE LA
BOULTERS LA
Islington Farm
CV9
Fields Farm
DANGER AREA
Edge Hill Wood
Wood End Fst Sch
Wood End
Lower Ridding
TAMWORTH RD
GREEN LA
BIRCHMOOR RD
WATLING ST
THE GREEN
OVERWOODS RD

35

23
38

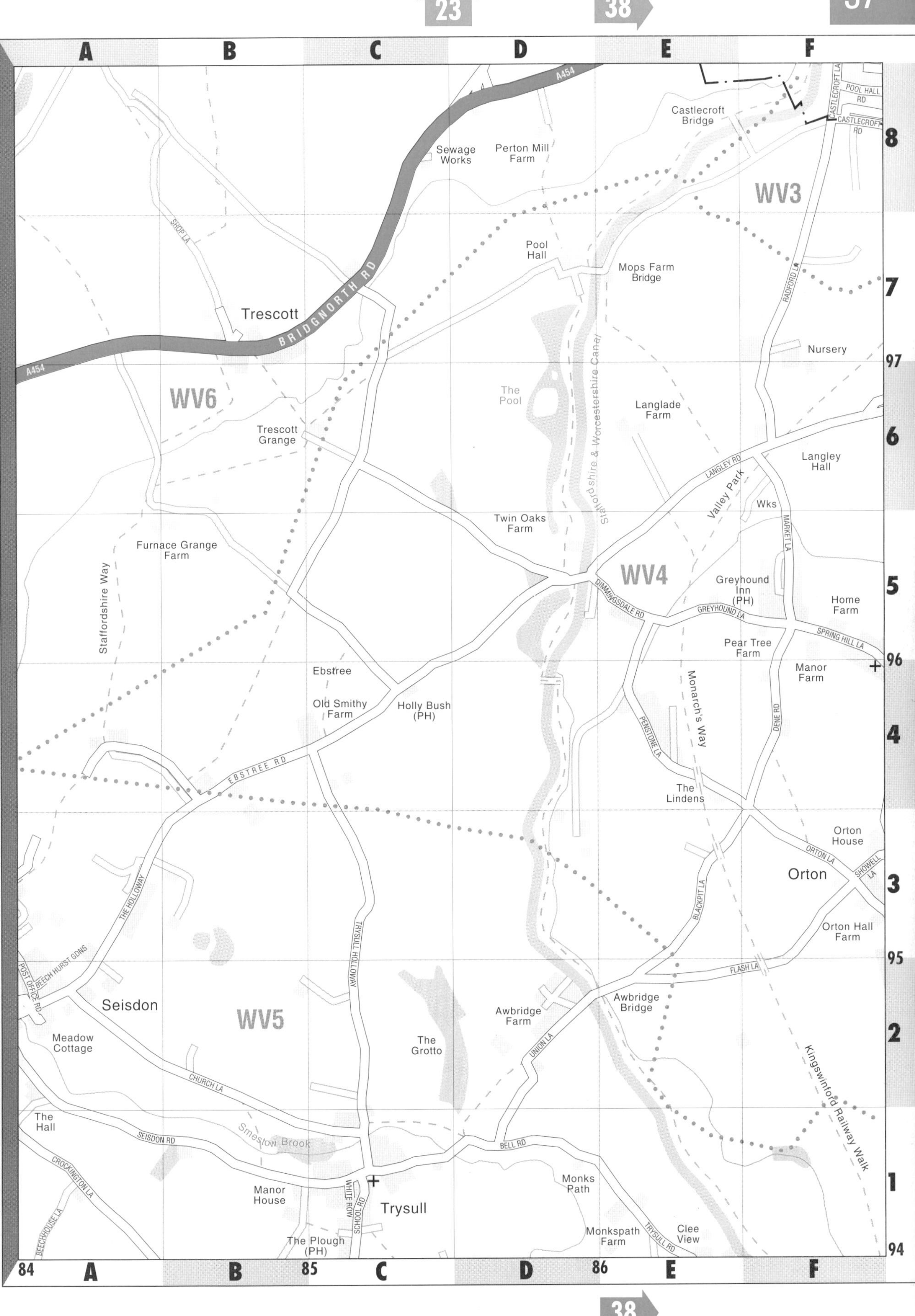
A
B
C
D
E
F
8
7
97
6
5
96
4
3
95
2
1
94
84
85
86
A454
BRIDGNORTH RD
Castlecroft Bridge
CASTLECROFT LA
POOL HALL RD
CASTLECROFT RD
Sewage Works
Perton Mill Farm
WV3
SHOP LA
Pool Hall
Mops Farm Bridge
RADFORD LA
Trescott
Nursery
WV6
The Pool
Staffordshire & Worcestershire Canal
Langlade Farm
Trescott Grange
LANGLEY RD
Langley Hall
Valley Park
Wks
Twin Oaks Farm
MARKET LA
Furnace Grange Farm
Staffordshire Way
WV4
Greyhound Inn (PH)
DIMMINGSDALE RD
GREYHOUND LA
Home Farm
Pear Tree Farm
SPRING HILL LA
Manor Farm
Ebstree
Monarch's Way
Old Smithy Farm
Holly Bush (PH)
DENE RD
PENSTONE LA
EBSTREE RD
The Lindens
Orton House
ORTON LA
SHOWELL LA
Orton
THE HOLLOWAY
BLACKPIT LA
TRYSULL HOLLOWAY
Orton Hall Farm
BEECH HURST GDNS
POST OFFICE RD
FLASH LA
Awbridge Bridge
Seisdon
WV5
Awbridge Farm
Meadow Cottage
The Grotto
UNION LA
Kingswinford Railway Walk
CHURCH LA
The Hall
Smestow Brook
SEISDON RD
BELL RD
CROCKINGTON LA
Monks Path
Manor House
WHITE ROW
SCHOOL RD
Trysull
Monkspath Farm
TRYSULL RD
Clee View
BEECHHOUSE LA
The Plough (PH)

38

37
24

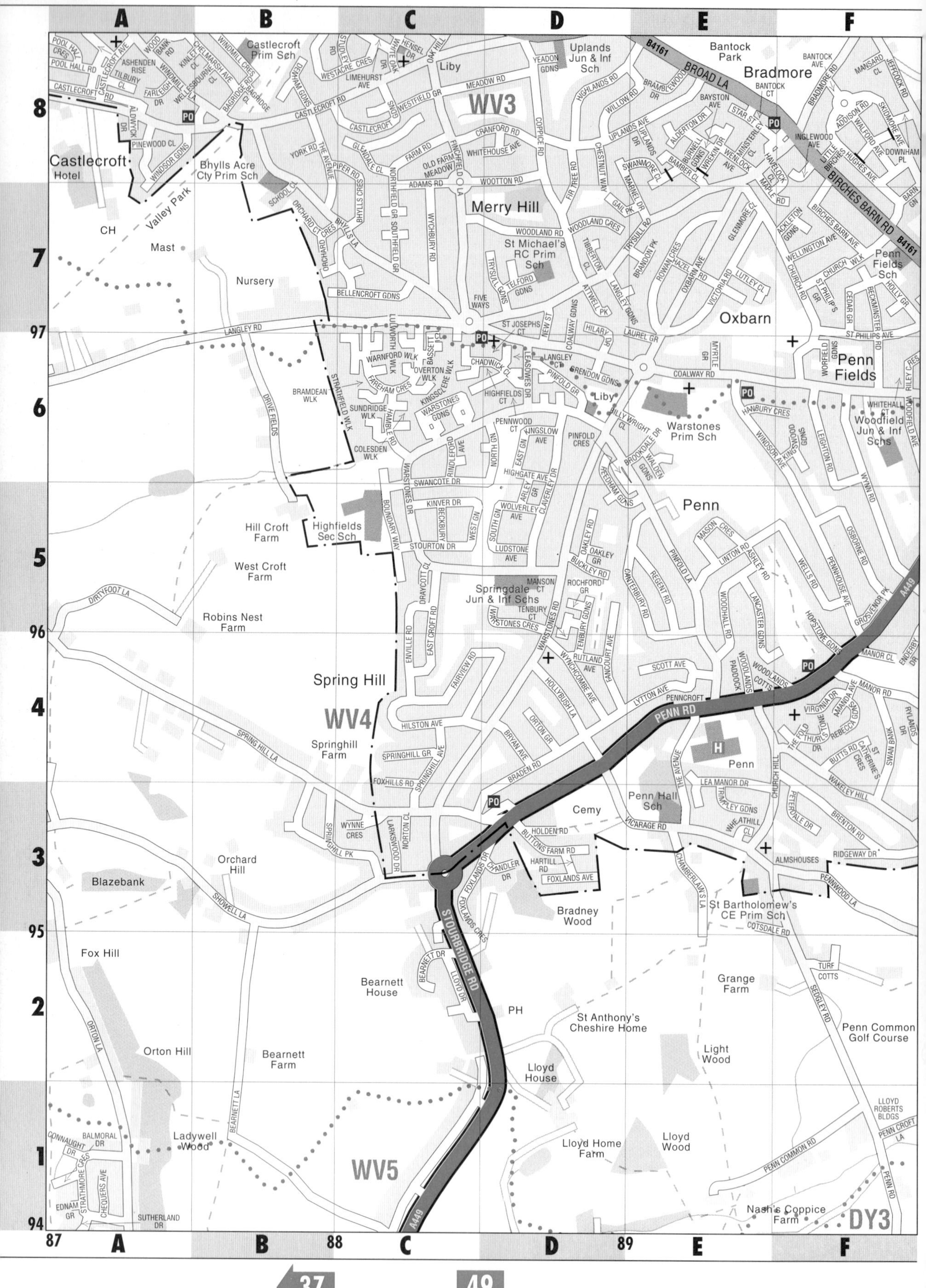
Castlecroft Prim Sch
Uplands Jun & Inf Sch
Bantock Park
Bradmore
Liby
WV3
Castlecroft Hotel
Bhylls Acre Cty Prim Sch
Valley Park
Merry Hill
St Michael's RC Prim Sch
Mast
Nursery
Oxbarn
Penn Fields
Penn Fields Sch
Warstones Prim Sch
Woodfield Jun & Inf Schs
Penn
Hill Croft Farm
Highfields Sec Sch
West Croft Farm
Springdale Jun & Inf Schs
Robins Nest Farm
Spring Hill
WV4
Springhill Farm
Penn Hall Sch
Cemy
Orchard Hill
Blazebank
Bradney Wood
St Bartholomew's CE Prim Sch
Fox Hill
Bearnett House
Grange Farm
PH
St Anthony's Cheshire Home
Penn Common Golf Course
Orton Hill
Bearnett Farm
Light Wood
Lloyd House
Ladywell Wood
Lloyd Home Farm
Lloyd Wood
WV5
Nash's Coppice Farm
DY3
PENN RD
STOURBRIDGE RD
BROAD LA
BIRCHES BARN RD
LANGLEY RD
COALWAY RD
SPRING HILL LA
SHOWELL LA
DIRTYFOOT LA
ORTON LA
BEARNETT LA
PENN COMMON RD
SEDGLEY RD

37
49

For full street detail of the highlighted area see page 163.

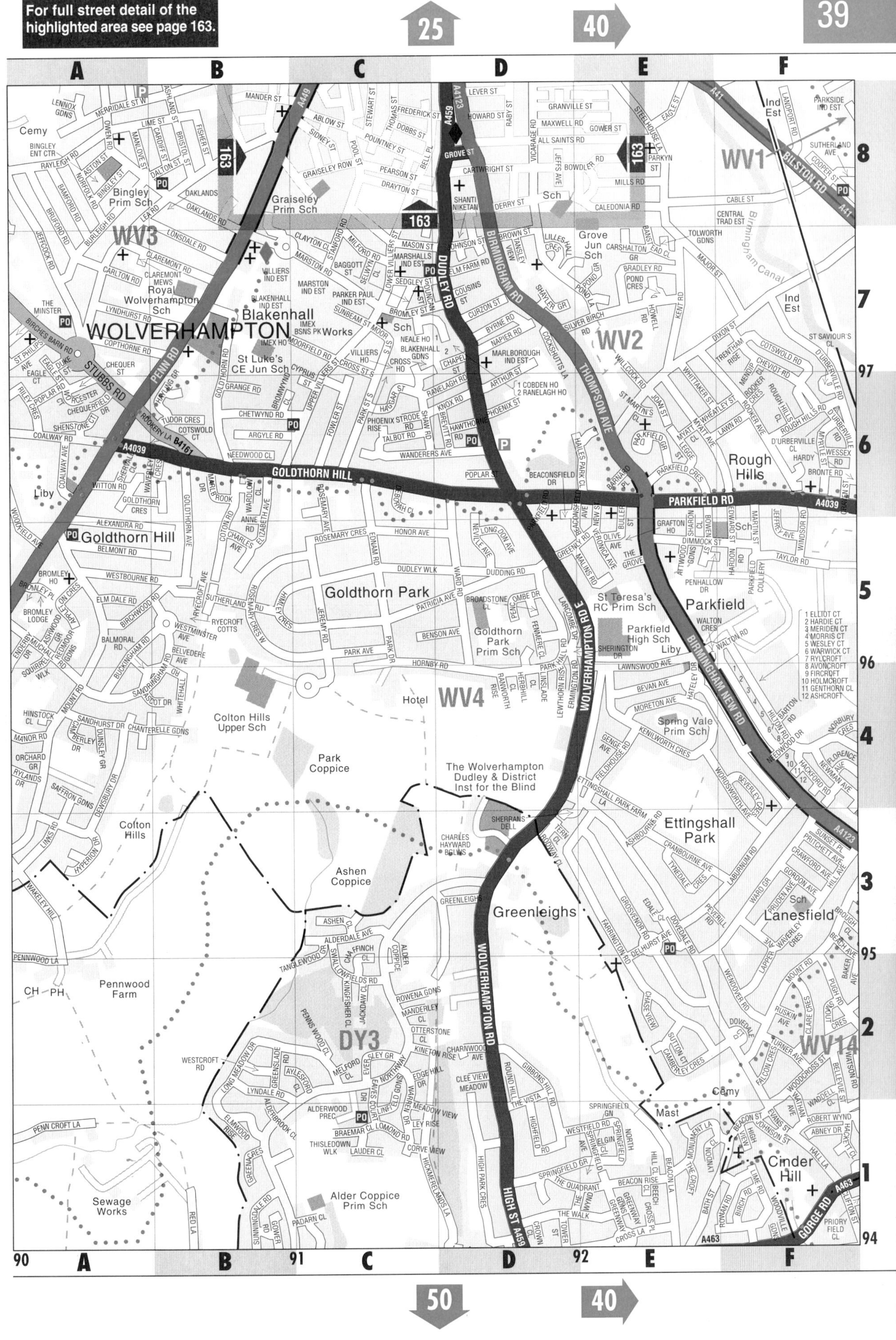

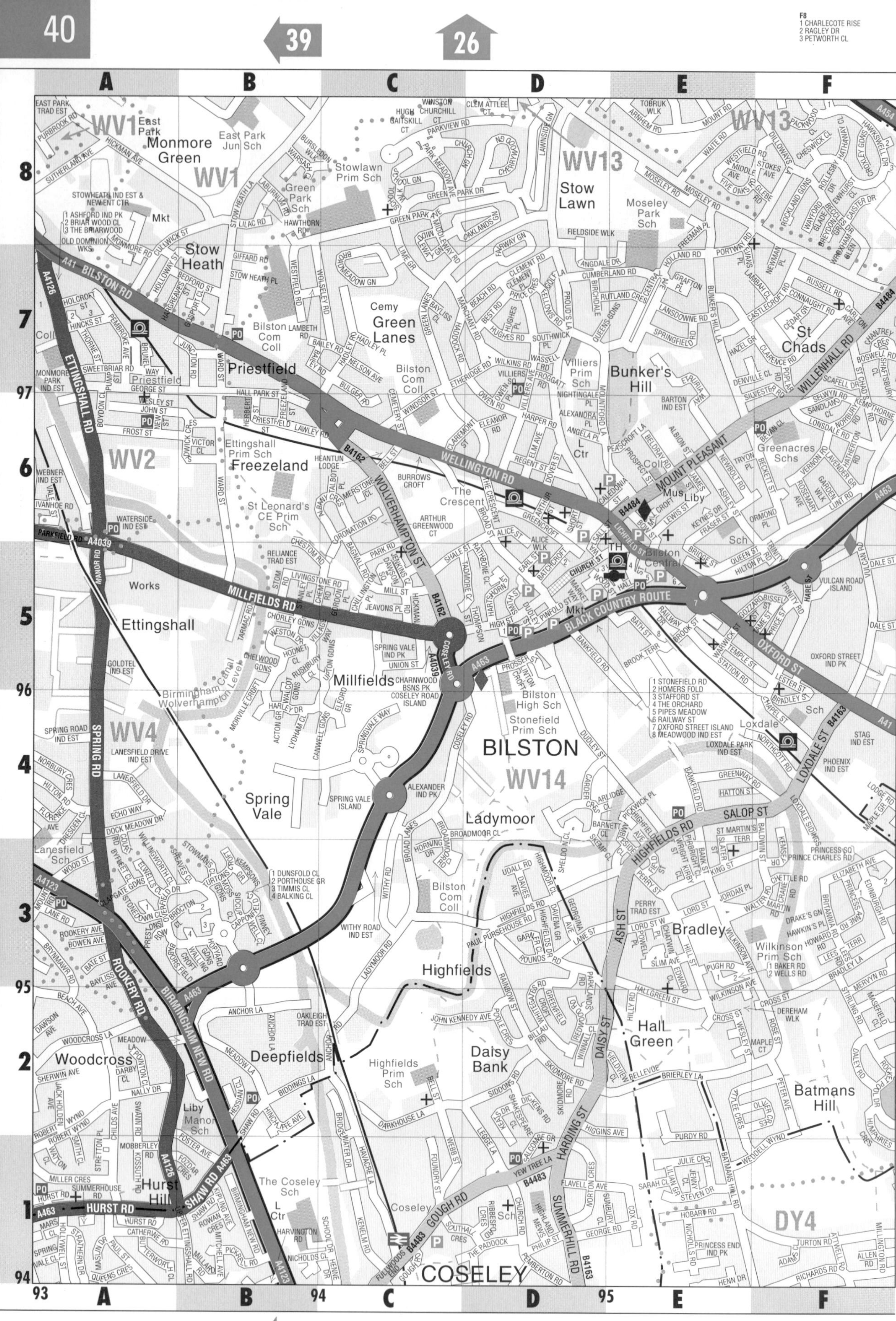
39
26
F8
1 CHARLECOTE RISE
2 RAGLEY DR
3 PETWORTH CL
A
B
C
D
E
F
8
7
97
6
5
96
4
3
95
2
1
94
93
94
95
WV1
East Park
Monmore Green
East Park Jun Sch
WV13
Stow Lawn
Moseley Park Sch
Stowlawn Prim Sch
Green Park Sch
STOWHEATH IND EST & NEW ENT CTR
1 ASHFORD IND PK
2 BRIAR WOOD CL
3 THE BRIARWOOD
OLD DOMINION WKS
Mkt
Stow Heath
BILSTON RD
A41
A4126
ETTINGSHALL RD
Bilston Com Coll
Priestfield
Cemy
Green Lanes
Bilston Com Coll
Villiers Prim Sch
Bunker's Hill
St Chads
WILLENHALL RD
B4484
WV2
Ettingshall Prim Sch
Freezeland
St Leonard's CE Prim Sch
WELLINGTON RD
The Crescent
MOUNT PLEASANT
Greenacres Schs
Mus
Liby
Coll
TH
Bilston Central
L Ctr
WEBNER IND EST
WATERSIDE IND EST
PARKFIELD RD
A4039
MILLFIELDS RD
WOLVERHAMPTON ST
B4162
Works
Ettingshall
BLACK COUNTRY ROUTE
Mkt
OXFORD ST
VULCAN ROAD ISLAND
OXFORD STREET IND PK
GOLDTEL IND EST
Birmingham Wolverhampton Level Canal
Millfields
CHARNWOOD BSNS PK
COSELEY ROAD ISLAND
SPRING VALE IND PK
A463
Bilston High Sch
Stonefield Prim Sch
1 STONEFIELD RD
2 HOMERS FOLD
3 STAFFORD ST
4 THE ORCHARD
5 PIPES MEADOW
6 RAILWAY ST
7 OXFORD STREET ISLAND
8 MEADWOOD IND EST
Loxdale
LOXDALE PARK IND EST
Sch
STAG IND EST
PHOENIX IND EST
SPRING ROAD IND EST
WV4
LANESFIELD DRIVE IND EST
SPRING RD
BILSTON
WV14
Spring Vale
SPRING VALE ISLAND
ALEXANDER IND PK
Ladymoor
HIGHFIELDS RD
SALOP ST
LOXDALE ST
B4163
Lanesfield Sch
1 DUNSFOLD CL
2 PORTHOUSE GR
3 TIMMIS CL
4 BALKING CL
Bilston Com Coll
PERRY TRAD EST
Bradley
Wilkinson Prim Sch
1 BAKER RD
2 WELLS RD
WITHY ROAD IND EST
Highfields
ASH ST
ROOKERY RD
BIRMINGHAM NEW RD
OAKLEIGH TRAD EST
Woodcross
Deepfields
Highfields Prim Sch
Daisy Bank
DAISY ST
Hall Green
Batmans Hill
Liby
Manor Sch
HARDING ST
Hurst Hill
HURST RD
A463
SHAW RD
A4123
The Coseley Sch
L Ctr
Coseley
GOUGH RD
B4483
SUMMERHILL RD
DY4
PRINCESS END IND PK
COSELEY

27
42

D6
1 THE LEYS
2 HIGH ST
3 GREAT CROFT HO
4 JOHN WOOTON HO
5 GREAT CROFT ST
6 PICTUREDROME WAY

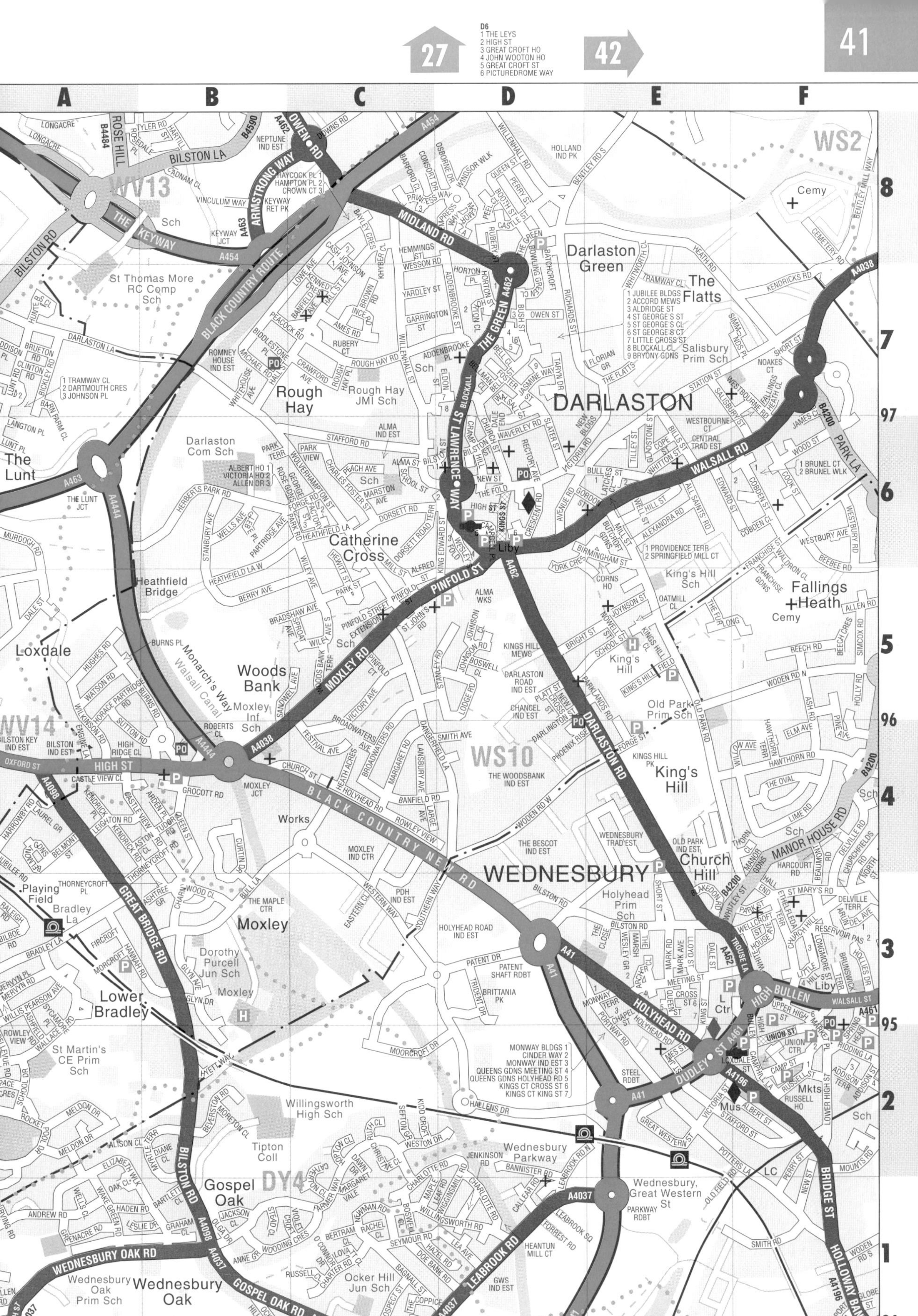

F2
1 UPPER RUSSELL ST
2 SHAMBLES
3 GREGORY CL
4 RAILWAY TERR

F3
1 CHURCH HILL CT
2 GEORGIAN GDNS
3 ST BARTHOLOMEW TERR
4 PARTRIDGE CT
5 LOVER'S WLK
6 CHURCH HILL

52
42

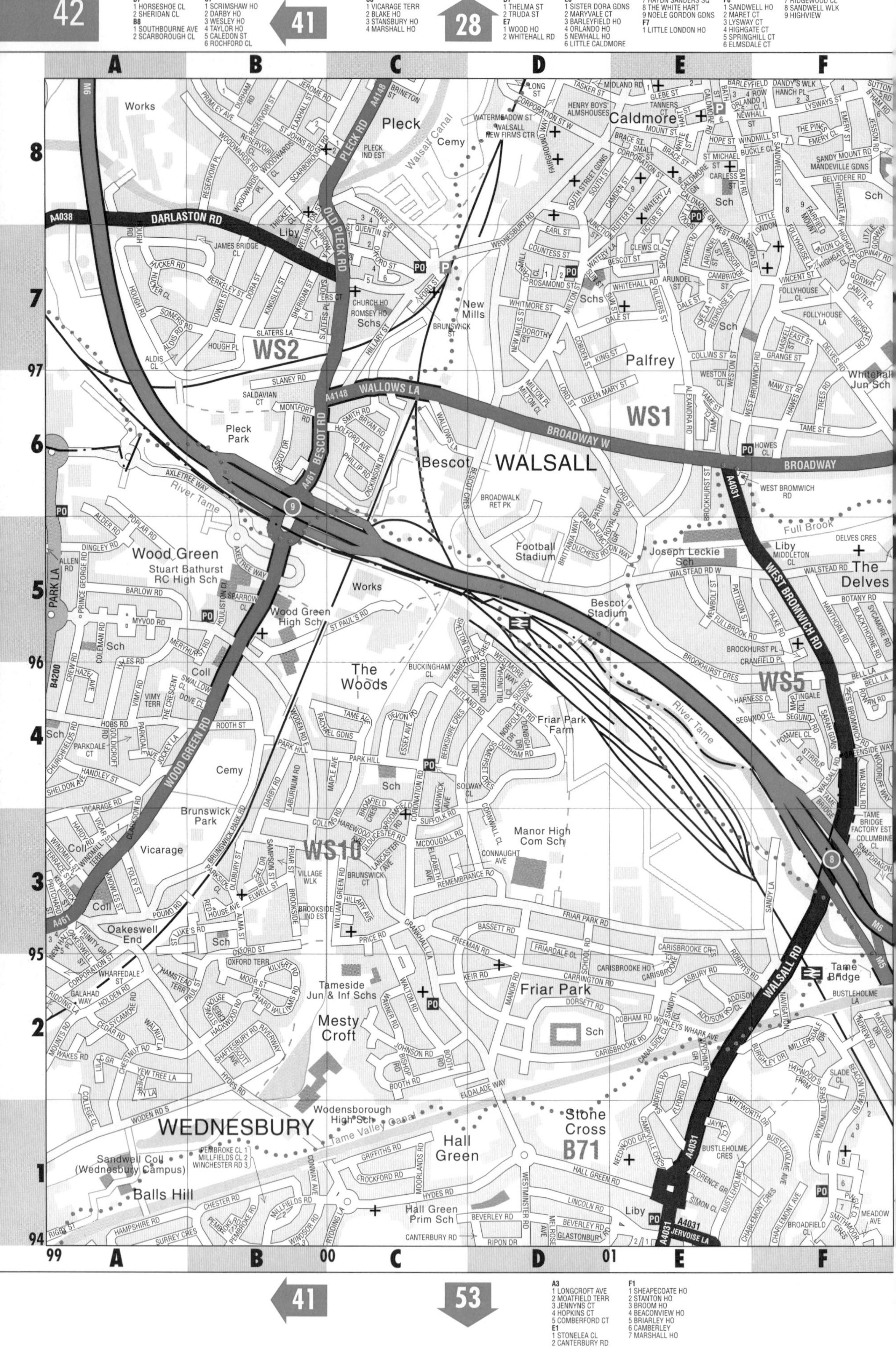
B7
1 HORSESHOE CL
2 SHERIDAN CL
B8
1 SOUTHBOURNE AVE
2 SCARBOROUGH CL
C7
1 SCRIMSHAW HO
2 DARBY HO
3 WESLEY HO
4 TAYLOR HO
5 CALEDON ST
6 ROCHFORD CL
41
C8
1 VICARAGE TERR
2 BLAKE HO
3 STANSBURY HO
4 MARSHALL HO
28
D7
1 THELMA ST
2 TRUDA ST
E7
1 WOOD HO
2 WHITEHALL RD
E8
1 SISTER DORA GDNS
2 MARYVALE CT
3 BARLEYFIELD HO
4 ORLANDO HO
5 NEWHALL HO
6 LITTLE CALDMORE
7 HAYDN SANDERS SQ
8 THE WHITE HART
9 NOELE GORDON GDNS
F7
1 LITTLE LONDON HO
F8
1 SANDWELL HO
2 MARET CT
3 LYSWAY CT
4 HIGHGATE CT
5 SPRINGHILL CT
6 ELMSDALE CT
7 RIDGEWOOD CL
8 SANDWELL WLK
9 HIGHVIEW
A B C D E F
8 7 97 6 5 96 4 3 95 2 1 94
99 00 01
Pleck
Caldmore
WS2
Palfrey
WS1
WALSALL
Bescot
Wood Green
WS5
The Delves
The Woods
WS10
Friar Park
Oakeswell End
Mesty Croft
WEDNESBURY
Hall Green
Stone Cross
B71
Balls Hill
DARLASTON RD
WALLOWS LA
BROADWAY W
BROADWAY
WEST BROMWICH RD
WALSALL RD
WOOD GREEN RD
BESCOT RD
OLD PLECK RD
PLECK RD
Football Stadium
Bescot Stadium
Tame Valley Canal
River Tame
41
53
A3
1 LONGCROFT AVE
2 MOATFIELD TERR
3 JENNYNS CT
4 HOPKINS CT
5 COMBERFORD CT
E1
1 STONELEA CL
2 CANTERBURY RD
F1
1 SHEAPECOATE HO
2 STANTON HO
3 BROOM HO
4 BEACONVIEW HO
5 BRIARLEY HO
6 CAMBERLEY
7 MARSHALL HO

29
44

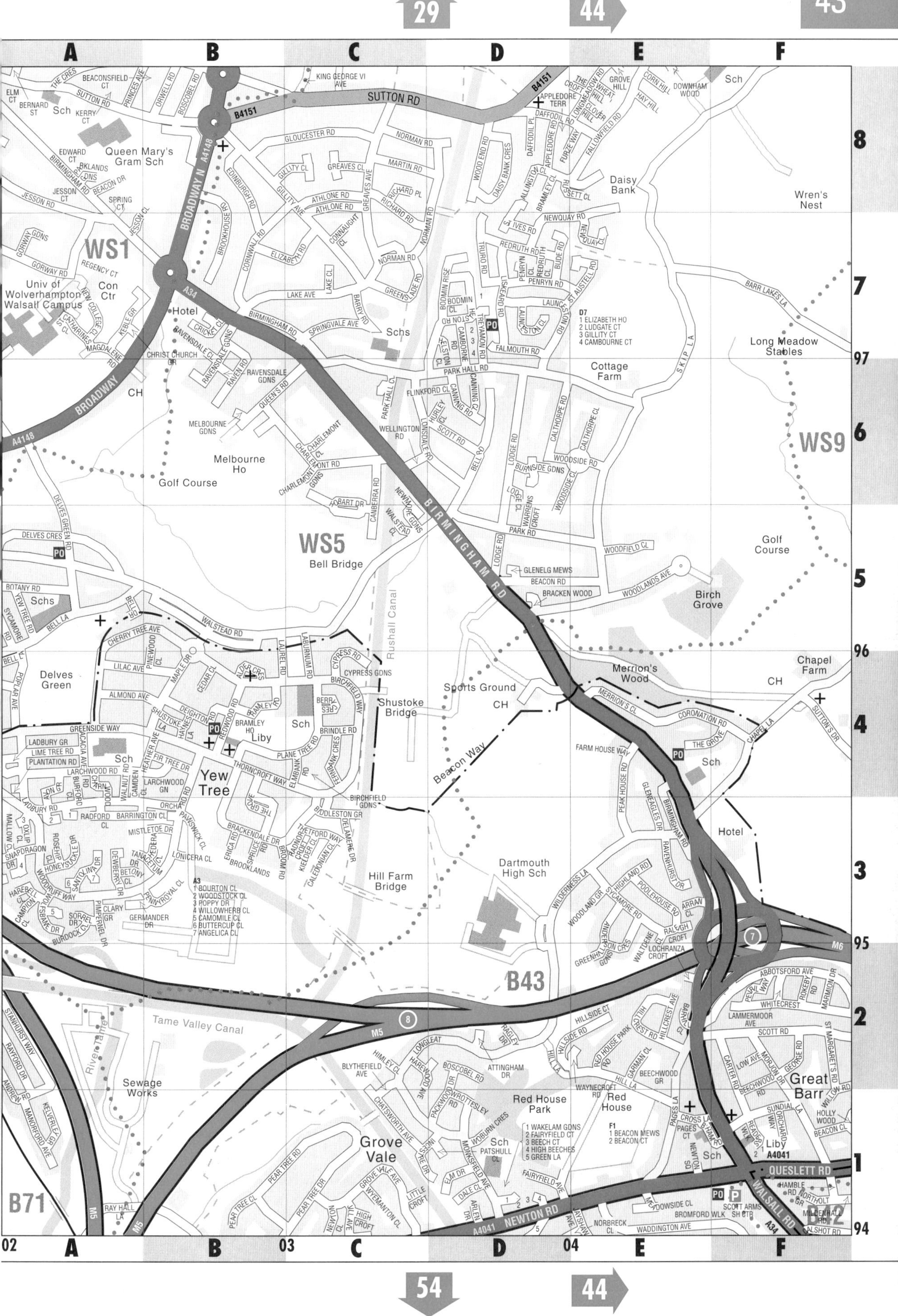
A
B
C
D
E
F
8
7
97
6
5
96
4
3
95
2
1
94
02
03
04
WS1
WS5
WS9
B43
B71
B42
SUTTON RD
B4151
A4148
BROADWAY N
BROADWAY
A34
BIRMINGHAM RD
Queen Mary's Gram Sch
Univ of Wolverhampton Walsall Campus
Con Ctr
Hotel
CH
Melbourne Ho
Golf Course
Bell Bridge
Rushall Canal
Daisy Bank
Wren's Nest
Cottage Farm
Long Meadow Stables
Birch Grove
Merrion's Wood
Chapel Farm
Delves Green
Yew Tree
Liby
Sch
Schs
Shustoke Bridge
Sports Ground
Beacon Way
Hill Farm Bridge
Dartmouth High Sch
Tame Valley Canal
River Tame
Sewage Works
M5
M6
Red House Park
Red House
Grove Vale
Great Barr
QUESLETT RD
A4041
NEWTON RD
WALSALL RD
D7
1 ELIZABETH HO
2 LUDGATE CT
3 GILLITY CT
4 CAMBOURNE CT
A3
1 BOURTON CL
2 WOODSTOCK CL
3 POPPY DR
4 WILLOWHERB CL
5 CAMOMILE CL
6 BUTTERCUP CL
7 ANGELICA CL
1 WAKELAM GDNS
2 FAIRYFIELD CT
3 BEECH CT
4 HIGH BEECHES
5 GREEN LA
F1
1 BEACON MEWS
2 BEACON CT

54
44

43
30

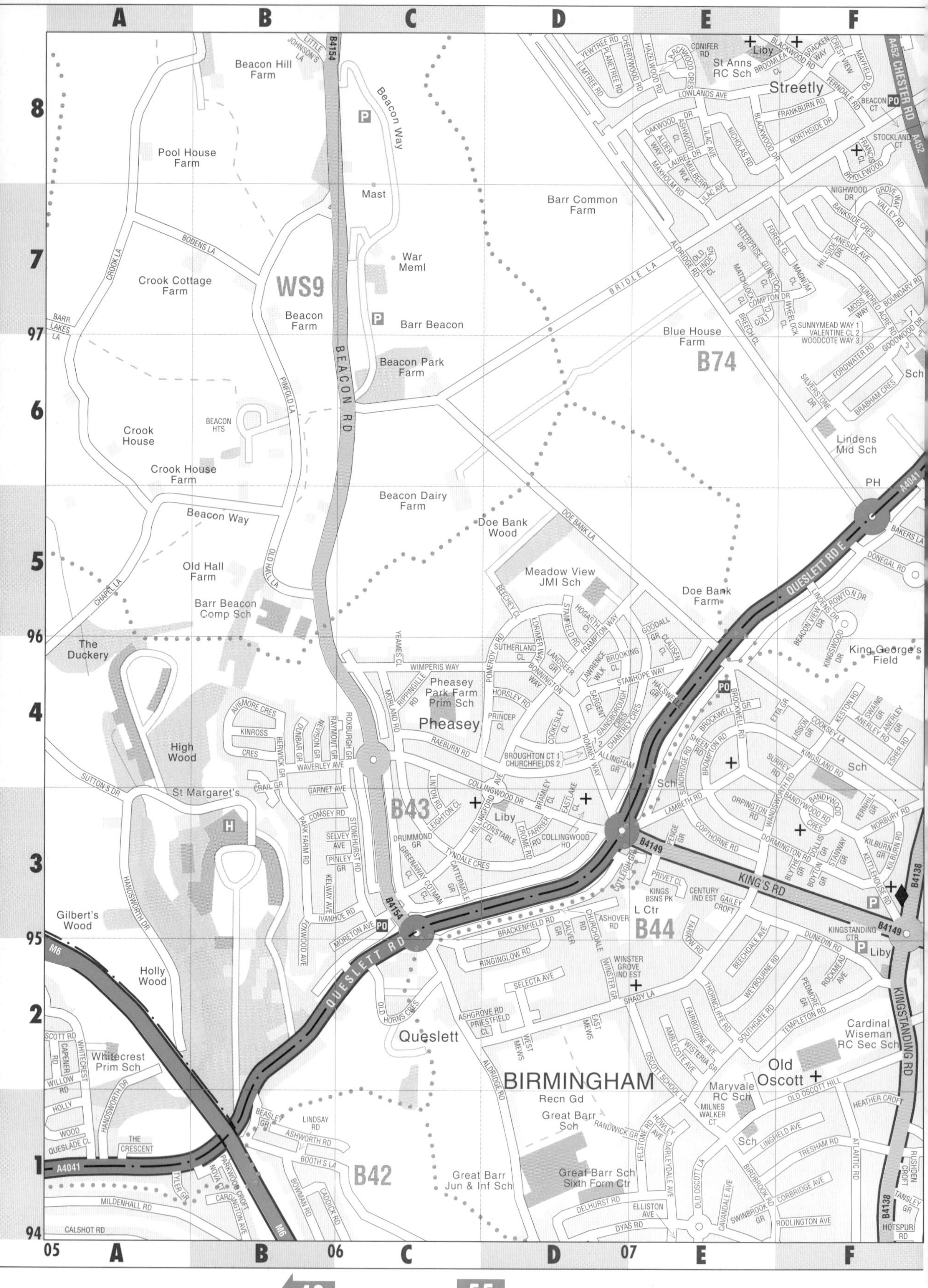
A
B
C
D
E
F
8
7
97
6
5
96
4
3
95
2
1
94
05
06
07
Beacon Hill Farm
LITTLE JOHNSON'S LA
B4154
Beacon Way
Pool House Farm
Mast
Barr Common Farm
BODENS LA
War Meml
CROOK LA
Crook Cottage Farm
WS9
BARR LAKES LA
Beacon Farm
Barr Beacon
BEACON RD
Beacon Park Farm
BRIDLE LA
PINFOLD LA
BEACON HTS
Crook House
Crook House Farm
Beacon Dairy Farm
Beacon Way
Doe Bank Wood
DOE BANK LA
Old Hall Farm
OLD HALL LA
CHAPEL LA
Meadow View JMI Sch
Barr Beacon Comp Sch
Doe Bank Farm
The Duckery
WIMPERIS WAY
Pheasey Park Farm Prim Sch
Pheasey
High Wood
SUTTON'S DR
St Margaret's
B43
Liby
COLLINGWOOD DR
QUESLETT RD E
King George's Field
B4149
KING'S RD
Gilbert's Wood
HANDSWORTH DR
Holly Wood
M6
QUESLETT RD
B44
L Ctr
KINGS BSNS PK
CENTURY IND EST
WINSTER GROVE IND EST
SHADY LA
Queslett
Whitecrest Prim Sch
BIRMINGHAM
Recn Gd
Great Barr Sch
Great Barr Sch Sixth Form Ctr
Great Barr Jun & Inf Sch
B42
A4041
MILDENHALL RD
CALSHOT RD
Old Oscott
Maryvale RC Sch
OLD OSCOTT HILL
Cardinal Wiseman RC Sec Sch
KINGSTANDING RD
KINGSTANDING CTR
B4138
Streetly
St Anns RC Sch
A452 CHESTER RD
LOWLANDS AVE
Blue House Farm
B74
Lindens Mid Sch
PH
A4041
Sch

Pool Hollies
Darnel Hurst
Lady Wood
Golf Course
Upper Nut Hurst
Blackroot Pool
B74
Meml
Lower Nut Hurst
Keeper's Pool
Sutton Park
Hill Hurst
Rowton's Well
Holly Hurst
The Streetly Sch
Hotel
Westwood Coppice
Banners Gate
Longmoor Pool
King's Standing
Banners Gate Jun & Inf Schs
Liby
Longmoor Sch
B73
Golf Course
SUTTON COLDFIELD
La Reserve
Wyndley Wood
Powell's Pool
New Oscott Jun & Inf Schs
CH
1 WINDLEY HO
2 BRACEBRIDGE HO
3 BLACKROOT HO
4 KEEPERS HO
5 POWELLS HO
New Oscott
Superstore
Sch
B44
Kingstanding
Twickenham Prim Sch
Boldmere Jun & Inf Schs
Kingsthorne Sch
Oscott Coll
B23
CHESTER RD
KINGS RD
JOCKEY RD
COLLEGE RD
SUTTON OAK RD
KINGSTANDING RD
BOLDMERE RD
THORNHILL RD
MONMOUTH DR
Warden's Belt

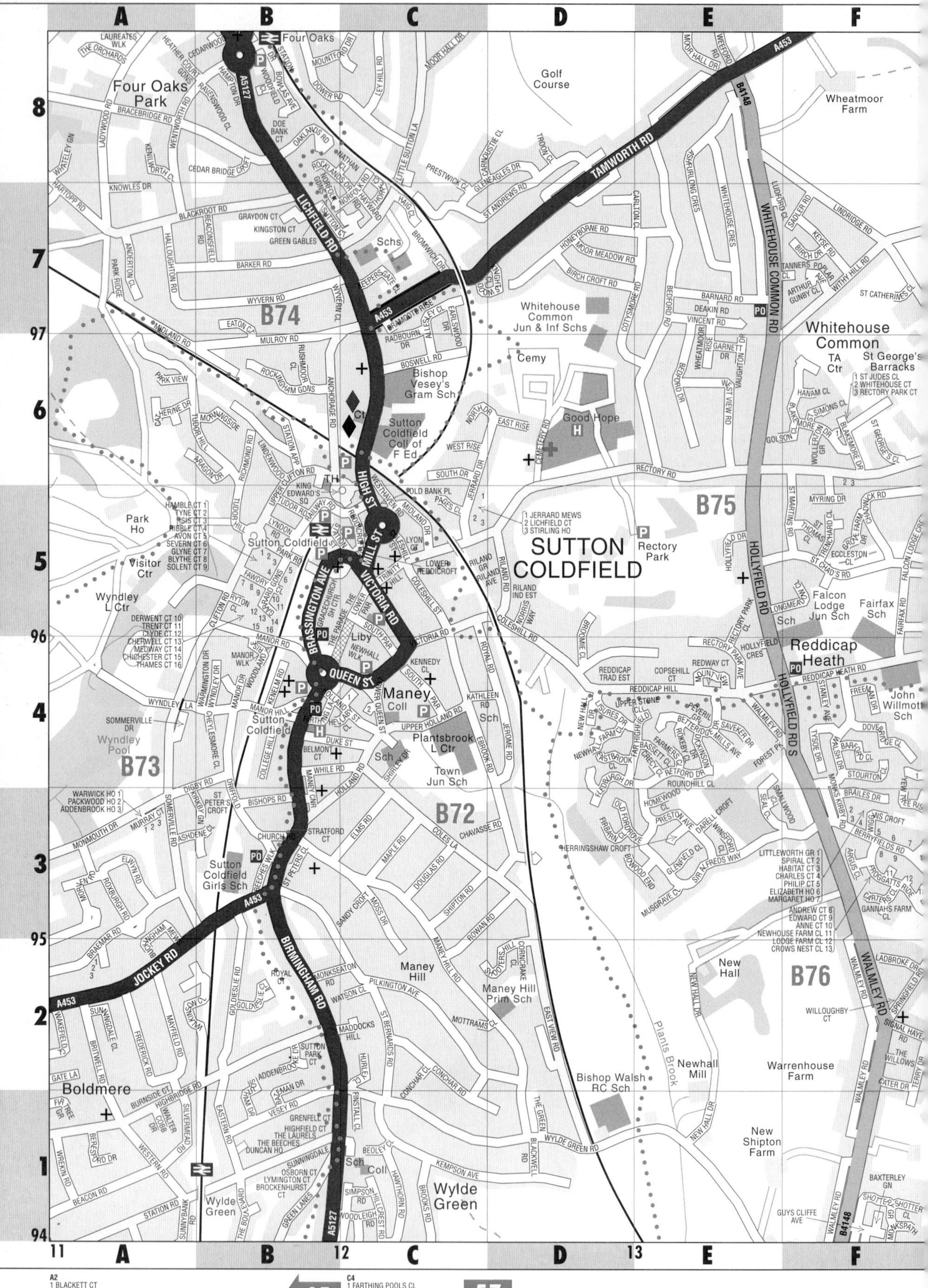

A2
1 BLACKETT CT
2 SOMERVILLE CT
3 BIDDULPH CT

C4
1 FARTHING POOLS CL
2 DEEPLOW CL

45 57

33
48
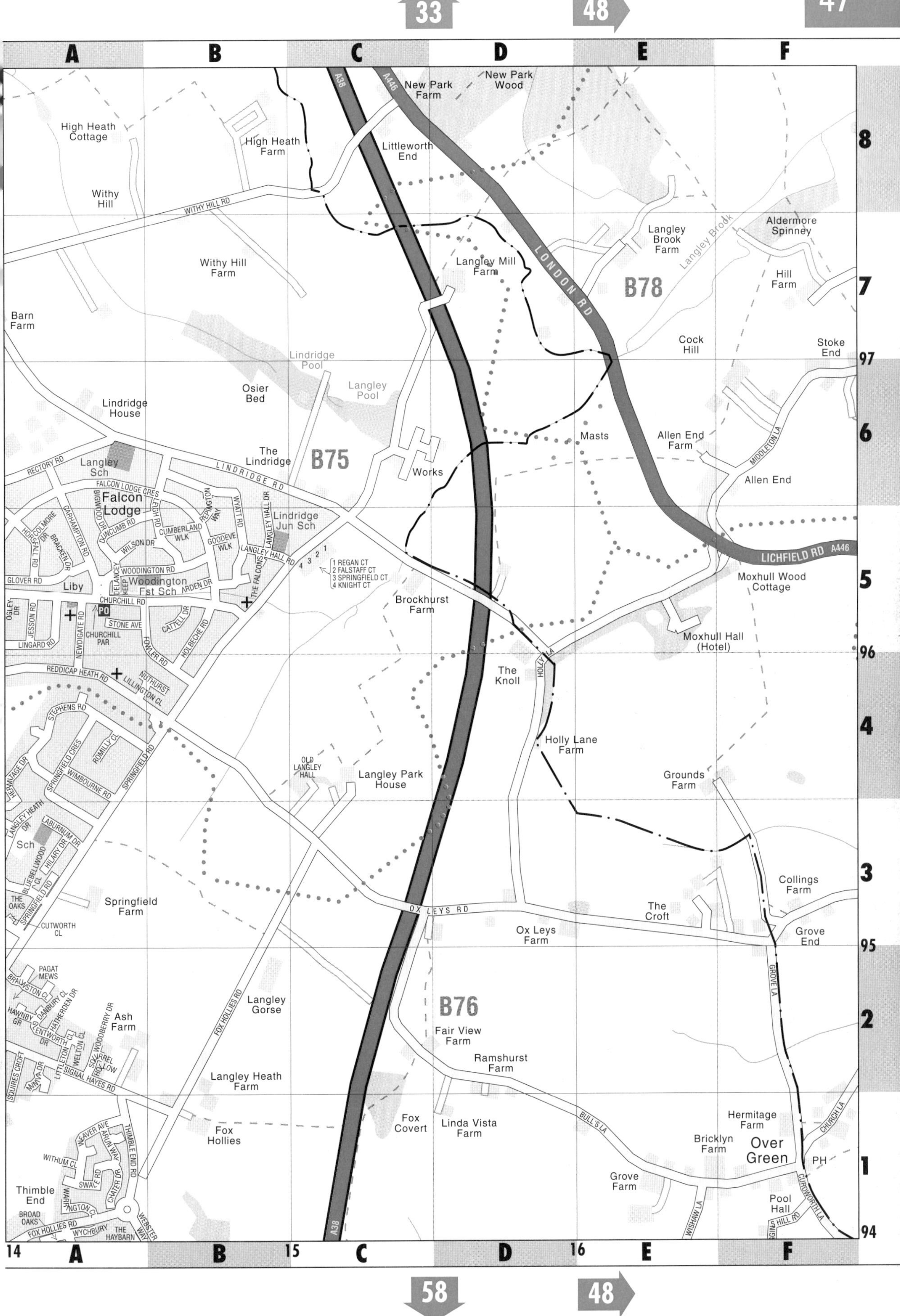
A
B
C
D
E
F
8
7
97
6
5
96
4
3
95
2
1
94
14
15
16
High Heath Cottage
High Heath Farm
New Park Farm
New Park Wood
Littleworth End
Withy Hill
WITHY HILL RD
Withy Hill Farm
Langley Mill Farm
LONDON RD
Langley Brook Farm
Langley Brook
Aldermore Spinney
Hill Farm
B78
Barn Farm
Lindridge Pool
Langley Pool
Cock Hill
Stoke End
Lindridge House
Osier Bed
Masts
Allen End Farm
MIDDLETON LA
Allen End
RECTORY RD
Langley Sch
The Lindridge
B75
Works
LINDRIDGE RD
FALCON LODGE CRES
Falcon Lodge
Lindridge Jun Sch
LICHFIELD RD
A446
A38
1 REGAN CT
2 FALSTAFF CT
3 SPRINGFIELD CT
4 KNIGHT CT
Moxhull Wood Cottage
GLOVER RD
Liby
Woodington Fst Sch
CHURCHILL RD
PO
Brockhurst Farm
Moxhull Hall (Hotel)
JESSON RD
NEWDIGATE RD
STONE AVE
CHURCHILL PAR
LINGARD RD
REDDICAP HEATH RD
LILLINGTON CL
HOLLY LA
The Knoll
STEPHENS RD
SPRINGFIELD CRES
ROMILLY CL
Holly Lane Farm
HERMITAGE DR
WIMBOURNE RD
SPRINGFIELD RD
OLD LANGLEY HALL
Langley Park House
Grounds Farm
LANGLEY HEATH DR
LABURNUM DR
Sch
HILARY DR
BLUEBELLWOOD CL
SPRINGFIELD RD
THE OAKS
CUTWORTH CL
Springfield Farm
OX LEYS RD
The Croft
Collings Farm
Ox Leys Farm
Grove End
PAGAT MEWS
FOX HOLLIES RD
Langley Gorse
B76
GROVE LA
Ash Farm
Fair View Farm
Ramshurst Farm
SIGNAL HAYES RD
Langley Heath Farm
BULL'S LA
Fox Hollies
Fox Covert
Linda Vista Farm
Hermitage Farm
Bricklyn Farm
Over Green
CHURCH LA
PH
WEAVER AVE
THIMBLE END RD
Grove Farm
Thimble End
BROAD OAKS
FOX HOLLIES RD
WYCHBURY RD
THE HAYBARN
WEBSTER WAY
WISHAW LA
Pool Hall
CURDWORTH LA
58
48

47
34

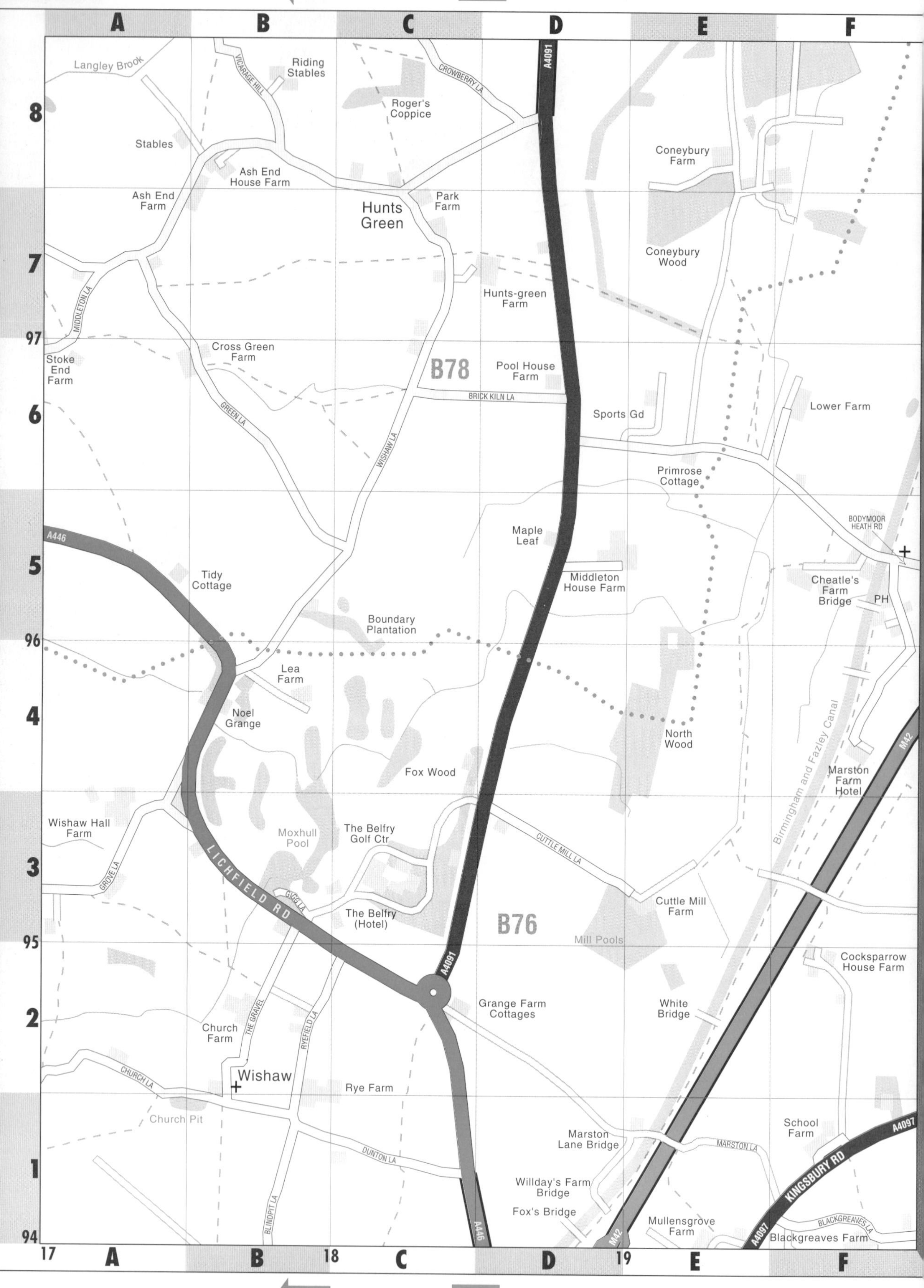
A
B
C
D
E
F
Langley Brook
Riding Stables
Roger's Coppice
CROWBERRY LA
VICARAGE HILL
A4091
8
Stables
Ash End House Farm
Coneybury Farm
Ash End Farm
Hunts Green
Park Farm
Coneybury Wood
7
MIDDLETON LA
Hunts-green Farm
97
Stoke End Farm
Cross Green Farm
B78
Pool House Farm
BRICK KILN LA
Sports Gd
Lower Farm
6
GREEN LA
WISHAW LA
Primrose Cottage
BODYMOOR HEATH RD
A446
Maple Leaf
5
Tidy Cottage
Middleton House Farm
Cheatle's Farm Bridge
PH
Boundary Plantation
96
Lea Farm
Noel Grange
4
North Wood
M42
Fox Wood
Birmingham and Fazley Canal
Marston Farm Hotel
Wishaw Hall Farm
Moxhull Pool
The Belfry Golf Ctr
CUTTLE MILL LA
3
GROVE LA
LICHFIELD RD
GIGG LA
Cuttle Mill Farm
The Belfry (Hotel)
B76
95
Mill Pools
Cocksparrow House Farm
A4091
Grange Farm Cottages
White Bridge
2
Church Farm
THE GRAVEL
RYEFIELD LA
CHURCH LA
Wishaw
Rye Farm
Church Pit
Marston Lane Bridge
School Farm
A4097
1
DUNTON LA
MARSTON LA
KINGSBURY RD
Willday's Farm Bridge
BLINDPIT LA
Fox's Bridge
A446
Mullensgrove Farm
BLACKGREAVES LA
94
M42
A4097
Blackgreaves Farm
17
18
19

47
59

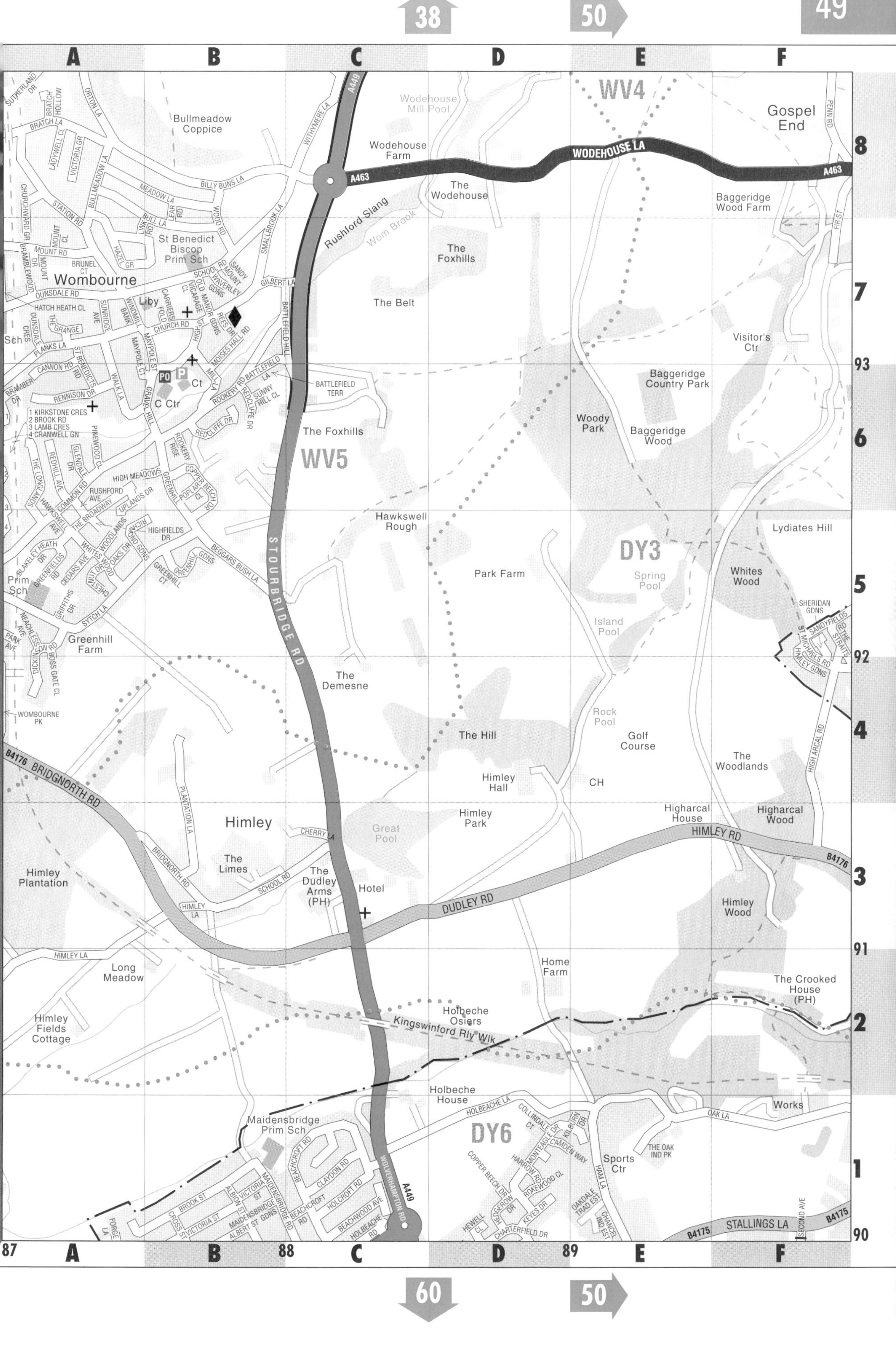

38
50
Wombourne
Bullmeadow Coppice
Wodehouse Mill Pool
Wodehouse Farm
WV4
Gospel End
WODEHOUSE LA
A463
A449
The Wodehouse
Baggeridge Wood Farm
Rushford Slang
Wom Brook
St Benedict Biscop Prim Sch
The Foxhills
The Belt
Liby
Visitor's Ctr
Baggeridge Country Park
Woody Park
Baggeridge Wood
C Ctr
The Foxhills
WV5
Hawkswell Rough
Lydiates Hill
DY3
Park Farm
Spring Pool
Whites Wood
Island Pool
Greenhill Farm
The Demesne
Rock Pool
The Hill
Golf Course
The Woodlands
STOURBRIDGE RD
B4176 BRIDGNORTH RD
Himley Hall
CH
Himley
Himley Park
Higharcal House
Higharcal Wood
Great Pool
HIMLEY RD
Himley Plantation
The Limes
The Dudley Arms (PH)
Hotel
DUDLEY RD
Himley Wood
Long Meadow
Home Farm
The Crooked House (PH)
Himley Fields Cottage
Holbeche Osiers
Kingswinford Rly Wlk
Holbeche House
Works
Maidensbridge Prim Sch
DY6
Sports Ctr
WOLVERHAMPTON RD
B4175 STALLINGS LA
A B C D E F
8 7 93 6 5 92 4 3 91 2 1 90
87 88 89
60
50

49
39

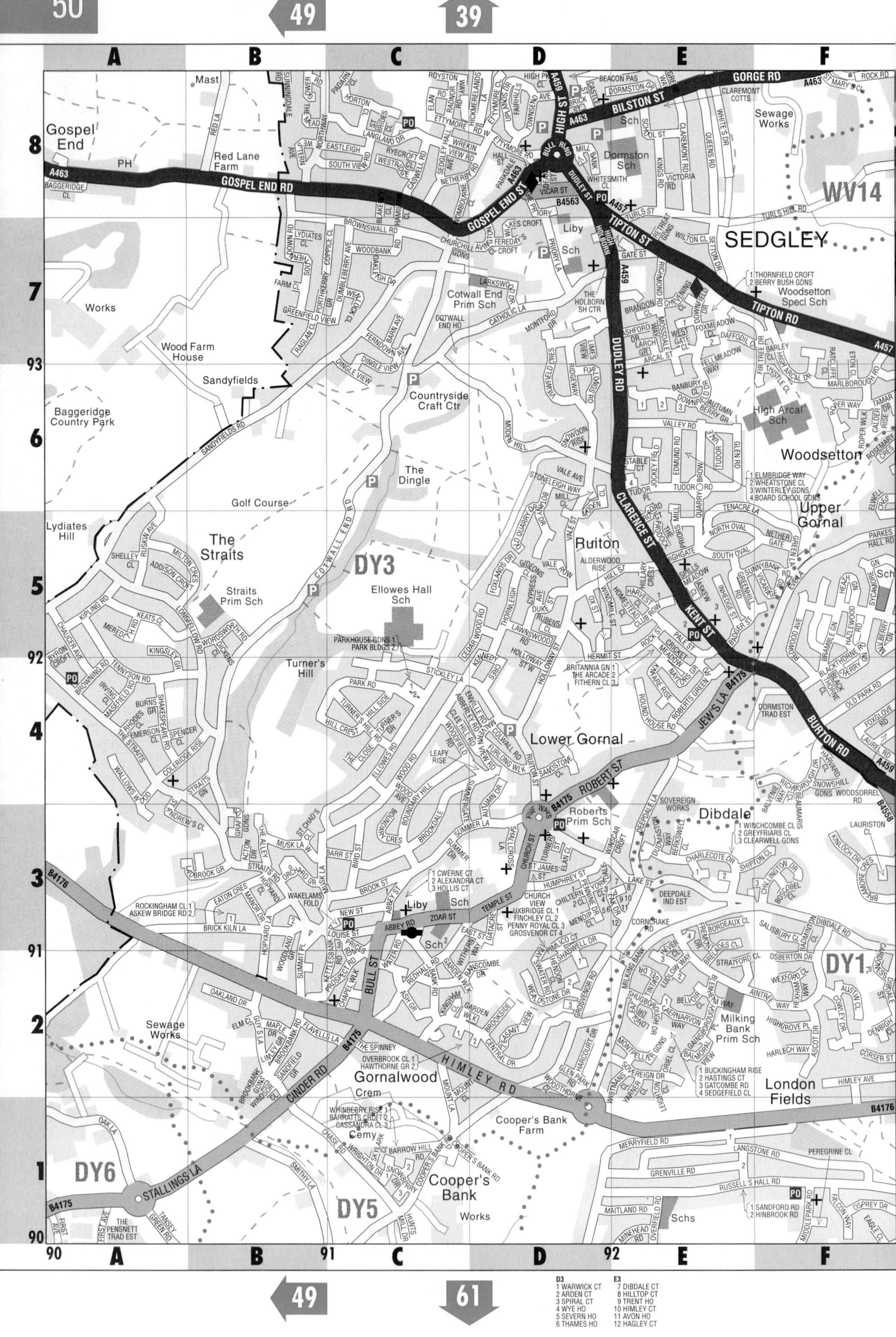

49
61

D3
1 WARWICK CT
2 ARDEN CT
3 SPIRAL CT
4 WYE HO
5 SEVERN HO
6 THAMES HO

E3
7 DIBDALE CT
8 HILLTOP CT
9 TRENT HO
10 HIMLEY CT
11 AVON HO
12 HAGLEY CT

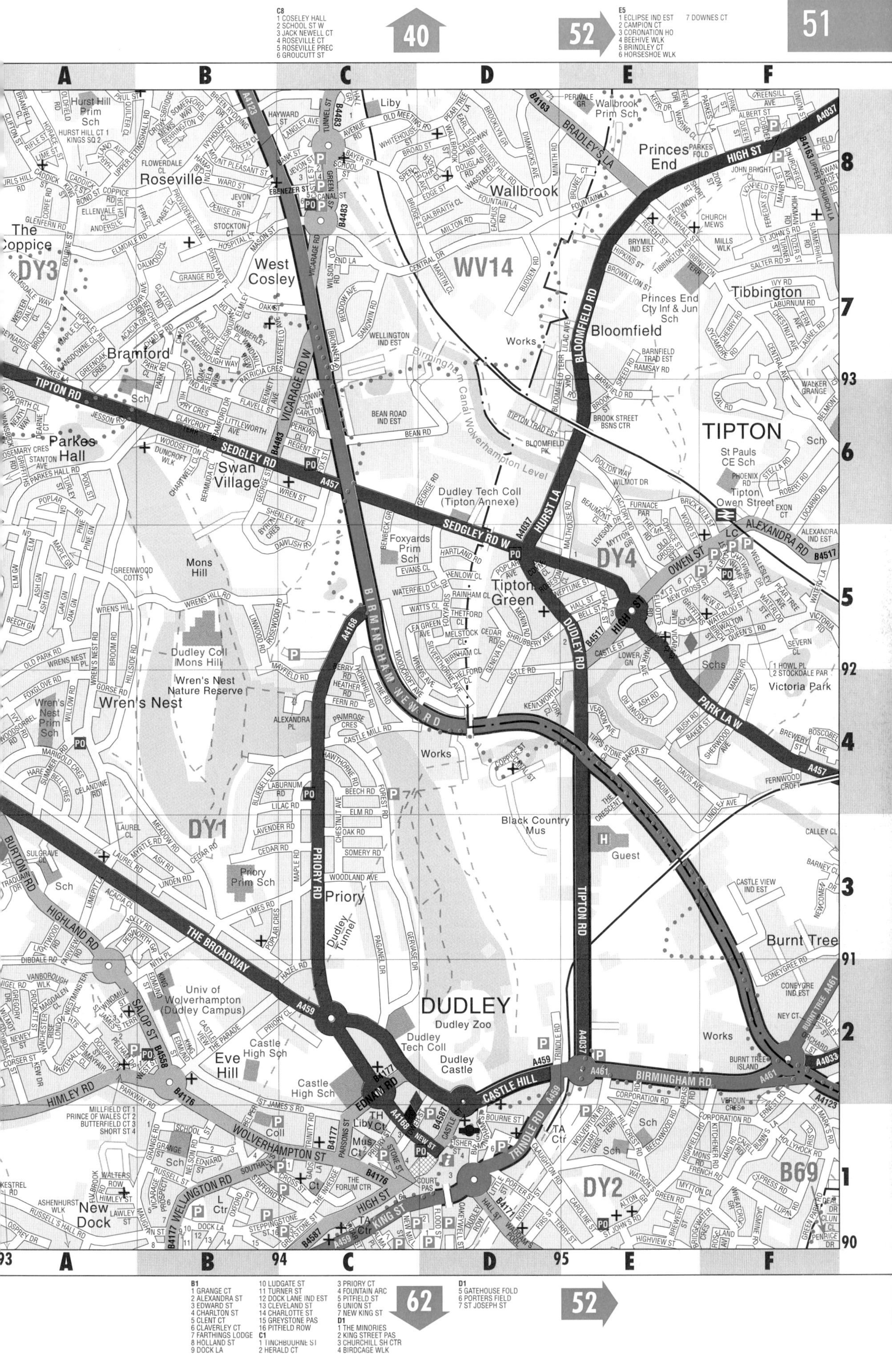

51
40
52
62
C8
1 COSELEY HALL
2 SCHOOL ST W
3 JACK NEWELL CT
4 ROSEVILLE CT
5 ROSEVILLE PREC
6 GROUCUTT ST
E5
1 ECLIPSE IND EST
2 CAMPION CT
3 CORONATION HO
4 BEEHIVE WLK
5 BRINDLEY CT
6 HORSESHOE WLK
7 DOWNES CT
A
B
C
D
E
F
8
7
93
6
5
92
4
3
91
2
1
90
93
94
95
Hurst Hill Prim Sch
HURST HILL CT 1
KINGS SQ 2
Roseville
The Coppice
DY3
West Cosley
Liby
WV14
Wallbrook
Wallbrook Prim Sch
Princes End
HIGH ST
CHURCH MEWS
MILLS WLK
Tibbington
Princes End Cty Inf & Jun Sch
Bloomfield
BLOOMFIELD RD
Works
WELLINGTON IND EST
BARNFIELD TRAD EST
Bramford
TIPTON RD
Sch
Parkes Hall
BEAN ROAD IND EST
TIPTON TRAD EST
BROOK STREET BSNS CTR
TIPTON
St Pauls CE Sch
Tipton Owen Street
SEDGLEY RD
Swan Village
A457
Dudley Tech Coll (Tipton Annexe)
SEDGLEY RD W
Foxyards Prim Sch
Tipton Green
DY4
ALEXANDRA RD
ALEXANDRA IND EST
Mons Hill
GREENWOOD COTTS
HURST LA
DUDLEY RD
OWEN ST
HIGH ST
BIRMINGHAM NEW RD
Dudley Coll Mons Hill
Wren's Nest Nature Reserve
Wren's Nest
Wren's Nest Prim Sch
Schs
1 HOWL PL
2 STOCKDALE PAR
Victoria Park
PARK LA W
ALEXANDRA PL
Works
Black Country Mus
DY1
PRIORY RD
Priory Prim Sch
Priory
Dudley Tunnel
Guest
CASTLE VIEW IND EST
TIPTON RD
Burnt Tree
THE BROADWAY
Univ of Wolverhampton (Dudley Campus)
DUDLEY
Dudley Zoo
Dudley Tech Coll
Dudley Castle
CONEYGRE IND EST
Works
BURNT TREE ISLAND
Castle High Sch
Eve Hill
CASTLE HILL
BIRMINGHAM RD
HIMLEY RD
MILLFIELD CT 1
PRINCE OF WALES CT 2
BUTTERFIELD CT 3
SHORT ST 4
Coll
Castle High Sch
WOLVERHAMPTON ST
TH
Liby
Mus Ct
TA Ctr
Sch
Sch
DY2
B69
WELLINGTON RD
New Dock
L Ctr
THE FORUM CTR
KING ST
HIGH ST
TA Ctr
B1
1 GRANGE CT
2 ALEXANDRA ST
3 EDWARD ST
4 CHARLTON ST
5 CLENT CT
6 CLAVERLEY CT
7 FARTHINGS LODGE
8 HOLLAND ST
9 DOCK LA
10 LUDGATE ST
11 TURNER ST
12 DOCK LANE IND EST
13 CLEVELAND ST
14 CHARLOTTE ST
15 GREYSTONE PAS
16 PITFIELD ROW
C1
1 TINCHBOURNE ST
2 HERALD CT
3 PRIORY CT
4 FOUNTAIN ARC
5 PITFIELD ST
6 UNION ST
7 NEW KING ST
D1
1 THE MINORIES
2 KING STREET PAS
3 CHURCHILL SH CTR
4 BIRDCAGE WLK
D1
5 GATEHOUSE FOLD
6 PORTERS FIELD
7 ST JOSEPH ST

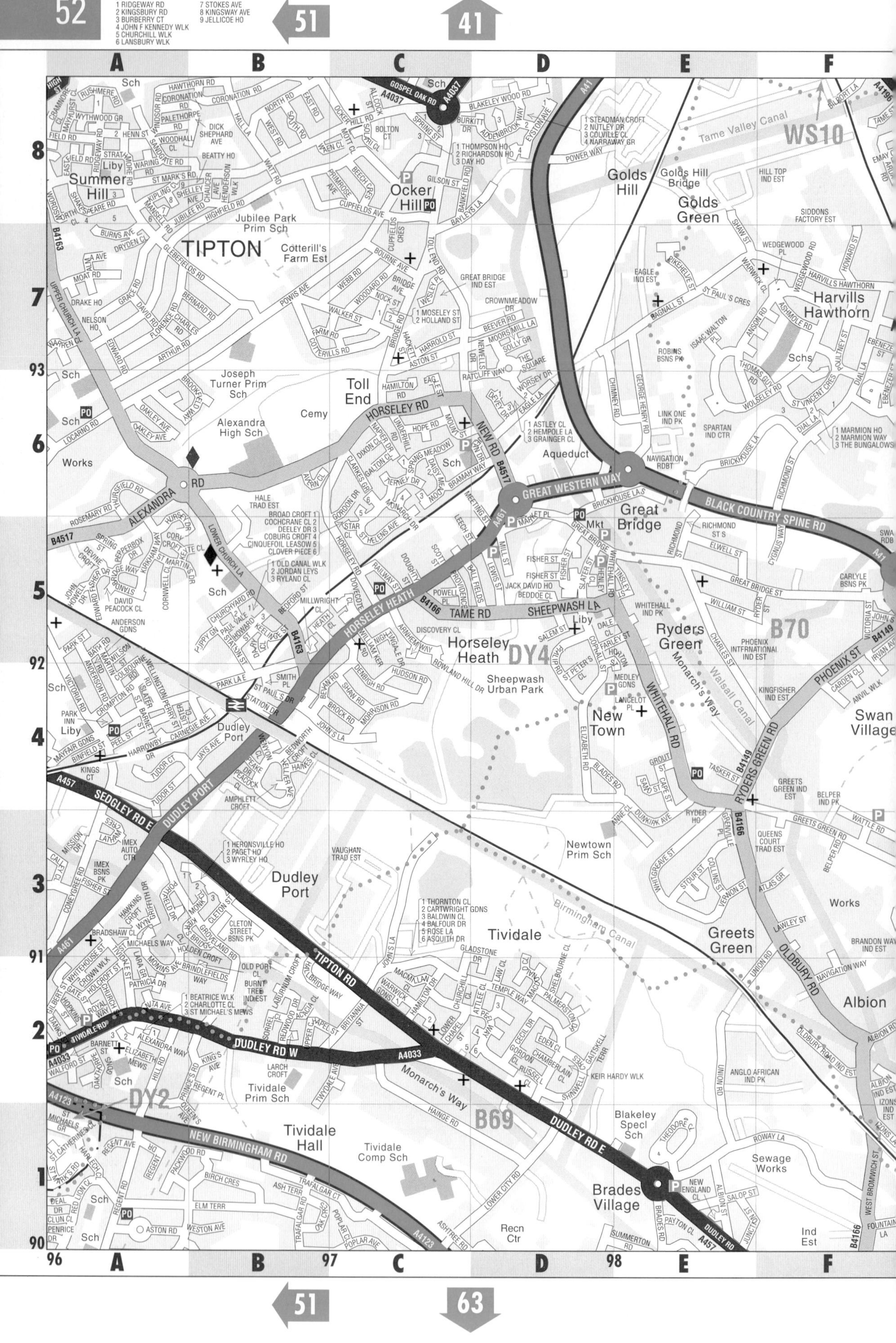
A
B
C
D
E
F
8
7
93
6
5
92
4
3
91
2
1
90
96
97
98
Summer Hill
TIPTON
Jubilee Park Prim Sch
Cotterill's Farm Est
Ocker Hill
Golds Hill
Golds Hill Bridge
Golds Green
Tame Valley Canal
WS10
HILL TOP IND EST
SIDDONS FACTORY EST
Harvills Hawthorn
GREAT BRIDGE IND EST
EAGLE IND EST
ROBINS BSNS PK
LINK ONE IND PK
SPARTAN IND CTR
Joseph Turner Prim Sch
Toll End
Cemy
Alexandra High Sch
Works
Aqueduct
NAVIGATION RDBT
GREAT WESTERN WAY
BLACK COUNTRY SPINE RD
Great Bridge
Mkt
HALE TRAD EST
Horseley Heath
DY4
Sheepwash Urban Park
Ryders Green
B70
WHITEHALL IND PK
PHOENIX INTERNATIONAL IND EST
KINGFISHER IND EST
Swan Village
New Town
Dudley Port
Walsall Canal
Monarch's Way
GREETS GREEN IND EST
BELPER IND PK
QUEENS COURT TRAD EST
Newtown Prim Sch
Dudley Port
VAUGHAN TRAD EST
IMEX BSNS PK
CLETON STREET BSNS PK
Tividale
Birmingham Canal
Greets Green
BRANDON WAY IND EST
Albion
OLDBURY ROAD IND EST
ANGLO AFRICAN IND PK
Tividale Prim Sch
DY2
B69
Tividale Hall
Tividale Comp Sch
Blakeley Specl Sch
Sewage Works
Brades Village
Recn Ctr
Ind Est
TIPTON RD
DUDLEY RD W
DUDLEY RD E
NEW BIRMINGHAM RD
SEDGLEY RD E
DUDLEY PORT
HORSELEY HEATH
HORSELEY RD
NEW RD
TAME RD
SHEEPWASH LA
WHITEHALL RD
RYDERS GREEN RD
PHOENIX ST
OLDBURY RD
GREAT BRIDGE ST
ALEXANDRA RD
POWIS AVE
UPPER CHURCH LA
LOWER CHURCH LA
OCKER HILL RD
GOSPEL OAK RD
A4037
A41
A461
B4517
B4163
B4166
B4149
A457
A4033
A4123

42
54

F8
1 BROADFIELD CL
2 GORSTY CL
3 EDNAM CL
4 BROGDEN CL
5 SPENCER CL

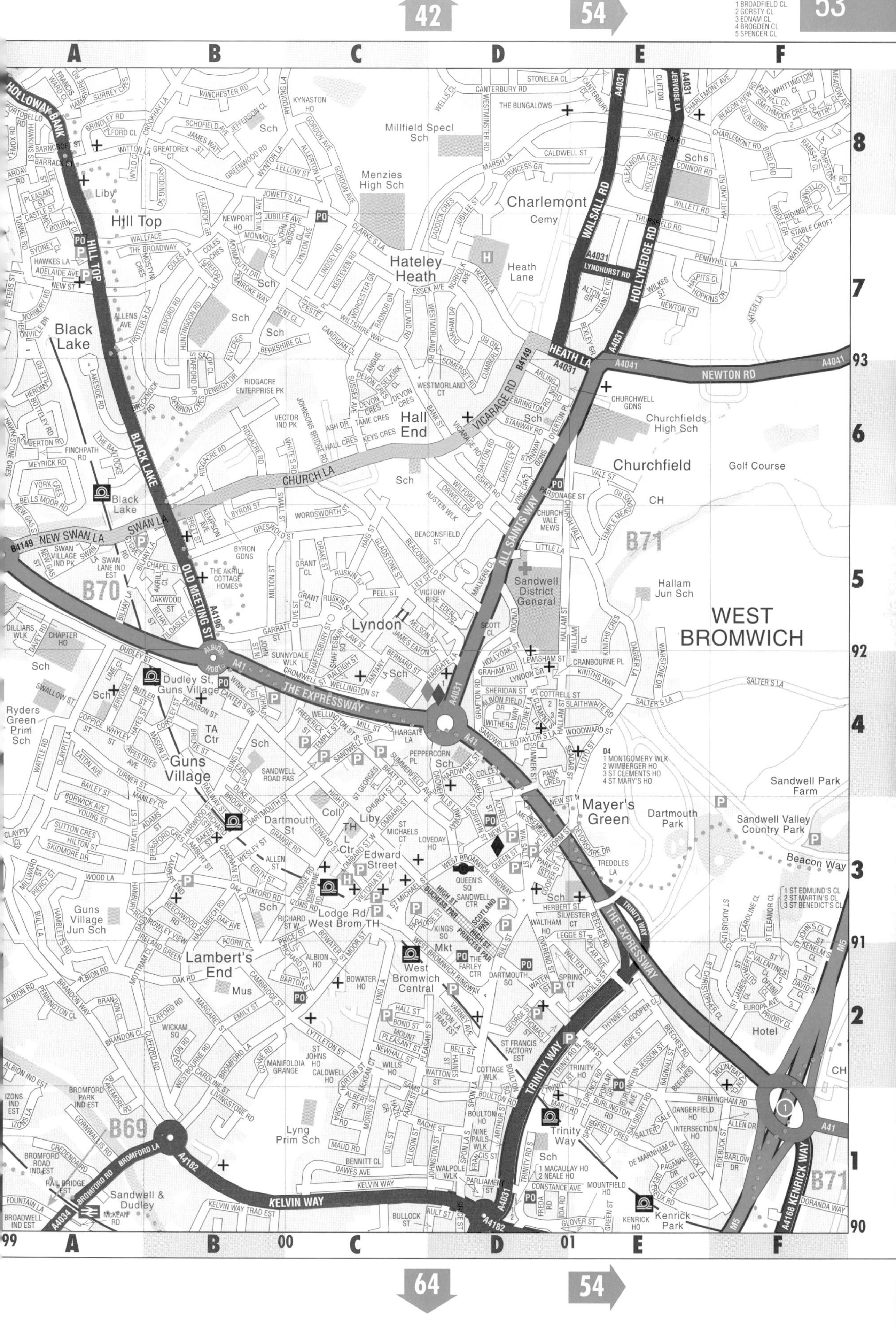

64
54

A   B   C   D   E   F

8

CHARLEMONT RD
HORSECROFT DR
WIGMORE LA
TURNERS CROFT
WATER LA
M5
Brook Bridge
CEDAR CT
BISHOP PEAR TREE CT
NEWTON RD
RAY HALL
BOWSTOKE RD
MARSTON RD
PO
B4167
HEATHER RD
BROOMHILL
BROOMHILL RD
GREEN LA
HAVEN CROFT
CHUDLEIGH GR
ROUSDON
AMBURY WAY
MANOR RD
CELBURY WAY
EARLSTON WAY
INDEN AVE
GREEN LA
CALVERTON GR
GORSTIE CROFT
JAYSHAW AVE
ALLENDALE
FARNHAM CL
A34 WALSALL RD
B4124
HOLLYWOOD
CEDARWOOD CROFT
CHARNWOOD RD

7

A4041
Crem
Haypits
FORGE LA
Newton
STELLA GR
JOHNS GR
HOWARD RD
HEMUS CRES
VALLEY GR
VALLEY RD
WINSTER RD
BLENHEIM DR
BAKER HOUSE LA
HIGHFIELD RD
GREENFIELD RD
TANHOUSE AVE
LINGFIELD CT
DENTON GR
CATERTON ST
CONWAY
VENNING
HOLLAND RD
JAMES RD
STANTON RD
TEMPLEMORE DR
APPLETON AVE
WOODFORT
WEST RD
ALLEN RD
WELSBY AVE
WATERSIDE
WEST RD
START
ORD
BANKSIDE
BRADFORD CT
LANGDALE RD
GRASMERE RD
ENNERDALE RD
ASTON CRES
LEITH AVE
LANGFORD AVE
SHENSTONE RD
EASTWOOD RD
GORSE FARM RD
COLERIDGE
FERNDALE LA
OLD WALSALL RD
KINGSDOWN AVE
DYAS AVE
ALMOND
LILAC
Ferndale Prim Sch
FERNDALE AVE
B43
Sch
B42
CHARNWOOD RD

93

A4041
Forge Farm
FORGE LA
Forge Mill Farm
Sandwell Valley Nature Ctr
P
EADGAR CT
Hamstead Jun & Inf Sch
P
BROOKSIDE
AMBERLEY GN
HAMSTEAD RD
Hamstead
WALCOT DR
FARRAN WAY 1
CROMANE SQ 2
FREEMOUNT SQ 3
HOLMES CL 4
LATHAM AVE 5
STAFFORD CT 6
RUSHALL CT 7
ALLEN HO 8
PEPYS CT 9
SUTTON CT 10
BOLDMERE CT 11
Garden Grove
HAMSTEAD HO 1
SCOTT HO 2
GROVE CT 3
GREENWAY
WOODEND
GARDEN
B4167
INTERLINK
Superstore
PO
ROCKY LA
Hamstead Wks

6

B71
Sandwell Valley Country Park
Beacon Way
P
River Tame
Golf Course
Golf Course
WOODEND
PARKSIDE
THE CROFTWAY
ACFOLD RD
CHALCOT GR
HAMSTEAD HALL RD
BEAUCHAMP AVE
MILLFIELD RD
DEERHURST RD
LEOPOLD AVE
GREENRIDGE RD
MANWAY CL

5

P
Golf Course
Hamstead Hall Sec Sch
ELMBANK CRES
CAMPLIN CRES
UNDERWOOD RD
CRAYTHORNE AVE
BEWLYS AVE
SEDGLEY RD
GREENRIDGE RD
VERNON AVE
WESTOVER RD
WEST AVE
Liby
ST DAVIDS GR

92

Swan Pool
Park Farm
CH
MEDCROFT AVE
PARK HILL DR
HAMSTEAD HILL
ST CHRISTOPHER
Grestone Jun & Inf Schs
B20
THE SPINNEY
BEECH
ST ANNES CL
Brown's Green
FRIARY CL
HIGH TREE
FRIARY RD
ENGLESTEDE CL
HANDSWORTH WOOD RD
B4124
TAVERNER'S GN

4

M5
Golf Course
P
CH
SILVERCROFT AVE
Sports Gd
Allot Gdns
BROSIL AVE
MENTONE CT
HAWTHORN PK
WHEATON VALE
GRESTONE AVE
ASHCOMBE AVE
SHIREHALL CL
WOODCROFT AVE
SILVERCROFT
FRIARY RD
BROWNS GN
OFTHOUSE RD
Handsworth Univ Village (Univ of Aston)
Handsworth Hall
DEVONSHIRE RD
SOMERSET RD
ORCHARD
OVAL RD
OAKLANDS
Schs

3

B70
CRADLEY CROFT
WILKS GN
POSEY CL
THE LEVER
SILLY
St John Wall RC Sch
OXHILL RD
LARCH AVE
St Augustine's RC Prim Sch
FRIARY GDNS
COLLEGE DR
WINDERMERE RD
STOCKDALE RD
COTMORE RD
BRIGHTON RD
CORNWALL RD
DENECRE
ROSEMORE DR
CALDER DR

2

Golf Course
Cemy
B21
COPTHALL RD
LINCHMERE RD
RALEIGH IND EST
CAMP LA
LANDGATE RD
CAMBROOK RD
PELGR
BUSH GR
SANDWELL RD
PO
OXHILL RD
CLENT RD
GREENHILL RD
FARNHAM RD
UPLANDS RD
NEWCOMBE RD
ASTLEY RD
FARCROFT GR
FARCROFT
AVE
MERVYN RD
FORD RD
ALBION RD
GROVE GDNS
HURSTWAY
MOUNT PLEASANT AVE
LAUREL GDNS
PO
CHURCH LA A4040
KILBYS
PHILIP VICTOR RD
GROVE HILL RD
ALBERT RD
GOLDEN CROFT
HINSTOCK RD
RIBERT RD

1

A41
BIRMINGHAM RD
B71
B66
BOUNDARY
WILLOW GR
COLLIERY RD
HALFORD'S LA
Park Lane Ind Est
The Hawthorns
RALEIGH IND EST
CRANKHALL
HOLYHEAD RD
A4040 ISLAND RD
SAMPSON
AUSTIN
A41
B66
Handsworth
Recn Gd
GRAFTON RD
HOLLYCR
St James CE Prim Sch
FARCROFT
ONIBURY RD
WESTBOURNE RD
NIXON CL
FARCROFT
CARLTON AVE
ROOKERY RD
ANTROBUS RD
Schs
MAPLE RD
BRUNSWICK RD
Wilkes Green Sch
CENT
A4040

90

Albion Jun Sch
MALVERN RD 1
PADDINGTON RD 2
MIDDLEMORE RD

02   A   B   03   C   D   04   E   F

F3
1 HAWTHORN PARK DR
2 CASSOWARY RD
3 QUORN HO
4 ALBRIGHTON RD
5 MEYNELL HO
6 PYTCHLEY HO
7 COTTESMORE HO

A8
1 BARDFIELD CL
2 HARRIS DR
3 BLOOMFIELD CT
4 MOLHAY GDNS

44
56

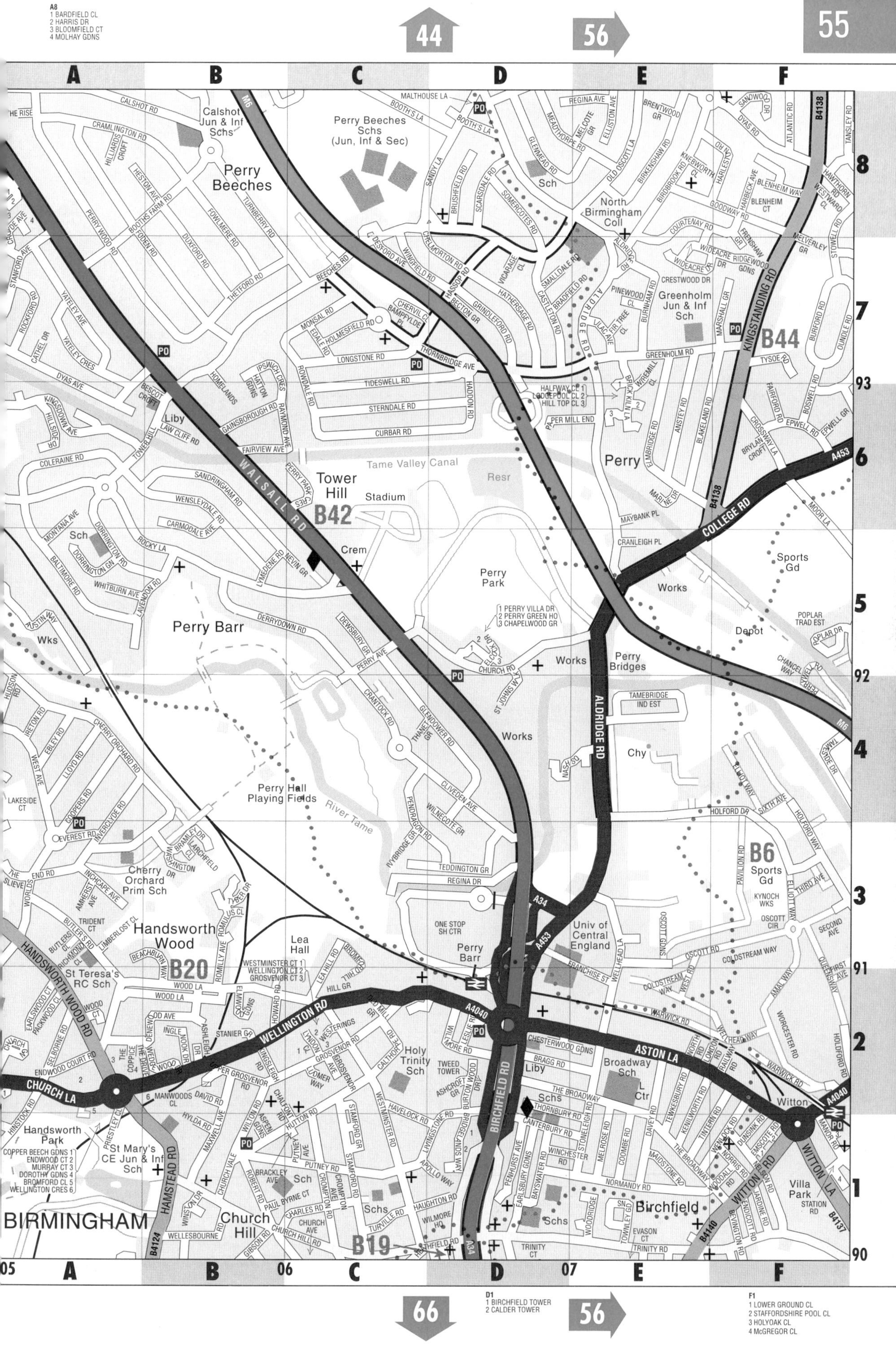

D1
1 BIRCHFIELD TOWER
2 CALDER TOWER

F1
1 LOWER GROUND CL
2 STAFFORDSHIRE POOL CL
3 HOLYOAK CL
4 McGREGOR CL

66
56

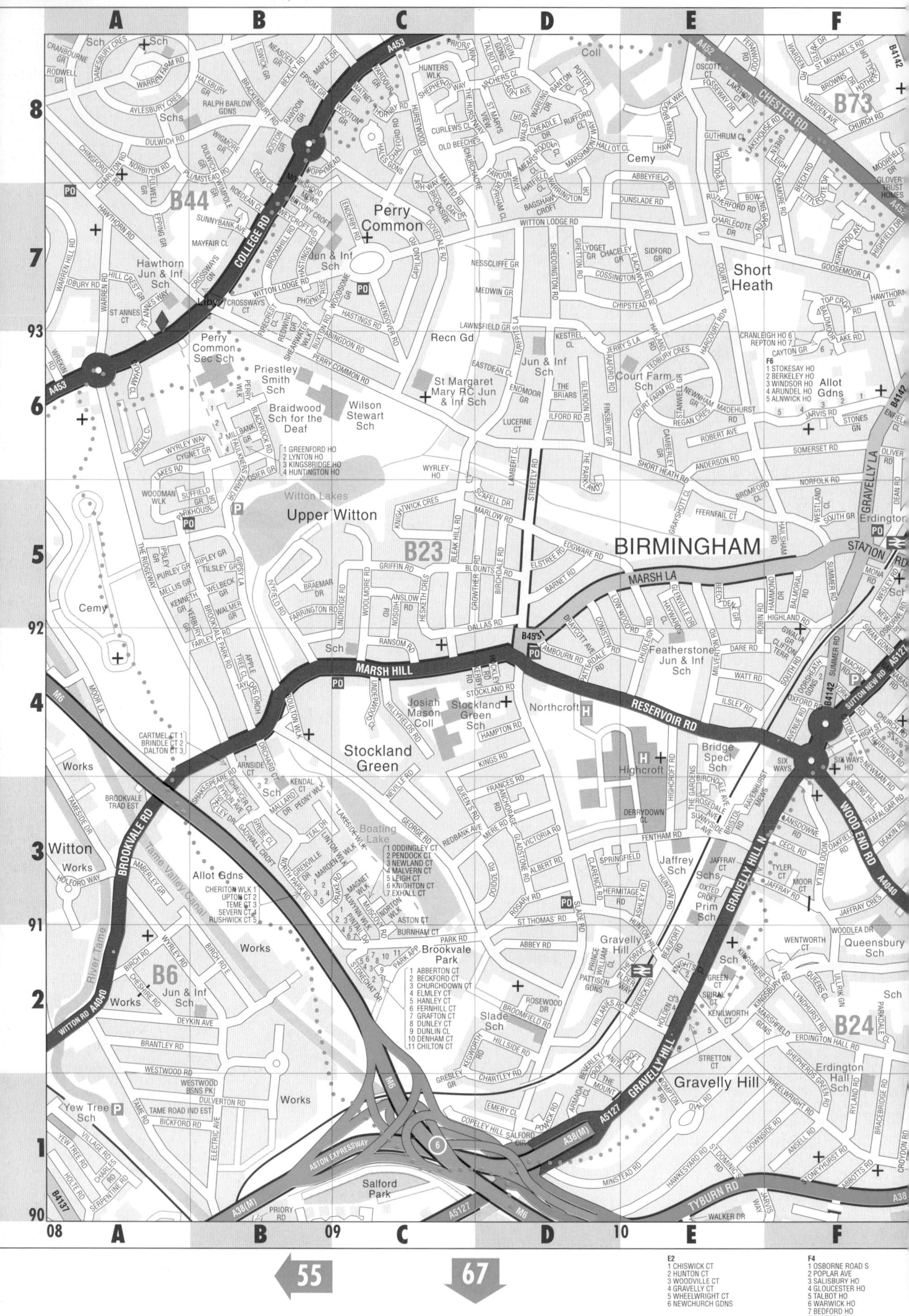

E2
1 CHISWICK CT
2 HUNTON CT
3 WOODVILLE CT
4 GRAVELLY CT
5 WHEELWRIGHT CT
6 NEWCHURCH GDNS

F4
1 OSBORNE ROAD S
2 POPLAR AVE
3 SALISBURY HO
4 GLOUCESTER HO
5 TALBOT HO
6 WARWICK HO
7 BEDFORD HO
8 EXETER HO

A6
1 NORMANTON TOWER
2 FAIRBOURNE TOWER

B7
1 THE LANES SHOPPING CTR
2 RICHMOND CT
3 HERON CT
4 FLORENCE DR
5 FLORENCE AVE

46
58

68
58

57
47

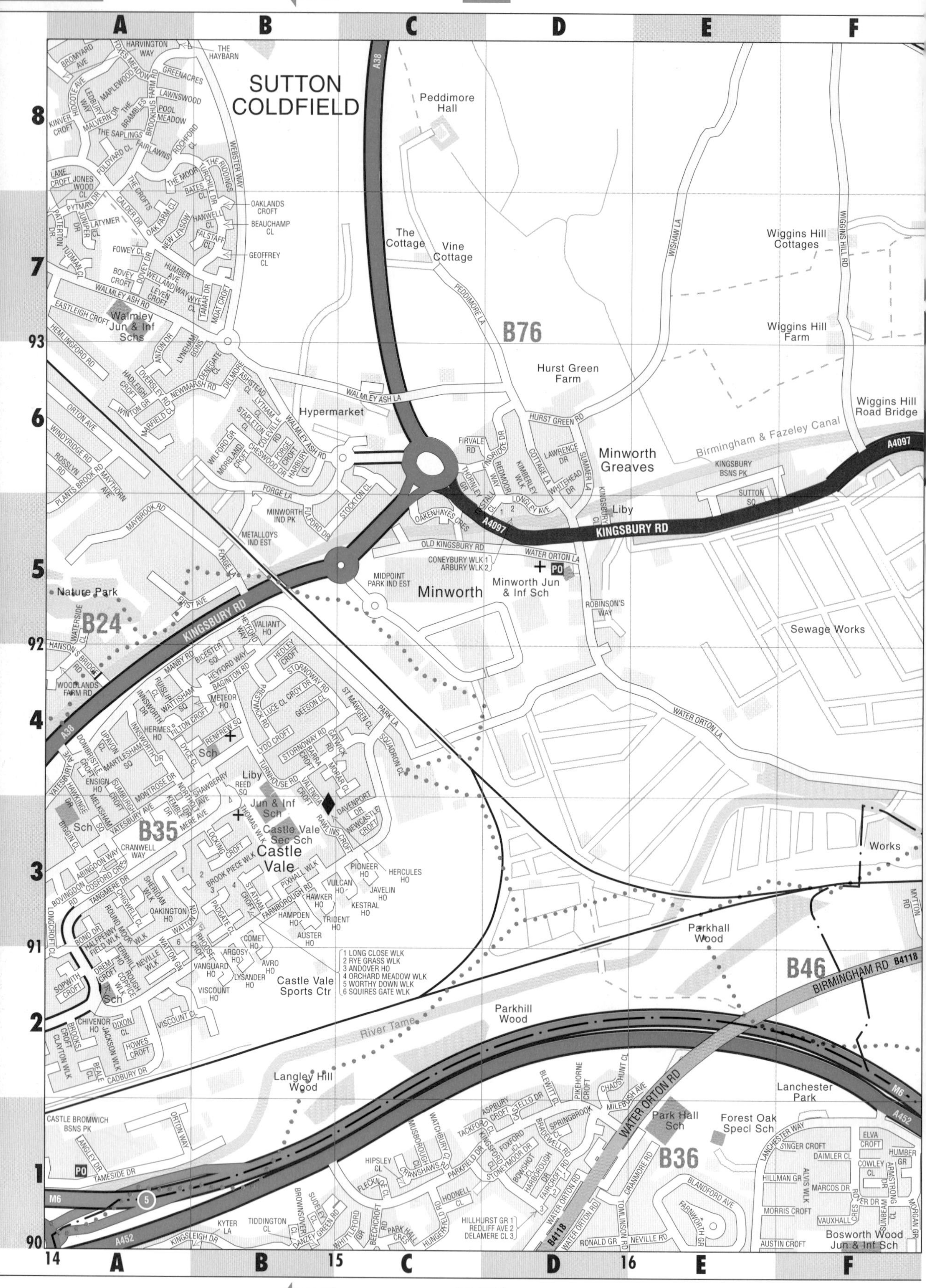
A
B
C
D
E
F
8
7
93
6
5
92
4
3
91
2
1
90
14
15
16
SUTTON COLDFIELD
Peddimore Hall
The Cottage
Vine Cottage
B76
Hurst Green Farm
Wiggins Hill Cottages
Wiggins Hill Farm
Wiggins Hill Road Bridge
Birmingham & Fazeley Canal
Minworth Greaves
Hypermarket
KINGSBURY BSNS PK
SUTTON SQ
Liby
KINGSBURY RD
A4097
A38
WALMLEY ASH LA
WISHAW LA
WIGGINS HILL RD
PEDDIMORE LA
HURST GREEN RD
Walmley Jun & Inf Schs
MINWORTH IND PK
METALLOYS IND EST
MIDPOINT PARK IND EST
Minworth
Minworth Jun & Inf Sch
OLD KINGSBURY RD
WATER ORTON LA
CONEYBURY WLK 1
ARBURY WLK 2
ROBINSON'S WAY
Nature Park
B24
Sewage Works
B35
Castle Vale
Castle Vale Sec Sch
Jun & Inf Sch
Sch
Liby
Works
Parkhall Wood
B46
BIRMINGHAM RD
B4118
Parkhill Wood
River Tame
Langley Hill Wood
Castle Vale Sports Ctr
1 LONG CLOSE WLK
2 RYE GRASS WLK
3 ANDOVER HO
4 ORCHARD MEADOW WLK
5 WORTHY DOWN WLK
6 SQUIRES GATE WLK
CASTLE BROMWICH BSNS PK
TAMESIDE DR
M6
A452
Lanchester Park
Park Hall Sch
Forest Oak Specl Sch
B36
WATER ORTON RD
HILLHURST GR 1
REDLIFF AVE 2
DELAMERE CL 3
Bosworth Wood Jun & Inf Sch
A
B
15
C
D
16
E
F

57
69

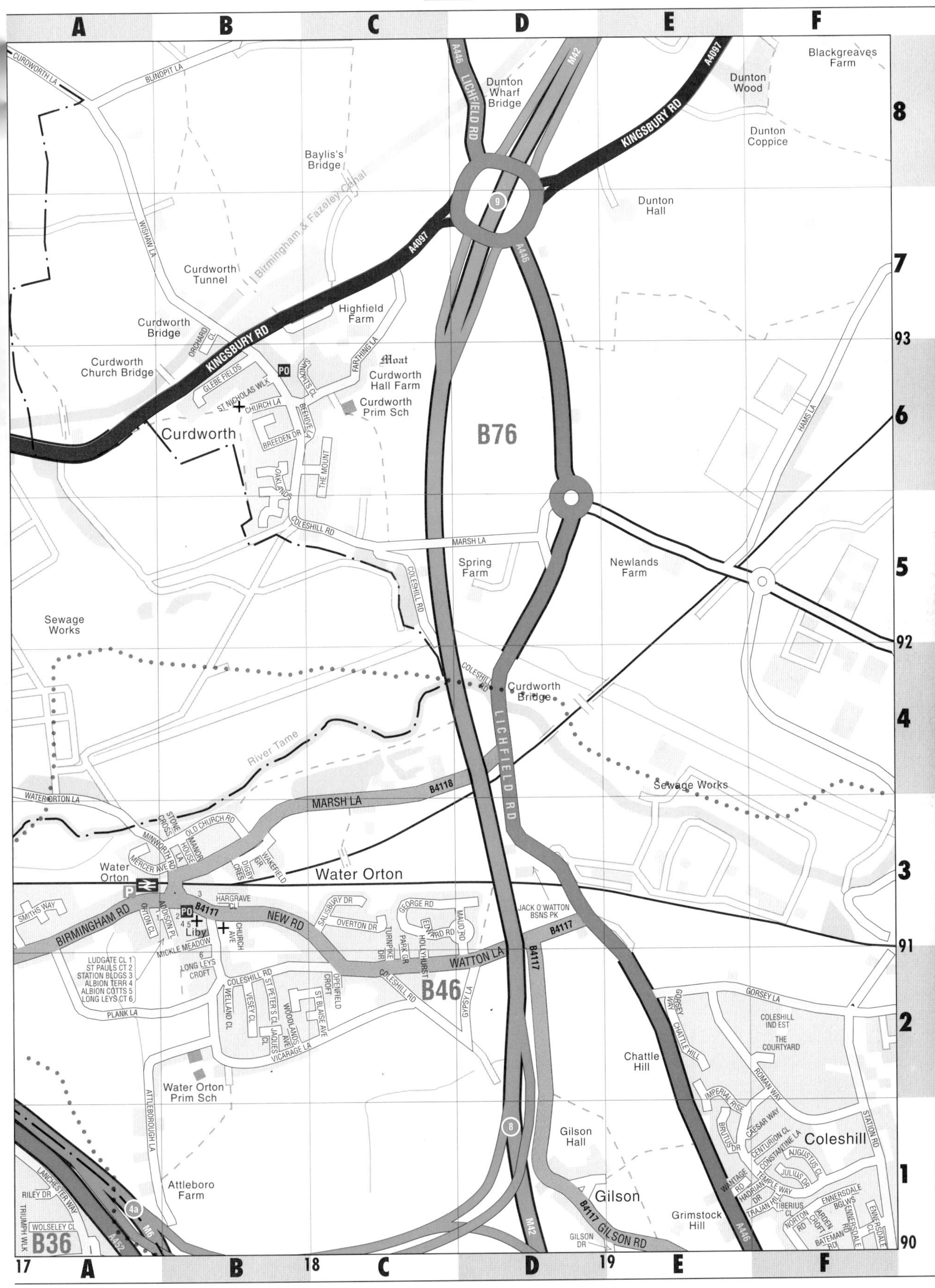

A B C D E F

8

7

93

6

5

92

4

91

2

1

90

17 18 19

Blackgreaves Farm

Dunton Wood

Dunton Coppice

CURDWORTH LA

BLINDPIT LA

Baylis's Bridge

KINGSBURY RD

Dunton Wharf Bridge

LICHFIELD RD

M42

KINGSBURY RD

A4097

A4097

Dunton Hall

A446

WISHAW LA

Curdworth Tunnel

Highfield Farm

Curdworth Bridge

KINGSBURY RD

ORCHARD CL

GLEBE FIELDS

St Nicholas

CHURCH LA

FARTHING LA

ST NICHOLAS WLK

PO

Moat
Curdworth Hall Farm

Curdworth Prim Sch

Curdworth Church Bridge

Curdworth

OAKLANDS

BREEDEN DR

PERIWINKLE LA

THE MOUNT

COLESHILL RD

B76

HAMS LA

MARSH LA

COLESHILL RD

Spring Farm

Newlands Farm

Sewage Works

COLESHILL RD

LICHFIELD RD

Curdworth Bridge

Sewage Works

River Tame

WATER ORTON LA

B4118

MARSH LA

B4118

STONE CROSS

OLD CHURCH RD

OLD MANORS HOUSE

DIGBY CRES

WANGFIELD

Water Orton

Water Orton

MINWORTH RD

MERCER AVE

P

B4117

BIRMINGHAM RD

ORTON CL

ADDISON PL

PO

1 2 3 4 5 6

HARGRAVE CL

NEW RD

MICKLE MEADOW

Lib'y

CHURCH AVE

SALISBURY DR

OVERTON DR

GEORGE RD

MAUD RD

EDWARD RD

TURNPIKE DR

HOLLYHURST RD

JACK O'WATTON BSNS PK

WATTON LA

B4117

B4117

GORSEY LA

COLESHILL IND EST

THE COURTYARD

LUDGATE CL 1
ST PAULS CT 2
STATION BLDGS 3
ALBION TERR 4
ALBION COTTS 5
LONG LEYS CT 6

LONG LEYS CROFT

COLESHILL RD

ST PETER'S CL

ST BLAISE AVE

CROFT

OPENFIELD

COLESHILL RD

B46

GYPSY LA

PLANK LA

WELLAND CL

VESEY CL

JAQUES CL

WOODLANDS

VICARAGE LA

GORSEY LA

GORSEY WAY

CHATTLE HILL

Chattle Hill

ROMAN WAY

IMPERIAL RISE

BRUTUS DR

CAESAR WAY

CENTURION CL

CONSTANTINE LA

AUGUSTUS CL

Coleshill

STATION RD

ATTLEBOROUGH LA

Water Orton Prim Sch

Attleboro Farm

M42

8

Gilson Hall

Gilson

GILSON RD

B4117

GILSON DR

Grimstock Hill

A446

WANTAGE DR

HADRIAN'S WAY

HADRIAN'S WAY

TRAJAN RISE

TIBERIUS

JULIUS CL

NORTON RD

JASPER CL

BATEMAN RD

ENNERSDALE RD

ENNERSDALE BGLWS

LANCHESTER WAY

RILEY DR

TRIUMPH WLK

WOLSELEY CL

B36

M6

A452

4a

49

D8
1 GARRET CL
2 FLANDERS DR
3 CHARTERFIELD SH CTR

E8
1 BROADMEADOW
2 BIRCHWOOD WLK
3 OAKLEIGH WLK
4 WOODTHORNE WLK
5 ROSEDALE WLK
6 PINEWOOD WLK
7 BLOSSOMFIELD CL
8 MIMOSA WLK
9 GREENLAND CL

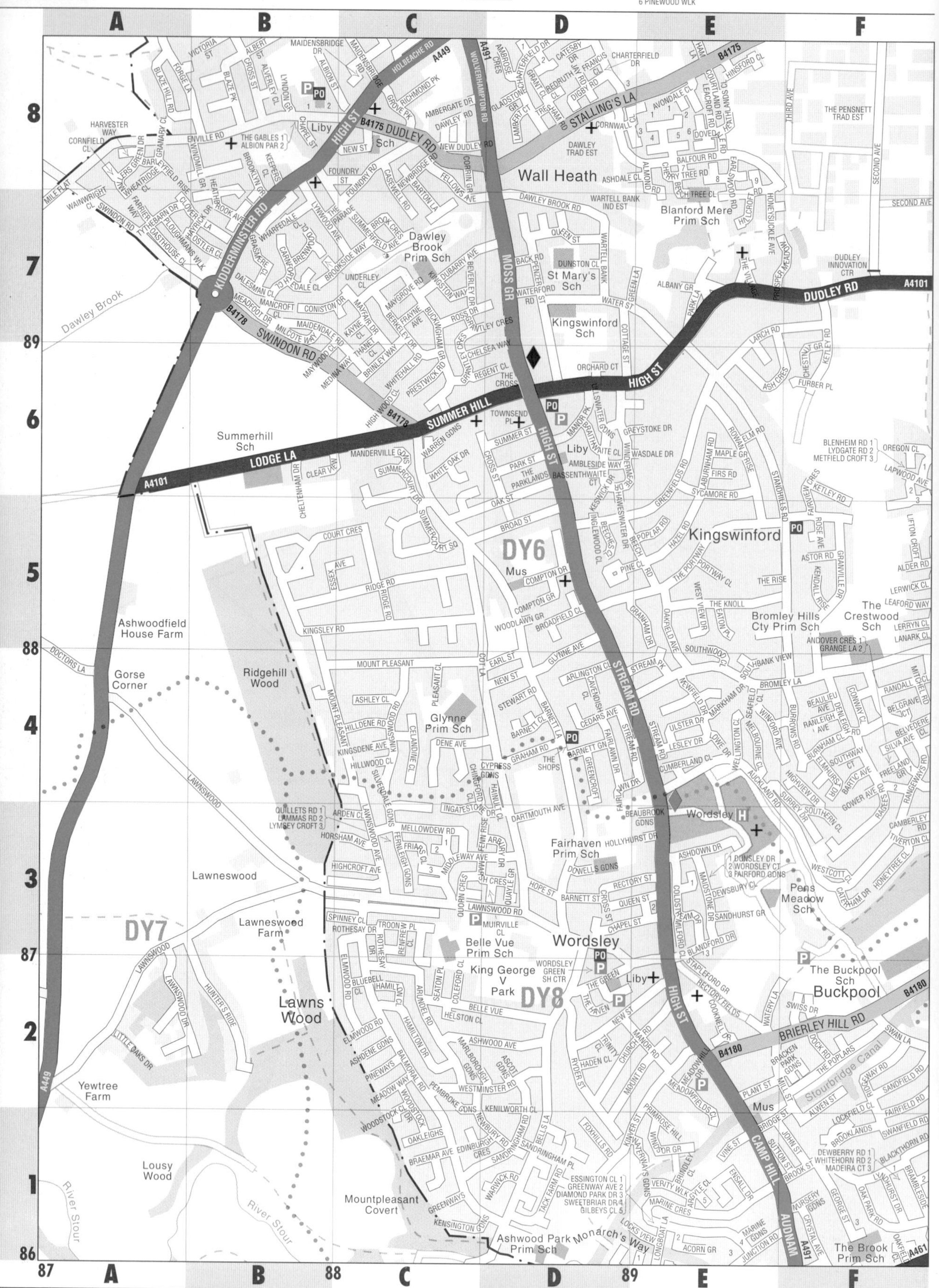

80

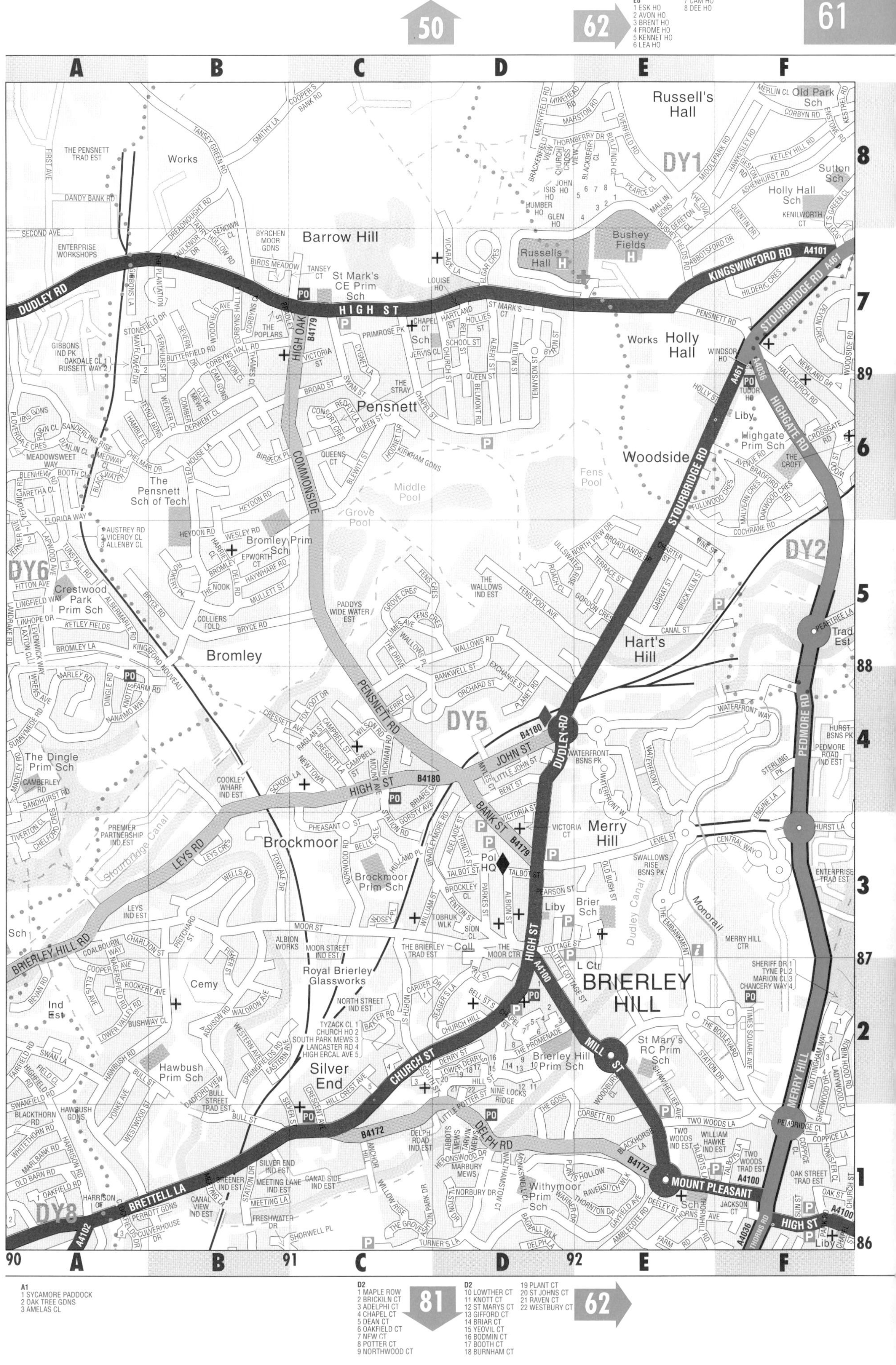

A1
1 SYCAMORE PADDOCK
2 OAK TREE GDNS
3 AMELAS CL

D2
1 MAPLE ROW
2 BRICKILN CT
3 ADELPHI CT
4 CHAPEL CT
5 DEAN CT
6 OAKFIELD CT
7 NEW CT
8 POTTER CT
9 NORTHWOOD CT

D2
10 LOWTHER CT
11 KNOTT CT
12 ST MARYS CT
13 GIFFORD CT
14 BRIAR CT
15 YEOVIL CT
16 BODMIN CT
17 BOOTH CT
18 BURNHAM CT
19 PLANT CT
20 ST JOHNS CT
21 RAVEN CT
22 WESTBURY CT

B8
1 HOLLAND ST
2 TURNER ST
3 CLIFFORD ST
4 CLEVELAND ST
5 CHARLOTTE ST
6 WESTLEY ST
7 WYCHBURY CT
8 ROMSLEY CT
9 HIGH ST

61

51

D8
1 OAKEYWELL ST
2 CAMPBELL ST
3 NEW BOND ST
4 SHEDDEN ST
5 SPRING GDNS
6 ROLLASON RD

E8
1 OLIVER CL
2 PRICE ST
3 SHARINGTON CL
4 LAMBERT FOLD
5 LEVESON WLK
6 HARLEY GRANGE
7 DIXONS GREEN CT
8 ASHLEIGH CT
9 OAKHAM CT

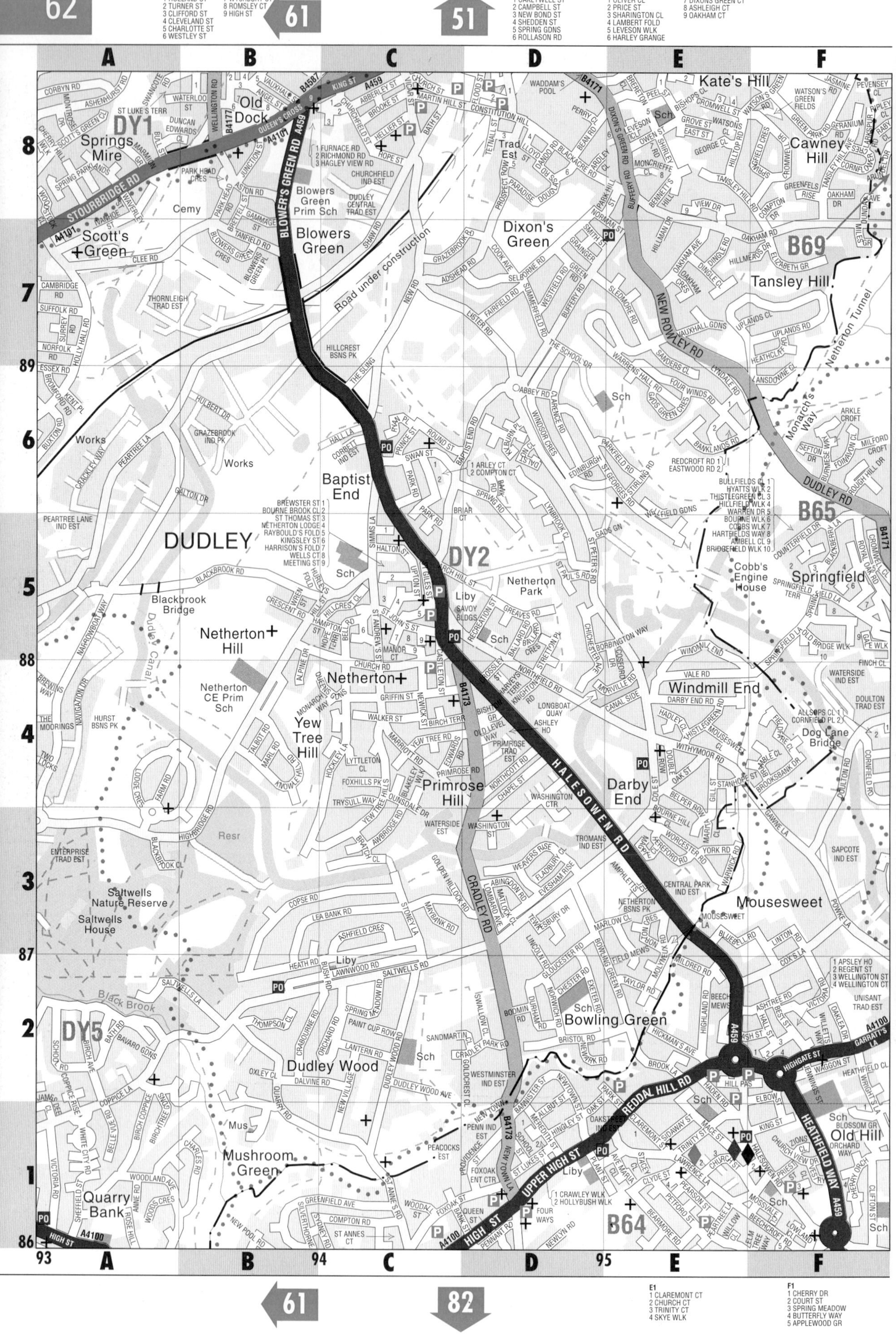

61

82

E1
1 CLAREMONT CT
2 CHURCH CT
3 TRINITY CT
4 SKYE WLK

F1
1 CHERRY DR
2 COURT ST
3 SPRING MEADOW
4 BUTTERFLY WAY
5 APPLEWOOD GR

Grid columns: A B C D E F (top and bottom)

Grid rows (right side): 8 7 89 6 5 88 4 87 3 2 87 1 86

Major place names and features:

Oakham · Darby's Hill · Grace Mary Estate · Round's Green · Ind Est

Warrens Hall Farm · Oakham Prim Sch · Bury Hill Park · B69 · OLDBURY · Civic Ctr

Golf Course · Rough Hill · Turner's Hill · Portway · Sports Ctr · Birchley Park

The Knowle · Tippity Green · Whiteheath Gate · Langley · Titford

Rowley Regis · Hawes Hill · B65 · Playing Fields

Britannia Park · Rowley Village · Causeway Green · B68

B64 · Powke La · High St A4100 · Rowley Regis · BLACKHEATH · B62 · B68

Monarch's Way · Waterfall Lane Ind Est

Roads: A4123 NEW BIRMINGHAM RD · A457 DUDLEY RD · WOLVERHAMPTON RD · A4034 CHURCHBRIDGE · OLDBURY RING WAY · A457 · A4182 · B4166 · A4123 · CAKEMORE RD · OLDBURY RD · STATION RD B4169 · NIMMINGS RD · HALESOWEN ST · LONG LA · HIGH ST A4100 · GARRATT'S LA · DUDLEY RD · HAWES LA · ROWLEY VILLAGE · B4171 · A4099 A4034 · B4163

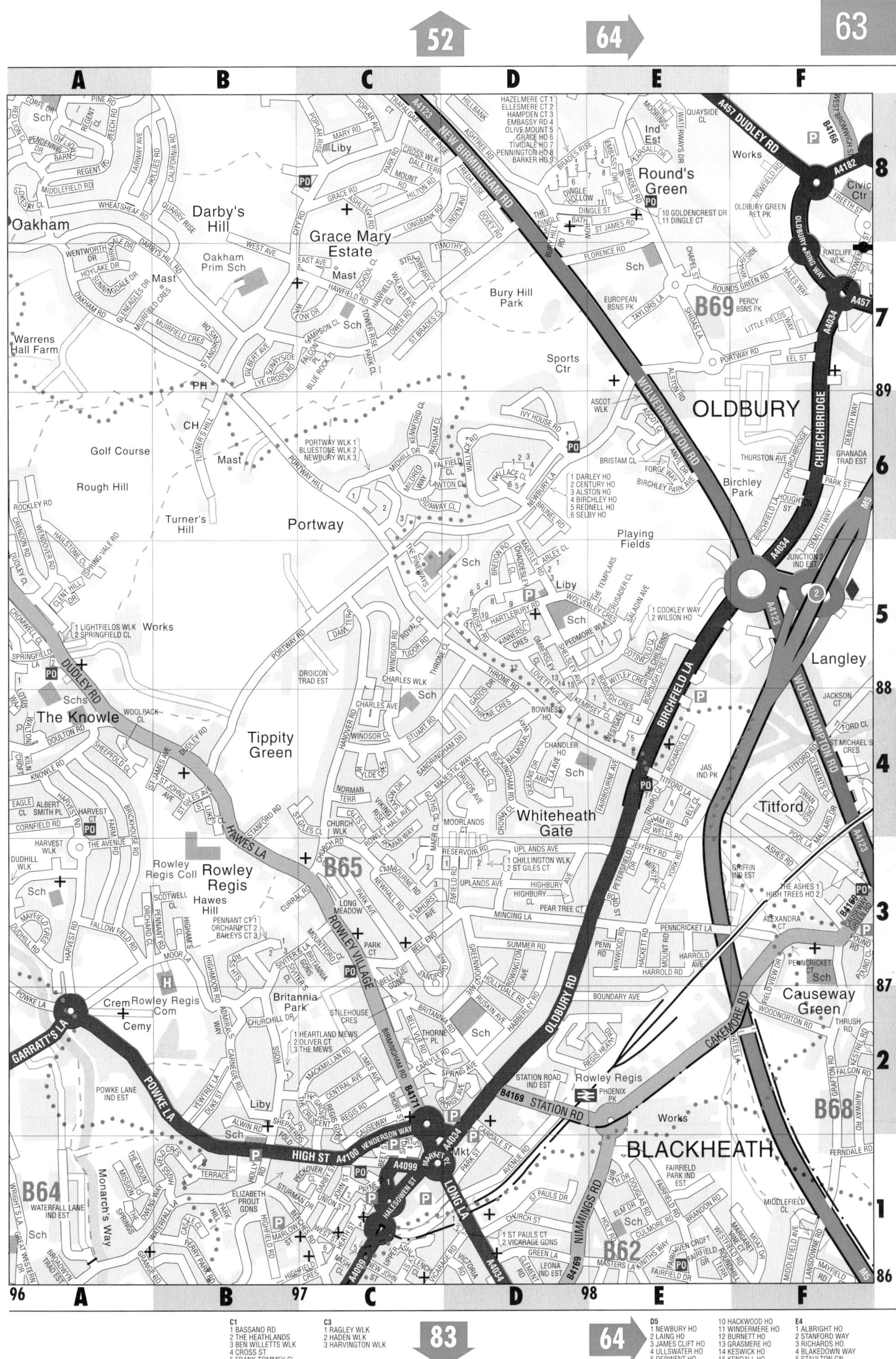

C1
1 BASSANO RD
2 THE HEATHLANDS
3 BEN WILLETTS WLK
4 CROSS ST
5 FRANK TOMMEY CL
6 DOWNING CL

C3
1 RAGLEY WLK
2 HADEN WLK
3 HARVINGTON WLK

D5
1 NEWBURY HO
2 LAING HO
3 JAMES CLIFT HO
4 ULLSWATER HO
5 DERWENT HO
6 RYDAL HO
7 CONISTON HO
8 WALLACE HO
9 HARRY PRICE HO
10 HACKWOOD HO
11 WINDERMERE HO
12 BURNETT HO
13 GRASMERE HO
14 KESWICK HO
15 KENDALL HO

E4
1 ALBRIGHT HO
2 STANFORD WAY
3 RICHARDS HO
4 BLAKEDOWN WAY
5 STAULTON GN
6 WHITEHEATH CT
7 LANCASTER HO
8 WINCHESTER CL
9 CANTERBURY CL

A7
1 DE SOMERLEY HO
2 HACKETT CT
3 RATCLIFF WLK
4 CHURCH SQ
5 LADY BRADES HO
6 LOW TOWN
7 DAVIES HO
8 PARKES HO
9 JACKSON HO
10 SHOWELL HO
11 JEFFRIES HO
12 WHEELER HO

63
53

E7
1 SANDFIELD
2 MALTHOUSE
3 LIZAFIELD CT

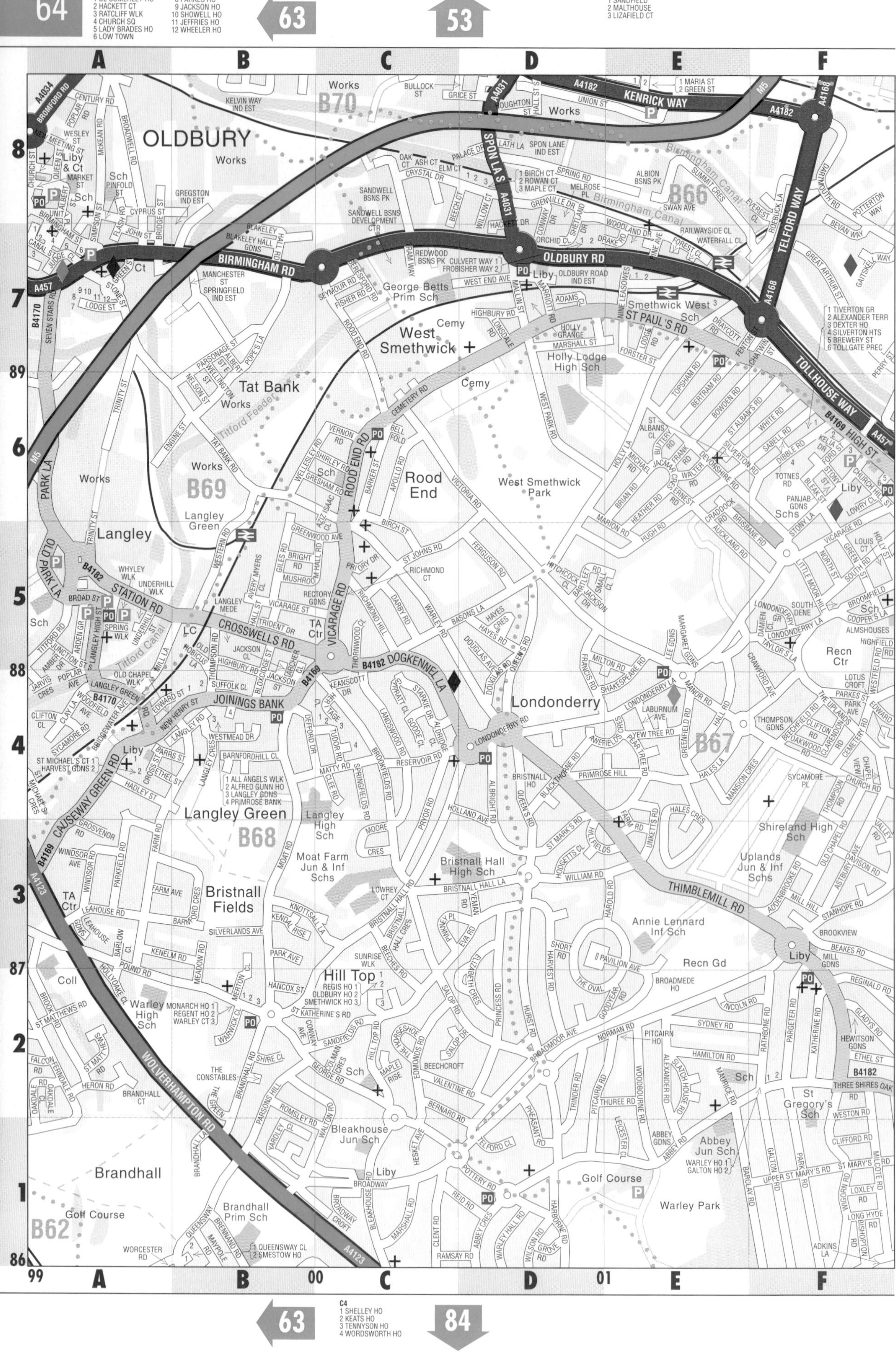

C4
1 SHELLEY HO
2 KEATS HO
3 TENNYSON HO
4 WORDSWORTH HO

63
84

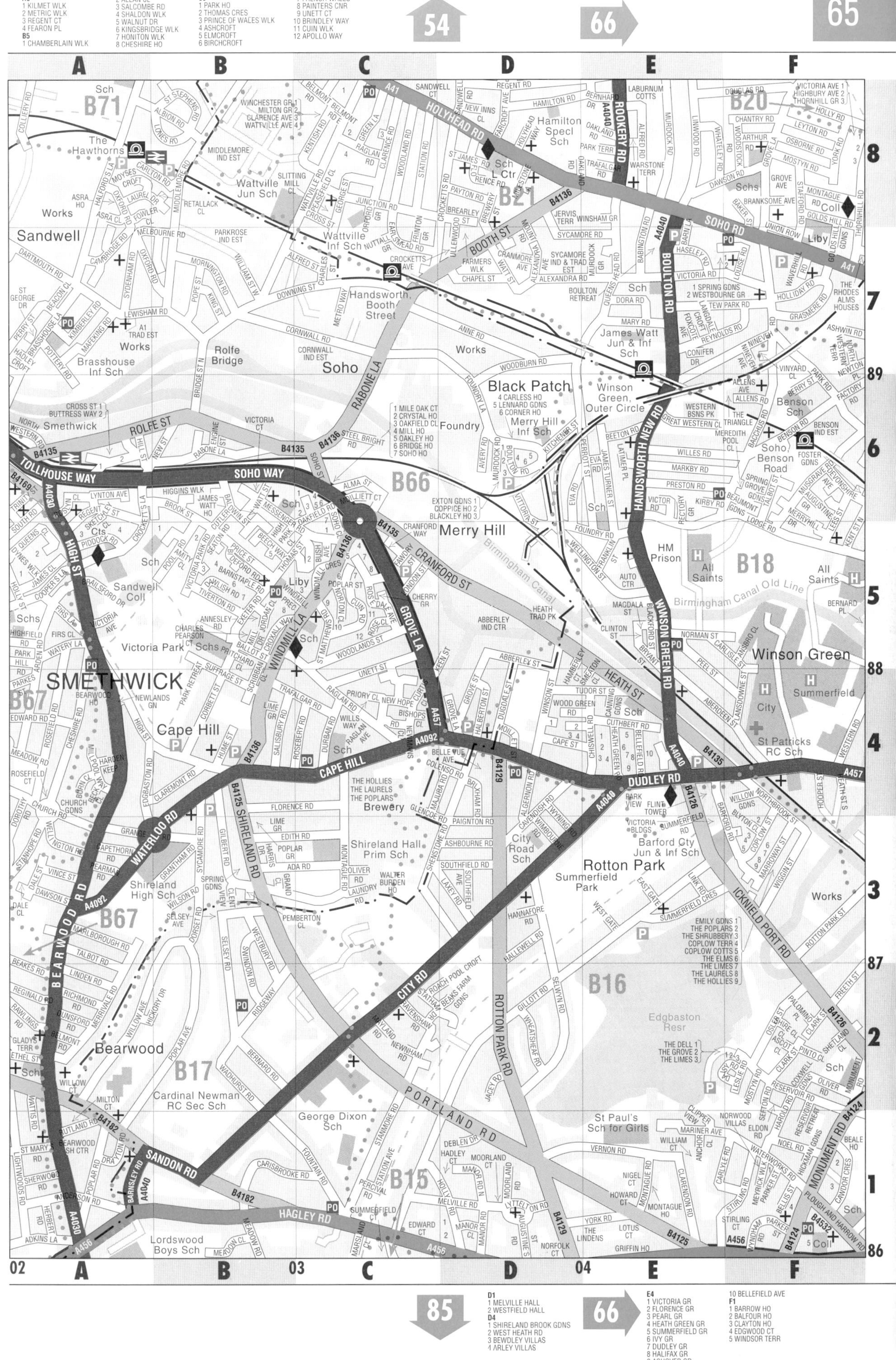

A5
1 KILMET WLK
2 METRIC WLK
3 REGENT CT
4 FEARON PL
B5
1 CHAMBERLAIN WLK
2 ALLAN CL
3 SALCOMBE RD
4 SHALDON WLK
5 WALNUT DR
6 KINGSBRIDGE WLK
7 HONITON WLK
8 CHESHIRE HO
C5
1 PARK HO
2 THOMAS CRES
3 PRINCE OF WALES WLK
4 ASHCROFT
5 ELMCROFT
6 BIRCHCROFT
7 FRENCH WALLS
8 PAINTERS CNR
9 UNETT CT
10 BRINDLEY WAY
11 CUIN WLK
12 APOLLO WAY
54
66
65
A
B
C
D
E
F
B71
The Hawthorns
Sandwell
Works
Wattville Jun Sch
Wattville Inf Sch
Handsworth, Booth Street
HOLYHEAD RD
Hamilton Specl Sch
B21
ROOKERY RD
SOHO RD
B20
BOULTON RD
Soho
Rolfe Bridge
Brasshouse Inf Sch
Black Patch
Winson Green, Outer Circle
James Watt Jun & Inf Sch
Merry Hill Inf Sch
Foundry
Benson Sch
Soho, Benson Road
North Smethwick
ROLFE ST
TOLLHOUSE WAY
SOHO WAY
B66
Merry Hill
CRANFORD ST
Birmingham Canal
Sandwell Coll
HM Prison
All Saints
B18
Birmingham Canal Old Line
Winson Green
Victoria Park
SMETHWICK
HIGH ST
GROVE LA
WINDMILL LA
HANDSWORTH NEW RD
WINSON GREEN RD
HEATH ST
Summerfield
City
St Patricks RC Sch
Cape Hill
CAPE HILL
DUDLEY RD
Brewery
Shireland Hall Prim Sch
City Road Sch
Rotton Park
Summerfield Park
Barford City Jun & Inf Sch
WATERLOO RD
Shireland High Sch
B67
SHIRELAND RD
ICKNIELD PORT RD
CITY RD
B16
Edgbaston Resr
BEARWOOD RD
Bearwood
B17
ROTTON PARK RD
Cardinal Newman RC Sec Sch
George Dixon Sch
PORTLAND RD
St Paul's Sch for Girls
SANDON RD
B15
HAGLEY RD
Lordswood Boys Sch
MONUMENT RD
8
7
89
6
5
88
4
3
87
2
1
86
02
03
04
85
66
D1
1 MELVILLE HALL
2 WESTFIELD HALL
D4
1 SHIRELAND BROOK GDNS
2 WEST HEATH RD
3 BEWDLEY VILLAS
4 ARLEY VILLAS
E4
1 VICTORIA GR
2 FLORENCE GR
3 PEARL GR
4 HEATH GREEN GR
5 SUMMERFIELD GR
6 IVY GR
7 DUDLEY GR
8 HALIFAX GR
9 ASHOVER GR
10 BELLEFIELD AVE
F1
1 BARROW HO
2 BALFOUR HO
3 CLAYTON HO
4 EDGWOOD CT
5 WINDSOR TERR

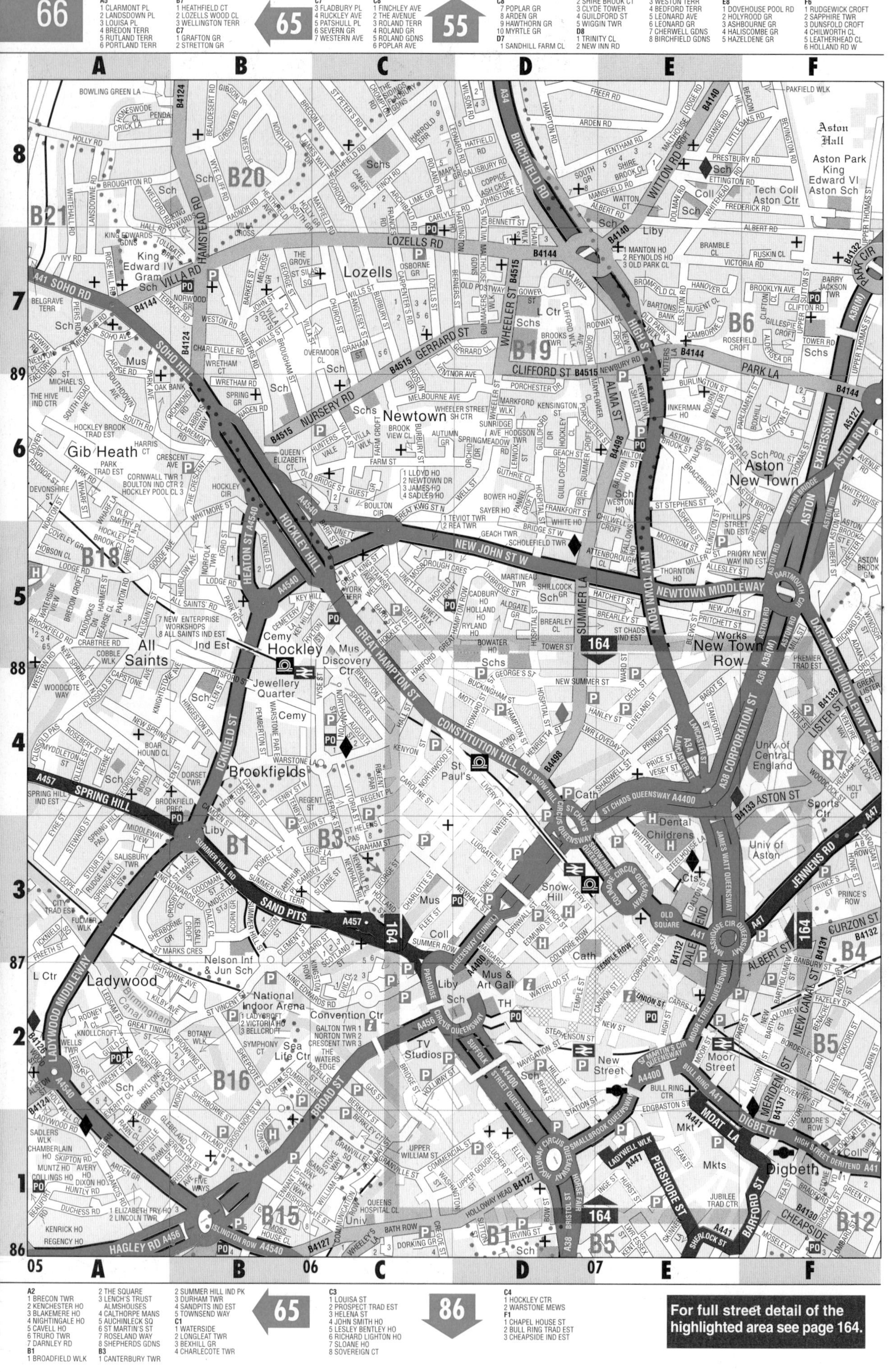
66
A5
1 CLARMONT PL
2 LANDSDOWN PL
3 LOUISA PL
4 BREDON TERR
5 RUTLAND TERR
6 PORTLAND TERR
B7
1 HEATHFIELD CT
2 LOZELLS WOOD CL
3 WELLINGTON TERR
C7
1 GRAFTON GR
2 STRETTON GR
65
C7
3 FLADBURY PL
4 RUCKLEY AVE
5 PATSHULL PL
6 SEVERN GR
7 WESTERN AVE
C8
1 FINCHLEY AVE
2 THE AVENUE
3 ROLAND TERR
4 ROLAND GR
5 ROLAND GDNS
6 POPLAR AVE
55
C8
7 POPLAR GR
8 ARDEN GR
9 HAWTHORN GR
10 MYRTLE GR
D7
1 SANDHILL FARM CL
2 SHIRE BROOK CT
3 CLYDE TOWER
4 GUILDFORD ST
5 WIGGIN TWR
D8
1 TRINITY CL
2 NEW INN RD
3 WESTON TERR
4 BEDFORD TERR
5 LEONARD AVE
6 LEONARD GR
7 CHERWELL GDNS
8 BIRCHFIELD GDNS
E8
1 DOVEHOUSE POOL RD
2 HOLYROOD GR
3 ASHBOURNE GR
4 HALISCOMBE GR
5 HAZELDENE GR
F6
1 RUDGEWICK CROFT
2 SAPPHIRE TWR
3 DUNSFOLD CROFT
4 CHILWORTH CL
5 LEATHERHEAD CL
6 HOLLAND RD W
A B C D E F
8 7 89 6 5 88 4 3 87 2 1 86
05 06 07
B21 B20 B19 B18 B6 B7 B1 B3 B16 B15 B5 B4 B12
Lozells
Newtown
Gib Heath
All Saints
Hockley
Jewellery Quarter
Brookfields
Ladywood
Aston Hall
Aston Park
Aston New Town
New Town Row
Univ of Central England
Univ of Aston
Snow Hill
National Indoor Arena
Convention Ctr
Sea Life Ctr
TV Studios
Mus & Art Gall
New Street
Moor Street
Digbeth
Mkts
Five Ways
HAGLEY RD A456
SOHO RD
SOHO HILL
HOCKLEY HILL
GREAT HAMPTON ST
CONSTITUTION HILL
NEW JOHN ST W
NEWTOWN MIDDLEWAY
SPRING HILL
SAND PITS
LADYWOOD MIDDLEWAY
BROAD ST
ASTON EXPRESSWAY
CORPORATION ST
DIGBETH
164
A2
1 BRECON TWR
2 KENCHESTER HO
3 BLAKEMERE HO
4 NIGHTINGALE HO
5 CAVELL HO
6 TRURO TWR
7 DARNLEY RD
B1
1 BROADFIELD WLK
2 THE SQUARE
3 LENCH'S TRUST ALMSHOUSES
4 CALTHORPE MANS
5 AUCHINLECK SQ
6 ST MARTIN'S ST
7 ROSELAND WAY
8 SHEPHERDS GDNS
B3
1 CANTERBURY TWR
2 SUMMER HILL IND PK
3 DURHAM TWR
4 SANDPITS IND EST
5 TOWNSEND WAY
C1
1 WATERSIDE
2 LONGLEAT TWR
3 BEXHILL GR
4 CHARLECOTE TWR
65
C3
1 LOUISA ST
2 PROSPECT TRAD EST
3 HELENA ST
4 JOHN SMITH HO
5 LESLEY BENTLEY HO
6 RICHARD LIGHTON HO
7 SLOANE HO
8 SOVEREIGN CT
86
C4
1 HOCKLEY CTR
2 WARSTONE MEWS
F1
1 CHAPEL HOUSE ST
2 BULL RING TRAD EST
3 CHEAPSIDE IND EST
For full street detail of the highlighted area see page 164.

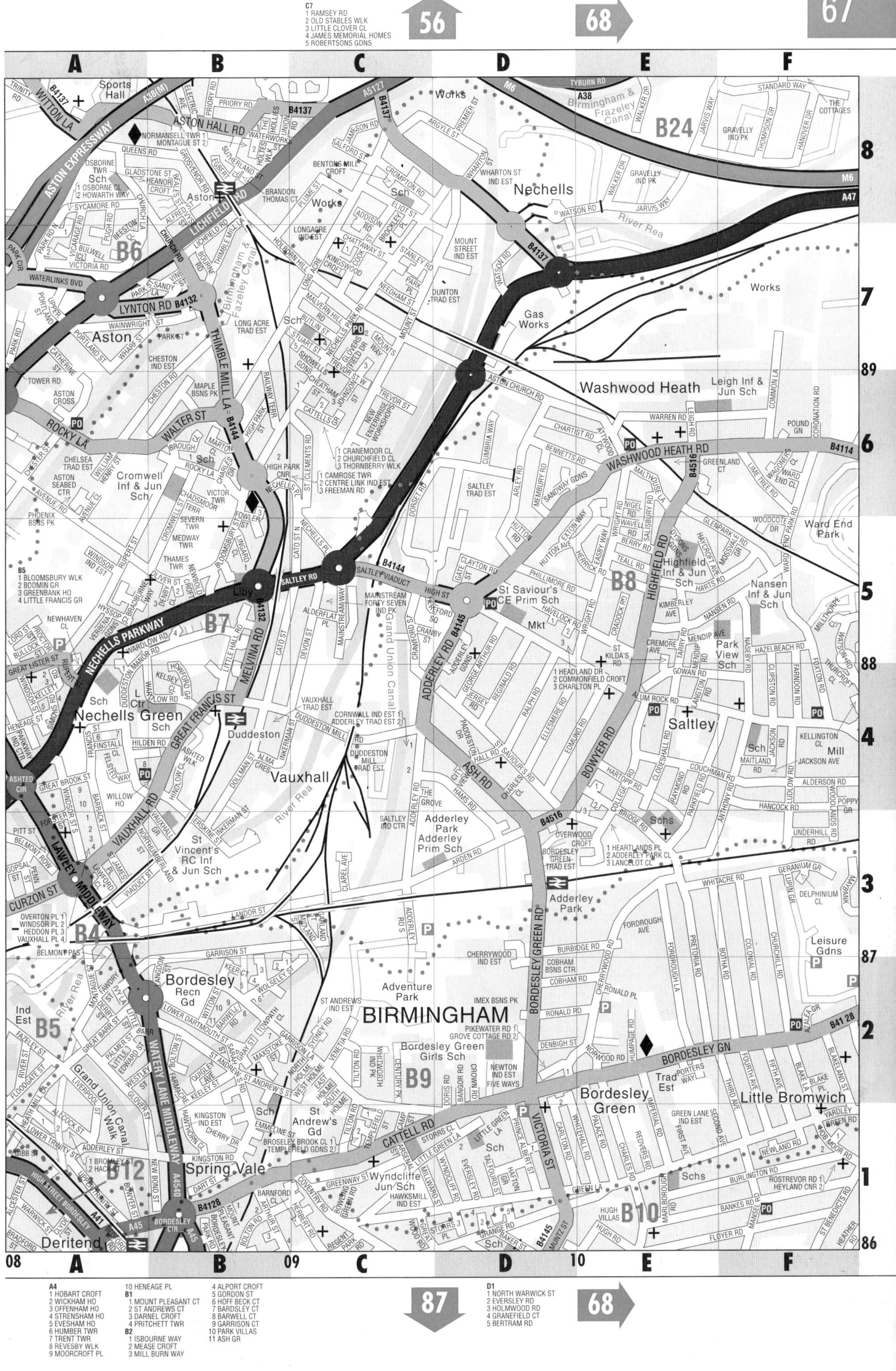

56

68

A4
1 HOBART CROFT
2 WICKHAM HO
3 OFFENHAM HO
4 STRENSHAM HO
5 EVESHAM HO
6 HUMBER TWR
7 TRENT TWR
8 REVESBY WLK
9 MOORCROFT PL
10 HENEAGE PL

B1
1 MOUNT PLEASANT CT
2 ST ANDREWS CT
3 DARNEL CROFT
4 PRITCHETT TWR

B2
1 ISBOURNE WAY
2 MEASE CROFT
3 MILL BURN WAY

4 ALPORT CROFT
5 GORDON ST
6 HOFF BECK CT
7 BARDSLEY CT
8 BARWELL CT
9 GARRISON CT
10 PARK VILLAS
11 ASH GR

D1
1 NORTH WARWICK ST
2 EVERSLEY RD
3 HOLMWOOD RD
4 GRANEFIELD CT
5 BERTRAM RD

67
57

E8
1 VANGUARD CL
2 AYALA CROFT
3 BAYLEY TOWER
4 STONEYCROFT TOWER
5 BRIDGEMEADOW HO
6 KINGSPIECE HO

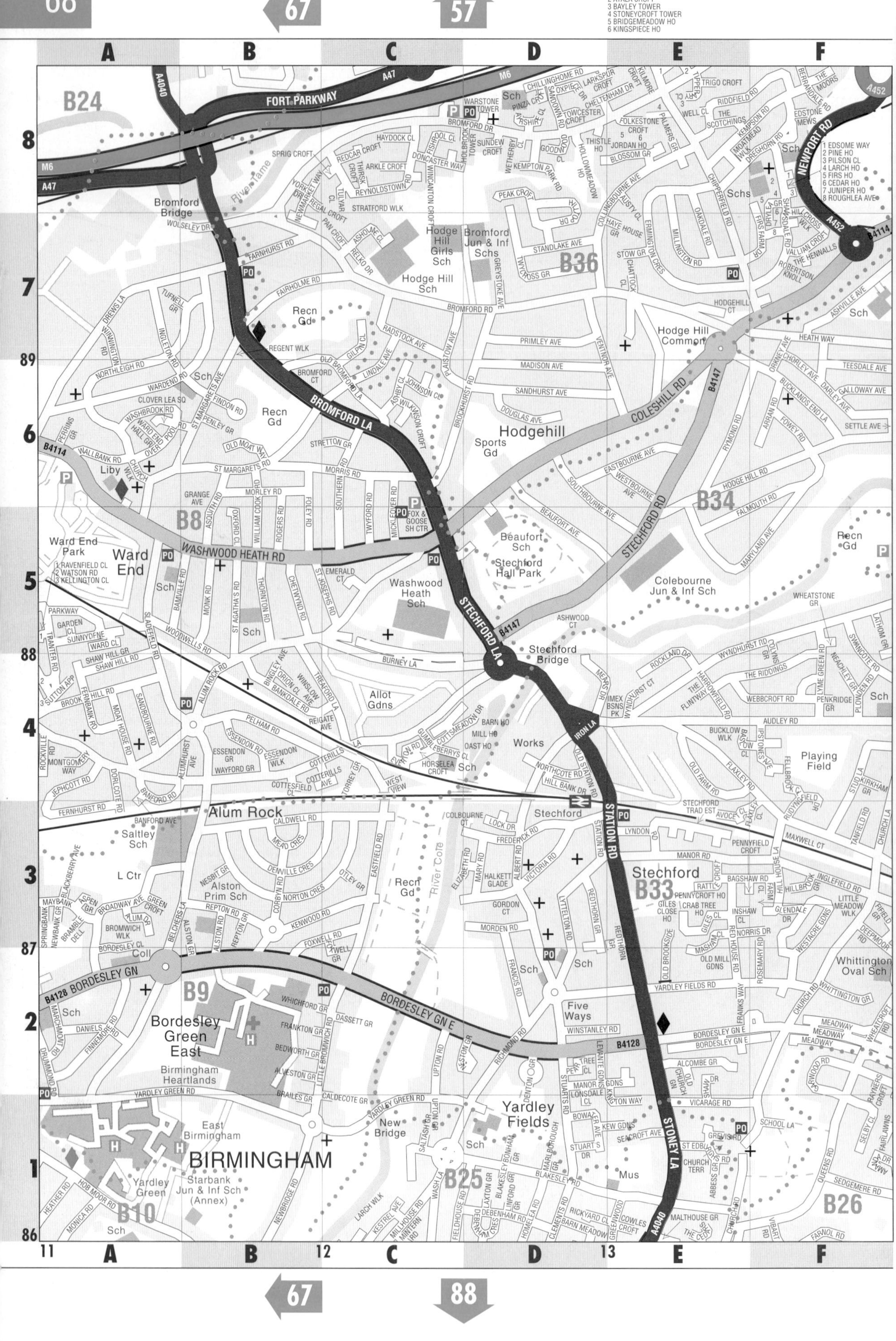

67
88

58
70

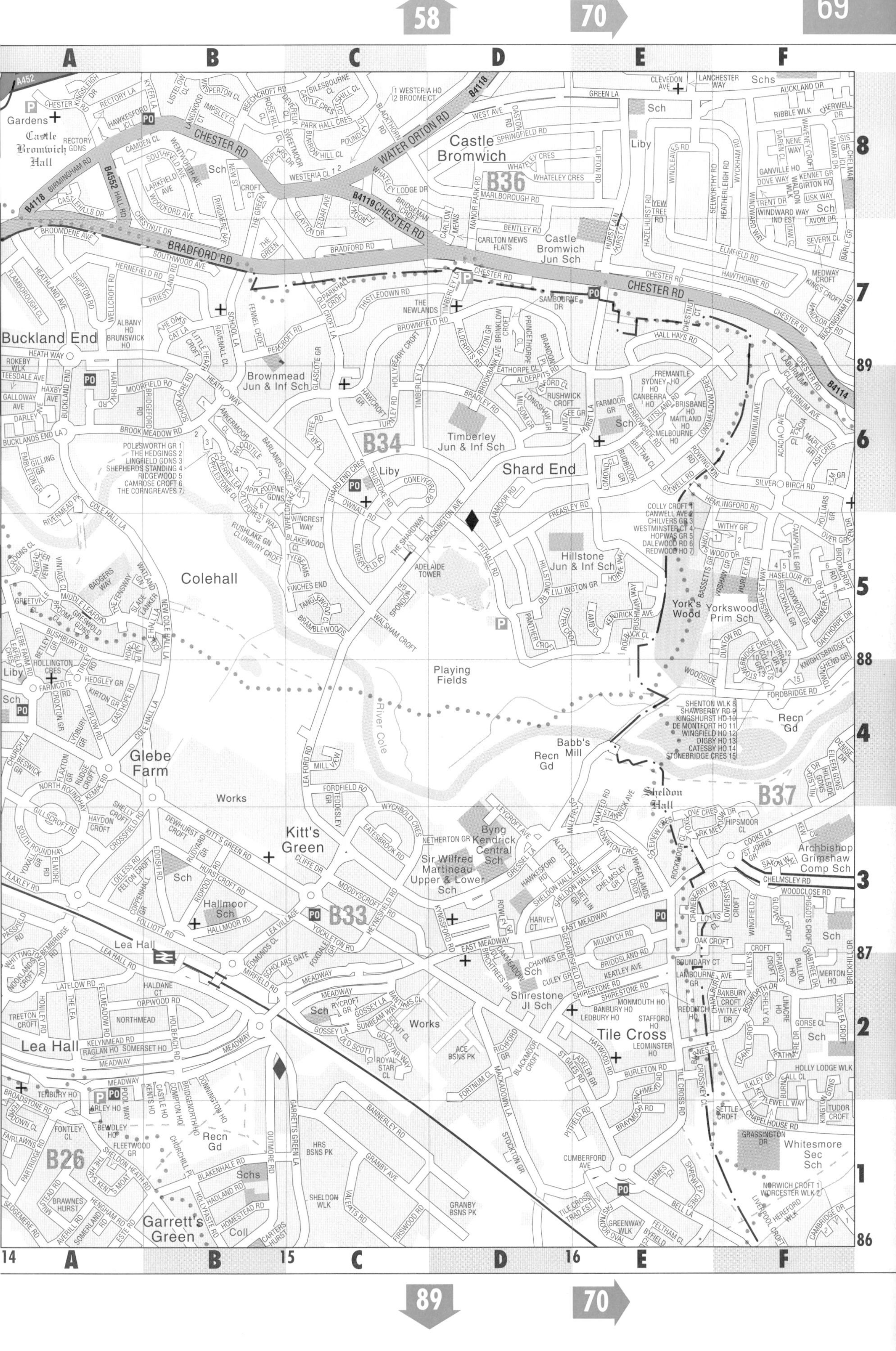
A
B
C
D
E
F
1
2
3
4
5
6
7
8
86
87
88
89
14
15
16
A452
Gardens
Castle Bromwich Hall
RECTORY GDNS
CHESTER RD
BIRMINGHAM RD
B4118
B4552 HALL RD
WATER ORTON RD
B4118
B4119 CHESTER RD
Castle Bromwich
B36
WEST AVE
SPRINGFIELD RD
WHATELEY CRES
MARLBOROUGH RD
BENTLEY RD
CARLTON MEWS FLATS
Castle Bromwich Jun Sch
CLIFTON RD
GREEN LA
Sch
Liby
Schs
AUCKLAND DR
RIBBLE WLK
CHERWELL DR
LANCHESTER WAY
CLEVEDON AVE
WINDLEAVES RD
SELWORTHY RD
HEATHERLEIGH RD
WYCKHAM RD
HAZELHURST RD
YEW TREE RD
ELMFIELD RD
HAWTHORNE RD
CHESTER RD
MEDWAY CROFT
KINGS CROFT
BUCKINGHAM RD
BRADFORD RD
BROOMDENE AVE
SOUTHWOOD AVE
HERNEFIELD RD
Buckland End
HEATH WAY
ROKEBY WLK
TEESDALE AVE
GALLOWAY AVE
DARLEY AVE
BUCKLANDS END LA
HAXBY AVE
MOORFIELD RD
BROOK MEADOW RD
Brownmead Jun & Inf Sch
THISTLEDOWN RD
THE NEWLANDS
BROWNFIELD RD
HOLLYBERRY CROFT
BRADLEY RD
Timberley Jun & Inf Sch
B34
Shard End
Liby
SHARD END CRES
CONEYFORD RD
PACKINGTON AVE
THE SHARDWAY
ADELAIDE TOWER
PITHALL RD
FREASLEY RD
Hillstone Jun & Inf Sch
LILLINGTON GR
KENDRICK AVE
HALL HAYS RD
FREMANTLE
SYDNEY HO
CANBERRA HO
BRISBANE HO
MAITLAND HO
MELBOURNE HO
FARMOOR GR
HEMLINGFORD RD
SILVER BIRCH RD
LABURNUM AVE
B4114
COLLY CROFT 1
CANWELL AVE 2
CHILVERS GR 3
WESTMINSTER CT 4
HOPWAS GR 5
DALEWOOD RD 6
REDWOOD HO 7
York's Wood
Yorkswood Prim Sch
WOODSIDE
FORDBRIDGE RD
KNIGHTSBRIDGE CT
SHENTON WLK 8
SHAWBERRY RD 9
KINGSHURST HO 10
DE MONTFORT HO 11
WINGFIELD HO 12
DIGBY HO 13
CATESBY HO 14
STONEBRIDGE CRES 15
Recn Gd
POLESWORTH GR 1
THE HEDGINGS 2
LINGFIELD GDNS 3
SHEPHERDS STANDING 4
RIDGEWOOD 5
CAMROSE CROFT 6
THE CORNGREAVES 7
RIVERMEAD PK
COLE HALL LA
Colehall
BADGERS WAY
NEW COLE HALL LA
Playing Fields
River Cole
Babb's Mill
Recn Gd
Sheldon Hall
B37
Liby
Sch
HOLLINGTON CRES
FARMCOTE
HEDGLEY GR
Glebe Farm
NORTH ROUNDHAY
SOUTH ROUNDHAY
Works
Kitt's Green
KITT'S GREEN RD
Byng Kendrick Central Sch
Sir Wilfred Martineau Upper & Lower Sch
Archbishop Grimshaw Comp Sch
CHELMSLEY RD
WOODCLOSE RD
Hallmoor Sch
HALLMOOR RD
B33
Lea Hall
LEA HALL RD
EAST MEADWAY
MEADWAY
Shirestone Jl Sch
SHIRESTONE RD
Tile Cross
BURLETON RD
TILE CROSS RD
Works
ACE BSNS PK
HRS BSNS PK
GRANBY BSNS PK
SHELDON WLK
GARRETTS GREEN LA
Recn Gd
Schs
Garrett's Green
Coll
B26
Whitesmore Sec Sch
GRASSINGTON DR
NORWICH CROFT 1
WORCESTER WLK 2
CUMBERFORD AVE
TILE CROSS TRAD EST
GREENWAY WLK

89
70

69
59

A B C D E F

8
7
89
6
5
88
4
3
87
2
1
86

Green La
The Belt
Cole End
High Meadow Fst Sch
B4117 GILSON RD
LICHFIELD RD
NORTON RD
ROSE RD
JAMES RD
DORIS RD
COLEBRIDGE CRES
STATION RD
PROSSERS WLK
HIGH ST
GILSON DR
M42
M6
A452
A446

SWIFT CL
RED WING WLK
GOLDCREST CROFT
NIGHTINGALE AVE
PHEASANT CROFT
SWALLOW AVE
JACKDAW DR
FIELDFARE CROFT
KINGFISHER DR
ISIS GR
LANDRAIL WLK
ROBIN CL
EAGLE GR
NUFFIELD HO
WORCESTER HO
Sch
Burtons Farm Prim Sch
DEE WLK
HEATHER CL
CORNCRAKE DR
GREENFINCH RD
WHEATFIELD CL
CHAFFINCH DR
BARLE GR
WOODPECKER GR
BLACKBIRD CROFT
GREENFINCH CL
MULL CROFT
AUCKLAND DR
BALMORAL RD
WESTFIELD HO
ARRAN WAY
ELLICE DR
PO
P
B36
Prim Sch
ORKNEY CROFT
Smiths Wood Sch
BELL CL
SKYE CL
CROFT
MEWS
AVE
ANGLESEY AVE
SARK DR
SANDA CROFT
B4114
WINDWARD WAY
JERSEY CROFT
GUERNSEY DR
SHETLAND WLK
Sch
BEDFORD HO
SCHOOL CL
BALLARD WLK
MERIDEN DR
Kingshurst Jun & Inf Schs
CHURCH CL
BIRBECK HO
RATHLIN CROFT
SHERARD CROFT
ANDY VIEW
COLLING WALK
THE PARADE
MARSTON DR
Liby
Kingshurst
GILSON WAY
MULLINSGROVE RD
OLD TOWN
MOXHULL
CHESTER RD
FALKLAND WAY
NEWNHAM HO
SHEPPEY DR
DIDGLEY GR
OAKTHORPE DR
WHEELEY MOOR RD
TILE GR
BELGRAVIA CT
SCHOFIELD RD
FORDBRIDGE RD
St Antony's RC Prim Sch
Fordbridge Inf Sch
WATERLOO IND EST
BURHILL WAY
NEWBY GR

The Catmore
The Decoy
Cemy
Coleshill Hall Bridge
BIRMINGHAM RD
B46
SOUTH DR
Coleshill Hall Farm
Hall Wlk
BIRMINGHAM
River Cole
Green La
B37
Solihull Coll Chelmsley Campus

F7
1 RIVERSIDE CT
2 SERVITE HO
3 BRIDGE VIEW
4 WINDMILL AVE
5 ST PAUL'S CRES
6 BRAMBLE CL
7 BLYTHE RD
8 ANGEL MEWS
9 FAIRVIEW MEWS
10 CHAMBERLAIN WLK
11 PARKFIELD CT
12 DUNCOMBE GN

OLD MILL RD
ORCHARD AVE
HIGH BRINK RD
KENDAL AVE
WOOD CROFT
COLLEMEADOW RD
RAVENSWOOD HILL
PENNS LA
B4114
B4117
PARK RD
L Ctr
PARKFIELD RD
Ct
SUMNER RD
PARK AVE
Coleshill
WHEATLEY GRANGE
CHELMSLEY AVE
CLINTON RD
WILMOT AVE
Prim Sch
DIGBY RD
WINGFIELD RD
HUDSON AVE
MOAT WALL AVE
MOUNTFORT RD
GREEN LA
OAK RISE
STONEBRIDGE RD
GREEN LA
CASTLE DR
BURMAN DR
SPRINGFIELDS
THE HALL GROVE
HALL WLK

CORINNE CROFT
COOKS LA
BANGOR HO
MENAI WLK
TOWER CROFT
WATERLOO AVE
TYNE CL
CLOPTON CRES
RUNCORN CL
TAY CROFT
EILEEN GDNS
KEELE HO
Bacon's End
LAMBETH CL
The City Tech Coll
FENCOTE AVE
FORTH DR
WESTHAM HO
WEDGEWOOD HO
STAPLETON DR
CONWAY RD
PUTNEY WLK
Sch
Sports Ctr
Fordbridge
CONWAY RD
Bacon's End Bridge

C3
1 BRACKEN CROFT
2 RICHMOND WAY
3 SWANSWOOD GR

B2
1 BEAUCHAMP CL
2 CHESTNUT WLK
3 CHESHUNT HO
4 MAPLE WLK
5 GREENWOOD SQ
6 CEDAR WLK
7 COPPICE WAY
8 DILLINGTON HO
9 WOODBROOK HO

1 SOMERVILLE HO
2 SELWYN HO
3 WADHAM HO
4 MANSFIELD HO

Bishop Wilson CE Prim Sch
CHESTER RD
BUSHBURY CROFT
HEATHGREEN CL
RYECROFT
WHEATEN CL
PARTRIDGE CL
YORKMINSTER DR
FRAMPTON CL
WATERSON CROFT
CORNFIELD CROFT
Wheeley Moor Farm
7a
WOODCLOSE RD
SHEEPCOTE CL
ORIEL HO
BLACKCAT CL
ACRES DR
PERCH AVE
GRANTLEY DR
Pol HQ
Liby
Chelmsley Wood
PIKE DR
ROACH CL
WALMER WAY
WOODLANDS WAY
TRAVELLERS WAY
ASHWOOD DR
FOXLAND CL
BRICKHILL DR
Prim Sch
PENDRELL CL
GEOLMUND CRES
STEPHENSON DR
WAUGH CL
PO
GREENWOOD WAY
CHELMSLEY CIRC
MOORESD AVE
GRAYLING WLK
CHELMSLEY RD
BREAM CL
CHILHAM DR
LUDLOW
CULEY WLK
BROOK FARM WLK
LYECROFT AVE
CHISWICK WLK
MAYTREE CL
CAMPLEA CROFT
COLEFORD DR
BOSWORTH DR
KINGSGATE HO
FIRCROFT HO
DERBY DR
LARCH CROFT
HEDGETREE CROFT
PENRITH GR
DRUMMOND WAY
WARDOUR DR
Prim Sch
CROFT IND EST
Prim Sch
WOODBINE WLK
CLOVER AVE
FRIARS WLK
BRAESIDE CROFT
BLUEBELL DR
MOAT CROFT
KEBLE HO
HOLLY LODGE WLK
CHESTER CL
AVONCROFT
DURHAM CROFT
IPSWICH WLK
PINE SQ
YEW WLK
CORALIN CL
CIRCUS AVE
Chelmsley Wood
CRAIG CROFT
DUNSTER RD
HEDINGHAM GR
LUMLEY GR
Recn Gd
COLESHILL HEATH RD
M6
4
KELSULL CROFT
ARDERNE
CHAPELHOUSE RD
Kingshurst Brook
WINCHESTER DR
TRURO WLK
ELY CL
STELLA CROFT
FRENSHAM CL
CARISBROOKE AVE
STARKEY CROFT
LANGLEY WLK
BLAIR GR
RAGLAN WAY
WILLOW WAY
HAZEL CROFT
DOWNING HO
LIME GR
ALDER DR
ARBOR WAY
GREENLANDS RD
Sch
MARLENE CROFT
COMPTON CROFT
ELLINGHAM
BARNARD CL

D2
1 HAREBELL WLK
2 MULLINERS CL
3 HIKER GR
4 CHESTER CT
5 WARWICK CT
6 PICTON CROFT

Brickfield Farm
7
Alcott Wood
CHICHESTER GR
BEECH AVE
Alcott Hall Prim Sch
HATCHFORD WLK
PICCADILLY CL
WORCESTER WLK
GUILLEMARD CT
ELFORD GR
CAMBRIDGE DR
GLOUCESTER WAY
HAMAR WAY
DAWLEY CRES
BERWICKS LA
WALNUT CL
PEACE WLK
BIRCH CROFT
NEVADA WAY
EDEN GR
Coleshill Pool
Sch
WELLS WLK
LINCOLN GR
PINBURY CROFT
PLANE GR
POPLAR AVE
ROWAN WAY
WHEATCROFT DR
HELMSWOOD DR
WHITE BEAM RD
BIRMINGHAM BSNS PK
A452
Pool Wood

17 A B 18 C D 19 E F

69
90

C1
1 TREVELYAN HO
2 RICHMOND HO
3 DARWIN HO

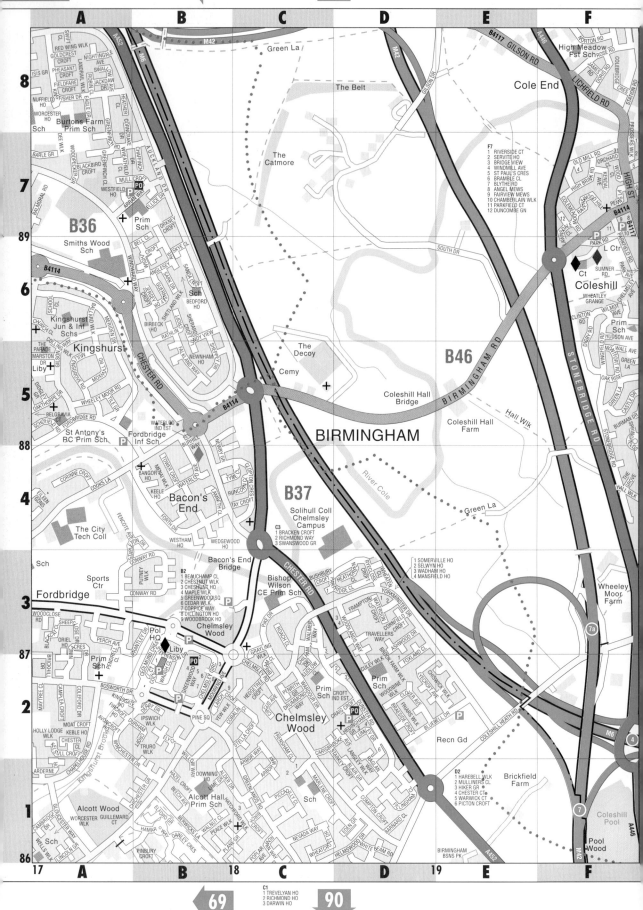

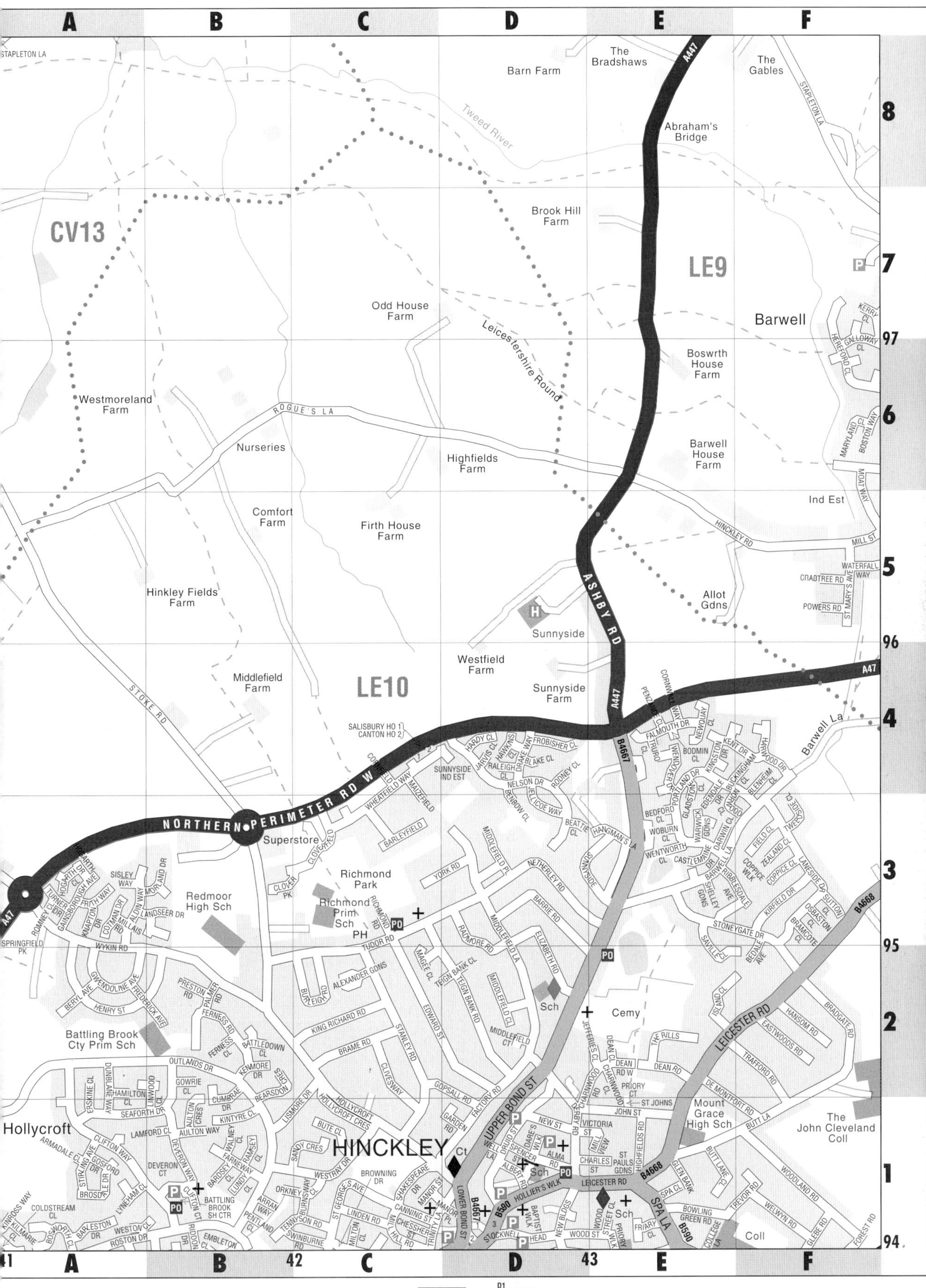

D1
1 BAINES' LA
2 KING ST
3 COUNCIL RD
4 EALES YD

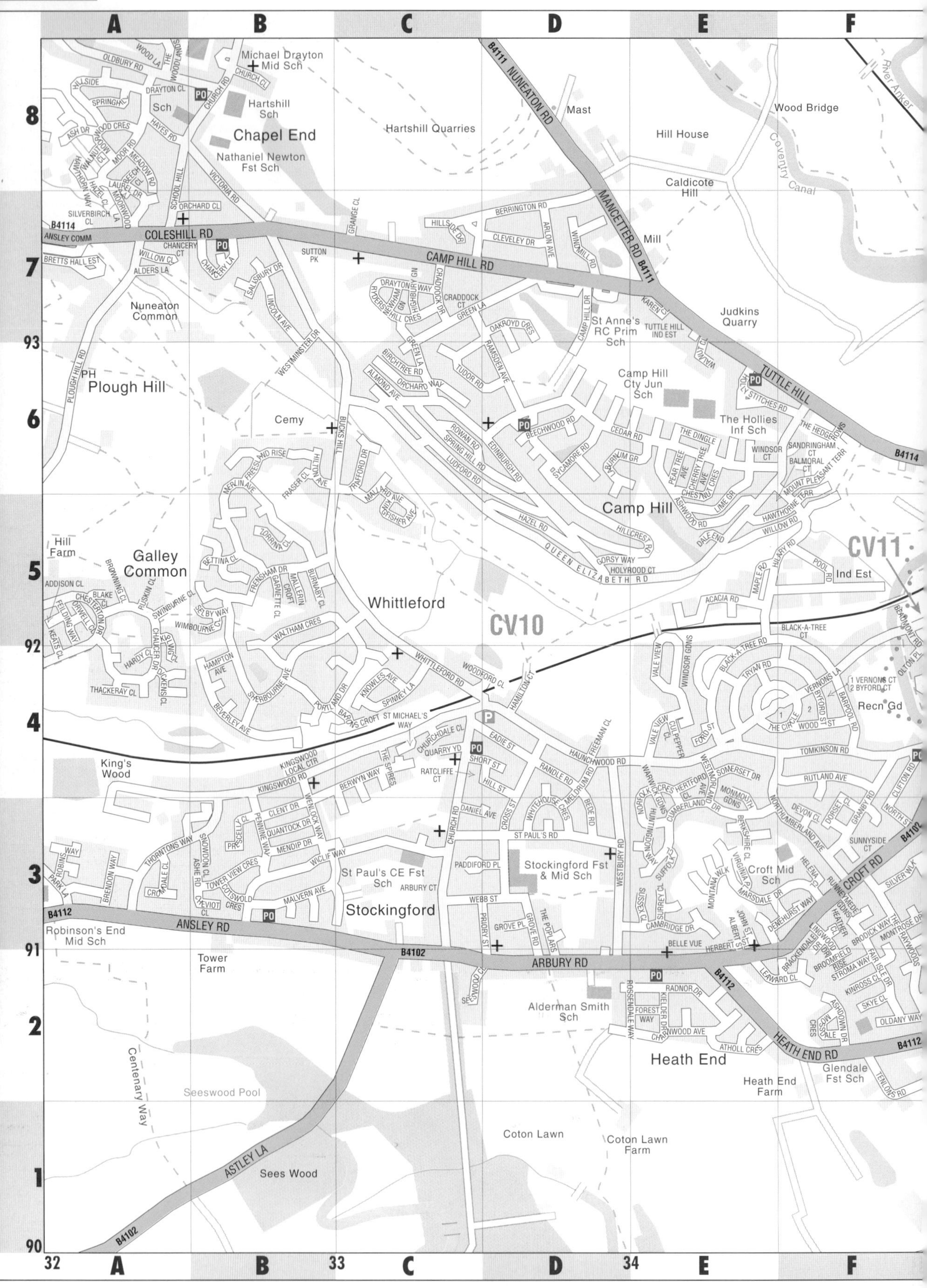
Chapel End
Hartshill Quarries
Nuneaton Common
Plough Hill
Galley Common
Whittleford
CV10
Camp Hill
CV11
Stockingford
Heath End
Coton Lawn
Sees Wood
Seeswood Pool
Centenary Way
Tower Farm
King's Wood
Hill Farm
Judkins Quarry
Caldicote Hill
Hill House
Wood Bridge
Coventry Canal
River Anker
COLESHILL RD
CAMP HILL RD
ANSLEY RD
ARBURY RD
HEATH END RD
ASTLEY LA
NUNEATON RD
MANCETTER RD
TUTTLE HILL
CROFT RD
QUEEN ELIZABETH RD

77

A B C D E F

8 7 93 6 5 92 4 3 91 2 1 90

NUNEATON

Top Farm
Milby Fst & Mid Sch
Canal Farm
Lingfield
CV10
River Anker
Sandon Park
Weddington Fst Sch
Weddington
Higham Lane Sch
St Nicolas CE Fst Sch
North Warwickshire & Hinckley Coll
Coventry Canal
Manor Park Sch
Nuneaton Trent Valley
Etone Com Sch
Sports Ctr
Horeston Grange
L Ctr
King Edward VI Coll
Cemy
Whitacre Rd Ind Est
CV11
Liby
TH
Mus
Crem
Jubilee Sports Ctr
St Thomas More Sch
Schs
The Pingles
Sports Ctr
Wem Brook
Chilvers Coton Craft Ctr
Swinnerton Mid Sch
Attleborough
Centenary Bsns Ctr
Hammond Bsns Ctr
Pioneer Units
The Quadrant
Attleborough Fields Ind Est
Exis Ct
Trident Bsns Pk
James Diskin Ct
Everard Ct
Closers Bsns Ctr
Centrovell Ind Est
Chilvers Coton
George Eliot
Middlemarch Mid Sch
Hill Top
All Saints' CE Fst Sch
Shepperton Bsns Pk
George Eliot Sch
Leyland Spec Sch
The Hollows
CV10
Ind Est
Centenary Way

A444 WEDDINGTON RD
A47 HINCKLEY RD
A47 OLD HINCKLEY RD
LEICESTER RD
B4114 MIDLAND RD
TUTTLE HILL
B4102 QUEEN'S RD
ROANNE RINGWAY
A444 NEWTOWN RD
CHURCH ST
VICARAGE ST
COTON RD
A4254 AVENUE RD
EASTBORO WAY
HIGHFIELD RD
ATTLEBOROUGH RD
LUTTERWORTH RD
B4114
HEATH END RD
B4112
B4113 COVENTRY RD

1 ST MARY'S CT
2 EDYVEAN WALKER CT
3 LEXINGTON CT
4 DILLON CT

CORONATION CT 5
WHATELEY CT 6
KING'S CT 7

8 TEMPLAR CT
9 DUGDALE HO
10 CHILVERS CT
11 ALDERSGATE
12 STONELEIGH GDNS
13 STONELEIGH CT
14 LYDGATE CT
15 MILBY CT

THE SQUARE 1
THE GREEN 2
WEMBROOK HO 3

35 36 37

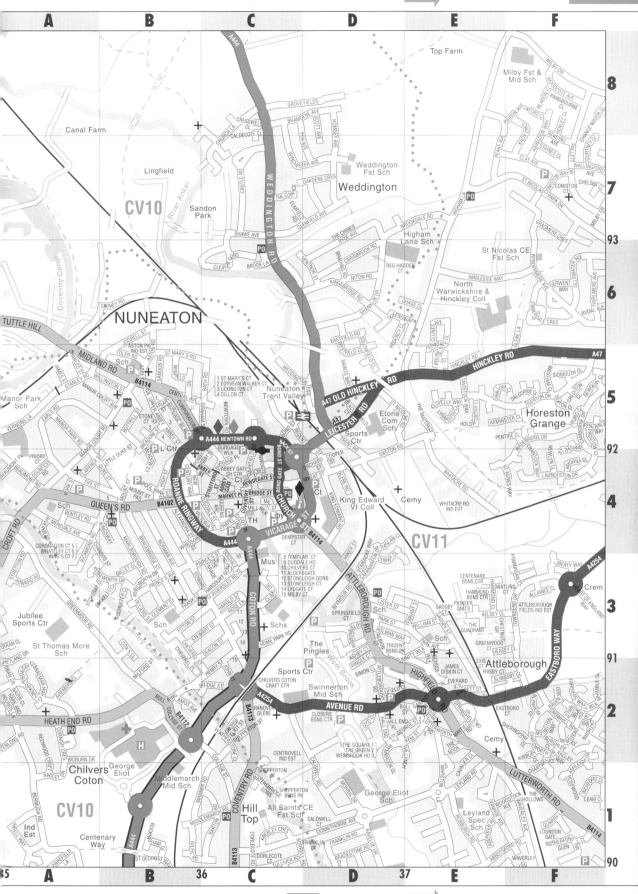

73

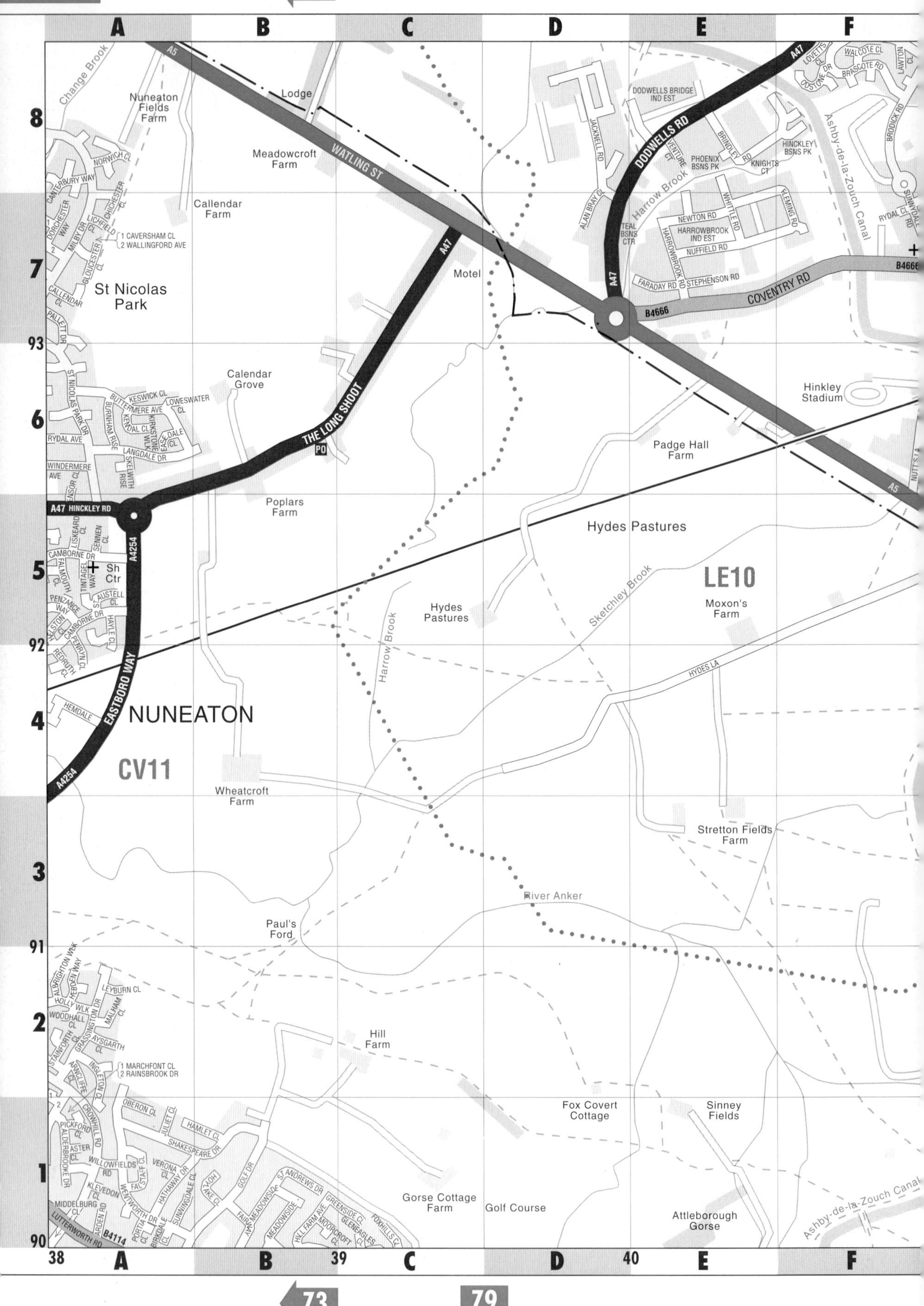

A
B
C
D
E
F
8
7
93
6
5
92
4
3
91
2
1
90
38
39
40
Nuneaton Fields Farm
Lodge
Meadowcroft Farm
WATLING ST
A5
Callendar Farm
St Nicolas Park
Motel
A47
DODWELLS BRIDGE IND EST
DODWELLS RD
PHOENIX BSNS PK
KNIGHTS CT
HINCKLEY BSNS PK
Ashby-de-la-Zouch Canal
Harrow Brook
NEWTON RD
HARROWBROOK IND EST
NUFFIELD RD
FARADAY RD
STEPHENSON RD
COVENTRY RD
B4666
TEAL BSNS CTR
Calendar Grove
THE LONG SHOOT
PO
Hinckley Stadium
Padge Hall Farm
Poplars Farm
Hydes Pastures
A47 HINCKLEY RD
A4254
Sh Ctr
Hydes Pastures
Sketchley Brook
LE10
Moxon's Farm
HYDES LA
EASTBORO WAY
NUNEATON
CV11
Wheatcroft Farm
Stretton Fields Farm
River Anker
Paul's Ford
Hill Farm
Fox Covert Cottage
Sinney Fields
Gorse Cottage Farm
Golf Course
Attleborough Gorse
LUTTERWORTH RD
B4114
1 CAVERSHAM CL
2 WALLINGFORD AVE
1 MARCHFONT CL
2 RAINSBROOK DR

73
79

71

D8
1 MANSION ST
2 HANSON CT
3 BRITTANIA SH CTR
4 BLOCKLEY'S YD
5 REGENT CT
6 THE PARADE

76

7 EDWARDS CTR
8 THE HORSEFAIR
E8
1 THE NARROWS
2 QUEEN'S PARK FLATS
3 QUEEN'S PARK TERR
4 CLARENCE CT

75

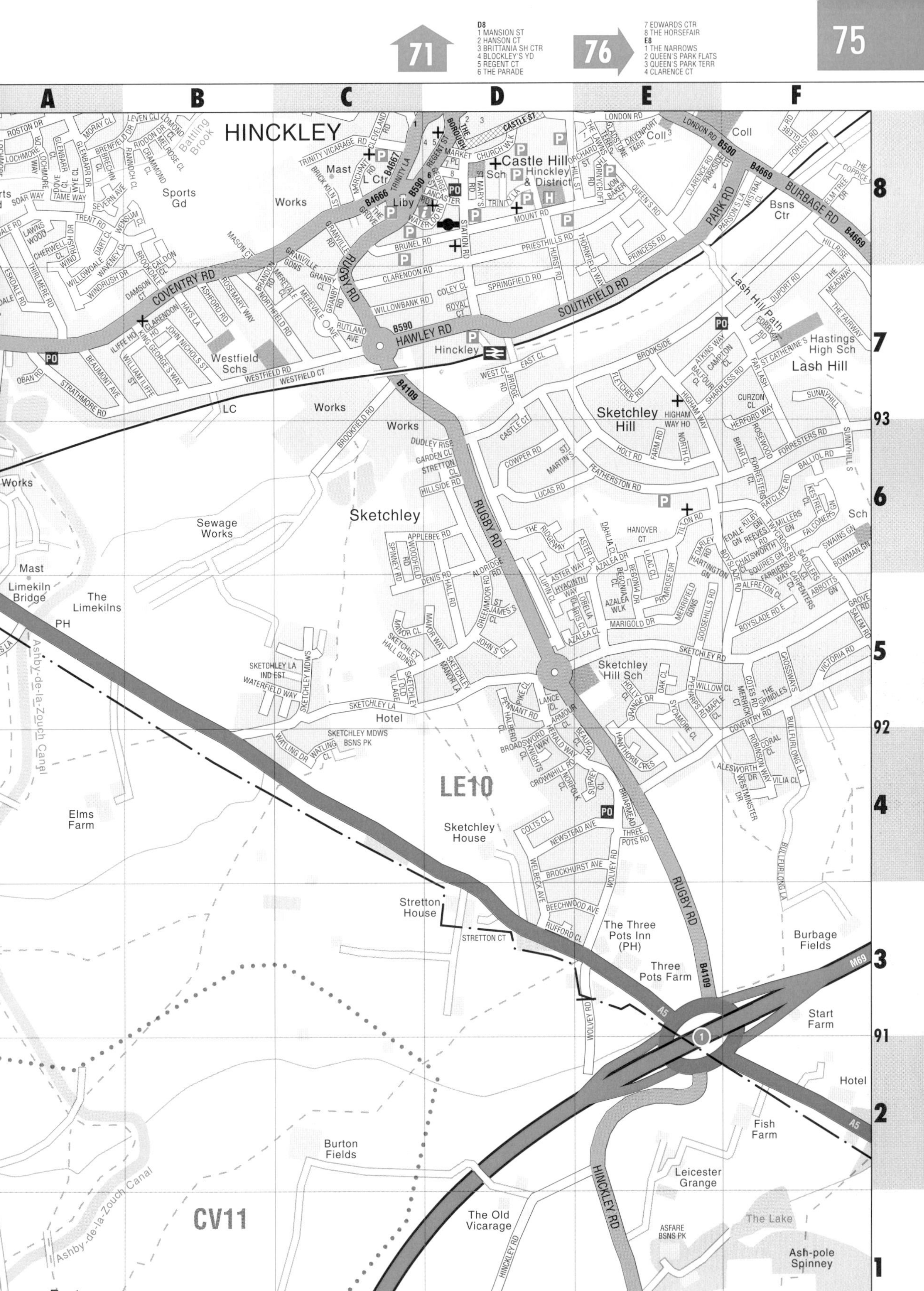

HINCKLEY

LE10

CV11

75

A
B
C
D
E
F
8
7
93
6
5
92
4
3
91
2
1
90
44
45
46
Caravan Site
Brickyard Farm
Aston Firs
HINCKLEY RD
B4669
LE9
The Homestead
Threeways Farm
SAPCOTE RD
ASTON FLAMVILLE RD
BURBAGE RD
B578
HINCKLEY RD
Manor House
MANOR HOUSE CL
Pond Spinney
SHARNFORD RD
Aston Flamville
Cottage Farm
Burbage
CHURCH ST
Liby
LYCHGATE LA
Oak Farm
Lychgate Farm
LUTTERWORTH ROAD COMMERCIAL EST
White House Farm
Deepdale Farm
LE10
Mickle Hill Spinney
Mickle Hill
Fields Farm
WORKHOUSE LA
LUTTERWORTH RD
Mickle Hill Farm
Orchard Farm
Burbage House
Soar Brook
Soar Brook Spinney
Hogue Hall
Three Corner Spinney
Ash-pole Spinney
Crab-tree Spinney
Lodge Farm
A5
M69
B4114
CHURCH LA

75

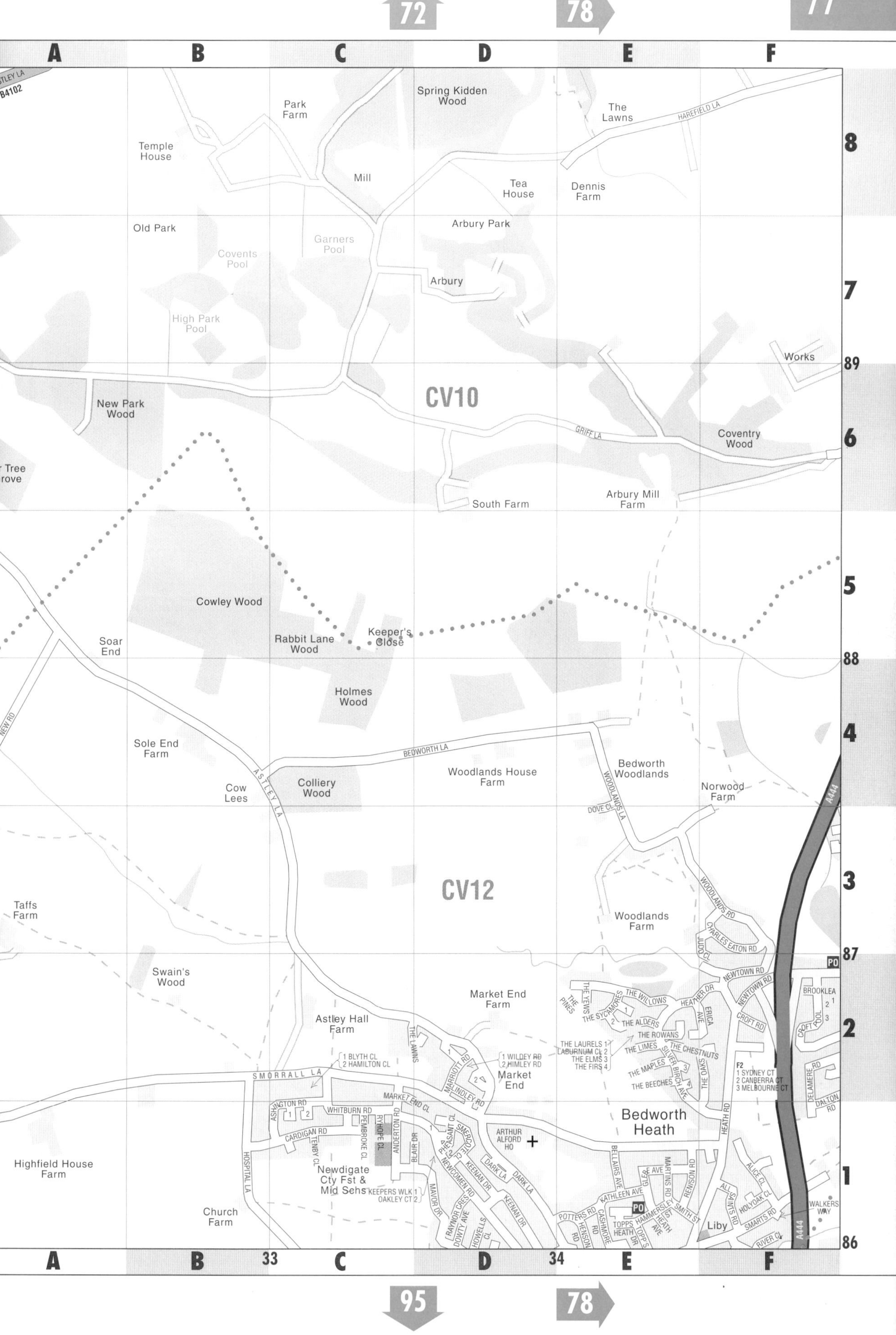

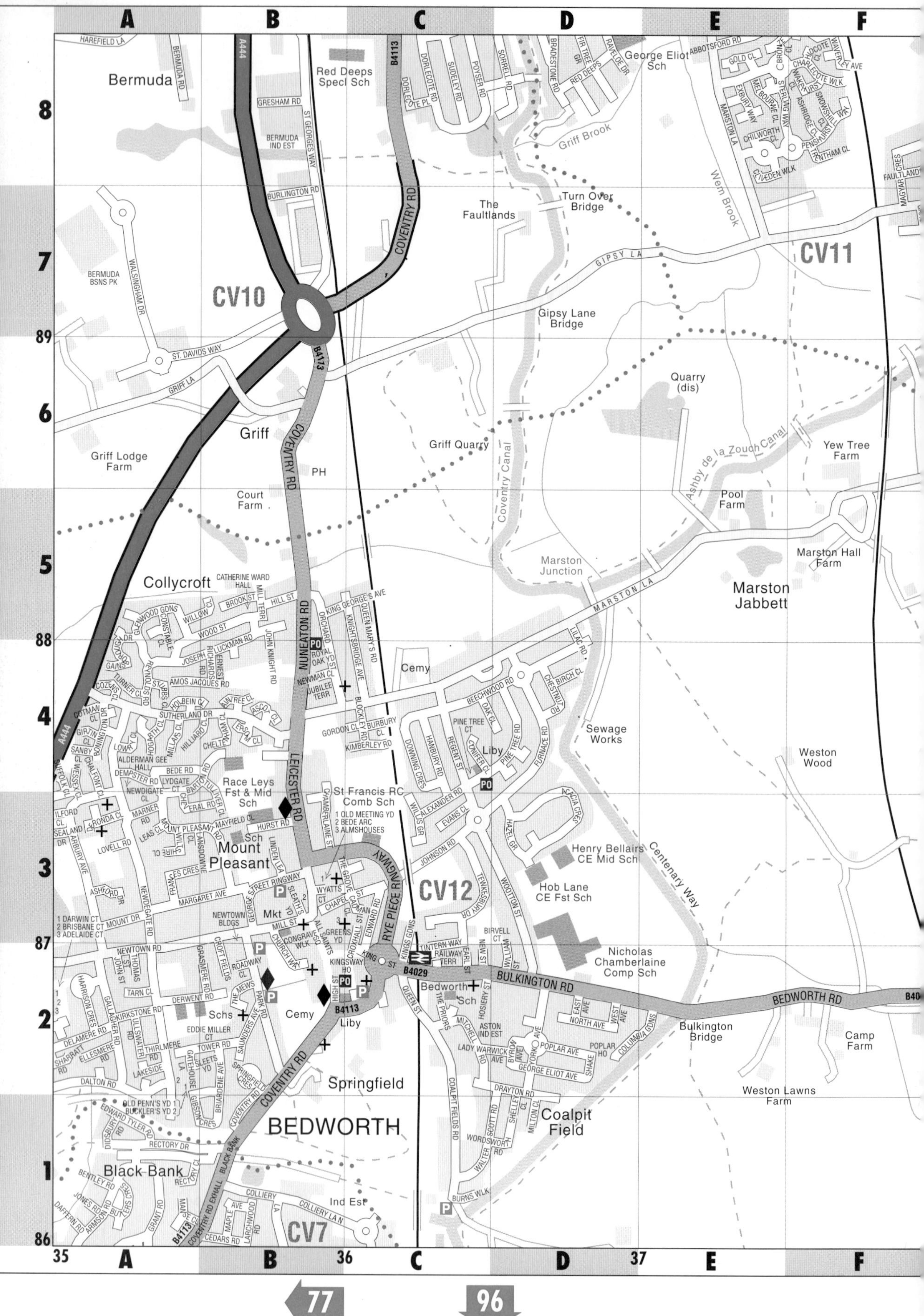
A
B
C
D
E
F
8
7
89
6
5
88
4
3
87
2
1
86
35
36
37
Bermuda
Red Deeps
Specl Sch
George Eliot
Sch
Griff Brook
BERMUDA
IND EST
The
Faultlands
Turn Over
Bridge
Wem Brook
CV11
CV10
BERMUDA
BSNS PK
GIPSY LA
Gipsy Lane
Bridge
ST. DAVIDS WAY
GRIFF LA
Quarry
(dis)
Griff
Griff Lodge
Farm
Griff Quarry
Coventry Canal
Ashby de la Zouch Canal
Yew Tree
Farm
PH
Court
Farm
Pool
Farm
Marston
Junction
Marston Hall
Farm
Collycroft
CATHERINE WARD
HALL
Marston
Jabbett
MARSTON LA
NUNEATON RD
COVENTRY RD
Cemy
Sewage
Works
Weston
Wood
Race Leys
Fst & Mid
Sch
LEICESTER RD
St Francis RC
Comb Sch
Liby
1 OLD MEETING YD
2 BEDE ARC
3 ALMSHOUSES
Henry Bellairs
CE Mid Sch
Centenary Way
Mount
Pleasant
Sch
RYE PIECE RINGWAY
CV12
Hob Lane
CE Fst Sch
1 DARWIN CT
2 BRISBANE CT
3 ADELAIDE CT
Mkt
Nicholas
Chamberlaine
Comp Sch
BULKINGTON RD
BEDWORTH RD
Bedworth
Sch
Schs
Cemy
Liby
Bulkington
Bridge
Camp
Farm
Springfield
Weston Lawns
Farm
OLD PENN'S YD 1
BUCKLER'S YD 2
BEDWORTH
Coalpit
Field
Black Bank
Ind Est
CV7
A444
B4113
B4029

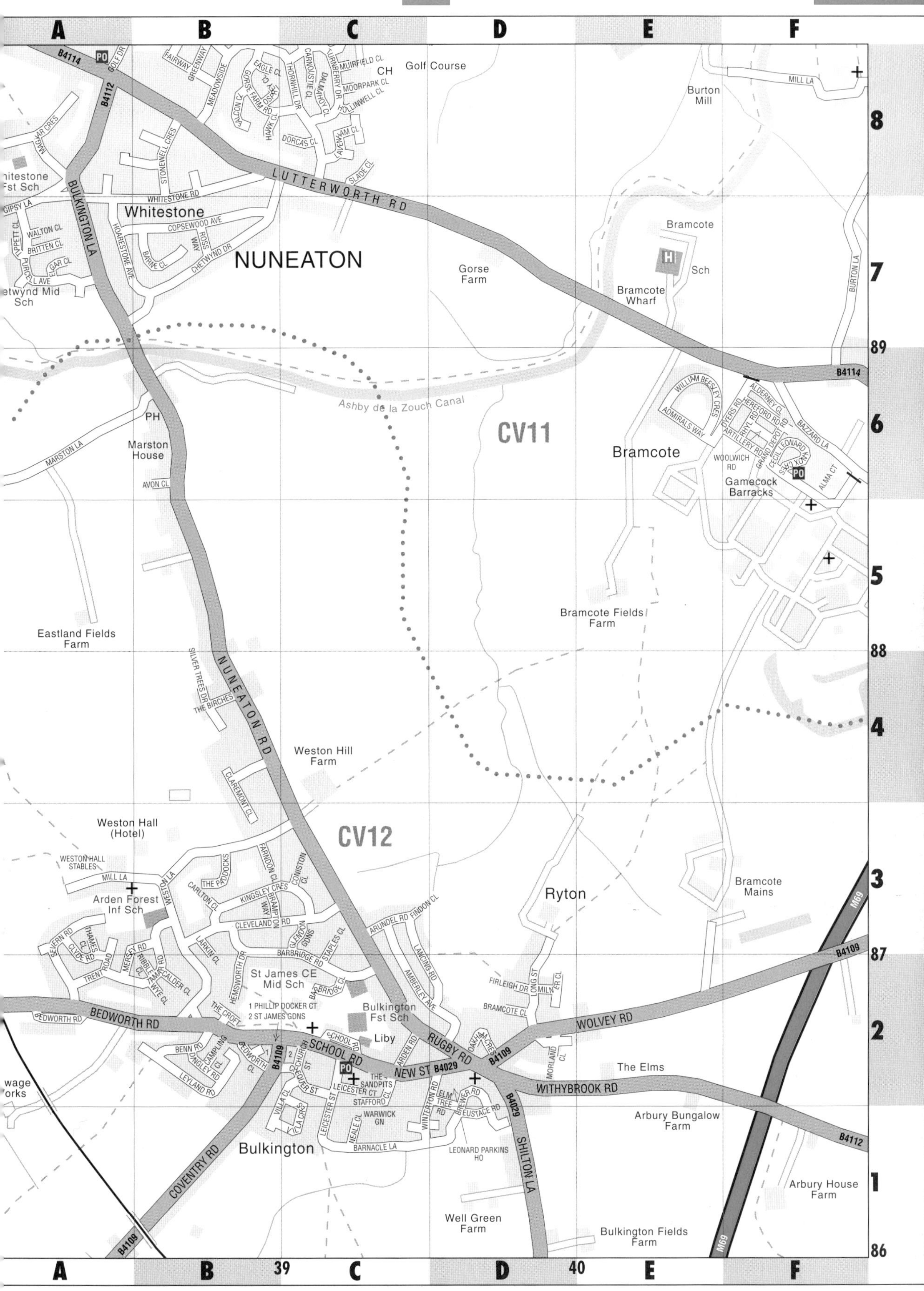
A
B
C
D
E
F
8
7
89
6
5
88
4
3
87
2
1
86
39
40
NUNEATON
Whitestone
CV11
CV12
Bramcote
Bulkington
Ryton
LUTTERWORTH RD
BULKINGTON LA
NUNEATON RD
Golf Course
Burton Mill
Bramcote Sch
Bramcote Wharf
Gorse Farm
Marston House
Ashby de la Zouch Canal
Gamecock Barracks
Bramcote Fields Farm
Eastland Fields Farm
Weston Hill Farm
Weston Hall (Hotel)
Arden Forest Inf Sch
St James CE Mid Sch
Bulkington Fst Sch
Liby
Bramcote Mains
The Elms
Arbury Bungalow Farm
Arbury House Farm
Well Green Farm
Bulkington Fields Farm
BEDWORTH RD
SCHOOL RD
NEW ST
RUGBY RD
WOLVEY RD
WITHYBROOK RD
SHILTON LA
COVENTRY RD
MARSTON LA
WHITESTONE RD
M69
B4114
B4112
B4109
B4029

60

F5
1 SUMMER ST
2 HEMMINGS CL
3 BALLARAT WLK
4 HOLLY GR
5 KENNEDY CT
6 BAYLIE CT
7 ENVILLE PL
8 SHORT ST
9 HEMPLANDS RD
10 CROWN LA
11 NEW ST

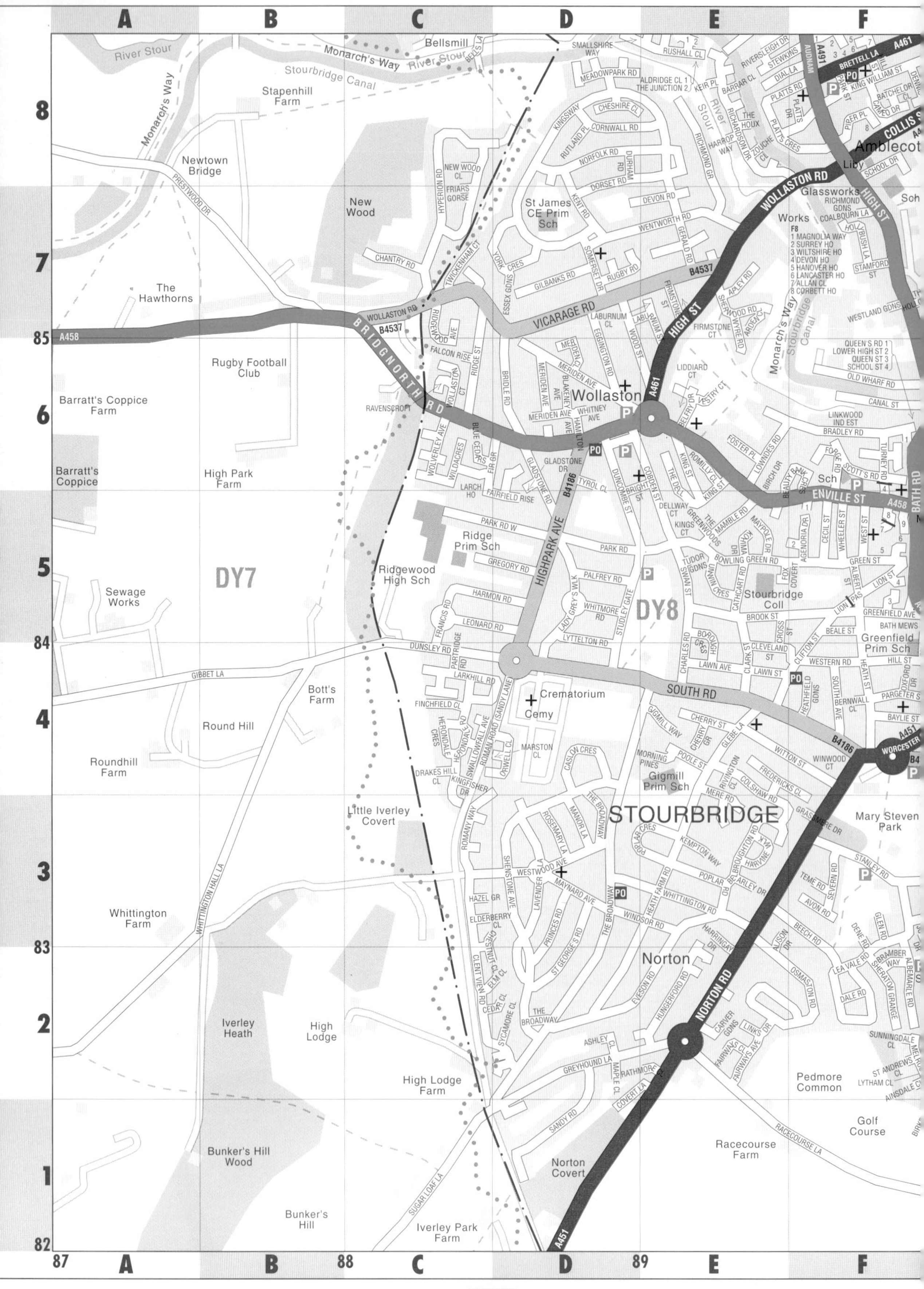

98

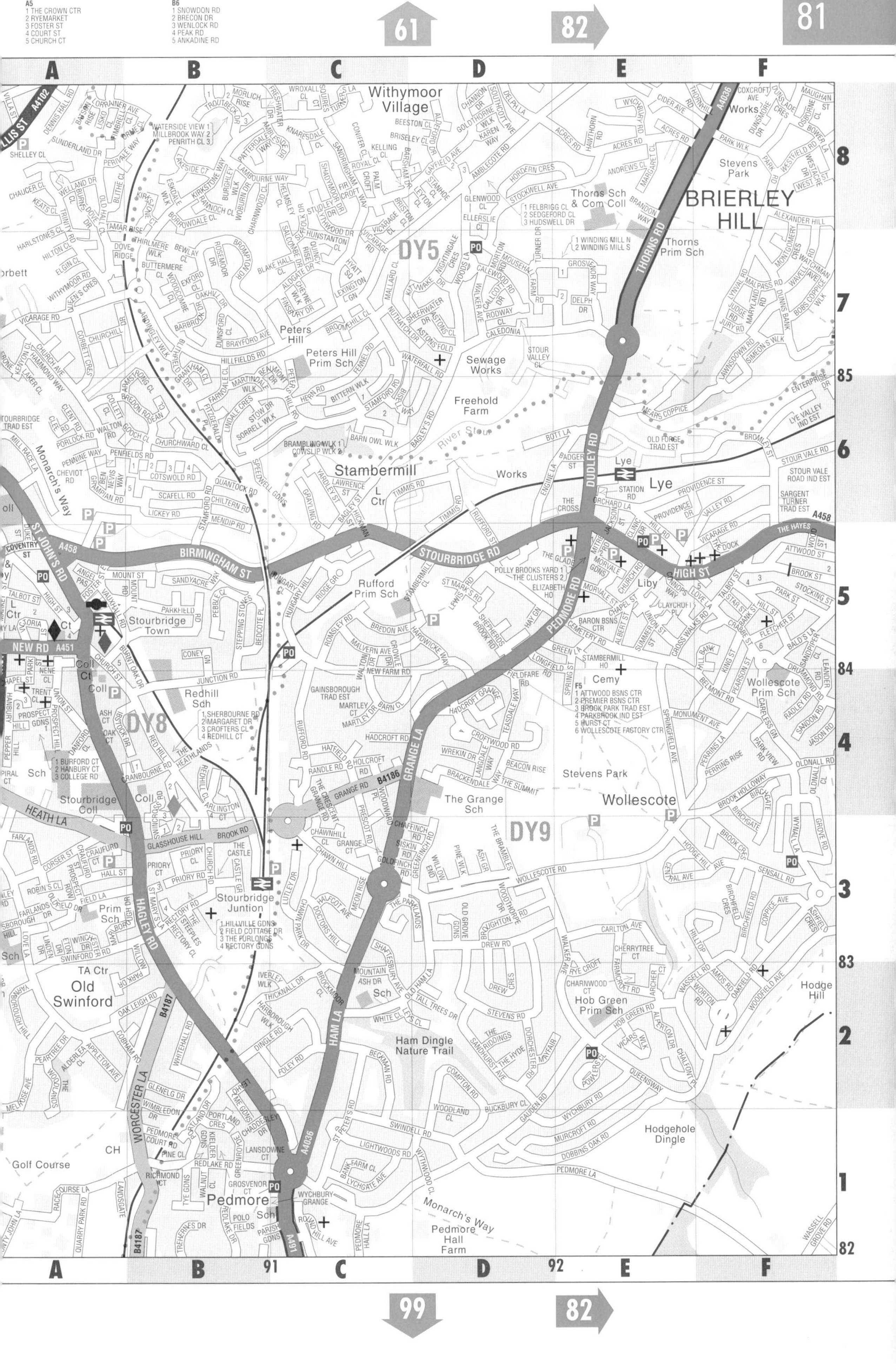
A5
1 THE CROWN CTR
2 RYEMARKET
3 FOSTER ST
4 COURT ST
5 CHURCH CT
B6
1 SNOWDON RD
2 BRECON DR
3 WENLOCK RD
4 PEAK RD
5 ANKADINE RD
61
82
A
B
C
D
E
F
8
7
85
6
5
84
4
3
83
2
1
82
91
92
Withymoor Village
BRIERLEY HILL
Stevens Park
Thorns Sch & Com Coll
Thorns Prim Sch
DY5
Peters Hill
Peters Hill Prim Sch
Sewage Works
Freehold Farm
River Stour
Stambermill
Works
Lye
Liby
Rufford Prim Sch
Stourbridge Town
Redhill Sch
DY8
Stourbridge Coll
Cemy
Wollescote Prim Sch
Stevens Park
Wollescote
The Grange Sch
DY9
Stourbridge Junction
Old Swinford
Hob Green Prim Sch
Hodge Hill
Ham Dingle Nature Trail
Hodgehole Dingle
Golf Course
Pedmore
Pedmore Hall Farm
Monarch's Way
Monarch's Way
THORNS RD
DUDLEY RD
PEDMORE RD
GRANGE LA
HAM LA
HAGLEY RD
WORCESTER LA
STOURBRIDGE RD
BIRMINGHAM ST
ST JOHN'S RD
HIGH ST
NEW RD
HEATH LA
GLASSHOUSE HILL
WOLLESCOTE RD
GRANGE RD
PEDMORE LA
QUEENSWAY
A4036
A458
A451
A491
B4186
B4187
A4102
F5
1 ATTWOOD BSNS CTR
2 PREMIER BSNS CTR
3 BROOK PARK TRAD EST
4 PARKBROOK IND EST
5 HURST CT
6 WOLLESCOTE FACTORY CTR
1 SHERBOURNE RD
2 MARGARET DR
3 CROFTERS CL
4 REDHILL CT
1 HILLVILLE GDNS
2 FIELD COTTAGE DR
3 THE FURLONGS
4 RECTORY GDNS
1 BURFORD CT
2 HANBURY CT
3 COLLEGE RD
1 FELBRIGG CL
2 SEDGEFORD CL
3 HUDSWELL DR
1 WINDING MILL N
2 WINDING MILL S
WATERSIDE VIEW 1
MILLBROOK WAY 2
PENRITH CL 3
POLLY BROOKS YARD 1
THE CLUSTERS 2
BRAMBLING WLK 1
COWSLIP WLK 2

81
62

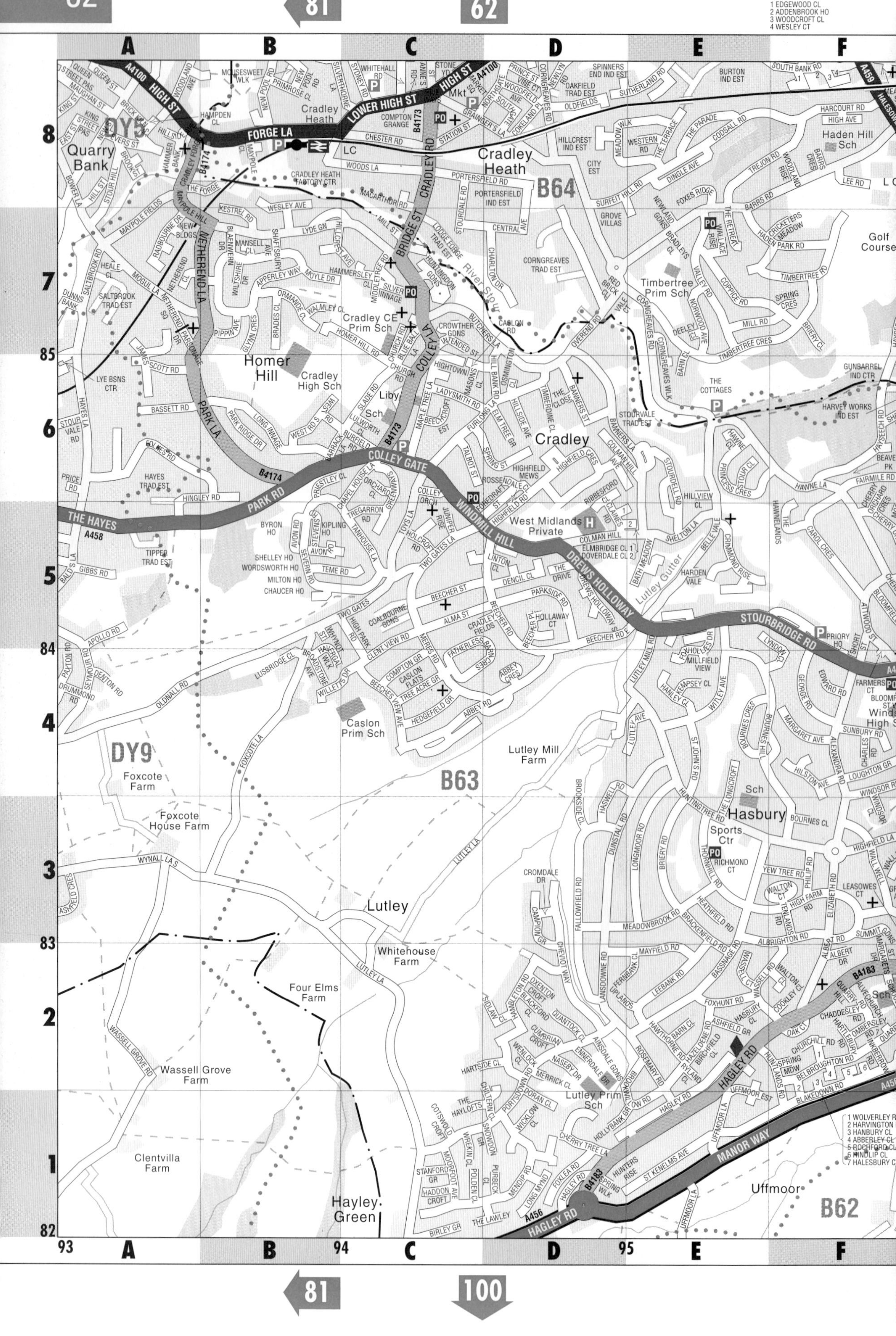
F8
1 EDGEWOOD CL
2 ADDENBROOK HO
3 WOODCROFT CL
4 WESLEY CT
Quarry Bank
Cradley Heath
Cradley
Homer Hill
Lutley
Hasbury
Uffmoor
Hayley Green
DY5
DY9
B64
B63
B62
FORGE LA
LOWER HIGH ST
HIGH ST
COLLEY GATE
PARK RD
THE HAYES
WINDMILL HILL
DREWS HOLLOWAY
STOURBRIDGE RD
HAGLEY RD
MANOR WAY
West Midlands Private
Cradley High Sch
Caslon Prim Sch
Timbertree Prim Sch
Haden Hill Sch
Lutley Prim Sch
Cradley CE Prim Sch
Foxcote Farm
Foxcote House Farm
Lutley Mill Farm
Whitehouse Farm
Four Elms Farm
Wassell Grove Farm
Clentvilla Farm
1 WOLVERLEY RD
2 HARVINGTON RD
3 HANBURY CL
4 ABBERLEY CL
5 ROCHFORD CL
6 HINDLIP CL
7 HALESBURY CT

81
100

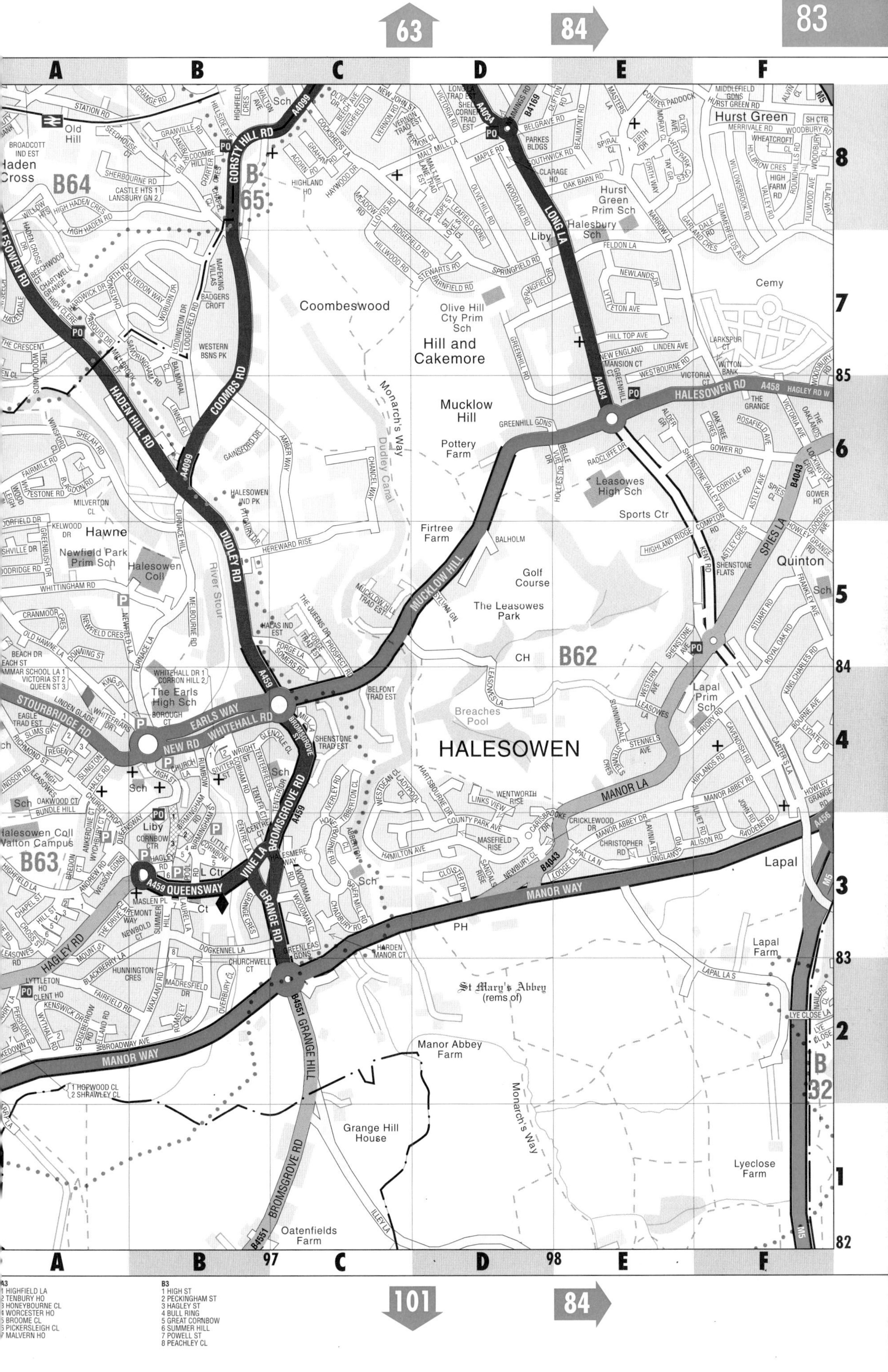
63
84
A
B
C
D
E
F
Old Hill
Haden Cross
B64
B65
GORSTY HILL RD
Hurst Green
Hurst Green Prim Sch
Halesbury Sch
Liby
LONG LA
Coombeswood
Olive Hill Cty Prim Sch
Hill and Cakemore
Cemy
Mucklow Hill
Pottery Farm
Monarch's Way
Dudley Canal
HALESOWEN RD
Leasowes High Sch
Sports Ctr
Hawne
Newfield Park Prim Sch
Halesowen Coll
HADEN HILL RD
COOMBS RD
DUDLEY RD
River Stour
Firtree Farm
Golf Course
The Leasowes Park
MUCKLOW HILL
B62
Quinton
SPIES LA
The Earls High Sch
Breaches Pool
HALESOWEN
Lapal Prim Sch
EARLS WAY
WHITEHALL RD
STOURBRIDGE RD
NEW RD
BROMSGROVE RD
MANOR LA
Halesowen Coll Walton Campus
B63
QUEENSWAY
GRANGE RD
MANOR WAY
Lapal
Lapal Farm
St Mary's Abbey (rems of)
HAGLEY RD
Manor Abbey Farm
B4551 GRANGE HILL
Grange Hill House
Monarch's Way
B32
Lyeclose Farm
BROMSGROVE RD
Oatenfields Farm
8
7
85
6
5
84
4
3
83
2
1
82
97
98
101
84
A3
1 HIGHFIELD LA
2 TENBURY HO
3 HONEYBOURNE CL
4 WORCESTER HO
5 BROOME CL
6 PICKERSLEIGH CL
7 MALVERN HO
B3
1 HIGH ST
2 PECKINGHAM ST
3 HAGLEY ST
4 BULL RING
5 GREAT CORNBOW
6 SUMMER HILL
7 POWELL ST
8 PEACHLEY CL

84
A6
1 BEVERLEY CT
2 HICKMANS CL
3 LOMBARDY CROFT
4 THE GREEN
B7
1 BRINDLEY CT
2 VERNON CT
3 HINCKLEY CT
4 ASTBURY CT
5 DOWNING CT
6 AVERY CT
83
B8
1 ARROW HO
2 STOUR HO
3 AVON HO
4 SEVERN HO
5 RUSKIN CT
6 LAWRENCE CT
7 HENDERSON CT
8 BRANDHALL CTR
9 FOLEY HO
10 REYNOLDS CT
11 OLD CRESCENT CT
64
A B C D E F
8 7 85 6 5 84 4 3 83 2 1 82
Warley Woods
Golf Course
B67
Lightwood Park
WOLVERHAMPTON RD
Perryfields High Sch
Perryfields Prim Sch
Liby
B68
HAGLEY RD W
Beech Lanes
B17
WOLVERHAMPTON RD S
A4123
COURT OAK RD
Ridgacre
Lenches Trust
QUINTON EXPRESSWAY
Quinton
World's End
Worlds End Jun & Inf Schs
WEST BVD
B62
Four Dwellings Schs
L Ctr
QUINTON RD W
SIMMONS DR
Welsh House Farm Prim Sch
B32
Bourn Brook
Golf Course
Woodgate Valley Country Park
Woodgate Valley
Hillcrest Sch
Hole Farm
Visitor Ctr
Nonsuch Sch
California
RSPCA Hospl
CLAPGATE LA
WOODGATE BSNS PK
BARNES HILL
Woodgate
Bartley Green Sec Sch
Woodgate Jun & Inf Sch
Senneleys Park
B31
B29
1 WESTSIDE DR
2 MODBURY AVE
3 FASTLEA RD
4 TANTALLAN DR
5 DUNBAR CL
99 00 01
83
102

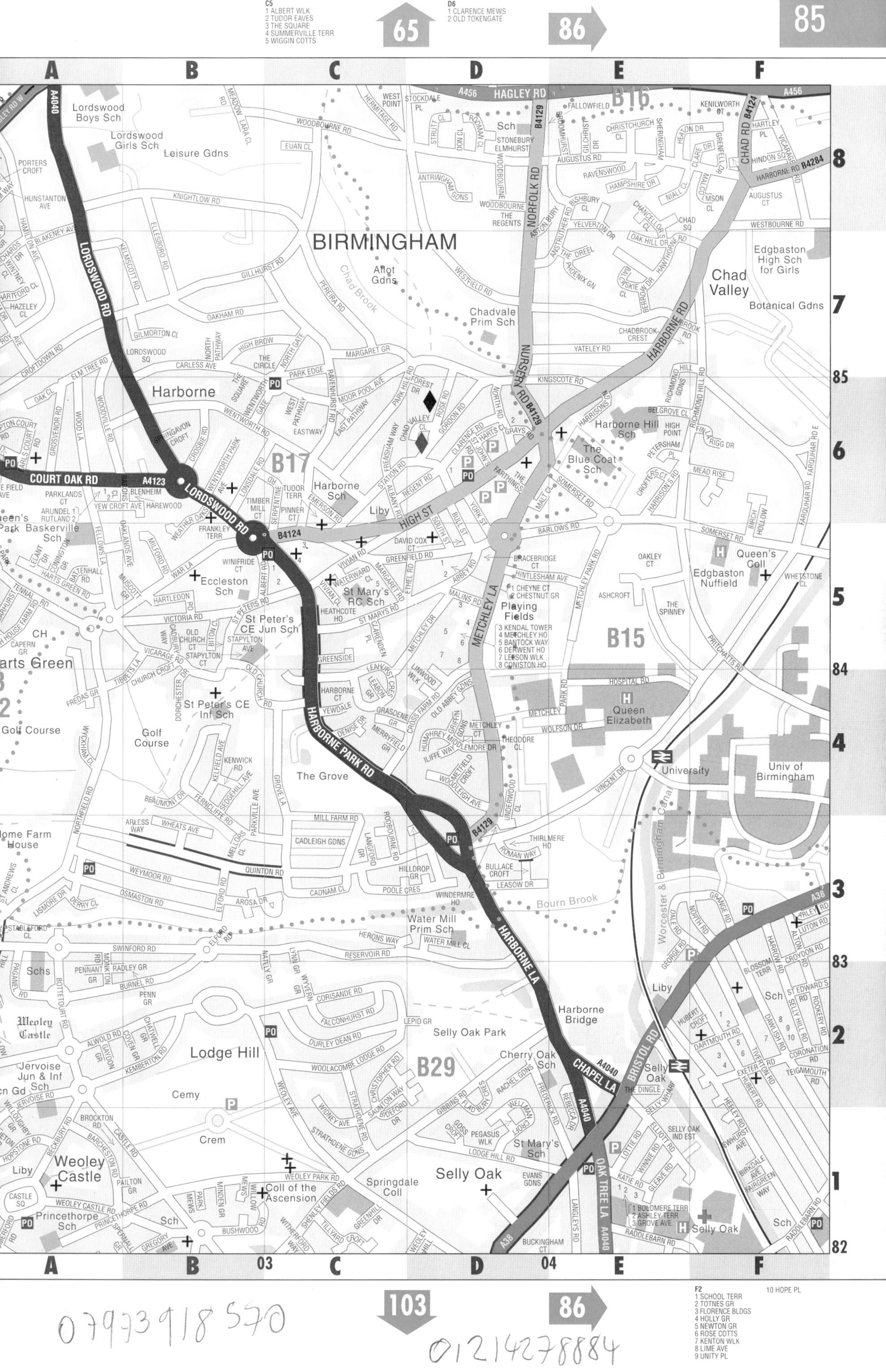

85
65
86
103
C5
1 ALBERT WLK
2 TUDOR EAVES
3 THE SQUARE
4 SUMMERVILLE TERR
5 WIGGIN COTTS
D6
1 CLARENCE MEWS
2 OLD TOKENGATE
BIRMINGHAM
Harborne
Chad Valley
B17
B15
B16
B29
HAGLEY RD
LORDSWOOD RD
COURT OAK RD
HARBORNE PARK RD
HARBORNE LA
HARBORNE RD
HIGH ST
NORFOLK RD
NURSERY RD
METCHLEY LA
BRISTOL RD
CHAPEL LA
OAK TREE LA
Lordswood Boys Sch
Lordswood Girls Sch
Leisure Gdns
Allot Gdns
Chadvale Prim Sch
Edgbaston High Sch for Girls
Botanical Gdns
Harborne Hill Sch
The Blue Coat Sch
Harborne Sch
Queen's Coll
Edgbaston Nuffield
Eccleston Sch
St Mary's RC Sch
St Peter's CE Jun Sch
St Peter's CE Inf Sch
Playing Fields
Queen Elizabeth
University
Univ of Birmingham
Golf Course
The Grove
Water Mill Prim Sch
Harborne Bridge
Selly Oak Park
Cherry Oak Sch
Lodge Hill
Cemy
Crem
Weoley Castle
Jervoise Jun & Inf Sch
Princethorpe Sch
Coll of the Ascension
Springdale Coll
Selly Oak
St Mary's Sch
Worcester & Birmingham Canal
Bourn Brook
Chad Brook
F2
1 SCHOOL TERR
2 TOTNES GR
3 FLORENCE BLDGS
4 HOLLY GR
5 NEWTON GR
6 ROSE COTTS
7 KENTON WLK
8 LIME AVE
9 UNITY PL
10 HOPE PL
07973918570
01214278884

C8
1 AUDLEIGH HO
2 CHISWICK HO
3 LEOFRIC CT
4 ALFRYTH CT
5 FARADAY HO
6 HOGARTH HO
7 CHATSWORTH TOWER
8 BELL BARN SH CTR

D7
1 QUEBEC HO
2 OTTAWA TOWER
3 HAMILTON HO

85

D8
1 DOVERCOURT HO
2 INGLETON HO
3 PAYNTON WLK
4 HADDON TOWER

66

E5
1 CANNON HILL PL
2 CANNON HILL GR
3 BEACONSFIELD CRES
3 CUMBERLAND AVE

E7
1 EARLSWOOD HO
2 ELMSTEAD TOWER

E8
1 HIGHGATE HO
2 CHARLBURY TOWER
3 WELLESBOURNE TOWER
4 DUNCHURCH HO

F5
1 PARK AVE
2 HEATH CT
3 MINTON HO

F7
1 BASKERVILLE HO
2 KENSTONE CROFT
3 CANTLOW HO
4 LENCH'S TRUST ALMSHOUSES
5 BRINKLOW TOWER
6 WILMCOTE TOWER
7 UPPER CONYBERE ST

F8
1 HANWOOD HO
2 DARFIELD WLK
3 RADCLIFFE TOW
4 CANBERRA WAY

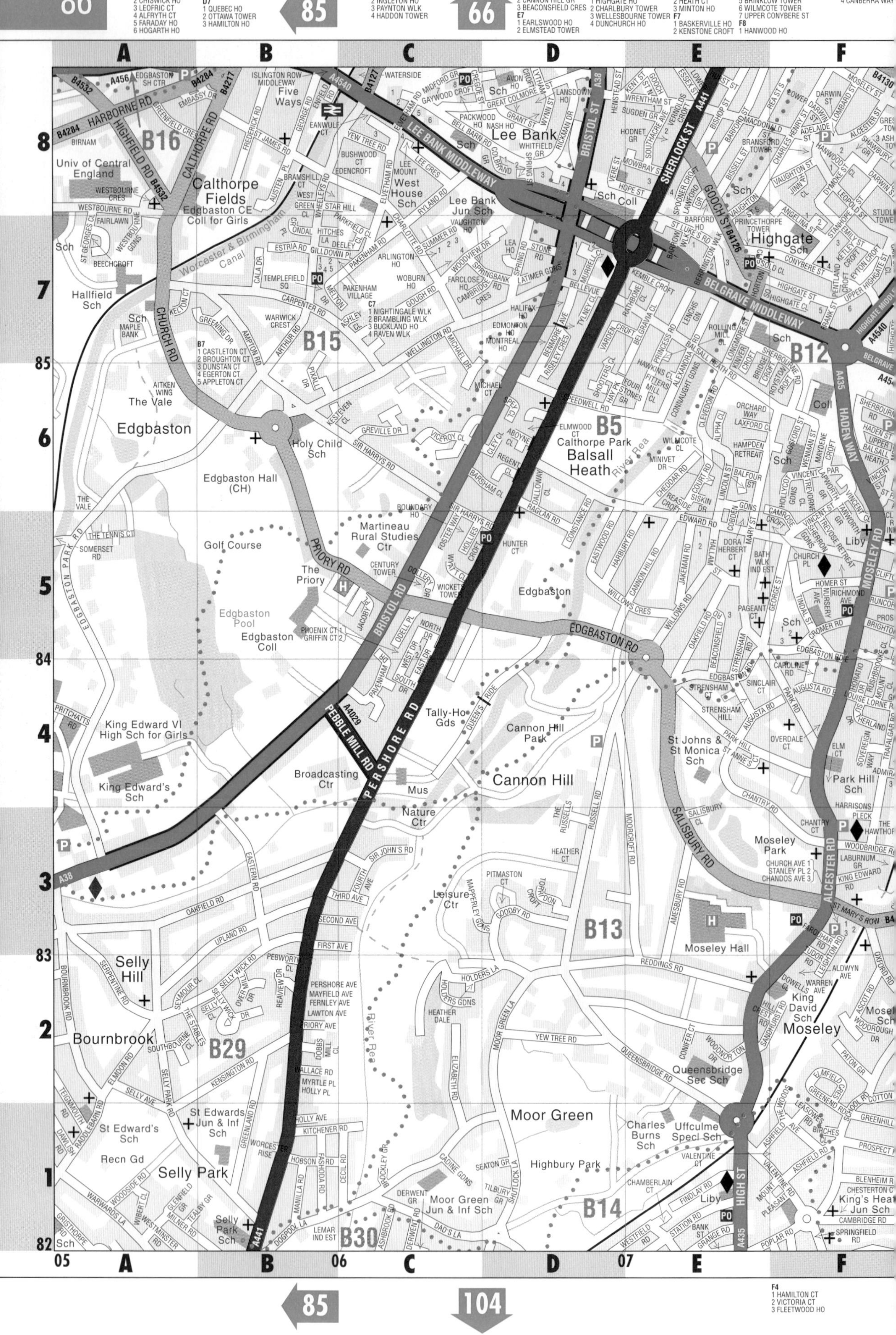

85

104

F4
1 HAMILTON CT
2 VICTORIA CT
3 FLEETWOOD HO

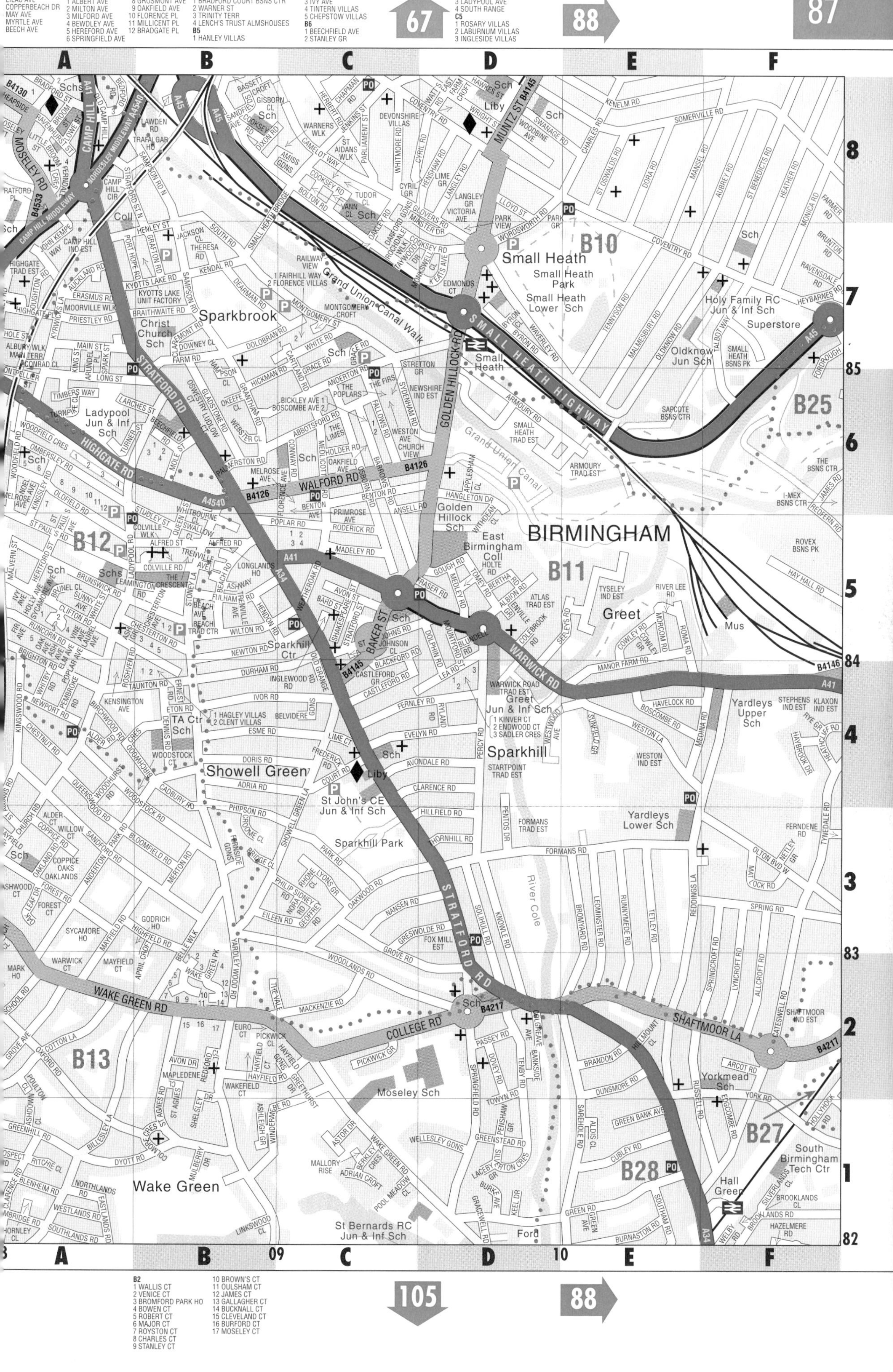

5
LILAC AVE
COPPERBEACH DR
MAY AVE
MYRTLE AVE
BEECH AVE
A6
1 ALBERT AVE
2 MILTON AVE
3 MILFORD AVE
4 BEWDLEY AVE
5 HEREFORD AVE
6 SPRINGFIELD AVE
7 CARPENTER PL
8 GROSMONT AVE
9 OAKFIELD AVE
10 FLORENCE PL
11 MILLICENT PL
12 BRADGATE PL
A8
1 BRADFORD COURT BSNS CTR
2 WARNER ST
3 TRINITY TERR
4 LENCH'S TRUST ALMSHOUSES
B5
1 HANLEY VILLAS
2 MATLOCK VILLAS
3 IVY AVE
4 TINTERN VILLAS
5 CHEPSTOW VILLAS
B6
1 BEECHFIELD AVE
2 STANLEY GR
67
B6
3 LADYPOOL AVE
4 SOUTH RANGE
C5
1 ROSARY VILLAS
2 LABURNUM VILLAS
3 INGLESIDE VILLAS
4 ORIEL VILLAS
88
A B C D E F
8 7 85 6 5 84 4 3 83 2 1 82
BIRMINGHAM
Small Heath
Sparkbrook
Sparkhill
Greet
Showell Green
Wake Green
Hall Green
B10
B11
B12
B13
B25
B27
B28
SMALL HEATH HIGHWAY
STRATFORD RD
HIGHGATE RD
WALFORD RD
GOLDEN HILLOCK RD
WARWICK RD
WAKE GREEN RD
COLLEGE RD
SHAFTMOOR LA
COVENTRY RD
MUNTZ ST
MOSELEY RD
CAMP HILL
Grand Union Canal Walk
Grand Union Canal
River Cole
Small Heath Park
Sparkhill Park
East Birmingham Coll
Moseley Sch
St Bernards RC Jun & Inf Sch
St John's CE Jun & Inf Sch
Yardleys Upper Sch
Yardleys Lower Sch
South Birmingham Tech Ctr
09 10
B2
1 WALLIS CT
2 VENICE CT
3 BROMFORD PARK HO
4 BOWEN CT
5 ROBERT CT
6 MAJOR CT
7 ROYSTON CT
8 CHARLES CT
9 STANLEY CT
10 BROWN'S CT
11 OULSHAM CT
12 JAMES CT
13 GALLAGHER CT
14 BUCKNALL CT
15 CLEVELAND CT
16 BURFORD CT
17 MOSELEY CT
105
88

← 87

C5
1 SYCAMORE WAY
2 CYPRESS SQ
3 BRAMLEY RD
4 LAUREL GDNS
5 ASH MEWS
6 CHERRY TREE CROFT

68

C5
7 SNOWBERRY GDNS
8 RYE CROFT
9 HONEYSUCKLE GR
10 BLOSSOMVILLE WAY

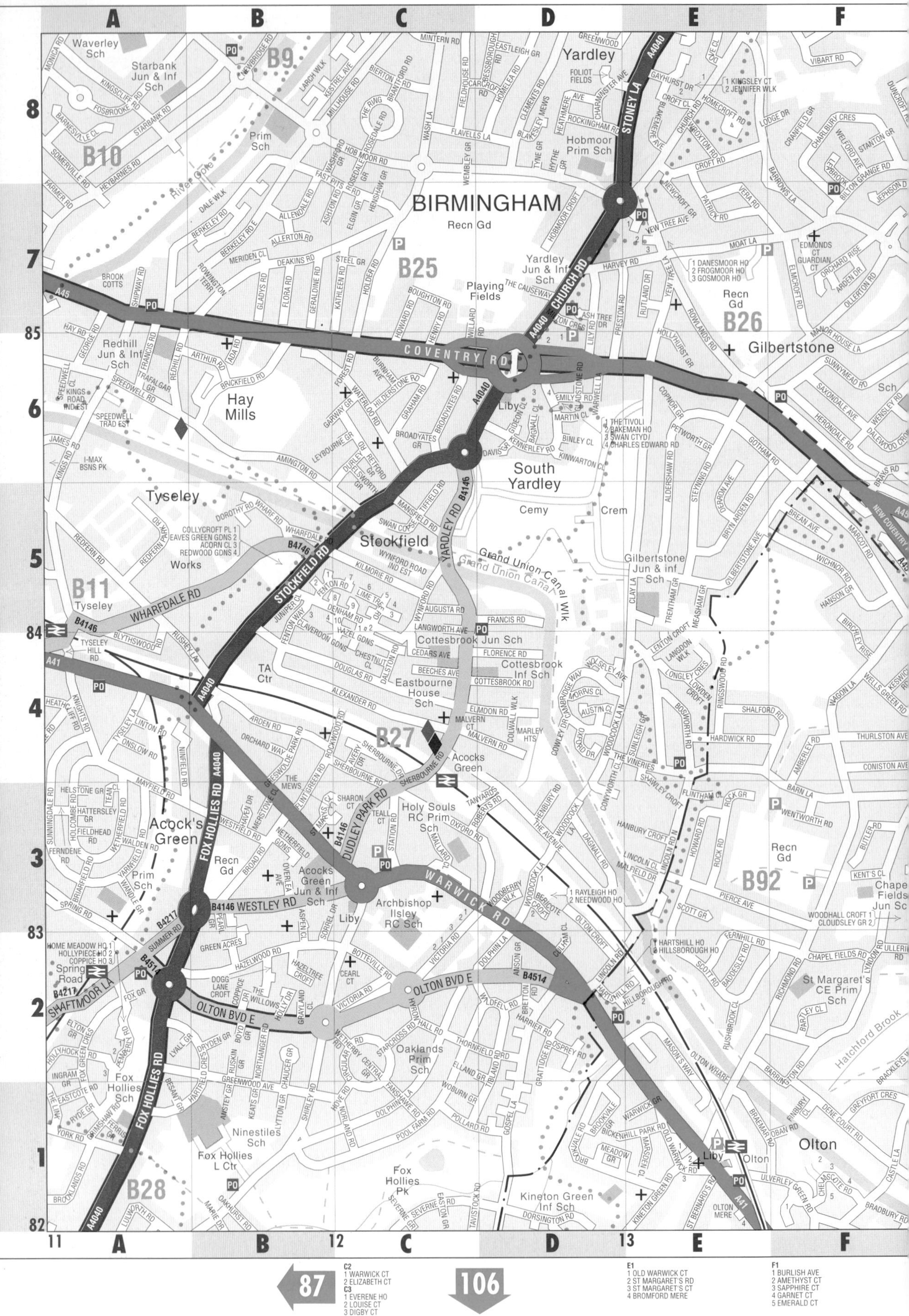

E1
1 OLD WARWICK CT
2 ST MARGARET'S RD
3 ST MARGARET'S CT
4 BROMFORD MERE

F1
1 BURLISH AVE
2 AMETHYST CT
3 SAPPHIRE CT
4 GARNET CT
5 EMERALD CT

C2
1 WARWICK CT
2 ELIZABETH CT
C3
1 EVERENE HO
2 LOUISE CT
3 DIGBY CT

69
90

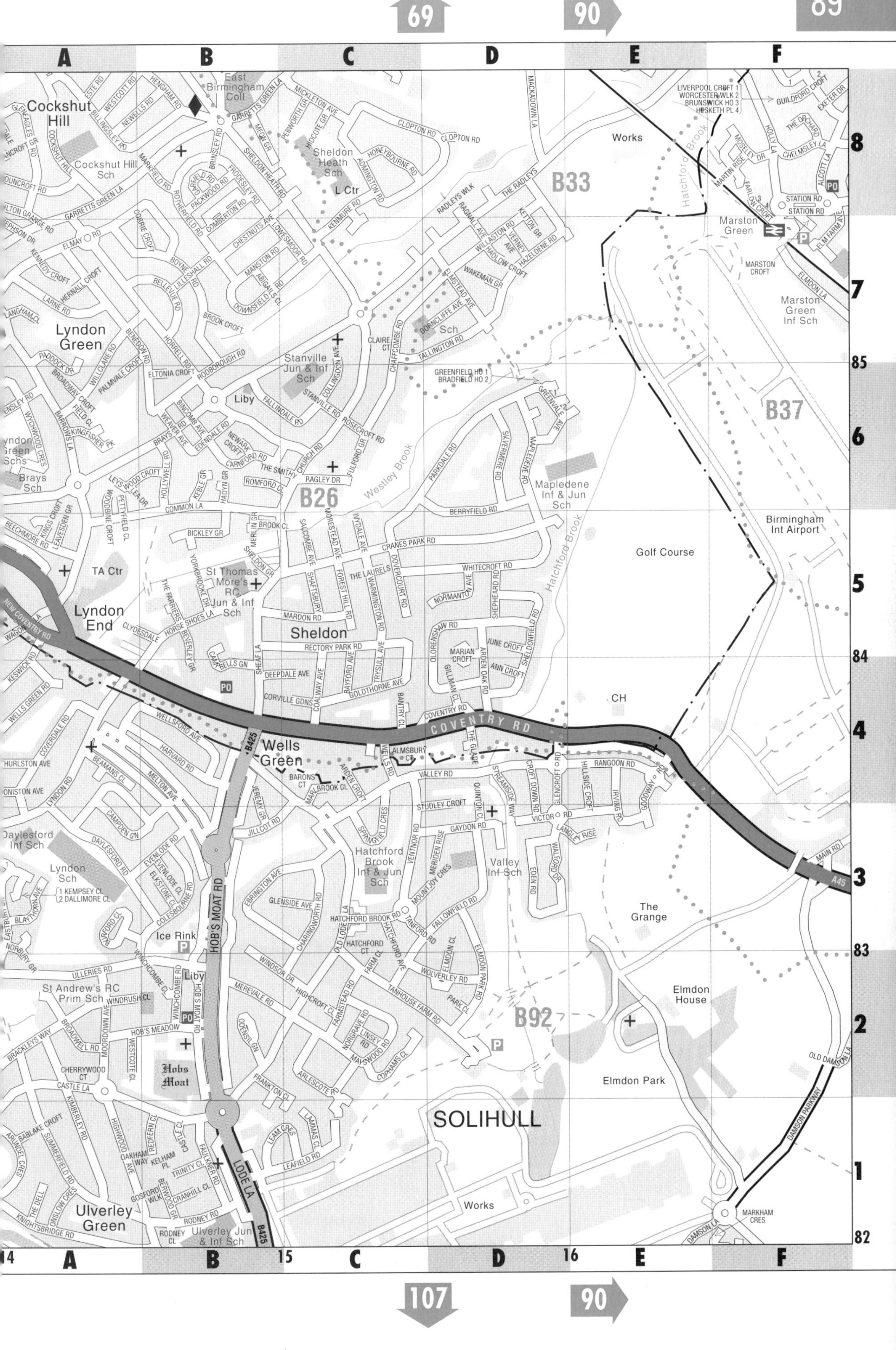
A
B
C
D
E
F
Cockshut Hill
East Birmingham Coll
Cockshut Hill Sch
Sheldon Heath Sch
L Ctr
Works
B33
Marston Green
Marston Croft
Marston Green Inf Sch
Lyndon Green
Stanville Jun & Inf Sch
Liby
Sch
B37
Lyndon Green Schs
Brays Sch
B26
Westley Brook
Mapledene Inf & Jun Sch
Birmingham Int Airport
Golf Course
TA Ctr
St Thomas More's RC Jun & Inf Sch
Lyndon End
Sheldon
Hatchford Brook
Marian Croft
CH
Wells Green
COVENTRY RD
NEW COVENTRY RD
B425
A45
Daylesford Inf Sch
Lyndon Sch
Hatchford Brook Inf & Jun Sch
Valley Inf Sch
The Grange
Ice Rink
St Andrew's RC Prim Sch
Elmdon House
B92
Hobs Moat
Elmdon Park
SOLIHULL
Works
Ulverley Green
Ulverley Jun & Inf Sch
HOB'S MOAT RD
LODE LA
DAMSON PARKWAY
LIVERPOOL CROFT 1
WORCESTER WLK 2
BRUNSWICK HO 3
HESKETH PL 4
GREENFIELD HO 1
BRADFIELD HO 2
1 KEMPSEY CL
2 DALLIMORE CL
MACKADOWN LA
CLOPTON RD
STATION RD
ELMDON LA
GARRETTS GREEN LA
WESTLEY BROOK
VALLEY RD
RANGOON RD
CRANES PARK RD
WHITECROFT RD
BERRYFIELD RD
RECTORY PARK RD
MARKHAM CRES
DAMSON LA
OLD DAMSON LA
8
7
85
6
5
84
4
3
83
2
1
82
14
15
16

107
90

89
70
A
B
C
D
E
F
8
7
85
6
5
84
4
3
83
2
1
82
17
18
19
MOOREND AVE
HAMAR WAY
NEWINGTON RD
POPLAR AVE
ASPEN DR
CORNEL CL
ROWAN WAY
HELMSWOOD DR
BOX RD
TULIP WLK
WHITE BEAM RD
BERWICKS LA
LEAF DR
MAPLE
Sports Ctr
Coleshill Heath
Heath Farm
THE CRESCENT
SOLIHULL PARKWAY
PARK SQ
BIRMINGHAM BSNS PK
CHESTER RD
A452
M42
SYCAMORE CRES
ELMWOOD LA
CHELMSLEY LA
WAYSIDE
MALTHOUSE ROW
STATION RD
Marston Green
COLESHILL RD
IVY LODGE CL
Marston Green Jun Sch
ELMDON CT
LAND LA
HALL DR
Liby
THE OAKLANDS
ST LEONARDS CL
BROOK CROFT
MOWE CROFT
LYNDON CROFT
BICKENHILL RD
B37
School Rough
COLESHILL HEATH RD
HEMLINGFORD CROFT
AYLESFORD DR
THE RISE
ELMDON RD
HIDCOTE GR
FARNDON AVE
SOMERTON DR
1 ROTHERBY GR
2 WOLVERTON RD
CANTERBURY DR
THE GREENWAY
ELMDON LA
BLACKFIRS LA
B4438
A452
Cemy
BICKENHILL LA
BICKENHILL PARKWAY
NEWLANDS LA
DIGBY DR
STARLEY WAY
B46
Bickenhill Plantations
THE FORDRIFT
ELMDON TRAD EST
FIRE STATION RD
Low Brook
NORTH AVE
NORTHWAY
B40
RAMP RD
MAIN AVE
NOVOTEL WAY
PARK LA
INTERNATIONAL DR
EUROPA WAY
BICKENHILL LA
STATION WAY
EXHIBITION WAY
THIRD EXHIBITION AVE
SECOND EXHIBITION AVE
FIRST EXHIBITION AVE
PERIMETER RD
THE UNDERPASS
National Exhibition Ctr
PO
Birmingham International
PERIMETER RD
HARBET DR
PENDIGO WAY
EAST CAR PARK RD
Hotel
Birmingham International Airport
AIRPORT WAY
HANGER RD
COMMISSARY RD
FORWARD RD
WORKS RD
B26
Mast
ELMDON LA
EASTWAY
PENDIGO WAY
FORUM RD
SOUTH CAR PARK RD
SOUTH WAY
6
A45
Hotels
AIRPORT WAY
Depot
BICKENHILL LA
B4438
Hotel
A45
CH
OLD DAMSON LA
COVENTRY RD
PO
The Clock Inn (PH)
CLOCK LA
Wyckhams Close
Dunston Farm
OLD STATION RD
CATHERINE DE BARNES LA
B92
PITT LA
CHURCH LA
The Jungle
Caravan Park
BICKENHILL GREEN CT
Castle Hills
Grange Farm
ST PETERS LA
B4438
Bickenhill
M42
A
B
C
D
E
F
89
108

A
B
C
D
E
F
A446
The Bogs Farm
Bannerley Rough
Depot
Todd's Rough
Mulliner's Rough
M6
8
Golf Course
Broadwater
Nursery Farm
STONEBRIDGE RD
B46
Nursery
Ford
7
Golf & Country Club
Foxes Den
Brook Farm
85
Fish Breeding Farm
Refuse Tip
Little Packington
PACKINGTON LA
The Ash Beds
6
DENBIGH CNR
Butler's Moors
A446
Packington Park
Park Meadow
FISHPOOL LA
Church Farm
Denbigh Spinney
River Blythe
5
Deer Park
Garden Spinney
CHESTER RD
84
CV7
Park Farm
Siding Wood
Packington Hall
Hall Pool
MIDDLE BICKENHILL LA
4
Great Pool
The Wilderness
Mill Shrubbery
Beech Lodge
Middle Bickenhill
The Mill Farm
Little Dayhouse Wood
B92
3
PH
Dials Pool
EAST WAY
COVENTRY RD
BIRMINGHAM RD
COVENTRY RD
Stonebridge
83
Works
A45
The National Motorcycle Mus
Geary's Heath
Pasture Farm
2
Mills Gorse
Golf Course
Diddington Hill
KENILWORTH RD
CH
DIDDINGTON LA
Diddington Hall
SOMERS RD
Shadow Brook
OLD STATION RD
1
The Somers
Mouldings Green Farm
A452
Molands Bridge
HE GROVE
B4102
82
0
21
22

91

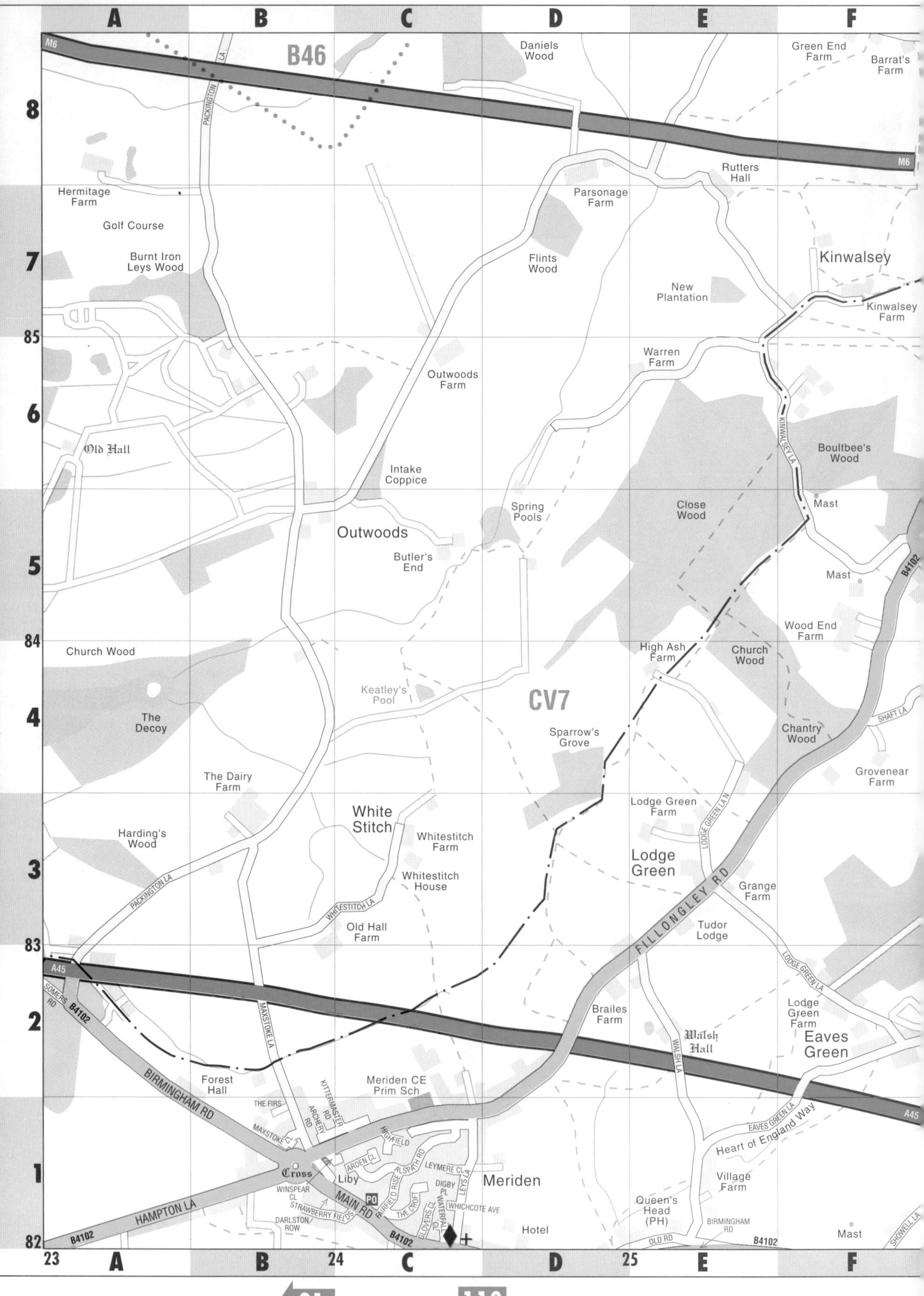
A
B
C
D
E
F
M6
B46
PACKINGTON LA
Daniels Wood
Green End Farm
Barrat's Farm
8
Rutters Hall
Hermitage Farm
Parsonage Farm
Golf Course
Burnt Iron Leys Wood
Flints Wood
Kinwalsey
7
New Plantation
Kinwalsey Farm
85
Warren Farm
Outwoods Farm
6
KINWALSEY LA
Old Hall
Boultbee's Wood
Intake Coppice
Spring Pools
Close Wood
Mast
Outwoods
Butler's End
5
B4102
Mast
84
Church Wood
Wood End Farm
High Ash Farm
Church Wood
Keatley's Pool
CV7
The Decoy
4
Sparrow's Grove
Chantry Wood
SHAFT LA
Grovenear Farm
The Dairy Farm
White Stitch
Lodge Green Farm
LODGE GREEN LA
Harding's Wood
Whitestitch Farm
3
Lodge Green
Whitestitch House
PACKINGTON LA
WHITESTITCH LA
Old Hall Farm
Grange Farm
FILLONGLEY RD
Tudor Lodge
83
A45
SOMERS RD
B4102
LODGE GREEN LA
MAXSTOKE LA
2
Brailes Farm
Lodge Green Farm
Walsh Hall
WALSH LA
Eaves Green
Forest Hall
Meriden CE Prim Sch
BIRMINGHAM RD
THE FIRS
KITTERMASTER RD
ARCHERY RD
MAXSTOKE CL
HIGHFIELD
A45
EAVES GREEN LA
Heart of England Way
ARDEN CL
ALSPATH RD
LEYMERE CL
LEYS LA
1
Cross
Liby
Meriden
Village Farm
WINSPEAR CL
FAIRFIELD RISE
DIGBY PL
STRAWBERRY FIELDS
MAIN RD
PO
THE CROFT
WHICHCOTE AVE
Queen's Head (PH)
HAMPTON LA
GLOVERS CL
WATERFALL CL
DARLSTON ROW
BIRMINGHAM RD
B4102
B4102
Hotel
OLD RD
B4102
Mast
SHOWELL LA
82
23
24
25

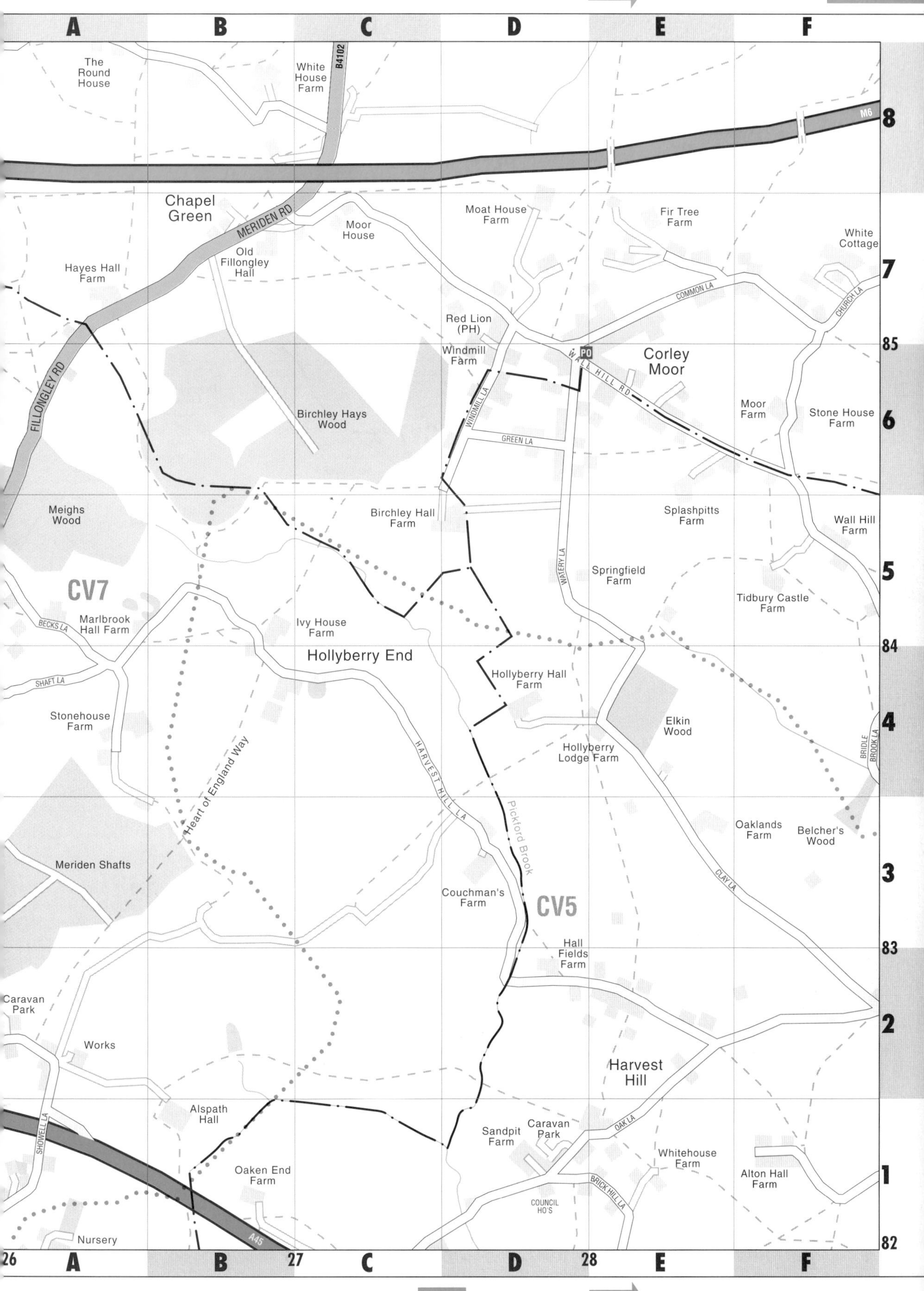
A
B
C
D
E
F
The Round House
White House Farm
B4102
M6
8
Chapel Green
MERIDEN RD
Moat House Farm
Fir Tree Farm
White Cottage
Moor House
Old Fillongley Hall
Hayes Hall Farm
7
COMMON LA
CHURCH LA
Red Lion (PH)
85
Windmill Farm
PO
WALL HILL RD
Corley Moor
FILLONGLEY RD
Birchley Hays Wood
WINDMILL LA
Moor Farm
Stone House Farm
6
GREEN LA
Meighs Wood
Birchley Hall Farm
Splashpitts Farm
Wall Hill Farm
CV7
Springfield Farm
WATERY LA
5
Marlbrook Hall Farm
BECKS LA
Ivy House Farm
Tidbury Castle Farm
Hollyberry End
84
SHAFT LA
Hollyberry Hall Farm
Stonehouse Farm
Elkin Wood
4
Hollyberry Lodge Farm
BRIDLE BROOK LA
Heart of England Way
HARVEST HILL LA
Pickford Brook
Oaklands Farm
Belcher's Wood
Meriden Shafts
3
CLAY LA
Couchman's Farm
CV5
Hall Fields Farm
83
Caravan Park
2
Works
Harvest Hill
Alspath Hall
Sandpit Farm
Caravan Park
OAK LA
Whitehouse Farm
SHOWELL LA
Oaken End Farm
BRICK HILL LA
Alton Hall Farm
1
COUNCIL HO'S
Nursery
A45
82
26
27
28

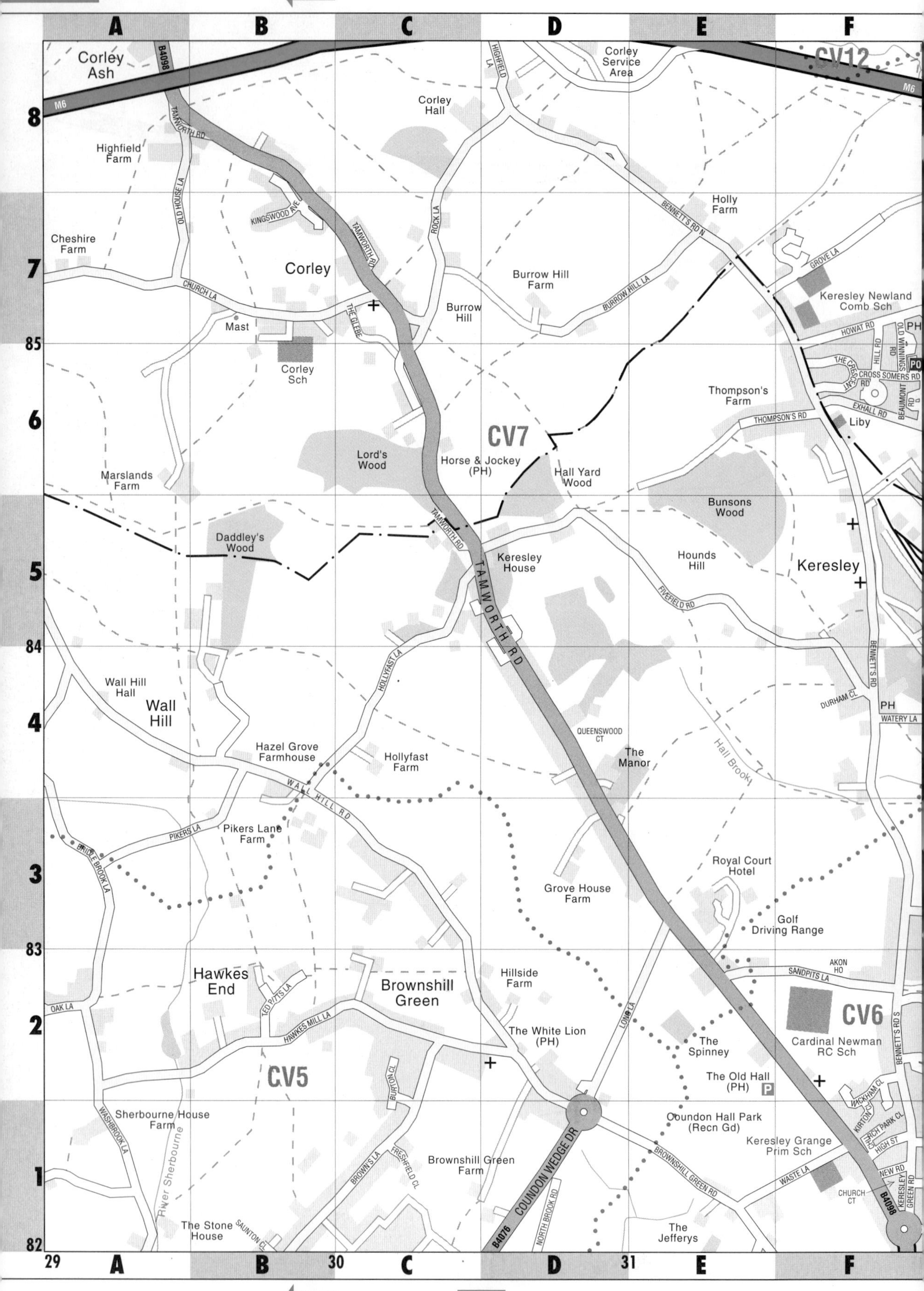

93

CV12

Corley Ash

Highfield Farm

Cheshire Farm

Corley

CHURCH LA

Mast

Corley Sch

Marslands Farm

Daddley's Wood

Wall Hill Hall

Wall Hill

Hazel Grove Farmhouse

Pikers Lane Farm

Hawkes End

CV5

Sherbourne House Farm

The Stone House

Corley Hall

Highfield Farm

Burrow Hill Farm

Burrow Hill

Lord's Wood

Keresley House

Hollyfast Farm

Pikers Lane Farm

Brownshill Green

Hillside Farm

The White Lion (PH)

Brownshill Green Farm

Corley Service Area

Holly Farm

Thompson's Farm

CV7

Horse & Jockey (PH)

Hall Yard Wood

Bunsons Wood

Hounds Hill

Keresley

Queenswood CT

The Manor

Grove House Farm

The Spinney

The Old Hall (PH)

Coundon Hall Park (Recn Gd)

The Jefferys

Keresley Newland Comb Sch

Liby

Royal Court Hotel

Golf Driving Range

CV6

Cardinal Newman RC Sch

Keresley Grange Prim Sch

B4098

TAMWORTH RD

TAMWORTH RD

BURROW HILL LA

BENNETT'S RD N

FIVEFIELD RD

HALL BROOK

THOMPSON'S RD

DURHAM CL

BENNETT'S RD

WATERY LA

SANDPITS LA

AKON HO

GROVE LA

HOWAT RD

HILL RD

EXHALL RD

CROSS SOMERS RD

KINGSWOOD AVE

ROCK LA

HIGHFIELD LA

THE GLEBE

HOLLYFAST LA

WALL HILL RD

PIKERS LA

BRIDLE BROOK LA

OAK LA

WASHBROOK LA

HAWKES MILL LA

ED PITS LA

BURTON CL

FRESFIELD CL

BROWN'S LA

SAUNTON CT

LONG LA

COUNDON WEDGE DR

NORTH BROOK RD

B4076

BROWNSHILL GREEN RD

WASTE LA

CHURCH CT

HIGH ST

NEW RD

KERESLEY RD

B4098

BEAUMONT CRES

77
96

A
B
C
D
E
F
8
7
85
6
5
84
4
3
83
2
1
82
33
34
Moat Farm
Hospital La
Swallow Ct 1
Jackwood Gn 2
Larkspur Ct 3
Bede Village
Newey Ave
Mayor Dr
Robinson Rd
Maynard Ave
Jeffrey Cl
Newcomen Rd
Melrose Ave
Dark La
McMahon Rd
The Tea Garden
Goodyers End La
Goodyers End
Field Gate
CV12
Goodyers End Fst & Mid Schs
Bowling Green La
Garden Gr
Constance Cl
Florence Cl
Marshall Rd
Hayes Green Rd
Hayes La
St Giles Cty Mid Sch
A444
Newland Farm
Alandale Ct
Newland Hall Farm
Breach Brook
The Royal Oak (PH)
Royal Oak La
Hall Farm
Tudor Ct
School La
Robert Rd
David Rd
High Ash Cl
Davies Rd
Startin Cl
Bruce Rd
Exhall Gn
Exhall Fst Sch
Barker's Farm
Newland La
High View Dr
Corley View
Vicarage La
Church La
Bell Dr
Winster Cl
De-Compton Cl
Hope Cl
Charity Rd
Shaftesbury Ave
Jackson Cl
Le Hanche Cl
Alwynne Freeman Ct
Addenbrooke Rd
Somers Rd
Colyere Cl
Beaumont Rd
Schofield Rd
Parkfield Rd
Synkere Cl
Exhall Rd
Ash Green
Ash Green Sch
Flude Rd
Ash Green La
Canon Dr
Deans Way
Shortlands
St Giles Rd
New Rd
M6
McDonnell Dr
B4113
CV7
River Sowe
Keresley Newlands
Coventry Colliery
Neal's Green
Exhall Grange Sch
Woodford Cl
Barratt's Farm
Hotel
Wilson's La
Greenodd Dr
Woodshires Green
Glenmount Ave
Slenmore Dr
Glenridding Cl
Grange Farm
Blackberry La
Wheelwright Lane Comb Sch
Carsal Cl
Exhall Grange Sch
Silverstone Dr
Gallagher Bsns Pk
Bramwell Gdns
Cargill Cl
Raymond Cl
Woodshires Rd
Wks
Blackberry La
Mallory Way
Cope Arnolds Cl
Basford Brook Dr
Oban Rd
Union Pl
Grindle Rd
Sydnall Rd
Amy Cl
Nolans Cl
Basley Way
Burbages La
Rowleys Green Lane Ind Est
Rowleys Green La
Oakey Cl
COVENTRY
Ladyfields Way
Wheelwright La
LC
President Kennedy Sch & Com Coll
Houldsworth Cres
Hales Park Ind Est
Lady La
Marlwood Cl
Sydnall Fields
The Croft
Hedgerow Wlk
Rookery La
Meadow Rd
Bentley Ct
Masser Rd
Alder Meadow Cl
Coronel Ave
Judds La
John Shelton Prim Sch
Gospel Oak Rd
Orpington Dr
Redcap Croft
Gas Works
Longford
Liby
Watery La
Nunts Park Ave
Nunts La
Elphin Cl
Butlin Rd
Briscoe Rd
Orton Rd
Hall Brook Rd
Bantam Gr
Albert Cres
Parkville Cl
Dymond Rd
Hen La
Farndale Ave
Rowley's Green
Vinecote Rd
Doyle Dr
Broome Croft
Parkville Highway
Forge Way
Lauderdale Ave
Bransdale Ave
Langdale Ave
Glaisdale Ave
Brookford Ave
Farm Cl
Roland Mount
Blackburn Rd
Stonebrook Way
Roland Ave
Glenn St
Pendrel Ct
Parkland Cl
Park Ave
Kirkdale Ave
Marshdale Ave
Edward Rd
Parkgate Rd
Whitmore Park Rd
St Luke's Rd
Selworthy Rd
Coventry Canal
Parkgate Prim Sch
CV6
Holbrooks
Dunster Pl
Brinsway
Penny Park La
Holy Family Sch
Berkett Rd
Hattam Rd
Morland Rd
Blenheim Ave
Beacon Rd
Crummock Cl
Leyburn Cl
Windmill Rd
Foreland Way
Malmesbury Rd
Cheshire Rd
Wood Hill Rise
Stadium Cl
Phoenix Way
Longford Rd
Leacrest Rd
Charlecote Rd
Harborough Rd
Romford Rd
Holborn Ave
Cherry Cl
Branstree Dr
Compton Rd
Marlissa Dr
Bedlam La
Astley Ave
Evelyn Ave
Dovedale Ave
Glentworth Ave
Rotherham Rd
Alderney Cl
Ladymead Dr
Peyto Cl
Leeder Cl
Foxglove Cl
Finch Cl
Pembrook Rd
Arbury Ave
Keresley Brook Rd
Cawnpore Rd
Deerhurst Rd
Lythalls La
Sandown Ave
Achal Cl
Parkstone Rd
Keresley Gutteridge Ave
Halford La
Headington Ave
Langlodge Rd
Braytoft Cl
Giles Cl
Lilley Cl
Midland Oak Trad Est 1
Fairview Wlk 2
Alexandra Terr 3
Bartlett Cl
Congleton Cl
Booths Fields
Elmsdale Ave
Benthall Rd
Clinton Rd
Ivor Rd
Lowe Rd
Wingfield Way
Cottage Farm Rd
Derwent Rd
Greycoat Rd
Beake Ave
Charlewood Rd
Paynell Cl
Sharp Cl
Richard Joy Cl
Esterton Cl
Holbrook La
Sunningdale Ave
Gateside Rd
Bartons Rd
King George's Ave
Foleshill Rd
Chillaton Rd
Greensleeves Cl
Buckland Rd
Penrith Cl
Rylston Ave
Monks Park
Cemy
Three Shires Jct
Holbrook Prim Sch
Lythalls Lane Ind Est
Little Heath
Halford Lodge
Cottage Farm Lodge
Greens Rd
TA Ctr
Whitmore Park Prim Sch
Whitmore Park
Holbrook Way
Jackson Rd
Newport Rd
Copper Beech Cl
B4082
Benson Rd
Swallow Rd
Berwyn Ave
Works
Coleridge Rd
Beresford Ave
Medina Rd
Lawrence's Rd
Lynton Rd
Teneriffe Rd
Carlton Rd
Old Church Rd
Locke Cl
Fraser Rd
Morton Cl
Sadler Rd
Instone Rd
The Scotchill
Burnaby Rd
B4118
Kingswood Cl
Durbar Ave
Delhi Ave
Churchill Ave
Victory Rd
Mason Rd
Spring Rd
Sch

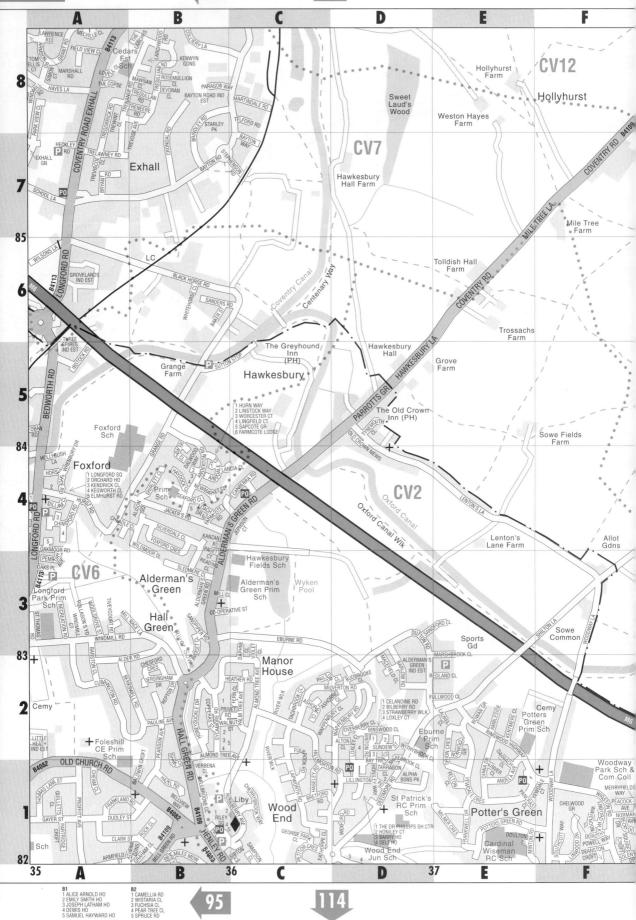

B1
1 ALICE ARNOLD HO
2 EMILY SMITH HO
3 JOSEPH LATHAM HO
4 DEWIS HO
5 SAMUEL HAYWARD HO

B2
1 CAMELLIA RD
2 WISTARIA CL
3 FUCHSIA CL
4 PEAR TREE CL
5 SPRUCE RD

79

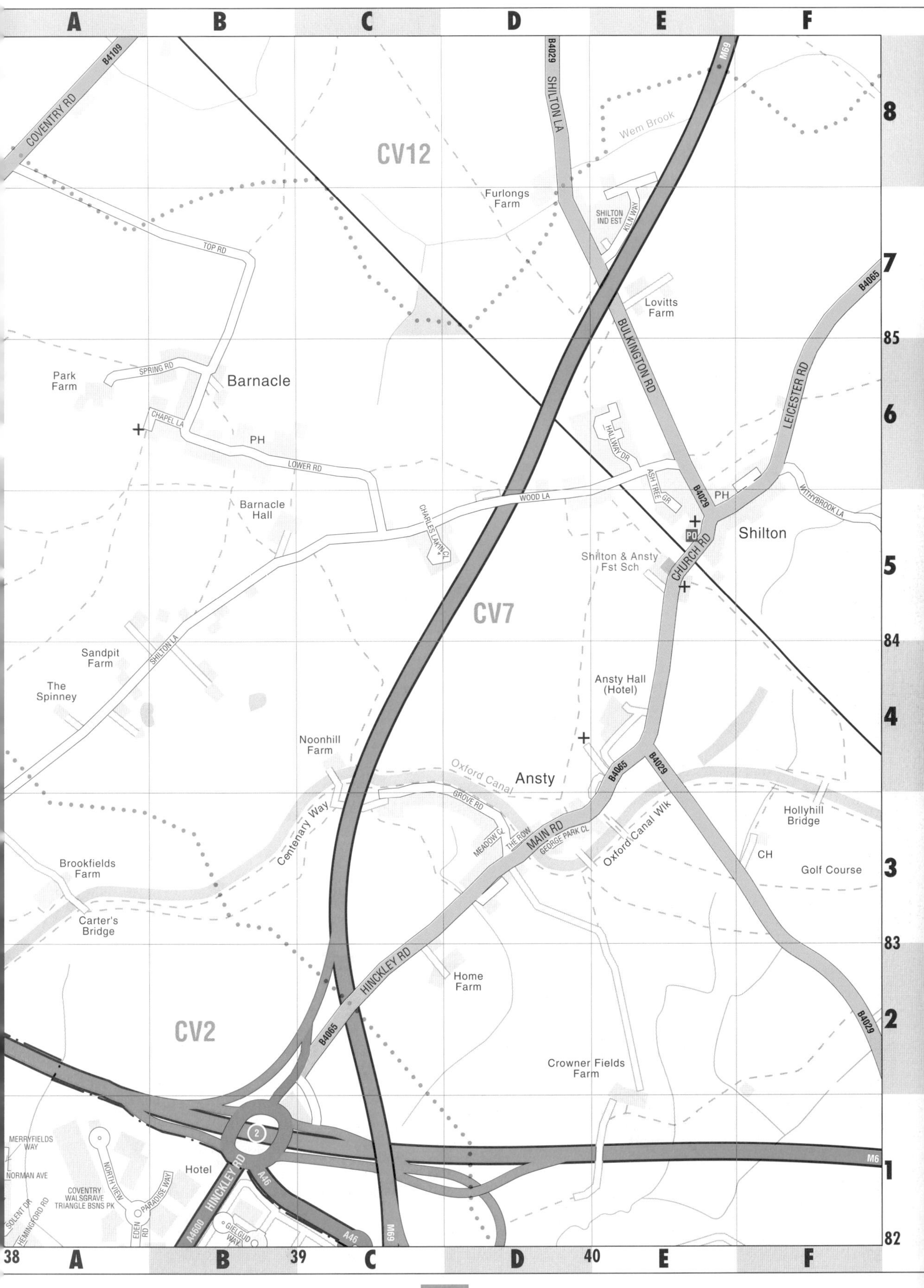

A B C D E F
8 7 6 5 4 3 2 1
85 84 83 82
38 39 40
CV12
CV7
CV2
COVENTRY RD
B4109
TOP RD
SPRING RD
CHAPEL LA
LOWER RD
SHILTON LA
WOOD LA
CHARLES LAKIN CL
B4029 SHILTON LA
Wem Brook
M69
Furlongs Farm
SHILTON IND EST
KILN WAY
Lovitts Farm
BULKINGTON RD
B4065
LEICESTER RD
HALLWAY DR
ASH TREE GR
PH
WITHYBROOK LA
Shilton
CHURCH RD
Shilton & Ansty Fst Sch
Park Farm
Barnacle
Barnacle Hall
Sandpit Farm
The Spinney
Noonhill Farm
Ansty Hall (Hotel)
Ansty
Oxford Canal
Centenary Way
GROVE RD
MEADOW CL
THE ROW
MAIN RD
GEORGE PARK CL
Oxford Canal Wlk
Hollyhill Bridge
CH
Golf Course
Brookfields Farm
Carter's Bridge
HINCKLEY RD
Home Farm
Crowner Fields Farm
MERRYFIELDS WAY
NORMAN AVE
SOLENT DR
HEMINGFORD RD
COVENTRY WALSGRAVE TRIANGLE BSNS PK
NORTH VIEW
EDEN RD
PARADISE WAY
Hotel
A4600
A46
GIELGUD WAY
M6

80

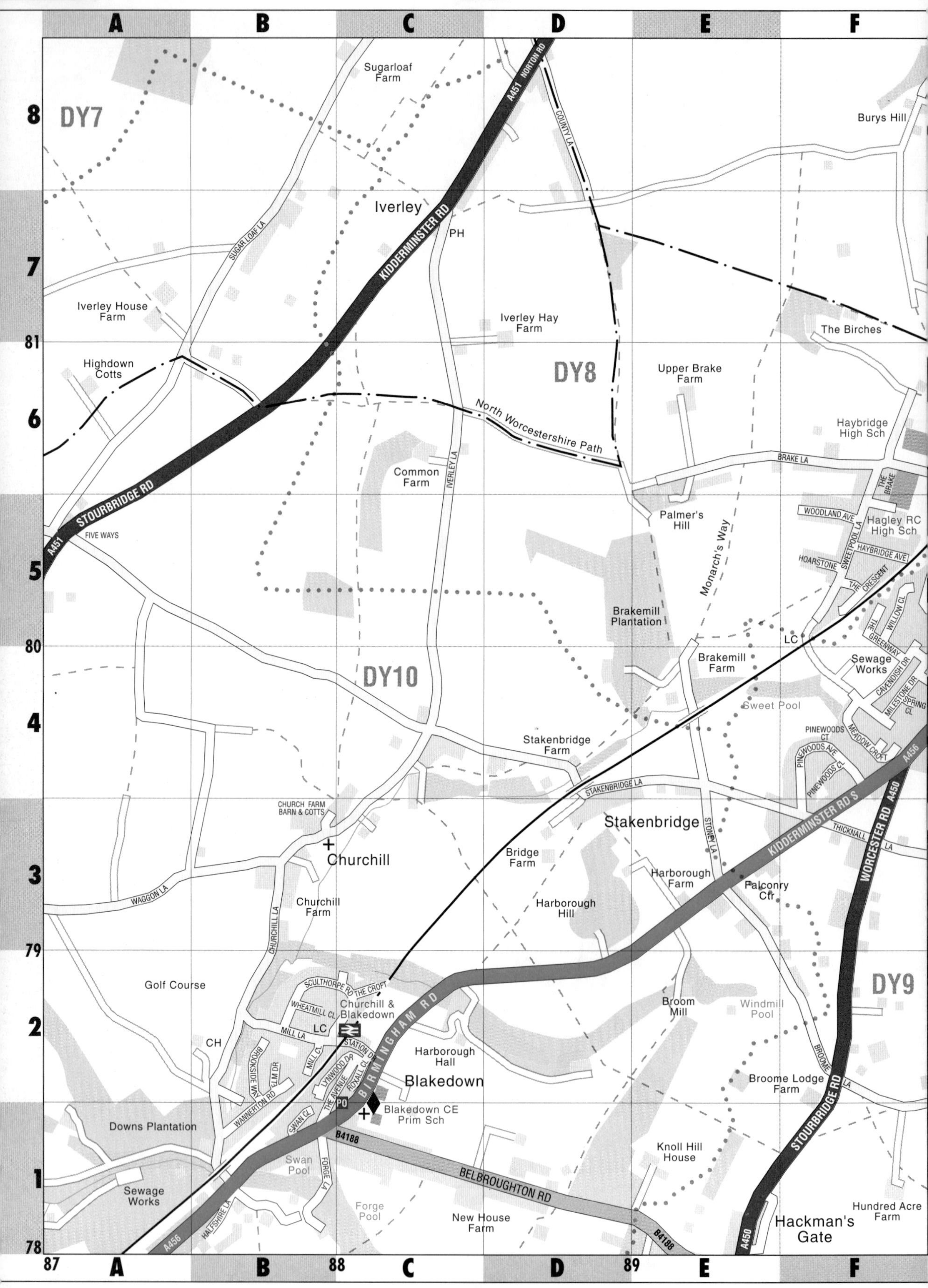

A
B
C
D
E
F
8
7
81
6
5
80
4
3
79
2
1
78
87
88
89
DY7
DY8
DY10
DY9
Sugarloaf Farm
Burys Hill
Iverley
PH
Iverley House Farm
Iverley Hay Farm
The Birches
Highdown Cotts
Upper Brake Farm
Haybridge High Sch
North Worcestershire Path
Common Farm
Palmer's Hill
Hagley RC High Sch
Monarch's Way
Brakemill Plantation
Brakemill Farm
Sewage Works
Sweet Pool
LC
Stakenbridge Farm
Stakenbridge
CHURCH FARM BARN & COTTS
Churchill
Bridge Farm
Harborough Farm
Falconry Ctr
Churchill Farm
Harborough Hill
Golf Course
Churchill & Blakedown
Broom Mill
Windmill Pool
CH
Harborough Hall
Blakedown
Broome Lodge Farm
Blakedown CE Prim Sch
Downs Plantation
Knoll Hill House
Swan Pool
Sewage Works
Forge Pool
New House Farm
Hundred Acre Farm
Hackman's Gate
A451 NORTON RD
COUNTY LA
KIDDERMINSTER RD
SUGAR LOAF LA
STOURBRIDGE RD
A451
FIVE WAYS
IVERLEY LA
BRAKE LA
THE BRAKE
WOODLAND AVE
SWEETPOOL LA
HAYBRIDGE AVE
HOARSTONE
THE CRESCENT
WILLOW CL
THE GREENWAY
CAVENDISH DR
MILESTONE DR
SPRING CL
PINEWOODS CT
PINEWOODS AVE
PINEWOODS CL
MEADOW CROFT
A456
STAKENBRIDGE LA
KIDDERMINSTER RD S
A450
WORCESTER RD
THICKNALL LA
STONEY LA
WAGGON LA
CHURCHILL LA
SCULTHORPE RD
THE CROFT
WHEATMILL CL
MILL LA
BIRMINGHAM RD
STATION DR
MILL CL
LYNWOOD DR
ROXALL CL
THE AVENUE
BROOKSIDE WAY
ELM DR
WANNERTON RD
SWAN CL
PO
B4188
BELBROUGHTON RD
FORGE LA
HALFSHIRE LA
BROOME LA
STOURBRIDGE RD

118

A
B
C
D
E
F
DY8
DY9
West Hagley
Hagley
Pedmore Hall
Roundhill Wood
Wychbury Hill
Wychbury
Obelisk
Badgers Sett (PH)
Round Hill
HAGLEY CSWY
A456
HAGLEY HILL
BIRMINGHAM RD
Hagleyhill Farm
Treherns's Farm
Hollier's Farm
Monarch's Way
North Worcestershire Path
Hagley Grange
HAGLEY RD
A491
WORCESTER LA
B4187
STOURBRIDGE RD
KIDDERMINSTER RD
PARK RD
MIDDLEFIELD LA
HALL DR
HALL LA
Hagley Hall
Hagley Park
Gallows Brook
Stocking Hill
Cemy
Hagley Cty Prim Inf & Jun Sch
Liby
Sch
Clent Grove
Lower Clent
Home Farm
Woodsman Hotel (PH)
Clent House
Country Park
Adam's Hill
Clent
Clent Hall
The Field House
Thicknall Farm
THICKNALL LA
Thicknall
BROOME LA
Broome Farm
Oldmill Farm
Holy Cross
Green Farm
Clent Fst Sch
Mousehole Farm
Walton House
Broome
Broome House
HOSSIL LA
Clent Grange
White Lodge Farm
Red Hall Farm
WORCESTER RD
WESTERN RD
NEWFIELD RD
FIELD LA
BROMSGROVE RD
VIOLET LA
WOODMAN LA
ADAM'S HILL
HILL LA
ODNALL LA
VINE LA
CHURCH AVE
KING'S MEADOW
HOLY CROSS GN
SUMMERFIELD RD
BELBROUGHTON RD
POOL FURLONG
HOLY CROSS LA
WALTON POOL LA
PEDMORE LA
WASSELL GROVE RD
MONUMENT LA
8
7
81
6
5
80
4
3
79
2
1
78
90
91
92

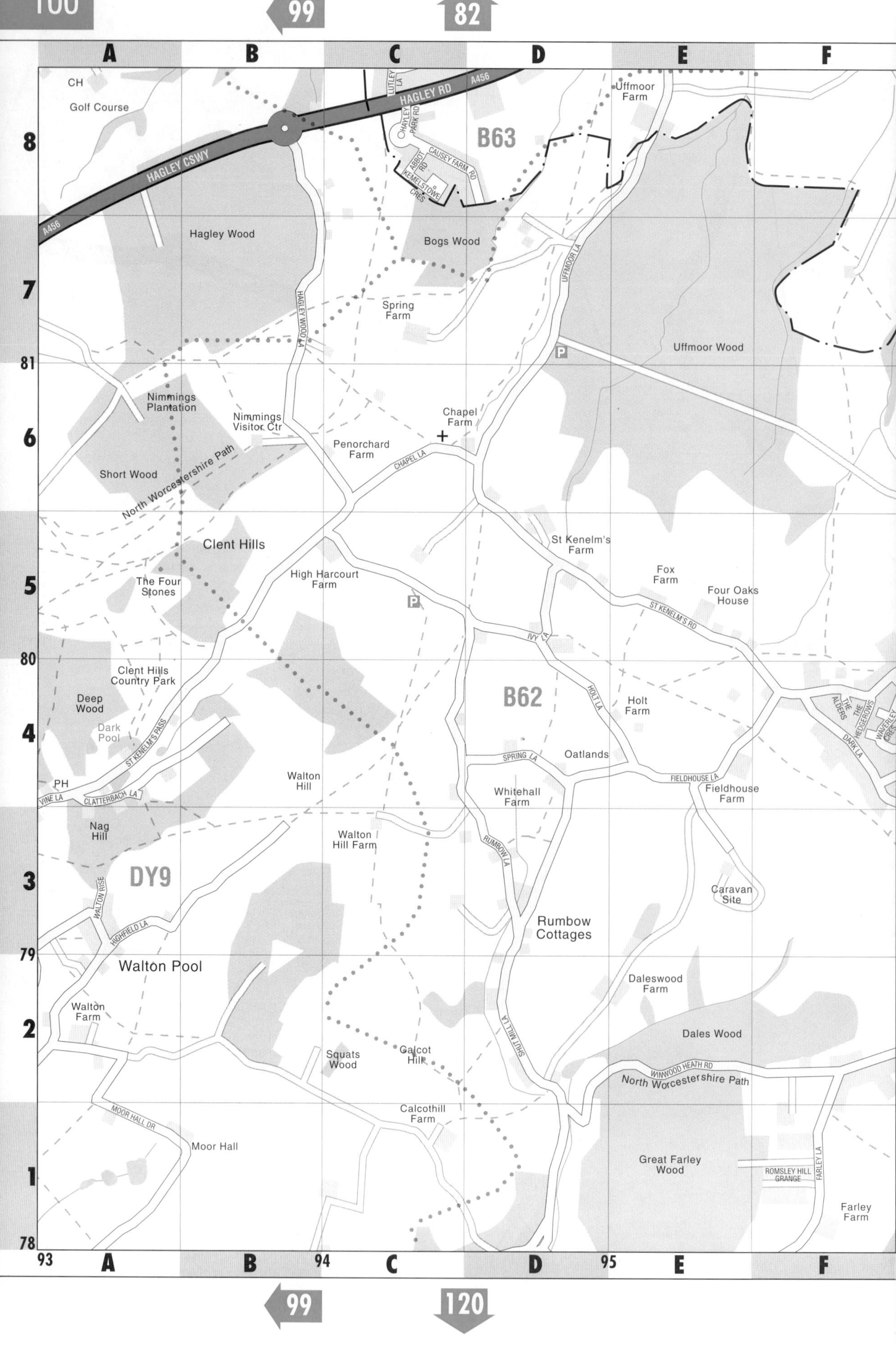

99
82
A
B
C
D
E
F
8
7
81
6
5
80
4
3
79
2
1
78
93
94
95
CH
Golf Course
HAGLEY CSWY
HAGLEY RD
A456
LUTLEY LA
HAYLEY PARK RD
ABBOT RD
CAUSEY FARM RD
KEMELSTOWE CRES
B63
Uffmoor Farm
Hagley Wood
Bogs Wood
UFFMOOR LA
HAGLEY WOOD LA
Spring Farm
Uffmoor Wood
Nimmings Plantation
Nimmings Visitor Ctr
Chapel Farm
Penorchard Farm
CHAPEL LA
Short Wood
North Worcestershire Path
Clent Hills
St Kenelm's Farm
The Four Stones
High Harcourt Farm
Fox Farm
Four Oaks House
ST KENELM'S RD
IVY LA
Clent Hills Country Park
Deep Wood
Dark Pool
B62
HOLT LA
Holt Farm
THE ALDERS
THE HEDGEROWS
WAVERLEY CRES
DARK LA
ST KENELM'S PASS
SPRING LA
Oatlands
PH
VINE LA
CLATTERBACH LA
Walton Hill
Whitehall Farm
FIELDHOUSE LA
Fieldhouse Farm
Nag Hill
Walton Hill Farm
RUMBOW LA
DY9
WALTON RISE
Caravan Site
HIGHFIELD LA
Rumbow Cottages
Walton Pool
Daleswood Farm
Walton Farm
SHUT MILL LA
Dales Wood
Squats Wood
Calcot Hill
WINWOOD HEATH RD
North Worcestershire Path
Calcothill Farm
MOOR HALL DR
Moor Hall
Great Farley Wood
ROMSLEY HILL GRANGE
FARLEY LA
Farley Farm
99
120

A B C D E F

8
81
7
6
80
5
4
79
3
2
78

Dovehousefields Farm

Hunnington

Goodrest Farm

BLUE BIRD PK

B4551

Illeybrook Farm

Innage Farm

PH

Illey

Potters Farm

Illey House Farm

ILLEY LA

Lower Illey

Frankley Service Area

Breach Farm

THE CLOSE

RED HILL PL

Hotties Farm

Twiland Wood

Kettles Wood

Raven Hays Wood

Hunnington Farm

Horsepool Farm

Brookhouse Farm

Long Kettles Wood

Yew Tree Farm

Porch House Farm

FRANKLEY GN

FRANKLEY GREEN LA

PH

YEW TREE

BROMSGROVE RD

ST KENELM'S RD

KENELM'S CL

PO

B62

Romsley

Monarch's Way

B32

OXWOOD LA

Newbrook Farm

WINSTON DR

DARK LA

St Kenelm's CE Fst Sch

PH

POPLAR LA

Penny Fields

Ell Wood

Dayhouse Wood

Long Saw Croft

Round Saw Croft

Yew Tree Farm

YEW TREE LA

Frankley Hill Farm

FRANKLEY HILL LA

POUND LA

Frankley Hill

Lower Hill Farm

Romsley Manor Farm

Mast

FARLEY LA

Sandhills Farm

1 CHADDERSLEY CL
2 RUBERY LA S
3 HOLLY HILL
4 CALDY WLK
5 BRYHER WLK
6 PRINCESS ANNE DR
7 FISHER CL

NEWTOWN LA

Newtown Farm

NEW SI

Romsley Hill

Mast

PUTNEY LA

Dayhouse Farm

OLD HOUSE LA

Gannow Green Farm

Gannow Green

B45

Holly Hill Methodist & CE Inf Sch

Frankley Sch

HIGH TIMBERS

ORDWAY

P
PO

Dayhouse Bank

North Worcestershire Path

B4551

M5

DAYHOUSE BANK

FORDRAUGHT LA

CHAPMAN'S HILL

P

Visitor Ctr

Duck Pool Farm

GANNOW GREEN LA

Jun Sch

QUARRY HOUSE CL

CHALYBEATE

GANNOW MANOR GDNS

MITTEN AVE

NEW INNS LA

CROSS FARMS LA

RUBERY LA

A B C D E F

96 97 98

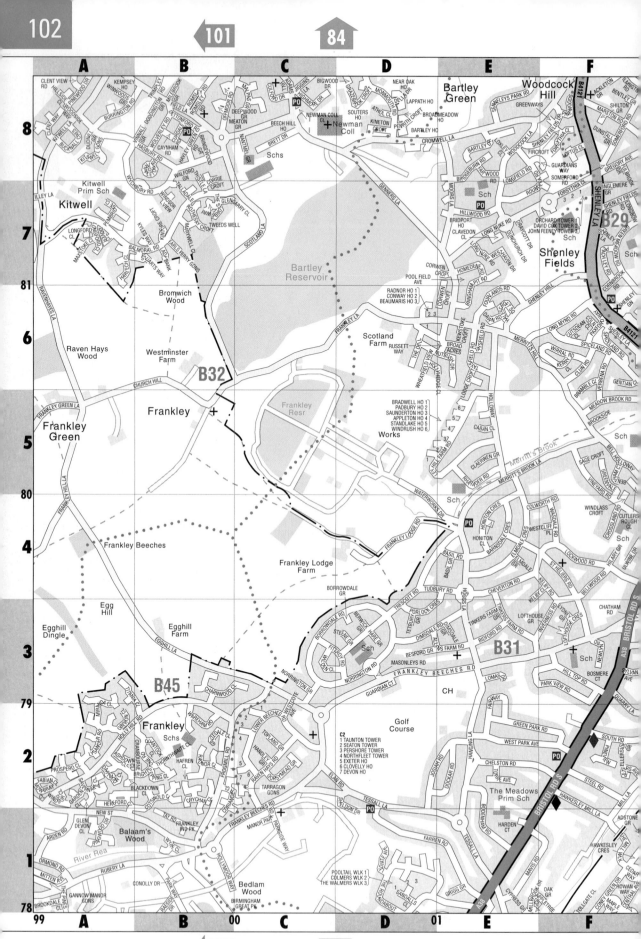
A
B
C
D
E
F
8
7
81
6
5
80
4
3
79
2
1
78
99
00
01
Bartley Green
Woodcock Hill
Kitwell
Kitwell Prim Sch
Newman Coll
Schs
Sch
Bartley Reservoir
Bromwich Wood
Raven Hays Wood
Westminster Farm
B32
Frankley
Frankley Green
Frankley Resr
Scotland Farm
Works
Shenley Fields
B29
Frankley Beeches
Frankley Lodge Farm
Egg Hill
Egghill Dingle
Egghill Farm
B45
B31
CH
Golf Course
The Meadows Prim Sch
Balaam's Wood
River Rea
Bedlam Wood
Merritt's Brook
C2
1 TAUNTON TOWER
2 SEATON TOWER
3 PERSHORE TOWER
4 NORTHFLEET TOWER
5 EXETER HO
6 CLOVELLY HO
7 DEVON HO
BRADWELL HO 1
PADBURY HO 2
SAUNDERTON HO 3
APPLETON HO 4
STANDLAKE HO 5
WINDRUSH HO 6
RADNOR HO 1
CONWAY HO 2
BEAUMARIS HO 3
ORCHARD TOWER 1
DAVID COX TOWER 2
JOHN FEENEY TOWER 3
POOLTAIL WLK 1
COLMERS WLK 2
THE WALMERS WLK 3
BRISTOL RD S
A38
B4121
SHENLEY LA
FRANKLEY BEECHES RD
CHURCH HILL
FRANKLEY LA
SCOTLAND LA
GENNERS LA
CROMWELL LA
WATERWORKS DR
MERRITT'S BROOK LA
FRANKLEY LODGE RD
EGGHILL LA
FRANKLEY HILL LA
RAVENHAYES LA
TESSALL LA
ELAN RD
HOLLYMOOR WAY
RUBERY LA
NEW ST
HOLLOWAY
MERRITTS HILL

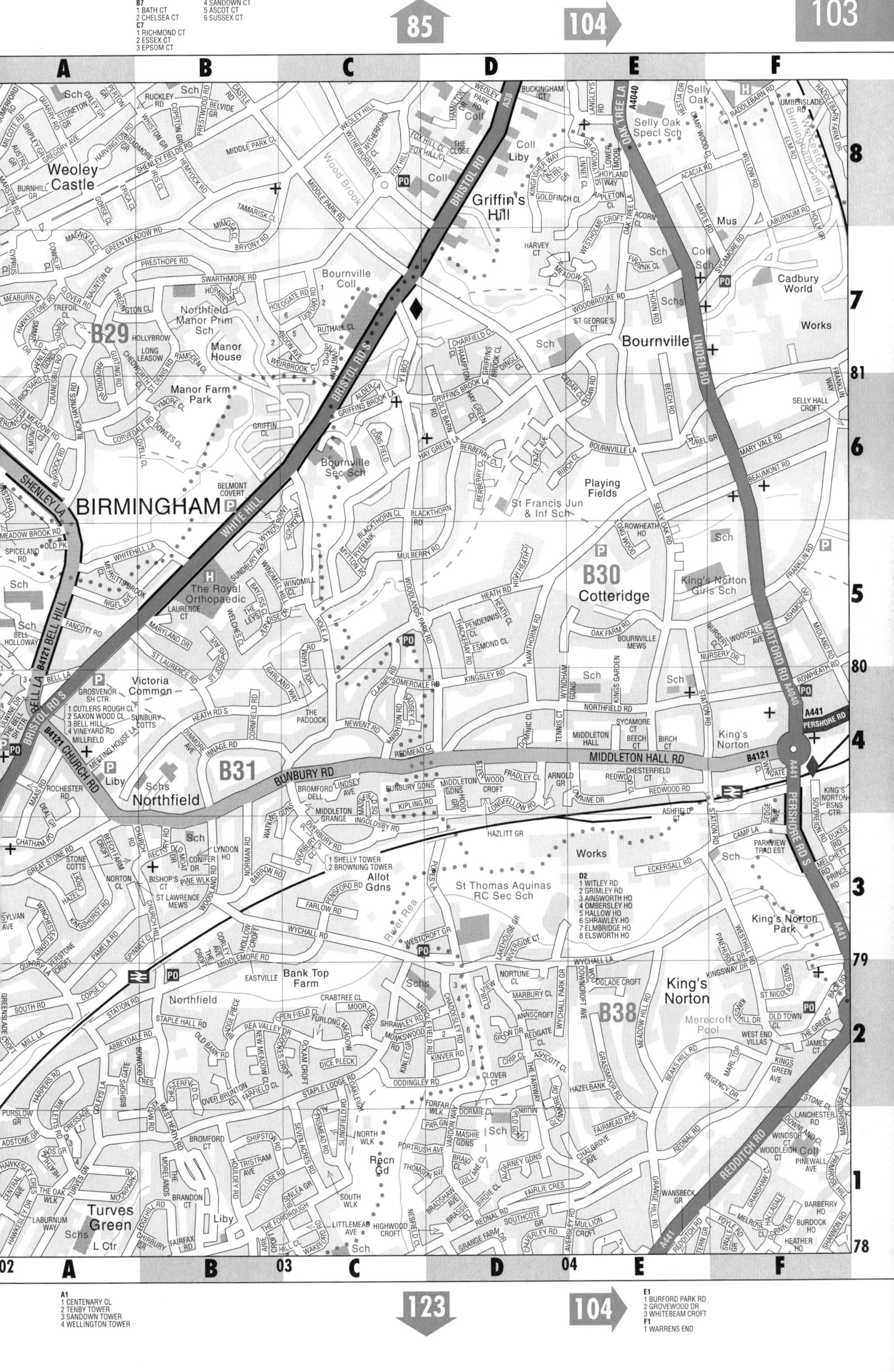
B7
1 BATH CT
2 CHELSEA CT
C7
1 RICHMOND CT
2 ESSEX CT
3 EPSOM CT
4 SANDOWN CT
5 ASCOT CT
6 SUSSEX CT
85
104
A
B
C
D
E
F
8
7
81
6
5
80
4
3
79
2
1
78
02
03
04
Weoley Castle
Sch
Selly Oak
Selly Oak Specl Sch
Worcester & Birmingham Canal
Wood Brook
BRISTOL RD
Griffin's Hill
Coll
Liby
Mus
Cadbury World
Works
Bournville Coll
Northfield Manor Prim Sch
Manor House
Manor Farm Park
B29
Bournville
LINDEN RD
OAK TREE LA
A4040
A38
BRISTOL RD S
Bournville Sec Sch
St Francis Jun & Inf Sch
Playing Fields
BIRMINGHAM
WHITE HILL
The Royal Orthopaedic
B30
Cotteridge
King's Norton Girls Sch
WATFORD RD
Victoria Common
B31
Northfield
BUNBURY RD
MIDDLETON HALL RD
King's Norton
PERSHORE RD S
A441
B4121
SHENLEY LA
BELL HILL
CHURCH RD
Works
St Thomas Aquinas RC Sec Sch
Allot Gdns
River Rea
D2
1 WITLEY RD
2 GRIMLEY RD
3 AINSWORTH HO
4 OMBERSLEY HO
5 HALLOW HO
6 SHRAWLEY HO
7 ELMBRIDGE HO
8 ELSWORTH HO
King's Norton Park
Bank Top Farm
Northfield
B38
King's Norton
Merecroft Pool
Recn Gd
REDDITCH RD
Turves Green
Liby
Schs
L Ctr
A1
1 CENTENARY CL
2 TENBY TOWER
3 SANDOWN TOWER
4 WELLINGTON TOWER
123
104
E1
1 BURFORD PARK RD
2 GROVEWOOD DR
3 WHITEBEAM CROFT
F1
1 WARRENS END

103
86

103

C3
1 BEECHWOOD CT
2 LINDSWORTH CT
3 ASHBURY COVERT
4 TAYNTON COVERT

124

A
B
C
D
E
F
Springfield
Billesley
Billesley Common
Warstock
Yardley Wood
Highter's Heath
Solihull Lodge
Hasluck's Green
Shirley
Peterbrook
Swanhurst Park
Chinn Brook Recn Gd
B13
B14
B28
B90
SWANSHURST LA
COLDBATH RD
BROOK LA
WHEELER'S LA
COLE BANK RD
ROBIN HOOD LA
HIGHFIELD RD
STRATFORD RD
FOX HOLLIES RD A4040
SCHOOL RD
WARSTOCK RD
MAYPOLE LA
Stratford-upon-Avon Canal
River Cole
Chinn Brook
Golf Course
Playing Fields
Allot Gdns
Mereside Cottage
Eversleigh
Hollywood Inf & Jun Sch
Peterbrook Prim Sch
Mill Lodge Prim Sch
Hall Green Sec Sch
Hall Green Inf & Jun Schs
Swanshurst Girls Sch
Billesley Inf & Jun Schs
Our Lady of Lourdes RC Inf & Jun Sch
Yardley Wood Inf & Jun Sch
Grendon Inf & Jun Sch
A3
1 LITTLECOTE CROFT
2 TIDWORTH CROFT
3 CLAYDON GR
4 NASEBY HO
5 LAMPORT HO
6 COTSWOLD HO
7 OAKHAM HO
8 DESBOROUGH HO
9 DICKENS GR
10 SHAWBROOK GR
8
7
81
6
5
80
4
3
79
2
1
78
08
09
10

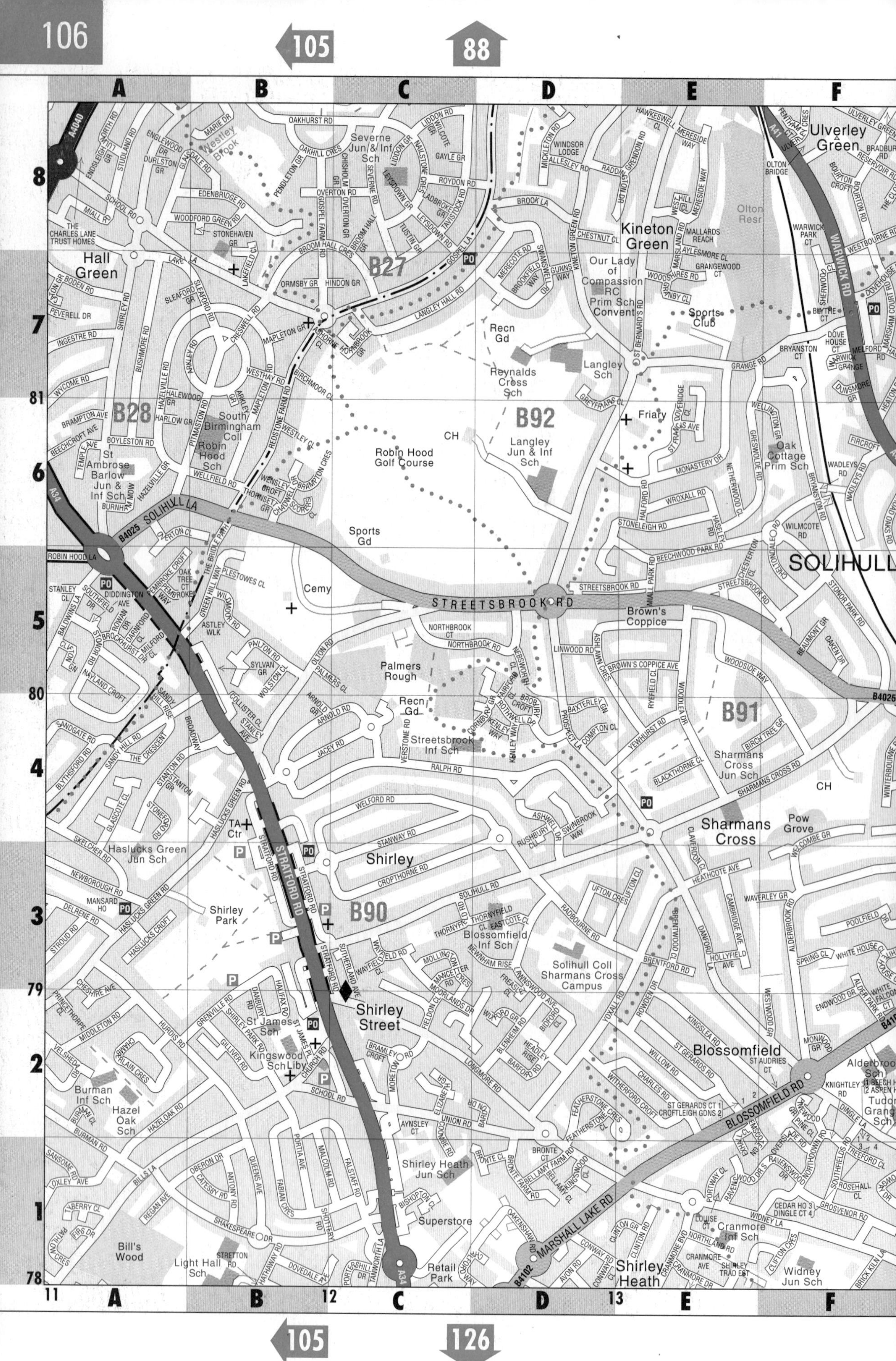

89
108
A
B
C
D
E
F
8
7
81
6
5
80
4
3
79
2
1
78
15
16
127
108
B92
B91
B93
B425
B4102
B4025
A41
M42
Works
Billsmore Wood
Damson Wood Inf Sch
Olton Golf Course
Mill Pool Spinney
CH
Worlds End
Lode Heath Sch
VULCAN HOUSE IND EST
Mast
Lode Heath
THE HERMITAGE
Cold Lands Wood
Greswold Prim Sch
Elmdon Heath
Coppice Jun Sch
Hampton Coppice
Yew Tree Prim Sch
Solihull Parkway
Field Farm
Eversfield Prep Sch
Ruckleigh Sch
Solihull
Solihull Sch
The Rookery
Berry Hall
Colwall Lodge
River Blythe
Stadium
Liby
St Alphege CE Inf Sch
Mon
St Martins
Sandals Bridge
Solihull Coll
Tudor Grange Park
Malvern Park
St Peter's RC Sch
St Augustine's Prim Sch
Tudor Grange Sch
St Alphege CE Jun Sch
Solihull Sixth Form Coll
Malvern Park Farm
Great Hytall
Hillfield
Hillfield Hall
Grand Union Canal
Low Brook
WARWICK RD
SEVEN STAR RD
LODE LA
STREETSBROOK RD
HAMPTON LA
SOLIHULL BY-PASS
BYPASS LINK
BLOSSOMFIELD RD
DAMSON PARKWAY
LUGTROUT LA
BURYFIELD RD
DOVE HOUSE LA
HENLEY CRES
ROWLANDS CRES
ALSTON RD
MOAT LA
REDLANDS RD
CALDWELL GR
ELMS CL
GROVE RD
STATION RD
HIGH ST
POPLAR RD
HOMER RD
HERBERT RD
PRINCE'S WAY
CHURCH HILL
RECTORY RD
LADBROOK RD
PARK AVE
BRUETON AVE
BLYTHEWAY
WARWICK RD
MONKSPATH HALL RD
WIDNEY MANOR RD
HILLFIELD RD
B2
1 HAZELTON CL
2 STONEYTHORPE CL
3 WOODBURY GR

107
90

A   B   C   D   E   F

8

Hampton
Coppice

B4438

St Peters La

Heath
Farm

Home
Farm

7

Woodhouse
Farm

Four
Winds

CATHERINE DE BARNES LA

SHADOW BROOK LA

81

Shadow Brook

6

Bunts
Wood

Catherine
de Barnes

Barber's
Coppice

Hampton Lane
Farm

SOLIHULL RD

B41

The
Limes

LUGTROUT LA

BICKENHILL LA

B4438

BARBERS LA

BRANSFORD RISE

OAKFIELD

LOCUS WAY

APPLETREE CL

PO

Aspbury's
Copse

B92

5

HAMPTON LA

FIELD LA

Boat Inn
(PH)

Walford Hall
Farm

80

B4102

Berry Hall La

Bogay
Hall

Grand Union Canal

FRIDAY LA

4

Berry
Hall

Brick Kiln Hole
Wood

B91

CATHERINES CL

HENWOOD LA

The
Woodlands

Sewage
Works

EASTCOTE LA

RAVENSHAW LA

Henwood Mill
(dis)

BARSTON LA

Eastcote
House

WALSAL END LA

Ford

Eastcote
Hall

Eastcote

Eastcote
Paddocks

3

Ravenshaw
Hall

BARSTON LA

Wharley
Hall

BARSTON LA

79

RAVENSHAW WAY

Copt Heath
Wharf
Cow
Hayes

BARSTON LA

KNOWLE RD

Wood
Lane
Farm

WOOD LA

PH

Th
Fi

2

A41

M42

5

Henwood Hall
Farm

B37

River Blythe

JACOBEAN LA

A4141

Sports
Gd

Grove
Farm

B93

HAMPTON RD

1

WARWICK RD A4141

WARWICK RD

LADY BYRON LA

Copt
Heath

WYCHWOOD AVE

WOOD LA

78

17   A   18   B   C   18   D   19   E   F

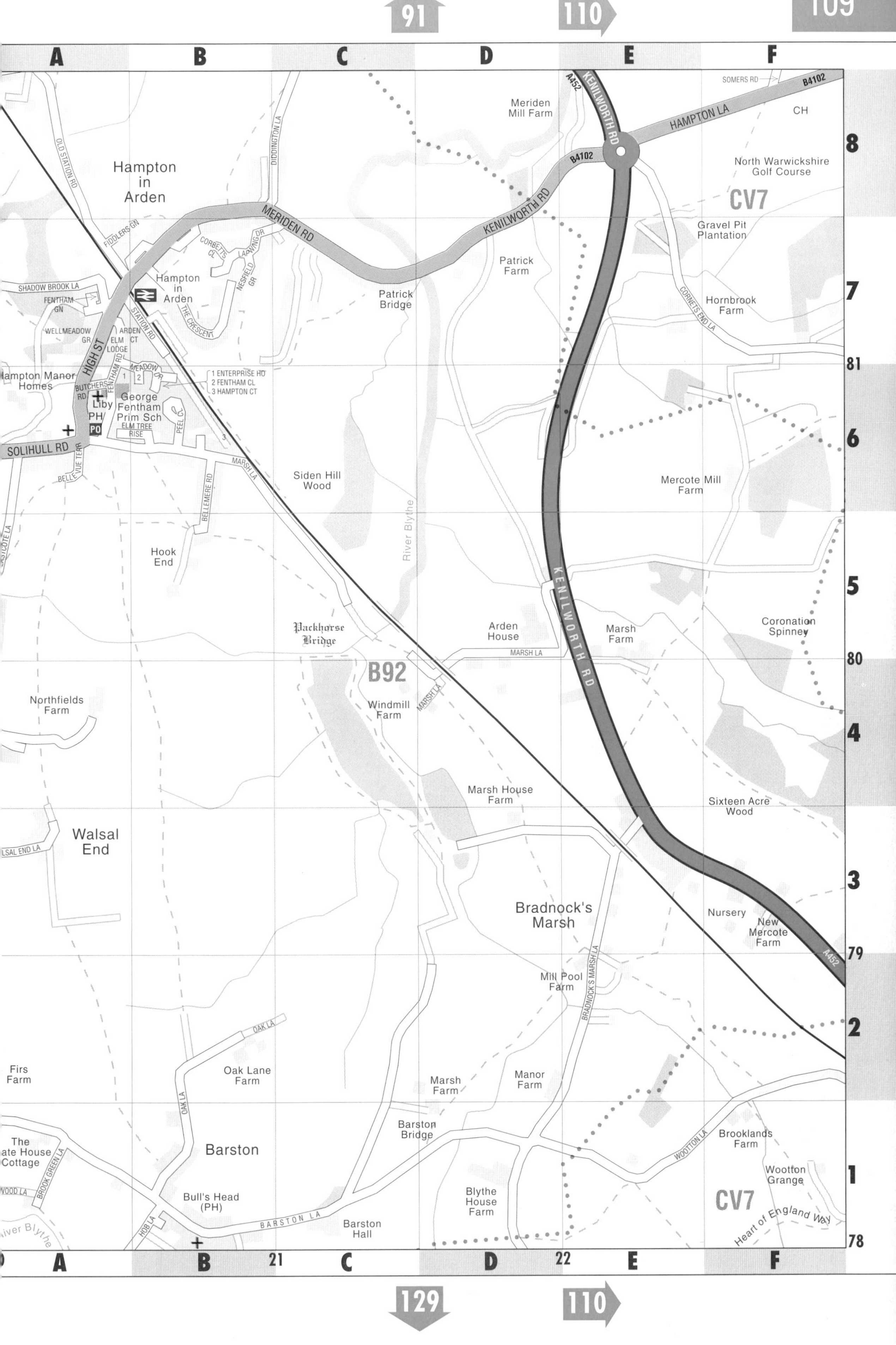
A B C D E F
8 7 81 6 5 80 4 3 79 2 1 78
21 22
Hampton in Arden
Meriden Mill Farm
North Warwickshire Golf Course
CV7
Gravel Pit Plantation
Patrick Farm
Patrick Bridge
Hornbrook Farm
Hampton Manor Homes
George Fentham Prim Sch
Liby
PH
PO
Siden Hill Wood
Mercote Mill Farm
Hook End
River Blythe
Packhorse Bridge
Arden House
Marsh Farm
Coronation Spinney
B92
Northfields Farm
Windmill Farm
Marsh House Farm
Sixteen Acre Wood
Walsal End
Bradnock's Marsh
Nursery
New Mercote Farm
Mill Pool Farm
Firs Farm
Oak Lane Farm
Marsh Farm
Manor Farm
Barston Bridge
Brooklands Farm
The Gate House Cottage
Barston
Wootton Grange
Bull's Head (PH)
Blythe House Farm
CV7
Barston Hall
Heart of England Way
KENILWORTH RD
HAMPTON LA
B4102
MERIDEN RD
KENILWORTH RD
A452
SOMERS RD
CH
DIDDINGTON LA
OLD STATION RD
FIDDLERS GN
SHADOW BROOK LA
FENTHAM GN
WELLMEADOW GR
HIGH ST
STATION RD
ARDEN CT
ELM LODGE
FENTHAM RD
MEADOW DR
BUTCHERS RD
ELM TREE RISE
PEEL CL
CORBETTS CL
LAPWING DR
NESFIELD GR
THE CRESCENT
1 ENTERPRISE HO
2 FENTHAM CL
3 HAMPTON CT
SOLIHULL RD
BELLE VUE TERR
MARSH LA
BELLEMERE RD
CORNETS END LA
MARSH LA
MARSH LA
BRADNOCK'S MARSH LA
OAK LA
OAK LA
BROOK GREEN LA
WOOTTON LA
BARSTON LA
HOB LA

109
92

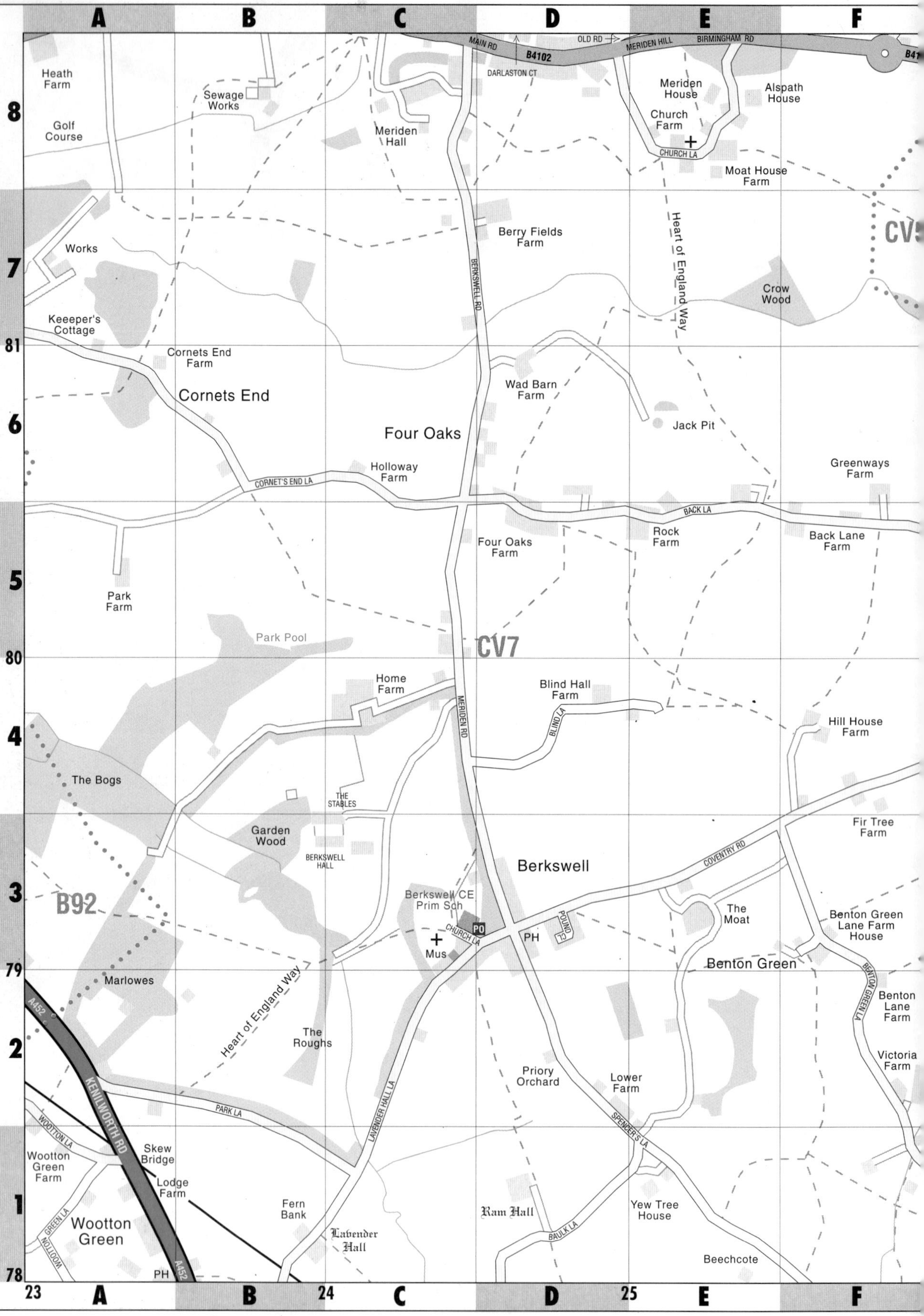

A B C D E F

8

Heath Farm

Golf Course

Sewage Works

Meriden Hall

MAIN RD
B4102
DARLASTON CT

OLD RD
MERIDEN HILL
BIRMINGHAM RD

Meriden House

Church Farm

Alspath House

CHURCH LA

Moat House Farm

CV

7

Works

Berry Fields Farm

Heart of England Way

Crow Wood

81

Keeeper's Cottage

Cornets End Farm

BERKSWELL RD

Wad Barn Farm

6

Cornets End

Four Oaks

Jack Pit

Greenways Farm

Holloway Farm

CORNET'S END LA

Four Oaks Farm

Rock Farm

BACK LA

Back Lane Farm

5

Park Farm

Park Pool

CV7

Home Farm

80

Blind Hall Farm

MERIDEN RD

BLIND LA

Hill House Farm

4

The Bogs

THE STABLES

Fir Tree Farm

Garden Wood

BERKSWELL HALL

Berkswell

COVENTRY RD

3

B92

Berkswell CE Prim Sch

PO

CHURCH LA

PH

PD/NO

The Moat

Benton Green Lane Farm House

Mus

PH

Benton Green

BENTON GREEN LA

79

Marlowes

Heart of England Way

The Roughs

LAVENDER HALL LA

Benton Lane Farm

A452

KENILWORTH RD

Priory Orchard

Lower Farm

SPENCER'S LA

Victoria Farm

2

PARK LA

WOOTTON LA

Wootton Green Farm

Skew Bridge

Lodge Farm

Fern Bank

Ram Hall

BAULK LA

Yew Tree House

1

Wootton Green

GREEN LA

MCLLOOM

Lavender Hall

Beechcote

A452

PH

78

23 A B 24 C D 25 E F

109
130

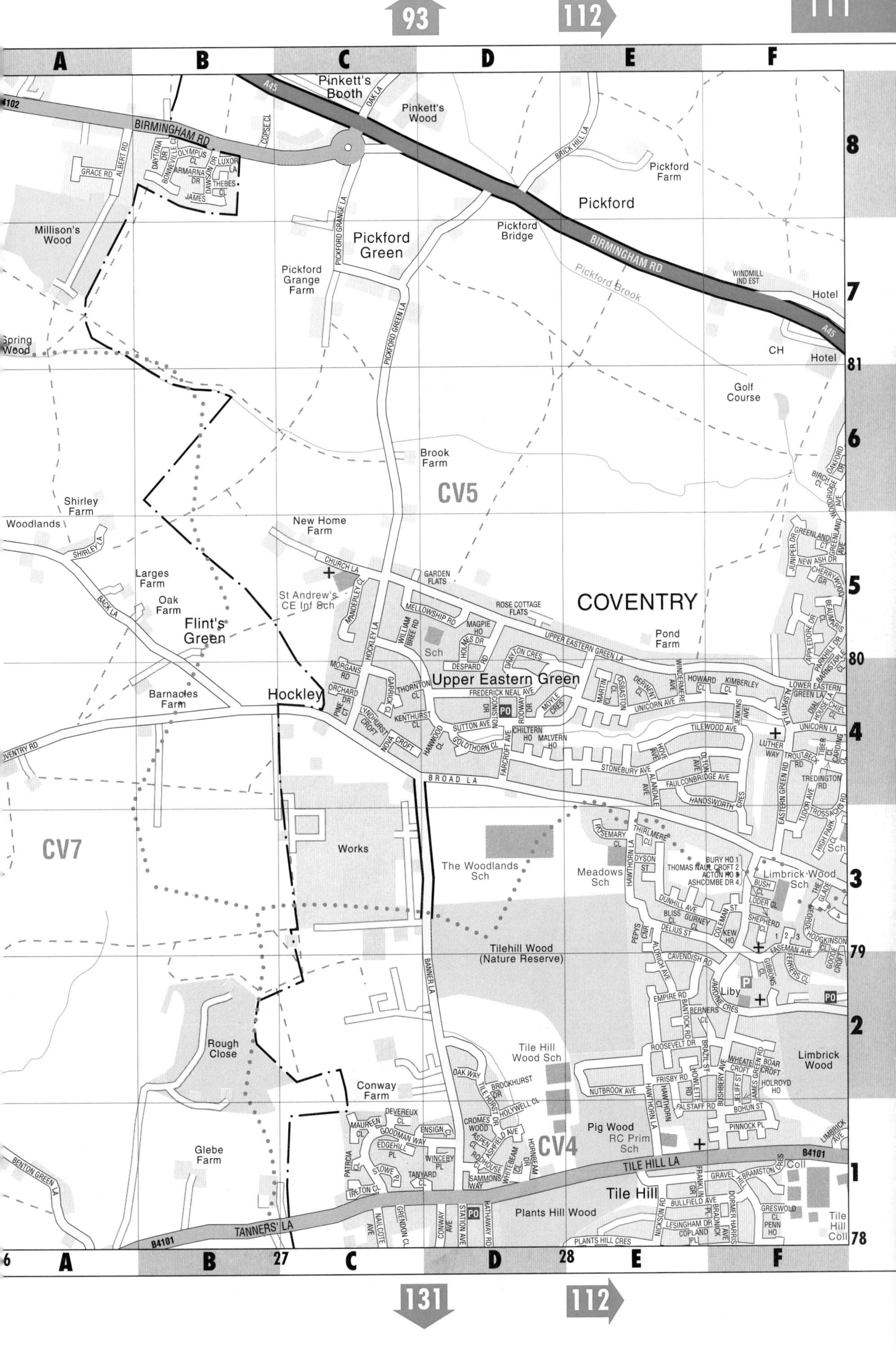

A B C D E F

8

Coundon Green

Motor Works

Rookery Farm

Coundon Lodge

MARYSHOW CL
SAUNTON CL
RYDAL CL
BROWN'S LA

7

Townfields

Northfield Farm

Allesley

COUNDON WEDGE DR

Church Farm

Coundon Court Sch & Com Coll

Hollyfast Prim Sch

Allesley Cty Prim Sch

Christ the King RC Jun Sch

81

M6

Hotel

River Sherbourne

Three Spires Sch

Coundon

CV6

Thistley Field S

6

Cemy

Church Wlk Farm

Paybody H

Christ the King RC Inf Sch

1 RECTDRY CL
2 FROGMERE CL

5

PICKFORD WAY
A4114

Allesley Park

Pickford Brook

Sherbourne Fields Sch

Hotel

Tiverton Sch

MORFA GDNS

Allesley Hall

1 BRADFIELD CL
2 BARN CL

The Dovecotes

A4106
B4106

HOLYHEAD RD

Sch

80

Shetland Cl

Sch

Allesley Hall Dr

VICTORIA CT

The Chilterns 1 2

PANGFIELD PK

WESTBURY RD

4

CV5

Sch

TORBAY RD

Allot Gdns

Sch

St Christopher Prim Sch

ALLESLEY OLD RD

1 COBURG HO
2 CROWN HO
3 PARISIENNE HO
4 VIENNA HO

River Sherbourne

Chapel Fields

3

Lower Eastern Green

Sch

Sch

Sch

Whoberley

KILBURN DR

SUNNYSIDE CL

79

BROAD LA

DUNCHURCH HIGHWAY

Hearsall Common

All Souls RC Prim Sch

HEARSALL COMM

2

Lime Tree Park

Windsor Ct

BROADMEAD CT

TILE HILL LA

HEARSALL COMM

QUEENSLAND AVE

HEARSALL LA

EARLSDON AVE N

1

B4101

TILE HILL LA
CV4

FLETCHAMSTEAD HIGHWAY

B4101

Superstore

Canley LC

B4101

Coll of F Ed

Templars Prim Sch

Works

A45

PILKINGTON RD
AINSBURY RD

78

29 A 30 B C 30 D 31 E F

A5
1 NETHERMILL RD
2 CHILTERN CT
3 PAKE'S CROFT
4 HUMBERSTONE RD
B3
1 HAWKSWORTH DR
2 COLLETT WLK
3 RIVER CT
4 COMPASS CT
5 MEADOW HO
B2
1 WELLINGTON GDNS
2 MILESTONE HO
3 TRAFALGAR HO
4 KERRY'S HO
5 GRINDLEY HO
6 GEORGE POOLE HO
7 DRINKWATER HO
8 GARDNER HO
9 GIVENS HO
10 FENNELL HO
11 WINSLOW HO
12 ST THOMAS'S HO
13 ST THOMAS'S CT
95
114
113
A
B
C
D
E
F
8
7
81
6
5
80
4
3
79
2
1
78
Radford
Sports Gd
CV6
Joseph Cash Prim Sch
St Augustine's RC Prim Sch
Hill Farm Prim Sch
Edgwick
Great Heath
Paradise
Bishopgate Green
Works
Coventry Canal
CENTRAL CITY IND EST
COVENTRY
Draper's Fields
Barrs Hill Sch & Com Coll
Moseley Prim Sch
Spon End
CV1
Hillfields Sch
CV2
Football Gd
Sports Ctr
Univ
Cath
Art Gall
Mkt
Coventry Tech Coll
Spencer Park
Earlsdon
King Henry VIII Sch
Gosford Green
CV3
All Saints CE Prim Sch
The Charterhouse
Blue Coat CE Sch
Cemy
CV5
RINGWAY ST NICHOLAS
RINGWAY SWANSWELL
RINGWAY WHITEFRIARS
RINGWAY ST JOHNS
RINGWAY QUEENS
RINGWAY HILL CROSS
RINGWAY ST PATRICKS
SKY BLUE WAY
FOLESHILL RD
STONEY STANTON RD
LONDON RD
WARWICK RD
BINLEY RD
165
32
33
34
For full street detail of the highlighted area see page 165.
133
114
E4
1 CAWTHORNE CL
2 PENSILVA WAY
3 JACQUARD HO
4 LEIGH ST
5 CLARENCE ST
6 THOMAS KING HO
7 NELSON ST
8 WATERLOO ST
9 VERNON CT
E3
1 HILLFIELDS HO
2 JEPHCOTT HO
3 GILBERT CL
4 VAUXHALL CL
5 VERNON CL
6 SPRING CL
7 RAGLAN CT

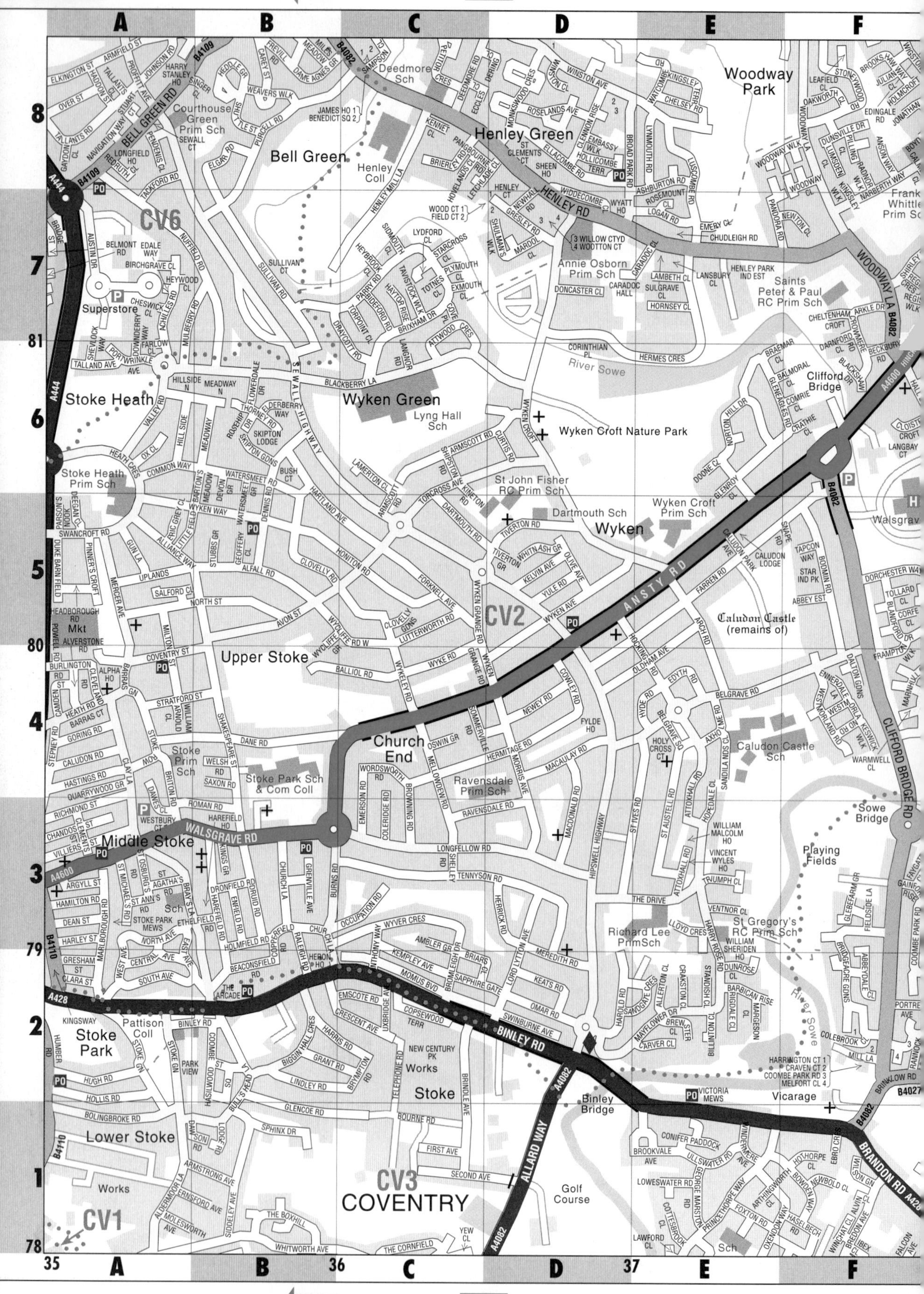
Woodway Park
Henley Green
Bell Green
Courthouse Green Prim Sch
Deedmore Sch
Henley Coll
CV6
Superstore
Annie Osborn Prim Sch
Saints Peter & Paul RC Prim Sch
Frank Whittle Prim Sch
Stoke Heath
Wyken Green
Lyng Hall Sch
Clifford Bridge
Wyken Croft Nature Park
Stoke Heath Prim Sch
St John Fisher RC Prim Sch
Dartmouth Sch
Wyken Croft Prim Sch
Wyken
Walsgrave
Caludon Castle (remains of)
CV2
Upper Stoke
Mkt
Church End
Caludon Castle Sch
Stoke Prim Sch
Stoke Park Sch & Com Coll
Ravensdale Prim Sch
Middle Stoke
Sowe Bridge
Playing Fields
Richard Lee PrimSch
St Gregory's RC Prim Sch
River Sowe
Stoke Park
Pattison Coll
Works
Stoke
Binley Bridge
Vicarage
Lower Stoke
CV3
COVENTRY
Golf Course
CV1
A444
B4109
B4082
A4600
ANSTY RD
WALSGRAVE RD
BINLEY RD
A428
A4082
ALLARD WAY
B4110
HENLEY RD
WOODWAY LA
CLIFFORD BRIDGE RD
BRANDON RD
BELL GREEN RD
SEWALL HIGHWAY
HIPSWELL HIGHWAY
A B C D E F
8 7 6 5 4 3 2 1
81 80 79 78
35 36 37

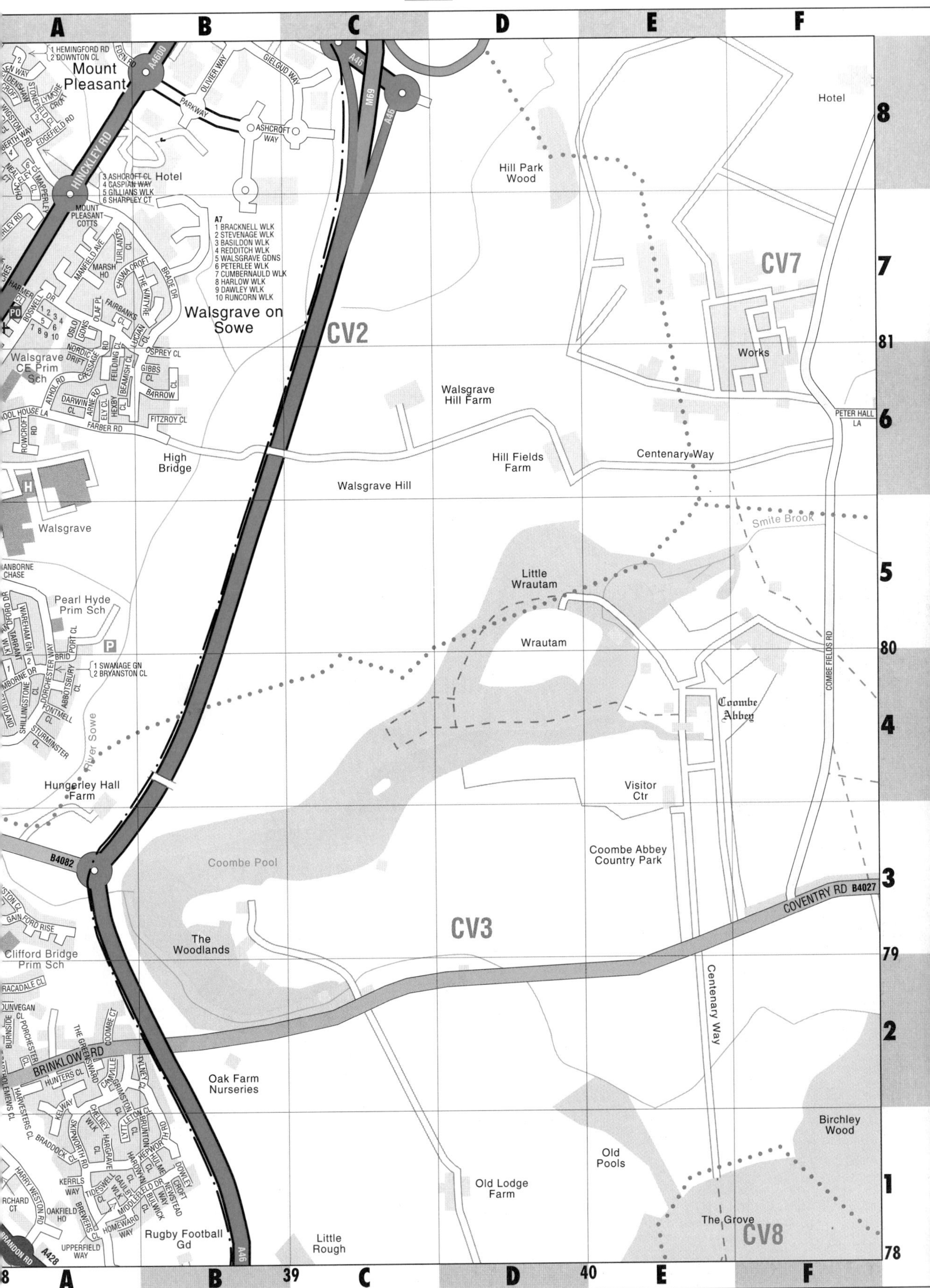
A
B
C
D
E
F
Mount Pleasant
Hotel
Walsgrave on Sowe
Walsgrave CE Prim Sch
High Bridge
Walsgrave
Pearl Hyde Prim Sch
Hungerley Hall Farm
Clifford Bridge Prim Sch
CV2
Hill Park Wood
Walsgrave Hill Farm
Hill Fields Farm
Walsgrave Hill
Centenary Way
CV7
Works
Hotel
Smite Brook
Little Wrautam
Wrautam
Coombe Abbey
Visitor Ctr
Coombe Abbey Country Park
Coombe Pool
The Woodlands
CV3
Oak Farm Nurseries
Old Lodge Farm
Old Pools
Birchley Wood
The Grove
CV8
Little Rough
Rugby Football Gd
HINCKLEY RD
BRINKLOW RD
COVENTRY RD B4027
COMBE FIELDS RD
PETER HALL LA
B4082
A46
M69
A4600
River Sowe
Centenary Way
8
7
81
6
5
80
4
3
79
2
1
78
39
40
A
B
C
D
E
F

C6
1 HABBERLEY ST
2 BENNETT ST
3 ADAMS HO
4 WOODFIELD ST
5 ST JOHN'S ST
6 ST JOHN'S CL

D6
1 MILLERS CT
2 MILLFIELD GDNS
3 RUTH CHAMBERLAIN CT
4 PATERNOSTER ROW
5 PERRETT WLK
6 NEW BLDGS

7 IDEAL BLDGS
E5
1 BRIDGE ST
2 MARLBOROUGH ST
3 WORCESTER CROSS
E6
1 BLACK HORSE LA

2 CALLOWS LA
3 FREDA EDDY CT
4 KING CHARLES SQ
5 DERICK BURCHER'S MALL
6 SIR GEORGE'S MALL
7 THE SWAN CTR
8 SIR WALTER'S MALL

9 ROWLAND HILL CTR
10 SIR GEORGES CT
F6
1 TRINITY CT
2 VICTORIA CT
3 SHORT ST

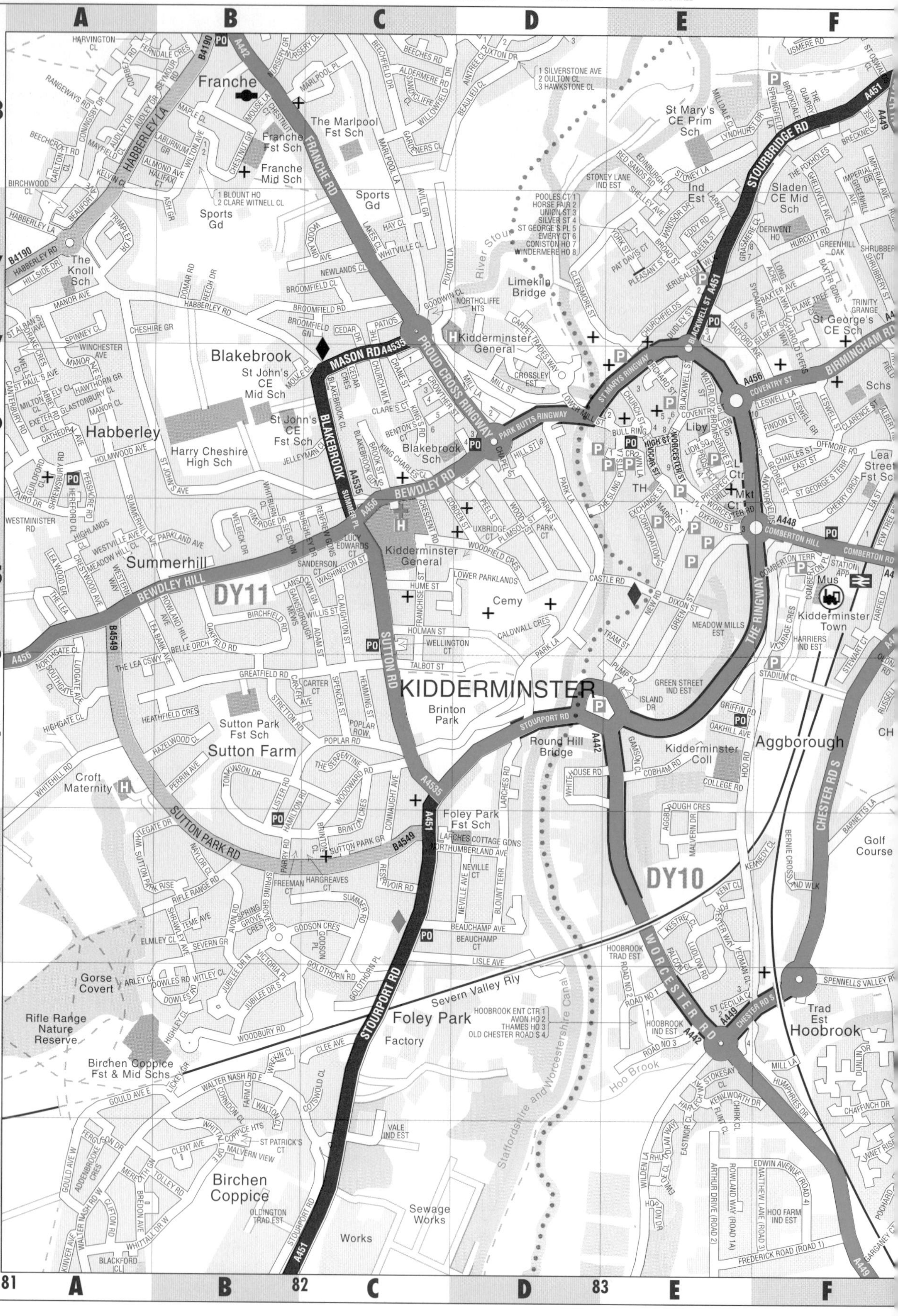

118

5
THE HAWTHORNS
CHADDERSLEY GDNS
SOMERLEYTON CT
COMBERTON MANS
COMBERTON CT

B6
1 HASEFIELD GDNS
2 GEORGE DANCE CL
3 KIPLING WLK
4 CHATTERTON WLK

5 ELIOT WLK
6 HOUSMAN WLK
7 COWPER WLK

8 CARROLL WLK
9 GOLDSMITH WLK
10 ROCHESTER WLK

1 THE LINKS
2 CYPRESS CT
3 LIME CT
4 JUNIPER CT

1 KINGFISHER GR
2 LITTLE GREBE RD

1 SWIFT PARK GR
2 SANDPIPER CL
3 STONECHAT CL
4 NIGHTINGALE DR

1 SHEARWATER CL
2 PLOVER GR

1 FIELDFARE CT
2 MORILLON CT

DY10

117
98

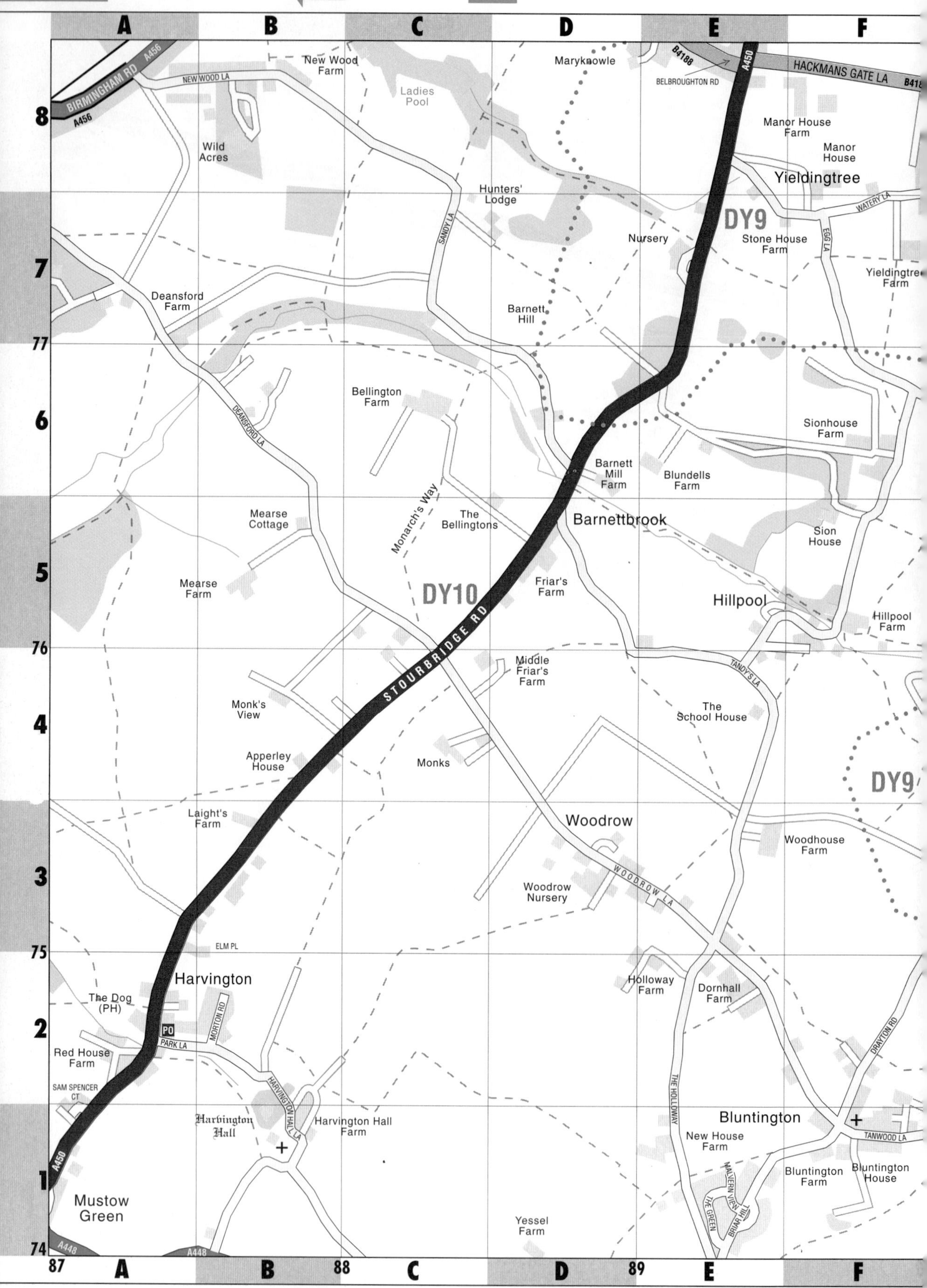

A
B
C
D
E
F
8
7
77
6
5
76
4
3
75
2
1
74
87
88
89
New Wood Farm
NEW WOOD LA
BIRMINGHAM RD
A456
Ladies Pool
Maryknowle
B4188
BELBROUGHTON RD
A450
HACKMANS GATE LA
Manor House Farm
Manor House
Wild Acres
Hunters' Lodge
Yieldingtree
WATERY LA
DY9
Nursery
Stone House Farm
EGG LA
SANDY LA
Yieldingtree Farm
Deansford Farm
Barnett Hill
Bellington Farm
Sionhouse Farm
DEANSFORD LA
Barnett Mill Farm
Blundells Farm
Monarch's Way
The Bellingtons
Barnettbrook
Mearse Cottage
Sion House
Mearse Farm
DY10
Friar's Farm
Hillpool
Hillpool Farm
STOURBRIDGE RD
Middle Friar's Farm
TANDY'S LA
Monk's View
The School House
Apperley House
Monks
DY9
Laight's Farm
Woodrow
Woodhouse Farm
WOODROW LA
Woodrow Nursery
ELM PL
Harvington
Holloway Farm
Dornhall Farm
The Dog (PH)
MORTON RD
PO
PARK LA
DRAYTON RD
Red House Farm
SAM SPENCER CT
HARVINGTON HALL LA
THE HOLLOWAY
Harbington Hall
Harvington Hall Farm
Bluntington
TANWOOD LA
New House Farm
MALVERN VIEW
Bluntington Farm
Bluntington House
Mustow Green
THE GREEN
BRIAR HILL
Yessel Farm
A448

117

99
120

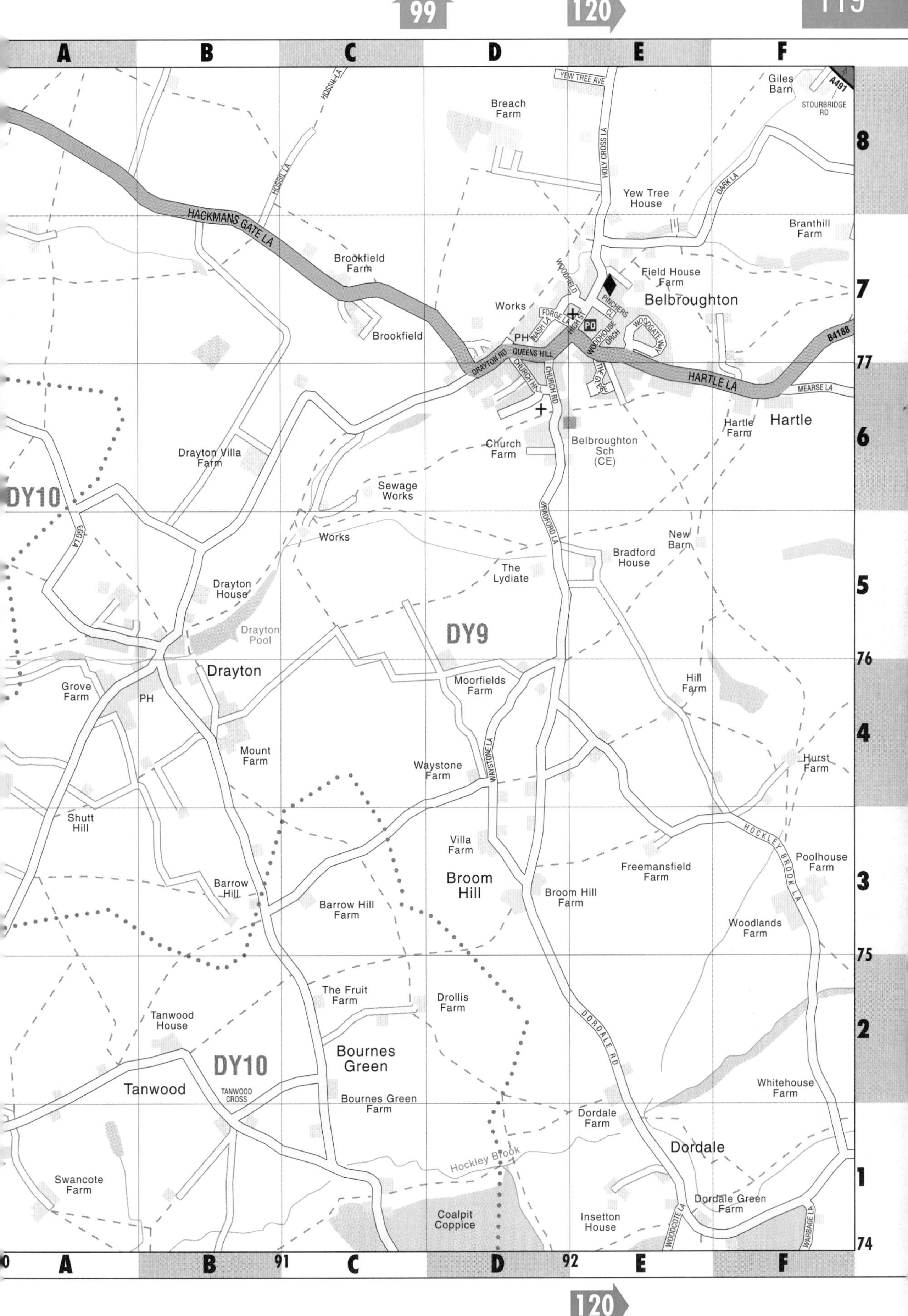
A
B
C
D
E
F
8
7
77
6
5
76
4
3
75
2
1
74
91
92
YEW TREE AVE
HOSSIL LA
Breach Farm
Giles Barn
A491
STOURBRIDGE RD
HOLY CROSS LA
Yew Tree House
DARK LA
Branthill Farm
HACKMANS GATE LA
Brookfield Farm
WOODFIELD
Field House Farm
Belbroughton
PINCHERS CL
Works
FORGE LA
HIGH ST
PO
WOODHOUSE ORCH
WOODGATE WAY
Brookfield
PH
NASH LA
DRAYTON RD
QUEENS HILL
CHURCH HILL
CHURCH RD
THE GLEBE
HARTLE LA
B4188
MEARSE LA
Hartle Farm
Hartle
Church Farm
Belbroughton Sch (CE)
Drayton Villa Farm
DY10
Sewage Works
BRADFORD LA
EGG LA
Works
New Barn
Bradford House
The Lydiate
Drayton House
Drayton Pool
DY9
Drayton
Grove Farm
PH
Moorfields Farm
Hill Farm
Mount Farm
Waystone Farm
WAYSTONE LA
Hurst Farm
Shutt Hill
Villa Farm
HOCKLEY BROOK LA
Poolhouse Farm
Barrow Hill
Broom Hill
Freemansfield Farm
Broom Hill Farm
Barrow Hill Farm
Woodlands Farm
The Fruit Farm
Drollis Farm
Tanwood House
DORDALE RD
DY10
Bournes Green
Tanwood
TANWOOD CROSS
Bournes Green Farm
Whitehouse Farm
Dordale Farm
Dordale
Hockley Brook
Swancote Farm
Coalpit Coppice
Insetton House
Dordale Green Farm
WOODCOTE LA
WARBAGE LA

120

A
B
C
D
E
F
8
7
77
6
5
76
4
3
75
2
1
74
93
94
95
Holly Bush (PH)
Gorse Farm
Sling Common
B62
Hayes Farm
Bell Heath
Gorse Green La
Dark La
Newtown La
Woodfield La
Farley La
Newtown
Gorse Grove
Galtons La
Mill Pond
Quantry La
Study Ctr
Bell End
Heath End Rd
The Gutter
Upper Madeley Farm
Hartle La
Stourbridge Rd
B4188
A491
Moor Hall Dr
Bell Inn (PH)
Coalyard Farm
Chapel La
Madeley Heath
Bell Hall
Fenn Brook
Chadwich La
Bell Hall Farm
Bonfire Hill
Fenn Farm
Madeley Rd
Lower Madeley Farm
DY9
Lawn Barn House
Castle Bourne
Harbours Hill
Mearse La
Stoneybridge Farm
Hagley Hill Farm
Mearse Farm
Stoneybridge
A49
Fairfield Court
B4091
Sandy La
Sand Pit
Wildmoor
Wildmoor Farmhouse
Third Rd
Cross Coppice
Crabtree Coppice
Swan Inn (PH)
Wildmoor Mill Farm
Fairfield House
Swan La
Pepperwood Cl
Fairfield
New Barn Farm
Poolhouse Dingle
Gorsey Piece
Mill La
Monarch's Way
Wood La
PO
Fairfield Cty Prim Sch
Glovers Meadow Farm
B61
Pepper Wood
Orchard Villas
Meadow Farm
Yew Tree La
Fir Tree Farm
Brook Rd
Bournheath Rd
Yewtree Farm
Merchants Farm
Mount Rd
New Rd
Snuff Hill
Dordale Rd
Mayfield Farm
Little Royal Farm
Parish Hill
Woodrow Cl
Mayfield
Fairfield Rd
Nursery
Royal Content Farm
Hilltop Farm
Claypit La
Hillborough
Varnold La
Doctors Hill
Dodford Rd
PH
M5
Chadcote Way
M5

A
B
C
D
E
F
B62
DY9
B61
B45
B60
Chapman's Hill Farm
Chapman's Hill
Waste Site
Thistle Grove Farm
Windmill Hill
Waseley Hills Country Park
Waseley Hill
Waseleyhill Farm
Segbourne Coppice
Barnes Close
Chadwich Grange Farm
Gannow Mid Sch
Waseley Hills High Sch
North Worcestershire Path
Monarch's Way
Hollywell Farm
Chadwich Manor Estate
Redwell Farm
Chadwich Manor
Spring Pools
Callowbrook Fst Sch
Liby
Eachway
Beaconside Fst & Mid Sch
L Ctr
Yewtree Farm
Money Lane Farm
Keys Hill Farm
Brookhouse Farm
Wildmoor Oak (PH)
Chadwich Farm
Sand Pit
Chadwick Wood
Stock Hill
Heanor
Golf Course
Beacon Hill
Beaconwood
Beacon Farm
High House Farm
Lydiate Ash
The Lickey Fst & Mid Sch
Upper Cottage Farm
Bellevue
Upper Marlbrook
Lower Marlbrook
Upper Catshill
Firs Farm
MONEY LA
SANDY LA
BIRMINGHAM RD
HALESOWEN RD
OLD BIRMINGHAM RD
ALVECHURCH HIGHWAY
GOLDEN CROSS LA
WILDMOOR LA
MARLBROOK LA
BEACON LA
MONUMENT LA
B4551
B4096
B 4185
A 491
A38
M 5
8
7
77
6
5
76
4
3
75
2
1
74
96
97
98

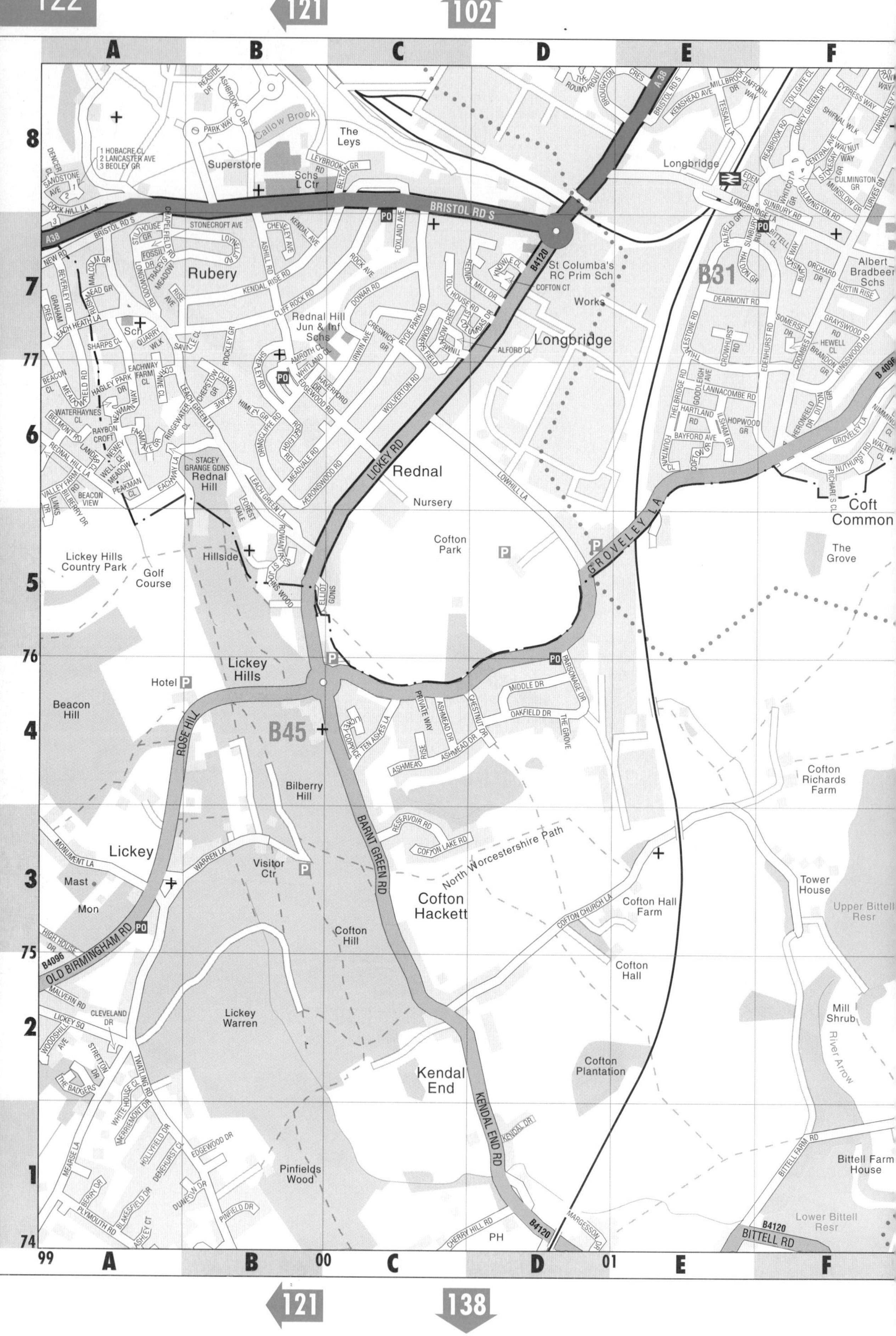

E8
1 CAMPION HO
2 SAFFRON HO
3 SEDGEBERROW COVERT
4 LYDBROOK COVERT
5 OFFENHAM COVERT
6 TARRINGTON COVERT
7 BILTON IND EST
8 REDBROOK COVERT

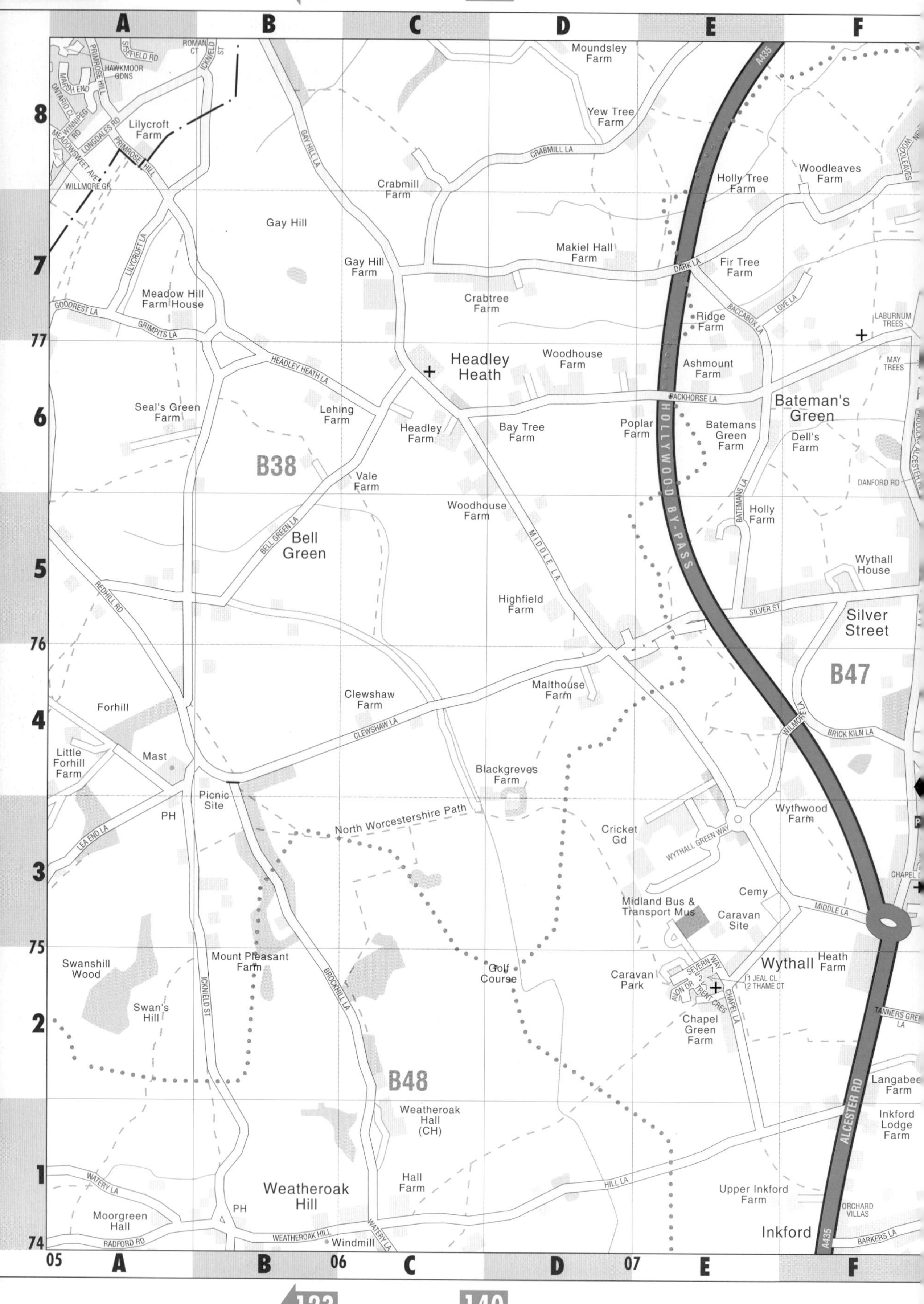

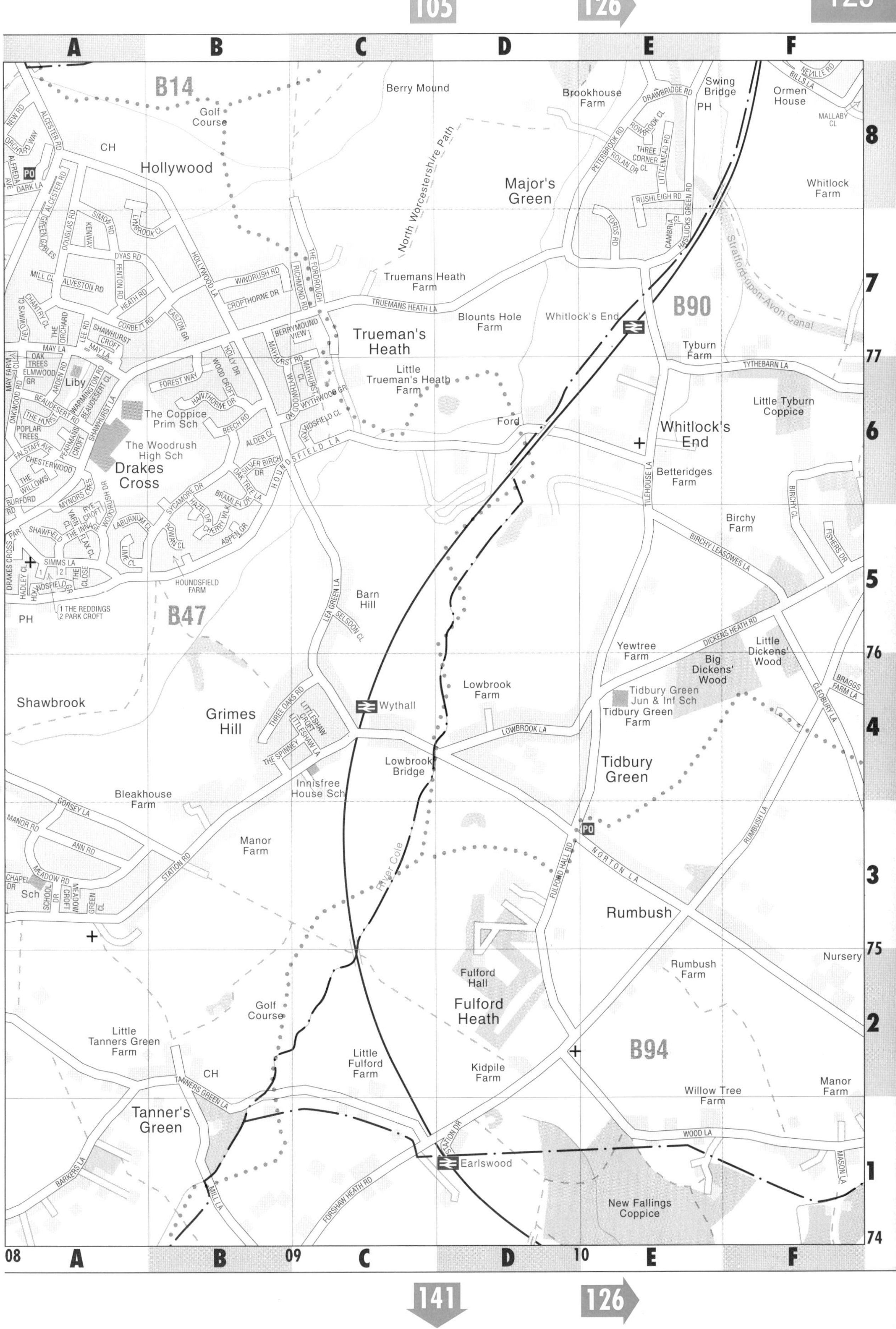

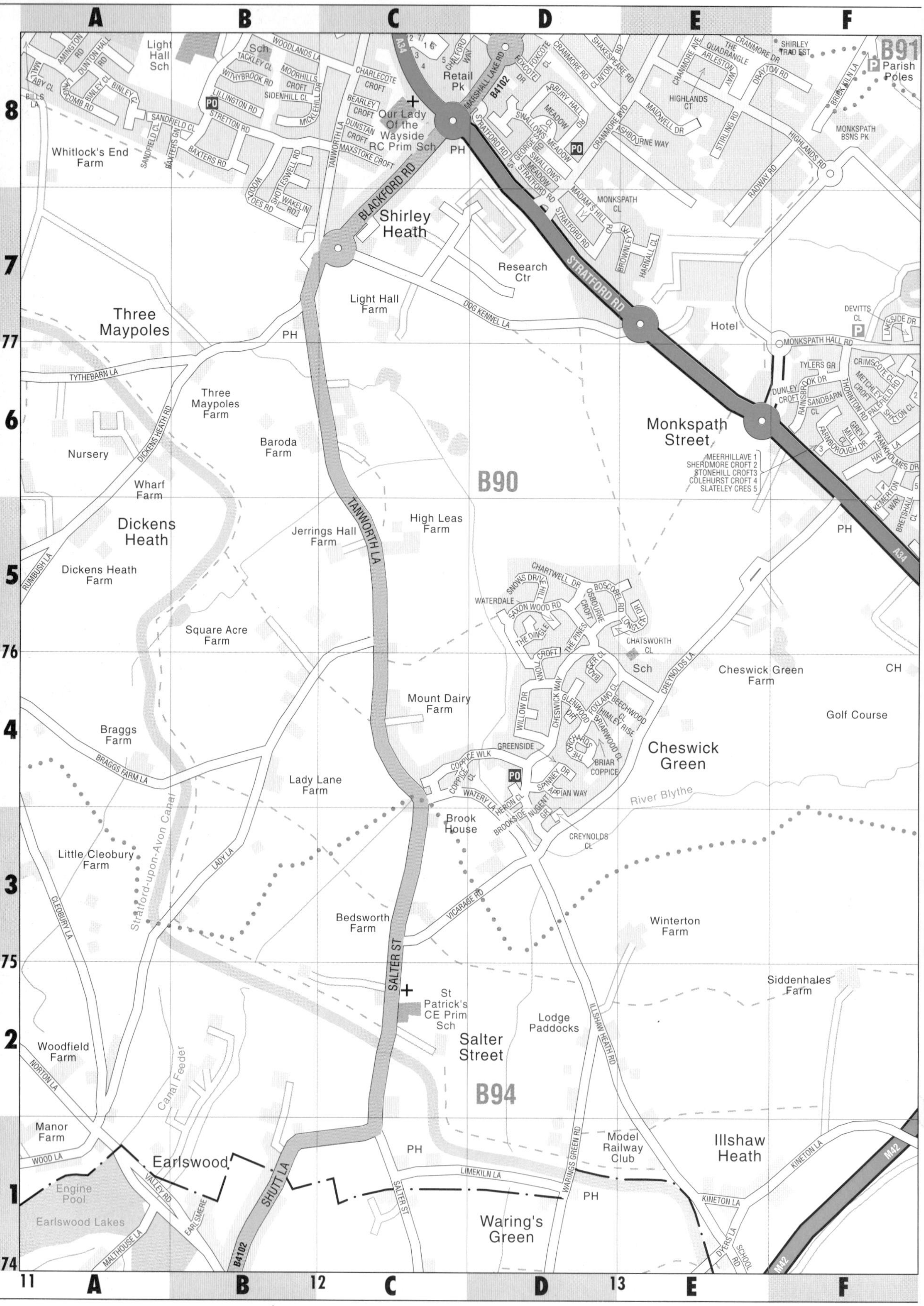

125
106

C8
1 HARWOOD GR
2 SHIRLEYDALE
3 CHELTONDALE
4 HENLEYDALE
5 QUINTONDALE
6 ARDENDALE

C8
7 YARNINGDALE

A B C D E F

8 7 77 6 5 76 4 3 75 2 1 74

B91
Parish Poles

Shirley Trad Est

Whitlock's End Farm

Light Hall Sch

Woodlands La
Tackley Cl
Moorhills
Withybrook Rd
Sidenhill Cl
Charlecote Croft
Bearley Croft
Dunstan Croft
Maxstoke Croft

Our Lady Of the Wayside RC Prim Sch

Retail Pk

PH

Shirley Heath

Research Ctr

Stratford Rd
B4102
A34

The Quadrangle
Cranmore
Arleston Way
Shakespeare Rd
Clinton Rd
Cranmore Ave
Highlands Ct
Maxwell Rd
Stirling Rd
Highlands Rd

Monkspath Bsns Pk

Three Maypoles

Light Hall Farm

Dog Kennel La

Three Maypoles Farm

Tythebarn La

Baroda Farm

Nursery

Dickens Heath Rd

Wharf Farm

Hotel

Monkspath Hall Rd

Devitts Cl

Lakeside Rd

Tylers Gr
Dunley Croft

Monkspath Street

Meerhill Ave 1
Sherdmore Croft 2
Stonehill Croft 3
Colehurst Croft 4
Slateley Cres 5

PH

B90

Dickens Heath

Dickens Heath Farm

Rumbush La

Tanworth La

Jerrings Hall Farm

High Leas Farm

Square Acre Farm

Chartwell Dr
Waterdale
Saxon Wood Rd
The Dingle
The Tynes

Chatsworth Cl

Sch

Cheswick Green Farm

CH

Golf Course

Braggs Farm

Braggs Farm La

Lady Lane Farm

Mount Dairy Farm

Greenside
Coppice Wlk

Cheswick Green

River Blythe

Little Cleobury Farm

Cleobury La

Brook House

Watery La
Heron Cl
Appian Way

Creynolds Cl

Vicarage Rd

Bedsworth Farm

Winterton Farm

Stratford-upon-Avon Canal

Salter St

St Patrick's CE Prim Sch

Lodge Paddocks

Siddenhales Farm

Woodfield Farm

Canal Feeder

Salter Street

B94

Illshaw Heath Rd

Manor Farm

Wood La

Earlswood

Shutt La

PH

Model Railway Club

Illshaw Heath

Kineton La

M42

Engine Pool

Valley Rd

Malthouse La

B4102

Limekiln La

Salter St

PH

Waring's Green

Kineton La

School Rd

Earlswood Lakes

Norton La

Peps La

11 A B 12 C D 13 E F

125
142

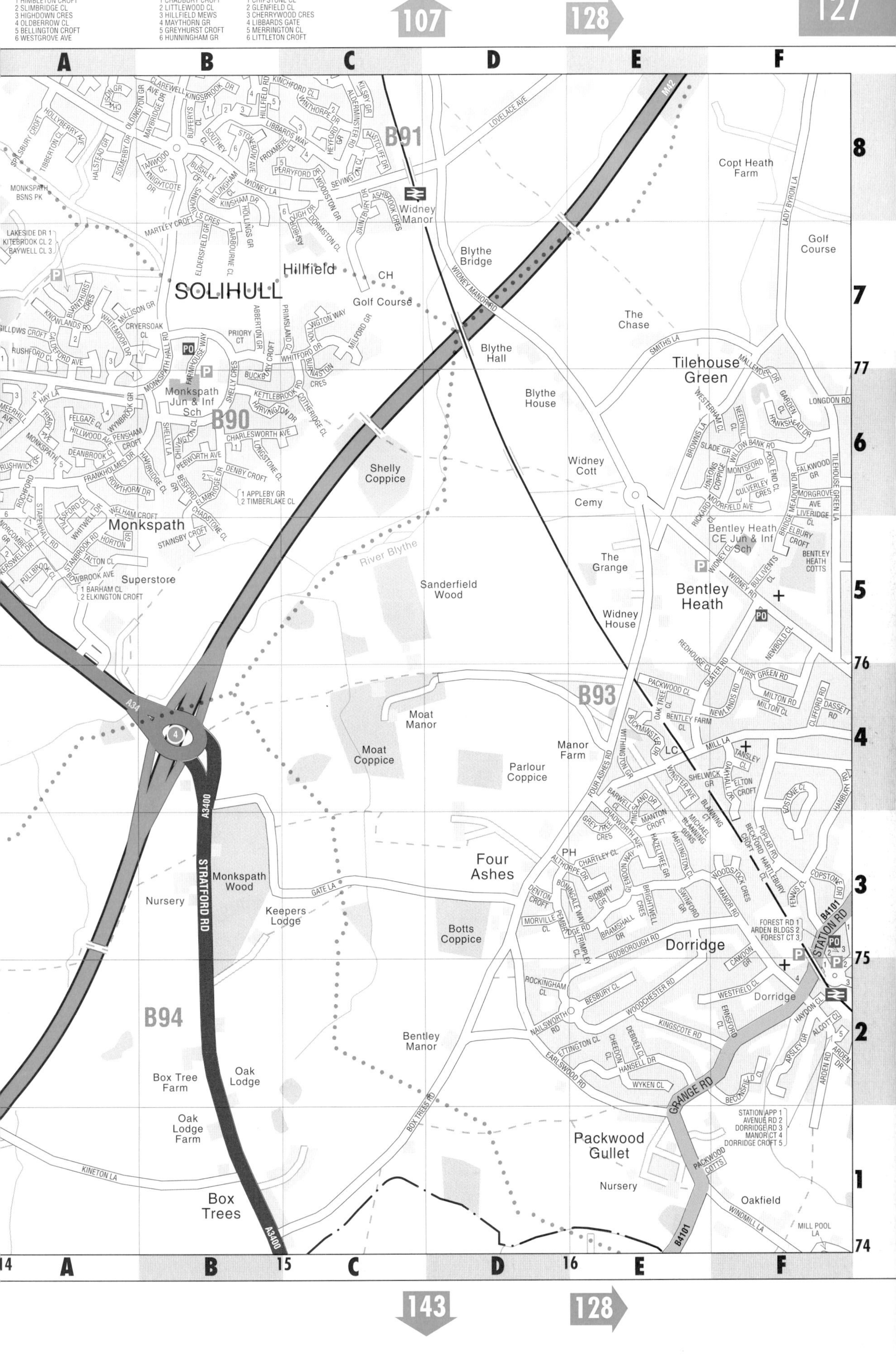

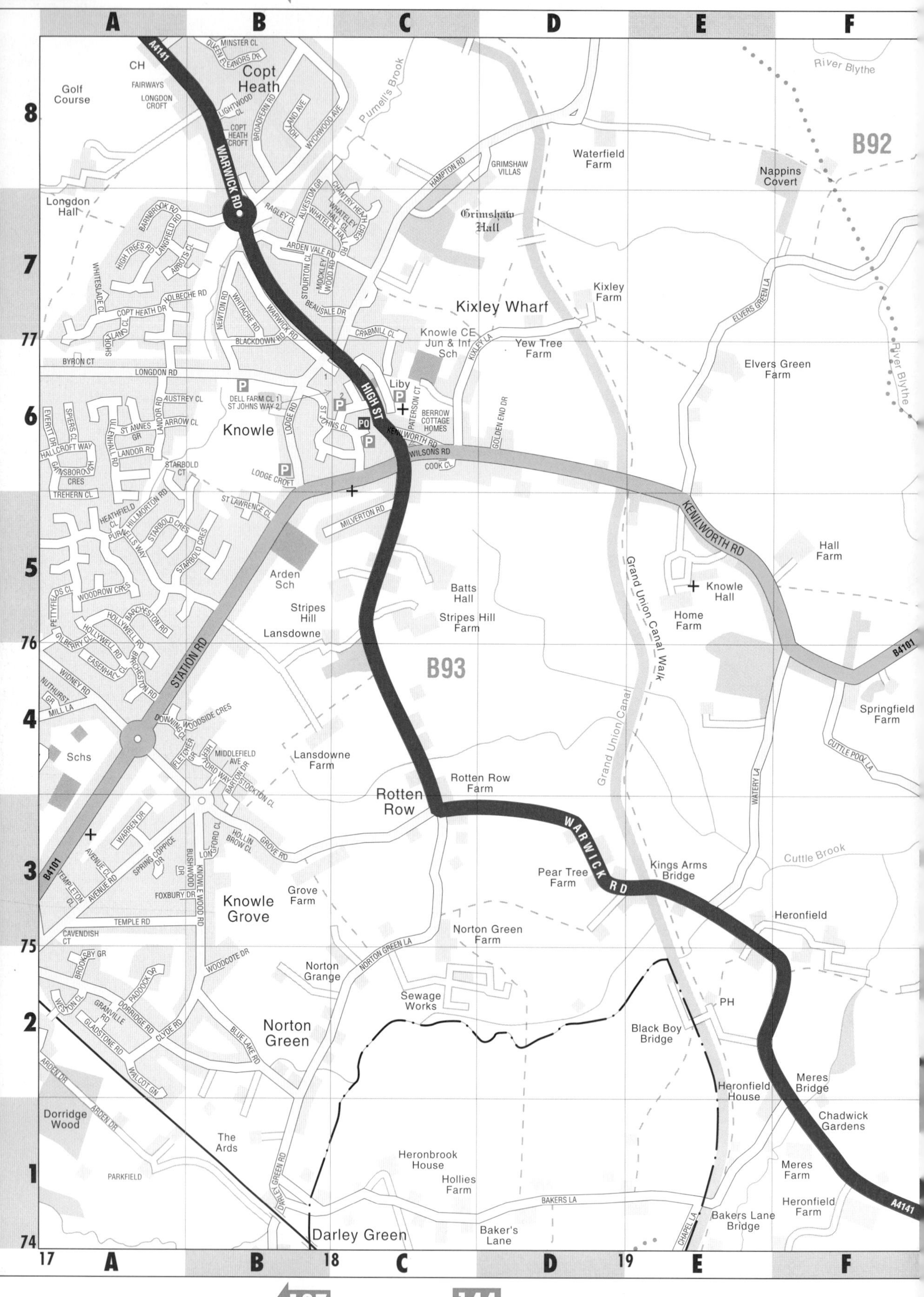

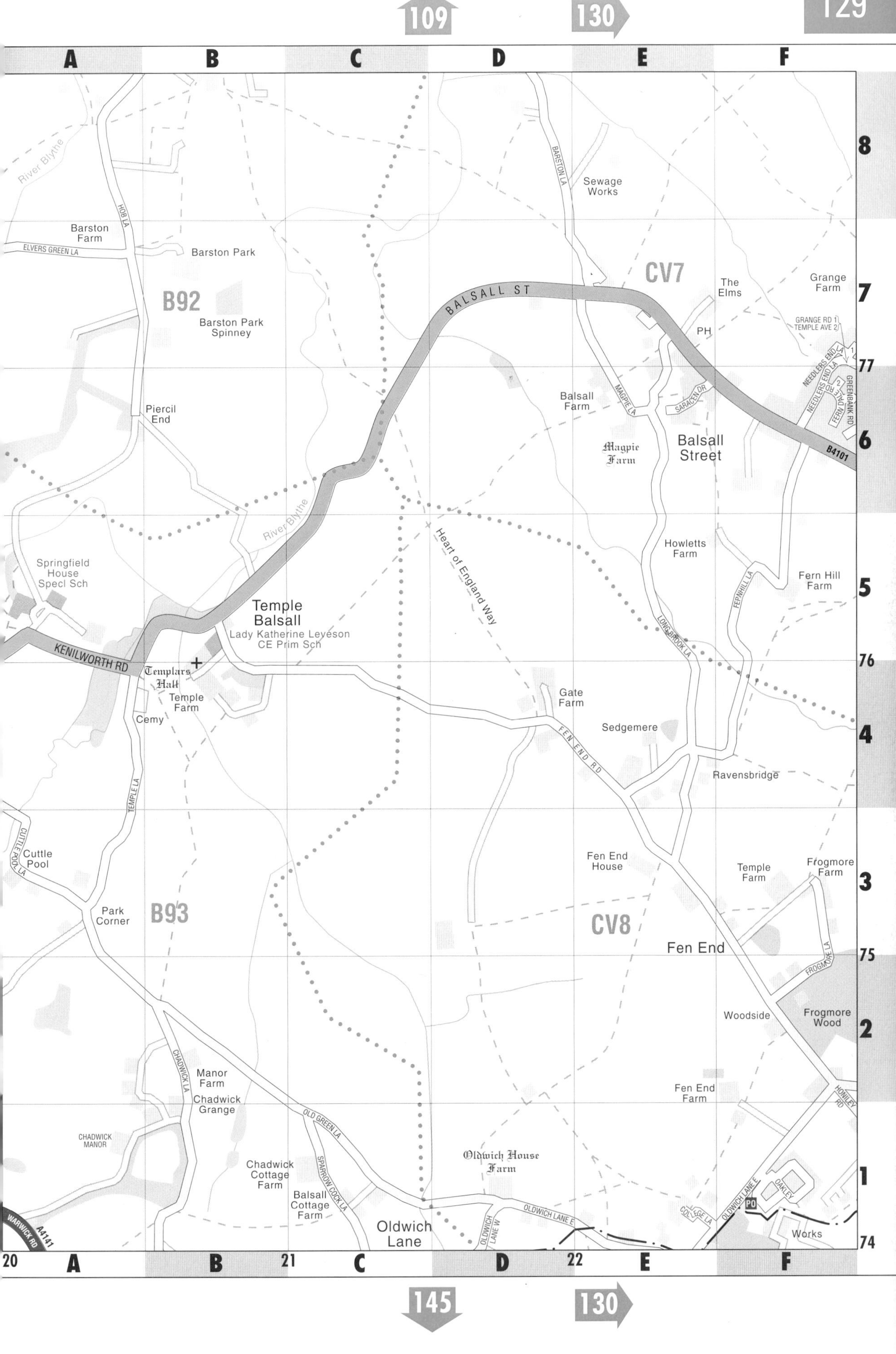

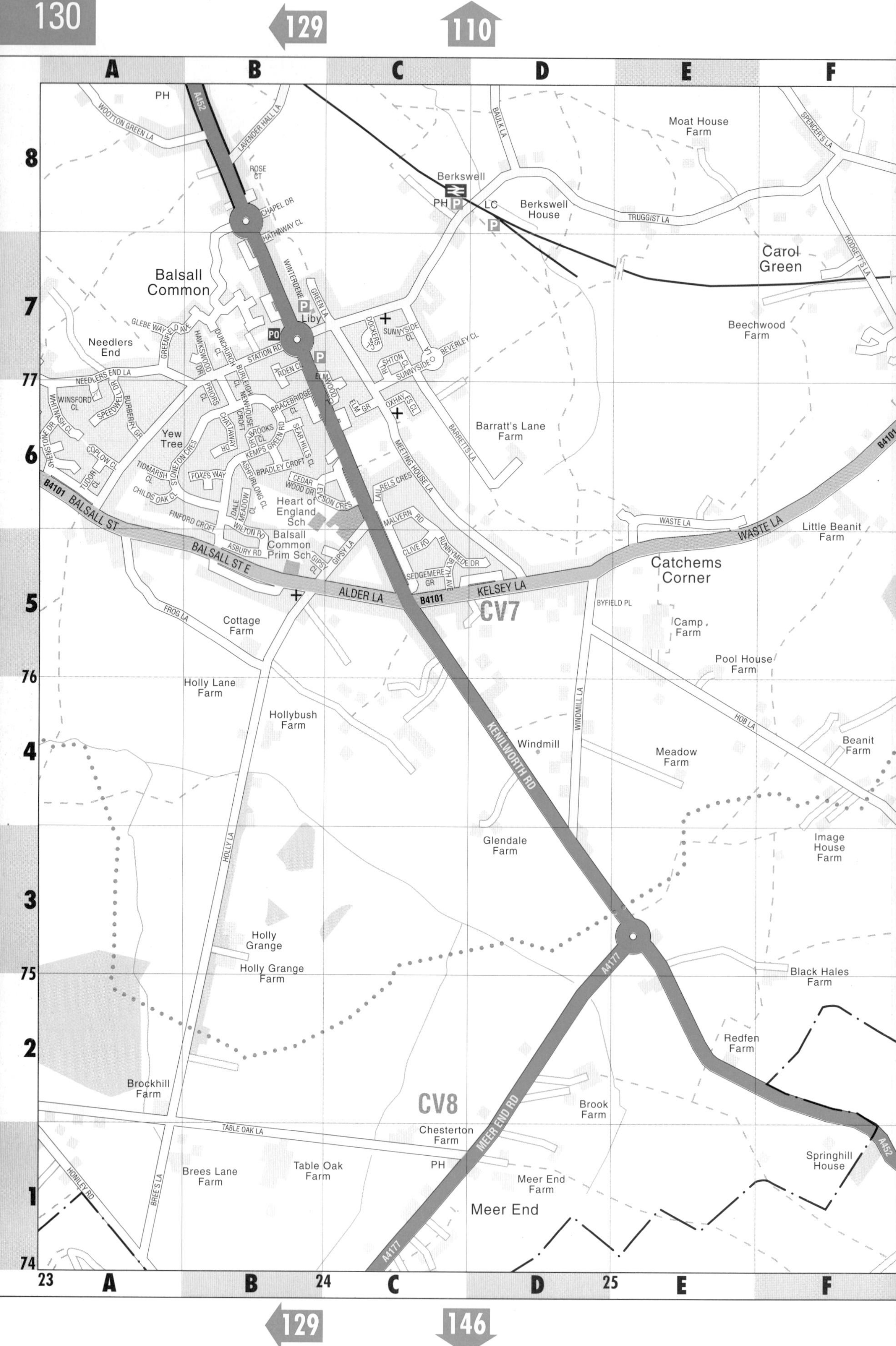

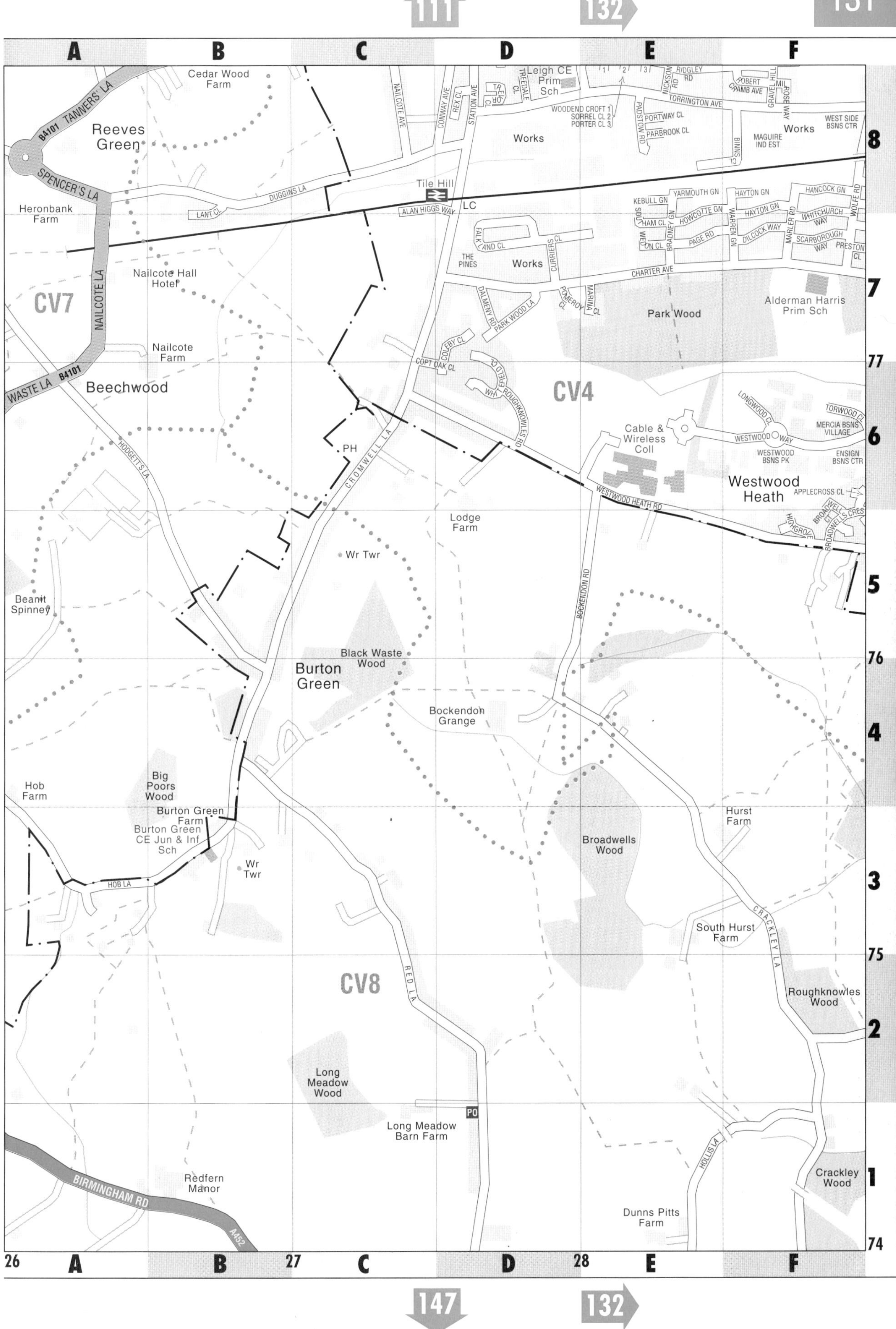
111
132
Cedar Wood Farm
Reeves Green
Heronbank Farm
Leigh CE Prim Sch
Works
Tile Hill
LC
Nailcote Hall Hotel
CV7
Nailcote Farm
Beechwood
Park Wood
Alderman Harris Prim Sch
CV4
Cable & Wireless Coll
Westwood Heath
PH
Lodge Farm
Wr Twr
Beanit Spinney
Black Waste Wood
Burton Green
Bockendon Grange
Hob Farm
Big Poors Wood
Burton Green Farm
Burton Green CE Jun & Inf Sch
Hurst Farm
Broadwells Wood
South Hurst Farm
CV8
Roughknowles Wood
Long Meadow Wood
Long Meadow Barn Farm
Redfern Manor
Crackley Wood
Dunns Pitts Farm
147
132

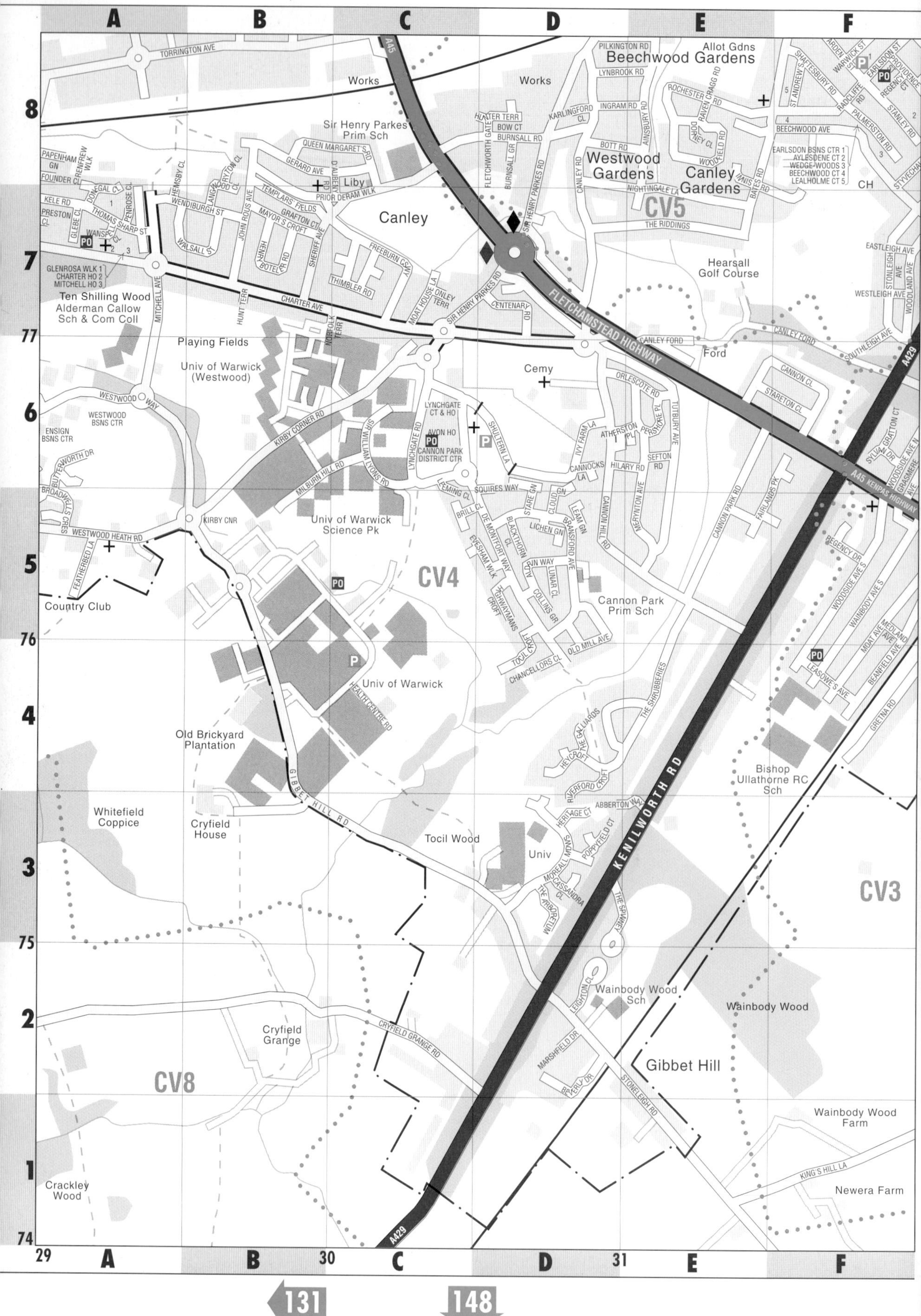

COVENTRY
CV5
KENILWORTH RD
Coventry Prep Sch
War Meml
Stivichall Common
War Memorial Park
Coat of Arms Bridge
Stivichall Prim Sch
Mon
LEAMINGTON RD
Manor Park Jun & Inf Sch
Quinton Park
Cheylesmore
Cemy
LONDON RD
Allot Gdns
Whitley Common
Sports Ctr
St Thomas More RC Prim Sch
Stivichall
Howes Prim Sch
Whitley Abbey Comp Sch
Works
Grange Farm Prim Sch
Green Lane
KENPAS HIGHWAY
CV3
Finham Park Comp Sch
Leasowes Farm
STONEBRIDGE HIGHWAY
River Sherbourne
River Sowe Bridge
Finham
Finham Prim Sch
Liby
Hotel
The Lunt
Nurseries
CV8
Baginton
Hill Farm
CH
King's Hill
Coventry Golf Course
River Sowe
PH
Sewage Works
Coventry Airport
Finham Bridge
A B C D E F
8 7 6 5 4 3 2 1
77 76 75 74
33 34

133
114

F8
1 CARDALE CROFT
2 KESTREL CROFT
3 RUTLAND CROFT
4 JIM FORREST CL
5 WILLOWHERB CL
6 WASPERTON CL
7 JOE WILLIAMS CL
A
B
C
D
E
F
8
7
77
6
5
76
4
3
75
2
1
74
35
36
37
Works
Pinley Gardens
Stoke Aldermoor
Ernesford Grange Sch & Com Coll
Binley
Sowe Valley Prim Sch
Corpus Christi RC Prim Sch
SEVERN STARS IND EST
Pinley
Superstore
Sports Gd
CV3
COVENTRY
ALLARD WAY
HUMBER RD
A4082
B4110
St Anne's RC Prim Sch
River Sowe
Chace Prim Sch
Whitley Abbey Prim Sch
Willenhall
Willenhall Wood Prim Sch
Alice Stevens Sch
Sch
St John the Divine CE Prim Sch
Willenhall Bridge
LONDON RD
Playing Field
Whitley Grove
Hotel
Willenhall Wood
Recn Gd
Black Spinney
Baginton Fields Sch
Lower Farm
BRANDON LA
STONEBRIDGE HIGHWAY
A45
A46
Tollbar End
STONEBRIDGE TRAD EST
River Avon
Ryton Bridge
Hotel
Midland Air Mus
Sewage Works
Bird Sanctuary
CV8
A423
Coventry Airport
MIDDLEMARCH BSNS PK
SISKIN PARKWAY E
OXFORD RD
Works
Coney Grey Farm
CV8

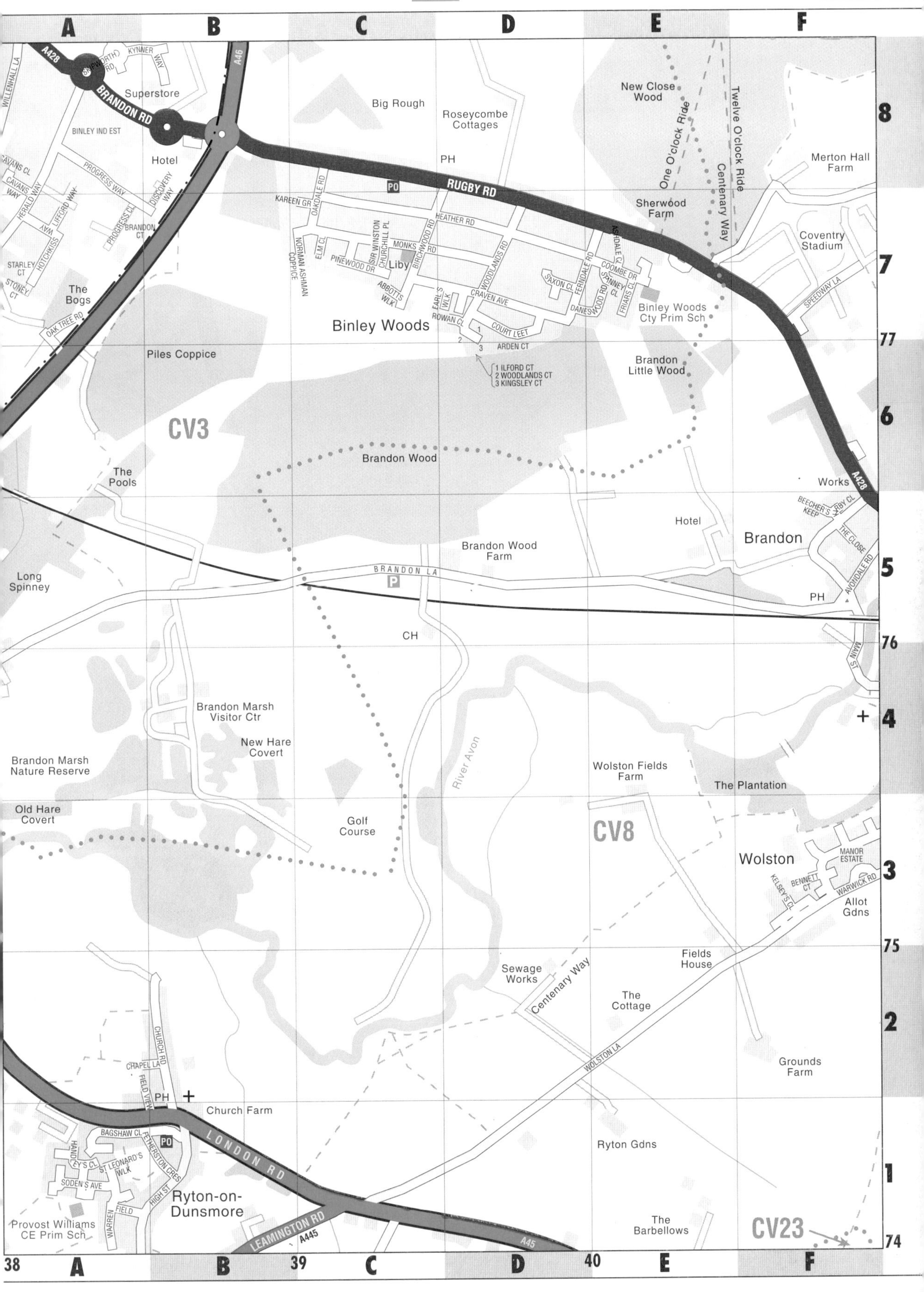

A B C D E F

8

WILLENHALL LA
A428
KYNNER WAY
BRANDON RD
Superstore
Hotel
BINLEY IND EST
PROGRESS WAY
PROGRESS CL
DISCOVERY WAY
BRANDON CT
HERALD WAY
LIFFORD WAY
AVM
HOTCHKISS
CAVANS CL
CAVANS WAY
STARLEY CT
STONEY CT
The Bogs
OAK TREE RD

Big Rough
Roseycombe Cottages
PH
RUGBY RD
PO

New Close Wood
One O'clock Ride
Twelve O'clock Ride
Centenary Way
Sherwood Farm

Merton Hall Farm
Coventry Stadium
SPEEDWAY LA

7

KAREEN GR
OAKDALE RD
NORMAN ASHMAN COPPICE
ELM CL
PINEWOOD DR
SIR WINSTON CHURCHILL PL
MONKS
BIRCHWOOD RD
HEATHER RD
WOODLANDS RD
FERNDALE RD
COOMBE DR
SPINNEY CL
FRIARS CL
KERSDALE CT
Liby
ABBOTTS WLK
EARLS WLK
ROWAN CL
CRAVEN AVE
COURT LEET
DANES WLK
SAXON CL
WOOD END
Binley Woods Cty Prim Sch

77

Binley Woods
2
3
ARDEN CT
1 ILFORD CT
2 WOODLANDS CT
3 KINGSLEY CT
Brandon Little Wood

Piles Coppice

6

CV3

Brandon Wood

A428
Works
BEECHER'S KEEP
RBY CL
THE CLOSE
AVONDALE RD

The Pools

Hotel
Brandon

5

Long Spinney

BRANDON LA
P
Brandon Wood Farm
PH
MAIN ST

76

CH

Brandon Marsh Visitor Ctr
New Hare Covert
Brandon Marsh Nature Reserve
Old Hare Covert

River Avon
Wolston Fields Farm
The Plantation

+ 4

CV8

Golf Course

Wolston
MANOR ESTATE
KELSEY'S CL
BENNETT CT
WARWICK RD
Allot Gdns

3

75

Sewage Works
Centenary Way
Fields House
The Cottage
WOLSTON LA

Grounds Farm

2

CHURCH RD
CHAPEL LA
FIELD VIEW
PH
+
Church Farm
Ryton Gdns
BAGSHAW CL
PO
HANDLEY'S CL
ST LEONARD'S WLK
PENNYSTON CRES
HIGH ST
SODEN'S AVE
FIELD
WARREN
Provost Williams CE Prim Sch
Ryton-on-Dunsmore
LONDON RD
LEAMINGTON RD
A445
The Barbellows
CV23

1

74

38 A B 39 C D 40 E F

120

A
B
C
D
E
F
8
7
73
6
5
72
4
3
71
2
1
70
93
94
95
Bournheath
Cottage Farm
DOCTORS HILL
FAIRFIELD RD
M5
CHURCH RD
MINSTER WLK
B4091
Catshill
MEADOW RD
BROOKSIDE DR
PO
WESTFIELDS
B4185
TALL TREES CL
Sch
PH
CHURCHSTONE CL
WOODBANK DR
POPLAR CL
Yarnold Lane Farm
Hilltop Poutlry Farm
YARNOLD LA
WOODLAND RD
WARBAGE LA
Hill Farm
ROCKY LA
Valley Farm
VALLEY RD
STOURBRIDGE RD
Holbourne Wood
CHURCH RD
VICTORIA RD
NIBLETTS HILL
DALE CL
HINTON FIELDS
Valley Wood
The Clock House
BUMBLE HOLE LA
Washingstocks Farm
Sunnyhill Coppice
BRIMSTONE LA
COCKSHUTT LA
Mast
WHINFIELD RD
PH
Worms Ash
BROMSGROVE RD
4a
M42
Priory
PRIORY RD
ALFREDS WELL
M42
Monarch's Way
Snakes Lake
SNAKES LAKE LA
KEITH WINTER CL
H
Dodford
BUMBLE HOLE LA
Forest Farm
SHEEPCOTE GRANGE
PAPWORTH DR
FOCKBURY RD
Fockbury Farm
Fockbury Mill Farm
Dodford Fst Sch
Little Dodford Farm
Crowfields Farm
BARTHOLEMEWS LA
Spout House
FOCKBURY MILL LA
MANDEVILLE WAY
B4091
B61
KING EDWARD RD
PERRYFIELDS CRES
KING GEORGE AVE
KING EDWARD AVE
ORCHARD RD
Perryfields
PERRYFIELDS RD
KING GEORGE CL
MIDDLETON RD
KING GEORGE CL
BEWELL HEAD
A448
Sidemoor
Park Farm
BEWELL CT
Battlefield Brook
MELBOURNE AVE
CHESTNUT RD
BROAD ST
LAUREL GR
LIME GR
YORK AVE
YORK RD
Array Fruit Farm
LINCOLN RD
BEECH RD
PH
JASMINE GR
LABURNUM GR
DURHAM
SILVERDALE
YORK CL
HOLLY RD
Battlefield Farm
LYNDEN CL
MELBOURNE RD
MELBOURNE CL
Park Gate
FALLOWFIELDS CL
THE FLATS
JUNCTION RD
SYDNEY RD
PO
CONIFER GR
HOLLY GR
GREENACRES RD
PROVIDENCE RD
HOWARD AVE
Sch
CRABTREE LA
CHURCHFIELDS GDNS
KIDDERMINSTER RD
GRAYSHOTT CL
MALCOLM AVE
CRABTREE DR
CHURCHFIELDS RD
SPIRE VIEW
Monsieurs Hall
Red Cross Farm
LARCHMERE DR
MONSIEURS HALL LA
Red Cross
CAROL AVE
CHERRY ORCHARD DR
WILLOW RD
WILLOW CT
NEW RD
WILLOW GDNS
FORGE DR
P
RECREATION RD
Warridge Lodge Farm
Hotel
CHERRY CRES
ROWAN CL
CHURCH RD
F2
1 GEORGE ST
2 ELGAR MEWS
3 NAILERS CT
MILL LA
P
P
Cemy
Whitford Hall Sch
COTTON POOL RD
PAGET CL
WILLOW CL
CHURCH ST
A448
ECHELLS CL
LEADBETTER DR
DAWSON RD
CHURCH LA
MARKET PL
MARKET ST
CROWN CL
Monarch's Way
Cemy
TIMBERHONGER LA
WHITFORD RD
BROMSGROVE
Tickeridge Farm
Whitford Farm
WHITFORD RD
ST JOHN ST
HIGH ST
B4184
SANDERS IND EST 1
WESTBOURNE TERR 2
WESTBOURNE CL 3
DEANSWAY
TINTERN CL
WALTHAM CL
St John's Sch
PERRY LA
HANOVER ST
WORCESTER RD
PO
P
PARADE ROW
STATION ST
Ct
BUCKFAST CL
MEDIBURN CL
WESTMINSTER CL
HIGH FIELDS
FACTORY LA
GAS SQ
SANDERS RD
B4091
HILL LA
HANOVER PL
OLD STATION RD
GUILD RD 1
THE CRESCENT 2
CARDINAL CRES
BYLANDS
MILLFIELD RD
BARNFIELD RD
SHRUBBERY RD
BROOK RD
FORD RD
WORCESTER RD
PETER'S FINGER
Bromsgrove Sch
CONWAY RD
DOVEDALE RD
MARTIN CL
Sch
B4091
B60
Bromsgrove Lower Sch
M5
93
A
B
94
C
D
95
E
F

150

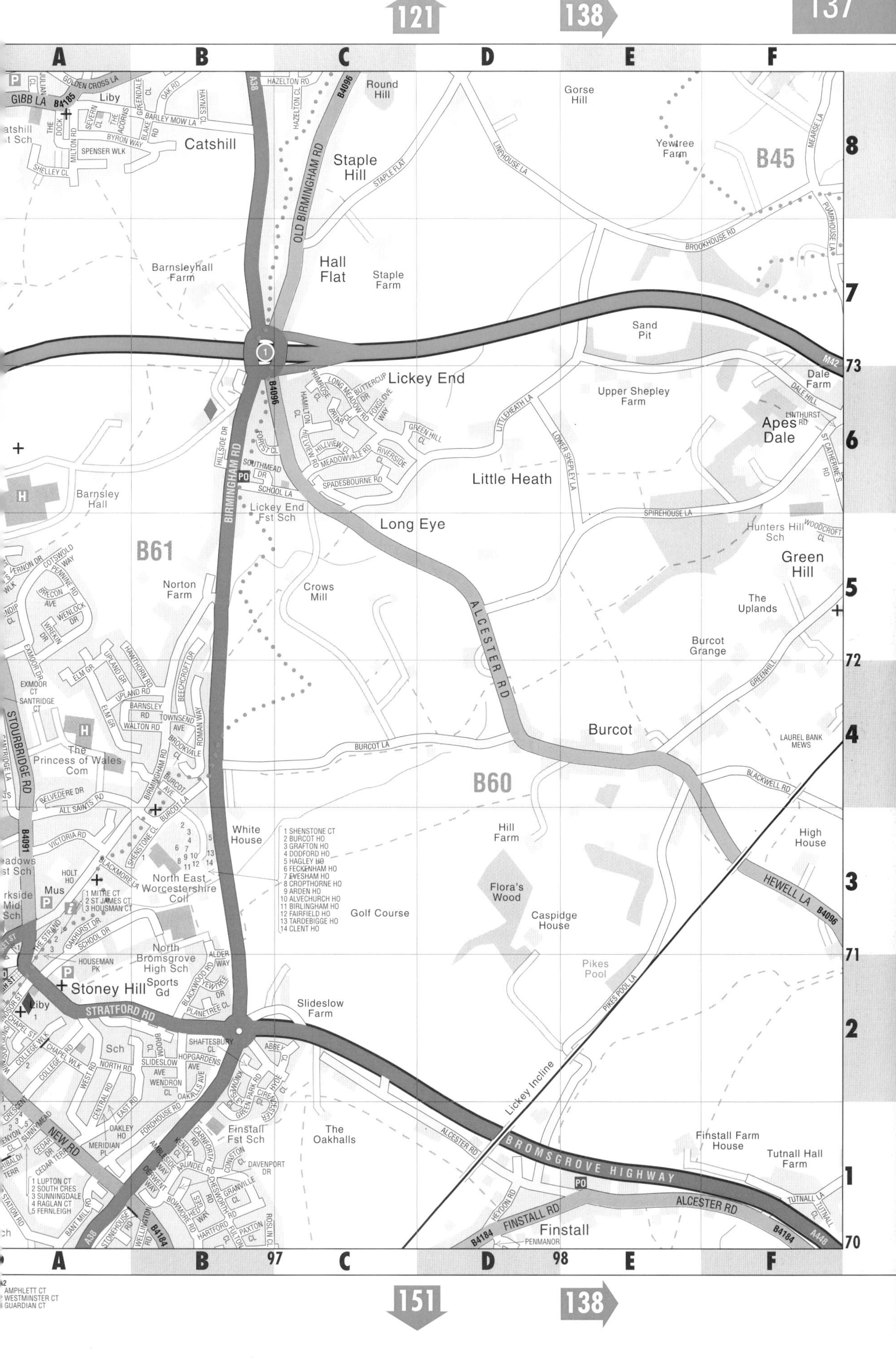

137 122

A B C D E F

8

Brook House

Plymouth Dr
WOOD WD LA
PLYMOUTH RD
WOODSIDE DR
GORSE MEADOW DR
TWATLING RD

Fiery Hill

CHERRY HILL RD
CHERRY HILL DR
CHERRY HILL AVE
OAKDENE DR
FIERY HILL RD
BELGE PARK DR
WILLOW TREE DR

B4120
BITTELL RD
B4120

St Andrew's Sch
GREENBANK
PENZER DR
POPLAR DR
ORCHARD PL
HEWELL RD
RIDGE TERR
BITTELL LA

PO

BROOKHOUSE RD

Barnt Green

SHEPLEY RD

B45

Barnt Green

HEWELL LA

SANDHILLS RD

SANDHILLS LA

The Paddocks

B4120
BITTELL RD

7

BILLY LA

FROGMOOR DR

THE LONGLANDS

Sandhills Gn

SANDHILLS LA

Sandhills Farm

M

PIKE HILL

LINTHURST RD

Linthurst Court

AQUEDUCT LA

73

M42

PIKE HILL

Masts

COOPERS HILL

Uplands

BIRCHES LA

WITHYBED LA

6

THE AVENUE

High Croft

Withybed Green

REAR COTTS
FRONT COTTS
FORWARD COTTS

Linthurst Prim Sch

Linthurst

TANGLEWOOD CL

THE GLEN

BADGERS WAY

PIPES CL

LINTHURST NEWTOWN

BLACKWELL RD

FOXHILL BARNS

B48

FOXHILL LA

ST CATHERINES CL

ST CATHERINE'S RD

Blackwell

GLENEAGLES DR

BIRKDALE AVE

WENTWORTH DR

FARMERS CL

AGMORE RD

Wheeley Farm

WHEELEY RD

Gorsey Lane Farm

Foxhill House

SCARFIELD HILL

Scarfields Farm

PO

5

CH

Golf Course

COBLEY HILL

Scarfields Dingle

72

STATION COTTS

STATION RD

Mast

Cobley Hill Farm

Cobley Hill

GRANGE LA

4

Blackwell Court

AGMORE RD

B60

Andrew's Coppice

3

Vigo

HOLLOW TREE LA

Hollow Tree Farm

Cattespool

Sunny Bank Farm

Worcester and Birmingham Canal

71

B4096

Robin Hill Farm

AGMORE LA

STONEY LA

Stoney Lane Farm

Shortwood Rough Grounds

2

HEWELL LA

Stoney Lane Cottage

Tunnel

Little Shortwood

The Lower House

WHARF LA

Bromsgrove Private

H

1

TUTNALL LA

Broad Green

Works

Oxleasows Farm

B97

B4096

BROCKHILL LA

70

99 A 00 B C 01 D E F

123
140
A
B
C
D
E
F
Hopwood Park Service Area
Little Radford Farm
PESTILENCE LA
A441
BITTELL RD
REDDITCH RD B4120
Lane House
AQUEDUCT LA
OLD BIRMINGHAM RD
The Leys
Radford Farm
RADFORD RD
The Old Rectory
OLD RECTORY LA
M42
The Lightwoods
Longfield Manor
Playing Field
Alvechurch
Fst & Mid Schs
Liby
Robin Hill Farm
The Moat House
THE SQUARE
TANYARD LA
TANYARD CL
MEADOW LA
RED LION ST
BEARHILL DR
Mill Farm
SWAN ST
ST LAURENCE CL
SCHOOL LA
River Arrow
B48
Rowney Green Farm
Rowney Green Court
Alpine Lodge Farm
High House Farm
STATION RD
SCARFIELD HILL
THE LEWKNER ALMSHOUSES
Alvechurch
Worcester and Birmingham Canal
Lodge Farm
Lye Meadows
Newbourne Hill
ROWNEY GREEN LA
ROCKWELL LA
Rowney Green
NEWBOURNE HILL
CHAPEL LA
Lye Bridge Farm
Lye Bridge
GRAVEL PIT LA
REDDITCH RD
Peck Wood
Woodlands Farm
Lower Rowney Green
GRANGE LA
THE HOLLOWAY
STORRAGE LA
Grange Farm
Bordesley Hall Farm
Bordesley Hall
Shortwood Dingle
Cobb's Barn Farm
Bordesley Park
B97
Road under construction
BIRMINGHAM RD
Bordesley
B98
Butler's Wood Cottage
8
7
73
6
5
72
4
3
71
2
1
70
02
03
04
153
140

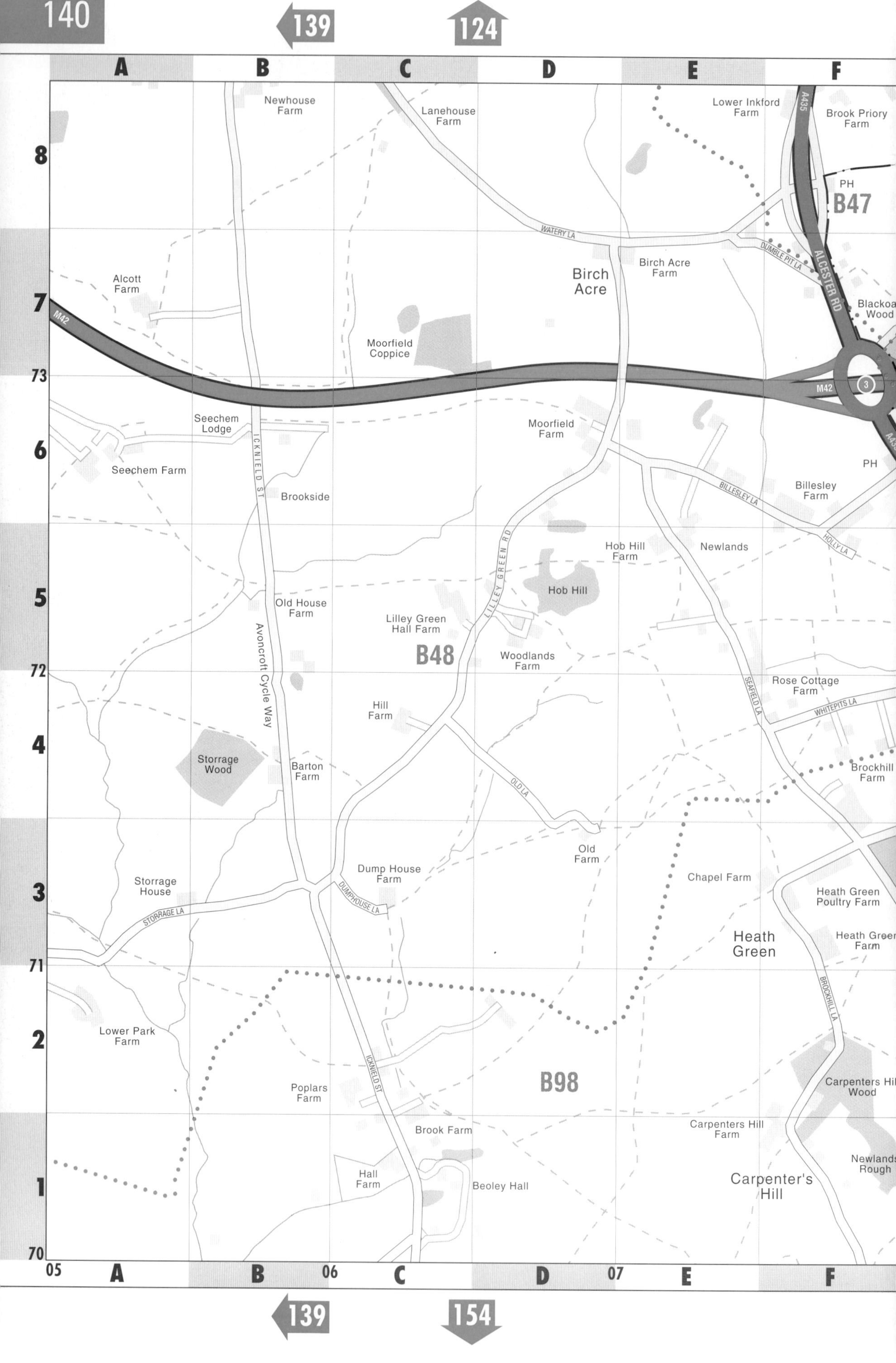

125
142

A
B
C
D
E
F
River Cole
MILL LA
FORSHAW HEATH RD
The Poplars
Terry's Pool
Clowes Wood
8
47
Pound Close Farm
CLOWESWOOD LA
The Lakes
Forshaw Heath
Terry's Green
Graves Coppice
POOLHEAD LA
MALTHOUSE LA
SPRINGBROOK LA
White House Farm
FORSHAW HEATH LA
JUGGINS LA
OAKTREE FARM MOBILE HOMES PK
7
Springbrook Farm
Yew Tree Farm
Forshaw Park Farm
Glebe Farm
Checkley's Coppice
73
The Plantation
The Lyndons
Small Lane Farm
SMALL LA
Spring Brook
EARLSWOOD TRAD EST
Sewage Works
Rugby Football Ground
BIDDLES HILL
6
M42
Tyler's Grove
Windmill Naps
B48
Portway
5
POOLHEAD LA
Ladbrookpark Coppice
Poolhead Farm
B94
WOOD END LA
Holly Farm
72
Golf Course
ALCESTER RD
Cottage Farm
Ladbrooke Hall Farm
Little Ladbrooke Farm
Ladbrooke Hall
Wood End
PH
B4101
4
Lion Wood
PENN LA
CH
ALCESTER RD
BROCKHILL LA
Wood End
Hill Barn
WOODCOCK CL
3
RUSHBROOK LA
Rushbrook
Rushbrook Farm
VICARAGE HILL
High Park Farm
BROAD LA
Gilbert's Green
71
Spring Brook
Highpark Wood
B98
SEAFIELD LA
2
ASPLEY HEATH LA
ARDEN LEYS
Park Farm
River Alne
Branson's Cross
Aspley Heath
ASPLEY HEATH
PH
Baylis Green
BLIND LA
BEOLEY LA
BROAD LA
CHERRY PIT LA
Pinkfield Wood
1
BATES LA
Branson's Cross Farm
Aspley Farm
B4101
A435
Alderhanger Wood
70
A
B
09
C
D
10
E
F

142

141
126

A
B
C
D
E
F
8
7
73
6
5
72
4
3
71
2
1
70
11
12
13
MALTHOUSE LA
VALLEY RD
SHUTT LA
PH
PO
P
B4102
Warren Farm
Windmill Pool
Earlswood Court
SALTER ST
Waring's Green Farm
WARINGS GREEN RD
Waring's Green
DYERS LA
M42
SCHOOL RD
TINKERS LA
Stratford-upon-Avon Canal
High Chimneys Farm
Rotheram's Farm
SCHOOL
The Old Moathouse
Terry's Green
Flower Knott Cottage
TINKERS LA
Clay Bank Farm
CUT THROAT LA
Acorn Coppice
Woodlands Farm
Mast
ROTHERHAMS OAK LA
Cottage Farm
SPRINGBROOK LA
EARLSWOOD COMM
UMBERSLADE RD
Old Grove Wood
Heath Far
Wychpitts Farm
Arnold's Wood
Old Grove
The Beeches
TITHE BARN LA
3a
Three Gables Wood Farm
Abbey Farm
The Priory
Chamber's Coppice
Chalcot Wood
Jonathan's Farm
M42
Wood's Coppice
Bissell's Coppice
M42
M40
Clarksland Coppice
B94
Birchy Cross
B4102
Beaumont Hill Farm
BROAD LA
Birchy Cross Farm
Brown's Green
B4101
POUND HOUSE LA
Works
Brown's Green
Tom Hill
Brook House Farm
Brown's Green Wood
Umberslade Hall
UMBERSLADE RD
TOM HILL
South Lodge
Knowlebury Cross
VICARAGE HILL
The Vicarage
BELLFIELD
BUTTS LA
Tanworth-in-Arden
Tanworth-in-Arden CE Sch
The Leasowes Children's Farm
Dairy House Farm
BATES LA
PO
OVERBARE CL
WELL LA
Oxstalls Farm House
Cank Farm
KEMPS GREEN
Sewage Works
DANZEY GREEN LA
Robin Hood Farm

141

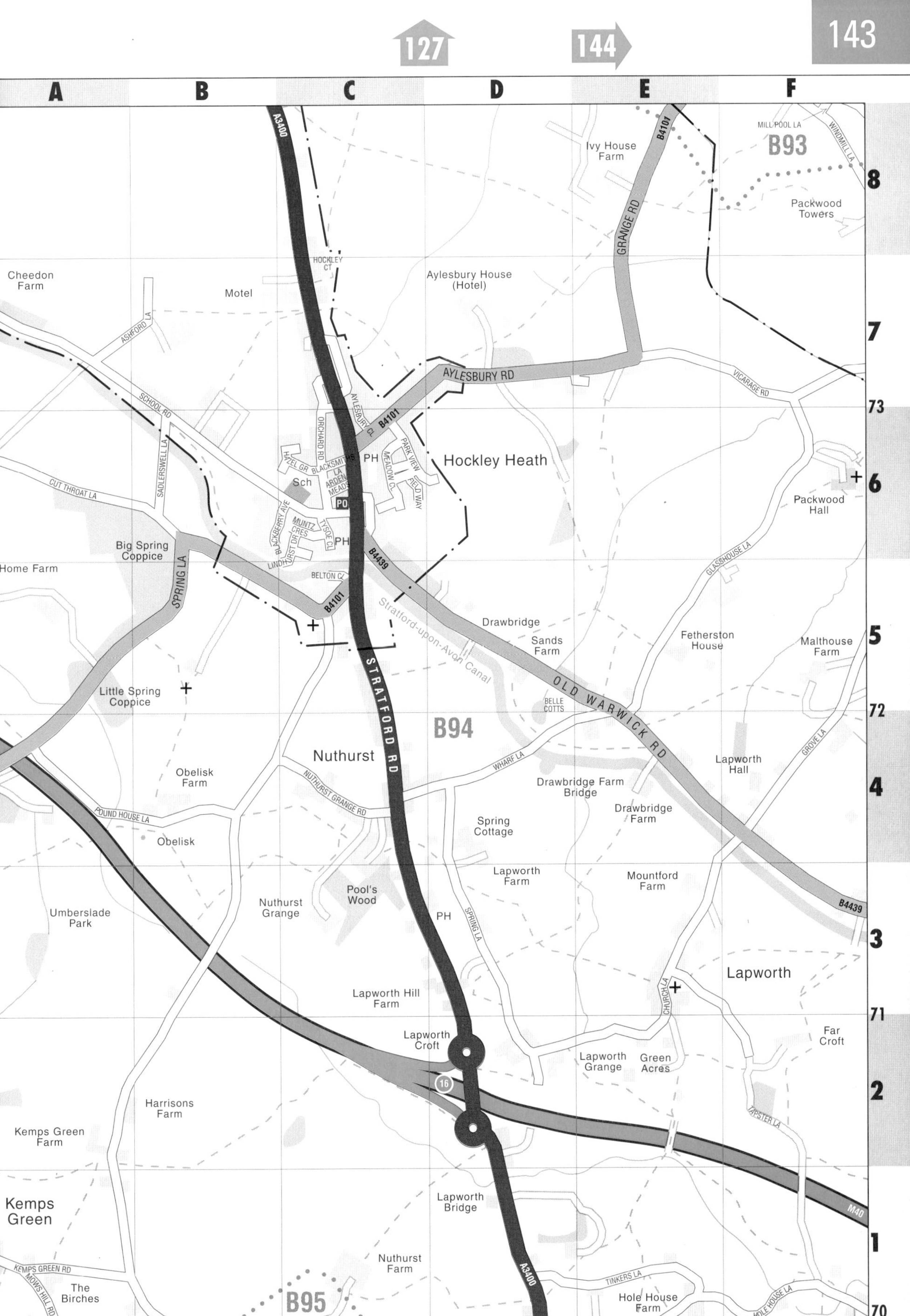

A B C D E F

8

7

73

B93

MILL POOL LA

WINDMILL LA

Packwood
Towers

Ivy House
Farm

GRANGE RD

B4101

VICARAGE RD

Cheedon
Farm

Motel

ASHFORD LA

SCHOOL RD

HOCKLEY
CT

Aylesbury House
(Hotel)

AYLESBURY RD

Hockley Heath

AYLESBURY CL

ORCHARD RD

B4101

PARK VIEW

MEADOW CL

FIELD WAY

PH

SADLERSWELL LA

CUT THROAT LA

HAZEL GR

BLACKSMITHS
LA

ARDEN
MEAD

Sch

PO

MUNTZ
CRES

GORSE CL

BLACKBERRY LANE

LINDHURST DRIVE

PH

+

Packwood
Hall

6

Home Farm

Big Spring
Coppice

SPRING LA

BELTON CL

B4101

B4439

Stratford-upon-Avon Canal

Drawbridge

Sands
Farm

Fetherston
House

GLASSHOUSE LA

Malthouse
Farm

5

Little Spring
Coppice

+

+

STRATFORD RD

B94

Nuthurst

NUTHURST GRANGE RD

WHARF LA

BELLE
COTTS

OLD WARWICK RD

Lapworth
Hall

GROVE LA

72

Obelisk
Farm

POUND HOUSE LA

Drawbridge Farm
Bridge

Drawbridge
Farm

B4439

4

Obelisk

Spring
Cottage

Lapworth
Farm

Mountford
Farm

Umberslade
Park

Nuthurst
Grange

Pool's
Wood

PH

SPRING LA

Lapworth

3

Harrisons
Farm

Lapworth Hill
Farm

CHURCH LA

+

Lapworth
Grange

Green
Acres

Far
Croft

71

Kemps Green
Farm

16

Lapworth
Croft

TAPSTER LA

2

Kemps
Green

KEMPS GREEN RD

MORRS HILL RD

The
Birches

B95

Nuthurst
Farm

Lapworth
Bridge

A3400

TINKERS LA

Hole House
Farm

MOLE HOUSE LA

M40

1

70

4 A B 15 C D 16 E F

143

128

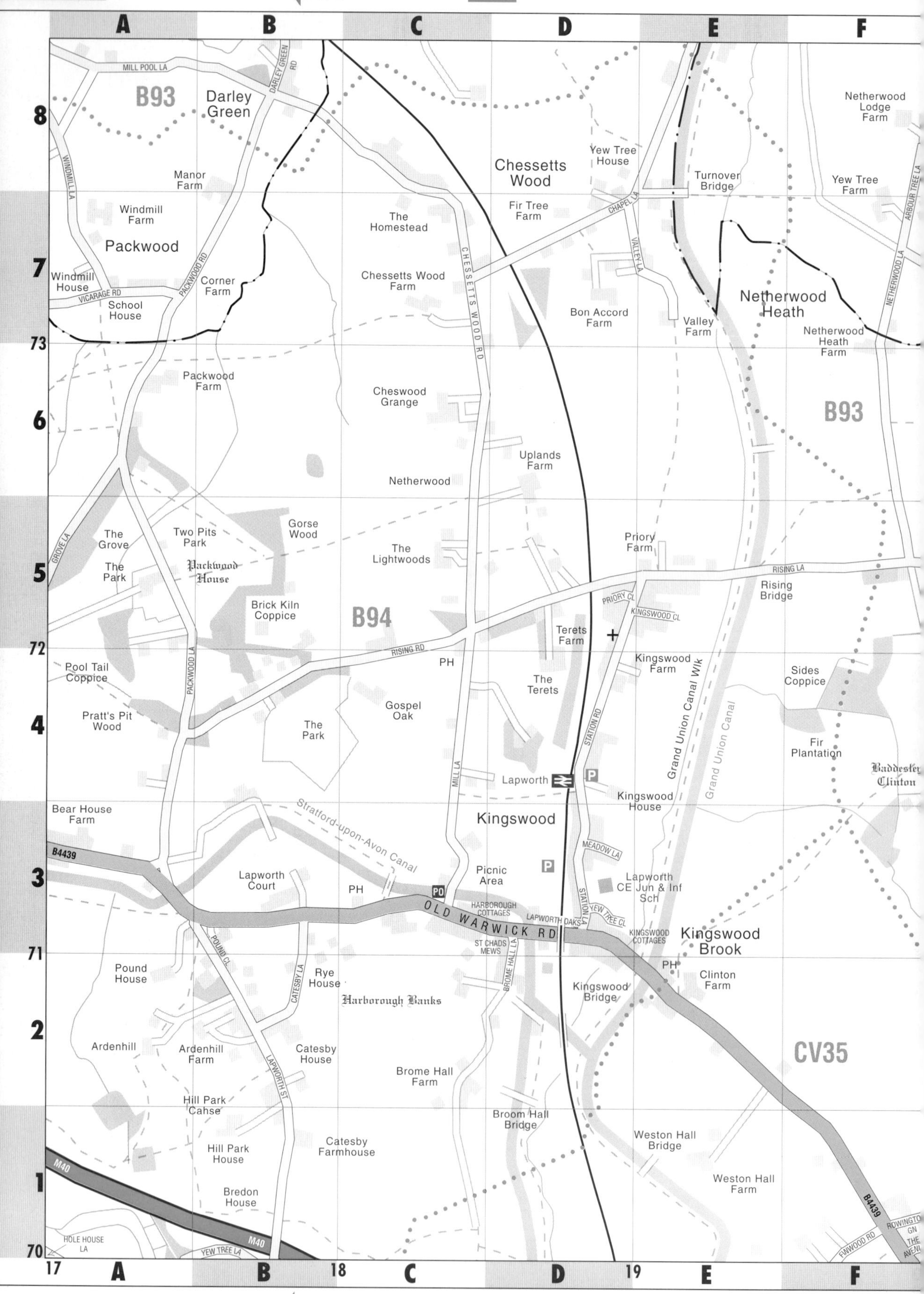
A
B
C
D
E
F
8
7
73
6
5
72
4
3
71
2
1
70
17
18
19
MILL POOL LA
DARLEY GREEN RD
B93
Darley Green
Manor Farm
WINDMILL LA
Windmill Farm
Packwood
Windmill House
VICARAGE RD
School House
PACKWOOD RD
Corner Farm
The Homestead
Chessetts Wood
Fir Tree Farm
Yew Tree House
CHAPEL LA
VALLEY LA
Turnover Bridge
Netherwood Lodge Farm
Yew Tree Farm
ARBOUR TREE LA
NETHERWOOD LA
Chessetts Wood Farm
CHESSETTS WOOD RD
Bon Accord Farm
Valley Farm
Netherwood Heath
Netherwood Heath Farm
Packwood Farm
Cheswood Grange
B93
Uplands Farm
Netherwood
GROVE LA
The Grove
Two Pits Park
Gorse Wood
The Lightwoods
Priory Farm
RISING LA
The Park
Packwood House
Brick Kiln Coppice
B94
PRIORY CL
KINGSWOOD CL
Rising Bridge
Terets Farm
RISING RD
PH
Pool Tail Coppice
PACKWOOD LA
Kingswood Farm
The Terets
Sides Coppice
Pratt's Pit Wood
The Park
Gospel Oak
STATION RD
Grand Union Canal Wlk
Grand Union Canal
Fir Plantation
MILL LA
Lapworth
Baddesley Clinton
Kingswood House
Bear House Farm
Stratford-upon-Avon Canal
Kingswood
B4439
MEADOW LA
Picnic Area
Lapworth Court
PH
PO
Lapworth CE Jun & Inf Sch
HARBOROUGH COTTAGES
OLD WARWICK RD
LAPWORTH OAKS
STATION LA
YEW TREE CL
KINGSWOOD COTTAGES
Kingswood Brook
POUND CL
ST CHADS MEWS
BROME HALL LA
PH
Clinton Farm
Pound House
CATESBY LA
Rye House
Harborough Banks
Kingswood Bridge
Ardenhill
Ardenhill Farm
Catesby House
LAPWORTH ST
CV35
Brome Hall Farm
Hill Park Cahse
Broom Hall Bridge
Weston Hall Bridge
Hill Park House
Catesby Farmhouse
M40
Weston Hall Farm
Bredon House
B4439
HOLE HOUSE LA
M40
YEW TREE LA
FINWOOD RD
ROWINGTON GN
THE AVENUE

143

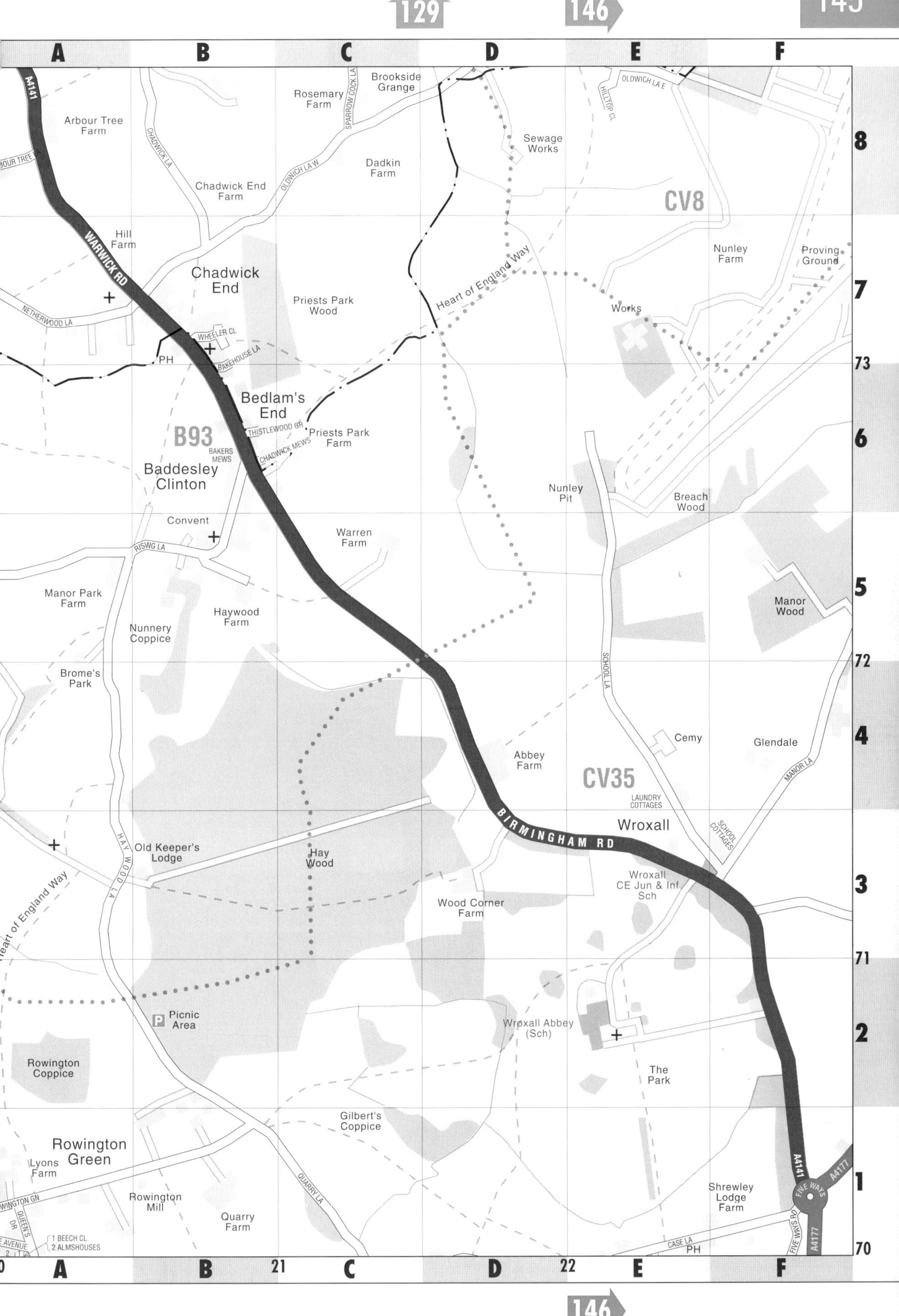
A
B
C
D
E
F
Brookside Grange
Rosemary Farm
SPARROW COCK LA
OLDWICH LA E
HILLTOP CL
Arbour Tree Farm
A4141
CHADWICK LA
Sewage Works
Dadkin Farm
OLDWICH LA W
Chadwick End Farm
CV8
Hill Farm
WARWICK RD
Chadwick End
Nunley Farm
Proving Ground
Priests Park Wood
Heart of England Way
NETHERWOOD LA
WHEELER CL
Works
BAKEHOUSE LA
PH
Bedlam's End
THISTLEWOOD GR
Priests Park Farm
B93
BAKERS MEWS
CHADWICK MEWS
Baddesley Clinton
Nunley Pit
Breach Wood
Convent
Warren Farm
RISWG LA
Manor Park Farm
Haywood Farm
Manor Wood
Nunnery Coppice
SCHOOL LA
Brome's Park
Cemy
Glendale
Abbey Farm
CV35
MANOR LA
LAUNDRY COTTAGES
BIRMINGHAM RD
Wroxall
SCHOOL COTTAGES
HAY WOOD LA
Old Keeper's Lodge
Hay Wood
Wroxall CE Jun & Inf Sch
Heart of England Way
Wood Corner Farm
Picnic Area
Wroxall Abbey (Sch)
Rowington Coppice
The Park
Gilbert's Coppice
Rowington Green
Lyons Farm
QUARRY LA
A4177
FIVE WAYS
Shrewley Lodge Farm
ROWINGTON GN
Rowington Mill
Quarry Farm
QUEEN'S DR
1 BEECH CL
2 ALMSHOUSES
CASE LA
PH
FIVE WAYS RD
8
7
73
6
5
72
4
3
71
2
1
70
21
22

← 145

↑ 130

A **B** **C** **D** **E** **F**

8

Proving Ground

Pear Tree Farm

HONILEY RD

MEER END RD A4177

Blenheim Farm

Runway Farm

Croft Farm

Black Hill Wood

Rudfyn Manor

Poors Wood

7

HOLLY FARM BSNS PK

Wattcote Farm

73

Warriors Lodge Farm

CHASE LA

HONILEY RD

6

CV8

Chase Wood

Honiley Boot (PH)

Yew Tree Cottage

Church Farm

Honiley

5

MANOR LA

Honiley Hall

Featherstons Grove

72

Clattyland Wood

Thorny Coppice

Grove Farm

4

Grove Cottage

Wakefield Wood

PO

3

Haseley Knob

CV35

Hill Farm Cottage

71

Cheyneys Farm

SCHOOL CROFT

Hill Farm

Fernwood Farm

2

HEATH TERR

BUTLERS END

BARRACKS LA

ROUNOIL LA

The Glade

Haseleygreen Farm

Beausale

Lyon Farm

Elmwood Farm

A4177

Holly Farm

KITES NEST LA

Camphill Farm

1

70

23 **A** **B** 24 **C** **D** 25 **E** **F**

A B C D E F

8 Crackley Wood

Engadine House

Camp Farm

Spring Farm

BIRMINGHAM RD
A452

RED LA

Finham Brook

Little Chase Farm

South Chase Farm

St Augustine's RC Comb Sch

The Spring

7

CHASE LA

East Chase Farm

Priors Field Comb Sch

BEEHIVE HILL

Upper Spring La

73

COVENTRY RD A429

B4103

Pleasance Farm

CLINTON LA

KENILCOURT

Grange Ave

PRIORSFIELD RD

COBBS TERR

DE MONTFORT RD

WOODCOTE AVE

Quarry Rd

Rose Croft

Amherst Rd

Malthouse La

Fernhill

FIELDGATE LA

FIELDGATE LAWN

Water Tower La

6

Castle Green

AVENUE RD

CLINTON AVE

Bromley Cl

Berkeley Rd

Elmbank Rd

Fancott Dr

MONMOUTH DR

NEW ST

PO

A429

Sch

MANOR RD

GLOUCESTER ST

LAWRENCE GDNS

SCHOOL LA

The Pleasance

Castle Green

HAMMONDS TERR

PURLIEU LA

ELIZABETH WAY

CASTLE HILL

High St

Pears Ct

BRIDGE ST

Avon Ct

PRESCELLY CT

5

High House Farm

Kenilworth Castle

Finham Brook

Abbey Fields

Kenilworth Hall Mews 1
Holmes Ct 2

ROSEMARY MEWS 3
RICHARDS CL 4
THE ABBEY 5
FIELD HO 6
MONTPELIER HO 7
CHURCH DR 8
CONISTON GRANGE 9

ROSEMARY HILL

ROSEMARY HILL

Upper

PRIORY RD A452

B4104

72

CV8

CASTLE RD

CASTLE GR

B4104

FORREST RD

BORROWELL LA

ABBEY HILL

ABBEY END

LADY LA

Belmont Mews

HIBBERD RD

SOUTHBANK RD

TANNERY

PRIORY HO

Quail Cottage

BORROWELL TERR

SMALLEY PL

THE SQUARE

HIGHFIELD CL

i

Margetts

BARROWFIELD LA

Station Rd

Talisman Sq

P

4

Grounds Farm

KENILWORTH

BROOKSIDE AVE

MERCIA AVE

GREVILLE RD

Liby

BARROWFIELD CT

WARWICK RD

BERTIE RD

HAGER CT

B4103

A452

Centenary Way

Clinton Comb Sch

FISHPONDS RD

WILLOUGHBY AVE

ARCHER RD

AVON RD

ANGLESS WAY

SIDDELEY AVE

BARROW RD

TALISMAN CL

RANDALL RD

QUEENS RD

REGENCY DR

John Nash Sq

Servite Ho

3

Cemy

ST NICHOLAS AVE

DRYDEN AVE

QUEENS ST

MOORLANDS AVE

Moorlands Lodge

Oaks Farm

JOHN O GAUNT RD

CAESAR RD

THE MEWS

PO

Oaks Prec

SCOTT RD

OAKS RD

CHESTNUT AVE

STANLEY RD

FAIRCROFT

ROSELAND RD

GUY RD

LEYCESTER RD

71

PERCY CRES

FARM RD

PERCY RD

LANCASTER RD

BEAUCHAMP RD

St Johns Mid Sch

MORTIMER RD

2

Fernhill Farm

ESSEX CL

DUDLEY RD

Bulkington

Ford

ROUNDS HILL

BEECHWOOD CROFT

COUNCIL LA

SOVEREIGN CL

Kenilworth Sch Castle Sixth Form Ctr

GYPSY LA

TOWERS CL

Roundshill Farm

1

HUNT PADDOCKS

70

A B 27 C D 28 E F

Crackley Farm
Ind Est
Crackley
Millburn Grange
CV4
West Brid
Kingswood House
The Dalehouse
Four Winds
Kingswood Riding School
Ladyes Hills
St Joseph's Sch
Ind Est
Finham Brook
DALEHOUSE LA
Centenary Way
Golf Course
Mill End
CH
Park Hill
South Crest
Park Hill Cty Mid Sch
Southcrest Farm
KENILWORTH
CV8
Whitemoor
Crewe Gardens
Crewe Farm
Kenilworth Sch
Woodside
Glasshouse Wood
Grecian Lodges
River Avon
Thorns Cty Fst Sch
Windy Arbour
The Grove
Thickthorn Wood
Abbey Farm
Ashow
Grove Farm House
Bullimore Wood
River Avon
Bericote Farm
CV32
Dial House Farm
KENILWORTH RD
COVENTRY RD
LEAMINGTON RD
WARWICK RD
WAVERLEY RD
PRIORY RD
ROCKY LA
CREW LA
COMMON LA

A   B   C   D   E   F

8

7

73

6

5

72

4

3

71

2

1

70

A   33   C   34   E   F

CV3

Pypes Mill House

The Rough

A46

B4115

B4113

Works

Manor Fields

COVENTRY RD

Gospel Oak

Chantry Heath Wood

Stoneleigh Grange

River Sowe

Kings Wood

ACORN CL

HALL CL

DUDLEY TERR

BIRMINGHAM RD

STONELEIGH CL

Stoneleigh

Stoneleigh Bridge

Chantry Heath Cottages

THE BANK

THE GREEN

WALKERS ORCH

VICARAGE RD

CHURCH LA

SCHOOL BELL MEWS

Sowe Mouth

Motslow Hill

Motslowhill Spinney

River Avon

Coach Bridge

CH

Cloud Bridge

Golf Course

Tantara Lodge

CV8

Gilbert's Spinney

Centenary Way

Sewage Works

Stoneleigh Deer Park

Waverley Farm

National Agricultural Ctr

Starr Bridge

STONELEIGH RD

Stoneleigh Park

Park Farm

Stareton

Ticknell Spinney

Home Farm

Hares Parlour

River Avon

Brick Kiln Spinney

A445

Decoy Spinney

Stone House Farm

CV32

LEICESTER LA

COVENTRY RD

Furzen Hill Farm

Bericote Wood

B4113

Leicester Lane Cotts

A445

136

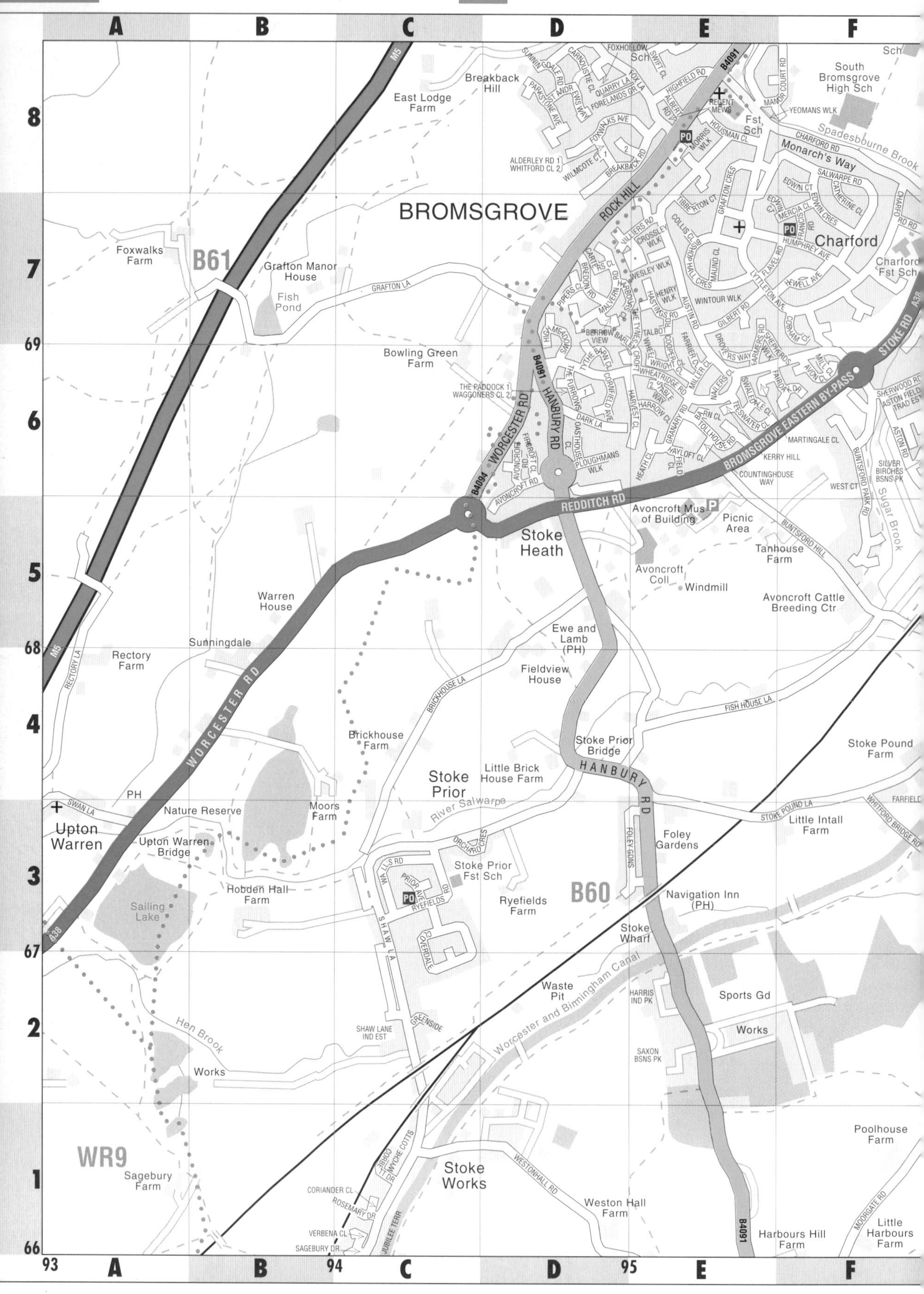
A
B
C
D
E
F
8
7
69
6
5
68
4
3
67
2
1
66
93
94
95
M5
B61
B60
WR9
A38
BROMSGROVE
Breakback Hill
East Lodge Farm
Foxhollow Sch
South Bromsgrove High Sch
Fst Sch
Spadesbourne Brook
Monarch's Way
Charford
Charford Fst Sch
Foxwalks Farm
Grafton Manor House
Fish Pond
GRAFTON LA
Bowling Green Farm
ROCK HILL
B4091
B4094
HANBURY RD
WORCESTER RD
REDDITCH RD
BROMSGROVE EASTERN BY-PASS
STOKE RD
Avoncroft Mus of Building
Picnic Area
Stoke Heath
Tanhouse Farm
Avoncroft Coll
Windmill
Avoncroft Cattle Breeding Ctr
BUNTSFORD HILL
Sugar Brook
Warren House
Sunningdale
Rectory Farm
RECTORY LA
Ewe and Lamb (PH)
Fieldview House
BRICKHOUSE LA
FISH HOUSE LA
Brickhouse Farm
Stoke Prior Bridge
Stoke Pound Farm
Stoke Prior
Little Brick House Farm
River Salwarpe
Moors Farm
Nature Reserve
PH
SWAN LA
Upton Warren
Upton Warren Bridge
Hobden Hall Farm
Sailing Lake
Stoke Prior Fst Sch
Ryefields Farm
STOKE POUND LA
Little Intall Farm
Foley Gardens
Navigation Inn (PH)
Stoke Wharf
Waste Pit
Worcester and Birmingham Canal
HARRIS IND PK
Sports Gd
Works
SAXON BSNS PK
SHAW LA
SHAW LANE IND EST
GREENSIDE
Hen Brook
Works
Sagebury Farm
Stoke Works
WESTONHALL RD
Weston Hall Farm
CORIANDER CL
ROSEMARY DR
VERBENA CL
SAGEBURY DR
JUBILEE TERR
Harbours Hill Farm
Poolhouse Farm
MOORGATE RD
Little Harbours Farm
WHITFORD BRIDGE RD
FARFIELD

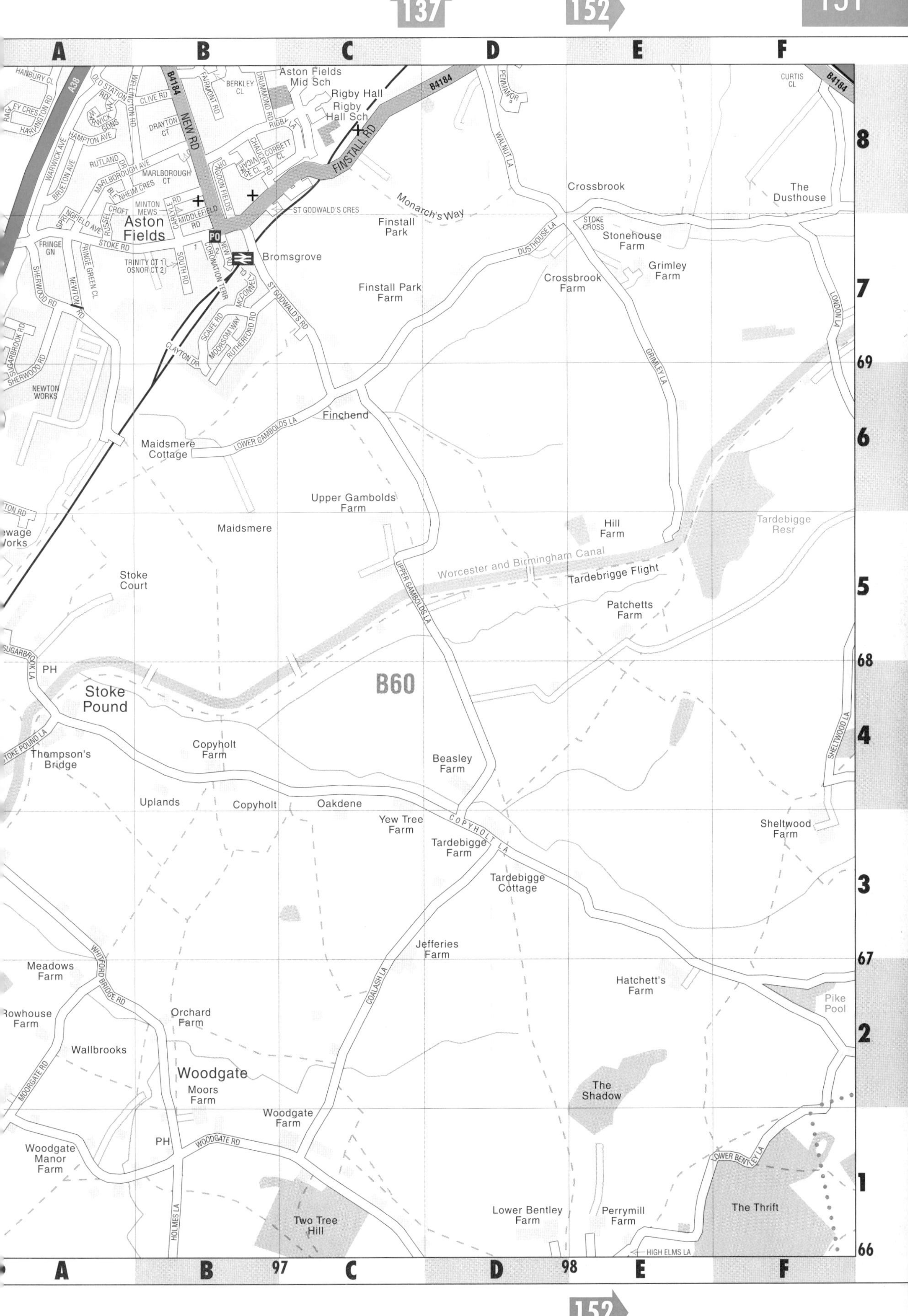
A
B
C
D
E
F
Aston Fields Mid Sch
Rigby Hall
Rigby Hall Sch
FINSTALL RD
B4184
NEW RD
A38
Aston Fields
Bromsgrove
Monarch's Way
Finstall Park
Crossbrook
The Dusthouse
Stonehouse Farm
Grimley Farm
Crossbrook Farm
Finstall Park Farm
NEWTON WORKS
Finchend
Maidsmere Cottage
Upper Gambolds Farm
Maidsmere
Hill Farm
Tardebigge Resr
Worcester and Birmingham Canal
Tardebigge Flight
Stoke Court
Patchetts Farm
PH
Stoke Pound
B60
Copyholt Farm
Thompson's Bridge
Beasley Farm
Uplands
Copyholt
Oakdene
Yew Tree Farm
Tardebigge Farm
Sheltwood Farm
Tardebigge Cottage
Jefferies Farm
Meadows Farm
Hatchett's Farm
Pike Pool
Orchard Farm
Wallbrooks
Woodgate
Moors Farm
The Shadow
Woodgate Farm
PH
Woodgate Manor Farm
The Thrift
Two Tree Hill
Lower Bentley Farm
Perrymill Farm
97
98
8
7
69
6
5
68
4
3
67
2
1
66

151 138

A **B** **C** **D** **E** **F**

B60

Great Shortwood Farm

The Elbows

Hewell Farm

HM Prison

Laurel Covert

Brockhill HM Remand Ctr

Brockhill Farm

A448
B4184

B4096

Tunnel

ALCESTER RD

NEW WHARF COTTS

Hall

Hewell Park

THE PARK

THE DRIVE

LAKESIDE

The Lake

Cladshill

Tardebigge

Tardebigge CE Fst Sch

Worcester & Birmingham Canal

Dialhouse Farm

B4184

PH

HEWELL CL

HM Young Offender Institution (Hewell Grange)

BROMSGROVE HIGHWAY

HEWELL LA

Hewell Kennels

High House Farm

HIGH HOUSE LA

LONDON LA

Nursery

Park Cottages

Batchley Brook

Paper Mill Cottages

B60

Monarch's Way

SHELTWOOD LA

Holyoakes Barn

HOLYOAKES LA

GYPSY LA

Oxstalls Farm

Holyoake's Pit

B97

Tack Farm

B4096

SALTER'S LA

B4...

Sheltwood Range

Cocksian Covert

Foxlydiate Wood

Brotherton's Wood

Sheltwood Cottages

SHELTWOOD LA

Banks Green Farm

Bartles Wood

CUR LA

PH

Hawthorn Pit

BIRCHFIELD RD

A4...

Foxlydiate

Bank's Green

COPYHOLT LA

Lane House Farm

Monarch's Way

REYNARDS CL

HENNALS AVE

MALTBY CL

FOXLYDIATE LA

GRAFTON LA

SHIRE CL

HAMPTON CL

BROTHERTON CL

ISHARE CL

TYNSALL AVE

SANDYGATE CL

Bentley House

Springhill Farm

KNIGHTSFORD CL

MICHAELWOOD CL

LIGHT LA

SHERRY...

MIDDLE RD

BANKS GN

Hennals Wood

Spring Brook

Boxnot Farm

SYDNALL CL

LORDSWOOD CL

SPRINGVALE RD

MEGGY RD

New House Farm

BLACK LAKE LA

Swans Brook

PUMPHOUSE LA

CHURCH RD

HILL TOP

BLACKSTITCH LA

CRUMPFIELDS LA

GREEN LA

Upper Bentley

MANOR RD

ANGEL ST

Callow Farm

Raglis Cottage

Brownlas Farm

99 **A** 00 **B** **C** 01 **D** **E** **F** 66

8

Bordesley

Bordesley Park Farm

7

69

6

DAGNELL END RD   B4101

B4101

BIRMINGHAM RD

Bordesley Bridge

River Arrow

HITHER GREEN LA

Sports & L Ctr

Cemy

Crem

Bordesley Abbey (rems of)

BORDESLEY LA

Visitor Ctr   Riverside

NEEDLE MILL LA

ALVECHURCH HIGHWAY

Mus

FORGE MILL RD

St Stephen's CE Fst & Mid Sch

MEADOW HILL CRES

MEADOWHILL RD

ABBEY GDNS

ST STEPHENS

TERRS CL

5

Works

Red Ditch

B4184   MIDDLEHOUSE LA

Superstore

WINDSOR RD

Enfield

Enfield IND EST

BIRMINGHAM RD

FISHING (ICE RD)

Abbey Trad Ind Area

PROSPECT HILL

ALBERT ST

WELLESBOURNE

LYDNALL CL

MABEY AVE

MALLORD

DALE END

SEDGLEY CL

Abbeydale

B4160   B98   A4023

68

CLADSWORTH HO 1
RADFORD HO 2
WEETHLEY HO 3
ABBERTON HO 4
HADZOR HO 5
STRETTON HO 6
RAGLEY HO 7
ELMLEY HO 8

SALTER'S LA

ASH TREE RD

BIRCHENSALE

HAZEL RD

BRIDLEY MOOR RD

CEDAR VIEW

CEDAR PARK

CEDAR RD

ELM RD

ELM CT

MILL ST

MELEN ST

ABBEY RD

HEWELL RD

CHURCH RD

FIST

ABBEY

CLIVE RD

Coll

Coll

St George's

The Abbey High Sch

A4023

A4023

COVENTRY HIGHWAY

A441

4

Pitcher Oak Sch

B97

1 KEMERTON HO
2 WILMCOTE HO
3 HANBURY HO
4 WOODGATE HO
5 LEDBURY HO

Birchensale Mid Sch

Holyoakes Field Fst Sch

IZOD ST 1
KINGFISHER WLK 2

ADELAIDE ST

BATES HILL

EDWARD ST

BRITTEN ST

BRIDGE ST

REDDITCH

UNICORN

Liby

VINE ST

SILVER ST

MARKET PL

ALCESTER ST

PEAKMAN ST

QUEEN ST

WILLIAM ST

CHURCH GREEN E

Ct

ST GEORGES RD

B4160

OTHER RD

PHILLIPS CL

TERR

BEDLEY RW

TEMPLE RD

Sch

Rowan Cres

FOXLYDIATE CRES

HAWTHORN RD

CADY

CHERRY TREE WK

Queen's Cotts

WILLOW RD

PO

Bridley Moor High Sch

Owans Hill View

Redditch

RINGWAY

STATION WAY

DAILY RD

EVESHAM

IPSLEY ST

THE TRAFFORD PK SMALLWOOD

HOLLOWAY LA

BURTON CL

Sch

BATTENS

3

Batchley Fst Sch

PRIORS OAK

Batchley

PINVIN HO
MORTON HO

PITCHEROAK COTTS

POPLAR RD

WOODLAND RD

BROMSGROVE RD

VICARAGE CRES

VICARAGE HILL

FERNEY HILL AVE

HOLMWOOD DR

VICARAGE VIEW

PROPHETS CL

Cemy

BENTLEY CL

LUDLOW

SOUTH CREST

MOUNT PLEASANT

SOUTH ST

SOUTH WEST AVE

ORCHARD

OSWALD ST

MOUNT ST

MARSDEN RD

GLOVER ST

UNION ST

SUMMER ST

LODGE RD

MILLSBRO RD

Smallwood

SOUTHMEAD CRES

3

67

Foxlydiate Wood

Pitcher Oak Wood

CH

REDDITCH

Golf Course

Cemy

HOLMWOOD HO

MARLPOOL DR

PURSHALL CL

SALOP RD

PLYMOUTH RD

BROMFIELD RD

IVOR RD

HARESFIELD

PARSONS RD

Almshouses

SMALLWOOD

DINGLESIDE

TUNNEL DR

NAILSWORTH RD

SOUTHCREST

HILL

BARLICH WAY

2

Webheath

REYDE

LYNDEWOOD

DINKNALL RD

Sch

Webheath Fst Sch

HELTWOOD

COLEFORD CL

PRINSVALE RD

HEATHFIELD RD

PO

BROMSGROVE

B4504

HIGHWAY

WOODSIDE AVE

MINWORTH CL

WOODEND CL

BIRCHFIELD RD

WOODEND RD

BIRCHILL CL

BASCOTE

ASHTON

ALTON

CARLTON CL

DORRIDGE CL

St Luke's CE Fst Sch

PLYMOUTH CL

PLYMOUTH CT

St Luke's Cotts

RECTORY RD

SOUDAN

TIFFHOUSE

THE MAYFIELDS

GREENFIELD

LILAC RD

LABURNUM

POOL BANK

MYRTLE AVE

PO

Southcrest

Southcrest Wood

COMPTON RD

FORDROAD CT

EASTNOR

ASHPERTON CL

DULAIS CL

BYFORD

BERRYSTONE

BELBROUGHTON RD

ALLINGTON DR

GREENLANDS DR

COLDFIELD DR

DORNSTON DR

EVERLODE

CHADDESLEY CL

Lodge Pool

Lodge Park

LODGE POOL DR

SKILTS AVE

TWINERS RD

CRABTREE CL

HUMBLETON

WIREHILL DR

GRIMLEY

GAYDON

1

Marlpit Farm

Golf Course

WINDMILL DR

BELMONT CL

MARLPIT LA

FECKENHAM RD

MALVERN HO

CHARLES RD

FORDBRIDGE RD

MIDDLE PIECE DR

SHELLEY CL

SPINNEY MEWS

STONEHOUSE CL

CHAPEL CL

ROOKERY CL

HEADLESS CROSS DR

EVESHAM RD

A441

A441

A4189

B4504

GREAT BARN LA

CRANHAM CL

THE MEADWAY

HALLOWFIELD'S

66

E3	E4	
1 CLARKE ST	1 WORCESTER SQ	2 GRANGE RD
2 KINGFISHER SH CTR	2 EVESHAM WLK	3 ST GEORGE'S GDNS
3 EVESHAM SQ	3 NEW WLK	
4 PARK WLK	4 MARKET WLK	
5 GEORGE WLK	5 SMALLWOOD ARCH	
6 ROYAL SQ	6 WELLINGTON ST	
7 WALFORD WLK	7 VICTORIA ST	
8 MILWARD SQ	F4	
9 EVESHAM MEWS	1 GRANGE CT	

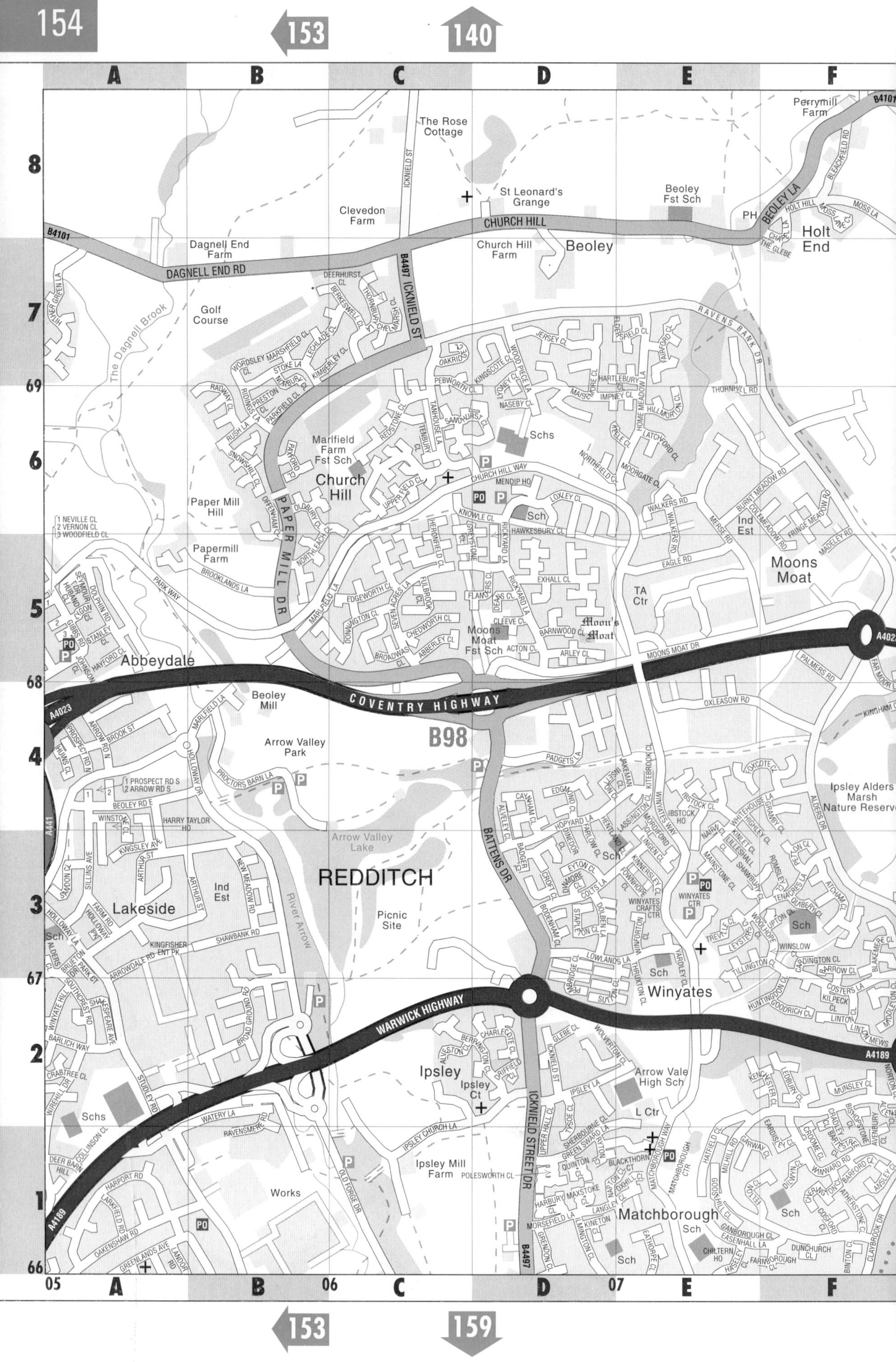

E1
1 NEWSHOLME CL
2 ADDINGHAM CL
3 WATSON CL
4 RYLSTONE WAY
5 KILDWICK WAY

F1
1 HETTON CL
2 BUCKDEN CL
3 LEYBURN CL
4 ARNCLIFFE WAY
5 HUDDISDON CL
6 PHILLIPPES RD

A   B   C   D   E   F

8

CV8

Chesford
Bridge

Field Barn
Farm

Hotel

Hotel

Blackdown
Manor

Bericote
Wood

Cattle Brook

New Farm

BERICOTE RD

Tiger's
Island

7

Wootton
Spinnies

Works

Blackdown

B44

69

THE
MEADOWS

THE HAMLET

THE CROFT RD

TIDMARSH RD

Tower
House

Meadow
Cottage

Stoneleigh RD

SANDY LA

Blackdown
Hill

Hote

HILL WOOTTON RD

Hill Wootton

6

Leek
Wootton

CV35

Sewage
Works

Hill Wootton
Farm

KENILWORTH RD

Woodland
Grange

New House
Farm

5

WARWICK RD

Leek Wootton
CE Fst Sch

The
Warwickshire
Nuffield

H

Cranford

OLD MILVERTON LA

68

Gaveston
Lodge

River Avon

Sandy Lane
Farm

North
Leamington
Sch

GARW

4

B4115

A29

A46

Church
Farm

SANDY LA

CV32

3

COVENTRY RD

Old
Milverton

OLD
MILVERTON

**ROYAL
LEAMINGTON SPA**

VERNON

BRAMBLING GR

THE CLOISTERS 1
BELL TOWER MEWS 2
AMBASSADOR CT 3.

CLOISTER CROFTS

CLOISTER WAY

Manor
Farm

Allot
Gdns

FAIRHURST DR

WOODCOTE RD

WARW

67

A29

RANGE MEADOW CL

HOPTON CROFTS

RAVENSDALE

OLD MILVERTON RD

LAMINTONE DR
COLBOURNE
GROVE DR

OVERELL GR

AVONLEA

DAVIS CL
RISE

EATON
CL

NORTHUMBERLAND RD

LOVEDAY CL

SPILSBURY CL

COLLEGES RD

ONSLOW

STRACHEY AVE

THE MALTINGS

BARLEY
CT

BELL CT

2

Guy's
Well

Guy's
Cave

Guy's
Cliffe

Patten's
Grove

CV34

MILLBANK

KENDAL
AVE

PENRITH

BORROWDALE CL

ENNERDALE CL

WINDERMERE DR

MOSS CL

ASTLEY CL

S WAYS

BEVERLEY RD

WHEATHILL

GREATHEED RD

The Trinity
RC Sch

Milverton

Sch

LILLINGTON AVE

B4087 KENILWORTH RD

A452

LUCAS
HO
9 10   11

B4087

1

Sch

THE SHOPPING
PREC

MAPLE GR

P.O

WINSLOW CL 4
EDWARD ST 3
BIRCHWAY CL 2
BLANDFORD RD 1

WEIR

ST JAMES MEADOW RD

KING DR

ULLSWATER

ST ALBANS

STEPHENSON DR

TROUT ROAD

RYDAL CL

BROOKHURST

SAXON MEADOWS

BEVERLEY RD

ST MARK'S

OLD STONE

RUGBY RD

FREEMANS CL

TRAVERSTON CL

Cemy

Sch

ALBERT
ST

RIDGEWAY

ROCK MILL LA

QUARRY

DERWENT CL

KESWICK CL

CLIFFE

ST MARK'S RD

EATON CL

APLEY MEWS

BEAUCHAMP HILL

UNION RD

HEATH TERR

GULISTAN RD

BINSWOOD ST

WARWICK
TERR

ALBANY
TERR

CLARENDON PL

RATHENA RD

STAMFORD
GDNS

CLARENDON
SQ

RUSSELL ST

WARWICK PL

Schs

Sch

TAVISTOCK ST

CLARENDON AVE

PARADE

CHANDOS ST

BEAUCHAMP AVE

MORRELL ST

PARMITER HO

66

SCH

THE RAILWAY

ARDEN CT

DICKENS RD

CRESFORD CRES

ALL SAINTS RD

A445

B4099 WARWICK RD

P.O

WARWICK ST

A452

WARWICK ST

B4087

29   A   30   B   C   30   D   31   E   F

D1
1 THE GRANGE MEWS
2 CONISTON CT
3 GUNNERY TERR
4 CROSS RD
5 PERCY TERR

E1
1 MILVERTON CRES
2 MILVERTON LODGE
3 MILVERTON CRES W
4 HENRY TANDAY CT
5 VODENA CT
6 GULISTAN CT
7 STUART CT
8 UPPER GROVE ST
9 GROVE ST

F1
1 BEAUCHAMP CT
2 GROSVENOR CT
3 LUNN POLY HO
4 POWERS CT
5 WATERLOO PL
6 CLARENCE TERR
7 CLARENCE MANS
8 WINDSOR PL
9 BEDFORD ST

10 GUY PL W
11 GUY PL E
12 OXFORD PL
13 CHANDOS CT
14 OXFORD ROW
15 WHITEHEADS CT
16 KENILWORTH ST
17 KIMMOND CT

F2
1 CLEVELAND CT
2 ARLINGTON CT
3 RIPLINGHAM
4 WHITE ROSE HO
5 ARLINGTON MEWS
6 WOOTTON CT
7 FININGS CT
8 PEMBROKE CT
9 ENGLAND HO

10 SAUNDERS HO
11 NORWOOD HO
12 BINSWOOD MEWS
13 DORMER HO

149

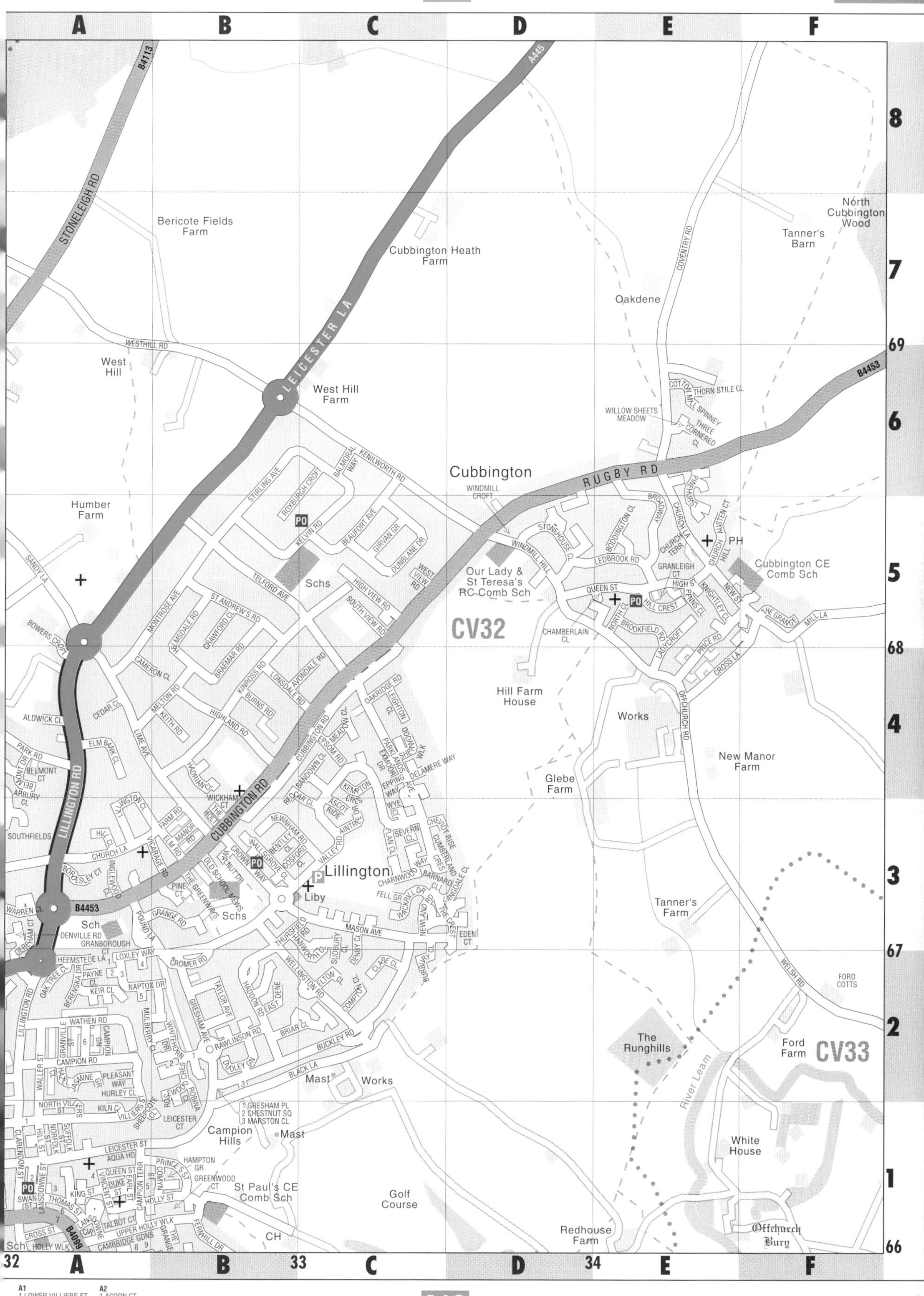

A1
1 LOWER VILLIERS ST
2 LANSDOWNE RD
3 KENNEDY SQ
4 ST PAUL'S SQ
5 MERCHANTS CT
6 LANSDOWNE CRES
7 WILLES RD
8 HANOVER GDNS
9 WHITTLE CT

A2
1 ACORN CT
2 STOCKTON GR
3 WHITACRE RD
4 SHUCKBURGH GR
5 HELLIDON CL
6 BROWNLOW ST

162

153

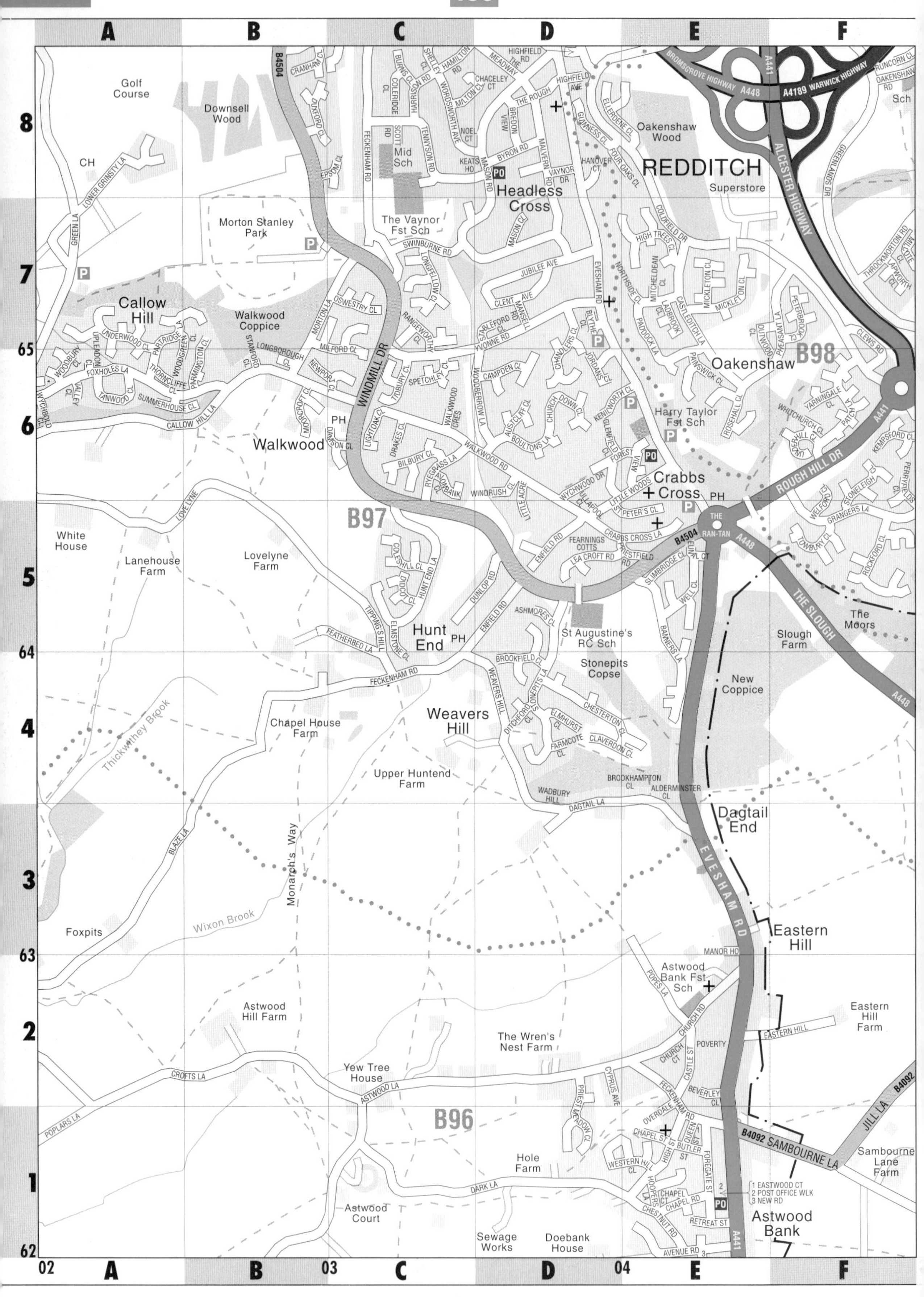

A
B
C
D
E
F
8
7
65
6
5
64
4
3
63
2
1
62
02
03
04
Golf Course
Downsell Wood
CH
Morton Stanley Park
Callow Hill
Walkwood Coppice
Walkwood
White House
Lanehouse Farm
Lovelyne Farm
Mid Sch
The Vaynor Fst Sch
Headless Cross
REDDITCH
Oakenshaw Wood
Superstore
Oakenshaw
B98
Harry Taylor Fst Sch
Crabbs Cross
PH
THE RAN-TAN
B97
Hunt End
St Augustine's RC Sch
Stonepits Copse
Slough Farm
The Moors
New Coppice
Weavers Hill
Chapel House Farm
Upper Huntend Farm
Dagtail End
Thickwithey Brook
Monarch's Way
Foxpits
Wixon Brook
Eastern Hill
Astwood Bank Fst Sch
Astwood Hill Farm
Eastern Hill Farm
The Wren's Nest Farm
Yew Tree House
B96
Hole Farm
Sambourne Lane Farm
Astwood Court
Sewage Works
Doebank House
Astwood Bank
B4504
B4092 SAMBOURNE LA
BROMSGROVE HIGHWAY A448
A4189 WARWICK HIGHWAY
ALCESTER HIGHWAY
A441
A448
WINDMILL DR
EVESHAM RD
ROUGH HILL DR
THE SLOUGH
FECKENHAM RD
CALLOW HILL LA
CROFTS LA
ASTWOOD LA
DARK LA
POPLARS LA
BLAZE LA
LOVE LYNE
JILL LA
1 EASTWOOD CT
2 POST OFFICE WLK
3 NEW RD

A
B
C
D
E
F
Park Farm
Arrow Valley Park
Dingleside Mid Sch
Liby
B98
The Old Forge
Washford
RC Fst Sch
Woodrow
Woodrow Sch
Red Hill
PH
Washford Farm
Hill Crest
L Ctr
The Leys High Sch
Green Lane
Tanhouse Farm
The Alexandra
Wirehill Wood
Wirehill
Washford Bridge
Green Lane Farm
Priory Farm and remains of Priory
Rough Hill Wood
Wapping
Studley Common
Studley Bridge
B97
Ind Est
THE SLOUGH
Works
STATION RD
B80
Studley
Studley High Sch
Thomas Town
The Park
Sch
TROY IND EST
JILL LA
Littlewood Green
BROMSGROVE RD
ALCESTER RD
Holt Farm
Spinney Cottage
Littlewood Green Farm
Reins Farm
Sambourne Reins
B96
Middletown
Elmdale House
Perrymill Farm
Sperrnal Ash
B49
Haydon Way Farm
Sambourne
8
7
65
6
5
64
4
3
63
2
1
62
06
07

155

E6
1 OLD SQ
2 MARKET PL
3 WESTGATE HO
4 PUCKERING'S LA
5 TIBBITS CT
6 THE GUILD COTTS

7 LEYCESTER CT
8 MARKS MEWS
9 EASTGATE MEWS
10 EASTGATE HO
11 ALMSHOUSES
12 GERRARD ST

F7
1 ALEXANDER CT
2 BARTLETT CL
3 JAMES CT
4 ST JOHN'S CT
5 CASTLEGATE MEWS
6 AVERY CT

8 GOODWAY CT
9 PRIORY WLK
10 CROSS ST
11 GARDEN CT
12 YEOMANRY CL

F7
1 FAIRFAX CT

F8
1 PEMBROKE CL
2 ARUNDEL CL
3 CORNWALL CL
4 CROSS FIELDS RD
5 MULBERRY DR
6 ROWAN DR

7 GAVESTON C

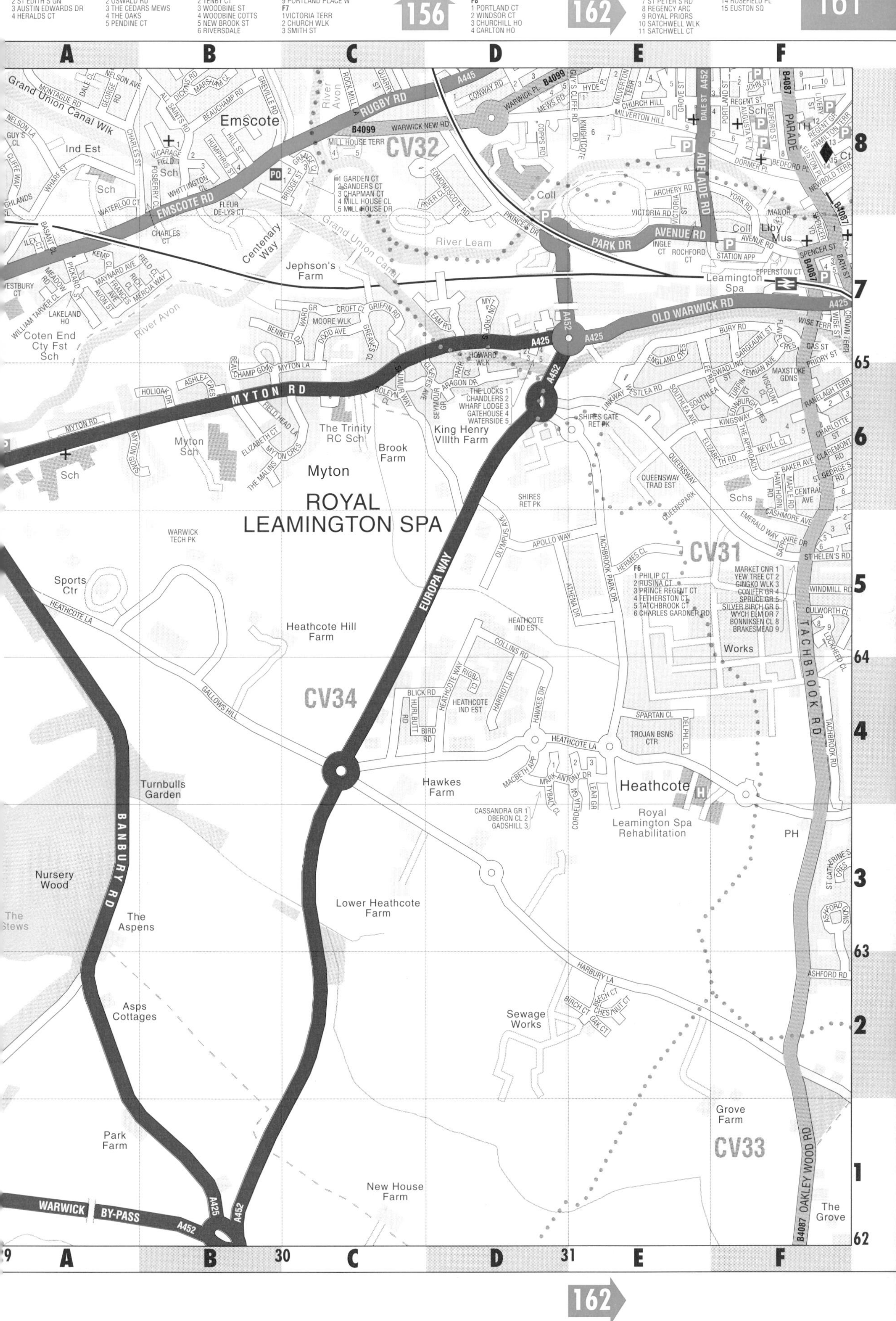

161
B8
1 ST EDITH'S HO
2 ST EDITH'S GN
3 AUSTIN EDWARDS DR
4 HERALDS CT
D8
1 WESTGROVE TERR
2 OSWALD RD
3 THE CEDARS MEWS
4 THE OAKS
5 PENDINE CT
E8
1 LYNDON CT
2 TENBY CT
3 WOODBINE ST
4 WOODBINE COTTS
5 NEW BROOK ST
6 RIVERSDALE
7 MILVERTON CT
8 SOMERS PL
9 PORTLAND PLACE W
F7
1 VICTORIA TERR
2 CHURCH WLK
3 SMITH ST
156
4 BATH PL
5 ABBOTTS ST
F8
1 PORTLAND CT
2 WINDSOR CT
3 CHURCHILL HO
4 CARLTON HO
162
5 PORTLAND PL E
6 PORTLAND PL
7 ST PETER'S RD
8 REGENCY ARC
9 ROYAL PRIORS
10 SATCHWELL WLK
11 SATCHWELL CT
12 DENBY BLDGS
13 ROSEFIELD WLK
14 ROSEFIELD PL
15 EUSTON SQ
A
B
C
D
E
F
Grand Union Canal Wlk
Emscote
Ind Est
RUGBY RD
B4099
CV32
EMSCOTE RD
1 GARDEN CT
2 SANDERS CT
3 CHAPMAN CT
4 MILL HOUSE CL
5 MILL HOUSE DR
River Leam
PARK DR
AVENUE RD
ADELAIDE RD
PARADE
Leamington Spa
Centenary Way
Jephson's Farm
Grand Union Canal
River Avon
OLD WARWICK RD
A425
A452
Coten End Cty Fst Sch
MYTON RD
The Trinity RC Sch
Brook Farm
King Henry VIIIth Farm
Myton Sch
Myton
ROYAL LEAMINGTON SPA
QUEENSWAY TRAD EST
SHIRES RET PK
CV31
F6
1 PHILIP CT
2 RUSINA CT
3 PRINCE REGENT CT
4 FETHERSTON CT
5 TATCHBROOK CT
6 CHARLES GARDNER RD
MARKET CNR 1
YEW TREE CT 2
GINGKO WLK 3
CONIFER GR 4
SPRUCE GR 5
SILVER BIRCH GR 6
WYCH ELM DR 7
BONNIKSEN CL 8
BRAKESMEAD 9
WARWICK TECH PK
Sports Ctr
HEATHCOTE LA
Heathcote Hill Farm
EUROPA WAY
HEATHCOTE IND EST
Works
TACHBROOK RD
CV34
GALLOWS HILL
TROJAN BSNS CTR
Heathcote
Royal Leamington Spa Rehabilitation
Turnbulls Garden
Hawkes Farm
CASSANDRA GR 1
OBERON CL 2
GADSHILL 3
BANBURY RD
Nursery Wood
The Aspens
Lower Heathcote Farm
HARBURY LA
Asps Cottages
Sewage Works
Grove Farm
CV33
Park Farm
New House Farm
OAKLEY WOOD RD
The Grove
WARWICK BY-PASS
8
7
65
6
5
64
4
3
63
2
1
62
30
31
162

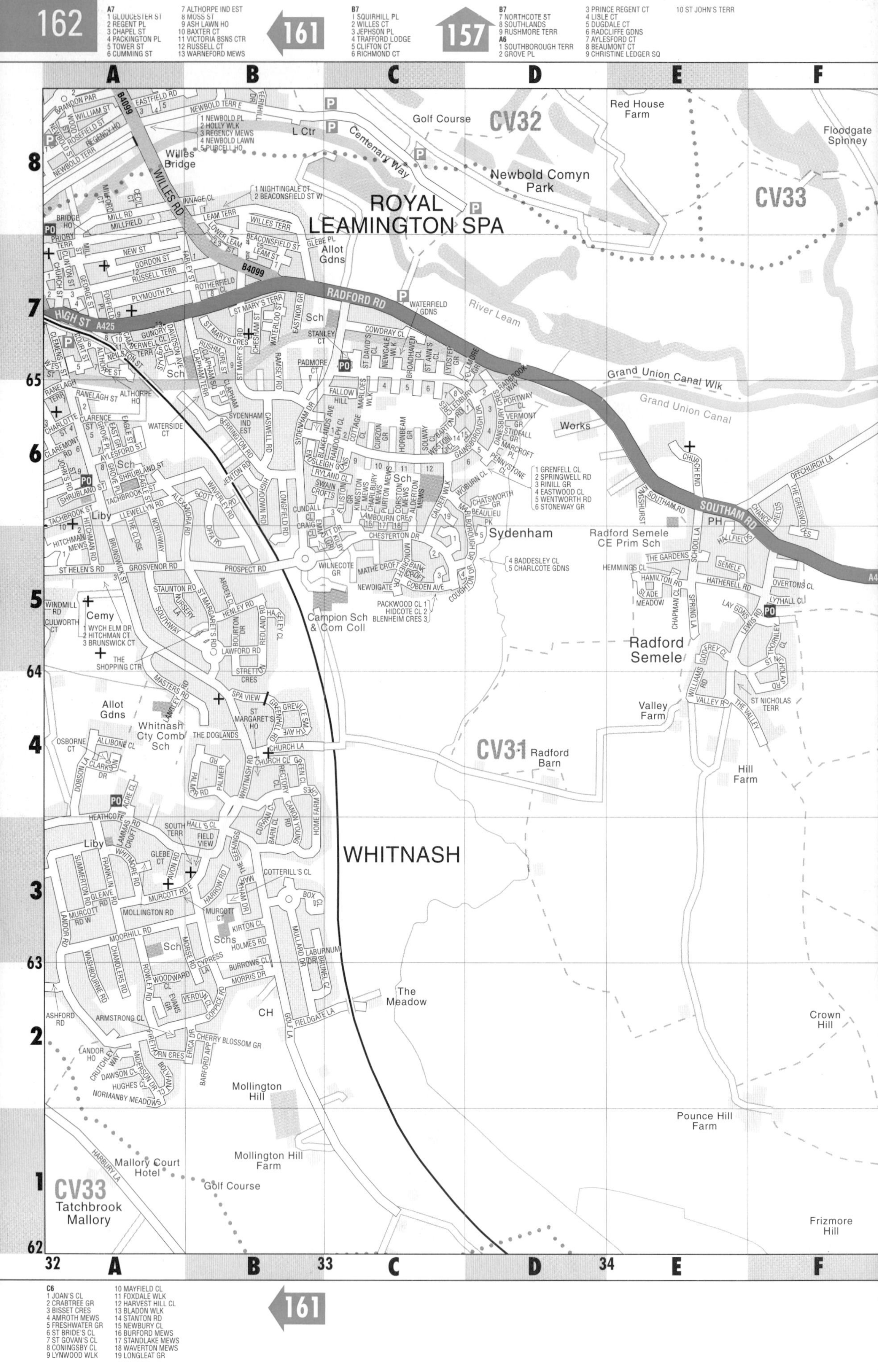

162
A7
1 GLOUCESTER ST
2 REGENT PL
3 CHAPEL ST
4 PACKINGTON PL
5 TOWER ST
6 CUMMING ST
7 ALTHORPE IND EST
8 MOSS ST
9 ASH LAWN HO
10 BAXTER CT
11 VICTORIA BSNS CTR
12 RUSSELL CT
13 WARNEFORD MEWS
161
B7
1 SQUIRHILL PL
2 WILLES CT
3 JEPHSON PL
4 TRAFFORD LODGE
5 CLIFTON CT
6 RICHMOND CT
157
B7
7 NORTHCOTE ST
8 SOUTHLANDS
9 RUSHMORE TERR
A6
1 SOUTHBOROUGH TERR
2 GROVE PL
3 PRINCE REGENT CT
4 LISLE CT
5 DUGDALE CT
6 RADCLIFFE GDNS
7 AYLESFORD CT
8 BEAUMONT CT
9 CHRISTINE LEDGER SQ
10 ST JOHN'S TERR
A
B
C
D
E
F
8
7
65
6
5
64
4
3
63
2
1
62
32
33
34
ROYAL LEAMINGTON SPA
CV32
CV33
CV31
Golf Course
Red House Farm
Floodgate Spinney
Newbold Comyn Park
Centenary Way
L Ctr
Willes Bridge
WILLES RD
B4099
RADFORD RD
HIGH ST A425
River Leam
Grand Union Canal Wlk
Grand Union Canal
Works
SOUTHAM RD
Sydenham
Radford Semele CE Prim Sch
Radford Semele
Valley Farm
Radford Barn
Hill Farm
Campion Sch & Com Coll
Cemy
Allot Gdns
Whitnash Cty Comb Sch
WHITNASH
The Meadow
Crown Hill
Mollington Hill
Pounce Hill Farm
Mallory Court Hotel
Mollington Hill Farm
Golf Course
Tatchbrook Mallory
Frizmore Hill
OFFCHURCH LA
HARBURY LA
C6
1 JOAN'S CL
2 CRABTREE GR
3 BISSET CRES
4 AMROTH MEWS
5 FRESHWATER GR
6 ST BRIDE'S CL
7 ST GOVAN'S CL
8 CONINGSBY CL
9 LYNWOOD WLK
10 MAYFIELD CL
11 FOXDALE WLK
12 HARVEST HILL CL
13 BLADON WLK
14 STANTON RD
15 NEWBURY CL
16 BURFORD MEWS
17 STANDLAKE MEWS
18 WAVERTON MEWS
19 LONGLEAT GR
161

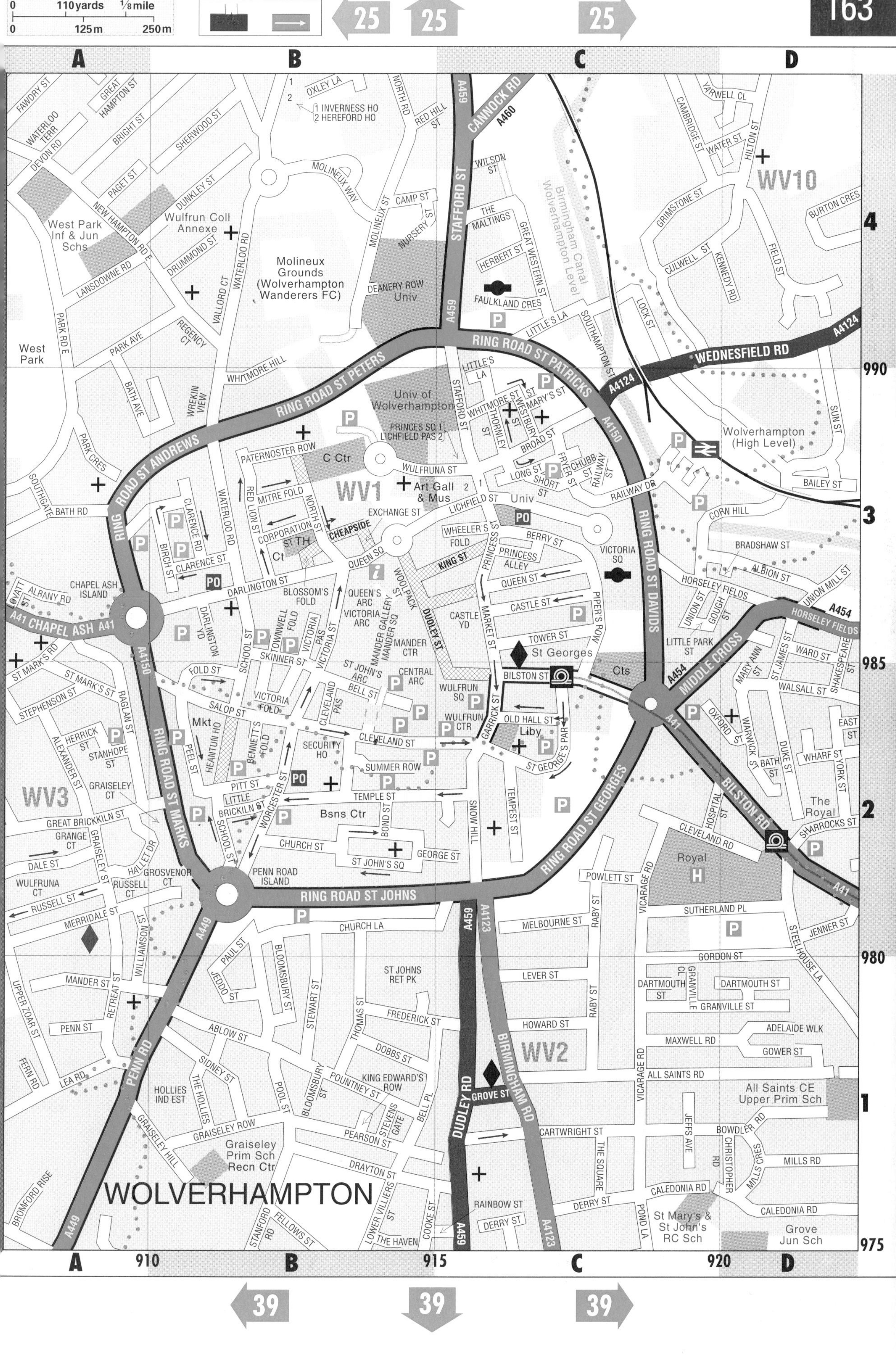

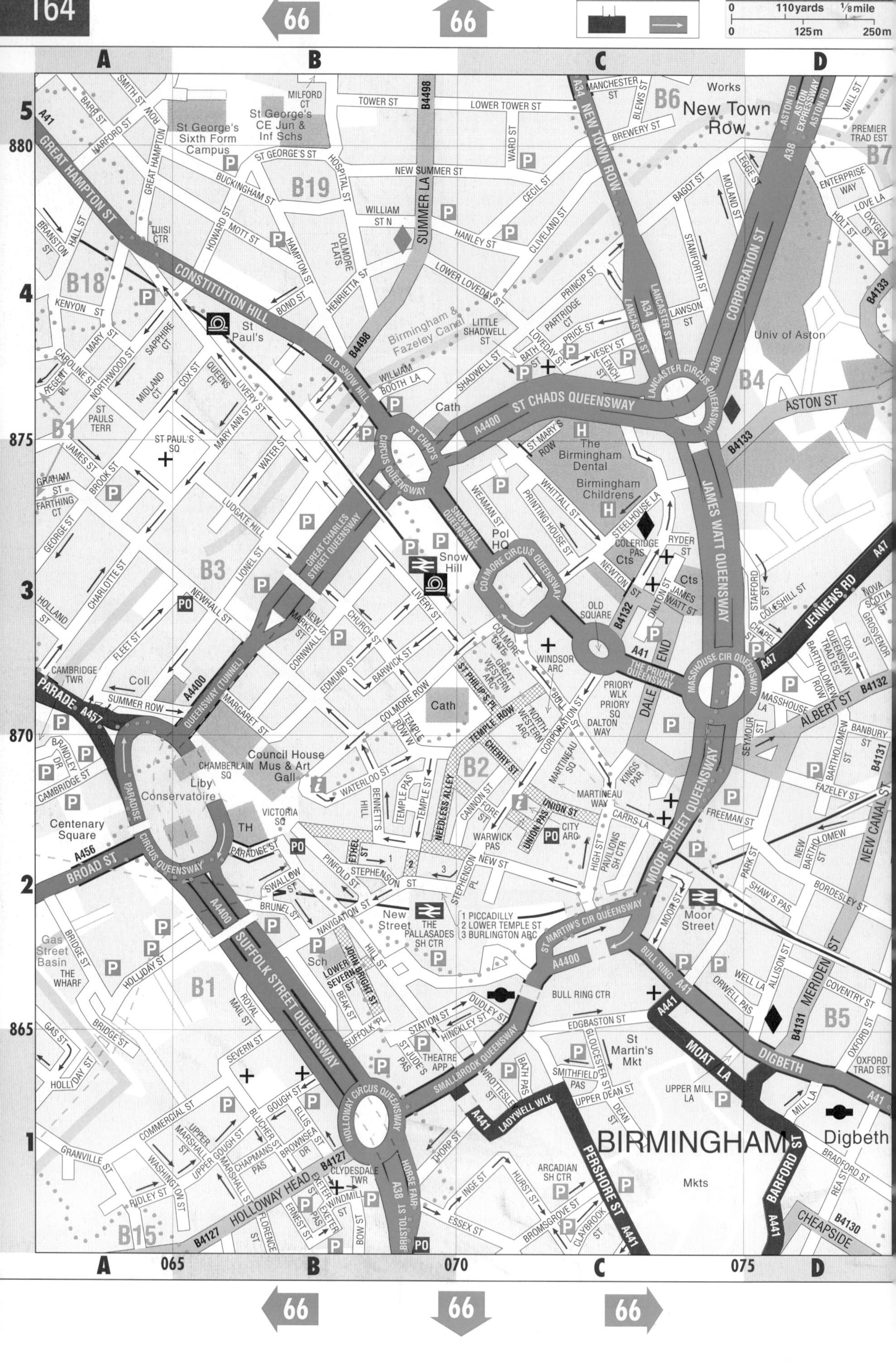
66
66
One-way streets
Scale: 7 inches to 1 mile
0
110yards
1/8 mile
0
125m
250m
A
B
C
D
5
880
4
875
3
870
2
865
1
065
070
075
New Town Row
St George's Sixth Form Campus
St George's CE Jun & Inf Schs
B19
B18
B6
B7
B4
B3
B1
B2
B5
B15
GREAT HAMPTON ST
CONSTITUTION HILL
St Paul's
Birmingham & Fazeley Canal
ST CHADS QUEENSWAY
JAMES WATT QUEENSWAY
CORPORATION ST
Univ of Aston
ASTON ST
The Birmingham Dental
Birmingham Childrens
Snow Hill
Pol HQ
OLD SQUARE
COLMORE CIRCUS QUEENSWAY
GREAT CHARLES STREET QUEENSWAY
Cath
Council House Mus & Art Gall
Liby
Conservatoire
Centenary Square
BROAD ST
PARADE
TH
New Street
THE PALLASADES SH CTR
1 PICCADILLY
2 LOWER TEMPLE ST
3 BURLINGTON ARC
Moor Street
MOOR STREET QUEENSWAY
BULL RING CTR
St Martin's Mkt
SUFFOLK STREET QUEENSWAY
HOLLOWAY HEAD
PERSHORE ST
BIRMINGHAM
Mkts
DIGBETH
Digbeth
MOAT LA
JENNENS RD
ALBERT ST
NEW CANAL ST
Gas Street Basin
THE WHARF
CHEAPSIDE
BARFORD ST

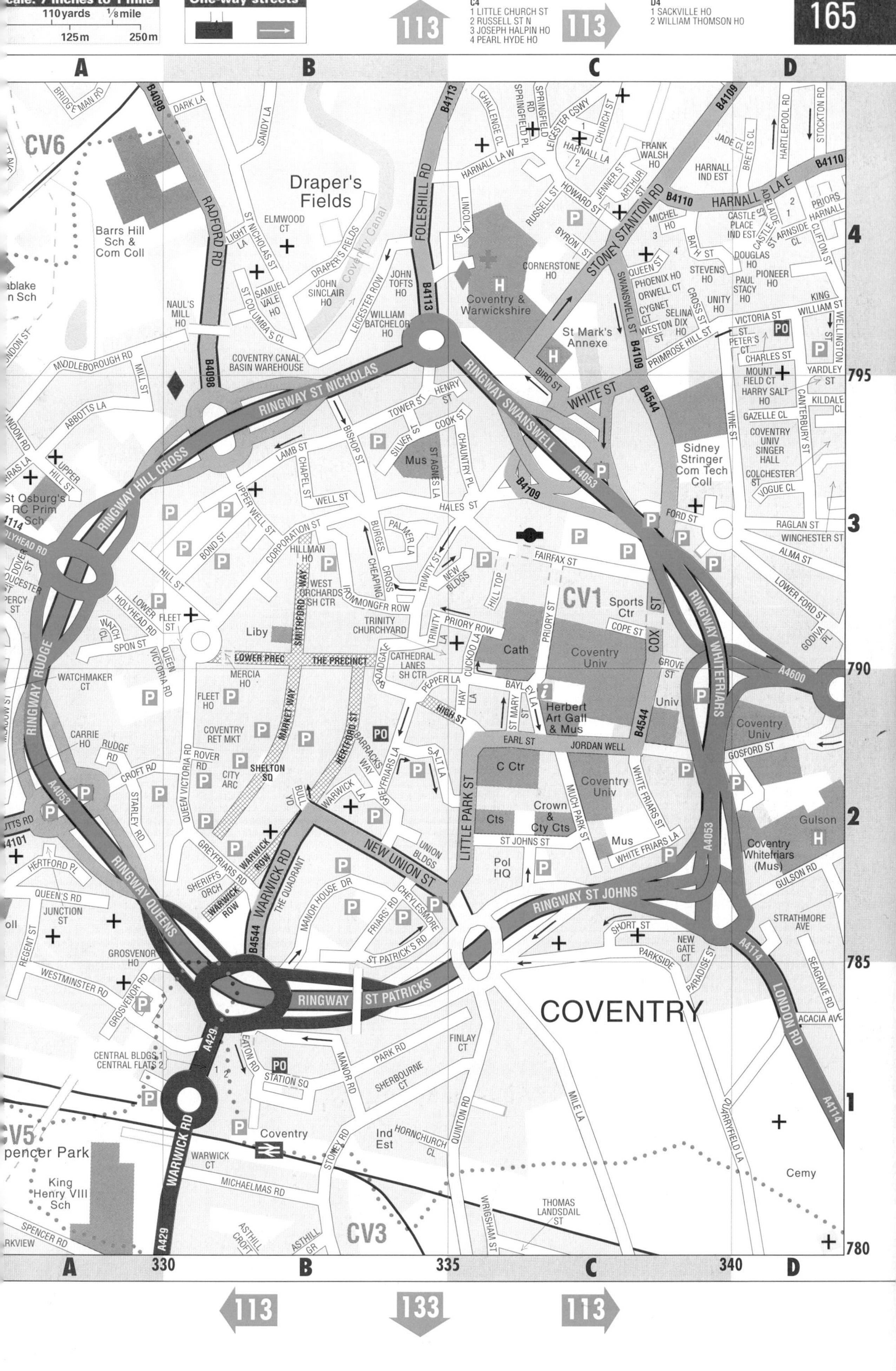
Scale: 7 inches to 1 mile
110 yards
1/8 mile
125m
250m
One-way streets
113
C4
1 LITTLE CHURCH ST
2 RUSSELL ST N
3 JOSEPH HALPIN HO
4 PEARL HYDE HO
113
D4
1 SACKVILLE HO
2 WILLIAM THOMSON HO
A
B
C
D
CV6
Draper's Fields
Barrs Hill Sch & Com Coll
RADFORD RD
B4098
DARK LA
SANDY LA
ELMWOOD CT
ST NICHOLAS ST
LIGHT LA
SAMUEL VALE HO
ST COLUMBA'S CL
NAUL'S MILL HO
DRAPER'S FIELDS
JOHN SINCLAIR HO
Coventry Canal
LEICESTER ROW
JOHN TOFTS HO
WILLIAM BATCHELOR HO
FOLESHILL RD
B4113
CHALLENGE CL
SPRINGFIELD RD
HARNALL LA W
LINCOLN ST
LEICESTER CSWY
CHURCH ST
HARNALL LA
RUSSELL ST
HOWARD ST
JENNER ST
ARTHUR ST
FRANK WALSH HO
B4109
HARNALL IND EST
JADE CL
BRETTS CL
HARTLEPOOL RD
STOCKTON RD
B4110
HARNALL LA E
STONEY STANTON RD
MICHEL HO
BYRON ST
CORNERSTONE HO
Coventry & Warwickshire
QUEEN ST
PHOENIX HO
ORWELL CT
CYGNET CT
WESTON ST
SELINA DIX HO
CROSS ST
SWANSWELL ST
BATH ST
STEVENS HO
UNITY HO
PAUL STACY HO
CASTLE PLACE IND EST
ADELAIDE ST
DOUGLAS HO
PIONEER HO
ARNSIDE CL
CLIFTON ST
PRIORS HARNALL
KING WILLIAM ST
WELLINGTON ST
St Mark's Annexe
PRIMROSE HILL ST
VICTORIA ST
ST PETER'S CT
CHARLES ST
MOUNT FIELD CT
HARRY SALT HO
YARDLEY ST
KILDALE CL
GAZELLE CL
COVENTRY UNIV SINGER HALL
CANTERBURY ST
COLCHESTER ST
VOGUE CL
VINE ST
Sidney Stringer Com Tech Coll
COVENTRY CANAL BASIN WAREHOUSE
MIDDLEBOROUGH RD
MILL ST
ABBOTTS LA
B4098
RINGWAY ST NICHOLAS
RINGWAY SWANSWELL
BIRD ST
WHITE ST
B4544
TOWER ST
HENRY ST
BISHOP ST
SILVER ST
COOK ST
Mus
ST AGNES LA
CHAUNTRY PL
LAMB ST
CHAPEL ST
WELL ST
HALES ST
B4709
A4053
FORD ST
RINGWAY HILL CROSS
UPPER HILL ST
St Osburg's RC Prim Sch
UPPER WELL ST
BOND ST
CORPORATION ST
HILLMAN HO
PALMER LA
BURGES
TRINITY ST
NEW BLDGS
HILL TOP
FAIRFAX ST
CV1
Sports Ctr
COX ST
RAGLAN ST
WINCHESTER ST
ALMA ST
LOWER FORD ST
GODIVA PL
HOLYHEAD RD
HILL ST
LOWER HOLYHEAD RD
FLEET ST
SMITHFORD WAY
WEST ORCHARDS SH CTR
CHEAPING
CROSS
IRONMONGER ROW
TRINITY CHURCHYARD
PRIORY ROW
PRIORY ST
COPE ST
RINGWAY WHITEFRIARS
Liby
Cath
Coventry Univ
WATCH CL
SPON ST
QUEEN VICTORIA RD
LOWER PREC
THE PRECINCT
CATHEDRAL LANES SH CTR
TRINITY LA
CUCKOO LA
GROVE ST
A4600
RINGWAY RUDGE
WATCHMAKER CT
MERCIA HO
FLEET HO
PEPPER LA
HAY LA
HIGH ST
BAYLEY LA
ST MARY ST
Herbert Art Gall & Mus
Univ
COVENTRY RET MKT
MARKET WAY
HERTFORD ST
BARRACKS WAY
GREYFRIARS LA
SALT LA
EARL ST
JORDAN WELL
Coventry Univ
GOSFORD ST
CARRIE HO
RUDGE RD
CROFT RD
ROVER RD
CITY ARC
SHELTON SQ
BULL YD
WARWICK LA
LITTLE PARK ST
C Ctr
MUCH PARK ST
WHITE FRIARS ST
A4053
Gulson
A4053
STARLEY RD
Cts
Crown & Cty Cts
ST JOHNS ST
WHITE FRIARS LA
Mus
Coventry Whitefriars (Mus)
GULSON RD
HERTFORD PL
GREYFRIARS RD
WARWICK ROW
WARWICK RD
THE QUADRANT
NEW UNION ST
UNION BLDGS
Pol HQ
QUEEN'S RD
SHERIFFS ORCH
MANOR HOUSE DR
FRIARS RD
CHEYLESMORE
RINGWAY QUEENS
RINGWAY ST JOHNS
JUNCTION ST
REGENT ST
SHORT ST
STRATHMORE AVE
B4544
ST PATRICK'S RD
GROSVENOR HO
NEW GATE CT
PARKSIDE
PARADISE ST
A4114
SEAGRAVE RD
WESTMINSTER RD
GROSVENOR RD
RINGWAY ST PATRICKS
COVENTRY
LONDON RD
ACACIA AVE
CENTRAL BLDGS 1
CENTRAL FLATS 2
A429
EATON RD
STATION SQ
MANOR RD
PARK RD
SHERBOURNE CT
FINLAY CT
WARWICK RD
Coventry
Ind Est
HORNCHURCH CL
QUINTON RD
MILE LA
QUARRYFIELD LA
A4114
CV5
Spencer Park
King Henry VIII Sch
WARWICK CT
MICHAELMAS RD
STONEY RD
Cemy
SPENCER RD
ASTHILL CROFT
ASTHILL GR
CV3
WRIGSHAM ST
THOMAS LANDSDAIL ST
A429
795
790
785
780
4
3
2
1
330
335
340
113
133
113

Index

Street names are listed alphabetically and show the locality, the Postcode District, the page number and a reference to the square in which the name falls on the map page

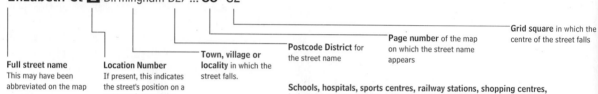

Full street name
This may have been abbreviated on the map

Location Number
If present, this indicates the street's position on a congested area of the map instead of the name

Town, village or locality in which the street falls.

Postcode District for the street name

Page number of the map on which the street name appears

Grid square in which the centre of the street falls

Schools, hospitals, sports centres, railway stations, shopping centres, industrial estates, public amenities and other places of interest are also listed. These are highlighted in magenta

Abbreviations used in the index

App	Approach	Comm	Common	Est	Estate	N	North	Sq	Square
Arc	Arcade	Cnr	Corner	Gdns	Gardens	Orch	Orchard	Strs	Stairs
Ave	Avenue	Cotts	Cottages	Gn	Green	Par	Parade	Stps	Steps
Bvd	Boulevard	Ct	Court	Gr	Grove	Pk	Park	St	Street, Saint
Bldgs	Buildings	Ctyd	Courtyard	Hts	Heights	Pas	Passage	Terr	Terrace
Bsns Pk	Business Park	Cres	Crescent	Ho	House	Pl	Place	Trad Est	Trading Estate
Bsns Ctr	Business Centre	Dr	Drive	Ind Est	Industrial Estate	Prec	Precinct	Wlk	Walk
Bglws	Bungalows	Dro	Drove	Intc	Interchange	Prom	Promenade	W	West
Cswy	Causeway	E	East	Junc	Junction	Ret Pk	Retail Park	Yd	Yard
Ctr	Centre	Emb	Embankment	La	Lane	Rd	Road		
Cir	Circus	Ent	Enterprise	Mans	Mansions	Rdbt	Roundabout		
Cl	Close	Espl	Esplanade	Mdw	Meadows	S	South		

Town and village index

Aldridge 30 A6	Brandon 135 F5	Earlswood 126 A2	Meriden 92 C1	Stourbridge 80 F5
Allesley 112 B7	Brierley Hill 61 E2	Essington 13 A4	Middleton 34 C1	Studley 159 F4
Alvechurch 139 B6	Brinsford 11 D7	Fairfield 120 D3	Mile Oak 20 D1	Sutton Coldfield 46 D5
Alvecote 22 D6	Bromsgrove 136 E1	Fazeley 20 F1	Minworth 58 D5	Tamworth 21 B3
Ansty 97 D4	Brownhills 16 B6	Featherstone 12 C7	Mustow Green 117 F1	Tanworth-In-Arden 142 A2
Ash Green 95 C6	Bulkington 79 C1	Finstall 137 D1	Norton Canes 5 F5	Tardebigge 152 B7
Aston Flamville 76 E6	Burcot 137 E4	Great Wyrley 5 B2	Nuneaton 73 C4	Tidbury Green 125 E4
Astwood Bank 158 E1	Burntwood 7 D6	Hagley 99 C7	Nurton 23 A3	Tipton 51 F6
Baginton 133 F2	Burton Green 131 C4	Halesowen 83 C3	Oldbury 63 B8	Trescott 37 C7
Balsall Common 130 B7	Burton Hastings 75 A1	Hampton in Arden 109 A7	Outwoods 92 C5	Trysull 37 C1
Barnacle 97 B6	Cannock 1 D2	Harvington 118 A2	Perton 23 D4	Upper Bentley 152 A1
Barnt Green 138 D8	Catherine de Barnes 108 B5	Himley 49 C3	Piccadilly 35 F1	Upper Marlbrook 121 D1
Barston 109 B1	Catshill 137 B8	Hinckley 74 C8	Polesworth 22 E1	Upton Warren 150 A3
Barwell 71 F7	Chadwick End 145 B7	Hockley Heath 143 C6	Portway 141 A5	Walsall 28 B3
Beausale 146 C2	Cheslyn Hay 4 D3	Hollywood 125 B8	Radford Semele 162 E5	Warwick 160 C6
Bedworth 78 B1	Cheswick Green 126 D4	Honiley 146 D5	Redditch 153 C2	Water Orton 59 C3
Belbroughton 119 E7	Churchill 98 B3	Hopwas 20 B7	Romsley 101 A4	Wedges Mills 4 B8
Bentley Heath 127 F5	Clayhanger 15 E6	Hopwood 123 B3	Rowington Green 145 A1	Wednesbury 41 F1
Beoley 154 D7	Clent 99 F3	Hunnington 101 B7	Rowney Green 139 F4	Wednesfield 26 D5
Berkswell 110 D3	Cliff 35 B1	Huntington 1 D8	Royal Leamington Spa 156 C6	Weeford 19 A4
Bickenhill 90 D1	Codsall 10 A3	Iverley 98 C7	Ryton-on-Dunsmore 135 A1	West Bromwich 53 F5
Bilston 40 D4	Coleshill 70 F6	Kenilworth 148 B5	Sambourne 159 B1	Whateley 35 F3
Binley Woods 135 C7	Corley 94 B7	Keresley 94 F5	Sedgley 50 E7	White Stitch 92 C5
Birchmoor 36 D7	Coseley 40 C1	Kidderminster 116 D4	Seisdon 37 A2	Whitnash 162 A4
Birmingham 67 C2	Coven Heath 11 C6	Kingswinford 60 E5	Shenstone 18 A6	Wildmoor 120 F4
Birmingham 164 C1	Coventry 113 C4	Knowle 128 B6	Shilton 97 E5	Willenhall 27 C1
Blackdown 156 F6	Coventry 165 C1	Lapworth 143 E3	Shuttington 22 E7	Wishaw 48 B2
Blackheath 63 E1	Cubbington 157 E5	Leek Wootton 155 F6	Smethwick 65 A4	Wolston 135 F3
Blackwell 138 A5	Curdworth 59 B6	Lichfield 9 D5	Solihull 106 F5	Wolverhampton 25 B3
Blakedown 98 B2	Darlaston 41 D7	Lickey End 137 B6	Stoke Heath 150 D5	Wolverhampton 163 B1
Bloxwich 14 C1	Dodford 136 A5	Little Aston 31 B4	Stoke Pound 151 A4	Wombourne 49 C5
Bluntington 118 E1	Dordon 36 F6	Little Packington 91 C6	Stoke Prior 150 C4	Wood End 36 C1
Bournheath 136 D8	Dorridge 127 F2	Lower Marlbrook 121 C1	Stone 117 D3	Wroxall 145 E3
Bradnock's Marsh 109 E3	Drayton Bassett 34 E5	Lydiate Ash 121 C3	Stoneleigh 149 B6	Wythall 124 E2
Bramcote 79 E6	Dudley 51 D2	Meer End 130 D1	Stonnall 16 E4	

A B Row B4 66 F3
A1 Trad Est B66 65 A7
Abberley B77 22 C2
Abberley Cl Halesowen B63 82 F2
Redditch B98 154 C5
Abberley Ind Ctr B66 65 D5
Abberley Rd Dudley DY3 50 D4
Oldbury B68 84 B8
Abberley St Dudley DY2 62 C8
Smethwick B66 65 D5
Abberton Cl B63 83 C3
Abberton Ct B23 56 C2
Abberton Gr B90 127 B7
Abberton Ho B97 153 A4
Abberton Way CV4 132 E3
Abbess Gr B25 68 E1
Abbey CE Fst Sch CV11 73 B5
Abbey Cl B60 137 C2
Abbey Cres Halesowen B63 82 D4
Oldbury B68 64 D1
Abbey Ct CV3 134 B6
Abbey Dr WS3 15 A5
Abbey End CV8 147 F4
Abbey Est CV2 114 F5
Abbey Gate CV11 73 C4
Abbey Gate Sh Ctr CV11 73 C4
Abbey Gdns B67 64 E1
Abbey Gn CV11 73 B5
Abbey High Sch The B98 153 F4
Abbey Hill CV8 147 F5
Abbey Inf Sch B67 64 E2
Abbey Jun Sch B67 64 E1
Abbey Mans 2 B24 57 B6
Abbey Prim Sch WS3 13 E2
Abbey RC Jun & Inf Sch B23 57 A5
Abbey Rd
Birmingham, Edgbaston B17 85 D5
Birmingham, Gravelly Hill B23 56 D2
Coventry CV3 134 A6
Dudley, Gornalwood DY3 50 C3
Dudley, Netherton DY2 62 D6
Halesowen B63 82 C4
Kidderminster DY11 116 A6
Redditch B97 153 E4
Smethwick B67 64 E1
Tamworth B77 21 D3
Abbey Sq WS3 13 E2
Abbey St Cannock WS12 2 B7
Dudley DY3 50 C3
Nuneaton CV11 73 B5
Abbey St N B18 66 A5
Abbey The CV8 147 F5
Abbey Trad Ind Area B97 153 E5
Abbey Way CV3 133 F6
Abbeydale Cl CV3 114 F2
Abbeydale Rd B31 103 A2
Abbeyfield Rd
Birmingham B23 56 E8
Wolverhampton WV10 11 E4
Abbeyfields Dr B80 159 E6
Abbot Rd B62 100 C8
Abbots Cl Knowle B93 128 A7
Walsall WS4 29 C6
Abbots Field WS11 1 E5
Abbots Mews DY5 61 D1
Abbots Rd B14 104 E7
Abbots Way Birmingham B18 66 B6
Warwick CV34 160 D6
Wolverhampton WV3 24 E1
Abbotsbury Cl CV2 115 A4
Abbotsford Ave B43 43 F2
Abbotsford Dr DY1 61 E7
Abbotsford Rd
Birmingham B11 87 C6
Lichfield WS14 9 E7
Nuneaton CV11 73 E1
Abbotsford Sch CV8 147 F6
Abbotts Gn LE10 75 F5
Abbotts La CV1 165 A3
Abbotts Pl WS3 14 D1
Abbotts Rd B24 56 F1
Abbotts St
5 Royal Leamington Spa CV31 161 F7
Walsall WS3 14 D2
Abbotts Wlk CV3 135 C7
Abdon Ave B29 103 C7
Abelia B77 21 F3
Abercorn Rd CV5 112 E2
Aberdeen Cl CV5 112 A5
Aberdeen Rd CV11 73 E1
Aberdeen St B18 65 E4
Aberford Cl WV12 27 D4
Abergavenny Wlk CV3 134 F6
Abigails Cl B26 89 B7
Abingdon Cl WV1 26 B2
Abingdon Rd
Birmingham B23 56 C6
Dudley DY2 62 D3
Walsall WS3 13 F2
Wolverhampton WV1 26 B2
Abingdon Way
Birmingham B35 58 A3
Nuneaton CV11 73 F7
Walsall WS3 13 F2
Ablewell St WS1 28 F1
Ablow St WV2 163 B1
Abnalls La WS13 8 B8
Abney Dr WV14 39 F1
Aboyne Cl B5 86 D6
Acacia Ave Birmingham B37 69 F6
Coventry CV1 113 E1
Walsall WS5 43 A4
Acacia Cl Birmingham B37 69 C5
Dudley DY1 51 A3
Tipton B69 52 B2
Acacia Cres WV8 10 B4
Acacia Dr WV14 51 B7
Acacia Gr WS12 2 F3
Acacia Rd Birmingham B30 103 E8
Nuneaton CV10 72 E5
Royal Leamington Spa CV32 156 D1
Accord Mews WS10 41 D7
Ace Bsns Pk B33 69 D2
Acfold Rd B20 54 E5
Achal Cl CV6 95 F2
Acheson Rd B28 105 F3
Achilees Cl WS6 4 F1
Achilles Rd CV6 114 A7
Ackleton Gdns WV3 38 F7
Ackleton Gr B29 84 F1
Acocks Green Inf Sch B27 88 B3
Acocks Green Jun Sch B27 88 B3
Acocks Green Sta B27 88 C4
Acorn Cl Bedworth CV12 95 C8
Birmingham, Bournville B30 103 E6
Birmingham, Stockfield B27 88 B5
Cannock WS11 2 C2
Great Wyrley WS6 5 A1
Stoneleigh CV8 149 B7
West Bromwich B70 53 B2
Acorn Ct 1 CV32 157 A2
Acorn Ctr 1 WS1 28 F1
Acorn Gdns B30 104 A7
Acorn Gr Birmingham B1 66 B3
Stourbridge DY8 60 E1
Acorn Rd Halesowen B62 83 C8
Wolverhampton WV11 13 A1
Acorn St Coventry CV3 134 B8
Willenhall WV13 27 C2
Acorn Starter Units WS7 6 D7
Acorns The B61 137 A8
Acre Cl CV31 162 A4
Acre Rise WV12 27 B5
Acres Rd DY5 81 E8
Acres The WV3 24 C1
Acton Cl B98 154 D5
Acton Dr DY3 50 B3
Acton Gr Bilston WV14 40 B4
Birmingham B44 45 A2
Acton Ho CV4 111 F3
Ada Rd Birmingham B25 88 B6
Smethwick B66 65 C3
Ada Wrighton Cl WV12 27 C7
Adam Ct WS11 1 D1
Adam Rd CV6 113 F7
Adam St DY11 116 C5
Adam's Hill DY9 99 F4
Adams Brook Dr B32 84 B1
Adams Cl Smethwick B66 64 D7
Tipton DY4 40 F1
Adams Ct DY10 117 A7
Adams Hill B32 84 B1
Adams Ho 3 DY11 116 C6
Adams Rd Brownhills WS8 16 B5
Water Orton WV3 38 C8
Adams St Birmingham B7 66 F5
Walsall WS2 28 D2
West Bromwich B70 53 B3
Adamson Cl WS11 1 B1
Adare Dr CV3 133 C8
Adcock Dr CV8 148 B5
Addenbrook Ho
2 Blackheath B64 82 F8
Sutton Coldfield B73 46 A3
Addenbrook Way DY4 52 D8
Addenbrooke Cres DY11 116 A1
Addenbrooke Dr B73 46 B2
Addenbrooke Pl WS10 41 D7
Addenbrooke Rd
Keresley CV7 95 A6
Smethwick B67 64 F3
Addenbrooke St
Darlaston WS10 41 D7
Walsall WS3 28 C7
Adderley Gdns B8 67 D5
Adderley Park Cl B8 67 E4
Adderley Park Sta B8 67 D3
Adderley Prim Sch The B8 67 D3
Adderley Rd B8 67 C4
Adderley Rd S B8 67 C3
Adderley St Birmingham B9 67 A1
Coventry CV1 113 E4
Adderley Trad Est B8 67 C4
Addingham Cl 2 CV34 155 E1
Addison Cl Cannock WS11 1 E5
Nuneaton CV10 72 A5
Wednesbury WS10 42 E2
Addison Croft DY3 50 A5
Addison Gr WV11 12 F1
Addison Pl Bilston WV14 41 A7
Water Orton B46 59 B3
Addison Rd
Birmingham, King's Heath B14 104 F7
Birmingham, Nechells B7 67 C8
Brierley Hill DY5 61 B2
Coventry CV6 113 A8
Wednesbury WS10 42 E2
Wolverhampton WV3 38 F8
Addison St WS10 41 F2
Addison Terr WS10 41 F2
Adelaide Ave B70 53 A7
Adelaide Ct CV12 78 A2
Adelaide Rd CV31 161 E8
Adelaide St Birmingham B12 86 F8
Brierley Hill DY5 61 D3
Coventry CV1 165 D4
Redditch B97 153 D4
Adelaide Tower B34 69 C5
Adelaide Wlk WV2 163 D1
Adelphi Ct 3 DY5 61 D2
Adey Rd WV11 26 F8
Adkins La B67 65 A1
Admington Rd B33 89 C8
Admiral Gdns CV8 148 C6
Admiral Parker Dr WS14 17 F5
Admiral Pl B13 86 F4
Admirals Way Blackheath B65 63 B2
Bramcote CV11 79 E6
Adonis Cl B79 21 C6
Adria Rd B11 87 B4
Adrian Croft B13 87 C1
Adrian Ct 1 B24 57 B6
Adshead Rd DY2 62 C7
Adstone Gr B31 103 A1
Advance Bsns Pk WS11 2 B3
Adwalton Rd WV6 23 F3
Aethelred Ct WV10 25 C6
Affleck Ave B78 20 D1
Agenoria Dr DY8 80 F5
Aggborough Cres DY10 116 E3
Agincourt Rd CV3 133 E7
Agmore La B60 138 B3
Agmore Rd B60 138 B4
Aiden Ct WS13 9 C7
Ainsbury Rd CV5 132 E8
Ainsdale Cl Coventry CV6 96 B4
Stourbridge DY8 80 F2
Ainsdale Gdns
Birmingham B24 57 C5
Halesowen B63 82 D2
Ainsworth Ho 3 B38 103 D2
Ainsworth Rd WV10 11 E4
Aintree Cl Bedworth CV12 78 B4
Cannock WS12 2 F6
Catshill B61 121 A1
Coventry CV6 113 E5
Kidderminster DY11 116 D8
Aintree Dr CV32 157 C3
Aintree Gr B34 69 D6
Aintree Rd WV10 11 D4
Aintree Way DY1 50 F2
Aire Croft B31 103 B1
Airfield Dr WS4 29 E3
Airport Way B26 90 C3
Aitken Cl B78 21 A2
Aitken Wing B15 86 A6
Ajax Cl WS6 4 F1
Akdene Cl WS6 4 D2
Akon Ho CV6 94 F2
Akrill Cl B70 53 B5
Akrill Cottage Homes The B70 53 B5
Al Hira Sch & Coll B12 87 A6
Alamein Rd WV13 26 E1
Alan Bray Cl LE10 74 D7
Alan Higgs Way CV4 131 C8
Alandale Ave CV5 111 E4
Alandale Ct CV12 95 C8
Albany Cl DY10 117 B6
Albany Cres WV14 40 C6
Albany Ct CV1 113 A2
Albany Gdns B91 107 E4
Albany Gr Kingswinford DY6 60 E7
Willenhall WV11 13 C1
Albany Ho B34 69 A7
Albany Rd Birmingham B17 85 C6
Coventry CV5 113 A1
Wolverhampton WV1 163 A3
Albany Terr CV32 156 E1
Albemarle Rd DY8 80 F2
Albermarle Rd DY6 61 A5
Albert Ave 1 B12 87 A6
Albert Bradbeer Inf Sch B31 122 F7
Albert Bradbeer Jun Sch B31 122 F7
Albert Bradford Specl Sch B66 64 E7
Albert Cl B80 159 E4
Albert Clarke Dr WV12 27 C7
Albert Cres CV6 95 B3
Albert Davie Dr WS12 2 E4
Albert Dr B63 82 F2
Albert Ho WS10 41 C6
Albert Pritchard Inf Sch WS10 42 A5
Albert Rd Allesley CV5 111 A8
Birmingham, Aston B6 66 F8
Birmingham, Gravelly Hill B23 56 D3
Birmingham, Handsworth B21 54 E1
Birmingham, Harborne B17 85 B5
Birmingham, King's Heath B14 104 F7
Birmingham, Stechford B33 68 D3
Bromsgrove B61 150 E8
Fazeley B78 35 A8
Halesowen B63 82 F3
Hinckley LE10 71 D1
Kidderminster DY10 116 F6
Oldbury B68 84 C8
Tamworth B79 21 B5
Wolverhampton WV6 25 A3
Albert Smith Pl B65 63 A4
Albert St Birmingham B5 164 D3
Brierley Hill DY5 61 D7
Cannock, Broomhill WS11 1 E4
Cannock, Hednesford WS12 2 D5
Coventry CV1 113 E4
Kingswinford DY6 60 B8
Nuneaton CV10 72 E2
Oldbury B69 64 A8
Redditch B97 153 E5
Royal Leamington Spa CV32 156 C1
Stourbridge, Lye DY9 81 E5
Stourbridge, Wollaston DY8 80 F5
Albert St continued
Tipton DY4 51 F8
Walsall WS1 28 E2
Warwick CV34 160 D7
Wednesbury WS10 41 F2
West Bromwich B70 53 C1
Albert St E B69 64 B7
Albert Wlk 1 B17 85 C5
Albion Ave WV13 27 C2
Albion Bsns Pk B66 64 E8
Albion Cotts B46 59 B3
Albion Ct CV11 73 D3
Albion Field Dr B71 53 D4
Albion Ho B70 53 C2
Albion Ind Est Coventry CV6 113 D7
West Bromwich B70 52 F2
Albion Jun Sch B71 54 A1
Albion Par DY6 60 B8
Albion Pl WS11 1 E4
Albion Rd
Birmingham, Handsworth B21 54 E1
Birmingham, Sparkhill B11 87 D5
Brownhills WS8 15 E8
West Bromwich, Albion B70 53 A2
West Bromwich, Handsworth B71 65 B8
Albion Rdbt B70 53 B4
Albion St Bilston WV14 40 E6
Birmingham B1 66 C3
Brierley Hill DY5 61 D3
Kenilworth CV8 148 A5
Kingswinford DY6 60 B8
Oldbury B69 52 E1
Tamworth B79 21 C5
Tipton DY4 51 F5
Willenhall WV13 27 B2
Wolverhampton WV1 163 D3
Albion Terr B46 59 B3
Albion Works DY5 61 B3
Alborn Cres B38 123 D8
Albright Ho 1 B69 63 E4
Albright Rd B68 64 D4
Albright & Wilson Ho B68 84 E7
Albrighton Ho 4 B20 54 F3
Albrighton Rd B63 82 F3
Albrighton Wlk CV11 74 A2
Albury Rd B80 159 E4
Albury Wlk B11 87 A7
Albutts Rd WS11, WS8 6 B3
Alcester Dr
Sutton Coldfield B73 45 D3
Willenhall WV13 26 D1
Alcester Gdns B14 104 F7
Alcester Highway B98 158 F8
Alcester Rd Birmingham B13 86 F3
Burcot B60 137 D5
Finstall B60 137 F1
Hollywood B47 124 F5
Portway B48 140 F7
Studley B80 159 E3
Tardebigge B60 152 B7
Alcester Rd S
Birmingham, Alcester Lane's End B14 104 E6
Birmingham, Highter's Heath B14 104 F2
Alcester St Birmingham B12 86 F8
Redditch B98 153 E4
Alcombe Gr B33 68 E2
Alcott Cl B93 127 F2
Alcott Gr B33 69 E3
Alcott Hall Prim Sch B37 70 B1
Alcott La B37 89 F8
Alcove The WS3 14 D2
Aldborough La B97 153 B5
Aldbourne Rd CV1 113 C5
Aldbourne Way B38 123 E7
Aldbury Rd B14 105 A3
Aldbury Rise CV5 112 C4
Aldeburgh Cl WS3 14 A3
Aldeford Dr DY5 81 D8
Alden Hurst WS7 6 F8
Alder Cl Hollywood B47 125 B6
Lichfield WS14 9 F7
Sutton Coldfield B76 57 E7
Alder Coppice DY3 39 C2
Alder Coppice Prim Sch DY3 39 C1
Alder Cres WS5 43 B4
Alder Ct B13 87 A3
Alder Dale WV3 24 E2
Alder Dr B37 70 B1
Alder Gr B62 83 E6
Alder Ho WV10 25 F3
Alder La
Balsall Common CV7 130 C5
Birmingham B30 103 C6
Alder Meadow Cl CV6 95 D4
Alder Park Rd B91 106 F2
Alder Rd Birmingham B12 87 A4
Coventry CV6 96 A2
Kingswinford DY6 60 F5
Wednesbury WS10 42 A5
Alder Way Bromsgrove B60 137 B2
Sutton Coldfield B74 44 E8
Alderbrook Cl Redditch B97 153 B5
Sedgley DY3 39 B1
Alderbrook Rd B91 106 F3
Alderbrook Sch B91 106 F2
Alderbrooke Dr CV11 74 A1
Alderdale Ave DY3 39 C3
Alderdale Cres B92 107 E7
Alderflat Pl B7 67 C5
Alderford Cl WV8 24 F8
Aldergate B79 21 B5
Alderham Cl B91 107 D4
Alderhithe Gr B74 31 B3
Alderlea Cl DY8 81 A2
Alderley Rd B61 150 D8
Alderman Callow Sch & Com Coll CV4 132 A6
Alderman Gee Hall CV12 78 A4
Alderman Harris Prim Sch CV4 131 F7
Alderman Smith Sch CV10 72 D2
Alderman's Green Ind Est CV2 96 D2
Alderman's Green Prim Sch CV2 96 C3
Alderman's Green Rd CV2 96 B3
Aldermere Rd DY11 116 C8
Alderminster Cl B97 158 E4
Alderminster Rd
Coventry CV5 112 A4
Solihull B91 107 C1
Aldermoor Farm Prim Sch CV3 134 B8
Aldermoor La CV3 114 A1
Alderney Cl Bramcote CV11 79 F6
Coventry CV6 95 B2
Alderney Gdns B38 103 D1
Alderpits Rd B34 69 D6
Alders Cl B98 154 A3
Alders Dr B98 154 F4
Alders Gr CV34 160 D4
Alders La Nuneaton CV10 72 A7
Tamworth B79 20 E6
Alders The Bedworth CV12 77 E2
Romsley B62 100 F4
Aldersea Dr B6 66 F7
Aldersgate CV11 73 C3
Aldershaw Rd B26 88 E6
Aldershawe Craft Ctr WS14 8 E3
Aldersley Ave WV6 24 E7
Aldersley Cl WV6 24 F7
Aldersley High Sch WV8 10 E1
Aldersley Rd WV6 24 F6
Aldersmead Rd B31 103 C1
Alderson Rd B8 67 F4
Alderton Cl B91 107 B1
Alderton Dr WV3 38 E8
Alderton Mews CV31 162 C6
Alderwood Pl B91 107 C3
Alderwood Prec DY3 39 C1
Alderwood Rise DY3 50 D5
Aldgate Dr DY5 81 C7
Aldgate Gr B19 66 D5
Aldin Cl B78 20 E2
Aldin Way LE10 71 A3
Aldington Cl B98 153 F1
Aldis Cl Birmingham B28 87 E1
Walsall WS2 42 A7
Aldis Rd WS2 42 A7
Aldrich Ave CV4 111 E2
Aldridge By-Pass WS9 30 A6
Aldridge Cl Birchmoor B78 36 F8
Oldbury B68 64 C4
Stourbridge DY8 80 E8
Aldridge Rd Birmingham B42 55 E4
Hinckley LE10 75 D6
Little Aston B74 31 B6
Oldbury B68 84 B8
Sutton Coldfield B74 44 E7
Walsall WS4 29 C3
Aldridge Sch WS9 30 A4
Aldridge St WS10 41 D7
Aldrin Way CV4 132 D5
Aldwick Cl CV32 157 A4
Aldwych Cl WS9 30 B8
Aldwyck Dr WV3 38 A8
Aldwyn Ave B13 86 F2
Alesworth Dr LE10 75 F4
Alex Grierson Cl CV3 134 E7
Alexander Cl B61 121 A1
Alexander Ct 1 CV34 160 F7
Alexander Gdns LE10 71 C2
Alexander Hill DY5 81 F8
Alexander Ind Pk WV14 40 C4
Alexander Rd Bedworth CV12 78 C3
Birmingham B27 88 C4
Codsall WV8 10 C3
Smethwick B67 64 E2
Walsall WS2 27 F2
Alexander St WV3 163 A2
Alexander Terr B67 64 F6
Alexandra Ave B21 65 D7
Alexandra Cres B71 53 E8
Alexandra Ct Dudley DY3 50 C3
Kenilworth CV8 148 A4
Oldbury B68 63 F3
Alexandra High Sch DY4 52 B6
Alexandra Hospl The B98 159 C6
Alexandra Ind Est DY4 51 F5
Alexandra Mews B79 21 C5
Alexandra Pl Bilston WV14 40 D6
Dudley DY1 51 C4
Alexandra Rd
Birmingham, Handsworth B21 65 D7
Birmingham, Highgate B5 86 E7
Birmingham, Stirchley B30 104 A7
Coventry CV1 113 F4
Darlaston WS10 41 E6
Halesowen B63 82 F4
Royal Leamington Spa CV31 162 B6
Tipton DY4 52 A6
Walsall WS1 42 E6
Wolverhampton WV4 39 A5
Alexandra St 2 Dudley DY1 51 B1
Nuneaton CV11 73 B4
Alexandra Terr CV6 95 E2
Alexandra Way Aldridge WS9 30 B5
Tipton B69 52 A2

Alfall Rd CV2 114 B5
Alford Cl B45 122 C7
Alfred Gunn Ho B68 64 B4
Alfred Rd
Birmingham, Handsworth B21 65 E8
Birmingham, Sparkhill B11 87 B5
Coventry CV1 113 F4
Alfred Squire Rd WV11 26 D5
Alfred St
Birmingham, Aston B6 67 B8
Birmingham, King's Heath B14 104 F7
Birmingham, Sparkbrook B12 87 B5
Darlaston WS10 41 C5
Smethwick B66 65 C7
Tamworth B79 21 A5
Walsall WS3 14 B1
West Bromwich B70 53 D3
Alfreda Ave B47 125 A8
Alfreds Well B61 136 C6
Alfreton Cl LE10 75 F5
Alfriston Rd CV3 133 C4
Alfryth Ct 4 B15 86 C8
Algernon Rd B16 65 D4
Algernon St WS2 28 D2
Alice Arnold Ho 1 CV2 96 B1
Alice Cl CV12 77 F1
Alice St WV14 40 D6
Alice Stevens Sch CV3 134 A6
Alice Wlk WV14 40 D6
Alison Cl DY4 41 A2
Alison Dr DY8 80 E3
Alison Rd B62 83 F3
Alison Sq CV6 96 B4
All Angels Wlk B68 64 B4
All Saints CE Fst Sch
Bedworth CV12 78 C2
Nuneaton CV10 73 C1
All Saints CE Mid Sch CV34 156 A1
All Saints CE Prim Sch
Coventry CV1 113 E1
West Bromwich B71 53 C6
All Saints CE Upper Prim Sch WV2 163 D1
All Saints Dr B74 32 A2
All Saints Hospl B18 65 E5
All Saints Ind Est B18 66 A5
All Saints La CV1 113 F3
All Saints Rd CV12 77 F1
All Saints' Rd B18 66 B5
All Saints Rd B14 104 E7
All Saints' Rd
Bromsgrove B61 137 A3
Darlaston WS10 41 E6
All Saints Rd Warwick CV34 161 B8
Wolverhampton WV2 163 C1
All Saints Sq CV12 78 B3
All Saints' St B18 66 A5
All Saints Way B71 53 D5
All Souls RC Prim Sch CV5 112 E2
Allan Cl
2 Smethwick B66 65 B5
7 Stourbridge DY8 80 F8
Allan Rd CV6 112 F4
Allard B77 21 E2
Allard Ho CV3 134 B6
Allard Way CV3 134 C7
Allbut St B64 62 D1
Allcock St Birmingham B9 67 A1
Tipton DY4 52 C8
Allcroft Rd B11 87 F2
Allen Cl Birmingham B43 54 E7
Studley B80 159 E3
Allen Dr Darlaston WS10 41 C6
West Bromwich B70 53 F1
Allen Ho B43 54 E7
Allen Rd Tipton DY4 40 F1
Wednesbury WS10 41 F5
Wolverhampton WV6 25 A3
Allen St Tamworth B77 21 C1
West Bromwich B70 53 B3
Allen's Rough Jun Mix Sch WV12 13 C1
Allenby Cl DY6 61 A5
Allendale Ave B80 159 E3
Allendale Cres B80 159 E3
Allendale Ct B80 159 E3
Allendale Gr B43 54 E8
Allendale Rd Birmingham B25 88 B7
Sutton Coldfield B76 57 E8
Allens Ave Birmingham B18 65 F6
West Bromwich B71 53 A7
Allens Cl WV12 27 B5
Allens Croft Rd B14 104 C6
Allens Farm Rd B31 102 E3
Allens La WS3 14 F2
Allens Rd B18 65 F6
Allensmead B77 21 C2
Allensmore Cl B98 154 F2
Allerdale Rd WS8 15 E6
Allerton Cl CV2 114 E2
Allerton La B71 53 C8
Allerton Rd B25 88 B7
Allesley Cl B74 46 C7
Allesley Croft CV5 112 A7
Allesley Ct CV5 112 A6
Allesley Cty Prim Sch CV5 112 A7
Allesley Hall Dr CV5 112 C5
Allesley Hall Prim Sch CV5 112 B4
Allesley Old Rd CV5 112 D4
Allesley Rd B92 106 D8
Allesley St B6 66 E5
Alleston Rd WV10 11 D1
Alleston Wlk WV10 11 D2
Alley The DY3 50 B3
Alleyne Gr B24 57 A2
Alleyne Rd B24 57 A1
Alliance Cl CV11 73 F3
Alliance Way CV2 114 A5
Allibone Cl CV31 162 A4
Allied Cl CV6 95 D2
Allingham Gr B43 44 E4
Allington Cl WS5 43 D8
Allison St B5 164 D2
Allitt Gr CV8 148 B5
Allman Rd B24 57 B4
Allmyn Dr B74 45 A6
Allport Mews WS11 1 E1
Allport Rd WS11 1 E1
Allport St WS11 1 E2
Allsops Cl B65 62 F4
Allton Ave B78 20 D1
Allwell Dr B14 104 F2
Allwood Gdns B32 84 A2
Alma Ave DY4 52 A7
Alma Cres B7 67 B4
Alma Ct CV11 79 F6
Alma Ind Est WS10 41 C6
Alma Pl DY2 51 C1
Alma Rd LE10 71 D1
Alma St Birmingham B19 66 E6
Coventry CV1 165 D3
Darlaston WS10 41 C6
Halesowen B63 82 C5
Smethwick B66 65 C6
Walsall WS2 28 D4
Wednesbury WS10 42 B3
Willenhall WV13 27 B2
Wolverhampton WV10 25 F2
Alma Way B19 66 D7
Alma Wks WS10 41 D5
Almond Ave
Kidderminster DY11 116 B8
Nuneaton CV10 72 C6
Royal Leamington Spa CV32 156 F3
Walsall, Bentley WS2 27 E4
Walsall, Yew Tree WS5 43 A4
Almond Cl Birmingham B29 103 A6
Cannock WS11 2 C2
Walsall WS3 14 F2
Almond Croft B42 54 F7
Almond Gr Warwick CV34 156 A1
Wolverhampton WV6 25 C4
Almond Rd Huntington WS12 1 D8
Kingswinford DY6 60 E8
Almond Tree Ave CV2 96 C2
Almsbury Ct B26 89 C4
Almshouses Bedworth CV12 78 B3
Middleton B78 34 B1
Rowington Green CV35 145 A1
Smethwick B67 64 F5
11 Warwick CV34 160 E6
Wolverhampton WV4 38 F3
Alnwick Cl WS12 2 E2
Alnwick Ho 5 B23 56 F6
Alnwick Rd WS3 14 A4
Alperton Dr DY9 81 E2
Alpha Bsns Pk CV2 96 D1
Alpha Cl B12 86 E6
Alpha Ho CV2 114 A4
Alpha Way WS6 14 A8
Alpine Ct CV8 148 A6
Alpine Dr Cannock WS12 2 D4
Dudley DY2 62 B4
Alpine Rise CV3 133 A5
Alpine Way WV3 24 C2
Alport Croft 4 B9 67 B2
Alspath La CV5 111 F4
Alspath Rd CV7 92 C1
Alston Cl Cannock WS12 2 E2
Solihull B91 107 D6
Sutton Coldfield B74 32 A2
Alston Gr B9 68 B2
Alston Ho B69 63 D6
Alston Prim Sch B9 68 B3
Alston Rd Birmingham B9 68 B3
Oldbury B69 63 E7
Solihull B91 107 D6
Alston St B16 66 A2
Althorpe Dr B93 127 E3
Althorpe Ho CV31 162 A6
Althorpe Ind Est
7 CV31 162 A7
Althorpe St CV31 162 A7
Alton Ave WV12 27 B5
Alton Cl Coventry CV2 96 D2
Redditch B97 153 B1
Wolverhampton WV10 11 F3
Alton Gr Cannock WS11 1 B1
Dudley DY2 51 E1
West Bromwich B71 53 E7
Alton Rd B29 85 F3
Alum Cl CV6 113 D8
Alum Dr B9 68 A3
Alum Rock Rd B8 68 B4
Alum Well Rd WS2 28 B1
Alumhurst Ave B8 68 B4
Alumwell Cl WS2 28 B1
Alumwell Comp Sch WS2 28 A1
Alumwell Jun & Inf Schs WS2 28 B2
Alvaston Cl WS3 14 C3
Alvechurch CE Mid Sch B48 139 B6
Alvechurch Crown Meadow Fst Sch B48 139 B6
Alvechurch Highway
Lydiate Ash B60 121 D2
Redditch B98 153 F3
Alvechurch Ho B60 137 B3
Alvechurch Rd
Birmingham B31 123 B7
Halesowen B63 82 F2
Alvechurch Sta B48 139 A4
Alvecote Cotts B79 22 D6
Alvecote Pools Nature Reserve B79 22 D7
Alveley Cl B98 154 D4
Alverley Cl DY6 60 B8
Alverstoke Cl WV9 11 A2
Alverstone Rd CV2 114 A4
Alveston Cl B98 154 C2
Alveston Gr Birmingham B9 68 B2
Knowle B93 128 B7
Alveston Rd B47 125 A7
Alvin Cl Coventry CV3 114 F1
Halesowen B62 83 F8
Alvington Cl WV12 27 D4
Alvis Cl B79 20 F7
Alvis Ret Pk CV5 113 A3
Alvis Wlk B36 58 F1
Alwen St DY8 60 F2
Alwin Rd B65 63 B2
Alwold Ct B29 84 F2
Alwold Rd B29 85 A2
Alwyn B77 35 E7
Alwyn Cl WS6 5 A3
Alwynn Wlk B23 56 C3
Alwynne Freeman Ct CV7 95 A6
Amal Way B6 55 F2
Amanda Ave WV4 38 F4
Amanda Dr B26 68 F1
Ambassador Ct CV32 156 F3
Ambell Cl B65 62 F5
Amber Bsns Village B77 22 B3
Amber Cl B77 22 B3
Amber Dr B69 64 A5
Amber Gr WS11 2 C2
Amber Terr DY10 116 F5
Amber Way B62 83 C6
Ambergate Cl Redditch B97 153 B5
Walsall WS3 14 C3
Ambergate Dr DY6 60 C8
Amberley Ave CV12 79 C2
Amberley Gn B43 54 E6
Amberley Gr B6 56 A3
Amberley Rd B92 88 F4
Amberley Way B74 30 E1
Amberwood Cl WS2 27 D3
Amblecote Ave B44 44 E2
Amblecote Prim Sch DY8 80 F7
Amblecote Rd
Brierley Hill DY5 81 D8
Kidderminster DY10 117 B5
Ambler Gr CV2 114 C3
Ambleside Birmingham B32 84 C1
Coventry CV2 96 E2
Ambleside Cl WV14 40 E3
Ambleside Dr DY5 81 C8
Ambleside Way
Bromsgrove B60 137 B1
Kingswinford DY6 60 D6
Nuneaton CV11 73 E6
Ambrose Cl WV13 26 E2
Ambrose Cres DY6 60 D8
Ambury Way B43 54 D8
Amelas Cl 3 DY5 61 A1
Amersham Cl
Birmingham B32 84 E5
Coventry CV5 112 B4
Ames Rd WS10 41 C7
Amesbury Rd B13 86 E3
Amethyst Ct 2 B92 88 F1
Amherst Ave B20 55 A3
Amherst Rd CV8 147 E6
Amhurst Bsns Ctr CV34 160 B7
Amicombe B77 22 C1
Amington Cl B75 32 D3
Amington Heath Prim Sch B77 22 B4
Amington Ind Est B77 22 B2
Amington Rd
Birmingham B25 88 B6
Solihull B90 126 A8
Tamworth B77 21 D4
Amiss Gdns B10 87 C8
Amity Cl B66 65 B5
Amos Ave Nuneaton CV10 73 B2
Wolverhampton WV11 26 C7
Amos Jacques Rd CV12 78 A4
Amos La WV11 26 C6
Amos Rd DY9 81 F2
Amphlett Croft DY4 52 B4
Amphlett Ct 1 B60 137 A2
Amphletts Cl DY2 62 E3
Ampton Rd B15 86 B7
Amroth Cl B45 122 B7
Amroth Mews 4 CV31 162 C6
Amwell Gr B14 104 F3
Amy Cl CV6 95 F4
Anchor Cl Birmingham B16 65 E1
Tamworth B77 21 E4
Anchor Hill DY5 61 C1
Anchor La WV14 40 B2
Anchor Par WS9 30 B6
Anchor Rd Aldridge WS9 30 B6
Dudley WV14 40 C2
Anchorage Rd
Birmingham B23 56 D3
Sutton Coldfield B74 46 B6
Anchorfields DY10 116 F6
Anchorway Rd CV3 133 B4
Anders B79 21 A6
Anders Sq WV6 23 E4
Andersleigh Dr WV14 51 A8
Anderson Cres B43 43 E2
Anderson Dr CV31 162 A2
Anderson Gdns DY4 52 A4
Anderson Rd Birmingham B23 56 E6
Smethwick B66 65 A1
Tipton DY4 52 A4
Anderton Cl B74 46 A7
Anderton Park Jun & Inf Sch B12 87 B4
Anderton Park Rd B13 87 A3
Anderton Rd Bedworth CV12 77 C1
Birmingham B11 87 C6
Coventry CV6 96 B4
Anderton St B1 66 B3
Andover Cres DY6 60 F4
Andover Ho B35 58 B3
Andover Pl WS11 2 A4
Andover St B5 66 F2
Andrew Cl WV12 27 D6
Andrew Ct B76 46 F3
Andrew Dr WV12 27 D6
Andrew Gdns B21 54 E1
Andrew Rd Halesowen B63 83 A3
Tipton DY4 41 A1
West Bromwich B71 42 F2
Andrews Cl DY5 81 E8
Andrews Ho WS13 9 A7
Andrews Rd WS9 16 B4
Anerley Gr B44 44 F4
Anerley Rd B44 44 F4
Angel Mews 8 B46 70 F7
Angel Pas DY8 81 A5
Angel St Dudley DY2 62 B8
Upper Bentley B97 152 B1
Angela Ave Blackheath B65 63 D4
Coventry CV2 96 E1
Angela Pl WV14 40 D6
Angelica B77 21 F4
Angelica Cl 7 WS5 43 A3
Angelina St B12 86 F7
Angelo Ho B13 105 D7
Anglesey Ave B36 70 B6
Anglesey Bsns Pk WS12 2 E4
Anglesey Cl Allesley CV5 112 B7
Burntwood WS7 6 F4
Anglesey Cres Brownhills WS8 6 F2
Cannock WS12 2 C5
Anglesey Inf Sch B19 66 C7
Anglesey Jun Sch B19 66 C6
Anglesey Mews WS12 2 C5
Anglesey Rd Brownhills WS8 6 F2
Lichfield WS13 3 B2
Anglesey St Birmingham B19 66 C7
Cannock WS12 2 B5
Angless Way CV8 147 F3
Anglia Rd WS11 1 D3
Anglian Rd WS9 29 D6
Anglo African Ind Pk B69 52 E2
Angorfa Cl WS13 8 F7
Angus Cl Coventry CV5 112 A4
Kenilworth CV8 148 C6
West Bromwich B71 53 C6
Anita Ave DY4 52 A2
Anita Croft B23 56 E2
Ankadine Rd 5 DY8 81 B6
Anker Cl WS7 7 D6
Anker St CV11 73 D3
Anker View B77 21 C3
Ankerdine Ct B63 83 A3
Ankerdrive B77, B79 21 B4
Ankermoor Cl B34 69 B6
Ankermoor Ct B77 21 E5
Ankermoor Prim Sch B77 21 E5
Ankerside Sh Ctr B79 21 B4
Ann Cres WS11 1 E6
Ann Croft B26 89 D4
Ann Rd B47 125 A3
Ann St WV13 27 B3
Annan Ave WV10 25 F7
Anne Cl B70 52 E3
Anne Cres CV3 134 C5
Anne Ct B76 46 F3
Anne Gr DY4 41 B1
Anne Rd Brierley Hill DY5 62 A1
Smethwick B66 65 D7
Wolverhampton WV4 39 B6
Annesley Rd B66 65 B5
Annie Lennard Inf Sch B67 64 E3
Annie Osborn Prim Sch CV2 114 D7
Annscroft B38 103 D2
Ansbro Cl B18 65 F5
Ansell Rd
Birmingham, Gravelly Hill B24 56 F1
Birmingham, Sparkbrook B11 87 C6
Warwick CV34 160 D7
Ansley Cl B98 154 F1
Ansley Comm CV10 72 A7
Ansley Rd CV10 72 B3
Ansley Way B92 107 D7
Anslow Rd B23 56 C5
Anson Ave WS13 3 A1
Anson Cl Burntwood WS7 7 C7
Great Wyrley WS6 4 F1
Perton WV6 23 E5
Anson Ct 3 B78 35 B8
Anson Gr B27 88 D2
Anson Junc WS2 27 E1
Anson Rd Great Wyrley WS6 4 F1
Walsall WS2 27 E1
West Bromwich B70 52 E7
Anson Way CV2 114 F8
Anstey Gr B27 88 B1
Anstey Rd B44 55 E6
Anston Way WV11 26 D7
Anstree Cl WS6 4 D1
Anstruther Rd B15 85 E8
Ansty Dr WS12 2 D1
Ansty Rd CV2 114 E5
Antelope Gdns CV34 160 C8
Anthony Rd B8 67 F4
Anthony Way CV2 114 C2
Anton Dr B76 58 A6
Antony Rd B90 106 B1
Antrim Cl CV5 112 B7
Antringham Gdns B15 85 D8
Antrobus Rd Birmingham B21 54 E1
Sutton Coldfield B73 45 F1
Anvil Dr B69 63 E6
Anvil Wlk B70 52 F4
Apex Bsns Pk WS11 5 F4
Apex Rd WS8 15 C7
Apley Rd DY8 80 E7
Apollo B79 20 F6
Apollo Cl WS11 2 A5
Apollo Croft B24 57 D3
Apollo Rd Oldbury B68 64 C6
Stourbridge DY9 82 A5
Apollo Way Birmingham B20 55 D1
Royal Leamington Spa CV34 161 D5
12 Smethwick B66 65 C5
Apperley Way B63 82 B7
Appian Cl Birmingham B14 104 E5
Tamworth B77 35 D7
Appian Way B90 126 D4
Apple Tree Cl
Birmingham B23 56 B4
Kidderminster DY10 117 B7
Apple Wlk WS11 2 C2
Applebee Rd LE10 75 D6
Appleby Cl B14 104 D5
Appleby Gr B90 127 B6
Applecross B74 31 F1
Applecross Cl CV4 131 F6
Appledore Cl Cannock WS12 2 E3
Great Wyrley WS6 5 A3
Appledore Ct 3 WS3 28 B8
Appledore Dr CV5 111 F5
Appledore Rd WS5 43 D8
Appledore Terr WS5 43 D8
Appledorne Gdns B34 69 B6
Applesham Cl B11 87 D6
Appleton Ave
Birmingham B43 54 E8
Stourbridge DY8 81 A2
Appleton Cl B30 103 E8
Appleton Cres WV4 39 A5
Appleton Ct 5 B15 86 B7
Appleton Ho B31 102 E5
Appletree Cl
Birmingham B31 102 F1
Catherine de B B91 108 B5
Appletree Gr Aldridge WS9 30 B5
Wolverhampton W6 25 C5
Appletree La B97 153 B5
Applewood Gr 5 B64 62 F1
Approach The CV31 161 F6
April Croft B13 87 B3
Apsley Cl B68 84 A7
Apsley Croft B38 104 B2
Apsley Gr Birmingham B24 57 A2
Dorridge B93 127 F2
Apsley Ho B64 62 F2
Apsley Rd B68 84 A7
Aqua Ho CV32 157 A1
Aqueduct La B48 138 F7
Aqueduct Rd B90 105 E1
Aragon Dr
Royal Leamington Spa CV34 161 D6
Sutton Coldfield B73 46 B6
Arbor Cl B77 21 D3
Arbor Gate WS9 16 B4
Arbor Way B37 70 C1
Arboretum Rd WS1 29 A3
Arboretum The CV4 132 D3
Arbour Cl CV8 148 B3
Arbour Tree La B93 144 F7
Arbury Ave Bedworth CV12 78 A3
Coventry CV6 95 F2
Arbury Cl CV32 157 A4
Arbury Ct CV10 72 C3
Arbury Dr DY8 60 D3
Arbury Hall Rd B90 126 D8
Arbury Rd CV10 72 D2
Arbury Wlk B76 58 D5
Arcade WS1 28 E1
Arcade The CV3 114 B2
Arcadian Sh Ctr B5 164 C1
Arcal St DY3 50 E7
Arch Hill St DY2 62 C5
Arch Rd CV2 114 E5
Archbishop Grimshaw Comp Sch B37 69 F3
Archbishop Ilsley RC Sch B27 88 C3
Archer Cl Oldbury B68 64 B4
Studley B80 159 D4
Wednesbury WS10 41 E3
Archer Ct DY9 81 E2
Archer Rd Birmingham B14 105 C4
Kenilworth CV8 147 E3
Redditch B98 153 E4
Walsall WS3 28 E6
Archers Cl B23 56 D8
Archery Fields CV34 160 F6
Archery Rd Meriden CV7 92 B1
Royal Leamington Spa CV31 161 E8
Arches Ind Est The CV5 113 A3
Archibald Rd B19 66 C8

Archway The 2 WS4 28 F3
Arcot Rd B28 87 F2
Ardarth Rd B38 104 A2
Ardav Rd B70 52 F8
Arden Bldgs B93 127 F3
Arden Cl
Balsall Common CV7 130 B7
Meriden CV7 92 C1
Royal Leamington Spa CV31 162 B5
Stourbridge, Wollaston DY8 80 E7
Stourbridge, Wordsley DY8 60 C3
Tamworth B77 21 E5
Warwick CV34 156 A1
Arden Croft Coleshill B46 59 F1
Solihull B92 89 C4
Arden Ct Binley Woods CV3 135 D6
2 Dudley DY3 50 D3
Hampton in A B92 109 A7
Sutton Coldfield B72 57 C8
Arden Dr Birmingham B26 88 F7
Dorridge B93 128 A1
Sutton Coldfield, Falcon Lodge B75 47 B5
Sutton Coldfield, Wylde Green B73 57 B8
Arden Forest Inf Sch CV12 79 B3
Arden Gr
Birmingham, Ladywood B16 66 A1
8 Birmingham, Lozells B19 66 C8
Oldbury B69 64 A5
Arden Ho B60 137 B3
Arden Jun & Inf Sch B11 87 C5
Arden Leys B94 141 D2
Arden Meads B94 143 C6
Arden Oak Rd B26 89 D4
Arden Pl WV14 41 B4
Arden Rd
Birmingham, Acock's Green B27 88 B4
Birmingham, Aston B6 66 D8
Birmingham, Rubery B45 102 A1
Birmingham, Saltley B8 67 D3
Bulkington CV12 79 C2
Dorridge B93 127 F2
Hollywood B47 125 A6
Kenilworth CV8 148 B3
Nuneaton CV11 74 A1
Smethwick B67 65 A5
Tamworth B77 35 F5
Arden Sch B93 128 B5
Arden Specl Sch B67 65 A5
Arden St CV5 132 F8
Arden Vale Rd B93 128 B7
Ardencote Rd B13 105 A6
Ardendale 6 B90 126 C8
Arderne Dr B37 70 A1
Ardgay Dr WS12 1 F7
Ardingley Wlk DY5 81 B7
Ardley Cl DY2 62 D8
Ardley Rd B14 105 A5
Aretha Cl DY6 61 A6
Argosy Ho B35 58 B2
Argus Cl B76 46 F3
Argyle Ave B77 21 D4
Argyle Cl Stourbridge DY8 60 E1
Walsall WS4 29 B3
Argyle Rd Walsall WS4 29 B3
Wolverhampton WV2 39 B6
Argyle St Birmingham B7 67 D8
Tamworth B77 21 E4
Argyll Ho 5 WV3 25 C4
Argyll St CV2 114 A3
Ariane B79 20 E7
Arion Cl B77 21 D5
Arkall Cl B79 21 C7
Arkle B77 35 D4
Arkle Croft Birmingham B36 68 C8
Blackheath B65 62 F6
Arkle Dr CV2 114 F7
Arkley Gr B28 106 B7
Arkley Rd B28 106 B7
Arkwright Rd
Birmingham B32 84 C5
Walsall WS2 28 B5
Arlen Dr B43 43 D1
Arlescote Cl B75 32 C2
Arlescote Rd B92 89 C2
Arless Way B17 85 B3
Arleston Way B90 126 E8
Arley Cl Kidderminster DY11 116 A2
Oldbury B69 63 D5
Redditch B98 154 D5
Arley Ct DY2 62 C6
Arley Dr DY8 80 E3
Arley Gr WV4 38 D5
Arley Ho B26 69 A1
Arley Mews CV32 156 E1
Arley Rd Birmingham B29 85 F3
Birmingham, Saltley B8 67 D6
Solihull B91 107 A4
Arley Villas 4 B18 65 D4
Arlidge Cl WV14 40 D4
Arlidge Cres CV8 148 C5
Arlington Ave CV32 156 F2
Arlington Cl DY6 60 D4
Arlington Ct 2
Royal Leamington Spa CV32 156 F2
Stourbridge DY8 81 B4
Arlington Gr B14 105 B2
Arlington Ho B15 86 C7
Arlington Mews 5 CV32 156 F2
Arlington Rd
Birmingham B14 105 B3
West Bromwich B71 53 D6
Arlington Way CV11 73 F2
Arlon Ave CV10 72 D7
Armada Cl B23 56 D1
Armadale Cl LE10 71 A1
Armarna Dr CV5 111 B8
Armfield St CV6 114 A8
Armitage Ho WS13 3 E1
Armorial Rd CV3 133 B7
Armour Cl LE10 75 D5
Armoury Rd B11 87 D6
Armoury Trad Est B11 87 E6
Armscott Rd CV2 114 C6
Armside Cl WS3 15 B4
Armson Rd CV7 78 A1
Armstead Rd WV9 11 A3
Armstrong B79 20 F6
Armstrong Ave CV3 114 B1
Armstrong Cl
Stourbridge DY8 81 B6
Whitnash CV31 162 A2
Armstrong Dr
Birmingham B36 58 F1
Walsall WS2 28 A4
Wolverhampton WV6 25 A5
Armstrong Way WV13 41 B8
Arna Ho CV3 134 B6
Arncliffe Cl CV11 74 A2
Arncliffe Way 4 CV34 155 F1
Arne Rd CV2 115 A6
Arnhem Cl WV11 26 B8
Arnhem Cnr CV3 134 D6
Arnhem Rd WV13 40 E8
Arnhem Way DY4 52 C5
Arnold Ave CV3 133 C5
Arnold Cl Tamworth B79 21 A6
Walsall WS2 27 F3
Arnold Gr Birmingham B30 103 D4
Solihull B90 106 B4
Arnold Lodge Prep Sch CV32 156 F2
Arnold Rd B90 106 C4
Arnotdale Dr WS12 1 F7
Arnside Cl CV1 165 D4
Arnside Ct B23 56 B4
Arnwood Cl WS2 27 F2
Arosa Dr B17 85 B3
Arran Cl Birmingham B43 43 E3
Cannock WS11 2 A3
Nuneaton CV10 73 A3
Arran Rd B34 68 F6
Arran Way Birmingham B36 70 B7
Hinckley LE10 71 B1
Arras Bvd CV35 160 A7
Arras Rd DY2 51 E2
Arrow Cl B93 128 A6
Arrow Ho 1 B68 84 B8
Arrow Rd WS3 28 E6
Arrow Rd N B98 154 A4
Arrow Rd S B98 154 A4
Arrow Vale High Sch B98 154 E2
Arrow Valley Park B98 154 B4
Arrow Wlk B38 104 B1
Arrowcrest Fst Sch B98 154 A2
Arrowdale Rd B98 154 A3
Arrowfield Gn B38 123 D7
Arsenal St B9 67 C1
Arthingworth Cl CV3 114 E1
Arthur Alford Ho CV12 77 D1
Arthur Dr (Road 2) DY10 116 E1
Arthur Greenwood Ct WV14 40 C6
Arthur Gunby Cl B75 46 F7
Arthur Pl B1 66 B3
Arthur Rd
Birmingham, Edgbaston B15 86 B7
Birmingham, Erdington B24 57 B4
Birmingham, Handsworth B21 65 F8
Birmingham, Hay Mills B25 88 B6
Tipton DY4 52 A7
Arthur St Bilston WV14 40 D6
Birmingham B10 67 B1
Cannock, Chadsmoor WS11 1 F4
Cannock, Wimblebury WS12 2 F3
Coventry CV1 165 C4
Kenilworth CV8 148 A5
Redditch B98 154 B3
West Bromwich B70 53 D1
Wolverhampton WV2 39 D6
Arthur Terry Sch B74 32 A3
Artillery Rd CV11 79 F6
Artingstall Ho B30 104 B8
Arton Croft B24 57 A2
Arun Way B76 47 A1
Arundel Birmingham B17 85 A6
Tamworth B77 35 C7
Arundel Ave WS10 41 F3
Arundel Cl 2 CV34 160 F8
Arundel Cres B92 89 A1
Arundel Dr B69 62 F8
Arundel Gr WV6 23 F3
Arundel Ho 4 B23 56 F6
Arundel Pl B11 87 A6
Arundel Rd Birmingham B14 105 A1
Bromsgrove B60 137 B1
Bulkington CV12 79 C3
Coventry CV3 133 D6
Stourbridge DY8 60 C2
Willenhall WV12 27 C7
Wolverhampton WV10 11 B2
Arundel St WS1 42 E7
Asbury Rd
Balsall Common CV7 130 B5
Wednesbury WS10 42 E2
Ascot Cl Bedworth CV12 78 B4
Birmingham B16 65 F2
Coventry CV3 134 C6
Lichfield WS14 9 D7
Oldbury B69 63 E6
Ascot Ct B29 103 C7
Ascot Dr Cannock WS11 4 C8
Dudley DY1 50 F2
Wolverhampton WV4 39 A4
Ascot Gdns DY8 60 D2
Ascot Rd B13 86 F2
Ascot Ride CV32 157 C3
Asfare Bsns Pk LE10 75 E1
Ash Ave B12 87 A5
Ash Cl WV8 10 A3
Ash Cres Birmingham B37 69 F6
Kingswinford DY6 60 E6
Ash Ct Oldbury B66 64 C8
Stourbridge DY8 81 A4
Ash Dr Catshill B61 121 B1
Kenilworth CV8 148 A4
Nuneaton CV10 72 A8
West Bromwich B71 53 C6
Ash Gn DY1 51 A5
Ash Gr Ash Green CV7 95 C7
Birmingham, Balsall Heath B12 87 A5
11 Birmingham, Bordesley B9 67 B2
Cannock WS11 1 F4
Dudley DY3 50 C2
Kidderminster DY11 116 B7
Lichfield WS13 9 E8
Stourbridge DY9 81 D3
Tamworth B77 35 F5
Ash Green La CV7 95 D6
Ash Green Sch CV7 95 D6
Ash Hill WV3 24 D2
Ash La Alvechurch B48 123 D2
Great Wyrley WS6 5 A3
Ash Lawn Ho 9 CV31 162 A7
Ash Mews 5 B27 88 C5
Ash Park Ind Est WS11 2 B3
Ash Priors Cl CV4 112 B1
Ash Rd Birmingham B8 67 D4
Dudley DY1 51 B3
Tipton DY4 51 E4
Wednesbury WS10 41 F5
Ash St Bilston WV14 40 E3
Blackheath B64 62 F2
Walsall WS3 14 D1
Wolverhampton WV3 25 A1
Ash Terr B69 52 B1
Ash Tree Ave CV4 112 A2
Ash Tree Dr B26 88 D7
Ash Tree Gr CV7 97 E5
Ash Tree Rd
Birmingham B30 104 A6
Redditch B97 153 B5
Ash View WS12 1 D8
Ash Way B23 56 C7
Ashborough Dr B91 127 C8
Ashbourne Cl WS11 2 A4
Ashbourne Gr 3 B6 66 E8
Ashbourne Rd
Birmingham B16 65 D3
Walsall WS3 14 C3
Wolverhampton, Ettingshall Park WV4 39 E3
Wolverhampton, Heath Town WV1 26 A3
Ashbourne Way B90 126 E8
Ashbridge Rd CV5 112 C4
Ashbrook Cres B91 127 C8
Ashbrook Gr B30 104 C8
Ashbrook Rd B30 104 C8
Ashburn Gr WV13 27 C2
Ashburton Cl LE10 76 A6
Ashburton Rd
Birmingham B14 104 D5
Coventry CV2 114 E8
Ashbury Covert 3 B30 104 C3
Ashby Cl Birmingham B8 68 C6
Coventry CV3 134 F8
Ashby Ct Nuneaton CV11 73 D3
Solihull B91 107 C1
Ashby Rd Hinckley LE9, LE10 71 E5
Tamworth B79 21 C8
Ashcombe Ave B20 54 E3
Ashcombe Dr CV4 111 F3
Ashcombe Gdns B24 57 D3
Ashcott Cl B38 103 D2
Ashcroft Birmingham B15 85 E5
4 Smethwick B66 65 C5
Wolverhampton WV4 39 F4
Ashcroft Cl CV2 115 A8
Ashcroft Cty Inf Sch B79 21 C7
Ashcroft Gr B20 55 D2
Ashcroft La Lichfield WS14 8 E1
Shenstone WS14 17 E7
Ashcroft Way CV2 115 B8
Ashdale Cl
Binley Woods CV3 135 E7
Huntington WS12 1 C7
Kingswinford DY6 60 E8
Ashdale Dr B14 105 A1
Ashdale Gr B26 89 A8
Ashdale Rd B77 21 D5
Ashdene Cl
Kidderminster DY10 117 C5
Sutton Coldfield B73 46 A3
Ashdene Gdns
Kenilworth CV8 148 B4
Stourbridge DY8 60 C2
Ashdown Cl
Birmingham, Frankley B45 102 A2
Birmingham, Highgate B13 87 A1
Coventry CV3 134 D8
Ashdown Dr Nuneaton CV10 72 F2
Stourbridge DY8 60 E3
Ashe Rd CV10 72 B3
Ashen Cl DY3 39 C3
Ashenden Rise WV3 38 A8
Ashenhurst Rd DY1 61 F8
Ashenhurst Wlk DY1 51 A1
Ashes Rd B69 63 F3
Ashes The Oldbury B69 63 F3
Wolverhampton WV11 26 B6
Ashfern Dr B76 57 F7
Ashfield Ave Birmingham B14 86 F1
Coventry CV4 111 D1
Ashfield Cl WS3 28 F4
Ashfield Cres Dudley DY2 62 C3
Stourbridge DY9 82 A3
Ashfield Ct B38 103 E4
Ashfield Gr Halesowen B63 82 E2
Wolverhampton WV10 11 C3
Ashfield Ho B28 105 E3
Ashfield Rd Bilston WV14 41 A2
Birmingham B14 86 F1
Kenilworth CV8 148 B4
Wolverhampton, Compton WV3 24 D2
Wolverhampton, Fordhouses WV10 11 C3
Ashford Dr Bedworth CV12 78 A3
Sedgley DY3 50 E7
Sutton Coldfield B76 57 F5
Ashford Gdns CV31 161 F3
Ashford Ind Pk WV2 40 A7
Ashford La B94 143 B7
Ashford Rd Hinckley LE10 75 B7
Whitnash CV31 161 F2
Ashford St B6 66 E6
Ashford Tower B12 86 F8
Ashfurlong Cl CV7 130 B6
Ashfurlong Cres B75 46 E8
Ashgrove WS7 6 F5
Ashgrove Cl B60 121 D1
Ashgrove Rd B44 44 C2
Ashill Rd B45 122 B7
Ashington Gr CV3 134 A5
Ashington Rd CV12 77 C1
Ashland St WV3 25 B1
Ashlands Cl B79 21 C7
Ashlawn Cres B91 106 D5
Ashlea B78 36 F5
Ashleigh Ct 8 DY2 62 E8
Ashleigh Dr Birmingham B20 55 B2
Nuneaton CV11 73 F1
Tamworth B77 35 E8
Ashleigh Gr B13 87 B1
Ashleigh Rd Solihull B91 107 B4
Tipton B69 63 C8
Ashley Cl Birmingham B15 86 C7
Kingswinford DY6 60 C4
Stourbridge DY8 80 D2
Ashley Cres CV34 161 B6
Ashley Ct B45 122 A1
Ashley Ho DY2 62 D4
Ashley Mount WV6 24 D5
Ashley Rd Birmingham B23 56 E3
Walsall WS3 27 F8
Wolverhampton WV4 38 E5
Ashley St WV14 40 E6
Ashmall WS7 7 D4
Ashmead Dr B45 122 C4
Ashmead Gr B24 57 A2
Ashmead Rd WS7 7 A8
Ashmead Rise B45 122 C4
Ashmole Cl WS14 9 E6
Ashmole Rd B70 52 F7
Ashmore Ave WV11 13 A1
Ashmore Lake Rd WV12 27 B4
Ashmore Lake Way WV12 27 B4
Ashmore Rd
Birmingham B30 103 F5
Coventry CV6 113 B4
Ashmores Cl B97 158 D5
Ashold Farm Rd B24 57 D2
Asholme Cl B36 68 C7
Ashorne Cl Birmingham B28 106 B7
Coventry CV2 96 C2
Redditch B98 159 D8
Ashover Gr 9 B18 65 E4
Ashover Rd B44 44 D3
Ashow Cl CV8 148 B4
Ashperton Cl B98 153 E1
Ashridge Cl CV11 78 F8
Ashstead Cl B76 58 B6
Ashted Cir B7 67 A4
Ashted Lock B7 66 F4
Ashted Wlk B7 67 B4
Ashton Cl B97 153 B1
Ashton Croft Birmingham B16 66 A2
Solihull B91 107 A1
Ashton Dr WS4 15 C2
Ashton Park Dr DY5 61 C1
Ashton Rd B25 88 C7
Ashtree Gr WV14 41 B3
Ashtree Rd Blackheath B64 62 F2
Oldbury B69 63 D8
Tipton B69 52 C1
Walsall WS3 15 A3
Ashurst Rd B76 57 F7
Ashville Ave B34 68 F7
Ashville Dr B63 83 A5
Ashwater Dr B14 104 D2
Ashway B11 87 B5
Ashwell Dr B90 106 D4
Ashwells Gr WV9 10 F2
Ashwin Rd B21 66 A7
Ashwood Ave Coventry CV6 112 F5
Stourbridge DY8 60 D2
Ashwood Cl B74 44 E8
Ashwood Ct Birmingham B13 87 A3
Birmingham, Stechford B34 68 D5
Ashwood Dr B37 70 D3
Ashwood Gr WV4 39 A5
Ashwood Park Prim Sch DY8 60 D1
Ashwood Rd CV10 72 E5
Ashworth Ho Cannock WS11 2 A4
Lichfield WS13 9 B8
Ashworth Rd B42 44 B1
Askew Bridge Rd DY3 50 B3
Askew Cl DY3 50 E5
Aspbury Croft B36 58 D1
Aspen Cl Birmingham B27 88 B2
Coventry CV4 111 D1
Aspen Dr B37 90 C8
Aspen Gdns B20 55 B1
Aspen Gr Birmingham B9 68 A3
Burntwood WS7 6 F8
Hollywood B47 125 B5
Willenhall WV12 27 E7
Aspen Ho B91 106 F2
Aspen Way WV3 25 A1
Asplen Ct CV8 148 C4
Aspley Heath B94 141 D2
Aspley Heath La B94 141 D2
Asquith Dr Cannock WS11 2 C2
Tipton B69 52 D2
Asquith Rd B8 68 B5
Asra Cl Coventry CV2 113 F4
Smethwick B66 65 A8
Asra Ho B66 65 A8
Astbury Ave B67 64 F3
Astbury Cl Walsall WS3 14 A4
Wolverhampton WV1 26 A1
Astbury Ct 4 B68 84 B7
Aster Cl Hinckley LE10 75 E6
Nuneaton CV11 74 A1
Aster Way LE10 75 D6
Aster Wlk WV9 11 A3
Asthill Croft CV3 133 C8
Asthill Gr CV3 133 C8
Astley Ave Coventry CV6 95 E2
Halesowen B62 83 F6
Astley Cl Redditch B98 159 A7
Royal Leamington Spa CV32 156 D2
Tipton DY4 52 D6
Astley Cres B62 83 F5
Astley La Bedworth CV12 77 C4
Nuneaton CV10 72 B1
Astley Rd B21 54 D1
Astley Wlk B90 106 B5
Aston Bridge B6 66 F6
Aston Brook Gn B6 66 F5
Aston Brook St B6 66 F6
Aston Brook St E B6 66 F5
Aston Bury B15 85 D7
Aston Church Rd B7, B8 67 D6
Aston Cl Bilston WV14 41 A4
Shenstone WS14 17 F6
Aston Cross B6 67 A6
Aston Ct B23 56 C3
Aston Expressway B6 66 F6
Aston Expressway (Elevated Rd) B6 67 A8
Aston Fields Mid Sch B60 151 C8
Aston Fields Trad Est B60 150 F6
Aston Flamville Rd LE10 76 C7
Aston Hall B6 66 F8
Aston Hall Rd B6 67 B8
Aston Ind Est CV12 78 C2
Aston La Birmingham B20 55 E2
Hinckley LE10 76 A6
Aston Manor Sch B6 66 F6
Aston Pk Ind Est CV11 73 B5
Aston Rd Birmingham B6 66 F5
Bromsgrove B60 150 F6
Coventry CV5 112 F1
Dudley DY2 62 B8
Nuneaton CV11 73 B5
Tipton B69 52 A1
Willenhall WV13 26 E2
Aston Rd N B6 66 F6
Aston Seabed Ctr B7 67 A6
Aston St Birmingham B4 164 D4
Tipton DY4 52 C7
Wolverhampton WV3 39 A8
Aston Sta B6 67 B8
Aston Tower Inf & Jun Schs B6 66 F7
Astons Cl DY5 81 D7
Astons Fold DY5 81 D7
Astor Dr B13 87 C1
Astor Rd Aldridge B74 31 A1
Kingswinford DY6 60 F5
Astoria Cl WV12 13 D1
Astoria Gdns WV11 13 D1
Astwell Prep Sch B20 66 B8
Astwood Bank Fst Sch B96 158 E2
Astwood La B96 158 C2
Atcham Cl B98 154 F3
Atcheson Cl B80 159 E4
Athelney Ct WS3 15 A3
Athelstan Gr WV6 23 F5
Athelstan Way B79 20 F7
Athena Dr CV34 161 E5
Athena Gdns CV6 96 A1
Atherston Pl CV4 132 D6
Atherstone Cl Redditch B98 154 F1
Solihull B90 105 E2
Atherstone Rd WV1 26 B2
Atherstone St B78 35 B8
Athlone Rd WS5 43 C8
Athol Cl B32 102 D8
Athol Rd CV2 115 A6

Athole St B12 .... 87 A7
Atholl Cres CV10 .... 72 E2
Atkins Way LE10 .... 75 E7
Atkinson Ct WV10 .... 25 D6
Atlantic Ct 4 WV13 .... 27 A1
Atlantic Rd B44 .... 44 F1
Atlas Croft WV10 .... 25 C6
Atlas Gr B70 .... 52 F3
Atlas Trad Est B11 .... 87 D5
Attenborough Cl B19 .... 66 E5
Attingham Dr
Birmingham B43 .... 43 D2
Cannock WS11 .... 2 B2
Attleborough Fields Ind Est CV11 .... 73 F3
Attleborough Fst Sch CV11 73 E3
Attleborough La B46 .... 59 A1
Attleborough Rd CV11 .... 73 D3
Attlee Cl B69 .... 52 D2
Attlee Cres WV14 .... 40 E2
Attlee Gr WS11 .... 2 C2
Attlee Rd WS2 .... 27 E3
Attoxhall Rd CV2 .... 114 E4
Attwell Pk WV3 .... 38 D7
Attwell Rd DY4 .... 40 F1
Attwood Bsns Ctr 1 DY9 .... 81 F5
Attwood Cl B8 .... 67 E6
Attwood Cres CV2 .... 114 C7
Attwood Gdns WV4 .... 39 E5
Attwood Rd WS7 .... 6 C7
Attwood St DY9 .... 81 F5
Aubrey Rd
Birmingham, Beech Lanes B32 .... 84 E7
Birmingham, Small Heath B10 .... 87 F8
Auchinleck Dr WS13 .... 3 C1
Auchinleck Sq 5 B15 .... 66 B1
Auckland Dr B36 .... 70 B7
Auckland Ho B32 .... 84 F4
Auckland Rd Birmingham B11 .... 87 A7
Kingswinford DY6 .... 60 E4
Smethwick B67 .... 64 E5
Auden Ct WV6 .... 23 F4
Audleigh Ho 1 B15 .... 86 C8
Audlem Wlk WV10 .... 26 A5
Audley Dr DY11 .... 116 A8
Audley Jun Sch B33 .... 68 F4
Audley Rd B33 .... 68 F4
Audnam DY8 .... 60 F1
Augusta Pl CV32 .... 161 F8
Augusta Rd
Birmingham, Acock's Green B27 .... 88 C5
Birmingham, Moseley B13 .... 86 E4
Augusta Rd E B13 .... 86 F4
Augusta St B18 .... 66 C4
Augustine Ave B80 .... 159 D4
Augustine Gr Birmingham B18 .... 65 F6
Sutton Coldfield B74 .... 31 F5
Augustines Wlk WS13 .... 3 A3
Augustus Cl B46 .... 59 F1
Augustus Ct B15 .... 85 F8
Augustus Rd Birmingham B15 .... 85 E8
Coventry CV1 .... 113 F4
Augustus St WS2 .... 28 D1
Ault St B70 .... 53 D1
Aulton Cres LE10 .... 71 B1
Aulton Rd B75 .... 32 E2
Aulton Way LE10 .... 71 B1
Austcliff Cl B97 .... 158 D6
Austcliff Dr B91 .... 127 C8
Austen Ct CV32 .... 157 E5
Austen Pl B15 .... 86 B8
Austen Wlk B71 .... 53 D6
Auster Ho B35 .... 58 B3
Austey Ct B73 .... 57 A7
Austin Cl Birmingham B27 .... 88 D4
Dudley DY1 .... 50 F2
Austin Cote La WS14 .... 9 E7
Austin Croft B36 .... 58 E1
Austin Dr CV6 .... 114 A7
Austin Edwards Dr
3 CV34 .... 161 B8
Austin Ho WS4 .... 28 F3
Austin Rd Birmingham B21 .... 54 C1
Bromsgrove B60 .... 150 E7
Austin Rise B31 .... 122 F7
Austin St WV6 .... 25 B4
Austin Way B42 .... 55 A5
Austrey Cl B93 .... 128 A6
Austrey Gr B29 .... 103 A8
Austrey Rd DY6 .... 61 A5
Austwick Cl CV34 .... 155 E1
Austy Cl B36 .... 68 E8
Auto Ctr B18 .... 65 E5
Autumn Berry Gr DY3 .... 50 E6
Autumn Cl WS4 .... 15 C1
Autumn Dr Dudley DY3 .... 50 D4
Lichfield WS13 .... 3 D2
Walsall WS4 .... 15 C2
Autumn Gr B19 .... 66 C6
Auxerre Ave B98 .... 159 B8
Avalon Cl B24 .... 57 B4
Ave Maria Cl B64 .... 62 E1
Avebury Cl CV11 .... 73 F2
Avebury Gr B30 .... 104 C7
Avebury Rd B30 .... 104 C8
Avenbury Cl B98 .... 154 F1
Avenbury Dr B91 .... 107 E4
Avenue Cl Birmingham B7 .... 67 A6
Dorridge B93 .... 128 A3
Avenue Rd
Astwood Bank B96 .... 158 E1
Birmingham, Aston B7, B6 .... 67 A6
Birmingham, Erdington B23 .... 56 F4
Birmingham, Handsworth B21 .... 54 D2
Birmingham, King's Heath B14 .... 104 D8
Blackheath B65 .... 63 D1
Cannock WS12 .... 2 E2
Darlaston WS10 .... 41 D6
Dorridge B93 .... 128 A3
Dudley, Roseville WV14 .... 51 C8
Dudley, Woodside DY2 .... 61 F6
Kenilworth CV8 .... 147 D6
Nuneaton CV11 .... 73 D2
Royal Leamington Spa CV31 .... 161 F7
Wolverhampton WV3 .... 24 E2
Avenue The
Birmingham, Acock's Green B27 .... 88 D3
Birmingham, Eachway B45 .... 121 E7
2 Birmingham, Lozells B19 .... 66 C8
Blackheath B65 .... 63 A3
Blackwell B60 .... 138 A6
Blakedown DY10 .... 98 B2
Coventry CV3 .... 134 A6
Featherstone WV10 .... 12 C7
Rowington Green CV35 .... 145 A1
Wolverhampton, Castlecroft WV3 .... 38 B8
Wolverhampton, Penn WV4 .... 38 E4
Averill Rd B26 .... 69 A1
Avern Cl DY4 .... 52 B6
Aversley Rd B38 .... 123 E8
Avery Croft B35 .... 57 F2
Avery Ct 6 Oldbury B68 .... 84 B7
6 Warwick CV34 .... 160 F7
Avery Dell Ind Est B30 .... 104 A6
Avery Dr B27 .... 88 C4
Avery Ho B16 .... 66 A1
Avery Myers Cl B68 .... 64 B5
Avery Rd Smethwick B66 .... 65 D6
Sutton Coldfield B73 .... 45 D3
Aviemore Cl CV10 .... 73 A2
Aviemore Cres B43 .... 44 B4
Avill B77 .... 36 A5
Avill Gr DY11 .... 116 C7
Avington Cl DY3 .... 50 D7
Avion Cl WS1 .... 42 F7
Avion Ctr W6 .... 25 A4
Avocet Cl Birmingham B33 .... 68 E3
Coventry CV2 .... 96 B3
Avocet Dr DY10 .... 117 A2
Avon B77 .... 36 A5
Avon Bsns Pk WS11 .... 4 C7
Avon Cl Brierley Hill DY5 .... 61 B7
Bromsgrove B60 .... 150 F6
Bulkington CV12 .... 79 B6
Perton WV6 .... 23 F4
Avon Cres WS3 .... 15 A1
Avon Ct Kenilworth CV8 .... 147 F5
Sutton Coldfield B73 .... 46 B5
Avon Dr
Birmingham, Castle Bromwich B36 .... 69 F7
Birmingham, Moseley B13 .... 87 B2
Willenhall WV13 .... 27 C2
Wythall B47 .... 124 E2
Avon Gr WS5 .... 43 A4
Avon Ho Birmingham B15 .... 86 D8
Coventry CV4 .... 132 C6
11 Dudley, Dibdale DY3 .... 50 E3
2 Dudley, Russell's Hall DY1 .... 61 E8
3 Oldbury B68 .... 84 B8
Avon Rd Burntwood WS7 .... 6 F5
Cannock WS11 .... 4 D7
Halesowen B63 .... 82 B5
Kenilworth CV8 .... 147 E3
Kidderminster DY11 .... 116 B3
Solihull B90 .... 106 D1
Stourbridge DY8 .... 80 F3
Walsall WS3 .... 14 E1
Whitnash CV31 .... 162 A3
Avon St Birmingham B11 .... 87 C5
Coventry CV2 .... 114 B5
Warwick CV34 .... 161 A7
Avonbank Cl B97 .... 158 C6
Avoncroft WV4 .... 39 F4
Avoncroft Coll B60 .... 150 E5
Avoncroft Ho B37 .... 70 A2
Avoncroft Mus of Building B60 .... 150 E5
Avoncroft Rd B60 .... 150 D6
Avondale Cl DY6 .... 60 E8
Avondale Rd Birmingham B11 .... 87 D4
Brandon CV8 .... 135 F5
Coventry CV5 .... 133 A8
Royal Leamington Spa CV32 .... 157 C4
Wolverhampton WV6 .... 25 A3
Avonlea Rise CV32 .... 156 D2
Avro Ho B35 .... 58 B2
Awbridge Rd DY2 .... 62 C3
Awefields Cres B67 .... 64 E4
Awson St CV6 .... 113 F6
Axholme Rd CV2 .... 114 E4
Axletree Way WS10 .... 42 B6
Axminster Cl CV11 .... 73 F5
Ayala Croft 2 B36 .... 68 E8
Aylesbury Cl B94 .... 143 C6
Aylesbury Cres B44 .... 56 A8
Aylesbury Rd B94 .... 143 D7
Aylesdene Ct CV5 .... 132 F8
Aylesford Cl DY3 .... 39 C2
Aylesford Ct 7 CV31 .... 162 A6
Aylesford Dr Birmingham B37 90 A7
Sutton Coldfield B74 .... 31 E5
Aylesford Rd B21 .... 54 D1
Aylesford Sch CV34 .... 160 C4
Aylesford St Coventry CV1 .... 113 E4
Royal Leamington Spa CV31 162 A6
Aylesmore Cl
Birmingham B32 .... 84 C1
Solihull B92 .... 106 E8
Aynho Cl CV5 .... 112 A3
Aynsley Ct B90 .... 106 C2
Ayre Rd B24 .... 57 B4
Ayrshire Cl B36 .... 68 D8
Ayrton Cl WV6 .... 24 A4
Aysgarth Cl CV11 .... 74 A2
Azalea Cl Codsall WV8 .... 10 B3
Hinckley LE10 .... 75 E5
Azalea Dr LE10 .... 75 E6
Azalea Gr B9 .... 67 F2
Azalea Wlk LE10 .... 75 E5
Aziz Isaac Cl B68 .... 64 C6

Babbacombe Rd CV3 .... 133 D5
Babington Rd B21 .... 65 E7
Bablake Cl CV6 .... 112 F8
Bablake Croft B92 .... 89 A1
Bablake Jun Sch CV1 .... 165 A4
Bablake Sch CV1 .... 113 B4
Babors Field WV14 .... 40 A3
Babworth Cl WV9 .... 11 A2
Baccabox La B47 .... 124 E7
Bacchus Rd B18 .... 65 F6
Bach Mill Dr B28 .... 105 D3
Bache St B70 .... 53 D1
Back La Aldridge WS9 .... 30 F8
Meriden CV7 .... 110 E5
Shenstone WS14 .... 17 E1
Warwick CV34 .... 160 E6
Back Rd Birmingham B38 .... 103 F2
Kingswinford DY6 .... 60 D7
Back St CV11 .... 73 C5
Backcester La WS13 .... 9 B8
Backcrofts 7 WS11 .... 1 E1
Backhouse La WV11 .... 26 C4
Badbury Cl B80 .... 159 D4
Baddesley Cl CV31 .... 162 D5
Baddesley Clinton B93 .... 144 F3
Baddesley Rd B92 .... 88 E2
Bader Rd Perton WV6 .... 23 E3
Walsall WS2 .... 27 F2
Bader Wlk B35 .... 57 F2
Badger Cl
Cheswick Green B90 .... 126 D4
Redditch B98 .... 154 D3
Badger Ct WV10 .... 25 D4
Badger Dr WV10 .... 25 D4
Badger Rd CV3 .... 134 D8
Badger St Dudley DY3 .... 50 E5
Stourbridge DY9 .... 81 E6
Badger Way B60 .... 138 B5
Badgers Bank Rd B74 .... 31 F5
Badgers Cl WS3 .... 15 A5
Badgers Croft B62 .... 83 B7
Badgers The B45 .... 122 A2
Badgers Way
Birmingham B34 .... 69 A5
Cannock WS12 .... 2 D1
Badminton Cl DY1 .... 50 F3
Badon Covert B14 .... 104 D2
Badsey Cl B31 .... 103 C4
Badsey Rd B69 .... 63 D5
Baggeridge Cl DY3 .... 50 A8
Baggeridge Cty Pk DY3 .... 49 E6
Baggott St WV2 .... 39 C7
Baginton Cl B91 .... 107 B5
Baginton Fields Sch CV3 .... 134 B4
Baginton Rd Birmingham B35 .... 58 B4
Coventry CV3 .... 133 C5
Bagley Rd DY5 .... 81 D6
Bagley St DY9 .... 81 C6
Bagnall Cl B25 .... 88 D6
Bagnall Rd WV14 .... 40 C5
Bagnall St Tipton DY4 .... 41 C1
Walsall WS3 .... 28 C6
West Bromwich, Goids Hill B70 .... 52 E7
West Bromwich, Mayer's Green B70 .... 53 E2
Bagnall Wlk DY5 .... 61 D1
Bagnell Rd B13 .... 104 F7
Bagot St B4 .... 164 C4
Bagridge Cl WV3 .... 38 B8
Bagridge Rd WV3 .... 38 B8
Bagshaw Cl CV8 .... 135 A1
Bagshaw Rd B33 .... 68 E3
Bagshawe Croft B23 .... 56 D7
Bailey Ave B77 .... 35 F5
Bailey Cl WS11 .... 2 A4
Bailey Rd WV14 .... 40 B7
Bailey St West Bromwich B70 .... 53 A4
Wolverhampton WV10 .... 163 D3
Baileys Ct B65 .... 63 B3
Bailye Cl WS13 .... 3 F1
Baines' La 1 LE10 .... 71 D1
Bakehouse La B93 .... 145 B6
Bakeman Ho B26 .... 88 D6
Baker Ave
Royal Leamington Spa CV31 .... 161 F6
Wolverhampton WV14 .... 39 F2
Baker House Gr B43 .... 54 D7
Baker Rd WV14 .... 40 E3
Baker St Bedworth CV6 .... 96 B6
Birmingham, Handsworth B21 .... 65 F8
Birmingham, Small Heath B10 67 D1
Birmingham, Sparkhill B11 .... 87 C5
Burntwood WS7 .... 6 F6
Tipton DY4 .... 51 E4
West Bromwich B70 .... 53 B3
Baker's La Aldridge WS9 .... 30 B6
Lichfield WS13 .... 9 B7
Bakers La Coventry CV5 .... 112 E2
Knowle B93 .... 128 D1
Sutton Coldfield B73, B74 .... 45 A5
Bakers Mews B93 .... 145 B6
Bakers Wlk B77 .... 35 F6
Bakewell Cl Coventry CV3 .... 134 F8
Walsall WS3 .... 14 C3
Balaclava Rd B14 .... 104 E8
Balcaskie Cl B15 .... 85 E7
Bald's La DY9 .... 81 F5
Balden Rd B32 .... 84 F7
Baldmoor Lake Rd B23 .... 56 F6
Baldwin Cl B69 .... 52 D2
Baldwin Croft CV6 .... 96 B1
Baldwin Gr WS11 .... 2 C2
Baldwin Ho B19 .... 66 E6
Baldwin Rd Birmingham B30 .... 104 A3
Kidderminster DY10 .... 117 B7
Baldwin St Bilston WV14 .... 40 F4
Smethwick B66 .... 65 B6
Baldwins La B28 .... 105 F4
Balfour B79 .... 21 A4
Balfour Cl LE10 .... 75 E7
Balfour Cres WV6 .... 24 F4
Balfour Ct
Sutton Coldfield B74 .... 32 A3
Wolverhampton WV6 .... 24 F4
Balfour Dr B69 .... 52 D2
Balfour Ho 2 B16 .... 65 F1
Balfour Rd DY6 .... 60 E8
Balfour St B12 .... 86 E6
Balham Gr B44 .... 45 A2
Balholm B62 .... 83 D5
Balking Cl WV14 .... 40 B3
Ball Fields DY4 .... 52 D5
Ball Ho 5 WS3 .... 28 B8
Ball La WV10 .... 11 C6
Ballantine Rd CV6 .... 113 B6
Ballarat Wlk 3 DY8 .... 80 F5
Ballard Cres DY2 .... 62 D5
Ballard Rd DY2 .... 62 D5
Ballard Wlk B37 .... 70 A6
Ballingham Cl CV4 .... 112 A2
Balliol Bsns Pk WV9 .... 10 E3
Balliol Ho B37 .... 69 F2
Balliol Rd Coventry CV2 .... 114 C4
Hinckley LE10 .... 75 F6
Ballot St B66 .... 65 B5
Balls Hill WS1 .... 28 F2
Balls St WS1 .... 28 F2
Balmain Cres WV11 .... 12 B1
Balmoral Cl Coventry CV2 .... 114 E6
Halesowen B62 .... 83 B7
Lichfield WS14 .... 9 D6
Walsall WS4 .... 29 D7
Balmoral Ct Cannock WS11 .... 2 A5
Kidderminster DY10 .... 117 A5
Nuneaton CV10 .... 72 E6
Balmoral Dr Cannock WS12 .... 1 F7
Willenhall WV12 .... 27 C7
Wombourne WV5 .... 38 A1
Balmoral Rd
Birmingham, Erdington B23 .... 56 F5
Birmingham, Kingshurst B36 .... 70 A7
Birmingham, Kitwell B32 .... 102 B7
Stourbridge DY8 .... 60 C2
Sutton Coldfield B74 .... 31 F5
Wolverhampton WV4 .... 39 A5
Balmoral View DY1 .... 50 E2
Balmoral Way
Blackheath B65 .... 63 D4
Royal Leamington Spa CV32 157 C6
Balsall Common Prim Sch CV7 .... 130 B5
Balsall Heath Rd B12 .... 86 E7
Balsall St B93, CV7 .... 129 D7
Balsall St E CV7 .... 130 B5
Baltic Cl WS11 .... 1 E2
Baltimore Rd B42 .... 55 A5
Balvenie Way DY1 .... 50 F4
Bamber Cl WV3 .... 38 E8
Bamburgh B77 .... 35 C7
Bamburgh Gr CV32 .... 156 E3
Bamford Cl WS3 .... 14 C3
Bamford Ho WS3 .... 14 C3
Bamford Rd Walsall WS3 .... 14 C3
Wolverhampton WV3 .... 39 A8
Bamford St B77 .... 21 D3
Bampfylde Pl B42 .... 55 C7
Bampton Ave WS7 .... 7 A8
Bamville Rd B8 .... 68 A5
Banbrook Cl B92 .... 107 D8
Banbury Cl DY3 .... 50 E6
Banbury Croft B37 .... 69 F2
Banbury Ho B33 .... 69 E2
Banbury Rd Cannock WS11 .... 4 C8
Warwick CV34 .... 161 A3
Banbury St B5 .... 66 F2
Bancroft B77 .... 21 F3
Bancroft Cl WV14 .... 51 B7
Bandywood Cres B44 .... 44 F3
Bandywood Rd B44 .... 44 F3
Baneberry Dr WV10 .... 12 B7
Banfield Ave WS10 .... 41 C7
Banfield Rd WS10 .... 41 C4
Banford Ave B8 .... 68 A4
Banford Rd B8 .... 68 A4
Bangham Pit Rd B31 .... 102 E6
Bangley La
Drayton Bassett B78 .... 33 E6
Mile Oak B78 .... 34 A8
Bangor Ho B37 .... 70 B4
Bangor Rd B9 .... 67 D2
Bank Cres WS7 .... 6 F5
Bank Croft CV31 .... 162 C5
Bank Farm Cl DY9 .... 81 C1
Bank Rd
Dudley, Gornalwood DY3 .... 50 C2
Dudley, Netherton DY2 .... 62 D6
Bank St Bilston WV14 .... 40 E3
Birmingham B14 .... 86 E1
Blackheath B64 .... 62 C1
Brierley Hill DY5 .... 61 D3
Cannock WS12 .... 2 E1
Dudley WV14 .... 51 C8
Stourbridge DY9 .... 81 F5
Walsall WS1 .... 28 F1
West Bromwich B71 .... 53 D6
Wolverhampton WV10 .... 25 E5
Bank The CV8 .... 149 C6
Bankdale Rd B8 .... 68 B4
Bankes Rd B10 .... 67 F1
Bankfield Dr CV32 .... 156 C1
Bankfield Rd Bilston WV14 .... 40 D5
Tipton DY4 .... 52 C8
Banklands Rd DY2 .... 62 E6
Banks Gn B60, B97 .... 152 B2
Banks Rd CV6 .... 113 A5
Banks St WV13 .... 27 A2
Bankside
Birmingham, Great Barr B43 .... 54 E7
Birmingham, Moseley B13 .... 87 D2
Bankside Cl CV3 .... 134 A6
Bankside Cres B74 .... 44 F7
Bankside Way WS9 .... 16 B2
Bankwell St DY5 .... 61 D4
Banky Mdw LE10 .... 76 A7
Banner La CV4 .... 111 D2
Bannerlea Rd B37 .... 69 F5
Bannerley Rd B33 .... 69 C1
Banners Ct B73 .... 45 B3
Banners Gate Inf Sch B73 .... 45 A4
Banners Gate Jun Sch B73 .... 45 A4
Banners Gate Rd B73 .... 45 B3
Banners Gr B23 .... 57 A6
Banners La Halesowen B63 .... 82 D6
Redditch B97 .... 158 E5
Banners St B63 .... 82 D6
Banners Wlk B44 .... 45 B2
Bannington Ct WV12 .... 27 D4
Bannister Rd WS10 .... 41 D2
Bannister St B64 .... 62 D2
Banstead Cl WV2 .... 39 E7
Bant Mill Rd B60 .... 137 A1
Bantam Gr CV6 .... 95 A3
Bantams Cl B33 .... 69 C2
Bantock Ave WV3 .... 38 F8
Bantock Ct WV3 .... 38 E8
Bantock Gdns WV3 .... 24 E1
Bantock House Mus WV3 .... 24 F1
Bantock Rd CV4 .... 111 E2
Bantock Way B17 .... 85 D5
Bantocks The B70 .... 53 A6
Banton Cl B23 .... 56 D8
Bantry Cl B26 .... 89 C4
Baptist End Rd DY2 .... 62 C6
Baptist Wlk LE10 .... 71 D1
Bar Wlk WS9 .... 16 C1
Barbara Rd B28 .... 105 E4
Barbara St B79 .... 21 A5
Barber Cl WS12 .... 2 E2
Barberry Ho B38 .... 103 F1
Barbers La B91 .... 108 C6
Barbican Rise CV2 .... 114 E2
Barbourne Cl B91 .... 127 B7
Barbridge Cl CV12 .... 79 C2
Barbridge Rd CV12 .... 79 C3
Barbrook Dr DY5 .... 81 B7
Barcheston Rd
Birmingham B29 .... 85 A1
Knowle B93 .... 128 A4
Barclay Ct WV3 .... 25 A2
Barclay Rd B67 .... 64 E1
Barcliff Ave B77 .... 21 E3
Barcroft WV13 .... 27 C2
Bard St B11 .... 87 C5
Bardfield Cl 1 B42 .... 55 A8
Bardon Dr B90 .... 106 D2
Bardsey Cl LE10 .... 71 B1
Bardsley Ct 7 B9 .... 67 B2
Bardwell Cl WV8 .... 24 F8
Barford App CV31 .... 162 B2
Barford Cl Coventry CV3 .... 134 D8
Darlaston WS10 .... 41 C8
Redditch B98 .... 154 F1
Sutton Coldfield B76 .... 46 F4
Barford Cres 5 B38 .... 104 C2
Barford Cty Jun & Inf Sch B16 .... 65 F3
Barford Ho B5 .... 86 E8
Barford Rd Birmingham B16 .... 65 F3
Kenilworth CV8 .... 148 B3
Solihull B90 .... 106 D2
Barford St B5 .... 86 E8
Bargate Dr W6 .... 25 A4
Bargery Rd WV11 .... 13 A1
Barham Cl B90 .... 127 A5
Bark Piece B32 .... 84 C3
Barker Ho B69 .... 63 E8
Barker Rd B74 .... 46 B7
Barker St Birmingham B19 .... 66 B7
Oldbury B68 .... 64 C6
Barker's Butts La CV6 .... 113 A4
Barkers' Butts La CV1 .... 113 A5
Barkers La B47 .... 125 A1
Barlands Croft B34 .... 69 C6
Barle Gr B36 .... 70 A7
Barleston Dr LE10 .... 71 A1
Barley Cl Aldridge WS9 .... 30 E2
Dudley DY3 .... 50 F7
Wolverhampton WV8 .... 10 E1
Barley Croft Perton WV6 .... 23 D3
Stoke Heath B60 .... 150 E6

Barley Ct CV32 156 F2
Barley Lea Ho CV3 134 B8
Barley Lea The CV3 134 C8
Barley Mow La B61 137 B8
Barleyfield LE10 71 C3
Barleyfield Ho 3 WS1 42 E8
Barleyfield Rise DY6 60 A8
Barleyfield Row WS1 42 E8
Barlich Way B98 154 A2
Barlow Cl Birmingham B45 101 E2
Oldbury B68 64 A3
Tamworth B77 21 E4
Barlow Dr B70 53 F1
Barlow Rd Coventry CV2 96 D2
Wednesbury WS10 42 A5
Barlows Rd B15 85 E5
Barmouth Cl WV12 27 C6
Barn Ave DY3 50 C7
Barn Cl Birmingham B30 104 B6
Blackheath B64 82 E6
Coventry CV5 112 C5
Dordon B78 36 F6
Halesowen B63 82 E2
Stoke Heath B60 150 E6
Stourbridge DY9 81 C4
Whitnash CV31 162 B3
Wolverhampton WS13 3 B3
Barn Croft Birmingham B32 84 E1
Burntwood WS7 7 A4
Great Wyrley WS6 5 A3
Barn Farm Cl WV14 41 A7
Barn Gn WV3 38 F7
Barn Ho B8 68 D4
Barn La
Birmingham, Handsworth B21 65 E7
Birmingham, King's Heath B13 105 A7
Solihull B92 88 F3
Barn Mdw B25 68 D1
Barn Owl Cl DY10 117 A2
Barn Owl Wlk DY5 81 C6
Barn Piece B32 84 B4
Barn St B5 66 F2
Barnabas Rd B23 56 F4
Barnaby Sq WV10 11 F4
Barnack Ave CV3 133 B5
Barnack Dr CV34 155 E1
Barnacle La CV12 79 C1
Barnard Cl Birmingham B37 70 D1
Royal Leamington Spa CV32 157 C3
Barnard Pl WV2 39 E6
Barnard Rd
Sutton Coldfield B75 46 E7
Wolverhampton WV11 12 F1
Barnard Way WS11 1 F2
Barnbridge B77 21 C2
Barnbrook Rd B93 128 A7
Barncroft Rd B69 63 A8
Barncroft St B70 53 A8
Barne Cl CV11 79 B7
Barnes Cl B37 69 E2
Barnes Hill B29 84 F2
Barnes Rd WS14 18 A6
Barnesville Cl B10 88 A8
Barnet Rd B23 56 D5
Barnett Cl Bilston WV14 40 D4
Kingswinford DY6 60 D4
Barnett Gn DY6 60 D4
Barnett La DY6 60 D4
Barnett Rd WV13 26 E1
Barnett St Stourbridge DY8 60 D3
Tipton, Tipton Green DY4 52 A4
Tipton, Tividale B69 52 A2
Barnetts Cl DY10 117 B4
Barnetts Gr DY10 117 A4
Barnetts La Brownhills WS8 15 F8
Kidderminster DY10 117 A4
Barney Cl DY4 51 F3
Barnfield Ave CV5 112 B6
Barnfield Cl WS14 9 B6
Barnfield Dr B92 107 F6
Barnfield Gr B20 54 E5
Barnfield Rd
Bromsgrove B61 136 E1
Halesowen B62 83 D7
Tipton DY4 51 E6
Wolverhampton WV1 26 A2
Barnfield Trad Est DY4 51 E7
Barnford Cl B10 67 C1
Barnford Cres B68 64 B3
Barnfordhill Cl B68 64 B4
Barnhurst La WV8 10 E2
Barnmoor Rise B91 107 C7
Barnpark Covert 9 B14 104 C2
Barns Cl WS9 15 F4
Barns Croft B74 31 B4
Barns La WS4 29 D7
Barnsbury Ave B72 57 C6
Barnsdale Cres B31 102 E4
Barnsley Hall Hospl B61 137 A6
Barnsley Rd Birmingham B17 65 A1
Bromsgrove B61 137 B4
Barnstaple Cl CV5 111 F5
Barnstaple Rd B66 65 B5
Barnswood Cl WS11 4 B8
Barnt Green Junc B45 138 D8
Barnt Green Rd B45 122 C3
Barnwood Cl B98 154 D5
Barnwood Rd
Birmingham B32 84 F4
Wolverhampton WV8 10 E1
Baron Bsns Ctr DY9 81 E5
Baron's Croft CV3 133 E7
Baron's Field Rd CV3 133 E8
Barons Cl B17 85 B6
Barons Croft CV10 72 C4
Barons Ct B92 89 C4
Barpool Rd CV10 72 F4
Barr Beacon Comp Sch WS9 44 B5
Barr Common Cl WS9 30 B3
Barr Common Rd WS9 30 B3
Barr Lakes La
Birmingham WS9 44 A7
Walsall WS5, WS9 43 F7
Barr St Birmingham B19 66 C5
Dudley DY3 50 C3
Barra Croft B35 58 B4
Barrack La B63 82 B6
Barrack St Birmingham B7 67 A3
Warwick CV34 160 E7
West Bromwich B70 53 A8
Barracks Cl WS3 28 E8
Barracks La Beausale CV35 146 C2
Brownhills WS9 16 C8
Walsall WS3 28 E8
Barracks Pl WS3 28 E8
Barracks Way CV1 165 B2
Barrar Cl DY8 80 E8
Barras Ct CV2 114 A4
Barras Gn CV2 114 A4
Barras La CV1 113 B3
Barratts Croft DY5 50 C1
Barratts Ho B14 104 E2
Barratts Rd B38 104 A1
Barrett Cl DY10 117 B6
Barretts La CV7 130 C6
Barrhill Cl B43 43 E2
Barrie Ave DY10 117 C7
Barrie Rd LE10 71 D3
Barrington Cl Walsall WS5 43 A3
Wolverhampton WV10 11 C1
Barrington Rd
Birmingham B45 121 E7
Solihull B92 88 F1
Barron Rd B31 103 B3
Barrow Cl Coventry CV2 115 B6
Redditch B98 154 F3
Barrow Hill Rd DY5 50 C1
Barrow Ho 1 B16 65 F1
Barrow Rd CV8 147 F4
Barrow Wlk B5 86 E7
Barrowfield Ct CV8 147 F4
Barrowfield La CV8 147 F4
Barrows La B26 89 A6
Barrows Rd B11 87 C6
Barrs Cres B64 82 F8
Barrs Hill Sch & Com Coll CV1 165 A4
Barrs Rd B64 82 E8
Barrs St B68 64 A4
Barry Ho CV2 96 D1
Barry Jackson Tower B6 66 F7
Barry Rd WS5 43 C7
Barsham Cl B5 86 C6
Barsham Dr DY5 81 C8
Barston Cl CV6 96 A2
Barston La
Balsall Common CV7 129 D8
Barston B92 109 C1
Cathrine de Barnes B91 108 B2
Hampton in A B92 108 D3
Solihull B91 107 F2
Barston Rd B68 84 B7
Bartestree Cl B98 154 F1
Bartholemews La B61 136 F5
Bartholomew Row B5 164 D3
Bartholomew St B5 164 D2
Bartic Ave DY6 60 F4
Bartleet Rd Redditch B98 159 E8
Smethwick B67 64 D5
Bartlett Cl Coventry CV6 95 E2
Tipton DY4 41 B1
2 Warwick CV34 160 F7
Bartley Cl B92 88 F2
Bartley Dr B31 102 E8
Bartley Green Sec Sch B32 84 C1
Bartley Ho B32 102 D8
Bartley Woods B32 84 B2
Barton Coll Of F Ed Annexe WV14 40 E6
Barton Cres CV31 162 C6
Barton Croft B28 105 F4
Barton Dr B93 128 B4
Barton Ind Est WV14 40 E6
Barton La DY6 60 C8
Barton Lodge Rd B28 105 E4
Barton Rd Bedworth CV12 78 A4
Coventry CV6 95 F2
Nuneaton CV10 73 C1
Wolverhampton WV4 39 F4
Barton St B70 53 C2
Barton's Mdw CV2 114 B6
Bartons Bank B6 66 E7
Barwell Cl Dorridge B93 127 E4
Royal Leamington Spa CV32 156 F3
Barwell Ct 8 B9 67 B2
Barwell La LE10 71 E3
Barwell Rd B9 67 B2
Barwick St B3 164 B3
Basalt Cl WS2 28 A3
Basant Cl CV34 161 A7
Bascote Cl B97 153 B1
Basford Brook Dr CV6 95 F4
Basil Gr B31 102 E4
Basil Rd B31 102 E4
Basildon Wlk 3 CV2 115 A7
Basin La B77 21 D3
Baskerville Ho 1 B12 86 F7
Baskerville Sch B17 85 A5
Baskeyfield Cl WS14 9 D7
Basley Way CV6 95 D4
Baslow Cl Birmingham B33 68 E4
Walsall WS3 14 C3
Baslow Rd WS3 14 B3
Basons La B68 64 D5
Bassano Rd 1 B65 63 C1
Bassenthwaite Ct DY6 60 D6
Bassett Cl Sutton Coldfield B76 46 E4
Willenhall WV12 27 D4
Wolverhampton WV4 38 C6
Bassett Croft B10 87 B8
Bassett Rd Coventry CV6 113 A5
Halesowen B63 82 A6
Wednesbury WS10 42 D3
Bassett St WS2 28 C2
Bassetts Gr B37 69 E5
Bassnage Rd B63 82 E2
Batchcroft Bilston WV14 40 D5
Darlaston WS10 41 D8
Batchelor Cl DY8 80 F8
Batchley Fst Sch B97 153 B4
Batchley Rd B97 153 C4
Bate St 3 Walsall WS2 28 E3
Wolverhampton WV4 40 A3
Bateman Dr B73 46 B1
Bateman Rd B46 59 F1
Bateman's Acre S 1 CV6 113 A4
Batemans La B47 124 E5
Bates Cl B76 58 B8
Bates Gr WV10 26 A4
Bates Hill B97 153 D4
Bates La B94 141 F1
Bates Rd CV5 132 E8
Bath Ave WV1 163 A3
Bath Ct 1 B29 103 B7
Bath Mdw B63 82 E5
Bath Mews DY8 80 F5
Bath Pas B5 164 C1
Bath Pl 4 CV31 161 F7
Bath Rd Brierley Hill DY5 62 A2
Cannock WS11 1 E5
Nuneaton CV11 73 C5
Stourbridge DY8 80 F5
Tipton DY4 52 A5
Walsall WS1 42 E8
Wolverhampton WV1 163 A3
Bath Row Birmingham B15 66 C1
Oldbury B69 63 D8
Bath St Bilston WV14 40 E5
Birmingham B4 164 C4
Coventry CV1 165 C4
Dudley DY2 62 C8
Royal Leamington Spa CV31 161 F7
Sedgley DY3 39 E1
Walsall WS1 42 E8
Willenhall WV13 27 B1
Wolverhampton WV1 163 D2
Bath Wlk Ind Est B12 86 E5
Batham Rd DY10 117 A8
Batheaston Cl B38 123 D7
Bathurst Rd CV6 113 A6
Bathway Rd CV3 133 A4
Batmans Hill Rd WV14, DY4 40 E1
Batsford Cl B98 159 B5
Batsford Rd CV6 112 F4
Batson Rise DY5 81 A8
Battenhall Rd B17 85 A5
Battens Cl B98 153 F3
Battens Dr B98 154 D3
Battledown Cl LE10 71 B2
Battlefield Hill WV5 49 C7
Battlefield La WV5 49 B6
Battlefield Terr WV5 49 B6
Battling Brook Cty Prim Sch LE10 71 B2
Battling Brook Sh Ctr LE10 71 B1
Baughan Ho B24 57 D3
Baulk La CV7 110 D1
Bavaro Gdns DY5 61 D1
Baverstock Rd B14 104 E2
Baverstock Sch B14 104 F2
Baxter Ave DY10 116 F7
Baxter Cl CV4 112 A2
Baxter Ct 10 CV31 162 A7
Baxter Gdns DY10 116 F7
Baxter Rd DY5 61 C2
Baxterley Gn Solihull B91 106 D4
Sutton Coldfield B76 46 F1
Baxters Gn B90 126 B8
Baxters Rd B90 126 B8
Bay Tree Cl Birmingham B38 123 D8
Coventry CV2 96 D1
Bayer St WV14 51 C8
Bayford Ave
Birmingham, Coft Common B31 122 E6
Birmingham, Sheldon B26 89 C4
Bayley Cres WS10 41 C8
Bayley Ho WS8 16 A6
Bayley La CV1 165 C2
Bayley Tower 3 B36 68 E8
Bayleys La DY4 52 C8
Baylie Ct 6 DY8 80 F5
Baylie St DY8 80 F4
Bayliss Ave
Wednesfield WV11 26 F8
Wolverhampton WV4 40 A3
Bayliss Cl Bilston WV14 40 C7
Birmingham B31 103 B5
Bayliss Ct WV3 24 E2
Baynton Rd WV12 27 C8
Bayston Ave WV3 38 E8
Bayston Rd B14 104 E3
Bayswater Rd
Birmingham B20 55 D1
Dudley DY3 50 D2
Bayton Rd CV7 96 B7
Bayton Road Ind Est CV7 96 B8
Bayton Way CV7 96 C7
Baytree Cl WS3 14 A2
Baytree Rd WS3 14 A2
Baywell Cl B90 127 A7
Bazzard La CV11 79 F6
Beach Ave Birmingham B12 87 B5
Wolverhampton WV14 40 A2
Beach Dr B63 83 A5
Beach Rd Bilston WV14 40 D7
Birmingham B11 87 B5
Beach St B63 83 A5
Beach Trad Ctr B12 87 B5
Beachburn Way B20 55 B3
Beachcroft Rd DY6 49 C1
Beachwood Ave DY6 49 C1
Beacon Cl
Birmingham, Great Barr B43 43 F1
Birmingham, Rubery B45 122 A6
Smethwick B66 65 A7
Beacon Ct 2 Birmingham B43 43 F1
Sutton Coldfield B74 44 F8
Beacon Dr WS1 43 A8
Beacon Gdns WS13 3 A1
Beacon Hill Aldridge WS9 30 C1
Birmingham, Aston B6 66 E8
Birmingham, Eachway B45 121 F5
Beacon Hts WS9 44 B6
Beacon Inf & Jun Schs WV12 27 D8
Beacon La Marlbrook B45 121 E4
Sedgley DY3 39 E1
Beacon Mews 1 B43 43 F1
Beacon Pas DY3 50 D8
Beacon Rd
Birmingham, Kingstanding B44 45 A3
Birmingham, Pheasey WS9, B43 44 C6
Coventry CV6 95 D3
Sutton Coldfield B73 46 A1
Walsall WS5 43 D5
Willenhall WV12 27 C8
Beacon Rise Aldridge WS9 30 B3
Sedgley DY3 39 E1
Stourbridge DY9 81 D4
Beacon St Lichfield WS13 9 A8
Walsall WS1 29 A1
Wolverhampton WV14 39 F1
Beacon View
Birmingham B45 122 A6
Walsall WS2 27 F2
Beacon View Dr B74 44 F5
Beacon View Rd B71 42 F2
Beacon Way Brownhills WS9 16 A3
Cannock WS12 2 F3
Beaconfields WS13 9 A8
Beaconsfield Ave WV4 39 D5
Beaconsfield Cres 3 B12 86 E5
Beaconsfield Ct
Nuneaton CV11 73 D5
Walsall WS1 43 B8
Beaconsfield Dr WV4 39 D6
Beaconsfield Rd
Birmingham B12 86 E5
Coventry CV2 114 B2
Sutton Coldfield B74 46 B7
Beaconsfield St
Royal Leamington Spa CV31 162 B7
West Bromwich B71 53 C5
Beaconsfield St W CV31 162 B8
Beaconside Fst & Mid Sch B45 121 E6
Beaconview Ho 4 B71 42 F1
Beak St B1 164 B2
Beake Ave CV6 113 B7
Beakes Rd B67 64 F3
Beaks Farm Gdns B16 65 D2
Beaks Hill Rd B38 103 E2
Beale Cl B35 58 A2
Beale Ho B16 65 F1
Beale St DY8 80 F5
Beales St B6 67 B8
Bealeys Ave WV11 26 C8
Bealeys Ct WV11 26 C8
Bealeys La WS3 14 A2
Beamans Cl B92 89 A4
Beaminster Rd B91 107 A4
Beamish Cl CV2 115 A6
Bean Croft B32 84 C2
Bean Rd
Dudley, Dixon's Green DY2 62 D8
Dudley, Swan Village DY4 51 C6
Bean Road Ind Est DY4 51 C6
Beanfield Ave CV3 132 F4
Bear Hill B48 139 B6
Beardmore Rd B72 57 C8
Bearhill Dr B48 139 B6
Bearley Croft B90 126 C8
Bearmore Rd B64 62 E1
Bearnett Dr WV4 38 C2
Bearnett La WV4 38 B1
Bearsdon Cres LE10 71 B2
Bearwood Ho B66 65 A4
Bearwood Jun & Inf Sch B66 65 A2
Bearwood Rd B66 65 A3
Bearwood Sh Ctr B66 65 A1
Beasley Gr B43 44 B1
Beaton Cl WV13 26 E2
Beaton Rd B74 32 A3
Beatrice St WS3 28 C6
Beatrice Wlk B69 52 A2
Beattie Cl LE10 71 D3
Beatty Ho DY4 52 B8
Beau Ct WS11 1 F1
Beaubrook Gdns DY8 60 E3
Beauchamp Ave
Birmingham B20 54 F5
Kidderminster DY11 116 D3
Royal Leamington Spa CV32 156 F1
Beauchamp Cl 1
Birmingham B37 70 B2
Sutton Coldfield B76 58 B7
Beauchamp Ct
Kidderminster DY11 116 D3
1 Royal Leamington Spa CV32 156 F1
Beauchamp Gdns CV34 161 B6
Beauchamp Hill CV32 156 E1
Beauchamp Ind Pk B77 35 D8
Beauchamp Rd
Birmingham B13 105 C5
Kenilworth CV8 147 F2
Royal Leamington Spa CV32 156 F1
Solihull B91 107 B5
Tamworth B77 35 F5
Warwick CV34 161 B8
Beaudesert Cl B47 125 A6
Beaudesert Rd
Birmingham B20 66 B8
Coventry CV5 113 A1
Hollywood B47 125 A6
Beaufell Cl CV34 155 E1
Beaufort Ave
Birmingham B34 68 D5
Kidderminster DY11 116 A7
Royal Leamington Spa CV32 157 C5
Beaufort Cl LE10 75 E4
Beaufort Dr CV3 134 F7
Beaufort Rd
Birmingham, Gravelly Hill B23 56 E2
Birmingham, Ladywood B16 66 A1
Beaufort Sch B34 68 D5
Beaufort St B98 153 E3
Beaufort Way WS9 30 B4
Beaulieu Ave DY6 60 F4
Beaulieu Cl DY11 116 D8
Beaulieu Pk CV31 162 D6
Beaumaris Cl Coventry CV5 111 F5
Dudley DY1 50 F4
Beaumaris Ho B32 102 D6
Beaumont Ave LE10 75 A7
Beaumont Cl
Great Wyrley WS6 4 F2
Tipton DY4 51 E6
Beaumont Cres CV6 113 A4
Beaumont Ct
9 Coventry CV6 113 A4
8 Royal Leamington Spa CV31 162 A6
Beaumont Dr
Birmingham B17 85 B4
Brierley Hill DY5 81 B7
Beaumont Gdns B18 65 F6
Beaumont Gr B91 106 F5
Beaumont Lawns B60 121 D1
Beaumont Pl CV11 73 A4
Beaumont Rd
Birmingham B30 103 F6
Great Wyrley WS6 4 F2
Halesowen B62 83 E8
Keresley CV7 95 A6
Nuneaton CV11 73 A4
Wednesbury WS10 41 F4
Beausale Croft CV5 112 A3
Beausale Dr B93 128 C7
Beauty Bank B64 83 A8
Beauty Bank Cres DY8 80 F6
Beauty Bank Prim Sch DY8 80 F6
Beaver Cl WV11 26 F5
Beaver Pk B63 82 F6
Bebington Cl WV8 24 F8
Beccles Dr WV13 40 F8
Beck Cl B66 65 A4
Beckbury Ave WV4 38 C5
Beckbury Rd Birmingham B29 85 A1
Coventry CV2 114 F6
Beckenham Ave B44 45 B1
Becket Cl B74 31 F6
Beckett St WV14 40 F6
Beckfield Cl
Birmingham B14 104 E2
Walsall WS4 29 C8
Beckfoot Dr CV2 96 F1
Beckford Croft B93 127 F3
Beckford Ct B23 56 C2
Beckman Rd DY9 81 C2
Beckminster Rd WV3 38 F7
Becks La CV7 93 A5
Becks The B48 139 A7
Beconsfield Cl B93 127 F2
Becton Gr B42 55 D7
Bedale Ave LE10 71 F2
Bedcote Pl DY8 81 B5
Beddoe Cl DY4 52 D5
Beddow Ave WV14 51 C7
Beddows Rd WS3 28 E5
Bede Arc CV12 78 B3
Bede Rd Bedworth CV12 78 A4
Coventry CV6 113 B6
Nuneaton CV10 72 D3
Bedford Cl LE10 71 E3
Bedford Dr B75 46 E6
Bedford Ho
7 Birmingham, Erdington B24 56 F4
Birmingham, Kingshurst B36 70 B6
6 Wolverhampton WV3 25 C4

Bedford Pl Cannock WS12 .... 2 B4
Royal Leamington Spa CV32 . 161 F8
Bedford Rd Birmingham B11 . 87 A8
Sutton Coldfield B75 .... 46 E7
West Bromwich B71 .... 53 B7
Bedford St Coventry CV1 ..... 113 A2
Royal Leamington Spa CV32 . 161 F8
Tipton DY4 .... 52 B5
Wolverhampton WV1 .... 40 B7
Bedford Terr 4 B19 .... 66 D8
Bedlam La CV6 .... 95 E2
Bedworth Cl CV12 .... 79 B2
Bedworth Croft DY4 .... 52 B4
Bedworth Gr B9 .... 68 B2
Bedworth La CV12 .... 77 D4
Bedworth Rd Bedworth
CV12 .... 78 F2
Bulkington CV12 .... 79 A2
Coventry CV6 .... 96 A5
Bedworth Sta CV12 .... 78 C2
Bee La WV10 .... 11 D3
Beebee Rd WS10 .... 41 F6
Beech Ave
Birmingham,
Chelmsley Wood B37 .... 70 B1
Birmingham, Quinton B32 .... 84 D7
5 Birmingham,
Showell Green B12 .... 87 A5
Halesowen B62 .... 83 C8
Tamworth B77 .... 21 E3
Beech Cl Nuneaton CV10 .... 72 A8
Rowington Green CV35 .... 145 A1
Sedgley DY3 .... 39 E1
Wolverhampton WV10 .... 25 B8
Beech Cliffe CV34 .... 160 F8
Beech Cres Burntwood WS7 ..... 6 F6
Tipton DY4 .... 52 C8
Wednesbury WS10 .... 41 F5
Beech Ct
Birmingham, Bournville B30 . 103 E4
Birmingham, Great Barr B43 .. 43 D1
Cannock WS12 .... 2 B7
Oldbury B66 .... 64 C8
Royal Leamington Spa CV34 . 161 E2
Beech Dene Gr B23 .... 56 E5
Beech Dr Kenilworth CV8 ..... 148 B5
Kidderminster DY11 .... 116 B7
Beech Farm Croft B31 .... 103 A3
Beech Gate B74 .... 31 C5
Beech Gdns WS14 .... 9 C6
Beech Gn DY1 .... 51 A5
Beech Gr Birmingham B14 ... 105 A5
Huntington WS12 .... 1 D8
Warwick CV34 .... 156 B1
Beech Hill Ct B72 .... 57 C8
Beech Hill Ho B32 .... 102 C8
Beech Ho B91 .... 106 F2
Beech Hurst B38 .... 123 E8
Beech Hurst Gdns WV5 .... 37 A2
Beech Mews B64 .... 62 E2
Beech Park Dr B45 .... 138 C8
Beech Pine Cl WS12 .... 2 A8
Beech Rd
Birmingham, Bournville B30 . 103 E6
Birmingham, Erdington B23 .... 56 F8
Bromsgrove B61 .... 136 F4
Coventry CV6 .... 113 B5
Dudley DY1 .... 51 C4
Hollywood B47 .... 125 B6
Kingswinford DY6 .... 60 E5
Stourbridge DY8 .... 80 F3
Tamworth B79 .... 21 A8
Tipton B69 .... 63 A8
Wednesbury WS10 .... 41 F5
Willenhall WV13 .... 26 E2
Wolverhampton WV10 .... 25 B8
Beech Tree Ave
Coventry CV4 .... 112 B2
Wolverhampton WV11 .... 26 C8
Beech Tree Cl
Kingswinford DY6 .... 60 E8
Redditch B97 .... 153 B4
Beech Tree La WS11 .... 4 D8
Beech Way B66 .... 65 B5
Beech Wlk B38 .... 123 F8
Beecham Cl WS9 .... 30 A8
Beechcroft Birmingham B15 .. 86 A7
Oldbury B68 .... 64 C2
Beechcroft Ave B28 .... 106 A6
Beechcroft Cres B74 .... 30 D1
Beechcroft Ct B74 .... 32 A1
Beechcroft Dr B61 .... 137 B4
Beechcroft Est B63 .... 82 C6
Beechcroft Pl WV10 .... 25 C6
Beechcroft Rd
Birmingham B36 .... 69 B8
Blackheath B64 .... 62 F1
Kidderminster DY11 .... 116 A8
Beechdale Ave B44 .... 44 E2
Beechdale Prim Sch WS2 ... 28 C5
Beechdale Rd WS3 .... 27 F8
Beechen Gr WS7 .... 6 F8
Beecher Pl B63 .... 82 D5
Beecher Rd B63 .... 82 D5
Beecher Rd E B63 .... 82 D5
Beecher St B63 .... 82 C5
Beecher's Keep CV8 .... 135 F5
Beeches Ave B27 .... 88 C4
Beeches Cl Birmingham B45 121 D8
Kingswinford DY6 .... 60 D5
Beeches Dr B24 .... 57 C5
Beeches Farm Dr B31 .... 123 A7
Beeches Inf Sch B70 .... 53 D3
Beeches Inf Sch The B45 .. 102 B2
Beeches Pl WS3 .... 28 D6
Beeches Rd Birmingham B42 . 55 C7
Blackheath B65 .... 63 C1
Kidderminster DY11 .... 116 C8
Oldbury B68 .... 64 C3
Walsall WS3 .... 28 D6
West Bromwich B70 .... 53 E2
Beeches The Bedworth
CV12 .... 77 E2
Sutton Coldfield, Little Aston
B74 .... 31 D4
Sutton Coldfield, Wylde Green
B73 .... 46 B1
West Bromwich B70 .... 53 E2
Wolverhampton, New Cross
WV11 .... 26 B5
Wolverhampton, Newbridge
WV1 .... 25 A3
Beeches View Ave B63 .... 82 C4
Beeches Way B31 .... 123 A7
Beeches Wlk B73 .... 46 B3
Beechey Cl B43 .... 44 D5
Beechfield Ave 1 B11 .... 87 B6
Beechfield Cl B62 .... 83 C8
Beechfield Dr DY11 .... 116 C8
Beechfield Gr WV14 .... 51 B7
Beechfield Rd
Birmingham B11 .... 87 B6
Smethwick B67 .... 64 F4
Beechfield Rise WS13 .... 9 D8
Beechglade B20 .... 54 F4
Beechhouse La WV5 .... 37 A1
Beechmore Rd B26 .... 89 A5
Beechmount Dr B23 .... 57 A6
Beechnut Cl B91 .... 107 D5
Beechnut La B91 .... 107 E4
Beechtree Rd WS9 .... 15 F3
Beechwood Ave
Coventry CV5 .... 132 F8
Hinckley LE10 .... 75 D3
Wolverhampton WV11 .... 26 B8
Beechwood Bsns Pk WS11 .... 2 B3
Beechwood Cl
Cheswick Green B90 .... 126 D4
Walsall WS3 .... 14 B3
Beechwood Cres B77 .... 21 F5
Beechwood Croft
Kenilworth CV8 .... 147 F2
Little Aston B74 .... 31 D5
Beechwood Ct
1 Birmingham B30 .... 104 C3
Blackheath B64 .... 83 A7
Coventry CV5 .... 132 F8
Wolverhampton WV6 .... 24 C3
Beechwood Dr WV6 .... 24 A2
Beechwood Gr B43 .... 43 E2
Beechwood Park Rd B91 .. 106 E5
Beechwood Rd
Bedworth CV12 .... 78 D4
Birmingham, Great Barr B43 .. 43 F2
Birmingham, King's Heath
B14 .... 104 F5
Dudley DY2 .... 51 E1
Nuneaton CV10 .... 72 D6
Smethwick B67 .... 84 F8
West Bromwich B70 .... 53 B3
Beecroft Ave WS13 .... 3 B1
Beecroft Hill Specl Sch WS11 1 E2
Beecroft Rd WS11 .... 1 E1
Beehive Cl B61 .... 121 A1
Beehive Hill CV8 .... 147 E7
Beehive La B76 .... 59 C6
Beehive Wlk 4 DY4 .... 51 E5
Beeston Cl Birmingham B6 ..... 67 A7
Brierley Hill DY5 .... 81 D8
Coventry CV3 .... 134 F8
Beet St B65 .... 63 C1
Beeton Rd B18 .... 65 E6
Beever Rd DY4 .... 52 D7
Beggars Bush La WV5 .... 49 B5
Begonia Cl LE10 .... 75 E5
Begonia Dr LE10 .... 75 E5
Beighton Cl B74 .... 31 F6
Beilby Rd B30 .... 104 B5
Belbroughton CE Sch DY9 119 E6
Belbroughton Cl B98 .... 153 F2
Belbroughton Rd
Blakedown DY9, DY10 .... 98 D1
Clent DY9 .... 99 E2
Halesowen B63 .... 82 F2
Stourbridge DY8 .... 80 E3
Belchers La B8 .... 68 A3
Beldray Rd WV14 .... 40 E6
Belfont Trad Est B62 .... 83 C4
Belfry Cl WS3 .... 14 A3
Belfry Dr DY8 .... 80 E6
Belfry The WV6 .... 23 D4
Belgrade Rd WV10 .... 11 B1
Belgrave Ct DY6 .... 60 F4
Belgrave Cty High Sch B77 21 E1
Belgrave Ho WS11 .... 1 D1
Belgrave Middleway
B5, B12 .... 86 E7
Belgrave Rd Birmingham
B12 .... 86 F6
Coventry CV2 .... 114 E4
Halesowen B62 .... 83 D8
Tamworth B77 .... 35 E8
Belgrave Sq CV2 .... 114 E4
Belgrave Terr B21 .... 66 A7
Belgrave Wlk WS2 .... 28 B3
Belgravia Cl B5 .... 86 E7
Belgravia Ct B37 .... 70 A5
Belgrove Cl B15 .... 85 E6
Belinda Cl WV13 .... 26 F3
Bell Barn Rd B15 .... 86 C8
Bell Barn Sh Ctr 8 B15 .... 86 C8
Bell Cl Birmingham B36 .... 70 B6
Darlaston WS10 .... 41 D7
Bell Ct CV32 .... 156 F2
Bell Dr Cannock WS12 .... 2 C7
Coventry CV7 .... 95 E7
Walsall WS5 .... 43 A5
Bell End B65 .... 63 C3
Bell Fold B68 .... 64 C6
Bell Green La B38 .... 124 B5
Bell Green Rd CV6 .... 114 A8
Bell Heath Way B32 .... 84 B2
Bell Heather Rd WS8 .... 15 D6
Bell Hill B31 .... 103 A5
Bell Holloway B31 .... 102 F5
Bell La
Birmingham, Kitt's Green B33 69 E1
Birmingham, Northfield B31 103 A4
Studley B80 .... 159 E4
Walsall, Wallington Heath
WS3 .... 14 B1
Walsall, Yew Tree WS5 .... 43 A5
Bell Mdw DY9 .... 99 B8
Bell Mead B80 .... 159 E4
Bell Meadow Way B14 .... 104 E1
Bell Pl WV2 .... 163 B1
Bell Rd Dudley DY2 .... 62 C5
Trysull WV5 .... 37 D1
Walsall WS5 .... 43 D6
Bell Sh Ctr The B31 .... 103 A4
Bell St Bilston WV14 .... 40 C6
Brierley Hill, Barrow Hill DY5 . 61 D7
Brierley Hill, Silver End DY5 .... 61 D2
Darlaston WS10 .... 41 D7
Dudley WV14 .... 40 C2
Stourbridge DY8 .... 81 A5
Tipton DY4 .... 51 E5
West Bromwich B70 .... 53 D2
Wolverhampton WV1 .... 163 B2
Bell St S DY5 .... 61 D2
Bell Tower Mews CV32 ...... 156 F3
Bell Vue Rd B65 .... 63 C2
Bellairs Ave CV12 .... 77 E1
Bellamy Cl B90 .... 106 D1
Bellamy Farm Rd B90 .... 106 D1
Bellamy La WV11 .... 26 C7
Bellbrooke Cl CV6 .... 96 B1
Bellcroft B16 .... 66 B2
Belle Cotts B94 .... 143 E5
Belle Isle DY5 .... 61 C3
Belle Orch DY11 .... 116 B5
Belle Vale B63 .... 82 E5
Belle Vue Nuneaton CV10 ...... 72 E3
Stourbridge DY8 .... 60 D2
Belle Vue Ave B16 .... 65 D4
Belle Vue Cl B61 .... 121 C1
Belle Vue Dr B62 .... 83 E6
Belle Vue Gdns B65 .... 63 C3
Belle Vue Prim Sch DY8 .... 60 C3
Belle Vue Rd DY5 .... 62 A1
Belle Vue Terr B92 .... 109 A6
Belle Wlk B13 .... 87 B3
Bellefield Ave 10 B18 .... 65 E4
Bellefield Rd B18 .... 65 E4
Bellemere Rd B92 .... 109 B6
Bellencroft Gdns WV3 .... 38 C7
Bellevue Birmingham B5 .... 86 D7
Dudley WV14 .... 40 E2
Bellevue Rd Bilston WV14 ..... 41 A2
Birmingham B26 .... 89 B7
Bellevue St WV14 .... 39 F2
Bellfield B94 .... 142 A2
Bellfield Ho B14 .... 104 D1
Bellfield Jun &
Inf Sch B31 .... 102 F4
Bellflower Cl WV10 .... 12 A7
Bellingham B77 .... 22 D1
Bellington Croft 5 B90 ...... 127 A6
Bellis St B16 .... 65 F1
Bellman Cl WS10 .... 41 D7
Bells Farm Cl B14 .... 104 C2
Bells Farm Inf & Jun
Sch B14 .... 104 C2
Bells La Birmingham B14 ...... 104 D2
Stourbridge DY8 .... 60 D1
Bells Moor Rd B70 .... 53 A6
Bellsize Cl WS11 .... 5 F5
Bellview Way CV6 .... 96 B1
Bellwood Rd B31 .... 102 F4
Belmont Ave WS11 .... 1 C2
Belmont Cl Aldridge WS9 .... 30 B7
Great Wyrley WS11 .... 5 A4
Redditch B97 .... 153 B1
Tipton DY4 .... 51 F6
Belmont Covert B31 .... 103 B6
Belmont Ct
Royal Leamington Spa CV32 157 A4
Sutton Coldfield B72 .... 46 B4
Belmont Dr CV32 .... 157 A4
Belmont Gdns WV14 .... 41 A4
Belmont Mews CV8 .... 147 F4
Belmont Pas B4 .... 67 A3
Belmont Rd
Birmingham,
Handsworth B21 .... 65 C8
Birmingham, Rubery B45 ...... 122 A6
Brierley Hill DY5 .... 61 D6
Coventry CV6 .... 114 A7
Smethwick B66 .... 65 A2
Stourbridge DY9 .... 81 F4
Tamworth B77 .... 35 E7
Wolverhampton WV4 .... 39 A5
Belmont Rd E B21 .... 65 C8
Belmont Row B4 .... 67 A3
Belmont St WV14 .... 41 A4
Belper DY1 .... 51 B1
Belper Ind Pk B70 .... 52 F4
Belper Rd Walsall WS3 .... 14 C3
West Bromwich B70 .... 52 F3
Belper Row DY2 .... 62 E4
Belsize B77 .... 21 E2
Belstone Cl B14 .... 104 D6
Belt Rd WS12 .... 2 A5
Belton Ave WV11 .... 12 B1
Belton Cl B94 .... 143 C5
Belton Gr B45 .... 122 C8
Belvedere Ave WV4 .... 39 B5
Belvedere Cl Burntwood
WS7 .... 6 F5
Kidderminster DY10 .... 117 A5
Kingswinford DY6 .... 60 F4
Tamworth B79 .... 21 C7
Belvedere Dr B61 .... 137 A4
Belvedere Gdns WV6 .... 24 E7
Belvedere Rd
Birmingham B24 .... 57 B2
Coventry CV5 .... 133 A8
Belvide Gr B29 .... 103 B8
Belvidere Gdns B11 .... 87 C4
Belvidere Rd WS1 .... 42 F8
Belvoir B77 .... 35 C7
Belvoir Cl DY1 .... 50 E2
Belwell Dr B74 .... 32 A2
Belwell La B74 .... 32 A2
Bembridge Cl WV12 .... 27 B8
Bembridge Rd B33 .... 69 A3
Ben Nevis Way DY8 .... 81 A6
Ben Willetts Wlk 3 B65 .... 63 C1
Benacre Dr B5 .... 66 F2
Benbeck Gr DY4 .... 51 C6
Benbow Cl LE10 .... 71 D4
Benches Cl WS7 .... 6 D6
Bendall Rd B44 .... 45 B2
Benedict Sq CV2 .... 114 C8
Benedictine Rd CV3 .... 133 C8
Benedon Rd B26 .... 89 B7
Bengrove Cl B98 .... 159 A7
Benion Rd WS11 .... 1 F5
Benmore Ave B5 .... 86 D7
Benn Rd CV12 .... 79 B2
Bennett Ave DY1 .... 51 B6
Bennett Ct CV8 .... 135 F3
Bennett Dr CV34 .... 161 C7
Bennett Rd B74 .... 31 D3
Bennett St Birmingham B19 ... 66 D8
2 Kidderminster DY11 .... 116 C6
Bennett's Fold WV3 .... 163 B2
Bennett's Hill
Birmingham B2 .... 164 B2
Dudley DY2 .... 62 E8
Bennett's Rd CV7 .... 94 F4
Bennett's Rd N CV7 .... 94 E7
Bennett's Rd S CV6 .... 94 F2
Bennetts Rd B8 .... 67 D6
Bennetts Well Jun &
Inf Sch B37 .... 69 F3
Bennetts Well Prim Sch
B37 .... 69 F3
Bennitt Cl B70 .... 53 C1
Benson Ave WV4 .... 39 D5
Benson Cl Lichfield WS13 .... 3 D1
Perton WV6 .... 23 E5
Benson Ind Est B18 .... 65 F6
Benson Jun & Inf Sch B18 .. 65 F6
Benson Rd
Birmingham,
Highter's Heath B14 .... 105 B1
Birmingham, Hockley B18 .... 65 F6
Coventry CV6 .... 95 A1
Benson View B79 .... 21 C8
Bent Ave B32 .... 84 D6
Bent St DY5 .... 61 D4
Benthall Rd CV6 .... 95 F2
Bentham Ct B31 .... 102 F5
Bentley Cl Redditch B97 ...... 153 D3
Royal Leamington Spa CV32 . 157 B3
Bentley Ct Coventry CV6 .... 95 C4
Sutton Coldfield B76 .... 57 F8
Bentley Dr WS2 .... 28 B3
Bentley Drive Jun Sch
WS2 .... 28 B2
Bentley Farm Cl B93 .... 127 E4
Bentley Gr B29 .... 102 F8
Bentley Heath CE Jun &
Inf Sch B93 .... 127 F5
Bentley Heath Cotts B93 ... 127 F5
Bentley La
Walsall, Birchills WS2 .... 28 B3
Walsall, Leamore WS2 .... 28 A5
Willenhall WV12 .... 27 E5
Bentley Lane Bsns Pk WS2 . 28 B3
Bentley Mill Cl WS2 .... 27 F1
Bentley Mill La WS2 .... 27 F1
Bentley Mill Way WS2 .... 27 F1
Bentley New Dr WS2 .... 28 B3
Bentley Pl WS2 .... 28 B2
Bentley Rd Bedworth CV7 ...... 78 A1
Birmingham B36 .... 69 D7
Nuneaton CV11 .... 73 A4
Wolverhampton WV10 .... 11 E2
Bentley Rd N WS2 .... 27 E1
Bentley Rd S Darlaston
WS10 .... 41 E8
Walsall WS10 .... 27 E1
Bentley Way B79 .... 20 F7
Bentley West JMI Sch
WS2 .... 27 E3
Bentleybridge Way WV11 .... 26 C4
Bentmead Gr B38 .... 104 A1
Benton Ave B11 .... 87 C6
Benton Cl WV12 .... 27 D4
Benton Cres WS3 .... 14 D2
Benton Green La CV7 .... 110 F2
Benton Rd B11 .... 87 C6
Benton's Ct DY11 .... 116 C6
Benton's La WS6 .... 5 A1
Bentons Mill Croft B7 .... 67 C8
Bentree The CV3 .... 134 B8
Benyon Ctr The WS2 .... 28 A7
Beoley Cl B72 .... 46 C1
Beoley Fst Sch B98 .... 154 E8
Beoley Gr B45 .... 122 A7
Beoley La Beoley B98 .... 154 F8
Portway B98 .... 141 B1
Beoley Rd E B98 .... 154 A4
Beoley Rd W B98 .... 153 F4
Berberry Cl B30 .... 103 D6
Berenska Dr CV32 .... 157 A2
Beresford Ave CV6 .... 95 E1
Beresford Cres B70 .... 53 B3
Beresford Dr B73 .... 46 A1
Beresford Rd Oldbury B69 ..... 64 C7
Walsall WS3 .... 28 E8
Bericote Croft B27 .... 88 D3
Bericote Rd CV32 .... 156 E8
Berkeley Cl Nuneaton CV11 ... 73 B3
Perton WV6 .... 23 F3
Walsall WS2 .... 27 F3
Berkeley Dr DY6 .... 60 C7
Berkeley Ho 2
Birmingham B23 .... 56 F6
Sutton Coldfield B76 .... 57 F8
Berkeley Prec B14 .... 104 F2
Berkeley Rd Birmingham
B25 .... 88 B7
Kenilworth CV8 .... 147 E6
Solihull B90 .... 105 F3
Berkeley Rd E B25 .... 88 B7
Berkeley Rd N CV5 .... 113 A1
Berkeley Rd S CV5 .... 133 A8
Berkeley St WS2 .... 42 B7
Berkeswell Cl B98 .... 154 C7
Berkett Rd CV6 .... 95 B2
Berkley Cl B60 .... 151 B8
Berkley Cres B13 .... 87 C1
Berkley Ct B1 .... 66 C1
Berkley St B1 .... 66 C1
Berkshire Cl Nuneaton CV10 . 72 E3
West Bromwich B71 .... 53 B7
Berkshire Cres WS10 .... 42 C4
Berkshire The WS3 .... 14 A3
Berkswell CE Prim Sch
CV7 .... 110 C3
Berkswell Cl Dudley DY1 .... 50 E3
Solihull B91 .... 107 B8
Sutton Coldfield B74 .... 31 E4
Berkswell Hall CV7 .... 110 C3
Berkswell Rd
Birmingham B24 .... 57 B4
Coventry CV6 .... 96 B2
Meriden CV7 .... 110 C7
Berkswell Sta CV7 .... 130 C8
Bermuda Bsns Pk CV10 .... 78 A7
Bermuda Cl DY1 .... 51 B6
Bermuda Ind Est CV10 .... 78 B8
Bermuda Rd CV10 .... 73 A1
Bernard Pl B18 .... 65 F5
Bernard Rd Birmingham B17 . 65 B2
Oldbury B68 .... 64 C2
Tipton DY4 .... 52 B7
Bernard St Walsall WS1 .... 29 A1
West Bromwich B71 .... 53 C4
Berners Cl CV4 .... 111 E2
Berners St B19 .... 66 D7
Bernhard Dr B21 .... 65 E8
Bernie Crossland Wlk
DY10 .... 116 F3
Bernwall Cl DY8 .... 80 F4
Berrandale Rd B36 .... 57 F1
Berrington Cl B98 .... 154 D2
Berrington Dr WV14 .... 51 B8
Berrington Rd
Nuneaton CV10 .... 72 D7
Royal Leamington Spa CV31 . 162 B6
Berrington Wlk B5 .... 86 E7
Berrow Cottage Homes
B93 .... 128 C6
Berrow Dr B15 .... 85 E7
Berrow View B61 .... 150 D7
Berrowside Rd B34 .... 69 E6
Berry Ave WS10 .... 41 B5
Berry Cres WS5 .... 43 C4
Berry Dr Aldridge WS9 .... 29 E5
Barnt Green B45 .... 122 A1
Berry Hall La B91 .... 108 B4
Berry Hill WS12 .... 2 C4
Berry Rd Birmingham B8 .... 67 E5
Dudley DY1 .... 51 C5
Berry St Birmingham B18 .... 65 F6
Coventry CV1 .... 113 E4
Wolverhampton WV1 .... 163 C3
Berrybush Gdns DY3 .... 50 E7
Berryfield Rd B26 .... 89 D5
Berryfields Aldridge WS9 .... 29 E5
Stonnall WS9 .... 16 E5
Berryfields Rd B76 .... 46 F3
Berrymound View B47 ...... 125 C7
Bertha Rd B11 .... 87 D5
Bertie Rd CV8 .... 148 A4
Bertie Terr CV32 .... 156 E1
Bertram Cl DY4 .... 41 C1
Bertram Rd
5 Birmingham B10 .... 67 D1
Smethwick B67 .... 64 E6
Berwick Cl Coventry CV5 ..... 112 B4
Warwick CV34 .... 155 E2
Berwick Dr WS11 .... 4 C8
Berwick Gr
Birmingham, Frankley B31 ... 102 D3
Birmingham, Pheasey B43 ...... 44 B4
Berwicks La B37 .... 70 B1
Berwood Farm Rd B72 .... 57 C6
Berwood Gdns B24 .... 57 C5
Berwood Gr B92 .... 89 B1
Berwood La B24 .... 57 E3
Berwood Rd B72 .... 57 D6
Berwyn Ave CV6 .... 95 A1

erwyn Gr WS6 .... 4 F3
erwyn Way CV10 .... 72 C4
eryl Ave LE10 .... 71 A2
esant Gr B27 .... 88 A1
esbury Cl B93 .... 127 E2
escot Cres WS1 .... 42 D6
escot Croft B42 .... 55 B6
escot Dr WS2 .... 42 B6
escot Ind Est The WS10 .... 41 D4
escot St WS1 .... 42 E7
escot Stadium Sta WS5 .... 42 D5
esford Gr Birmingham B31 .... 102 D3
  Solihull B90 .... 127 B6
essborough Rd B25 .... 88 C8
est Ave CV8 .... 148 C7
est Rd WV14 .... 40 D7
est St B64 .... 62 F2
Beswick Gr B33 .... 69 A4
Beta Gr B14 .... 105 C4
Betjeman Ct DY10 .... 117 B5
Betjeman Pl WV10 .... 12 A1
Betley Gr B33 .... 69 A5
Betony Cl WS5 .... 43 A3
Betsham Cl B44 .... 45 B1
Bett Rd B20 .... 54 F3
Bettany Glade WV10 .... 11 E4
Betteridge Dr B76 .... 46 E4
Bettina Cl CV10 .... 72 B5
Bettman Cl CV3 .... 133 E6
Betton Rd B14 .... 104 E5
Betty's La WS11 .... 6 A4
Bevan Ave WV4 .... 39 E4
Bevan Cl Bilston WV14 .... 40 F6
  Walsall WS4 .... 15 C1
Bevan Lee Rd WS11 .... 1 D3
Bevan Rd Brierley Hill DY5 .... 61 A2
  Tipton DY4 .... 52 B4
Bevan Way B66 .... 64 F7
Beverley Ave CV10 .... 72 B4
Beverley Cl
  Astwood Bank B96 .... 158 E2
  Balsall Common CV7 .... 130 C7
  Sutton Coldfield B72 .... 57 D7
Beverley Court Rd B32 .... 84 C6
Beverley Cres WV4 .... 39 F4
Beverley Croft B23 .... 56 D2
Beverley Ct [1] B62 .... 84 A6
Beverley Dr DY6 .... 60 C7
Beverley Gr B26 .... 89 B5
Beverley Hill WS12 .... 2 D6
Beverley Rd
  Birmingham B45 .... 122 A7
  Royal Leamington Spa CV32 .... 156 D1
  West Bromwich B71 .... 42 D1
Beverly Dr CV4 .... 132 D2
Beverston Rd Perton WV6 .... 24 A4
  Tipton DY4 .... 41 B2
Bevin Rd WS2 .... 27 E3
Bevington Cres CV6 .... 112 E5
Bevington Rd B6 .... 66 F8
Bewdley Ave [4] B12 .... 87 A6
Bewdley Dr WV1 .... 26 B2
Bewdley Hill DY11 .... 116 B5
Bewdley Ho B69 .... 69 A1
Bewdley Rd
  Birmingham B30 .... 104 B8
  Kidderminster DY11 .... 116 C6
Bewdley Villas [3] B18 .... 65 D4
Bewell Cl B61 .... 136 F4
Bewell Head B61 .... 136 F4
Bewlay Cl DY5 .... 81 B7
Bewley Rd WV12 .... 27 D4
Bewlys Ave B20 .... 54 E4
Bexfield Cl CV5 .... 112 A6
Bexhill Gr [3] B15 .... 66 C1
Bexley Gr B71 .... 53 E7
Bexley Rd B44 .... 56 B8
Bexmore Dr WS13 .... 3 F1
Beyer Cl B77 .... 22 A2
Bhylls Acre Cty Prim Sch WV3 .... 38 B8
Bhylls Cres WV3 .... 38 C7
Bhylls La WV3 .... 38 C7
Bibbey's Gn WV10 .... 11 F4
Bibsworth Ave B13 .... 105 D8
Bibury Rd B28 .... 105 E2
Bicester Sq B35 .... 58 B4
Bickenhill Green Ct B92 .... 90 D1
Bickenhill La
  Birmingham B37 .... 90 C6
  Birmingham B40 .... 90 D4
  Catherine de B B91 .... 108 C6
Bickenhill Park Rd B92 .... 88 E1
Bickenhill Parkway B37 .... 90 D6
Bickenhill Rd B37 .... 90 B7
Bickford Rd Birmingham B6 .... 56 A1
  Wolverhampton WV10 .... 25 F5
Bickington Rd B32 .... 84 D2
Bickley Ave Birmingham B11 .... 87 C6
  Sutton Coldfield B74 .... 31 E5
Bickley Gr B26 .... 89 B5
Bickley Ho B74 .... 31 E5
Bickley Rd Bilston WV14 .... 41 A7
  Walsall WS4 .... 29 C7
Bicknell Croft B14 .... 104 E2
Bickton B24 .... 57 C5
Biddings La WV14 .... 40 B2
Biddles Hill B94 .... 141 C6
Biddlestone Gr WS5 .... 43 C3
Biddlestone Pl WS10 .... 41 B7
Biddulph Ct [3] B73 .... 46 A2
Bideford Dr B29 .... 85 C1
Bideford Rd Coventry CV2 .... 114 C4
  Smethwick B66 .... 65 B5
Bideford Way WS11 .... 4 B8
Bidford Cl B90 .... 106 D2

Bidford Rd B31 .... 102 E3
Bierton Rd B25 .... 88 C8
Bigbury Cl CV3 .... 133 E5
Biggin Cl Birmingham B35 .... 58 A3
  Perton WV6 .... 23 E5
Biggin Hall Cres CV3 .... 114 B2
Bigwood Dr Birmingham B32 .... 84 D1
  Sutton Coldfield B75 .... 47 A5
Bilberry Bank WS11 .... 1 E6
Bilberry Cres WS12 .... 1 C5
Bilberry Dr B45 .... 122 A6
Bilberry Rd Birmingham
  B14 .... 104 C6
  Coventry CV2 .... 96 D2
Bilboe Rd WV14 .... 41 A3
Bilbrook Cl WV8 .... 10 B3
Bilbrook Gr Birmingham B29 .... 84 F2
  Codsall WV8 .... 10 B3
Bilbrook Mid CE Sch WV8 .... 10 B3
Bilbrook Rd WV8 .... 10 B4
Bilbrook Sta WV8 .... 10 A2
Bilbury Cl B97 .... 158 C6
Bilhay La B70 .... 53 B5
Bilhay St B70 .... 53 B5
Billau Rd WV14 .... 40 D2
Billesden Cl CV3 .... 134 E8
Billesley Inf Sch B13 .... 105 C6
Billesley Jun Sch B13 .... 105 C6
Billesley La Birmingham B13 .... 87 A1
  Portway B48 .... 140 E6
Billing Rd CV5 .... 112 D3
Billingham Cl B91 .... 127 B8
Billingsley Rd B26 .... 89 A8
Billinton Cl CV2 .... 114 E2
Bills La B90 .... 106 A1
Bills St WS10 .... 41 E6
Billsmore Gn B92 .... 107 C7
Billy Buns La WV5 .... 49 B8
Billy La B45 .... 138 A7
Billy Wright Cl WV4 .... 38 D6
Bilport La WS10 .... 52 F8
Bilston Central Sta WV14 .... 40 E5
Bilston Coll of F Ed
  Annexe WV14 .... 40 E6
Bilston Com Coll WV14 .... 40 B7
Bilston Com Coll
  Broad Lanes Site WV14 .... 40 C3
Bilston Com Coll
  Devonshire Ho WV2 .... 40 A7
Bilston Com Coll
  Green Lanes WV14 .... 40 C6
Bilston High Sch WV14 .... 40 D5
Bilston Ind Est WV14 .... 41 A4
Bilston Key Ind Est WV14 .... 41 A4
Bilston La WV13 .... 41 B8
Bilston Rd Tipton DY4 .... 52 B5
  Wednesbury WS10 .... 41 E3
  Willenhall WV13 .... 41 A8
  Wolverhampton WV2 .... 39 F8
Bilston St Darlaston WS10 .... 41 D6
  Sedgley DY3 .... 50 E8
  Willenhall WV13 .... 27 A1
  Wolverhampton WV1 .... 163 C2
Bilton Grange Rd B26 .... 88 F8
Bilton Ind Est
  [7] Birmingham B38 .... 123 E8
  Coventry CV3 .... 113 F1
Binbrook Rd WV12 .... 27 D4
Bincomb Ave B26 .... 89 B6
Binfield St DY4 .... 52 A4
Bingley Ave B8 .... 68 B4
Bingley Ent Ctr WV3 .... 39 A8
Bingley Prim Sch WV3 .... 39 A8
Bingley St WV3 .... 39 A8
Binley Ave CV3 .... 134 F7
Binley Cl Birmingham B26 .... 88 D6
  Solihull B90 .... 126 A8
Binley Gr CV3 .... 134 F7
Binley Ind Est CV3 .... 135 A8
Binley Rd CV2, CV3 .... 114 D1
Binley Woods Cty
  Prim Sch CV3 .... 135 E7
Binns Cl CV4 .... 131 F8
Binstead Rd B44 .... 45 A2
Binswood Ave CV32 .... 156 F2
Binswood Cl CV2 .... 96 D2
Binswood Mans [12] CV32 .... 156 F2
Binswood Rd B62 .... 84 A7
Binswood St CV32 .... 156 E1
Binton Cl B98 .... 154 F1
Binton Croft B13 .... 104 F8
Binton Rd Coventry CV2 .... 96 D2
  Solihull B90 .... 105 F1
Birbeck Ho B36 .... 70 B6
Birbeck Pl DY5 .... 61 A6
Birch Ave Brierley Hill DY5 .... 62 A2
  Brownhills WS8 .... 15 E8
  Burntwood WS7 .... 6 F6
  Cannock WS11 .... 4 C8
Birch Brook La WS14 .... 17 E6
Birch Cl Bedworth CV12 .... 78 D4
  Birmingham B30 .... 103 E6
  Coventry CV5 .... 111 F6
Birch Coppice DY5 .... 62 A1
Birch Cres B69 .... 52 E1
Birch Croft Aldridge WS9 .... 30 C8
  Birmingham B37 .... 70 C1
  Sutton Coldfield B24 .... 57 D5
Birch Croft Rd B75 .... 46 D7
Birch Ct Birmingham B30 .... 103 E4
  Oldbury B66 .... 64 D8
  Royal Leamington Spa CV34 .... 161 E2
  Walsall WS4 .... 29 A4
  [11] Wolverhampton WV3 .... 38 F8
Birch Dr Halesowen B62 .... 63 E1
  Little Aston B74 .... 31 D5
  Stourbridge DY8 .... 80 E6
  Sutton Coldfield B75 .... 46 F7

Birch Gr Birchmoor B78 .... 36 D7
  Lichfield WS13 .... 9 D8
  Oldbury B68 .... 84 D7
Birch Hollow B15 .... 85 F6
Birch La Aldridge WS9 .... 16 D1
  Oldbury B68 .... 84 D7
  Walsall WS4 .... 15 C1
Birch Rd
  Birmingham, Eachway B45 .... 121 E6
  Birmingham, Witton B6 .... 56 A2
  Oldbury B68 .... 84 D7
  Sedgley DY3 .... 39 F1
  Wednesfield WV11 .... 26 F8
Birch Rd E B6 .... 56 B2
Birch St Oldbury B68 .... 64 C5
  Tipton DY4 .... 51 F5
  Walsall WS2 .... 28 D3
  Wolverhampton WV1 .... 163 B3
Birch Terr [7] DY2 .... 62 C4
Birch Tree Gr B91 .... 106 F4
Birch Wlk B68 .... 84 D8
Birchall St B12 .... 66 F1
Birchbrook Ind Pk WS14 .... 17 E6
Birchcoppice Gdns WV12 .... 27 E4
Birchcroft [6] B66 .... 65 C5
Birchdale WV14 .... 40 D7
Birchdale Ave B23 .... 56 E3
Birchdale Rd B23 .... 56 E4
Birchen Coppice Fst Sch DY11 .... 116 B2
Birchen Coppice Mid Sch DY11 .... 116 B2
Birchensale Mid Sch B97 .... 153 C4
Birchensale Rd B97 .... 153 C5
Birches Ave WV8 .... 10 C1
Birches Barn Ave WV3 .... 38 F7
Birches Barn Rd WV3 .... 38 F7
Birches Cl B13 .... 86 F1
Birches Fst Sch WV8 .... 10 B1
Birches Green Inf Sch B24 .... 57 B2
Birches Green Jun Sch B24 .... 57 B3
Birches Green Rd B24 .... 57 B2
Birches La Alvechurch B48 .... 138 F6
  Kenilworth CV8 .... 148 B3
Birches Park Rd WV8 .... 10 A2
Birches Rd WV8 .... 10 B2
Birches Rise WV13 .... 26 F1
Birches The CV12 .... 79 B4
Birchfield Cl Halesowen B63 .... 82 E2
  Wood End CV9 .... 36 C1
Birchfield Cres DY9 .... 81 F3
Birchfield Ct B97 .... 153 B2
Birchfield Gdns
  [8] Birmingham B6 .... 66 D8
  Walsall WS5 .... 43 C4
Birchfield Jun & Inf Sch B20 .... 55 D1
Birchfield La B69 .... 63 E4
Birchfield Rd
  Birmingham B20 .... 55 D2
  Coventry CV6 .... 112 F8
  Kidderminster DY11 .... 116 B5
  Redditch B97 .... 153 B2
  Stourbridge DY9 .... 81 F3
Birchfield Tower [1] B20 .... 55 D1
Birchfield Way WS5 .... 43 C4
Birchfields Dr WS12 .... 2 D1
Birchfields Rd WV12 .... 27 A5
Birchgate DY9 .... 81 F4
Birchglade WV3 .... 24 D1
Birchgrave Cl CV6 .... 114 A7
Birchills CE Com Prim Sch WS2 .... 28 D2
Birchills St WS2 .... 28 D2
Birchley Ho B69 .... 63 D6
Birchley Park Ave B69 .... 63 E6
Birchley Rise B92 .... 88 F4
Birchley Spec Sch B65 .... 63 D4
Birchmoor Cl B28 .... 106 B7
Birchmoor Rd B78 .... 36 F8
Birchover Rd WS2 .... 28 A4
Birchtree Gdns DY5 .... 62 A1
Birchtree Hollow WV12 .... 27 D5
Birchtree Rd CV10 .... 72 C6
Birchtrees Dr B33 .... 69 D2
Birchway Cl CV32 .... 156 C1
Birchwood Ave B78 .... 36 F7
Birchwood Cl
  Essington WV11 .... 13 A3
  Kidderminster DY11 .... 116 A7
Birchwood Cres B12 .... 87 A4
Birchwood Prim Sch B78 .... 36 F7
Birchwood Rd
  Binley Woods CV3 .... 135 C7
  Birmingham B12 .... 87 A4
  Lichfield WS14 .... 9 C7
  Wolverhampton WV4 .... 39 A5
Birchwood Wlk [2] DY6 .... 60 E8
Birchwoods B32 .... 84 B2
Birchy Cl B90 .... 125 F6
Birchy Leasowes La B90 .... 125 E5
Bird End B71 .... 53 F8
Bird Grove Ct CV1 .... 113 D5
Bird Rd CV34 .... 161 D4
Bird St Coventry CV1 .... 165 C3
  Dudley DY3 .... 50 C3
  Lichfield WS13 .... 9 B8
Birdbrook Rd B44 .... 55 E8
Birdcage Wlk [4] DY2 .... 51 D1
Birdhope B77 .... 22 C1
Birdie Cl B38 .... 103 D1
Birdlip Gr B32 .... 84 C6
Birds Bush Cty Prim Sch B77 .... 35 E4
Birds Bush Rd B77 .... 35 F8
Birds Mdw DY5 .... 61 C7
Birdwell Croft B13 .... 104 F6

Birkdale Ave Birmingham B29 .... 85 F1
  Blackwell B60 .... 138 A5
Birkdale Cl Nuneaton CV11 .... 74 A1
  Stourbridge DY8 .... 80 F2
  Wolverhampton WV1 .... 26 A2
Birkdale Dr B69 .... 63 A8
Birkdale Gr B29 .... 104 A8
Birkdale Rd WS3 .... 14 A3
Birkenshaw Rd B44 .... 55 E8
Birley Gr B63 .... 82 C1
Birlingham Ho B60 .... 137 B3
Birmingham Bsns Pk B37 .... 90 E8
Birmingham
  Childrens Hospl B4 .... 164 C3
Birmingham Coll of Food
  Tourism &
  Creative Studies B3 .... 164 A3
Birmingham
  Conservatoire B1 .... 164 B2
Birmingham Dental
  Hospl The B4 .... 164 C4
Birmingham Great Pk B31 .... 102 B1
Birmingham Heartlands
  Hospl B9 .... 68 B2
Birmingham Int Airport B40 .... 90 B4
Birmingham Int
  Convention Ctr B1 .... 66 C2
Birmingham Int Sta B40 .... 90 D4
Birmingham New Rd
  Dudley WV14, DY4 .... 51 C4
  Wolverhampton WV4 .... 39 E4
Birmingham Rd
  Aldridge WS9 .... 30 A4
  Allesley CV5 .... 111 E2
  Alvechurch B48 .... 139 B7
  Birmingham B36 .... 69 A8
  Blackheath B65 .... 63 C2
  Blakedown DY10 .... 98 C2
  Burton Green CV8 .... 131 A1
  Coleshill B46 .... 70 E5
  Dudley DY1 .... 51 E2
  Hagley DY9 .... 99 D7
  Halesowen B63 .... 83 B4
  Hopwood B38, B48 .... 123 B4
  Kenilworth CV8 .... 147 C8
  Kidderminster DY10 .... 117 D7
  Lichfield WS14 .... 9 A4
  Lickey End B60, B61 .... 137 B6
  Little Packington CV7 .... 91 E3
  Lydiate Ash B45, B61 .... 121 D5
  Marlbrook B61 .... 121 B1
  Oldbury B69 .... 64 B7
  Redditch B97 .... 153 E8
  Shenstone WS14 .... 18 A5
  Stoneleigh CV8 .... 149 B6
  Studley B80 .... 159 E7
  Sutton Coldfield B72 .... 46 B2
  Walsall WS5 .... 43 D5
  Warwick CV34 .... 160 C8
  Water Orton B46 .... 59 A3
  West Bromwich B71 .... 54 A1
  Wolverhampton WV2 .... 39 D7
  Wroxall B93, CV35 .... 145 D3
Birmingham Sch of
  Speech & Drama
  Birmingham, Edgbaston B15 .... 86 A7
  Birmingham, Ladywood B1 .... 164 B2
Birmingham St
  Darlaston WS10 .... 41 E6
  Dudley DY2 .... 51 D1
  Halesowen B63 .... 83 B3
  Oldbury B69 .... 64 A7
  Stourbridge DY8 .... 81 B5
  Walsall WS1 .... 28 F1
  Willenhall WV13 .... 27 C2
Birnam B15 .... 86 A8
Birnham Cl DY4 .... 51 D5
Birstall Wlk B38 .... 123 C8
Birvell Ct CV12 .... 78 D3
Bisell Way DY5 .... 81 C6
Biset Ave DY10 .... 117 B5
Bishbury Cl B15 .... 85 E8
Bishop Asbury Cres B43 .... 54 C8
Bishop Challoner RC Sch
  B14 .... 104 F8
Bishop Cl B45 .... 101 E1
Bishop Hall Cres B60 .... 150 E7
Bishop Milner RC Sec Sch
  DY1 .... 51 A3
Bishop Rd WS10 .... 42 C2
Bishop St Birmingham B5 .... 86 E8
  Coventry CV1 .... 165 B3
Bishop Ullathorne RC Sch
  CV3 .... 132 F4
Bishop Vesey's Gram Sch
  B74 .... 46 C6
Bishop Walsh RC Sch B72 .... 46 D1
Bishop Wilson CE Prim
  Sch B37 .... 70 C3
Bishop's Ct B31 .... 103 B3
Bishopgate Bsns Pk CV1 .... 113 D5
Bishopgate Ind Est CV1 .... 113 D5
Bishops Cl Dudley DY2 .... 62 E8
  Smethwick B66 .... 65 C4
Bishops Gate B31 .... 103 A2
Bishops Mdw B75 .... 32 E3
Bishops Rd B73 .... 46 B3
Bishops Way B74 .... 31 F6
Bishops Wlk CV5 .... 133 B8
Bishopstone B98 .... 154 F2
Bishopton Cl Coventry
  CV5 .... 112 B3
  Solihull B90 .... 106 C1
Bishopton Rd B67 .... 64 F1

Bishton Gr DY2 .... 62 D4
Bisley Gr B24 .... 57 B2
Bissel Dr WS10 .... 42 B3
Bissel St WV14 .... 40 F5
Bissell Cl B28 .... 105 F6
Bissell St
  Birmingham, Highgate B5 .... 86 E8
  Birmingham, Quinton B32 .... 84 A6
Bisset Cres [3] CV31 .... 162 C6
Biton Cl B17 .... 85 B5
Bittell Cl Birmingham B31 .... 122 F7
  Wolverhampton WV10 .... 11 E4
Bittell Farm Rd B48 .... 123 A2
Bittell La B45 .... 138 E8
Bittell Rd Alvechurch B48 .... 139 A8
  Barnt Green B45 .... 138 E5
Bittern Wlk DY5 .... 81 C6
Bittern Wood Rd DY10 .... 117 B3
Bitterne Dr W6 .... 25 A4
Bitterscote La B78 .... 21 A2
Black Bank CV7 .... 78 B1
Black Country Mus DY1 .... 51 D3
Black Country New Rd
  WS10 .... 41 C4
Black Country Route
  Bilston WV14 .... 40 E5
  Darlaston WV13, WS10 .... 41 B7
  Walsall WS2, WS10 .... 27 E1
Black Country Spine Rd
  B70 .... 52 F6
Black Haynes Rd B29 .... 103 A6
Black Horse La [1] DY10 .... 116 E6
Black Horse Rd CV6 .... 96 B6
Black La CV32 .... 157 C2
Black Lake B70 .... 53 A6
Black Lake La B60 .... 152 A2
Black Lake Sta B70 .... 53 A6
Black Prince Ave CV3 .... 133 E6
Black-a-Tree Ct CV10 .... 72 F5
Black-A-Tree Rd CV10 .... 72 E4
Blackacre Rd DY2 .... 62 D8
Blackberry Ave
  Birmingham B9 .... 68 A3
  Tanworth-in-A B94 .... 143 C6
Blackberry Cl DY1 .... 61 E8
Blackberry La Ash Green
  CV7 .... 95 C5
  Blackheath B65 .... 62 F5
  Brownhills WS9 .... 16 B4
  Coventry CV2 .... 114 C6
  Halesowen B63 .... 83 A2
  Sutton Coldfield B74 .... 31 E4
Blackbird Croft B36 .... 70 A7
Blackbrook Cl DY2 .... 62 A3
Blackbrook Rd DY2 .... 62 B5
Blackbrook Way WV10 .... 11 E4
Blackburn Ave WV6 .... 24 F7
Blackburn Rd CV6 .... 95 F3
Blackburne Rd B28 .... 105 F6
Blackbushe Cl B17 .... 84 F7
Blackcat Cl B37 .... 70 A3
Blackdown B77 .... 22 C1
Blackdown Cl B45 .... 102 A2
Blackdown Rd B93 .... 128 B6
Blackett Ct [1] B73 .... 46 A2
Blackfirs La B37, B46 .... 90 D7
Blackford Cl Halesowen
  B63 .... 82 D2
  Kidderminster DY11 .... 116 A1
Blackford Rd
  Birmingham B11 .... 87 C4
  Solihull B90 .... 126 C8
Blackford St B18 .... 65 E5
Blackgreaves La B76 .... 48 F1
Blackhalve La WV11 .... 12 D2
Blackham Dr B73 .... 57 A7
Blackham Rd WV11 .... 26 F8
Blackheath Mkt B65 .... 63 B1
Blackheath Prim Sch B65 .... 63 B1
Blackhorse La DY5 .... 61 E1
Blackley Ho B66 .... 65 D6
Blacklow Rd CV34 .... 156 A1
Blackmoor Croft B33 .... 69 D2
Blackmore La B60 .... 137 A3
Blackpit La WV4 .... 37 E3
Blackrock Rd B23 .... 56 B6
Blackroot Cl WS7 .... 7 D4
Blackroot Ho B23 .... 45 C2
Blackroot Rd B74 .... 46 B7
Blackshaw Dr CV2 .... 114 F6
Blacksmiths La B94 .... 143 C6
Blackstick La B94 .... 153 A1
Blackstitch La B97 .... 152 F1
Blackthorn Ave WS7 .... 6 F4
Blackthorn Cl
  Birmingham B30 .... 103 C6
  Coventry CV4 .... 132 D5
Blackthorn Ct B98 .... 154 E1
Blackthorn Gr CV11 .... 73 F2
Blackthorn Rd
  Birmingham, Bournville
  B30 .... 103 D6
  Birmingham,
  Castle Bromwich B36 .... 69 C8
  Stourbridge DY8 .... 61 A1
Blackthorne Cl Dudley DY1 .... 50 F4
  Solihull B91 .... 106 E4
Blackthorne Rd Dudley DY1 .... 50 F4
  Kenilworth CV8 .... 148 A3
  Lichfield WS14 .... 9 D7
  Smethwick B67 .... 64 D4
  Walsall WS5 .... 42 F5
Blackwatch Rd CV6 .... 113 C8
Blackwater Cl DY5 .... 61 A6
Blackwell La B97 .... 153 B5

Blackwell Rd
Barnt Green B45, B60 .... 138 B5
Coventry CV6 .... 113 E8
Sutton Coldfield B72 .... 46 D1
Blackwell St DY10 .... 116 E6
Blackwood Ave WV11 .... 26 C8
Blackwood Dr B74 .... 44 E8
Blackwood Rd Aldridge B74 .. 30 E1
Bromsgrove B60 .... 137 B2
Tamworth B77 .... 35 C7
Blades Rd B70 .... 52 D4
Bladon Cl CV11 .... 73 F8
Bladon Wlk 13 CV31 .... 162 C6
Blaenwern Dr B63 .... 82 B7
Blagdon Rd B63 .... 83 A6
Blair Dr CV12 .... 77 D1
Blair Gr B37 .... 70 D1
Blake Cl Cannock WS11 .... 2 A5
Hinckley LE10 .... 71 D4
Nuneaton CV10 .... 72 A5
Blake Hall Cl DY5 .... 81 C7
Blake High Sch WS12 .... 1 F6
Blake Ho 2 WS2 .... 42 C8
Blake La B9 .... 67 F2
Blake Pl B9 .... 67 F2
Blake Rd B61 .... 137 B8
Blake St B74 .... 31 E6
Blake Street Sta B74 .... 31 F6
Blakebrook DY11 .... 116 C6
Blakebrook Cl DY11 .... 116 C6
Blakebrook Day Special Sch DY11 .... 116 C6
Blakebrook Gdns DY11 .... 116 C6
Blakedon Rd WS10 .... 41 E3
Blakedown CE Prim Sch DY10 .... 98 C1
Blakedown Rd B63 .... 82 F1
Blakedown Way 4 B69 .... 63 E4
Blakeland Rd B44 .... 55 E6
Blakeland St B9 .... 67 F2
Blakelands Ave CV31 .... 162 B6
Blakeley Ave WV6 .... 24 F7
Blakeley Ct B72 .... 57 C8
Blakeley Hall Gdns B69 .... 64 B7
Blakeley Hall Rd B69 .... 64 B7
Blakeley Heath Cty Prim Sch WV5 .... 49 A5
Blakeley Heath Dr WV5 .... 49 A5
Blakeley Rise WV6 .... 24 F7
Blakeley Specl Sch B69 .... 52 E1
Blakeley Wood Rd DY4 .... 52 D8
Blakemere Ave B25 .... 88 E8
Blakemere Cl B98 .... 154 F3
Blakemere Ho 3 B16 .... 66 A2
Blakemore Cl B32 .... 84 F3
Blakemore Dr B75 .... 46 F6
Blakemore Rd
Brownhills WS9 .... 16 A3
West Bromwich B70 .... 53 A1
Blakenall Cl 1 WS3 .... 28 D8
Blakenall Heath WS3 .... 28 D8
Blakenall Heath Jun Sch WS3 .... 28 C8
Blakenall La WS3 .... 28 D8
Blakenall Row WS3 .... 28 D8
Blakeney Ave
Birmingham B17 .... 85 A7
Stourbridge DY8 .... 80 D6
Blakeney Cl DY3 .... 50 C8
Blakenhale J & I Schs B33 .... 69 B1
Blakenhale Rd B33 .... 69 B1
Blakenhall Gdns WV2 .... 39 C7
Blakenhall Ind Est WV2 .... 39 B7
Blakesfield Dr B45 .... 122 A1
Blakesley Cl B76 .... 57 F5
Blakesley Gr B25 .... 68 D1
Blakesley Hall Jun & Inf Sch B25 .... 68 D1
Blakesley Mews B25 .... 88 D8
Blakesley Rd B25 .... 68 D1
Blakewood Cl B34 .... 69 C5
Blandford Ave B36 .... 58 E1
Blandford Dr Coventry CV2 .... 114 F5
Stourbridge DY8 .... 60 E3
Blandford Gdns WS7 .... 7 C6
Blandford Rd
Birmingham B32 .... 84 F5
Royal Leamington Spa CV32 156 C1
Blandford Way CV35 .... 160 A7
Blanefield WV8 .... 10 E2
Blanford Mere Prim Sch DY6 .... 60 E7
Blanning Ct B93 .... 127 E3
Blay Ave WS2 .... 28 B2
Blaydon Ave B75 .... 32 E2
Blaydon Rd WV9, WV10 .... 11 A1
Blaythorn Ave B92 .... 89 A3
Blaze Hill Rd DY6 .... 60 A8
Blaze La B96, B97 .... 158 A3
Blaze Pk DY6 .... 60 B8
Bleachfield Rd B98 .... 154 F8
Bleak Hill Rd B23 .... 56 C5
Bleak House Dr WS7 .... 6 D8
Bleak St B67 .... 64 F6
Bleakhouse Jun Sch B68 .... 64 C1
Bleakhouse Rd B68 .... 64 C1
Bleakman Ct B30 .... 104 A6
Blenheim B17 .... 85 B6
Blenheim Ave CV6 .... 95 C2
Blenheim Cl Hinckley LE10 .... 71 F4
Nuneaton CV11 .... 73 F2
Tamworth B77 .... 21 C4
Walsall WS4 .... 29 D7
Blenheim Cres
Bromsgrove B60 .... 151 A8
Royal Leamington Spa CV31 162 C5
Blenheim Ct B44 .... 55 F8
Blenheim Dr B43 .... 54 D8
Blenheim Rd Birmingham B13 .... 86 F1
Burntwood WS7 .... 7 A8
Kingswinford DY6 .... 61 A6
Norton Canes WS11 .... 6 B4
Solihull B90 .... 106 D2
Willenhall WV12 .... 27 B6
Blenheim Way
Birmingham B44 .... 55 F8
Dudley DY1 .... 50 E2
Bletchley Dr CV5 .... 112 B4
Bletchley Rd B24 .... 57 E4
Blewitt Cl B36 .... 58 D2
Blewitt St Brierley Hill DY5 .... 61 C6
Cannock WS12 .... 2 B7
Blews St B6 .... 66 E5
Blick Rd CV34 .... 161 C4
Blind La Berkswell CV7 .... 110 D4
Tanworth-In-A B94 .... 141 D1
Blindpit La B76 .... 59 B8
Bliss Cl CV4 .... 111 E3
Blithe Cl DY8 .... 81 A8
Blithfield Dr DY5 .... 81 B7
Blithfield Gr B24 .... 57 C5
Blithfield Pl WS11 .... 2 B1
Blithfield Rd WS8 .... 6 C2
Blockall WS10 .... 41 D7
Blockall Cl WS10 .... 41 D7
Blockley Rd CV12 .... 78 C4
Blockley's Yd 4 LE10 .... 75 D8
Blondvil St CV3 .... 133 D7
Bloomfield Cres WS13 .... 3 B2
Bloomfield Ct 3 B42 .... 55 A8
Bloomfield Dr WV12 .... 13 D1
Bloomfield Pk DY4 .... 51 D6
Bloomfield Rd
Birmingham B13 .... 87 B3
Tipton DY4 .... 51 E7
Bloomfield St N B63 .... 82 F5
Bloomfield St W B63 .... 82 F4
Bloomfield Terr DY4 .... 51 E7
Bloomfield Way B79 .... 20 F7
Bloomsbury Gr B14 .... 104 C7
Bloomsbury St
Birmingham B7 .... 67 B5
Wolverhampton WV2 .... 163 B1
Bloomsbury Way WS14 .... 9 E7
Bloomsbury Wlk 1 B7 .... 67 B5
Blossom Gr Birmingham B36 . 68 E8
Blackheath B64 .... 62 F1
Blossom Hill B24 .... 57 A4
Blossom Terr B29 .... 85 F2
Blossom's Fold WV1 .... 163 B3
Blossomfield Cl
Birmingham B38 .... 123 D8
7 Kingswinford DY6 .... 60 E8
Blossomfield Ct B38 .... 123 D8
Blossomfield Inf Sch B90 . 106 D3
Blossomfield Rd B91 .... 106 F2
Blossomville Way 10 B27 .... 88 C5
Blount Ho DY11 .... 116 B8
Blount Terr DY11 .... 116 D3
Blounts Rd B23 .... 56 C5
Blower's Green Rd DY2 .... 62 B8
Blowers Green Cres DY2 .... 62 B7
Blowers Green Pl DY2 .... 62 B7
Blowers Green Prim Sch DY2 .... 62 B8
Bloxcidge St B68 .... 64 B4
Bloxwich Bsns Pk WS2 .... 28 A7
Bloxwich Hospl WS3 .... 28 B8
Bloxwich Jun & Mixed Inf Sch WS3 .... 14 B1
Bloxwich L Ctr WS3 .... 28 C8
Bloxwich La WS2 .... 28 A4
Bloxwich North Sta WS3 .... 13 F3
Bloxwich Rd WS2, WS3 .... 28 D5
Bloxwich Rd N WV12 .... 27 D6
Bloxwich Rd S WV13 .... 27 A3
Bloxwich Sta WS3 .... 14 A1
Blucher St B1 .... 164 B1
Blue Ball La B63 .... 82 C7
Blue Bird Pk B62 .... 101 B7
Blue Cedars DY8 .... 80 C6
Blue Coat CE Comp Sch WS1 .... 28 F1
Blue Coat CE Inf Sch WS1 .. 28 F1
Blue Coat CE Jun Sch WS1 .... 28 F1
Blue Coat CE Sch CV1 .... 113 F1
Blue Coat Sch The B17 .... 85 E6
Blue La E WS2 .... 28 E3
Blue La W WS2 .... 28 D2
Blue Lake Rd B93 .... 128 B2
Blue Rock Pl B69 .... 63 C7
Bluebell Cl Cannock WS12 .... 2 B6
Stourbridge DY8 .... 60 C2
Bluebell Cres WV11 .... 26 D5
Bluebell Dr B37 .... 70 E2
Bluebell La WS6 .... 5 A1
Bluebell Rd Blackheath B64 .. 62 E3
Brownhills WS9 .... 16 B3
Dudley DY1 .... 51 B4
Bluebellwood Cl B76 .... 47 A3
Bluebird Cl WS14 .... 9 D8
Bluebird Trad Est WV10 .... 25 E5
Bluestone Wlk B65 .... 63 C6
Blundell Rd B11 .... 87 D5
Blundells The CV8 .... 148 A5
Blyth Ave CV7 .... 130 C5
Blyth Cl CV12 .... 77 C1
Blythe Cl Burntwood WS7 .... 7 D6
Redditch B97 .... 158 D7
Blythe Ct Solihull B91 .... 106 F7
Sutton Coldfield B73 .... 46 B5
Blythe Gdns WV8 .... 10 A4
Blythe Gr B44 .... 44 F3
Blythe Rd 7 Coleshill B46 .... 70 F7
Coventry CV1 .... 113 E4
Blythe St B77 .... 21 C4
Blythefield Ave B43 .... 43 C2
Blythesway B48 .... 139 A6
Blytheway B91 .... 107 E3
Blythewood Cl B91 .... 107 F1
Blythsford Rd B28 .... 106 A4
Blythswood Rd B11 .... 88 A4
Blyton Cl B16 .... 65 F3
Boar Croft CV4 .... 111 F2
Boar Hound Cl B18 .... 66 A4
Board School Gdns DY3 .... 50 E6
Boat La Burntwood WS14 .... 7 F1
Lichfield WS14 .... 8 A1
Boatman's La WS9 .... 15 E2
Bobbington Way DY2 .... 62 E5
Bobs Coppice Wlk DY5 .... 81 F7
Bockendon Rd CV4 .... 131 E5
Boddington Cl CV32 .... 157 E5
Boden Rd B28 .... 106 A7
Bodenham Cl B98 .... 154 D3
Bodenham Rd
Birmingham B31 .... 102 E1
Oldbury B68 .... 84 B8
Bodens La WS9 .... 44 B7
Bodiam Ct WV6 .... 24 A3
Bodicote Gr B75 .... 32 E3
Bodington Rd B75 .... 32 C3
Bodmin Cl Hinckley LE10 .... 71 E4
Walsall WS5 .... 43 D7
Bodmin Ct 16 DY5 .... 61 D2
Bodmin Gr 2 B7 .... 67 B5
Bodmin Rd Coventry CV2 .... 114 F5
Dudley DY2 .... 62 D2
Bodmin Rise WS5 .... 43 D7
Bodnant Way CV8 .... 148 C6
Bodymoor Heath Rd B76 .... 48 F5
Bognop Rd WV11 .... 12 D4
Bohun St CV4 .... 111 F1
Boldmere Cl B73 .... 57 A7
Boldmere Ct B43 .... 54 E7
Boldmere Dr B73 .... 57 A8
Boldmere Gdns B73 .... 57 A8
Boldmere Inf Sch B73 .... 45 F1
Boldmere Jun Sch B73 .... 45 F1
Boldmere Rd B73 .... 57 A8
Bolebridge Mews B79 .... 21 B5
Bolebridge St B79 .... 21 C4
Boley Cl WS14 .... 9 D7
Boley Cottage La WS14 .... 9 E7
Boley La WS14 .... 9 D7
Boley Park Ctr WS14 .... 9 E7
Boleyn Cl Cheslyn Hay WS6 .... 4 D2
Warwick CV34 .... 161 C6
Boleyn Rd B45 .... 101 E2
Bolingbroke Rd CV3 .... 114 A1
Bolney Rd B32 .... 84 E4
Bolton Cl CV3 .... 133 E5
Bolton Ct DY4 .... 52 C8
Bolton Rd Birmingham B10 .... 87 C8
Wednesfield WV11 .... 26 D5
Bolton St B9 .... 67 B2
Bolton Way WS3 .... 13 F3
Bolyfant Cl CV31 .... 162 A2
Bomers Field B45 .... 122 C7
Bond Dr B35 .... 58 A3
Bond Gate CV11 .... 73 C4
Bond Sq B18 .... 66 A4
Bond St
Birmingham, Ladywood B19 . 164 B4
Birmingham, Stirchley B30 .. 104 A7
Blackheath B65 .... 63 E3
Coventry CV1 .... 165 B3
Dudley WV14 .... 51 A8
Nuneaton CV11 .... 73 C5
West Bromwich B70 .... 53 C2
Wolverhampton WV2 .... 163 B2
Bondfield Rd B13 .... 105 B6
Bondway WS12 .... 1 F8
Bone Mill La WV1 .... 25 D4
Bonehill Rd B78 .... 20 E3
Boney Hay Rd WS7 .... 7 B7
Bonfire Hill DY9 .... 120 E6
Bonham Gr B25 .... 68 D1
Boningale Way B93 .... 127 E3
Bonington Dr CV12 .... 78 A4
Bonner Dr B76 .... 57 F5
Bonner Gr WS9 .... 29 F5
Bonneville Cl CV5 .... 111 B8
Bonniksen Cl CV31 .... 161 F5
Bonnington Way B43 .... 44 D4
Bonsall Rd B23 .... 57 A6
Bonville Gdns WV10 .... 11 E4
Boot Piece La B97 .... 153 B5
Booth Cl Kingswinford DY6 .... 61 A6
Lichfield WS13 .... 3 A2
Walsall WS3 .... 28 D8
Booth Ct 17 DY5 .... 61 D2
Booth Ho WS4 .... 28 F3
Booth Rd WS10 .... 42 C2
Booth St Birmingham B21 .... 65 D7
Cannock WS12 .... 2 B6
Darlaston WS10 .... 41 D8
Walsall WS3 .... 28 C8
Booth's La B42 .... 44 B1
Booths Farm Rd B42 .... 55 B8
Booths Fields CV6 .... 95 E2
Bordeaux Cl DY1 .... 50 E3
Borden Cl WV8 .... 24 F8
Bordesley Abbey B98 .... 153 F6
Bordesley Cir B10 .... 67 B1
Bordesley Cl B9 .... 68 A2
Bordesley Ct CV32 .... 157 A3
Bordesley Gn B9 .... 67 F2
Bordesley Gn E B9 .... 68 C2
Bordesley Green Girls Sch B9 .... 67 D2
Bordesley Green Jun & Inf Sch B9 .... 68 A2
Bordesley Green Rd B8 .... 67 D2
Bordesley Green Trad Est B9 .... 67 D3
Bordesley La B98 .... 153 E6
Bordesley Middleway B12 .. 87 A8
Bordesley Park Rd B10 .... 67 B1
Bordesley St B5 .... 164 D2
Bordesley Sta B10 .... 67 A1
Bore St WS13 .... 9 B7
Borman B79 .... 20 F5
Borneo St WS4 .... 28 F4
Borough Cres Oldbury B69 .... 63 E5
Stourbridge DY8 .... 80 E5
Borough Ct B63 .... 83 B4
Borough Rd B79 .... 21 C7
Borough The LE10 .... 75 D8
Borrington Rd DY10 .... 117 B5
Borrow St WV13 .... 27 A3
Borrowcop Ho WS14 .... 9 C6
Borrowcop La WS14 .... 9 C5
Borrowdale Cl
Brierley Hill DY5 .... 81 B8
Coventry CV6 .... 113 A8
Borrowdale Dr CV32 .... 156 D2
Borrowdale Gr B31 .... 102 D3
Borrowdale Rd B31 .... 102 C3
Borrowell La CV8 .... 147 E4
Borrowell Terr CV8 .... 147 E4
Borwick Ave B70 .... 53 A3
Bosbury Terr B30 .... 104 B7
Boscobel Ave DY4 .... 51 F4
Boscobel Cl DY1 .... 50 F3
Boscobel Cres WV1 .... 25 C4
Boscobel Rd Birmingham B43 .... 43 D2
Cheswick Green B90 .... 126 D5
Walsall WS1 .... 43 B8
Boscombe Ave B11 .... 87 C6
Boscombe Rd B11 .... 87 E4
Bosmere Ct B31 .... 102 F3
Boss Gate Cl WV5 .... 49 A5
Boston Cl WS12 .... 2 E1
Boston Gr B44 .... 56 B8
Boston Pl CV6 .... 113 D8
Boston Way LE9 .... 71 F6
Bosty La WS9 .... 29 E5
Boswell Cl Darlaston WS10 .... 41 D5
Tipton WS10 .... 41 C1
Boswell Dr CV2 .... 115 A7
Boswell Gr CV34 .... 155 D1
Boswell Rd Bilston WV14 .... 40 F7
Birmingham B44 .... 55 F6
Cannock WS11 .... 1 D4
Sutton Coldfield B74 .... 46 C6
Bosworth Cl Dudley DY3 .... 51 A6
Hinckley LE10 .... 71 A1
Bosworth Dr B37 .... 70 A2
Bosworth Rd B26 .... 88 E4
Bosworth Wood Jun & Inf Sch B36 .... 58 F1
Botany Dr DY3 .... 50 D6
Botany Rd WS5 .... 43 A5
Botany Wlk B16 .... 66 A2
Botha Rd B9 .... 67 F2
Botoner Rd CV1 .... 113 F2
Bott La Stourbridge DY9 .... 81 E6
Walsall WS1 .... 28 F1
Bott Rd CV5 .... 132 D8
Botteley Rd B70 .... 53 A6
Bottetourt Rd B29 .... 85 A2
Botteville Rd B27 .... 88 C2
Bottrill St CV11 .... 73 B5
Boughton Rd B25 .... 88 C7
Boulevard The
Brierley Hill DY5 .... 61 F2
Sutton Coldfield B73 .... 57 B8
Boultbee Rd B72 .... 57 C7
Boulters La CV9 .... 36 D1
Boulton Cir B19 .... 66 C6
Boulton Cl WS7 .... 7 C8
Boulton Ind Ctr B18 .... 66 B5
Boulton Jun & Inf Sch B21 . 65 E7
Boulton Rd Birmingham B21 .. 65 E7
Smethwick B66 .... 65 D6
Solihull B91 .... 107 C7
West Bromwich B70 .... 53 D1
Boulton Retreat B21 .... 65 E7
Boulton Sq B70 .... 53 D1
Boulton Wlk B23 .... 56 B4
Boultons La B97 .... 158 D6
Boundary Ave B65 .... 63 E2
Boundary Cres DY3 .... 50 C3
Boundary Ct B37 .... 69 E2
Boundary Hill DY3 .... 50 C4
Boundary Ho B5 .... 86 C5
Boundary Ind Est WV10 .... 11 C5
Boundary Pl B21 .... 54 B1
Boundary Rd Brownhills WS9 .... 15 F3
Sutton Coldfield B74 .... 44 F7
Wolverhampton WV13 .... 26 C1
Boundary Way
Wolverhampton, Compton WV6 .... 23 F2
Wolverhampton, Penn WV4 .... 38 C5
Bourlay Cl B45 .... 101 E2
Bourn Mill Dr B6 .... 66 E6
Bournbrook Rd B29 .... 86 A2
Bourne Ave Catshill B61 .... 120 F1
Fazeley B78 .... 20 E1
Halesowen B62 .... 83 F4
Tipton DY4 .... 52 C7
Bourne Cl Birmingham B13 .. 105 D
Cannock WS12 .... 2 E
Solihull B91 .... 107 E
Bourne Gn B32 .... 84 E
Bourne Hill Cl DY2 .... 62 E
Bourne Rd Birmingham B6 .... 67 B
Coventry CV3 .... 114 C
Bourne St Dudley DY2 .... 51 D
Dudley, Bramford WV14 .... 51 A
Bourne Vale WS9 .... 30 D
Bourne Way Gdns B29 .... 104 A
Bourne Wlk B65 .... 62 F
Bournebrook Cl DY2 .... 62 C
Bournebrook Cres B62 .... 84 A
Bournes Cl B63 .... 82 F
Bournes Cres B63 .... 82 E
Bournes Hill B63 .... 82 E
Bourneville Sta B30 .... 104 A
Bournheath Rd B61 .... 120 D
Bournville Coll B31 .... 103 C
Bournville Coll of F Ed B30 .... 103 F
Bournville Inf Sch B30 .... 103 E
Bournville Jun Sch B30 .... 103 E
Bournville La B30 .... 103 E
Bournville Mews B30 .... 103 E
Bournville Sch of Art B30 . 103 E
Bournville Sec Sch B30 .... 103 C
Bourton Cl 1 WS5 .... 43 A
Bourton Croft B92 .... 106 F
Bourton Dr CV31 .... 162 B
Bourton Rd B92 .... 106 F
Bovey Croft B76 .... 58 A
Bovingdon Rd B35 .... 58 A
Bow Ct CV5 .... 132 D
Bow St Bilston WV14 .... 40 E
Birmingham B1 .... 164 B
Willenhall WV13 .... 27 A
Bowater Ave B33 .... 68 D
Bowater Ho Birmingham B19 . 66 D
West Bromwich B70 .... 53 C
Bowater St B70 .... 53 C
Bowbrook Ave B90 .... 127 A
Bowcroft Gr B24 .... 57 C
Bowden Rd B67 .... 64 E
Bowden Way CV3 .... 114 F
Bowdler Rd WV2 .... 163 D
Bowen Ave WV4 .... 40 A
Bowen Ct 4 B13 .... 87 B
Bowen St WV4 .... 39 E
Bowen-Cooke Ave WV6 .... 23 E
Bower Cl WS13 .... 3 D
Bower Ho B19 .... 66 D
Bower La DY5 .... 82 A
Bowercourt Cl B91 .... 107 B
Bowers Croft CV32 .... 157 A
Bowes Dr WS11 .... 1 F
Bowes Rd B45 .... 121 E
Bowfell Cl CV5 .... 112 B
Bowker St WV13 .... 26 C1
Bowlas Ave B74 .... 46 B8
Bowling Green Ave B77 .... 35 F7
Bowling Green Cl
Birmingham B23 .... 56 F7
Darlaston WS10 .... 41 D7
Bowling Green La
Bedworth CV7, CV12 .... 95 E8
Birmingham B20 .... 66 A8
Bowling Green Rd
Birmingham B9 .... 67 C1
Dudley DY2 .... 62 E2
Hinckley LE10 .... 71 E1
Stourbridge DY8 .... 80 E5
Bowling Green St CV34 .... 160 D6
Bowls Ct CV5 .... 112 F3
Bowman Gn LE10 .... 75 F6
Bowman Rd B42 .... 44 B1
Bowman's Rise WV1 .... 26 B3
Bowmore Rd B60 .... 137 B1
Bowness Cl CV6 .... 113 A8
Bowness Ho B65 .... 63 D4
Bowood Cres B31 .... 103 B2
Bowood Dr WV6 .... 24 D6
Bowood End B76 .... 46 E3
Bowshot Cl B36 .... 58 D1
Bowstoke Rd B43 .... 54 C8
Bowyer Rd B8 .... 67 E4
Bowyer St B10 .... 67 A1
Box Cl CV31 .... 162 B3
Box Rd B37 .... 90 C8
Box St WS1 .... 28 F1
Box Trees Rd B93 .... 127 C1
Boxhill Cl B6 .... 66 F6
Boxhill The CV3 .... 114 B1
Boxnott Cl B97 .... 153 A2
Boyd Cl CV2 .... 115 A8
Boyd Gr B27 .... 88 B2
Boyden Cl WS11 .... 1 B1
Boydon Cl WV2 .... 40 A6
Boyleston Rd B28 .... 106 A6
Boyne Rd B26 .... 89 B7
Boyslade Rd LE10 .... 75 F6
Boyslade Rd E LE10 .... 75 F5
Boyton Gr B44 .... 44 F3
Brabazon Gr B35 .... 57 F3
Brabham Cres B74 .... 44 F6
Bracadale Ave B24 .... 57 A4
Bracadale Cl CV3 .... 115 A2
Brace St WS1 .... 42 E8
Bracebridge Cl CV7 .... 130 B6
Bracebridge Ct B17 .... 85 D5
Bracebridge Ho B73 .... 45 C2
Bracebridge Rd
Birmingham B24 .... 56 F1
Sutton Coldfield B74 .... 46 A8
Bracebridge St
Birmingham B6 .... 66 E6
Nuneaton CV11 .... 73 B3

Bra – Bri 175

Braceby Ave B13 105 C6
Braces La B60 121 C1
Bracken Cl Burntwood WS7 7 C7
Cannock WS12 2 D8
Lichfield WS14 9 E6
Wolverhampton WV8 10 E1
Bracken Croft 1 B37 70 C3
Bracken Dr B75 47 A5
Bracken Gr B61 121 A1
Bracken Park Gdns DY8 60 F2
Bracken Rd Birmingham B24 57 C2
Huntington WS12 1 C5
Bracken Way
Birmingham B38 123 D6
Sutton Coldfield B74 44 F8
Bracken Wood WS5 43 D5
Brackenbury Rd B44 56 B8
Brackendale Dr
Nuneaton CV10 72 F3
Walsall WS5 43 B3
Brackendale Sh Ctr WV12 27 D4
Brackendale Way DY9 81 D4
Brackenfield Rd
Birmingham B44 44 D3
Halesowen B63 82 E3
Brackenfield View DY1 61 D8
Brackenhill Rd WS7 7 A8
Brackenhurst Rd CV6 113 A7
Brackenwood Dr WV11 26 F5
Bracklesham Way B77 22 A6
Brackley Ave B20 55 C1
Brackley Cl CV6 112 F7
Brackleys Way B92 89 A2
Bracknell Wlk 1 CV2 115 A7
Bradburn Rd WV11 26 B8
Bradburne Way B7 67 A5
Bradbury Cl WS8 15 F5
Bradbury La WS12 2 B7
Bradbury Rd B92 107 A8
Braddock Cl CV3 115 A1
Brade Dr CV2 115 B7
Braden Rd WV4 38 D4
Brades Cl B63 82 B7
Brades Rd B69 63 E8
Brades Rise B69 63 D8
Bradestone Rd CV11 73 D1
Bradewell Rd B36 58 D1
Bradfield Cl CV5 112 C5
Bradfield Ho B26 89 D6
Bradfield Rd B42 55 D7
Bradford Cl B43 54 F7
Bradford Court Bsns Ctr
1 B12 87 A8
Bradford La
Belbroughton DY9 119 D5
Walsall WS1 28 E1
Bradford Mall WS1 28 E1
Bradford Pl WS1 28 E1
Bradford Rd Birmingham B36 69 B7
Brownhills WS8 15 E8
Dudley DY2 61 F6
Bradford St
Birmingham B12, B5 66 F1
Cannock WS11 2 A5
Tamworth B79 20 F5
Walsall WS1 28 E1
Bradgate Cl WV12 27 C6
Bradgate Dr B74 31 E5
Bradgate Pl 12 B12 87 A6
Bradgate Rd LE10 71 F2
Brading Rd CV10 73 D6
Bradley Croft CV7 130 B6
Bradley La WV14 41 A3
Bradley La Sta WV14 41 A3
Bradley Rd Birmingham B34 69 D6
Stourbridge DY8 80 F6
Wolverhampton WV2 39 E7
Bradley St Bilston WV14 40 F4
Brierley Hill DY5 61 C7
Tipton DY4 51 F2
Bradley's La WV14 51 E8
Bradleymore Rd DY5 61 D3
Bradleys Cl B64 82 E7
Bradmore Cl B91 107 A1
Bradmore Gr B29 103 A8
Bradmore Rd WV3 38 F8
Bradney Gn CV4 131 E7
Bradnick Pl CV4 111 F1
Bradnock Cl B13 105 C7
Bradnock's Marsh La
B92 109 E2
Bradshaw Ave
Birmingham B38 103 D1
Darlaston WS10 41 C5
Bradshaw Cl DY4 52 A3
Bradshaw St WV1 163 D3
Bradshawe Cl B28 105 D3
Bradstock Rd B30 104 C4
Bradwell Croft B75 32 E3
Bradwell Ho B31 102 D5
Braemar Ave DY8 60 C1
Braemar Cl Coventry CV2 114 E6
Sedgley DY3 39 C1
Willenhall WV12 27 B5
Braemar Dr B23 56 B5
Braemar Gdns WS12 1 F7
Braemar Rd
Norton Canes WS11 6 B4
Royal Leamington Spa CV32 157 B4
Solihull B92 88 E1
Sutton Coldfield B73 46 A2
Braemar Way CV10 73 A2
Braeside Croft B37 70 D2
Braeside Way WS3 14 F3
Bragg Rd B20 55 D2
Braggs Farm La B90 126 A4
Braham B79 20 D6
Braid Cl B38 103 D1
Braidwood Sch for the Deaf
B23 56 B6
Brailes Cl B92 107 E7
Brailes Dr B76 46 F3
Brailes Gr B9 68 B1
Brailsford Cl WV11 26 E8
Brailsford Dr B66 65 A5
Brain St B77 22 A2
Braithwaite Cl DY6 60 D6
Braithwaite Rd B11 87 B7
Brake La DY8 98 F6
Brake The DY8 98 F6
Brakesmead CV31 161 F5
Bramah Way DY4 52 C6
Bramber B77 21 D1
Bramber Dr WV5 49 A6
Bramber Way DY8 80 F2
Bramble Cl
Birmingham, Aston B6 66 E7
Birmingham, Shenley Fields
B31 102 F6
Blackheath B64 62 F4
Clayhanger WS8 15 E5
6 Coleshill B46 70 F7
Nuneaton CV11 73 F2
Willenhall WV12 27 C7
Bramble Dell B9 68 A3
Bramble Dr WS12 2 C7
Bramble Gn DY1 50 F5
Bramble La WS7 7 B8
Bramble St CV1 113 E2
Brambles The Lichfield
WS14 9 D6
Stourbridge DY9 81 D3
Sutton Coldfield B76 58 A8
Brambleside DY8 60 F1
Bramblewood WV5 49 A7
Bramblewood Dr WV3 38 E8
Bramblewoods B34 69 C5
Brambling B77 36 A7
Brambling Rise DY10 117 B1
Brambling Wlk 2
Birmingham B15 86 C7
Brierley Hill DY5 81 C6
Bramcote Cl Bulkington
CV12 79 D2
Hinckley LE10 71 F3
Bramcote Dr B91 107 C7
Bramcote Hospl CV11 79 E7
Bramcote Rd B32 84 C5
Bramcote Rise B75 46 C7
Bramdean Wlk WV4 38 C6
Bramdene Ave CV10 73 D8
Brame Rd LE10 71 C2
Bramerton Cl WV11 26 A6
Bramford Dr DY1 51 B6
Bramford Park Ind Est B70 53 A1
Bramford Prim Sch DY1 51 B6
Bramley Cl Birmingham B43 44 D3
Walsall WS5 43 D8
Bramley Croft B90 106 C2
Bramley Ct WV11 26 C6
Bramley Dr Birmingham B20 55 B3
Hollywood B47 125 B6
Bramley Ho WS5 43 B4
Bramley Rd 3
Birmingham B27 88 C5
Walsall WS5 43 B4
Brampton Ave B28 106 A6
Brampton Cres B90 106 B6
Brampton Dr WS12 2 E2
Brampton Way CV12 79 B3
Bramshall Dr B93 127 E3
Bramshaw Cl B14 104 F2
Bramshill Ct B15 86 B8
Bramstead Ave WV6 24 B2
Bramston Cres CV4 111 F1
Bramwell Gdns CV6 95 F5
Brancaster Cl B77 22 A5
Branch Rd B38 123 E8
Branchal Rd WS9 16 C1
Branden Rd B48 139 A5
Brandfield Rd CV6 112 F8
Brandhall Ct B68 64 A2
Brandhall Ct 8 B68 84 B8
Brandhall La B68 64 B1
Brandhall Prim Sch B68 64 B1
Brandhall Rd B68 64 B2
Brandon Cl Aldridge WS9 30 F3
Sedgley DY3 50 E7
West Bromwich B70 53 A2
Brandon Ct Birmingham B31 103 B1
Coventry CV3 135 A7
Brandon Gr B31 122 F7
Brandon La CV3, CV8 135 C5
Brandon Marsh Nature
Reserve CV8 135 A4
Brandon Marsh Visitor
Ctr CV8 135 B4
Brandon Par CV32 162 A8
Brandon Pk WV3 38 E7
Brandon Pl B34 69 D7
Brandon Rd Birmingham B28 87 E2
Coventry CV3 135 A8
Halesowen B62 63 E1
Hinckley LE10 75 B7
Solihull B91 107 C7
Brandon Thomas Ct B6 67 B8
Brandon Way
Brierley Hill DY5 81 E8
West Bromwich B70 53 A2
Brandon Way Ind Est B70 52 F3
Brandwood Gr B14 104 D5
Brandwood Ho B14 104 D7
Brandwood Park Rd B14 104 C4
Brandwood Rd B14 104 D5
Branfield Cl WV14 51 A8
Branksome Ave B21 65 F8
Branksome Rd CV6 112 E6
Branscombe Cl B14 104 D5
Bransdale Ave CV6 95 D3
Bransdale Cl WV6 25 A5
Bransdale Rd WS8 15 E6
Bransford Ave CV4 132 D5
Bransford Rise B91 108 B5
Bransford Tower B12 86 F8
Branston St B18 66 C4
Branstree Dr CV6 95 D2
Brantford Rd B25 88 C8
Branthill Croft B91 107 B1
Brantley Ave WV3 24 C1
Brantley Rd B6 56 A2
Branton Hill La WS9 30 C5
Brantwood Ave WS7 7 A5
Brascote Rd LE10 74 F8
Brasshouse Inf Sch B66 65 A7
Brasshouse La B66 65 A7
Brassie Cl B38 103 D1
Brassington Ave B73 46 B5
Bratch Cl DY2 62 C3
Bratch Hollow WV5 49 A8
Bratch La WV5 49 A8
Brathay Cl CV3 133 D6
Bratt St B70 53 C4
Braunston Cl B76 47 A2
Brawnes Hurst B26 69 A1
Bray Ho WV11 26 C5
Bray St WV13 27 B2
Bray's La CV2 114 A3
Brayford Ave Brierley Hill
DY5 81 B7
Coventry CV3 133 C6
Braymoor Rd B33 69 E1
Brays Rd B26 89 B6
Brays Sch B26 89 A6
Braytoft Cl CV6 95 C2
Brazil St CV4 111 E2
Breaches La B98 159 D8
Breadmarket St WS13 9 B8
Breakback Rd B61 150 D8
Bream B77 35 D7
Bream Cl B37 70 C2
Breamore Cres DY1 50 F3
Brean Ave B92 88 F5
Brearley Cl B19 66 E5
Brearley St
Birmingham,
Handsworth B21 65 D8
Birmingham, Hockley B19 66 E5
Brechin Cl LE10 75 A8
Brecknell Rise DY10 116 F8
Brecknock Rd B71 53 A6
Brecon Ave B61 137 A5
Brecon Dr 2 DY8 81 B6
Brecon Rd B20 66 B8
Brecon Tower 1 B16 66 A2
Bredon Ave Coventry CV3 134 F8
Kidderminster DY11 116 A1
Stourbridge DY9 81 C5
Bredon Croft B18 66 A5
Bredon Ct Halesowen B63 83 A3
Sutton Coldfield B75 32 A4
Bredon Rd Bromsgrove
B61 150 D7
Oldbury B69 63 D5
Stourbridge DY8 81 B6
Bredon Terr 4 B18 66 A5
Bredon View B97 158 D8
Bree Cl CV5 112 A7
Bree's La CV8 130 A1
Breech Cl B74 44 E7
Breeden Dr B76 59 B6
Breedon Rd B30 104 A5
Breedon Way WS4 15 C1
Breen Rydding Dr WV14 51 B8
Breener Ind Est DY5 61 B1
Breeze Ave WS11 6 B5
Brelades Cl DY1 50 E3
Brendon B77 22 B1
Brendon Way CV10 72 A3
Brenfield Dr LE10 75 A8
Brennand Cl B68 84 C8
Brennand Rd B68 84 B8
Brent B77 35 E7
Brent Ho 3 DY1 61 E8
Brent Rd B30 104 D8
Brentford Rd
Birmingham B14 105 A5
Solihull B91 106 E3
Brentmill Cl WV10 11 F4
Brentnall Dr B75 32 B3
Brenton Rd WV4 38 F3
Brentwood Ave CV3 133 C3
Brentwood Cl B91 106 E3
Brentwood Gdns CV3 133 C3
Brentwood Gr B44 55 E8
Brenwood Cl DY6 60 B7
Brereton Cl DY2 62 E8
Brereton Rd WV12 27 D7
Brese Ave CV34 155 F1
Bretby Gr B23 57 A6
Bretford Rd CV2 96 C1
Bretshall Cl B90 126 F5
Brett Dr B32 102 C8
Brett St B71 53 B5
Brett Young Cl DY10 117 B5
Brettell La
Brierley Hill DY5, DY8 61 B1
Stourbridge DY8 60 F1
Brettell St 5 DY2 62 B8
Bretton Gdns WV10 25 F6
Bretton Rd B27 88 D2
Bretts Cl CV1 165 D4
Bretts Hall Est CV10 72 A7
Brevitt Rd WV2 39 D6
Brewer Rd CV12 79 D2
Brewer St WS2 28 E4
Brewers Cl CV3 115 A1
Brewers Dr WS3 15 A1
Brewers Terr WS3 15 A2
Brewery St
Birmingham,
Handsworth B21 65 D8
Birmingham,
New Town Row B6 164 C5
Dudley DY2 51 E1
Smethwick B67 64 F6
Tipton DY4 51 F4
Brewins Way DY6 62 A4
Brewster Cl Coventry CV2 114 E2
Fazeley B78 20 E1
Brewster St DY2 62 C5
Breydon Gr WV13 40 F8
Brian Rd B67 64 E6
Briansway CV6 95 E3
Briar B77 22 A3
Briar Ave B74 31 A1
Briar Cl Birmingham B24 57 A4
Cannock WS12 2 A8
Hinckley LE10 75 F6
Lickey End B60 137 C6
Royal Leamington Spa CV32 157 B2
Briar Coppice B90 126 D4
Briar Ct 14 Brierley Hill DY5 61 D2
Dudley DY2 62 C6
Briar Hill DY10 118 E1
Briar Hill Cty Fst Sch
CV31 162 B3
Briar Wood Cl WV2 40 A7
Briarbeck WS4 29 C8
Briardene Ave CV12 78 B2
Briarfield Rd B11 88 A3
Briarley Ho 5 B71 42 F1
Briarmead LE10 75 E4
Briars Cl Brierley Hill DY5 61 C4
Coventry CV2 114 C2
Nuneaton CV11 73 E5
Briars The B23 56 D6
Briarwood Cl B90 126 D4
Briarwood The WV2 40 A7
Brick Hill La CV5 111 E8
Brick Kiln La Birmingham
B44 55 E6
Dudley DY3 50 B3
Middleton B78 48 D6
Solihull B90 126 F8
Wythall B47 124 F4
Brick Kiln St
Brierley Hill, Hart's Hill DY5 61 E5
Brierley Hill,
Quarry Bank DY5 82 A8
Hinckley LE10 75 C8
Tipton DY4 51 F6
Brick St DY3 50 D8
Brickfield Rd B25 88 B6
Brickheath Rd WV1 26 A3
Brickhill Dr B37 70 A2
Brickhouse La
Stoke Prior B60 150 C4
West Bromwich B70 52 E6
Brickhouse La S DY4 52 E6
Brickhouse Prim Sch B65 63 A3
Brickhouse Rd B65 63 A4
Brickiln Ct 2 DY5 61 D2
Brickiln St WS8 15 F7
Brickkiln Prim Sch WV3 25 B1
Brickkiln St WV13 26 F1
Brickyard La B80 159 C4
Brickyard Rd WS9 15 F1
Bridal Path The CV5 112 B6
Briddsland Rd B33 69 E2
Bridge Ave Cheslyn Hay WS6 4 E4
Tipton DY4 52 C7
Bridge Cl Birmingham B11 87 B3
Clayhanger WS8 15 E6
Bridge Croft B12 86 E6
Bridge Cross Rd WS7 6 F7
Bridge End CV34 160 F6
Bridge Ho
Royal Leamington Spa
CV31 162 A8
Smethwick B66 65 C6
Bridge Ind Est B91 107 C7
Bridge Meadow Dr B93 127 F6
Bridge Piece B31 103 B2
Bridge Rd Birmingham B8 67 E3
Hinckley LE10 75 D7
Tipton DY4 52 C7
Walsall WS4 15 B1
Bridge Specl Sch B23 56 E4
Bridge St Bilston WV14 40 E5
Birmingham B1 164 A2
Cannock WS11 4 E5
Clayhanger WS8 15 E6
Coventry CV6 114 A7
Dudley WV14 51 C8
Halesowen B63 82 C7
Kenilworth CV8 147 F5
1 Kidderminster DY10 116 E5
Nuneaton CV11 73 C4
Nuneaton, Chilvers Coton
CV11 73 C2
Oldbury B69 64 A8
Redditch B97 153 D4
Stourbridge DY8 60 E1
Tamworth B77 21 E5
Walsall WS1 28 F2
Warwick CV34 161 C8
Wednesbury WS10 41 F1
West Bromwich B70 53 B4
Willenhall WV13 26 F1
Wolverhampton WV10 25 E5
Bridge St N B66 65 B7
Bridge St W B19 66 D5
Bridge View Baginton CV8 133 D3
3 Coleshill B46 70 F7
Bridge Way WS8 15 E6
Bridgeacre Gdns CV3 114 F2
Bridgeburn Rd B31 102 E8
Bridgecote CV3 134 E6
Bridgefield Wlk B65 62 F5
Bridgefoot Wlk WV8 10 F1
Bridgeford Rd B34 69 B6
Bridgelands Way B20 55 D1
Bridgeman Croft B36 69 C8
Bridgeman Rd CV6 113 B4
Bridgeman St WS2 28 D1
Bridgemary Cl WV10 11 E4
Bridgemeadow Ho 5 B36 68 E8
Bridgenorth Ho B33 69 B2
Bridges Cres WS11 5 F5
Bridges Rd WS11 5 F5
Bridgewater Ave B69 64 A4
Bridgewater Cres DY2 51 E1
Bridgewater Dr WV14 40 C2
Bridgewater St B77 21 D5
Bridgnorth Gr WV12 27 B6
Bridgnorth Rd Himley DY3 49 B3
Stourbridge DY7, DY8 80 C6
Trescott WV6 37 C7
Wolverhampton WV6 24 B2
Wombourne WV5 49 A4
Bridgtown Bsns Ctr WS11 4 E6
Bridgtown Cty Prim Sch
WS11 4 E6
Bridgwater Cl WS9 15 F3
Bridle Brook La CV5, CV7 94 A3
Bridle Gr B71 53 F7
Bridle La B74 44 E7
Bridle Mead B38 123 D8
Bridle Path The B90 106 B6
Bridle Rd DY8 80 D6
Bridlewood B74 44 F8
Bridley Moor High Sch
B97 153 C4
Bridley Moor Rd B97 153 C5
Bridport Cl CV2 115 A4
Bridport Ho B31 102 E7
Brier Mill Rd B62 83 C3
Brier Sch DY5 61 E3
Brierley Hill Prim Sch DY5 61 D2
Brierley Hill Rd DY8 60 F2
Brierley La WV14 40 E2
Brierley Rd CV2 114 C8
Brierley Trad Est The DY5 61 C3
Briery Cl B64 82 F7
Briery Rd B63 82 E3
Brigfield Cres B13 105 B5
Brigfield Rd B13 105 B5
Bright Cres B77 21 C2
Bright Rd B68 64 B5
Bright St Coventry CV6 113 E6
Darlaston WS10 41 D5
Stourbridge DY8 80 D6
Wolverhampton WV1 163 A4
Brightmere Rd CV6 113 B4
Brighton Cl WS2 28 D3
Brighton Mews 8 WV3 25 A2
Brighton Rd B12 87 A5
Brighton St CV2 113 F3
Brightstone Cl WV10 11 F4
Brightstone Rd B45 102 B2
Brightwalton Rd CV3 133 D7
Brightwell Cres B93 127 E3
Brill Cl CV4 132 C5
Brimfield Pl WV6 24 F4
Brimstone La B61 136 D7
Brindle Ave CV3 114 C2
Brindle Ct B23 56 B3
Brindle Rd WS5 43 C4
Brindlefields Way DY4 52 B2
Brindley Ave WV11 13 A1
Brindley Cl Stourbridge DY8 60 E1
Walsall WS2 27 F5
Brindley Cres WS12 2 C8
Brindley Ct 1 Oldbury B68 84 B7
5 Tipton DY4 51 E5
Brindley Dr B1 164 A2
Brindley Heath Rd WS12 2 D8
Brindley Rd Bedworth CV7 96 B8
Hinckley LE10 74 E8
West Bromwich B71 53 A8
Brindley Way 10 B66 65 C5
Brindleys Bsns Pk WS11 2 B3
Brineton Gr B29 85 A1
Brineton Ind Est 1 WS2 28 C1
Brineton St WS2 28 C1
Bringewood Gr B32 102 B8
Brinklow Cl B98 159 D8
Brinklow Croft B34 69 D7
Brinklow Rd Birmingham
B29 84 F2
Coventry CV3 115 A2
Brinklow Tower 5 B12 86 F7
Brinley Way DY6 60 C6
Brinsford La WV10 11 D7
Brinsford Rd WV10 11 C3
Brinsley Cl B91 107 B2
Brinsley Rd B26 89 B8
Brinton Cl DY11 116 C3
Brinton Cres DY11 116 C3
Brisbane Cl CV3 133 E6
Brisbane Ct CV12 78 A2
Brisbane Ho B34 69 E6
Brisbane Rd B67 64 E5
Briscoe Rd CV6 95 D4
Briseley Cl DY5 81 D8
Bristam Cl B69 63 E6
Bristnall Hall Cres B68 64 C3

Bristnall Hall High Sch
B68 64 D3
Bristnall Hall La B68 64 D3
Bristnall Hall Rd B68 64 C3
Bristnall Ho B67 64 D4
Bristol Cl WS11 2 B1
Bristol Rd
Birmingham,
Balsall Heath B5 86 C5
Birmingham, Gravelly Hill B23 56 E3
Coventry CV5 112 F2
Dudley DY2 62 D2
Bristol Rd S B31, B45 102 F2
Bristol St Birmingham B15 86 D8
Wolverhampton WV3 39 B8
Briston Cl DY5 81 C8
Britannia Gdns B65 63 C3
Britannia High Sch B65 63 D2
Britannia Rd Bilston WV14 40 F3
Blackheath B65 63 C2
Hinckley LE10 76 A5
Britannia St Coventry CV2 113 F3
Tipton B69 52 C2
Britannia Way WS14 9 F8
Britford Cl B14 104 F3
Briton Rd CV2 114 A4
Brittan Cl B34 69 E6
Brittania Pk WS10 41 D3
Brittania Sh Ctr 3 LE10 75 D8
Brittania Way WS5 42 D5
Britten Cl CV11 79 A7
Britten St B97 153 D4
Britton Dr B72 57 C8
Britwell Rd B73 46 A2
Brixham Cl CV11 73 F5
Brixham Dr CV2 114 C7
Brixham Rd B16 65 D4
Brixworth Cl CV3 134 E8
Broad Acres B31 102 E6
Broad Croft DY4 52 C6
Broad Ground Rd B98 154 B2
Broad Heath Cl B97 153 B5
Broad Heath Com Prim Sch CV6 113 E7
Broad La Birmingham B14 104 E4
Coventry CV5 111 D4
Lichfield WS14 9 D6
Tanworth-In-A B98 141 E3
Walsall, Essington
WV11, WS3 13 E4
Walsall, Pelsall WS4 15 C2
Wolverhampton, Penn WV3 38 E8
Wolverhampton, Wall WS13 8 B5
Broad La N WV12 27 B7
Broad La S WV11 27 A5
Broad Lane Gdns WS3 14 A2
Broad Lanes WV14 40 C3
Broad Mdw WS9 30 B8
Broad Meadow La
Birmingham B30, B38 104 B3
Great Wyrley WS6 5 A2
Broad Oaks B76 47 A1
Broad Oaks Rd B91 107 A5
Broad Park Rd CV2 114 D8
Broad Rd B27 88 B3
Broad St Bilston WV14 40 D6
Birmingham B15, B1 66 C2
Brierley Hill DY5 61 C6
Bromsgrove B61 136 F4
Cannock WS11 4 E6
Coventry CV6 113 E7
Dudley WV14 51 C8
Kidderminster DY10 116 E7
Kingswinford DY6 60 D5
Oldbury B69 64 A5
Warwick CV34 160 F7
Wolverhampton WV1 163 C3
Broad Street Jetty CV6 113 E7
Broad Way WS4 15 C2
Broadcott Ind Est B64 83 A8
Broadfern Rd B93 128 B8
Broadfield Cl
Kingswinford DY6 60 D5
West Bromwich B71 42 F1
Broadfield House Glass Mus DY6 60 D5
Broadfield Wlk 1 B16 66 B1
Broadfields DY9 99 A6
Broadfields Rd B23 57 B7
Broadgate CV1 165 B3
Broadhaven Cl CV31 162 C7
Broadheath Dr WS4 29 D8
Broadhidley Dr B32 84 B1
Broadhurst Gn WS12 2 A8
Broadlands Cl CV5 112 C2
Broadlands Dr DY5 61 E5
Broadlands Rise WS14 9 D7
Broadlee B77 22 C1
Broadmead Ct CV4 112 C2
Broadmeadow 1 DY6 60 E8
Broadmeadow Cl B30 104 B3
Broadmeadow Gn WV14 40 C7
Broadmeadow Ho B32 102 D8
Broadmeadow Inf Sch
B30 104 B2
Broadmeadow Jun Sch
B30 104 B2
Broadmeadows Cl WV12 27 E8
Broadmeadows Rd WV12 27 E8
Broadmede Ho B67 64 E2
Broadmere Rise CV5 112 A2
Broadmoor Ave B68 64 D2
Broadmoor Cl WV14 40 C4
Broadmoor Rd WV14 40 C3
Broadoaks Cl WS11 5 F6
Broadsmeath B77 21 C1
Broadstone Ave
Halesowen B63 82 B4
Walsall WS3 28 D7
Broadstone Cl WV4 39 D5
Broadstone Rd B26 69 A1
Broadsword Way LE10 75 D4
Broadwalk Ret Pk WS1 42 D6
Broadwas Cl B98 154 C5
Broadwater CV5 133 A8
Broadwaters Ave WS10 41 C4
Broadwaters Dr Hagley DY9 99 B4
Kidderminster DY10 117 A8
Broadwaters Rd WS10 41 C4
Broadway Cannock WS12 1 F6
Coventry CV5 113 A1
Cubbington CV32 157 E5
Oldbury B68 64 C1
Solihull B90 106 B4
Walsall WS5 43 A6
Wolverhampton, Bushbury
WV10 11 E2
Wolverhampton, Compton
WV3 24 C1
Broadway Ave
Birmingham B9 68 A3
Halesowen B63 83 A2
Broadway Croft
Birmingham B26 89 A6
Oldbury B68 64 C1
Broadway Gdns WV10 11 E2
Broadway Lower Sch The
B6 66 E8
Broadway Mans CV5 113 A1
Broadway N WS1 29 B2
Broadway Sch B20 55 E2
Broadway Sch The B20 55 D1
Broadway The
Birmingham B20 55 E2
Dudley DY1 51 B3
Stourbridge DY8 80 D3
West Bromwich B71 53 B7
Wombourne WV5 49 A5
Broadway W WS1 42 D6
Broadwell Ct CV4 131 F6
Broadwell Ind Est B69 53 A1
Broadwell Rd Oldbury B69 64 A8
Solihull B92 89 A2
Broadwells Cres CV4 132 A5
Broadyates Gr B25 88 C6
Broadyates Rd B25 88 C6
Brobury Croft B91 106 D4
Brock Rd DY4 52 C4
Brockenhurst Ct B73 46 B1
Brockeridge Cl WV12 13 C1
Brockfield Ho WV10 25 F4
Brockhall Gr B37 69 F5
Brockhill La Alvechurch
B48 124 B2
Beoley B98 140 F2
Tardebigge B97 152 E8
Brockhurst Ave LE10 75 D4
Brockhurst Cres WS5 42 E4
Brockhurst Dr
Birmingham B28 106 A5
Coventry CV4 111 D2
Wolverhampton W6 25 A4
Brockhurst Ho 4 WS2 28 D3
Brockhurst La B75 33 B7
Brockhurst Pl WS5 42 F5
Brockhurst Rd
Birmingham B36 68 D6
Sutton Coldfield B75 32 D1
Brockhurst St WS1 42 E6
Brockley Cl DY5 61 D3
Brockley Gr B13 86 C1
Brockley Pl B7 67 C7
Brockmoor Cl DY9 81 C2
Brockmoor Prim Sch DY5 61 C3
Brockton Rd B29 85 A1
Brockwell Gr B44 44 E4
Brockwell Rd B44 44 E4
Brockworth Rd B14 104 C2
Brocton Cl WV14 40 A3
Brodick Cl LE10 75 A8
Brodick Rd LE10 74 F8
Brodick Way CV10 72 F3
Brogden Cl 4 B71 53 F8
Brome Hall La B94 144 D2
Bromfield Cl B6 66 E7
Bromfield Cres WS10 42 C4
Bromfield Ct WV6 24 B3
Bromfield Rd B97 153 D2
Bromford Cl
Birmingham, Erdington B23 56 E5
Birmingham,
Handsworth B20 55 A2
Bromford Cres B24 57 A2
Bromford Ct
Birmingham,
Turves Green B31 103 B1
Birmingham,
Washwood Heath B8 68 B6
Bromford Dale WV6 24 F3
Bromford Dell B31 103 C4
Bromford Dr B36 68 D8
Bromford Hill B20 55 C3
Bromford Ho B73 45 F2
Bromford Jun & Inf Schs
B36 68 D7
Bromford La Birmingham B8 68 C6
West Bromwich B70 53 B2
Bromford Mere 4 B92 88 E1
Bromford Park Ho 3 B13 87 B2
Bromford Rd
Birmingham B36 68 D7
Dudley DY2 62 A6
West Bromwich B69, B70 53 A1
Bromford Rise WV3 163 A1
Bromford Road Ind Est B70 53 A1
Bromford Wlk B43 43 F1
Bromleigh Dr CV2 114 C2
Bromleigh Villas CV8 133 F2
Bromley DY5 61 B5
Bromley Cl CV8 147 E6
Bromley Gdns WV8 10 A4
Bromley Hills Cty Prim Sch
DY6 60 F5
Bromley Ho WV4 39 A5
Bromley La DY6 60 E4
Bromley Lodge WV4 39 A5
Bromley Pl WV4 39 A5
Bromley Prim Sch DY5 61 B5
Bromley St Birmingham B9 67 A1
Stourbridge DY9 81 F6
Wolverhampton WV2 39 C7
Brompton Dr DY5 81 B7
Brompton Lawns WV6 24 A3
Brompton Pool Rd B28 105 E3
Brompton Rd B44 44 E4
Bromsgrove Eastern By-Pass B60 150 E6
Bromsgrove Highway
Bromsgrove B60 137 D1
Redditch B97 153 B2
Tardebigge B97 152 C6
Bromsgrove Lower Sch
B60 136 F1
Bromsgrove Pre-Prep Sch B60 137 A2
Bromsgrove Private Hospl B60 138 B1
Bromsgrove Rd
Bournheath B61 136 D6
Clent DY9 99 D4
Halesowen B63 83 C4
Kidderminster DY10 117 F2
Redditch B97 153 B3
Romsley B62 101 A5
Studley B80 159 D2
Bromsgrove Sch B61 136 F1
Bromsgrove St
Birmingham B5 164 C1
Halesowen B63 83 C4
Kidderminster DY10 116 E6
Bromsgrove Sta B60 151 B7
Bromwall Rd B13 105 B6
Bromwich Cl CV3 134 F8
Bromwich Dr B75 46 C7
Bromwich La DY9 99 B8
Bromwich Wlk B9 68 A3
Bromwynd Cl WV2 39 B6
Bromyard Ave B76 58 A8
Bromyard Rd B11 87 E3
Bronte Cl B90 106 D1
Bronte Ct Solihull B90 106 D1
Tamworth B79 21 A6
Bronte Dr Cannock WS11 2 C2
Kidderminster DY10 117 C6
Bronte Farm Rd B90 106 D1
Bronte Rd WV2 39 F6
Bronwen Rd WV14 51 C7
Bronze Cl CV11 78 E8
Brook Ave B77 36 A7
Brook Cl Birmingham B26 89 B5
Brownhills WS9 16 A3
Coventry CV1 113 E4
Lichfield WS13 3 A1
Solihull B90 105 F1
Brook Cotts B25 88 A7
Brook Cres Hagley DY9 99 B5
Kingswinford DY6 60 C7
Stourbridge DY9 81 F3
Brook Croft
Birmingham,
Lyndon Green B26 89 B7
Birmingham,
Marston Green B37 90 B7
Brook Dr B32 84 D1
Brook End Burntwood WS7 7 A4
Fazeley B78 35 B8
Brook Farm Wlk B37 70 D2
Brook Fields Cl B60 121 C1
Brook Gr WV8 10 B2
Brook Green La B92 109 A1
Brook Hill Rd B8 68 A4
Brook Holloway DY9 81 F4
Brook House Cl WV10 12 B6
Brook House La WV10 12 B7
Brook La Birmingham B13 105 B7
Blackheath B64 62 E2
Brownhills WS9 15 F3
Great Wyrley WS6 5 A3
Nuneaton CV10 73 C6
Solihull B92 106 D8
Brook Meadow Rd
Birmingham B34 69 B6
Walsall WS4 29 D8
Brook Park Trad Est
3 DY9 81 F5
Brook Piece Wlk B35 58 B3
Brook Prim Sch The DY8 60 F1
Brook Rd
Birmingham, Chad Valley B15 85 E7
Birmingham, Eachway B45 121 E7
Bromsgrove B61 136 E1
Cheslyn Hay WS6 4 E4
Fairfield B61 120 C2
Oldbury B68 64 A2
Stourbridge DY8 81 B3
Willenhall WV13 26 E1
Wombourne WV5 49 A6
Brook St Bedworth CV12 78 B5
Bilston WV14 40 E5
Birmingham B3 164 A3
Brierley Hill DY5 82 A8
Brook St continued
Dudley, Gornalwood DY3 50 C3
Dudley, Woodsetton DY3 51 A7
Kidderminster DY11 116 C6
Kingswinford DY6 49 B1
Redditch B98 154 A4
Smethwick B66 65 B6
Stourbridge, Amblecote DY8 60 F1
Stourbridge, Lye DY9 81 F5
Stourbridge, Wollaston DY8 80 E5
Tipton DY4 51 E6
Walsall WS2 28 D1
Warwick CV34 160 E6
West Bromwich B70 53 B3
Brook Street Bsns Ctr DY4 51 E6
Brook Terr WV14 40 E5
Brook View Cl B19 66 C6
Brook Wlk B32 84 D2
Brookbank Ave B34 69 D6
Brookbank Gdns DY3 50 B2
Brookbank Rd DY3 50 B2
Brookdale Dudley DY3 50 C3
Hinckley LE10 75 B7
Kidderminster DY10 116 F8
Brookdale Cl B45 102 A1
Brookdale Dr WV4 38 E6
Brookdale Rd CV10 73 E7
Brooke Cl CV34 160 F5
Brooke Rd Cannock WS12 1 F6
Kenilworth CV8 148 B4
Brooke St DY2 62 C8
Brookend Dr B45 121 F7
Brookes Ho 3 WS1 28 F1
Brookfield Cl Aldridge WS9 16 A1
Redditch B97 158 D4
Brookfield Dr WS11 4 E7
Brookfield Prec B18 66 B4
Brookfield Rd Aldridge WS9 16 A1
Birmingham B18 66 A5
Codsall WV8 10 B3
Cubbington CV32 157 E5
Hinckley LE10 75 C6
Brookfield Way Solihull
B92 106 D7
Tipton DY4 52 B6
Brookfields Inf & Jun Sch
B18 66 B4
Brookfields Rd B68 64 C4
Brookford Ave CV6 95 A3
Brookhampton Cl B97 158 E4
Brookhill Cl WV12 13 D1
Brookhill Way WV12 13 D1
Brookhouse La WV10 11 F6
Brookhouse Rd
Barnt Green B45 137 F7
Walsall WS5 43 B7
Brookhurst Ct CV32 156 D1
Brookhurst Cty Comb Sch CV32 156 C1
Brookhus Farm Rd B76 58 A8
Brooking Cl B43 44 D4
Brookland Rd Brownhills
WS9 15 F3
Hagley DY9 99 A5
Brooklands Stourbridge DY8 60 F1
Walsall WS5 43 B3
Brooklands Ave WS6 4 F4
Brooklands Cl B28 87 F1
Brooklands Dr B14 104 E5
Brooklands Gr WS9 15 F3
Brooklands La B98 154 B5
Brooklands Par WV1 26 B2
Brooklands Rd
Birmingham B28 87 F1
Cannock WS11 2 A4
Brooklea CV12 77 F2
Brooklea Gr B38 104 A1
Brooklime Gdns WV10 12 B7
Brooklyn Ave B6 66 F7
Brooklyn Gr Dudley WV14 51 D8
Kingswinford DY6 60 B8
Brooklyn Rd Burntwood WS7 7 A4
Cannock WS12 2 D1
Coventry CV1 113 D6
Brookmans Ave B32 84 D4
Brookmeadow Ct B28 105 D6
Brooks Croft B35 58 A2
Brooks Rd B72 57 C8
Brooks Tower B19 66 D7
Brooksbank Dr B64 62 F4
Brooksby Gr B93 128 A2
Brookshaw Way CV2 114 F8
Brookside
Birmingham, Great Barr B43 54 D7
Birmingham, Northfield B31 102 F5
Cheswick Green B90 126 D3
Dudley DY3 50 D2
Hinckley LE10 75 E7
Brookside Ave
Birmingham B13 105 B7
Coventry CV5 112 C3
Kenilworth CV8 147 E4
Brookside Cl
Alvechurch B48 139 B6
Birmingham B23 56 C7
Halesowen B63 82 D3
Brookside Dr B61 136 F8
Brookside Ind Est WS10 42 B3
Brookside Rd B78 20 E1
Brookside Way
Blakedown DY10 98 B2
Kingswinford DY6 60 C7
Tamworth B77 36 A6
Brookstray Flats CV5 112 B3
Brookthorpe Dr WV12 27 C4
Brookvale Ave CV3 114 E1
Brookvale Cl B61 137 B4
Brookvale Gr B92 88 D1
Brookvale Jun & Inf Sch
B23 56 B3
Brookvale Park Rd B23 56 B4
Brookvale Rd
Birmingham B23, B6 56 A3
Solihull B92 88 D1
Brookvale Trad Est B6 56 A3
Brookview B67 64 F3
Brookweed B77 22 A3
Brookwillow Rd B63 82 E1
Brookwood Ave B28 105 D5
Broom Cl B60 137 B2
Broom Covert Rd WS14 18 E8
Broom Cres DY10 117 A6
Broom Dr B14 104 E4
Broom Hall Cres B27 106 B8
Broom Hall Gr B27 106 C8
Broom Ho 3 B71 42 F1
Broom Rd Dudley DY1 51 A5
Walsall WS5 43 B3
Broom St B12 87 A8
Broomcroft Rd B37 69 F5
Broomdene Ave B34 69 A7
Broome Ave B43 54 C7
Broome Cl 5 B63 83 A3
Broome Croft CV6 95 B3
Broome Ct B36 69 C8
Broome La Blakedown DY10 98 F2
Hagley DY9 99 B2
Broome Rd WV10 25 E7
Broomehill Cl DY5 81 C7
Broomfield B67 64 F5
Broomfield Ave B78 35 A8
Broomfield Cl DY11 116 C7
Broomfield Gn DY11 116 C7
Broomfield Pl CV5 113 A2
Broomfield Rd
Birmingham B23 56 D2
Coventry CV5 113 A1
Kidderminster DY11 116 C7
Wednesbury WS10 42 C3
Broomfield Rise CV10 72 F2
Broomfields Ave B91 107 D5
Broomfields Cl B91 107 D5
Broomfields Farm Rd
B91 107 D5
Broomhall Ave WV11 26 D6
Broomhill Bank WS11 1 E3
Broomhill Cl
Birmingham B43 54 D8
Cannock WS11 1 E4
Broomhill La B43 54 D8
Broomhill Rd B23 56 B7
Broomhurst B15 85 E8
Broomie Cl B75 46 D4
Broomlea Cl B74 44 E8
Broomy Cl B34 69 A5
Broomybank CV8 148 B6
Brosdale Dr LE10 71 A1
Broseley Ave B31 123 B8
Broseley Brook Cl B9 67 C1
Brosil Ave B20 54 E3
Brotherton Ave B97 152 F2
Brough Cl Birmingham B7 67 B6
Wolverhampton WV4 39 F3
Brougham St B19 66 B7
Broughton Cres B31 122 D8
Broughton Ct
2 Birmingham,
Edgbaston B15 86 B7
Birmingham, Pheasey B43 44 D4
Perton WV6 24 A3
Broughton Rd
Birmingham B20 66 A8
Stourbridge DY9 81 D3
Wolverhampton WV3 24 C1
Browett Rd CV6 113 A5
Brown Lion St DY4 51 E7
Brown Rd WS10 41 C7
Brown St WV2 39 D7
Brown's Coppice Ave B91 106 E5
Brown's Ct 10 B13 87 B2
Brown's La Allesley CV5 94 C1
Dordon B78 36 F5
Tamworth B79 21 C8
Brownfield Rd B34 69 C7
Brownhills Rd
Brownhills WS9 16 A4
Norton Canes WS11 6 A5
Brownhills Sch WS8 6 F1
Brownhills West JMI Sch
WS8 6 C2
Browning Ave CV34 160 C5
Browning Cl
Kidderminster DY10 117 B6
Nuneaton CV10 72 A5
Tamworth B79 20 F8
Willenhall WV12 27 E7
Browning Cres WV10 11 C2
Browning Dr LE10 71 C1
Browning Gr WV6 23 E4
Browning Rd Burntwood WS7 7 C7
Coventry CV2 114 C3
Dudley DY3 50 A4
Browning St B16 66 B2
Browning Tower B31 103 C3
Brownley Rd B90 126 E7
Brownlow St 6 CV32 157 A2
Brownmead Jun & Inf Sch
B34 69 B7
Browns Dr B73 56 F8
Browns Gn B20 54 F3
Browns La Knowle B93 127 E6
Tamworth B79 21 C8
Brownsea Cl B45 101 F1
Brownsea Dr B1 164 B1
Brownsfield Rd WS13 3 D1
Brownshill Ct CV6 112 F8

Brownshill Green Rd CV6 .... 94 E1
Brownshore La WV11 .... 13 B3
Brownsover Cl B36 .... 58 B1
Brownswall Rd DY3 .... 50 C7
Browsholme B79 .... 20 D6
Broxell Cl CV34 .... 155 C1
Broxwood Pk WV6 .... 24 C3
Bruce Rd Bedworth CV7 .... 95 F7
Coventry CV6 .... 113 B8
Kidderminster DY10 .... 117 B7
Brueton Ave
Bromsgrove B60 .... 151 A8
Solihull B91 .... 107 D3
Brueton Dr Birmingham B24 .. 57 A3
Redditch B98 .... 154 A3
Brueton Rd WV14 .... 41 A7
Bruford Rd WV3 .... 39 A8
Brunel Cl Birmingham B12 ..... 87 A5
Burntwood WS7 .... 7 B8
Coventry CV2 .... 113 F3
Tamworth B79 .... 21 B6
Whitnash CV31 .... 162 B2
Brunel Ct Darlaston WS10 ..... 41 F6
Dudley WV14 .... 51 E8
Wombourne WV5 .... 49 A7
Brunel Gr WV6 .... 23 E6
Brunel Rd Hinckley LE10 .... 75 C8
Oldbury B69 .... 63 D6
Brunel St B1 .... 164 B2
Brunel Way WV2 .... 40 A7
Brunel Wlk WS10 .... 41 F6
Brunslow Cl Willenhall
WV13 .... 27 C1
Wolverhampton WV10 .... 11 C1
Brunswick Ct
Royal Leamington Spa
CV31 .... 162 A5
Wednesbury WS10 .... 42 C3
Brunswick Gdns B21 .... 54 F1
Brunswick Ho
Birmingham,
Buckland End B34 .... 69 A7
Birmingham,
Marston Green B37 .... 89 F8
Brunswick Park Rd WS10 .... 42 B3
Brunswick Rd
Birmingham,
Handsworth B21 .... 54 F1
Birmingham, Sparkbrook B12 . 87 A5
Cannock WS11 .... 1 E2
Coventry CV1 .... 113 B2
Brunswick St
Royal Leamington Spa
CV31 .... 162 A5
Walsall WS2 .... 42 C7
Brunswick Terr WS10 .... 41 F3
Bruntingthorpe Way CV3 .. 134 E8
Brunton Cl CV3 .... 115 B1
Brunton Rd B10 .... 87 F7
Brushfield Rd B42 .... 55 D8
Brutus Dr B46 .... 59 E1
Bryan Ave WV4 .... 38 D4
Bryan Rd WS2 .... 42 C6
Bryans Way WS12 .... 2 F4
Bryanston Cl CV2 .... 115 A4
Bryanston Ct B92 .... 106 F7
Bryanston Rd B91 .... 106 F6
Bryant Rd CV7 .... 96 A7
Bryant St B18 .... 65 E5
Bryce Rd DY5 .... 61 B5
Bryher Wlk B45 .... 101 E1
Brylan Croft B44 .... 55 F6
Brymill Ind Est DY4 .... 51 E7
Brympton Rd CV3 .... 114 C2
Bryn Arden Rd B26 .... 88 E5
Bryn Jones Cl CV3 .... 134 F7
Bryn Rd CV6 .... 113 F7
Bryndale Ave B14 .... 104 C4
Brynmawr Rd WV14 .... 40 A3
Brynside Cl B14 .... 104 D2
Bryony Croft B23 .... 56 B7
Bryony Gdns WS10 .... 41 D7
Bryony Rd B29 .... 103 B7
Bsns Ctr The B11 .... 87 F6
Buchanan Ave WS4 .... 29 A3
Buchanan Cl WS4 .... 29 A3
Buchanan Rd WS4 .... 29 A3
Buckbury Cl DY9 .... 81 D2
Buckbury Croft B90 .... 127 B6
Buckden B77 .... 22 C1
Buckden Cl 2 CV34 .... 155 F1
Buckfast Cl Bromsgrove
B61 .... 136 D1
Coventry CV3 .... 133 E5
Buckhold Dr CV5 .... 112 B5
Buckingham Cl Hinckley
LE10 .... 71 F4
Nuneaton CV10 .... 73 B1
Wednesbury WS10 .... 42 D4
Buckingham Ct
Birmingham,
Griffin's Hill B29 .... 103 D8
Birmingham, Selly Oak B29 ..... 85 D1
Buckingham Dr WV12 .... 27 B7
Buckingham Gdns WS13 .... 9 B6
Buckingham Gr DY6 .... 60 C7
Buckingham Mews B73 .... 46 A3
Buckingham Pl WS12 .... 2 C1
Buckingham Rd
Birmingham B36 .... 69 F7
Blackheath B65 .... 63 D4
Tamworth B79 .... 20 E6
Wolverhampton WV4 .... 39 A5
Buckingham Rise
Coventry CV5 .... 112 B4
Dudley DY1 .... 50 E2
Buckingham St B19 .... 164 B4
Buckland Cl WS12 .... 2 D1
Buckland End B34 .... 69 A6
Buckland Ho 3 B15 .... 86 C7
Buckland Rd CV6 .... 95 B2
Bucklands End La B34 .... 68 F6
Buckle Cl WS1 .... 42 E8
Buckler's Yd CV12 .... 78 A2
Buckley Ho CV5 .... 112 F1
Buckley Rd
Royal Leamington Spa CV32 157 C2
Wolverhampton WV4 .... 38 D5
Buckleys Gn B48 .... 139 A6
Buckleys The B48 .... 139 A6
Bucklow Wlk B33 .... 68 E4
Buckminster Dr B93 .... 127 E4
Bucknall Cres B32 .... 102 A8
Bucknall Ct 14 B13 .... 87 B2
Bucknall Ho B14 .... 104 E6
Bucknall Rd WV11 .... 13 B1
Bucknell Cl B91 .... 107 C5
Buckpool Sch The DY8 .... 60 F2
Buckridge Cl B38 .... 123 D7
Bucks Hill CV10 .... 72 C6
Buckthorn Cl WS12 .... 1 F8
Buckton Cl B75 .... 32 E2
Budbrook Gr B34 .... 69 E6
Budbrooke Cl CV2 .... 96 D2
Budbrooke Ind Est CV34 .... 160 B7
Budbrooke Rd CV34 .... 160 B7
Budden Rd WV14 .... 51 D7
Bude Rd WS5 .... 43 D7
Buffery Rd DY2 .... 62 D7
Bufferys Cl B91 .... 127 B8
Buildwas Cl WS3 .... 13 F2
Bulford Cl B14 .... 104 F2
Bulger Rd WV14 .... 40 C7
Bulkington Fst Sch CV12 ...... 79 C2
Bulkington La CV11 .... 79 A7
Bulkington Rd
Bedworth CV12 .... 78 D2
Shilton CV7 .... 97 E6
Bull La Bilston WV14, WS10 .... 41 B3
West Bromwich B70 .... 53 A3
Wombourne WV5 .... 49 B7
Bull Ring Birmingham B5 ..... 164 C2
4 Halesowen B63 .... 83 B3
Kidderminster DY10 .... 116 E6
Nuneaton CV10 .... 73 B2
Sedgley DY3 .... 50 D8
Willenhall WV13 .... 27 A3
Bull Ring Ctr B5 .... 164 C2
Bull Ring Trad Est 2 B12 ... 66 F1
Bull St
Birmingham, Brookfields B4 164 C3
Birmingham, Harborne B17 .... 85 D5
Brierley Hill DY5 .... 61 B1
Darlaston WS10 .... 41 E6
Dudley, Gornalwood DY3 .... 50 C2
Dudley, Springs Mire DY1 .... 62 A8
Nuneaton CV11 .... 73 D2
West Bromwich B70 .... 53 D3
Bull Street Trad Est DY5 ..... 61 B2
Bull Yd CV1 .... 165 B2
Bull's Head La CV3 .... 114 B2
Bull's La B76 .... 47 E1
Bullace Croft B15 .... 85 D3
Bulldog La WS13 .... 3 B1
Buller St WV4 .... 39 E6
Bullfield Ave CV4 .... 111 E1
Bullfields Cl B65 .... 62 F5
Bullfinch Cl DY1 .... 61 E8
Bullfurlong La LE10 .... 75 F4
Bullimore Gr CV8 .... 148 A2
Bullivents Cl B93 .... 127 F5
Bullmeadow La WV5 .... 49 A8
Bullmoor La WS14 .... 8 B1
Bullock St Birmingham B7 ..... 67 A5
West Bromwich B70 .... 53 D1
Bullock's Row WS1 .... 28 F1
Bullows Rd WS8 .... 15 C6
Bulwell Cl B6 .... 67 A7
Bulwer Rd CV6 .... 113 A6
Bulwick Cl CV3 .... 115 B1
Bumble Hole La B61 .... 136 E7
Bunbury Gdns B30 .... 103 D4
Bunbury Rd B31 .... 103 C4
Bundle Hill B63 .... 83 A4
Bungalows The
West Bromwich,
Charlemont B71 .... 53 E8
West Bromwich,
Swan Village B70 .... 52 F6
Bunker's Hill La WV14 .... 40 E7
Bunn's La DY1, DY2 .... 51 F1
Bunny Stile La WV11 .... 26 B6
Buntsford Hill B60 .... 150 F5
Buntsford Park Rd B60 .... 150 F6
Bunyan Pl WS11 .... 1 E4
Burbage Cl WV10 .... 25 E6
Burbage Cty Jun Sch
Hinckley LE10 .... 75 F6
Hinckley LE10 .... 76 A5
Burbage Rd LE10 .... 76 A7
Burbages La CV6 .... 95 D4
Burberry Ct 3 DY4 .... 52 A8
Burberry Gr CV7 .... 130 A6
Burbidge Rd B9 .... 67 E3
Burbury Cl Bedworth CV12 .... 78 C4
Royal Leamington Spa
CV32 .... 157 C2
Burbury St
Birmingham, Lozells B19 .... 66 C7
Birmingham, Newtown B19 ..... 66 C6
Burcombe Twr B23 .... 57 B6
Burcot Ave Bromsgrove
B60 .... 137 B4
Wolverhampton WV1 .... 26 A2
Burcot Ct B74 .... 31 F2
Burcot Ho B60 .... 137 B3
Burcot La
Bromsgrove, Burcot B60 ...... 137 B3
Bromsgrove, Stoney Hill B60 137 C4
Burcote Rd B24 .... 57 D3
Burdock Cl Cannock WS11 .... 2 B3
Walsall WS5 .... 43 A3
Burdock Ho B38 .... 103 F1
Burdock Rd B29 .... 103 A6
Burdons Cl B34 .... 69 A5
Burfield Rd B63 .... 82 C6
Burford Cl Solihull B92 .... 89 A3
Walsall WS5 .... 43 A4
Burford Ct 16
Birmingham B13 .... 87 B2
Stourbridge DY8 .... 81 A4
Burford Mews 16 CV31 ...... 162 C6
Burford Park Rd B38 .... 123 E8
Burford Rd Birmingham B44 .. 55 F7
Hollywood B47 .... 125 A6
Burgage Pl CV11 .... 73 C4
Burgage Wlk CV11 .... 73 B5
Burges CV1 .... 165 B3
Burges Gr CV34 .... 155 F1
Burgess Croft B92 .... 107 F7
Burghley Cl CV11 .... 73 F2
Burghley Dr
Kidderminster DY11 .... 116 C5
West Bromwich B71 .... 42 F2
Burghley Wlk DY5 .... 81 B8
Burgoyne St WS11 .... 2 A5
Burhill Way B37 .... 70 B5
Burke Ave B13 .... 87 D1
Burkitt Dr DY4 .... 52 C8
Burland Ave WV6 .... 24 E6
Burleigh Cl
Balsall Common CV7 .... 130 B7
Cannock WS12 .... 2 A8
Willenhall WV12 .... 27 B6
Burleigh Croft WS7 .... 7 A4
Burleigh Rd Hinckley LE10 ..... 71 C2
Wolverhampton WV3 .... 39 A8
Burleigh St WS1 .... 29 A1
Burleton Rd B33 .... 69 E2
Burley Cl B90 .... 105 F2
Burley Wlk B38 .... 123 C8
Burlington Arc B2 .... 164 B2
Burlington Ave B70 .... 53 E1
Burlington Cl DY10 .... 117 B4
Burlington Ct 1 B78 .... 35 B8
Burlington Rd
Birmingham B10 .... 67 F1
Coventry CV2 .... 113 F4
Nuneaton CV10 .... 78 B7
West Bromwich B70 .... 53 E1
Burlington St B6 .... 66 E6
Burlish Ave 1 B92 .... 88 F1
Burman Cl B90 .... 106 A2
Burman Dr B46 .... 70 F5
Burman Inf Sch B90 .... 106 A2
Burman Rd B90 .... 106 A2
Burmarsh Wlk WV8 .... 24 F8
Burmese Way B65 .... 62 F6
Burn Cl B66 .... 65 A4
Burnaby Cl CV10 .... 72 B5
Burnaby Rd CV6 .... 95 B1
Burnaston Cres B90 .... 127 C6
Burnaston Rd B28 .... 87 E1
Burnbank Gr B24 .... 57 B4
Burncross Way WV10 .... 25 F6
Burnel Rd B29 .... 85 B2
Burnell Gdns WV3 .... 38 E8
Burnet Gr WV10 .... 12 B8
Burnett Ho 12 B69 .... 63 D5
Burnett Rd B74 .... 31 B2
Burney La B8 .... 68 C4
Burnfields Cl WS9 .... 30 A7
Burnham Ave
Birmingham B25 .... 88 C6
Wolverhampton WV10 .... 25 C8
Burnham Cl DY6 .... 60 F4
Burnham Ct Birmingham
B23 .... 56 C2
10 Brierley Hill DY5 .... 61 D2
Burnham Gn WS11 .... 4 B8
Burnham Mdw B28 .... 106 A6
Burnham Rd Birmingham
B44 .... 55 E7
Coventry CV3 .... 134 A6
Burnham Rise CV11 .... 74 A6
Burnhill Gr B29 .... 103 A8
Burnlea Gr B31 .... 103 C1
Burns Ave Tipton DY4 .... 52 A7
Warwick CV34 .... 160 C5
Wolverhampton WV10 .... 11 D2
Burns Cl Kidderminster
DY10 .... 117 B6
Lichfield WS14 .... 9 B6
Redditch B97 .... 158 C8
Stourbridge DY8 .... 81 A8
Burns Dr WS7 .... 7 C7
Burns Gr DY3 .... 50 A4
Burns Pl WS10 .... 41 B5
Burns Rd Coventry CV2 .... 114 B3
Royal Leamington Spa CV32 . 157 B4
Tamworth B79 .... 21 A6
Wednesbury WS10 .... 41 B5
Burns St WS11 .... 2 A3
Burns Wlk CV12 .... 78 C1
Burnsall Cl Birmingham B37 .. 69 F2
Wolverhampton WV9 .... 11 A3
Burnsall Gr CV5 .... 132 D8
Burnsall Rd CV5 .... 132 D8
Burnside CV3 .... 115 A2
Burnside Ct B73 .... 46 A1
Burnside Gdns WS5 .... 43 D6
Burnside Way B31 .... 122 F7
Burnsway LE10 .... 71 C1
Burnt Meadow Rd B98 ...... 154 F6
Burnt Oak Dr DY8 .... 81 B5
Burnt Tree DY4 .... 51 F2
Burnt Tree Ind Est B69 .... 52 B2
Burnt Tree Island DY4 .... 51 F2
Burnt Tree Prim Sch B69 .... 52 A2
Burnthurst Cres B90 .... 127 A7
Burntwood Rd
Burntwood WS7 .... 7 D4
Norton Canes WS11 .... 6 A6
Burntwood Town Sh Ctr
WS7 .... 6 E7
Burrelton Way 1 B43 .... 54 D8
Burrington Rd B32 .... 102 A8
Burrow Hill Cl B36 .... 69 C8
Burrow Hill La CV7 .... 94 D7
Burrowes St WS2 .... 28 D3
Burrows Cl CV31 .... 162 B2
Burrows Croft WV14 .... 40 C6
Burrows Ho 7 WS2 .... 28 D3
Burrows Rd DY6 .... 60 F4
Bursledon Wlk WV1 .... 40 B8
Burslem Cl WS3 .... 14 A3
Bursnips Rd WV11 .... 13 C4
Burton Ave WS4 .... 29 B8
Burton Cl Allesley CV5 .... 94 C2
Tamworth B79 .... 21 C7
Burton Cres WV10 .... 163 D4
Burton Farm Rd WS4 .... 29 B3
Burton Green CE Jun &
Inf Sch CV8 .... 131 B3
Burton Ind Est B64 .... 82 E8
Burton La Bramcote CV11 ...... 79 F7
Redditch B98 .... 153 F3
Burton Old Rd WS14 .... 9 F8
Burton Old Rd E WS14 .... 9 E8
Burton Old Rd W WS13 .... 9 D8
Burton Rd Dudley DY1 .... 50 F4
Lichfield WS13 .... 3 F1
Wolverhampton WV10 .... 25 E3
Burton Wood Dr B20 .... 55 D2
Burtons Farm Prim Sch
B36 .... 70 A8
Bury Hill Rd B69 .... 63 D8
Bury Ho CV4 .... 111 F3
Bury Mound Ct B90 .... 105 C2
Bury Rd CV31 .... 161 F7
Buryfield Rd B91 .... 107 B6
Busby Cl CV3 .... 134 F7
Bush Ave B66 .... 65 C5
Bush Cl CV4 .... 111 F3
Bush Ct CV2 .... 114 B6
Bush Gr Birmingham B21 .... 54 C1
Walsall WS3 .... 15 A2
Bush Rd Dudley DY2 .... 62 C2
Tipton DY4 .... 51 E4
Bush St WS10 .... 41 D7
Bushbery Ave CV4 .... 111 F2
Bushbury Croft B37 .... 70 C3
Bushbury Hill Jun &
Inf Schs WV10 .... 11 F1
Bushbury La WV10 .... 25 D7
Bushbury Rd Birmingham
B33 .... 69 A5
Wolverhampton WV10 .... 26 A5
Bushell Dr B91 .... 107 D4
Bushey Cl B74 .... 30 F2
Bushey Fields Hospl DY5 ...... 61 E7
Bushey Fields Rd DY1 .... 61 E7
Bushley Cl B98 .... 159 A7
Bushley Croft B91 .... 127 B8
Bushman Way B34 .... 69 E5
Bushmore Rd B28 .... 106 A7
Bushway Cl DY5 .... 61 B2
Bushwood Ct B15 .... 86 C8
Bushwood Dr B93 .... 128 B3
Bushwood Rd B29 .... 85 B1
Busill Jones Jun Mixed
Inf Sch WS3 .... 27 F8
Bustleholme Ave B71 .... 42 F1
Bustleholme Cres B71 .... 42 E1
Bustleholme La B71 .... 42 E1
Butcher's La CV5 .... 112 C6
Butchers La B63 .... 82 C7
Butchers Rd B92 .... 109 A6
Butcroft Gdns WS10 .... 41 E6
Bute Cl Birmingham B45 ...... 101 E1
Hinckley LE10 .... 71 C1
Willenhall WV12 .... 27 B6
Butler Cl CV8 .... 148 C7
Butler Rd B92 .... 88 F3
Butler St Astwood Bank B96 . 158 E1
West Bromwich B70 .... 53 A4
Butler's Hill La B97 .... 153 C5
Butler's Rd B20 .... 55 A3
Butlers Cl
Birmingham,
Handsworth B20 .... 55 A3
Birmingham,
Perry Common B73 .... 45 D1
Butlers Cres CV7 .... 78 A1
Butlers End CV35 .... 146 C2
Butlers La B74 .... 32 A3
Butlers Lane Sta B74 .... 32 A3
Butlers Prec 2 WS1 .... 28 E2
Butlin Rd CV6 .... 95 C4
Butlin St B7 .... 67 C7
Butt La Allesley CV5 .... 112 B7
Hinckley LE10 .... 71 F1
Butt Lane Cl LE10 .... 71 E1
Butter Wlk B38 .... 123 C8
Buttercup Cl 6 WS5 .... 43 A3
Buttercup Dr B60 .... 137 C6
Butterfield Cl WV6 .... 23 D3
Butterfield Ct DY1 .... 51 A2
Butterfield Rd DY5 .... 61 B7
Butterfly Way 4 B64 .... 62 F1
Buttermere B77 .... 36 B7
Buttermere Ave CV11 .... 74 A6
Buttermere Cl
Brierley Hill DY5 .... 81 B7
Cannock WS11 .... 2 A3
Coventry CV3 .... 134 F7
Wolverhampton WV6 .... 24 D8
Buttermere Ct WV6 .... 23 F4
Buttermere Dr
Birmingham B32 .... 84 F3
Essington WV11 .... 13 A2
Buttermere Gr WV12 .... 13 B1
Butterworth Cl WV14 .... 40 A1
Butterworth Dr CV4 .... 132 A6
Buttery Rd B67 .... 64 E6
Buttons Farm Rd WV4 .... 38 D3
Buttress Way B66 .... 65 A6
Butts CV1 .... 113 A2
Butts Cl WS11 .... 5 E4
Butts JMI Sch WS4 .... 28 F3
Butts La Norton Canes WS11 ..... 5 E4
Stone DY10 .... 117 D1
Tanworth-In-A B94 .... 142 B2
Butts Rd Coventry CV1 .... 113 B2
Walsall WS4 .... 28 F3
Wolverhampton WV4 .... 38 F4
Butts St WS4 .... 28 F3
Butts The Lichfield WS14 .... 8 D2
Walsall WS4 .... 28 F3
Warwick CV34 .... 160 E7
Butts Way WS11 .... 5 E4
Buxton Ave B78 .... 35 B8
Buxton Cl WS3 .... 14 C3
Buxton Rd Birmingham B23 ... 56 B6
Dudley DY2 .... 62 A6
Sutton Coldfield B73 .... 57 A8
Walsall WS3 .... 14 C3
By Pass Rd B77 .... 22 A5
Byfield Cl B33 .... 69 E1
Byfield Pl CV7 .... 130 D5
Byfield Rd CV6 .... 112 E5
Byfleet Cl WV14 .... 40 A3
Byford Cl B98 .... 153 E2
Byford Ct CV10 .... 72 F4
Byford St CV10 .... 72 F4
Byland B77 .... 21 D3
Byland Way WS3 .... 13 F2
Bylands Cl B61 .... 136 E1
Byng Kendrick Central
Sch B33 .... 69 D3
Bypass Link B91 .... 107 F3
Byrchen Moor Gdns DY5 ...... 61 B7
Byrne Rd WV2 .... 39 D7
Byron Ave Bedworth CV12 ...... 78 D2
Birmingham B23 .... 56 B3
Lichfield WS14 .... 9 B5
Warwick CV34 .... 160 C4
Byron Cl Birmingham B10 ...... 87 D7
Kidderminster DY10 .... 117 B5
Byron Cres DY1 .... 51 B6
Byron Croft Dudley DY3 .... 50 A4
Sutton Coldfield B74 .... 31 F6
Byron Ct Knowle B93 .... 128 A6
Sutton Coldfield B75 .... 32 A5
Byron Gdns B71 .... 53 B5
Byron Ho B63 .... 82 B5
Byron Pl WS11 .... 1 F5
Byron Rd Birmingham B10 ..... 87 D7
Redditch B97 .... 158 D8
Tamworth B79 .... 21 A7
Willenhall WV12 .... 27 E7
Wolverhampton WV10 .... 12 A1
Byron St Brierley Hill DY5 ..... 61 D7
Coventry CV1 .... 165 C4
West Bromwich B71 .... 53 B5
Byron Way B61 .... 137 A8
Bywater Cl CV3 .... 133 B5
Bywater Ho 5 WS1 .... 28 F1
Byways WS3 .... 14 C3

Caban Cl B31 .... 102 E5
Cable Dr WS2 .... 28 C5
Cable St WV2 .... 39 F8
Cable & Wireless Coll
CV4 .... 131 E6
Cabot Gr WV6 .... 23 E4
Cadbury Dr B35 .... 58 A2
Cadbury Ho B19 .... 66 D5
Cadbury Rd B13 .... 87 B4
Cadbury Sixth Form Coll
B38 .... 103 F1
Cadbury Way B17 .... 85 B5
Cadbury World B30 .... 103 F7
Cadden Dr CV4 .... 112 B2
Caddick Cres B71 .... 53 D7
Caddick Rd B42 .... 44 B1
Caddick St WV14 .... 51 A8
Cadine Gdns B13 .... 86 C1
Cadle Rd WV10 .... 25 E7
Cadleigh Gdns B17 .... 85 C3
Cadman Cl CV12 .... 78 C3
Cadman Cres WV10 .... 26 A7
Cadman's La WS6, WS3 .... 14 D7
Cadnam Cl Birmingham B17 .. 85 C3
Willenhall WV13 .... 41 B8
Cadogan Rd B77 .... 35 D5
Caen Cl CV35 .... 160 A7
Caernarfon Dr CV11 .... 73 D3
Caernarvon Cl WV12 .... 27 C7
Caernarvon Way DY1 .... 50 E2
Caesar Rd CV8 .... 147 E3
Caesar Way B46 .... 59 E1
Cairn Dr WS2 .... 27 F2
Cairndhu Dr DY10 .... 117 B7
Cairns St WS2 .... 28 C3
Caister B77 .... 22 A6
Caister Dr WV13 .... 40 F8

Caistor Cl B78 34 B8
Caithness Cl CV5 112 A4
Cakemore Rd B65 63 F2
Cala Dr B15 86 B7
Calcot Dr WV6 24 E7
Calcott Ho CV3 134 B5
Caldecote Cl CV10 73 C8
Caldecote Gr B9 68 C1
Caldecote Rd CV6 113 C5
Caldeford Ave B90 127 A7
Calder B77 22 B2
Calder Ave WS1 29 A2
Calder Cl Bulkington CV12 79 B2
Coventry CV3 133 E7
Calder Dr B76 58 A7
Calder Gr B20 54 F2
Calder Rise DY3 50 F6
Calder Tower 2 B20 55 D1
Calder Wlk CV31 162 C6
Calderfields Cl WS4 29 A3
Caldmore Gn WS1 42 E8
Caldmore Prim Sch WS1 42 E8
Caldmore Rd WS1 42 E8
Caldon Cl LE10 75 B8
Caldwall Cres DY11 116 D5
Caldwell Ct Nuneaton CV11 73 D1
Solihull B91 107 C5
Caldwell Gr B91 107 C5
Caldwell Ho B70 53 C2
Caldwell Rd Birmingham B9 68 B3
Nuneaton CV11 73 D1
Caldwell St B71 53 D8
Caldy Wlk B45 101 F1
Cale Cl B77 21 C2
Caledon St 5 WS2 42 C7
Caledonia DY5 81 D7
Caledonia Rd WV2 163 D1
Caledonia St WV14 40 E6
Caledonian B77 21 F2
Caledonian Cl WS5 43 C3
Calewood Rd DY5 81 D7
California Ho B32 84 E2
California Rd B69 63 B8
California Way B32 84 F3
Californian Gr WS7 6 F8
Callaghan Gr WS11 2 C2
Callcott Dr DY5 81 D7
Callear Rd WS10 41 D1
Callendar Cl CV11 74 A7
Calley Cl DY4 52 A3
Callow Hill La B97 158 B6
Callow Hill Rd B48 139 A6
Callowbridge Rd B45 121 F7
Callowbrook Fst Sch B45 121 E7
Callowbrook La B45 121 F7
Callows La 2 DY10 116 E6
Calmere Cl CV2 114 F8
Calshot Jun & Inf Schs B42 55 B8
Calshot Rd B42 55 A8
Calstock Rd WV12 27 D4
Calthorpe Cl WS5 43 E6
Calthorpe Mans 4 B15 66 B1
Calthorpe Rd Birmingham, Edgbaston B15 86 B8
Birmingham Handsworth Wood B20 55 C2
Walsall WS5 43 D6
Calthorpe Specl Sch B12 87 A8
Caludon Castle Sch CV2 114 E4
Caludon Lodge CV2 114 E5
Caludon Park Ave CV2 114 E5
Caludon Rd CV2 114 A4
Calver Cres WV11 26 F5
Calver Gr B44 44 D3
Calverley Rd B38 123 D8
Calvert Cl CV3 133 D6
Calverton Gr B43 54 E8
Calves Croft WV13 27 A3
Calvin Cl WV10 11 D3
Calving Hill WS11 1 E2
Cam Gdns DY5 61 B6
Cam Ho 7 DY1 61 E8
Camberley 6 B71 42 F1
Camberley Cres WV4 39 E2
Camberley Dr WV4 39 A4
Camberley Gr B23 56 E6
Camberley Rd DY6 61 A4
Camberwell Terr CV31 162 A7
Camborne Cl B6 66 E7
Camborne Dr CV11 73 F5
Camborne Rd WS5 43 D7
Cambourne Ct 4 WS5 43 D7
Cambourne Rd Blackheath B65 63 C3
Hinckley LE10 76 A6
Cambrai Dr B28 105 F8
Cambria Cl B90 125 E7
Cambria St WS11 1 D4
Cambrian B77 22 A2
Cambridge Ave Solihull B91 106 E3
Sutton Coldfield B73 57 B8
Cambridge Cl WS9 30 B8
Cambridge Cres B15 86 D7
Cambridge Dr Birmingham B37 69 F1
Nuneaton CV10 72 E3
Cambridge Gdns CV32 157 A1
Cambridge Rd Birmingham B13 86 F1
Dudley DY2 62 A7
Smethwick B66 65 A7
Cambridge St Birmingham B1 164 A2
Coventry CV1 113 E5
Walsall WS1 42 E7
West Bromwich B70 53 B2
Wolverhampton WV10 163 C4
Cambridge Tower B1 164 A2
Cambridge Way B27 88 D4
Camden Cl Birmingham B36 69 A8
Walsall WS5 43 A4
Camden Dr Birmingham B1 66 C3
Tamworth B77 21 E3
Camden St Birmingham B18, B1 66 B4
Brownhills WS9 15 F4
Coventry CV2 114 A4
Walsall WS1 42 E8
Camden Way DY6 49 D1
Camellia Gdns WV9 10 F3
Camellia Rd 1 CV2 96 B2
Camelot Cl WS11 1 F4
Camelot Gr CV8 148 C5
Camelot Way B10 87 C8
Cameo Dr DY8 80 F8
Cameron Cl Allesley CV5 112 A7
Royal Leamington Spa CV32 157 A4
Cameron Rd WS4 29 B3
Camford Gr B14 104 F3
Camhouses B77 22 B1
Camino Rd B32 84 F3
Camomile Cl 5 WS5 43 A3
Camp Hill Birmingham B12 87 A8
Stourbridge DY8 60 E1
Camp Hill Cir B12 87 A8
Camp Hill Cty Jun Sch CV10 72 E6
Camp Hill Dr CV10 72 D7
Camp Hill Middleway B12 87 A7
Camp Hill Rd CV10 72 C7
Camp La Birmingham, Handsworth B21 54 C2
Birmingham, King's Norton B38 103 F3
Camp Rd WS14, B75 32 D6
Camp St Birmingham B9 67 C1
Wednesbury WS10 41 F2
Wolverhampton WV1 163 B4
Camp Wood Cl B30 103 F8
Campbell Cl Tamworth B79 20 F8
Walsall WS4 29 A3
Campbell Pl WS10 41 D6
Campbell St Brierley Hill DY5 61 C4
2 Dudley DY2 62 D8
Campbells Gn B26 89 B4
Campden Cl B97 158 D6
Campden Gn B92 89 A3
Camphill La WS10 41 F2
Campian's Ave WS6 4 D2
Campion Cl Coventry CV3 133 D6
Walsall WS5 43 A3
Campion Ct 2 DY4 51 E5
Campion Dr Featherstone WV10 12 A7
Tamworth B77 21 C3
Campion Gn CV32 157 A2
Campion Gr B63 82 D3
Campion Ho 1 Birmingham B38 123 E8
Wolverhampton WV10 25 F4
Campion Rd CV32 157 A2
Campion Sch & Com Coll CV31 162 C5
Campion Terr CV32 157 A1
Camplea Croft B37 70 A2
Camplin Cres B20 54 E5
Campling Cl CV12 79 B2
Campton Cl LE10 75 E7
Campville Cres B71 42 E1
Campville Gr B37 69 F5
Camrose Croft Birmingham Balsall Heath B12 86 F5
Birmingham, Castle Bromwich B34 69 B6
Camrose Gdns WV9 11 A3
Camrose Tower B7 67 B6
Camsey La WS7 7 E8
Camville CV3 115 A2
Canal La B24 57 A1
Canal Rd CV6 113 F8
Canal Side Dudley DY2 62 E4
Hopwood B48 123 B2
Canal Side Ind Est DY5 61 C1
Canal St Brierley Hill DY5 61 E5
Dudley, Roseville WV14 51 C8
Dudley, Tipton Green DY1 51 D4
Oldbury B69 64 A7
Stourbridge DY8 80 F6
Canal View Ind Est DY5 61 B1
Canalside Cl Walsall WS3 14 F1
Wednesbury WS10 42 E2
Canary Gr B19 66 C8
Canberra Ct 2 CV12 77 F2
Canberra Ho B34 69 E6
Canberra Rd Coventry CV2 96 C4
Walsall WS5 43 C6
Canberra Way 4 B12 86 F8
Canford Cl Birmingham B12 86 F7
Coventry CV3 133 C3
Canley Ford CV5 132 E7
Canley Rd CV5 132 D8
Canley Sta CV5 112 D1
Cannel Rd WS7 6 D6
Canning Cl WS5 43 D6
Canning Gdns B18 65 E4
Canning Rd Tamworth B77 21 F4
Walsall WS5 43 D6
Canning St LE10 71 C1
Cannock Chase High Sch WS11 1 E2
Cannock Chase Tech Coll Cannock, Blackfords WS11 1 D1
Cannock, Bridgton WS11 4 E7
Cannock Com Hospl WS11 1 E2
Cannock Ind Ctr WS11 4 D5
Cannock Motor Village WS11 2 B3
Cannock Rd Burntwood WS7 7 B7
Cannock WS11 2 A5
Featherstone WV10 12 C7
Norton Canes WS7 6 C8
Willenhall WV12 27 C7
Wolverhampton WV10 26 A8
Cannock Sh Ctr 3 WS11 1 E1
Cannock Sta WS11 4 F8
Cannocks La CV5 132 D6
Cannon Cl CV4 132 F6
Cannon Hill Gr 2 B12 86 E5
Cannon Hill Pl 1 B12 86 E5
Cannon Hill Rd Birmingham B12 86 E5
Coventry CV4 132 D5
Cannon Park District Ctr CV4 132 C6
Cannon Park Prim Sch CV4 132 D5
Cannon Park Rd CV4 132 E5
Cannon Rd WV5 49 A6
Cannon St Birmingham B2 164 C2
Walsall WS2 28 E4
Willenhall WV13 27 B2
Cannon St N WS2 28 E4
Canon Dr CV7 95 D6
Canon Evans CE Fst Sch CV12 78 A2
Canon Hudson Cl CV3 134 C6
Canon Maggs CE Mid Sch CV12 78 B2
Canon Young Rd CV31 162 B3
Canterbury Ave WV13 27 D2
Canterbury Cl Blackheath B65 63 E4
Kenilworth CV8 148 C3
Lichfield WS13 3 C3
9 Oldbury B65 63 E4
Studley B80 159 C4
Walsall WS3 15 A4
West Bromwich B71 53 E8
Canterbury Cross Prim Sch B20 55 D1
Canterbury Dr Birmingham B37 90 A7
Burntwood WS7 7 D7
Perton WV6 23 E4
Canterbury Rd Birmingham B20 55 D1
Kidderminster DY11 116 A6
West Bromwich B71 53 D8
Wolverhampton WV4 38 E5
Canterbury St CV1 165 D3
Canterbury Tower 1 B1 66 B3
Canterbury Way Cannock WS12 2 B1
Nuneaton CV11 74 A8
Cantlow Cl CV5 112 A3
Cantlow Ho 3 B12 86 F7
Cantlow Rd B13 105 A6
Canton Ho LE10 71 C4
Canute Cl WS1 42 F7
Canvey Cl B45 101 E1
Canwell Ave B37 69 F5
Canwell Dr B75 33 B5
Canwell Gdns WV14 40 C4
Capcroft Rd B13 105 B6
Cape Cl WS8 16 A6
Cape Hill B66 65 C4
Cape Ind Est CV34 160 E7
Cape Prim Sch B66 65 C4
Cape Rd CV34 160 D8
Cape St Birmingham B18 65 D4
West Bromwich B70 52 E4
Capener Rd B43 44 A2
Capern Gr B32 84 F5
Capethorn Rd B66 65 A3
Capilano Rd B23 56 C7
Capmartin Rd CV6 113 C7
Cappers La WS13, WS14 9 F8
Capponfield Cl WV14 40 B3
Capstone Ave Birmingham B18 66 A4
Wolverhampton WV10 25 C8
Captain's Cl WV3 24 D2
Captain's Pool Rd DY10 117 B2
Captains Pool Rd DY10 117 A1
Capulet Cl CV3 134 C6
Caradoc B77 22 A2
Caradoc Cl CV2 114 D7
Caradoc Hall CV2 114 D7
Carcroft Rd B25 88 D8
Cardale Croft 1 CV3 134 F8
Cardale St B65 63 D1
Carden Cl B70 52 F4
Carder Cres WV14 40 D4
Carder Dr DY5 61 C2
Cardiff Cl CV3 134 D5
Cardiff St WV3 39 B8
Cardigan Cl B71 53 C7
Cardigan Dr WV12 27 B6
Cardigan Pl WS12 2 C5
Cardigan Rd CV12 77 C1
Cardigan St B4 66 F3
Cardinal Cres B61 136 D1
Cardinal Dr DY10 117 B3
Cardinal Griffin RC Sch WS11 1 D3
Cardinal Newman RC Sch CV6 94 F2
Cardinal Newman RC Sec Sch B17 65 A2
Cardinal Way WS11 1 D2
Cardinal Wiseman RC Sch CV2 96 E1
Cardinal Wiseman RC Sec Sch B44 44 F2
Carding Cl CV5 111 F4
Cardington Ave B42 44 B1
Cardington Cl B98 154 F3
Cardoness Pl DY1 50 F2
Cardy Cl B97 153 B4
Careless Gn DY9 81 F4
Carey B77 36 A5
Carey St CV6 114 B8
Carfax WS11 4 E8
Cargill Cl CV6 95 F5
Carhampton Rd B75 47 A5
Carisbroke B77 22 A2
Carisbrook Rd CV10 73 D6
Carisbrooke Ave B37 70 C2
Carisbrooke Cl WS10 42 E2
Carisbrooke Cres WS10 42 E3
Carisbrooke Dr B62 83 D3
Carisbrooke Gdns WV10 11 E3
Carisbrooke Ho WS10 42 E2
Carisbrooke Rd Birmingham B17 65 B1
Perton WV6 24 A3
Wednesbury WS10 42 E2
Wolverhampton WV10 11 E3
Carl Eynon Ct 2 WS3 28 B8
Carl St WS2 28 D5
Carlcroft B77 22 B2
Carless Ave B17 85 B7
Carless Ho B66 65 D6
Carless St WS1 42 E8
Carlisle Rd WS11 4 B7
Carlisle St B18 65 F5
Carlton Ave Aldridge B74 31 A2
Bilston WV14 40 F7
Birmingham B21 54 E1
Stourbridge DY9 81 E3
Wolverhampton WV11 26 A7
Carlton Cl Bulkington CV12 79 B3
Cannock WS12 2 D1
Dudley DY1 51 C6
Kidderminster DY11 116 A8
Redditch B97 153 B1
Sutton Coldfield B75 46 E7
Carlton Cres Burntwood WS7 7 A8
Tamworth B79 20 F8
Carlton Croft B74 31 A2
Carlton Ct CV5 112 F2
Carlton Gdns CV5 133 A8
Carlton Ho 4 Royal Leamington Spa CV32 161 F8
Sutton Coldfield B75 32 B2
Carlton Mews B36 69 D7
Carlton Mews Flats B36 69 D7
Carlton Rd Birmingham B9 67 D1
Coventry CV6 95 F1
Smethwick B66 65 B8
Wolverhampton WV3 39 A7
Carlyle Ave DY10 117 B6
Carlyle Bsns Pk B70 52 F5
Carlyle Gr WV10 26 A8
Carlyle Rd Birmingham, Edgbaston B16 65 E1
Birmingham, Lozells B19 66 C8
Blackheath B65 63 C2
Bromsgrove B60 151 B8
Wolverhampton WV10 26 A8
Carmel Cl WS12 2 C5
Carmel Gr B32 84 B1
Carmelite Rd CV1 113 E2
Carmichael Cl WS14 9 D7
Carmodale Ave B42 55 B5
Carnbroe Ave CV3 134 F7
Carnegie Ave DY4 52 B4
Carnegie Cl CV3 134 B5
Carnegie Rd B65 63 B2
Carnford Rd B26 89 B6
Carnforth Cl DY6 60 B7
Carnforth Rd B60 137 B1
Carnoustie B77 22 C5
Carnoustie Cl Bromsgrove B61 150 D8
Nuneaton CV11 79 C8
Sutton Coldfield B75 46 C8
Walsall WS3 14 A3
Carnwath Rd B73 45 E2
Carol Ave B61 136 D3
Carol Cres Halesowen B63 82 F5
Wednesfield WV11 26 E6
Caroline Cl CV11 78 F7
Caroline Rd B13 86 F4
Caroline St Birmingham B3 164 A4
Dudley DY2 51 E1
West Bromwich B70 53 B2
Carpenter Pl 7 B12 87 A6
Carpenter Rd B15 86 B7
Carpenter's Rd B19 66 C7
Carpenters Cl LE10 75 F5
Carpet Trades Way DY11 116 D7
Carrick Cl WS3 15 A5
Carrie Ho CV1 165 A2
Carriers Cl WS2 27 F1
Carriers Fold WV5 49 B7
Carrington Rd WS10 42 D2
Carroll Wlk DY10 117 C5
Carroway Head Hill B78 33 D4
Carrs La B4 164 C2
Carsal Cl CV7 95 D5
Carshalton Gr WV2 39 E7
Carshalton Rd B44 45 A2
Cartbridge Cres WS3 28 F6
Cartbridge La WS4 29 A6
Cartbridge La S WS4 29 A5
Cartbridge Wlk WS3 29 A6
Carter Ave Codsall WV8 10 B3
Kidderminster DY11 116 B4
Carter Ct DY11 116 C4
Carter Rd Birmingham B43 43 F2
Coventry CV3 134 A8
Wolverhampton W6 25 B5
Carter's Gn B70 53 B4
Carter's La Birmingham B62 84 A3
Halesowen B62 83 F4
Carters Cl Bromsgrove B61 150 D7
Sutton Coldfield B76 46 F3
Carters Hurst B33 69 B1
Cartersfield La WS9 16 E6
Carthusian Rd CV3 133 C7
Cartland Rd Birmingham, Sparkbrook B11 87 C6
Birmingham, Stirchley B14, B30 104 C7
Cartmel Cl CV5 112 A4
Cartmel Ct B23 56 B4
Cartway The WV6 23 D4
Cartwright Gdns B69 52 C2
Cartwright Ho 2 WS3 14 B1
Cartwright Rd B75 32 C3
Cartwright St WV2 163 C1
Carver Cl CV2 114 E2
Carver Ct B24 57 C6
Carver Gdns DY8 80 E2
Carver St B1 66 B4
Casa Mio Ct WS12 2 C5
Cascade Cl CV3 133 E6
Case La CV35 145 E1
Casewell Rd DY6 60 C8
Casey Ave B23 56 D8
Cash Joynson Ave WS10 41 C8
Cash's Bsns Ctr CV1 113 D5
Cash's La CV1 113 D6
Cashmore Ave CV31 161 F5
Cashmore Mid Sch CV31 161 F6
Cashmore Rd Bedworth CV12 77 E1
Kenilworth CV8 148 C4
Casia Gr CV8 148 C4
Caslon Cres DY8 80 D4
Caslon Flats B63 82 C4
Caslon Prim Sch B63 82 C4
Caslon Rd B63 82 C6
Caspian Way CV2 115 A8
Cassandra Cl Brierley Hill DY5 50 C1
Coventry CV4 132 D3
Cassandra Gr CV34 161 D4
Cassowary Rd 2 B20 54 F3
Castello Dr B36 58 D1
Castle Bromwich Bsns Pk B35 58 A1
Castle Bromwich Hall Gdns B36 69 A8
Castle Bromwich Inf Sch B36 69 E8
Castle Bromwich Jun Sch B36 69 E7
Castle Cl Blackheath B64 63 B1
Brownhills WS8 6 F2
Coventry CV3 133 D6
Solihull B92 89 B1
Tamworth B77 21 E4
Warwick CV34 160 E6
Castle Cres B36 69 C8
Castle Croft B68 84 D8
Castle Ct Hinckley LE10 75 D6
Kenilworth CV8 148 A6
Castle Dr Coleshill B46 70 F5
Willenhall WV12 27 B5
Castle Dyke 5 WS13 9 B7
Castle Gn CV8 147 D5
Castle Gr Kenilworth CV8 147 E4
Stourbridge DY8 81 B3
Castle High Sch DY1 51 C2
Castle Hill Dudley DY1 51 D2
Kenilworth CV8 147 E5
Warwick CV34 160 F6
Castle Ho B33 69 B2
Castle Hts B64 83 B8
Castle La Solihull B92 89 A2
Warwick CV34 160 E6
Castle Mews CV34 160 E6
Castle Mill Rd DY1 51 C4
Castle Place Ind Est CV1 165 D4
Castle Rd Birmingham B29 85 B1
Brownhills WS9 16 A3
Kenilworth CV8 147 E5
Kidderminster DY11 116 E5
Nuneaton CV10 73 C7
Studley B80 159 F4
Tamworth B77 35 F5
Tipton DY4 51 D4
Castle Rd E B68 84 D8
Castle Rd W B68 84 C8
Castle Sch WS3 28 B7
Castle Sq B29 85 A1
Castle St Astwood Bank B96 158 E2
Brownhills WS8 6 F2
Coventry CV1 165 D4
Darlaston WS10 41 D8
Dudley DY1 51 D1
Dudley, Roseville WV14 51 C8

astle St continued
Hinckley LE10 .... 75 D8
Sedgley DY3 .... 50 D8
Tipton DY4 .... 51 E5
Warwick CV34 .... 160 E6
West Bromwich B70 .... 53 A8
Wolverhampton WV1 .... 163 C3
astle The DY8 .... 81 B3
astle Vale Sec Sch B35 .... 58 B3
astle Vale Sh Ctr B35 .... 57 F3
astle Vale Sports Ctr
B35 .... 58 B2
Castle View Dudley DY1 .... 51 B2
Tamworth B77 .... 21 C3
astle View Cl WS10 .... 41 A4
astle View Ind Est DY4 .... 51 F3
astle View Rd WV14 .... 41 B4
astle Yd WV1 .... 163 C3
astlebridge Gdns WV11 .... 26 F7
astlebridge Rd WV11 .... 27 A6
astlecroft WS11 .... 5 E5
astlecroft Ave WV3 .... 38 A8
astlecroft Gdns WV3 .... 38 C8
astlecroft La WV3 .... 23 F1
astlecroft Prim Sch WV3 ... 38 B8
astlecroft Rd Bilston
WV14 .... 40 F7
Wolverhampton WV3 .... 38 B8
astleditch La B98 .... 158 E7
astleford Gr B11 .... 87 C4
astleford Rd B11 .... 87 C4
astlefort JMI Sch WS9 .... 16 B3
astlefort Rd WS9 .... 16 A3
astlegate Mews
5 CV34 .... 160 F1
astlehall B77 .... 22 A2
astlehill Rd WS9 .... 16 C3
astlehills Dr B36 .... 69 A8
astlemaine Dr LE10 .... 71 E3
astlereagh Cl WV10 .... 25 C6
astleton Ct 1 B15 .... 86 B7
astleton Rd Birmingham
B42 .... 55 D7
Walsall WS3 .... 14 C3
astleton Dr DY2 .... 62 C4
aswell Rd
Royal Leamington Spa CV31 . 162 B6
Sedgley DY3 .... 50 C8
at and Kittens La WV10 .... 11 E6
at La B34 .... 69 B7
ater Dr B76 .... 46 F2
aterham Dr DY6 .... 60 F3
atesby Dr DY6 .... 60 D8
atesby Ho B37 .... 69 F4
atesby La B94 .... 144 B2
atesby Rd Coventry CV6 ..... 113 B8
Solihull B90 .... 106 B1
ateswell Rd B28 .... 87 F2
athcart Rd DY8 .... 80 E5
athcart Rd Birmingham
B42 .... 55 D7
Walsall WS3 .... 14 C3
athedral Ave DY11 .... 116 A6
athedral Cl WS13 .... 9 B8
athedral Ct WS13 .... 9 B8
athedral Lanes Sh Ctr
CV1 .... 165 B3
athedral Rise WS13 .... 9 A8
athel Dr B42 .... 55 A7
atherine Cl B60 .... 150 F8
atherine Ct B24 .... 57 C4
atherine de Barnes La
Bickenhill B92 .... 90 D1
Catherine de B B92 .... 108 C7
atherine Dr B73 .... 46 A6
atherine Rd WV14 .... 40 A1
atherine St Birmingham
B6 .... 67 A7
Coventry CV2 .... 113 F3
atherine Ward Hall CV12 .. 78 B5
atherines Cl B91 .... 108 B4
atherton Cl DY4 .... 41 C1
atholic La DY3 .... 50 D7
atisfield Cres WV8 .... 10 F1
ato St B7 .... 67 C5
ato St N B7 .... 67 C5
aton Gr B28 .... 106 A7
atshill Fst Sch B61 .... 137 A8
atshill Mid Sch B61 .... 136 F8
atshill Rd WS8 .... 16 A7
attell Dr B75 .... 47 B5
attell Rd Birmingham B9 ... 67 C1
Warwick CV34 .... 160 E7
attells Gr B37 .... 67 C6
attermole Gr B43 .... 44 C3
attock Hurst Dr B72 .... 57 D7
atwall End Prim Sch DY3 . 50 D7
auseway B65 .... 63 C2
auseway Green Prim Sch
B68 .... 63 F3
Causeway Green Rd B68 ..... 64 A4
auseway Rd WV14 .... 51 D8
auseway The B25 .... 88 D7
ausey Farm Rd B63 .... 100 C8
avalier Cir WV10 .... 11 E4
avalier Cl CV11 .... 73 E2
avan's Cl WS11 .... 1 E4
avandale Ave B44 .... 44 E1
avans Cl CV3 .... 135 A8
avans Way CV3 .... 135 A8
avans Wood Mobile
Homes WS12 .... 1 D5
avell Cl WS2 .... 28 D2
avell Ho 5 B16 .... 66 A2
avell Rd DY2 .... 51 F1
avendish B79 .... 20 E7
avendish Cl
Birmingham B38 .... 104 B1
Kingswinford DY6 .... 60 D4
Marlbrook B60 .... 121 C1
avendish Ct B93 .... 128 A3

Cavendish Dr Hagley DY9 .... 98 F4
Kidderminster DY10 .... 117 B7
Cavendish Gdns Walsall
WS2 .... 28 A4
Wolverhampton WV1 .... 26 C1
Cavendish Rd
Birmingham B16 .... 65 D4
Coventry CV4 .... 111 E2
Halesowen B62 .... 83 F4
Walsall WS2 .... 28 B5
Wolverhampton WV1 .... 26 B1
avendish Way WS9 .... 30 B5
aversham Cl CV11 .... 74 A7
aversham Rd B44 .... 45 A2
awdon Gr B93 .... 127 F3
awdor Cres B16 .... 65 F1
awnpore Rd CV6 .... 95 B2
awthorne Cl 1 CV1 .... 113 E4
axton Cl WS11 .... 4 E8
axton Gr B44 .... 45 C1
axton St WS11 .... 4 E8
aynham Cl B98 .... 154 D4
aynham Rd B32 .... 102 B8
ayton Gr B23 .... 56 F6
CE Prim Sch of St Edmund
& St John The DY2 .... 51 E1
Cearl Ct B27 .... 88 C2
Cecil Ct CV31 .... 162 A8
Cecil Dr B69 .... 52 D2
Cecil Leonard Knox Cres
CV11 .... 79 F6
Cecil Rd
Birmingham,
Gravelly Hill B24 .... 56 F3
Birmingham,
Selly Park B13 .... 86 C1
Cecil St Birmingham B19 ..... 164 C4
Cannock WS11 .... 1 F4
Stourbridge DY8 .... 80 F5
Walsall WS4 .... 28 F3
Cecily Rd CV3 .... 133 E7
Cedar Ave Birmingham B36 .. 69 C8
Brownhills WS8 .... 16 A8
Dudley WV14 .... 51 B7
Cedar Bridge Croft B74 ...... 46 B8
Cedar Cl Birmingham B30 .. 103 E6
Burntwood WS7 .... 7 A6
Cannock WS12 .... 2 A8
Lichfield WS14 .... 9 F7
Oldbury B68 .... 84 C8
Royal Leamington Spa
CV32 .... 157 A4
Stourbridge DY8 .... 80 D2
Walsall WS5 .... 43 B4
Cedar Cres DY11 .... 116 C6
Cedar Ct Allesley CV5 .... 112 A6
Birmingham B43 .... 54 B8
Hinckley LE10 .... 76 A6
Tamworth B77 .... 35 E6
Cedar Dr Aldridge B74 .... 30 E1
Birmingham B24 .... 57 C5
Bromsgrove B60 .... 137 A1
Kidderminster DY11 .... 116 C7
Tamworth B79 .... 21 A8
Cedar Gr Bilston WV14 .... 40 F7
Codsall WV8 .... 10 B3
Warwick CV34 .... 156 A1
Wolverhampton WV3 .... 38 B8
Cedar Ho Birmingham B36 ... 68 F8
Solihull B91 .... 106 F1
Cedar Park Rd
Redditch B97 .... 153 D4
Willenhall WV12 .... 13 C1
Cedar Rd Birmingham B30 .. 103 E6
Burntwood WS7 .... 7 A6
Dudley DY1 .... 51 B3
Nuneaton CV10 .... 72 D6
Redditch B97 .... 153 D4
Tipton DY4 .... 51 D5
Wednesbury WS10 .... 42 A2
Willenhall WV13 .... 26 E2
Cedar Terr B97 .... 137 A1
Cedar View B97 .... 153 C4
Cedar Way Birmingham
B31 .... 102 F1
Wolverhampton WV11 .... 26 C7
Cedar Wlk 3 B37 .... 70 B2
Cedar Wood Dr CV7 .... 130 B6
Cedar Wood Rd DY3 .... 50 D5
Cedarhill Dr WS11 .... 1 F3
Cedarhurst Birmingham
B32 .... 85 A5
Solihull B91 .... 107 C3
Cedars Ave Birmingham B27 .. 88 C4
Coventry CV6 .... 112 F5
Kingswinford DY6 .... 60 D4
Wombourne WV5 .... 49 A5
Cedars Fst Sch CV7 .... 96 A8
Cedars Mews The
3 CV32 .... 161 D8
Cedars Rd CV7 .... 78 B1
Cedars The Birmingham
B25 .... 68 E1
Wolverhampton,
Heath Town WV11 .... 26 B5
Wolverhampton,
Newbridge WV6 .... 24 F3
Wolverhampton,
Tettenhall WV6 .... 24 D5
Cedarwood B74 .... 46 B8
Cedarwood Croft B42 .... 54 F8
Cedric Cl CV3 .... 134 C5
Celandine Cl DY6 .... 60 C4
Celandine Rd Coventry CV2 .. 96 D2
Dudley DY1 .... 51 A4
Celbury Way B43 .... 54 D8
Celendine B77 .... 21 C3
Celtic Rd WS11 .... 1 E3

Celts Cl B65 .... 63 C4
Cemetery La B18 .... 66 B5
Cemetery Rd Cannock WS11 .. 1 F5
Darlaston WS10 .... 41 F8
Oldbury B68 .... 64 C6
Redditch B97 .... 153 D3
Smethwick B67 .... 64 F4
Stourbridge DY9 .... 81 E5
Sutton Coldfield B75 .... 46 D6
Walsall WS3 .... 27 A2
Cemetery St Bilston WV14 ... 40 C6
Cheslyn Hay WS6 .... 4 C2
Cemetery Way WS3 .... 14 B1
Centaur Rd CV5 .... 112 F2
Centenary Bsns Ctr CV11 ... 73 E3
Centenary Cl 1 B31 .... 103 A1
Centenary Dr B21 .... 54 E1
Centenary Rd CV4 .... 132 D2
Central Ave Bilston WV14 .... 40 E7
Birmingham B31 .... 122 F8
Blackheath,
Cradley Heath B64 .... 82 D7
Blackheath,
Rowley Regis B65 .... 63 C2
Cannock WS11 .... 1 F5
Coventry CV2 .... 114 A4
Nuneaton CV11 .... 73 B5
Royal Leamington Spa CV31 . 161 F6
Stourbridge DY9 .... 81 E3
Tipton DY4 .... 51 F7
Central Bldgs CV1 .... 165 B1
Central City Ind Est CV6 ... 113 F5
Central Cl WS3 .... 14 A1
Central Dr
Dudley, Gornalwood DY3 ...... 50 D2
Dudley, West Cosley WV14 ... 51 D7
Walsall WS3 .... 14 A1
Central Flats CV1 .... 165 B1
Central Gr B27 .... 88 C2
Central Park Ind Est DY2 .... 62 E3
Central Rd B60 .... 137 A2
Central Sq B23 .... 57 A4
Central Trad Est
Darlaston WS10 .... 41 E6
Wolverhampton WV2 .... 39 F8
Central Way DY5 .... 61 F3
Centre Ct B63 .... 83 B3
Centre La B63 .... 83 B3
Centre Link Ind Est B7 .... 67 B6
Centreway The B14 .... 105 D4
Centrovell Ind Est CV11 ..... 73 C2
Centurion Cl B46 .... 59 F1
Centurion Pk B77 .... 36 B6
Centurion Way B77 .... 36 B6
Century Ho B69 .... 63 D6
Century Ind Est B44 .... 44 E3
Century Pk B9 .... 67 C2
Century Rd B69 .... 64 A8
Century Tower B5 .... 86 C5
Ceolmund Cres B37 .... 70 B2
Chace Ave CV3 .... 134 C6
Chace Prim Sch CV3 .... 134 C6
Chaceley Cl CV2 .... 115 A8
Chaceley Ct B97 .... 158 D8
Chaceley Gr B23 .... 56 E7
Chad Rd Birmingham B15 ... 85 F8
Dudley WV14 .... 51 B7
Chad Sq B15 .... 85 E8
Chad Valley Cl B17 .... 85 D6
Chadbrook Crest B15 .... 85 E7
Chadbury Croft 1 B91 ...... 127 B8
Chadbury Rd B63 .... 83 C3
Chadcote Way B61 .... 120 F1
Chaddersley Cl B45 .... 101 F1
Chaddersley Gdns
2 B98 .... 117 A5
Chaddesley Cl Oldbury B69 .. 63 D5
Redditch B98 .... 153 F1
Chaddesley Dr DY9 .... 81 B1
Chaddesley Rd
Birmingham B31 .... 103 D2
Halesowen B63 .... 82 F2
Kidderminster DY10 .... 117 A5
Chadley Cl B91 .... 107 A6
Chadsgrove Sch B61 .... 136 F8
Chadshunt Cl B36 .... 58 D2
Chadsmead Prim Sch
WS13 .... 3 A1
Chadsmoor CE Jun Sch
WS11 .... 2 A3
Chadsmoor Inf Sch WS11 .... 2 A4
Chadstone Terr B7 .... 67 B6
Chadstone Cl B69 .... 127 B6
Chadvale Prim Sch B15 ...... 85 D7
Chadwell Dr B90 .... 106 B6
Chadwich La CV7 .... 120 F7
Chadwick Ave B45 .... 122 B6
Chadwick Cl Coventry CV5 .. 112 B3
Wolverhampton WV4 .... 38 D6
Chadwick La
Chadwick End B93 .... 145 B8
Knowle B93 .... 129 B2
Chadwick Manor B93 .... 129 A1
Chadwick Mews B93 .... 145 B6
Chadwick Rd B75 .... 46 F5
Chadworth Ave B93 .... 127 E3
Chaffcombe Rd B26 .... 89 C7
Chaffinch Cl Cannock WS12 .. 2 A7
Sedgley DY3 .... 39 C2
Chaffinch Dr Birmingham
B36 .... 70 B7
Kidderminster DY10 .... 116 F2
Chaffinch Rd DY9 .... 81 D3
Chain Wlk B19 .... 66 D1
Chainshop Mus DY2 .... 62 B1
Chalcot Dr WS12 .... 2 A7

Chalcot Gr B20 .... 54 E5
Chaldon Cl WV9 .... 11 A1
Chale Gr B14 .... 105 A3
Chalfield B79 .... 20 D6
Chalfont Ave WS11 .... 4 C7
Coventry CV5 .... 112 B4
Chalfont Pl DY9 .... 81 E2
Chalfont Rd B20 .... 55 C1
Chalford Rd B23 .... 56 C8
Chalford Way B90 .... 106 C1
Chalgrove Ave B38 .... 103 E1
Chalgrove Cres B91 .... 107 B1
Challenge Bsns Pk CV1 .... 113 D5
Challenge Cl CV1 .... 165 C4
Challenge Way WV10 .... 25 E5
Challenor Ave WV13 .... 26 D1
Chalybeate Cl B45 .... 101 F1
Chamberlain Cl
Cubbington CV32 .... 157 E5
Tipton B69 .... 52 D2
Chamberlain Cres B90 ...... 106 A2
Chamberlain Ct B14 .... 86 E1
Chamberlain Ho B66 .... 66 A1
Chamberlain Rd B13 .... 105 A6
Chamberlain Sq B3 .... 164 B2
Chamberlain Wlk
10 Coleshill B46 .... 70 F7
1 Smethwick B66 .... 65 B5
Chamberlain's La WV4 .... 38 E3
Chamberlaine St CV12 .... 78 B3
Chance Croft B68 .... 84 B8
Chance Fields CV31 .... 162 F6
Chancel Ind Est
Darlaston WS10 .... 41 D5
Kingswinford DY6 .... 49 E1
Willenhall WV13 .... 27 B2
Chancel Ind Est The WV1 ... 26 A1
Chancel Way Birmingham
B6 .... 55 F5
Halesowen B62 .... 83 C6
Chancellor's Cl B15 .... 85 E8
Chancellors Cl CV4 .... 132 D4
Chancery Ct CV10 .... 72 A7
Chancery Dr WS12 .... 2 C7
Chancery La CV10 .... 72 B7
Chancery Way DY5 .... 61 F2
Chanders Rd CV34 .... 155 D1
Chandler Dr WV4 .... 38 D3
Chandler Ho B65 .... 63 D4
Chandlers CV31 .... 161 D7
Chandlers Cl Redditch B97 .. 158 D7
Wolverhampton WV9 .... 11 A1
Chandlers Dr B77 .... 22 B5
Chandlers Keep WS8 .... 16 A6
Chandos Ave B13 .... 86 F3
Chandos Ct 13 CV32 .... 156 F1
Chandos Jun & Inf Sch
B12 .... 86 E8
Chandos St Coventry CV2 .. 114 A3
Nuneaton CV11 .... 73 A4
Royal Leamington Spa CV32 . 156 F1
Change Brook Cl CV11 .... 73 F8
Channon Dr DY5 .... 81 D8
Chanston Ave B14 .... 104 E4
Chanterelle Gdns WV4 .... 39 B4
Chantrey Cres Bilston
WV14 .... 40 F7
Birmingham B43 .... 44 D4
Chantries The CV1 .... 113 E5
Chantry Ave WS3 .... 28 D8
Chantry Cl B47 .... 125 A7
Chantry Ct B13 .... 86 F3
Chantry Dr B62 .... 84 A6
Chantry Heath Cres B93 ... 128 C7
Chantry Rd
Birmingham,
Handsworth B21 .... 65 F8
Birmingham, Moseley B13 .... 86 E4
Stourbridge DY7 .... 80 C7
Chantry The CV34 .... 156 A1
Chapel Ash WV3 .... 25 B2
Chapel Ash Island WV1 .... 163 A3
Chapel Ave WS8 .... 6 F2
Chapel Cl B64 .... 83 B8
Chapel Ct Astwood Bank
B96 .... 158 E1
Brierley Hill, Barrow Hill
DY5 .... 61 C7
4 Brierley Hill,
Silver End DY5 .... 61 D2
Chapel Dr
Balsall Common CV7 .... 130 B8
Brownhills WS8 .... 6 E2
Wythall B47 .... 124 F3
Chapel Fields Jun Sch
B92 .... 88 F3
Chapel Fields Rd B92 .... 88 F2
Chapel Gn WV13 .... 27 B2
Chapel House La B63 .... 82 C6
Chapel House St 1 B12 ..... 66 F1
Chapel La Barnacle CV7 ..... 97 B6
Belbroughton DY9 .... 120 D7
Beoley B98 .... 154 F8
Birmingham,
Great Barr B43 .... 44 A5
Birmingham, Selly Oak B29 ... 85 E2
Lapworth B94 .... 144 D7
Lichfield WS14 .... 9 B6
Romsley B62 .... 100 C6
Rowney Green B48 .... 139 F4
Ryton-on-D CV8 .... 135 B2
Walsall B47 .... 43 F4
Wythall B47 .... 124 F3
Chapel Rd B96 .... 158 E1
Chapel Row CV34 .... 160 E7
Chapel Sq WS6 .... 4 D3

Chapel St Astwood Bank
B96 .... 158 E1
Bedworth CV12 .... 78 C3
Bilston WV14 .... 40 F4
Birmingham B5 .... 164 D3
Birmingham,
Handsworth B21 .... 65 D7
Brierley Hill,
Barrow Hill DY5 .... 61 C6
Brierley Hill,
Quarry Bank DY5 .... 61 F1
Brierley Hill,
Silver End DY5 .... 61 D2
Bromsgrove B60 .... 137 A2
Brownhills WS8 .... 6 E2
Burntwood WS7 .... 6 E8
Cannock WS12 .... 2 E1
Coventry CV1 .... 165 B3
Dudley DY2 .... 62 D4
Hagley DY9 .... 99 A5
Halesowen B63 .... 83 A3
Kidderminster DY11 .... 116 D6
Kingswinford DY6 .... 60 B8
Norton Canes WS11 .... 5 F5
Nuneaton CV11 .... 73 C4
Oldbury B69 .... 63 E7
Redditch B97 .... 153 D1
3 Royal Leamington Spa
CV31 .... 162 A7
Stourbridge, Lye DY9 .... 81 E5
Stourbridge, Wollaston DY8 .. 81 A4
Stourbridge, Wordsley DY8 ... 60 D3
Tipton DY4 .... 51 E5
Walsall,
Blakenall Heath WS3 .... 28 D8
Walsall, Pelsall WS3 .... 15 A3
Warwick CV34 .... 160 E7
Wednesbury WS10 .... 41 E3
West Bromwich B70 .... 53 B5
Wolverhampton WV2 .... 39 D7
Chapel View B67 .... 64 F4
Chapel Wlk Birmingham
B30 .... 104 A2
Bromsgrove B60 .... 137 A2
Dudley B60 .... 50 C2
Chapelfield Rd B45 .... 122 A7
Chapelhouse Rd B37 .... 69 F1
Chapelon B77 .... 22 A2
Chapelwood Gr B42 .... 55 D5
Chaplain Rd WS12 .... 2 E2
Chapman Cl CV31 .... 162 E5
Chapman Ct CV34 .... 161 C8
Chapman Rd B10 .... 87 C8
Chapman St B70 .... 53 B3
Chapman's Hill B62 .... 101 B1
Chapmans Pas 1 B1 .... 164 B1
Chapter Ho B70 .... 53 A8
Chard Rd CV3 .... 134 D8
Charfield Cl B30 .... 103 D7
Charford Fst Sch B60 .... 150 F7
Charford Rd B60 .... 150 F7
Charingworth Rd B92 .... 89 C3
Charity Rd CV7 .... 95 A7
Charlbury Ave B37 .... 69 F2
Charlbury Cres B26 .... 88 F8
Charlbury Mews CV31 .... 162 C6
Charlbury Tower 2 B5 .... 86 E8
Charlecote Cl B98 .... 154 D2
Charlecote Croft B90 .... 126 C8
Charlecote Dr
Birmingham B23 .... 56 E7
Dudley DY1 .... 50 E3
Charlecote Gdns
Royal Leamington Spa
CV31 .... 162 D5
Sutton Coldfield B73 .... 57 A8
Charlecote Rd CV6 .... 95 A2
Charlecote Rise 1 WV13 .... 40 F8
Charlecote Tower 4 B15 ... 86 C1
Charlecote Wlk CV11 .... 78 E1
Charlecott Cl B13 .... 105 D7
Charlemont Ave B71 .... 53 E8
Charlemont Cl WS5 .... 43 C6
Charlemont Cres B71 .... 42 E1
Charlemont Gdns WS5 .... 43 C6
Charlemont Prim Sch B71 .. 53 E8
Charlemont Rd Walsall
WS5 .... 43 C6
West Bromwich B71 .... 53 F8
Charlemonte Cl WS12 .... 2 D3
Charles Ave Blackheath B65 .. 63 C4
Essington WV11 .... 12 F4
Wolverhampton WV4 .... 39 B5
Charles Burns Sch B13 .... 86 E1
Charles Cl Birmingham B8 ... 67 D4
Cheslyn Hay WS6 .... 4 D1
Charles Cres WS3 .... 15 A5
Charles Ct
8 Birmingham B13 .... 87 B2
Sutton Coldfield B76 .... 46 F3
Warwick CV34 .... 161 B8
Charles Dr B7 .... 67 B6
Charles Eaton Rd CV12 .... 77 F3
Charles Edward Rd B26 ...... 88 D6
Charles Foster St WS10 ...... 41 C6
Charles Gardner Rd
6 CV31 .... 161 F6
Charles Hayward Bglws
WV4 .... 39 D3
Charles Henry St B12 .... 86 F8
Charles Holland St WV13 ... 27 B2
Charles Lakin Cl CV7 .... 97 C5
Charles Lane Trust Homes
The B28 .... 106 A8
Charles Pearson Ct B66 ..... 65 B5

Charles Rd
Birmingham, Aston B6 .... 56 A1
Birmingham, Bordesley Green B9, B10 .... 67 E1
Birmingham, Handsworth B20 .... 55 C1
Brierley Hill DY5 .... 62 B1
Halesowen B63 .... 82 F4
Solihull B91 .... 106 E2
Stourbridge DY8 .... 80 E4
Tipton DY4 .... 52 A7
Charles St Coventry CV1 .... 165 D4
Hinckley LE10 .... 71 E1
Kidderminster DY10 .... 116 F6
Nuneaton CV11 .... 73 A5
Redditch B97 .... 153 C1
Smethwick B66 .... 65 C7
Walsall WS2 .... 28 D2
Warwick CV34 .... 161 A8
West Bromwich B70 .... 52 E5
Willenhall WV13 .... 27 C3
Charles The W6 .... 25 B5
Charles Wlk B65 .... 63 C5
Charlesdale Dr WS9 .... 30 B4
Charlesworth Ave B90 .... 127 B6
Charleville Rd B19 .... 66 B7
Charlewood Rd CV6 .... 95 B2
Charlock Gr WS11 .... 2 C3
Charlotte Cl B69 .... 52 A2
Charlotte Rd
Birmingham, Edgbaston B15 .... 86 C7
Birmingham, Stirchley B30 .... 104 A6
Tipton WS10 .... 41 C2
Charlotte St Birmingham B3 .... 164 A3
14 Dudley DY1 .... 51 B1
Royal Leamington Spa CV31 .... 161 F6
Walsall WS1 .... 29 A2
Charlton Dr B64 .... 82 D7
Charlton Pl B8 .... 67 D5
Charlton Rd B44 .... 56 A8
Charlton St Brierley Hill DY5 .... 61 A3
4 Dudley DY1 .... 51 B1
Charminster Ave B25 .... 88 D8
Charminster Dr CV3 .... 133 D4
Charnley Dr B75 .... 32 E2
Charnwood Ave
Nuneaton CV10 .... 72 E2
Sedgley DY3 .... 39 D2
Charnwood Bsns Pk WV14 .... 40 C5
Charnwood Cl Bilston WV14 .... 41 B3
Birmingham B45 .... 102 B3
Brierley Hill DY5 .... 81 B8
Cannock WS12 .... 2 C3
Hinckley LE10 .... 71 E2
Lichfield WS13 .... 3 C1
Charnwood Ct DY9 .... 81 E2
Charnwood Ho WS13 .... 3 B2
Charnwood Prim Sch WS13 .... 3 C2
Charnwood Rd
Birmingham B42 .... 54 F7
Hinckley LE10 .... 71 D2
Walsall WS5 .... 43 A4
Charnwood Way CV32 .... 157 C3
Charter App CV34 .... 160 D5
Charter Ave CV4 .... 132 B7
Charter Cl WS11 .... 5 E4
Charter Cres B64 .... 83 B8
Charter Ho CV4 .... 132 A7
Charter House Dr B91 .... 107 C1
Charter Rd DY4 .... 41 C1
Charter St DY5 .... 61 E5
Charterfield Dr Cannock WS12 .... 2 C1
Kingswinford DY6 .... 60 D8
Charterfield Sh Ctr 3 DY6 .... 60 D8
Charterhouse Dr B91 .... 107 C1
Charterhouse Rd CV1 .... 113 E2
Charters Ave WV8 .... 10 B1
Charters The WS13 .... 3 B1
Chartist Rd B8 .... 67 D6
Chartley Cl Dorridge B93 .... 127 E3
Perton WV6 .... 23 F4
Chartley Rd Birmingham B23 .... 56 D1
West Bromwich B71 .... 53 D6
Chartway The WS3 .... 15 B4
Chartwell B79 .... 20 D7
Chartwell Cl Dudley DY1 .... 51 B6
Nuneaton CV11 .... 73 F1
Chartwell Ct B72 .... 57 C8
Chartwell Dr
Cheswick Green B90 .... 126 D5
Sutton Coldfield B74 .... 31 D4
Wolverhampton WV10 .... 11 E1
Chartwell Grange B64 .... 83 A7
Chase Ave WS6 .... 4 E3
Chase Cl CV11 .... 73 E6
Chase Gr B24 .... 57 D6
Chase L Ctr WS11 .... 1 D2
Chase La CV8 .... 147 B7
Chase Park Ind Est WS7 .... 6 D7
Chase Rd Brierley Hill DY5 .... 50 C1
Brownhills WS8 .... 7 A1
Burntwood WS7 .... 7 B6
Walsall WS3 .... 28 A8
Chase Terrace High Sch WS7 .... 7 A7
Chase Terrace HighSch (Annexe) WS7 .... 6 F8
Chase Terrace Prim Sch WS7 .... 6 F8
Chase The
Sutton Coldfield B76 .... 57 D7
Wolverhampton WV6 .... 25 B6
Chase Vale WS7 .... 6 E6
Chase View WV4 .... 39 E2
Chase Wlk WS12 .... 1 C4
Chaselands WS7 .... 6 D7
Chaseley Ave WS11 .... 1 C2
Chaseley Croft WS11 .... 1 C2
Chaseley Gdns WS7 .... 7 C7
Chaseside Dr WS11 .... 2 B3
Chaseside Ind Est WS11 .... 2 B3
Chasetown High Sch WS7 .... 6 E4
Chasetown Ind Est WS7 .... 6 E6
Chasetown Prim Sch WS7 .... 6 E5
Chasewater Light Rlwy WS8 .... 6 C3
Chasewater Raceway WS8 .... 6 E2
Chasewater Way WS11 .... 5 F5
Chasewood Park Bsns Ctr WS12 .... 2 E1
Chater Dr B76 .... 47 A1
Chatham Cl CV3 .... 134 C8
Chatham Rd B31 .... 103 A3
Chatsworth B79 .... 20 C7
Chatsworth Ave B43 .... 43 C1
Chatsworth Cl
Cheswick Green B90 .... 126 E5
Hinckley LE10 .... 75 F6
Sutton Coldfield B72 .... 57 D7
Willenhall WV12 .... 27 B5
Chatsworth Cres WS4 .... 29 D7
Chatsworth Dr Cannock WS11 .... 2 A4
Nuneaton CV11 .... 73 F2
Chatsworth Gdns WV6 .... 24 A7
Chatsworth Gr
Kenilworth CV8 .... 148 C5
Royal Leamington Spa CV31 .... 162 D6
Chatsworth Rd B62 .... 83 A7
Chatsworth Rise CV3 .... 133 E6
Chatsworth Tower 7 B15 .... 86 C8
Chattaway Dr CV7 .... 130 B6
Chattaway St B7 .... 67 C7
Chatterton Wlk 4 DY10 .... 117 B6
Chattle Hill B46 .... 59 E2
Chattock Ave B91 .... 107 E3
Chattock Cl B36 .... 68 E7
Chatwell Gr B29 .... 85 B2
Chatwin Pl WV14 .... 40 E3
Chatwin St B66 .... 64 F7
Chatwins Wharf DY4 .... 51 F5
Chaucer Ave Dudley DY3 .... 50 A5
Tipton DY4 .... 52 B8
Willenhall WV12 .... 27 E8
Chaucer Cl Birmingham B23 .... 56 B3
Dudley WV14 .... 51 D8
Lichfield WS14 .... 9 B6
Stourbridge DY8 .... 81 A8
Tamworth B79 .... 21 A6
Chaucer Cres DY10 .... 117 C5
Chaucer Dr CV10 .... 72 A4
Chaucer Gr B27 .... 88 B2
Chaucer Ho B63 .... 82 B5
Chaucer Rd Bromsgrove B60 .... 151 B8
Walsall WS3 .... 28 E8
Chauntry Pl CV1 .... 165 C3
Chauson Gr B91 .... 127 A8
Chavasse Rd B72 .... 46 D3
Chawn Hill DY9 .... 81 C3
Chawn Park Dr DY9 .... 81 C3
Chawnhill Cl DY9 .... 81 C3
Chaynes Gr B33 .... 69 D2
Cheadle Cl CV2 .... 96 A4
Cheadle Dr B23 .... 56 D8
Cheam Cl CV6 .... 96 A1
Cheam Gdns WV6 .... 24 E8
Cheapside
Birmingham B5, B12 .... 164 D1
3 Willenhall WV13 .... 27 A1
Wolverhampton WV1 .... 163 B3
Cheapside Ind Est 3 B12 .... 66 F1
Cheatham St B7 .... 67 C6
Cheatle Ct B77 .... 35 D5
Checketts St WS2 .... 28 C2
Checkley Croft B76 .... 57 F8
Cheddar Rd B12 .... 86 E6
Chedworth Cl
Birmingham B29 .... 103 B6
Redditch B98 .... 154 C5
Cheedon Cl B93 .... 127 E2
Chelford Cres DY6 .... 61 A3
Chells Gr B13 .... 105 B5
Chelmar Cl B36 .... 69 F8
Chelmar Dr DY5 .... 61 A6
Chelmarsh Ave WV3 .... 38 B8
Chelmarsh Cl B98 .... 154 C7
Chelmorton Rd B42 .... 55 D7
Chelmscote Rd B92 .... 88 F1
Chelmsley Ave B46 .... 70 F6
Chelmsley Circ B37 .... 70 B3
Chelmsley Gr B33 .... 69 E3
Chelmsley La B37 .... 90 A8
Chelmsley Rd B37 .... 70 C2
Chelney Wlk CV3 .... 115 A1
Chelsea Cl Birmingham B32 .... 84 F4
Nuneaton CV11 .... 73 F7
Chelsea Ct B29 .... 103 B7
Chelsea Dr B74 .... 31 F4
Chelsea Trad Est B7 .... 67 A6
Chelsea Way DY6 .... 60 C6
Chelsey Rd CV2 .... 114 E8
Chelston Dr WV6 .... 24 E4
Chelston Rd B31 .... 102 E2
Cheltenham Cl
Bedworth CV12 .... 78 B4
Wolverhampton W6 .... 25 B5
Cheltenham Croft CV2 .... 114 F7
Cheltenham Dr
Birmingham B36 .... 68 D8
Kingswinford DY6 .... 60 B6
Chelthorn Way B91 .... 107 C2
Cheltondale 3 B90 .... 126 C8
Cheltondale Rd B91 .... 106 F6
Chelveston Cres B91 .... 107 B1
Chelveston Rd CV6 .... 112 E5
Chelwood Gdns WV14 .... 40 B5
Chelwood Gr CV2 .... 96 F1
Chelworth Rd B38 .... 104 B2
Chem Rd WV14 .... 40 C5
Chenies Cl CV5 .... 112 B3
Cheniston Rd WV12 .... 27 C7
Chepstow Cl Coventry CV3 .... 134 C5
Perton WV6 .... 23 F4
Chepstow Gr B45 .... 122 B6
Chepstow Rd Walsall WS3 .... 13 F1
Wolverhampton WV10 .... 11 D5
Chepstow Villas 5 B12 .... 87 B5
Chepstow Way WS3 .... 13 F1
Chequer St Bulkington CV12 .... 79 C2
Wolverhampton WV3 .... 39 A6
Chequerfield Dr WV3 .... 39 A6
Chequers Ave WV5 .... 38 A1
Chequers Ct WS11 .... 6 A5
Chequers The 1 WS13 .... 9 C8
Cherhill Covert 7 B14 .... 104 C2
Cherington Cl B98 .... 154 F1
Cherington Rd B29 .... 104 A8
Cheriton Cl CV5 .... 112 D4
Cheriton Gr WV6 .... 23 E3
Cheriton Wlk B23 .... 56 B3
Cherrington Dr WS6 .... 4 F4
Cherrington Gdns
Stourbridge DY9 .... 99 C7
Wolverhampton WV6 .... 24 B2
Cherrington Way B91 .... 107 B1
Cherry Bank WS12 .... 2 C6
Cherry Blossom Gr CV31 .... 162 B2
Cherry Cl Burntwood WS7 .... 6 F6
Coventry CV6 .... 95 D2
Cherry Cres B61 .... 136 E2
Cherry Dr Birmingham B9 .... 67 B1
1 Blackheath B64 .... 62 F1
Cherry Gn DY1 .... 50 F4
Cherry Gr Smethwick B66 .... 65 C5
Stourbridge DY8 .... 80 E4
Wolverhampton WV11 .... 26 C7
Cherry Hill Ave B45 .... 138 C8
Cherry Hill Dr B45 .... 138 C8
Cherry Hill Rd B45 .... 138 C8
Cherry Hill Wlk DY1 .... 62 A8
Cherry La Himley DY3 .... 49 C3
Sutton Coldfield B73 .... 57 A7
Wednesbury WS10 .... 42 A2
Cherry Lea B34 .... 69 B6
Cherry Oak Sch B29 .... 85 D2
Cherry Orch Blackheath B64 .... 62 F1
Kenilworth CV8 .... 148 A5
Kidderminster DY10 .... 116 F6
Lichfield WS14 .... 9 C7
Cherry Orchard Ave B63 .... 82 F5
Cherry Orchard Cres B63 .... 82 F6
Cherry Orchard Dr B61 .... 136 E3
Cherry Orchard Prim Sch B20 .... 55 A3
Cherry Orchard Rd B20 .... 55 A4
Cherry Pit La B98 .... 141 A1
Cherry Rd DY4 .... 51 F7
Cherry St Birmingham B2 .... 164 C2
Halesowen B63 .... 82 F5
Stourbridge DY8 .... 80 E4
Tamworth B79 .... 21 B5
Warwick CV34 .... 160 F7
Wolverhampton WV3 .... 25 B1
Cherry Tree Ave
Nuneaton CV10 .... 72 E6
Walsall WS5 .... 43 A5
Cherry Tree Croft 6 B27 .... 88 C5
Cherry Tree Gdns WV8 .... 10 B3
Cherry Tree La Codsall WV8 .... 10 B3
Halesowen B63 .... 82 D1
Cherry Tree Rd
Huntington WS12 .... 1 D8
Kingswinford DY6 .... 60 E8
Norton Canes WS11 .... 6 B5
Cherry Tree Wlk
Redditch B97 .... 153 B4
Tamworth B79 .... 21 A8
Cherry Way CV8 .... 148 A5
Cherry Wlk B47 .... 125 B5
Cherrybrook Way CV2 .... 96 C1
Cherryl Ho B74 .... 31 E2
Cherrytree Ct DY9 .... 81 E3
Cherrywood Cres 3 B91 .... 127 C8
Cherrywood Ct B92 .... 89 A2
Cherrywood Gn WV14 .... 40 D8
Cherrywood Gr CV5 .... 111 F5
Cherrywood Ind Est B9 .... 67 D3
Cherrywood Rd
Birmingham B9 .... 67 E2
Sutton Coldfield B74 .... 44 D8
Cherrywood Way B74 .... 31 D4
Chervil Cl B42 .... 55 C7
Chervil Rise WV10 .... 25 F3
Cherwell B77 .... 21 D1
Cherwell Cl LE10 .... 75 A8
Cherwell Ct B73 .... 46 B5
Cherwell Dr Birmingham B36 .... 69 F8
Brownhills WS8 .... 6 C2
Cherwell Gdns 7 B6 .... 66 D8
Chesford Cres Coventry CV6 .... 96 B2
Warwick CV34 .... 156 B1
Chesham St CV31 .... 162 B7
Cheshire Ave B90 .... 106 A2
Cheshire Cl DY8 .... 80 D8
Cheshire Gr
Kidderminster DY11 .... 116 A7
Perton WV6 .... 23 E4
Cheshire Ho 8 B66 .... 65 B5
Cheshire Rd Birmingham B6 .... 56 A2
Smethwick B67 .... 65 A4
Walsall WS2 .... 27 F2
Chesholme Rd CV6 .... 95 B2
Cheshunt Ho 3 B37 .... 70 B2
Chesils The CV3 .... 133 D6
Cheslyn Dr WS6 .... 4 D2
Cheslyn Gr B14 .... 105 A3
Cheslyn Hay Cty Prim Sch WS6 .... 4 C3
Cheslyn Hay High Sch WS6 .... 4 C3
Chessetts Gr B13 .... 105 A6
Chessetts Wood Rd B94 .... 144 C7
Chessher St LE10 .... 71 C1
Chester Ave WV6 .... 24 F7
Chester Cl Birmingham B37 .... 70 A2
Cannock WS11 .... 2 B1
Lichfield WS13 .... 3 C3
Willenhall WV13 .... 27 D2
Chester Ct 4 B37 .... 70 D2
Chester Hayes Ct B24 .... 57 C5
Chester Pl WS2 .... 28 B1
Chester Rd Aldridge WS9 .... 30 E4
Birmingham, Castle Bromwich B36 .... 69 E7
Birmingham, Chelmsley Wood B37 .... 90 F8
Blackheath B64 .... 82 C8
Dudley DY2 .... 62 D2
Hampton In A B46, B92, CV7 .... 91 B5
Stonnall WS9 .... 16 D3
Sutton Coldfield B24, B35, B23, B73 .... 57 E4
West Bromwich B71 .... 42 B1
Chester Rd N
Birmingham B73 .... 45 B4
Brownhills WS8 .... 6 D1
Kidderminster DY10 .... 117 A7
Chester Rd S DY10 .... 116 F4
Chester Rise B68 .... 84 B8
Chester Road Sta B73 .... 57 A7
Chester St Birmingham B6 .... 67 A6
Coventry CV1 .... 113 B3
Wolverhampton WV6 .... 25 B4
Chesterfield Cl B31 .... 103 B2
Chesterfield Ct B38 .... 103 E4
Chesterfield Rd WS14 .... 9 A5
Chestergate Croft B24 .... 57 D4
Chesterton Ave B12 .... 87 B5
Chesterton Cl Redditch B97 .... 158 D4
Solihull B91 .... 106 E5
Chesterton Ct B13 .... 86 F1
Chesterton Dr
Nuneaton CV10 .... 72 A5
Royal Leamington Spa CV31 .... 162 C5
Chesterton Rd
Birmingham B12 .... 87 B5
Coventry CV6 .... 113 A7
Wolverhampton WV10 .... 26 A8
Chesterton Way B79 .... 21 A6
Chesterwood Aldridge WS9 .... 30 F2
Hollywood B47 .... 125 A6
Chesterwood Gdns B20 .... 55 D2
Chesterwood Rd B13 .... 104 F6
Chestnut Ave Dudley DY1 .... 51 C3
Kenilworth CV8 .... 147 F3
Tamworth B79 .... 21 B7
Tipton DY4 .... 51 F7
Chestnut Cl Aldridge B74 .... 31 A3
Birmingham B27 .... 88 C4
Cannock WS11 .... 2 C2
Solihull B92 .... 106 D8
Stourbridge DY8 .... 80 C3
Chestnut Cres CV10 .... 72 E5
Chestnut Ct Birmingham B36 .... 69 E7
Coventry CV3 .... 134 B8
Royal Leamington Spa CV34 .... 161 E2
Chestnut Dr
Birmingham, Buckland End B36 .... 69 B7
Birmingham, Erdington B24 .... 57 C4
Birmingham, Rednal B45 .... 122 D4
Cheslyn Hay WS6 .... 4 D3
Great Wyrley WS6 .... 4 F3
Nuneaton CV11 .... 73 E3
Shenstone WS14 .... 17 F5
Walsall WS4 .... 29 B8
Wombourne WV5 .... 49 A5
Chestnut Gr Birmingham B17 .... 85 D5
Coventry CV4 .... 112 A2
Kidderminster DY11 .... 116 B8
Kingswinford DY6 .... 60 F6
Tamworth B77 .... 21 C3
Wolverhampton WV11 .... 26 C7
Chestnut Pl Birmingham B14 .... 104 E8
Walsall WS3 .... 28 D6
Chestnut Rd
Astwood Bank B96 .... 158 E1
Bedworth CV12 .... 78 D4
Birmingham B13 .... 87 A4
Bromsgrove B61 .... 136 F4
Oldbury B68 .... 84 C7
Walsall WS3 .... 28 E6
Wednesbury WS10 .... 42 A2
Chestnut Sq CV32 .... 157 B2
Chestnut Tree Ave CV4 .... 112 A2
Chestnut Way WV3 .... 38 D8
Chestnut Wlk 2 B37 .... 70 B2
Chestnuts Ave B26 .... 89 B7
Chestnuts The
Bedworth CV12 .... 77 E2
Wolverhampton WV11 .... 26 B6
Cheston Rd WV14 .... 40 B5
Cheston Ind Est B7 .... 67 B7
Cheston Rd B7 .... 67 B6
Cheswell Cl WV6 .... 24 B
Cheswick Cl Coventry CV6 .... 114 A
Willenhall WV13 .... 40 F
Cheswick Green Jun & Inf Sch B94 .... 126 E
Cheswick Way B90 .... 126 D
Cheswood Dr B76 .... 58 B
Chesworth Rd B60 .... 137 B
Chetland Croft B92 .... 107 F
Chettle Rd WV14 .... 40 F
Chetton Gn WV10 .... 11 B
Chetwode Cl CV5 .... 112 B
Chetwood Cl WV6 .... 25 A
Chetwynd Cl WS2 .... 27 D
Chetwynd Dr CV11 .... 79 B
Chetwynd Gdns WS11 .... 1 D
Chetwynd Mid Sch CV11 .... 79 A
Chetwynd Rd Birmingham B8 .... 68 B
Wolverhampton WV2 .... 39 B
Cheveley Ave B45 .... 122 B
Chevening Cl DY3 .... 50 E
Cheveral Ave CV6 .... 113 B
Cheveral Rd CV12 .... 78 A
Cheverel Pl CV11 .... 73 B
Cheverel St CV11 .... 73 B
Cheveridge Cl B91 .... 107 A
Cheverton Rd B31 .... 102 E
Cheviot B77 .... 22 C
Cheviot Cl CV10 .... 72 B
Cheviot Ct B75 .... 32 A
Cheviot Rd Stourbridge DY8 .... 81 A
Wolverhampton WV2 .... 39 F
Cheviot Rise Cannock WS12 .... 2 C
Royal Leamington Spa CV32 .... 157 C
Cheviot Way B63 .... 82 D
Cheylesmore CV1 .... 165 B
Cheylesmore Cl B73 .... 46 B
Cheyne Ct B17 .... 85 D
Cheyne Gdns B28 .... 105 E
Cheyne Wlk DY5 .... 81 C7
Cheyney Cl WV6 .... 25 A5
Cheywynd House Prep Sch B74 .... 31 F2
Chichester Ave DY2 .... 62 D5
Chichester Cl CV11 .... 74 A7
Chichester Ct B73 .... 46 B5
Chichester Dr
Birmingham B32 .... 84 A5
Cannock WS12 .... 2 C1
Chichester Gr B37 .... 70 B1
Chideock Hill CV3 .... 133 B6
Chiel Cl CV5 .... 111 F4
Chigwell Cl B35 .... 58 A3
Chilcote Cl B28 .... 105 F4
Chilcote Inf & Jun Sch B28 .... 105 F4
Childs Ave WV14 .... 40 A2
Childs Oak Cl CV7 .... 130 A6
Chilgrove Gdns WV6 .... 24 C5
Chilham Dr B37 .... 70 C2
Chillaton Rd CV6 .... 95 B2
Chillenden Ct WV13 .... 27 C2
Chillingham B77 .... 35 C7
Chillinghome Rd B36 .... 68 D8
Chillinghome Tower 1 B36 .... 57 F1
Chillington Cl WS6 .... 4 F1
Chillington Dr Codsall WV8 .... 10 A4
Dudley DY1 .... 50 F3
Chillington Fields WV1 .... 26 A1
Chillington Ho WV6 .... 24 E5
Chillington Pl WV14 .... 40 C5
Chillington Rd DY4 .... 41 C1
Chillington St WV1 .... 25 F1
Chillington Wlk B65 .... 63 D3
Chillington Works Ind Est WV1 .... 25 F1
Chiltern Cl Dudley DY3 .... 50 D3
Halesowen B63 .... 82 D1
Chiltern Ct 2 Coventry CV6 .... 113 A5
Sutton Coldfield B75 .... 32 A4
Chiltern Dr WV13 .... 26 D1
Chiltern Ho Coventry CV5 .... 111 D4
Redditch B98 .... 154 E1
Chiltern Leys 2 CV6 .... 113 A4
Chiltern Rd Stourbridge DY8 .... 81 B6
Tamworth B77 .... 22 C1
Chilterns The Coventry CV5 .... 112 B4
Oldbury B69 .... 63 E5
Chilton Ct B23 .... 56 C2
Chilton Rd B14 .... 105 D4
Chilvers Coton Craft Ctr CV11 .... 73 C2
Chilvers Coton Fst Sch CV11 .... 73 B3
Chilvers Ct CV11 .... 73 C4
Chilvers Gr B37 .... 69 F5
Chilwell Cl B91 .... 107 B1
Chilwell Croft B19 .... 66 E6
Chilworth Ave WV11 .... 26 F7
Chilworth Cl 4
Birmingham B6 .... 66 F6
Nuneaton CV11 .... 78 E8
Chimes Cl B33 .... 69 E1
Chimney Rd DY4 .... 52 D6
Chines The CV10 .... 73 D7
Chingford Cl DY8 .... 60 C4
Chingford Rd
Birmingham B44 .... 56 A8
Coventry CV6 .... 96 A4
Chinley Gr B44 .... 45 C1
Chinn Brook Rd B13 .... 105 C5
Chip Cl B38 .... 103 D2
Chipperfield Rd B36 .... 68 E8

Chipstead Rd B23 56 E7
Chipstone Cl B91 107 C1
Chirbury Gr B31 103 B1
Chirk Cl DY10 116 E2
Chirton Gr B14 104 D6
Chiseldon Croft B14 105 A3
Chisholm Gr B27 106 C8
Chiswell Rd B18 65 E4
Chiswick Ct 1 B23 56 E2
Chiswick Ho 2 B15 86 C8
Chiswick Wlk B37 70 E2
Chivenor Ho B35 58 A2
Chivenor Prim Sch B35 58 A2
Chivington Cl B90 127 B6
Chorley Ave B34 68 F6
Chorley Gdns WV14 40 B5
Christ Church CE Inf Sch
Wolverhampton,
Dunstall Hill WV6 25 B4
Wolverhampton,
Tettenhall Wood WV6 24 B3
Christ Church CE Jun Sch
WV6 24 C4
Christ Church CE Prim Sch
Dudley WV14 40 D1
Lichfield WS13 8 F7
Oldbury B69 64 A8
Walsall WS3 28 D7
Christ Church Gdns WS13 8 F7
Christ Church Gr WS1 43 A7
Christ Church Jun & Inf
Sch B11 87 B7
Christ the King RC Inf
Sch CV6 112 F6
Christ the King RC Jun
Sch CV6 112 F7
Christ The King RC Prim
Sch B44 56 A8
Christchurch Cl B15 85 E8
Christchurch La WS13 8 F7
Christchurch Rd CV6 113 A5
Christine Cl DY4 41 C2
Christine Ledger Sq
9 CV31 162 A6
Christopher Hooke Ho
CV6 113 E8
Christopher Rd
Birmingham B29 85 C2
Halesowen B62 83 E3
Wolverhampton WV2 163 D1
Christopher Wlk WS13 3 A3
Chub B77 35 D7
Chubb St WV1 163 C3
Chuckery Jun & Inf Schs
WS1 29 A1
Chuckery Rd WS1 29 A1
Chudleigh Gr B43 54 D8
Chudleigh Rd
Birmingham B23 56 E4
Coventry CV2 114 E7
Church Ave
Birmingham,
Handsworth B20 55 C1
Birmingham, Moseley B13 86 F3
Clent DY9 99 F3
Stourbridge DY8 81 A7
Water Orton B46 59 B3
Church Cl Birmingham B37 70 A6
Drayton Bassett B78 34 E5
Hinckley LE10 76 A5
Nuneaton CV10 72 B8
Shenstone WS14 18 A5
Whitnash CV31 162 B4
Wood End CV9 36 C1
Wythall B47 124 F3
Church Cres WV11 12 F3
Church Croft Birmingham
B17 85 B4
Halesowen B63 83 A4
Church Cross View DY1 61 D8
Church Ct
Astwood Bank B96 158 E2
2 Blackheath B64 62 E1
Coventry CV6 94 F1
5 Stourbridge DY8 81 A5
Church Down Cl B97 158 D6
Church Dr Birmingham B30 104 B7
Hopwas B78 20 B7
Kenilworth CV8 147 F5
Church End CV31 162 E6
Church Farm Barn & Cotts
DY10 98 B3
Church Gdns Smethwick B67 65 A4
Wolverhampton WV10 26 A4
Church Gn Bilston WV14 40 D8
Birmingham B20 55 A2
Church Gn E B98 153 E4
Church Gn W B97 153 E4
Church Gr B13 105 C5
Church Hill
Belbroughton DY9 119 D6
Beoley B98 154 D8
Birmingham,
Frankley Green B32 102 B6
Birmingham,
Northfield B31 103 B3
Brierley Hill DY5 61 D2
Cannock WS12 2 D5
Cubbington CV32 157 E5
Royal Leamington Spa
CV32 161 E8
8 Walsall WS1 28 F1
6 Wednesbury WS10 41 F3
Wolverhampton WV4 38 F4
Church Hill Cl B91 107 C2
Church Hill Ct 1 WS10 41 F3
Church Hill Dr WV6 24 E5
Church Hill Mid Sch B98 154 D6
Church Hill Rd
Birmingham B20 55 C1
Solihull B91 107 C3
Wolverhampton WV6 24 D5
Church Hill St B67 64 F6
Church Hill Way B98 154 D6
Church Ho Brierley Hill DY5 61 C2
Walsall WS2 42 C7
Church La Ash Green CV7 95 E7
Aston Flamville LE10 76 F1
Berkswell CV7 110 C3
Bickenhill B92 90 E2
Birmingham, Aston B6 67 A8
Birmingham,
Handsworth B20 55 A2
Birmingham,
Kitt's Green B33 69 A4
Bromsgrove B61 136 F2
Burntwood WS7 7 D3
Corley CV7 94 B7
Coventry, Middle Stoke CV2 114 B3
Coventry,
Upper Eastern Green CV5 111 C5
Cubbington CV32 157 E5
Curdworth B76 59 B6
Halesowen B63 83 B4
Lapworth B94 143 E3
Meriden CV7 110 E8
Middleton B78 34 C1
Nuneaton CV10 73 C7
Royal Leamington Spa
CV32 157 A3
Seisdon WV5 37 B2
Shuttington B79 22 E7
Stoneleigh CV8 149 C6
Stonnall WS9 16 E4
Tamworth B79 21 B5
West Bromwich B71 53 C6
Whitnash CV31 162 B4
Wishaw B76 48 A2
Wolverhampton WV2 163 B2
Church Mews DY4 51 E8
Church Moat Way 1 WS3 28 B8
Church of the Ascension
CE Prim Sch DY6 60 C8
Church Park Cl CV6 94 F1
Church Pl Birmingham B12 86 F5
Walsall WS3 28 D8
Church Rd
Astwood Bank B96 158 E2
Baginton CV8 133 F2
Belbroughton DY9 119 D6
Birmingham, Aston B6 67 B7
Birmingham, Edgbaston B15 86 A7
Birmingham, Erdington B24 57 A4
Birmingham, Moseley B13 87 A3
Birmingham,
Northfield B31 103 A4
Birmingham, Perry Barr B42 55 D5
Birmingham, Sheldon B26 89 C6
Birmingham,
South Yardley B25 88 E8
Birmingham, Stechford B33 68 F2
Blackheath B65 63 C3
Bromsgrove B61 136 F2
Brownhills WS8 15 F7
Burntwood WS7 7 D7
Catshill B61 136 F8
Dodford B61 136 A7
Dudley, Daisy Bank WV14 40 D1
Dudley, Netherton DY2 62 C4
Halesowen B63 82 C7
Huntington WS11 1 A2
Norton Canes WS11 5 E4
Nuneaton, Chapel End CV10 72 B8
Nuneaton, Stockingford CV10 72 C3
Perton WV6 23 E4
Redditch, St George's B97 153 E4
Redditch, Webheath B97 152 F2
Ryton-on-D CV8 135 B2
Shenstone WS14 17 F5
Shilton CV7 97 E5
Smethwick B67 65 A4
Solihull B90 106 B2
Stonnall WS9 16 E3
Stourbridge, Lye DY9 81 E5
Stourbridge,
Old Swinford DY8 81 B3
Stourbridge, Wordsley DY8 60 D2
Sutton Coldfield,
Erdington B73 56 F8
Sutton Coldfield, Maney B73 46 B3
Tamworth B77 35 C4
Walsall WS3 15 A3
Willenhall WV12 27 D6
Wolverhampton, Bradmore
WV3 38 F7
Wolverhampton, Oxley WV10 11 C1
Wolverhampton,
Tettenhall WV6 24 E5
Wolverhampton,
Tettenhall Wood WV6 24 B3
Wombourne WV5 49 B7
Church Row B78 34 B1
Church Sq 4 B69 64 A7
Church St Bilston WV14 40 D5
Birmingham B3 164 B3
Birmingham, Lozells B19 66 C7
Blackheath B64 62 E1
Brierley Hill, Barrow Hill DY5 61 D7
Brierley Hill,
Quarry Bank DY5 61 F1
Brierley Hill, Silver End DY5 61 C2
Bromsgrove B61 136 F2
Bulkington CV12 79 C2
Burntwood WS7 6 E5
Cannock WS11 1 E1
Cannock, Bridgtown WS11 4 D6
Church St continued
Cannock, Chadsmoor WS11 2 A4
Clayhanger WS8 15 E6
Coventry CV1 165 C4
Darlaston WS10 41 D6
Darlaston, Moxley WS10 41 C4
Dudley, Gornalwood DY3 50 D3
Dudley, Kate's Hill DY2 62 C8
Hagley DY9 99 A5
Halesowen B62 63 D1
Hinckley LE10 76 A5
Kidderminster DY10 116 E6
Lichfield WS13 9 C8
Nuneaton CV11 73 D4
Oldbury B69 64 A8
Royal Leamington Spa
CV31 162 A7
Stourbridge DY8 81 A5
Studley B80 159 E3
Tamworth B79 21 B5
Tipton DY4 52 A2
Walsall WS1 28 F1
Walsall,
Blakenall Green WS3 28 B8
Warwick CV34 160 E6
West Bromwich B70 53 C4
Willenhall WV13 27 B2
Wolverhampton WV2 163 B2
Wolverhampton,
Heath Town WV10 26 A4
Wolverhampton,
New Cross WV11 26 C5
Church Terr
Cubbington CV32 157 E5
Royal Leamington Spa
CV31 162 A7
Sutton Coldfield B75 32 C3
Church Vale Birmingham
B20 55 B1
Norton Canes WS11 5 E4
West Bromwich B71 53 D5
Church Vale Mews B71 53 D5
Church View Aldridge WS9 30 B6
Birmingham B11 87 C6
Brownhills WS9 15 F3
Dudley DY3 50 D3
Tamworth B77 35 F7
Church View Cl WS3 28 D8
Church View Dr B64 62 F1
Church Way Bedworth CV12 78 B2
Walsall WS4 15 C2
Church Wlk Allesley CV5 112 C6
Birmingham B8 68 A6
Hinckley LE10 75 D8
Kidderminster DY11 116 C6
2 Royal Leamington Spa
CV31 161 F7
Wolverhampton, Penn WV3 38 F7
Wolverhampton,
Tettenhall WV6 24 E5
Churchacre B23 56 C8
Churchbridge B69 63 F6
Churchdale Cl CV10 72 C4
Churchdale Rd B44 44 D3
Churchdown Ct B23 56 C2
Churchfield Ave DY4 51 F8
Churchfield Cl B7 67 C6
Churchfield Ind Est DY2 62 C8
Churchfield Rd WV10 25 B8
Churchfield St DY2 62 C8
Churchfields Birmingham
B43 44 D4
Bromsgrove B61 136 F3
Kidderminster DY10 116 E7
Churchfields Cl B61 136 F3
Churchfields Gdns B61 136 F3
Churchfields High Sch
B71 53 E6
Churchfields Rd
Bromsgrove B61 136 F3
Wednesbury WS10 42 A4
Churchill Ave Coventry CV6 113 E8
Kenilworth CV8 148 A6
Churchill & Blakedown
Sta DY10 98 C2
Churchill Cl B69 52 C2
Churchill Dr Blackheath B65 63 B2
Stourbridge DY8 81 A7
Churchill Gdns DY3 50 C7
Churchill Ho 3 CV32 161 F8
Churchill La DY10 98 B3
Churchill Par B75 47 A5
Churchill Pl B33 69 B1
Churchill Rd Birmingham B9 67 F3
Catshill B61 121 A1
Halesowen B63 82 F2
Shenstone WS14 18 A5
Sutton Coldfield B75 47 A5
Walsall WS2 27 E3
Churchill Sh Ctr 3 DY2 51 D1
Churchill Wlk 5 DY4 52 A8
Churchover Cl B76 57 D6
Churchside Way WS9 16 B2
Churchstone Cl B61 136 F8
Churchward Cl DY8 81 B6
Churchward Gr WV5 49 A8
Churchwell Ct B63 83 B2
Churchwell Gdns B71 53 E6
Churchyard Rd DY4 52 B5
Churn Hill Rd WS9 30 B4
Churnet Gr WV6 23 F4
Churston Cl WS3 14 A3
Chylds Ct CV5 112 A5
Cider Ave DY5 81 E8
Cinder Bank DY2 62 C6
Cinder Rd Burntwood WS7 6 E7
Dudley DY3 50 B2
Cinder Way WS10 41 E3
Cinquefoil Leasow DY4 52 C6
Circle The Birmingham
B17 85 C6
Nuneaton CV10 72 E4
Circuit Cl WV13 27 B3
Circular Rd B27 88 C2
Circus Ave B37 70 C2
Cirencester Cl B60 137 B2
City Arc Birmingham B2 164 C2
Coventry CV1 165 B2
1 Lichfield WS13 9 B7
City Est B64 82 D8
City Hospl B18 65 F4
City Rd Birmingham B16 65 C2
Tipton B69 63 C8
City Road Prim Sch B16 65 D3
City Tech Coll The B37 70 A4
City Trad Est B16 66 A3
City View B8 67 D4
Civic Cl B1 66 C2
Cladsworth Ho B97 153 A4
Claerwen Gr B31 102 E5
Claines Cres DY10 117 B5
Claines Rd Birmingham
B31 103 C4
Halesowen B63 82 D5
Claire Ct B26 89 C7
Clandon Cl B14 104 C2
Clanfield Ave WV11 26 F7
Clapgate Gdns WV14 40 A3
Clapgate La
Birmingham, Woodgate B32 84 A2
Birmingham,
Woodgate Valley B32 84 C2
Clapham Sq CV31 162 B7
Clapham St CV31 162 B6
Clapham Terr CV31 162 B7
Clapham Terrace Com
Prim Sch CV31 162 B7
Clapton Gr B44 45 B1
Clara St CV2 114 A2
Clarage Ho B62 83 D8
Clare Ave WV11 12 F1
Clare Cl CV32 157 C2
Clare Cres WV14 39 F2
Clare Ct B90 105 D2
Clare Dr B15 85 F8
Clare Rd Walsall WS3 29 A6
Wolverhampton WV10 25 E7
Clare Witnell Cl DY11 116 B8
Clare's Ct DY11 116 C6
Claregate Prim Sch WV6 24 F7
Clarel Ave B8 67 C3
Claremont Cl CV12 79 B4
Claremont Cotts DY3 50 E8
Claremont Ct 1 B64 62 E1
Claremont Mews WV3 39 A7
Claremont Rd
Birmingham, Hockley B18 66 B6
Birmingham, Sparkbrook B11 87 B7
Royal Leamington Spa CV31 161 F6
Sedgley DY3 50 E8
Smethwick B66 65 B4
Tamworth B79 21 A8
Wolverhampton WV3 39 B7
Claremont St Bilston WV14 40 C6
Blackheath B64 62 E1
Claremont Way B63 83 A3
Claremont Wlk CV5 112 C6
Clarence Ave B21 65 C8
Clarence Ct 4 LE10 75 E8
Clarence Gdns B74 31 F2
Clarence Mans 7 CV32 156 F1
Clarence Mews 1 B17 85 D6
Clarence Rd Bilston WV14 40 F7
Birmingham,
Gravelly Hill B23 56 D3
Birmingham,
Handsworth B21 65 C8
Birmingham, Harborne B17 85 D6
Birmingham,
King's Heath B13 87 A1
Birmingham, Sparkhill B11 87 D4
Dudley DY2 62 D6
Hinckley LE10 75 E8
Sutton Coldfield B74 31 F4
Wolverhampton WV1 163 B3
Clarence St
5 Coventry CV1 113 E4
Dudley DY3 50 E5
Kidderminster DY10 116 F6
Nuneaton CV11 73 A4
Royal Leamington Spa
CV31 162 A6
Wolverhampton WV1 163 B3
Clarence Terr 6 CV32 156 F1
Clarenden Pl B17 85 C5
Clarendon Ave CV32 156 F1
Clarendon Cres CV32 156 E1
Clarendon Ho LE10 75 B7
Clarendon Pl Halesowen
B62 84 A6
Royal Leamington Spa CV32 156 E1
Walsall WS3 14 F3
Clarendon Rd
Birmingham B16 65 E1
Hinckley LE10 75 C7
Kenilworth CV8 148 A3
Smethwick B67 64 F4
Sutton Coldfield B75 32 C3
Walsall WS4 15 C2
Wolverhampton WV3 25 A2
Clarendon Sq CV32 156 F1
Clarendon St Coventry CV5 112 F1
Royal Leamington Spa
CV32 157 A1
Walsall WS3 14 B1
Wolverhampton WV3 25 A2
Clarewell Ave B91 127 B8
Clarion Way WS11 1 E5
Clark Rd WV3 24 F2
Clark St Birmingham B16 65 F2
Coventry CV6 96 A1
Stourbridge DY8 80 E4
Clarke Ho 3 WS3 14 B1
Clarke St 1 B97 153 E3
Clarke's Ave CV8 148 A3
Clarke's La B71 53 C7
Clarkes Gr DY4 52 C6
Clarkes La WV13 27 C3
Clarkson Dr CV31 162 A4
Clarkson Rd WS10 42 A3
Clarmont Pl 1 B18 66 A5
Clarry Dr B74 45 F8
Clary Gr WS5 43 A3
Clatterbach La DY9 100 A4
Claughton Rd DY2 51 D1
Claughton St DY11 116 C5
Clausen Cl B43 44 E4
Clavedon Cl B31 102 E7
Claverdon Cl Redditch B97 158 D4
Solihull B91 106 E3
Claverdon Dr
Birmingham B43 54 D7
Little Aston B74 31 B4
Claverdon Gdns B27 88 B5
Claverdon Ho B13 105 A7
Claverdon Rd CV5 112 B3
Claverley Ct 6 DY1 51 B1
Claverley Dr WV4 38 D5
Clay Ave CV11 73 F7
Clay Dr B32 84 A5
Clay La Allesley CV5 93 E3
Birmingham B26 88 E5
Coventry CV2 114 A4
Oldbury B69 64 A4
Clay Pit La WS14 8 F3
Claybrook Dr B98 159 F7
Claybrook Fst Sch B98 154 F1
Claybrook St B5 164 C1
Claycroft Pl DY9 81 E5
Claycroft Terr DY1 51 B6
Claydon Gr 3 B14 105 A3
Claydon Rd DY6 49 C1
Claygate Rd WS12 2 E3
Clayhanger La WS8 15 D7
Clayhanger Rd WS8 15 F6
Claymore B77 35 D7
Claypit Cl B70 53 A3
Claypit La Bournheath B61 120 E1
West Bromwich B70 53 A4
Clayton Cl WV2 39 C7
Clayton Dr Birmingham B36 69 C7
Bromsgrove B60 151 B7
Clayton Ho 3 B16 65 F1
Clayton Rd Birmingham B8 67 D5
Coventry CV6 112 E5
Dudley WV14 51 B7
Clayton Wlk B35 58 A2
Clear View DY6 60 B6
Clearwell Gdns DY1 50 F3
Cleasby B77 22 C1
Cleaver Gdns CV10 73 C6
Clee Ave DY11 116 C2
Clee Hill Dr WV3 24 A1
Clee Hill Rd DY3 50 D4
Clee Rd Birmingham B31 123 A8
Dudley DY2 62 A7
Oldbury B68 64 C4
Stourbridge DY8 81 A6
Clee View Mdw DY3 39 D2
Cleeton St WS12 2 D1
Cleeve B77 21 D3
Cleeve Cl B98 154 D5
Cleeve Dr B74 31 F6
Cleeve Ho B24 57 A2
Cleeve Rd Birmingham B14 105 C4
Walsall WS3 13 F3
Cleeve Way WS3 13 F3
Cleeves Ave CV34 161 D6
Clem Attlee Ct WV13 40 D8
Clematis B77 21 F3
Clematis Dr WV9 10 F3
Clemens St CV31 162 A7
Clement Pl WV14 40 D7
Clement Rd Bilston WV14 40 D7
Halesowen B62 63 D1
Clement St Birmingham B1 66 B3
Nuneaton CV11 73 B3
Walsall WS2 28 D1
Clements Cl B69 63 F4
Clements Rd B25 88 D8
Clements St CV2 114 A3
Clemson St WV13 27 A2
Clennon Rise CV2 114 D8
Clensmore St DY10 116 D7
Clent Ave
Kidderminster DY11 116 B1
Redditch B97 158 D7
Clent Ct 5 DY1 51 B1
Clent Dr Hagley DY9 99 D6
Nuneaton CV10 72 B3
Clent Fst Sch DY9 99 E2
Clent Hill Dr B65 63 A5
Clent Hills Ctry Pk DY9 100 A4
Clent Ho Bromsgrove B60 137 B3
Halesowen B63 83 A2
Clent Rd
Birmingham,
Handsworth B21 54 D1
Birmingham, Rubery B45 121 E8
Oldbury B68 64 C1
Stourbridge DY8 81 A6
Clent View B66 65 B3

Clent View Rd
Birmingham B32 ... 84 A1
Halesowen B63 ... 82 C5
Stourbridge DY8 ... 80 C2
Clent Villas B12 ... 87 B4
Clent Way B32 ... 102 A8
Cleobury La B94 ... 126 A3
Cleton St DY4 ... 52 B3
Cleton Street Bsns Pk DY4 . 52 B3
Clevedon Ave B36 ... 69 E8
Clevedon Rd B12 ... 86 E6
Cleveland Cl Willenhall WV13 ... 26 D1
Wolverhampton WV11 ... 12 F1
Cleveland Ct
15 Birmingham B13 ... 87 B2
1 Royal Leamington Spa CV32 ... 156 F2
Cleveland Dr
Barnt Green B45 ... 122 A2
Cannock WS11 ... 2 B4
Cleveland Pas WV1 ... 163 B2
Cleveland Rd Bulkington CV12 ... 79 B3
Coventry CV2 ... 114 A4
Hinckley LE10 ... 75 C8
Wolverhampton WV2 ... 163 C2
Cleveland St
13 Dudley, New Dock DY1 ... 51 B1
3 Dudley, Old Dock DY2 ... 62 B8
Stourbridge DY8 ... 80 E4
Wolverhampton WV1 ... 163 B2
Cleveley Dr CV10 ... 72 D7
Cleves Cres WS6 ... 4 D1
Cleves Dr B45 ... 121 E7
Cleves Rd B45 ... 121 E8
Clewley Dr WV9 ... 11 B3
Clewley Gr B32 ... 84 B5
Clews Cl WS1 ... 42 E7
Clews Rd B98 ... 158 F7
Clewshaw La B38 ... 124 C4
Cley Cl B5 ... 86 D6
Clifden Gr CV8 ... 148 C6
Cliff Hall La B78 ... 35 C1
Cliff Rock Rd B45 ... 122 B7
Cliffe Ct CV32 ... 156 D1
Cliffe Dr B33 ... 69 C3
Cliffe Rd CV32 ... 156 D1
Cliffe Way CV34 ... 161 A8
Clifford Bridge Prim Sch CV3 ... 115 A3
Clifford Bridge Rd CV3 ... 114 F4
Clifford Cl B77 ... 21 F3
Clifford Rd
Bentley Heath B93 ... 127 F4
Smethwick B67 ... 64 F1
West Bromwich B70 ... 53 B2
Clifford St Birmingham B19 ... 66 D7
Dudley DY2 ... 62 B8
Tamworth B77 ... 21 E3
Wolverhampton WV6 ... 25 A3
Clifford Wlk B19 ... 66 D7
Clift Cl WV12 ... 27 C6
Clifton Ave Aldridge WS9 ... 16 C1
Cannock WS11 ... 4 C7
Clayhanger WS8 ... 15 D7
Tamworth B79 ... 21 A7
Clifton Cl Birmingham B6 ... 66 F7
Oldbury B69 ... 64 A4
Redditch B98 ... 159 E8
Clifton Cres B91 ... 106 F1
Clifton Ct Hinckley LE10 ... 71 B1
5 Royal Leamington Spa CV31 ... 162 B7
Clifton Gdns WV8 ... 10 C3
Clifton Gn B28 ... 106 A5
Clifton Inf Sch B12 ... 87 A5
Clifton Jun Sch B12 ... 87 A5
Clifton La B71 ... 53 E8
Clifton Rd
Birmingham, Aston B6 ... 66 F7
Birmingham, Balsall Heath B12 ... 87 A5
Birmingham, Castle Bromwich B36 ... 69 E8
Halesowen B62 ... 83 E8
Kidderminster DY11 ... 116 A1
Nuneaton CV10 ... 72 F4
Smethwick B67 ... 64 F4
Sutton Coldfield B73 ... 46 B5
Wolverhampton WV6 ... 24 D5
Clifton Road Ind Est B12 ... 86 F5
Clifton St Blackheath B64 ... 62 F1
Coventry CV1 ... 165 D4
Dudley WV14 ... 51 A8
Stourbridge DY8 ... 80 F4
Wolverhampton WV3 ... 25 B2
Clifton Terr B23 ... 56 F4
Clifton Way LE10 ... 71 A1
Clinic Dr Nuneaton CV11 ... 73 C3
Stourbridge DY9 ... 81 E5
Clinton Ave Kenilworth CV8 147 D6
Warwick CV35 ... 160 A7
Clinton Comb Sch CV8 ... 147 E3
Clinton Cres 2 WS7 ... 7 B8
Clinton Gr B90 ... 106 E1
Clinton La CV8 ... 147 D6
Clinton Rd Bilston WV14 ... 41 A7
Coleshill B46 ... 70 F6
Coventry CV6 ... 95 F2
Solihull B90 ... 106 E1
Clinton St Birmingham B18 ... 65 E5
Royal Leamington Spa CV31 162 A7
Clipper View B16 ... 65 E1
Clipston Rd B8 ... 67 F4
Clipstone Rd CV6 ... 112 E6
Clissold Cl B12 ... 86 E7
Clissold Pas B18 ... 66 A4
Clissold St B18 ... 66 A4
Clive Cl B75 ... 32 D2
Clive Rd Balsall Common CV7 ... 130 C5
Birmingham B32 ... 84 D7
Bromsgrove B60 ... 151 B8
Burntwood WS7 ... 7 A7
Redditch B97 ... 153 D5
Clive St B71 ... 53 C5
Cliveden Ave Aldridge WS9 ... 16 B1
Birmingham B42 ... 55 D4
Cliveden Coppice B74 ... 31 F1
Cliveden Wlk CV11 ... 78 E8
Clivedon Way B62 ... 83 B7
Cliveland St B19 ... 164 C4
Clivesway LE10 ... 71 C2
Clock La B92 ... 90 D2
Clockfields Dr DY5 ... 61 A1
Clockmill Ave WS3 ... 14 E3
Clockmill Pl WS3 ... 14 F3
Clockmill Rd WS3 ... 14 E3
Clodeshall Rd B8 ... 67 E4
Cloister Croft CV2 ... 114 F6
Cloister Crofts CV32 ... 156 F3
Cloister Dr B62 ... 83 D3
Cloister Way CV32 ... 156 F3
Cloisters The
Royal Leamington Spa CV32 . 156 F3
Studley B80 ... 159 D4
Clonmel Rd B30 ... 104 A6
Clopton Cres B37 ... 70 C4
Clopton Rd B33 ... 89 C8
Close The
Birmingham, Beech Lanes B17 ... 84 F7
Birmingham, Griffin's Hill B29 ... 103 D8
Brandon CV8 ... 135 F5
Dudley DY3 ... 50 C4
Halesowen B63 ... 82 D6
Hollywood B47 ... 125 A5
Hunnington B62 ... 101 A7
Kenilworth CV8 ... 148 A6
Royal Leamington Spa CV31 162 A5
Solihull B92 ... 106 F8
Wednesbury WS10 ... 41 E3
Closers Bsns Ctr CV11 ... 73 D2
Clothier Gdns WV13 ... 27 A3
Clothier St WV13 ... 27 A3
Clothier Street Prim Sch WV13 ... 27 A3
Cloud Gn CV4 ... 132 D5
Cloudbridge Dr B92 ... 107 F7
Cloudsley Gr B92 ... 88 F3
Clovelly Gdns CV2 ... 114 C5
Clovelly Ho 6 B31 ... 102 C2
Clovelly Rd CV2 ... 114 B5
Clovelly Way CV11 ... 73 E5
Clover Ave B37 ... 70 D2
Clover Ct B38 ... 103 D2
Clover Dr B32 ... 84 D2
Clover Hill WS5 ... 43 E8
Clover La DY6 ... 60 B7
Clover Lea Sq B8 ... 68 A6
Clover Ley WV10 ... 25 F3
Clover Mdws WS12 ... 2 C1
Clover Piece DY4 ... 52 C6
Clover Pk LE10 ... 71 B3
Clover Rd B29 ... 103 A7
Clover Ridge WS6 ... 4 C3
Cloverdale Perton WV6 ... 23 D4
Stoke Prior B60 ... 150 C3
Cloverfield LE10 ... 71 C3
Cloweswood La B94 ... 141 F8
Club Bldgs WV10 ... 11 C6
Club La WV10 ... 11 C6
Club Row DY3 ... 50 E5
Club View B38 ... 103 D2
Clun Cl B69 ... 52 A1
Clun Rd B31 ... 102 F6
Clunbury Croft B34 ... 69 B5
Clunbury Rd B31 ... 123 A8
Clunes Ave CV11 ... 73 E6
Clusters The DY9 ... 81 E5
Clyde Ave B62 ... 83 E8
Clyde Ct B73 ... 46 B5
Clyde Mews DY5 ... 61 B6
Clyde Rd Bulkington CV12 ... 79 A2
Dorridge B93 ... 128 A2
Clyde St Birmingham B12 ... 67 A1
Blackheath B64 ... 62 E1
Clyde Tower 3 B19 ... 66 D7
Clydesdale B26 ... 89 B5
Clydesdale Rd
Birmingham B32 ... 84 B6
Clayhanger WS8 ... 15 E6
Clydesdale Tower B1 ... 164 B1
Co-Operative St CV2 ... 96 B3
Coach House Rise B77 ... 35 F7
Coal Haulage Rd WS11 ... 5 D7
Coal Pool La
Walsall, Coal Pool WS3 ... 28 F5
Walsall, Harden WS3 ... 28 F6
Coalash La B60 ... 151 C2
Coalbourn La DY8 ... 80 F7
Coalbourn Way DY5 ... 61 A3
Coalbourne Gdns B63 ... 82 C5
Coalheath La WS4 ... 29 C8
Coalmeadow Cl WS3 ... 13 F3
Coalpit Fields Rd CV12 ... 78 C1
Coalpool Pl WS3 ... 28 F6
Coalport Rd WV1 ... 26 A1
Coalway Ave Birmingham B26 89 C4
Wolverhampton WV3 ... 39 A6
Coalway Gdns WV3 ... 38 D7
Coalway Rd Walsall WS3 ... 28 A8
Wolverhampton WV3 ... 38 E6
Coat Of Arms Bridge Rd CV3 ... 133 A6
Coates Rd DY10 ... 117 B7
Coatsgate Wlk WV8 ... 10 F1
Cob La B30 ... 103 C6
Cobbett Rd WS7 ... 6 D7
Cobble Wlk B18 ... 66 A5
Cobbles The B72 ... 57 C7
Cobbs Rd CV8 ... 147 D6
Cobbs Wlk B65 ... 62 F5
Cobden Ave CV31 ... 162 C5
Cobden Cl Cannock WS12 ... 2 C7
Darlaston WS10 ... 41 F6
Tipton DY4 ... 51 F8
Cobden Gdns B12 ... 86 E6
Cobden Ho WV2 ... 39 D7
Cobden St Coventry CV6 ... 113 E5
Darlaston WS10 ... 41 F6
Kidderminster DY11 ... 116 D5
Stourbridge DY8 ... 80 E6
Walsall WS1 ... 42 D7
Cobham Bsns Ctr B9 ... 67 D2
Cobham Cl Birmingham B35 .. 57 F3
Bromsgrove B60 ... 150 F7
Cobham Court Mews DY9 ... 99 D6
Cobham Rd Birmingham B9 ... 67 D2
Halesowen B63 ... 83 B4
Kidderminster DY10 ... 116 E4
Stourbridge DY8 ... 81 B2
Wednesbury WS10 ... 42 E2
Cobia B77 ... 35 D7
Cobley Hill B48 ... 138 E4
Cobnall Rd B61 ... 121 A2
Cobs Field B30 ... 103 C6
Coburg Croft DY4 ... 52 C6
Coburg Ho CV5 ... 112 E3
Coburn Dr B75 ... 32 D2
Cochrane Cl Stourbridge DY9 ... 99 C8
Tipton DY4 ... 52 C6
Cochrane Rd DY2 ... 61 F5
Cock Hill La B45 ... 121 F8
Cockermouth Cl CV32 ... 156 D2
Cocksheds La B62 ... 83 C8
Cockshut Hill B26 ... 89 A8
Cockshut Hill Sch B26 ... 89 A8
Cockshutt La B61 ... 136 D7
Cockshutts La WV2 ... 39 D7
Cocksmead Croft B14 ... 104 D5
Cocksmoor Ho B14 ... 104 D7
Cocksparrow La ST19, WS12 ... 1 B5
Cocksparrow St CV34 ... 160 D7
Cockspur St B78 ... 36 E7
Cockthorpe Cl B17 ... 84 F7
Cocton Cl WV6 ... 23 E5
Codsall Cty High Sch WV8 .. 10 A4
Codsall Cty Mid Sch WV8 ... 10 A3
Codsall Rd Blackheath B64 ... 82 E8
Codsall WV8 ... 10 C1
Wolverhampton WV6 ... 24 D7
Cofield Rd B73 ... 45 F1
Cofton Church La B45 ... 122 D3
Cofton Ct B45 ... 122 D7
Cofton Gr B31 ... 122 E6
Cofton Jun & Inf Sch B31 123 A6
Cofton Lake Rd B45 ... 122 C3
Cofton Rd B31 ... 123 B7
Cokeland Pl B64 ... 82 D8
Colaton Cl WV10 ... 25 E4
Colbourne Ct B33 ... 68 D3
Colbourne Grove Dr CV32 ... 156 D2
Colbourne Rd Tamworth B78 ... 21 A2
Tipton DY4 ... 52 A4
Colbrand Gr B15 ... 86 D8
Colbrook B77 ... 21 D1
Coldbath Rd B13 ... 105 B8
Coldfield Dr B98 ... 158 E7
Coldridge Cl WV8 ... 10 F1
Coldstream Cl LE10 ... 71 A1
Coldstream Dr DY8 ... 60 E3
Coldstream Rd B76 ... 57 E8
Coldstream Way B42, B6 ... 55 F3
Cole Bank Rd B28 ... 105 E8
Cole Ct B37 ... 70 B2
Cole Gn B90 ... 105 F2
Cole Hall La B34 ... 69 A5
Cole St DY2 ... 62 E4
Cole Valley Rd B28 ... 105 D6
Colebourne Jun & Inf Sch B33 ... 68 E5
Colebourne Rd B13 ... 105 D6
Colebridge Cres B46 ... 70 F8
Colebrook Cl CV3 ... 114 F2
Colebrook Croft B90 ... 105 F2
Colebrook Rd
Birmingham B11 ... 87 D5
Solihull B90 ... 105 F2
Coleby Cl CV4 ... 131 D7
Coleford Cl Redditch B97 ... 153 A2
Stourbridge DY8 ... 60 C2
Coleford Dr B37 ... 70 A2
Colehill B79 ... 21 B5
Colehurst Croft B90 ... 126 F6
Coleman Rd WS10 ... 42 A5
Coleman St Coventry CV4 ... 111 F3
Wolverhampton WV6 ... 24 F4
Colemeadow Rd
Birmingham B13 ... 105 B6
Coleshill B46 ... 70 F7
Redditch B98 ... 154 F6
Colenso Rd B16 ... 65 D4
Coleraine Rd B42 ... 55 A6
Coleridge Cl Redditch B97 .. 158 C8
Tamworth B79 ... 21 A6
Walsall WS3 ... 15 A5
Willenhall WV12 ... 27 E7
Coleridge Dr WV6 ... 23 E4
Coleridge Pas B4 ... 164 C3
Coleridge Rd
Birmingham B43 ... 54 E7
Coventry CV2 ... 114 C3
Coleridge Rise DY3 ... 50 A4
Coles Cres B71 ... 53 B7
Coles La Sutton Coldfield B72 . 46 C3
West Bromwich B71 ... 53 B7
Colesbourne Ave B14 ... 104 C2
Colesbourne Rd B92 ... 89 B3
Colesden Wlk WV4 ... 38 C6
Coleshill CE Prim Sch B46 . 70 F6
Coleshill Cl B97 ... 158 C5
Coleshill Heath Rd
Birmingham B37 ... 90 C7
Coleshill B37, B46 ... 70 E2
Coleshill Heath Sch B37 ... 70 C1
Coleshill Ind Est B46 ... 59 F2
Coleshill Rd
Birmingham, Hodgehill B36 ... 68 E6
Birmingham, Marston Green B37 ... 90 B8
Curdworth B76 ... 59 C5
Fazeley B78 ... 35 A7
Nuneaton CV10 ... 72 A7
Sutton Coldfield B75 ... 46 D5
Water Orton B46 ... 59 B2
Coleshill St Birmingham B5 ... 164 D3
Fazeley B78 ... 35 A8
Sutton Coldfield B72 ... 46 C5
Coleside Ave B13 ... 105 D7
Coleview Cres B33 ... 69 E3
Coleville Rd B76 ... 58 B6
Coley Cl LE10 ... 75 D7
Coleys La B31 ... 103 A2
Colgreave Ave B13 ... 87 D2
Colina Cl CV3 ... 134 C5
Colindale Rd B44 ... 45 A3
Colinwood Cl WS6 ... 4 F1
Coll of the Ascension B29 .. 85 C1
Colledge Rd CV6 ... 95 D1
Colleen Ave B30 ... 104 B3
College Cl WS10 ... 42 A1
College Ct WV6 ... 24 D4
College Dr Birmingham B20 ... 54 F2
Royal Leamington Spa CV32 . 156 F2
College Farm Dr B73 ... 45 D1
College Hill B73 ... 46 B4
College La
Balsall Common CV8 ... 129 E1
Hinckley LE10 ... 71 E1
Tamworth B79 ... 21 B5
College Rd
Birmingham, Alum Rock B8 ... 67 E4
Birmingham, Handsworth B20 ... 54 E2
Birmingham, Moseley B13 ... 87 C2
Birmingham, Perry Common B44 ... 56 B7
Birmingham, Quinton B32 ... 84 A6
Bromsgrove B60 ... 137 A2
Kidderminster DY10 ... 116 E4
Stourbridge DY8 ... 81 A4
Wolverhampton WV6 ... 24 D4
College St Birmingham B18 ... 66 A4
Nuneaton CV10 ... 73 C1
College View WV6 ... 24 D3
College Wlk B60 ... 137 A2
Collet Rd WV6 ... 23 E5
Collets Brook B75 ... 33 A2
Collett B77 ... 22 A1
Collett Cl DY8 ... 81 A6
Collett Wlk 2 CV1 ... 113 B3
Colletts Gr B37 ... 69 F4
Colley Ave WV10 ... 25 F7
Colley Gate B63 ... 82 C6
Colley La B63 ... 82 C6
Colley Lane Prim Sch B63 .. 82 C6
Colley Orch B63 ... 82 C6
Colley St B70 ... 53 D4
Collier Cl Cheslyn Hay WS6 ... 4 D2
Walsall WS8 ... 15 C7
Colliers Cl WV12 ... 27 B6
Colliers Fold DY5 ... 61 B5
Colliery Dr WS3 ... 13 F3
Colliery La CV7 ... 78 B1
Colliery La N CV7 ... 78 B1
Colliery Rd Smethwick B71 ... 65 A8
West Bromwich B71 ... 54 A1
Wolverhampton WV1 ... 25 F2
Collindale Ct DY6 ... 49 D1
Colling Wlk B37 ... 70 A5
Collingbourne Ave B36 ... 68 E8
Collingdon Ave B26 ... 89 C6
Collings Ho B16 ... 66 A1
Collingwood Dr B43 ... 44 D3
Collingwood Ho B43 ... 44 D3
Collingwood Jun & Inf Sch WV10 ... 11 E2
Collingwood Rd
Coventry CV5 ... 113 A2
Wolverhampton WV10 ... 11 E2
Collins Cl B32 ... 84 A5
Collins Gr CV4 ... 132 D5
Collins Hill WS13 ... 3 A2
Collins Rd Brownhills WS8 ... 16 A5
Royal Leamington Spa CV34 161 D5
Wednesbury WS10 ... 42 C3
Collins St Walsall WS1 ... 42 E7
West Bromwich B70 ... 52 E3
Collinson Cl B98 ... 154 A1
Collis Cl B60 ... 150 E7
Collis St DY8 ... 80 F8
Collister Cl B90 ... 106 B4
Collumbine Cl WS5 ... 42 F3
Colly Croft B37 ... 69 F5
Collycroft Pl B27 ... 88 B5
Colman Ave WV11 ... 26 F6
Colman Cres B68 ... 64 C2
Colman Hill B63 ... 82 D5
Colman Hill Ave B63 ... 82 D6
Colmers Farm Inf Sch B45 122 B8
Colmers Farm Jun Sch B45 ... 122 B8
Colmers Farm L Ctr B45 ... 122 B8
Colmers Farm Sch B45 ... 122 B8
Colmers Wlk B31 ... 102 D1
Colmore Ave B14 ... 104 D7
Colmore Circus Queensway B4 ... 164 C3
Colmore Cres B13 ... 87 B1
Colmore Dr B75 ... 47 A5
Colmore Flats B19 ... 164 B4
Colmore Gate B2 ... 164 C3
Colmore Inf Sch B14 ... 104 D7
Colmore Jun Sch B14 ... 104 D7
Colmore Rd B14 ... 104 D7
Colmore Row B3 ... 164 B3
Coln Cl B31 ... 102 F6
Colonial Rd B9 ... 67 F2
Colshaw Rd DY8 ... 80 E4
Colston Rd B24 ... 57 B2
Colt Cl B74 ... 44 E7
Coltham Rd WV12 ... 27 D7
Coltishall Croft B35 ... 57 F2
Coltman Cl WS14 ... 9 D7
Colton Hills Upper Sch WV4 ... 39 B4
Colts Cl LE10 ... 75 D4
Colts La B98 ... 154 D3
Coltsfoot Cl WV11 ... 26 E5
Coltsfoot View WS6 ... 4 E1
Columbia Gdns CV12 ... 78 E2
Columbian Cres WS7 ... 6 F8
Columbian Dr WS11 ... 1 F3
Columbian Way WS11 ... 1 F3
Colville Cl DY4 ... 52 D8
Colville Rd B12 ... 87 B5
Colville Wlk B12 ... 87 B5
Colwall Rd DY3 ... 50 D4
Colwall Wlk B27 ... 88 D4
Colworth Rd B31 ... 102 F4
Colyere Cl CV7 ... 95 A6
Colyns Gr B33 ... 68 F5
Combe Fields Rd CV3 ... 115 F4
Comber Croft B13 ... 105 D8
Comber Dr DY5 ... 61 B6
Comberford Ct 5 WS10 ... 42 A3
Comberford Dr WS10 ... 42 D4
Comberford Rd B79 ... 21 A7
Comberton Ave DY10 ... 117 B5
Comberton Ct 5 DY10 ... 117 A5
Comberton Fst Sch DY10 .. 117 B4
Comberton Hill DY10 ... 116 F5
Comberton Mans 4 DY10 117 A5
Comberton Mid Sch DY10 . 117 B4
Comberton Park Rd DY10 . 117 B4
Comberton Pl DY10 ... 116 F5
Comberton Rd
Birmingham B26 ... 89 B8
Kidderminster DY10 ... 117 B4
Comberton Terr DY10 ... 116 F5
Comet Ho B35 ... 58 B3
Commainge Cl CV34 ... 160 D7
Commercial Rd Walsall WS2 ... 28 A7
Wolverhampton WV1 ... 25 E1
Commercial St B1 ... 164 A1
Commissary Rd B26 ... 90 A3
Common La
Birmingham, Sheldon B26 ... 89 B6
Birmingham, Washwood Heath B8 ... 67 F6
Cannock WS11 ... 2 A3
Corley CV7 ... 93 E7
Kenilworth CV8 ... 148 B7
Tamworth B79 ... 21 B4
Common Rd WV5 ... 49 A6
Common Side WS8 ... 16 A6
Common View WS12 ... 2 B7
Common Way CV2 ... 114 A6
Common Wlk WS12 ... 1 C5
Commonfield Croft B8 ... 67 D5
Commonside
Brierley Hill DY5 ... 61 C6
Walsall WS3 ... 15 A2
Communication Row B15 ... 66 C1
Compass Ct 4 CV1 ... 113 B3
Compton Cl Redditch B98 ... 153 E2
Royal Leamington Spa CV32 157 C2
Solihull B91 ... 106 D4
Compton Croft B37 ... 70 D1
Compton Ct Dudley DY2 ... 62 C6
Sutton Coldfield B74 ... 31 E3
7 Wolverhampton WV3 ... 25 A2
Compton Dr Dudley DY2 ... 62 F8
Kingswinford DY6 ... 60 D5
Sutton Coldfield B74 ... 44 E7
Compton Gr Halesowen B63 . 82 C4
Kingswinford DY6 ... 60 D5
Compton Grange B64 ... 82 C8
Compton Hill Dr WV3 ... 24 D2
Compton Ho B33 ... 69 B2
Compton Rd Birmingham B24 56 E1
Blackheath B64 ... 62 C1
Coventry CV6 ... 95 D2
Halesowen B62 ... 83 F5
Stourbridge DY9 ... 81 D2
Tamworth B79 ... 20 F7
Wolverhampton WV3 ... 24 F2

Compton Rd W WV3 .... 24 D2
Comrie Cl CV2 .... 114 F6
Comsey Rd B43 .... 44 B3
Comwall Cl WS3 .... 28 C6
Comyn St CV32 .... 157 B1
Conchar Rd B72 .... 46 C2
Conchar St B72 .... 46 C2
Concorde Tower B35 .... 57 F2
Condor Gr CV11 .... 2 C1
Condover Cl WS2 .... 27 D3
Condover Rd B31 .... 123 B8
Conduit Cl WS11 .... 6 A4
Conduit St WS13 .... 9 B8
Coney Gn DY8 .... 81 B5
Coney Green Dr B31 .... 122 F8
Coneybury Wlk B76 .... 58 D5
Coneyford Rd B34 .... 69 C6
Coneygre Ind Est DY4 ...... 51 F2
Coneygree Rd DY4 .... 52 A3
Congleton Cl Coventry CV6 .. 95 E2
Redditch B97 .... 153 B5
Congrave Wlk CV12 .... 78 B2
Congreve Cl CV34 .... 155 F2
Conifer Cl Bedworth CV12 ..... 78 C4
Brierley Hill DY5 .... 81 C8
Cannock WS12 .... 2 A8
Conifer Ct B13 .... 86 E2
Conifer Dr
Birmingham,
Handsworth B21 .... 65 E7
Birmingham, Northfield B31 . 103 B3
Conifer Gr Bromsgrove B61 ... 136 F3
Royal Leamington Spa CV31 . 161 F5
Conifer Paddock
Coventry CV3 .... 114 E1
Halesowen B62 .... 83 E8
Conifer Rd B74 .... 44 E8
Coningsby Cl **8** CV31 ...... 162 C6
Coningsby Dr DY11 .... 116 A8
Conington Gr B17 .... 85 A5
Coniston B77 .... 36 B7
Coniston Ave B92 .... 88 F4
Coniston Cl Birmingham
B28 .... 105 F7
Bromsgrove B60 .... 137 B1
Bulkington CV12 .... 79 C3
Coniston Cres B43 .... 54 F7
Coniston Ct Nuneaton CV11 .. 73 F7
2 Royal Leamington Spa
CV32 .... 156 D1
Coniston Dr Coventry CV5 .. 111 D4
Kingswinford DY6 .... 60 B7
Coniston Grange CV8 ...... 147 F5
Coniston Ho Birmingham
B17 .... 85 D5
Kidderminster DY10 .... 116 F7
7 Oldbury B69 .... 63 D5
Coniston Rd Aldridge B74 ... 30 F3
Birmingham B23 .... 56 D4
Coventry CV5 .... 112 F1
Royal Leamington Spa CV32 156 D1
Wolverhampton WV6 .... 24 D8
Coniston Way
1 Cannock WS11 .... 1 E1
Nuneaton CV11 .... 73 F7
Connaught Ave
Kidderminster DY11 .... 116 C4
Wednesbury WS10 .... 42 C3
Connaught Cl WS5 .... 43 C7
Connaught Dr WV5 .... 38 A1
Connaught Gdns B5 .... 86 E6
Connaught Ho **1** WV3 .... 25 A2
Connaught Rd Bilston WV14 . 40 F1
Wolverhampton WV1 .... 25 A2
Connops Way DY9 .... 81 E5
Connor Rd B71 .... 53 E8
Conolly Dr B45 .... 102 B1
Conrad Cl B11 .... 87 A7
Conrad Rd CV6 .... 113 A7
Consort Cres DY5 .... 61 C6
Consort Dr WS10 .... 41 C8
Consort Rd B30 .... 104 A3
Constable Cl Bedworth
CV12 .... 78 A5
Birmingham B43 .... 44 D3
Constables The B68 .... 64 B2
Constance Ave B70 .... 53 D1
Constance Cl CV12 .... 95 F8
Constance Rd B5 .... 86 D5
Constantine La B46 .... 59 F1
Constitution Hill
Birmingham B19 .... 164 B4
Dudley DY2 .... 62 D8
Convent Cl Cannock WS11 .. 4 D8
Kenilworth CV8 .... 148 A7
Conway Ave Birmingham
B32 .... 84 B6
Coventry CV4 .... 131 D8
Oldbury B68 .... 64 B2
West Bromwich B71 .... 42 B1
Conway Cl Dudley DY1 ...... 51 C6
Kingswinford DY6 .... 60 F4
Solihull B90 .... 106 D1
Conway Cres WV12 .... 27 C7
Conway Dr B66 .... 64 D7
Conway Gr B43 .... 54 D7
Conway Ho Birmingham
B32 .... 102 D6
Walsall WS3 .... 28 D6
Conway Jun & Inf Sch B11 . 87 C6
Conway Rd
Birmingham, Fordbridge B37 . 70 B3
Birmingham, Sparkbrook B11 . 87 C6
Bromsgrove B60 .... 136 F1
Cannock WS11 .... 4 B8
Perton WV6 .... 23 F3
Royal Leamington Spa CV32 161 D8
Solihull B90 .... 106 D1

Conwy Cl Nuneaton CV11 ... 73 D3
Walsall WS2 .... 28 A4
Conybere St B12 .... 86 F7
Conyworth Cl B27 .... 88 D4
Cook Ave DY2 .... 62 D7
Cook Cl Knowle B93 .... 128 C6
Perton WV6 .... 23 E4
Cook Rd WS3 .... 14 D2
Cook St Birmingham B7 ..... 67 C7
Coventry CV1 .... 165 C3
Darlaston WS10 .... 41 F6
Cooke Cl CV34 .... 155 F2
Cooke St WV2 .... 163 B1
Cookes Croft B31 .... 103 B2
Cookesley Cl B43 .... 44 D4
Cookley Cl B63 .... 82 F2
Cookley Way B69 .... 63 E5
Cookley Wharf Ind Est
DY5 .... 61 B4
Cooknell Dr DY8 .... 60 E2
Cooks Cl B37 .... 70 A4
Cooksey La B44 .... 44 F4
Cooksey Rd Birmingham
B10 .... 87 B8
Birmingham B10 .... 87 C8
Birmingham,
Small Heath B10 .... 87 D7
Coombe Abbey Ctry Pk
CV3 .... 115 E4
Coombe Ave CV3 .... 134 F7
Coombe Croft WV9 .... 11 A3
Coombe Ct CV3 .... 115 A2
Coombe Dr CV3 .... 135 E7
Coombe Hill B64 .... 83 B8
Coombe Park Rd CV3 ..... 114 F2
Coombe Pk B74 .... 45 F7
Coombe Rd Birmingham
B20 .... 55 E1
Solihull B90 .... 106 C2
Coombes La B31 .... 122 F7
Coombes Rd B62 .... 83 B7
Coombs Rd B62 .... 83 B7
Cooper Ave B5 .... 61 A2
Cooper Cl Bromsgrove
B60 .... 150 E6
West Bromwich B70 .... 53 E2
Cooper & Jordan CE
Jun & Inf Schs WS9 .... 30 C6
Cooper St Nuneaton CV11 .. 73 D4
West Bromwich B70 .... 53 D3
Wolverhampton WV2 .... 39 F8
Cooper's Bank Rd DY5 ..... 50 C1
Coopr's La B67 .... 65 A5
Coopers Hill B48 .... 138 E6
Coopers Rd B20 .... 55 A4
Cope Arnolds Cl CV6 .... 95 F4
Cope St Birmingham B18 ... 66 A3
Coventry CV1 .... 165 C3
Darlaston WS10 .... 41 E6
Walsall WS3 .... 28 C6
Cope's Dr B79 .... 21 B7
Copeley Hill B23 .... 56 D1
Copes Cres WV10 .... 26 A7
Cophall St DY4 .... 52 D5
Cophams Cl B92 .... 89 C2
Copland Pl CV4 .... 111 E1
Coplow Cl CV7 .... 130 A6
Coplow Cotts B16 .... 65 E3
Coplow St B16 .... 65 F3
Coplow Terr B16 .... 65 F3
Copnor Gr B26 .... 88 E6
Coppenhall Gr B33 .... 69 A3
Copper Beech Cl CV6 ...... 95 E1
Copper Beech Dr
Kingswinford DY6 .... 49 D1
Wombourne WV5 .... 49 B6
Copper Beech Gdns B20 ... 55 A2
Copperas St **2** B12 ...... 87 A5
Copperbeach Dr **2** B12 . 87 A5
Copperbeech Cl B32 .... 84 F5
Copperfield Rd CV2 .... 114 B3
Copperfields WS14 .... 9 D7
Copperkins Rd WS12 .... 2 E4
Coppermill Cl WS12 .... 1 F7
Coppice Ash Croft B19 .... 66 D8
Coppice Ave DY9 .... 81 F3
Coppice Cl Birmingham
B45 .... 121 F7
Brierley Hill DY5 .... 61 F1
Burntwood WS7 .... 7 D2
Cheswick Green B90 .... 126 C4
Hinckley LE10 .... 71 F3
Redditch B97 .... 153 C3
Sedgley DY3 .... 50 C7
Solihull B92 .... 107 A7
Wolverhampton WV11 .... 13 A1
Coppice Com High Sch
WV11 .... 27 A8
Coppice Cres WS8 .... 15 D7
Coppice Ct WS11 .... 4 B7
Coppice Dr Birmingham
B27 .... 88 B2
Dordon B78 .... 36 F7
Coppice Farm Way WV12 .. 27 B8
Coppice Gr WS14 .... 9 F7
Coppice Ho
Birmingham,
Acock's Green B27 .... 88 A2
Birmingham,
Handsworth B66 .... 65 D6
Willenhall WV12 .... 27 C6
Coppice Hollow B32 .... 84 A1
Coppice Hts DY11 .... 116 B1
Coppice Inf & Jun Schs
B75 .... 32 B1
Coppice Jun Sch B92 .... 107 E7

Coppice La Aldridge WS9 .. 15 F1
Brierley Hill DY5 .... 62 A1
Brownhills WS8 .... 15 D8
Burntwood WS7 .... 8 A3
Cheslyn Hay WS6 .... 4 D4
Middleton B78 .... 33 D2
Willenhall WV12 .... 27 C6
Wolverhampton WV6 .... 24 C7
Coppice Oaks B13 .... 87 A3
Coppice Prim Sch The B47 125 A6
Coppice Rd Birmingham B13 . 87 A3
Blackheath B64 .... 82 E7
Brownhills WS9 .... 15 F4
Dudley WV14 .... 51 A8
Solihull B92 .... 107 E7
Whitnash CV31 .... 162 B2
Wolverhampton WV3 .... 38 D8
Coppice Rise DY5 .... 62 A2
Coppice Side WS8 .... 15 C8
Coppice Side Ind Est WS8 . 15 C7
Coppice St Dudley DY1 ..... 51 D4
Tipton DY4 .... 51 E5
West Bromwich B70 .... 53 A4
Coppice The Birmingham
B20 .... 55 A2
Cannock WS12 .... 2 E1
Coventry CV3 .... 134 B8
Hinckley LE10 .... 75 F8
Nuneaton CV10 .... 73 C7
Tipton DY4 .... 41 C1
Willenhall WV12 .... 27 C6
Coppice View Rd B73 ...... 45 A4
Coppice Way **7** B37 ...... 70 B2
Coppice Wlk
Cheswick Green B90 .... 126 C4
Hinckley LE10 .... 71 F3
Copplestone Cl B34 .... 69 B6
Copps Rd CV32 .... 161 D8
Coppy Hall Gr WS9 .... 16 B1
Coppy Nook La WS7 .... 7 C5
Copse Cl Allesley CV5 ...... 111 B8
Birmingham B31 .... 103 A2
Copse Cres WS3 .... 15 A4
Copse Rd DY2 .... 62 B3
Copse The Bedworth CV7 ... 96 A8
Sutton Coldfield B74 .... 31 F1
Copsehill Ct B75 .... 46 C4
Copsewood Ave CV11 .... 79 B7
Copsewood Terr CV3 ...... 114 C2
Copston Gr B29 .... 103 B8
Copstone Dr B93 .... 127 F3
Copt Heath Croft B93 .... 128 B8
Copt Heath Dr B93 .... 128 A7
Copt Oak Cl CV4 .... 131 C6
Copthall Rd B21 .... 54 C2
Copthorne Ave WS7 .... 6 F4
Copthorne Rd
Birmingham B44 .... 44 E3
Coventry CV6 .... 112 F3
Wolverhampton WV3 .... 39 A7
Copyholt La Stoke Prior
B60 .... 151 D3
Upper Bentley B60, B97 ... 152 A3
Coral Cl Coventry CV5 .... 112 C2
Hinckley LE10 .... 75 F4
Coralin Cl B37 .... 70 C2
Corbett Cl B60 .... 151 B8
Corbett Cres DY8 .... 81 A7
Corbett Dr B60 .... 150 C1
Corbett Ho **8** DY8 .... 80 F8
Corbett Hospl DY8 .... 81 A7
Corbett Ind Est DY2 .... 62 C6
Corbett Inf Sch B66 .... 65 B5
Corbett Rd Brierley Hill
DY5 .... 61 E1
Hollywood B47 .... 125 A7
Kidderminster DY11 .... 116 A8
Corbett St B66 .... 65 B4
Corbetts Cl B92 .... 109 B7
Corbin Way B78 .... 36 F6
Corbison Cl CV34 .... 155 D1
Corbizum Ave B80 .... 159 D4
Corbridge Ave B44 .... 44 F1
Corbridge Rd B73 .... 45 F2
Corbyn Rd Birmingham B9 . 68 B3
Dudley DY1 .... 61 F8
Corbyns Cl DY5 .... 61 B7
Corbyns Hall La DY5 .... 61 B7
Corbyns Hall Rd DY5 .... 61 B7
Cordelia Gn CV34 .... 161 E4
Cordley St B70 .... 53 B4
Corfe Cl Birmingham B32 ... 84 F5
Coventry CV2 .... 114 F5
Perton WV6 .... 23 F3
Corfe Dr B69 .... 63 A8
Corfe Rd WV14 .... 51 A8
Corfton Dr WV6 .... 24 C3
Coriander Cl
Birmingham B45 .... 102 B2
Stoke Prior B60 .... 150 C1
Corinne Cl B45 .... 122 A6
Corinne Croft B37 .... 70 A4
Corinthian Pl CV2 .... 114 D6
Corisande Rd B29 .... 85 C2
Corley Ave B31 .... 103 B3
Corley Cl B90 .... 105 E1
Corley Sch CV7 .... 94 B6
Corley View CV7 .... 95 C6
Corn Exchange WS13 .... 9 B8
Corn Hill Walsall WS5 ...... 43 E8
Wolverhampton WV10 ..... 163 D3
Corn Mill Cl B32 .... 84 E1
Cornbow Ctr B63 .... 83 B3
Cornbrook Rd B29 .... 102 F7
Cornbury Gr B91 .... 106 D4
Corncrake Cl B72 .... 46 D2
Corncrake Dr B36 .... 70 A7
Corncrake Rd DY3 .... 50 E2

Corndon Cl DY11 .... 116 B2
Cornel B77 .... 21 F4
Cornel Cl B37 .... 90 C8
Corner Ho B66 .... 65 D6
Cornerstone Ho CV1 ...... 165 C1
Cornerway B38 .... 123 F7
Cornelius St CV3 .... 133 D8
Cornet's End La CV7 ...... 110 B6
Cornets End La CV7 .... 109 E7
Cornfield Hinckley LE10 .... 71 C4
Wolverhampton WV8 .... 10 F2
Cornfield Ave B60 .... 150 D6
Cornfield Cl DY6 .... 60 A8
Cornfield Croft B37 .... 70 D3
Cornfield Dr WS14 .... 9 E7
Cornfield Pl B65 .... 62 F4
Cornfield Rd
Birmingham B31 .... 103 B4
Blackheath B65 .... 62 F4
Cornfield The CV3 .... 114 C1
Cornflower Cl WV10 .... 12 A7
Cornflower Cres DY2 .... 62 F8
Cornflower Rd WS5 .... 15 D6
Corngreaves Prim Sch
B64 .... 62 D1
Corngreaves Rd B64 .... 82 E7
Corngreaves The B34 ...... 69 C6
Corngreaves Trad Est B64 . 82 D7
Corngreaves Wlk B64 ...... 82 E7
Cornhampton Cl B97 ...... 153 B5
Cornhill WS11 .... 1 E5
Cornhill Gr Birmingham
B30 .... 104 C7
Kenilworth CV8 .... 148 C5
Cornish Cres CV10 .... 73 A2
Cornmill Cl WS1 .... 42 D7
Cornmill Gr WV6 .... 23 D3
Cornovian Cl WV6 .... 23 E5
Corns Ho WS10 .... 41 E6
Cornwall Ave Oldbury B68 . 84 B8
Tamworth B78 .... 21 A1
Cornwall Cl Aldridge WS9 .. 16 A1
Kingswinford DY6 .... 60 D8
3 Warwick CV34 .... 160 F8
Wednesbury WS10 .... 42 D3
Cornwall Gate WV12 .... 27 B5
Cornwall Ind Est
Birmingham B8 .... 67 C4
Smethwick B66 .... 65 C7
Cornwall Pl
Royal Leamington Spa
CV32 .... 156 D1
Walsall WS2 .... 27 E3
Cornwall Rd
Birmingham,
Handsworth B20 .... 54 F7
Birmingham, Rubery B45 .. 101 C1
Cannock WS12 .... 2 A5
Coventry CV1 .... 113 C1
Smethwick B66 .... 65 C7
Stourbridge DY8 .... 80 D8
Walsall WS5 .... 43 B7
Wolverhampton WV6 .... 24 C4
Cornwall St B3 .... 164 B3
Cornwall Tower B18 .... 66 B5
Cornwall Way LE10 .... 71 C4
Cornwallis Rd B70 .... 53 A1
Cornwell Cl Redditch B98 . 159 B5
Tipton DY4 .... 52 A5
Cornyx La DY9 .... 107 D6
Coronation Ave Mile Oak
B78 .... 20 D1
Willenhall WV13 .... 27 D2
Coronation Cres B79 .... 22 F7
Coronation Ct CV11 .... 73 B4
Coronation Ho **3** DY4 .... 51 E5
Coronation Rd Bilston
WV14 .... 40 C6
Birmingham,
Great Barr B43 .... 43 E4
Birmingham, Selly Oak B29 . 85 E7
Birmingham,
Washwood Heath B8 .... 67 F6
Brownhills WS9 .... 16 A3
Coventry CV1 .... 113 F4
Tipton DY4 .... 52 B8
Walsall WS4 .... 15 B2
Wednesbury WS10 .... 42 C4
Wolverhampton WV10 ...... 26 A5
Coronation St B79 .... 21 A5
Coronation Terr B60 ...... 151 B7
Coronation Way DY10 ..... 117 B5
Coronel Ave CV6 .... 95 A4
Corporation Rd DY2 .... 51 F1
Corporation St
Birmingham B4 .... 66 F4
Birmingham B2 .... 164 C3
Coventry CV1 .... 165 B3
Kidderminster DY10 .... 116 C5
Nuneaton CV11 .... 73 B5
Tamworth B79 .... 21 B5
Walsall WS1 .... 42 E8
Wednesbury WS10 .... 42 A2
Wolverhampton WV1 ...... 163 B3
Corporation St W WS1 ..... 42 D8
Corpus Christi RC Jun &
Inf Sch B33 .... 68 D2
Corpus Christi RC Prim
Sch Coventry CV3 .... 134 D7
Wednesbury WS10 .... 27 A1
Correen B77 .... 22 C2
Corrie Croft
Birmingham,
Bartley Green B32 .... 102 B7
Birmingham,
Lyndon Green B26 .... 89 B7
Corrin Gr DY6 .... 60 C8
Corron Hill B63 .... 83 B4

Corser St Dudley DY1 ...... 51 A2
Stourbridge DY8 .... 81 A3
Wolverhampton WV1 .... 25 F1
Corsican Cl **5** Burntwood
WS7 .... 7 A8
Wolverhampton WV12 ...... 27 F1
Corsican Dr WS12 .... 2 A8
Corston Mews CV31 ...... 162 C6
Cort Dr B77 .... 7 B8
Corve Gdns WV6 .... 24 C5
Corve View DY3 .... 39 C1
Corvedale Ho WV1 .... 26 B1
Corvedale Rd B29 .... 103 A6
Corville Gdns B26 .... 89 C4
Corville Rd B62 .... 83 F6
Corwen Croft
Birmingham B31 .... 102 E6
Birmingham B31 .... 102 E7
Cory Croft DY4 .... 52 A5
Coseley Hall **1** WV14 ... 51 C8
Coseley Rd WV14 .... 40 C4
Coseley Road Island WV14 . 40 C4
Coseley Sch The WV14 ..... 40 B1
Coseley Sta WV14 .... 40 C1
Cosford Cl Redditch B98 .. 154 F1
Royal Leamington Spa CV32 . 157 B3
Cosford Cres B35 .... 58 A3
Cosford Ct WV6 .... 23 E5
Cosford Dr DY2 .... 62 E5
Cosgrove Wlk WV8 .... 10 F1
Cossington Rd B23 .... 56 E7
Costers La B98 .... 154 F2
Cot La DY6 .... 60 C4
Coten End DY4 .... 160 F7
Coten End Cty Fst Sch
CV34 .... 161 A7
Coten End Prim Sch CV34 . 160 F7
Cotes Rd LE10 .... 75 F5
Cotford Rd B14 .... 105 A2
Cotheridge Cl B90 .... 127 C6
Cotleigh Gr B43 .... 44 D3
Cotman Cl Bedworth CV12 . 78 A4
Birmingham B43 .... 44 C3
Cotman Dr LE10 .... 71 A3
Coton Gr B90 .... 105 E2
Coton Green Cty Prim Sch
B79 .... 20 F8
Coton Green Prec B79 ...... 20 F7
Coton La Birmingham B23 .. 56 F4
Tamworth B79 .... 20 E8
Coton Rd Nuneaton CV11 .. 73 C3
Wolverhampton WV4 .... 39 B5
Cotsdale Rd WV4 .... 38 E3
Cotsford B91 .... 107 A3
Cotswold Ave WS6 .... 4 F3
Cotswold Cl Aldridge WS9 . 16 A1
Birmingham B45 .... 102 B2
Kidderminster DY11 .... 116 C2
Oldbury B69 .... 63 E5
Cotswold Cres CV10 .... 72 B3
Cotswold Croft B63 .... 82 C1
Cotswold Ct
Sutton Coldfield B75 .... 32 A4
Wolverhampton WV2 .... 39 B6
Cotswold Dr CV3 .... 133 C6
Cotswold Gr WV12 .... 13 B1
Cotswold Ho **6** B14 ..... 105 A3
Cotswold Rd Cannock WS12 . 2 A8
Stourbridge DY8 .... 81 B6
Wolverhampton WV2 .... 39 F7
Cotswold Way B61 .... 137 A5
Cottage Cl Burntwood WS7 . 6 F5
Cannock WS12 .... 2 D5
Royal Leamington Spa CV32 162 C6
Wolverhampton WV11 ...... 26 C6
Cottage Ct WS7 .... 6 F5
Cottage Dr B60 .... 121 D1
Cottage Farm La B60 ..... 121 C1
Cottage Farm Lodge CV6 .. 95 A1
Cottage Farm Rd
Coventry CV6 .... 95 A2
Tamworth B79 .... 35 D7
Cottage Gdns B45 .... 121 F6
Cottage La Burntwood WS7 . 6 F5
Marlbrook B60 .... 121 C1
Minworth B76 .... 58 D6
Wolverhampton WV10 ...... 11 D3
Cottage St Brierley Hill DY5 . 61 D3
Kingswinford DY6 .... 60 D7
Cottage View WV8 .... 10 B4
Cottage Wlk B77 .... 35 F6
Cottages The
Birmingham B24 .... 67 F8
Halesowen B63 .... 82 E6
Cotterell Ct **3** WS4 ...... 28 F3
Cotteridge Inf & Jun Sch
B30 .... 104 A5
Cotteridge Rd B30 .... 104 A4
Cotterill's Cl CV31 .... 162 B3
Cotterills Ave B8 .... 68 C4
Cotterills La B8 .... 68 B4
Cotterills Rd DY4 .... 52 B7
Cottesbrook Cl CV3 .... 114 E1
Cottesbrook Inf Sch B27 ... 88 B4
Cottesbrook Jun Sch B27 . 88 B4
Cottesbrook Rd B27 .... 88 B4
Cottesfield Cl B8 .... 68 B4
Cottesmore Cl B71 .... 53 F8
Cottesmore Ho **7** B20 ... 54 F3
Cottle Cl WS2 .... 27 F3
Cotton Dr CV8 .... 148 C6
Cotton La B13 .... 87 A2
Cotton Mill Spinney CV32 . 157 C6
Cotton Pool Rd B61 .... 136 E2
Cottrell St B71 .... 53 D4

Cottrells Cl B14 105 C4
Cottsmeadow Dr B8 68 C4
Cotwall End Ho DY3 50 C7
Cotwall End Prim Sch DY3 50 D7
Cotwall End Rd DY3 50 C5
Cotysmore Rd B75 46 D7
Couchman Rd B8 67 E4
Coughton Dr CV31 162 D5
Coulter Gr WV6 23 D4
Coulter La WS7 7 E8
Council Cres WV12 27 C4
Council Ho, Art Gall B3 164 B2
Council Ho's CV5 93 D1
Council House Mus B3 164 B2
Council Rd 3 LE10 71 D1
Coundon Court Sch & Com Coll CV6 112 E7
Coundon Gn CV6 112 E8
Coundon Prim Sch CV6 112 E5
Coundon Rd CV1 113 B3
Coundon St CV1 165 A4
Coundon Wedge Dr CV5 112 D7
Counterfield Dr B65 62 F5
Countess Dr WS4 29 D7
Countess Rd CV11 73 A4
Countess St WS1 42 D7
Countess's Croft The CV3 133 D7
Countinghouse Way B60 150 E6
County Bridge Jun Mixed Inf Sch WS2 27 E1
County Cl
Birmingham, Stirchley B30 104 C6
Birmingham, Woodgate B32 84 D3
County Dr B78 21 A2
County La DY8 98 D8
County Park Ave B62 83 D3
Court Cres DY6 60 C5
Court Dr WS14 17 F4
Court Farm Rd B23 56 E6
Court Farm Sch B23 56 E6
Court La B23 56 E7
Court Leet CV3 135 D7
Court Leet Rd CV3 133 E7
Court Oak Gr B32 84 F6
Court Oak Rd B17 85 A6
Court Par WS9 30 B6
Court Pas DY1 51 C1
Court Rd
Birmingham, Balsall Heath B12 86 E6
Birmingham, Sparkhill B11 87 C4
Wolverhampton, Lanesfield WV4 40 A3
Wolverhampton, Newbridge WV6 24 F4
Court St 2 Blackheath B64 62 F1
Royal Leamington Spa CV31 162 A7
4 Stourbridge DY8 81 A5
Court Way WS2 28 E2
Courtaulds Way CV6 113 D6
Courtenay Rd B44 55 E8
Courthouse Croft CV8 148 C4
Courthouse Green Prim Sch CV6 114 A8
Courtland Ave CV6 112 F5
Courtland Rd DY6 60 E8
Courtlands The WV6 24 E4
Courtney Cl CV11 73 F7
Courtway Ave B14 105 B1
Courtyard The Coleshill B46 59 F2
Solihull B91 107 C4
Cousins St WV2 39 D7
Cove Pl CV2 114 C7
Coveley Gr B18 66 A5
Coven Cl WS3 15 A5
Coven Gr B29 85 B2
Coven St WV10 25 D4
Coventry Airport CV8 134 B2
Coventry Canal Basin Warehouse CV1 165 B4
Coventry Cath Church of St Michael CV1 165 C3
Coventry City FC CV1 113 F3
Coventry Golf Course CV8 133 D1
Coventry Highway B98 154 C4
Coventry Prep Sch CV3 133 B8
Coventry Rd Baginton CV8 133 F2
Barnacle CV12 97 A8
Bedworth, Hawkesbury CV2, CV7 96 E6
Bedworth, Springfield CV12 78 B2
Berkswell CV7 110 E3
Birmingham B10, B25, B26 88 C6
Bulkington CV12 79 B1
Coventry CV3 115 F3
Cubbington CV32 157 E7
Hampton In A B92 91 B3
Hinckley LE10 75 B7
Hinckley, Sketchley LE10 75 F5
Kenilworth CV8 148 A7
Nuneaton CV10 78 C7
Solihull B26, B92 90 C2
Stoneleigh CV8 149 C7
Warwick CV34 160 F8
Wigston Parva LE10 76 F1
Coventry Ret Mkt CV1 165 B2
Coventry Road Exhall CV7 96 A8
Coventry St Birmingham B5 164 D2
Coventry CV2 114 A4
Kidderminster DY10 116 F6
Nuneaton CV11 73 C4
Stourbridge DY8 81 A5
Wolverhampton WV1 26 A2
Coventry Sta CV1 165 B1
Coventry Tech Coll
Coventry CV1 113 A2
Coventry CV1 113 B1
Coventry CV1 165 A2
Coventry Univ Coventry CV1 165 C2
Coventry CV1 165 C3
Coventry CV1 165 D2
Coventry Univ Singer Hall CV1 165 D3
Coventry Walsgrave Triangle Bsns Pk CV2 97 A1
Coventry & Warwickshire Hospl CV1 165 C4
Coventry Whitefriars (Mus) CV1 165 D2
Coverdale Rd B92 89 A4
Covers The B80 159 E6
Covert La DY8 80 D2
Covert The WV8 10 E1
Covey Cl WS13 3 D1
Cow La B78 35 F3
Cowdray Cl CV31 162 C7
Cowles Croft B25 68 E1
Cowley B77 21 E2
Cowley Cl B36 58 F1
Cowley Dr Birmingham B27 88 D4
Dudley DY1 50 F2
Cowley Gn WS12 1 F8
Cowley Gr B11 87 E5
Cowley Rd Birmingham B11 87 E5
Coventry CV2 114 D4
Cowper Cl Warwick CV34 155 E1
Willenhall WV12 27 E7
Cowper Rd LE10 75 D6
Cowper Wlk DY10 117 C6
Cowslip Cl
Birmingham, King's Norton B38 123 F8
Birmingham, Selly Oak B29 103 A7
Cowslip Wlk DY5 81 C6
Cox Rd WV14 40 E1
Cox St Birmingham B3 164 B4
Coventry CV1 165 C3
Cox's Cl CV10 73 B3
Cox's La B64 62 F2
Coxcroft Ave DY5 81 F8
Coxmoor Cl WS3 13 F3
Coxwell Gdns B16 65 F2
Coyne Cl DY4 51 D5
Coyne Rd B70 53 B2
Cozens Cl CV12 78 A4
Crab La Cannock WS11 2 A3
Willenhall WV12 13 D1
Crab Mill Cl B38 123 E7
Crab Tree Ho B33 68 E3
Crabbe St DY9 81 F5
Crabbs Cross La B97 158 E5
Crabmill Cl B93 128 C7
Crabmill La Birmingham B38 124 D8
Coventry CV6 113 F7
Crabourne Rd DY2 62 B2
Crabtree Cl Birmingham B31 103 C2
Hagley DY9 99 B6
Redditch B98 154 A2
West Bromwich B71 53 F8
Crabtree Dr Birmingham B37 69 F2
Bromsgrove B61 136 F3
Crabtree Gr 2 CV31 162 C6
Crabtree La B61 136 E3
Crabtree Rd Barwell LE9 71 F5
Birmingham B18 66 A5
Crackley Cotts CV8 148 B8
Crackley Cres CV8 148 B8
Crackley La Coventry CV4 131 F3
Kenilworth CV8 148 A7
Crackley Way DY2 62 A6
Craddock Ct CV10 72 C7
Craddock Dr CV10 72 C7
Craddock Rd B67 64 E6
Craddock St WV6 25 B4
Cradley CE Prim Sch B63 82 C7
Cradley Cl B98 154 F2
Cradley Croft B21 54 C3
Cradley Fields B63 82 C8
Cradley Forge DY5 82 A8
Cradley Heath Factory Ctr B64 82 B8
Cradley Heath Sta B64 82 B8
Cradley High Sch B63 82 B6
Cradley Park Rd DY2 62 D2
Cradley Rd Blackheath B64 82 C8
Dudley DY2 62 D3
Cradock Rd B8 67 E5
Craig Cl CV31 162 B6
Craig Croft B37 70 D2
Craigends Ave CV3 134 E6
Crail Gr B43 44 B4
Crakston Cl CV2 114 E2
Cramlington Rd B42 55 A8
Crammond Cl LE10 75 B8
Cramnore Cl DY4 52 A8
Cramp Hill WS10 41 D6
Cramper's Field CV6 113 A5
Cranborne Chase CV2 115 A5
Cranbourne Ave WV4 39 E3
Cranbourne Cl B45 102 B2
Cranbourne Gr B44 56 A8
Cranbourne Pl B71 53 D4
Cranbourne Rd
Birmingham B44 45 A1
Stourbridge DY8 81 B4
Cranbrook Ct WV13 27 C2
Cranbrook Gr WV6 23 F3
Cranbrook Rd B21 54 C2
Cranby St B8 67 C5
Crane Cl CV34 155 D1
Crane Ct WS1 29 A3
Crane Dr WS7 7 A4
Crane Field WS13 3 B1
Crane Rd WV14 40 F3
Crane St DY11 116 C6
Crane Terr WV6 24 E5
Craneberry Rd B37 69 E3
Cranebrook Hill B78 33 E5
Cranebrook La WS14 16 F7
Cranemoor Cl B7 67 C6
Craner's Rd CV1 113 F4
Cranes Park Rd B26 89 C5
Cranesbill Cl WV10 12 C7
Cranesbill Rd B29 103 A6
Cranfield Gr B26 88 F8
Cranfield Pl WS5 42 F5
Cranfield Rd WS7 7 A7
Cranford Gr B91 107 B1
Cranford Pl WS11 1 F1
Cranford Rd Coventry CV5 112 D4
Wolverhampton WV3 38 D8
Cranford St B66 65 C5
Cranford Way B66 65 C5
Cranham Cl B97 153 B1
Cranham Dr DY6 60 E5
Cranhill Cl B92 89 B1
Crankhall La WS10 42 C3
Cranleigh Cl Aldridge WS9 30 B5
Willenhall WV12 13 C1
Cranleigh Ho B23 56 F6
Cranleigh Pl B44 55 E5
Cranleigh Way WS14 9 E7
Cranmer Ave WV12 27 D7
Cranmer Cl WS6 4 D1
Cranmer Gr B74 31 F6
Cranmere Ave WV6 24 A6
Cranmere Ct WV6 24 A6
Cranmoor Cres B63 83 A5
Cranmore Ave
Birmingham B21 65 D7
Solihull B90 126 E8
Cranmore Bvd B90 126 D8
Cranmore Dr B90 106 E1
Cranmore Inf Sch B90 106 E1
Cranmore Rd
Birmingham B36 58 E1
Solihull B90 126 D8
Wolverhampton WV3 24 F3
Cransley Gr B91 107 A1
Crantock Cl WV11 13 C1
Crantock Rd B42 55 C4
Crantock Way CV11 73 F4
Cranwell Gn WV5 49 A5
Cranwell Gr B24 57 D3
Cranwell Rise B78 20 C1
Cranwell Way B35 58 A3
Crathie Cl CV2 114 F6
Crathorne Ave WV10 11 C1
Craufurd Ct DY8 81 A3
Craufurd St DY8 81 A3
Craven B77 22 B1
Craven Ave CV3 135 D7
Craven Ct CV3 114 F2
Craven St Coventry CV5 112 F2
Wolverhampton WV2 39 F6
Crawford Ave
Darlaston WS10 41 C7
Smethwick B67 64 F4
Wolverhampton WV4 39 F3
Crawford Cl CV32 157 B5
Crawford Rd
Sutton Coldfield B76 57 F8
Wolverhampton WV3 25 A2
Crawford St B8 67 C5
Crawley Wlk B64 62 D1
Crawshaws Rd B36 58 C1
Crayford Rd B44 45 A1
Craythorne Ave B20 54 E4
Crecy Cl B76 46 E4
Crecy Rd CV3 133 E7
Credenda Rd B70 53 A1
Crediton Cl CV11 73 F5
Cregoe St B15 86 C8
Cremore Ave B8 67 E5
Cremorne Rd B75 32 B2
Cremorne Wlk B75 32 B2
Crendon Cl B80 159 E5
Crendon Rd B65 63 A6
Crescent Ave
Birmingham B18 66 B6
Brierley Hill DY5 61 C1
Coventry CV3 114 C2
Crescent Grange Rd The DY9 81 C4
Crescent Rd Darlaston WS10 41 D6
Dudley DY2 62 B5
Kidderminster DY11 116 C5
Willenhall WV13 27 C2
Crescent Sta The WV14 40 D6
Crescent The Bilston WV14 40 D6
Birmingham, Coleshill Heath B37 90 E8
Birmingham, Great Barr B43 44 A1
Birmingham, Hockley B18 66 B6
Birmingham, Sparkbrook B12 87 B5
Blackheath, Cradley Heath B64 83 A7
Blackheath, Rowley Regis B65 63 C2
Crescent The continued
Bromsgrove B60 136 F1
Dudley DY1 51 E4
Great Wyrley WS6 5 A2
Hagley DY8 98 F5
Hampton in A B92 109 B7
Keresley CV7 94 F6
Solihull, Lode Heath B91 107 B4
Solihull, Shirley B90 106 A4
Walsall WS1 43 A8
Wednesbury WS10 42 A4
Willenhall WV13 27 C1
Wolverhampton WV6 24 B3
Crescent Tower B1 66 C2
Cressage Ave B31 103 A1
Cressage Rd CV2 115 A6
Cressett Ave DY5 61 C4
Cressett La DY5 61 C4
Cressington Dr B74 32 A1
Cresswell Cl CV10 73 C8
Cresswell Cres WS3 13 F2
Cresswell Ct WV9 11 A3
Cresswell Ho CV6 113 B7
Crest The Birmingham B31 123 C7
Royal Leamington Spa CV32 157 D3
Crest View Birmingham B14 105 B4
Sutton Coldfield B74 44 F8
Crestwood B77 22 A5
Crestwood Ave DY11 116 A5
Crestwood Dr B44 55 E7
Crestwood Glen WV6 24 E7
Crestwood Park Prim Sch DY6 61 A5
Crestwood Sch The DY6 60 F5
Creswell Rd B28 106 B7
Creswick Gr B45 122 C7
Crew La CV8 148 E6
Crew Rd WS10 42 A4
Creynolds Cl B90 126 D3
Creynolds La B90 126 E4
Crick La B20 66 A8
Cricket Cl Coventry CV5 112 F3
Walsall WS5 43 B7
Cricket La WS14 9 C5
Cricket Mdw Dudley DY3 50 E5
Wolverhampton WV10 11 D4
Cricketers Mdw B64 82 F7
Cricklewood Dr B62 83 D3
Crigdon B77 22 C2
Crimmond Rise B63 82 E5
Crimscote Cl B90 126 F6
Cringlebrook B77 21 D1
Cripps Rd WS2 27 E3
Crockett St DY1 51 A2
Crockett's La B66 65 A6
Crocketts Ave B21 65 D7
Crocketts Lane Inf Sch B66 65 B5
Crocketts Rd B21 65 D8
Crockford Dr B75 32 B3
Crockford Rd B71 42 C1
Crockington La WV5 37 A1
Crocus Cres WV9 11 A3
Croft Apartments 2 WV13 27 A2
Croft Cl Birmingham B25 88 E8
Redditch B98 154 D3
Warwick CV34 161 C7
Croft Cres WS8 15 D7
Croft Ct B36 69 B8
Croft Down Rd B92 89 D4
Croft Fields CV12 78 B2
Croft Gdns WS7 7 A8
Croft Ho 2 WS1 28 F1
Croft Ind Est Birmingham B37 70 D2
3 Willenhall WV13 27 A2
Croft La WV10 26 A7
Croft Mid Sch CV10 72 F3
Croft Par WS9 30 B6
Croft Pool CV12 77 F2
Croft Rd Bedworth CV12 77 F2
Birmingham B26 88 E8
Coventry CV1 165 A2
Leek Wootton CV35 156 A7
Nuneaton CV10 72 F3
Croft St Tamworth B79 21 B6
Walsall WS2 28 D3
Willenhall WV13 27 A2
Croft Street JMI Sch WS2 28 D3
Croft The Birmingham B31 103 B2
Blakedown DY10 98 C2
Bulkington CV12 79 B2
Cheslyn Hay WS6 4 E2
Coventry CV6 95 F4
Dudley DY2 61 F6
Meriden CV7 92 C1
Sedgley DY3 39 E1
Walsall WS5 43 E8
Willenhall WV13 27 A2
Croftdown Rd B17 85 A7
Crofters Cl DY8 81 B4
Crofters Ct B15 85 E6
Crofters Wlk WV8 10 E1
Croftleigh Gdns B91 106 E2
Crofts La B96 158 B2
Crofts The B76 58 A8
Croftway The B20 54 E6
Croftwood Rd DY9 81 D4
Cromane Sq B43 54 E7
Cromarty Cl CV5 112 A5
Cromdale B77 22 C1
Cromdale Cl CV10 72 A3
Cromdale Dr B63 82 D3
Crome Rd B43 44 D3
Cromer Gdns WV6 24 F5
Cromer Rd Birmingham B12 86 F5
Royal Leamington Spa CV32 157 B2
Cromes Wood CV4 111 D1
Crompton Ave B20 55 C1
Crompton Cl WS2 28 A5
Crompton Ct CV34 160 D6
Crompton Rd
Birmingham, Handsworth B20 55 C1
Birmingham, Nechells B7 67 C8
Birmingham, Rubery B45 101 D1
Tipton DY4 52 A4
Crompton St CV34 160 D6
Cromwell Cl Blackheath B65 63 A5
Walsall WS2 27 E4
Cromwell Ct WS6 5 A1
Cromwell Dr DY2 62 F8
Cromwell Inf & Jun Sch B7 67 B6
Cromwell La
Birmingham B31 102 E8
Coventry CV4 131 C6
Cromwell Rd Cannock WS12 2 E1
Tamworth B79 20 E8
Wolverhampton WV10 11 E4
Cromwell St Birmingham B7 67 B5
Coventry CV6 113 F6
Dudley DY2 62 E8
West Bromwich 53 C4
Cromwells Mdw WS14 9 C5
Crondal Pl B15 86 B7
Crondal Rd CV7 96 B7
Cronehills Linkway B70 53 D3
Cronehills Prim Sch B70 53 D4
Cronehills St B70 53 D4
Crook La WS9 44 A7
Crookham Cl B17 84 F7
Crookhay La B71 53 B8
Crooks La B80 159 D3
Croome Cl Birmingham B11 87 B3
Coventry CV6 112 F4
Redditch B98 154 F1
Cropredy Rd B31 123 B8
Cropthorne Cl B98 159 B7
Cropthorne Dr B47 125 B7
Cropthorne Ho B60 137 B3
Cropthorne Rd B90 106 C3
Crosbie Rd Birmingham B17 85 B6
Coventry CV5 112 E3
Crosby Cl Birmingham B1 66 B3
Wolverhampton WV6 24 F5
Cross Cheaping CV1 165 B3
Cross Cl B64 62 F2
Cross Farm Rd B17 85 D4
Cross Farms La B45 101 F1
Cross Fields Rd 4 CV34 160 F8
Cross Ho WV2 39 C7
Cross Keys WS13 9 B8
Cross La Birmingham B43 43 E1
Cubbington CV32 157 E4
Lichfield WS14 9 D6
Sedgley DY3 39 E1
Cross Pl DY3 39 E1
Cross Rd Coventry CV6 113 F8
Keresley CV7 94 F6
4 Royal Leamington Spa CV32 156 D1
Cross Road Ind Est CV6 113 F7
Cross St Bilston WV14 40 F2
Birmingham B21 65 C8
4 Blackheath B65 63 C1
Burntwood WS7 6 E8
Cannock, Bridgtown WS11 4 E5
Cannock, Heath Hayes WS12 2 E1
Cheslyn Hay WS6 4 D2
Coventry CV1 165 C4
Dudley DY1 51 C1
Halesowen B63 83 A3
Kingswinford DY6 60 D6
Kingswinford, Wall Heath DY6 60 B8
Nuneaton CV10 72 D3
Oldbury B68 64 A4
Royal Leamington Spa CV32 157 A1
Smethwick B66 65 A6
Stourbridge DY8 80 E5
Tamworth B79 21 B5
Tamworth, Kettlebrook B77 21 C3
Walsall WS3 15 A1
10 Warwick CV34 160 F7
Wednesbury WS10 41 E3
2 Willenhall WV13 27 A1
Wolverhampton WV1 25 F1
Cross St N WV1 25 D4
Cross St S WV2 39 C7
Cross The Kingswinford DY6 60 D6
Stourbridge DY9 81 E6
Cross Walks Rd DY9 81 E5
Cross Wlk B69 63 C8
Crossfell B77 22 B1
Crossfield Ind Est WS13 9 E8
Crossfield Rd
Birmingham B33 69 A3
Lichfield WS13 9 E8
Crossgate Rd Dudley DY2 61 F6
Redditch B98 159 C7
Crossings Ind Est The 4 WS3 28 B8
Crossings The WS14 9 E8
Crosskey Cl B33 69 E2
Crossland Cres WV6 24 F7
Crossland Rd B31 102 F4
Crossland Row LE10 76 A6
Crossley Ct CV6 113 F7
Crossley St DY2 62 D4
Crossley Wlk B60 150 E7
Crossway La B44 55 F6

Crossway Rd CV3 133 B4
Crossways LE10 75 F5
Crossways Ct B44 56 B7
Crossways Gn B44 56 B7
Crosswells Rd B68 64 B5
Crowberry Cl WS8 15 D6
Crowberry La B78 48 C8
Crowden Rd B77 22 A1
Crowesbridge Mews WV14 51 B8
Crowhill Rd CV11 74 A1
Crowhurst Rd B31 122 E7
Crowland Ave WV6 23 E4
Crowle Dr DY9 81 C5
Crowmere Rd CV2 114 F7
Crown Cl Blackheath B65 63 D4
Bromsgrove B61 136 F2
Sedgley DY3 39 D1
Crown Ct Darlaston WS10 41 C8
Sutton Coldfield B74 31 E2
Crown Ctr The 1 DY8 81 A5
Crown Ho CV5 112 E3
Crown La
Kidderminster DY10 116 E6
10 Stourbridge DY8 80 F5
Sutton Coldfield B74 31 E3
Crown Mdw B48 139 A7
Crown Rd
Birmingham, Bordesley Green B9 67 D2
Birmingham, King's Heath B30 104 A4
Crown St WV1 25 D4
Crown Terr CV31 161 F7
Crown Way CV32 157 B3
Crown Wlk DY4 52 A2
Crownhill Rd LE10 75 D4
Crownmeadow Dr DY4 52 D7
Crows Nest Cl B76 46 F3
Crowther Gdns B63 82 C7
Crowther Gr WV6 24 F4
Crowther Rd Birmingham B23 56 D5
Wolverhampton WV6 24 F5
Crowther St
Kidderminster DY11 116 C6
Wolverhampton WV10 25 E4
Croxall Way B66 65 B5
Croxdene Ave WS3 14 A1
Croxhall St CV12 78 C3
Croxley Dr WS12 2 C3
Croxley Gdns WV13 40 F8
Croxstalls Ave WS3 28 A8
Croxstalls Cl WS3 14 A1
Croxstalls Pl WS3 28 A8
Croxstalls Rd WS3 28 A8
Croxton Gr B33 69 A4
Croy Dr B35 58 B4
Croyde Ave B42 55 A8
Croydon Cl CV3 133 E6
Croydon Rd
Birmingham, Bournbrook B29 85 F3
Birmingham, Erdington B24 57 A2
Crummock Cl CV6 95 D3
Crump Ho WS1 28 F1
Crumpfields La B97 152 F1
Crusader Cl B69 63 E5
Crutchley Ave B78 21 A2
Crutchley Way CV31 162 A2
Crychan Cl B45 102 B2
Cryersoak Cl B90 127 B7
Cryfield Grange Rd CV4 132 C2
Crystal Ave DY8 60 F1
Crystal Dr B66 64 C8
Crystal Ho B66 65 C6
Crystal L Ctr DY8 81 A5
Cubbington CE Comb Sch CV32 157 F5
Cubbington Rd Coventry CV6 96 A2
Royal Leamington Spa CV32 157 B3
Cubley Rd B28 87 E1
Cuckoo Cl WS11 2 C2
Cuckoo La CV1 165 C3
Cuin Rd B66 65 C5
Cuin Wlk 11 B66 65 C5
Culey Gr B33 69 D2
Culey Wlk B37 70 D2
Culford Dr B32 102 C8
Culham Cl B27 88 D2
Cullwick St WV1 40 A8
Culmington Gr B31 122 F8
Culmington Rd B31 122 F8
Culmore Cl WV12 27 D4
Culmore Rd B62 63 E1
Culpepper Cl CV10 72 E4
Culverhouse Dr DY5 61 A1
Culverley Cres B93 127 F6
Culvert Way B66 64 D7
Culwell St WV10 163 C4
Culwell Trad Est WV10 25 F4
Culworth Cl CV31 161 F5
Culworth Ct Coventry CV6 113 E7
Royal Leamington Spa CV31 162 A5
Culworth Row CV6 113 E8
Cumberford Ave B33 69 E1
Cumberland Ave 3 B5 86 E7
Cumberland Cl DY6 60 E4
Cumberland Cres 6
Burntwood WS7 7 A8
Royal Leamington Spa CV32 157 C3
Cumberland Dr
Nuneaton CV10 72 E3
Tamworth B78 21 A1
Cumberland Ho 7 WV3 25 C4
Cumberland Rd
Bilston WV14 40 D7
Cannock WS11 2 A4
Oldbury B68 84 B7
West Bromwich B71 53 D7
Willenhall WV13 27 D2
Cumberland St B1 66 B2
Cumberland Wlk B75 47 B5
Cumbernauld Wlk 7 CV2 115 A7
Cumbrae Dr LE10 71 B2
Cumbria Cl CV1 113 A3
Cumbria Way B8 67 D6
Cumbrian Croft B63 82 D2
Cumming St 6 CV31 162 A7
Cundall Cl CV31 162 B6
Cunningham Rd Perton WV6 23 E4
Walsall WS2 27 E2
Cupfields Ave DY4 52 C8
Cupfields Cres DY4 52 C7
Cur La B97 152 D3
Curbar Rd B42 55 C6
Curborough Rd WS13 3 B2
Curdale Rd B32 102 B8
Curdworth La B76 59 A8
Curdworth Prim Sch B76 59 C6
Curlew B77 36 A7
Curlew Cl
Kidderminster DY10 117 B2
Lichfield WS14 9 E7
Curlew Hill WS11 2 A4
Curlews Cl B23 56 C8
Curlieu Cl CV35 160 A7
Curral Rd B65 63 C3
Curran Cl CV31 162 B4
Curriers Cl CV4 131 D7
Cursley La DY10 117 F1
Curtin Dr WS10 41 B4
Curtis Cl Smethwick B66 65 C4
Tutnall B60 151 F8
Curtis Rd CV2 114 D6
Curzon Ave CV6 113 E8
Curzon Cl LE10 75 F7
Curzon Gr CV31 162 C6
Curzon St Birmingham B4 67 A3
Wolverhampton WV2 39 D7
Cut Throat La B94 142 D7
Cuthbert Rd B18 65 E4
Cutler St B66 65 B6
Cutlers Rough Cl B31 102 F5
Cutsdean Cl B31 102 F6
Cutshill Cl B36 69 C8
Cutting The WS4 28 F4
Cuttle Mill La B76 48 D3
Cuttle Pool La B93 128 F4
Cutworth Cl B76 47 A3
Cwerne Ct DY3 50 C3
Cygnet Cl Alvechurch B48 139 A7
Cannock WS12 2 C7
Cygnet Ct CV1 165 C4
Cygnet Gr B23 56 B6
Cygnet La DY5 61 C7
Cygnet Rd B70 53 A5
Cygnus Way B70 52 F5
Cypress Ave DY3 50 D5
Cypress Croft CV3 134 F8
Cypress Gdns
Kingswinford DY6 60 D4
Walsall WS5 43 C4
Cypress Gr B31 102 E1
Cypress La CV31 162 B2
Cypress Rd Dudley DY2 51 F1
Walsall WS5 43 C4
Cypress Sq 2 B27 88 C5
Cypress Way B31 122 F8
Cyprus Ave B96 158 D2
Cyprus Cl B29 103 A7
Cyprus St Oldbury B69 64 A8
Wolverhampton WV2 39 C6
Cyril Gr B10 87 C8
Cyril Rd B10 87 D8

D'aubeny Rd CV4 132 C8
D'Eyncourt Prim Sch WV11 26 B7
D'Eyncourt Rd WV10 26 A7
D'urberville Cl WV2 39 F6
D'urberville Rd WV2 39 F6
D'urberville Wlk WS11 2 A2
Dace B77 35 D7
Dacer Cl B30 104 B5
Dad's La B13 86 C1
Dadford View DY5 61 B2
Daffern Rd CV7 78 A1
Daffodil Cl DY3 50 E7
Daffodil Pl WS5 43 D8
Daffodil Rd WS5 43 D8
Daffodil Way B31 122 E8
Dagger La B71 53 E4
Dagnall Rd B27 88 D3
Dagnell End Rd B98 154 B7
Dagtail La B97 158 D3
Dahlia Cl LE10 75 E6
Daimler Cl B36 58 F1
Daimler Rd Birmingham B14 105 D3
Coventry CV6 113 C5
Dainton Gr B32 84 C1
Daintree Croft CV3 133 C7
Daintry Dr B78 20 B7
Dairy Cl DY4 52 B5
Dairy Ct B68 84 D7
Daisy Bank WS12 1 F8
Daisy Bank Cl WS3 15 B2
Daisy Bank Cres WS5 43 D8
Daisy Farm Rd B14 105 B3
Daisy Mdw DY4 52 C6
Daisy Rd B16 65 F2
Daisy St Dudley WV14 40 D2
Wolverhampton W6 25 A4
Daisy Wlk WV9 11 A3
Dalbeg Cl WV8 24 E8
Dalbury Rd B28 105 E5
Dalby Cl CV3 134 E8
Dalby Rd WS3 28 F6
Dale Cl Birmingham B43 43 D1
Catshill B61 136 F7
Smethwick B66 65 A3
Tipton DY4 52 D5
Warwick CV34 161 A8
Dale Ct WV1 25 A3
Dale Dr WS7 7 B7
Dale End Birmingham B4 164 C3
Darlaston WS10 41 D6
Nuneaton CV10 72 E5
Dale End Cl LE10 75 A7
Dale Hill B60 137 F6
Dale Meadow Cl CV7 130 B6
Dale Rd Birmingham B29 85 E3
Halesowen B62 83 F8
Redditch B98 153 F5
Stourbridge DY8 80 F2
Dale St Bilston WV14 41 A5
Royal Leamington Spa CV32 161 E8
Smethwick B66 65 A3
Walsall WS1 42 F7
Wednesbury WS10 41 E3
Wolverhampton WV3 163 A2
Dale Terr B69 63 C8
Dale Wlk B25 88 B7
Dalecote Ave B92 107 E8
Dalehouse Flats CV8 148 B6
Dalehouse La CV8 148 D7
Dales Cl WV6 25 B6
Dales Cty Jun & Inf Schs The B77 36 B8
Dales La WS9 29 C5
Dalesman Cl DY6 60 B7
Daleview Rd B14 105 C4
Daleway Rd CV3 133 B4
Dalewood Croft B26 88 F6
Dalewood Rd B37 69 F5
Daley Cl B1 66 B3
Daley Rd WV14 40 F2
Dalkeith Rd B73 45 E2
Dalkeith St WS2 28 C3
Dallas Rd B23 56 D5
Dallimore Cl B92 89 A3
Dallington Rd CV6 112 E6
Dalloway Cl B5 86 D6
Dalmahoy Cl CV11 79 C8
Dalmeny Rd CV4 131 D7
Dalston Cl DY2 62 D6
Dalston Rd B27 88 C4
Dalton Ct B23 56 B3
Dalton Gdns CV2 114 F4
Dalton Rd Bedworth CV12 78 A2
Coventry CV5 113 B1
Walsall WS2 28 A3
Dalton St Birmingham B4 164 C3
Wolverhampton WV3 39 B8
Dalton Way B4 164 C3
Dalvine Rd DY2 62 B2
Dalwood Cl WV14 51 B7
Dalwood Way CV6 96 B4
Dam St WS13 9 B8
Dama Rd B78 34 F8
Damar Croft B14 104 D4
Dame Agnes Gr CV6 114 B8
Dame Elizabeth Cadbury Sec Sch B30 103 D7
Dame Ellen Pinsent Specl Sch B13 105 A7
Damien Cl B67 64 F5
Damson Cl B97 158 C6
Damson Ct LE10 75 B7
Damson La B91 107 E7
Damson Parkway B91, B92 107 F7
Damson Wood Inf Sch B92 107 D7
Danbury Cl B76 47 A2
Danbury Rd B90 106 B2
Danby Gr B24 57 B2
Dando Rd DY2 62 D8
Dandy Bank Rd DY6 61 A8
Dandy's Wlk WS1 42 F8
Dane Gr B13 104 D8
Dane Rd CV2 114 B4
Dane Terr B65 63 C5
Danelagh Cl B79 20 F7
Danes Cl WV11 12 F4
Danesbury Cres
Birmingham B44 56 A8
Royal Leamington Spa CV31 162 D6
Danescourt Rd WV6 24 C6
Daneshill Wlk WV8 24 F8
Danesmoor Ho B26 88 E7
Danesmore Park Prim Sch WV11 13 A1
Daneswood Dr WS9 15 F3
Daneswood Rd CV3 135 E7
Daneways Cl B74 45 A8
Danford Cl DY8 81 A4
Danford Gdns B10 87 C8
Danford La B91 106 E3
Danford Rd B47 124 F6
Danford Way B43 54 D8
Dangerfield Ho B70 53 E1
Dangerfield La WS10 41 C4
Daniel Ave CV10 72 C3
Daniels La WS9 30 C4
Daniels Rd B9 68 A2
Danilo Rd WS11 1 D1
Danks St DY4 52 A2
Danzey Cl B98 159 B5
Danzey Gr B14 104 C3
Danzey Green La B94 142 B1
Danzey Green Rd B36 58 B1
Daphne Cl CV2 96 C3
Darby Cl WV14 40 A2
Darby End Rd DY2 62 E4
Darby Ho 2 WS2 42 C7
Darby Rd Oldbury B68 64 C5
Wednesbury WS10 42 B4
Darby St B65 63 C1
Darbys Hill Rd B69 63 B7
Dare Rd B23 56 E4
Dare's Wlk LE10 71 D1
Darell Croft B76 46 E3
Daren Cl B36 69 F8
Darfield Wlk 2 B12 86 F8
Darges La WS6 4 F4
Dark La Astwood Bank B96 158 D1
Bedworth CV12 77 D1
Belbroughton DY9 119 F8
Birchmoor B78 36 E8
Brinsford WV10 11 D8
Coventry CV1 165 B4
Featherstone WV10 12 D7
Great Wyrley WS6 5 C1
Hollywood B47 124 E7
Lichfield WS13 8 B8
Romsley B62 100 F4
Stoke Heath B60 150 D6
Darkhouse La WV14 40 C2
Darlaston Com Sch WS10 41 B6
Darlaston Ct CV7 110 D8
Darlaston La WV14 41 A7
Darlaston Rd Walsall WS2 42 B8
Wednesbury WS10 41 E4
Darlaston Road Ind Est WS10 41 D5
Darley Ave B34 68 F6
Darley Dr W6 25 B5
Darley Green Rd B93 128 B1
Darley Ho B69 63 D6
Darley Mead Ct B91 107 E4
Darley Rd LE10 75 E6
Darley Way B74 45 A7
Darleydale Ave B44 44 E1
Darlington St
Darlaston WS10 41 D5
Wolverhampton WV1 163 B3
Darlington Yd WV1 163 B3
Darlston Row CV7 92 B1
Darnbrook B77 22 C1
Darnel Croft 3 B10 67 B1
Darnel Hurst Rd B75 32 D3
Darnford Cl
Birmingham B28 106 A5
Coventry CV2 114 F7
Sutton Coldfield B72 57 D7
Darnford La WS14 9 F6
Darnford Moors WS14 9 E6
Darnford View WS13 3 E1
Darnick Rd B73 45 D2
Darnley Rd 7 B16 66 A2
Darrach Cl CV2 96 E1
Darris Rd B29 104 A8
Dart B77 36 A5
Dart Cl LE10 75 A8
Dart St B9 67 B1
Dartford Rd WS3 13 F1
Dartmoor Cl B45 102 A2
Dartmouth Ave Cannock WS11 4 C8
Stourbridge DY8 60 D3
Walsall WS3 28 E6
Willenhall WV13 27 A2
Dartmouth Cir B6 66 F5
Dartmouth Cl WS3 28 E5
Dartmouth Cres WV14 41 A7
Dartmouth Dr WS9 30 A5
Dartmouth High Sch B43 43 D3
Dartmouth Ho 2 WS3 28 F6
Dartmouth Middleway B7 66 F4
Dartmouth Pl WS3 28 F6
Dartmouth Rd
Birmingham B29 85 F2
Cannock WS11 1 D1
Coventry CV2 114 C5
Smethwick B66 64 F8
Dartmouth Sch CV2 114 D5
Dartmouth Sq B70 53 D2
Dartmouth St
West Bromwich B70 53 B3
Wolverhampton WV2 163 C1
Wolverhampton WV2 163 D1
Dartmouth Street Sta B70 53 B3
Darvel Rd WV12 27 D4
Darwall St WS1 28 E2
Darwell Pk B77 22 B2
Darwin Cl Burntwood WS7 7 B7
Cannock WS12 2 E2
Coventry CV2 115 A6
Hinckley LE10 71 E3
Lichfield WS13 9 A8
Darwin Ct Bedworth CV12 78 A2
Perton WV6 23 E4
Darwin Ho 3 B37 70 C1
Darwin Pl WS2 28 B6
Darwin Rd WS2 28 B6
Darwin St B12 86 F8
Dassett Gr B9 68 C2
Dassett Rd B93 127 F4
Datchet Cl CV5 112 C4
Datteln Rd WS11 2 A4
Dauntsey Covert B14 104 D2
Davena Dr B29 84 E2
Davena Gr WV14 40 D3
Davenport Dr
Birmingham B35 58 C3
Bromsgrove B60 137 B1
Davenport Rd Coventry CV5 133 B8
Wednesfield WV11 26 E6
Wolverhampton WV6 24 B5
Davenport Terr LE10 75 E8
Daventry Gr B32 84 D6
Daventry Rd CV3 133 D7
Davey Rd Birmingham B20 55 E1
West Bromwich B70 53 A5
David Cox Ct B17 85 D5
David Cox Tower B31 102 F7
David Garrick Gdns WS13 3 B2
David Peacock Cl DY4 52 A5
David Rd Bedworth CV7 95 F8
Birmingham B20 55 B2
Coventry CV1 113 F2
Tipton DY4 52 A7
Davids The B31 103 C5
Davidson Ave CV31 162 A7
Davidson Rd WS14 9 B7
Davies Ave WV14 40 D3
Davies Ho 7 Oldbury B69 64 A7
1 Walsall WS3 14 B1
Davies Rd CV7 95 F7
Davis Ave DY4 51 E4
Davis Cl CV32 156 D2
Davis Gr B25 88 D6
Davis Rd Tamworth B77 21 F4
Willenhall WV12 27 D8
Davison Rd B67 64 F3
Davy Rd WS2 28 A5
Daw End WS4 29 C6
Daw End La WS4 29 C6
Daw End Specl Sch WS4 29 C6
Dawberry Cl B14 104 D5
Dawberry Fields Rd B14 104 D5
Dawberry Rd B14 104 C6
Dawes Ave B70 53 C1
Dawes Cl CV2 114 A3
Dawes La WS8 7 A1
Dawley Brook Prim Sch DY6 60 C7
Dawley Brook Rd DY6 60 D7
Dawley Cres B37 70 B1
Dawley Rd DY6 60 C8
Dawley Trad Est DY6 60 D8
Dawley Wlk 9 CV2 115 A7
Dawlish Cl CV11 73 E5
Dawlish Dr CV3 133 D5
Dawlish Rd Birmingham B29 85 F2
Dudley DY1 51 C5
Smethwick B66 65 B5
Dawn Dr DY4 41 C2
Dawn Rd B31 102 E6
Dawney Dr B75 32 A4
Dawson Ave WV14 40 A2
Dawson Cl Redditch B97 158 C6
Whitnash CV31 162 A2
Dawson Rd Birmingham B21 65 F8
Bromsgrove B61 136 E2
Coventry CV3 114 A1
Dawson Sq WV14 40 C5
Dawson St Smethwick B66 65 A3
Walsall WS3 28 D8
Day Ave WV11 26 E7
Day Ho DY4 52 C8
Day St WS2 28 E3
Day's La CV2 113 F3
Daybrook Cl B97 153 B5
Dayhouse Bank B62 101 B1
Daylesford Inf Sch B92 89 A3
Daylesford Rd B92 89 A3
Days Cl CV1 113 E3
Daytona Dr CV5 111 B8
De Marnham Cl B70 53 E1
De Montfort Ho B37 69 F5
De Montfort Rd
Hinckley LE10 71 E1
Kenilworth CV8 147 E6
De Montfort Way CV4 132 D5
De Moram Gr B92 107 F7
De Somerley Ho 1 B69 64 A7
De-Compton Cl CV7 95 A7
De-La-Bere Cres LE10 76 A6
Deacon St CV11 73 C3
Deakin Ave WS8 6 F1
Deakin Rd Birmingham B24 57 A3
Sutton Coldfield B75 46 E7
Deakins Rd B25 88 B7
Deal Ave WS7 7 A8
Deal Dr B69 52 A1
Deal Gr B31 103 A3
Dean Cl Birmingham B44 56 B8
Hinckley LE10 71 E2
Stourbridge DY8 81 B6
Sutton Coldfield B72 57 B7
Dean Ct 5 Brierley Hill DY5 61 D2
Perton WV6 23 E6
Dean Rd Birmingham B23 56 F5
Hinckley LE10 71 E2
Walsall WS4 29 C7
Dean Rd W LE10 71 E2
Dean St Birmingham B5 164 C1
Coventry CV2 114 A3
Sedgley DY3 50 D8
Dean's Rd WV1 26 B2
Deanbrook Cl B90 127 A6
Deanery Jun Sch B76 57 F8
Deanery Row WV1 163 B4
Deans Cl B98 154 D5
Deans Croft WS13 9 C8
Deans Pl WS3 28 F6

Deans Way CV7 95 D6
Deansfield High Sch WV1 26 C2
Deansfield Rd WV1 26 A2
Deansford La DY10 118 B6
Deanston Croft CV2 96 F1
Deansway Bromsgrove B61 136 E2
Warwick CV34 155 E1
Deansway Ho DY10 117 A7
Deansway The DY10 117 A7
Dearman Rd B11 87 B7
Dearmont Rd B31 122 E7
Dearne Ct DY3 51 A6
Deasy Ho CV3 134 B5
Deavall Way WS11 2 B2
Debden Cl B93 127 E2
Debenham Cres B25 68 D1
Debenham Rd B25 68 D1
Deblen Dr B16 65 D1
Deborah Cl WV2 39 C6
Dee Gr Birmingham B38 123 E8
Cannock WS11 4 D8
Dee Ho 8 DY1 61 E8
Dee Rd WS3 14 E1
Dee Wlk B36 70 A7
Deedmore Rd CV2 96 D1
Deedmore Sch CV2 114 C8
Deegan Cl CV2 114 A5
Deelands Rd B45 121 F8
Deeley B77 22 A1
Deeley Cl Birmingham B15 86 C7
Blackheath B64 82 E7
Deeley Dr DY4 52 C6
Deeley Pl WS3 28 B8
Deeley St Brierley Hill DY5 61 E1
Walsall WS3 28 B8
Deepdale B77 22 D1
Deepdale Ave B26 89 B4
Deepdale Ind Est DY1 50 E3
Deepdale La DY3 50 E3
Deeplow Cl 2 B72 46 C4
Deepmoor Rd B33 68 F3
Deepmore Ave WS2 28 B2
Deepwood Cl WS4 29 B8
Deer Barn Hill B98 154 A1
Deer Cl Norton Canes WS11 6 A7
Walsall WS3 14 C1
Deer Leap The CV8 148 B6
Deer Park Rd B78 20 E1
Deer Park Way B91 107 C1
Deer Wlk WV8 10 F2
Deerdale Way CV3 134 F8
Deerfold Cres WS7 7 B7
Deerham Cl B23 56 D7
Deerhill B77 22 C1
Deerhurst Cl B98 154 C7
Deerhurst Ct B91 107 D4
Deerhurst Rd
Birmingham B20 54 F5
Coventry CV6 95 B2
Deerhurst Rise WS12 2 F6
Deerpark Dr CV34 160 E8
Defford Ave WS4 15 C1
Defford Dr B68 64 B4
Deighton Rd WS5 43 B4
Delage Cl CV6 96 B4
Delamere Cl B36 58 D1
Delamere Dr WS5 43 C3
Delamere Rd Bedworth CV12 77 F2
Birmingham B28 105 F7
Willenhall WV12 27 C7
Delamere Way CV32 157 C4
Delancey Keep B75 47 A5
Delaware Rd CV3 133 C5
Delf Ho CV2 96 D1
Delhi Ave CV6 95 D1
Delhurst Ave WV4 39 E3
Delhurst Rd B44 44 D1
Delius St CV4 111 E3
Dell Cl CV3 134 C5
Dell Farm Cl B93 128 B6
Dell Rd Birmingham B30 104 A5
Brierley Hill DY5 61 B5
Dell The Birmingham B31 102 D6
Birmingham, Edgbaston B16 65 F2
Cannock WS12 2 F4
Lichfield WS13 8 F7
Solihull B92 89 A1
Stourbridge DY8 80 E6
Tamworth B79 21 B6
Della Dr B32 102 D8
Dellow Gr B48 139 A5
Dellows Cl B38 123 D7
Dellway Ct DY8 80 E5
Delmore Way B76 58 B6
Delph Dr DY5 81 E7
Delph La DY5 81 D8
Delph Rd DY5 61 D1
Delph Road Ind Est DY5 61 C1
Delphinium Cl B69 67 F3
Delphl Cl CV34 161 E4
Delrene Rd B28 105 F3
Delta Way WS11 4 D7
Delta Way Bsns Ctr WS11 4 D6
Deltic B77 22 A1
Delves Cres Walsall WS5 43 A5
Wood End CV9 36 D1
Delves Green Rd WS5 43 A5
Delves Inf Sch WS5 43 A5
Delves Jun Mix Sch WS5 43 A5
Delves Rd WS1 42 F7
Delville Rd WS10 41 F4
Delville Terr WS10 41 F3
Dempster Ct CV11 73 C4
Dempster Rd CV12 78 A4
Demuth Way B69 63 F6
Denaby Gr B14 105 D4
Denbigh Cl DY1 50 F2
Denbigh Cnr B46 91 A6
Denbigh Cres B71 53 B6
Denbigh Dr
Wednesbury WS10 42 D4
West Bromwich B71 53 B6
Denbigh Rd Coventry CV6 112 E5
Tipton DY4 52 C4
Denbigh St B9 67 D2
Denbury Cl WS12 2 D1
Denby Bldgs 12 CV32 161 F8
Denby Cl Birmingham B7 67 B5
Royal Leamington Spa CV32 157 C3
Denby Croft B90 127 B6
Dencer Cl B45 122 A8
Dencer Dr CV8 148 C4
Dencil Cl B63 82 D5
Dene Ave DY6 60 C4
Dene Court Rd B92 88 F1
Dene Hollow B13 105 C7
Dene Rd Stourbridge DY8 80 F3
Wombourne WV4 37 F4
Denegate Cl B76 58 B6
Denehurst Cl B45 122 A1
Denehurst Way CV10 72 F3
Denewood Ave B20 55 B2
Denewood Way CV8 148 C6
Denford Gr B14 104 D5
Denham Ave CV5 112 C4
Denham Ct B23 56 C2
Denham Gdns WV3 38 B8
Denham Rd B27 88 C5
Denholm Rd B73 45 D2
Denholme Gr B14 105 A3
Denis Rd LE10 75 D5
Denise Dr Birmingham B17 85 C4
Birmingham, Kingshurst B37 69 F4
Dudley WV14 51 B8
Denleigh Rd DY6 60 F4
Denmark Cl WV6 25 A4
Denmark Rise WS12 2 D7
Denmark Villas WS13 8 C5
Denmead Dr WV11 26 F8
Denmore Gdns WV1 26 C2
Dennett Cl CV34 155 F2
Dennis B77 21 E2
Dennis Hall Rd DY8 81 A8
Dennis Rd Birmingham B12 87 B4
Coventry CV2 114 B6
Dennis St DY8 80 F8
Denshaw Croft CV2 115 A8
Denshaw Rd B14 104 D6
Denston Ct B74 31 F2
Dent St B79 21 C5
Denton Cl CV8 147 D6
Denton Croft B93 127 D3
Denton Gr
Birmingham, Great Barr B43 54 D7
Birmingham, Stechford B33 68 D2
Denton Rd DY9 82 A4
Denver Rd B14 105 A2
Denville Cl WV14 40 E7
Denville Cres B9 68 B3
Denville Rd CV32 157 A3
Depwo Gr B32 102 B8
Derby Ave WV6 24 F7
Derby Dr B37 70 B2
Derby Rd LE10 71 D1
Derby St Birmingham B9 67 A2
Walsall WS2 28 E4
Dereham Ct CV32 157 A2
Dereham Wlk WV14 40 E2
Dereton Cl DY1 61 E8
Derick Burcher's Mall
5 DY10 116 E6
Dering Cl CV2 114 D8
Deronda Cl CV12 78 A3
Derron Ave B26 88 E5
Derry Cl B17 85 A3
Derry St Brierley Hill DY5 61 D2
Wolverhampton WV2 163 C1
Derrydown Cl B23 56 E3
Derrydown Rd B42 55 B5
Dersingham Dr CV6 96 B2
Derwent B77 21 D1
Derwent Cl Aldridge B74 30 F3
Brierley Hill DY5 61 B6
Coventry CV5 111 E4
Royal Leamington Spa CV32 156 D1
Willenhall WV13 27 C2
Derwent Ct B73 46 B5
Derwent Gr Birmingham B13 86 C1
Burntwood WS7 7 D6
Cannock WS11 4 D7
Derwent Ho Birmingham B17 85 D5
Kidderminster DY10 116 F7
5 Oldbury B69 63 D5
Derwent Rd Bedworth CV12 78 A2
Birmingham B30 104 C8
Coventry CV6 95 A2
Wolverhampton WV6 24 E8
Derwent Way
Bromsgrove B60 137 B1
Nuneaton CV11 73 F6
Desborough Ho 8 B14 105 A3
Desford Ave B42 55 C7
Despard Rd CV5 111 D4
Dettonford Rd B32 102 B8
Devereux Cl Birmingham B36 69 C8
Coventry CV4 111 C1
Devereux Ho B79 21 A4
Devereux Rd
Sutton Coldfield B75 32 C1
West Bromwich B70 53 E1
Deveron Cl LE10 71 B1
Deveron Way LE10 71 B1
Devey Dr DY4 52 D6
Devine Croft DY4 52 A5
Devitts Cl B90 126 F7
Devon Cl Birmingham B20 54 F2
Nuneaton CV10 72 F3
Devon Cres Aldridge WS9 16 A1
Dudley DY2 61 F7
West Bromwich B71 53 C6
Devon Ct WS11 4 C8
Devon Gn WS11 4 F8
Devon Gr CV2 114 B6
Devon Ho
7 Birmingham B31 102 C2
4 Stourbridge DY8 80 F8
Devon Rd Birmingham B45 101 F1
Cannock WS11 4 F8
Smethwick B67 84 E7
Stourbridge DY8 80 E7
Wednesbury WS10 42 C4
Willenhall WV13 27 D1
Wolverhampton WV1 163 A4
Devon St B7 67 C5
Devonshire Ave B18 65 F6
Devonshire Ct B74 32 A2
Devonshire Dr Tamworth B78 21 A1
West Bromwich B71 53 E3
Devonshire Inf Sch B67 64 F5
Devonshire Jun Sch B67 64 F5
Devonshire Rd
Birmingham B20 54 F2
Smethwick B67 64 E6
Devonshire St B18 66 A6
Devonshire Villas B10 87 D8
Devoran Cl Bedworth CV7 96 B8
Wolverhampton WV6 25 B4
Dewberry Dr WS5 43 A3
Dewberry Rd DY8 60 F1
Dewhurst Croft B33 69 B3
Dewis Ho 4 CV2 96 B1
Dewsbury Ave CV3 133 B5
Dewsbury Cl DY8 60 E3
Dewsbury Dr Burntwood WS7 7 C6
Wolverhampton WV4 39 A4
Dewsbury Gr B42 55 C5
Dexter Ho B67 64 F6
Dexter Way B78 36 F8
Deykin Ave B6 56 B2
Deykin Avenue Jun & Inf Sch B6 56 B2
Dial Cl B14 104 E2
Dial House La CV5 111 F4
Dial La Stourbridge DY8 80 E8
West Bromwich B70 52 F6
Diamond Gr WS11 2 C2
Diamond Park Dr DY8 60 E1
Diana Cl WS9 16 B3
Diana Dr CV2 96 E1
Diane Cl DY4 41 B2
Dibble Cl WV12 27 D5
Dibble Rd B67 64 F6
Dibdale Ct 7 DY3 50 E3
Dibdale Rd DY1 50 F3
Dibdale St DY1 51 A2
Dice Pleck B31 103 C2
Dick Sheppard Ave DY4 52 B8
Dickens Cl Dudley DY3 50 B5
Nuneaton CV10 72 A4
Dickens Gr 9 B14 105 A3
Dickens Heath Rd B90 126 A6
Dickens Rd Coventry CV6 113 A8
Dudley WV14 40 D2
Wolverhampton WV10 12 A1
Dickins Rd CV34 156 B1
Dickinson Ave WV10 25 F8
Dickinson Dr
Sutton Coldfield B76 46 E4
Walsall WS2 42 C6
Dickinson Rd WV5 49 A5
Didcot Cl B97 158 C5
Diddington Ave B28 106 A5
Diddington La B92, CV7 91 C1
Didgley Gr B37 70 A5
Didsbury Rd CV7 78 A1
Digbeth Birmingham B5 164 D1
Walsall WS1 28 E1
Digbey Cl CV5 112 B6
Digby Cres B46 59 B3
Digby Ct 3 B27 88 C3
Digby Dr B37 90 B6
Digby Ho B37 69 F4
Digby Pl CV7 92 C1
Digby Rd Coleshill B46 70 F6
Kingswinford DY6 60 D8
Sutton Coldfield B73 46 B4
Dilcock Way CV4 131 F7
Dilke Rd WS9 29 F5
Dillam Cl CV6 96 A4
Dilliars Wlk B70 53 A5
Dillington Ho 8 B37 70 B2
Dillon Ct CV11 73 B5
Dillotford Ave CV3 133 D6
Dilloways La WV13 40 F8
Dilwyn Cl B98 154 F1
Dimbles Hill WS13 3 B1
Dimbles La WS13 3 A2
Dimmingsdale Bank B32 84 C4
Dimmingsdale Rd WV4 37 E5
Dimminsdale WV13 27 A1
Dimmock St WV4 39 E5
Dimmocks Ave WV14 51 D8
Dimsdale Gr B31 102 E3
Dimsdale Rd B31 102 D3
Dinedor Cl B98 154 D3
Dingle Ave B64 82 E8
Dingle Cl Birmingham B30 103 D7
Coventry CV6 113 A6
Dudley DY2 62 E7
Dingle Ct B91 106 F1
Dingle Hollow B69 63 D8
Dingle La Solihull B91 106 F2
Willenhall WV13 27 A4
Dingle Mead B14 104 C4
Dingle Prim Sch The DY6 61 A4
Dingle Rd Clayhanger WS8 15 E6
Dudley DY2 62 E7
Kingswinford DY6 61 A4
Stourbridge DY9 81 C2
Dingle St B69 63 E8
Dingle The Birmingham B29 85 E2
Cheswick Green B90 126 D5
Nuneaton CV10 72 E6
Oldbury B69 63 D8
Wolverhampton WV3 24 D1
Dingle View DY3 50 C6
Dingleside B98 153 E2
Dingleside Mid Sch B98 159 B8
Dingley Rd Bulkington CV12 79 B2
Wednesbury WS10 42 A5
Dinmore Ave B31 103 B4
Dinmore Cl B98 154 D3
Dinsdale Wlk WV6 25 A5
Dippons Dr WV6 24 A3
Dippons Ho WV6 24 A3
Dippons Mill Cl WV6 24 A3
Dirtyfoot La WV4 38 A5
Discovery Cl DY4 52 C5
Discovery Way CV3 135 B7
Ditch The WS1 28 F1
Ditchford Cl B97 158 D4
Ditton Gr B31 122 F6
Dixon Cl Birmingham B35 58 A2
Tipton DY4 52 C6
Dixon Ct DY10 117 C8
Dixon Ho B16 66 A1
Dixon Rd B10 87 B8
Dixon St Kidderminster DY10 116 E5
Wolverhampton WV2 39 F7
Dixon's Green Rd DY2 62 E8
Dixons Green Ct 7 DY2 62 E8
Dobbins Oak Rd DY9 81 E1
Dobbs Mill Cl B29 86 B2
Dobbs St WV2 163 B1
Dobson La CV31 162 A4
Dock La 9 DY1 51 B1
Dock Lane Ind Est 12 DY1 51 B1
Dock Meadow Dr WV4 40 A4
Dock Rd DY8 60 F2
Dock The Catshill B61 137 A8
Stourbridge DY9 81 F5
Dockar Rd B31 102 E2
Dockers Cl CV7 130 C7
Doctor's Piece WV13 27 B2
Doctors Hill
Bournheath B61 136 D8
Stourbridge DY9 81 C3
Doctors La Kingswinford DY6 60 A4
Shenstone WS14 18 A6
Dodd Ave CV34 161 C7
Doddington Gr B32 102 B8
Dodford Cl B45 121 F7
Dodford Fst Sch B61 136 A5
Dodford Ho B60 137 B3
Dodford Rd B61 120 D1
Dodwells Bridge Ind Est LE10 74 E8
Dodwells Rd LE10 74 E8
Doe Bank Ct B74 46 B8
Doe Bank La Birmingham B43 44 D5
Coventry CV1 113 A3
Doe Bank Rd DY4 41 C1
Dog Kennel La Solihull B90 126 D7
3 Walsall WS1 28 F2
Dog La Tamworth B77 22 B6
Weeford WS14 19 A4
Dogberry Cl CV3 134 C6
Dogge Lane Croft B27 88 B2
Dogkennel La Halesowen B63 83 B3
Oldbury B68 64 C5
Doglands The CV31 162 B4
Dogpool La B30 86 B1
Doidge Rd B23 56 D3
Dolben La B98 154 D3
Doll Mus CV34 160 E6
Dollery Dr B5 86 C5
Dollis Gr B44 44 F3
Dollman St B7 67 B4
Dolman Rd B6 66 E8
Dolobran Rd B11 87 B7
Dolphin Cl WS3 14 F1
Dolphin Ct WV12 27 D8
Dolphin La B27 88 C1
Dolphin Rd Birmingham B11 87 D5
Redditch B98 154 A5
Dolton Way DY4 51 E6
Domar Rd DY11 116 B7
Dominic Cl B30 103 D4
Don Cl B15 85 D8
Don Gr WS11 4 D7
Doncaster Cl CV2 114 D7
Doncaster Way B36 68 C8
Donegal Cl CV4 132 A7
Donegal Rd B74 44 F5
Dongan Rd CV34 160 E7
Donibristle Croft B35 58 A4
Donnington Ave CV6 112 E5
Donnington Cl B98 154 C5
Donnington Ho B33 69 B2
Donnithorne Ave CV10, CV11 73 D1
Dooley Cl WV13 26 E2
Doone Cl CV2 114 E6
Dora Herbert Ct B12 86 E5
Dora Rd Birmingham B10 87 E8
Birmingham, Handsworth B21 65 E7
West Bromwich B70 53 C1
Dora St WS2 42 B7
Dorado B77 35 D6
Doran Cl B63 82 D1
Doranda Way B71 53 F1
Dorcas Cl CV11 79 C8
Dorchester Cl WV12 27 C8
Dorchester Ct B91 107 A4
Dorchester Dr B17 85 B4
Dorchester Rd Cannock WS11 1 B1
Hinckley LE10 76 B7
Solihull B91 107 A4
Stourbridge DY9 81 D2
Willenhall WV12 13 C1
Dorchester Way
Coventry CV2 115 A4
Nuneaton CV11 74 A7
Dordale Rd B61, DY9 119 E2
Dordon Cl B90 105 E1
Dordon Rd B78 36 F8
Doreen Gr B24 57 B2
Doris Rd Birmingham B11 87 B4
Birmingham, Bordesley Green B9 67 D2
Coleshill B46 70 F8
Dorking Gr B15 66 C1
Dorlcote Rd B8 68 A4
Dorlecote Ct CV10 73 C1
Dorlecote Pl CV10 78 C8
Dorlecote Rd CV10 78 C8
Dormer Ave B77 21 E5
Dormer Harris Ave CV4 111 F1
Dormer Ho 13 CV32 156 F2
Dormer Pl CV32 161 F8
Dormie Cl B38 103 D1
Dormington Rd B44 44 F3
Dormston Cl Redditch B98 153 F1
Solihull B91 127 C8
Dormston Dr Birmingham B29 84 F2
Sedgley DY3 50 E8
Dormston Sch DY3 50 E8
Dormston Trad Est DY1 50 F4
Dormy Dr B31 123 A7
Dorncliffe Ave B33 89 D7
Dorney Cl CV5 132 E8
Dornie Dr B38 103 F1
Dornton Rd B30 104 C8
Dorothy Gdns B20 55 A2
Dorothy Goodman Specl Sch The LE10 71 D2
Dorothy Pattison Hospl WS2 28 B1
Dorothy Powell Way CV2 96 F1
Dorothy Purcell Jun Sch WV14 41 B3
Dorothy Rd Birmingham B11 88 B5
Smethwick B67 65 A4
Dorothy St WS1 42 D7
Dorridge Cl B97 153 B1
Dorridge Croft B93 127 F2
Dorridge Jun & Inf Schs B93 128 A4
Dorridge Rd B93 128 A2
Dorridge Sta B93 127 F2
Dorrington Gn B42 55 A5
Dorrington Jun & Inf Sch B42 55 A5
Dorrington Rd B42 55 A5
Dorset Cl Birmingham B45 101 F2
Nuneaton CV10 72 F3
Tamworth B78 21 A1
Dorset Cotts B30 104 A6
Dorset Dr WS9 16 B1
Dorset Pl WS3 28 C7
Dorset Rd Birmingham B8 67 C6
Cannock WS12 2 E1
Coventry CV1 113 C5
Smethwick B17 65 B3
Stourbridge DY8 80 D8
Dorset Tower B18 66 B4
Dorsett Rd Darlaston WS10 41 C6
Wednesbury WS10 42 D2
Dorsett Road Terr WS10 41 C6
Dorsheath Gdns B23 56 F4
Dorsington Rd B27 88 D1
Dorstone Covert B14 104 C2
Dorville Cl B38 123 D8
Dosthill Rd (Two Gates) B77 35 D7
Dosthill Sch B77 35 D5
Dotterel Pl DY10 117 A1
Douay Rd B24 57 B6
Double Row DY2 62 E4
Doughty St DY4 52 C5
Douglas Ave Birmingham B36 68 D6
Oldbury B68 64 D5
Douglas Davies Cl WV12 27 C4
Douglas Ho
5 Birmingham B36 57 F1
Coventry CV1 165 D4
Douglas Pl WV10 25 C6

Douglas Rd Birmingham B27 88 C4
Birmingham,
Handsworth B21 65 F8
Dudley WV14 51 D8
Halesowen B62 63 E1
Hollywood B47 125 A7
Oldbury B68 64 D4
Sutton Coldfield B72 46 C3
Douglass Rd DY2 62 D8
Doulton Cl Birmingham B32 84 F3
Coventry CV2 96 E1
Doulton Rd Blackheath B65 63 A4
Oldbury B64, B65 62 F4
Doulton Trad Est B65 62 F4
Dove Cl Bedworth CV12 77 E3
Birmingham B25 88 E8
Burntwood WS7 7 D6
Hinckley LE10 75 A8
Kidderminster DY10 117 B2
Wednesbury WS10 42 B4
Dove Dr DY8 81 A8
Dove Gdns B38 104 B2
Dove Hollow Cannock WS12 2 E4
Great Wyrley WS6 4 F1
Dove House Ct B92 106 F7
Dove House La B91 107 A8
Dove Ridge DY8 81 A7
Dove Way B36 69 F8
Dovebridge Cl B76 46 F4
Dovecote Cl Coventry CV6 112 D5
Solihull B91 107 B8
Tipton DY4 52 C5
Wolverhampton WV6 24 C4
Dovecote Rd B61 136 E1
Dovecotes Jun & Inf Schs
WV8 10 F1
Dovecotes The
Coventry CV5 112 B5
Sutton Coldfield B75 32 B3
Dovedale WS11 2 A5
Dovedale Ave Coventry CV6 95 F2
Solihull B90 106 B1
Walsall WS3 15 B5
Willenhall WV12 27 B4
Dovedale Ct WV4 39 F2
Dovedale Dr B28 105 F5
Dovedale Ho WV1 26 C1
Dovedale Rd Birmingham
B23 56 C7
Kingswinford DY6 60 E8
Wolverhampton wv4, WV14 39 E3
Dovehouse Fields WS14 9 B6
Dovehouse La B91 106 F7
Dovehouse Pool Rd 1 B6 66 E8
Dover Cl B32 102 A7
Dover Farm Cl B77 36 B8
Dover Ho WS3 28 C7
Dover St Bilston WV14 40 D6
Birmingham B18 66 A6
Coventry CV1 165 A3
Dovercourt Ho 1 B15 86 D8
Dovercourt Rd B26 89 C5
Doverdale Ave DY10 117 B5
Doverdale Cl Halesowen
B63 82 E5
Redditch B98 159 B7
Doveridge Cl B91 106 E6
Doveridge Rd B28 105 E5
Doversley Rd B14 104 C5
Dovestone B77 22 D1
Dovey Dr B76 58 A7
Dovey Rd Birmingham B13 87 D2
Tipton B69 63 D8
Dowar Rd B45 122 C7
Dowells Cl B13 86 F2
Dowells Gdns DY8 60 D3
Dower Rd B75 32 B1
Doweries The B45 121 F8
Dowler's Hill Cres B98 159 A8
Dowles Cl B29 103 B6
Dowles Rd DY11 116 B2
Dowley Croft CV3 115 B1
Downcroft Ave B38 103 E2
Downderry Way CV6 114 A6
Downend Cl WV10 11 F4
Downes Ct 7 DY4 51 E5
Downesway WS11 1 C2
Downey Cl B11 87 B7
Downfield Cl WS3 14 A4
Downfield Dr DY3 50 E6
Downham Cl WS5 29 E1
Downham Pl WV3 38 F8
Downham Wood WS5 43 E8
Downie Rd WV8 10 C3
Downing Cl 6
Blackheath B65 63 C1
Knowle B93 128 A4
Wednesfield WV11 27 A7
Downing Cres CV12 78 C4
Downing Ct 5 B68 84 B7
Downing Ho B37 70 B1
Downing St Halesowen B63 83 A5
Smethwick B66 65 C7
Downland Cl B38 103 F1
Downs Rd WV13 41 C8
Downs The Aldridge WS9 30 E2
Wolverhampton WV10 25 C6
Downsell Rd B97 153 A2
Downsfield Rd B26 89 B7
Downside Rd B24 56 E1
Downton Cl CV2 115 A8
Downton Cres B33 69 E3
Dowty Ave CV12 77 D1
Dowty Way WV9 11 A3
Doyle Dr CV6 95 F3
Dr Phillips Sh Ctr The CV2 96 D1
Dragoon Fields B60 151 B8
Drake Cl WS3 14 B1
Drake Cres DY11 116 A7
Drake Croft 3 WS13 9 C8
Drake Ho DY4 52 A7
Drake Rd Birmingham B23 56 C3
Smethwick B66 64 E7
Walsall WS3 14 B1
Drake St Coventry CV6 113 D7
West Bromwich B71 53 C5
Drake Way LE10 71 D4
Drake's Gn WV14 40 F3
Drakes Cl B97 158 C6
Drakes Hill Cl DY8 80 C4
Drancy Ave WV12 27 D6
Draper Cl CV8 148 C4
Draper's Fields CV1 165 B4
Drawbridge Rd B90 125 E8
Draycote Cl B92 107 D6
Draycott Ave B23 56 D5
Draycott Cl Redditch B97 153 B5
Wolverhampton WV4 38 C5
Draycott Cres B77 21 D1
Draycott Dr B31 102 E7
Draycott Rd Coventry CV2 114 C7
Smethwick B66 64 E7
Drayton Cl Nuneaton CV10 72 A8
Redditch B98 159 D8
Sutton Coldfield B75 32 B3
Drayton Cres CV5 111 D5
Drayton Ct Bromsgrove B60 151 B8
Warwick CV34 155 E2
Drayton La B78 34 C5
Drayton Manor Dr
Fazeley B78 34 F7
Fazeley B78 34 F8
Drayton Manor Pk B78 34 E7
Drayton Rd Bedworth CV12 78 D2
Belbroughton DY9 119 B5
Birmingham B14 104 F8
Smethwick B66 65 A1
Solihull B90 126 E8
Drayton St Walsall WS2 28 C2
Wolverhampton WV2 163 B1
Drayton St E WS2 28 C2
Drayton Way CV10 72 C7
Dreadnought Rd DY5 61 B8
Dreel The B15 85 E7
Dreghorn Rd B36 68 F8
Drem Croft B35 58 A2
Dresden Cl WV4 40 A4
Drew Cres Kenilworth CV8 148 A4
Stourbridge DY9 81 D2
Drew Rd DY9 81 D3
Drews Ho B14 104 D1
Drews Holloway B63 82 D5
Drews Holloway S B63 82 D5
Drews La B8 68 A7
Drews Meadow Cl
1 B14 104 C2
Driffield Cl B98 154 D2
Driffold B73 46 B3
Driftwood Cl B38 123 D7
Drinkwater Ho 7 CV1 113 B2
Drive Fields WV4 38 B6
Drive Prep Sch The WV6 24 C5
Drive The
Birmingham,
Gravelly Hill B23 56 E2
Birmingham,
Handsworth B20 55 B2
Brierley Hill DY5 61 C5
Coventry CV2 114 E3
Halesowen B63 83 A3
Hopwood B48 123 B3
Redditch B97 152 C7
Shenstone WS14 18 E8
Walsall, High Heath WS4 15 C1
Walsall, Pelsall WS3 14 E2
Wolverhampton WV6 24 C5
Droicon Trad Est B65 63 C5
Dronfield Rd CV2 114 B3
Drovers Way B60 150 E6
Droveway The WV8, WV9 10 F2
Droxford Wlk WV8 10 E1
Droylsdon Park Rd CV3 133 B3
Druid Park Rd WV12 13 C1
Druid Rd CV2 114 B3
Druid St LE10 71 D1
Druids Ave Aldridge WS9 30 C8
Blackheath B65 63 D4
Druids La B14 104 D1
Druids Wlk WS9 16 A3
Drummond Cl Coventry
CV6 112 F7
Wolverhampton WV11 13 A2
Drummond Gr B43 44 C3
Drummond Rd
Birmingham B9 68 A2
Bromsgrove B60 151 B8
Stourbridge DY9 81 F4
Drummond St WV1 163 B4
Drummond Way B37 70 C2
Drury La Solihull B91 107 C3
Stourbridge DY8 81 A5
Drybrook Cl B38 123 E8
Drybrooks Cl CV7 130 B6
Dryden Cl Kenilworth CV8 147 F3
Tipton DY4 52 A7
Willenhall WV12 27 E8
Dryden Ct B27 88 B2
Dryden Pl WS3 28 E7
Dryden Rd Tamworth B79 21 A6
Walsall WS3 28 E7
Wolverhampton WV10 11 F1
Drylea Gr B36 68 F8
Dual Way WS12 1 D8
Dubarry Ave DY6 60 C7
Duchess Rd Birmingham B16 66 A1
Walsall WS1 42 D5
Duck La WV8 10 B3
Duckhouse Rd WV11 26 D7
Duddeston Manor Rd B7 67 A4
Duddeston Mill Rd B7, B8 67 C4
Duddeston Mill Trad Est B8 67 C4
Duddeston Sta B7 67 B4
Dudding Rd WV4 39 D5
Dudhill Rd B65 63 A3
Dudhill Wlk B65 63 A4
Dudley Castle DY1 51 D2
Dudley Central Trad Est
DY2 62 C8
Dudley Cl B65 63 A5
Dudley Coll Mons Hill DY1 51 B5
Dudley Coll of Tech (The
Glass Ctr Annexe) DY5 61 D3
Dudley Cres WV11 26 E6
Dudley Gn CV32 157 B2
Dudley Gr 7 B18 65 F4
Dudley Innovation Ctr DY6 60 F7
Dudley L Ctr DY1 51 B1
Dudley Park Rd B27 88 C3
Dudley Port DY4 52 A3
Dudley Port Sta DY4 52 B4
Dudley Rd Birmingham B18 65 E4
Blackheath B65 63 A5
Brierley Hill DY5 61 D4
Dudley DY3 50 E6
Halesowen B63 83 B5
Himley DY3 49 D3
Kenilworth CV8 147 F2
Kingswinford,
Barrow Hill DY6 60 F7
Kingswinford,Wall Heath DY6 60 C8
Oldbury B69 63 F8
Stourbridge DY9 81 E6
Tipton DY4 51 E5
Wolverhampton WV2 39 D7
Dudley Rd E B69 52 D1
Dudley Rd W B69 52 B2
Dudley Rise LE10 75 D6
Dudley Row DY2 51 D1
Dudley St Bilston WV14 40 D4
Birmingham B5 164 C2
Coventry CV6 96 A1
Kidderminster DY10 116 E7
Sedgley DY3 50 D8
Walsall WS1 28 E1
Wednesbury WS10 41 E2
West Bromwich B70 53 A5
Wolverhampton WV1 163 B3
Dudley Street, Guns
Village Sta B70 53 B4
Dudley Tech Coll DY1 51 C2
Dudley Tech Coll Annexe
DY1 51 B1
Dudley Tech Coll (Tipton
Annexe) DY4 51 D6
Dudley Terr CV8 149 B6
Dudley Wlk WV4 39 C5
Dudley Wood Ave DY2 62 C2
Dudley Wood Prim Sch
DY2 62 C2
Dudley Wood Rd DY2 62 C2
Dudley Zoo DY1 51 D2
Dudmaston Way DY1 50 E3
Dudnill Gr B32 102 A8
Duffield Cl WV8 10 F1
Dufton Rd B32 84 E4
Dugdale Cl WS12 2 F3
Dugdale Cres B75 32 C3
Dugdale Ct 5 CV31 162 A6
Dugdale Ho CV11 73 C3
Dugdale Rd CV6 113 B6
Dugdale St Nuneaton CV11 73 C4
Smethwick B18 65 D4
Duggins La CV4, CV7 131 B8
Duke Barn Field CV2 114 A5
Duke St Blackheath B65 63 B2
Coventry CV5 112 F2
Dudley DY3 50 D5
Nuneaton CV11 73 B4
Royal Leamington Spa CV32 157 A1
Stourbridge DY8 81 A6
Sutton Coldfield B72 46 B4
Wednesfield WV11 26 D5
West Bromwich B70 53 B4
Wolverhampton,
Penn Fields WV3 39 A7
Wolverhampton,
Springfield WV1 163 D2
Dukes Rd Birmingham B30 104 A3
Dordon B78 36 F6
Dulais Cl B98 153 E1
Dulvern Gr B14 104 D5
Dulverton Ave CV5 112 D4
Dulverton Ct CV5 112 D4
Dulverton Rd B6 56 B1
Dulwich Gr B44 56 B8
Dulwich Rd B44 56 A8
Dumble Pit La B48 140 F7
Dumbleberry Ave DY3 50 C7
Dumbleberry Ct WS9 29 F5
Dumblederry La
Aldridge WS9 29 F6
Walsall WS9 29 E7
Dumolo's Cty Prim Sch
B77 21 F2
Dumolos La B77 21 F3
Dumphouse La B48 140 C3
Dunard Rd B90 105 F3
Dunbar Cl Birmingham B32 84 D1
Kidderminster DY10 117 C6
Dunbar Gr B43 44 B4
Dunblane Dr CV32 157 C5
Dunblane Way LE10 71 A2
Duncalfe Dr B75 32 B3
Duncan Edwards Cl DY1 62 A8
Duncan Ho B73 46 B1
Duncan St WV2 39 C7
Dunchurch Cl
Balsall Common CV7 130 B7
Redditch B98 154 F1
Dunchurch Cres B73 45 C3
Dunchurch Dr B31 102 E7
Dunchurch Highway CV5 112 A4
Dunchurch Ho 4 B5 86 E8
Dunclent Cres DY10 117 B5
Duncombe Gn 12 B46 70 F7
Duncombe Gr B17 85 A7
Duncombe St DY8 80 D5
Duncroft Ave CV6 112 F7
Duncroft Rd B26 89 A8
Duncroft Wlk DY1 51 B6
Duncumb Rd B75 47 A5
Dundalk La WS6 4 D2
Dundas Ave DY2 62 F8
Dundle Ct B74 31 F2
Dunedin B77 22 A1
Dunedin Dr B45 122 B1
Dunedin Ho B32 84 F4
Dunedin Rd B44 44 F3
Dunhill Ave CV4 111 E3
Dunkirk Ave B70 52 E3
Dunkley St WV1 163 B4
Dunley Croft B90 126 F6
Dunley Ct B23 56 C2
Dunlin Cl Birmingham B23 56 C2
Featherstone WV10 12 B7
Kingswinford DY6 61 A6
Dunlin Dr DY10 116 F2
Dunlop Rd B97 158 D5
Dunlop Way B35 57 F2
Dunnerdale Rd WS8 15 D6
Dunnigan Rd B32 84 F3
Dunnose Cl CV6 113 E8
Dunns Bank DY5 81 F7
Dunrose Cl CV2 114 E2
Dunsfold Cl WV14 40 A3
Dunsfold Croft 3 B6 66 F6
Dunsford Cl DY5 81 B7
Dunsford Rd B66 65 A2
Dunsink Rd B6 55 F1
Dunslade Cres DY5 81 F8
Dunslade Rd B23 56 E7
Dunsley Dr DY8 60 E3
Dunsley Gr WV4 39 A4
Dunsley Rd DY8 80 C4
Dunsmore Ave CV3 134 C6
Dunsmore Dr DY5 81 F8
Dunsmore Gr B91 106 F7
Dunsmore Rd B28 87 E2
Dunstall Ave WV6 25 C4
Dunstall Cl B97 153 B2
Dunstall Gr B29 102 F8
Dunstall Hill W6 25 C5
Dunstall Hill Prim Sch
WV6 25 C4
Dunstall Hill Trad Est W6 25 C5
Dunstall La Hopwas B78 20 D4
Wolverhampton W6 25 B5
Dunstall Park Race
Course WV6 25 A6
Dunstall Rd Halesowen B63 82 D3
Wolverhampton WV6 25 B4
Dunstan Croft B90 126 C8
Dunstan Ct 3 B15 86 B7
Dunster B77 35 C7
Dunster Cl B30 104 C4
Dunster Gr WV6 23 F3
Dunster Pl CV6 95 D3
Dunster Rd B37 70 D2
Dunston Cl Great Wyrley
WS6 13 E8
Kingswinford DY6 60 D7
Dunston Dr WS7 7 A8
Dunsville Dr CV2 114 F8
Dunton Cl B75 32 A4
Dunton Hall Rd B90 126 A8
Dunton La B76 48 C1
Dunton Rd B37 69 F5
Dunton Trad Est B7 67 D7
Dunvegan Cl Coventry CV3 115 A2
Kenilworth CV8 148 C4
Dunvegan Rd B24 57 A4
Duport Rd LE10 75 F7
Durant Cl B45 101 E1
Durban Rd B66 65 C4
Durbar Ave CV6 113 D8
Durham Ave WV13 27 D3
Durham Cl Bromsgrove
B61 136 E4
Keresley CV7 94 F4
Durham Cres CV5 112 B7
Durham Croft B37 70 B2
Durham Dr B71 53 D7
Durham Ho 1 WV3 25 C4
Durham Pl WS2 28 B1
Durham Rd Birmingham B11 87 B4
Blackheath B65 63 E4
Dudley DY2 62 D2
Stourbridge DY8 80 D8
Walsall WS2 42 B8
Wednesbury WS10 42 D4
Durham Tower 3 B1 66 B3
Durley Dean Rd B29 85 C2
Durley Dr B73 45 C3
Durley Rd B25 88 C6
Durlston Cl B77 21 F5
Durlston Gr B28 106 A8
Durnford Croft B14 104 E1
Dursley Cl Solihull B92 107 B8
Willenhall WV12 27 D4
Dursley Dr WS11 1 B2
Dursley Rd WS7 7 A7
Dusthouse La B60 151 D7
Dutton Rd CV2 96 D3
Dutton's La B75 32 E4
Duxford Cl B97 158 B8
Duxford Rd B42 55 B7
Dwarris Wlk CV34 155 E2
Dwellings La B32 84 B5
Dyas Ave B42 55 A7
Dyas Rd Birmingham B44 44 E1
Hollywood B47 125 A7
Dyce Cl B35 58 A4
Dyers La B94 142 D8
Dyers Rd CV11 79 F6
Dymoke St B12 86 F8
Dymond Rd CV6 95 D3
Dynes Wlk B67 65 A5
Dyott Rd B13 87 A1
Dysart Cl CV1 113 E4
Dyson Cl WS2 27 F3
Dyson St CV4 111 E3
Dysons Gdns B8 67 E5

Eachelhurst Rd B24, B76 57 F5
Eachus Rd WV14 51 D8
Eachway B45 121 F6
Eachway Farm Cl B45 122 A6
Eachway La B45 122 A6
Eacott Cl CV6 95 A3
Eadgar Ct B43 54 D7
Eadie St CV10 72 D4
Eagle Cl Blackheath B65 63 A4
Cheslyn Hay WS6 4 D2
Dudley DY1 50 F1
Nuneaton CV11 79 B8
Eagle Croft B14 104 E2
Eagle Ct WV3 39 A7
Eagle Dr B77 22 C4
Eagle Gdns B24 57 A2
Eagle Gr Birmingham B36 70 A8
Cannock WS12 2 C1
Eagle Ho CV1 113 D5
Eagle Ind Est DY4 52 E7
Eagle La Kenilworth CV8 147 F4
Tipton DY4 52 D6
Eagle Rd B98 154 E5
Eagle St Coventry CV1 113 D5
Royal Leamington Spa CV31 162 A6
Tipton DY4 52 C6
Wolverhampton,
Monmore Green WV2 39 E8
Wolverhampton,
Penn Fields WV3 39 A7
Eagle St E CV1 113 D5
Eagle Trad Est B63 83 A4
Eales Yd 4 LE10 71 D1
Ealing Gr B44 45 A1
Ealingham B77 22 B1
Eanwulf Ct B15 86 C8
Eardisley Cl B98 154 F1
Earl St Bedworth CV12 78 C2
Bilston WV14 40 D5
Coventry CV1 165 C2
Dudley WV14 51 D8
Kingswinford DY6 60 D4
Royal Leamington Spa CV32 157 A1
Walsall WS1 42 D7
West Bromwich B70 53 B4
Earl's Croft The CV3 133 D7
Earl's Wlk CV3 135 D7
Earls Court Rd B17 85 A6
Earls Ferry Gdns B32 102 B7
Earls High Sch The B63 83 B4
Earls Rd Nuneaton CV11 73 A5
Walsall WS4 29 D7
Earls Way B63 83 B4
Earlsbury Gdns B20 55 D1
Earlsdon Ave N CV5 112 F1
Earlsdon Ave S CV5 133 A8
Earlsdon Bsns Ctr CV5 132 F8
Earlsdon Prim Sch CV5 113 A1
Earlsdon St CV5 132 F8
Earlsmead Rd B21 65 C7
Earlsmere B94 126 B1
Earlston Way B43 54 D8
Earlswood Comm B94 142 A6
Earlswood Cres WV9 11 A3
Earlswood Ct B20 55 A2
Earlswood Dr B74 46 C7
Earlswood Ho 1 B5 86 E7
Earlswood Rd Dorridge
B93 127 D2
Kingswinford DY6 60 E8
Earlswood Sta B94 125 D1
Earlswood Trad Est B94 141 C6
Easby Way Birmingham B8 67 E5
Walsall WS3 13 F2
Easedale Cl Coventry CV3 133 B6
Nuneaton CV11 74 A6
Easemore Rd B98 153 F5
Easenhall Cl B93 128 A4
Easenhall La B98 154 E1
Easmore Cl B14 104 D2
East Ave Bedworth CV12 78 D2
Coventry CV2 114 A2
Tipton B69 63 C7
Wolverhampton WV11 26 C6
East Birmingham Coll
Birmingham B11 87 A7
Birmingham B33 89 B8
Birmingham, Sparkhill B11 87 D5
East Birmingham Coll
Bordesley Green Campus
B9 68 A2
East Birmingham Hospl
B9 68 B1
East Cannock Ind Est WS12 2 B3

East Cannock Rd WS12 .... 2 C4
East Car Park Rd B40 .... 90 F4
East Cl LE10 .... 75 D7
East Croft Rd WV4 .... 38 C5
East Dene CV32 .... 157 B2
East Dr B5 .... 86 C4
East Farm Croft B10 .... 87 D8
East Gate B16 .... 65 E3
East Gn WV4 .... 38 D6
East Gr CV31 .... 162 A6
East Holme B9 .... 67 C2
East Meadway B33 .... 69 E3
East Mews B44 .... 44 D2
East Park Inf Sch WV1 .... 26 B1
East Park Jun Sch WV1 .... 40 B8
East Park Trad Est WV1 .... 40 A8
East Park Way WV1 .... 26 A1
East Pathway B17 .... 85 C6
East Rd Bromsgrove B60 .... 137 A1
Featherstone WV10 .... 12 A6
Tipton DY4 .... 52 B8
East Rise B75 .... 46 D6
East St Brierley Hill DY5 .... 82 A8
Cannock WS11 .... 4 E6
Coventry CV1 .... 113 E3
Dudley, Gornalwood DY3 .... 50 D3
Dudley, Kate's Hill DY2 .... 62 E8
Kidderminster DY10 .... 116 F6
Tamworth B77 .... 35 D5
Walsall WS1 .... 42 F7
Wolverhampton WV1 .... 163 D2
East View B77 .... 21 E3
East View Rd B72 .... 46 D2
East Way B92 .... 91 B3
Eastboro Ct CV11 .... 73 E2
Eastboro Way CV11 .... 73 F2
Eastbourne Ave B34 .... 68 E6
Eastbourne Cl CV6 .... 112 E6
Eastbourne House Sch B27 .... 88 C4
Eastbourne St WS4 .... 28 F3
Eastbrook Cl B76 .... 46 D4
Eastbury Dr B92 .... 89 A3
Eastcote Cl B90 .... 106 D3
Eastcote Cres WS7 .... 7 A5
Eastcote La B92 .... 108 F4
Eastcote Rd Birmingham B27 .... 88 A1
Wolverhampton WV10 .... 25 F5
Eastcotes CV4 .... 112 B1
Eastdean Cl B23 .... 56 D6
Eastern Ave Brierley Hill DY5 .... 61 B2
Lichfield WS13 .... 3 C3
Eastern Cl WS10 .... 41 C3
Eastern Green Jun Sch CV5 .... 111 D5
Eastern Green Rd CV5 .... 111 F4
Eastern Hill B96 .... 158 F2
Eastern Rd Birmingham B29 .... 86 B3
Sutton Coldfield B73 .... 46 B1
Eastern Way WS11 .... 4 F6
Easterton Croft B14 .... 104 E2
Eastfield Dr B92 .... 107 E8
Eastfield Gr WV1 .... 25 F2
Eastfield Prim Sch WV1 .... 25 F2
Eastfield Rd Birmingham B9 .... 68 C3
Nuneaton CV10 .... 73 D6
Royal Leamington Spa CV32 .... 162 A8
Tipton DY4 .... 52 A8
Wolverhampton WV1 .... 25 F2
Eastfield Retreat WV1 .... 25 F2
Eastgate Ho 10 CV34 .... 160 E6
Eastgate Mews 9 CV34 .... 160 E6
Eastgate St WS7 .... 6 E8
Eastham Rd B13 .... 105 C6
Easthope Rd B33 .... 69 A4
Eastlake Cl B43 .... 44 D3
Eastlands Gr CV5 .... 112 E4
Eastlands Rd B13 .... 87 A1
Eastleigh DY3 .... 50 C8
Eastleigh Ave CV5 .... 132 F7
Eastleigh Croft B76 .... 58 A7
Eastleigh Dr B62 .... 101 A4
Eastleigh Gr B25 .... 88 D8
Eastley Cres CV34 .... 160 B8
Eastmoor Cl B74 .... 31 B2
Eastney Cres WV8 .... 24 F8
Eastnor Cl Kidderminster DY10 .... 116 E2
Redditch B98 .... 153 E1
Eastnor Gr CV31 .... 162 B7
Easton Gdns WV11 .... 26 F5
Easton Gr Birmingham B27 .... 88 C1
Hollywood B47 .... 125 B7
Eastridge Croft WS14 .... 18 A5
Eastville B31 .... 103 B3
Eastward Glen WV8 .... 10 C1
Eastway
Birmingham, Bickenhill B40 .... 90 F3
Birmingham, Harborne B17 .... 85 C6
Eastwood Ave WS7 .... 7 A8
Eastwood Cl CV31 .... 162 D6
Eastwood Ct B96 .... 158 E1
Eastwood Dr DY10 .... 117 B5
Eastwood Rd
Birmingham, Balsall Heath B12 .... 86 D5
Birmingham, Great Barr B43 .... 54 F8
Dudley DY2 .... 62 E6
Eastwoods Rd LE10 .... 71 F2
Eatesbrook Rd B33 .... 69 C3
Eathorpe Cl Birmingham B34 .... 69 D6
Coventry CV2 .... 96 C1
Redditch B98 .... 154 E1
Eaton Ave B70 .... 53 A4
Eaton Cl CV32 .... 156 D2
Eaton Cres DY3 .... 50 B3
Eaton Ct
Royal Leamington Spa CV32 .... 156 D1
Sutton Coldfield B74 .... 46 B7
Eaton Pl DY6 .... 60 E5
Eaton Rd CV1 .... 165 B1
Eaton Rise WV12 .... 27 B6
Eaves Court Dr DY3 .... 39 C1
Eaves Green Gdns B27 .... 88 B5
Eaves Green La CV7 .... 92 E1
Ebbw Vale Terr CV3 .... 133 D7
Ebenezer St Cannock WS12 .... 2 A7
Dudley WV14 .... 51 C8
West Bromwich B70 .... 52 F6
Ebley Rd B20 .... 55 A4
Ebmore Dr B14 .... 104 D2
Eborall Cl CV34 .... 155 E2
Ebourne Cl CV8 .... 148 A4
Ebrington Ave B92 .... 89 B3
Ebrington Cl B14 .... 104 D4
Ebrington Rd B71 .... 53 D6
Ebro Cres CV3 .... 114 F1
Ebrook Rd B72 .... 46 C4
Ebstree Rd WV4 .... 37 B4
Eburne Prim Sch CV2 .... 96 D2
Eburne Rd CV2 .... 96 C3
Ebury Rd B30 .... 104 B4
Eccles Cl CV2 .... 114 C8
Eccleshall Ave WV10 .... 25 C8
Eccleston Cl B75 .... 46 F5
Eccleston Sch B17 .... 85 B5
Ecclestone Rd WV11 .... 27 A8
Echells Cl B61 .... 136 D2
Echo Way WV4 .... 40 A4
Eckersall Rd B38 .... 103 E3
Eckington Cl B98 .... 159 B8
Eckington Wlk B38 .... 123 E7
Eclipse Ind Est 1 DY4 .... 51 E5
Edale B77 .... 22 B1
Edale Cl Kingswinford DY6 .... 60 B7
Wolverhampton WV4 .... 39 E3
Edale Gn LE10 .... 75 F6
Edale Rd B42 .... 55 C7
Edale Way CV6 .... 114 A7
Eddenswood Cl B78 .... 34 E5
Eddie Miller Ct CV12 .... 78 B2
Eddish Rd B33 .... 69 B3
Eddy Rd DY10 .... 116 E7
Eden Cl Birmingham B31 .... 122 E8
Cannock WS12 .... 2 E2
Studley B80 .... 159 D3
Tipton B69 .... 52 D2
Eden Croft CV8 .... 148 B3
Eden Ct CV32 .... 157 D3
Eden Gr Birmingham B37 .... 70 D1
West Bromwich B71 .... 53 D5
Eden Rd Coventry CV2 .... 115 A8
Solihull B92 .... 89 D3
Eden St CV6 .... 113 F7
Edenbridge Rd B28 .... 106 B8
Edencroft B15 .... 86 C8
Edendale Dr LE10 .... 71 E4
Edendale Rd B26 .... 89 B6
Edenhall Rd B32 .... 84 B6
Edenhurst Rd B31 .... 122 F7
Edensor Cl WV10 .... 25 E4
Edgar Cl B79 .... 20 F7
Edgar Stammers Jun & Inf Schs WS3 .... 28 F6
Edgbaston CE Coll for Girls B15 .... 86 B8
Edgbaston Coll B5 .... 86 B5
Edgbaston High Sch for Girls B15 .... 85 F7
Edgbaston Nuffield Hospl B15 .... 85 F5
Edgbaston Park Rd B15 .... 86 A5
Edgbaston Rd
Birmingham B12 .... 86 D5
Smethwick B66 .... 65 A4
Edgbaston Rd E B12 .... 86 F5
Edgbaston Sh Ctr B16 .... 86 A8
Edgbaston St B5 .... 164 C2
Edgbaston (The Warwickshire Cty Cricket Club) B12 .... 86 D5
Edgcombe Rd B28 .... 87 F1
Edge Hill CV9 .... 36 B2
Edge Hill Ave WV10 .... 12 B2
Edge Hill Dr Perton WV6 .... 23 E3
Sedgley DY3 .... 39 C2
Edge Hill Rd B74 .... 31 E4
Edge St WV14 .... 51 D8
Edgefield Rd CV2 .... 115 A8
Edgehill Pl CV4 .... 111 C1
Edgehill Rd B31 .... 103 B1
Edgemond Ave B24 .... 57 F4
Edgemoor Mdw WS12 .... 2 C1
Edgewick Com Prim Sch CV6 .... 113 E8
Edgewood Cl 1 B64 .... 82 F8
Edgewood Dr B45 .... 122 B1
Edgewood Rd
Birmingham, King's Norton B38 .... 123 F7
Birmingham, Rednall B45 .... 122 B6
Edgeworth Cl Redditch B98 .... 154 C5
Willenhall WV12 .... 27 C4
Edgeworth Ho WS13 .... 3 A2
Edgmond Cl B98 .... 154 D4
Edgware Rd B23 .... 56 D5
Edgwick Park Ind Est CV6 .... 113 F8
Edgwick Rd CV6 .... 113 F7
Edgwood Ct 4 B16 .... 65 F1
Edinburgh Ave WS2 .... 27 F3
Edinburgh Cl DY10 .... 116 E8
Edinburgh Cres
Royal Leamington Spa CV31 .... 161 F6
Stourbridge DY8 .... 60 C1
Edinburgh Ct B24 .... 57 D4
Edinburgh Dr Walsall WS4 .... 29 D7
Willenhall WV12 .... 27 B6
Edinburgh La WS2 .... 28 A4
Edinburgh Rd Bilston WV14 .... 40 F3
Dudley DY2 .... 62 D6
Nuneaton CV10 .... 72 D6
Oldbury B68 .... 84 B8
Walsall WS5 .... 43 B8
Edinburgh Villas CV8 .... 133 F2
Edingale Rd CV2 .... 114 F8
Edison Cl WS12 .... 2 C7
Edison Ct WV12 .... 27 D7
Edison Gr B32 .... 84 D5
Edison Rd WS2 .... 28 B5
Edison Wlk WS2 .... 28 B5
Edith Rd B66 .... 65 C3
Edith St B70 .... 53 B3
Edmondes Cl CV34 .... 155 F1
Edmonds Cl B33 .... 69 B2
Edmonds Ct
Birmingham, Gilbertsone B26 .... 88 F7
Birmingham, Small Heath B10 .... 87 D7
Edmonds Rd B68 .... 64 C2
Edmondscote Rd CV32 .... 161 D8
Edmonton Ave B44 .... 45 B1
Edmonton Cl WS11 .... 2 B2
Edmonton Ho B5 .... 86 D7
Edmoor Cl WV12 .... 27 C6
Edmund Rd Birmingham B8 .... 67 D4
Coventry CV1 .... 113 D5
Dudley DY3 .... 50 E6
Edmund St B3 .... 164 B3
Ednall La B60 .... 136 F1
Ednam Cl 3 B71 .... 53 F8
Ednam Gr WV5 .... 38 A1
Ednam Rd Dudley DY1 .... 51 C2
Wolverhampton WV4 .... 39 C5
Edsome Way B36 .... 68 F8
Edstone Cl B93 .... 127 F4
Edstone Mews B36 .... 68 F8
Edward Ave WS9 .... 30 A7
Edward Bailey Cl CV3 .... 134 E7
Edward Cl WV14 .... 40 E3
Edward Ct Birmingham B16 .... 65 C1
Sutton Coldfield B76 .... 46 F3
Tamworth B77 .... 21 F4
Walsall WS1 .... 43 A8
Edward Fisher Dr DY4 .... 52 A5
Edward Rd Bedworth CV12 .... 78 C3
Birmingham, Balsall Heath B12 .... 86 E5
Birmingham, Highter's Heath B14 .... 105 A1
Coventry CV6 .... 95 A3
Halesowen B63 .... 82 F4
Oldbury B68 .... 84 C8
Perton WV6 .... 23 E5
Smethwick B67 .... 65 A4
Tipton DY4 .... 52 A7
Water Orton B46 .... 59 C3
Edward St Birmingham B1 .... 66 C3
Cannock WS11 .... 1 E4
Coventry CV6 .... 113 E5
Darlaston WS10 .... 41 E6
3 Dudley DY1 .... 51 B1
Hinckley LE10 .... 71 C2
Nuneaton CV11 .... 73 C3
Oldbury B68 .... 64 A4
Redditch B97 .... 153 D4
Royal Leamington Spa CV32 .... 156 C1
Tamworth B79 .... 21 A5
Walsall WS2 .... 28 C3
Warwick CV34 .... 160 D7
West Bromwich B70 .... 53 C3
Wolverhampton WV4 .... 39 F5
Edward Street Hospl B70 .... 53 C3
Edward Tyler Rd CV7 .... 78 A1
Edwards Ctr 7 LE10 .... 75 D8
Edwards Gr CV8 .... 148 C5
Edwards Rd Birmingham B24 .... 57 A4
Burntwood WS7 .... 6 F5
Dudley DY2 .... 62 C4
Sutton Coldfield B75 .... 32 D3
Edwin Ave (Road 4) DY10 .... 116 F1
Edwin Cres B60 .... 150 F7
Edwin Ct Bromsgrove B60 .... 150 F7
Bromsgrove B60 .... 150 F8
Edwin Rd B30 .... 104 B7
Edyth Rd CV2 .... 114 E4
Edyvean Walker Ct CV11 .... 73 B5
Eel St B69 .... 63 F7
Effingham Rd B13 .... 105 C7
Egbert Cl B6 .... 67 B8
Egelwin Cl WV6 .... 23 E5
Egerton Ct 4 B15 .... 86 B7
Egerton Rd Aldridge B74 .... 30 F1
Birmingham B24 .... 57 E3
Wolverhampton WV10 .... 11 E3
Egg La DY9, DY10 .... 119 A5
Egghill La B31, B45 .... 102 B3
Eggington Rd DY8 .... 80 D6
Egginton Rd B28 .... 105 E5
Egmont Gdns WV11 .... 26 F5
Egret Ct DY10 .... 117 A1
Eider Cl DY10 .... 117 B1
Eileen Gdns B37 .... 69 F4
Eileen Rd B11 .... 87 C3
Elan Cl Dudley DY3 .... 50 D3
Royal Leamington Spa CV32 .... 157 C3
Elan Rd Birmingham B31 .... 102 D2
Sedgley DY3 .... 50 C8
Elbow St B64 .... 62 F2
Elbury Croft B93 .... 127 F5
Elcock Dr B42 .... 55 D5
Eld Rd CV6 .... 113 E7
Eldalade Way WS10 .... 42 D2
Elder Cl WS11 .... 2 C2
Elder La WS7 .... 7 C7
Elder Way B23 .... 56 E2
Elderberry Cl DY8 .... 80 C3
Elderberry Way CV2 .... 114 B6
Elderfield Rd B30 .... 104 B3
Eldersfield Cl B98 .... 154 E7
Eldersfield Gr B91 .... 127 B7
Eldon Ct WS1 .... 28 F1
Eldon Dr B76 .... 57 E7
Eldon Rd
Birmingham, Edgbaston B16 .... 65 F2
Birmingham, Woodgate B32 .... 84 A3
Halesowen B62 .... 83 F3
Eldon St Darlaston WS10 .... 41 D7
Walsall WS1 .... 28 F1
Eldorado Cl B80 .... 159 D4
Eldridge Cl WV9 .... 10 F2
Eleanor Rd WV14 .... 40 D6
Electric Ave B6 .... 56 B1
Elford Cl B14 .... 104 E5
Elford Gr Bilston WV14 .... 40 C4
Birmingham B37 .... 70 B1
Elford Rd
Birmingham B17, B29 .... 85 B3
West Bromwich B71 .... 42 E2
Elgar Cl Cannock WS11 .... 1 E5
Lichfield WS13 .... 3 B2
Nuneaton CV11 .... 79 A7
Elgar Cres DY5 .... 61 D7
Elgar Mews 2 B60 .... 136 F2
Elgar Rd CV6 .... 114 B8
Elgin Cl Sedgley DY3 .... 39 E1
Stourbridge DY8 .... 81 A7
Elgin Ct WV6 .... 23 E4
Elgin Gr B25 .... 88 C7
Elgin Rd WS3 .... 14 A4
Elias Cl WS14 .... 9 E6
Eliot Cl Tamworth B79 .... 21 A7
Warwick CV34 .... 155 E2
Eliot St B7 .... 67 C8
Eliot Wlk DY10 .... 117 C6
Elizabeth Ave Bilston WV14 .... 40 F3
Wednesbury WS10 .... 42 C3
Wolverhampton WV4 .... 39 B5
Elizabeth Cres B68 .... 64 D2
Elizabeth Ct
2 Birmingham B27 .... 88 C2
8 Coventry CV6 .... 113 A4
Warwick CV34 .... 161 B6
Elizabeth Dr B79 .... 21 A6
Elizabeth Fry Ho B16 .... 66 A1
Elizabeth Gr Dudley DY2 .... 62 F7
Solihull B90 .... 106 C2
Elizabeth Ho Stourbridge DY9 .... 81 E5
Sutton Coldfield B76 .... 46 F3
1 Walsall WS5 .... 43 D7
Elizabeth Mews B69 .... 52 A2
Elizabeth Prout Gdns B65 .... 63 B1
Elizabeth Rd
Birmingham, Moseley B13 .... 86 C2
Birmingham, New Oscott B73 .... 45 D1
Birmingham, Stechford B33 .... 68 D3
Cannock WS11 .... 1 E6
Halesowen B63 .... 82 F3
Hinckley LE10 .... 71 D2
Royal Leamington Spa CV31 .... 161 F6
Walsall WS5 .... 43 C7
West Bromwich B70 .... 52 D4
Elizabeth Way CV8 .... 147 E5
Elizabeth Wlk DY4 .... 41 A2
Elkington Croft B90 .... 127 A5
Elkington St Birmingham B6 .... 66 E5
Coventry CV6 .... 113 F8
Elkstone Cl B92 .... 89 B3
Elkstone Covert B14 .... 104 C2
Ellacombe Rd CV2 .... 114 D8
Ellards Dr WV11 .... 26 F5
Ellen St B18 .... 66 B4
Ellenvale Cl WV14 .... 51 A8
Ellerbeck B77 .... 22 B1
Ellerby Gr B24 .... 57 E4
Ellerdene Cl B98 .... 158 D8
Ellerside Gr B31 .... 102 F2
Ellerslie Cl DY5 .... 81 D8
Ellerslie Rd B13 .... 105 C7
Ellerton Rd B44 .... 45 B1
Ellerton Wlk WV10 .... 25 F5
Ellesboro' Rd B17 .... 85 B7
Ellesmere Ct B69 .... 63 D8
Ellesmere Rd Bedworth CV12 .... 78 A2
Birmingham B8 .... 67 D4
Cannock WS11 .... 4 B8
Ellice Dr B36 .... 70 B7
Elliot Ct WV4 .... 39 F4
Elliot Gdns B45 .... 122 B5
Elliot Way B6 .... 55 F4
Elliott Rd B29 .... 85 E1
Elliott Way B6 .... 55 F3
Elliott's Rd DY4 .... 51 E5
Elliotts La WV8 .... 10 A3
Ellis Ave DY5 .... 61 A2
Ellis St B1 .... 164 B1
Ellis Wlk WS11 .... 4 F8
Ellison St B70 .... 53 C1
Elliston Ave B44 .... 55 E8
Elliston Gr CV31 .... 162 C6
Ellowes Hall Sch DY3 .... 50 C5
Ellowes Rd DY3 .... 50 C4
Ellys Rd CV1 .... 113 C5
Elm Ave Bilston WV14 .... 40 D6
Birmingham B12 .... 87 A5
Wednesbury WS10 .... 41 F4
Wolverhampton WV11 .... 26 B8
Elm Bank Cl CV32 .... 157 A4
Elm Cl Binley Woods CV3 .... 135 C7
Dudley DY3 .... 50 B2
Stourbridge DY8 .... 80 C2
Elm Croft B68 .... 84 C7
Elm Ct Birmingham B13 .... 86 F4
Oldbury B66 .... 64 C8
Redditch B97 .... 153 D4
Walsall WS1 .... 43 A8
Elm Dale Rd WV4 .... 39 A5
Elm Dr Birmingham B43 .... 43 D1
Blakedown DY10 .... 98 B2
Halesowen B62 .... 63 E1
Elm Farm Ave B37 .... 89 F7
Elm Farm Rd WV2 .... 39 D7
Elm Gdns WS14 .... 9 C7
Elm Gn DY1 .... 51 A5
Elm Gr Balsall Common CV7 .... 130 C6
Birmingham B37 .... 69 F6
Bromsgrove B61 .... 137 A4
Codsall WV8 .... 10 A3
Huntington WS12 .... 1 D8
Elm Lodge B92 .... 109 A7
Elm Pl DY10 .... 118 B3
Elm Rd Birmingham B30 .... 103 F8
Dudley DY1 .... 51 C4
Kidderminster DY10 .... 117 A6
Kingswinford DY6 .... 60 E6
Norton Canes WS11 .... 6 B5
Redditch B97 .... 153 D4
Royal Leamington Spa CV32 .... 157 B3
Walsall WS3 .... 28 D6
Elm St Willenhall WV13 .... 27 C2
Wolverhampton WV3 .... 25 A1
Elm Street Inf Sch WV13 .... 27 C2
Elm Terr B69 .... 52 B1
Elm Tree Ave CV4 .... 112 B2
Elm Tree Dr LE10 .... 75 F8
Elm Tree Gr B63 .... 82 D6
Elm Tree Rd
Birmingham, Harborne B17 .... 85 A7
Birmingham, Stirchley B30 .... 104 A6
Bulkington CV12 .... 79 D2
Elm Tree Rise B92 .... 109 B6
Elm Tree Way B64 .... 62 F1
Elmay Rd B26 .... 89 A7
Elmbank Gr B20 .... 54 E5
Elmbank Rd Kenilworth CV8 .... 147 E6
Walsall WS5 .... 43 C4
Elmbridge Cl B63 .... 82 D5
Elmbridge Dr B90 .... 127 B6
Elmbridge Ho 7 B38 .... 103 D2
Elmbridge Rd B44 .... 55 E6
Elmbridge Way DY3 .... 50 E6
Elmcroft 5 B66 .... 65 C5
Elmcroft Ave B32 .... 84 A1
Elmcroft Gdns WV10 .... 11 E3
Elmcroft Rd B26 .... 88 F7
Elmdale B62 .... 84 A7
Elmdale Cres B31 .... 102 E4
Elmdale Dr Aldridge WS9 .... 30 C8
Kidderminster DY10 .... 117 C5
Elmdale Gr B31 .... 102 E4
Elmdale Rd WV14 .... 51 A7
Elmdene Rd CV8 .... 148 B4
Elmdon Cl Solihull B92 .... 89 D2
Wolverhampton WV10 .... 11 A1
Elmdon Coppice B92 .... 107 F7
Elmdon Ct B37 .... 90 A7
Elmdon La Birmingham B37 .... 90 A6
Solihull B26 .... 90 A3
Elmdon Park Rd B92 .... 89 D2
Elmdon Rd
Birmingham, Acock's Green B27 .... 88 D4
Birmingham, Marston Green B37 .... 90 A7
Birmingham, Selly Park B29 .... 86 A2
Wolverhampton WV10 .... 11 A1
Elmdon Trad Est B37 .... 90 C5
Elmfield Ave B24 .... 57 F4
Elmfield Cres B13 .... 86 F2
Elmfield Rd Birmingham B36 .... 69 F7
Nuneaton CV10 .... 73 C7
Elmfield Rudolf Steiner Sch DY8 .... 81 A3
Elmhurst B15 .... 85 D8
Elmhurst Ave B65 .... 63 C3
Elmhurst Cl B97 .... 158 D4
Elmhurst Dr Burntwood WS7 .... 7 A4
Kingswinford DY6 .... 60 F4
Elmhurst Rd Birmingham B21 .... 54 E1
Coventry CV6 .... 96 A4
Elmley Cl Dudley WV14 .... 51 B7
Kidderminster DY11 .... 116 B3
Elmley Ct B23 .... 56 C2
Elmley Gr Birmingham B30 .... 104 B2
Perton WV6 .... 23 F3
Elmley Ho B97 .... 153 A4
Elmore Cl CV3 .... 134 D8
Elmore Green Cl WS3 .... 28 B8
Elmore Green Cty Prim Sch WS3 .... 14 B1

Elmore Green Rd WS3 14 B1
Elmore Rd B33 69 A3
Elmore Row WS3 14 B1
Elms Cl Birmingham B38 123 C8
Solihull B91 107 D5
Elms Dr WS11 1 C1
Elms Farm Inf & Jun Sch B33 89 C7
Elms Rd B72 46 C3
Elms The Bedworth CV12 77 E2
Birmingham B16 65 F3
Leek Wootton CV35 155 F6
Wolverhampton WV11 26 B5
Elmsdale WV6 24 A2
Elmsdale Ave CV6 95 F2
Elmsdale Ct 6 WS1 42 F8
Elmstead Ave B33 89 D7
Elmstead Cl WS5 29 E1
Elmstead Tower 2 B5 86 E7
Elmstead Wood WS5 29 E1
Elmstone Cl B97 158 C5
Elmtree Rd B74 44 D8
Elmwood Ave Coventry CV6 112 F5
Essington WV11 13 A3
Elmwood Cl
Balsall Common CV7 130 B6
Cannock WS11 2 A3
Elmwood Ct Birmingham B5 86 D6
Coventry CV1 165 B4
Sutton Coldfield B74 45 A5
Elmwood Gdns B20 55 B2
Elmwood Gr B47 125 A6
Elmwood Rd Birmingham B24 57 C2
Stourbridge DY8 60 C2
Sutton Coldfield B74 45 A5
Elmwood Rise DY3 39 B1
Elmwoods B32 84 B2
Elphin Cl CV6 95 A4
Elphinstone End B24 57 C6
Elsma Rd B68 84 C8
Elston Hall Jun & Inf Schs WV10 11 C2
Elston Hall La WV10 11 D1
Elstree Rd B23 56 D5
Elswick Gr B44 56 B8
Elswick Pl B44 45 B1
Elsworth Gr B25 88 C6
Elsworth Ho 8 B38 103 D2
Eltham Gr B44 45 B1
Eltham Rd CV3 133 E7
Elton Cl
Royal Leamington Spa CV32 157 C2
Wolverhampton WV10 11 E4
Elton Croft B93 127 F4
Elton Gr B27 88 A2
Eltonia Croft B26 89 B6
Elunda Gr WS7 6 E5
Elva Croft B36 58 F1
Elvers Green La B93 128 E7
Elvetham Rd B15 86 C8
Elviron Dr WV6 24 B5
Elwell Cres DY1 50 F5
Elwell St Wednesbury WS10 42 B3
West Bromwich B70 52 E5
Elwells Cl WV14 40 A3
Elwy Circ CV7 95 C6
Elwyn Rd B73 46 A3
Ely Cl Birmingham B37 70 B2
Blackheath B65 63 E4
Cannock WS11 2 B1
Coventry CV2 115 A6
Kidderminster DY11 116 A6
Ely Cres B71 53 B7
Ely Gr B32 84 F4
Ely Pl WS2 28 B1
Ely Rd WS2 28 B1
Emay Cl B70 52 F8
Embankment The DY5 61 E3
Embassy Dr Birmingham B15 86 B8
Oldbury B69 63 E8
Embassy Rd B69 63 E8
Embassy Wlk CV2 114 D8
Emberton Way B77 21 F5
Embleton Cl LE10 71 B1
Embleton Gr B34 69 A6
Emerald Ct Birmingham B8 68 C5
5 Solihull B92 88 F1
Emerald Way CV31 161 F5
Emerson Cl DY3 50 A4
Emerson Gr WV10 25 F8
Emerson Rd Birmingham B17 85 C6
Coventry CV2 114 C3
Wolverhampton WV10 26 A8
Emery Cl Birmingham B23 56 D1
Coventry CV2 114 E7
Walsall WS1 42 F8
Emery Ct DY10 116 E7
Emery St WS1 42 F8
Emily Gdns B16 65 F3
Emily Rd B26 88 D6
Emily Smith Ho 2 CV2 96 B1
Emily St Birmingham B12 86 F7
West Bromwich B70 53 B2
Emmanuel Rd Burntwood WS7 7 B7
Sutton Coldfield B73 57 B8
Emmeline St B9 67 B1
Emmott Dr CV31 162 B5
Empire Cl WS9 29 F8
Empire Ind Pk WS9 29 F8
Empire Rd CV4 111 E2
Empress Way WS10 41 D8
Emscote Cty Fst Sch CV34 161 B8
Emscote Dr B73 57 B7
Emscote Gn B91 106 E2
Emscote Lawn Prep Sch CV34 161 A8
Emscote Rd Birmingham B6 55 F1
Coventry CV3 114 C2
Warwick CV34 161 B8
Emsworth Cres WV9 11 A2
Emsworth Gr B14 104 D6
Ena Rd CV1 113 D5
End Hall Rd WV6 24 A3
Endemere Rd CV6 113 D7
Enderby Dr WV4 39 A4
Enderby Rd B23 56 C7
Enderley Cl WS3 14 B3
Enderley Dr WS3 14 B3
Endhill Rd B44 45 A3
Endicott Rd B6 55 F1
Endmoor Gr B23 56 D6
Endsleigh Gdns CV31 162 B6
Endsleigh Gr B28 106 A8
Endwood Court Rd B20 55 A2
Endwood Ct Birmingham B11 87 D4
Birmingham, Handsworth Wood B20 55 A2
Endwood Dr Little Aston B74 31 C4
Solihull B91 106 F2
Enfield Cl B23 56 F6
Enfield Ind Est B97 153 D5
Enfield Rd Birmingham B15 86 B8
Coventry CV2 114 B3
Redditch B97 158 D5
Enford Cl B34 69 D6
Engine La Bilston WS10 41 A4
Brierley Hill DY5 61 F4
Stourbridge DY9 81 D6
Tamworth B77 22 A2
Walsall WS8 15 C8
Engine St Oldbury B69 64 B6
Smethwick B66 65 B6
England Cres CV31 161 E7
England Ho 9 CV32 156 F2
Englestede Cl B20 54 F3
Engleton Rd CV6 113 A6
Englewood Dr B28 106 A8
English Martyrs Jun & Inf Sch B11 87 C4
Ennerdale Cl CV32 156 D2
Ennerdale Cres CV11 73 F6
Ennerdale Dr Halesowen B63 82 D2
Perton WV6 23 F4
Ennerdale La CV2 114 F4
Ennerdale Rd
Birmingham B43 54 F6
Wolverhampton WV6 24 D8
Ennersdale Bglws B46 59 F1
Ennersdale Cl B46 59 F1
Ennersdale Rd B46 59 F1
Ennnerdale Cl WS8 15 E7
Enright Cl CV32 156 E2
Ensall Dr DY8 60 E1
Ensbury Cl WV12 27 D4
Ensdale Row WV13 27 A1
Ensdon Gr B44 45 B1
Ensford Cl B74 31 E5
Ensign Bsns Ctr CV4 131 F6
Ensign Cl CV4 111 D1
Ensign Ho B35 58 A4
Ensor Cl CV11 74 A6
Ensor Dr B78 22 F1
Enstone Rd Birmingham B23 57 A7
Dudley DY1 61 F8
Enterprise Dr
Stourbridge DY9 81 F6
Sutton Coldfield B74 44 E7
Enterprise Gr WS3 15 B5
Enterprise Ho B92 109 A6
Enterprise Ind Pk WS14 9 F8
Enterprise Trad Est
Brierley Hill DY5 61 F3
Dudley DY5 62 A3
Enterprise Way B7 164 D4
Enterprise Workshops DY6 61 A7
Enville Cl WS3 14 A3
Enville Gr B11 87 D5
Enville Pl 7 DY8 80 F5
Enville Rd Dudley DY3 50 D4
Kingswinford DY6 60 E8
Wolverhampton WV4 38 C4
Enville St DY8 80 F5
Epperston Ct CV31 161 F7
Epping Cl Birmingham B45 102 B2
Walsall WS3 28 F6
Epping Gr B44 56 A7
Epping Way CV32 157 C4
Epsom Cl Bedworth CV12 78 B4
Lichfield WS14 9 D7
Perton WV6 23 F4
Redditch B97 158 C8
Epsom Ct B29 103 C7
Epsom Gr B44 56 B8
Epsom Rd Catshill B61 121 A1
Royal Leamington Spa CV32 157 C4
Epwell Gr B44 55 F6
Epwell Rd B44 55 F6
Epworth Ct DY5 61 B5
Erasmus Rd B11 87 A7
Erasmus Way WS13 9 A8
Ercall Cl B23 56 A6
Erdington Hall Jun & Inf Sch B24 56 F1
Erdington Hall Rd B24 56 F2
Erdington Ind Pk B24 57 F4
Erdington Rd WS9 30 C3
Erdington Sta B23 56 F5
Erdington Tech Coll B24 57 A4
Eric Grey Cl CV2 114 A5
Erica Ave CV12 77 F2
Erica Cl B29 103 A8
Erica Dr CV31 162 B2
Erica Rd WS5 43 B3
Eringden B77 22 B1
Erithway Rd CV3 133 B4
Ermington Cres B36 68 E7
Ermington Rd WV4 39 E4
Ernesford Grange Prim Sch CV3 114 E1
Ernesford Grange Sch & Com Coll CV3 134 D8
Ernest Clarke Cl WV12 27 C4
Ernest Ct B38 104 A1
Ernest Rd Birmingham B12 87 B4
Dudley DY2 51 F1
Smethwick B67 64 E6
Ernest Richards Rd CV12 78 B4
Ernest St B1 164 B1
Ernsford Ave CV3 114 B1
Ernsford Cl B93 127 F2
Erskine Cl LE10 71 A2
Erskine St B7 67 B3
Erwood Cl B97 153 B2
Esher Dr CV3 133 E7
Esher Rd Birmingham B44 44 F4
West Bromwich B71 53 D6
Esk Ho 1 DY1 61 E8
Eskdale Cl WV1 26 A2
Eskdale Rd LE10 75 A7
Eskdale Wlk Brierley Hill DY5 81 B8
Coventry CV3 134 D7
Eskrett St WS12 2 C5
Esme Rd B11 87 B4
Esmond Cl B30 103 D5
Essendon Gr B8 68 B4
Essendon Rd B8 68 B4
Essendon Wlk B8 68 B4
Essex Ave Kingswinford DY6 60 B5
Wednesbury WS10 42 C4
West Bromwich B71 53 D7
Essex Cl Coventry CV5 112 B3
Kenilworth CV8 147 E2
Essex Ct Birmingham B29 103 C7
Warwick CV34 160 E8
Essex Dr WS12 2 B4
Essex Gdns DY8 80 D7
Essex Ho 2 WV3 25 C4
Essex Rd Dudley DY2 62 A6
Sutton Coldfield B75 32 D2
Essex St Birmingham B5 164 C1
Walsall WS2 28 E5
Essington Cl Lichfield WS14 9 A5
Shenstone WS14 18 A6
Stourbridge DY8 60 E1
Essington Ind Est WV11 12 F4
Essington Rd WV12 13 B1
Essington St B16 66 B1
Essington Way WV1 26 B1
Este Rd B26 69 A1
Esterton Cl CV6 95 C2
Estria Rd B15 86 B7
Estridge La WS6 5 A2
Ethel Rd B17 85 D5
Ethel St Birmingham B2 164 B2
Oldbury B68 64 A4
Smethwick B67 64 F2
Ethelfield Rd CV2 114 B3
Ethelfleda Rd B77 35 F5
Ethelfleda Terr WS10 41 F3
Ethelred Cl B74 32 A3
Etheridge Rd WV14 40 D7
Eton Cl DY3 50 F6
Eton Ct Lichfield WS14 9 B6
Sutton Coldfield B74 31 F2
Eton Dr DY8 81 A3
Eton Rd B12 87 B4
Eton Wlk DY9 99 A6
Etone Com Sch CV11 73 D5
Etone Ct CV11 73 B5
Etruria Way WV14 40 E7
Etta Gr B44 44 F4
Ettingley Cl B98 159 B5
Ettingshall Park Farm La WV4 39 E4
Ettingshall Prim Sch WV14 40 B6
Ettingshall Rd WV2 40 A7
Ettington Cl B93 127 D2
Ettington Rd Birmingham B6 66 E8
Coventry CV5 112 A3
Ettymore Cl DY3 50 D8
Ettymore Rd DY3 50 D8
Ettymore Rd W DY3 50 C8
Etwall Rd B28 105 E6
Euan Cl B17 85 C8
Eunal Ct B97 158 E5
Euro Ct B13 87 B2
Europa Ave B70 53 F2
Europa Way Birmingham B26 90 C4
Lichfield WS14 9 F8
Royal Leamington Spa CV34 161 D5
European Bsns Pk B69 63 E7
Eustace Rd CV12 79 D1
Euston Cres CV3 134 C6
Euston Pl CV32 161 F8
Euston Sq 15 CV32 161 F8
Eva Rd Birmingham B18 65 D6
Oldbury B68 64 D3
Evans Cl Bedworth CV12 78 C3
Dudley DY4 51 C5
Evans Croft B78 21 A1
Evans Gdns B29 85 D1
Evans Gr CV31 162 A2
Evans Pl WV14 40 E7
Evans St Willenhall WV13 26 D1
Wolverhampton, Cinder Hill WV14 39 F1
Wolverhampton, Dunstall Hill WV6 25 B4
Evason Ct B6 55 E1
Eve La DY1 50 F5
Evelyn Ave CV6 95 F2
Evelyn Croft B73 57 A8
Evelyn Rd B11 87 D4
Evenlode Cl Redditch B98 153 F1
Solihull B92 89 B3
Evenlode Cres CV6 112 F5
Evenlode Rd B92 89 B3
Everard Ct CV11 73 E2
Everdon Rd CV6 95 B2
Everene Ho 1 B27 88 C3
Everest Cl B66 64 F8
Everest Rd Birmingham B20 55 A3
Walsall WS2 27 F3
Everglade Rd CV9 36 C1
Evergreen Cl WV14 51 B8
Evergreen Hts WS12 2 A8
Everitt Cl B16 66 A1
Everitt Dr B93 128 A6
Evers St DY5 82 A8
Eversfield Prep Sch B91 107 B4
Eversleigh Rd CV6 112 E7
Eversley Dale B24 57 A2
Eversley Gr Sedgley DY3 39 C2
Wolverhampton WV11 26 C6
Eversley Rd 2 B9 67 D1
Everton Rd B8 68 C4
Eves Croft B32 84 C1
Evesham Cres WS3 13 F3
Evesham Ho 5
Birmingham B7 67 A4
Bromsgrove B60 137 B3
Evesham Mews 9 B97 153 E3
Evesham Rd B96, B97 158 E3
Evesham Rise DY2 62 D3
Evesham Sq 8 B97 153 E3
Evesham St B97 153 E3
Evesham Wlk Coventry CV4 132 D5
2 Redditch B98 153 E4
Eveson Rd DY8 80 E2
Ewart Rd WS2 27 E3
Ewell Rd B24 57 B4
Ewhurst Ave B29 85 F1
Ewhurst Cl WV13 40 F8
Ewloe Cl DY10 116 E1
Exbury Cl WV9 10 F2
Exbury Way CV11 78 E8
Excelsior Gr WS3 15 B5
Exchange Ind Est The WS11 4 E5
Exchange St Brierley Hill DY5 61 D4
Kidderminster DY10 116 E6
Wolverhampton WV1 163 B3
Exchange The 7 WS3 14 B1
Exe Croft B31 123 B8
Exeter Cl Coventry CV3 134 D8
Kidderminster DY11 116 A6
Exeter Dr B37 89 F8
Exeter Ho
5 Birmingham B31 102 C2
8 Birmingham, Erdington B24 56 F4
Exeter Pas B1 164 B1
Exeter Pl WS2 28 B1
Exeter Rd Birmingham B29 85 F2
Cannock WS11 4 B8
Dudley DY2 62 D2
Smethwick B66 65 B5
Exeter St B1 164 B1
Exford Cl DY5 81 B7
Exhall Cl Redditch B98 154 D5
Solihull B91 106 E2
Exhall Ct B23 56 C2
Exhall Fst Sch CV7 95 F7
Exhall Gn CV7 95 F7
Exhall Grange Sch CV7 95 C5
Exhall Rd CV7 95 A6
Exham Cl CV34 155 E1
Exhibition Way B40 90 D4
Exis Ct CV11 73 E2
Exley B77 21 D1
Exminster Rd CV3 133 E5
Exmoor Ct B61 137 A4
Exmoor Dr Bromsgrove B61 137 A4
Royal Leamington Spa CV32 157 C4
Exmoor Gn WV11 26 C7
Exmouth Cl CV2 114 C7
Exon Ct DY4 51 F6
Exonbury Wlk WS11 1 F2
Expressway The B70 53 C4
Exton Cl Ash Green CV7 95 C6
Wednesfield WV11 26 F8
Exton Gdns B66 65 D6
Exton Way B8 67 D5
Eyffler Cl CV34 160 D7
Eyland Gr WS1 28 F2
Eymore Cl B29 103 B6
Eynsham Ct WV6 24 E5
Eyre St B18 66 A3
Eyston Ave DY4 52 D8
Eyton Cl B98 154 D3
Eyton Croft B12 86 F7
Ezekiel La WV12 27 C6
Fabian Cl Birmingham B45 102 A2
Coventry CV3 134 D7
Fabian Cres B90 106 B1
Facet Rd B38 104 A2
Factory La B61 136 F1
Factory Rd Birmingham B18 66 A6
Hinckley LE10 71 D1
Tipton DY4 51 E6
Factory St WS10 41 C6
Fair Isle Dr CV10 72 F2
Fair Lady Dr WS7 6 D8
Fair Oaks Dr WS6 14 A8
Fairbanks Cl CV2 115 A7
Fairbourne Ave
Birmingham B44 44 E2
Blackheath B65 63 E4
Fairbourne Tower 2 B23 57 A6
Fairbourne Way CV6 112 E8
Fairburn Cres WS3 15 B5
Faircroft CV8 147 F3
Faircroft Ave B76 57 F6
Faircroft Rd B36 58 D1
Fairdene Way 3 B43 54 D8
Fairfax Ct 7 CV34 160 F7
Fairfax Rd Birmingham B31 123 A8
Sutton Coldfield B75 46 F5
Wolverhampton WV10 11 E3
Fairfax Sch B75 46 F5
Fairfax St CV1 165 C3
Fairfield Cl WS12 2 D1
Fairfield Ct CV3 134 A7
Fairfield Cty Prim Sch B61 120 D3
Fairfield Dr Halesowen B62 63 E1
Walsall WS3 15 B4
Fairfield Gr B62 63 E1
Fairfield Ho B60 137 B3
Fairfield Mount WS1 42 F8
Fairfield Park Ind Est B62 63 E1
Fairfield Rd Birmingham B14 104 E8
Bournheath B61 120 D1
Dudley DY2 62 D7
Halesowen B63 83 A2
Halesowen, Hurst Green B62 63 E1
Stourbridge DY8 60 F2
Fairfield Rise Meriden CV7 92 C1
Stourbridge DY8 80 D5
Fairfield Studios DY10 116 F5
Fairfields Hill B78 36 F8
Fairford Cl Redditch B98 154 E7
Solihull B91 106 D5
Fairford Gdns Burntwood WS7 7 C6
Stourbridge DY8 60 E3
Fairford Rd B44 55 F6
Fairgreen Way Aldridge B74 31 A1
Birmingham B29 85 F1
Fairground Way WS1 42 D8
Fairhaven Croft B62 63 E1
Fairhaven Prim Sch DY8 60 D3
Fairhill Way B11 87 C7
Fairhills DY3 50 D8
Fairholme Rd B36 68 B7
Fairhurst Dr CV32 156 E3
Fairlands Pk CV4 132 F6
Fairlawn B15 86 A7
Fairlawn Cl
Royal Leamington Spa CV32 156 D1
Willenhall WV12 13 C1
Fairlawn Dr DY6 60 D4
Fairlawn Way WV12 13 C1
Fairlawns Birmingham B26 69 A1
Sutton Coldfield B76 58 A8
Fairlie Cres B38 103 D1
Fairmead Rise B38 103 E1
Fairmile Cl CV3 134 C8
Fairmile Rd B63 83 A6
Fairmont Rd B60 151 B8
Fairmount Dr WS11 4 E8
Fairoak Dr Bromsgrove B60 150 F6
Wolverhampton WV6 24 B3
Fairview Ave B42 55 B6
Fairview Cl Cheslyn Hay WS6 4 D2
Tamworth B77 21 F5
Wolverhampton WV11 26 B7
Fairview Cres
Kingswinford DY6 60 F6
Wolverhampton WV11 26 B7
Fairview Ct WS2 27 D2
Fairview Gr WV11 26 B7
Fairview Mews 9 B46 70 F7
Fairview Rd Dudley DY1 51 A3
Wolverhampton, Penn WV4 38 C4
Wolverhampton, Scotlands WV11 26 B7
Fairview Wlk CV6 95 E2
Fairway Birmingham B31 102 E3
Cannock WS11 4 D6
Nuneaton CV11 79 B8
Tamworth B77 35 F5
Walsall WS4 15 D1
Fairway Ave B69 63 A8
Fairway Ct B77 22 B3
Fairway Dr B45 121 F6
Fairway Gn WV14 40 D8
Fairway Jun &Inf Sch B38 103 D1
Fairway Rd B68 63 F2
Fairway Rise CV8 148 C6

Fairway The
Birmingham B38 103 D2
Hinckley LE10 75 F7
Fairways B93 128 A8
Fairways Ave DY8 80 E2
Fairways Cl Coventry CV5 112 A6
Stourbridge DY8 80 E2
Fairways Dr B60 138 B5
Fairways The CV32 156 D2
Fairyfield Ave B43 43 D1
Fairyfield Ct B43 43 D1
Fakenham Croft B17 84 F7
Falcon B77 36 A6
Falcon Ave CV3 134 F8
Falcon Cl Cannock WS11 1 C2
Cheslyn Hay WS6 4 C2
Kidderminster DY10 116 E2
Nuneaton CV11 79 B8
Falcon Cres WV14 39 F2
Falcon Lodge Cres B75 47 A6
Falcon Lodge Jun Sch B75 46 F5
Falcon Pl B69 63 C7
Falcon Rd B68 63 F2
Falcon Rise DY8 80 C6
Falcon View B30 104 A4
Falcon Way DY1 50 F1
Falcondale Rd WV12 13 C1
Falconers Gn LE10 75 F6
Falconhurst Rd B29 85 C2
Falcons The B75 47 B5
Falfield Cl B65 63 D6
Falfield Gr B31 122 E7
Falkener Ho CV6 113 E7
Falkland Cl CV4 131 D7
Falkland Croft B30 104 B6
Falkland Way B36 70 B5
Falkwood Gr B93 127 F6
Fallindale Rd B26 89 C6
Fallings Heath Cl WS10 41 F7
Fallings Park Ind Est
WV10 25 F5
Fallow Field Cannock WS11 1 E3
Lichfield WS13 3 C3
Little Aston B74 31 B3
Fallow Field Rd B65 63 A3
Fallow Hill CV31 162 C6
Fallow Rd B78 20 F1
Fallow Wlk B32 84 A2
Fallowfield Birmingham B15 85 E8
Perton WV6 23 D4
Wolverhampton WV8 10 E2
Fallowfield Ave B28 105 F5
Fallowfield Rd
Halesowen B63 82 D3
Solihull B92 89 D3
Walsall WS5 43 E8
Fallowfields Cl B61 136 E3
Fallows Ho B19 66 E5
Fallows Rd B11 87 C6
Falmouth Cl CV11 74 B5
Falmouth Dr Hinckley LE10 71 E4
Tamworth B77 21 F5
Falmouth Rd Birmingham
B34 68 F6
Walsall WS5 43 D7
Falna Cres B79 20 F7
Falstaff Ave B47 125 A6
Falstaff Cl Nuneaton CV11 74 A1
Sutton Coldfield B76 58 B7
Falstaff Ct B75 47 C5
Falstaff Ho B13 105 D7
Falstaff Rd Coventry CV4 111 E1
Solihull B90 106 C1
Falstone Rd B73 45 D2
Fancott Dr CV8 147 F6
Fancott Rd B31 103 A5
Fancourt Ave WV4 38 D4
Fane Rd WV11 13 B2
Fanshawe Rd B27 88 C1
Far Gosford St CV1 113 E2
Far Highfield B76 46 E4
Far Hill Cl B71 53 F8
Far Lash LE10 75 F7
Far Moor La B98 154 F5
Far View WS9 16 B2
Far Wood Rd B31 102 E8
Faraday Ave B32 84 D5
Faraday Ct B32 84 D5
Faraday Ho 5 B15 86 C8
Faraday Rd Hinckley LE10 74 E7
Walsall WS2 28 B6
Farber Rd CV2 115 A6
Farbrook Way WV12 27 B6
Farclose Ho B15 86 C7
Farcroft Ave Birmingham
B21 65 D8
Coventry CV5 111 D4
Farcroft Gr B21 54 D1
Farcroft Rd B21 54 D1
Fardon Way B23 56 D8
Fareham Cres WV4 38 C6
Farewell La WS7 7 E6
Farfield Kidderminster
DY10 116 F5
Stoke Prior B60 150 F4
Farfield Cl B31 103 B2
Faringdon B77 21 F1
Farlands Dr DY8 81 A3
Farlands Gr B43 54 F7
Farlands Rd DY8 81 A3
Farleigh Dr WV3 38 A8
Farleigh Rd WV6 24 A3
Farley Ctr The B70 53 D2
Farley La B62 100 F1
Farley Rd B23 56 B4
Farley St
Royal Leamington Spa CV31 162 B7
Tipton DY4 52 D5
Farlow Cl Coventry CV6 114 A6
Redditch B98 154 D3
Farlow Croft B37 89 F8
Farlow Rd B31 103 C3
Farm Ave B68 64 A3
Farm Cl Birmingham B33 68 F3
Cannock WS12 2 C3
Codsall WV8 10 B2
Coventry CV6 95 B3
Kidderminster DY11 116 B2
Sedgley DY3 50 B7
Solihull B92 89 C2
Tamworth B79 21 C7
Farm Croft B19 66 C6
Farm House Way B43 43 E4
Farm Rd Birmingham B11 87 B7
Blackheath B65 63 A4
Brierley Hill DY5 61 E1
Dudley DY2 62 A4
Hinckley LE10 75 E6
Kenilworth CV8 147 E2
Oldbury B68 64 A3
Redditch B98 154 A3
Royal Leamington Spa CV32 157 B3
Smethwick B67 64 E3
Tipton DY4 52 B7
Wolverhampton WV3 38 C8
Farm St Birmingham B19 66 C6
Walsall WS2 28 E4
West Bromwich B70 53 C1
Farmacre B9 67 B2
Farman Rd CV5 113 A2
Farmbridge Cl WS2 27 D3
Farmbridge Rd WS2 27 D3
Farmbridge Way WS2 27 D3
Farmbrook Ave WV10 11 D3
Farmcote Cl B97 158 D4
Farmcote Lodge CV6 96 B4
Farmcote Rd Birmingham
B33 69 A4
Coventry CV2 96 B4
Farmcroft Rd DY9 81 E2
Farmdale Gr B45 122 A6
Farmer Rd B10 88 A8
Farmer Ward Rd CV8 148 A3
Farmer Way DY4 41 C1
Farmers Cl B76 46 E4
Farmers Ct B63 82 F4
Farmers Rd B60 150 E7
Farmers Wlk B21 65 D7
Farmhouse Rd WV12 27 D5
Farmhouse Way
Solihull B90 127 B7
Willenhall WV12 27 D5
Farmoor Gr B34 69 E6
Farmoor Way WV10 11 E4
Farmside CV3 134 D5
Farmside Gn WV9 10 F2
Farmstead Rd B92 89 C2
Farmstead The CV3 134 B8
Farnborough Cl B98 154 F1
Farnborough Ct B75 32 C2
Farnborough Dr B90 126 F6
Farnborough Rd B35 58 B3
Farnbury Croft B38 104 B2
Farncote Dr B74 31 F3
Farndale Ave Coventry CV6 95 D3
Wolverhampton WV6 25 A5
Farndale Cl DY5 81 B6
Farndale Jun Sch W6 25 A4
Farndon Ave B37 90 B7
Farndon Cl CV12 79 B3
Farndon Rd B8 67 F4
Farneway LE10 71 B1
Farnham Cl B43 54 F8
Farnham Rd B21 54 E2
Farnhurst Rd B36 68 B7
Farnol Rd B26 68 F1
Farnworth Gr B36 58 E1
Farquhar Rd
Birmingham, Edgbaston B15 85 F6
Birmingham, Moseley B13 86 F3
Farquhar Rd E B15 85 F6
Farr Dr CV4 112 B2
Farran Way B43 54 E7
Farren Rd Birmingham B31 102 D1
Coventry CV2 114 E5
Farrier Cl Bromsgrove B60 150 E6
Sutton Coldfield B76 57 F8
Farrier Rd B43 44 D3
Farrier Way DY6 60 A7
Farriers The B26 89 B5
Farriers Way Hinckley LE10 75 F6
Nuneaton CV11 73 F2
Farringdon Ho 5 WS2 28 D3
Farringdon St WS2 28 D3
Farrington Rd
Birmingham B23 56 B5
Wolverhampton WV4 39 E3
Farrow Rd B44 44 E3
Farthing Ct B3 164 A3
Farthing La Curdworth B76 59 C6
Sutton Coldfield B72 46 B4
Farthing Pools Cl 1 B72 46 C4
Farthings Lodge 7 DY1 51 B1
Farthings The B17 85 D6
Farvale Rd B76 58 C6
Faseman Ave CV4 111 F3
Fashoda Rd B29 86 B1
Fast Pits Rd B25 88 C7
Fastlea Rd B32 84 D1
Fastmoor Oval B33 69 E1
Fatherless Barn Cres B63 82 D5
Faulconbridge Ave CV5 111 E4
Faulkland Cres WV1 163 C4
Faulkner Cl DY8 80 F4
Faulkner Rd B92 89 B1
Faulkners Farm Dr B23 56 B6
Faulknor Dr DY5 61 B7
Faultlands Cl CV11 78 F8
Faversham Cl Willenhall
WS2 27 D3
Wolverhampton WV8 24 E8
Fawdry Cl B73 46 B5
Fawdry St Birmingham B9 67 A2
Smethwick B66 65 C5
Wolverhampton WV1 163 A4
Fawley Cl Coventry CV3 134 C6
Willenhall WV13 26 F1
Fawley Gr B14 104 B5
Faygate Cl CV3 114 F3
Fazeley Rd B78 21 B2
Fazeley St B5 66 F2
Fearnings Cotts B97 158 D5
Fearon Pl 4 B66 65 A5
Featherbed La
Coventry CV4 132 A5
Redditch B97 158 C5
Featherston Rd Aldridge
B74 31 A2
Hinckley LE10 75 E6
Featherstone Cl
Nuneaton CV10 73 C2
Solihull B90 106 D2
Featherstone Cres B90 106 D2
Featherstone Jun & Inf
Sch B23 56 E4
Featherstone La WV10 12 B8
Featherstone Rd B14 104 E6
Feckenham Ho B60 137 B3
Feckenham Rd
Astwood Bank B96 158 E2
Redditch,
Headless Cross B97 158 C8
Redditch, Hunt End B97 158 C4
Fecknam Way WS13 3 C1
Feilding Cl CV2 115 A6
Feilding Way CV10 72 A5
Felbrigg Cl DY5 81 D8
Feldings The B24 57 C4
Feldon La B62 83 E7
Felgate Cl B90 127 A6
Fell Gr Birmingham B21 54 C2
Royal Leamington Spa
CV32 157 C3
Fellbrook Cl B33 68 F4
Fellmeadow Rd B33 69 A2
Fellmeadow Way DY3 50 E7
Fellmore Gr CV31 162 D7
Fellows Ave DY6 60 C8
Fellows La B17 85 A5
Fellows Rd WV14 40 D7
Fellows St WV2 163 B1
Felspar Rd B77 22 B3
Felsted Way B7 67 A4
Felstone Rd B44 44 E1
Feltham Cl B33 69 E1
Felton Cl Coventry CV2 96 E1
Redditch B98 154 E1
Felton Croft B33 69 A3
Felton Gr B91 107 C1
Fen End Rd CV8 129 E4
Fenbourne Cl WS4 29 C8
Fenchurch Cl WS2 28 D4
Fencote Ave B37 70 A4
Fenmere Cl WV4 39 D5
Fenn Rise Stourbridge DY8 60 D3
Willenhall WV12 27 B5
Fenn St B77 21 E1
Fennel Cl WS6 4 D3
Fennel Croft B34 69 B7
Fennel Rd DY5 81 C7
Fennell Ho 10 CV1 113 B2
Fennis Cl B93 127 F3
Fens Cres DY5 61 C5
Fens Pool Ave DY5 61 D5
Fenside Ave CV3 133 D4
Fensway The B34 69 A5
Fenter Cl B13 86 F5
Fentham Cl B92 109 B6
Fentham Ct B92 106 F8
Fentham Gn B92 109 A7
Fentham Rd
Birmingham, Aston B6 66 E8
Birmingham,
Gravelly Hill B23 56 E3
Hampton in A B92 109 A6
Fenton Rd Birmingham B27 88 B5
Hollywood B47 125 A7
Fenton St Brierley Hill DY5 61 D3
Smethwick B66 64 E7
Fenton Way B27 88 B5
Fenwick Cl B97 153 B1
Fereday Rd WS9 16 B3
Fereday St DY4 51 F8
Fereday's Croft DY3 50 D7
Ferguson Dr DY11 116 A1
Ferguson Rd B68 64 D5
Ferguson St WV11 13 A1
Fern Ave DY4 51 F7
Fern Cl Coventry CV2 96 C2
Dudley WV14 51 B8
Walsall WS4 15 D1
Fern Dale Rd CV7 129 F6
Fern Dell Cl WS11 1 C2
Fern Dr WS6 5 A4
Fern Leys WV3 24 D1
Fern Rd Birmingham B24 57 A4
Dudley DY1 51 C4
Huntington WS12 1 D5
Wolverhampton WV3 163 A1
Fernbank Cl B63 82 E2
Fernbank Cres WS5 43 C4
Fernbank Rd B8 68 A4
Ferncliffe Rd B17 85 B4
Ferndale Ave B43 54 F7
Ferndale Cl Burntwood WS7 7 B6
Catshill B61 121 A1
Hagley DY9 99 A5
Nuneaton CV11 73 E5
Ferndale Cres
Birmingham B12 87 A8
Kidderminster DY11 116 B8
Ferndale Dr CV8 148 A2
Ferndale Pk DY9 99 C8
Ferndale Prim Sch B43 54 E8
Ferndale Rd
Binley Woods CV3 135 D7
Birmingham B28 105 F8
Essington WV11 13 B3
Oldbury B68 64 A2
Sutton Coldfield B74 44 F8
Ferndene Rd B11 88 A3
Ferndown Ave DY3 50 C7
Ferndown Cl Birmingham
B26 69 A1
Coventry CV4 112 A3
Walsall WS3 14 B4
Ferndown Gdns WV11 26 F5
Ferndown Rd B91 107 C5
Ferness Cl LE10 71 B2
Ferness Rd LE10 71 B2
Ferney Hill Ave B97 153 C3
Fernhill Cl CV8 147 E6
Fernhill Ct B23 56 C2
Fernhill Dr CV32 157 B1
Fernhill Gr B44 44 F3
Fernhill La CV7 129 F5
Fernhill Rd B92 88 E2
Fernhurst Dr DY5 61 B7
Fernhurst Rd B8 68 A3
Fernleigh B60 137 A1
Fernleigh Ave WS7 7 A8
Fernleigh Gdns DY8 60 C3
Fernleigh Rd WS4 29 B3
Fernley Ave B29 86 B2
Fernley Rd B11 87 C4
Fernside Gdns B13 87 B3
Fernwood Cl Redditch B98 159 B5
Sutton Coldfield B73 45 E1
Fernwood Croft
Birmingham B14 104 E6
Tipton DY4 51 F4
Fernwood Rd B73 56 E8
Fernwoods B32 84 B2
Ferrers Cl Coventry CV4 111 F2
Sutton Coldfield B75 32 D2
Ferrers Rd B77 21 D4
Ferrie Gr WS8 15 E8
Ferris Gr B27 88 A1
Festival Ave WS10 41 C4
Festival Ct WS11 1 E5
Festival Mews WS12 1 F6
Festival Way W6 25 B5
Fetherston Cres CV8 135 B1
Fetherston Ct 4 CV31 161 F6
Ffernfail Ct B23 56 E5
Fibbersley WV13, WV11 26 F4
Fibbersley Bank WV13 26 F4
Fiddlers Gn B92 109 A7
Field Barn Rd CV35 160 A7
Field Cl Birmingham B26 89 A6
Bromsgrove B60 150 E6
Hinckley LE10 71 F3
Kenilworth CV8 148 B5
Stourbridge DY8 61 A2
Walsall,
Blakenall Heath WS3 28 C8
Walsall, Pelsall WS4 15 B2
Warwick CV34 161 B7
Field Cottage Dr DY8 81 B3
Field Ct Coventry CV2 114 D7
Walsall WS4 15 B2
Field Farm Rd B77 21 D1
Field Head La CV34 161 B6
Field Head Pl WV6 24 B4
Field Ho CV8 147 F5
Field La Birmingham B32 102 B8
Clent DY9 99 D4
Great Wyrley WS6 4 F3
Solihull B91 108 A5
Stourbridge DY8 81 A3
Walsall WS4 15 B2
Field March CV3 134 E5
Field Mews DY2 62 E2
Field Rd Dudley DY2 51 E2
Tipton DY4 52 A8
Walsall WS3 14 C1
Wolverhampton WS13 3 B3
Field St Bilston WV14 40 E3
Cannock WS11 1 F3
Willenhall WV13 27 A2
Wolverhampton WV10 163 D4
Field Trad Est WS11 4 D6
Field View Ryton-on-D CV8 135 A1
Whitnash CV31 162 B3
Field View Cl CV7 96 A8
Field View Dr B65 63 F3
Field Way B94 143 C6
Field Wlk WS9 30 B7
Fieldfare WS7 7 D5
Fieldfare Cl B64 62 F4
Fieldfare Croft B36 70 A8
Fieldfare Ct DY10 117 A1
Fieldfare Rd DY9 81 D4
Fieldgate La Kenilworth
CV8 147 F6
Whitnash CV31 162 B2
Fieldgate Lawn CV8 147 F6
Fieldgate Trad Est WS1 28 F1
Fieldhead Rd B11 88 A3
Fieldhouse La B62 100 E4
Fieldhouse Rd
Birmingham B25 88 C8
Burntwood WS7 7 A7
Cannock WS12 1 F7
Wolverhampton WV4 39 E4
Fieldon Cl B90 106 C2
Fields Ct CV34 160 F8
Fieldside La CV3 114 F3
Fieldside Wlk WV14 40 D8
Fieldview Cl WV14 40 E2
Fieldways Cl B47 125 A7
Fiery Hill Rd B45 138 C8
Fife Rd CV5 112 F2
Fife St CV11 73 A4
Fifield Cl CV11 73 D2
Fifield Gr B33 68 F3
Fifth Ave Birmingham B9 67 F2
Wolverhampton WV10 25 E7
Filey B77 21 F6
Filey Cl WS11 4 C8
Filey Rd WV10 11 B2
Fillingham Cl B37 70 D1
Fillongley Rd CV7 92 E3
Filton Ave WS7 7 A8
Filton Croft B35 58 A4
Fimbrell Cl DY5 81 A8
Finbury Cl B92 88 F1
Finch Cl Blackheath B65 62 F4
Coventry CV6 95 C2
Finch Dr B74 45 A6
Finch Rd B19 66 C8
Finchall Croft B92 107 E7
Fincham Cl WV9 11 A3
Finchdene Gr WV3 24 D1
Finches End B34 69 C5
Finchfield Cl DY8 80 C4
Finchfield Gdns WV3 24 E1
Finchfield Hill WV3 24 C1
Finchfield La WV3 38 C8
Finchfield Rd WV3 24 E1
Finchfield Rd W WV3 24 D1
Finchley Ave 1 B19 66 C8
Finchley Cl DY3 50 D2
Finchley Rd B44 45 B1
Finchmead Rd B33 69 E2
Finchpath Rd B70 53 A6
Findlay Rd B14 86 E1
Findon Cl CV12 79 C3
Findon Rd B8 68 B6
Findon St DY10 116 F6
Finford Croft CV7 130 B6
Fingal Cl CV3 134 C6
Finger Post Dr WS3 15 A5
Fingest Cl CV5 112 B4
Finham Cres CV8 148 B6
Finham Flats CV8 148 B6
Finham Gr CV3 133 C3
Finham Green Rd CV3 133 B3
Finham Park Comp Sch
CV3 133 A4
Finham Prim Sch CV3 133 B3
Finham Rd CV8 148 B6
Finings Ct 7 CV32 156 F2
Finlarigg Dr B15 85 F6
Finlay Ct CV1 165 C1
Finmere Rd B28 105 F8
Finnemore Cl CV3 133 B5
Finnemore Rd B9 68 A2
Finney Well Cl WV14 40 B3
Finsbury Dr DY5 81 C7
Finsbury Gr B23 56 D6
Finstall Cl Birmingham B7 67 A4
Sutton Coldfield B72 46 C1
Finstall Fst Sch B60 137 B1
Finstall Rd Bromsgrove
B60 151 C8
Finstall B60 137 D1
Finwood Cl B92 107 E8
Finwood Rd CV35 144 F1
Fir Ave B12 87 A5
Fir Cl WS12 1 D8
Fir Croft DY5 81 C8
Fir Gr Birmingham B14 104 F5
Coventry CV4 112 A2
Stourbridge DY8 80 C6
Wolverhampton WV3 25 A1
Fir St DY3 49 F7
Fir Tree Ave CV4 112 B2
Fir Tree Cl Birmingham B44 55 E7
Tamworth B79 20 E7
Fir Tree Dr Dudley DY3 50 F7
Walsall WS5 43 B4
Fir Tree Gr Nuneaton CV11 78 D8
Sutton Coldfield B73 45 F1
Fir Tree Prim Sch WS5 43 A4
Fir Tree Rd WV3 38 D8
Firbank Cl B30 103 E7
Firbank Way WS3 14 F2
Firbarn Cl B76 46 D3
Firbeck Gr B44 45 A1
Firbeck Rd B44 45 A1
Fircroft Bilston WV14 41 A3
Birmingham B31 102 F8
Solihull B91 106 F6
Wolverhampton WV4 39 F4
Fircroft Cl Cannock WS11 2 A3
Stoke Heath B60 150 D6
Fircroft Coll B29 103 D8
Fircroft Ho B37 70 A2
Fire Station Rd B26 90 C5
Firecrest Cl Birmingham B23 56 B7
Cannock WS11 2 C2
Firecrest Way DY10 117 B1
Firethorn Cres CV31 162 A2
Firhill Croft B14 104 D2
Firleigh Dr CV12 79 D2
Firmstone Ct DY8 80 E7

Firmstone St DY8 80 E7
Firs Cl Kidderminster DY10 .. 117 A5
Marlbrook B60 121 D1
Smethwick B67 65 A5
Firs Dr B90 106 A1
Firs Farm Dr B36 68 F7
Firs Ho B36 68 F8
Firs Inf Sch The B36 68 F8
Firs La B67 65 A5
Firs Rd DY6 60 E6
Firs Sch The B67 65 A5
Firs St DY2 51 D1
Firs The Bedworth CV12 77 E2
Birmingham B11 87 C6
Cannock WS11 2 A2
Coventry CV5 133 B8
Meriden CV7 92 B1
Wolverhampton WV11 26 B5
Firsbrook Cl WV6 25 A5
Firsbrook Ho WV6 25 A5
Firsholm Cl B73 57 A7
First Ave
Birmingham, Selly Oak B29 86 B3
Birmingham, Smallheath B9 67 E1
Birmingham, Tyburn B76 58 A5
Birmingham, Witton B6 55 F2
Brownhills WS8 16 A8
Coventry CV3 114 C1
Kingswinford DY6 61 A8
Wolverhampton WV10 25 E6
First Exhibition Ave B40 90 D4
First Meadow Piece B32 84 E4
Firsvale Rd WV11 26 F5
Firsway WV6 24 A2
Firswood Rd B33 69 C1
Firth Dr Birmingham B14 105 B5
Halesowen B62 83 E8
Firth Park Cres B62 83 E8
Firtree Rd B24 57 B2
Fish Hill B98 153 E4
Fish House La B60 150 E4
Fisher Cl B45 101 E2
Fisher Rd Coventry CV6 113 E8
Oldbury B69 64 C7
Walsall WS3 13 F2
Fisher St Brierley Hill DY5 61 B2
Cannock WS12 1 F8
Dudley DY2 51 D1
Tipton, Burnt Tree DY4 52 A3
Tipton, Great Bridge DY4 52 D5
Willenhall WV13 27 C2
Wolverhampton WV3 39 B8
Fisher's Ct CV34 160 D4
Fishers Dr B90 125 F5
Fishing Line Rd B97 153 E5
Fishley Cl WS3 14 C4
Fishley La WS3 14 D5
Fishponds Rd CV8 147 E3
Fishpool Cl B36 68 C8
Fishpool La CV7 91 B5
Fitters Mill Cl B5 86 E6
Fitton Ave DY6 61 A5
Fitton St CV11 73 B3
Fitz Roy Ave B17 84 F7
Fitzgerald Pl DY5 81 B6
Fitzguy Cl B70 53 E1
Fitzmaurice Rd WV11 27 A7
Fitzroy Cl CV2 115 B6
Fitzroy Rd B31 102 D3
Fitzwarren Specl Sch
DY4 52 A6
Five Fields Rd WV12 27 A5
Five Oaks Rd WV13 40 E8
Five Ways
Birmingham,
Bordesley Green B9 67 D2
Birmingham, Ladywood B16 66 B1
Blackheath B64 82 C8
Churchill DY10 98 A5
Dudley DY3 50 D3
Wolverhampton,
Dunstall Hill WV3 25 C4
Wolverhampton,
Merry Hill WV3 38 C7
Wroxall CV35 145 F1
Five Ways Cty Prim Sch
WS12 2 D2
Five Ways Rd CV35 145 F1
Five Ways Sta B15 86 B8
Fivefield Rd CV7 94 E5
Flackwell Rd B23 56 E7
Fladbury Cl Dudley DY2 62 D3
Redditch B98 159 B8
Fladbury Cres B29 85 D1
Fladbury Gdns B20 66 C8
Fladbury Pl 3 B19 66 C7
Flamboro' Cl CV3 134 F8
Flamborough Cl B34 69 A7
Flamborough Way WV14 51 B7
Flamville Rd LE10 76 B5
Flanders Cl B98 154 D5
Flanders Dr 2 DY6 60 D8
Flash La WV4 37 F2
Flash Rd B69 64 A7
Flats La WS14 19 A6
Flats The B61 136 F3
Flatts The WS10 41 E7
Flaunden Cl CV5 112 B4
Flavel Cres CV31 161 F7
Flavel Rd B60 150 E7
Flavell Ave WV14 40 D1
Flavell Cl B32 84 B1
Flavell St DY1 51 B6
Flavells La Birmingham B25 88 C8
Dudley DY3 50 B2
Flax Cl B47 125 A5
Flax Gdns B38 123 F8
Flax Hill Jun Sch B79 21 B7
Flaxhall St WS2 42 B8
Flaxley Cl B33 68 F3
Flaxley Rd B33 68 E4
Flaxton Gr B33 69 A4
Flaxton Wlk WV6 25 A5
Flecknoe Cl B36 58 C1
Flecknose St CV3 134 C6
Fledburgh Dr B76 46 D4
Fleet Ho CV1 165 B2
Fleet St Birmingham B3 164 A3
Coventry CV1 165 B3
Fleetwood Gr B26 69 A1
Fleetwood Ho 3 B13 86 F4
Fleming Pl WS2 28 A6
Fleming Rd Birmingham B32 84 D5
Hinckley LE10 74 F7
Walsall WS2 28 A6
Fletchamstead Highway
CV5 132 D7
Fletcher Gr B93 128 B4
Fletcher Rd Hinckley LE10 75 E7
Willenhall WV12 27 D8
Fletcher St DY9 81 F5
Fletcher's La WV13 27 C2
Fletchworth Gate CV5 132 D8
Fletton Gr B14 105 A3
Fleur de-lys Ct CV34 161 B8
Flinkford Cl WS5 43 D6
Flinn Cl WS14 9 D7
Flint Cl DY10 116 E2
Flint Green Rd B27 88 B3
Flint Ho 3 WV3 25 C4
Flint Tower B18 65 E4
Flintham Cl B92 88 E3
Flintway The B33 68 E4
Flood St DY2 51 D1
Floodgate St B5 66 F1
Flora Cl B79 21 C7
Flora Rd B25 88 B7
Florence Ave
Birmingham B11 87 C5
5 Sutton Coldfield B73 57 B7
Wolverhampton WV4 40 A4
Florence Bldgs 3 B29 85 F2
Florence Cl CV12 95 F8
Florence Dr 4 B73 57 B7
Florence Gr 2
Birmingham B18 65 E4
West Bromwich B71 42 E1
Florence Pl 10 B12 87 A6
Florence Rd
Birmingham,
Acock's Green B27 88 D4
Birmingham,
Handsworth B21 65 D8
Birmingham,
King's Heath B14 104 F8
Codsall WV8 10 C3
Oldbury B69 63 E7
Smethwick B66 65 B4
Sutton Coldfield B73 57 B7
Tipton DY4 52 A7
West Bromwich B70 53 E1
Florence St Birmingham B1 164 B1
Cannock WS12 2 B7
Walsall WS1 29 A1
Florence Villas B11 87 C7
Florendine Cty Prim Sch
B77 21 F5
Florendine St B77 21 F5
Florian Gr WS10 41 E7
Florida Way DY6 61 A6
Flowerdale Cl WV14 51 B8
Flowerdale Dr CV2 114 B6
Floyds La WS4 29 C6
Floyer Rd B10 67 F1
Flude Rd CV7 95 C6
Flyford Cl B98 153 F1
Flyford Croft B29 84 F2
Flynt Ave CV5 112 B6
Fockbury Mill La B61 136 E5
Fockbury Rd B61 136 B5
Foden Cl WS14 17 F6
Foden Rd B42 55 A7
Foinavon Cl B65 62 F6
Fold St WV1 163 B2
Fold The Birmingham B38 104 A1
Darlaston WS10 41 D6
Wolverhampton WV4 38 F4
Foldyard Cl B76 58 A8
Foleshill CE Prim Sch CV6 96 A1
Foleshill Rd CV1, CV6 113 D6
Foley Ave WV6 24 C3
Foley Church Cl B74 31 A2
Foley Dr WV6 24 C3
Foley Gdns B60 150 E3
Foley Ho 9 B68 84 B8
Foley Park Fst Sch DY11 116 D3
Foley Rd Birmingham B8 68 B5
Stourbridge DY9 81 C2
Foley Rd E B74 31 A2
Foley Rd W B74 30 E1
Foley St WS10 42 A3
Foley Wood Cl B74 30 E1
Foliot Fields B25 88 D8
Folkes Rd DY9 82 A6
Folkestone Croft B36 68 E8
Folkland Gn CV6 113 A7
Folliott Rd B33 69 B3
Follyhouse Cl WS1 42 F7
Follyhouse La WS1 42 F7
Fontenaye Rd B79 20 F7
Fontley Cl B26 69 A2
Fontmell Cl CV2 115 A4
Fontwell Rd WV10 11 D4
Footherley La WS14 17 E4
Footherley Rd WS14 17 E4
Ford Brook La WS4 15 B2
Ford Cotts CV33 157 F2
Ford Rd B61 136 E1
Ford St Birmingham B18 66 B5
Coventry CV1 165 C3
Nuneaton CV10 72 E4
Smethwick B67 64 F6
Walsall WS2 42 C7
Fordbridge Cl B97 153 C1
Fordbridge Inf Sch B37 70 A5
Fordbridge Rd B37 70 A5
Forde Way Gdns B38 123 D7
Forder Gr B14 105 A2
Fordfield Rd B33 69 C4
Fordham Gr WV9 11 A3
Fordhouse La B30 104 B6
Fordhouse Rd
Bromsgrove B60 137 B1
Wolverhampton WV10 11 D1
Fordhouse Road Ind Est
WV10 25 D8
Fordraught La B62 101 B1
Fordrift The B37 90 A6
Fordrough B25 87 F7
Fordrough Ave B9 67 E3
Fordrough La B9 67 E2
Fordrough The
Birmingham B31 103 C1
Hollywood B90 125 C7
Sutton Coldfield B74 32 A1
Fords Rd B90 125 E7
Fordwater Rd B74 44 F6
Fordwell Cl CV5 112 F3
Fore St B2 164 C2
Foredraft Cl B32 84 C2
Foredraft St B63 82 D5
Foredraught B80 159 E4
Foredrift Cl B98 153 E2
Foredrove La B92 107 E7
Foregate St B96 158 E1
Foreland Way CV6 95 A3
Forelands Gr B61 150 D8
Forest Ave WS3 28 D7
Forest Cl Lickey End B60 137 B6
Smethwick B66 64 E7
Sutton Coldfield B74 44 E7
Forest Ct Birmingham B13 87 A3
Coventry CV5 112 A4
Dorridge B93 127 F3
Willenhall WV12 27 C8
Forest Dale B45 122 B6
Forest Dr B17 85 D6
Forest Gate WV12 27 D8
Forest Hill Rd B26 89 C5
Forest La WS2 28 D5
Forest Lawns B74 31 C3
Forest Oak Specl Sch B36 58 E1
Forest Pk B76 46 E4
Forest Pl WS3 28 E6
Forest Rd
Birmingham, Moseley B13 87 A3
Birmingham,
South Yardley B25 88 C6
Dorridge B93 127 F3
Dudley DY1 51 C4
Hinckley LE10 75 F8
Oldbury B68 84 C7
Forest View B97 158 E6
Forest Way Great Wyrley
WS6 5 A1
Hollywood B47 125 B6
Nuneaton CV10 72 E2
Forester Way DY10 116 E3
Forester's Rd CV3 133 E6
Forfar Wlk B38 103 D2
Forfield Pl CV31 162 A7
Forfield Rd CV6 112 E5
Forge Cl Burntwood WS7 7 D5
Wolverhampton WV8 10 E1
Forge Croft B76 58 B6
Forge Dr B61 136 F3
Forge La
Aldridge, Leighswood WS9 30 A5
Aldridge, Mill Green WS9 30 F7
Belbroughton DY9 119 D7
Blackheath B64 82 B8
Blakedown DY10 98 B1
Burntwood WS7 7 F6
Halesowen B62 83 C5
Kingswinford DY6 60 A8
Lichfield WS13 3 A1
Shenstone WS14 31 C8
Sutton Coldfield B76 58 B5
West Bromwich B71 54 A6
Forge Mill Farm B71 54 B6
Forge Mill Rd B98 153 F6
Forge Rd Darlaston WS10 41 C6
Kenilworth CV8 148 A6
Stourbridge DY8 80 F6
Walsall WS3 14 F5
Willenhall WV12 27 C4
Forge St Cannock WS12 2 C4
Wednesbury WS10 41 E4
Forge The B63 82 B8
Forge Trad Est B62 83 C5
Forge Way Coventry CV6 95 C3
Oldbury B69 63 E6
Forhill Ho B38 123 F3
Forknell Ave CV2 114 C5
Formans Rd B11 87 E3
Formans Trad Est B11 87 D3
Formby Ave WV6 23 D4
Formby Way WS3 14 A3
Forrell Gr B31 123 B7
Forrest Ave Cannock WS11 4 E8
Essington WV11 13 A4
Forrest Ct 9 WS13 9 B7
Forrest Rd Kenilworth CV8 147 E4
Wednesbury WS10 41 D1
Forrester St WS2 28 C2
Forrester Street Prec
3 WS2 28 C2
Foresters Cl LE10 75 F6
Foresters Rd LE10 75 F6
Forryan Rd LE10 75 F7
Forshaw Heath La B94 141 A7
Forshaw Heath Rd B94 125 C1
Forster St Birmingham B7 67 A3
Smethwick B67 64 E7
Forsythia Cl
Birmingham,
Shenley Fields B31 102 F7
Birmingham,
Woodcock Hill B31 102 F8
Forsythia Gr WV8 10 A3
Fort Cres WS9 16 A3
Fort Ind Pk The B35 57 F1
Fort Parkway B35, B36 57 D1
Fort The B24 57 C1
Forth Dr B37 70 B4
Forth Gr B38 123 E8
Forth Way B62 83 E8
Forties B77 35 E7
Fortnum Cl B33 69 D2
Forton Cl WV6 24 B2
Forum Ctr The DY1 51 C1
Forum Rd B40 90 E3
Forward Cotts B48 138 F6
Forward Rd B26 90 A3
Fosberry Cl CV34 161 B8
Fosbrooke Rd B10 88 A8
Fossdale Rd B77 36 A8
Fosseway WS14 9 A5
Fosseway Dr B23 56 E8
Fosseway La WS13 8 E4
Fosseway Rd CV3 133 B4
Fossil Dr B45 122 A7
Foster Ave Cannock WS12 1 F6
Studley B80 159 E3
Wolverhampton WV14 40 B1
Foster Gdns B18 65 F6
Foster Gn WV6 23 E3
Foster Pl DY8 80 E6
Foster Rd Coventry CV6 113 B7
Wolverhampton WV10 25 E7
Foster St Darlaston WS10 41 D7
3 Stourbridge DY8 81 A5
Walsall WS3 28 D8
Foster St E DY8 81 A5
Foster Way B5 86 C5
Fotherley Brook Rd WS9 30 F5
Founder Cl CV4 132 A8
Foundry La Smethwick B66 65 D6
Walsall WS3 14 E3
Foundry Rd Birmingham
B18 65 E5
Kingswinford DY6 60 C8
Foundry Road Prim Sch
B18 65 E6
Foundry St Dudley WV14 40 C1
Kingswinford DY6 60 C8
Tipton DY4 51 E8
Fountain Arc 4 DY1 51 C1
Fountain Cl B31 122 E6
Fountain La Dudley WV14 51 E8
West Bromwich B69 53 A1
Fountain Rd B17 65 C1
Fountains Rd WS3 13 E2
Fountains Way WS3 13 E2
Four Acres B32 84 C4
Four Ashes Rd B93 127 E4
Four Crosses Rd WS4 15 C1
Four Dwellings High Sch
B32 84 B5
Four Dwellings Inf Sch
B32 84 C5
Four Dwellings Jun Sch
B32 84 B5
Four Oaks Cl B98 158 D8
Four Oaks Common Rd
B74 31 F3
Four Oaks Ct B74 32 B1
Four Oaks Inf Sch B74 31 E4
Four Oaks Jun Sch B74 31 E4
Four Oaks Rd B74 32 A1
Four Oaks Sta B74 46 B8
Four Pounds Ave CV5 112 F3
Four Stones Cl B91 107 A1
Four Stones Gr B5 86 D6
Four Winds Rd DY2 62 E6
Fourlands Ave B72 57 D7
Fourlands Rd B31 102 E6
Fourth Ave
Birmingham,
Bordesley Green B9 67 F2
Birmingham, Selly Oak B29 86 C3
Brownhills WS8 7 A1
Wolverhampton WV10 25 E6
Fowey Cl B76 58 A7
Fowey Rd B34 68 F6
Fowgay Dr B91 106 F1
Fowler Cl Perton WV6 23 E6
Smethwick B66 65 A8
Fowler Rd Coventry CV6 113 B4
Sutton Coldfield B75 47 B5
Fowler St Birmingham B7 67 B6
Wolverhampton WV2 39 C6
Fowlmere Rd B42 55 B8
Fownhope Cl B98 154 E3
Fox Ave CV10 73 D7
Fox Covert DY8 80 E5
Fox Foot Dr DY5 61 C4
Fox & Goose Sh Ctr B8 68 C5
Fox Gr B27 88 A2
Fox Green Cres B27 88 A2
Fox Hill B29 103 C8
Fox Hill Cl B29 103 C8
Fox Hill Rd B75 32 F2
Fox Hollies L Ctr B27 88 B1
Fox Hollies Rd
Birmingham B27, B28 88 A1
Sutton Coldfield B76 47 B2
Fox Hollies Sch B27 88 A1
Fox Hollow WV6 24 C2
Fox La Bromsgrove B61 150 E8
Lichfield WS13 3 A5
Fox Mill Est B11 87 D3
Fox St Birmingham B5 164 D3
Dudley DY1 51 C6
Fox Wlk WS9 16 B3
Fox's La WV6 25 C4
Foxbury Dr B93 128 B3
Foxcote Ave B21 65 E7
Foxcote Cl Redditch B98 154 F4
Solihull B90 126 D8
Foxcote Dr B90 126 D8
Foxcote La B63, DY9 82 B4
Foxcroft Cl WS7 7 B5
Foxdale Dr DY5 61 B3
Foxdale Gr B33 69 C3
Foxdale Wlk 11 CV31 162 C6
Foxes Cl B60 138 B5
Foxes Mdw B76 58 A8
Foxes Rake WS11 1 E3
Foxes Ridge B64 82 E8
Foxes Way
Balsall Common CV7 130 B6
Warwick CV34 160 D4
Foxfields Way WS12 1 C7
Foxford Cl Birmingham B36 58 D1
Sutton Coldfield B72 57 D7
Foxford Cres CV2 96 B4
Foxford Sch CV6 96 A5
Foxglove B77 22 A4
Foxglove Cl Coventry CV6 95 C2
Featherstone WV10 12 B7
Walsall WS3 15 A5
Wednesfield WV11 26 E5
Foxglove Cres B37 69 E3
Foxglove Rd DY1 51 A4
Foxglove Way B60 137 C6
Foxglove Wlk WS12 2 C7
Foxhill Barns B48 138 E5
Foxhill Cl WS12 2 D2
Foxhill La B48 138 E5
Foxhill's Cl WS7 7 A5
Foxhills Cl CV11 74 C1
Foxhills Pk DY2 62 C4
Foxhills Rd Stourbridge
DY8 60 D1
Wolverhampton WV4 38 C3
Foxholes La B97 158 A6
Foxholes The DY10 116 F8
Foxhollies Dr B63 82 E4
Foxhollow B61 150 D8
Foxhope Cl B38 104 B2
Foxhunt Rd B63 82 E2
Foxland Ave
Birmingham B45 122 C7
Great Wyrley WS6 5 A3
Foxland Cl Birmingham B37 70 D2
Cheswick Green B90 126 D4
Foxlands Ave WV4 38 D3
Foxlands Cres WV4 38 C3
Foxlands Dr Dudley DY3 50 D5
Sutton Coldfield B72 57 D7
Wombourne WV4 38 D3
Foxlea Rd B63 82 D1
Foxlydiate Cres B97 153 A3
Foxlydiate La B97 152 F3
Foxmeadow Cl DY3 50 E7
Foxoak Ent Ctr B64 62 D1
Foxoak St B64 62 C1
Foxton Rd Birmingham B8 67 F4
Coventry CV3 114 E1
Foxwalks Ave B61 150 D8
Foxwell Gr B9 68 C3
Foxwell Rd B9 68 C3
Foxwood Ave B43 44 B2
Foxwood Gr B37 69 F5
Foxwood Rd Birchmoor B78 36 F8
Polesworth B78 22 F1
Foxyards Cl DY4 51 D5
Foxyards Prim Sch DY4 51 C5
Foxyards Rd DY4 51 D5
Foyle Rd B38 103 F1
Fozdar Cres WV14 40 B1
Fradley Cl B30 103 D4
Framefield Dr B91 107 F6
Framlingham Gr
Kenilworth CV8 148 C6
Perton WV6 24 A3
Frampton Cl
Birmingham,
Bournville B30 103 D7
Birmingham,
Chelmsley Wood B37 70 D3
Frampton Way B43 44 D5
Frampton Wlk CV2 114 F4
Frances Ave CV34 161 A7
Frances Cres CV12 78 A3
Frances Dr WS3 14 B2
Frances Rd Baginton CV8 133 F3
Birmingham,
Balsall Heath B30 104 A5
Birmingham, Lozells B19 66 C8
Birmingham,
Stockland Green B23 56 D3
Franche Fst Sch DY11 116 C8
Franche Mid Sch DY11 116 C8
Franche Rd DY11 116 C8
Franchise Gdns WS10 41 F6

Franchise St Birmingham
B42 .... 55 E2
Darlaston WS10 .... 41 F6
Kidderminster DY11 ...... 116 C5
Francis Cl Kingswinford
DY6 .... 60 D8
Sutton Coldfield B74 ..... 44 F8
Francis Rd
Birmingham,
Acock's Green B27 ...... 88 D5
Birmingham, Edgbaston B16 .. 66 A1
Birmingham,
South Yardley B25 ...... 88 A6
Birmingham, Stechford B33 .... 68 D2
Bromsgrove B60 .... 150 F7
Lichfield WS13 .... 3 A2
Smethwick B67 .... 64 D4
Stourbridge DY8 .... 80 C5
Francis St Birmingham B7 .. 67 A4
Coventry CV6 .... 113 E7
West Bromwich B70 ..... 53 D1
Wolverhampton WV1 .... 25 C4
Francis Ward Cl B71 ..... 53 A8
Franciscan Rd CV3 ...... 133 D8
Francis Wlk B31 .... 123 A7
Frank F Harrison Comp Sch WS2 .... 27 F7
Frank Rd B67 .... 64 E6
Frank St Birmingham B12 .. 86 F7
Nuneaton CV11 .... 73 B3
Frank Tommey Cl 5 B65 .. 63 C1
Frank Walsh Ho CV1 ..... 165 C4
Frank Whittle Prim Sch CV2 .... 114 F8
Frankburn Rd B74 ...... 44 F8
Frankfort St B19 .... 66 D6
Frankholmes Dr B90 ..... 127 A6
Frankland Rd CV6 ...... 96 A1
Frankley Ave B62 .... 83 F5
Frankley Beeches Rd B31 .... 102 D3
Frankley Com Sch B45 .... 101 F1
Frankley Gn B45 .... 101 D5
Frankley Green La B45 .... 101 E5
Frankley Hill La B32 ..... 102 A4
Frankley Ind Pk B45 ...... 102 B1
Frankley La B31, B32 .... 102 D6
Frankley Lodge Rd B31 .... 102 D4
Frankley Rd B68 .... 84 B8
Frankley Terr B17 .... 85 B5
Franklin Ct CV11 .... 73 D1
Franklin Dr WS7 .... 7 B7
Franklin Gr CV4 .... 111 E1
Franklin Rd Birmingham
B30 .... 103 F5
Nuneaton CV11 .... 73 D1
Whitnash CV31 .... 162 A3
Franklin St B18 .... 65 E5
Franklin Way B30 .... 103 F6
Franklyn Cl WV6 .... 23 E5
Frankpledge Rd CV3 ..... 133 E7
Franks Way B33 .... 68 E2
Frankton Ave CV3 ...... 133 C5
Frankton Cl Redditch B98 .. 159 E8
Solihull B92 .... 89 B2
Frankton Gr B9 .... 68 B2
Frankwell Dr CV2 .... 96 E1
Frannkley Hill La B45 .... 101 F3
Fraser Cl CV10 .... 72 B6
Fraser Rd Birmingham B11 .. 87 D5
Coventry CV6 .... 95 A1
Fraser St WV14 .... 40 E6
Frayne Ave DY6 .... 60 C7
Freasley Cl B90 .... 106 D3
Freasley Rd B34 .... 69 D6
Fred Lee Gr CV3 .... 133 D4
Freda Eddy Ct 3 DY10 .. 116 E6
Freda Rd B70 .... 53 D1
Freda Rise B69 .... 63 D8
Fredas Gr B17 .... 85 A4
Frederick Ave LE10 ..... 71 B2
Frederick Bird Prim Sch CV1 .... 113 F5
Frederick Neal Ave CV5 ... 111 D4
Frederick Rd
Birmingham, Aston B6 .... 66 F8
Birmingham, Edgbaston B15 .. 86 B8
Birmingham,
Gravelly Hill B23 ...... 56 E2
Birmingham, Selly Oak B29 ... 85 D2
Birmingham, Sparkhill B11 ... 87 C4
Birmingham, Stechford B33 .... 68 D3
Oldbury B68 .... 84 D7
Sutton Coldfield B73 .... 46 A2
Wolverhampton WV11 .... 26 C5
Frederick Rd (Road 1) DY10 .... 116 F1
Frederick St Birmingham
B1 .... 66 C4
Walsall WS2 .... 28 D1
West Bromwich B70 ..... 53 C4
Wolverhampton WV2 .... 163 B1
Frederick William St WV13 .... 27 B2
Fredericks Cl DY8 ...... 80 E4
Freeburn Cswy CV4 ..... 132 C2
Freeford Gdns WS14 .... 9 E6
Freehold St CV1 .... 113 F4
Freeland Gr DY6 .... 60 F4
Freeman Cl CV10 .... 72 D4
Freeman Dr B76 .... 46 F4
Freeman Pl WV14 ...... 40 E8
Freeman Rd Birmingham B7 .. 67 B6
Wednesbury WS10 ..... 42 D3

Freeman St Birmingham
B5 .... 164 C2
Coventry CV6 .... 113 F6
Wolverhampton WV10 .... 25 F2
Freeman's La LE10 ...... 76 A5
Freemans Cl CV32 ...... 156 E2
Freemantle Ho B24 ..... 57 D3
Freemount Sq B43 ..... 54 E7
Freer Rd B6 .... 66 E8
Freer St Nuneaton CV11 ... 73 E2
Walsall WS1 .... 28 F2
Freesland Rise CV10 .... 72 B6
Freeth Rd WS8 .... 7 A1
Freeth St Birmingham B16 .. 65 F2
Oldbury B69 .... 63 F8
Freezeland St WV14 .... 40 B6
Fremantle Ho B34 ..... 69 E6
Fremont Dr DY1 .... 50 E3
French Ave B78 .... 20 C1
French Rd DY2 .... 51 F1
French Walls 7 B66 .... 65 C5
Frensham Cl Birmingham
B37 .... 70 C2
Cheslyn Hay WS6 ...... 4 E4
Frensham Dr CV10 ..... 72 B5
Frensham Way B17 ..... 85 C6
Frenshaw Gr B44 ...... 55 F7
Freshfield Cl CV5 ...... 94 C1
Freshwater Gr 5 CV31 .. 162 C6
Fretton Cl CV6 .... 113 F7
Frevill Rd CV6 .... 114 B8
Freville Cl B79 .... 21 A6
Friar Park Rd WS10 .... 42 D3
Friar St WS10 .... 42 B3
Friardale Cl WS10 ..... 42 D3
Friars Cl Binley Woods CV3 .. 135 E7
Stourbridge DY8 .... 60 C3
Friars Gorse DY7 ...... 80 C7
Friars' Rd CV1 .... 165 B2
Friars St CV34 .... 160 D6
Friars Wlk B37 .... 70 D2
Friary Ave Lichfield WS13 .. 9 A6
Solihull B90 .... 127 A6
Friary Cl Birmingham B20 .. 54 F3
Hinckley LE10 .... 71 E1
Friary Cres WS4 .... 29 D7
Friary Gdns Birmingham B21 .. 54 D2
Lichfield WS13 .... 9 A7
Friary Rd Birmingham B20 .. 54 F3
Lichfield WS13 .... 9 A7
Friary St CV11 .... 73 B5
Friary The WS13 .... 9 A7
Friday Acre WS13 ...... 3 A2
Friday La B92 .... 108 D4
Friesland Dr WV1 ...... 26 B3
Friezeland Rd WS2 ..... 28 B2
Friezland La WS8 ...... 16 A5
Friezland Way WS8 ..... 16 A5
Frilsham Way CV5 ...... 112 B4
Fringe Gn B60 .... 151 A7
Fringe Green Cl B60 .... 151 A7
Fringe Meadow Rd B98 ... 154 F6
Frinton Gr B21 .... 65 C7
Frisby Ct CV11 .... 73 E2
Frisby Rd Birmingham B32 .. 84 E5
Coventry CV4 .... 111 E2
Friston Ave B16 .... 66 B1
Friswell Dr CV6 .... 113 F8
Friswell Ho 3 CV2 ..... 114 D8
Frith Way B11 .... 71 A3
Frobisher Cl Great Wyrley
WS6 .... 4 F1
Hinckley LE10 .... 71 D4
Frobisher Rd CV3 ...... 133 C5
Frobisher Way B66 ..... 64 D7
Frodesley Rd B26 ...... 89 B8
Frog La Balsall Common
CV7 .... 130 A5
Lichfield WS13 .... 9 B7
Froggatt Rd WV14 ..... 40 D7
Froggatts Ride B76 .... 46 F3
Frogmere Cl CV5 ...... 112 C6
Frogmill Mid Sch B45 .... 102 B2
Frogmill Rd B45 .... 102 B2
Frogmoor Ho B26 ...... 88 E7
Frogmore La CV8 ...... 129 F2
Frome Dr WV11 .... 26 C5
Frome Ho 4 DY1 ...... 61 E8
Frome Way B14 .... 104 D6
Front Cotts B48 .... 138 F6
Frost St WV2 .... 40 A6
Froxmere Cl B91 ...... 127 C8
Froyle Cl WV6 .... 24 C5
Froysell St WV13 ...... 27 B2
Fryer Ave CV32 .... 156 E3
Fryer Rd B31 .... 123 B7
Fryer St WV1 .... 163 C3
Fryers Cl WS3 .... 28 B7
Fryers Rd WS2 .... 28 A7
Frythe Cl CV8 .... 148 C6
Fuchsia Cl 3 CV2 ..... 96 B2
Fuchsia Dr WV9 .... 10 F3
Fugelmere Cl B17 ...... 84 F7
Fulbrook Cl B98 .... 154 C5
Fulbrook Gr B29 ...... 102 F8
Fulbrook Rd Coventry CV2 .. 96 B2
Dudley DY1 .... 51 A1
Fulfen Prim Sch WS7 .... 7 D7
Fulford Dr B76 .... 58 B5
Fulford Gr B26 .... 89 C6
Fulford Hall Rd B94 ..... 125 D3
Fulham Rd B11 .... 87 B5
Fullbrook Cl B90 ...... 127 A5
Fullbrook Rd WS5 ..... 42 E5
Fullelove Rd WS8 ...... 16 A7
Fullers Cl CV6 .... 112 F2
Fullerton Cl WV8 ...... 24 E8

Fullwood Cl CV2 .... 96 E2
Fullwood Cres DY2 ..... 61 F6
Fullwoods End WV14 .... 40 C1
Fulmar Cres DY10 ..... 117 B2
Fulmer Wlk B18 .... 66 A3
Fulton Cl B60 .... 137 B1
Fulwell Gr B44 .... 56 A8
Fulwood Ave B62 ...... 83 F8
Furber Pl DY6 .... 60 F6
Furlong La B63 .... 82 D6
Furlong Mdw B31 ...... 103 C2
Furlong The WS10 ..... 41 E5
Furlong Wlk DY3 ...... 50 D4
Furlongs Rd DY3 ...... 50 D6
Furlongs The
Stourbridge DY8 ...... 81 B3
Wolverhampton WV11 ... 26 B5
Furnace Hill B63 ...... 83 B5
Furnace La B63 .... 83 B5
Furnace Par DY4 ...... 51 E6
Furnace Rd Bedworth CV12 .. 78 D4
Dudley DY2 .... 62 C8
Furness B77 .... 21 D3
Furness Cl WS3 .... 13 F3
Furnivall Cres WS13 .... 3 D1
Furrows The B60 ...... 150 D6
Furst St WS8 .... 16 A8
Furze Way WS5 .... 43 E8
Furzebank Way WV12 ... 27 E4
Fylde Ho CV2 .... 114 D4
Fynford Rd CV6 .... 113 B5

Gable Croft WS14 ..... 9 F6
Gables The DY6 ...... 60 B8
Gaddesby Rd B14 ..... 104 F8
Gadds Dr B65 .... 63 D4
Gads Gn DY2 .... 62 D5
Gads Green Cres DY2 ... 62 E6
Gads La Dudley DY1 .... 51 C1
West Bromwich B70 .... 53 A3
Gadsby Ave WV11 ..... 27 A7
Gadsby Ct CV11 ...... 73 E3
Gadsby St CV11 ...... 73 E3
Gadshill CV31 .... 161 E4
Gadwall Croft B23 .... 56 B3
Gaelic Rd WS11 ...... 1 D4
Gagarin B79 .... 20 F5
Gaia La WS13 .... 9 B8
Gaiafields Rd WS13 .... 3 B1
Gaialands Cres WS13 ... 3 B1
Gaiastowe WS13 ..... 3 B1
Gail Cl WS9 .... 16 B4
Gail Pk WV3 .... 38 D7
Gailey Croft B44 ..... 44 E3
Gainford Cl WV8 ..... 10 F1
Gainford Rd B44 ..... 45 C1
Gainford Rise CV3 .... 115 A3
Gains La WS11 .... 5 D3
Gainsborough Ave LE10 .. 71 A3
Gainsborough Cres
Birmingham B43 ...... 44 D4
Knowle B93 .... 128 A6
Gainsborough Dr
Bedworth CV12 ...... 78 A4
Mile Oak B78 .... 34 B8
Perton WV6 .... 24 A4
Royal Leamington Spa
CV31 .... 162 D6
Gainsborough Hill DY8 ... 81 A3
Gainsborough Mews DY11 .... 116 B5
Gainsborough Pl DY1 ... 50 E2
Gainsborough Rd B42 ... 55 B6
Gainsborough Trad Est DY9 .... 81 C4
Gainsbrook Cres WS11 ... 5 F5
Gainsford Dr B62 ..... 83 B6
Gairloch Rd WV12 .... 13 B1
Gaitskell Terr B69 .... 52 D2
Gaitskell Way B66 .... 64 F7
Galahad Way WS10 .... 42 A2
Galbraith Cl WV14 .... 51 D8
Gale Wlk B65 .... 62 F5
Galey's Rd CV3 ...... 133 D8
Gallagher Bsns Pk CV6 .. 95 E5
Gallagher Ct 15 B13 .. 87 B2
Gallagher Rd CV12 .... 78 A2
Galliards The CV4 ..... 132 D4
Galloway Ave B34 .... 68 F6
Galloway Cl LE9 ..... 71 F7
Gallows Hill CV34 .... 161 B4
Galmington Dr CV3 .... 133 B6
Galton Cl Sutton Coldfield
B24 .... 57 F4
Tipton DY4 .... 52 C6
Galton Dr DY2 .... 62 B6
Galton Ho B67 .... 64 F2
Galton Rd B67 .... 64 F1
Galton Tower B1 ..... 66 C2
Galtons La DY9 ...... 120 A7
Galway Rd WS7 ...... 7 A7
Gamesfield Gn WV3 ... 24 F1
Gammage St DY2 ..... 62 B8
Gamson Cl DY10 ..... 116 E4
Ganborough Cl B98 ... 154 E1
Gandy Rd WV12 ..... 27 A7
Gannahs Farm Cl B76 ... 46 F3
Gannow Green La B45 ... 101 D1
Gannow Manor Cres B45 .. 101 E2
Gannow Manor Gdns B45 .... 101 F1
Gannow Mid Sch B45 ... 121 D7
Gannow Rd B45 ...... 121 E7
Gannow Wlk B45 ..... 121 E7
Ganton Rd WS3 ...... 14 A4
Ganton Wlk WV8 ..... 24 D7
Ganville Ho B36 ..... 69 F8
Garage Cl B77 .... 21 D5

Garden Cl
Birmingham, Frankley B45 .. 102 A2
Birmingham, Ward End B8 .. 68 A5
Hinckley LE10 .... 75 D6
Knowle B93 .... 127 F6
Garden Cres WS3 ..... 14 F3
Garden Croft WS9 .... 30 B7
Garden Ct
Warwick, Emscote CV34 .. 161 C8
11 Warwick, Packmores
CV34 .... 160 F7
Garden Flats CV5 ..... 111 D5
Garden Gr Bedworth CV12 .. 95 F8
Birmingham B20 ...... 54 E6
Garden Rd LE10 ...... 71 D1
Garden St WS2 .... 28 E3
Garden Wlk Bilston WV14 .. 40 F6
Dudley DY2 .... 50 C2
Gardeners Cl DY11 .... 116 C8
Gardeners Wlk B91 ... 107 C3
Gardenia Dr CV5 ..... 112 B6
Gardens The Birmingham
B23 .... 56 E3
Kenilworth CV8 ...... 148 A3
Radford Semele CV31 ... 162 E5
Gardner Ho 8 CV1 ... 113 B2
Garfield Rd B26 ...... 89 B8
Garganey Ct DY10 .... 116 F1
Garibaldi Terr B60 .... 137 A1
Garland Cres B62 .... 83 E8
Garland St B9 .... 67 C3
Garland Way B31 ..... 103 C4
Garlick Dr CV8 ...... 148 C6
Garman Cl B43 ...... 43 E2
Garner Cl WV14 ..... 40 D3
Garnet Ave B43 ..... 44 B3
Garnet Cl WS9 ...... 16 E4
Garnet Ct 4 B92 ... 88 F1
Garnett Dr B75 ..... 46 E6
Garnette Cl CV10 .... 72 B5
Garrard Gdns B73 ... 46 B5
Garrat St B71 ...... 53 B5
Garratt Cl B68 ..... 64 C4
Garratt's La B65 .... 63 A2
Garratts Wlk B14 ... 104 E2
Garret Cl 1 DY6 ... 60 D8
Garrett St CV11 .... 73 E2
Garretts Green La B26 .. 89 A8
Garrick Cl CV5 ...... 111 C4
Garrick Rd WS11 .... 1 D4
Garrick Rise WS7 .... 7 B7
Garrick St WV1 ..... 163 C2
Garrigill B77 .... 22 B1
Garrington St WS10 ... 41 C7
Garrison Ct 9 B9 ... 67 B2
Garrison La B9 ..... 67 C2
Garrison St B9 ..... 67 B3
Garston Way 4 B43 ... 54 D8
Garth Cres CV3 ..... 134 D8
Garth Ho CV3 ...... 134 D8
Garth The Birmingham B14 .. 105 D4
Lichfield WS13 ...... 3 B2
Garway Cl Redditch B98 .. 154 E1
Royal Leamington Spa CV32 .. 156 F4
Garway Gr B25 ..... 88 C6
Garwood Rd B26 .... 88 F2
Gas Sq B61 .... 136 F1
Gas St Birmingham B1 .. 66 C2
Royal Leamington Spa CV31 .. 161 F7
Gas Street Basin B1 ... 164 A2
Gatacre St DY3 ..... 50 D3
Gatcombe Cl WV10 ... 11 F4
Gatcombe Dr DY1 .... 50 E2
Gate La Dorridge B93 .. 127 C3
Sutton Coldfield B73 ... 45 F2
Gate St Birmingham B8 .. 67 D5
Sedgley DY3 .... 50 E7
Tipton DY4 .... 52 A2
Gatehouse CV31 ..... 161 D7
Gatehouse Fold 5 DY2 .. 51 D1
Gatehouse La CV12 ... 78 A2
Gatehouse Trad Est WS8 .. 7 A1
Gateley Rd B68 ..... 84 D7
Gateside Rd CV6 .... 95 E2
Gatis St WV6 ...... 25 A5
Gatwick Rd B35 .... 58 B4
Gauden Rd DY9 .... 81 D2
Gaulby Wlk CV3 .... 115 A1
Gaunts The B48 .... 139 B6
Gaveston Cl 7 CV34 .. 160 F8
Gaveston Rd Coventry CV6 .. 112 F6
Royal Leamington Spa CV32 .. 156 E1
Gawne La B64 ...... 62 F3
Gawsworth B79 .... 20 D7
Gay Hill La B38 .... 124 B8
Gaydon Cl Coventry CV6 .. 114 A8
Perton WV6 .... 23 E5
Redditch B98 .... 153 F1
Gaydon Gr B29 ..... 85 A2
Gaydon Rd Aldridge WS9 .. 30 A4
Solihull B92 .... 89 D3
Gayer St CV6 .... 96 A1
Gayfield Ave DY5 .... 61 E1
Gayhurst Cl CV3 .... 134 E8
Gayhurst Dr B25 .... 88 E8
Gayle B77 .... 22 A1
Gayle Gr B27 .... 106 C3
Gayton Rd B71 ..... 53 D6
Gaywood Croft B15 ... 86 C8
Gaza Cl CV4 .... 112 A1
Gazelle Cl CV1 ..... 165 D3
Geach St B19 ...... 66 D6
Geach Tower B19 ... 66 D5
Gedney Cl B90 ..... 105 C3
Gee St B19 .... 66 D6
Geeson Cl B35 ..... 58 B4
Gemini Dr WS11 .... 4 F6

Geneva Rd DY4 ...... 51 D5
Genge Ave WV4 ..... 39 E4
Genners La B32 ..... 102 D7
Genthorn Cl WV4 ... 39 F4
Gentian B74 .... 31 F4
Gentian Cl B31 ..... 102 F6
Geoffery Cl CV2 .... 114 B5
Geoffrey Cl B76 .... 58 B7
Geoffrey Rd Birmingham
B11 .... 87 C3
Solihull B90 .... 105 F3
George Arthur Rd B8 ... 67 D5
George Auden Specl Sch B31 .... 102 F5
George Ave Blackheath B65 .. 63 D2
Mile Oak B78 .... 20 C1
George Betts Prim Sch B66 .... 64 C7
George Cl DY2 ...... 62 C8
George Dance Cl 2 DY10 .. 117 B6
George Dixon Jun & Inf Sch B17 .... 65 C2
George Dixon Sec Sch B17 .... 65 C2
George Eliot Ave CV12 .. 78 D2
George Eliot Hospl CV10 .. 73 B2
George Eliot Rd CV1 ... 113 D5
George Eliot Sch
Nuneaton CV11 ...... 73 D1
Nuneaton CV11 ...... 78 D8
George Eliot St CV11 ... 73 C2
George Fentham Prim Sch B92 .... 109 B6
George Frederick Rd B73 .. 45 A4
George Henry Rd DY4 ... 52 E6
George Hodgkinson Cl CV4 .... 111 F3
George La WS13 ..... 9 C8
George Marston Rd CV3 .. 114 C1
George Park Cl Ansty CV7 .. 97 D3
Coventry CV2 .... 96 C1
George Poole Ho 6 CV1 .. 113 B2
George Rd Alvechurch B48 .. 139 A5
Birmingham, Edgbaston B15 .. 86 B8
Birmingham, Great Barr B43 .. 43 F2
Birmingham,
Perry Common B73 .... 45 D1
Birmingham,
Selly Oak B29 .... 85 E3
Birmingham,
South Yardley B25 .... 88 A6
Birmingham,
Stockland Green B23 ... 56 C3
Dudley, Daisy Bank WV14 .. 40 D1
Dudley, Tipton Green DY4 .. 51 F6
Halesowen B63 ...... 82 F4
Oldbury B68 .... 64 C2
Solihull B91 .... 107 D3
Warwick CV34 ...... 161 A8
Water Orton B46 .... 59 C3
George Robertson Cl CV3 .. 134 E7
George Rose Gdns WS10 .. 41 C6
George Salter High Sch B70 .... 53 A4
George St
Birmingham,
Balsall Heath B12 .... 86 F5
Birmingham,
Brookfields B3 ...... 164 A3
Birmingham,
Handsworth B21 ..... 65 C8
Birmingham, Lozells B19 .. 66 B7
1 Bromsgrove B61 ... 136 F2
Cannock WS12 ...... 2 D4
Coventry CV1 .... 113 E5
Dudley DY1 .... 51 B6
Hinckley LE10 ...... 75 D8
Kidderminster DY10 ... 116 F6
Nuneaton CV11 ...... 73 E2
Royal Leamington Spa
CV31 .... 162 A7
Stourbridge DY8 ..... 60 F1
Tamworth B79 ...... 21 B4
Walsall WS1 .... 28 E1
West Bromwich B70 ... 53 D2
Willenhall WV13 .... 27 A4
Wolverhampton WV2 .. 163 C2
Wolverhampton,
Ettingshall WV2 ..... 40 A7
George St W B18 .... 66 A4
George Street Ringway CV12 .... 78 B3
George Wlk 5 B97 ... 153 E3
Georgian Gdns 2 WS10 .. 41 F3
Georgian Pl WS11 .... 1 E2
Georgina Ave WV14 ... 40 D3
Gerald Rd DY8 ...... 80 E7
Geraldine Rd B25 .... 88 B7
Geranium Gr B9 ..... 67 F3
Geranium Rd DY2 .... 62 F8
Gerard B79 .... 20 E7
Gerard Ave CV4 ..... 132 B8
Gerardsfield Rd B33 ... 69 E2
Germander Dr WS5 ... 43 A3
Gerrard Cl B19 ..... 66 D7
Gerrard Rd WV13 .... 26 F1
Gerrard St Birmingham B19 .. 66 C7
12 Warwick CV34 .... 160 E6
Gervase Dr DY1 .... 51 C3
Geston Rd DY1 .... 61 F8
Gheluvelt Ave DY10 .. 116 F7
Gibb La B61 .... 137 A8
Gibb St B9 .... 66 F1
Gibbet Hill Rd CV4 .. 132 B3
Gibbet La DY7 ..... 80 B4
Gibbins Rd B29 .... 85 D2
Gibbons Cl CV4 .... 111 F2
Gibbons Gr WV6 .... 24 F4
Gibbons Hill Rd DY3 .. 39 D2

Gibbons Ind Pk DY6 61 A7
Gibbons La DY5 61 A7
Gibbons Rd
Sutton Coldfield B75 32 B3
Wolverhampton WV6 24 F4
Gibbs Cl CV2 115 B6
Gibbs Hill Rd B31 123 C7
Gibbs Rd Redditch B98 154 A5
Stourbridge DY9 82 A5
Gibbs St W6 25 A4
Gibson Cres CV12 78 A1
Gibson Dr B20 66 B8
Gibson Rd Birmingham B20 66 B8
Perton WV6 23 E3
Gidcon Cl B25 88 D6
Gideons Cl DY3 50 D5
Gielgud Way CV2 115 B8
Giffard RC Prim Sch WV6 24 F5
Giffard Rd Bilston WV1 40 B7
Wolverhampton WV10 11 F3
Giffard Way CV34 155 E1
Gifford Ct 13 DY5 61 D2
Giffords Croft WS13 3 A1
Gigg La B76 48 B3
Gigmill Prim Sch DY8 80 E4
Gigmill Way DY8 80 E4
Gilbanks Rd DY8 80 D7
Gilberry Cl B93 128 A4
Gilbert Ave B69 63 B7
Gilbert Cl 3 Coventry CV1 113 E3
Wednesfield WV11 27 A7
Gilbert La WV5 49 B7
Gilbert Rd Bromsgrove B60 150 E7
Lichfield WS13 3 C2
Smethwick B66 65 B3
Gilbert Scott Way DY10 116 F7
Gilbert St DY4 52 A2
Gilbert Wlk WS13 3 C2
Gilberts Ct WS4 29 A4
Gilbertstone Ave B26 88 E5
Gilbertstone Cl B98 153 E1
Gilbertstone Jun & Inf Sch
B26 88 E5
Gilbeys Cl DY8 60 E1
Gilby Rd B16 66 A1
Gilchrist Dr B15 85 E8
Gildas Ave B38 104 A1
Giles Cl Birmingham B33 68 E3
Coventry CV6 95 C2
Solihull B92 107 F7
Giles Close Ho B33 68 E3
Giles Rd Lichfield WS13 3 A3
Oldbury B68 64 B5
Gilfil Rd CV10 73 B1
Gill St Dudley DY2 62 E4
West Bromwich B70 53 C1
Gilldown Pl B15 86 B7
Gillespie Croft B6 66 F7
Gillet Cl CV11 73 B3
Gillhurst Rd B17 85 C7
Gillians Wlk CV2 115 A8
Gilling Gr B34 69 A6
Gillingham Cl WS10 42 D4
Gillity Ave WS5 43 C8
Gillity Cl WS5 43 C8
Gillity Ct 3 WS5 43 D7
Gilliver Rd B90 106 B2
Gillman Cl B26 89 D4
Gillott Cl B91 107 E3
Gillott Rd B16 65 D2
Gillows Croft B90 127 A7
Gillscroft Rd B33 69 A3
Gillway B79 21 B8
Gilmorton Cl Birmingham
B17 85 B7
Solihull B91 107 C1
Gilpin Cl B8 68 C7
Gilpin Cres WS3 15 A4
Gilpins Croft WS6 4 D1
Gilson Dr B46 70 D8
Gilson Rd B46 70 E8
Gilson St DY4 52 C8
Gilson Way B37 70 A5
Gilwell Rd B34 69 E6
Gingko Wlk CV31 161 F5
Gipsy Cl CV7 130 B5
Gipsy La
Balsall Common CV7 130 C5
Birmingham B23 56 B5
Nuneaton CV10, CV11 78 D7
Willenhall WV13 27 B1
Girdlers Cl CV3 133 B5
Girtin Cl CV12 78 A4
Girton Ho B36 69 F8
Girton Rd WS11 4 F8
Girvan Gr CV32 157 C5
Gisborn Cl B10 87 B8
Gisburn Cl CV34 155 F1
Givens Ho 9 CV1 113 B2
Glade The Aldridge B74 30 E1
Birmingham B26 89 D4
Cannock WS11 1 C2
Coventry CV5 111 F3
Stourbridge DY9 81 E5
Wolverhampton WV8 10 E1
Glades The WS9 30 B7
Gladeside Cl WS4 29 D8
Gladstone Cl LE10 71 E4
Gladstone Dr
Stourbridge DY8 80 D6
Tipton B69 52 D3
Gladstone Gr DY6 60 D8
Gladstone Rd
Birmingham,
Gravelly Hill B23 56 D3
Birmingham,
South Yardley B26 88 D6
Birmingham, Sparkbrook B11 87 B6
Gladstone Rd continued
Cannock WS12 2 E1
Dorridge B93 128 A2
Stourbridge DY8 80 D6
Gladstone St Birmingham B6 67 B8
Darlaston WS10 41 E6
Walsall WS2 28 D4
West Bromwich B71 53 C5
Gladstone Terr LE10 75 E8
Gladys Rd Birmingham B25 88 B7
Smethwick B67 64 F2
Gladys Terr B67 65 A2
Glaisdale Ave CV6 95 E3
Glaisdale Gdns WV6 25 A5
Glaisdale Rd B28 106 B8
Glaisedale Gr WV13 27 C2
Glamis Rd WV12 27 B7
Glamorgan Cl CV3 134 D5
Glanville Dr B75 32 A4
Glasbury Croft B38 123 E7
Glascote Cl B90 106 A4
Glascote Ct B77 21 E4
Glascote Gr B34 69 C6
Glascote Heath Prim Sch
B77 22 A2
Glascote La B77 35 F7
Glascote Rd B77 22 B2
Glasscroft Cotts WS7 7 F7
Glasshouse Hill DY8 81 B3
Glasshouse La
Kenilworth CV8 148 D4
Tanworth-in-A B94 143 F6
Glaston Dr B91 107 A1
Glastonbury Cl DY11 116 A6
Glastonbury Cres WS3 13 E2
Glastonbury Rd
Birmingham B14 105 C5
West Bromwich B71 42 D1
Glastonbury Way WS3 13 E1
Gleads Croft B62 84 A3
Gleaston Wlk WV1 26 C1
Gleave Rd Birmingham B29 85 E1
Whitnash CV31 162 A3
Glebe Ave CV12 77 E1
Glebe Cl Coventry CV4 132 A7
Redditch B98 154 D2
Glebe Cres CV8 148 A3
Glebe Ct CV31 162 A3
Glebe Dr B73 56 F8
Glebe Farm Rd B33 69 A5
Glebe Fields B76 59 B6
Glebe La Nuneaton CV11 73 F6
Stourbridge DY8 80 E4
Glebe Pl Darlaston WS10 41 B6
Royal Leamington Spa CV31 162 B7
Glebe Rd Alvechurch B48 139 A7
Hinckley LE10 71 F1
Nuneaton CV11 73 D4
Solihull B91 107 D5
Willenhall WV13 40 F8
Glebe St WS1 42 E8
Glebe The Belbroughton
DY9 119 E6
Beoley B98 154 F7
Corley CV7 94 C7
Glebe Way CV7 130 A7
Glebefarm Gr CV3 114 F3
Glebefields Prim Sch DY4 52 A8
Glebefields Rd DY4 52 A7
Glebeland Cl B16 66 B1
Gledhill Pk WS14 9 C5
Gleeson Dr CV34 155 E1
Glen Bank LE10 71 E1
Glen Cl Cannock WS11 1 E5
Walsall WS4 29 A3
Glen Ct Codsall WV8 10 A4
Wolverhampton WV3 24 E2
Glen Devon Cl B45 102 A2
Glen Ho DY1 61 D8
Glen Park Rd DY3 50 D2
Glen Rd Dudley DY3 50 E6
Stourbridge DY8 80 F3
Glen Rise B13 105 C6
Glen Side B32 84 D2
Glen The B60 138 A5
Glenavon Rd B14 105 A3
Glenbarr Cl LE10 75 A8
Glenbarr Dr LE10 75 A8
Glencoe Dr WS11 2 A4
Glencoe Rd Birmingham B16 65 C4
Coventry CV3 114 B1
Glencroft Rd B92 89 D4
Glendale Ave CV8 148 A6
Glendale Cl Halesowen B63 83 B4
Wolverhampton WV3 38 C8
Glendale Dr Birmingham
B33 68 F3
Wombourne WV5 49 A6
Glendale Fst Sch CV10 72 F2
Glendale Tower 5 B23 57 B6
Glendawn Cl WS11 2 A3
Glendene Cres B38 123 C7
Glendene Dr 2 B43 54 D8
Glendene Rd WS12 2 D6
Glendon Gdns CV12 79 C3
Glendon Rd B23 56 D6
Glendon Way B93 127 E3
Glendower Ave CV5 112 D3
Glendower Rd Aldridge
WS9 16 B1
Birmingham B42 55 D4
Gleneagles B77 22 B5
Gleneagles Cl CV11 74 C1
Gleneagles Dr
Birmingham B43 43 E3
Blackwell B60 138 A5
Sutton Coldfield B75 46 D8
Tipton B69 63 A7
Gleneagles Rd
Birmingham B26 89 A8
Coventry CV2 114 E6
Perton WV6 23 D5
Walsall WS3 13 F3
Glenelg Dr DY8 81 B2
Glenelg Mews WS5 43 D5
Glenfern Rd WV14 51 A8
Glenfield Tamworth B77 21 C1
Wolverhampton WV8 10 E2
Glenfield Ave CV10 73 D7
Glenfield Cl Redditch B97 158 D6
2 Solihull B91 127 C8
Sutton Coldfield B76 46 E3
Glenfield Gr B29 86 A1
Glengarry Cl B32 102 B7
Glengarry Gdns WV3 24 F1
Glenhurst Cl WS2 27 D3
Glenmead Jun & Inf Sch
B44 55 D8
Glenmead Rd B44 55 D8
Glenmore Ave WS7 7 A6
Glenmore Cl WV3 38 E7
Glenmore Dr
Birmingham B38 103 D2
Coventry CV6 95 F5
Glenmount Ave CV6 95 F5
Glenn St CV6 95 D3
Glenpark Rd B8 67 F5
Glenridding Cl CV6 95 F5
Glenrosa Wlk CV4 132 A7
Glenroy Cl CV2 114 E6
Glenroyde B38 123 E7
Glenside Ave B92 89 C3
Glenthorne Dr WS6 4 E3
Glenthorne Ho WS6 4 D2
Glenthorne Prim Sch WS6 4 E3
Glenthorne Rd B24 57 A2
Glenthorne Way B24 57 A2
Glentworth Ave CV6 95 A2
Glentworth Dr B76 47 A2
Glentworth Gdns W6 25 B5
Glenvale Specl Sch B70 53 A4
Glenville Ave CV9 36 C1
Glenville Dr B23 56 E5
Glenwood Cl DY5 81 D8
Glenwood Dr B90 126 D4
Glenwood Gdns CV12 78 A5
Glenwood Rd B38 123 D8
Glenwood Rise WS9 16 D3
Globe St WS10 41 F1
Gloster Dr CV8 147 F6
Gloucester Cl Nuneaton
CV11 74 A7
Wolverhampton WS13 3 B3
Gloucester Ho
4 Birmingham B24 56 F4
4 Wolverhampton WV3 25 C4
Gloucester Pl WV13 27 A2
Gloucester Rd Dudley DY2 62 D2
Walsall WS5 43 C8
Wednesbury WS10 42 C3
Gloucester St
Birmingham B5 164 C1
Coventry CV1 113 B3
1 Royal Leamington Spa
CV31 162 A7
Wolverhampton WV6 25 B4
Gloucester Way
Birmingham B37 70 A1
Cannock WS11 2 B1
Glover Cl Birmingham B28 105 F6
Warwick CV34 160 B4
Glover Rd B75 47 A5
Glover St Birmingham B9 67 A2
Cannock WS12 2 F3
Coventry CV3 133 D8
Redditch B98 153 E3
West Bromwich B70 53 D1
Glover's Trust Homes B73 56 F7
Glovers Cl CV7 92 C1
Glovers Croft B37 69 F3
Glovers Field Dr B7 67 C7
Glovers Rd B10 87 D8
Glyme Dr WV6 24 E5
Glyn Ave WV14 41 B3
Glyn Dr WV14 41 B3
Glyn Farm Rd B32 84 C6
Glyn Rd B32 84 D6
Glyndebourne B79 20 D7
Glyne Ct B73 46 B5
Glynn Cres B63 82 B7
Glynne Ave DY6 60 D4
Glynne Prim Sch DY6 60 C4
Glynside Ave B32 84 D6
Godfrey Cl CV31 162 E5
Godiva Pl CV1 165 D3
Godiva Trad Est CV6 113 F8
Godolphin B79 20 D6
Godrich Ho B13 87 B3
Godson Cres DY11 116 C3
Godson Pl DY11 116 C3
Goffs Cl B32 84 F3
Gofton B77 36 A8
Gold Cl CV11 78 E8
Goldcrest B77 36 A6
Goldcrest Cl DY2 62 D2
Goldcrest Croft B36 70 A8
Goldcrest Dr DY10 117 B2
Golden Acres La CV3 134 F7
Golden Croft B20 54 F1
Golden Cross La B61 121 B1
Golden End Dr B93 128 D6
Golden Hillock Rd
Birmingham B11 87 D6
Dudley DY2 62 C3
Golden Hillock Sch B11 87 D5
Goldencrest Dr B69 63 E8
Goldfinch Cl B30 103 D8
Goldfinch Rd DY9 81 C3
Goldicroft Rd WS10 42 A4
Goldieslie Cl B73 46 B2
Goldieslie Rd B73 46 B2
Golds Hill Gdns B21 65 F7
Golds Hill Rd B21 65 F8
Goldsborough B77 22 A1
Goldsmith Ave CV34 160 C5
Goldsmith Pl B79 21 A7
Goldsmith Rd
Birmingham B14 104 F8
Walsall WS3 28 E7
Goldsmith Wlk DY10 117 C5
Goldstar Way B33 69 C2
Goldtel Ind Est WV4 40 A5
Goldthorn Ave WV4 39 B6
Goldthorn Cl CV5 111 D4
Goldthorn Cres WV4 39 A6
Goldthorn Hill WV2, WV4 39 C6
Goldthorn Park Prim Sch
WV4 39 D5
Goldthorn Pl DY11 116 C2
Goldthorn Rd
Kidderminster DY11 116 C2
Wolverhampton WV2 39 B6
Goldthorne Ave
Birmingham B26 89 C4
Cannock WS11 1 F2
Goldthorne Cl B97 153 C1
Goldthorne Wlk DY5 81 D8
Golf Dr CV11 74 B1
Golf La Bilston WV14 40 D7
Whitnash CV31 162 B2
Golson Cl B75 46 F6
Gomeldon Ave B14 104 F3
Gomer St WV13 27 A2
Gomer St W WV13 27 A2
Gooch Cl DY8 81 B6
Gooch St B5 86 E8
Gooch St N B5 86 E8
Good Hope Hospl B75 46 D6
Good Shepherd Prim Sch
CV6 95 F1
Goodall Gr B43 44 E5
Goodall St WS1 28 F1
Goodby Rd B13 86 D3
Goode Ave B18 66 A5
Goode Cl B68 64 C4
Goode Croft CV4 111 F2
Goodeve Wlk B75 47 B5
Goodfellow St CV32 156 C1
Goodison Gdns B24 57 B5
Goodleigh Ave B45 122 E6
Goodman Cl B28 105 F6
Goodman St B1 66 B3
Goodman Way CV4 111 C1
Goodrest Ave B62 84 A5
Goodrest Croft B14 105 C4
Goodrest La B38 123 F6
Goodrich Ave WV6 24 A3
Goodrich Cl B98 154 F2
Goodrich Covert 10 B14 104 C2
Goodway Ct 8 CV34 160 F7
Goodway Rd Birmingham
B44 55 F8
Solihull B92 89 E4
Goodwin Cl DY11 116 C7
Goodwood Cl
Birmingham B36 68 D8
Lichfield WS14 9 D7
Goodwood Dr B74 44 F7
Goodwyn Ave B68 84 C7
Goodyear Ave WV10 25 E7
Goodyear Rd B67 64 E2
Goodyers End Fst & Mid
Schs CV12 95 E8
Goodyers End La CV12 95 D8
Goosehill Cl B98 154 E1
Goosehills Rd LE10 75 E5
Goosemoor La B23 56 F7
Goostry Cl B77 21 D5
Goostry Rd B77 21 D5
Gopsal St B4 67 A3
Gopsall Rd LE10 71 D2
Gordon Ave Birmingham B19 66 D7
West Bromwich B71 53 C8
Wolverhampton WV4 39 F3
Gordon Cl Bedworth CV12 78 C4
Tipton B69 52 D2
Gordon Cres DY5 61 E5
Gordon Ct B33 68 D3
Gordon Dr DY4 52 C6
Gordon Pl WV14 40 C5
Gordon Rd
Birmingham, Harborne B17 85 D6
Birmingham, Lozells B19 66 C8
Gordon St
5 Birmingham B9 67 B2
Coventry CV1 113 B2
Darlaston WS10 41 E6
Royal Leamington Spa
CV31 162 A7
Wolverhampton WV2 163 C2
Gorey Cl WV12 27 B8
Gorge Rd WV14, DY3 39 F1
Goring Rd CV2 114 A4
Gorleston Gr B14 105 B2
Gorleston Rd B14 105 B2
Gorse Cl
Birmingham,
Fordbridge B37 69 F2
Birmingham, Selly Oak B29 103 A8
Gorse Dr WS12 1 D5
Gorse Farm Rd
Birmingham B43 54 E8
Nuneaton CV11 79 B8
Gorse Green La DY9 120 C8
Gorse La Lichfield WS14 9 E6
Lichfield, Curborough WS13 3 F6
Gorse Meadow Dr B45 138 B8
Gorse Rd Dudley DY1 51 A4
Wednesfield WV11 27 A8
Gorse Way WS12 2 C8
Gorsebrook Rd W6 25 B5
Gorsefield Rd B34 69 C5
Gorsemoor Cty Prim Sch
WS12 2 D1
Gorsemoor Rd WS12 2 D1
Gorsemoor Way WV11 13 B3
Gorseway Burntwood WS7 7 B5
Coventry CV5 112 C3
Gorsey La Cannock WS11 1 C1
Coleshill B46 59 F2
Great Wyrley WS6 4 F1
Norton Canes WS3 5 E1
Wythall B47 125 A3
Gorsey Way Aldridge WS9 29 E5
Coleshill B46 59 E2
Gorsly Piece B32 84 C4
Gorstey Lea WS7 7 C7
Gorstie Croft B43 54 E8
Gorsty Ave DY5 61 C3
Gorsty Bank WS14 9 E8
Gorsty Cl 3 B71 53 F8
Gorsty Hill Rd B65 83 B8
Gorsy Bank Rd B77 35 F5
Gorsy Rd B32 84 D5
Gorsy Way CV10 72 D5
Gorsymead Gr B31 102 C2
Gorway Cl WS1 42 F7
Gorway Gdns WS1 43 A7
Gorway Rd WS1 43 A7
Goscote Cl WS3 28 F7
Goscote Hospl WS3 28 F8
Goscote Ind Est WS3 14 E1
Goscote La WS3 28 F8
Goscote Lodge Cres WS3 29 A7
Goscote Pl WS3 29 A7
Goscote Rd WS3 15 A1
Gosford Dr LE10 71 A1
Gosford Ind Est CV1 113 F2
Gosford Park Prim Sch
CV1 113 F2
Gosford St Birmingham B12 86 F6
Coventry CV1 165 D2
Gosford Wlk B92 89 B1
Gosmoor Ho B26 88 E7
Gospel End Rd DY3 50 B8
Gospel End St DY3 50 D8
Gospel Farm Rd B27 106 B8
Gospel La B27 106 C8
Gospel Oak Rd Coventry
CV6 95 B4
Tipton DY4 41 B1
Gosport Cl WV1 40 B7
Gosport Rd CV6 113 E8
Goss Croft B29 85 D1
Goss The DY5 61 D1
Gossey La B33 69 C2
Gossey Lane Jun & Inf Sch
B33 69 C2
Gotham Rd B26 88 E6
Goths Cl B65 63 C4
Gough Ave WV11 26 B8
Gough Rd
Birmingham, Edgbaston B15 86 C7
Birmingham, Sparkhill B11 87 D5
Dudley WV14 40 F1
Gough St Birmingham B1 164 B1
Willenhall WV13 27 C2
Wolverhampton WV1 163 C3
Gould Ave E DY11 116 A2
Gould Ave W DY11 116 A1
Gould Firm La WS9 30 E6
Gould Rd CV35 160 A7
Governor's Ct CV34 160 D8
Gowan Rd B8 67 E4
Gower Ave DY6 60 F4
Gower Ho B62 83 F6
Gower Rd Halesowen B62 83 F6
Sedgley DY3 50 B8
Gower St Birmingham B19 66 D7
Walsall WS2 42 B7
Willenhall WV13 27 A2
Wolverhampton WV2 163 D1
Gowland Dr WS11 1 B1
Gowrie Cl LE10 71 B2
Goya Cl WS11 2 C2
Gozzard St WV14 40 E5
Grace Ho B69 63 D8
Grace Mary Prim Sch B69 63 C7
Grace Moore Ct WS11 1 F4
Grace Rd Allesley CV5 111 A8
Birmingham B11 87 C7
Tipton, Summer Hill DY4 52 A7
Tipton, Tividale B69 63 C8
Gracechurch Sh Ctr B72 46 B5
Gracemere Cres B28 105 E3
Gracewell Homes B13 105 D8
Gracewell Rd B13 87 D1
Grafton Cl B98 159 B7
Grafton Cres B60 150 E8
Grafton Ct Birmingham B23 56 C2
Coventry CV4 132 B7
Wolverhampton WV6 24 F4
Grafton Dr WV13 26 D1
Grafton Gdns DY3 50 B3
Grafton Gr 1 B19 66 C7
Grafton Ho Bromsgrove
B60 137 B3
Wolverhampton WV4 39 E5
Grafton La B61 150 C7

Grafton Pl WV14 40 E7
Grafton Rd
Birmingham, Handsworth B21 54 D1
Birmingham, Sparkbrook B11 . 87 B7
Oldbury B68 63 F2
Solihull B90 105 C2
West Bromwich B71 53 D4
Grafton St CV1 113 F2
Graham Cl Coventry CV6 96 B1
Tipton DY4 41 B1
Graham Cres B45 122 A7
Graham Ho B74 30 F2
Graham Rd Birmingham B25 .. 88 C6
Halesowen B62 83 C8
Stourbridge DY8 60 D4
West Bromwich B71 53 D4
Graham St
Birmingham, Hockley B1 66 C3
Birmingham, Lozells B19 66 C7
Nuneaton CV11 73 C5
Grainger Cl DY4 52 D6
Grainger St DY2 62 D7
Grainger's La B64 82 D8
Graiseley Ct WV3 163 B2
Graiseley Hill WV2 163 B1
Graiseley La WV11 26 C5
Graiseley Prim Sch WV2 163 B1
Graiseley Row WV2 163 B1
Graiseley St WV3 163 A2
Graith Cl B28 105 E3
Grammar School La B63 83 A4
Grampian Rd DY8 81 A6
Granada Trad Est B69 63 F6
Granary Cl DY6 60 A8
Granary Rd Stoke Heath
B60 150 E6
Wolverhampton WV8 10 E1
Granary The WS9 30 B6
Granborough Cl CV3 134 F8
Granborough Ct CV32 157 A3
Granbourne Rd WS2 27 D4
Granby Ave B33 69 C1
Granby Bsns Pk B33 69 D1
Granby Cl Hinckley LE10 75 C7
Redditch B98 154 F4
Solihull B92 106 E7
Granby Rd Hinckley LE10 75 C7
Nuneaton CV10 72 F3
Grand Cl B66 65 B3
Grand Depot Rd CV11 79 F6
Grand Junction Way WS1 42 D5
Grandborough Dr B91 107 A1
Grandys Croft B37 69 F2
Granefield Ct [4] B9 67 D1
Grange Ave Aldridge WS9 16 A1
Birmingham B8 68 B6
Burntwood WS7 7 B7
Coventry, Binley CV3 134 F7
Coventry, Finham CV3 133 C3
Kenilworth CV8 147 E7
Sutton Coldfield B75 32 C3
Grange Cl Nuneaton CV10 72 C7
Tamworth B77 35 C8
Warwick CV34 161 C8
Grange Cres
Birmingham B45 121 F8
Halesowen B63 83 B3
Walsall WS4 29 B8
Grange Ct [1] Dudley DY1 51 B1
[1] Redditch B98 153 F4
Stourbridge DY9 81 C3
Willenhall WS2 27 D2
Wolverhampton WV3 163 A2
Grange Dr Cannock WS11 1 F2
Hinckley LE10 75 E5
Grange Farm Dr B38 123 D8
Grange Farm Prim Sch
CV3 133 B5
Grange Hill B62 83 C2
Grange Hill Rd B38 103 E1
Grange La Alvechurch B48 139 B3
Kingswinford DY6 60 F4
Lichfield WS13 8 C5
Stourbridge DY9 81 D4
Sutton Coldfield B75 32 C3
Grange Mews The
[1] CV32 156 D1
Grange Rd
Balsall Common CV7 129 F7
Birmingham, Aston B6 66 E8
Birmingham,
Bordesley Green B10 67 D1
Birmingham, Erdington B24 57 C5
Birmingham,
King's Heath B14 104 E8
Birmingham, Selly Oak B29 85 F3
Blackheath B64 83 B8
Burntwood WS7 7 A5
Coventry CV6 96 B5
Dorridge B93 127 E2
Dudley, New Dock DY1 51 B1
Dudley, Roseville WV14 51 B7
Halesowen B63 83 C3
Norton Canes WS11 6 B6
[2] Redditch B98 153 F4
Royal Leamington Spa CV32 . 157 B3
Smethwick B66 65 A3
Solihull B91 106 E7
Stourbridge DY9 81 C4
Tanworth-in-A B94 143 E8
West Bromwich B70 53 B3
Wolverhampton,
Blakenhall WV2 39 B6
Wolverhampton,
TettenhallWV6 24C4
Grange Rise B38 123 F7
Grange Sch The DY9 81 D4
Grange St Dudley DY1 51 B1
Walsall WS1 42 F7
Grange The
Cubbington CV32 157 F5
Halesowen B62 83 F6
Royal Leamington Spa CV32 . 157 B1
Wombourne WV5 49 A7
Grangefield Cl WV8 10 F1
Grangehurst Prim Sch
CV6 96 B4
Grangemouth Rd CV6 113 B7
Grangers La B98 158 F5
Grangewood Ct Solihull
B92 106 E7
Sutton Coldfield B73 57 A7
Granhill Cl B98 159 A8
Granleigh Ct CV32 157 E5
Granoe Cl CV3 134 E8
Granshaw Cl B38 103 F1
Grant Cl Kingswinford DY6 60 D8
West Bromwich B71 53 C5
Grant Ct B30 104 A5
Grant Rd Bedworth CV7 78 A1
Coventry CV3 114 B2
Grant St Birmingham B15 86 D8
Walsall WS3 28 B8
Grantham Cl DY5 81 B7
Grantham Rd
Birmingham B11 87 B6
Smethwick B66 65 B3
Grantham St CV2 113 F3
Grantley Cres DY6 60 C6
Grantley Dr B37 70 B3
Granton Cl B14 104 D5
Granton Rd B14 104 D5
Grantown Gr WS3 14 A4
Granville B77 21 F1
Granville Cl Bromsgrove
B60 137 B1
Wolverhampton WV2 163 C1
Granville Crest DY10 117 B6
Granville Dr DY6 60 F5
Granville Gdns LE10 75 C8
Granville Rd Blackheath B64 . 83 B8
Dorridge B93 128 A2
Hinckley LE10 75 C8
Granville Sq B1 66 C1
Granville St Birmingham
B1 164 A1
Royal Leamington Spa
CV32 157 A2
Willenhall WV13 27 A3
Wolverhampton WV2 163 C1
Grapes Cl CV6 113 B5
Grasdene Gr B17 85 C4
Grasmere Ave Aldridge B74 .. 31 A2
Coventry CV3 132 F6
Perton WV6 23 F4
Grasmere Cl Birmingham
B43 54 F7
Kidderminster DY10 116 E7
Kingswinford DY6 60 B7
Wolverhampton,
Tettenhall WV6 24 E8
Wolverhampton,
Wood End WV11 26 C7
Grasmere Cres CV11 73 F7
Grasmere Ho [13] B69 63 D5
Grasmere Pl WS11 1 E5
Grasmere Rd Bedworth
CV12 78 B2
Birmingham B21 65 F7
Grasscroft Dr CV3 133 E6
Grassholme B77 36 A8
Grassington Ave CV34 155 F1
Grassington Dr
Birmingham B37 69 F1
Nuneaton CV11 74 A2
Grassmere Ct WS6 4 D3
Grassmere Dr DY8 80 F3
Grassmoor Rd B38 103 E2
Grassy La WV10 12 B1
Graston Cl B16 66 A2
Gratley Croft WS12 1 C4
Grattidge Rd B27 88 D2
Gratton Ct CV3 132 F6
Gravel Bank B32 84 E3
Gravel Hill Coventry CV4 111 F1
Wombourne WV5 49 B6
Gravel La Huntington WS12 1 B6
Huntington WS12 1 C5
Gravel Pit La B48 139 E3
Gravel The B76 48 B2
Gravelly Ct [4] B23 56 E2
Gravelly Hill B23 56 E2
Gravelly Hill N B23 56 E3
Gravelly Hill Sta B23 56 E2
Gravelly Ind Pk B24 67 F8
Gravelly La Birmingham B23 .. 56 F5
Stonnall WS9 16 F3
Gray Rd WS12 1 F6
Gray St B9 67 B2
Graydon Ct B74 46 B7
Grayfield Ave B13 87 A3
Grayland Cl B27 88 B2
Graylands The CV3 133 C4
Grayling B77 35 D6
Grayling Rd DY9 81 C6
Grayling Wlk B37 70 C3
Grays Cl DY10 117 B6
Grays Rd B17 85 D6
Grayshott Cl Birmingham B23 56 E5
Bromsgrove B61 136 E3
Grayston Ave B77 21 E4
Grayswood Ave CV5 112 D4
Grayswood Park Rd B32 84 C6
Grayswood Rd B31 122 F7
Grazebrook Croft B32 102 D8
Grazebrook Ind Pk DY2 62 B6
Grazebrook Rd DY2 62 C7
Grazewood Cl WV12 27 B7
Grazing La B97 152 F2
Greadier St WV12 27 C5
Great Arthur St B66 64 F7
Great Barn La B97 153 B1
Great Barr Jun & Inf Sch
B44 44 D1
Great Barr Sch B44 44 D1
Great Barr Sch Sixth Form
Ctr B44 44 D1
Great Barr St B9 67 A2
Great Brickkiln St WV3 25 B1
Great Bridge DY4 52 D5
Great Bridge Ind Est DY4 52 C7
Great Bridge Prim Sch
DY4 52 C6
Great Bridge Rd WV14 41 B3
Great Bridge St B70 52 E5
Great Brook St B7 67 A4
Great Charles St WS8 15 F8
Great Charles Street
Queensway B3 164 B3
Great Colmore St B15 86 D8
Great Cornbow [5] B63 83 B3
Great Croft Ho [3] WS10 41 D6
Great Croft St [5] WS10 41 D6
Great Francis St B7 67 B4
Great Hampton Row B19 . 164 A4
Great Hampton St
Birmingham B18 164 A4
Wolverhampton WV1 25 B4
Great King St B19 66 C5
Great King St N B19 66 C6
Great Lister St B7 67 A4
Great Moor Rd WV6 23 A3
Great Stone Rd B31 103 A3
Great Tindal St B16 66 A2
Great Western Arc B2 164 C3
Great Western Cl B18 65 E6
Great Western Dr B64 63 A1
Great Western St
Wednesbury WS10 41 E2
Wolverhampton WV1 163 C4
Great Western Way DY4 52 D6
Great Wood Rd B10 67 C1
Great Wyrley Cty High Sch
WS6 4 F4
Greatfield Rd DY11 116 B4
Greatheed Rd CV32 156 E2
Greatmead B77 21 C1
Greatorex Ct B71 53 B8
Greaves Ave WS5 43 C8
Greaves Cl Walsall WS5 43 C8
Warwick CV34 161 C7
Greaves Cres WV12 27 C8
Greaves Rd DY2 62 D5
Greaves Sq B38 104 B1
Grebe Cl B23 56 B3
Green Acres B27 88 B2
Green Acres Rd B38 123 D8
Green Ave B28 87 E1
Green Bank Ave B28 87 E1
Green Barns La WS14 32 C8
Green Cl Studley B80 159 E3
Whitnash CV31 162 B4
Wythall B47 125 A3
Green Croft B9 68 A3
Green Ct
Birmingham,
Gravelly Hill B24 56 E2
Birmingham,
Hall Green B28 105 F8
[10] Lichfield WS13 9 B7
Green Dr Birmingham B32 84 C1
Wolverhampton WV10 25 C7
Green Field The CV3 134 B8
Green Gables
Hollywood B47 125 A7
Sutton Coldfield B74 46 B7
Green Heath Rd WS12 2 A7
Green Hill Cl B60 137 D6
Green Hill Way B90 106 B5
Green La Aldridge WS9 30 E5
Balsall Common CV7 130 B7
Birmingham,
Bordesley Green B9 67 E1
Birmingham,
Castle Bromwich B36 69 E8
Birmingham,
Great Barr B43 43 D1
Birmingham,
Handsworth B21 65 C8
Birmingham,
Hawkesley B38 123 E8
Birmingham, Newton B43 54 D8
Birmingham, Quinton B32 84 C6
Brownhills WS8 7 B2
Cannock WS11 4 E6
Catshill B61 121 A1
Coleshill B46 70 F5
Corley CV7 93 D6
Coventry CV3 133 B4
Dudley DY3 50 F5
Halesowen B62 63 D1
Kingswinford DY6 60 D7
Lichfield WS14 8 D2
Middleton B78 48 B6
Nuneaton CV10 72 C7
Redditch B97 158 A7
Solihull B90 105 E1
Stourbridge DY9 81 E5
Studley B80 159 B5
Tamworth B78 36 C7
Walsall, Birchills WS3 28 C5
Green La continued
Walsall,
High Heath WS4, WS9 15 D3
Walsall, Pelsall WS3 15 A4
Warwick CV34 160 F8
Wolverhampton WV6 24 F7
Green Lane Ind Est B9 67 E1
Green Lane Venture Ctr
WS11 4 E6
Green Lanes Bilston WV14 40 C7
Sutton Coldfield B73 57 B8
Green Lanes Prim Sch
B36 69 F8
Green Lea B77 36 A8
Green Leigh B23 56 F8
Green Mdw Stourbridge
DY9 99 B7
Wednesfield WV11 26 E5
Green Mdws WS12 2 C1
Green Meadow Prim Sch
B29 102 F7
Green Meadow Rd
Birmingham B29 103 A7
Willenhall WV12 27 B7
Green Oak Rd WV8 10 B2
Green Park Ave WV14 40 C8
Green Park Dr WV14 40 C8
Green Park Rd
Birmingham B31 102 E2
Bromsgrove B60 137 B2
Dudley DY2 62 F8
Green Park Sch WV14 40 B8
Green Rd Birmingham B28 87 E1
Dudley DY2 62 D7
Green Rock Jun & Mixed
Inf Sch WS3 14 E1
Green Rock La WS3 14 D1
Green Slade Cres B60 121 C1
Green Slade Gr WS12 2 C7
Green St Birmingham B12 66 F1
Dudley WV14 51 C8
Kidderminster DY10 116 E5
Oldbury B69 64 A7
Smethwick B67 64 F5
Stourbridge DY8 80 F5
Walsall WS2 28 C3
West Bromwich B70 64 E8
Green Street Ind Est
DY10 116 E4
Green Sward La B98 154 D1
Green The Aldridge WS9 30 C6
Birmingham,
Castle Bromwich B36 69 B8
Birmingham, Erdington B23 57 A4
Birmingham,
King's Norton B38 103 F2
[4] Birmingham, Quinton B32 . 84 A6
Bluntington DY10 118 E1
Darlaston WS10 41 D7
Fazeley B78 20 E2
Nuneaton CV11 73 E2
Oldbury B68 64 B1
Solihull B91 107 D5
Stoneleigh CV8 149 C6
Stourbridge DY8 60 D2
Sutton Coldfield B72 46 D1
Tamworth B77 22 B5
Walsall WS3 14 B1
Wood End B78 36 C4
Green Way WS9 16 B2
Green Wickets B13 104 E6
Green Wlk B17 84 F7
Greenacre Cl B77 22 B5
Greenacre Dr WV8 10 B2
Greenacre Rd DY4 41 A1
Greenacres Sedgley DY3 39 B1
Sutton Coldfield B76 58 A8
Wolverhampton WV6 24 B5
Greenacres Ave WV10 12 B2
Greenacres Cl WS9 30 E2
Greenacres Jun & Inf Schs
WV14 40 F6
Greenacres Prim Sch B77 .. 22 B5
Greenacres Rd B61 136 E3
Greenaleigh Rd B14 105 D3
Greenaway Cl B43 44 C3
Greenbank B45 138 D8
Greenbank Ho [3] B7 67 B5
Greenbank Rd CV7 129 F6
Greenbush Dr B63 83 A5
Greencroft Bilston WV14 40 D6
Kingswinford DY6 60 D4
Lichfield WS13 3 A2
Greendale Cl B61 137 B8
Greendale Rd CV5 112 D3
Greenend Rd B13 86 F2
Greenfels Rise DY2 62 F8
Greenfield Ave
Balsall Common CV7 130 A7
Blackheath B64 62 B1
Marlbrook B60 121 D1
Stourbridge DY8 80 F5
Greenfield Cotts B48 139 A5
Greenfield Cres B15 86 A8
Greenfield Croft WV14 40 D2
Greenfield Ho B26 89 D6
Greenfield La WV10 11 E5
Greenfield Prim Sch
Stourbridge DY8 80 F4
Walsall WS4 29 C8
Greenfield Rd
Birmingham, Harborne B17 85 D5
Birmingham, Newton B43 54 D7
Smethwick B67 64 E4
Greenfield View DY3 50 B7
Greenfields Aldridge WS9 30 B7
Cannock WS11 1 E2
Redditch B98 153 E2
Greenfields Rd
Kingswinford DY6 60 E6
Walsall WS4 15 D2
Wombourne WV5 49 A5
Greenfinch Cl
Birmingham B36 70 A7
Kidderminster DY10 117 B3
Greenfinch Rd
Birmingham B36 70 A7
Stourbridge DY9 81 D3
Greenford Ho B23 56 B6
Greenford Rd B14 105 C3
Greenhart B77 22 A4
Greenhill Blackwell B60 137 F4
[7] Lichfield WS13 9 C8
Wombourne WV5 49 B6
Greenhill Ave DY10 116 F7
Greenhill Cl Tamworth B77 35 C5
Willenhall WV12 27 B5
Greenhill Ct Halesowen B62 .. 83 E7
Sutton Coldfield B72 57 C8
Wombourne WV5 49 B5
Greenhill Dr B29 85 C1
Greenhill Gdns
Birmingham B43 43 E2
Halesowen B62 83 D6
Wombourne WV5 49 B5
Greenhill Oak DY10 116 F7
Greenhill Rd
Birmingham,
Handsworth B21 54 E2
Birmingham, Moseley B13 87 A1
Dudley DY3 50 E5
Halesowen B62 83 D7
Sutton Coldfield B72 57 C8
Whitnash CV31 162 B4
Greenhill Way WS9 16 B1
Greenholm Jun & Inf Sch
B44 55 E7
Greenholm Rd B44 55 E7
Greenhough Rd WS13 9 A8
Greening Dr B15 86 B7
Greenland Ave CV5 111 F5
Greenland Cl [9] DY6 60 E8
Greenland Ct Birmingham
B8 67 E6
Coventry CV5 111 F5
Greenland Rd B29 86 B1
Greenland Rise B92 107 D7
Greenlands Ave B98 154 A1
Greenlands Dr B98 158 F8
Greenlands Rd B37 70 C1
Greenleaf Cl CV5 112 A3
Greenleas Gdns B62 83 C3
Greenleighs DY3 39 D3
Greenly Rd WV4 39 D5
Greenmoor Rd Hinckley
LE10 75 D5
Nuneaton CV10 73 A3
Greenoak Cres
Birmingham B30 104 C8
Dudley WV14 51 A7
Greenodd Dr CV6 95 F5
Greenridge Rd B20 54 E5
Greenroyde DY9 81 B1
Greens Ind Est WS12 2 C7
Greens Rd CV6 95 A1
Greens The WV6 23 E3
Greens Yd CV12 78 C3
Greenside Birmingham B17 85 C5
Cheswick Green B90 126 D4
Stoke Prior B60 150 C2
Greenside Cl CV11 74 C1
Greenside Rd B24 57 C5
Greenside Way WS5 43 A4
Greensill Ave DY4 51 F8
Greenslade Croft B31 103 A2
Greenslade Rd Sedgley DY3 .. 39 B2
Solihull B90 105 C2
Walsall WS5 43 C7
Greensleeves B74 32 A1
Greensleeves Cl CV6 95 B2
Greenstead Rd B13 87 D1
Greensward Cl CV8 148 B6
Greensward The CV3 115 A2
Greensway WV11 26 B8
Greenvale B31 102 F5
Greenvale Ave B26 89 D6
Greenway Birmingham B20 54 F6
Nuneaton CV11 79 B8
Sedgley DY3 39 E1
Warwick CV34 155 E1
Greenway Ave DY8 60 E1
Greenway Dr B73 45 C3
Greenway Gdns
Birmingham B38 123 E7
Sedgley DY3 39 E1
Greenway Rd WV14 40 E4
Greenway St B9 67 C1
Greenway The
Birmingham,
Marston Green B37 90 A6
Birmingham,
New Oscott B73 45 B3
Hagley DY9 98 F5
Greenway Wlk B33 69 E1
Greenways Birmingham
B31 102 F8
Halesowen B63 82 C6
Stourbridge DY8 60 C1
Greenways The CV32 157 B3
Greenwood B25 88 D8
Greenwood Ave
Birmingham B27 88 B1
Blackheath B65 63 D3
Oldbury B68 64 C5
Greenwood Cl B14 104 E5
Greenwood Cotts DY1 51 A5

Greenwood Ct
 Nuneaton CV11 .... 73 E3
 Royal Leamington Spa CV32 . 157 B1
Greenwood Dr WS14 .... 9 B6
Greenwood Pk Aldridge
 WS9 .... 16 C2
 Cannock WS12 .... 2 B8
Greenwood Pl B44 .... 45 B1
Greenwood Rd Aldridge
 WS9 .... 16 B2
 West Bromwich B71 .... 53 B8
 Wolverhampton WV10 .... 25 C7
Greenwood Sq B37 .... 70 B2
Greenwood Way B37 .... 70 B2
Greenwoods The DY8 .... 80 E5
Greet Jun & Inf Sch B11 ... 87 D4
Greethurst Dr B13 .... 87 C2
Greets Green Ind Est B70... 52 F4
Greets Green Rd B70 .... 52 F3
Greetville Cl B34 .... 69 A5
Gregory Ave
 Birmingham B29 .... 103 A8
 Coventry CV3 .... 133 A6
Gregory Cl 3 WS10 .... 41 F2
Gregory Ct WV11 .... 26 E5
Gregory Dr DY1 .... 51 A2
Gregory Hood Rd CV3 ...... 133 E2
Gregory Rd DY8 .... 80 D5
Gregston Ind Est B69 ...... 64 B8
Greig Ct WS11 .... 2 C2
Grendon Cl Coventry CV4 .... 111 C1
 Redditch B98 .... 154 D1
Grendon Dr B73 .... 45 D3
Grendon Gdns WV3 .... 38 D6
Grendon Inf & Jun Sch
 B14 .... 105 A3
Grendon Rd
 Birmingham B14 .... 105 A3
 Solihull B92 .... 106 E8
Grenfell Cl CV31 .... 162 D6
Grenfell Ct B73 .... 46 B1
Grenfell Dr B15 .... 85 F8
Grenfell Rd WS3 .... 14 D3
Grenville Ave CV2 .... 114 B3
Grenville Cl WS2 .... 27 D3
Grenville Dr Birmingham
 B23 .... 56 B3
 Smethwick B66 .... 64 D8
Grenville Pl B70 .... 52 E3
Grenville Rd Dudley DY1 .... 51 A2
 Solihull B90 .... 106 B2
Gresham Ave CV32 .... 157 B2
Gresham Pl CV32 .... 157 B2
Gresham Rd
 Birmingham B28 .... 105 F6
 Cannock WS11 .... 1 F3
 Nuneaton CV10 .... 78 B8
 Oldbury B68 .... 64 C6
Gresham St CV2 .... 114 A2
Gresham Tower B12 .... 86 F8
Gresley B77 .... 21 F1
Gresley Cl B75 .... 32 A4
Gresley Gr B23 .... 56 C2
Gresley Rd CV2 .... 114 D7
Gresley Row 8 Lichfield
 WS13 .... 9 B7
 6 Lichfield WS13 .... 9 C8
Gressel La B33 .... 69 D3
Grestone Ave B20 .... 54 E3
Grestone Jun & Inf Schs
 B20 .... 54 E4
Greswold Cl CV4 .... 111 F1
Greswold Gdns B34 .... 68 F5
Greswold Prim Sch B91 ... 107 C6
Greswold St B71 .... 53 B5
Greswolde Dr B24 .... 57 B4
Greswolde Park Rd B27 .... 88 B4
Greswolde Rd
 Birmingham B11 .... 87 D3
 Solihull B91 .... 106 E6
Greswoldes The CV31 .... 162 F6
Gretna Rd CV3 .... 132 F4
Gretton Cres WS9 .... 29 E5
Gretton Rd Aldridge WS9 .... 29 F5
 Birmingham B23 .... 56 D7
Greville Dr B15 .... 86 C6
Greville Rd Kenilworth CV8 .. 147 F4
 Warwick CV34 .... 156 B1
Greville Smith Ave CV31 ... 162 B4
Grevis Cl B13 .... 86 F4
Grevis Rd B25 .... 68 E1
Grey Mill Cl B90 .... 126 F6
Grey Tree Cres B93 .... 127 E3
Grey's Rd B80 .... 159 E3
Greycoat Rd CV6 .... 95 A2
Greyfort Cres B92 .... 88 F1
Greyfriars Cl Dudley DY1 .. 50 E3
 Solihull B92 .... 106 D6
Greyfriars Cres CV6 .... 113 A7
Greyfriars La CV1 .... 165 B2
Greyfriars Rd CV1 .... 165 B2
Greyhound La
 Stourbridge DY8 .... 80 D2
 Wombourne WV4 .... 37 E5
Greyhurst Croft 5 B91 ... 127 B8
Greysbrooke WS14 .... 18 A5
Greysbrooke Cty Prim Sch
 WS14 .... 18 A6
Greystoke Ave B36 .... 68 D7
Greystoke Dr DY6 .... 60 D6
Greystone Cl B98 .... 154 C5
Greystone Pas 15 DY1 .... 51 B1
Grice St B70 .... 64 D8
Griff La CV10 .... 77 E6
Griffin Cl Birmingham B31 ... 103 B6
 Burntwood WS7 .... 6 E8
Griffin Ct B5 .... 86 C5
Griffin Gdns B17 .... 85 D4

Griffin Ho B16 .... 65 E1
Griffin Ind Est B65 .... 63 F3
Griffin Rd Birmingham B23 ... 56 C5
 Kidderminster DY10 .... 116 E4
 Warwick CV34 .... 161 C7
Griffin St Dudley DY2 .... 62 C4
 West Bromwich B70 .... 53 D3
 Wolverhampton WV1 .... 25 F1
Griffins Brook Cl B30 .... 103 D7
Griffins Brook La B30 .... 103 D6
Griffiths Dr
 Wolverhampton WV11 .... 13 A1
 Wombourne WV5 .... 49 A5
Griffiths Rd Dudley DY1 .... 51 A6
 West Bromwich B71 .... 42 C1
 Willenhall WV12 .... 27 D8
Griffiths St DY4 .... 51 E5
Grigg Gr B31 .... 102 E1
Grimley Cl B98 .... 153 F1
Grimley La B60 .... 151 E6
Grimley Rd 2 B31 .... 103 D2
Grimley Way WS11 .... 1 F4
Grimshaw Rd B27 .... 88 A1
Grimshaw Villas B93 .... 128 D8
Grimston Cl CV3 .... 115 A2
Grimstone St WV10 .... 163 C4
Grindle Rd CV6 .... 95 F4
Grindleford Rd B42 .... 55 D7
Grindley Ho 5 CV1 .... 113 B2
Grindsbrook B77 .... 36 A8
Gristhorpe Rd B29 .... 104 A8
Grizebeck Dr CV5 .... 112 A5
Grizedale Cl B45 .... 102 B2
Grocott Rd WS10 .... 41 B4
Grosmont 8 B42 .... 87 A1
Grosvenor Ave Aldridge B74 . 30 F1
 Birmingham B20 .... 55 C2
 Kidderminster DY10 .... 117 A6
Grosvenor Cl Lichfield WS14 ... 9 D6
 Sutton Coldfield B75 .... 32 C1
 Wolverhampton WV10 .... 11 D2
Grosvenor Cres
 Hinckley LE10 .... 76 A6
 Wolverhampton WV10 .... 11 D2
Grosvenor Ct
 Birmingham, Erdington B24 ... 57 A5
 Birmingham,
 Handsworth B20 .... 55 C2
 Dudley DY3 .... 50 D2
 2 Royal Leamington Spa
 CV32 .... 156 F1
 Shenstone WS14 .... 17 F6
 Stourbridge DY9 .... 81 B1
 Wednesfield WV11 .... 26 E5
 Wolverhampton WV3 .... 163 B2
 Wolverhampton,
 Tettenhall WV6 .... 24 A3
Grosvenor Ho CV1 .... 165 A2
Grosvenor Pk WV4 .... 38 F5
Grosvenor Rd
 Birmingham, Aston B6 .... 67 B8
 Birmingham,
 Handsworth B20 .... 55 C2
 Birmingham, Harborne B17 ... 85 A6
 Coventry CV1 .... 165 A1
 Dudley DY3 .... 50 D2
 Oldbury B68 .... 64 A3
 Royal Leamington Spa
 CV31 .... 162 A5
 Solihull B91 .... 106 F1
 Wolverhampton,
 Bushbury WV10 .... 11 D2
 Wolverhampton,
 Ettingshall Park WV4 .... 39 E3
Grosvenor Sh Ctr B31 ...... 103 A4
Grosvenor Sq B28 .... 105 F5
Grosvenor St
 Birmingham B5 .... 164 D3
 Wolverhampton WV10 .... 25 F3
Grosvenor St W B16 .... 66 B1
Grosvenor Way DY5 .... 81 E7
Grotto La WV6 .... 24 E5
Groucutt St 6 WV14 .... 51 E4
Grounds Dr B74 .... 31 F3
Grounds Rd B74 .... 31 F3
Grout St B70 .... 52 E4
Grove Ave
 Birmingham,
 Handsworth B21 .... 65 F8
 Birmingham, Moseley B13 ...... 87 A2
 Halesowen B63 .... 82 F3
 Solihull B91 .... 107 C5
Grove Cl WS11 .... 5 F5
Grove Cottage Rd B9 .... 67 D2
Grove Cres Brierley Hill DY5 .. 61 C5
 Walsall WS3 .... 14 F3
Grove Ct Birmingham B43 .... 54 F6
 Coventry CV5 .... 133 B8
Grove Farm Dr B75 .... 46 F5
Grove Fields CV10 .... 73 D8
Grove Gdns B20 .... 54 F2
Grove Hill WS5 .... 29 E1
Grove Hill Rd B21 .... 54 F1
Grove Jun Sch WV2 .... 163 D1
Grove La
 Birmingham,
 Handsworth B20 .... 54 F1
 Birmingham, Harborne B17 ... 85 C4
 Keresley CV7 .... 94 F7
 Lapworth B94 .... 143 F4
 Norton Canes WS3 .... 5 E1
 Smethwick B66 .... 65 C5
 Wishaw B76 .... 47 F2
 Wolverhampton WV6 .... 24 B2
Grove Mews B31 .... 123 B8
Grove Pk Hinckley LE10 ...... 76 A6
 Kingswinford DY6 .... 60 C8

Grove Pl Nuneaton CV10 .... 72 D3
 2 Royal Leamington Spa
 CV31 .... 162 A6
Grove Prim Sch B21 .... 65 F8
Grove Rd Ansty CV7 .... 97 D4
 Birmingham, King's Heath
 B14 .... 104 D6
 Birmingham, Sparkhill B11 .... 87 C2
 Dorridge B93 .... 128 B3
 Hinckley LE10 .... 76 A6
 Nuneaton CV10 .... 72 D3
 Oldbury B68 .... 64 D1
 Solihull B91 .... 107 C5
 Stourbridge DY9 .... 81 F3
Grove St Coventry CV1 ...... 165 C3
 Dudley DY2 .... 62 E8
 Redditch B98 .... 153 E4
 Royal Leamington Spa CV32 . 161 E8
 Smethwick B66 .... 65 D4
 Wolverhampton WV2 .... 163 C1
 Wolverhampton,
 Springfield WV10 .... 25 F3
Grove Terr WS1 .... 28 F1
Grove The Bedworth CV12 ... 78 C3
 Birmingham, Edgbaston B16 .. 65 F2
 Birmingham, Great Barr B43 ... 43 E4
 Birmingham, Lozells B19 ...... 66 B7
 Birmingham, Rednall B45 ...... 122 D4
 Birmingham, Saltley B8 .... 67 C4
 Birmingham,
 West Heath B31 .... 123 B8
 Blackheath B65 .... 63 C2
 Brierley Hill DY5 .... 61 C1
 Burntwood WS7 .... 6 D8
 Coleshill B46 .... 70 F4
 Hampton In A B92 .... 91 A1
 Hinckley LE10 .... 75 C8
 Little Aston B74 .... 31 D5
 Studley B80 .... 159 D3
 Walsall WS5 .... 43 B3
 Wolverhampton,
 Lanesfield WV4 .... 39 E5
 Wolverhampton,
 New Cross WV11 .... 26 B6
Grove Vale Ave B43 .... 43 C1
Grove Vale Prim Sch B43 .... 43 D1
Grove Villas B64 .... 82 D7
Grove Way B74 .... 44 F7
Groveland Dr DY4 .... 52 B3
Grovelands Cres WV10 ...... 11 D3
Grovelands Ind Est CV7 ...... 96 A6
Groveley La B31, B45 .... 122 E5
Grovelley La R31, B45 .... 122 E5
Groveside Way WS3 .... 15 A5
Grovewood Dr 2 B38 ...... 103 E1
Guardhouse Rd CV6 .... 113 B8
Guardian Angels RC
 Jun & Inf Sch B34 .... 69 E6
Guardian Ct
 Birmingham, Frankley B31 ... 102 D3
 Birmingham,
 Gilbertstone B26 .... 88 F7
 3 Bromsgrove B60 .... 137 A2
 Solihull B91 .... 107 D3
Guardian Ho B68 .... 84 C7
Guardians Way B31 .... 102 E8
Guernsey Dr B36 .... 70 B6
Guest Ave WV11 .... 26 C8
Guest Gr B19 .... 66 C6
Guest Hospl DY1 .... 51 E3
Guild Ave WS3 .... 28 D8
Guild Cl B16 .... 66 A2
Guild Cotts The 6 CV34 .... 160 E6
Guild Croft B19 .... 66 D6
Guild Rd Bromsgrove B60 .... 136 F1
 Coventry CV6 .... 113 D7
Guildford Cl DY11 .... 116 A6
Guildford Croft B37 .... 89 F8
Guildford Ct CV6 .... 113 D7
Guildford Dr B19 .... 66 D6
Guildford St 4 B19 .... 66 D7
Guildhall Mews The
 7 WS1 .... 28 F1
Guillemard Ct B37 .... 70 B1
Guilsborough Rd CV3 .... 134 E8
Guinness Cl B98 .... 158 D8
Guiting Cl B97 .... 153 B1
Guiting Rd B29 .... 103 A2
Gulistan Ct 6 CV32 .... 156 E1
Gulistan Rd CV32 .... 156 E1
Gullane Cl B38 .... 103 D1
Gullet The B78 .... 22 F1
Gullswood Cl B14 .... 104 D2
Gulson Hospl CV1 .... 165 D2
Gulson Rd CV1 .... 113 E2
Gumbleberrys Cl B8 .... 68 C4
Gun La CV2 .... 114 A5
Gunbarrel Ind Ctr B63 ...... 82 F6
Gundry Cl CV31 .... 162 A7
Gungate B79 .... 21 B5
Gunmakers Wlk B19 .... 66 D7
Gunner La B80 .... 121 D7
Gunners La B80 .... 159 E4
Gunnery Terr 3 CV32 ...... 156 D1
Gunns Way B92 .... 106 D7
Guns La B70 .... 53 B4
Guns Village Inf Sch B70 .. 53 B4
Guns Village Jun Sch B70 .. 53 A3
Gunstock Cl B74 .... 44 F7
Gunter Jun & Inf Sch B24 ... 57 E3
Gunter Rd B24 .... 57 F3
Gunton Ave CV3 .... 134 C6
Guphill Ave CV5 .... 112 C2
Guphill La CV5 .... 112 D3
Gurnard B77 .... 35 D6
Gurnard Cl WV12 .... 13 B1
Gurney Cl CV4 .... 111 E3
Gurney Pl WS2 .... 28 A5

Gurney Rd WS2 .... 28 A5
Guthrie Cl B19 .... 66 D6
Guthrum Cl Birmingham B23 .. 56 E8
 Perton WV6 .... 23 F5
Gutter The DY9 .... 120 E7
Gutteridge Ave CV6 .... 95 A2
Guy Ave WV10 .... 25 E6
Guy Pl E 11 CV32 .... 156 F1
Guy Pl W 10 CV32 .... 156 F1
Guy Rd CV8 .... 147 F2
Guy St
 Royal Leamington Spa CV32 . 156 F1
 Warwick CV34 .... 161 A8
Guy's Almshouses R79 ...... 21 B5
Guy's Cl CV34 .... 161 A8
Guy's Cliffe Ave CV32 ...... 156 D2
Guy's Cliffe Rd CV32 .... 161 E8
Guy's Cliffe Terr CV34 ...... 160 F7
Guy's Cross Park Rd CV34 160 F8
Guy's La DY3 .... 50 B2
Guys Cl B61 .... 137 A5
Guys Cl 2 B77 .... 20 F7
Guys Cliffe Ave B76 .... 46 F1
Gwalia Gr B19 .... 66 D7
Gwendoline Ave LE10 .... 71 A2
Gwendoline Way WS9 .... 16 B4
GWS Ind Est WV1 .... 41 D1
Gypsy La Kenilworth CV8 .... 147 F2
 Redditch B97 .... 152 C5
 Water Orton B46 .... 59 D2

Habberley La DY11 .... 116 A8
Habberley Rd Blackheath
 B63 .... 63 D2
 Kidderminster DY11 .... 116 B7
Habberley St 1 DY11 ...... 116 C6
Habberly Croft B91 .... 107 B5
Habitat Ct B76 .... 46 F3
Hack St B9 .... 67 A1
Hackett Cl WV14 .... 39 F1
Hackett Ct 2 B69 .... 64 A7
Hackett Dr B66 .... 64 D7
Hackett Rd B63 .... 63 E3
Hackett St DY4 .... 52 C7
Hackford Rd WV4 .... 39 F4
Hackmans Gate La DY9 .... 119 B7
Hackwood Ho 10 B69 ...... 63 D5
Hackwood Rd WS10 .... 42 B2
Hadcroft Grange DY9 .... 81 D4
Hadcroft Rd DY9 .... 81 C4
Haddock Rd WV14 .... 40 C7
Haddon Cres WV12 .... 27 C7
Haddon Croft B63 .... 82 C1
Haddon End CV3 .... 133 E6
Haddon Rd Birmingham
 B42 .... 55 D6
 Royal Leamington Spa CV32 . 157 B2
Haddon St CV6 .... 114 A8
Haddon Tower 4 B15 ...... 86 D8
Haden Cl Blackheath B64 .... 83 A7
 Stourbridge DY8 .... 60 D2
Haden Cres WV11 .... 26 F6
Haden Cross Dr B64 .... 83 A7
Haden Ct 5 WV3 .... 25 A2
Haden Hill WV3 .... 25 A2
Haden Hill Rd B63 .... 83 B6
Haden Hill Sch B64 .... 82 F8
Haden Park Rd B64 .... 82 F7
Haden Rd Blackheath B64 .... 82 F7
 Tipton DY4 .... 41 A1
Haden St B12 .... 86 F6
Haden Way B12 .... 86 F6
Haden Wlk 2 B65 .... 63 C3
Hadendale B64 .... 83 A7
Hadfield Croft B19 .... 66 C5
Hadland Rd B33 .... 69 B1
Hadleigh Croft B76 .... 58 A6
Hadleigh Rd CV3 .... 133 C4
Hadley Cl Dudley DY2 .... 62 E4
 Hollywood B47 .... 125 A5
Hadley Croft B66 .... 65 A7
Hadley Ct B16 .... 65 D1
Hadley Pl WV14 .... 40 C7
Hadley Rd Bilston WV14 ...... 40 C7
 Walsall WS2 .... 27 F6
Hadley St B68 .... 64 A4
Hadley Way WS2 .... 28 A6
Hadlow Croft B33 .... 89 D7
Hadrian Cl CV32 .... 157 B4
Hadrian Dr B46 .... 59 F1
Hadrians Cl B77 .... 35 D8
Hadyn Gr B26 .... 89 B6
Hadzor Ho B97 .... 153 A4
Hadzor Rd B68 .... 84 D8
Hafren Cl B45 .... 102 B2
Hafton Gr B9 .... 67 D1
Haggar St WV2 .... 39 C6
Hagley Cswy DY9 .... 100 B8
Hagley Ct DY9 .... 99 C6
Hagley Ct 12 DY3 .... 50 E3
Hagley Cty Prim Inf &
 Jun Sch DY9 .... 99 B5
Hagley Hall DY9 .... 99 D6
Hagley Hill DY9 .... 99 E7
Hagley Ho B60 .... 137 B3
Hagley Park Dr B45 .... 122 A6
Hagley RC High Sch DY8 .. 98 F6
Hagley Rd Birmingham B16 .. 65 C1
 Halesowen B63 .... 82 E2
 Stourbridge DY9 .... 81 B3
Hagley Rd W B32 .... 84 D7
Hagley St 3 B63 .... 83 B3
Hagley Sta DY9 .... 99 A6
Hagley View Rd DY2 .... 62 C8
Hagley Villas B12 .... 87 B4
Hagley Wood La B62 .... 100 B7
Haig Cl Cannock WS11 .... 2 A5
 Sutton Coldfield B75 .... 46 C7

Haig Pl B13 .... 105 A7
Haig Rd DY2 .... 51 F1
Haig St B71 .... 53 C5
Hailes Park Cl WV4 .... 39 E6
Hailsham Rd B23 .... 56 F5
Hailstone Cl B65 .... 63 A5
Haines Cl DY4 .... 52 B4
Haines St B70 .... 53 D2
Hainfield Dr B91 .... 107 E5
Hainge Rd B69 .... 52 C1
Hainult Cl DY8 .... 60 D4
Halas Ind Est B62 .... 83 C5
Halberd Cl LE10 .... 75 D5
Halberton St B66 .... 65 D4
Haldane Ct B33 .... 69 B2
Haldon Gr B31 .... 122 E7
Hale Gr B24 .... 57 D4
Halecroft Ave WV11 .... 26 D5
Hales Cres B67 .... 64 E4
Hales Gdns B23 .... 56 C8
Hales La B67 .... 64 E4
Hales Park Ind Est CV6 ...... 95 E4
Hales Rd Halesowen B63 .... 83 A4
 Wednesbury WS10 .... 42 A5
Hales St CV1 .... 165 C3
Hales Way B69 .... 63 F7
Halesbury Ct B63 .... 82 F2
Halesbury Sch B62 .... 83 E7
Halescroft Sq B31 .... 102 E6
Halesmere Way B63 .... 83 C3
Halesowen CE Prim Sch
 B63 .... 83 B4
Halesowen Coll B62 .... 83 B5
Halesowen Coll Walton
 Campus B62 .... 83 A3
Halesowen Ind Pk B62 ...... 83 B6
Halesowen Rd Dudley DY2 .... 62 D4
 Halesowen B62 .... 83 F6
 Lydiate Ash B61 .... 121 C3
Halesowen St Blackheath
 B65 .... 63 C1
 Oldbury B69 .... 63 F7
Halesworth Rd WV9 .... 10 F3
Halewood Gr B28 .... 106 A7
Haley St WV12 .... 27 C5
Halfcot Ave DY9 .... 81 C3
Halford Cres WS3 .... 28 F5
Halford Gr B24 .... 57 E4
Halford La CV6 .... 95 A2
Halford Lodge CV6 .... 95 A2
Halford Rd B91 .... 106 E6
Halford St B79 .... 21 A5
Halford's La B66 .... 65 A8
Halfpenny Field Wlk B35 ... 58 A3
Halfshire La DY10 .... 98 B1
Halfway Cl B44 .... 55 E6
Halifax Cl CV5 .... 112 A7
Halifax Gr 8 B18 .... 65 E4
Halifax Ho B76 .... 86 D7
Halifax Rd B90 .... 106 B2
Haliscombe Gr 4 B6 .... 66 E8
Halkett Glade B33 .... 68 D3
Hall Cl CV8 .... 149 B6
Hall Cres B71 .... 53 C6
Hall Dale Cl B28 .... 105 F5
Hall Dr Baginton CV8 .... 133 E3
 Birmingham B37 .... 90 A7
 Hagley DY9 .... 99 D6
Hall End Nuneaton CV11 ...... 73 D2
 Wednesbury WS10 .... 41 F3
Hall End Pl CV11 .... 73 D2
Hall Gr WV14 .... 51 C8
Hall Green Inf Sch B28 ...... 105 F6
Hall Green Prim Sch B71 ... 42 D1
Hall Green Rd Coventry CV6 . 96 B2
 West Bromwich B71 .... 42 D1
Hall Green Sec Sch B28 .... 105 E8
Hall Green Sta B28 .... 87 F1
Hall Hays Rd B34 .... 69 E5
Hall La Brownhills WS9 ...... 15 E3
 Burntwood, Hammerwich WS7 .. 7 E4
 Burntwood,
 Muckley Corner WS7, WS14 ... 7 F2
 Coventry CV2 .... 114 F6
 Dudley DY2 .... 62 C6
 Great Wyrley WS6 .... 5 A3
 Hagley DY9 .... 99 D6
 Lichfield WS14 .... 8 A2
 Tipton DY4 .... 52 B8
 Walsall WS3 .... 14 F3
 Wolverhampton WV14 .... 39 F1
Hall Mdw Hagley DY9 .... 99 D7
 Wedges Mills WS11 .... 4 B6
Hall Park St WV14 .... 40 B7
Hall Rd
 Birmingham,
 Castle Bromwich B36 .... 69 A8
 Birmingham,
 Handsworth B20 .... 66 A8
 Birmingham, Saltley B8 .... 67 D4
 Hinckley LE10 .... 75 D5
 Royal Leamington Spa CV32 . 156 F1
 Smethwick B67 .... 64 E4
Hall St Bilston WV14 .... 40 E5
 Birmingham B18 .... 164 A4
 Blackheath B64 .... 62 F2
 Darlaston WS10 .... 41 B2
 Dudley DY2 .... 51 D1
 Oldbury B68 .... 64 B5
 Sedgley DY3 .... 50 D8
 Stourbridge DY8 .... 81 A3
 Tipton DY4 .... 51 E5
 Walsall WS2 .... 28 D3

Hall St continued
West Bromwich B70 53 C2
Willenhall WV13 27 B1
Wolverhampton WV11 26 C5
Hall St E WS10 41 C7
Hall St S B70 64 D8
Hall Wlk B46 70 F4
Hall's Cl CV31 162 B3
Halladale B38 103 F1
Hallam Cl B71 53 E5
Hallam Cres WV10 25 E6
Hallam Jun Sch B71 53 E5
Hallam Rd CV6 95 B2
Hallam St Birmingham B12 86 E5
West Bromwich B71 53 D5
Hallbridge Cl WS3 14 F2
Hallbridge Way B69 52 B2
Hallchurch Rd DY2 61 F6
Hallcourt Cl WS11 4 E8
Hallcourt Cres WS11 4 E8
Hallcourt La WS11 4 E8
Hallcroft Cl B72 57 C7
Hallcroft Way Aldridge WS9 30 C5
Knowle B93 128 A6
Hallens Dr WS10 41 D2
Hallet Dr WV3 163 A2
Hallewell Rd B16 65 D3
Hallfield Sch B15 86 A7
Hallfields CV31 162 E5
Hallgreen St WV14 40 E2
Hallmoor Rd B33 69 B3
Hallmoor Sch B33 69 B3
Hallot Cl B23 56 D8
Halloughton Rd B74 46 A7
Hallow Ho 5 B38 103 D2
Hallowfields Cl B98 153 E1
Hallstead Rd B13 105 B5
Hallway Dr CV7 97 E6
Halsbury Gr B44 56 B8
Halstead Gr B91 127 A8
Halston Rd 3 WS7 7 B8
Halswelle Gr B43 44 E4
Halton Rd B73 45 E2
Halton St DY2 62 C5
Haltonlea B77 36 A8
Ham Dingle Prim Sch DY9 81 C2
Ham La Kingswinford DY6 49 E1
Stourbridge DY9 81 C2
Hamar Way B37 70 B1
Hamberley Ct B18 65 D5
Hamble B77 21 D2
Hamble Cl DY5 61 A6
Hamble Ct B73 46 B5
Hamble Gr WV6 23 F4
Hamble Rd Birmingham B42 43 F1
Wolverhampton WV4 38 C6
Hambledon Cl WV9 11 A2
Hambleton Rd B63 82 D2
Hambletts Rd B70 53 A3
Hambrook Cl WV6 25 A5
Hambury Dr B14 104 D7
Hamelin St WS11 1 E3
Hamilton Ave
Birmingham B17 85 A7
Halesowen B62 83 C3
Stourbridge DY8 80 D6
Hamilton Cl Bedworth CV12 77 C1
Cannock WS12 2 F4
Hinckley LE10 71 A2
Lickey End B60 137 C6
Sedgley DY3 50 C8
Stourbridge DY8 60 C2
Hamilton Ct
1 Birmingham B13 86 F4
Nuneaton CV10 72 D4
Hamilton Dr
Birmingham B29 103 D8
Stourbridge DY8 60 C2
Studley B80 159 D3
Tipton B69 52 C2
Hamilton Gdns WV10 11 F3
Hamilton Ho 3
Birmingham B5 86 D7
Walsall WS3 14 C1
Hamilton Lea WS11 6 A6
Hamilton Rd Birmingham
B21 65 D8
Coventry CV2 114 A3
Kidderminster DY11 116 B3
Radford Semele CV31 162 E5
Redditch B97 158 C8
Smethwick B67 64 E2
Tipton DY4 52 C6
Hamilton Specl Sch B21 65 D8
Hamilton St WS3 14 D1
Hamilton Terr CV32 161 F8
Hamlet Cl CV11 74 B1
Hamlet Gdns B28 105 F8
Hamlet Rd B28 105 F8
Hamlet The
Leek Wootton CV35 156 A7
Norton Canes WS11 5 E5
Hammer Bank DY5 82 A8
Hammersley Cl B63 82 C7
Hammersley St CV12 77 E1
Hammerwich Hospl WS7 7 B5
Hammerwich La WS7 7 F3
Hammerwich Rd WS7 7 D5
Hammond Ave WV10 25 E8
Hammond Bsns Ctr CV11 73 E3
Hammond Cl CV11 73 E3
Hammond Dr B23 56 F5
Hammond Rd CV2 113 F4
Hammond Way DY8 81 A7
Hammonds Terr CV8 147 D5
Hampden Cl DY5 82 A8
Hampden Ct B69 63 E8
Hampden Ho B35 58 B3
Hampden Retreat B12 86 E6
Hamps Cl WS7 7 D7
Hampshire Cl Coventry CV3 134 F8
Tamworth B78 20 F2
Hampshire Dr B15 85 E8
Hampshire Rd B71 42 A1
Hampson Cl B11 87 B6
Hampstead Cl WV11 26 D6
Hampton Ave
Bromsgrove B60 151 A8
Nuneaton CV10 72 B4
Hampton Cl Coventry CV6 113 F6
Redditch B98 159 A7
Tamworth B79 21 C7
Hampton Court Rd B17 85 A6
Hampton Ct B92 109 B6
Hampton Dr B74 46 B8
Hampton Gn WS11 4 E7
Hampton Gr
Royal Leamington Spa CV32 157 B1
1 Walsall WS3 15 A4
Hampton in Arden Sta
B92 109 B7
Hampton La Meriden CV7 109 E8
Solihull B91 108 B5
Hampton Pl WS10 41 C8
Hampton Rd
Birmingham, Aston B6 66 D8
Birmingham,
Stockland Green B23 56 D4
Coventry CV6 113 F6
Knowle B93 128 C8
Warwick CV34 160 B5
Wolverhampton WV10 11 B1
Hampton St
Birmingham B19 164 B4
Cannock WS11 4 D7
Dudley, Netherton DY2 62 C5
Dudley, Roseville WV14 51 B8
Warwick CV34 160 D6
Hams La B76 59 F6
Hams Rd B8 67 D4
Hamstead Hall Ave B20 54 E5
Hamstead Hall Rd B20 54 F4
Hamstead Hall Sec Sch
B20 54 E6
Hamstead Hill B20 54 F4
Hamstead Ho B43 54 F7
Hamstead Jun & Inf Sch
B43 54 D7
Hamstead Rd
Birmingham, Hanmtead B43 54 D7
Birmingham,
Lozells B19, B20 66 B7
Hamstead Sta B42 54 F6
Hamstead Terr WS10 42 A2
Hanam Cl B75 46 F6
Hanbury Cl Bromsgrove
B60 151 A8
Halesowen B63 82 F1
Hanbury Cres WV4 38 E6
Hanbury Croft B27 88 E3
Hanbury Ct DY8 81 A4
Hanbury Hill DY8 81 A4
Hanbury Ho B97 153 B4
Hanbury Rd Bedworth CV12 78 C4
Brownhills WS8 6 F2
Dorridge B93 127 F4
Norton Canes WS11 5 F5
Stoke Heath B60 150 D4
Tamworth B77 21 F4
West Bromwich B70 53 A3
Hanbury's Farm Prim Sch
B77 21 D1
Hanch Pl WS1 42 F8
Hancock Gn CV4 131 F8
Hancock Rd B8 67 F4
Hancox St B68 64 B2
Handcross Gr CV3 133 A5
Handel Ct WS11 2 C2
Handel Wlk WS13 3 C2
Handley Gr Birmingham B31 102 C2
Warwick CV34 155 D1
Handley St WS10 42 A4
Handley's Cl CV8 135 A1
Handsworth, Booth Street
Sta B21 65 C7
Handsworth Coll B21 65 F8
Handsworth Coll
(Corporation)
Aston Ctr B6 66 E8
Handsworth Coll F Ed B6 66 E8
Handsworth Cres CV5 111 E4
Handsworth Dr B43 44 A3
Handsworth Gram Sch B21 65 F8
Handsworth New Rd B18 65 E6
Handsworth Univ Village
(Univ of Aston) B21 54 E2
Handsworth Wood Boys' Sch
B20 54 F2
Handsworth Wood Girls'
Sch B20 54 F2
Handsworth Wood Rd B20 55 A2
Hanford Cl CV6 113 E6
Hanger Rd B26 90 A3
Hanging La B31 102 E2
Hangleton Dr B11 87 D6
Hangman's La LE10 71 E3
Hanley Cl B63 82 E4
Hanley Ct B23 56 C2
Hanley St B19 164 C4
Hanley Villas 1 B12 87 B5
Hanlith B77 36 A8
Hannaford Way WS11 1 F2
Hannafore Rd B16 65 D3
Hannah Rd WV14 41 A3
Hanney Hay Rd WS7 7 B3
Hannon Rd B14 104 E5
Hanover Cl B6 66 E7
Hanover Ct Hinckley LE10 75 E6
Redditch B98 158 D8
Tamworth B79 20 E7
Walsall WS2 27 E1
Wolverhampton WV6 24 C4
Hanover Dr B24 67 F8
Hanover Gdns 8 CV32 157 A1
Hanover Glebe CV11 73 C2
Hanover Ho 5 DY8 80 F8
Hanover Pl Bromsgrove
B60 136 F1
Cannock WS11 1 E2
Hanover Rd B65 63 C4
Hanover St B61 136 F1
Hans Cl CV2 113 F4
Hansell Dr B93 127 E2
Hansom Rd Birmingham B32 84 C5
Hinckley LE10 71 F2
Hanson Ct 2 LE10 75 D8
Hanson Gr B92 88 F5
Hanson's Bridge Rd B24 57 F5
Hanwell Cl B76 58 B7
Hanwood Cl Birmingham B12 86 F8
Coventry CV5 111 D4
Hanwood Ho 1 B12 86 F8
Hanworth Cl CV32 157 C2
Hanworth Rd CV34 160 D8
Harald Cl WV6 23 E5
Harbeck Ave B44 55 F8
Harberrow Cl DY9 99 A6
Harbet Dr B40 90 E4
Harbinger Rd B38 104 B2
Harbington Hall DY10 118 B1
Harborne Ct B17 85 C4
Harborne Hill Sch B15 85 E6
Harborne Inf Sch B17 85 C6
Harborne Jun Sch B17 85 C6
Harborne La B17 85 D3
Harborne Park Rd B17 85 C4
Harborne Rd Birmingham
B15 85 E7
Oldbury B68 84 E8
Harborough Cotts B94 144 D3
Harborough Ct B74 32 A2
Harborough Dr Aldridge
WS9 30 B5
Birmingham B36 58 D1
Harborough Rd CV6 95 B2
Harborough Wlk DY9 81 B2
Harbours Cl B61 150 D7
Harbours Hill DY9 120 E6
Harbury Cl Redditch B98 154 D1
Sutton Coldfield B76 58 B6
Harbury La CV33, CV34 161 E2
Harbury Rd B12 86 D5
Harcourt CV3 134 E5
Harcourt Dr Dudley DY3 50 D2
Sutton Coldfield B74 31 F4
Harcourt Gdns CV11 73 C3
Harcourt Ho B79 21 A4
Harcourt Rd Birmingham
B23 56 E7
Blackheath B64 82 F8
Wednesbury WS10 41 F4
Harden Cl WS3 28 E7
Harden Ct B31 102 E1
Harden Gr WS3 28 E7
Harden Keep B66 65 A4
Harden Manor Ct B62 83 C3
Harden Prim Sch WS3 28 E7
Harden Rd WS3 28 E7
Harden Vale B63 82 E5
Hardie Ct WV4 39 F4
Hardie Gn WS11 1 F3
Harding St WV14 40 D2
Hardon Rd WV4 39 F5
Hardware St B70 53 D4
Hardwick Cl CV5 112 A4
Hardwick Ct B74 30 F2
Hardwick Dr B62 83 A7
Hardwick La B80 159 F4
Hardwick Rd Aldridge B74 31 A2
Solihull B92 88 E4
Hardwicke Way DY9 81 D5
Hardwike Wlk B14 104 D2
Hardwyn Cl CV3 115 A1
Hardy Ave DY10 117 A6
Hardy Cl Hinckley LE10 71 D4
Nuneaton CV10 72 A4
Hardy Rd Coventry CV6 113 A8
Walsall WS3 28 E8
Wednesbury WS10 42 A3
Hardy Sq WV2 39 F6
Hare And Hounds La CV10 73 A2
Hare Gr B31 102 D3
Hare St WV14 40 F5
Harebell B77 22 A4
Harebell Cl Cannock WS12 2 D2
Featherstone WV10 12 A7
Walsall WS5 43 A3
Harebell Cres DY1 51 A4
Harebell Gdns B38 123 F8
Harebell Wlk 1 B37 70 D2
Harefield Ho CV2 114 B3
Harefield La CV12 77 F8
Harefield Rd Coventry CV2 114 B3
Nuneaton CV11 73 C4
Haresfield Cl B97 153 D3
Harewell Dr B75 32 C1
Harewood B17 85 B6
Harewood Ave
Birmingham B43 43 C2
Wednesbury WS10 42 C3
Harewood Cl B28 105 E5
Harewood Rd CV5 112 C2
Harford St B19 164 A5
Hargate La B71 53 D4
Hargate Prim Sch B71 53 C4
Harger Ct CV8 147 F4
Hargrave Cl Coventry CV3 115 A1
Water Orton B46 59 B3
Hargrave Rd B90 105 D1
Hargreave Cl B76 57 F8
Hargreaves Ct DY11 116 C3
Hargreaves St WV1 40 A7
Harington Rd CV6 113 A5
Harland Rd B74 32 A3
Harlech Cl Birmingham
B32 102 A7
Kenilworth CV8 148 C5
Tipton B69 52 A1
Harlech Ho 2 WS3 28 C6
Harlech Rd WV12 27 C6
Harlech Tower B23 57 A6
Harlech Way Dudley DY1 50 F2
Kidderminster DY10 116 E2
Harleston Rd B44 55 F8
Harley Cl WS8 16 A6
Harley Dr WV14 40 B4
Harley Grange 6 DY2 62 E8
Harley St CV2 114 A3
Harlow Gr B28 106 A6
Harlow Wlk 8 CV2 115 A7
Harlstones Cl DY8 81 A8
Harman Rd B72 57 B6
Harmar Cl CV34 155 D1
Harmer Cl CV2 115 A7
Harmer St B18 66 A5
Harmon Rd DY8 80 C5
Harnall Cl B90 126 E7
Harnall Ind Est CV1 165 C4
Harnall La CV1 165 C4
Harnall La E CV1 113 E4
Harnall La W CV1 165 C4
Harnall Row Coventry CV1 113 E2
Coventry CV1 113 E3
Harness Cl WS5 42 F4
Harold Evers Way DY10 116 F7
Harold Rd Birmingham B16 65 F1
Coventry CV2 114 D2
Smethwick B67 64 E3
Harold St CV11 73 C3
Harpenden Dr CV5 112 A5
Harper Ave WV11 26 C7
Harper Bell Sch The B12 87 A8
Harper Rd Bilston WV14 40 D6
Coventry CV1 113 E2
Harper St WV13 27 A2
Harpers Rd B31 103 A2
Harport Rd B98 154 A1
Harpur Cl WS4 29 A4
Harpur Rd WS4 29 A4
Harrier Rd B27 88 D2
Harriers Gn DY10 117 B8
Harriers Ind Est DY10 116 F5
Harriet Cl DY5 61 B5
Harringay Dr DY8 80 E3
Harringay Rd B44 45 A2
Harrington Ct CV3 114 F2
Harringworth Ct WS4 29 C8
Harriott Dr CV34 161 D4
Harris Ct B18 66 A6
Harris Dr 2 Birmingham
B42 55 A8
Smethwick B66 65 B3
Harris Ind Pk B60 150 E2
Harris Rd Coventry CV3 114 B2
Warwick CV34 160 C8
Harrison Cl Cheslyn Hay WS6 4 D1
Walsall WS3 14 C1
Harrison Cres CV12 78 A2
Harrison Ct DY8 61 A1
Harrison Ho B14 104 F3
Harrison Rd Birmingham B24 56 F4
Cannock WS11 4 E7
Redditch B97 158 C8
Stourbridge DY8 61 A1
Sutton Coldfield B74 31 E5
Walsall WS4 15 C2
Harrison St WS3 14 C1
Harrison's Fold DY2 62 C5
Harrison's Rd B15 85 E6
Harrisons Gn B15 85 E6
Harrisons Pleck B13 86 F3
Harrold Ave B65 63 E3
Harrold Rd B65 63 E3
Harrold St DY4 52 C7
Harrold Terr B19 66 C8
Harrop Way DY8 80 E8
Harrow Cl Hagley DY9 99 A6
Stoke Heath B60 150 E6
Harrow Ct B74 31 F2
Harrow Rd Birmingham B29 85 F3
Kingswinford DY6 49 D1
Whitnash CV31 162 B3
Harrow St WV1 25 B4
Harrowbrook Ind Est LE10 74 E7
Harrowbrook Rd LE10 74 E7
Harrowby Dr DY4 52 A4
Harrowby Pl WV13 27 D1
Harrowby Rd Bilston WV14 41 A4
Wolverhampton WV10 11 C2
Harrowfield Rd B33 68 E4
Harry Caplan Ho CV5 112 B6
Harry Cheshire High Sch
DY11 116 B6
Harry Edwards Ho 2 CV2 114 D8
Harry Perks St WV13 27 A3
Harry Price Ho 9 B69 63 D5
Harry Rose Rd CV2 114 E3
Harry Salt Ho CV1 165 D3
Harry Stanley Ho CV6 114 A8
Harry Taylor Fst Sch B97 158 E6
Harry Taylor Ho B98 154 A4
Harry Truslove Cl CV6 113 A7
Harry Weston Rd CV3 115 A1
Hart Dr B73 57 A8
Hart Rd Birmingham B24 57 A5
Willenhall WV11 26 D4
Hart St WS1 42 E8
Hartfield Cres B27 88 B2
Hartfields Way B65 62 F5
Hartford Cl B17 85 A7
Hartford Rd B60 137 B1
Hartill Rd WV4 38 D3
Hartill St WV13 41 B8
Hartington Cl B93 127 E3
Hartington Cres CV5 112 F1
Hartington Gn LE10 75 E6
Hartington Rd B19 66 D7
Hartland Ave Coventry
CV2 114 B5
Dudley WV14 51 A8
Hartland Rd
Birmingham B31 122 E6
Dudley DY4 51 D5
West Bromwich B71 53 F8
Hartland St DY5 61 D7
Hartle La DY9 119 F6
Hartlebury Cl Cannock
WS11 2 C2
Dorridge B93 127 F3
Redditch B98 154 E7
Hartlebury Rd
Halesowen B63 82 F2
Oldbury B69 63 D5
Hartledon Rd B17 85 B5
Hartlepool Rd CV1 165 D4
Hartley Dr WS9 30 B4
Hartley Gr B44 45 B3
Hartley Pl B15 85 F8
Hartley Rd B44 45 B3
Hartley St WV3 25 A2
Hartleyburn B77 36 A8
Harton Way B14 104 C5
Hartopp Rd Birmingham B8 67 E4
Sutton Coldfield B74 45 F8
Hartridge Wlk CV5 112 B4
Harts Cl B17 85 D6
Harts Green Rd B17 85 A5
Harts Rd B8 67 E5
Hartsbourne Dr B62 83 D4
Hartshill Ho B27 88 E2
Hartshill Rd Birmingham
B34 69 A6
Solihull B27 88 D2
Hartshill Sch CV10 72 B8
Hartshorn St WV14 40 D5
Hartside Cl B63 82 D2
Hartslade WS14 9 E6
Hartswell Dr B13 104 F6
Hartwell Cl B91 107 B1
Hartwell La WS6 5 A3
Hartwell Rd B24 57 B2
Harvard Cl DY1 50 F4
Harvard Rd B92 89 B4
Harvest Cl Birmingham B30 104 B6
Dudley DY3 50 E5
Stoke Heath B60 150 E6
Harvest Ct B65 63 A4
Harvest Gdns B68 64 A4
Harvest Hill Cl 12 CV31 162 C6
Harvest Hill La CV5, CV7 93 C4
Harvest Rd Blackheath B65 63 A3
Smethwick B67 64 D3
Harvest Wlk B65 63 A4
Harvester Way DY6 60 A8
Harvesters Cl Aldridge WS9 30 E2
Coventry CV3 115 A2
Harvesters Rd WV12 27 D5
Harvesters Way WV12 27 D5
Harvesters Wlk WV8 10 E1
Harvey Cl CV5 112 A7
Harvey Ct
Birmingham,
Bournville B30 103 D7
Birmingham, Tile Cross B33 69 D3
Harvey Dr B75 32 C2
Harvey Rd Birmingham B26 88 D7
Walsall WS2 28 B5
Harvey Works Ind Est B63 82 F6
Harveys Terr DY2 62 D4
Harvills Hawthorn B70 52 F7
Harvills Hawthorn Jun &
Inf Sch B70 52 F7
Harvine Wlk DY8 80 E3
Harvington Cl DY11 116 A8
Harvington Dr B90 127 B6
Harvington Hall La DY10 118 B1
Harvington Rd
Birmingham B29 103 A8
Bromsgrove B60 151 A8
Dudley WV14 40 B1
Halesowen B63 82 F1
Oldbury B68 84 A8
Harvington Way B76 58 A8
Harvington Wlk 3 B65 63 C3
Harwell Cl B79 21 C7
Harwin Cl WV6 24 F7
Harwood Dr LE10 71 F4
Harwood Gr 1 B90 126 C8
Harwood Rd WS13 3 B3
Harwood St B70 53 B3
Hasbury CE Prim Sch B63 82 F2
Hasbury Cl B63 82 E2
Hasbury Rd B32 102 B8
Hasefield Gdns 1 DY10 117 B6
Haselbech Rd CV3 114 F1
Haseley Cl Redditch B98 154 E1
Royal Leamington Spa CV31 162 B5

Haseley Rd Birmingham B21 .... 65 E7
Coventry CV2 .... 96 C1
Solihull B91 .... 106 E6
Haselor Rd B73 .... 45 E1
Haselour Rd B37 .... 69 F5
Hasilwood Sq CV3 .... 114 B2
Haskell St WS1 .... 42 F7
Haslucks Croft B90 .... 106 A3
Haslucks Green Jun Sch
B90 .... 106 A3
Haslucks Green Rd
Hollywood B90 .... 125 E7
Solihull B90 .... 106 B4
Hassop Rd B42 .... 55 D7
Hastings Cl B77 .... 35 F6
Hastings Ct DY1 .... 50 E2
Hastings High Sch LE10 .... 75 F7
Hastings Rd Birmingham
B23 .... 56 B7
Bromsgrove B60 .... 150 E7
Coventry CV2 .... 114 A4
Haswell Rd B63 .... 82 D4
Hatch Heath Cl WV5 .... 49 A4
Hatcham Rd B44 .... 45 C2
Hatchett St B19 .... 66 E5
Hatchford Ave B92 .... 89 C3
Hatchford Brook Inf Sch
B92 .... 89 C3
Hatchford Brook Jun Sch
B92 .... 89 C3
Hatchford Brook Rd B92 ... 89 C3
Hatchford Ct B92 .... 89 C3
Hatchford Jun & Prim
Schs B37 .... 69 F2
Hatchford Prim Sch B37 .... 69 F2
Hatchford Wlk B37 .... 70 B1
Hateley Dr WV4 .... 39 E4
Hateley Heath Jun & Inf
Schs B71 .... 53 B7
Hately Heath Jun & Inf
Schs B71 .... 53 B7
Hatfield Cl Birmingham B23 .. 56 D8
Redditch B98 .... 154 E1
Hatfield Rd Birmingham B19 .. 66 D8
Stourbridge DY9 .... 81 C4
Hathaway Cl
Balsall Common CV7 .... 130 B7
Willenhall WV13 .... 40 F8
Hathaway Dr Nuneaton
CV11 .... 74 A1
Warwick CV34 .... 155 E2
Hathaway Rd Coventry
CV4 .... 111 D1
Solihull B90 .... 106 B1
Sutton Coldfield B75 .... 32 A4
Hatherden Dr B76 .... 47 A2
Hatherell Rd CV31 .... 162 E5
Hathersage Rd B42 .... 55 D7
Hatherton Croft WS11 .... 1 C1
Hatherton Gdns WV10 .... 11 E2
Hatherton Gr B29 .... 84 F1
Hatherton Lane JMI Sch
WS2 .... 28 A6
Hatherton Pl WS9 .... 30 A7
Hatherton Rd Bilston WV14 .. 40 F6
Cannock WS11 .... 1 C1
Walsall WS1 .... 28 E2
Hatherton St Cheslyn Hay
WS6 .... 4 C2
Walsall WS1, WS4 .... 28 E3
Hattersley Gr B11 .... 88 A3
Hatton Cres WV10 .... 26 A7
Hatton Gdns B42 .... 55 D8
Hatton Rd Cannock WS11 .... 1 A1
Wolverhampton WV6 .... 24 F3
Hatton St WV14 .... 40 E4
Hattons Gr WV8 .... 10 B2
Haughton Rd B20 .... 55 D1
Haunch La B13 .... 105 A5
Haunchwood Dr CV6 .... 57 F7
Haunchwood Rd CV10 .... 72 D4
Havacre La WV14 .... 40 C1
Havefield Ave WS14 .... 9 E7
Havelock Cl WV3 .... 38 F8
Havelock Rd
Birmingham,
Handsworth B20 .... 55 C1
Birmingham, Saltley B8 .... 67 D5
Birmingham, Sparkhill B11 ... 87 E4
Haven Croft B43 .... 54 D8
Haven Dr B27 .... 88 B3
Haven The Birmingham B14 .. 105 D4
Stourbridge DY8 .... 60 D2
Wolverhampton WV2 .... 163 B1
Havendale Cl CV6 .... 113 B5
Haverford Dr B45 .... 122 B6
Havergal Wlk B63 .... 82 B4
Haverhill Cl WS3 .... 14 A3
Hawbridge Cl B90 .... 127 B6
Hawbush Gdns DY5 .... 61 A1
Hawbush Prim Sch DY5 .... 61 B2
Hawbush Rd Brierley Hill DY5 61 A2
Walsall WS3 .... 28 E6
Hawcroft Gr B34 .... 69 C6
Hawes La B65 .... 63 B3
Hawes Rd WS1 .... 42 F6
Haweswater Dr DY6 .... 60 D6
Hawfield Cl B69 .... 63 C7
Hawfield Gr B72 .... 57 C7
Hawfield Rd B69 .... 63 C7
Hawfinch B77 .... 36 A5
Hawfinch Rise DY10 .... 117 A2
Hawford Ave DY10 .... 117 B6
Hawk Cl CV11 .... 79 B8
Hawker Dr B35 .... 57 F2
Hawker Ho B35 .... 58 B3
Hawkes Cl B30 .... 104 A7
Hawkes Dr CV34 .... 161 D4

Hawkes La B70 .... 53 A7
Hawkes Mill La CV5 .... 94 B2
Hawkes St B10 .... 87 D8
Hawkesbury Cl B98 .... 154 D5
Hawkesbury Fields Sch
CV2 .... 96 C3
Hawkesbury La CV2 .... 96 D5
Hawkesbury Rd B90 .... 105 F1
Hawkesford Cl
Birmingham B36 .... 69 A8
Sutton Coldfield B74 .... 32 B1
Hawkesford Rd B33 .... 69 D3
Hawkesley CE Inf Sch
B38 .... 123 E7
Hawkesley CE Jun Sch
B38 .... 123 E7
Hawkesley Cres B31 .... 103 A1
Hawkesley Dr B31 .... 122 F8
Hawkesley End B38 .... 123 E7
Hawkesley Mill La B31 .... 102 F2
Hawkesley Rd DY1 .... 61 F8
Hawkesmoor Dr
Lichfield WS14 .... 9 D8
Perton WV6 .... 23 D3
Hawkestone Cres B70 .... 53 A6
Hawkestone Rd B29 .... 103 A4
Hawkesville Dr WS11 .... 1 F2
Hawkeswell Cl B92 .... 106 E8
Hawkesworth Dr CV8 .... 148 A6
Hawkesyard Rd B24 .... 56 E1
Hawkhurst Rd B14 .... 104 F2
Hawkin's Pl WV14 .... 40 F3
Hawkinge Dr B35 .... 58 A4
Hawkins Cl Birmingham B5 .. 86 E6
Hinckley LE10 .... 71 D4
Lichfield WS13 .... 3 B2
Hawkins Croft DY4 .... 52 A3
Hawkins Dr WS11 .... 4 C4
Hawkins Rd CV5 .... 113 A2
Hawkins St B70 .... 53 A8
Hawkley Cl WV1 .... 26 B2
Hawkley Rd WV1 .... 26 B2
Hawkmoor Gdns B38 .... 124 A8
Hawks Cl WS6 .... 4 D2
Hawks Green La WS11 .... 2 A2
Hawksford Cres WV10 .... 25 E7
Hawkshead Dr B93 .... 127 F6
Hawkside B77 .... 36 B8
Hawksmill Ind Est B9 .... 67 C1
Hawkstone Cl DY11 .... 116 D8
Hawkstone Ct WV6 .... 23 D5
Hawkswell Ave WV5 .... 49 A5
Hawkswell Dr WV13 .... 40 F8
Hawkswood Dr CV7 .... 130 B7
Hawkswood Gr B14 .... 105 B3
Hawksworth B77 .... 21 F2
Hawksworth Dr 1 CV1 .... 113 B3
Hawkyard Ct WS11 .... 2 A4
Hawley Rd LE10 .... 75 D7
Hawnby Gr B76 .... 47 A2
Hawne Cl B63 .... 82 E6
Hawne La B63 .... 82 F6
Hawnelands The B63 .... 82 F5
Hawskford Cres WV10 .... 25 D7
Hawthorn Brook Way B23 .. 56 E8
Hawthorn Cl
Birmingham, Erdington B23 .. 56 F7
Birmingham, Spring Vale B9 ... 67 B1
Lichfield WS13 .... 9 D8
Hawthorn Coppice DY9 .... 99 A6
Hawthorn Cres LE10 .... 75 E4
Hawthorn Croft B68 .... 84 D7
Hawthorn Ct CV4 .... 111 E1
Hawthorn Gr 9
Birmingham B19 .... 66 C8
Kidderminster DY11 .... 116 A6
Hawthorn Jun & Inf Sch
B44 .... 56 A7
Hawthorn La CV4 .... 111 E1
Hawthorn Park Dr 1 B20 .. 54 F3
Hawthorn Pk B20 .... 54 E3
Hawthorn Pl WS2 .... 27 E3
Hawthorn Rd Aldridge B74 .... 31 A1
Bilston WV1 .... 40 B8
Birmingham B44 .... 56 A7
Brierley Hill DY5 .... 81 E8
Bromsgrove B61 .... 137 B4
Redditch B97 .... 153 A3
Royal Leamington Spa CV31 . 161 F6
Tipton DY4 .... 52 B8
Walsall, Bescot WS5 .... 42 F5
Walsall, Shelfield WS4 .... 29 B8
Wednesbury WS10 .... 41 F4
Wylde Green B72 .... 46 C1
Hawthorn Terr WS10 .... 41 F4
Hawthorn Way CV10 .... 72 A8
Hawthornden Ct B72 .... 57 D7
Hawthorne Ave B79 .... 21 B8
Hawthorne Cres WS7 .... 7 A6
Hawthorne Dr B47 .... 125 B6
Hawthorne Gr DY3 .... 50 D2
Hawthorne Ho WV10 .... 25 F3
Hawthorne Rd
Birmingham,
Castle Bromwich B36 .... 69 F7
Birmingham, Edgbaston B15 ... 85 E7
Birmingham,
King's Norton B30 .... 103 D5
Cannock WS12 .... 2 F3
Cheslyn Hay WS6 .... 4 C1
Dudley DY1 .... 51 C4
Essington WV11 .... 13 A3
Halesowen B63 .... 82 E2
Huntington WS12 .... 1 D8
Wednesfield WV11 .... 27 A5
Willenhall WV12 .... 27 D7
Wolverhampton WV2 .... 39 D6

Hawthorne Terr CV10 .... 72 F5
Hawthorns Sta The B71 .... 65 B8
Hawthorns The
Birmingham B13 .... 86 F3
1 Kidderminster DY10 ...... 117 A5
Oldbury B68 .... 84 D7
West Bromwich B21 .... 54 B1
Wolverhampton WV11 .... 26 B6
Haxby Ave B34 .... 69 A6
Hay Cl DY11 .... 116 C7
Hay Gn DY9 .... 81 D5
Hay Green Cl B30 .... 103 D6
Hay Green La B30 .... 103 D6
Hay Hall Rd B11 .... 87 F5
Hay Hill WS5 .... 43 E8
Hay La Coventry CV1 .... 165 C2
Solihull B90 .... 127 A6
Hay Pk B5 .... 86 D6
Hay Rd B25 .... 88 A7
Hay Wood La B93, CV35 ...... 145 A1
Haybarn The B76 .... 58 A8
Haybridge Ave DY8 .... 98 F5
Haybridge High Sch DY8 .... 98 F6
Haybrook Dr B11 .... 87 F4
Haycock Pl WS10 .... 41 C8
Haycroft Ave B8 .... 67 E5
Haycroft Dr B74 .... 32 A4
Haydn Sanders Sq 7 WS1 .. 42 E8
Haydock Cl Birmingham B36 .. 68 C8
Coventry CV6 .... 96 B4
Wolverhampton W6 .... 25 B5
Haydon Cl B93 .... 127 F2
Haydon Croft B33 .... 69 A3
Haydon Way B47 .... 159 F1
Haye House Gr B36 .... 68 E7
Hayes Cres B68 .... 64 D5
Hayes Croft B38 .... 123 F7
Hayes Gr B24 .... 57 D6
Hayes Green Rd CV12 .... 95 F8
Hayes La Bedworth CV7 .... 96 A8
Stourbridge DY9 .... 82 A6
Hayes Mdw B72 .... 57 D7
Hayes Rd Nuneaton CV10 ...... 72 A8
Oldbury B68 .... 64 D5
Hayes St B70 .... 53 A8
Hayes The Birmingham B31 .. 123 C7
Stourbridge DY9 .... 82 A5
Willenhall WV12 .... 27 B6
Hayes Trad Est DY9 .... 82 A6
Hayes View Dr WS6 .... 4 E4
Hayes Way WS11, WS12 .... 2 C1
Hayfield Cl B13 .... 87 B2
Hayfield Gdns B13 .... 87 C2
Hayfield Rd B13 .... 87 B2
Hayford Cl B98 .... 154 A5
Hayland Rd B23 .... 56 E6
Hayle B77 .... 21 D2
Hayle Ave CV34 .... 155 F1
Hayle Cl Birmingham B38 .... 104 B2
Nuneaton CV11 .... 74 A5
Hayley Ct B24 .... 57 C6
Hayley Green Rd B32 .... 102 B8
Hayley Park Rd B63 .... 100 C8
Hayling Cl B45 .... 101 F1
Hayling Gr WV2 .... 39 B6
Hayloft Cl B60 .... 150 E6
Haylofts The B63 .... 82 C1
Haymarket The WV8 .... 10 E1
Haymoor WS14 .... 9 E7
Haynes Cl B61 .... 137 B8
Haynes La WS5 .... 43 B4
Haynestone Rd CV6 .... 112 E6
Haypits Cl B71 .... 53 E7
Hayrick Dr DY6 .... 60 B7
Hays Kent's Moat The B26 . 69 A1
Hays La LE10 .... 75 B7
Hayseech B64 .... 83 A7
Hayseech Rd B63 .... 82 F6
Hayton Gn CV4 .... 131 F8
Haytor Ave B14 .... 104 D5
Haytor Rise CV2 .... 114 C7
Haywain Cl WV9 .... 10 F2
Hayward Rd B75 .... 46 C7
Hayward St WV14 .... 51 B8
Hayward's Gn CV6 .... 113 A7
Haywards Cl Birmingham
B23 .... 56 E5
Walsall WS3 .... 14 F3
Haywharf Rd DY5 .... 61 B5
Haywood Dr Halesowen B62 . 83 C8
Wolverhampton WV6 .... 24 D4
Haywood Rd B33 .... 69 E2
Haywood's Farm B71 .... 42 F2
Hayworth Cl B79 .... 20 F8
Hayworth Rd WS13 .... 3 C2
Hazel Ave Birmingham B73 .. 45 C1
Wednesbury WS10 .... 42 A4
Hazel Cl Nuneaton CV10 ...... 72 A8
Royal Leamington Spa
CV32 .... 157 A2
Hazel Croft
Birmingham,
Chelmsley Wood B37 .... 70 B1
Birmingham,
Northfield B31 .... 103 A3
Hazel Dr B47 .... 125 B5
Hazel Gdns Birmingham B27 .. 88 C5
Codsall WV8 .... 10 A4
Hazel Gr Bedworth CV12 ...... 78 D3
Bilston WV14 .... 40 E7
Lichfield WS14 .... 9 C7
Stourbridge DY8 .... 80 C3
Tanworth-in-A B94 .... 143 C6
West Bromwich B70 .... 53 C1
Wolverhampton WV5 .... 49 A7
Wombourne WV5 .... 49 A7
Hazel La WS6 .... 5 B2
Hazel Oak Sch B90 .... 106 A2

Hazel Rd Birmingham B45 .... 121 F6
Coventry CV6 .... 96 B1
Dudley DY1 .... 51 C2
Kingswinford DY6 .... 60 E5
Nuneaton CV10 .... 72 D5
Redditch B97 .... 153 C5
Tipton DY4 .... 41 D1
Wolverhampton WV3 .... 38 E7
Hazelbank B38 .... 103 E2
Hazelbeach Rd B8 .... 67 F5
Hazelbeech Rd B70 .... 53 B3
Hazeldene Gr 5 B6 .... 66 E8
Hazeldene Rd
Birmingham B33 .... 89 D7
Halesowen B63 .... 82 E2
Hazeley Cl B17 .... 85 A7
Hazelgarth B77 .... 36 B8
Hazelhead St Georges
(Ind Est) CV1 .... 113 F2
Hazelhurst Rd
Birmingham,
Castle Bromwich B36 .... 69 C7
Birmingham,
King's Heath B14 .... 104 E7
Hazell Way CV10 .... 73 A1
Hazelmead Ct B73 .... 57 A7
Hazelmere Ct B69 .... 63 D8
Hazelmere Dr WS7 .... 6 F4
Hazelmere Rd B28 .... 105 F8
Hazeloak Rd B90 .... 106 A2
Hazelton Cl Marlbrook B61 .. 137 C8
1 Solihull B91 .... 107 B1
Hazelton Rd B61 .... 121 C1
Hazeltree Croft B27 .... 88 B2
Hazeltree Gr B93 .... 127 E3
Hazelville Gr B28 .... 106 A6
Hazelville Rd B28 .... 106 A7
Hazelwell Cres B30 .... 104 B6
Hazelwell Fordrough B30 . 104 B6
Hazelwell La B30 .... 104 B7
Hazelwell Rd B30 .... 104 A6
Hazelwell St B30 .... 104 A7
Hazelwood Cl
Cheslyn Hay WS6 .... 4 D2
Kidderminster DY11 .... 116 B4
Hazelwood Dr WV11 .... 26 A5
Hazelwood Gr Cannock WS11 . 4 C8
Willenhall WV12 .... 27 D5
Hazelwood Rd Aldridge B74 .. 30 D1
Birmingham B27 .... 88 B2
Hazlemere Cl CV5 .... 112 B4
Hazlemere Dr B74 .... 32 B1
Hazlemere Gr WS11 .... 4 B8
Hazlewood Rd DY1 .... 50 F5
Hazlitt Gr B30 .... 103 D4
Headborough Rd CV2 .... 114 A5
Headborough Wlk WS9 .... 16 B1
Headingley Rd B21 .... 54 E2
Headington Ave CV6 .... 95 A2
Headland Dr B8 .... 67 D5
Headland Rd WV3 .... 24 A1
Headlands The
Coventry CV5 .... 112 D4
Little Aston B74 .... 31 C3
Headless Cross Dr B97 ...... 153 D1
Headley Croft B38 .... 123 D8
Headley Heath La B38 ...... 124 B6
Headley Rise B90 .... 106 D2
Heale Cl B63 .... 82 A7
Healey B77 .... 21 E2
Healey Ct CV34 .... 160 F7
Health Centre Rd CV8 .... 132 C4
Heanor Croft B6 .... 67 B8
Heantun Croft WV10 .... 26 A5
Heantun Ct WV3 .... 25 B1
Heantun Ho WV3 .... 163 B2
Heantun Lodge WV14 .... 40 C6
Heantun Mill Ct WS10 .... 41 D1
Heantun Rise WV3 .... 25 C4
Heantun Row WV11 .... 13 B2
Hearsall Com Prim Sch
CV5 .... 112 F2
Hearsall Comm CV5 .... 112 F2
Hearsall Ct CV4 .... 112 D2
Hearsall Golf Course CV5 . 132 E7
Hearsall La CV5 .... 112 F2
Heart of England Sch CV7 130 C6
Heart of England Way
CV11 .... 73 F3
Heartland Mews B65 .... 63 B2
Heartlands High Sch B7 .... 67 B4
Heartlands Pl B8 .... 67 E4
Heath Acres WS10 .... 41 C4
Heath Ave CV12 .... 77 E1
Heath Bridge Cl WS4 .... 29 A8
Heath Cl Birmingham B30 ... 103 D5
Bromsgrove B60 .... 150 E6
Stonnall WS9 .... 16 E5
Tipton DY4 .... 52 B5
Heath Cres CV2 .... 114 A6
Heath Croft B31 .... 123 A7
Heath Croft B75 .... 32 D1
Heath Ct 2 B12 .... 86 F5
Heath End Rd
Belbroughton DY9 .... 120 D7
Nuneaton CV10 .... 72 F2
Heath Farm Rd Codsall
WV8 .... 10 B2
Stourbridge DY8 .... 80 E3
Heath Gap Rd WS11 .... 1 F3
Heath Gdns B91 .... 107 B6
Heath Gn DY1 .... 50 F5
Heath Gn Wy WS8 .... 10 B3
Heath Green Gr 4 B18 .... 65 E4
Heath Green Rd B18 .... 65 E4
Heath Hayes Cty Prim Sch
WS12 .... 2 E1
Heath Hays Prim Sch WS12 . 2 F1

Heath Hill Rd WV6 .... 23 E1
Heath Ho B14 .... 104 F2
Heath House La WV8 .... 23 E8
Heath La
Kidderminster DY10 .... 117 C1
Stourbridge DY8 .... 81 A4
West Bromwich B71 .... 53 D7
Heath Lane Hospl B71 ...... 53 D7
Heath Mill La B9 .... 67 A1
Heath Park High Sch
WV11 .... 26 A5
Heath Rd Bedworth CV12 ..... 77 F1
Birmingham B30 .... 103 D5
Coventry CV2 .... 114 A4
Darlaston WS10 .... 41 E8
Dudley DY2 .... 62 C2
Hollywood B47 .... 125 A7
Solihull B91 .... 107 A6
Willenhall WV12 .... 13 C1
Heath Rd S B31 .... 103 B4
Heath Rise B14 .... 105 A1
Heath St Birmingham B18 .. 65 E4
Blackheath B65 .... 63 C1
Cannock WS12 .... 2 B7
Stourbridge DY8 .... 80 F4
Tamworth B79 .... 21 C5
Heath St S B18 .... 65 F4
Heath Terr Beausale CV35 .. 146 C2
Royal Leamington Spa CV32 . 156 E2
Heath Trad Pk B66 .... 65 D5
Heath View Cannock WS12 ... 5 E8
Walsall WS2 .... 27 F3
Heath Way Birmingham B34 .. 69 B6
Cannock WS11 .... 2 B2
Heath-Mount Jun & Inf Sch
B12 .... 86 F6
Heathbank Dr WS12 .... 1 C6
Heathbrook Ave DY6 .... 60 B7
Heathcliff Rd Birmingham
B11 .... 87 F4
Dudley DY2 .... 62 F7
Heathcote Ave B91 .... 106 E3
Heathcote Ct CV6 .... 113 A7
Heathcote Ho B11 .... 85 C5
Heathcote Ind Est CV34 ... 161 D5
Heathcote La
Royal Leamington Spa
CV34 .... 161 D4
Warwick CV34 .... 161 A5
Heathcote Rd
Birmingham B30 .... 104 A5
Whitnash CV31 .... 162 A4
Heathcote St CV6 .... 113 A7
Heathcote Way CV34 .... 161 D4
Heather Ave WS5 .... 43 B4
Heather Cl Birmingham B36 .. 70 A8
Nuneaton CV10 .... 72 F3
Walsall WS3 .... 28 A8
Wednesfield WV11 .... 26 E5
Heather Court Gdns B74 .. 46 A8
Heather Croft B44 .... 44 F1
Heather Ct B13 .... 86 D3
Heather Dale B13 .... 86 C2
Heather Dr Bedworth CV12 .. 77 E2
Birmingham B45 .... 121 F6
Huntington WS12 .... 1 D5
Heather Gr Solihull B91 ... 107 E6
Willenhall WV12 .... 27 E6
Heather Ho B38 .... 103 F1
Heather Mews WS12 .... 2 A8
Heather Rd
Binley Woods CV3 .... 135 D7
Birmingham, Great Barr B43 .. 54 D8
Birmingham,
Small Heath B10 .... 87 F8
Cannock WS12 .... 2 A8
Coventry CV2 .... 96 C2
Dudley DY1 .... 51 C4
Smethwick B67 .... 65 A5
Walsall WS3 .... 28 A8
Heather Valley WS12 .... 2 D6
Heatherleigh Rd B36 .... 69 F8
Heathfield Ave B20 .... 66 B8
Heathfield Cl Blackheath
B64 .... 62 F2
Knowle B93 .... 128 A5
Heathfield Cres DY11 .... 116 B4
Heathfield Ct 1 B19 ...... 66 B7
Heathfield Dr WS3 .... 14 B2
Heathfield Gdns DY8 .... 80 F4
Heathfield Inf & Jun Sch
B19 .... 66 C8
Heathfield La B10 .... 41 C6
Heathfield La W WS10 .... 41 B6
Heathfield Rd
Birmingham,
King's Heath B14 .... 104 F8
Birmingham, Lozells B19 ... 66 C8
Coventry CV5 .... 112 C2
Halesowen B63 .... 82 E3
Redditch B97 .... 153 A1
Sutton Coldfield B74 .... 31 F3
Heathfield Sch B74 .... 31 F3
Heathfield Way B64 .... 62 F1
Heathfields Cty Inf Sch
B77 .... 35 F6
Heathgreen Cl B37 .... 70 D3
Heathland Ave B34 .... 69 A7
Heathland Cl WS12 .... 2 D2
Heathlands DY6 .... 60 E8
Heathlands Cres B73 .... 45 F1
Heathlands Gr B31 .... 103 A1
Heathlands Jun & Inf Sch
B34 .... 68 F7
Heathlands Rd B73 .... 45 F1

Heathlands The
2 Blackheath B65 63 C1
Stourbridge DY8 81 B4
Heathleigh Rd B38 123 C8
Heathley La B78 34 E5
Heathmere Ave B25 88 D8
Heathmere Dr B37 69 F2
Heathside Dr
Birmingham B38 104 B2
4 Walsall WS3 15 A4
Heathy Farm Cl B32 84 B1
Heathy Rise B32 84 A2
Heaton Cl WV10 11 E5
Heaton Dr Birmingham B15 85 E8
Sutton Coldfield B73 45 F8
Heaton Rd B91 107 A7
Heaton St B18 66 B5
Hebden B77 36 B8
Hebden Ave CV34 155 F1
Hebden Gr Birmingham B28 105 E3
Willenhall WV12 13 B1
Hebden Way CV11 74 A2
Heckley Rd CV7 96 A7
Heddle Gr CV6 114 B8
Heddon Pl B7 67 A3
Hedera Cl WS5 43 B3
Hedgefield Gr B63 82 C4
Hedgerow Cl WS12 1 F7
Hedgerow Dr DY6 49 D1
Hedgerow Wlk Coventry CV6 95 B4
Wolverhampton WV8 10 E1
Hedgerows The Lichfield WS14 9 B5
Nuneaton CV10 72 F6
Romsley B62 100 F4
Hedges Way B60 137 B1
Hedgetree Croft B37 70 C2
Hedging La B77 35 E5
Hedging Lane Ind Est B77 35 E5
Hedgings The B34 69 B6
Hedgley Gr B33 69 A4
Hedingham Gr B37 70 D2
Hedley Croft B35 58 B4
Hednesford Rd
Brownhills WS8 6 C2
Cannock, Blackfords WS11 1 F2
Cannock, Heath Hayes WS12 2 E1
Norton Canes WS11 5 F7
Hednesford St WS11 1 E1
Hednesford Sta WS12 2 B5
Heeley Rd B29 85 F1
Heemstede La CV32 157 A2
Heera Cl CV6 113 D8
Hele Rd CV3 133 D6
Helen St CV6 113 F6
Helena Cl CV10 72 F3
Helena St 3 B1 66 C3
Helenny Cl WV11 26 A5
Helford Cl DY4 51 D4
Heligan Pl WS12 2 D2
Hellaby Cl B72 46 C4
Hellaby Ct B73 57 A7
Hellidon Cl 5 CV32 157 A2
Hellier Ave DY4 52 B4
Hellier Rd WV10 11 E2
Hellier St DY2 62 C8
Helming Dr WV1 26 B3
Helmingham B79 20 D7
Helmsdale Rd CV32 157 B5
Helmsdale Way DY3 51 A7
Helmsley Cl DY5 81 C8
Helmsley Rd WV11 26 C8
Helmswood Dr B37 90 C8
Helston Cl Nuneaton CV11 74 A5
Stourbridge DY8 60 C2
Tamworth B79 21 C8
Walsall WS5 43 D7
Helston Rd WS5 43 D7
Helstone Gr B11 88 A3
Hembs Cres B43 54 C8
Hemdale CV11 74 A4
Heming Rd B98 159 E8
Hemingford Rd CV2 115 A8
Hemlingford Croft B37 90 A7
Hemlingford Rd
Birmingham B37 69 F6
Sutton Coldfield B76 58 A6
Hemlock Way WS11 2 B3
Hemming St DY11 116 C4
Hemmings Cl
Radford Semele CV31 162 E5
2 Stourbridge DY8 80 F5
Wolverhampton WV10 25 E3
Hemmings St WS10 41 C8
Hemplands Rd 9 DY8 80 F5
Hempole La DY4 52 D6
Hemsby Cl CV4 132 A7
Hemsworth Dr CV12 79 B2
Hemyock Rd B29 103 B8
Hen La CV6 95 D3
Henbury Rd B27 88 D3
Henderson Cl WS14 9 D7
Henderson Ct 7 B68 84 B8
Henderson Way B65 63 C1
Henderson Wlk DY4 52 B8
Hendon Cl Dudley DY3 50 D2
Wolverhampton WV10 25 E7
Hendon Rd B11 87 B5
Hendre Cl CV5 112 D2
Heneage Pl 10 B7 67 A4
Heneage St B7 67 A4
Heneage St W B7 66 F4
Henfield Cl WV11 26 D7
Hengham Rd B26 69 A1
Henley Cl Burntwood WS7 7 B5
Nuneaton CV11 73 F8
Sutton Coldfield B73 57 B8
Tamworth B79 21 C6
Tipton DY4 52 D5
Walsall WS3 14 E1
Henley Coll CV2 114 C8
Henley Cres B91 107 B7
Henley Ct Coventry CV2 114 D7
Lichfield WS14 9 B6
Henley Dr B75 32 A3
Henley Mill La CV2 114 C7
Henley Park Ind Est CV2 114 E7
Henley Rd Coventry CV2 114 D7
Royal Leamington Spa CV31 162 B5
Wolverhampton WV10 11 B1
Henley St B11 87 B7
Henleydale 4 B90 126 C8
Henlow Cl DY4 51 D5
Henlow Rd B14 105 A2
Henn Dr DY4 40 E1
Henn St DY4 52 A8
Hennalls The B36 68 F7
Hennals Ave B97 152 F2
Henne Dr WV14 40 C1
Henrietta St
Birmingham B19 164 B4
Coventry CV6 113 E5
Henry Bellairs CE Mid Sch CV12 78 D3
Henry Boteler Rd CV4 132 B7
Henry Boys' Almshouses WS1 42 D8
Henry Rd B25 88 C7
Henry St Coventry CV1 165 B3
Hinckley LE10 71 A2
Kenilworth CV8 148 A5
Nuneaton CV11 73 C2
Walsall WS2 28 D1
Henry Tanday Ct 4 CV32 156 E1
Henry Wlk B60 150 E7
Hensel Dr WV3 38 C8
Henshaw Gr B25 88 C7
Henshaw Rd B10 87 D8
Henson Rd CV12 77 E1
Henstead St B5 86 D8
Hentland Cl B98 154 D4
Henwood Cl WV6 24 D3
Henwood La B91 108 B4
Henwood Rd WV6 24 D3
Hepburn Cl WS9 30 A4
Hepburn Edge B24 57 B4
Hepworth Cl WV6 23 F4
Hepworth Rd CV3 115 B1
Herald Bsns Pk CV3 134 F7
Herald Ct 2 DY1 51 C1
Herald Way Coventry CV3 135 A7
Hinckley LE10 75 D4
Heralds Ct 4 CV34 161 B8
Herbert Art Gall & Mus CV1 165 C2
Herbert Rd Aldridge WS9 16 A1
Birmingham, Handsworth B21 54 F1
Birmingham, Small Heath B10 87 C8
Smethwick B67 65 A1
Solihull B91 107 B4
Herbert St Bilston WV14 40 B6
Nuneaton CV10 72 E3
Redditch B98 153 E4
West Bromwich B70 53 D3
Wolverhampton WV1 163 C4
Herbert's La CV8 148 A5
Herberts Park Rd WS10 41 B6
Herbhill Cl WV4 39 D4
Hercules Ho B35 58 B3
Hereford Ave 5 B12 87 A6
Hereford Cl Aldridge WS9 30 A8
Barwell LE9 71 F6
Birmingham B45 102 A2
Kidderminster DY11 116 A5
Hereford Ho WV1 163 B4
Hereford Pl B71 53 B7
Hereford Rd Bramcote CV11 79 F6
Cannock WS12 2 B4
Dudley DY2 62 E3
Oldbury B68 84 B7
Hereford Sq B8 67 C5
Hereford St WS2 28 E4
Hereford Way B78 21 A2
Hereford Wlk B37 69 F1
Hereward Coll of FE CV4 111 F1
Hereward Rise B62 83 C5
Herford Way LE10 75 F6
Heritage Cl B68 64 C4
Heritage Ct Coventry CV4 132 D3
Lichfield WS14 9 D6
Heritage The 6 WS1 28 E1
Hermes Cl CV34 161 E5
Hermes Cres CV2 114 E6
Hermes Ct B74 31 F3
Hermes Ho B35 58 A4
Hermes Rd WS13 3 D1
Hermit St DY3 50 D5
Hermit's Croft CV3 133 D8
Hermitage Dr B76 47 A4
Hermitage La B78 22 E1
Hermitage Rd
Birmingham, Edgbaston B15 85 C8
Birmingham, Gravelly Hill B23 56 E3
Coventry CV2 114 D4
Solihull B91 107 C6
Hermitage The B91 107 C5
Hermitage Way CV8 148 A3
Hern Rd DY5 81 C6
Hernall Croft B26 89 A7
Herne Cl B18 66 A4
Hernefield Rd B34 69 A7
Hernehurst B32 84 C6
Heron Cl Alvechurch B48 139 A7
Cheswick Green B90 126 D4
Heron Ct 3 B73 57 B7
Heron Ho CV3 114 B2
Heron Rd B68 64 A2
Heron Way B45 121 F7
Herondale WS12 2 B4
Herondale Cres DY8 80 C4
Herondale Rd
Birmingham B26 88 F6
Stourbridge DY8 80 C4
Heronfield Cl B98 154 C5
Heronfield Dr B31 122 F6
Heronfield Way B91 107 E5
Heronry The WV6 23 F2
Herons Way B29 85 C3
Heronsville Ho DY4 52 B3
Heronswood Dr DY5 61 D1
Heronswood Rd
Birmingham B45 122 B6
Kidderminster DY10 117 A2
Heronville Dr B70 53 A7
Heronville Rd B70 53 A6
Herrick Rd Birmingham B8 67 E5
Coventry CV2 114 D3
Herrick St WV3 163 A2
Herringshaw Croft B76 46 E3
Hertford Cl CV10 72 E4
Hertford Pl CV1 165 A2
Hertford St Birmingham B12 87 A5
Coventry CV1 165 B2
Hertford Way B93 128 B4
Hervey Gr B24 57 D6
Hesket Ave B68 64 C1
Hesketh Cres B23 56 C5
Hesketh Pl B37 89 F8
Hesleden B77 36 B8
Heslop Cl CV3 134 F8
Hessian Cl WV14 40 B2
Hestia Dr B29 103 E8
Heston Ave B42 55 B8
Hetton Cl 1 CV34 155 F1
Hever Ave B44 45 A1
Hever Cl DY1 50 E3
Hewell Ave B60 150 F7
Hewell Cl Birmingham B31 122 F7
Kingswinford DY6 49 D1
Redditch B97 152 C6
Hewell La Barnt Green B45 138 D8
Redditch B97 152 D6
Hewell Rd Barnt Green B45 138 D8
Redditch B97 153 D4
Hewitson Gdns B67 64 F2
Hewitt Ave CV6 113 B4
Hewitt Cl WS13 3 A2
Hewitt St WS10 41 C5
Hewston Croft WS12 2 D4
Hexby Cl CV2 115 A6
Hexham Way DY1 50 F2
Hexton Cl B90 105 D2
Hexworthy Ave CV3 133 B5
Heybarnes Rd B10 88 A8
Heybrook Cl CV2 114 C7
Heycott Gr B38 104 C2
Heycroft CV4 132 D4
Heydon Rd Brierley Hill DY5 61 B6
Finstall B60 137 D1
Heyford Gr B91 127 C8
Heyford Way B35 58 B5
Heygate Way WS9 16 B1
Heyland Cnr B10 67 F1
Heynesfield Rd B33 69 C3
Heythrop Gr B13 105 D8
Heyville Croft CV8 148 C3
Heywood Cl CV6 114 A7
Hibberd Ct CV8 147 F4
Hickman Ave WV1, WV2 40 A8
Hickman Gdns B16 65 F1
Hickman Rd Bilston WV14 40 C5
Birmingham B11 87 B6
Brierley Hill DY5 61 C4
Tipton DY4 51 F8
Hickman St DY9 81 C6
Hickman's Ave B64 62 E2
Hickmans Cl 2 B62 84 A6
Hickmerelands La DY3 39 C1
Hickory Ct WS11 2 C2
Hickory Dr B17 65 A2
Hicks Cl CV34 155 E2
Hidcote Ave B76 58 A8
Hidcote Cl Nuneaton CV11 78 F8
Royal Leamington Spa CV31 162 C5
Hidcote Gr
Birmingham, Garret's Green B33 89 C8
Birmingham, Marston Green B37 90 A7
Hidcote Rd CV8 148 C6
Hidson Rd B23 56 C5
Higgins Ave WV14 40 D2
Higgins La B32 84 C5
Higgins Wlk B66 65 B6
Higgs Field Cres B64 63 B1
Higgs Rd WV11 13 A1
High Arcal Dr DY3 50 F6
High Arcal Rd DY3 49 F4
High Arcal Sch DY3 50 F6
High Ash Cl CV7 95 F7
High Ave B64 82 F8
High Bank WS11 4 E8
High Beech CV5 112 A6
High Beeches B43 43 D1
High Brink Rd B46 70 F7
High Brow B17 85 B7
High Bullen WS10 41 F3
High Clere B64 83 A7
High Croft Aldridge WS9 16 B2
Birmingham B43 43 C1
High Elms La B60 151 E1
High Ercal Ave DY5 61 C2
High Farm Rd
Halesowen, Hasbury B63 82 F3
Halesowen, Hurst Green B62 83 F8
High Gn WS11 1 D1
High Grange WS11 2 A5
High Haden Cres B64 83 A8
High Haden Rd B64 83 A8
High Heath Cl B30 103 D5
High Hill WV11 13 A2
High Holborn DY3 50 D7
High House Dr B45 121 F3
High House La B60 152 A6
High Land Rd WS9 16 B3
High Leasowes B63 83 A4
High Mdws Stoke Heath B60 150 D7
Wolverhampton WV6 24 C3
Wombourne WV5 49 B6
High Meadow Fst Sch B46 70 F8
High Meadow Rd B38 104 A2
High Mount St WS12 2 B6
High Oak DY5 61 C7
High Park Cl Coventry CV5 111 F3
Sedgley DY3 50 D8
Smethwick B66 65 B5
High Park Cnr B7 67 B6
High Park Cres DY3 39 D1
High Park Rd B63 82 C5
High Park St B7 67 B6
High Point B15 85 E6
High Rd WV12 27 C5
High Ridge WS9 29 F5
High Ridge Cl Aldridge WS9 29 E5
Bilston WS10 41 A4
High St Aldridge WS9 30 B6
Astwood Bank B96 158 E1
Bedworth CV12 78 B2
Belbroughton DY9 119 E7
Bilston WV14 40 D5
Bilston, Moxley WS10 41 A4
Birmingham B4 164 C2
Birmingham, Aston B6, B19 66 E7
Birmingham, Erdington B23 56 F4
Birmingham, Harborne B17 85 D6
Birmingham, King's Heath B14 104 E8
Birmingham, Quinton B32 84 A6
Birmingham, Saltley B8 67 D5
Blackheath, Cradley Heath B64 62 D1
Blackheath, Rowley Regis B65 63 C1
Brierley Hill, Barrow Hill DY5 61 C7
Brierley Hill, Brockmoor DY5 61 C4
Brierley Hill, Quarry Bank DY5 82 A8
Bromsgrove B61 137 A2
Brownhills WS8 15 F7
Brownhills, Walsall Wood WS9 15 F3
Burntwood, Chase Terrace WS7 6 E8
Burntwood, Chasetown WS7 6 F6
Cheslyn Hay WS6 4 D2
Clayhanger WS8 15 E6
Coleshill B46 70 F7
Coventry CV1 165 C2
Coventry, Keresley CV6 94 F1
Cubbington CV32 157 E5
2 Darlaston WS10 41 D6
Dudley DY1 51 C1
9 Dudley, Old Dock DY2 62 B8
1 Halesowen B63 83 B3
Hampton in A B92 109 A7
Kenilworth CV8 147 E5
Kidderminster DY10 116 E6
Kingswinford DY6 60 E6
Kingswinford, Wall Heath DY6 60 C8
Knowle B93 128 C6
Norton Canes WS11 6 B5
Nuneaton CV11 73 B4
Royal Leamington Spa CV31 162 A7
Ryton-on-D CV8 135 B1
Sedgley DY3 50 D8
Smethwick B66 65 A5
Solihull B91 107 C3
Solihull,Shirley B90 105 D2
Stourbridge DY8 81 A5
Stourbridge, Amblecote DY8 80 F7
Stourbridge, Lye DY9 81 E5
Stourbridge, Wordsley DY8 60 E2
Studley B80 159 E4
Sutton Coldfield B72 46 C5
Tamworth B77 35 C4
Tipton, Princes End DY4 51 F8
Tipton, Tipton Green DY4 51 E5
Walsall WS1 28 E1
Walsall, Pelsall WS3 15 A4
Walsall, Wallington Heath WS3 14 B1
Warwick CV34 160 E6
Wednesfield WV11 26 D5
West Bromwich B70 53 C3
Wolverhampton WV6 24 D4
Wombourne WV5 49 B7
High St Duchess Par B70 53 D3
High St Princess Par B70 53 D3
High Street Bordesley B12 67 A1
High Street Deritend B12 66 F1
High Timbers B45 101 F1
High Town Ragged Sch B63 82 C6
High Trees B20 54 F3
High Trees Cl B98 158 E7
High Trees Ho B69 63 F3
High Trees Rd B93 128 A7
High View WV14 39 F1
High View Dr CV7 95 C7
High View Rd CV32 157 C5
High Wood Cl DY6 60 C6
Higham La CV11 73 E7
Higham Lane Sch CV10 73 D6
Higham Way Hinckley LE10 75 E7
Wolverhampton WV10 25 E6
Higham Way Ho LE10 75 E7
Higham's Cl B65 63 B3
Highbridge Rd Dudley DY2 62 B3
Sutton Coldfield B73 46 A1
Highbrook Cl WV9 11 A2
Highbury Ave
Birmingham B21 65 F8
Blackheath B65 63 D3
Highbury Cl B65 63 D3
Highbury Gn CV10 72 C7
Highbury Rd
Birmingham B14 104 D8
Oldbury B68 64 B5
Smethwick B66 64 D7
Sutton Coldfield B74 31 C3
Highclare Sch B72 46 C1
Highcliffe Rd B77 35 D8
Highcrest Cl B31 123 A7
Highcroft WS3 15 B6
Highcroft Ave DY8 60 C3
Highcroft Cl B92 89 C2
Highcroft Cres Lichfield WS14 9 C7
Royal Leamington Spa CV32 156 C1
Highcroft Dr B74 31 E3
Highcroft Hospl B23 56 E4
Highcroft Rd B23 56 E3
Highdown Cres 3 B90 127 A6
Highdown Rd CV31 162 B6
Highfield CV7 92 C1
Highfield Ave Bilston WV14 40 E4
Burntwood WS7 7 B7
Redditch B97 158 D8
Tamworth B77 22 A5
Walsall WS4 29 C8
Wolverhampton WV10 12 A2
Highfield Cl
Birmingham B28 105 D5
1 Burntwood WS7 7 B7
Kenilworth CV8 147 E4
Highfield Cres
Blackheath B65 63 B1
Halesowen B63 82 D6
Wolverhampton WV11 26 B6
Highfield Ct Cannock WS11 2 B5
Sutton Coldfield B73 46 B1
Highfield Dr B73 56 F7
Highfield Gdns WS14 9 E6
Highfield Inf & Jun Sch B8 67 E5
Highfield La Birmingham B32 84 B4
Clent DY9 100 A3
Corley CV7 94 D8
1 Halesowen B63 83 A3
Highfield Mews B63 82 D6
Highfield Pl B14 105 D5
Highfield Rd
Birmingham, Edgbaston B15 86 A8
Birmingham, Moseley B13 87 B3
Birmingham, Newton B43 54 C7
Birmingham, Saltley B8 67 E5
Birmingham, Yardley Wood B14, B28 105 D5
Blackheath B65 63 B1
Bromsgrove B61 150 E8
Burntwood WS7 7 C7
Cannock WS12 2 E1
Coventry CV2 113 F4
Dudley DY2 51 E1
Halesowen B63 82 D5
Kidderminster DY10 117 A8
Nuneaton CV11 73 E2
Redditch B97 158 D8
Sedgley DY3 39 D1
Smethwick B67 65 A5
Stourbridge DY8 61 A2
Studley B80 159 D4
Tipton DY4 52 B8
Walsall WS3 15 A4
Highfield Rd N WS3 14 F5
Highfield Terr CV32 156 D1
Highfield Way WS9 16 B2
Highfields Bromsgrove B61 136 E1
Burntwood WS7 7 B7
Highfields Ct WV4 38 D6
Highfields Dr Dudley WV14 40 D3
Wombourne WV5 49 A5
Highfields Grange WS6 4 D1
Highfields Jun & Inf Sch B65 83 C8
Highfields Pk WS6 4 D1
Highfields Prim Sch
Burntwood WS7 7 C7
Dudley WV14 40 C2
Highfields Rd Burntwood WS7 6 F4
Dudley WV14 40 D3
Hinckley LE10 71 E1
Highfields Sec Sch WV4 38 C5
Highfields The WV6 24 A2
Highgate Aldridge B74 31 A1
Dudley DY3 50 E5
Highgate Ave Walsall WS1 42 F8
Wolverhampton WV4 38 D6

Highgate Cl Birmingham B12 86 F7
Kidderminster DY11 116 A4
Walsall WS1 42 F7
Highgate Ct 4 WS1 42 F8
Highgate Dr WS1 42 F7
Highgate Ho 1 B5 86 E8
Highgate Middleway B12 86 F7
Highgate Pl B12 87 A7
Highgate Prim Sch DY2 61 F6
Highgate Rd Birmingham B12 87 A6
Dudley DY2 61 F6
Walsall WS1 42 F7
Highgate Sq B12 86 F7
Highgate St Birmingham B12 86 F7
Blackheath B64 62 F2
Highgate Trad Est B11 87 A7
Highgrove Coventry CV4 131 F5
Wolverhampton WV6 24 C3
Highgrove Cl WV12 27 B7
Highgrove Pl DY1 50 F2
Highland Ho B62 83 C8
Highland Mews WV14 40 D1
Highland Rd
Birmingham, Erdington B23 56 F5
Birmingham, Great Barr B43 43 E3
Blackheath B64 62 E2
Cannock WS12 1 C4
Coventry CV5 112 F1
Dudley DY1 51 A3
Kenilworth CV8 148 C7
Royal Leamington Spa CV32 157 B4
Highland Ridge B62 83 E5
Highland Way B98 159 A7
Highlands Cl
Kidderminster DY11 116 A5
Warwick CV34 161 A8
Highlands Ct B90 126 E8
Highlands Rd Solihull B90 126 F8
Wolverhampton WV3 38 D8
Highley Cl
Kidderminster DY11 116 B2
Redditch B98 154 E4
Highmoor Cl Dudley WV14 40 D3
Willenhall WV12 27 B7
Highmoor Rd B65 63 B3
Highmore Dr B32 102 C8
Highpark Ave DY8 80 D5
Highter's Heath Inf & Jun Sch B14 105 B3
Highter's Heath La B14 105 A2
Highters Cl B14 105 B2
Highters Rd B14 105 A3
Hightown B63 82 C6
Hightree Cl B32 84 B1
Highview 9 WS1 42 F8
Highview Dr DY6 60 F4
Highview St DY2 51 E1
Highwaymans Croft CV4 132 D5
Highwood Ave B92 89 A1
Highwood Croft B38 103 D1
Hiker Gr 3 B37 70 D2
Hilary Cres DY1 51 B6
Hilary Dr Aldridge WS9 30 A5
Sutton Coldfield B76 47 A3
Wolverhampton WV3 38 D7
Hilary Gr B31 102 F4
Hilary Rd Coventry CV4 132 E6
Nuneaton CV10 72 F5
Hilden Rd B7 67 B4
Hilderic Cres DY1 61 F7
Hilderstone Rd B25 88 C6
Hildicks Cres WS3 28 F7
Hildicks Pl WS3 29 A7
Hill Ave WV4 39 F3
Hill Avenue Cty Prim Sch WV4 39 F3
Hill Bank DY9 81 F5
Hill Bank Dr B33 68 D4
Hill Bank Rd
Birmingham B38 104 A2
Halesowen B63 82 D6
Hill Cl Birmingham B31 103 C1
Royal Leamington Spa CV32 157 A3
Sedgley DY3 39 E1
Hill Crest Cubbington CV32 157 E5
Dudley DY3 50 C4
Hill Crest Ave DY5 61 C2
Hill Crest Dr WS13 3 A1
Hill Crest Gr B44 56 A7
Hill Crest Hospl B98 159 C6
Hill Crest Rd Birmingham B13 86 E2
Dudley DY2 51 E1
Hill Croft Rd B14 104 C6
Hill Dr WS11 2 A3
Hill Farm Ave CV11 74 B1
Hill Farm Prim Sch CV6 113 B7
Hill Fray Dr CV3 134 A5
Hill Gr B20 55 C2
Hill Grove Cres DY10 117 A4
Hill Hook Ho B74 31 E5
Hill Hook Rd B74 31 F5
Hill House La B33 68 F3
Hill La Alvechurch B47, B48 124 D1
Birmingham B43 43 E2
Bromsgrove B60 136 F1
Clent DY9 99 E4
Middleton B75 33 B2
Hill Pas B64 62 E2
Hill Pk WS9 16 A4
Hill Pl WV11 13 A1
Hill Rd Keresley CV7 94 F6
Stourbridge DY9 81 E5
Tipton B69 52 A2
Willenhall WV13 26 E1
Hill Side Coventry CV2 114 A6
Dudley DY3 50 C4
Hill St Bedworth CV12 78 B5
Bilston WV14 40 E3
Birmingham B5 164 B2
Brierley Hill, Quarry Bank DY5 82 A8
Brierley Hill, Silver End DY5 61 D2
Burntwood WS7 6 E5
Cannock WS12 2 C3
Cheslyn Hay WS6 4 C2
Coventry CV1 165 B3
Darlaston WS10 41 E6
Dudley, Netherton DY2 62 C5
Dudley, Upper Gornal DY3 50 E5
Essington WV11 12 F3
Halesowen B63 83 A3
Hinckley LE10 75 E8
Kidderminster DY11 116 D6
Norton Canes WS11 5 F6
Nuneaton CV10 72 D4
Royal Leamington Spa CV32 157 A1
Smethwick B66 65 A6
Stourbridge, Amblecote DY8 80 F8
Stourbridge, Lye DY9 81 F5
Stourbridge, Wollaston DY8 80 F4
Tipton DY4 51 F4
Walsall WS1 28 F1
Warwick CV34 161 B8
Hill The B32 84 E2
Hill Top Coventry CV1 165 C3
Redditch B97 152 F1
West Bromwich B70 53 A7
Hill Top Ave Halesowen B62 83 E7
Tamworth B79 21 B8
Hill Top Cl B44 55 E6
Hill Top Ind Est B70 52 F8
Hill Top Rd Birmingham B31 102 F3
Oldbury B68 64 C2
Hill Top Wlk WS9 16 C1
Hill View WS9 16 B2
Hill Village Rd B75 32 A4
Hill West Jun & Inf Schs B74 31 F4
Hill Wood WS3 14 F2
Hill Wood Rd B75 32 C5
Hill Wootton Rd CV35 156 C6
Hillaire Cl B38 104 C2
Hillaries Rd B23 56 D2
Hillary Ave WS10 42 C3
Hillary Crest DY3 50 E5
Hillary Inf & Jun Schs WS2 42 C7
Hillary St WS2 42 C7
Hillbank B69 63 D8
Hillborough Rd B27 88 D2
Hillbrook Gr B33 68 F3
Hillbrow Cres B62 83 F8
Hillbury Dr WV12 27 B8
Hillcrest Ave Birmingham B43 43 E2
Halesowen B63 82 B7
Wolverhampton WV10 11 E1
Hillcrest Bsns Pk DY2 62 C7
Hillcrest Cl Dudley DY2 62 C5
Tamworth B79 21 B6
Hillcrest Gdns WV12 27 D5
Hillcrest Ind Est B64 82 D8
Hillcrest Rd Birmingham B43 43 E2
Dordon B78 36 F7
Nuneaton CV10 72 E5
Romsley B62 101 A4
Sutton Coldfield B72 46 C1
Hillcrest Rise WS7 7 B4
Hillcrest Sch B32 84 E3
Hillcrest Sch & Com Coll DY2 62 C5
Hillcroft Ho B14 104 F2
Hillcroft Rd DY6 60 E7
Hillcross Wlk B36 68 F8
Hilldene Rd DY6 60 C4
Hilldrop Gr B17 85 D3
Hilleys Croft B37 69 F2
Hillfield Mews 3 B91 127 B8
Hillfield Rd Birmingham B11 87 D3
Solihull B91 107 B1
Solihull B91 107 C2
Hillfield Wlk B65 62 F5
Hillfields B67 64 D3
Hillfields Ho 1 CV1 113 E3
Hillfields Rd DY5 81 B7
Hillgrove Gdns DY10 117 A4
Hillhurst Gr B36 58 D1
Hilliard Cl CV12 78 B4
Hilliards Croft B42 55 A8
Hillingford Ave B43 44 D3
Hillman B77 21 E2
Hillman Dr DY2 62 E7
Hillman Gr B36 58 F1
Hillman Ho CV1 165 B3
Hillmeads Dr DY2 62 F7
Hillmeads Rd B38 104 A1
Hillmorton B74 31 F3
Hillmorton Cl B98 154 E6
Hillmorton Rd Coventry CV2 96 C1
Knowle B93 128 A5
Sutton Coldfield B74 31 F4
Hillmount Cl B28 87 E2
Hillrise LE10 75 F8
Hillsborough Ho B27 88 E2
Hillside Brownhills WS8 16 A6
Lichfield WS14 9 D6
Nuneaton CV10 72 A8
Redditch B98 153 D2
Hillside Ave Blackheath B65 83 B8
Brierley Hill DY5 82 A8
Halesowen B63 82 D6
Hillside Cl Birmingham B32 102 A8
Brownhills WS8 16 A6
Cannock WS12 2 A7
Kidderminster DY11 116 A7
Hillside Cres WS3 14 F2
Hillside Croft B92 89 E4
Hillside Ct B43 43 E2
Hillside Dr
Birmingham, Great Barr B42 55 A6
Birmingham, Kingshurst B37 69 F4
Kidderminster DY11 116 A7
Lickey End B61 137 B6
Nuneaton CV10 72 C7
Sutton Coldfield B74 44 F7
Hillside Gdns
Birmingham B37 69 F4
Wolverhampton WV1 26 A3
Hillside N CV2 114 A6
Hillside Rd
Birmingham, Gravelly Hill B23 56 D2
Birmingham, Great Barr B43 43 D2
Dudley DY1 51 A5
Hinckley LE10 75 D6
Sutton Coldfield B74 32 A4
Hillstone Gdns WV10 25 F8
Hillstone Jun & Inf Sch B34 69 D5
Hillstone Rd B34 69 D5
Hilltop DY9 81 F3
Hilltop Cl CV8 145 E8
Hilltop Ct 8 DY3 50 E3
Hilltop Dr B36 68 D7
Hilltop Rd DY2 62 E8
Hillview Cl Halesowen B63 82 E6
Lickey End B60 137 C6
Hillview Rd Birmingham B45 121 E8
Lickey End B60 137 C6
Hillville Gdns DY8 81 B3
Hillwood Ave B90 127 A6
Hillwood Cl DY6 60 C4
Hillwood Common Rd B75 32 B6
Hillwood Rd
Birmingham B31 102 E7
Halesowen B62 83 C7
Hilly Rd WV14 40 E2
Hillyfields Rd B23 56 C4
Hilmore Way B77 35 E8
Hilsea Cl WV8 10 F1
Hilston Ave Halesowen B63 82 F4
Wolverhampton WV4 38 C4
Hilton Ave Birmingham B28 105 F4
Nuneaton CV10 72 B6
Hilton Cl Stourbridge DY8 81 A7
Walsall WS3 14 A2
Hilton Cross WV10 12 B5
Hilton Cross Bsns Pk WV10 12 B5
Hilton Ct Coventry CV5 112 F2
Sutton Coldfield B72 57 C8
Hilton Dr B72 57 C8
Hilton La Essington WV11 12 E8
Great Wyrley WS6 5 A2
Hilton Main Ind Est WV10 12 C5
Hilton Pl WV14 40 F5
Hilton Rd Featherstone WV10 12 C7
Tipton B69 63 C8
Willenhall WV12 13 C1
Wolverhampton WV4 39 F4
Hilton St West Bromwich B70 53 A3
Wolverhampton WV10 163 D4
Himbleton Cl B98 153 F1
Himbleton Croft 1 B90 127 A6
Himley Ave DY1 50 F2
Himley Cl Birmingham B43 43 C2
Willenhall WV12 27 B5
Himley Cres WV4 39 B5
Himley Ct 10 DY3 50 E3
Himley Gdns DY3 49 F4
Himley Gr B45 122 B6
Himley La DY3 49 A2
Himley Rd Bedworth CV12 77 D2
Dudley DY1, DY3 50 D2
Himley Rise B90 126 E4
Himley St DY1 51 A1
Hinbrook Rd DY1 50 E1
Hinchliffe Ave WV14 40 B2
Hinckes Rd WV6 24 B5
Hinckley Bsns Pk LE10 74 F8
Hinckley CE Jun & Inf Sch LE10 75 D8
Hinckley Coll LE10 71 F1
Hinckley Ct 3 B68 84 B7
Hinckley & District Hospl LE10 75 D8
Hinckley & North Warwickshire Coll LE10 71 E1
Hinckley Rd Ansty CV2, CV7 97 C2
Aston Flamville LE10 76 D7
Aston Flamville LE10 76 D8
Barwell LE9 71 E5
Burton Hastings CV11 75 A1
Burton Hastings LE10 75 D1
Burton Hastings LE10 75 E3
Coventry CV2 115 A8
Hinckley LE10 76 A6
Nuneaton CV11 73 E5
Hinckley St B5 164 C2
Hinckley Sta LE10 75 D7
Hincks St WV2 40 A7
Hind Cl CV34 155 F2
Hindhead Rd B14 105 C4
Hindlip Cl B63 82 F2
Hindlow Cl B7 67 B4
Hindon Gr B27 106 C7
Hindon Sq B15 85 F8
Hindon Wlk B32 84 C2
Hingeston St B18 66 B4
Hingley Croft WS9 30 F3
Hingley Rd DY9 82 A6
Hingley St B64 62 D1
Hinsford Cl DY6 60 E8
Hinstock Cl WV4 39 A4
Hinstock Rd B20 54 F1
Hintlesham Ave B15 85 D5
Hinton Ave B48 139 A6
Hinton Fields B61 136 E7
Hinton Gr WV11 26 F5
Hintons Coppice B93 127 E6
Hints Ct B78 19 D2
Hints La Hopwas B78 20 B5
Weeford B78 19 F4
Hints Rd Hopwas B78 20 B6
Mile Oak B78 20 C2
Hipkins St DY4 51 E7
Hiplands Rd B62 83 F4
Hipsley Cl B36 58 C1
Hipsmoor Cl B37 69 F3
Hipswell Highway CV2 114 D3
Hiron Croft CV3 133 C8
Hiron The CV3 133 C8
Hiron Way CV34 160 B7
Histons Hill WV8 10 A3
Hitchcock Cl B67 64 D5
Hitches La B15 86 B7
Hitchman Ct CV31 162 A5
Hitchman Mews CV31 162 A5
Hitchman Rd CV31 162 A5
Hither Green La B98 153 F7
Hive Ind Ctr The B18 66 A6
Hoarestone Ave CV11 79 A7
Hoarstone DY8 98 F5
Hob Green Prim Sch DY9 81 E2
Hob Green Rd DY9 81 E2
Hob La Balsall Common CV7 130 E4
Burton Green CV8 131 A3
Knowle B92 129 A8
Hob Lane CE Fst Sch CV12 78 D3
Hob Moor Rd B10, B25 88 C8
Hob's Mdw B92 89 B2
Hob's Moat Rd B92 89 B3
Hob's Rd WS13 3 E1
Hobacre Cl B45 122 A8
Hobart Croft 1 B7 67 A4
Hobart Ct B74 32 A3
Hobart Dr WS5 43 C6
Hobart Rd Cannock WS12 2 E2
Tipton DY4 40 E1
Hobbis Ho B38 123 C7
Hobble End La WS6 14 B7
Hobgate Cl WV10 25 F4
Hobgate Rd WV10 25 F4
Hobley St WV13 27 C2
Hobmoor Croft B25 88 D7
Hobmoor Prim Sch B25 88 D8
Hobnock Rd WV11 13 B5
Hobs Hole La WS9 30 D7
Hobs Rd WS10 42 A4
Hobson Cl B18 66 A5
Hobson Rd B29 86 B1
Hockett St CV3 133 D8
Hocking Rd CV2 114 E4
Hockley Brook Cl B18 66 A5
Hockley Brook La DY9 119 F3
Hockley Brook Trad Est B18 66 A6
Hockley Cir B18 66 B6
Hockley Cl B19 66 D6
Hockley Ct B94 143 C7
Hockley Ctr 1 B18 66 C4
Hockley Heat Prim Sch B94 143 C6
Hockley Hill B18 66 B5
Hockley La Coventry CV5 111 C5
Dudley DY2 62 C4
Hockley Pool Cl B18 66 B5
Hockley Rd Birmingham B23 56 D4
Dudley WV14 51 A7
Tamworth B77 35 F6
Hockley St B19 66 C5
Hodge Hill Ave DY9 81 F3
Hodge Hill Girls Sch B36 68 C7
Hodge Hill Rd B34 68 E6
Hodge Hill Sch B36 68 C7
Hodge La B77 22 B6
Hodgehill Ct B36 68 E7
Hodgett's La Berkswell CV7 130 F7
Coventry CV7 131 A6
Hodgetts Cl B67 64 D3
Hodgkins Cl WS8 16 A6
Hodgson Tower B19 66 D6
Hodnell Cl B36 58 C1
Hodnet Cl Bilston WV14 40 B5
Kenilworth CV8 148 B5
Hodnet Dr DY5 61 C6
Hodnet Gr B5 86 E8
Hodnet Pl WS11 2 B2
Hodson Ave WV13 27 C1
Hodson Cl WV11 26 F8
Hodson Way WS11 2 B2
Hoff Beck Ct 6 B9 67 B2
Hogarth Cl Bedworth CV12 78 A4
Birmingham B43 44 D5
Hinckley LE10 71 A3
Willenhall WV13 26 E2
Hogarth Dr LE10 71 A3
Hogarth Ho 6 B15 86 C8
Hoggs La B31 102 E4
Holbeach Rd B33 69 B2
Holbeache La DY6 49 D1
Holbeache Rd DY6 60 C8
Holbeche Rd Knowle B93 128 A7
Sutton Coldfield B75 47 B5
Holbein Cl CV12 78 A4
Holberg Gr WV11 26 F5
Holborn Ave CV6 95 C2
Holborn Hill B6, B7 67 C7
Holborn Sh Ctr The DY3 50 E7
Holbrook La CV6 95 D2
Holbrook Park Est CV6 113 D8
Holbrook Prim Sch CV6 95 E1
Holbrook Tower B36 68 D8
Holbrook Way CV6 95 D1
Holbury Cl WV9 11 A2
Holcombe Rd B11 88 A3
Holcroft Rd Halesowen B63 82 C5
Kingswinford DY6 49 C1
Stourbridge DY9 81 C4
Holcroft St Tipton DY4 52 A2
Wolverhampton WV2 40 A7
Holden Cl B23 56 E2
Holden Cres WS3 28 F5
Holden Croft DY4 52 A3
Holden Pl WS3 28 E5
Holden Rd Wednesbur WS10 42 A2
Wolverhampton WV4 38 D3
Holder Dr WS11 1 B2
Holder Rd
Birmingham, South Yardley B25 88 C7
Birmingham, Sparkbrook B11 87 C6
Holders Gdns B13 86 C2
Holders La B13 86 C2
Holdford Rd B6 55 F2
Holdgate Rd B29 103 C7
Hole Farm Rd B31 103 C5
Hole Farm Way B38 123 F7
Hole House La B94 143 F1
Hole La B31 103 C5
Holford Ave WS2 42 C6
Holford Dr B42, B6 55 F4
Holford Way B6 55 F3
Holifast Rd B72 57 C7
Holioak Dr CV34 161 B6
Holland Ave Knowle B93 128 B8
Oldbury B68 64 D4
Holland Ho B19 66 D5
Holland House Inf Sch B72 46 C4
Holland Ind Pk WS10 41 D8
Holland Rd Bilston WV14 40 E7
Birmingham B43 54 D7
Coventry CV6 113 A6
Sutton Coldfield B72 46 C4
Holland Rd W 6 B6 66 F6
Holland St Birmingham B3 164 A3
1 Dudley DY2 62 B8
Sutton Coldfield B72 46 C4
Tipton DY4 52 C7
Holland's Way WS3 14 F4
Hollands Pl WS3 14 D1
Hollands Rd WS3 14 D1
Hollaway Ct B63 82 D5
Hollemeadow Ave WS3 28 D7
Holliars Gr B37 69 F5
Hollicombe Terr CV2 114 D8
Holliday Rd
Birmingham, Erdington B24 57 A4
Birmingham, Handsworth B21 65 F7
Holliday St Birmingham B1 66 C1
Birmingham B1 164 A2
Hollie Lucas Rd B13 104 F7
Hollier's Wlk LE10 71 D1
Holliers Walk Cty Prim Sch LE10 71 D1
Hollies Ave WS11 1 F1
Hollies Croft B5 86 C5
Hollies Dr Halesowen B62 83 E6
Wednesbury WS10 41 F3
Hollies Ind Est WV2 163 B1
Hollies Inf Sch The CV10 72 E6
Hollies La WV6 23 A4
Hollies Rd B69 63 B8
Hollies St DY5 61 D7
Hollies The
Birmingham, Aston B6 67 B8
Birmingham, Winson Green B16 65 F3
Smethwick B66 65 C4
Wolverhampton WV2 163 B1
Wolverhampton, New Cross WV11 26 B5
Hollin Brow Cl B93 128 B3
Hollings Gr B91 127 B8
Hollington Cres B33 69 A4
Hollington Rd WV1 26 B1
Hollington Way B90 127 C7
Hollinwell Cl Nuneaton CV11 79 C8
Walsall WS3 14 A3
Hollis Ct DY3 50 C3
Hollis La CV8 147 E8
Hollis Rd CV3 114 A2
Hollister Dr B32 84 F3
Hollow Cres CV6 113 B5
Hollow Croft B31 103 B3
Hollow Croft Rd WV12 27 B7
Holloway Birmingham B31 102 E5
Tamworth B79 21 B4
Holloway Bank
Wednesbury WS10 41 F1
West Bromwich B70 53 A8
Holloway Circus Queensway B1 164 B1

Holloway Dr B98 154 B4
Holloway Field CV6 113 A6
Holloway Head B1 164 B1
Holloway La B98 153 F3
Holloway Pk B98 154 A3
Holloway St Dudley DY3 50 D4
Wolverhampton WV1 40 A7
Holloway St W DY3 50 D4
Holloway The
Alvechurch B48 139 D3
Bluntington DY10 118 E2
Seisdon WV5 37 A3
Stourbridge DY8 80 F7
Warwick CV34 160 D6
Wolverhampton WV6 24 C2
Hollowmeadow Ho B36 68 D8
Hollows The CV11 73 F1
Hollowtree La B60 138 A3
Holly Ave
Birmingham, Balsall Heath B12 87 A5
Birmingham, Selly Oak B29 86 B1
Holly Bank CV5 133 A8
Holly Bush Gr B32 84 D7
Holly Cl Hinckley LE10 75 E5
Tamworth B79 21 B7
Willenhall WV12 27 C6
Holly Ct B24 57 A5
Holly Dell B38 104 B2
Holly Dr Birmingham B27 88 B2
Hollywood B47 125 B7
Holly Farm Bsns Pk CV8 146 B7
Holly Gr
Birmingham, Bournville B30 103 F8
Birmingham, Lozells B19 66 B8
4 Birmingham, Selly Oak B29 85 F2
Bromsgrove B61 136 F3
Coventry CV4 112 B2
4 Stourbridge DY8 80 F5
Wolverhampton WV3 38 F7
Holly Grange B66 64 D7
Holly Grove La WS7 6 E8
Holly Hall Rd DY2 62 A7
Holly Hall Sch DY1 61 F8
Holly Hill Birmingham B45 101 F1
Great Wyrley WS6 13 E8
Holly Hill Meth & CE Inf Sch B45 101 F2
Holly Hill Rd
Birmingham B45 102 A2
Shenstone WS14 17 F5
Holly La Aldridge WS9 30 F8
Balsall Common CV7 130 B3
Birmingham, Erdington B24 57 C4
Birmingham, Marston Green B37 89 F8
Brownhills WS9 16 B4
Great Wyrley WS6 13 F8
Huntington WS12 1 C7
Portway B48 140 F5
Smethwick B66 64 E6
Sutton Coldfield B75 32 B3
Wishaw B76 47 D4
Holly Lodge High Sch B67 64 D7
Holly Lodge Wlk B37 69 F2
Holly Park Dr B24 57 C4
Holly Park Ind Est B24 57 C2
Holly Pl B29 86 B2
Holly Rd
Birmingham, Edgbaston B16 65 D1
Birmingham, Handsworth B20 66 A8
Birmingham, King's Norton B30 104 A4
Blackheath B65 63 B1
Bromsgrove B61 136 F4
Dudley DY1 51 A3
Oldbury B68 84 C8
Wednesbury WS10 41 F5
West Bromwich B71 53 E8
Holly St Cannock WS11 1 F6
Dudley DY1 61 E6
Royal Leamington Spa CV32 157 B1
Smethwick B67 64 F5
Holly Stitches Rd CV10 72 E6
Holly Wlk Baginton CV8 133 E2
Nuneaton CV11 73 F2
Royal Leamington Spa CV32 157 A1
Holly Wood B43 44 A1
Hollybank Ave WV11 13 A3
Hollybank Cl WS3 14 A1
Hollybank Gr B63 82 D1
Hollybank Rd B13 105 A6
Hollyberry Ave B91 127 A8
Hollyberry Croft B34 69 C6
Hollybrow B29 103 B7
Hollybush La Coventry CV6 96 A4
Stourbridge DY8 80 F7
Wolverhampton WV4 38 D4
Hollybush Wlk B64 62 D1
Hollycot Gdns B12 86 F6
Hollycroft LE10 71 C1
Hollycroft Cres LE10 71 C1
Hollycroft Rd B21 54 D1
Hollydale Rd Birmingham B24 57 C3
Blackheath B65 63 D2
Hollyfast La CV7 94 C4
Hollyfast Prim Sch CV6 112 E7
Hollyfast Rd CV6 112 E6
Hollyfaste Rd B33 69 B1
Hollyfield Ave B91 106 E3
Hollyfield Cres B75 46 E4
Hollyfield Dr
Barnt Green B45 122 A1
Sutton Coldfield B75 46 E5
Hollyfield Rd B75 46 E5
Hollyfield Rd S B76 46 F4
Hollyhedge Cl
Birmingham B31 102 D6
Walsall WS2 28 C2
Hollyhedge La WS2 28 C2
Hollyhedge Prim Sch B71 53 E8
Hollyhedge Rd B71 53 E7
Hollyhill La WS14 17 E5
Hollyhock Rd
Birmingham B27 88 A2
Dudley DY2 51 F1
Hollyhurst B46 59 C2
Hollyhurst Dr DY8 60 E3
Hollyhurst Gr B26 88 E6
Hollyhurst Rd B73 45 B3
Hollymoor Way B31 102 B1
Hollymount B62 84 A7
Hollyoak Gr B91 107 A1
Hollyoak St B71 53 D4
Hollyoake Cl B68 64 A2
Hollypiece Ho B27 88 A2
Hollywell Rd Birmingham B26 89 B6
Knowle B93 128 A5
Hollywell St WV14 40 A1
Hollywood By-Pass
Birmingham B47 104 F1
Hollywood B47 124 E6
Hollywood Croft B42 54 F8
Hollywood Inf & Jun Sch B14 105 A1
Hollywood La B47 125 B7
Holm View Cl WS14 17 F6
Holman Cl WV13 26 E2
Holman Rd WV13 26 E2
Holman St DY11 116 C5
Holman Way CV11 73 D3
Holmcroft Coventry CV2 114 F8
Wolverhampton WV4 39 F4
Holmcroft Rd DY10 117 A5
Holme Mill WV10 11 D4
Holme Way WS4 29 B7
Holmes Cl B43 54 E7
Holmes Ct CV8 147 F5
Holmes Dr Birmingham B45 121 F6
Coventry CV5 111 D5
Holmes La B60 151 B1
Holmes Rd Whitnash CV31 162 B3
Willenhall WV12 27 D6
Holmes The WV10 11 D3
Holmesfield Rd B42 55 C7
Holmewood Cl CV8 148 B5
Holmewood Ct CV8 148 B5
Holmfield Rd CV2 114 B3
Holmsdale Rd CV6 113 E7
Holmwood Ave DY11 116 A6
Holmwood Dr B97 153 C3
Holmwood Ho B97 153 C3
Holmwood Rd 3 B10 67 D1
Holroyd Ho CV4 111 F2
Holston Cl WS12 2 F1
Holsworth Cl B77 21 D1
Holsworthy Cl CV11 73 E5
Holt Cres WS11 2 B2
Holt Ct B7 66 F4
Holt Farm Prim Sch B62 63 E1
Holt Gdns B80 159 E2
Holt Hill B98 154 F8
Holt Ho B61 137 A3
Holt La B62 100 D4
Holt Rd Halesowen B62 63 E1
Hinckley LE10 75 E6
Studley B80 159 E2
Holt St B7 164 D4
Holt The CV32 157 B3
Holte Dr B75 32 D2
Holte Rd
Birmingham, Aston B6 56 A1
Birmingham, Sparkhill B11 87 D5
Holte Sch B19 66 D7
Holtes Wlk B6 67 B8
Holton Ct WV13 27 C2
Holtshill La WS1 28 F2
Holwick B77 36 B8
Holy Child Sch B15 86 B6
Holy Cross Ct CV2 114 E4
Holy Cross Gn DY9 99 E2
Holy Cross La DY9 119 E8
Holy Cross RC Jun & Inf Sch B76 47 A3
Holy Family RC Jun & Inf Sch B10 87 F7
Holy Family RC Prim Sch CV6 95 B3
Holy Name RC Prim Sch B43 43 E1
Holy Rosary RC Prim Sch WV1 26 A1
Holy Souls RC Prim Sch B27 88 C3
Holy Trinity CE Inf Sch WS8 15 E6
Holy Trinity CE Prim Sch
Birmingham B20 55 C2
West Bromwich B70 53 D1
Holy Trinity RC Prim Sch WV14 40 E6
Holy Trinity RC Sec Sch B10 87 C8
Holy Well Cl B16 66 A2
Holyhead L Ctr B21 65 D8
Holyhead Prim Sch WS10 41 E3
Holyhead Rd Birmingham B21 65 D8
Codsall WV8 23 E8
Coventry CV5 112 E5
Darlaston WS10 41 C4
Wednesbury WS10 41 E3
Holyhead Road Ind Est WS10 41 D3
Holyhead Sch B21 65 D8
Holyhead Way B21 65 D8
Holyoak Cl Bedworth CV12 77 F1
3 Birmingham B6 55 F1
Holyoak Croft B31 123 B8
Holyoakes Field Fst Sch B97 153 D4
Holyoakes La B97 152 C5
Holyrood Ct CV10 72 D5
Holyrood Gr 2 B6 66 E8
Holywell Cl CV4 111 D1
Holywell La B45 121 D6
Holywell Rise WS14 9 D6
Home Farm CV35 155 F6
Home Farm Cres CV31 162 B4
Home Meadow Ct B13 105 A5
Home Meadow Ho B27 88 A2
Home Meadow La B98 154 E6
Home Park Rd CV11 73 C3
Homecroft Rd B26 88 E8
Homedene Rd B31 102 E7
Homefield Rd WV8 10 C3
Homelands B42 55 B7
Homelea Rd B25 88 D8
Homelodge Ho 4 WS13 9 B7
Homemead Gr B45 121 F7
Homer Hill Rd B63 82 C7
Homer Rd Solihull B91 107 B3
Sutton Coldfield B75 32 D2
Homer St B12 86 F5
Homers Fold WV14 40 D5
Homerton Rd B44 45 B1
Homestead Cl DY3 50 E5
Homestead Dr B75 32 C3
Homestead Rd B33 69 B1
Homeward Way CV3 115 A1
Homewood Cl B76 46 E3
Honesty Cl WS8 15 D6
Honeswode Cl B20 66 A8
Honeyborne Rd B75 46 D7
Honeybourne B77 21 D2
Honeybourne Cl
Coventry CV5 112 B3
3 Halesowen B63 83 A3
Honeybourne Rd
Birmingham B33 89 C8
Halesowen B63 83 C3
Honeybourne Sch B28 105 F8
Honeybourne Way WV13 27 C2
Honeyfield Rd CV1 113 D5
Honeysuckle Ave DY6 60 E7
Honeysuckle Cl B32 84 B5
Honeysuckle Dr
Coventry CV2 96 B2
Featherstone WV10 12 C7
Walsall WS5 43 A3
Honeysuckle Gr 9 B27 88 C5
Honeytree Cl DY6 60 F3
Honiley Ct CV2 96 D1
Honiley Dr B73 45 C2
Honiley Rd Birmingham B33 69 A2
Honiley CV8 146 B6
Meer End CV8 130 A1
Honiley Way CV2 96 D1
Honister Cl DY5 61 F1
Honiton Cl B31 102 E4
Honiton Cres B31 102 E4
Honiton Rd CV2 114 C5
Honiton Way WS9 29 F5
Honiton Wlk 7 B66 65 B5
Honor Ave WV4 39 C5
Hoo Farm Ind Est DY10 116 F1
Hoo Rd DY10 116 E4
Hoobrook Ent Ctr DY10 116 E2
Hoobrook Ind Est DY10 116 E2
Hoobrook Trad Est DY10 116 E3
Hood Gr B30 103 D4
Hood St CV1 113 E3
Hook Dr B74 31 F4
Hook La WS14 17 C3
Hooper St B18 65 F4
Hoopers La B96 158 E1
Hoosen Cl B62 84 A6
Hope Cl CV7 95 A7
Hope Pl 10 B29 85 F2
Hope Rd DY4 52 C6
Hope St Birmingham B5 86 E8
Coventry CV1 113 B2
Dudley DY2 62 C8
Halesowen B62 83 D8
Stourbridge DY8 60 D3
Walsall WS1 42 E8
West Bromwich B70 53 E2
Hope Terr DY2 62 C5
Hopedale Cl CV2 114 E3
Hopedale Rd B32 84 C5
Hopgardens Ave B60 137 B2
Hopkins Ct 4 WS10 42 A3
Hopkins Dr B71 53 E7
Hopkins Rd CV6 113 A4
Hopkins St DY4 52 A2
Hopleys Cl B77 21 E4
Hopstone Gdns WV4 38 F4
Hopstone Rd B29 85 A1
Hopton Cl Coventry CV5 112 A4
Perton WV6 23 F3
Tipton DY4 41 C2
Hopton Cres WV11 26 E6
Hopton Crofts CV32 156 C2
Hopton Dr DY10 116 E1
Hopton Gr B13 105 C5
Hopton Mdw WS12 2 C1
Hopwas Gr B37 69 F5
Hopwas Hill B78 20 A6
Hopwood Cl B63 83 A2
Hopwood Gr B31 122 E6
Hopyard Cl DY3 50 B3
Hopyard Gdns WV14 40 B3
Hopyard La Dudley DY3 50 B2
Redditch B98 154 D4
Hopyard Rd WS2 27 E2
Horace Partridge Rd WS10 41 A5
Horace St WV14 51 A8
Horatio Dr B13 86 F4
Hordern Cl WV6 24 F5
Hordern Cres DY5 81 D8
Hordern Gr WV6 24 F5
Hordern Rd WV6 24 F5
Hornbeam B77 22 A4
Hornbeam Cl B29 103 B7
Hornbeam Dr CV4 111 D1
Hornbeam Gr CV31 162 C6
Hornbeam Wlk WV3 25 A1
Hornbrook Gr B92 106 C7
Hornby Gr B14 105 C4
Hornby Rd WV4 39 C5
Hornchurch Cl CV1 165 B1
Horndean Cl CV6 113 E8
Horne Way B34 69 E5
Horning Dr WV14 40 C3
Horninghold Cl CV3 134 E8
Hornsey Cl CV2 114 E7
Hornsey Gr B44 45 A2
Hornsey Rd B44 45 A2
Hornton Cl B74 31 D5
Horrell Rd Birmingham B26 89 B7
Solihull B90 105 F2
Horse Fair Birmingham B1 164 B1
Kidderminster DY10 116 E7
Horse Shoe Rd CV6 96 A4
Horse Shoes La B26 89 B5
Horsecroft Dr B71 54 A8
Horsefair The 8 LE10 75 D8
Horsehills Dr WV3 24 E2
Horselea Croft B8 68 C4
Horseley Fields WV1 163 D3
Horseley Heath DY4 52 C5
Horseley Rd DY4 52 C5
Horsepool LE10 76 A5
Horseshoe Cl 1 WS2 42 B7
Horseshoe The B68 64 C2
Horseshoe Wlk 6 DY4 51 E5
Horsfall Rd B75 47 A5
Horsford Rd CV3 133 E6
Horsham Ave DY8 60 C3
Horsley La Lichfield WS14 8 D1
Shenstone WS14 17 D8
Horsley Rd B43 44 D4
Horticultural Training Sch B14 104 D8
Horticultural Unit Wulfrun Coll WV3 24 D2
Horton Cl Darlaston WS10 41 D7
Sedgley DY3 50 C8
Horton Gr B90 127 A5
Horton Pl WS10 41 D7
Horton Sq B12 86 E7
Horton St Darlaston WS10 41 D7
Tipton DY4 52 D5
West Bromwich B70 53 C2
Hosiery St CV12 78 C2
Hospital La Bedworth CV12 77 B1
Cheslyn Hay WS6 4 B2
Dudley WV14 51 B7
Hospital Rd Birmingham B15 85 E4
Burntwood WS7 7 B5
Hospital St Birmingham B19 66 D6
Birmingham B19 164 B4
Tamworth B79 21 B5
Walsall WS2 28 D4
Wolverhampton WV2 163 C2
Hossil La Belbroughton DY9 119 C8
Clent DY9 99 D1
Hotchkiss Way CV3 135 A7
Hothersall Dr B73 56 F8
Hothorpe Cl CV3 114 F1
Hotspur Rd B44 44 F1
Hough Pl WS2 42 B7
Hough Rd Birmingham B14 104 D6
Walsall WS2 42 A7
Houghton Ct B28 105 D4
Houghton St Oldbury B69 63 F6
West Bromwich B70 64 D8
Houlbrooke Ho 5 WS13 9 C8
Houldey Rd B31 103 B1
Houldsworth Cres CV6 95 C4
Houliston Cl WS10 42 B5
Houndsfield Cl B47 125 C6
Houndsfield Farm B47 125 B5
Houndsfield Gr B47 125 A5
Houndsfield La B47 125 C6
Houseman Pk B60 137 A2
Housman Cl B60 150 E8
Housman Ct B60 137 A3
Housman Wlk DY10 117 C6
Houting B77 35 D5
Houx The DY8 80 E8
Hove Ave CV5 111 E4
Hove Rd B27 88 C1
Hovelands Cl CV2 114 C8
Howard Ave B61 136 E3
Howard Cl CV5 111 E4
Howard Cres WS12 2 C7
Howard Ct B16 65 E1
Howard Rd Bilston WV14 40 F3
Birmingham, Handsworth B20 55 B2
Birmingham, King's Heath B14 104 E7
Birmingham, Newton B43 54 C8
Birmingham, South Yardley B25 88 C7
Nuneaton CV10 73 A3
Redditch B98 159 C8
Solihull B92 88 E3
Wednesfield WV11 26 F8
Howard Rd E B13 104 F7
Howard St Birmingham B19 164 B4
Coventry CV1 165 C4
Tipton DY4 52 B5
West Bromwich B70 52 F7
Wolverhampton WV2 163 C1
Howard Wlk CV31 161 D7
Howarth Way B6 67 A7
Howat Rd CV7 94 F7
Howcotte Gn CV4 131 E8
Howden Pl B33 69 A5
Howdle's La WS8 6 F2
Howe Cres WV12 27 C6
Howe St B4 66 F3
Howell Rd WV2 39 E7
Howells Cl CV12 77 D1
Howes Cl WS1 42 F6
Howes Croft B35 58 A2
Howes La CV3 133 D3
Howes Prim Sch CV3 133 E5
Howford Gr B7 67 B4
Howl Pl DY4 51 F5
Howland Cl WV9 10 F2
Howlette Rd CV4 111 E2
Howley Ave B44 44 E1
Howley Grange Prim Sch B62 83 F5
Howley Grange Rd B62 84 A4
Hoylake B77 22 B4
Hoylake Cl Nuneaton CV11 74 B1
Walsall WS3 14 B4
Hoylake Dr B69 63 A7
Hoylake Rd WV6 23 D5
Hoyland Way B30 103 E8
HRS Bsns Pk B33 69 C1
Huband Cl B98 154 A5
Hubert Croft B29 85 F2
Hubert Rd B29 85 F2
Hubert St B6 66 F5
Hucker Cl WS2 42 A7
Hucker Rd WS2 42 A7
Huddisdon Cl 5 CV34 155 F1
Huddlestone Cl WV10 12 B6
Huddocks View WS3 14 F5
Hudson Ave B46 70 F6
Hudson Cl WS11 2 B2
Hudson Dr WS7 7 C6
Hudson Gr WV6 23 E5
Hudson Rd Birmingham B20 55 A4
Tipton DY4 52 C4
Hudson's Dr B30 104 A4
Hudswell Dr DY5 81 D8
Hugh Gaitskill Ct WV14 40 C8
Hugh Rd Birmingham B10 67 E1
Coventry CV3 114 A2
Smethwick B67 64 E5
Hugh Villas B10 67 E1
Hughes Ave WV3 38 F8
Hughes Cl Warwick CV34 155 D2
Whitnash CV31 162 A2
Hughes Pl WV14 40 D7
Hughes Rd Bilston WV14 40 D7
Wednesbury WS10 41 A5
Huins Cl B98 154 A4
Hulbert Dr DY2 62 B6
Hulland Pl DY5 61 C3
Hullbrook Rd B13 105 C6
Hulme Cl CV3 115 B1
Humber Ave Coventry CV1 113 F1
Coventry CV3 113 F2
Sutton Coldfield B76 58 A7
Humber Gr B36 58 F1
Humber Ho DY1 61 D8
Humber Rd Coventry CV3 134 A8
Wolverhampton WV3 25 A1
Humber Tower 6 B7 67 A4
Humberstone Rd
4 Coventry CV6 113 A5
Sutton Coldfield B24 57 E4
Hume St Kidderminster DY11 116 C5
Smethwick B66 65 B4
Humpage Rd B9 67 E2
Humphrey Ave B60 150 F7
Humphrey Burton's Rd CV3 133 C8
Humphrey Middlemore Dr B17 85 D4
Humphrey St DY3 50 D3
Humphrey-Davy Rd CV12 95 D8
Humphreys Rd WV10 25 D6
Humphries Cres WV14 40 F2
Humphries Dr DY10 116 F2
Humphries Ho WS8 15 F7
Humphris St CV34 161 B8
Hundred Acre Rd B74 44 F7
Hungary Cl DY9 81 C5
Hungary Hill DY9 81 C5
Hungerfield Rd B36 58 C1
Hungerford Rd DY8 80 E2
Hungry La WS14 18 F5
Hunningham Gr 6 B91 127 B8
Hunnington Cl B32 84 A1
Hunnington Cres B63 83 B2
Hunscote Cl B90 105 F1
Hunscote Ho B90 105 F1

Hunslet Rd Birmingham B32 84 F4
Burntwood WS7 7 B8
Hunstanton Ave B17 84 F8
Hunstanton Cl DY5 81 C7
Hunt End La B97 158 C5
Hunt Paddocks CV8 147 E1
Hunt Terr CV4 132 B7
Hunt's La WV12 27 D6
Hunter Ave WS7 7 B7
Hunter Cl WS14 9 D6
Hunter Cres WS3 28 F7
Hunter Ct B5 86 D5
Hunter Rd WS11 4 E8
Hunter St W6 25 A4
Hunter Terr CV5 132 D8
Hunter's Ride DY7 60 B2
Hunters Cl Bilston WV14 41 A7
Coventry CV3 115 A2
Hunters Hill Sch B60 137 F6
Hunters Rd B19 66 B7
Hunters Rise B63 82 D1
Hunters Vale B19 66 C6
Hunters Wlk B23 56 C8
Huntingdon Cl Redditch B98 154 F2
Tamworth B78 20 F2
Huntingdon Gdns B63 82 C7
Huntingdon Rd
Coventry CV5 133 A8
West Bromwich B71 53 B7
Huntingdon Way CV10 72 E3
Huntington Ho B23 56 B6
Huntington Ind Est WS12 1 B6
Huntington Prim Sch WS12 1 C8
Huntington Rd WV12 27 D8
Huntington Terrace Rd WS11 1 F4
Huntingtree Prim Sch B63 82 E3
Huntingtree Rd B63 82 E3
Huntlands Rd B63 82 F2
Huntley Dr B91 107 B2
Huntly Rd B16 66 A1
Hunton Ct 2 B23 56 E2
Hunton Hill B23 56 E2
Hunton Rd B23 56 E3
Hunts Mill Dr DY5 50 C1
Hunts Rd B30 104 B7
Huntsmans Gate WS7 7 B8
Huntsmans Rise WS12 1 C8
Hurcott Ct DY10 117 A8
Hurcott La DY10 117 C8
Hurcott Rd DY10 117 B8
Hurdis Rd B90 106 A2
Hurdlow Ave B18 66 B5
Hurlbutt Rd CV34 161 C4
Hurley Cl
Royal Leamington Spa CV32 157 A2
Sutton Coldfield B72 46 C2
Walsall WS5 43 D6
Hurley Gr B37 69 F5
Hurleys Fold DY2 62 C5
Hurlingham Rd B44 45 A1
Hurn Way CV6 96 B4
Huron Cl WS11 2 B2
Hursey Dr DY4 52 A6
Hurst Bsns Pk DY6 62 A4
Hurst Cl B36 69 E7
Hurst Ct 5 DY9 81 F5
Hurst Green Prim Sch B62 83 E8
Hurst Green Rd
Bentley Heath B93 127 F4
Halesowen B62 83 F8
Minworth B76 58 D6
Hurst Hill Ct WV14 51 A8
Hurst Hill Prim Sch WV14 51 A8
Hurst La Birmingham B34 69 E6
Brierley Hill DY5 61 F3
Tipton DY4 51 D6
Hurst La N B36 69 E7
Hurst Rd Bedworth CV12 78 B3
Coventry CV6 96 A4
Dudley WV14 40 A1
Hinckley LE10 75 D8
Smethwick B67 64 D2
Hurst St B5 164 C1
Hurst The Birmingham B13 105 D7
Hollywood B47 125 A6
Hurstbourne Cres WV1 26 B1
Hurstcroft Rd B33 69 B3
Hurstway The B23 56 C8
Hurstwood Rd B23 56 C8
Huskisson Ct WV10 25 C6
Hussey Rd Brownhills WS8 15 E8
Norton Canes WS11 5 F5
Husum Way DY10 117 C7
Hut Hill La WS6 5 A4
Hutton Ave B8 67 D5
Hutton Rd
Birmingham, Handsworth B20 55 C1
Birmingham, Saltley B8 67 D5
Huxbey Dr B92 107 F8
Huxley Cl WV9 11 A3
Hyacinth Way LE10 75 D5
Hyatt Sq DY5 81 C7
Hyatts Wlk B65 62 F5
Hyde Cl B60 137 B2
Hyde Pl CV32 161 E8
Hyde Rd Coventry CV2 114 E4
Kenilworth CV8 148 A5
Wednesfield WV11 26 E6
Hyde The DY9 81 D2
Hydes La LE10 74 E4
Hydes Rd Wednesbury WS10 42 B2
West Bromwich B71 42 C1
Hydesville Tower Sch WS1 29 A2
Hyett Way WV14 41 B2
Hylda Rd B20 55 B1
Hylstone Cres WV11 26 D6
Hylton St B18 66 C5
Hyperion Dr WV4 39 A3
Hyperion Rd Birmingham B36 57 F1
Stourbridge DY7 80 C7
Hyron Hall Rd B27 88 C2
Hyssop Cl Birmingham B7 67 A5
Cannock WS11 2 B3
Hytall Rd B90 105 C2
Hythe Gr B25 88 D8

I-Max Bsns Pk B11 88 A6
Ibberton Rd B14 105 B3
Ibex Cl CV3 114 F1
Ibis Cl DY10 117 B3
Ibis Gdns DY6 61 A6
Ibstock Cl B98 154 E4
Ibstock Dr DY8 81 A4
Ibstock Ho B98 154 E4
Ibstock Rd CV6 96 A5
Icknield Cl B74 31 A1
Icknield Fst Sch B98 154 D1
Icknield Port Rd B16 65 F3
Icknield Sq B16 66 A3
Icknield St Alvechurch B38 124 B2
Beoley B98 140 C2
Birmingham B18 66 B4
Redditch, Church Hill B98 154 C7
Redditch, Ipsley B98 154 D2
Rowney Green B48 140 B6
Icknield Street Dr B98 159 D7
Ida Rd Walsall WS2 28 C1
West Bromwich B70 53 D1
Idbury Rd B44 56 A7
Ideal Bldgs 7 DY11 116 D6
Iden Rd CV1 113 E4
Idmiston Croft B14 104 F2
Idonia Rd WV6 23 F5
Ilam Pk CV8 148 C5
Ilex Ct CV34 161 A7
Ilford Cl CV12 78 A3
Ilford Ct CV3 135 D7
Ilford Dr CV3 133 B5
Ilford Rd B23 56 D6
Ilfracombe Gr CV3 133 A5
Iliffe Ho LE10 75 B7
Iliffe Way B17 85 D4
Ilkley Gr B37 69 F2
Illey La Birmingham B32 102 A7
Halesowen B62 101 E8
Illeybrook Sq B32 84 D2
Illshaw WV9 11 A3
Illshaw Heath Rd B94 126 D2
Ilmington Cl Coventry CV3 133 B5
Redditch B98 154 D1
Ilmington Dr B73 45 C3
Ilmington Rd B29 84 F1
Ilminster Cl LE10 76 B7
Ilsham Gr B31 122 E6
Ilsley Rd B23 56 E4
Imber Rd DY10 117 A1
Imex Auto Ctr DY4 52 A3
Imex Bsns Pk
Birmingham, Bordesley Green B9 67 D2
Birmingham, Stechford B33 68 E4
Tipton DY4 52 A3
Wolverhampton WV2 39 C7
Imex Ho WV2 39 B7
Imperial Ave DY10 116 F8
Imperial Gr DY10 116 F8
Imperial Rd B9 67 E1
Imperial Rise B46 59 E2
Impney Cl B98 154 E6
Impsley Cl B36 69 B8
Inca Cl CV3 134 F8
Ince Rd WS10 41 C7
Incestre Dr B43 43 D1
Inchbrook Rd CV8 148 C7
Inchcape Ave B20 55 A3
Inchford Ave CV34 155 E2
Inchford Cl CV11 73 F1
Inchford Rd B92 107 E7
Inchlaggan Rd WV10 25 F6
Ingatestone Dr DY8 60 C3
Inge St B5 164 C1
Ingestre Cl Cannock WS11 2 B1
Walsall WS3 13 F3
Ingestre Dr B43 43 C1
Ingestre Ho WV6 24 E5
Ingestre Rd Birmingham B28 106 A7
Wolverhampton WV10 11 C1
Ingham Way B17 85 A8
Ingle Ct CV31 161 E7
Ingleby Gdns WV6 25 A5
Ingledew Cl WS2 27 D3
Inglefield Rd B33 68 F3
Inglemere Gr B29 102 F7
Inglenook Dr B20 55 B2
Ingleside Villas 3 B11 87 C5
Ingleton Cl CV11 74 A2
Ingleton Ho 2 B15 86 D8
Ingleton Rd B8 68 A7
Inglewood Ave WV3 38 F8
Inglewood Cl
Kingswinford DY6 60 D5
Royal Leamington Spa CV32 157 A3
Inglewood Gr B74 30 F1
Inglewood Rd B11 87 C5
Ingoldsby Rd B31 103 C3
Ingot Cl WS2 28 B6
Ingram Gr B27 88 A2
Ingram Pit La B77 22 A5
Ingram Pl WS3 14 D1
Ingram Rd Coventry CV5 132 D8
Walsall WS3 14 D1
Inhedge St DY3 50 E5
Inhedge The DY1 51 C1
Inkberrow Rd B63 82 F2
Inkerman Gr WV10 25 F2
Inkerman Ho B19 66 E6
Inkerman St Birmingham B7 67 B4
Wolverhampton WV10 25 F3
Inland Rd B24 57 B2
Innage Cl CV31 162 B8
Innage Rd B31 103 B4
Innage The B47 125 A5
Innis Rd CV5 132 E8
Innisfree House Sch B47 125 C4
Innsworth Dr B35 58 A4
Insetton Cl B98 154 D4
Inshaw Cl B33 68 E3
Instone Rd Coventry CV6 95 A1
Halesowen B63 83 A3
Instow Cl WV12 27 B8
Insull Ave B14 105 B1
Intended St B63 82 C7
International Dr B26 90 C4
International Ho B43 54 F6
Intersection Ho B70 53 E1
Intown WS1 28 F2
Intown Row WS1 28 F2
Inveraray Cl CV8 148 C4
Inverclyde Rd B20 55 A3
Inverness Cl CV5 112 A4
Inverness Ho WV1 163 B4
Inverness Rd B31 102 F3
Invicta Rd CV3 134 F8
Inworth WV9 11 B3
Ipsley Church La B98 154 C1
Ipsley Fst Sch B98 158 F8
Ipsley Gr B23 56 A5
Ipsley La B98 154 D2
Ipsley St B98 153 E3
Ipstones Ave B33 68 F4
Ipswich Cres B42 55 B7
Ipswich Wlk B37 70 B2
Ireland Green Rd B70 53 B2
Ireton Cl CV4 111 C1
Ireton Rd Birmingham B20 55 A4
Wolverhampton WV10 11 E3
Iris Cl Birmingham B29 103 B8
Dudley DY2 51 F1
Hinckley LE10 75 E5
Tamworth B79 21 C6
Iris Dr B14 104 D3
Irnham Rd B74 32 B1
Iron Bridge Wlk DY9 99 B8
Iron La B33 68 D4
Ironmonger Row CV1 165 B3
Ironstone Rd WS7 6 E8
Irvan Ave B70 52 F5
Irvine Cl WS3 28 B7
Irvine Rd WS3 28 B7
Irving Cl DY3 50 A4
Irving Rd Coventry CV1 113 E2
Solihull B92 89 E3
Tipton DY4 41 A1
Irving St B1 66 D1
Irwell B77 21 E2
Irwin Ave B45 122 C7
Isaac Walton Pl B70 52 E7
Isbourne Way 1 B9 67 B2
Isis Ct B73 46 B5
Isis Gr Birmingham B36 69 F8
Willenhall WV13 27 C2
Isis Ho DY1 61 D8
Island Cl LE10 71 E2
Island Dr DY10 116 E4
Island Rd B21 54 C1
Island The B78 20 C1
Islington B63 83 A4
Islington Cres CV9 36 C1
Islington Row B15 66 B1
Islington Row Middleway B15 86 C8
Ismere Rd B24 57 B2
Itchen Gr WV6 23 E4
Ithon Gr B38 123 E8
Ivanhoe Ave CV11 73 E1
Ivanhoe Rd Birmingham B43 44 C3
Lichfield WS14 9 B6
Wolverhampton WV2 40 A6
Ivanhoe St DY2 62 A7
Ivatt B77 21 F2
Ivatt Cl WS4 29 B7
Iverley La DY10 98 C6
Iverley Rd B63 83 C4
Iverley Wlk DY9 81 C2
Ivor Rd Birmingham B11 87 B4
Coventry CV6 95 F2
Redditch B97 153 D2
Ivy Ave Birmingham B12 87 B5
3 Birmingham B12 87 B5
Ivy Cl WS11 4 D8
Ivy Croft WV9 10 F3
Ivy Farm La CV4 132 D6
Ivy Gr 6 B18 65 E4
Ivy House Rd B69 63 D6
Ivy La Birmingham B9 67 A2
Romsley B62 100 D5
Ivy Lodge Cl B37 90 A7
Ivy Rd
Birmingham, Handsworth B21 66 A7
Birmingham, Stirchley B30 104 A6
Dudley DY1 51 A4
Sutton Coldfield B73 45 F1
Tipton DY4 51 F7
Ivybridge Gr B42 55 C3
Ivybridge Rd CV3 133 D6
Ivydale Ave B26 89 C5
Ivyfield Rd B23 56 B5
Ivyhouse La WV14 51 B8
Ivyhouse Rd B38 123 C8
Ivyhouse Wlk B77 35 F6
Izod St B97 153 D4
Izons Ind Est B70 53 A1
Izons La B70 53 A1
Izons Rd B70 53 C3

Jacey Rd Birmingham B16 65 D2
Solihull B90 106 B4
Jack David Ho DY4 52 D5
Jack Holden Ave WV14 40 A2
Jack Newell Ct 3 WV14 51 C8
Jack O'Watton Bsns Pk B46 59 D3
Jackdaw Cl DY3 39 C2
Jackdaw Dr B36 70 A8
Jacker's Rd CV2 96 B4
Jacklin Dr CV3 133 C4
Jacknell Rd LE10 74 D8
Jackson Ave B8 67 F4
Jackson Cl Birmingham B11 87 B7
Featherstone WV10 12 A6
Keresley CV7 95 A7
Norton Canes WS11 5 E4
Oldbury B68 64 B5
Tipton DY4 41 B1
Jackson Ct Brierley Hill DY5 61 F1
Oldbury B69 63 F4
Jackson Dr B67 64 D5
Jackson Ho 9 B69 64 A7
Jackson Rd Birmingham B8 67 F4
Coventry CV6 95 D1
Wolverhampton WS13 3 B3
Jackson St Oldbury B68 64 B4
Stourbridge DY9 81 E6
Wolverhampton WV6 25 B4
Jackson Way B32 84 A5
Jackson Wlk B35 58 A2
Jackwood Gn CV12 95 C8
Jacmar Cres B67 64 E6
Jacob's Hall La WS6 5 B1
Jacobean La B93 108 B1
Jacoby Pl B5 86 C5
Jacox Cres CV8 148 C5
Jacquard Cl CV3 133 D4
Jacquard Ho 3 CV1 113 E4
Jade Cl CV1 165 D4
Jade Gr WS11 2 C2
Jaffray Cres B24 56 F3
Jaffray Ct B23 56 E3
Jaffray Rd B24 56 F3
Jaffray Jun Sch Annexe B23 56 E3
Jaffray Sch B23 56 E3
Jaguar B77 21 E2
Jakeman Cl B98 154 E4
Jakeman Rd B12 86 E5
James Bridge Cl WS2 42 B7
James Cl Darlaston WS10 41 F7
Smethwick B67 65 A5
James Clift Ho 3 B69 63 D5
James Ct
Birmingham, King's Norton B38 103 F2
12 Birmingham, Moseley B13 87 B2
3 Warwick CV34 160 F7
James Dawson Dr CV5 111 B8
James Dee Cl DY5 62 A1
James Diskin Ct CV11 73 E2
James Eaton Cl B71 53 C5
James Galloway Cl CV3 134 E7
James Green Rd CV4 111 F2
James Greenway WS13 3 A2
James Ho Birmingham B19 66 C6
Coventry CV2 114 C8
James Memorial Homes 4 B7 67 C7
James Rd
Birmingham, Great Barr B43 54 E7
Birmingham, Tyseley B11 87 F6
Coleshill B46 70 F8
Kidderminster DY10 117 A8
James Scott Rd B63 82 A6
James St Bilston WV14 40 E6
Birmingham B3 164 A3
Cannock WS11 1 F5
Nuneaton CV11 73 A5
Willenhall WV13 27 A3
James Turner St B18 65 E6
James Watt Dr B19 66 C8
James Watt Ho B66 65 B6
James Watt Jun & Inf Sch B21 65 E7
James Watt Queensway B4 164 C3
James Watt St
Birmingham B4 164 C3
West Bromwich B71 53 B8
Jamescroft CV3 134 E6
Jameson Rd B6 67 C8
Jameson St WV6 25 B4
Jane Lane Cl WS2 27 F4
Jane Lane Sch The WS2 27 F3
Janice Gr B14 105 B4
Janine Ave WV11 26 E7
Jaques Cl B46 59 B2
Jardine Cres CV4 111 F2
Jardine Rd B6 55 F1
Jarvis Cl LE10 71 D4
Jarvis Cres B69 64 A4
Jarvis Rd B23 56 F6
Jarvis Way B24 67 E8
JAS Ind Pk B65 63 E4
Jasmin Croft B14 104 E3
Jasmine Cl WV9 11 A3
Jasmine Gr Bromsgrove B61 136 F4
Codsall WV8 10 B3
Coventry CV3 134 C8
Royal Leamington Spa CV32 157 A2
Jasmine Rd Dudley DY2 51 F1
Tamworth B77 22 A4
Jasmine Way WS10 41 D7
Jason Cl B77 21 D5
Jason Rd DY9 81 F4
Javelin Ho B35 58 C3
Jay Park Cres DY10 117 B2
Jay Rd DY6 60 D8
Jayne Cl Wednesfield WV11 26 D7
West Bromwich B71 42 E1
Jays Ave DY4 52 B4
Jays Cres B48 123 B1
Jayshaw Ave B43 54 E8
Jeal Cl B47 124 E2
Jean Dr DY4 52 D6
Jeavons Pl WV14 40 C5
Jedburgh Ave WV6 23 E4
Jedburgh Gr CV3 133 A4
Jeddo St WV2 163 B1
Jeffcock Rd WV3 39 A7
Jefferies Cl LE10 71 E2
Jefferson Cl B71 53 B8
Jeffrey Ave WV4 39 F5
Jeffrey Cl CV12 95 D8
Jeffrey Rd B65 63 E3
Jeffrey Woods Cross CV1 113 F4
Jeffries Ho 11 B69 64 A7
Jeffs Ave WV2 163 C1
Jeliff St CV4 111 F2
Jelleyman Cl DY11 116 C6
Jellicoe Ho 9 DY4 52 A8
Jellicoe Way LE10 71 D3
Jenkins Ave CV5 111 F4
Jenkins Cl WV14 40 C5
Jenkins St B10 87 C8
Jenkinson Rd WS10 41 D1
Jenks Ave WV10 25 E8
Jennens Rd B4 66 F3
Jenner Cl WS2 28 A6
Jenner Ho WS2 27 F6
Jenner Rd WS2 28 A6
Jenner St Coventry CV1 165 C4
Wolverhampton WV2 163 D2
Jennifer Wlk B25 88 E8
Jennings St B64 62 F2
Jenny Cl WV14 40 E1
Jenny Walkers La WV6 23 D1
Jennyns Ct 3 WS10 42 A3
Jensen B77 21 E2
Jenton Rd CV31 162 B6
Jephcott Ho 2 CV1 113 E3
Jephcott Rd B8 68 A4
Jephson Ct CV2 96 C4
Jephson Dr B26 88 F7
Jephson Pl 3 CV31 162 B7
Jeremy Gr B92 89 B3
Jeremy Rd WV4 39 C5
Jerome Ct B74 30 F1
Jerome Dr WS11 6 A5
Jerome Prim Sch The WS11 5 F5
Jerome Rd Norton Canes WS11 6 A5
Sutton Coldfield B72 46 D4
Walsall WS2 28 B1
Jerome Way WS7 7 C7
Jerrard Dr B75 46 C6
Jerrard Mews B75 46 C5
Jerry's La Birmingham B23 56 E6
Weeford WS14 19 B8
Jersey Cl B98 154 D7
Jersey Croft B36 70 B6
Jersey Rd B8 67 D4
Jerusalem Wlk DY10 116 E7
Jervis Cl DY5 61 C7
Jervis Cres B74 31 D3
Jervis Ct 2 WS1 28 F2
Jervis Rd B77 35 F5
Jervis Terr B21 65 D8
Jervoise Dr B31 103 B5
Jervoise Jun & Inf Sch B29 85 A1
Jervoise La B71 42 E1
Jervoise Rd B29 85 A2
Jervoise St B70 53 A4
Jesmond Gr B24 57 E4
Jesmond Rd CV1 113 F4
Jessel Rd WS2 28 C2
Jessie Rd WS9 16 B1
Jesson Cl WS1 43 A7
Jesson Ct WS1 43 A8
Jesson Rd Dudley DY3 51 A6
Sutton Coldfield B75 47 A5
Walsall WS1 43 A8
Jesson St B70 53 E2
Jesson's CE Prim Sch DY1 51 B1
Jevon St WV14 51 B8
Jevons Rd B73 45 C3
Jew's La DY3 50 E4
Jewellery Quarter Sta B18 66 B4
Jiggins La B32 84 D1
Jill Ave B43 43 C1
Jill La B96 159 B2
Jillcot Rd B92 89 B3
Jim Forrest Cl 4 CV3 134 F8
Jinnah Cl B12 86 F8
Joan of Arc Ho CV3 133 E6
Joan St WV2 39 E6
Joan Ward St CV3 133 D8
Joan's Cl 1 CV31 162 C6
Joanna Dr CV3 133 C3
Job's La CV4 112 A2
Jockey Field DY3 50 E6

Jockey La WS10 42 A4
Jockey Rd B73 46 A2
Jodrell St CV11 73 B6
Joe Williams Cl 7 CV3 134 F8
Joeys La WV8 10 C3
John Bosco Cl B71 53 B7
John Bright Cl DY4 51 F8
John Bright St B1 164 B2
John Cleveland Coll The LE10 71 F1
John F Kennedy Wlk 4 DY4 52 A8
John Feeney Tower B31 102 F7
John Grace St CV3 133 D8
John Gulson Prim Sch CV1 113 D5
John Harper St WV13 27 B2
John Ho DY1 61 D8
John Howell Dr DY4 52 A5
John Kempe Way B12 87 A7
John Kennedy Ave WV14 40 D2
John Knight Rd CV12 78 B5
John McGuire Cres CV3 134 E7
John Nash Sq CV8 147 F3
John Nichols St LE10 75 B7
John O'Gaunt Rd CV8 147 E3
John of Gaunt Ho CV3 133 E6
John Rd B62 83 F3
John Riley Dr WV12 27 C8
John Rous Ave CV4 132 B7
John Shelton Prim Sch CV6 95 D4
John Sinclair Ho CV1 165 B4
John Smith Ho 4 B1 66 C3
John St Bedworth CV12 78 A2
Birmingham B19 66 B7
Blackheath B65 63 C1
Brierley Hill DY5 61 D4
Cannock, High Town WS11 2 A4
Cannock, Wimblebury WS12 2 F3
Hinckley LE10 71 E1
Nuneaton, Coton CV11 73 C2
Nuneaton, Stockingford CV10 72 E3
Oldbury B69 64 A7
Royal Leamington Spa CV32 161 F8
Stourbridge DY8 60 F1
Tamworth B77 21 E4
Walsall WS2 28 E3
West Bromwich, Guns Village B70 53 B4
West Bromwich, Swan Village B70 52 F5
Willenhall WV13 27 A1
Wolverhampton WV2 40 A6
John St N B71 53 B5
John Tofts Ho CV1 165 B4
John Willmott Sch B76 46 F4
John Wood CE Inf Sch WS11 4 D8
John Wooton Ho 4 WS10 41 D6
John's Cl LE10 75 D5
John's La
Tipton, Dudley Port DY4 52 B4
Tipton, Tividale B69 52 C3
Johndory B77 35 D6
Johns Cl B80 159 C4
Johns Gr B43 54 C8
Johns La WS6 4 F3
Johnson Ave WV11 26 F7
Johnson Cl
Birmingham, Sparkhill B11 87 C5
Birmingham, Ward End B8 68 C6
Darlaston WS10 41 D5
Lichfield WS13 3 C1
Redditch B98 154 A5
Johnson Dr B35 57 F3
Johnson Pl WV14 41 A7
Johnson Rd Bedworth CV12 78 C3
Birmingham B23 57 A6
Burntwood WS7 6 F8
Cannock WS11 1 D4
Coventry CV6 114 A8
Darlaston WS10 41 D5
Wednesbury WS10 42 C2
Willenhall WV12 27 D7
Johnson St Birmingham B7 67 C6
Wolverhampton WV2 39 D7
Wolverhampton, Cinder Hill WV14 39 F1
Wood End CV9 36 C1
Johnsons Bridge Rd B71 53 C6
Johnsons Gr B68 84 D8
Johnston St B70 53 D1
Johnstone St B19 66 D8
Joiners Croft B92 107 E8
Joinings Bank B68 64 B4
Jon Baker Ct LE10 75 E8
Jonathan Rd CV2 114 F8
Jones Field Cres WV1 26 B2
Jones Ho WS2 28 D3
Jones' La WS7 7 F7
Jones La WS6 5 B1
Jones Rd Bedworth CV7 78 A1
Willenhall WV12 27 D8
Wolverhampton WV10 25 C6
Jones Wood Cl B76 58 A7
Jonkel Ave B77 36 A5
Jordan Cl Kenilworth CV8 148 B2
Lichfield WS13 9 A8
Smethwick B66 65 B5
Sutton Coldfield B75 32 B1
Jordan Ho B36 68 E8
Jordan Leys DY4 52 B5
Jordan Pl WV14 40 E3
Jordan Rd B75 32 B2
Jordan Way WS9 16 B1
Jordan Well CV1 165 C2
Jordans Cl B97 158 D6
Jordans The CV5 112 C4
Joseph Cash Prim Sch CV6 113 C7
Joseph Chamberlain VI Form Coll B12 86 F6
Joseph Creighton Cl CV3 134 E7
Joseph Halpin Ho 3 CV1 165 C4
Joseph Latham Ho 3 CV2 96 B1
Joseph Leckie Sch WS5 42 E5
Joseph Luckman Rd CV12 78 B4
Joseph Turner Prim Sch DY4 52 B7
Josiah Mason Coll B23 56 C4
Josiah Rd B31 102 D2
Jowett B77 21 E2
Jowett's La B71 53 B8
Joyberry Dr DY8 81 A3
Joyce Pool CV34 160 E7
Joynson St WS10 41 E5
Jubilee Ave Redditch B97 158 D7
West Bromwich B71 53 B7
Jubilee Bldgs WS10 41 D7
Jubilee Cl Great Wyrley WS6 4 F2
Walsall WS3 28 E6
Jubilee Cres CV6 113 B7
Jubilee Dr N DY11 116 B2
Jubilee Dr S DY11 116 B2
Jubilee Park Prim Sch DY4 52 B8
Jubilee Rd Bilston WV14 41 A4
Birmingham B45 101 E2
Tipton DY4 52 B8
Jubilee St B71 53 D8
Jubilee Terr Bedworth CV12 78 B4
Stoke Prior B60 150 C1
Jubilee Trad Ctr B5 66 E1
Judd Cl CV12 77 F3
Judds La CV6 95 E4
Judge Cl B69 64 A7
Judge Rd DY5 81 F7
Juggins La B94 141 B7
Julia Ave B24 57 F4
Julia Gdns B71 53 F8
Julian Cl Catshill B61 137 A8
Coventry CV2 114 F8
Great Wyrley WS6 5 A3
Wolverhampton WV1 26 B2
Julian Rd WV1 26 B2
Julie Croft WV14 40 E1
Juliet Cl CV11 74 A1
Juliet Rd B62 83 F3
Julius Dr B46 59 F1
Junction 2 Ind Est B69 63 F5
Junction Rd Birmingham B21 65 C8
Bromsgrove B61 136 E3
Stourbridge DY8 81 B4
Stourbridge, Amblecote DY8 81 E1
Wolverhampton WV2 40 B7
Junction St Coventry CV1 165 A2
Dudley DY2 62 B8
Oldbury, Brades Village B69 52 E1
Walsall WS1 42 D7
Junction St S B69 64 A5
Junction The DY8 80 E8
June Cres B77 21 E5
June Croft B26 89 D5
Juniper B77 22 A4
Juniper Cl B27 88 B5
Juniper Dr Coventry CV5 111 F5
Sutton Coldfield B76 58 A7
Juniper Ho B36 68 F7
Juniper Rise B63 82 C5
Jury Rd DY5 81 F7
Jury St CV34 160 E6
Jutland Rd B13 105 B8

Kanzan Rd CV2 96 B4
Kareen Gr CV3 135 C7
Karen Cl CV10 72 E7
Karen Way DY5 81 D8
Karlingford Cl CV5 132 D8
Kate's Hill Prim Sch DY2 62 E8
Katherine Rd B67 64 F2
Kathleen Ave CV12 77 E1
Kathleen Rd Birmingham B25 88 C7
Sutton Coldfield B72 46 C4
Katie Rd B29 85 E1
Kayne Cl DY6 60 C7
Keanscott Dr B68 64 C4
Keasdon Gr WV13 27 C3
Keating Gdns B75 32 A4
Keatley Ave B33 69 E2
Keats Ave Birmingham B10 87 D7
Cannock WS11 1 E5
Keats Cl Dudley DY3 50 A5
Nuneaton CV10 72 A4
Stourbridge DY8 81 A8
Sutton Coldfield B74 31 F6
Tamworth B79 20 F8
Keats Dr WV14 40 D2
Keats Gr Birmingham B27 88 B1
Wolverhampton WV10 26 A8
Keats Ho 2 Oldbury B68 64 C4
Redditch B97 158 C8
Keats Pl DY10 117 B6
Keats Rd Coventry CV2 114 D2
Walsall WS3 28 E7
Willenhall WV12 27 E7
Wolverhampton WV10 12 A1
Keble Cl Burntwood WS7 7 C7
Cannock WS11 4 E8
Keble Gr Birmingham B26 89 B6
Walsall WS1 43 A7
Keble Ho B37 70 A2
Keble Wlk B79 21 A6
Kebull Gn CV4 131 E8
Kedleston Cl WS3 14 A3
Kedleston Ct B28 105 F4
Kedleston Rd B28 105 F5
Keegan Wlk WS2 27 F4
Keel Dr B13 87 D1
Keele Cl B98 154 E6
Keele Ho B37 70 B4
Keeley St B9 67 B2
Keeling Dr WS11 1 B1
Keeling Rd CV8 148 B5
Keelinge St DY4 52 B5
Keen St B66 65 D5
Keenan Dr CV12 77 D1
Keeper's Cl WS7 7 A6
Keepers Cl Brownhills WS9 15 F3
Kingswinford DY6 60 B8
Lichfield WS14 9 E7
Keepers Gate Cl B74 46 C7
Keepers Ho B73 45 C2
Keepers La Codsall WV8 10 A1
Wolverhampton WV6 24 A7
Keepers Rd B74 31 C5
Keepers Wlk CV12 77 D1
Keer Ct B9 67 B2
Kegworth Cl CV6 96 A4
Kegworth Rd B23 56 C2
Keir Cl CV32 157 A2
Keir Hardy Wlk B69 52 D2
Keir Pl DY8 80 E8
Keir Rd WS10 42 D2
Keith Rd CV32 157 B4
Keith Winter Cl B61 136 F6
Kelby Cl B31 102 E4
Kelby Rd B31 102 F4
Keldy Cl WV6 24 F5
Kele Rd CV4 132 A7
Kelfield Ave B17 85 B4
Kelham Pl B92 89 B1
Kelia Dr B67 64 F6
Kellett Rd B7 67 A4
Kelling Cl DY5 81 C8
Kellington Cl B8 67 F4
Kelmarsh Dr B91 107 B1
Kelmscote Rd CV6 112 F8
Kelmscott Rd B17 85 B7
Kelsall Cl WV1 26 B2
Kelsall Croft B1 66 B3
Kelsey Cl Birmingham B7 67 B4
Nuneaton CV11 73 E3
Kelsey La CV7 130 D5
Kelsey's Cl CV8 135 F3
Kelso Gdns WV6 23 D4
Kelsull Croft B37 70 A2
Kelton Ct B15 86 A7
Kelvedon Gr B91 107 C4
Kelverdale Gr B14 104 C4
Kelverley Gr B71 43 A1
Kelvin Ave CV2 114 D5
Kelvin Cl DY11 116 A8
Kelvin Dr WS11 2 A3
Kelvin Pl WS2 28 B6
Kelvin Rd Birmingham B31 103 B1
Royal Leamington Spa CV32 157 C5
Walsall WS2 28 B6
Kelvin Way B70 53 C1
Kelvin Way Trad Est B70 53 B1
Kelway CV3 115 A2
Kelway Ave B43 44 B3
Kelwood Dr B63 83 A5
Kelynmead Rd B33 69 A2
Kem St CV11 73 E2
Kemberton Cl WV3 24 C1
Kemberton Rd
Birmingham B29 85 B2
Wolverhampton WV3 24 C1
Kemble Cl WV12 27 D3
Kemble Croft B5 86 E7
Kemble Dr B35 58 A3
Kemelstowe Cres B63 100 C8
Kemerton Ho B97 153 B4
Kemerton Way B90 126 F6
Kemp Cl CV34 161 A7
Kempe Rd B33 69 A4
Kempley Ave CV2 114 C2
Kemps Green Rd
Balsall Common CV7 130 B6
Tanworth-in-A B94 143 A1
Kempsey Cl Halesowen B63 82 E4
Oldbury B69 63 E4
Redditch B98 159 B7
Solihull B92 89 A3
Kempsey Covert B38 123 E7
Kempsey Ho B32 102 A8
Kempsford Cl B98 158 F6
Kempson Ave
Sutton Coldfield B72 46 C1
West Bromwich B71 53 B5
Kempson Rd B36 68 F8
Kempsons Gr WV14 40 B3
Kempthorne Ave WV10 25 E8
Kempthorne Gdns WS3 14 A2
Kempthorne Rd WV14 40 F6
Kempton Cres CV32 157 C4
Kempton Ct B61 121 A1
Kempton Dr WS6 4 F2
Kempton Park Rd B36 68 D8
Kempton Way DY8 80 E3
Kemsey Dr WV14 40 F3
Kemshead Ave B31 122 E8
Kemsley Rd B14 104 F2
Kenchester Cl B98 154 F2
Kenchester Ho 2 B16 66 A2
Kendal Ave Birmingham B45 122 B7
Coleshill B46 70 F7
Royal Leamington Spa CV32 156 C2
Kendal Cl Bromsgrove B60 137 B1
Nuneaton CV11 74 A6
Wolverhampton WV6 24 F6
Kendal Ct Birmingham B23 56 B3
Cannock WS11 4 B8
Kendal Dr B45 122 D1
Kendal End Rd B45 122 D1
Kendal Gr B92 107 F8
Kendal Rd B11 87 B7
Kendal Rise Coventry CV5 112 C4
Oldbury B68 64 B3
Wolverhampton WV6 24 F6
Kendal Rise Rd B45 122 B7
Kendal Tower B17 85 D5
Kendall Ho 15 B69 63 D5
Kendall Rise DY6 60 F5
Kendon Ave CV6 112 E6
Kendrick Ave B34 69 E5
Kendrick Cl Coventry CV6 96 A4
Solihull B92 107 F6
Kendrick Pl WV14 41 A4
Kendrick Rd Bilston WV14 41 A4
Sutton Coldfield B76 57 F5
Wolverhampton WV10 25 E6
Kendrick St WS10 42 A3
Kendricks Rd WS10 41 F7
Kenelm Ct CV3 134 C5
Kenelm Rd Birmingham B10 87 E8
Dudley WV14 40 C1
Oldbury B68 64 A3
Sutton Coldfield B73 46 B4
Kenelm's Ct B62 101 A4
Kenilcourt CV8 147 D6
Kenilworth Castle CV8 147 D5
Kenilworth Cl Redditch B97 158 D6
Stourbridge DY8 60 D2
Sutton Coldfield B74 46 A8
Tipton DY4 51 D4
Kenilworth Cres
Walsall WS2 28 A4
Wolverhampton WV4 39 E4
Kenilworth Ct
Birmingham, Edgbaston B15 85 F8
Birmingham, Gravelly Hill B24 56 E2
10 Cannock WS11 1 E1
Coventry CV3 133 C8
Dudley DY1 61 F8
Kenilworth Dr Cannock WS11 1 D4
Kidderminster DY10 116 E2
Nuneaton CV11 73 B3
Kenilworth Hall Mews CV8 147 F5
Kenilworth Ho
Birmingham B13 105 A6
3 Walsall WS3 28 C6
Kenilworth Rd
Balsall Common CV7, CV8 130 D4
Birmingham B20 55 E2
Coventry CV3 132 E3
Cubbington CV32 157 C6
Hampton in A B92 109 E5
Kenilworth CV8 148 C8
Knowle B93 128 E5
Lichfield WS14 9 B6
Meriden CV7 91 D1
Oldbury B68 84 D7
Perton WV6 23 F4
Royal Leamington Spa CV32 156 E5
Tamworth B77 21 E4
Kenilworth Sch CV8 148 C5
Kenilworth Sch Castle Sixth Form Ctr CV8 147 F2
Kenilworth St 16 CV32 156 F1
Kenley Gr B30 104 B3
Kenley Way B91 106 D4
Kenmare Way WV11 26 C4
Kenmore Ave WS12 1 F7
Kenmore Dr LE10 71 B2
Kenmure Rd B33 89 C8
Kennan Ave CV31 161 F6
Kennedy Cl
Kidderminster DY10 116 F3
Sutton Coldfield B72 46 C4
Tamworth B77 21 C1
Kennedy Cres
Darlaston WS10 41 C7
Dudley DY3 50 D4
Kennedy Croft B26 89 A7
Kennedy Ct 5 DY8 80 F5
Kennedy Gr B30 104 B6
Kennedy Rd WV10 163 D4
Kennedy Sq 3 CV32 157 A1
Kennerley Rd B25 88 D6
Kennet Cl Brownhills WS8 6 C2
Coventry CV2 114 C8
Kennet Gr B36 69 F8
Kennet Ho 5 DY1 61 E8
Kenneth Gr B23 56 B5
Kennford Cl B65 63 C6
Kennington Rd WV10 25 F5
Kenpas Highway CV3 133 A5
Kenrick Croft B35 57 F2
Kenrick Ho B16 66 A1
Kenrick Park Sta B66 53 E1
Kenrick Way B70 64 E8
Kensington Ave B12 87 A4
Kensington Ct CV5 113 A1
Kensington Dr B74 31 F5
Kensington Gdns
Cannock WS11 1 C2
Stourbridge DY8 60 C1
Kensington Pl WS12 5 C8
Kensington Rd
Birmingham B29 86 B2
Coventry CV5 113 A1
Willenhall WV12 27 B7
Kensington St B19 66 D6
Kenstone Croft 2 B12 86 F7
Kenswick Dr B63 83 A2
Kent Ave Fazeley B78 20 F1
Walsall WS2 28 B3
Kent Cl Aldridge WS9 16 B1
Coventry CV3 133 E6
Kidderminster DY10 116 E3
Walsall WS2 28 E5
West Bromwich B71 53 C7
Kent Close Prim Sch B71 53 B7
Kent Dr LE10 71 F4
Kent Pl Cannock WS12 2 F1
Dudley DY2 62 A6
Kent Rd Birmingham B45 101 F1
Halesowen B62 83 F5
Stourbridge DY8 80 D7
Wednesbury WS10 42 D4
Wolverhampton WV2 39 E7
Kent St Birmingham B5 66 E1
Dudley DY3 50 E5
Walsall WS2 28 E5
Kent St N B18 65 F5
Kent's Cl B92 88 F3
Kenthurst Cl CV5 111 C4
Kentish Rd B21 65 C8
Kentmere Cl CV2 96 E2
Kentmere Tower 4 B23 57 B6
Kenton Ave WV6 24 F4
Kenton Wlk 7 B29 85 F2
Kents Ho B33 69 B2
Kentwell B79 20 D7
Kenward Croft B17 84 F7
Kenway B47 125 A7
Kenwick Rd B17 85 B4
Kenwood Rd B9 68 B3
Kenwyn Gdns CV7 96 B8
Kenyon Cl Bromsgrove B60 137 A1
Stourbridge DY8 81 A7
Kenyon St B18 164 A4
Kepler B79 20 E7
Keppel St CV1 113 E5
Kerby Rd B23 56 D4
Keresley Brook Rd CV6 95 A2
Keresley Cl Coventry CV6 95 A2
Solihull B91 107 C5
Keresley Gr B29 84 F2
Keresley Grange Prim Sch CV6 94 F1
Keresley Green Rd CV6 94 F1
Keresley Newland Comb Sch CV7 94 F7
Keresley Rd CV6 113 A8
Kernthorpe Rd B14 104 D4
Kerr Dr DY4 51 E8
Kerria Ctr B77 22 A4
Kerria Rd B77 22 B4
Kerridge Cl WV9 11 A2
Kerrls Way CV3 115 A1
Kerry Cl Barwell LE9 71 F7
Birmingham B31 102 F6
Brierley Hill DY5 61 C4
Kerry Ct WS1 43 A8
Kerry Hill B60 150 E6
Kerry's Ho 4 CV1 113 B2
Kersley Gdns WV11 26 F5
Kerswell Dr B90 127 A5
Kesterton Rd B74 31 E5
Kesteven Cl B15 86 B6
Kesteven Rd B71 53 C7
Keston Rd B44 44 F4
Kestral Ho B35 58 C3
Kestrel B77 36 A6
Kestrel Ave B25 88 C8
Kestrel Cl Birmingham B23 56 D6
Hinckley LE10 75 F6
Kidderminster DY10 116 E3
Kestrel Croft 2 CV3 134 F8
Kestrel Dr B74 31 F5
Kestrel Gr Birmingham B30 103 D8
Cannock WS12 2 C1
Willenhall WV12 27 C8
Kestrel Rd Dudley DY1 51 A1
Halesowen B63 82 B7
Oldbury B68 63 F2
Kestrel Rise WV6 24 F7
Kestrel Way WS6 4 C2
Keswick Cl CV11 74 A6
Keswick Dr DY6 60 D6
Keswick Gn CV32 156 D1
Keswick Gr B74 30 F2
Keswick Ho 14 B69 63 D5
Keswick Rd B92 89 A4
Keswick Wlk CV2 114 F4
Ketley Croft B12 86 F7
Ketley Fields DY6 61 A5
Ketley Hill Rd DY1 61 F8
Ketley Rd DY6 60 F7
Kettlebrook Rd Solihull B90 127 C6
Tamworth B77 21 C3
Kettlehouse Rd B44 44 F3
Kettles Wood Dr B32 84 C2
Kettlesbank Rd DY3 50 C2
Kettlewell Cl CV34 155 E1
Kettlewell Way B37 69 F1
Ketton Gr B33 89 D7
Keviliok St CV3 133 D6
Kew Cl Birmingham B37 69 F3
Kenilworth CV8 148 C5
Kew Dr DY1 51 A2
Kew Gdns B33 68 E1
Kew Ho CV4 111 F3

Kewstoke Cl WV12 13 B1
Kewstoke Croft B31 102 E6
Kewstoke Rd WV12 13 C1
Key Bsns Pk B24 57 E3
Key Cl WS12 2 C3
Key Hill B18 66 B5
Key Hill Dr B18 66 B5
Key Ind Pk WV13 26 D3
Keyes Dr DY6 49 D1
Keynell Covert B30 104 C2
Keynes Dr WV14 40 E6
Keys Cres B71 53 C6
Keyse Rd B75 46 F7
Keyspark Rd WS12 2 E4
Keyte Cl DY4 52 A5
Keyway Jct WV13 41 B8
Keyway Ret Pk WV13 41 B8
Keyway The WV13 41 A8
Khyber Cl WS10 41 C8
Kidd Croft DY4 41 C2
Kidderminster Coll DY10 116 E4
Kidderminster General Hospl DY11 116 C5
Kidderminster General Hospl Mill Street Branch DY11 116 C7
Kidderminster Rd
Bromsgrove B61 136 C3
Hagley DY9 99 B5
Iverley DY10 98 C7
Kingswinford DY6 60 B7
Kidderminster Rd S DY9 98 F3
Kidderminster Sta DY10 116 F5
Kidderminster Town Sta DY10 116 F5
Kidson Eventide Homes WV6 24 F5
Kielder Cl Cannock WS12 2 E2
Walsall WS5 43 C3
Kielder Dr CV10 72 E2
Kielder Gdns DY9 81 B1
Kier's Bridge Cl DY4 52 B3
Kilburn Dr Coventry CV5 112 F3
Kingswinford DY6 49 E1
Kilburn Gr B44 44 F3
Kilburn Pl DY2 62 D6
Kilburn Rd B44 44 F3
Kilby Ave B16 66 A2
Kilby Gn LE10 75 F6
Kilby Gr CV31 162 C5
Kilbye Cl B77 35 F5
Kilbys Gr B20 54 F2
Kilcote Rd B90 105 C2
Kildale Cl CV1 165 D3
Kildwick Way 5 CV34 155 E1
Kilmarie Cl LE10 71 A1
Kilmet Wlk 1 B67 65 A5
Kilmore Croft B36 68 E8
Kilmorie Rd Birmingham B27 88 C5
Cannock WS11 1 C2
Kiln Cl
Royal Leamington Spa CV32 157 A1
Studley B80 159 C4
Kiln Croft B65 63 A4
Kiln Way Polesworth B78 22 F1
Shilton CV12 97 E7
Kilnsey Gr CV34 155 E1
Kilpeck Cl B98 154 F2
Kilsall Ct 12 WV3 25 C4
Kilsby Gr B91 127 C8
Kilvert Rd WS10 42 B2
Kimberley B77 35 F7
Kimberley Ave B8 67 E5
Kimberley Cl Aldridge B74 31 A2
Coventry CV5 111 F4
Redditch B98 154 B7
Kimberley Pl WV14 51 B7
Kimberley Rd Baginton CV8 133 F2
Bedworth CV12 78 C4
Smethwick B66 65 A7
Solihull B92 89 A1
Kimberley St WV3 25 A1
Kimberley Wlk B76 58 D6
Kimble Cl CV5 112 B4
Kimble Gr B24 57 D3
King's Mdw DY9 99 E3
Kimmond Ct 17 CV32 156 F1
Kimpton Cl B14 104 E2
Kimsan Croft B74 45 A7
Kinchford Cl B91 127 B8
Kineton Cl B98 154 D1
Kineton Croft B32 102 D8
Kineton Green Inf Sch B92 88 D1
Kineton Green Rd B92 106 D8
Kineton Ho B13 105 A6
Kineton La B94 127 A1
Kineton Rd Birmingham B45 121 E7
Coventry CV2 114 C6
Kenilworth CV8 148 C4
Sutton Coldfield B73 45 E1
Kineton Rise DY3 39 C2
Kinfare Dr WV6 24 B4
Kinfare Rise DY3 50 E4
King Charles Ave WS2 27 E2
King Charles Cl DY11 116 C6
King Charles Ct B44 45 B2
King Charles Cty Prim Sch WS2 27 F2
King Charles I High Sch DY10 117 A5
King Charles Rd B62 83 F4
King Charles Sq 4 DY10 116 E6
King David Jun & Inf Sch B13 86 F2
King Edmund St DY1 51 B2
King Edward Ave B61 136 F5
King Edward IV Handsworth Sch B21 66 A7
King Edward Rd
Birmingham B13 86 F3
Bromsgrove B61 136 F5
Coventry CV1 113 F4
Nuneaton CV11 73 D4
King Edward St WS10 41 D6
King Edward VI Aston Sch B6 66 F8
King Edward VI Camp Hill Schs B14 104 D7
King Edward VI Coll
Nuneaton CV11 73 D4
Stourbridge DY8 81 A6
King Edward VI Cty Sch WS14 9 C6
King Edward VI Five Ways Sch B32 102 C8
King Edward VI High Sch for Girls B15 86 A4
King Edward's Row WV2 163 B1
King Edward's Sch B15 86 A4
King Edward's Sq B73 46 B5
King Edwards Cl B20 66 B8
King Edwards Gdns B20 66 B7
King Edwards Rd B1 66 B2
King George Ave B61 136 F4
King George Cl B61 136 F4
King George Cres WS4 29 B6
King George Pl WS4 29 B6
King George VI Ave WS5 29 C1
King George's Ave
Bedworth CV12 78 B5
Coventry CV6 95 F2
King George's Way LE10 75 B7
King Henry VIII Sch CV1 165 A1
King Richard Rd LE10 71 C2
King Richard St CV2 113 F3
King St Bedworth CV12 78 C2
Bilston WV14 40 E3
Birmingham B11 87 A7
Blackheath B64 62 F1
Brierley Hill DY5 82 A8
Brownhills WS9 15 F2
Burntwood WS7 6 F5
Dudley DY2 51 C1
Dudley, Roseville WV14 51 A8
Halesowen B63 83 A4
2 Hinckley LE10 71 D1
Royal Leamington Spa CV32 157 A1
Smethwick B66 65 B7
Stourbridge, Lye DY9 81 F5
Stourbridge, Wollaston DY8 80 E6
Tamworth B79 21 B5
Walsall WS1 42 D7
Wednesbury WS10 41 E3
Willenhall WV13 27 B2
Wolverhampton WV1 163 C3
King Street Pas
Brierley Hill DY5 82 A8
2 Dudley DY2 51 D1
King William St
Coventry CV1 113 E4
Stourbridge DY8 80 F8
King's Ave B69 52 B2
King's Ct CV11 73 B4
King's Heath Boys Sch B13 105 A6
King's Heath Jun Sch B14 86 F1
King's Hill Day Hospl WS10 41 E5
King's Hill Field WS10 41 E5
King's Hill La CV8 133 B2
King's Hill Rd WS14 9 C6
King's Hill Sch WS10 41 E5
King's Norton Boys Sch B30 103 E4
King's Norton Bsns Ctr B30 103 F4
King's Norton Girls Sch B30 103 F5
King's Norton Sta B38 103 F4
King's Rd Birmingham B44 44 E3
Kidderminster DY11 116 C6
King's Rise Com Prim Sch B44 45 A2
Kingfield Rd
Coventry CV1, CV6 113 D7
Solihull B90 105 C2
Kingfisher B77 36 A6
Kingfisher Ave CV10 72 C5
Kingfisher Cl DY3 39 C2
Kingfisher Ct B48 139 A7
Kingfisher Dr
Birmingham B36 70 A8
Cannock WS12 2 C5
Stourbridge DY8 80 C4
Kingfisher Ent Pk B98 154 A3
Kingfisher Gr
Kidderminster DY10 117 B3
Willenhall WV12 27 C8
Kingfisher Ind Est B70 52 F4
Kingfisher Pk B26 89 A6
Kingfisher Sh Ctr 2 B97 153 E3
Kingfisher Veiw B34 69 A5
Kingfisher Way B30 103 D8
Kingfisher Wlk B97 153 D4
Kingham Cl Dudley DY3 50 C2
Redditch B98 154 F4
Kingham Covert B14 104 D2
Kingland Dr CV32 156 C1
Kings Ave WS12 2 C4
Kings Bsns Pk B44 44 E3
Kings Centre Jaffrey Sch B23 56 E3
Kings Cl B14 104 C6
Kings Croft
Birmingham, Castle Bromwich B36 69 F7
Birmingham, Sheldon B26 89 A5
Kings Ct Stourbridge DY8 80 E5
Sutton Coldfield B75 32 B3
Tipton DY4 52 A4
Kings Ct Cross St WS10 41 E3
Kings Ct King St WS10 41 E3
Kings Garden B30 103 E4
Kings Gdns CV12 78 C2
Kings Gr CV2 114 B3
Kings Green Ave B38 103 F2
Kings High Sch for Girls CV34 160 E7
Kings Hill Cl WS10 41 E5
Kings Hill Mews WS10 41 D5
Kings Hill Pk WS10 41 E4
Kings Ho B24 57 A4
Kings Mews WS14 9 B5
Kings Norton Bsns Ctr B30 104 A4
Kings Norton High Sch B38 123 F8
Kings Norton Inf & Jun Sch B30 104 A2
Kings Norton L Ctr B38 123 F8
Kings Par B4 164 C2
Kings Rd
Birmingham, Kingstanding B44, B73 45 B2
Birmingham, Stirchley B14 104 C6
Birmingham, Stockland Green B23 56 D4
Birmingham, Tyseley B11 88 A6
Sedgley DY3 50 E8
Walsall WS4 29 C7
Kings Road Ind Est B25 88 A6
Kings Sq Dudley WV14 51 A8
West Bromwich B70 53 D3
Kings St WS10 41 D6
Kings Terr B14 104 C6
Kingsbridge Ho B23 56 B6
Kingsbridge Rd
Birmingham B32 84 D1
Nuneaton CV10 73 D6
Kingsbridge Wlk 6 B66 65 B5
Kingsbrook Dr B91 127 B8
Kingsbury Bsns Pk B76 58 E6
Kingsbury Cl Minworth B76 58 D5
Walsall WS4 29 B4
Kingsbury Rd
Birmingham, Birches Green B24 57 B3
Birmingham, Tyburn B24, B35 57 E3
Coventry CV6 112 E5
Curdworth B76 59 B7
Minworth B76 58 D5
Sutton Coldfield B35, B76 58 B5
2 Tipton DY4 52 A8
Kingsbury Sch B24 57 A2
Kingsclere Wlk WV4 38 C6
Kingscliff Rd B10 88 A8
Kingscote Cl B98 154 D7
Kingscote Gr CV3 133 A4
Kingscote Rd
Birmingham B15 85 E6
Dorridge B93 127 E2
Kingscroft Cl B74 45 A8
Kingscroft Rd B74 45 A8
Kingsdene Ave DY6 60 C4
Kingsdown Ave B42 55 A6
Kingsdown Rd B31 84 F1
Kingsfield Ind Est CV1 113 C6
Kingsfield Rd B14 104 E8
Kingsford Cl B36 58 D1
Kingsford Nouveau DY6 61 A5
Kingsgate Ho B37 70 A2
Kingshayes Rd WS9 16 B1
Kingshill Dr B38 103 F2
Kingshurst CV31 162 E6
Kingshurst Ho B37 69 F5
Kingshurst Inf Sch B37 70 A6
Kingshurst Jun Sch B37 70 A6
Kingshurst Rd
Birmingham B31 103 A3
Solihull B90 105 F1
Kingshurst Way B37 69 F5
Kingsland Ave CV5 112 F2
Kingsland Dr B93 127 E4
Kingsland Jun & Inf Sch B44 44 F4
Kingsland Rd
Birmingham B44 44 F4
Wolverhampton WV1 25 B3
Kingslea Rd B91 106 E2
Kingsleigh Dr B36 69 A8
Kingsleigh Rd B20 55 B2
Kingsley Ave Cannock WS12 2 C7
Redditch B98 154 A3
Wolverhampton WV6 24 B4
Kingsley Cl B79 21 A6
Kingsley Cres CV12 79 B3
Kingsley Ct
Binley Woods CV3 135 D6
Birmingham B25 88 E8
Kingsley Gr DY3 50 A5
Kingsley Prep Sch B93 128 A4
Kingsley Rd
Birmingham, Balsall Heath B12 87 A6
Birmingham, King's Norton B30 103 D4
Kingswinford DY6 60 B5
Kingsley Sch The CV32 156 F1
Kingsley St Dudley DY2 62 C5
Walsall WS2 42 B7
Kingsley Terr CV2 114 E8
Kingsley Wlk CV2 114 F7
Kingslow Ave WV4 38 D6
Kingsmead Coll B29 103 D8
Kingsmead Cty High Sch WS12 2 C4
Kingsmere Cl B24 56 F2
Kingspiece Ho 6 B36 68 E8
Kingstanding Ctr B44 44 F3
Kingstanding Rd B44 55 F7
Kingstanding Specl Sch B44 44 E1
Kingsthorne Jun & Inf Sch B44 45 A1
Kingsthorpe Rd B14 105 A3
Kingston Arc 8 WS11 1 E1
Kingston Cl B79 21 C7
Kingston Ct B74 46 B7
Kingston Dr LE10 71 E4
Kingston Ind Est B9 67 B1
Kingston Mews CV31 162 C6
Kingston Rd Birmingham B9 67 B1
Coventry CV5 112 F2
Kingston Row B1 66 C2
Kingston Way DY6 60 C7
Kingsway Cannock WS11 2 A4
Coventry CV2 114 A3
Essington WV11 13 A4
Nuneaton CV11 73 B4
Oldbury B68 84 B7
Royal Leamington Spa CV31 161 F6
Stourbridge DY8 80 D8
Wolverhampton WV10 26 A6
Kingsway Ave 8 DY4 52 A8
Kingsway Dr B38 103 F2
Kingsway Ho CV12 78 C2
Kingsway Rd WV10 26 A6
Kingswear Ave WV6 23 F3
Kingswinford Rd DY1 61 F7
Kingswinford Sch DY6 60 D7
Kingswood Ave Cannock WS11 4 C7
Corley CV7 94 B8
Kingswood Cl Coventry CV6 95 D1
Lapworth B94 144 E5
Solihull B90 106 D1
Kingswood Cotts B94 144 D3
Kingswood Croft B7 67 C7
Kingswood Dr
Great Wyrley WS6 5 A4
Norton Canes WS11 5 F5
Sutton Coldfield B74 44 F5
Kingswood Gdns WV4 38 F6
Kingswood Ho B14 104 E2
Kingswood Local Ctr CV10 72 B4
Kingswood Rd
Birmingham, Coft Common B31 122 F7
Birmingham, Moseley B13 87 A4
Kingswinford DY6 60 C4
Nuneaton CV10 72 B4
Kingswood Sch B90 106 B2
Kington Cl WV12 27 B8
Kington Gdns B37 69 F2
Kington Way B33 68 E1
Kiniths Cres B71 53 E5
Kiniths Way Halesowen B62 63 E1
West Bromwich B71 53 E4
Kinlet Cl Redditch B98 154 E3
Wolverhampton WV3 38 A8
Kinlet Gr B31 103 C2
Kinloch Dr DY1 50 F3
Kinnerley St WS1 29 A1
Kinnersley Cl B98 154 E3
Kinnersley Cres B69 63 D5
Kinnerton Cres B29 84 F2
Kinross Ave WS12 1 F7
Kinross Cl CV10 72 F2
Kinross Cres B43 44 B4
Kinross Rd CV32 157 B4
Kinross Way LE10 71 A1
Kinsall Gn B77 36 C6
Kinsey Gr B14 104 F4
Kinsham Dr B91 127 B8
Kintore Croft B32 102 B7
Kintyre Cl Birmingham B45 101 E1
Hinckley LE10 71 B1
Kintyre The CV2 115 B7
Kinver Ave
Kidderminster DY11 116 A1
Willenhall WV12 27 B5
Kinver Cl CV2 96 E1
Kinver Cres WS9 16 C1
Kinver Croft Birmingham B12 86 E7
Sutton Coldfield B76 58 A8
Kinver Ct B11 87 D4
Kinver Dr Hagley DY9 99 C7
Wolverhampton WV4 38 C5
Kinver Rd B31 103 D2
Kinver St DY8 60 E1
Kinwalsey La CV7 92 F6
Kinwarton Cl B26 88 D6
Kipling Ave Burntwood WS7 7 A8
Dudley WV14 40 B1
Warwick CV34 160 C4
Kipling Cl Nuneaton CV10 72 A5
Tipton DY4 52 A8
Kipling Ho B63 82 B5
Kipling Rd Birmingham B30 103 C4
Coventry CV6 113 A8
Dudley DY3 50 A5
Willenhall WV12 27 E8
Wolverhampton WV10 11 D2
Kipling Rise B79 20 F8
Kipling Wlk 3 DY10 117 B6
Kirby Ave CV34 155 F1
Kirby Cl Bilston WV14 40 E3
Brandon CV8 135 F5
Coventry CV1 113 D6
Kirby Cnr CV4 132 B5
Kirby Corner Rd CV4 132 B6
Kirby Rd Birmingham B18 65 E6
Coventry CV5 112 F2
Kirfield Dr LE10 71 F3
Kirkby Gn B73 46 B3
Kirkdale Ave CV6 95 D3
Kirkham Gdns DY5 61 C6
Kirkham Gr B33 68 F4
Kirkham Way DY4 52 A5
Kirkland Way B78 34 B8
Kirkside Gr WS8 15 F7
Kirkstall Cl WS3 13 F2
Kirkstall Cres WS3 13 F2
Kirkstone Cres
Birmingham B43 54 F6
Wombourne WV5 49 A6
Kirkstone Ct DY5 81 B8
Kirkstone Rd CV12 78 A2
Kirkstone Way DY5 81 B8
Kirkstone Wlk CV11 74 A6
Kirkwall Rd B32 84 D1
Kirkwood Ave B23 56 F7
Kirmond Wlk WV6 25 C5
Kirstead Gdns WV6 24 B3
Kirtley B77 21 E2
Kirton Cl Coventry CV6 94 F1
Whitnash CV31 162 B3
Kirton Gr Birmingham B33 69 A4
Solihull B91 107 A1
Wolverhampton WV6 24 C4
Kitchen La Wednesfield WV11 26 F8
Wolverhampton WV11 12 F1
Kitchener Rd
Birmingham B29 86 B1
Coventry CV6 113 E8
Dudley DY2 51 F1
Kitchener St B66 65 D6
Kitebrook Cl Redditch B98 154 E4
Solihull B90 127 A7
Kites Cl CV34 155 E2
Kites Nest La CV35 146 C1
Kitsland Rd B34 69 E6
Kitswell Gdns B32 102 A8
Kitt's Green Rd B33 69 B3
Kittermaster Rd CV7 92 C1
Kittiwake Dr Brierley Hill DY5 81 D7
Kidderminster DY10 117 B3
Kittoe Rd B74 32 A3
Kitwell La B32 102 A8
Kitwell Prim Sch B32 102 A7
Kitwood Ave B78 36 F6
Kitwood Dr B92 107 D7
Kixley La B93 128 C6
Klaxon Ind Est B11 87 F4
Klevedon Cl CV11 74 A1
Knapton Dr LE10 71 A3
Knaresdale Cl DY5 81 C8
Knaves Castle Ave WS8 6 F2
Knebley Cres CV10 73 C1
Knebworth Cl B44 55 E8
Knibbs Sh Ctr The CV34 160 E7
Knight Ave CV1 113 E1
Knight Ct B75 47 C5
Knight Ho B13 105 D7
Knightcote Dr
Royal Leamington Spa CV32 161 E8
Solihull B91 127 B8
Knightley Cl CV32 157 E5
Knightley Rd B91 106 F2
Knightlow Ave CV3 134 C6
Knightlow Cl CV8 148 C3
Knightlow Rd B17 85 B8
Knighton Cl B74 31 F3
Knighton Ct B23 56 C2
Knighton Dr B74 31 F3
Knighton Rd
Birmingham B31 103 C4
Cannock WS12 2 E3
Dudley DY2 62 D4
Sutton Coldfield B74 31 D5
Knights Ave WV6 24 E6
Knights Cl Birmingham B23 56 E2
Hinckley LE10 75 D4
Knights Cres WV6 24 E7
Knights Ct Hinckley LE10 74 E8
Norton Canes WS11 6 A4
Knights Hill WS9 30 B3
Knights Rd B11 88 A4
Knights Wood Cl B75 46 D7
Knightsbridge Ave CV12 78 C4
Knightsbridge Cl B74 31 F4
Knightsbridge Ct B37 69 F5
Knightsbridge La WV12 27 C6
Knightsbridge Rd B92 89 A1
Knightsford Cl B97 152 F2
Knightstone Ave B18 66 A4
Knightwick Cres B23 56 C5
Knipersley Rd B73 57 A7
Knoll Cl WS7 7 A5
Knoll Croft Aldridge WS9 16 C1
Cheswick Green B90 126 D4
Coventry CV3 133 C6
Knoll Dr Coventry CV3 133 C6
Warwick CV34 155 E1
Knoll Sch The DY11 116 A7
Knoll The Birmingham B32 84 C1
Kingswinford DY6 60 E5
Knollcroft B16 66 A2

Knott Ct 11 DY5 61 D2
Knottesford Cl B80 159 C3
Knotts Farm Rd DY6 61 A4
Knottsall La B68 64 B3
Knowesley Cl B60 137 B2
Knowlands Rd B90 127 A7
Knowle CE Jun & Inf Sch B93 128 C6
Knowle Cl Birmingham B45 122 D7
Redditch B98 154 C6
Knowle Hill CV8 148 C6
Knowle Hill Rd DY2 62 B4
Knowle La WS14 9 B3
Knowle Rd Birmingham B11 87 D3
Blackheath B65 63 A4
Hampton in A B92 108 E2
Knowle Sch The B65 63 A4
Knowle Wood Rd B93 128 B3
Knowles Ave CV10 72 C4
Knowles Dr B74 46 A7
Knowles Rd WV1 25 F1
Knowles St WS10 42 A3
Knox Cres CV11 73 F8
Knox Rd WV2 39 D6
Knox's Grave La WS14 19 D7
Knutswood Cl B13 105 D7
Kohima Dr DY8 80 E5
Kossuth Rd WV14 40 A1
Kurtus B77 35 D6
Kyle Cl WV10 11 B1
Kyles Way B32 102 B7
Kynaston Cres WV8 10 B2
Kynaston Ho B71 53 C8
Kyngsford Rd B33 69 D3
Kynner Way CV3 135 B8
Kynoch Wks B6 55 F3
Kyotts Lake Rd B11 87 B7
Kyotts Lake Unit Factory B11 87 B7
Kyrwicks La B11 87 A7
Kyter La B36 69 B8

Laburnham Ct WS14 9 C5
Laburnham Rd DY6 60 E6
Laburnum Ave
Birmingham B37 69 F6
Cannock WS11 4 E7
Coventry CV6 112 F5
Kenilworth CV8 148 A4
Smethwick B67 64 E4
Tamworth B79 21 B8
Laburnum Cl Bedworth CV12 77 E2
Birmingham B37 69 F6
Cannock WS11 4 E7
Hollywood B47 125 A5
Redditch B98 153 E2
Stourbridge DY8 80 E7
Walsall WS3 15 A2
Laburnum Cotts B21 65 E8
Laburnum Croft B69 52 B2
Laburnum Dr
Sutton Coldfield B76 47 A3
Whitnash CV31 162 B3
Laburnum Gr
Birmingham B13 86 F3
Bromsgrove B61 136 F4
Burntwood WS7 6 F6
Kidderminster DY11 116 B8
Nuneaton CV10 72 D6
Walsall WS2 27 F3
Warwick CV34 156 B1
Laburnum Ho WS4 15 D1
Laburnum Rd Bilston WV1 40 B8
Birmingham B30 103 F8
Brownhills WS9 16 A3
Dudley DY1 51 C4
Tipton DY4 51 F7
Walsall WS5 43 C4
Wednesbury WS10 42 B4
Wolverhampton WV4 39 F3
Laburnum St Stourbridge DY8 80 E7
Wolverhampton WV3 25 B1
Laburnum Trees B47 124 F7
Laburnum Villas 2 B11 87 C5
Laburnum Way B31 103 A1
Laceby Gr B13 87 D1
Lacell Cl CV34 155 E1
Ladbroke Dr B76 46 F2
Ladbroke Gr B27 106 C8
Ladbroke Pk CV34 155 E1
Ladbrook Cl B98 158 E7
Ladbrook Gr DY3 50 B3
Ladbrook Rd Coventry CV5 112 A4
Solihull B91 107 C2
Ladbury Gr WS5 43 A4
Ladbury Rd WS5 43 A3
Ladeler Gr B33 69 E2
Lady Bank Birmingham B32 102 B7
Tamworth B79 21 B4
Lady Brades Ho 5 B69 64 A7
Lady Byron La B93 127 F8
Lady Grey's Wlk DY8 80 D5
Lady Harriet's La B98 153 F4
Lady Katherine Leveson CE Prim Sch B93 129 B5
Lady La Coventry CV6 95 F4
Earlswood B90, B94 126 B3
Kenilworth CV8 147 F4
Lady Warwick Ave CV12 78 D2
Ladycroft Birmingham B16 66 B2
Cubbington CV32 157 E5
Ladyfields Way CV6 95 B4
Ladygrove Cl B98 159 A8
Ladymead Dr CV6 95 B2
Ladymoor Rd WV14 40 C3
Ladypool Ave 3 B11 87 B6
Ladypool Cl Halesowen B62 83 C4
Walsall WS4 29 A5
Ladypool Jun & Inf Sch B11 87 B6
Ladypool Rd B11, B12 87 A5
Ladysmith Rd B63 82 C6
Ladywell Cl WV5 49 A8
Ladywell Wlk B5 164 C1
Ladywood Cl DY5 61 F2
Ladywood Middleway B16 66 A2
Ladywood Rd
Birmingham B16 66 A1
Sutton Coldfield B74 46 A8
Lagonda B77 21 E3
Lagrange B79 20 E6
Laing Ho 2 B69 63 D5
Lair The B78 36 F8
Lake Ave WS5 43 C7
Lake Cl WS5 43 C7
Lake St DY3, DY1 50 E3
Lake View Rd CV5 112 F4
Lakedown Cl B14 104 E1
Lakefield Cl B28 106 B7
Lakefield Rd WV11 26 E5
Lakehouse Ct B23 56 E8
Lakehouse Gr B38 103 D3
Lakehouse Rd B73 56 F8
Lakeland Dr B77 36 A7
Lakeland Ho CV34 161 A7
Lakenheath B79 21 C7
Laker Cl DY8 81 A7
Lakes Cl DY11 116 C7
Lakes Rd B23 56 A6
Lakes Sta The B94 141 F8
Lakeside Bedworth CV12 78 A2
Little Aston B74 31 B5
Redditch B97 152 D7
Lakeside Cl WV13 26 E3
Lakeside Ct Birmingham B20 55 A4
Brierley Hill DY5 81 B8
Lakeside Dr
Norton Canes WS11 6 B6
Solihull B90 126 F7
Lakeside Inf Sch WV13 26 E3
Lakeside Prim Sch B77 21 E2
Lakeside Rd B70 53 A6
Lakeside Wlk B23 56 C3
Lakey La B28 106 A7
Lakey Lane Prim Sch B28 106 B7
Lakin Ct CV34 160 F8
Lakin Ho CV34 160 F8
Lakin Rd CV34 160 F8
Lamb Cl B34 69 E5
Lamb Cres WV5 49 A5
Lamb St CV1 165 B3
Lambah Cl WV14 40 F7
Lambert Cl B23 56 D6
Lambert Ct Kingswinford DY6 60 D8
Warwick CV34 160 D6
Lambert Dr WS7 7 A8
Lambert End B70 53 B3
Lambert Fold 4 DY2 62 E8
Lambert Rd WV10 25 F6
Lambert St B70 53 B3
Lambeth Cl Birmingham B37 70 B4
Coventry CV2 114 E7
Lambeth Rd Bilston WV14 40 B7
Birmingham B44 44 E3
Lambourn Cl WS3 14 C2
Lambourn Cres CV31 162 C6
Lambourn Rd B23 56 D4
Lambourne Cl Coventry CV5 112 A4
Great Wyrley WS6 4 F3
Lichfield WS14 9 E8
Lambourne Gr B37 69 E2
Lambourne Way DY5 81 B8
Lambscote Cl B90 105 C2
Lamerton Cl CV2 114 C6
Lamford Cl LE10 71 B1
Lamintone Dr CV32 156 D2
Lammas Cl B92 89 C1
Lammas Croft CV31 162 A3
Lammas Ct CV34 160 D6
Lammas Ho 6 CV6 113 A4
Lammas Rd Coventry CV6 112 F4
Stourbridge DY8 60 C3
Lammas Wlk CV34 160 D7
Lammermoor Ave B43 43 F2
Lamont Ave B32 84 F3
Lamorna Cl CV11 73 F4
Lamport Ho 5 B14 105 A3
Lamprey B77 35 D6
Lanark Cl DY6 60 F5
Lanark Croft B35 57 F3
Lancaster Ave Aldridge WS9 30 B8
Birmingham B45 122 A8
Wednesbury WS10 42 C3
Lancaster Circus Queensway B4 164 C4
Lancaster Cl B30 104 A6
Lancaster Gdns WV4 38 E5
Lancaster Ho Cannock WS12 2 D1
7 Oldbury B65 63 E4
6 Stourbridge DY8 80 F8
Lancaster Pl Kenilworth CV8 147 E2
Walsall WS3 14 C2
Lancaster Rd
Brierley Hill DY5 61 C2
Hinckley LE10 75 D8
Lancaster St B4 164 C4
Lance Cl LE10 75 D5
Lancelot Cl B8 67 E3
Lancelot Ho DY10 117 C8
Lancelot Pl B70 52 E4
Lanchester Cl B79 20 E7
Lanchester Rd
Birmingham B38 104 A1
Coventry CV6 113 B6
Lanchester Way B36 58 F1
Lancia Cl CV6 96 B4
Lancing Rd CV12 79 C2
Land La B37 90 A7
Land Oak Dr DY10 117 B7
Lander Cl B45 122 A6
Landgate Rd B21 54 C2
Landor Ho CV31 162 A2
Landor Rd Knowle B93 128 A6
Redditch B98 154 A1
Warwick CV34 160 D8
Whitnash CV31 162 A3
Landor St B8 67 B3
Landport Rd WV2 39 F8
Landrail Wlk B36 70 A8
Landrake Rd DY6 61 A5
Landsberg B79 20 F6
Landsdown Pl 2 B18 66 A5
Landseer Dr LE10 71 B3
Landseer Gr B43 44 D4
Landsgate DY8 81 A1
Landswood Cl B44 45 A1
Landswood Rd B68 64 C4
Landywood Ent Pk WS6 13 F8
Landywood Gn WS6 4 E2
Landywood La WS6 4 E2
Landywood Prim Sch WS6 13 F8
Landywood Sta WS6 4 F2
Lane Ave WS2 28 B3
Lane Cl WS2 28 B3
Lane Croft B76 58 A8
Lane Ct 8 WV3 25 C4
Lane Green Ave WV8 10 C1
Lane Green Ct WV8 10 B3
Lane Green Fst Sch WV8 10 B4
Lane Green Rd WV8 10 C2
Lane Green Sh Par WV8 10 B3
Lane Rd WV4 40 A3
Lane St WV14 40 D3
Lanes Sh Ctr The 1 B73 57 B7
Lanesfield Dr WV4 40 A4
Lanesfield Drive Ind Est WV4 40 A4
Lanesfield Prim Sch WV4 40 A4
Laneside CV3 134 E6
Laneside Ave B74 44 F7
Laneside Dr LE10 71 F3
Laneside Gdns WS2 28 B2
Langbank Ave CV3 134 D7
Langbay Ct CV2 114 F6
Langcliffe Ave CV34 155 F1
Langcomb Rd B90 126 A8
Langdale Ave CV6 95 D3
Langdale Cl Clayhanger WS8 15 E6
Royal Leamington Spa CV32 157 D3
Langdale Croft B21 65 E7
Langdale Dr Bilston WV14 40 D7
Cannock WS11 4 C7
Nuneaton CV11 74 A6
Langdale Gn WS11 4 C7
Langdale Rd Birmingham B43 54 F7
Hinckley LE10 75 A8
Langdale Way DY9 81 D4
Langdon St B9 67 B2
Langdon Wlk B27 88 E4
Langfield Rd B93 128 A7
Langford Ave B43 54 E8
Langford Croft B91 107 C2
Langford Gr B17 85 C3
Langham Cl B26 89 A7
Langham Gn B74 30 F1
Langholm Dr
Birmingham B44 45 D1
Cannock WS12 2 E2
Langland Dr DY3 50 C8
Langley Ave WV14 51 C8
Langley Cl B98 154 D1
Langley Cres B68 64 B4
Langley Croft CV4 112 A2
Langley Ct WV4 38 D6
Langley Dr B35 58 A1
Langley Gdns Oldbury B68 64 B4
Wolverhampton WV3 38 D7
Langley Green Rd B69 64 A4
Langley Green Sta B68 64 B5
Langley Hall Dr B75 47 B5
Langley Hall Rd
Solihull B92 106 C7
Sutton Coldfield B75 47 B5
Langley Heath Dr B76 47 A3
Langley High Sch B68 64 C4
Langley High St B69 64 A5
Langley Jun & Inf Sch B92 106 D6
Langley Mede B68 64 B5
Langley Prim Sch B69 64 A5
Langley Rd Birmingham B10 87 D8
Oldbury B68 64 B4
Whitnash CV31 162 A4
Wolverhampton WV3, WV4 38 B7
Langley Rise B92 89 E3
Langley Sch Solihull B92 106 D7
Sutton Coldfield B75 47 A6
Langley Wlk B37 70 D2
Langleys Rd B29 85 E1
Langlodge Rd CV6 95 B2
Langmead Cl WS2 27 D3
Langnor Rd CV2 114 C6
Langsett Rd WV10 25 E4
Langstone Rd
Birmingham B14 105 B3
Dudley DY1 50 F1
Langton Cl CV3 134 E8
Langton Ct WS13 3 A1
Langton Pl WV14 41 A6
Langton Rd B8 67 E4
Langtree Ave B91 107 B1
Langtree Cl WS12 2 D1
Langwood Cl CV4 132 B8
Langwood Ct B36 69 B8
Langworth Ave B27 88 C5
Lannacombe Rd B31 122 E6
Lansbury Ave WS10 41 C4
Lansbury Cl CV2 114 E7
Lansbury Dr WS11 1 E4
Lansbury Gn B64 83 B8
Lansbury Rd B64 83 B8
Lansbury Wlk 6 DY4 52 A8
Lansdale Ave B92 107 F8
Lansdown Gn DY11 116 C5
Lansdown Ho B15 86 D8
Lansdowne Cir CV32 157 A1
Lansdowne Cl
Bedworth CV12 78 A3
Dudley, Tansley Hill DY2 62 F6
Dudley, West Coseley WV14 51 A7
Lansdowne Cres
6 Royal Leamington Spa CV32 157 A1
Studley B80 159 D3
Tamworth B77 35 D8
Lansdowne Ct DY9 81 C1
Lansdowne Rd Bilston WV14 40 E7
Birmingham, Erdington B24 56 F3
Birmingham, Handsworth B21 66 A8
Halesowen, Hasbury B63 82 D2
Halesowen, Hurst Green B62 63 F1
2 Royal Leamington Spa CV32 157 A1
Studley B80 159 D3
Wolverhampton WV1 163 A4
Lansdowne St
Birmingham B18 65 F4
Coventry CV2 113 F3
Royal Leamington Spa CV32 157 A1
Lant Cl CV7 131 B7
Lantern Rd DY2 62 C2
Lapal La B68 84 A2
Lapal La N B62 83 E3
Lapal La S B62 83 F2
Lapal Prim Sch B62 83 F4
Lapley Cl WV1 26 B2
Lappath Ho B32 102 D8
Lapper Ave WV4 39 F2
Lapwing B77 36 A6
Lapwing Cl Cheslyn Hay WS6 4 C1
Kidderminster DY10 117 B1
Lapwing Dr B92 109 B7
Lapwood Ave DY6 61 A5
Lapworth CE Jun & Inf Sch B94 144 D3
Lapworth Cl B98 158 F7
Lapworth Dr B73 45 C3
Lapworth Gr B12 86 F6
Lapworth Oaks B94 144 D3
Lapworth Rd CV2 96 C1
Lapworth St B94 144 B2
Lapworth Sta B94 144 D4
Lara Cl B17 85 B8
Lara Gr DY4 52 A2
Larch Ave B21 54 D2
Larch Cl WS14 9 E7
Larch Croft Birmingham B37 70 B2
Tipton B69 52 B2
Larch Gr Sedgley DY3 50 E7
Warwick CV34 156 A1
Larch Ho Birmingham B36 68 F8
Stourbridge DY8 80 C6
Larch Rd DY6 60 E7
Larch Tree Ave CV4 112 A2
Larch Wlk B25 88 B8
Larches Cottage Gdns DY11 116 C3
Larches La WV3 25 A2
Larches Rd DY11 116 D4
Larches St B11 87 B6
Larches The Bedworth CV7 96 B8
Wolverhampton WV11 26 B5
Larchfield Cl B20 55 B3
Larchmere Dr
Birmingham B28 105 F8
Bromsgrove B61 136 E3
Essington WV11 13 B3
Larchwood Cres B74 44 E8
Larchwood Dr WS11 2 A4
Larchwood Gn WS5 43 B4
Larchwood Rd Bedworth CV7 78 B1
Walsall WS5 43 A4
Larcombe Dr WV4 39 E5
Large Ave WS10 41 C4
Lark Cl B14 105 A2
Lark Hall Cty Inf Sch B79 21 A8
Lark Meadow Dr B37 69 F3
Larkfield Ave B36 69 B8
Larkfield Rd B98 154 A1
Larkfield Way CV5 112 A6
Larkhill DY10 116 E7
Larkhill Rd DY8 80 D4
Larkhill Wlk B14 104 D1
Larkin Cl Bulkington CV12 79 B3
Wolverhampton WV10 12 A1
Larkspur B77 35 D4
Larkspur Ave WS7 7 A5
Larkspur Croft B36 68 D8
Larkspur Ct Bedworth CV12 95 C8
Halesowen B62 83 F7
Larkspur Dr WV10 12 B7
Larkspur Rd DY2 62 F8
Larkspur Way WS8 15 D6
Larkswood Dr Sedgley DY3 50 D7
Wolverhampton WV4 38 C3
Larne Rd B26 89 A7
Lashbrooke Ho B45 121 F7
Lassington Cl B98 154 E4
Latches Cl WS10 41 E6
Latchford Cl B98 154 E6
Latelow Rd B33 69 A2
Lath La B66 64 D8
Latham Ave B43 54 E7
Latham Cres DY4 52 A3
Latham Rd CV5 113 A2
Lathom Gr B33 68 F5
Latimer Cl CV8 147 F2
Latimer Gdns B15 86 D7
Latimer Pl B18 65 E6
Latimer Rd B48 139 A5
Latimer St WV13 27 B3
Latymer Cl B76 58 A7
Lauder Cl Sedgley DY3 39 C1
Willenhall WV13 26 D1
Lauderdale Ave CV6 95 D3
Lauderdale Cl WS8 15 E6
Lauderdale Gdns WV10 11 E3
Launceston Cl Tamworth B77 21 D2
Walsall WS5 43 D7
Launceston Dr CV11 73 F4
Launceston Rd WS5 43 D7
Launde The B28 105 E3
Laundry Cotts CV35 145 E4
Laundry Rd B66 65 C3
Laureates Wlk B74 46 A8
Laurel Ave B12 87 A5
Laurel Bank B79 21 B6
Laurel Bank Mews B60 137 F4
Laurel Cl Coventry CV2 96 E2
Dudley DY1 51 A3
Lichfield WS13 9 D8
Redditch B98 153 E2
Laurel Dr Burntwood WS7 7 C7
Cannock WS12 2 E4
Nuneaton CV10 72 A7
Smethwick B66 65 A8
Sutton Coldfield B74 44 E8
Laurel Gdns Birmingham B21 54 E1
4 Birmingham, Stockfield B27 88 C5
Laurel Gr Bilston WV14 41 A4
Birmingham B30 103 E6
Bromsgrove B61 136 F4
Wolverhampton WV3 38 E6
Laurel La B63 83 B3
Laurel Rd
Birmingham, Handsworth B21 54 F1
Birmingham, King's Norton B30 104 A4
Dudley DY1 51 A3
Tipton DY4 51 F7
Walsall WS5 43 B4
Laurels Cres CV7 130 C6
Laurels The Bedworth CV12 77 E2
Birmingham, Ladywood B16 65 F3
Birmingham, Sheldon B26 89 C5
Oldbury B68 84 B6
Smethwick B66 65 C4
Sutton Coldfield B73 46 B1
Laurence Ct B31 103 B5
Laurence Gr WV6 24 E7
Lauriston Cl DY1 50 F3
Lavender Ave CV6 112 F5
Lavender Cl WV9 10 F3
Lavender Gr WV14 40 F6
Lavender Hall La CV7 110 C2
Lavender Ho B38 123 F8
Lavender La DY8 80 D3
Lavender Rd Dudley DY1 51 B3
Tamworth B77 21 F4
Lavendon Rd B42 55 B5
Lavenham Cl CV11 79 C8
Lavinia Rd B62 83 E3
Law Cl B69 52 D2
Law Cliff Rd B42 55 B6
Law St B71 53 C5
Lawden Rd B10 87 B8
Lawford Ave WS14 9 E7
Lawford Cl Birmingham B7 67 A3
Coventry CV3 114 E1
Lawford Gr Birmingham B5 86 E8
Solihull B90 105 D2
Lawford Rd CV31 162 B5
Lawfred Ave WV11 26 D5
Lawley Cl Coventry CV4 112 A2
Walsall WS4 15 B1
Lawley Middleway B4 67 A3
Lawley Rd WV14 40 B6
Lawley St Dudley DY1 51 A1
West Bromwich B70 52 F3
Lawley The B63 82 D1
Lawn Ave DY8 80 E4
Lawn La Coven Heath WV9 11 A7
Wolverhampton WV9 10 F5
Lawn Rd WV2 39 F6
Lawn St DY8 80 E4
Lawnoaks Cl WS8 6 D2
Lawns The Bedworth CV12 77 C2
Hinckley LE10 75 E8
Lawnsdale Cl B46 70 F7
Lawnsdown Rd DY5 81 F6
Lawnsfield Gr B23 56 D7

Lawnside Gn WV14 40 D8
Lawnswood Hinckley LE10 75 A8
Stourbridge DY7 60 A2
Sutton Coldfield B76 58 A8
Lawnswood Ave
Burntwood WS7 6 F5
Solihull B90 106 D3
Stourbridge DY8 60 C3
Wolverhampton, Parkfields WV4 39 E4
Wolverhampton, Tettenhall WV6 24 E8
Lawnswood Cl WS12 2 D1
Lawnswood Dr
Brownhills WS9 16 A3
Stourbridge DY7 60 A2
Lawnswood Gr B21 54 C1
Lawnswood Rd Dudley DY3 50 D5
Stourbridge DY8 60 D3
Lawnswood Rise WV6 24 F8
Lawnwood Rd DY2 62 C2
Lawrence Ave
Wednesfield WV11 26 F6
Wolverhampton WV10 26 A4
Lawrence Ct 6 Oldbury B68 84 B8
Tamworth B79 21 A6
Lawrence Dr B76 58 D6
Lawrence Gdns CV8 148 A6
Lawrence La B64 62 E1
Lawrence Rd CV7 96 A8
Lawrence Saunders Rd CV6 113 B5
Lawrence St Stourbridge DY9 81 C6
Willenhall WV13 27 A3
Lawrence Wlk B43 44 D4
Lawson Cl WS9 30 B4
Lawson St B4 164 C4
Lawton Ave B29 86 B2
Lawton Cl Blackheath B65 63 D6
Hinckley LE10 74 F8
Lawton Ct WV3 25 B1
Laxey Rd B16 65 D3
Laxford Cl B12 86 E6
Laxton Cl DY6 61 A5
Laxton Gr B25 68 D1
Lay Gdns CV31 162 E5
Lazy Hill Birmingham B38 104 B2
Stonnall WS9 16 D2
Lazy Hill Rd WS9 16 C1
Le Hanche Cl CV7 95 A7
Le More B74 32 A2
Lea Ave WS10 41 D1
Lea Bank Ave DY11 116 B5
Lea Bank Rd DY2 62 C3
Lea Croft Rd B97 158 D5
Lea Cswy The DY11 116 A4
Lea Dr B26 89 A6
Lea End La B38, B48 123 D3
Lea Ford Rd B33 69 C4
Lea Green Ave DY4 51 D5
Lea Green La B47 125 C5
Lea Hall Rd B33 69 A2
Lea Hall Sta B33 69 B2
Lea Hill Rd B20 55 C2
Lea Ho Birmingham B15 86 D7
6 Dudley DY1 61 E8
Lea House Rd B30 104 A7
Lea La WS6 5 A3
Lea Manor Dr WV4 38 E4
Lea Park Rise B61 136 F5
Lea Rd Birmingham B11 87 D4
Wolverhampton WV3 39 B8
Lea St DY10 116 F6
Lea Street Fst Sch DY10 116 F6
Lea The Birmingham B33 69 A2
Kidderminster DY11 116 A5
Lea Vale Rd DY8 80 F2
Lea View Aldridge WS9 29 E5
Wednesfield WV12 27 A5
Lea Village B33 69 B3
Lea Wlk B45 121 F8
Lea Wood Gr DY11 116 A5
Lea Yield Cl B30 104 A7
Leabon Gr B17 85 C4
Leabrook B26 88 F8
Leabrook Rd DY4, WS14 41 D1
Leabrook Rd N WS10 41 D2
Leabrook Sq WS10 41 D1
Leach Green La B45 122 B6
Leach Heath La B45 122 A7
Leacliffe Way WS9 30 F3
Leacote Dr WV6 24 C4
Leacrest Rd CV6 95 A2
Leacroft WV12 27 C7
Leacroft Ave WV10 25 E8
Leacroft Cl WS9 16 B1
Leacroft Gr B71 53 B7
Leacroft La WS11 4 F5
Leacroft Rd DY6 60 E8
Leadbeater Ho 6 WS3 28 B8
Leadbetter Dr B61 136 D2
Leaf Ct CV3 133 D4
Leaf La Coventry CV3 133 E5
Coventry CV3 133 F6
Leafdown Cl WS12 2 D3
Leafenden Ave WS7 7 A6
Leafield Cl CV2 114 F8
Leafield Cres B33 69 A5
Leafield Gdns B62 83 D8
Leafield Rd B92 89 C1
Leaford Way DY6 60 F5
Leafy Glade B74 31 A3
Leafy Rise DY3 50 D4
Leagh Cl CV8 148 B7
Leahill Croft B37 69 F2
Leaholme Gdns DY9 81 B2
Leahouse Gdns B68 64 A3
Leahouse Rd B68 64 A3
Leahurst Cres B17 85 C4
Lealholme Ct CV5 132 F8
Leam Cl CV11 73 F1
Leam Cres B92 89 B1
Leam Dr WS7 7 D7
Leam Gn CV4 132 D5
Leam Rd CV31 161 D7
Leam St CV31 162 B7
Leam Terr CV31 162 B8
Leamington Cl WS11 4 C7
Leamington Rd
Birmingham B12 87 B5
Coventry CV3 133 C6
Kenilworth CV8 148 B2
Ryton-on-D CV8 135 B1
Leamington Spa Sta CV31 161 F7
Leamore Cl WS2 28 A7
Leamore Ind Est WS2 28 C6
Leamore JMI Sch WS3 28 C7
Leamore La WS2 28 B6
Leander Cl WS6 4 F1
Leander Gdns B14 104 F5
Leander Rd DY9 81 F4
Leandor Dr B74 45 A7
Lear Gr CV34 161 E4
Lear Rd WV5 49 B8
Leas Cl CV12 78 A3
Leas The WV10 12 C7
Leason La WV10 26 A7
Leasow Dr B15 85 D3
Leasow The WS9 29 E5
Leasowe Rd
Birmingham B45 121 F8
Tipton DY4 51 E4
Leasowe The WS13 3 A1
Leasowe's Ave CV3 132 F4
Leasowes Children's Farm The B94 142 C2
Leasowes Ct B63 82 F3
Leasowes Dr Perton WV6 23 D4
Wolverhampton WV4 38 D6
Leasowes High Sch B62 83 E6
Leasowes La B62 83 D4
Leasowes Rd B14 86 F1
Leatherhead Cl 5 B6 66 F6
Leavesden Gr B26 89 A5
Leaward Cl CV10 72 E2
Lebanon Gr WS7 6 F8
Lebanon Ho 6 B36 57 F1
Lechlade Cl B98 154 B7
Lechlade Rd B43 54 E8
Leckie Rd WS2 28 E4
Ledbrook Rd CV32 157 E5
Ledbury Cl Aldridge WS9 16 C1
Birmingham B16 66 A2
Redditch B98 154 F2
Ledbury Dr WV1 26 B1
Ledbury Ho Birmingham B33 69 E2
Redditch B97 153 B4
Ledbury Rd CV31 162 C6
Ledbury Way B76 58 A8
Ledsam Gr B32 84 F6
Ledsam St B16 66 A2
Lee Bank Jun Sch B15 86 C7
Lee Bank Middleway B15 86 C8
Lee Cl CV34 155 E2
Lee Cres B15 86 C8
Lee Ct WS9 15 F3
Lee Gdns B67 64 E5
Lee Mount B15 86 C8
Lee Rd Blackheath B64 82 F8
Hollywood B47 125 A7
Royal Leamington Spa CV31 161 E6
Lee St B70 53 A8
Lee The CV5 112 C4
Lee Wlk WS11 2 B4
Leebank Rd B63 82 E2
Leech St DY4 52 C5
Leeder Cl CV6 95 C2
Leedham Ave B77 21 D5
Leek Wootton CE Fst Sch CV35 156 A5
Leeming Cl CV4 132 C6
Lees Rd WV14 40 F3
Lees St B18 65 F6
Lees Terr WV14 40 F3
Leeson Wlk B17 85 D5
Legge La Birmingham B1 66 C3
Dudley WV14 40 D1
Legge St Birmingham B4 164 F4
West Bromwich B70 53 E3
Wolverhampton WV2 39 E6
Legion Cl WS11 6 A6
Legion Rd B45 121 E7
Legs La WV10 11 F3
Leicester Cl B67 64 E1
Leicester Cswy CV1 113 D5
Leicester Ct CV12 79 C2
Leicester La
Cubbington CV32 149 E1
Royal Leamington Spa CV32 157 C6
Leicester Pl B71 53 C7
Leicester Rd Bedworth CV12 78 B4
Hinckley LE10 71 F2
Nuneaton CV11 73 D5
Shilton CV7 97 F6
Leicester Row CV1 165 B4
Leicester St Bedworth CV12 78 B3
Bulkington CV12 79 C2
Royal Leamington Spa CV32 157 A1
Walsall WS1 28 E2
Wolverhampton WV6 25 B4
Leigh Ave Burntwood WS7 7 B7
Coventry CV3 133 C3
Leigh CE Prim Sch CV4 131 D8
Leigh Cl WS4 29 A4
Leigh Ct Birmingham B23 56 C2
Walsall WS4 29 A3
Leigh Inf & Jun Sch B8 67 E6
Leigh Rd Birmingham B8 67 E6
Sutton Coldfield B75 47 B5
Walsall WS4 29 A4
Leigh St 4 CV1 113 E4
Leigham Dr B17 85 A7
Leighs Cl WS4 15 C1
Leighs Rd WS4 15 C1
Leighswood Ave WS9 30 B7
Leighswood Cl WS11 5 F5
Leighswood Ct WS9 30 B6
Leighswood Gr WS9 30 A7
Leighswood Ind Est WS9 30 A8
Leighswood Inf Sch WS9 30 B8
Leighswood Jun Sch WS9 30 B7
Leighswood Rd WS9 30 A7
Leighton Cl Birmingham B43 44 C3
Coventry CV4 132 D2
Dudley DY1 50 E2
Royal Leamington Spa CV32 157 C4
Leighton Rd Bilston WV14 41 A4
Birmingham B13 86 F2
Wolverhampton WV4 38 F6
Leisure Wlk B77 35 F6
Leith Gr B38 123 E8
Lelant Gr B17 85 A5
Lellow St B71 53 C8
Lemar Ind Est B30 86 B1
Lemont Dr B44 45 C2
Lemox Rd B70 53 A8
Len Davies Rd WV12 27 B7
Lench Cl Birmingham B13 87 A3
Halesowen B62 63 C1
Lench St B4 164 C4
Lench's Trust Almshouses
4 Birmingham, Edgbaston B12 87 A8
4 Birmingham, Highgate B12 86 F7
3 Birmingham, Ladywood B16 86 F7
Lenches Trust B32 84 E6
Lenchs Gn B5 86 E7
Lennard Gdns B66 65 D6
Lennox Cl CV3 134 E6
Lennox Gdns WV3 39 A8
Lennox Gr B73 57 A7
Lennox St B19 66 D6
Lenton Croft B26 88 E4
Lenton's La CV2 96 E4
Lenwade Rd B68 84 D8
Leofric Ct 3 B15 86 C8
Leofric St CV6 113 A5
Leominster Ct B45 121 F8
Leominster Ho B33 69 E2
Leominster Rd B11 87 E3
Leominster Wlk B45 121 F8
Leomonsley Cl WS13 8 F7
Leomonsley Ct WS13 8 E7
Leomonsley Rd WS13 8 F7
Leomonsley View WS13 8 F7
Leona Ind Est B62 63 D1
Leonard Ave 5 B19 66 D8
Leonard Gr 6 B19 66 D8
Leonard Parkins Ho CV12 79 D2
Leonard Rd Birmingham B19 66 D8
Stourbridge DY8 80 C5
Leopold Ave B20 54 F5
Leopold Rd CV1 113 F4
Leopold St B12 86 F8
Lepid Gr B29 85 D2
Lerryn Cl DY6 60 F5
Lerwick Cl DY6 60 F5
Lesingham Dr CV4 111 E1
Lesley Bentley Ho 5 B1 66 C3
Lesley Dr DY6 60 E4
Leslie Dr DY4 41 B1
Leslie Rd
Birmingham, Edgbaston B16 65 F2
Birmingham, Handsworth B20 55 D2
Little Aston B74 31 B2
Wolverhampton WV10 25 F4
Leslie Rise B69 63 C8
Lesscroft Cl WV9 11 A3
Lester Gr WS9 30 E2
Lester St WV14 40 F5
Leswell Gr DY10 116 F6
Leswell La DY10 116 F6
Leswell St DY10 116 F6
Letchlade Cl CV2 114 C8
Levante Gdns B33 68 D2
Leve La WV13 27 B1
Level St DY5 61 E3
Leven Cl LE10 75 B8
Leven Croft B76 58 A7
Leven Dr WV12 13 B1
Leven Way CV2 115 A8
Levenwick Way DY6 61 A5
Lever St WV2 163 C1
Leverretts The B21 54 C3
Leverton Rise WV10 25 C6
Leveson Ave WS6 4 E2
Leveson Cl DY2 62 E8
Leveson Cres CV7 130 B6
Leveson Ct
1 Willenhall WV13 27 A2
Wolverhampton W6 25 A4
Leveson Dr DY4 51 E6
Leveson Rd WV11 26 F8
Leveson St WV13 27 A2
Leveson Wlk 5 DY2 62 E8
Levett Rd B77 22 B5
Levetts Fields WS13 9 C7
Levetts Hollow WS12 2 D3
Levetts Sq 6 WS13 9 B7
Levington Cl WV6 23 F4
Lewis Ave WV1 26 B2
Lewis Cl Lichfield WS14 9 E7
Willenhall WV12 27 D5
Lewis Gr WV11 26 D6
Lewis Rd Birmingham B30 104 C7
Coventry CV1 113 D5
Oldbury B68 84 B7
Radford Semele CV31 162 F5
Stourbridge DY9 81 D5
Lewis St Bilston WV14 40 E6
Tipton DY4 52 D5
Walsall WS2 28 D3
Lewisham Rd Smethwick B66 65 A7
Wolverhampton WV10 11 B2
Lewisham St B71 53 D4
Lewkner Almshouses The B48 139 A5
Lewthorn Rise WV4 39 D4
Lexington Ct CV11 73 B5
Lexington Gn DY5 81 C7
Ley Hill Farm Rd B31 102 D5
Ley Hill Prim Sch B31 102 E5
Ley Hill Rd B75 46 C8
Ley Rise DY3 39 C1
Leybourne Cres WV9 10 F2
Leybourne Gr B25 88 C6
Leybrook Rd B45 122 B8
Leyburn Cl Coventry CV6 95 E2
Nuneaton CV11 74 A2
3 Warwick CV34 155 F1
Willenhall WS2 27 D3
Leyburn Rd B16 66 A1
Leycester Cl B31 123 A7
Leycester Ct 7 CV34 160 E6
Leycester Pl CV34 160 E6
Leycester Rd CV8 148 A2
Leycroft Ave B33 69 D3
Leydon Croft B38 104 B2
Leyes La CV8 148 C5
Leyfields WS13 3 B2
Leyfields Cres CV34 160 D4
Leylan Croft B13 105 D7
Leyland Ave WV3 24 F1
Leyland Croft WS3 14 F4
Leyland Rd Bulkington CV12 79 B2
Coventry CV5 112 D4
Nuneaton CV11 73 E1
Tamworth B77 21 E3
Leyland Spec Sch CV11 73 E1
Leyman Cl B14 105 C4
Leymere Cl CV7 92 C1
Leys Cl DY9 81 C2
Leys Cres DY5 61 B3
Leys High Sch The B98 159 C6
Leys Ind Est DY5 61 A3
Leys La CV7 92 C1
Leys Rd DY5 61 B3
Leys The Birmingham B31 103 B5
1 Darlaston WS10 41 D6
Leys Wood Croft B26 89 B6
Leysdown Gr B27 106 C8
Leysdown Rd B27 106 C8
Leyside CV3 134 E5
Leysters Cl B98 154 E3
Leyton Cl DY5 81 D8
Leyton Gr B44 45 A1
Leyton Rd B21 65 F8
Libbards Gate 4 B91 127 C8
Libbards Way B91 127 B8
Liberty Rd B77 35 F5
Liberty Way CV11 73 F3
Libra Cl B79 20 F7
Library Cl LE10 76 A5
Library Way B45 121 F7
Lich Ave WV11 26 E7
Lichen Cl WS12 1 C6
Lichen Gn CV4 132 D5
Lichfield Bsns Ctr WS13 3 D1
Lichfield Cath WS13 9 B8
Lichfield Cath Sch (St Chads) WS13 9 B8
Lichfield City Sta WS13 9 B7
Lichfield Cl CV11 74 A7
Lichfield Coll WS13 9 B7
Lichfield Cres B78 20 B7
Lichfield Ct Solihull B90 105 D2
Sutton Coldfield B75 46 C5
Walsall WS4 29 A4
Lichfield Pas WV1 163 C3
Lichfield Rd Birmingham B6 67 B8
Brownhills, New Town WS8 7 C1
Brownhills, Shire Oak WS8, WS9 16 B5
Burntwood WS7 7 E6
Cannock WS11 5 B8
Coventry CV3 133 D8
Hopwas B78 20 B7
Sutton Coldfield B74 32 A3
Tamworth B79 20 D6
Walsall, Highbridge WS3 14 C2
Walsall, Rushall WS4 29 B6
Walsall, Wallington Heath WS3 15 B6
Water Orton B46, B76 59 D4
Wednesfield WV11 26 E6
Willenhall WV12 27 D8
Wishaw B76 48 B3
Lichfield Road Ind Est B79 20 E6
Lichfield St Bilston WV14 40 E5
Fazeley B78 20 F1
Tamworth B79 21 A5
Tipton DY4 51 F8
Walsall WS1 28 F2
Wolverhampton WV1 163 C3
Lichfield (Trent Valley) Sta WS14 9 F8
Lichwood Rd WV11 26 F7
Lickey Coppice B45 122 C4
Lickey End Fst Sch B60 137 C6
Lickey Fst & Mid Sch The B45 121 F3
Lickey Gr DY11 116 B2
Lickey Grange B45 121 E1
Lickey Hills Ctry Pk B45 122 A5
Lickey Rd Birmingham B45 122 C6
Stourbridge DY8 81 B6
Lickey Rock B60 121 D1
Lickey Sq B45 122 A2
Liddiard Ct DY8 80 E6
Liddon Gr B27 106 C8
Liddon Rd B27 106 C8
Lifford Cl B14 104 C4
Lifford La B30 104 B4
Lifford Way CV3 135 A7
Lifton Croft DY6 60 F5
Light Hall Sch B90 126 B8
Light La CV1 165 B4
Lightfields Wlk B65 63 A5
Lighthorne Ave B16 66 B2
Lighthorne Rd B91 107 C6
Lightning Way B31 123 B7
Lightoak Cl B97 158 C6
Lightwood Cl B93 128 B8
Lightwood Rd DY1 51 A3
Lightwoods Hill B67 84 E8
Lightwoods Jun & Inf Sch B68 84 D8
Lightwoods Prim Sch B68 84 D8
Lightwoods Rd
Smethwick B67 65 A1
Stourbridge DY9 81 C1
Lilac Ave
1 Birmingham, Balsall Heath B12 87 A5
Birmingham, Perry B44 55 E7
Cannock WS11 4 D7
Coventry CV6 112 F5
Sutton Coldfield B74 44 E8
Tipton DY4 51 E7
Walsall WS5 43 A4
Lilac Cl Hinckley LE10 75 E6
Redditch B98 153 E2
Lilac Gr Burntwood WS7 6 F7
Walsall WS2 27 E3
Warwick CV34 156 A1
Wednesbury WS10 42 A2
Lilac Ho WS4 15 D1
Lilac La WS6 14 A8
Lilac Rd Bedworth CV12 78 D5
Bilston WV1 40 B8
Dudley DY1 51 C4
Tamworth B79 21 A8
Willenhall WV12 27 E7
Lilac Way B62 83 F8
Lilian Gr WV14 40 E1
Lilleshall Cl B98 154 E3
Lilleshall Cres WV2 39 D7
Lilleshall Rd B26 89 B7
Lilley Cl CV6 95 C2
Lilley Green Rd B48 140 D5
Lilley La B31 123 B8
Lillington Ave CV32 156 F2
Lillington CE Fst Sch CV32 157 B3
Lillington Cl Lichfield WS13 9 A8
Royal Leamington Spa CV32 157 A3
Sutton Coldfield B75 47 A4
Lillington Gr B34 69 D5
Lillington Prim Sch CV32 157 B3
Lillington Rd Coventry CV2 96 D1
Royal Leamington Spa CV32 157 A3
Solihull B90 126 B8
Lily Rd B26 88 D7
Lily St B71 53 C5
Lilycroft La B38 124 A7
Limberlost Cl B20 55 A3
Limbrick Ave CV4 112 A1
Limbrick Cl B90 105 F2
Limbrick Wood Prim Sch CV4 111 F3
Limbury Gr B92 107 F8
Lime Ave 8 Birmingham B29 85 F2
Royal Leamington Spa CV32 157 A4
Walsall WS2 27 E3
Lime Cl Great Wyrley WS6 4 F4
Hollywood B47 125 A5
Tipton DY4 51 E5
Walsall WS2 27 E3
West Bromwich B70 53 A4
Lime Ct B11 87 C4
Lime Gr Bilston WV14 40 C7
Birmingham, Balsall Heath B12 86 F5
Birmingham, Chemsley Wood B37 70 B1
Birmingham, Lozells B19 66 C8
Birmingham, Small Heath B10 87 D8
Bromsgrove B61 136 F4
Burntwood WS7 7 C6
Coventry CV4 112 B2
Kenilworth CV8 148 A4
Lichfield WS13 9 D8
Nuneaton CV10 72 E5

Lime Gr continued
Smethwick B66 65 B3
Smethwick B66 65 B4
Sutton Coldfield B73 57 B7
Walsall WS4 29 C6
Lime Kiln Cl B38 123 D7
Lime La Norton Canes WS3 6 A1
Walsall WS3 15 A8
Lime Rd Huntington WS12 1 D8
Sedgley DY3 39 F1
Wednesbury WS10 41 F4
Lime St Dudley WV14 51 A8
Walsall WS1 29 A1
Wolverhampton WV3 39 B8
Lime Tree Ave
Coventry CV4 112 A2
Wolverhampton WV6 24 A3
Lime Tree Cres B97 153 B4
Lime Tree Gdns WV8 10 B3
Lime Tree Rd
Birmingham,
Acock's Green B27 88 C5
Birmingham, Saltley B8 67 F6
Codsall WV8 10 B4
Walsall WS5 43 A4
Limehurst Ave WV3 38 C8
Limehurst Rd WS4 29 C6
Limekiln La Birmingham
B14 105 A4
Tanworth-in-A B94 126 D1
Limepit La Dudley DY1 51 A3
Huntington WS11, WS12 1 D6
Limes Ave Blackheath B65 63 C2
Brierley Hill DY5 61 C5
Limes Rd Dudley DY1 51 B3
Wolverhampton WV6 24 D4
Limes The Bedworth CV12 77 E2
Birmingham, Ladywood B16 65 F2
Birmingham,
Rotton Park B16 65 F3
Birmingham, Sparkbrook B11 87 C6
Wolverhampton WV11 26 B5
Limes View DY3 50 D7
Limetree Rd B74 30 D1
Linacre Ho B37 69 F2
Linaker Rd CV3 134 C5
Linchmere Rd B21 54 C2
Lincoln Ave Nuneaton CV10 72 B7
Willenhall WV13 27 D2
Lincoln Cl Birmingham B27 88 E3
Lichfield WS13 3 C3
Warwick CV34 155 E1
Lincoln Croft WS14 17 F6
Lincoln Dr WS11 4 F8
Lincoln Gn WV10 11 D2
Lincoln Gr B37 70 A1
Lincoln Ho WV10 25 E3
Lincoln Rd Birmingham B27 88 D2
Bromsgrove B61 136 E4
Dudley DY2 62 D2
Smethwick B67 64 E2
Walsall WS1 29 A1
West Bromwich B71 42 D1
Lincoln Rd N B27 88 E3
Lincoln St Birmingham B12 86 E6
Coventry CV1 165 C4
Wolverhampton WV10 25 E3
Lincoln Tower B16 66 A1
Lincroft Cres CV5 112 E4
Lindale Ave B36 68 C6
Lindale Cres DY5 81 B6
Linden Ave Birmingham B43 54 D8
Burntwood WS7 7 A8
Halesowen B62 83 E7
Kidderminster DY10 117 A7
Tipton B69 63 D8
Linden Cl Tamworth B77 21 F4
Warwick CV34 155 E2
Willenhall WS2 27 D2
Linden Ct B91 107 E4
Linden Dr DY8 81 A3
Linden Gdns DY10 117 A6
Linden Glade B63 83 A4
Linden Gr DY10 117 A7
Linden La WV12 27 E6
Linden Lea Bedworth CV12 78 B3
Wolverhampton WV3 24 D1
Linden Rd Birmingham B30 103 E7
Dudley DY1 51 B3
Hinckley LE10 71 C1
Smethwick B66 65 A2
Linden View WS12 2 B4
Lindens Dr B74 44 F5
Lindens Mid Sch B74 44 F6
Lindens The
Birmingham,
Beech Lanes B32 84 E7
Birmingham, Edgbaston B16 65 D1
Wolverhampton WV6 24 E3
Lindenwood B73 46 B6
Lindera B77 22 A4
Lindfield The CV3 134 C8
Lindford Way B38 104 B2
Lindhurst Dr B94 143 C6
Lindisfarne B77 21 D3
Lindisfarne Dr CV8 148 C4
Lindley Ave DY4 51 F4
Lindley Rd Bedworth CV12 77 D2
Coventry CV3 114 B2
Lindon Cl WS8 16 A6
Lindon Dr WS8 15 F6
Lindon Rd WS8 15 F5
Lindon View WS8 16 A5
Lindrick Cl WS3 13 F3
Lindridge Dr B76 58 D6
Lindridge Jun Sch B75 47 B5
Lindridge Rd Birmingham
B23 56 C5
Solihull B90 105 F1
Sutton Coldfield B75 47 B6
Lindrosa Rd B74 30 F3
Lindsay Rd B42 44 B1
Lindsey Ave B31 103 C4
Lindsey Cres CV8 148 A1
Lindsey Pl DY5 61 C3
Lindsey Rd B71 53 C7
Lindsworth App B30 104 C3
Lindsworth Ct 2 B30 104 C3
Lindsworth Rd B30 104 C3
Lindsworth Specl Sch
B30 104 C3
Lineholt Cl B98 159 A6
Linehouse La
Lickey End B60 137 D8
Marlbrook B60 121 D1
Linen St CV34 160 D6
Linfield Gdns DY3 39 C1
Linford Gr B25 68 D1
Linford Wlk CV2 96 F1
Linforth Dr B74 45 A7
Ling Ho WV10 25 F3
Ling Rd WS12 1 C5
Lingard Cl B7 67 B5
Lingard Ho B76 57 F8
Lingard Rd B75 47 A5
Lingen Cl B98 154 E3
Lingfield Ave Birmingham
B44 44 F1
Wolverhampton WV10 11 D5
Lingfield Cl WS6 4 F2
Lingfield Ct Birmingham
B43 54 D7
Coventry CV6 96 B4
Lingfield Dr WS6 4 F2
Lingfield Gdns B34 69 B6
Lingfield Gr WV6 23 F4
Lingfield Way DY6 61 A5
Lingfield Wlk B61 121 B1
Lingham Cl B92 107 D7
Lingwood Dr CV10 72 F3
Linhope Dr DY6 61 A5
Link One Ind Pk DY4 52 E6
Link Rd Birmingham B16 65 E3
Brownhills WS9 16 B3
Wombourne WV5 49 A7
Link The B27 88 A1
Links Ave WV6 24 D7
Links Cres B68 84 B8
Links Dr Birmingham B45 122 A5
Solihull B91 107 B6
Stourbridge DY8 80 E2
Links Rd Birmingham B14 105 A1
Coventry CV6 113 B8
Oldbury B68 84 B8
Wolverhampton WV4 39 A3
Links Side Way WS9 30 C8
Links View Aldridge B74 31 B1
Halesowen B62 83 D4
Linkswood Cl B13 87 B1
Linkway CV31 161 E6
Linkway Ret Pk WS11 4 B6
Linkwood Ind Est DY8 80 F6
Linley Cl WS9 29 E5
Linley Dr WV10 11 E1
Linley Gr Birmingham B14 104 C6
Dudley DY3 50 B2
Linley Lodge Ind Est WS9 29 E6
Linley Rd WS4 29 D7
Linley Wood Rd WS9 29 E5
Linnet Cl Birmingham B30 103 E8
Coventry CV3 134 D5
Halesowen B62 83 B6
Huntington WS12 1 D7
Linnet Gr WV12 27 C8
Linnet Rise DY10 116 F1
Linpole Wlk B14 104 D2
Linsey Rd B92 89 C2
Linslade Cl WV4 39 D4
Linstock Way CV6 96 B4
Linthouse La WV11 26 E8
Linthouse Wlk B77 35 F6
Linthurst Newtown B60 138 B5
Linthurst Prim Sch B60 138 A6
Linthurst Rd B45, B60 138 A7
Lintly B77 22 B1
Linton Ave B91 107 A1
Linton Cl Halesowen B63 82 D5
Redditch B98 154 F2
Linton Croft WV14 40 D5
Linton Mews B98 154 F2
Linton Rd
Birmingham,
Acock's Green B11 88 A4
Birmingham, Great Barr B43 44 C3
Blackheath B64 62 F3
Wolverhampton WV4 38 E5
Linton Wlk B23 56 C3
Linwood Cl LE10 71 B2
Linwood Dr Cannock WS12 1 F7
Coventry CV2 96 F1
Linwood Rd Birmingham
B21 65 E8
Dudley DY1 51 B5
Solihull B91 106 D5
Linwood Wlk B17 85 D4
Lion Fields Ave CV5 112 B6
Lion Ind Est WS9 30 A8
Lion Pas DY8 80 F5
Lion Sq DY10 116 E6
Lion St Kidderminster DY10 116 E6
Stourbridge DY8 80 F5
Lion's Den WS14 7 E2
Lionel St B3 164 B3
Liskeard Cl CV11 74 A5
Liskeard Rd WS5 43 D7
Lisko Cl DY5 81 A8
Lisle Ave DY11 116 D3
Lisle Ct 4 CV31 162 A6
Lismore Cl B45 101 E1
Lismore Dr Birmingham B17 85 A3
Hinckley LE10 71 C1
Lisson Gr B44 44 F4
Listelow Cl B36 69 B8
Lister Cl Tipton DY4 52 A4
Walsall WS2 28 B5
Lister Rd Dudley DY2 62 D7
Kidderminster DY11 116 B4
Walsall WS2 28 B5
Lister St Birmingham B7 66 F4
Nuneaton CV11 73 D3
Willenhall WV13 27 B1
Listowel Rd B14 104 D6
Lisures Dr B76 46 D4
Little Acre B97 158 D6
Little Albert St WS2 28 E2
Little Ann St B5 66 F2
Little Aston Cty Prim Sch
B74 31 C6
Little Aston Hospl B74 31 B5
Little Aston La B74 31 D6
Little Aston Park Rd B74 31 A3
Little Aston Rd WS9 30 D6
Little Barr St B9 67 A2
Little Barrow Wlk WS13 3 A1
Little Birches WV3 38 F8
Little Bloxwich CE Prim
Sch WS3 14 D3
Little Brickiln St WV3 163 B2
Little Bromwich Rd B9 68 C2
Little Broom St B12 87 A8
Little Caldmore 6 WS1 42 E8
Little Church La B79 21 B5
Little Church St 1 CV1 165 C4
Little Clothier St WV13 27 A3
Little Clover Cl 3 B7 67 C7
Little Comm WS3 15 A4
Little Cornbow B63 83 B3
Little Cottage St DY5 61 D2
Little Croft B43 43 C1
Little Cross St WS10 41 D7
Little Duke St CV11 73 B4
Little Edward St B9 67 A2
Little Farm CV3 134 D5
Little Field CV2 114 A5
Little Fields Way B69 63 F7
Little Forge Rd B98 159 C8
Little Francis Gr 4 B7 67 B5
Little Gorway WS1 42 F7
Little Grebe Rd DY10 117 B3
Little Green La B9 67 C1
Little Green Lanes B73 57 B7
Little Hall Rd B7 67 B5
Little Hardwick Rd WS9 30 D2
Little Hay La WS14 18 C3
Little Heath Croft B34 69 B7
Little Heath Ind Est CV6 96 A2
Little Hill WS10 41 F3
Little Hill Gr B38 104 A1
Little Hill Way B32 84 D2
Little John St DY5 61 D4
Little Johnson's La WS9 44 B8
Little La West Bromwich B71 53 D5
Willenhall WV12 27 D7
Little Lawns Cl WS8 16 A4
Little London WS1 42 F8
Little London Ho 1 WS1 42 F7
Little London Jun Mixed
Inf Sch WV13 27 A2
Little Meadow Wlk B33 68 F3
Little Moor Hill B67 64 F5
Little Newport St 4 WS1 28 E1
Little Oaks Dr DY7 60 A2
Little Oaks Rd B6 66 E8
Little Park St Coventry CV1 165 C2
Wolverhampton WV1 163 C3
Little Pitts Cl B24 57 D5
Little Pk B32 84 B4
Little Potter St DY5 61 D2
Little Pountney St WV2 163 B1
Little Shadwell St B4 164 C4
Little South St CV1 113 E3
Little St DY2 51 D1
Little Station St WS2 28 E2
Little Sutton Fst, Jun &
Mid Schs B75 32 D4
Little Sutton La B75 46 C8
Little Sutton Rd B75 32 D2
Little Wood St WV13 27 A2
Little Woods B97 158 E6
Little's La
Wolverhampton WV1 163 C3
Wolverhampton WV1 163 C4
Littlecote B79 20 D7
Littlecote Croft 1 B14 105 A3
Littlecote Dr B23 56 F7
Littleheath La B60 137 D6
Littlemead Ave B31 103 C1
Littlemead Rd B90 125 E8
Littleover Ave B28 105 F6
Littleshaw Croft B47 125 C4
Littleshaw La B47 125 C4
Littlethorpe CV3 134 D6
Littleton Bsns Pk WS12 1 C7
Littleton Cl Kenilworth
CV8 148 A7
Sutton Coldfield B76 47 A2
Littleton Croft 6 B91 127 C8
Littleton Dr WS12 1 C7
Littleton Rd WV12 27 D7
Littleton St E WS1 28 F3
Littleton St W WS2 28 E2
Littlewood Cl 2 B91 127 B8
Littlewood Gn B80 159 D3
Littlewood La WS6 4 E4
Littlewood Rd WS6 4 E4
Littleworth Ave DY1 51 B6
Littleworth Gr B76 46 F4
Littleworth Hill WS12 2 D4
Littleworth Rd WS12 2 E4
Litton B77 22 C1
Liveridge Cl B93 127 F6
Liverpool Croft B37 89 F8
Liverpool St B9 67 A2
Livery St Birmingham B3 164 B3
Birmingham B3 164 B4
Royal Leamington Spa CV32 161 F8
Livingstone Ave WV6 23 E5
Livingstone Rd Bilston
WV14 40 B5
Birmingham,
Handsworth B20 55 D1
Birmingham,
King's Heath B14 104 E6
Coventry CV6 113 E7
Walsall WS3 14 E2
West Bromwich B70 53 B1
Lizafield Ct 3 B66 64 E7
Llewellyn Rd CV31 162 A6
Lloyd Cl CV11 73 D2
Lloyd Cres CV2 114 E3
Lloyd Dr WV4 38 C2
Lloyd George Gr WS11 2 C2
Lloyd Ho B19 66 C6
Lloyd Rd Birmingham B20 55 A4
Wolverhampton WV6 24 D5
Lloyd Roberts Bldgs WV4 38 F1
Lloyd St Birmingham B10 87 D8
Cannock WS11 1 D1
Dudley DY2 62 D8
Wednesbury WS10 41 E3
West Bromwich B71 53 E4
Wolverhampton WV6 24 F4
Lloyds Rd B62 83 C8
Loach Dr CV2 96 B4
Lobelia Cl LE10 75 E5
Locarno Jun & Inf Schs
DY4 52 A6
Locarno Rd DY4 52 A6
Lochalsh Gr WV12 13 B1
Lochmore Cl LE10 75 A8
Lochmore Dr LE10 75 A8
Lochmore Way LE10 75 A8
Lochranza Croft B43 43 E2
Lock Cl B97 153 A4
Lock Dr B33 68 D3
Lock La CV34 160 D8
Lock St WV1 163 C4
Locke Cl CV6 95 A1
Locket Cl WS2 27 F4
Lockfield Cl DY8 60 F2
Lockhart Cl CV8 148 A4
Lockhart Dr B75 32 C1
Lockheed Cl CV31 161 F5
Lockhurst La CV6 113 D7
Locking Croft B35 58 B3
Lockington Croft B62 83 F6
Lockley Cl WV10 25 F4
Locks The CV31 161 D7
Locks View DY8 60 E1
Lockside WS9 29 F7
Locksmith Cl WV13 27 B2
Lockton Rd B30 104 C8
Lockwood Rd B31 102 F4
Lode Heath Sch B91 107 C6
Lode La B91, B92 107 C6
Loder Cl CV4 111 F3
Lodge Cl Halesowen B62 83 E3
Hinckley LE10 76 A5
Walsall WS5 43 D6
Lodge Cres Dudley DY2 62 A4
Hagley DY9 99 B5
Warwick CV34 160 D4
Lodge Croft
Birmingham B31 102 E6
Knowle B93 128 B6
Lodge Dr B26 88 F8
Lodge Farm Cl B76 46 F3
Lodge Farm Mid Sch
B98 154 A2
Lodge Forge Trad Est B64 82 C7
Lodge Gr WS9 30 A5
Lodge Green La CV7 92 F2
Lodge Green La N CV7 92 E3
Lodge Hill Rd B29 85 D1
Lodge La Cheslyn Hay WS11 4 C5
Kingswinford DY6 60 B6
Lodge Pool Dr B98 153 F1
Lodge Prim Sch B70 53 B3
Lodge Rd Bilston WV14 40 F4
Birmingham B18 65 F5
Coventry CV3 114 B1
Darlaston WS10 41 D5
Knowle B93 128 B6
Redditch B98 153 E3
Smethwick B67 64 E7
Walsall, Pelsall WS4 15 B1
Walsall, THe Chuckery WS5 43 D6
West Bromwich B70 53 C3
Wolverhampton WV10 25 B8
Lodge Rd/ West Bromwich
TH Sta B70 53 C3
Lodge St Oldbury B69 64 A7
Willenhall WV12 27 C5
Lodge View WS6 4 C3
Lodgefarm Jun Mixed Inf
Sch WV12 27 E4
Lodgefield Rd B62 83 B7
Lodgepool Cl B44 55 E6
Loeless Rd B33 69 A3
Lofthouse Cres B31 102 F3
Lofthouse Gr B31 102 F3
Lofthouse Rd B20 54 F3
Loftus Cl B29 102 F8
Loftus Ct WS7 7 A5
Logan Cl WV10 25 C6
Logan Rd CV2 114 E7
Lollard Croft CV3 133 D8
Lomaine Dr B30 103 E4
Lomas Dr B31 102 E3
Lomas St WV1 25 C4
Lomax Cl WS13 3 A1
Lomax Rd WS12 2 B7
Lombard Ave DY2 62 D3
Lombard St Birmingham B12 86 F8
Lichfield WS13 9 B8
West Bromwich B70 53 C3
Lombard St W B70 53 C3
Lombardy Croft 3 B62 84 A6
Lombardy Gdns WV12 27 E7
Lombardy Gr WS7 6 F8
Lomita Cres B77 35 D8
Lomond Cl Birmingham B34 69 E6
Hinckley LE10 75 B8
Tamworth B79 20 F8
Lomond Rd DY3 39 C1
London Hts DY1 51 A2
London La Bromsgrove B60 151 F7
Tardebigge B60 152 A6
London Rd Birmingham B20 55 E2
Coventry, Cheylesmore CV3 133 E7
Coventry, Willenhall CV3 134 B5
Hinckley LE10 75 F8
Lichfield WS14 9 C5
Middleton B75, B78 47 D7
Ryton-on-D CV8 135 B1
Shenstone B75, WS14 32 F7
London St B66 65 C5
Londonderry Gr B67 64 F5
Londonderry La B67 64 E4
Londonderry Rd B68 64 D4
Lones Rd B71 65 B8
Long Acre Birmingham B7 67 C7
Kidderminster DY10 116 F7
Long Acre St WS2 28 D3
Long Acre Trad Est B7 67 B7
Long Bridge Rd WS14 9 C5
Long Brook La CV7 129 E5
Long Cl DY9 99 A4
Long Close Ave CV5 112 B6
Long Close Wlk B35 58 A3
Long Compton Dr DY9 99 A6
Long Croft WS12 1 C4
Long Furrow WV8 10 E1
Long Hyde Rd B67 64 F1
Long Innage B63 82 B6
Long Knowle La WV11 26 B8
Long Knowle Prim Sch
WV11 26 C8
Long La Allesley CV5, CV7 94 D2
Great Wyrley WV11, WS6 13 E6
Halesowen B62 83 E8
Long La Trad Est B62 83 D8
Long Leasow B29 103 B7
Long Ley WV10 25 F3
Long Ley Prim Sch WV10 25 F3
Long Leys Croft B46 59 B2
Long Leys Ct B46 59 B2
Long Mdw B65 63 C3
Long Meadow Dr DY3 39 B2
Long Meadow Rd B60 137 C6
Long Mill Ave WV11 26 B7
Long Mill N WV11 26 B7
Long Mill S WV11 26 B7
Long Mynd B63 82 D1
Long Mynd Cl WV12 13 B1
Long Mynd Rd B31 102 F6
Long Nuke Rd B31 102 E7
Long Shoot The CV11 74 C6
Long St Birmingham B11 87 A6
Bulkington CV12 79 D2
Walsall WS2 28 D1
Wolverhampton WV1 163 C3
Long Wood B30 103 E5
Longacre WS10 41 A8
Longacre Ind Est B7 67 C7
Longacres Cannock WS12 2 F5
Little Aston B74 31 C4
Longbank Rd B69 63 C8
Longboat La DY8 60 E1
Longboat Quay DY2 62 D4
Longborough Cl B97 158 B6
Longbow Rd B29 102 F7
Longbridge La B31 122 E8
Longbridge Sta B31 122 E8
Longcroft Ave 1 WS10 42 A3
Longcroft Cl B35 58 A2
Longcroft The
Halesowen B63 82 E4
Walsall WS4 29 C7
Longdales Rd B38 123 E7
Longdon Ave WV4 39 D5
Longdon Cl B98 159 B7
Longdon Croft B93 128 A8
Longdon Dr B74 31 E3
Longdon Rd B93 128 A6
Longfellow Ave CV34 160 C4
Longfellow Cl B97 158 C7
Longfellow Pl WS11 1 E4
Longfellow Rd
Birmingham B30 103 D4
Coventry CV2 114 C3
Dudley DY3 50 B5
Longfellow Wlk B79 20 F8
Longfield Cl
Birmingham B28 105 F6
Tamworth B77 21 E4
Longfield Dr B74 31 D4

Longfield Ho Coventry CV6 114 A8
Wolverhampton WV10 25 F3
Longfield Rd
Birmingham B31 102 E8
Royal Leamington Spa CV31 162 B6
Stourbridge DY9 81 D5
Longford Cl
Birmingham B32 102 A7
Dorridge B93 128 B3
Walsall WS1 29 A1
Longford Ct WS11 4 B8
Longford Cty Prim Sch WS11 4 C8
Longford Gn WS11 4 C7
Longford Gr B44 45 A3
Longford Ind Est WS11 4 D6
Longford Park Prim Sch CV6 96 A3
Longford Rd Bedworth CV7 96 A6
Birmingham B44 45 A2
Cannock WS11 4 D7
Coventry CV6 96 A4
Wolverhampton WV10 26 A4
Longford Sq CV6 96 A4
Longham Croft B32 84 F4
Longhurst Croft B31 123 B7
Longlake Ave WV6 24 B3
Longlands Cl B38 123 C8
Longlands Dr B77 21 F4
Longlands Ho B11 87 B5
Longlands Rd B62 83 E3
Longlands The
Barnt Green B45 138 D7
Wombourne WV5 49 A6
Longleat Birmingham B43 43 C2
Tamworth B79 20 D7
Longleat Dr
Cheswick Green B90 126 E5
Dudley DY1 50 E2
Longleat Gr 19 CV31 162 C6
Longleat Rd WS9 16 A1
Longleat Tower 2 B15 66 C1
Longley Ave B76 58 D5
Longley Cres B26 88 E4
Longmeadow Cl B75 46 F5
Longmeadow Cres B34 69 E6
Longmeadow Gr B31 123 A6
Longmeadow Rd WS5 43 E8
Longmoor Cl WV11 26 F5
Longmoor Rd
Birmingham B73 45 B3
Halesowen B63 82 E3
Longmoor Specl Sch B73 45 A4
Longmore Ave WS2 27 F1
Longmore Ho B73 45 C3
Longmore Rd B90 106 D2
Longmore St Birmingham B12 86 E7
Wednesbury WS10 41 F3
Longshaw Gr B34 69 D6
Longstone Cl B90 127 B6
Longstone Rd B42 55 C7
Longwill Specl Sch B31 103 A5
Longwood Cl CV4 131 F6
Longwood Jun & Inf Sch B78 20 D1
Longwood La WS5, WS4 29 E2
Longwood Rd Aldridge WS9 30 B2
Birmingham B45 122 A7
Longwood Rise WV12 27 D5
Lonicera Cl WS5 43 B3
Lonscale Dr CV3 133 B5
Lonsdale Cl Birmingham B33 68 D2
Willenhall WV12 27 B5
Lonsdale Rd Bilston WV14 40 F6
Birmingham B17 85 B6
Royal Leamington Spa CV32 157 B4
Smethwick B66 64 D7
Walsall WS5 43 C6
Wolverhampton WV3 39 B7
Lord Cromwell Ct WS11 2 A5
Lord Lytton Ave CV2 114 D2
Lord St Bilston WV14 40 E3
Birmingham B7 66 F5
Coventry CV5 112 F2
Walsall WS1 42 E6
Wolverhampton WV3 25 B1
Lord St W WV14 40 E3
Lord's Dr WS2 28 E3
Lords La B80 159 E2
Lordswood Boys Sch B17 65 A1
Lordswood Cl B97 152 F2
Lordswood Girls Sch B17 85 A8
Lordswood Rd B17 85 A7
Lordswood Sq B17 85 B7
Lorenzo Cl CV3 134 D6
Lorimer Way B43 44 D4
Lorne Gr DY10 117 A6
Lorne St Burntwood WS7 6 E8
Kidderminster DY10 117 A5
Tipton DY4 51 F8
Lorrainer Ave DY5 81 A8
Lorton B79 20 D7
Lothersdale B77 36 C8
Lothians Rd Walsall WS3 15 A5
Wolverhampton WV6 24 E6
Lottie Rd B29 85 E1
Lotus B77 21 E3
Lotus Croft B67 64 F4
Lotus Ct B16 65 E1
Lotus Dr WS11 1 E5
Lotus Way B65 63 A4
Loudon Ave CV6 113 A5
Loughshaw B77 22 C1
Loughton Gr B63 82 F4
Louis Ct B67 64 F5
Louisa Pl 3 B18 66 A5
Louisa St 1 B1 66 C3
Louise Croft B14 104 E2
Louise Ct 2 Birmingham B27 88 C3
Solihull B91 106 E1
Louise Ho DY5 61 D7
Louise Lorne Rd B13 86 F4
Louise Rd B21 65 F7
Louise St DY3 50 C3
Loundon Gate CV11 73 F1
Lovatt Cl DY4 41 C1
Lovatt Pl WS11 1 E5
Lovatt St WV1 163 A3
Love La Birmingham B7 66 F4
Great Wyrley WS6 5 B3
Hinckley LE10 76 A6
Hollywood B47 124 F7
Stourbridge, Lye DY9 81 F5
Stourbridge, Old Swinford DY8 81 A3
Walsall WS1 42 E7
Wolverhampton WV6 24 D6
Love Lyne B97 158 B5
Loveday Cl CV32 156 E2
Loveday Ho B70 53 D3
Loveday St B4 164 C4
Lovelace Ave B91 127 D8
Lovell B79 20 F6
Lovell Cl Bedworth CV7 96 A8
Birmingham B29 103 B6
Lovell Rd CV12 78 A3
Lover's Wlk 5 WS10 41 F3
Lovett Ave B69 63 D5
Lovetts Cl LE10 74 F8
Low Ave B43 43 F2
Low Hill Cres WV10 25 E8
Low St WS6 4 D3
Low Thatch B38 123 E7
Low Town 6 B69 64 A7
Low Wood Rd B23 56 E5
Lowans Hill View B97 153 C4
Lowbridge Cl WV12 27 C5
Lowbrook La B90 125 D4
Lowden Croft B26 88 E4
Lowdham B77 22 C1
Lowe Ave WS10 41 C7
Lowe Dr Kingswinford DY6 60 E4
Sutton Coldfield B73 45 C3
Lowe Rd CV6 95 A2
Lowe St Birmingham B12 87 A8
Wolverhampton WV6 25 B4
Lower Ave CV31 161 F7
Lower Beeches Rd B31 102 C2
Lower Bentley La B60 151 F1
Lower Bond St LE10 71 D1
Lower Cape CV34 160 D8
Lower Chapel St B69 52 C2
Lower Church La DY4 52 B5
Lower City Rd B69 52 D1
Lower Common La B97 153 B2
Lower Dartmouth St B9 67 B2
Lower Darwin St B12 86 F8
Lower Derry St DY5 61 D2
Lower Eastern Green La CV5 111 F4
Lower Essex St B5 66 E1
Lower Farm WS9 16 E4
Lower Farm Cty Prim Sch WS3 14 C3
Lower Ford St CV1 165 D3
Lower Forster St WS1 28 F2
Lower Gambolds La B60 151 B6
Lower Gn DY4 51 E5
Lower Grinsty La B97 158 A8
Lower Ground Cl 1 B6 55 F1
Lower Hall La WS1 28 E1
Lower Hall St WV13 27 B1
Lower High St
Blackheath B64 82 C8
Stourbridge DY8 80 F6
Wednesbury WS10 41 F2
Lower Higley Cl B32 84 E4
Lower Holyhead Rd CV1 165 A3
Lower Horseley Fields WV1 25 F2
Lower House La CV9 36 F2
Lower Ladyes Hills CV8 148 A6
Lower Leam St CV31 162 B7
Lower Lichfield St WV13 27 B2
Lower Loveday St B19 164 C4
Lower Mill St DY11 116 D6
Lower Moor B30 103 E8
Lower North St WS4 28 E3
Lower Par The B72 46 C5
Lower Parklands DY11 116 C5
Lower Prec CV1 165 B3
Lower Prestwood Rd WV11 26 C7
Lower Queen St B72 46 C4
Lower Rd Barnacle CV7 97 C6
Cannock WS12 2 C3
Lower Reddicroft B73 46 C5
Lower Rushall St WS1 28 F2
Lower Sandford St WS13 9 A7
Lower Severn St B1 164 B2
Lower Shepley La B60 137 E6
Lower St WV6 24 E5
Lower Temple St B2 164 B2
Lower Tower St B19 164 C5
Lower Trinity St B9 67 A1
Lower Valley Rd DY5 61 A2
Lower Vauxhall WV1 25 A3
Lower Villiers St
1 Royal Leamington Spa CV32 157 A1
Wolverhampton WV2 39 C7
Lower Walsall St WV1 25 F1
Lower White Rd B32 84 D5
Lowercroft Way B74 31 E6
Lowerpark B77 21 C1
Lowerstack Croft B37 69 F3
Lowes Ave CV34 155 E1
Lowesmoor Rd B26 89 C7
Loweswater Cl CV11 74 A6
Loweswater Rd CV3 114 E1
Lowfield Cl B62 84 A3
Lowfield La B97 153 B5
Lowforce B77 36 C8
Lowhill La B45 122 D6
Lowland Cl B64 62 F1
Lowland Rd WS12 1 C4
Lowlands Ave
Sutton Coldfield B74 44 E8
Wolverhampton WV6 24 E6
Lowlands Ct WV6 24 E6
Lowlands La B98 154 D3
Lowndes Rd DY8 80 E6
Lowrey Ct B68 64 C3
Lowry Cl Bedworth CV12 78 A4
Perton WV6 23 F4
Smethwick B67 64 F6
Willenhall WV13 26 E2
Lowswater Ho B38 104 B1
Lowther Ct 10 DY5 61 D2
Lowther St CV2 113 F4
Loxdale Park Ind Est WV14 40 E4
Loxdale Prim Sch WV14 40 F4
Loxdale Sidings WV14 40 F4
Loxdale St Bilston WV14 40 F4
Wednesbury WS10 41 E2
Loxdale Sta WV14 40 F4
Loxley Ave Birmingham B14 105 C3
Solihull B90 105 F1
Loxley Cl Birmingham B31 102 E8
Coventry CV2 96 D2
Redditch B98 154 D6
Loxley Ct CV2 96 D2
Loxley Rd Smethwick B67 64 F1
Sutton Coldfield B75 32 D3
Loxley Way CV32 157 A2
Loxton Cl B74 31 D5
Loynells Rd B45 122 B7
Loyns Cl B37 69 E3
Lozells Inf & Jun Sch B19 66 D7
Lozells Rd B19 66 C7
Lozells St B19 66 C7
Lozells Wood Cl 2 B19 66 B7
Lucas Ho CV32 156 F2
Lucas Rd LE10 75 D6
Luce Cl B35 58 B4
Luce Rd WV10 25 E6
Lucerne Ct B23 56 D6
Lucian Cl CV2 115 B7
Lucknow Rd WV12 27 B5
Lucy Edwards Ct DY11 116 C5
Lud La B79 21 A5
Luddington Rd B92 107 E8
Ludford Cl B75 46 E7
Ludford Rd Birmingham B32 84 A1
Nuneaton CV10 72 C6
Ludgate B79 21 A5
Ludgate Ave DY11 116 A4
Ludgate Cl B46 59 B3
Ludgate Ct Tamworth B77 22 A6
2 Walsall WS5 43 D7
Ludgate Hill B3 164 B3
Ludgate St 10 DY1 51 B1
Ludlow Cl Birmingham B37 70 C2
Cannock WS11 2 C2
Willenhall WV12 27 B6
Ludlow Ct B11 87 B6
Ludlow Ho Birmingham B13 105 A6
1 Walsall WS3 28 C6
Ludlow La WS2 28 A4
Ludlow Rd Birmingham B8 67 F4
Coventry CV5 113 A2
Kidderminster DY10 116 E3
Redditch B97 153 E3
Ludlow Way DY1 50 E2
Ludmer Way B20 55 C2
Ludstone Ave WV4 38 D5
Ludstone Rd B29 84 F1
Luff Cl CV3 134 B8
Lugtrout La
Catherine de B B91 108 A6
Solihull B91 107 F6
Lukes Wlk WS13 3 A2
Lulworth Cl B63 82 C6
Lulworth Pk CV8 148 C6
Lulworth Rd Birmingham B28 88 A1
Burntwood WS7 7 A7
Lulworth Wlk WV4 38 C6
Lumley Gr B37 70 D2
Lumley Rd WS1 29 A1
Lumsden Cl CV2 114 F8
Lunar Cl CV4 132 D5
Lundy Cl LE10 71 B1
Lundy View B36 70 B6
Lunn Ave CV8 147 E3
Lunn Poly Ho 3 CV32 156 F1
Lunns Croft WS13 9 C8
Lunt Jct The WV14 41 A6
Lunt Pl WV14 41 A6
Lunt Rd Bilston WV14 40 F6
Birmingham B32 84 D5
Lupin Cl LE10 75 D5
Lupin Gr B9 67 F3
Lupin Rd DY2 51 F1
Lupton Ave CV3 133 C7
Lupton Ct B60 137 A1
Lusbridge Cl B63 82 B4
Luscombe Rd CV2 114 E8
Luther Way CV5 111 F4
Lutley Ave B63 82 E4
Lutley Cl WV3 38 E7
Lutley Dr DY9 81 C3
Lutley Gr B32 84 B1
Lutley La B63 82 C2
Lutley Mill Rd B63 82 E4
Lutley Prim Sch B63 82 D1
Luton Rd B29 85 F3
Lutterworth Rd
Coventry CV2 114 C5
Hinckley LE10 76 C3
Nuneaton CV11 79 C8
Lutterworth Road Commercial Est LE10 76 A5
Luttrell Rd B74 32 A1
Luxor La CV5 111 B8
Lyall Gdns B45 101 E1
Lyall Gr B27 88 A2
Lychgate Ave DY9 81 C1
Lychgate Cl LE10 76 A5
Lychgate La LE10 76 C5
Lyd Cl WV11 26 B5
Lydate Rd B62 83 F4
Lydbrook Covert 4 B38 123 E8
Lydbury Gr B33 69 A4
Lydd Croft B35 58 B4
Lyddington Dr B62 83 B7
Lyde Gn B63 82 B7
Lydford Cl CV2 114 C7
Lydford Gr B24 57 A1
Lydford Rd WS3 14 B3
Lydgate Ct Bedworth CV12 78 A4
Nuneaton CV11 73 C3
Lydgate Rd Coventry CV6 113 B5
Kingswinford DY6 60 F6
Lydget Gr B23 56 D7
Lydham Cl Bilston WV14 40 B4
Birmingham B44 56 A6
Redditch B98 153 E5
Lydia Croft B74 31 E6
Lydian Cl WV6 25 B4
Lydiate Ash Rd B60 121 C3
Lydiate Ave B31 102 D1
Lydiates Cl DY3 50 B7
Lydney Cl Redditch B98 154 D7
Willenhall WV12 27 D4
Lydney Gr B31 102 F3
Lydstep Gr CV31 162 C7
Lye Ave B32 84 A2
Lye Bsns Ctr DY9 82 A6
Lye Close La B32 84 A2
Lye Cross Rd B69 63 B7
Lye Sta DY9 81 E6
Lye Valley Ind Est DY9 81 F6
Lyecroft Ave B37 70 D2
Lygon Cl B98 154 A5
Lygon Gr B32 84 E4
Lyme Green Rd B33 68 F4
Lymedene Rd B42 55 B5
Lymer Rd WV10 11 C1
Lymesy St CV3 133 D7
Lymington Cl CV6 113 D8
Lymington Ct B73 46 B1
Lymore Croft CV2 115 A8
Lymsey Croft DY8 60 C3
Lynbrook Cl Dudley DY2 62 D5
Hollywood B47 125 A7
Lynbrook Rd CV5 132 D8
Lynch The Nuneaton CV11 73 D2
Polesworth B78 22 F1
Lynchgate Ct CV4 132 C6
Lynchgate Ho CV4 132 C6
Lynchgate Rd CV4 132 C6
Lyncourt Gr B32 84 B6
Lyncroft House Sch WS11 4 E8
Lyncroft L Ctr WS11 4 E8
Lyncroft Rd B11 87 F2
Lyndale B77 35 F6
Lyndale Dr WV11 26 E6
Lyndale Rd Coventry CV5 112 C3
Dudley DY2 62 E6
Sedgley DY3 39 B2
Lynden Cl B61 136 E3
Lyndenwood B97 153 A2
Lyndholm Rd DY10 117 A6
Lyndhurst Cl LE10 76 A7
Lyndhurst Croft CV5 111 C4
Lyndhurst Dr
Kidderminster DY10 116 E8
Stourbridge DY8 60 F1
Lyndhurst Rd
Birmingham B24 56 F2
Cannock WS12 2 E1
West Bromwich B71 53 E7
Wolverhampton WV3 39 A7
Lyndon B71 53 D5
Lyndon Cl
Birmingham, Castle Bromwich B36 69 C8
Birmingham, Handsworth B20 55 C2
Halesowen B63 82 F4
Sedgley DY3 39 E1
Lyndon Croft B37 90 B7
Lyndon Ct 1 CV32 161 E8
Lyndon Gr Kingswinford DY6 60 B8
West Bromwich B71 53 D4
Lyndon Green Inf Sch B26 89 A6
Lyndon Green Jun Sch B26 89 A6
Lyndon Ho B31 103 B3
Lyndon Rd Birmingham B33 68 E3
Birmingham, Eachway B45 121 E7
Solihull B92 88 F2
Sutton Coldfield B73 46 B5
Lyndon Sch B92 89 A3
Lyndworth Rd B30 104 C8
Lyne Ho 1 CV2 114 D8
Lyneham Cl Hinckley LE10 71 A1
Tamworth B79 21 C8
Lyneham Gdns B76 58 B6
Lyneham Way B35 57 F3
Lynfield Cl B38 123 F7
Lyng Cl CV5 112 A4
Lyng Hall Sch CV2 114 C6
Lyng La B70 53 C2
Lyng Prim Sch B70 53 C1
Lynmouth Cl Aldridge WS9 30 A5
Nuneaton CV11 73 E5
Lynmouth Rd CV2 114 E8
Lynn Gr B29 85 C3
Lynn La WS14 17 C6
Lynton Ave Smethwick B66 65 A6
West Bromwich B71 53 C7
Wolverhampton WV6 24 F6
Lynton Cl CV34 155 E1
Lynton Ho B23 56 B6
Lynton Rd Birmingham B6 67 B7
Coventry CV6 95 F1
Lynval Rd DY5 81 F7
Lynwood Ave DY6 60 B7
Lynwood Cl WV12 27 E8
Lynwood Dr DY10 98 C2
Lynwood Wlk 9 CV31 162 C6
Lyon Ct B72 46 C5
Lyons Gr B11 87 C3
Lysander Ho B35 58 B2
Lysander Rd B45 102 A2
Lysander St CV3 134 D6
Lysander Way WS11 1 E3
Lyster Cl CV34 160 B8
Lysway Ct 3 WS1 42 F8
Lysways St WS1 42 F8
Lythall Cl CV31 162 F5
Lythalls La CV6 95 E2
Lythalls Lane Ind Est CV6 95 E1
Lytham B77 22 C5
Lytham Cl Stourbridge DY8 80 F2
Sutton Coldfield B76 58 B6
Lytham Croft B15 86 D8
Lytham Gr WS3 14 A4
Lytham Rd WV6 23 D4
Lythwood Dr DY5 81 C8
Lyttelton Rd
Birmingham, Edgbaston B16 65 D1
Birmingham, Stechford B33 68 D3
Stourbridge DY8 80 D5
Warwick CV34 160 E8
Lyttleton Ave
Bromsgrove B60 150 E7
Halesowen B62 83 E7
Lyttleton Cl Coventry CV3 115 A1
Dudley DY2 62 C4
Lyttleton Ho B63 83 A2
Lyttleton Pl DY9 99 C6
Lyttleton St B70 53 C2
Lytton Ave WV4 38 E4
Lytton Gr B27 88 B1
Lytton La B32 84 F3

Maas Rd B31 103 A4
Mabey Ave B98 153 F5
Mac Gregor Cres B77 21 F3
Macadam Cl WS7 7 B8
Macarthur Rd B64 82 C8
Macaulay Ho B70 53 D1
Macaulay Rd CV2 114 D4
Macbeth App CV34 161 D4
Macdonald Cl B69 52 D2
Macdonald Rd CV2 114 D3
Macdonald St B5 86 E8
Mace St B64 62 E1
Macefield Cl CV2 96 D2
Machin Rd B23 56 F4
Mackadown La B33 69 D2
Mackay Rd WS3 14 D2
Mackenzie Cl CV5 112 A7
Mackenzie Rd B11 87 C2
Mackmillan Rd B65 63 C2
Macmillan Cl B69 52 C2
Macrome Rd WV6 24 E8
Madam's Hill Rd B90 126 D7
Maddocks Hill B72 46 C2
Madehurst Rd B23 56 E6
Madeira Ave WV8 10 A2
Madeira Croft CV5 112 E2
Madeira Ct DY8 60 F1
Madeley Rd
Belbroughton DY9 120 D6
Birmingham B11 87 C5
Kingswinford DY6 61 A4
Redditch B98 154 F5
Madin Rd DY4 51 E4
Madinatul Uloom Islamic Coll DY10 117 D1
Madison Ave Birmingham B36 68 D6
Walsall WS2 28 B2
Madley Cl B45 121 E8
Madox Cl B79 20 E7
Madresfield Dr B63 83 B2
Madrona B77 22 B4
Maer Cl B65 63 C3
Mafeking Rd B66 65 A7
Mafeking Villas B62 83 B7
Magdala St B18 65 E5
Magdalen Cl DY1 51 A2
Magdalene Rd WS1 43 A7
Magee Cl LE10 71 C2
Magna Cl WS6 4 E3
Magness Cres WV12 27 C5
Magnet Wlk B23 56 C3
Magnolia B77 22 A4

Magnolia Cl
Birmingham B29 103 A7
Coventry CV3 133 B5
Magnolia Gr WV8 10 B3
Magnolia Way 1 DY8 80 F8
Magnum Cl B74 44 F7
Magnus B77 35 E6
Magpie Cl DY2 62 E3
Magpie Ho CV5 111 D5
Magpie La CV7 129 E6
Magpie Way DY10 117 B2
Maguire Ind Est CV4 131 F8
Magyar Cres CV11 79 A8
Maidavale Cres CV3 133 C4
Maidendale Rd DY6 60 B7
Maidensbridge Dr DY6 60 C8
Maidensbridge Gdns DY6 49 B1
Maidensbridge Prim Sch DY6 49 B1
Maidensbridge Rd DY6 49 B1
Maidstone Dr Burntwood WS7 7 D6
Stourbridge DY8 60 E3
Maidstone Rd B20 55 E1
Maidwell Dr B90 126 E8
Main Ave B26 90 C4
Main Rd Ansty CV7 97 D3
Birmingham B26 89 F3
Meriden CV7 110 D8
Main St Birmingham B11 87 A7
Brandon CV8 135 F4
Shenstone WS14 17 F6
Stonnall WS9 16 E4
Tamworth B79 21 B8
Main Terr B11 87 A7
Mainstone Cl B98 154 E3
Mainstream Forty Seven Ind Pk B7 67 C5
Mainstream Way B7 67 C5
Mainwaring Dr B75 32 E2
Maisemore Cl B98 154 D6
Maitland B77 21 F2
Maitland Ho B34 69 E6
Maitland Rd Birmingham B8 67 F4
Dudley DY1 50 E1
Maizefield LE10 71 C4
Majestic Way B65 63 D4
Major Ct 6 B13 87 B2
Major St WV2 39 E7
Majuba Rd B16 65 C4
Makepeace Ave CV34 155 F1
Malam Cl CV4 112 A1
Malcolm Ave Birmingham B24 57 C5
Bromsgrove B61 136 E3
Malcolm Ct WV1 25 A3
Malcolm Gr B45 122 A7
Malcolm Rd B90 106 B1
Malcolmson Cl B15 85 F8
Maldale B77 22 C1
Malfield Dr Birmingham B27 88 E3
Redditch B97 152 F3
Malham Cl CV11 74 A2
Malham Rd Tamworth B77 36 C8
Warwick CV34 155 F1
Malins Rd Birmingham B17 85 D5
Wolverhampton WV4 39 E5
Malins The CV34 161 B6
Malkit Cl WS2 27 F4
Mallaby Cl B90 126 A8
Mallard Ave
Kidderminster DY10 117 B3
Nuneaton CV10 72 C6
Mallard Cl Birmingham B27 88 C3
Brierley Hill DY5 81 C7
Redditch B98 153 F5
Walsall WS3 15 A5
Mallard Croft 2 WS13 9 C8
Mallard Dr Birmingham B23 56 B3
Oldbury B69 63 F4
Mallard Rd B80 159 F4
Mallards Reach B92 106 E8
Mallender Dr B93 127 F6
Mallerin Croft CV10 72 B5
Mallicot Cl WS13 3 D1
Mallin Gdns DY1 61 E8
Mallin St B66 64 D7
Mallory Cres WS3 14 D2
Mallory Dr
Kidderminster DY11 116 D8
Warwick CV34 160 D7
Mallory Rd WV6 23 E3
Mallory Rise B13 87 C1
Mallory Way CV6 95 E4
Mallow Cl WS5 43 A3
Malmesbury Rd
Birmingham B10 87 E7
Coventry CV6 95 A3
Malpas Dr B32 102 C8
Malpas Wlk WV10 26 A4
Malpass Rd DY5 81 F7
Malt Cl B17 85 D6
Malt Mill La B62 83 D8
Malt Mill Lane Trad Est B62 83 D8
Malthouse 2 B66 64 E7
Malthouse Croft B6 66 E8
Malthouse Gdns B19 66 D7
Malthouse Gr B25 68 E1
Malthouse La
Birmingham B8 67 E6
Birmingham, Great Barr B42 55 D8
Earlswood B94 141 E7
Kenilworth CV8 147 E6
Wolverhampton WV6 24 E6
Malthouse Rd DY4 51 E5
Malthouse Row B37 90 A8
Maltings The Aldridge WS9 30 C6
Nuneaton CV11 73 E5
Royal Leamington Spa CV32 156 F2
Studley B80 159 D4
Wolverhampton WV1 163 C4
Malton Gr B13 105 B7
Malvern Ave Nuneaton CV10 72 B3
Stourbridge DY9 81 C5
Malvern Cl
West Bromwich B71 53 D5
Willenhall WV12 27 B4
Malvern Cres DY2 61 F6
Malvern Ct
Birmingham, Acock's Green B27 88 C4
Birmingham, Stockland Green B23 56 C3
Sutton Coldfield B74 31 F2
Wolverhampton WV10 25 D8
Malvern Dr Aldridge WS9 30 C8
Kidderminster DY10 116 E3
Sutton Coldfield B76 58 A8
Wolverhampton WV1 26 B1
Malvern Hill Rd B7 67 C7
Malvern Ho Coventry CV5 111 D4
7 Halesowen B63 83 A3
Redditch B97 153 C1
Malvern Park Ave B91 107 D3
Malvern Rd
Balsall Common CV7 130 C6
Barnt Green B45 122 A2
Birmingham, Acock's Green B27 88 D4
Birmingham, Handsworth B21 54 C1
Bromsgrove B61 150 D7
Coventry CV5 112 F4
Oldbury B68 84 B8
Redditch B97 158 D8
Malvern St B12 87 A5
Malvern View
Bluntington DY10 118 E1
Kidderminster DY11 116 B1
Malvern View Rd DY3 50 D4
Mamble Rd DY8 80 E5
Manby Cl W6 25 A4
Manby Rd B35 58 A4
Manby St DY4 51 F8
Mancetter Rd Nuneaton CV10 72 D7
Solihull B90 106 C3
Manchester St
Birmingham B6 164 C5
Oldbury B69 64 B7
Mancroft Cl DY6 60 B7
Mancroft Gdns WV6 24 C5
Mancroft Rd WV6 24 C5
Mandale Rd WV10 25 F6
Mandarin Ave DY10 117 B3
Mander Ctr WV1 163 B3
Mander Gallery WV1 163 B3
Mander Gr CV34 160 C4
Mander Sq WV1 163 B3
Mander St WV3 163 A1
Manderley Cl Coventry CV5 111 C5
Sedgley DY3 39 C2
Manderville Gdns DY6 60 C6
Mandeville Gdns WS1 42 F8
Mandeville Way B61 136 F5
Maney Cnr B72 46 B4
Maney Hill Prim Sch B72 46 D2
Maney Hill Rd B72 46 C2
Manfield Ave CV2 115 A7
Manfield Rd WV13 26 C3
Manifold Cl WS7 7 D6
Manifoldia Grange B70 53 B2
Manilla Rd B29 86 B1
Manitoba Croft B38 123 F8
Manley Cl B70 53 A3
Manley Rd WS13 3 D1
Manlove St WV3 39 A8
Manningford Ct B14 104 F3
Manningford Rd B14 104 E3
Manor Abbey Dr B62 83 E3
Manor Abbey Rd B62 83 F4
Manor Ave Cannock WS11 1 D1
Great Wyrley WS6 5 A4
Kidderminster DY11 116 A7
Manor Ave S DY11 116 A6
Manor Cl Birmingham B16 65 D1
Codsall WV8 10 B4
Hinckley LE10 75 C5
Kidderminster DY11 116 A6
Willenhall WV13 26 F3
Wolverhampton WV4 38 F4
Manor Court Ave CV11 73 B5
Manor Court Rd
Bromsgrove B60 150 F8
Nuneaton CV11 73 A5
Manor Ct Dorridge B93 127 F2
Dudley DY2 62 C5
Kenilworth CV8 148 A6
Royal Leamington Spa CV31 161 F7
Walsall WS2 28 C1
Manor Cty Prim Sch B78 34 E5
Manor Dr Dudley DY3 50 B3
Sutton Coldfield B73 46 B4
Manor Est CV8 135 F3
Manor Farm Com Sch WS4 29 B6
Manor Farm Dr WV12 27 D5
Manor Farm Rd B11 87 E4
Manor Gdns Birmingham B33 68 D2
Wednesbury WS10 41 F4
Wombourne WV5 49 B7
Manor (General) Hospl The WS2 28 C1
Manor High Com Sch WS10 42 D3
Manor Hill B73 46 B4
Manor Ho Astwood Bank B96 158 E3
Wolverhampton WV6 24 D5
Manor House Cl
Aston Flamville LE10 76 E6
Birmingham B29 84 F1
Manor House Dr CV1 165 B2
Manor House La
Birmingham B26 88 F7
Water Orton B46 59 B3
Manor House Pk WV8 10 C4
Manor House Rd WS10 41 F4
Manor Ind Est WS2 28 C1
Manor La Halesowen B62 83 E4
Honiley CV8 146 A5
Lydiate Ash B61 121 C4
Stourbridge DY8 80 D3
Wroxall CV35 145 F4
Manor Mews B80 159 E4
Manor Park Gr B31 102 C1
Manor Park Jun & Inf Sch CV3 133 D7
Manor Park Prim Sch B6 67 A8
Manor Park Rd
Birmingham B36 69 D8
Nuneaton CV11 73 A5
Manor Park Sch CV11 73 A5
Manor Pk DY6 60 D6
Manor Pl LE10 71 D1
Manor Prim Sch
Aldridge B74 31 A1
Wolverhampton WV14 40 B2
Manor Rd
Birmingham, Birchfield B6 55 F1
Birmingham, Edgbaston B16 65 D1
Birmingham, Stechford B33 68 E3
Coventry CV1 165 B1
Dorridge B93 127 F3
Kenilworth CV8 147 F6
Mile Oak B78 20 D1
Royal Leamington Spa CV32 157 B3
Smethwick B67 64 E4
Solihull B91 107 C5
Stourbridge DY8 60 E2
Studley B80 159 E4
Sutton Coldfield, Maney B73 46 B4
Sutton Coldfield, Streetly B74 45 A8
Tamworth B77 21 D4
Tipton DY4 51 F4
Upper Bentley B60, B97 152 B1
Walsall WS2 28 C2
Wednesbury WS10 42 D2
Wolverhampton, Ettingshall WV4 40 A5
Wolverhampton, Oxley WV10 25 C7
Wolverhampton, Penn WV4 38 F4
Wythall B47 125 A3
Manor Rd N B16 65 D1
Manor Rise Burntwood WS7 7 A5
Lichfield WS14 9 C7
Manor Road Prec 2 WS2 28 C2
Manor St Hinckley LE10 71 C1
Wolverhampton WV6 24 D5
Manor Terr CV8 148 A6
Manor Way Birmingham B62 84 A3
Halesowen B62 83 D3
Hinckley LE10 75 D5
Manor Way Prim Sch B62 83 C3
Manor Wlk Solihull B91 107 C3
Sutton Coldfield B73 46 B4
Manorford Ave B71 43 A1
Mansard Cl
Wolverhampton, Bradmore WV3 38 F8
Wolverhampton, Scotland WV10 26 B8
Mansard Ho B90 106 A3
Manse Cl CV7 78 A1
Mansel Rd B10 87 E8
Mansel St CV6 113 E8
Mansell Cl B63 82 B7
Mansell Rd Redditch B97 158 D7
Tipton DY4 52 A8
Mansfield Green Inf & Jun Sch B6 66 E8
Mansfield Ho B37 70 D3
Mansfield Rd
Birmingham, Aston B6 66 E8
Birmingham, South Yardley B25 88 C5
Mansion Cres B67 64 E4
Mansion Ct B62 83 E7
Mansion Dr WS7 7 D4
Mansion St 1 LE10 75 D8
Manston Ct WV4 38 D5
Manston Dr WV6 23 E5
Manston Rd B26 89 B7
Manston View B79 21 C8
Manta Rd B77 35 D6
Mantilla Dr CV3 133 B5
Manton Croft B93 127 E3
Manton Ho B19 66 E7
Manway Cl B20 54 F4
Manwoods Cl B20 55 B2
Maple Ave Bedworth CV7 78 B1
Wednesbury WS10 42 C4
Maple Bank B15 86 A7
Maple Bsns Pk B7 67 B6
Maple Cl Birmingham B21 54 E1
Burntwood WS7 6 F7
Dudley WV14 51 A7
Hinckley LE10 75 E5
Kidderminster DY11 116 B8
Stourbridge DY8 80 D2
Maple Cres WS11 1 C1
Maple Croft B13 104 F5
Maple Ct Bilston WV14 40 F2
Lichfield WS14 9 C5
Oldbury B66 64 D8
Maple Ctr The WS10 41 B3
Maple Dr Birmingham B44 56 C8
Dudley DY3 50 B2
Huntington WS12 1 D8
Walsall, Shelfield WS4 29 B8
Walsall, Yew Tree WS5 43 B4
Maple Gn DY1 51 A5
Maple Gr Bilston WV14 40 F4
Birmingham, Aston B19 66 D8
Birmingham, Kingshurst B37 69 F6
Kingswinford DY6 60 E6
Lichfield WS14 9 F7
Warwick CV34 156 A1
Wolverhampton WV3 24 C2
Maple Hayes Dyslexia Sch The WS13 8 D8
Maple Ho WS4 15 D1
Maple Leaf Dr B37 90 C8
Maple Leaf Ind Est WS2 28 A3
Maple Leaf Rd WS10 41 C1
Maple Rd
Birmingham, Eachway B45 121 F6
Birmingham, Selly Oak B30 103 E8
Dudley DY1 51 C3
Halesowen B62 83 D8
Nuneaton CV10 72 E5
Royal Leamington Spa CV31 161 F6
Sutton Coldfield B72 46 C3
Walsall WS3 14 F2
Wolverhampton WV3 38 E7
Maple Rise Oldbury B68 64 C2
Tamworth B77 22 A4
Maple Row 1 DY5 61 D2
Maple St WS3 14 D2
Maple Tree La B63 82 C6
Maple Way B31 102 F1
Maple Wlk 4 B37 70 B2
Maplebeck Cl CV5 113 A3
Mapledene B13 87 B2
Mapledene Inf Sch B26 89 D6
Mapledene Jun Sch B26 89 D6
Mapledene Rd B26 89 D6
Maples The Bedworth CV12 77 E2
Wolverhampton WV11 26 B5
Mapleton Gr B28 106 B7
Mapleton Rd
Birmingham B28 106 B7
Coventry CV6 112 F8
Maplewood B76 58 A8
Mapperley Cl CV2 115 A8
Mapperley Gdns B13 86 C3
Mappleborough Rd B90 105 E1
Marans Croft B38 123 D7
Marble Alley B80 159 E4
Marbury Cl B38 103 D2
Marbury Mews DY5 61 D1
March Cl WS6 4 D1
March End Rd WV11 26 D5
March Way Aldridge WS9 16 C1
Coventry CV3 134 D7
Marchant Rd Bilston WV14 40 D7
Hinckley LE10 75 C8
Wolverhampton WV3 24 F2
Marchfont Cl CV11 74 A1
Marchmont Rd B9 68 A2
Marchmount Rd B72 57 C8
Marcliff Cres B90 105 C2
Marconi Pl WS12 2 C7
Marcos Dr B36 58 F1
Marcot Rd B92 88 F5
Marcroft Pl CV31 162 D6
Marden Cl WV13 26 F1
Marden Gr B31 123 A7
Marden Wlk B23 56 C3
Mardol Cl CV2 114 D7
Mardon Rd B26 89 C5
Maree Gr WV12 13 B1
Maret Ct 2 WS1 42 F8
Marfield Cl B76 58 A6
Margam Cres WS3 13 F2
Margam Terr WS3 13 F2
Margam Way WS3 13 F2
Margaret Ave Bedworth CV12 78 B3
Halesowen B63 82 F4
Margaret Cl DY5 81 E8
Margaret Dr Cannock WS11 1 E6
Stourbridge DY8 81 B4
Margaret Gdns B67 64 E5
Margaret Gr B17 85 C7
Margaret Ho B76 46 F3
Margaret Rd Birmingham B73 45 D1
Birmingham, Harborne B17 85 C5
Darlaston WS10 41 C4
Walsall WS2 27 E3
Margaret St Birmingham B3 164 B3
Walsall WS2 28 D2
West Bromwich B70 53 B2
Margaret Vale DY4 41 C1
Margaret Vine Ct B62 63 F1
Margeson Cl CV2 114 E2
Margesson Dr B45 122 D1
Margetts Cl CV8 147 F4
Marholm Cl WV9 10 F2
Maria St B70 64 E8
Marian Croft B26 89 D4
Marie Brock Cl CV4 112 B1
Marie Dr B27 106 B8
Marigold Cl WS11 2 C3
Marigold Cres DY1 51 A4
Marigold Dr LE10 75 E5
Marina Cl CV4 131 E7
Marina Cres WS12 2 A5
Marine Cres DY8 60 E1
Marine Dr B44 55 E6
Marine Gdns DY8 60 E1
Mariner B79 20 E6
Mariner Ave B16 65 E1
Marion Cl DY5 61 F2
Marion Rd Coventry CV6 113 D7
Smethwick B67 64 E5
Marion Way B28 105 E7
Marita Cl DY2 62 E3
Marjoram Cl B38 123 F8
Marjorie Ave B30 104 B3
Mark Antony Dr CV34 161 D4
Mark Ave WS10 41 E3
Mark Ct WS1 29 A3
Mark Rd B13 87 A2
Mark Rd WS10 41 E3
Markby Rd B18 65 E6
Market Cnr Baginton CV8 133 F2
Royal Leamington Spa CV31 161 F5
Market End Cl CV12 77 C2
Market Hall St WS11 1 E1
Market La Lichfield WS14 8 E2
Wombourne WV4 37 F5
Market Pl Blackheath B65 63 C1
Bromsgrove B61 136 F2
Cannock WS11 1 D1
Hinckley LE10 75 D8
Nuneaton CV11 73 C4
Redditch B98 153 E4
Tamworth B79 21 B4
Tipton DY4 52 D5
Walsall WS3 14 B1
2 Warwick CV34 160 E6
Wednesbury WS10 41 F2
Willenhall WV13 27 A1
Market Sq B64 82 C8
Market St Bromsgrove B61 136 F2
Cannock WS12 2 C5
Kidderminster DY10 116 E5
Lichfield WS13 9 B8
Oldbury B69 64 A8
Stourbridge DY8 81 A5
Tamworth B79 21 B4
Warwick CV34 160 D6
Wolverhampton WV1 163 C3
Market Way Bilston WV14 40 D5
Coventry CV1 165 B2
Hagley DY9 99 C6
Market Wlk 4 B98 153 E4
Markfield Rd B26 89 B8
Markford Wlk B19 66 D6
Markham Cres B92 89 F1
Markham Croft WV9 11 A2
Markham Dr
Kingswinford DY6 60 E4
Whitnash CV31 162 B3
Markham Rd B73 45 C3
Marklew Cl WS8 16 A5
Marklin Ave WV10 11 D1
Marks Mews 8 CV34 160 E6
Marks Wlk WS13 3 A2
Marksbury Cl WV6 25 A5
Marl Rd DY2 62 B4
Marl Top B38 103 F2
Marlbank Rd DY8 61 A1
Marlborough Ave B60 151 A8
Marlborough Cl
Hinckley LE10 76 B7
Sutton Coldfield B74 31 E6
Marlborough Ct
Bromsgrove B60 151 B8
Lichfield WS13 9 B7
Sutton Coldfield B74 31 F2
Marlborough Dr
Royal Leamington Spa CV31 162 D5
Stourbridge DY8 81 A3
Marlborough Gdns
Stourbridge DY8 60 D2
Wolverhampton WV6 24 E4
Marlborough Gr B25 68 D1
Marlborough Ind Est WV2 39 D7
Marlborough Inf Sch B10 67 E1
Marlborough Jun Sch B10 67 E1
Marlborough Rd
Birmingham, Castle Bromwich B36 69 D8
Birmingham, Small Heath B10 67 E1
Coventry CV2 114 A3
Dudley DY3 50 F6
Nuneaton CV11 73 B3
Smethwick B66 65 A3
Marlborough St
2 Kidderminster DY10 116 E5
Walsall WS3 14 B1
Marlborough Way B77 21 F2
Marlbrook Cl B92 89 C4
Marlbrook Dr WV4 39 B6
Marlbrook La B60 121 D2
Marlcliff Gr B13 105 A6
Marlcroft CV3 134 E5
Marldon Rd B14 104 E6
Marlene Croft B37 70 C1
Marler Rd CV4 131 F7
Marley Hts B27 88 D4
Marley Rd DY6 61 A4
Marlfield Farm Fst Sch B98 154 C6
Marlfield La Redditch B98 154 B4
Redditch B98 154 B5
Marlin B77 35 D6
Marling Croft B92 107 F7
Marlissa Dr CV6 95 E2
Marloes Wlk CV31 162 C6

Marlow Cl Coventry CV5 112 B4
Dudley DY2 62 E3
Marlow Rd Birmingham B23 56 D5
Tamworth B77 21 D5
Marlow St Blackheath B65 63 B1
Walsall WS2 28 E3
Marlowe Cl DY10 117 B6
Marlowe Dr WV12 27 A7
Marlpit La Redditch B97 153 C1
Sutton Coldfield B75 32 E3
Marlpool Dr Redditch B97 153 C3
Walsall WS3 15 A1
Marlpool Fst Sch The DY11 116 C8
Marlpool La DY11 116 C8
Marlpool Pl DY11 116 C8
Marlston Wlk CV5 112 B4
Marlwood Cl CV6 95 F4
Marmion Dr B43 43 F2
Marmion Gr DY1 62 A8
Marmion Ho B70 52 F6
Marmion Jun Sch B79 21 B6
Marmion St B79 21 B5
Marmion Way B70 52 F6
Marnel Dr WV3 38 E7
Marner Cres CV6 113 B5
Marner Rd Bedworth CV12 78 A3
Nuneaton CV10 73 B1
Marnhull Cl CV2 114 F4
Marquis Dr B62 83 A7
Marrick B77 22 C1
Marriners La CV5 112 B5
Marriott Rd Bedworth CV12 77 D2
Coventry CV6 113 A4
Dudley DY2 62 C4
Smethwick B66 64 D7
Marroway St B16 65 F3
Mars Cl WV14 40 A1
Marsdale Dr CV10 72 E3
Marsden Cl B92 88 E1
Marsden Rd B98 153 E3
Marsett B77 36 C8
Marsh Cres DY8 60 D3
Marsh End B38 124 A8
Marsh Hill B23 56 C4
Marsh Hill Jun & Inf Sch B23 56 C4
Marsh Ho CV2 115 A7
Marsh La Birmingham B23 56 E5
Bradnock's Marsh B92 109 D5
Curdworth B76 59 D5
Hampton in A B92 109 B6
Lichfield WS14 9 C5
Solihull B91 107 E3
Walsall WS2 28 E2
Water Orton B46 59 C3
West Bromwich B71 53 D8
Wolverhampton WV10 11 B2
Marsh Lane Par WV10 11 C2
Marsh St WS2 28 E2
Marsh The WS10 41 E3
Marshall Cl WS9 30 B4
Marshall Gr B44 55 F7
Marshall Ho 4 Walsall WS2 42 C8
7 West Bromwich B71 42 F1
Marshall Lake Rd B90 106 D1
Marshall Rd Bedworth CV7 95 F8
Oldbury B68 64 C1
Willenhall WV13 26 D1
Marshall St Birmingham B1 164 B1
Smethwick B67 64 D7
Tamworth B77 21 E5
Marshalls Ind Est WV2 39 C7
Marsham Cl CV34 161 B8
Marsham Court Rd B91 106 F7
Marsham Rd B14 104 F3
Marshbrook Cl CV2 96 E3
Marshbrook Rd B24 57 D4
Marshdale Ave CV6 95 E3
Marshfield Cl B98 154 B7
Marshfield Dr CV4 132 D2
Marshfield Gdns B24 56 F2
Marshland Way WS2 27 E1
Marshmont Way B23 56 D8
Marshwood Cl WS11 2 A2
Marshwood Croft B62 84 A3
Marsland Cl B17 65 C1
Marsland Rd B92 106 E8
Marston Ave WS10 41 C6
Marston Cl
Royal Leamington Spa CV32 157 B2
Stourbridge DY8 80 D4
Marston Croft B37 89 F7
Marston Dr B37 70 A5
Marston Gr B43 54 C8
Marston Green Inf Sch B37 89 F7
Marston Green Jun Sch B37 90 A7
Marston Green Sta B37 89 F7
Marston Ind Est WV2 39 C7
Marston La Bedworth CV12 78 D5
Nuneaton CV11 78 E8
Wishaw B76 48 E1
Marston Rd Birmingham B29 102 F8
Cannock WS12 1 F6
Dudley DY1 61 E8
Sutton Coldfield B73 46 F3
Wolverhampton WV2 39 C7
Marston St WV13 27 C2
Marten Cl CV35 160 A7
Martham Dr WV6 24 B2
Martin Cl Birmingham B26 88 D6
Bromsgrove B61 136 E1
Coventry CV5 111 E4
Dudley WV14 51 D7
Martin Croft WS13 3 A1
Martin Dr WV12 27 C5
Martin Hill St DY2 62 C8
Martin Rd Bilston WV14 40 F3
Tipton DY4 52 A4
Walsall WS5 43 C8
Martin Rise B37 89 F8
Martin St WV4 39 F5
Martindale WS11 2 A2
Martindale Rd CV7 96 C8
Martindale Trad Est WS11 2 A2
Martindale Wlk DY5 81 B6
Martineau Rural Studies Ctr B5 86 C5
Martineau Sq B2 164 C2
Martineau Tower B19 66 D5
Martineau Way B2 164 C2
Martingale Cl
Bromsgrove B60 150 E6
Walsall WS5 42 F4
Martins Rd CV12 77 E1
Martlesham Sq B35 58 A4
Martley Cl B98 159 B7
Martley Croft
Birmingham B32 84 E4
Solihull B91 127 B8
Martley Ct DY9 81 C4
Martley Dr DY9 81 C4
Martley Rd Oldbury B69 63 D5
Walsall WS4 15 C2
Marton Ave 7 WS7 7 A8
Marton Cl B7 67 B6
Martyrs' Cl The CV3 133 D8
Marwood Croft B74 31 A2
Mary Ann St Birmingham B3 164 B4
Wolverhampton WV1 163 D2
Mary Elliot Sch WS2 28 E4
Mary Herbert St CV3 133 D7
Mary Rd
Birmingham, Handsworth B21 65 E7
Birmingham, Stechford B33 68 D3
Tipton B69 63 C8
West Bromwich B70 53 D1
Mary Slessor St CV3 134 D7
Mary St
Birmingham, Balsall Heath B12 86 E5
Birmingham, Brookfields B3 164 A4
Cannock WS12 2 B7
Walsall WS2 28 D3
Mary Vale Rd B30 103 F6
Maryland Ave B34 68 F5
Maryland Cl LE9 71 F6
Maryland Dr B31 103 B5
Maryland Rd DY5 81 F7
Marylebone Cl DY8 81 A7
Marystow Cl CV5 112 B8
Maryvale Ct Lichfield WS14 9 D7
2 Walsall WS1 42 E8
Maryvale RC Jun & Inf Sch B44 44 E1
Marywell Cl B32 102 B7
Masefield Ave Dudley DY1 51 C7
Warwick CV34 160 C4
Masefield Cl Bilston WV14 40 F2
Lichfield WS14 9 B6
Masefield Dr B79 21 A7
Masefield Gr WS11 1 E4
Masefield Rd Dudley DY3 50 A4
Walsall WS3 28 E7
Wolverhampton WV10 12 A1
Masefield Rise B62 83 D3
Masefield Sq B31 103 C4
Masham Cl B33 68 E3
Mashie Gdns B38 103 D1
Maslen Pl B63 83 B3
Maslin Dr WV14 40 A1
Mason Ave CV32 157 C3
Mason Cl B97 158 D7
Mason Cotts B24 57 B5
Mason Cres WV4 38 E5
Mason Ct LE10 75 B8
Mason La B94 125 F1
Mason Rd Birmingham B24 57 A4
Coventry CV6 95 F1
Kidderminster DY11 116 C6
Redditch B97 158 D8
Walsall WS2 28 B5
Mason St Dudley WV14 51 B7
West Bromwich B70 53 B4
Wolverhampton WV2 39 C7
Mason's Way B92 88 E2
Masonleys Rd B31 102 D3
Masons Cl B63 82 C6
Masons Way B92 88 E2
Massbrook Gr WV10 25 F6
Massbrook Rd WV10 25 F6
Masser Rd CV6 95 D4
Masshouse Circus Queensway B4 164 C3
Masshouse La
Birmingham, Digbeth B5 164 D3
Birmingham, King's Norton B38 103 F1
Masters La B62 63 E1
Masters Rd CV31 162 A4
Matchborough Ctr B98 154 E1
Matchborough Way B98 154 E1
Matchlock Cl B74 44 E7
Matfen Ave B73 45 F2
Math Mdw B32 84 F5
Mathe Croft CV31 162 C5
Mathews Wlk WS13 3 A2
Matlock Cl Dudley DY2 62 D3
Walsall WS3 14 C3
Matlock Dr WS11 2 A4
Matlock Rd Birmingham B11 87 F3
Coventry CV1 113 D6
Walsall WS3 14 C3
Matlock Villas 2 B12 87 B5
Matterson Rd CV6 113 A5
Matthew Boulton Coll B15 86 D8
Matthew La (Road 3) DY10 116 F1
Mattox Rd WV11 26 D6
Matty Rd B68 64 C4
Maud Rd Water Orton B46 59 D3
West Bromwich B70 53 C1
Maudslay Rd CV5 112 E2
Maughan St Brierley Hill DY5 82 A8
Dudley DY1 51 B1
Maund Cl B60 150 E7
Maureen Cl CV4 111 C1
Maurice Gr WV10 26 A6
Maurice Rd Birmingham B14 104 E5
Smethwick B67 64 E2
Mavis Gdns B68 84 B8
Mavis Rd Birmingham B31 102 E1
Cannock WS12 2 B7
Mavor Dr CV12 77 D1
Maw St WS1 42 F6
Mawgan Dr WS14 9 D6
Mawnan Cl CV7 96 B8
Max Rd Birmingham B32 84 D5
Coventry CV6 112 F5
Maxholm Rd B74 44 E8
Maxstoke Cl
Birmingham B32 102 A7
Meriden CV7 92 B1
Redditch B98 154 D1
Sutton Coldfield B73 45 E2
Tamworth B77 35 C4
Walsall WS3 14 A3
Maxstoke Croft B90 126 C8
Maxstoke Gdns CV31 161 F6
Maxstoke La CV7 92 B2
Maxstoke Rd B73 45 E1
Maxstoke St B9 67 B2
Maxted Rd B23 56 C7
Maxwell Ave B20 55 B1
Maxwell Cl WS13 9 C7
Maxwell Ct B33 68 F3
Maxwell Rd WV2 163 C1
May Ave 3 B12 87 A5
May Farm Cl B47 125 A6
May La Birmingham B14 104 F5
Hollywood B47 125 A7
May St Coventry CV6 113 E8
Walsall WS3 28 D6
May Tree Gr B20 54 F3
May Trees B47 124 F5
Mayall Dr B75 32 D4
Mayama Rd B78 34 F8
Maybank B9 67 F3
Maybank Cl WS14 9 E8
Maybank Pl B44 55 E6
Maybank Rd DY2 62 C3
Mayberry Cl B14 105 B2
Maybridge Dr B91 127 B8
Maybrook Ind Est WS8 15 F5
Maybrook Rd Brownhills WS8 15 F5
Sutton Coldfield B76 58 A5
Maybush Gdns WV10 11 C1
Maycock Rd CV6 113 D7
Maycroft Cl WS12 1 F7
Maydene Croft B12 86 F6
Mayfair DY9 81 D2
Mayfair Cl Birmingham B44 56 B7
Dudley DY1 51 A2
Mayfair Dr DY6 60 C7
Mayfair Gdns Tipton DY4 52 A4
Wolverhampton WV3 24 D2
Mayfield B77 36 C8
Mayfield Ave B29 86 B2
Mayfield Cl Bedworth CV12 78 B3
Catshill B61 120 F1
Kidderminster DY11 116 A8
10 Royal Leamington Spa CV31 162 C6
Solihull B91 107 C1
Mayfield Cres B65 63 A3
Mayfield Ct B13 87 A2
Mayfield Dr CV8 148 C4
Mayfield Prep Sch WS1 43 A8
Mayfield Rd
Birmingham, Acock's Green B11 88 A3
Birmingham, Lozells B19 66 C8
Birmingham, Moseley B13 87 A3
Birmingham, Stirchley B30 104 A6
Coventry CV5 113 A1
Dudley DY1 51 C4
Halesowen B62 63 F1
Halesowen, Hasbury B63 82 E2
Nuneaton CV11 73 E2
Sutton Coldfield, Boldmere B73 46 A2
Sutton Coldfield, Streetly B74 44 F8
Wolverhampton WV1 26 B1
Mayfield Sch
Birmingham B19 66 C6
Birmingham B19 66 C8
Mayfield The WV1 26 B1
Mayfields Dr WS8 6 B2
Mayfields The B98 153 E2
Mayflower Cl B19 66 D6
Mayflower Dr
Brierley Hill DY5 61 A7
Coventry CV2 114 E2
Mayford Gr B13 105 B6
Maygrove Rd DY6 60 C7
Mayhurst Cl Hollywood B47 125 C6
Tipton DY4 52 A8
Mayhurst Rd B47 125 B6
Mayland Dr B74 45 A5
Mayland Rd B16 65 C2
Maynard Ave Bedworth CV12 95 D8
Stourbridge DY8 80 D3
Warwick CV34 161 A7
Mayo Dr CV8 148 A4
Mayor's Croft CV4 132 B7
Mayou Ct WS3 15 A4
Maypole Cl B64 82 B8
Maypole Ct WV5 49 A6
Maypole Dr DY8 80 E5
Maypole Fields B63 82 A7
Maypole Gr B14 105 B2
Maypole Hill B63 82 A7
Maypole La B14 105 A2
Maypole Rd B68 64 B1
Maypole St WV5 49 B7
Mayswood Dr WV6 23 F1
Mayswood Gr B32 84 D4
Mayswood Rd B92 89 C2
Maythorn Ave B76 58 A6
Maythorn Gdns WV6 24 C3
Maythorn Gr 4 B91 127 B8
Maytree Cl B37 70 A2
Maywell Dr B92 107 F8
Maywood Cl DY6 60 B6
McKean Ct B70 53 C1
McKean Rd Oldbury B69 64 A8
West Bromwich B70 53 C1
McBean Rd WV6 24 F4
McCalla Ho WV3 25 B1
McConnell Cl B60 151 B7
McDonnell Dr CV6 95 F6
McDougall Rd WS10 42 C3
McGeough Wlk WS11 2 B5
McGhie St WS12 2 B6
McGregor Cl 4 B6 55 F1
McLean Rd WV10 11 C1
McMahon Rd CV12 95 E8
Meaburn Cl B29 103 A7
Mead Cl WS9 30 B6
Mead Cres B9 68 B3
Mead Rise B15 85 F6
Mead The DY3 50 B8
Meadfoot Ave B14 104 F3
Meadfoot Dr DY6 60 B7
Meadfoot Rd CV3 134 E6
Meadow Ave B71 53 F8
Meadow Brook Rd B31 102 F5
Meadow Cl Aldridge B74 30 F2
Ansty CV7 97 D3
Birmingham B17 65 B1
Royal Leamington Spa CV32 157 C4
Tanworth-in-A B94 143 C6
Walsall WS4 29 C8
Meadow Croft Cannock WS12 1 C4
Hagley DY9 98 F4
Perton WV6 23 D3
Wythall B47 125 A3
Meadow Ct CV11 73 B4
Meadow Dr
Hampton in A B92 109 B7
Hinckley LE10 76 A7
Meadow Gr Great Wyrley WS6 5 A2
Solihull B92 88 D1
Meadow Grange Dr WV12 27 B7
Meadow Green Prim Sch B47 125 A3
Meadow Hill Cl DY11 116 A5
Meadow Hill Cres B98 153 F5
Meadow Hill Dr WS11 2 A2
Meadow Hill Rd B38 103 E2
Meadow Ho 5 CV1 113 B3
Meadow La Alvechurch B48 139 B6
Coven Heath WV10 11 C6
Lapworth B94 144 D3
Wednesfield WV12 27 A5
Wolverhampton WV14 40 B2
Wombourne WV5 49 B8
Meadow Lark Cl WS12 2 B4
Meadow Mills Est DY10 116 E5
Meadow Pk B79 20 F5
Meadow Rd Aldridge WS9 30 A4
Birmingham, Harborne B17 65 B1
Birmingham, Quinton B32 84 A6
Catshill B61 136 F8
Coventry CV6 95 B4
Dudley DY1 51 B3
Halesowen B62 83 C8
Nuneaton CV10 72 A8
Oldbury B68 64 B3
Smethwick B67 65 A4
Warwick CV34 161 A7
Wolverhampton WV3 38 D8
Wythall B47 125 A3
Meadow Rise B30 103 E7
Meadow St Blackheath B64 82 F8
Coventry CV1 165 A2
Nuneaton CV11 73 B5
Tamworth B77 21 C3
Walsall WS1 42 D8
1 Wolverhampton WV1 25 B2
Meadow Vale WV8 10 B2
Meadow View
Birmingham B13 105 C8
Burntwood WS7 7 D6
Sedgley DY3 39 C1
Meadow View JMI Sch B43 44 D5
Meadow View Terr WV6 24 E4
Meadow Way Cannock WS12 2 C1
Stourbridge DY8 60 C2
Meadow Wlk
Birmingham B14 104 E1
Blackheath B64 82 D8
Meadowbrook Rd
Halesowen B63 82 E3
Wolverhampton WS13 3 B3
Meadowfield Rd B45 122 A6
Meadowfields Cl DY8 60 E2
Meadowhill Dr DY8 60 E2
Meadowhill Rd B98 153 F5
Meadowlands Dr WS4 15 D1
Meadowpark Rd DY8 80 D8
Meadows Fst Sch B61 137 A3
Meadows Prim Sch The B31 102 E1
Meadows Sch CV4 111 E3
Meadows The Aldridge WS9 29 E5
Hinckley LE10 76 A7
Leek Wootton CV35 156 A7
Meadowside CV11 79 B8
Meadowside Cl B43 43 E1
Meadowside Rd B74 31 F3
Meadowsweet Ave B38 123 F8
Meadowsweet Way DY6 61 A6
Meadowvale Rd B60 137 C6
Meadthorpe Rd B44 55 D8
Meadvale Rd B45 122 B6
Meadway Birmingham B33 69 B2
Coventry CV2 114 B6
Meadway Cl WS12 2 C3
Meadway N CV2 114 B6
Meadway St WS7 7 A5
Meadway The Hinckley LE10 75 F7
Redditch B97 153 C1
Wolverhampton WV6 24 A5
Meadwood Ind Est WV14 40 E5
Mears Cl B23 56 D8
Mears Coppice DY5 81 E6
Mears Dr B33 68 D4
Mearse Cl B18 66 A5
Mearse La Barnt Green B45 122 A1
Belbroughton DY9 120 B6
Mease Ave WS7 7 D6
Mease Croft 2 B9 67 B2
Measham Gr B26 88 E5
Measham Way WV11 26 E7
Meaton Gr B32 102 B8
Medcroft Ave B20 54 E4
Medina B77 21 E1
Medina Rd Birmingham B11 87 E4
Coventry CV6 95 E1
Medina Way DY6 60 C6
Medland Ave CV3 132 F5
Medley Gdns DY4 52 E4
Medley Rd B11 87 D5
Medlicott Rd B11 87 C6
Medway B77 21 E1
Medway Cl DY5 61 A6
Medway Croft B36 69 F7
Medway Ct B73 46 B5
Medway Gr B38 123 E8
Medway Rd WS8 6 C2
Medway Tower B7 67 B5
Medway Wlk WS8 6 C2
Medwin Gr B23 56 D7
Meer End B38 123 D7
Meer End Rd CV8 130 D1
Meerash La WS7 7 C3
Meerhill Ave B90 127 A6
Meeting House La
Balsall Common CV7 130 C6
Birmingham B31 103 A4
Meeting La DY5 61 B1
Meeting Lane Ind Est DY5 61 B1
Meeting St Dudley DY2 62 C5
Tipton DY4 52 D5
Wednesbury WS10 41 E3
Meg La WS7 7 C8
Meir Rd B98 159 C8
Melbourne Ave
Birmingham B19 66 C6
Bromsgrove B61 136 E4
Melbourne Cl
Bromsgrove B61 136 E3
Kingswinford DY6 60 E4
Nuneaton CV11 78 E8
West Bromwich B70 53 A7
Melbourne Cres WS12 2 F2
Melbourne Ct 3 CV12 77 F2
Melbourne Gdns WS5 43 B6
Melbourne Ho B34 69 E6
Melbourne Rd
Bromsgrove B61 136 E3
Cannock WS12 2 F2
Coventry CV5 113 A2
Halesowen B63 83 B5
Smethwick B66 65 B7
Melbourne St WV2 163 C2
Melbury Cl WV3 25 A1
Melbury Gr B14 104 E5
Melbury Way WS11 1 F2
Melchester Wlk WS11 1 F2
Melchett Rd B30 104 A4
Melcote Gr B44 55 E8
Meldon Dr WV14 41 A2
Meldrum Rd CV10 72 D4
Melen St B97 153 D4
Melford B79 20 E6
Melford Cl DY3 39 C2
Melford Hall Rd B91 106 F7
Melfort Cl CV3 114 F2
Melfort Gr B14 105 A3
Melksham Sq B35 58 A3
Mell Sq B91 107 C4
Mellis Gr B23 56 A5

Mellish Ct WS4 29 A3
Mellish Dr WS4 29 B3
Mellish Rd WS4 29 A3
Mellor Dr B74 31 E3
Mellors Cl B17 85 B3
Mellowdew Rd
Coventry CV2 114 C4
Stourbridge DY8 60 C3
Mellowship Rd CV5 111 D5
Mellwaters B77 36 C8
Melmerby B77 36 C8
Melplash Ave B91 107 A4
Melrose Ave Bedworth CV12 95 D8
Birmingham, Sparkbrook B12 87 A6
Birmingham, Sparkhill B11 87 C6
Stourbridge DY8 81 A2
Sutton Coldfield B73 45 E2
West Bromwich B71 42 D1
Melrose Cl Birmingham B38 103 F1
Hinckley LE10 75 B8
Melrose Dr Cannock WS12 1 F7
Perton WV6 23 E4
Melrose Gr B19 66 B7
Melrose Pl B66 64 D8
Melrose Rd B20 55 E1
Melstock Cl DY4 51 D5
Melstock Rd B14 104 D7
Melton Ave B92 89 A4
Melton Dr B15 86 B7
Melton Rd Birmingham B14 104 F8
Royal Leamington Spa CV32 157 B4
Melverley Gr B44 55 F7
Melverton Ave WV10 25 E8
Melville Cl CV7 96 A8
Melville Hall [1] B16 65 D1
Melville Rd Birmingham B16 65 D1
Coventry CV1 113 A3
Melvina Rd B7 67 B5
Membury Rd B8 67 D6
Memorial Cl WV13 27 A2
Memory La Darlaston WS10 41 D8
Wolverhampton WV11 26 B5
Menai Cl WV12 27 C6
Menai Wlk B37 70 B4
Mendip Ave B8 67 E5
Mendip Cl Bromsgrove B61 137 A5
Dudley DY3 50 D3
Wolverhampton WV2 39 F7
Mendip Dr CV10 72 B3
Mendip Ho B98 154 D6
Mendip Rd Birmingham B8 67 E5
Halesowen B63 82 D1
Stourbridge DY8 81 B6
Mendip Way B77 22 C1
Menin Cres B13 105 B7
Menin Rd Birmingham B13 105 B8
Tipton DY4 51 D5
Mentone Ct B20 54 E3
Menzies High Sch B71 53 C8
Meon Gr Birmingham B33 89 B8
Perton WV6 23 F4
Meon Rise DY9 81 C3
Meon Way WV11 26 F7
Meranti Cl WV12 27 C8
Mercer Ave Coventry CV2 114 A5
Water Orton B46 59 A3
Mercer Gr WV11 26 D7
Merchants Ct [5] CV32 157 A1
Merchants Way WS9 30 A7
Mercia Ave CV8 147 F4
Mercia Bsns Village CV4 131 F6
Mercia Cl Bromsgrove B60 150 F7
Tamworth B79 20 E7
Mercia Dr WV6 23 E5
Mercia Ho CV1 165 B3
Mercia Way CV34 161 B7
Mercian Ct WS13 9 C7
Mercian Pk B77 22 B3
Mercian Way B77 22 B4
Mercot Cl B98 159 A6
Mercury Ct B77 22 B3
Mercury Rd WS11 2 A5
Mere Ave B35 58 B3
Mere Cl WV12 27 A5
Mere Dr B75 32 B2
Mere Green Cl B75 32 C2
Mere Green Comb Sch B75 32 B2
Mere Green Rd B75 32 C2
Mere Oak Rd WV6 23 E5
Mere Pool Rd B75 32 E2
Mere Rd Birmingham B23 56 D3
Stourbridge DY8 80 E3
Mere View WS4 29 C8
Merecote Rd B92 106 D7
Meredith Gn DY11 116 A1
Meredith Pool Cl B18 65 F6
Meredith Rd Coventry CV2 114 D2
Dudley DY3 50 A5
Wolverhampton WV11 26 C8
Meredith St B64 62 D1
Meres Rd B63 82 C5
Mereside Way B92 106 E8
Merevale Ave Hinckley LE10 75 C7
Nuneaton CV11 73 A4
Merevale Cl Hinckley LE10 75 C7
Redditch B98 159 D8
Merevale Rd B92 89 B2
Merganser B77 36 A6
Merganser Way DY10 117 B3
Meriden Ave DY8 80 D6
Meriden CE Prim Sch CV7 92 C1
Meriden Cl Birmingham B25 88 B7
Cannock WS11 4 B8
Stourbridge DY8 80 D6
Meriden Ct WV4 39 F4
Meriden Dr B37 70 A6
Meriden Hill CV7 110 E8
Meriden Rd Berkswell CV7 110 C4
Corley CV7 93 B7
Hampton in A B92 109 B8
Wolverhampton WV10 25 A8
Meriden Rise B92 89 D3
Meriden St Birmingham B5 164 D2
Coventry CV1 113 B3
Meridian Pl B60 137 A1
Merino Ave B31 123 A8
Merlin Ave CV10 72 B6
Merlin Cl Cannock WS11 1 C2
Dudley DY1 61 F8
Tamworth B77 36 A6
Merlin Dr DY10 117 B3
Merlin Gr B26 89 B5
Merrick Cl B63 82 D2
Merrick Ct LE10 75 F5
Merrick Rd WV11 27 A6
Merridale Ave WV3 24 F2
Merridale Cres WV3 25 A2
Merridale Ct WV3 24 F1
Merridale Gdns WV3 25 A1
Merridale Gr WV3 24 E1
Merridale La WV3 25 A2
Merridale Prim Sch WV3 25 A1
Merridale Rd WV3 25 A1
Merridale St WV3 163 A2
Merridale St W WV3 39 A8
Merriemont Dr B45 122 A1
Merrifield Gdns LE10 75 E5
Merrigold Bsns Pk WV11 26 C5
Merrill Cl WS6 4 E2
Merrill Gdns B60 121 D2
Merrill's Hall La WV11 26 E4
Merrington Cl [5] B91 127 C8
Merrion's Cl B43 43 E4
Merrishaw Rd B31 123 A8
Merritt's Brook La B31 102 E5
Merritts Brook Cl B29 103 A5
Merritts Hill B31 102 E6
Merrivale Rd Coventry CV5 112 E3
Halesowen B62 83 F8
Smethwick B66 65 A2
Merry Hill DY5 61 F2
Merry Hill Ctr DY5 61 F3
Merry Hill Inf Sch B66 65 D6
Merryfield Cl B92 107 D7
Merryfield Gr B17 85 C4
Merryfield Rd DY1 50 E1
Merryfields Way CV2 96 F1
Merryhill Dr B18 65 F6
Merse Rd B98 154 E6
Mersey Gr B38 123 E8
Mersey Rd Bulkington CV12 79 A3
Walsall WS3 14 E1
Merstal Dr B92 107 F7
Merstone Cl WV14 40 C6
Merstone Sch B37 70 A1
Merstowe Cl B27 88 B3
Merton Cl
Kidderminster DY10 117 B7
Oldbury B68 64 B2
Merton Ct WS7 6 F5
Merton Ho B37 69 F2
Merton Rd B13 87 B3
Mervyn Pl WV14 41 A3
Mervyn Rd Bilston WV14 41 A3
Birmingham B21 54 E1
Meryhurst Rd WS10 42 B5
Merynton Ave CV4 132 E5
Meschines St CV3 133 D6
Mesnes Gn WS14 9 C7
Messenger La B70 53 D3
Messenger Rd B66 65 B6
Mesty Croft Prim Sch WS10 42 B3
Metalloys Ind Est B76 58 B5
Metcalf Cl WS7 7 C8
Metcalfe Cl WS12 2 C6
Metchley Croft B90 126 F6
Metchley Ct B17 85 D4
Metchley Dr B17 85 D5
Metchley Ho B17 85 D5
Metchley La B17 85 D5
Metchley Park Rd B15 85 E4
Meteor Ho B35 58 B4
Metfield Cl B79 21 C8
Metfield Croft
Birmingham B17 85 D4
Kingswinford DY6 60 F6
Metlin Gr B33 69 E3
Metric Wlk [2] B67 65 A5
Metro Way B66 65 C7
Mews Rd CV32 161 D8
Mews The Bedworth CV12 78 B2
Birmingham B27 88 B3
Blackheath B65 63 B2
Kenilworth CV8 147 E3
Meynell Ho [5] B20 54 F3
Meyrick Rd B70 53 A6
Meyrick Wlk B16 65 F1
Miall Park Rd B91 106 E5
Miall Rd B28 106 A8
Mica Cl B77 22 B2
Michael Blanning Gdns B93 127 E3
Michael Ct B5 86 D6
Michael Dr B15 86 C6
Michael Drayton Mid Sch CV10 72 A8
Michael Rd Darlaston WS10 41 B7
Smethwick B67 64 E6
Michaelmas Rd CV3 165 B1
Michaelwood Cl B97 152 F2
Michel Ho CV1 165 C4
Michell Cl CV3 134 B8
Michigan Cl WS11 2 B2
Mickle Mdw B46 59 B3
Micklehill Dr B90 126 B8
Mickleover Rd B8 68 C5
Mickleton Ave B33 89 C8
Mickleton Cl B98 158 E7
Mickleton Rd Coventry CV5 133 A8
Solihull B92 106 D8
Mickley Ave WV10 25 E5
Midacre WV13 27 A1
Middelburg Cl CV11 74 A1
Middle Acre Rd B32 84 E2
Middle Ave WV13 40 E8
Middle Bickenhill La B92 91 A4
Middle Cres WS3 29 A7
Middle Cross WV1 163 D3
Middle Dr B45 122 D4
Middle Entry B79 21 B5
Middle Field Rd B31 103 D2
Middle Gdns WV13 27 B2
Middle House Dr B60 121 D1
Middle La
Wolverhampton WV9 11 A5
Wythall B38 124 D5
Middle Leaford B34 69 A5
Middle Leasowe B32 84 D4
Middle Meadow Ave B32 84 C5
Middle Park Cl B29 103 B8
Middle Park Rd B29 103 C8
Middle Piece Dr B97 153 B1
Middle Rd
Upper Bentley B60 152 A2
Wildmoor B61 120 F4
Middle Ride CV3 134 E5
Middle Vauxhall [4] WV1 25 A2
Middleborough Rd CV1 165 A4
Middlecotes CV4 112 B1
Middlefield WV8 10 E2
Middlefield Ave
Halesowen B62 63 F1
Knowle B93 128 B4
Middlefield Cl
Halesowen B62 63 F1
Hinckley LE10 71 D2
Middlefield Ct LE10 71 D2
Middlefield Dr CV3 115 B1
Middlefield Gdns B62 83 F8
Middlefield Ho B14 104 F3
Middlefield La Hagley DY9 99 B6
Hinckley LE10 71 D3
Middlefield Pl LE10 71 D3
Middlefield Rd
Bromsgrove B60 151 B7
Tipton B69 63 A8
Middlefleld Dr CV3 115 A1
Middlehill Rise B31 84 D3
Middlehouse La B98 153 E6
Middlemarch Bsns Pk CV3 134 C2
Middlemarch Mid Sch CV10 73 B1
Middlemarch Rd
Coventry CV6 113 C7
Nuneaton CV10 73 C1
Middlemist Gr B43 54 F6
Middlemore Bsns Pk WS9 29 E6
Middlemore Cl B80 159 D3
Middlemore Ind Est B66 65 B8
Middlemore La WS9 30 A6
Middlemore La W WS9 29 E6
Middlemore Rd
Birmingham B31 103 B3
Smethwick B66 65 B8
Middlepark Rd DY1 61 F8
Middlesmoor B77 36 C8
Middleton Cl Redditch B98 154 F2
Walsall WS5 42 F5
Middleton Fst Sch B78 34 B1
Middleton Gdns B30 103 D4
Middleton Grange B31 103 C4
Middleton Hall
Birmingham B30 103 E4
Middleton B78 34 E1
Middleton Hall Rd B30 103 E4
Middleton La B78 47 F6
Middleton Rd Aldridge B74 31 A1
Birmingham B14 104 F7
Bromsgrove B61 136 F4
Brownhills WS8 7 A1
Solihull B90 106 A2
Middleton Trad Est WV13 26 E1
Middletown B80 159 D1
Middletown La B96 159 D1
Middletree Rd B63 82 C7
Middleway Ave DY8 60 C3
Middleway Gn WV14 40 C8
Middleway Rd WV14 40 C7
Middleway View B18 66 A3
Midford Gr B15 86 C8
Midgley Dr B74 32 A2
Midhill Dr B65 63 C6
Midhurst Dr WS12 2 C7
Midhurst Gr WV6 24 C5
Midhurst Rd B30 104 B3
Midland Air Mus CV3 134 B3
Midland Bus & Transport Mus B47 124 E3
Midland Cl B21 65 F7
Midland Ct B3 164 A4
Midland Dr B72 46 C5
Midland Oak Trad Est CV6 95 E2
Midland Rd Birmingham B30 103 F5
Coventry CV6 113 E5
Darlaston WS10 41 C8
Nuneaton CV11 73 A5
Sutton Coldfield B74 46 A6
Walsall WS1 28 E1
Midland St B9 67 C3
Midpoint Park Ind Est B76 58 C5
Midvale Dr B14 104 D2
Milburn B77 36 C8
Milburn Hill Rd CV4 132 B6
Milburn Rd B44 45 A3
Milby Ct CV11 73 C3
Milby Dr CV11 74 A7
Milby Fst & Mid Sch CV11 73 F8
Milcote Cl B98 159 A7
Milcote Dr
Sutton Coldfield B73 45 C3
Willenhall WV13 26 D1
Milcote Rd Birmingham B29 103 A8
Smethwick B67 64 F1
Solihull B91 107 B4
Milcote Way DY6 60 B6
Mildenhall B79 21 C8
Mildenhall Rd B42 44 A1
Mildred Rd B64 62 E2
Mildred Way B65 63 C6
Mile Flat DY6 60 A7
Mile La CV1 165 C1
Mile Oak Cross Rds B78 20 C2
Mile Oak Ct B66 65 C6
Mile Tree La CV2 96 F7
Milebrook Gr B32 102 B8
Milebush Ave B36 58 D1
Miles Gr DY2 62 F7
Miles Mdw CV6 96 B1
Miles Meadow Cl WV12 27 C8
Milestone Ct WV6 24 A3
Milestone Dr DY9 98 F4
Milestone Ho [2] CV1 113 B2
Milestone La B21 65 D8
Milestone Way WV12 27 C8
Milford Ave
[3] Birmingham B12 87 A6
Willenhall WV12 27 A5
Milford Cl Allesley CV5 112 B6
Birmingham B28 106 A5
Redditch B97 158 C6
Stourbridge DY8 60 E3
Milford Croft B65 62 F6
Milford Ct Birmingham B19 164 B5
Royal Leamington Spa CV31 162 A8
Milford Gr B90 127 C7
Milford Pl B14 104 E8
Milford Rd Birmingham B17 85 B5
Wolverhampton WV2 39 C7
Milford St CV10 73 B2
Milhill Rd B98 154 E1
Milholme Gn B92 107 D8
Milk St B5 66 F1
Milking Bank DY1 50 E2
Milking Bank Prim Sch DY1 50 E2
Mill Bank DY3 50 D8
Mill Bank Mews CV8 148 B6
Mill Burn Way [3] B9 67 B2
Mill Cl Blakedown DY10 98 B2
Bromsgrove B60 150 F6
Coventry CV2 96 B3
Dudley DY3 50 D6
Hollywood B47 125 A7
Nuneaton CV11 73 F1
Mill Cres WS11 2 B2
Mill Croft WV14 40 E6
Mill Dr B66 65 B5
Mill End CV8 148 A6
Mill Farm Rd B17 85 C3
Mill Gdns Birmingham B14 105 D5
Smethwick B67 64 F3
Mill Gn WV10 11 D4
Mill Gr WV8 10 C3
Mill Green Nature Pk WS11 1 F1
Mill Hill Baginton CV8 133 D3
Smethwick B67 64 F3
Mill Hill Rd LE10 71 C1
Mill Ho Birmingham B8 68 D4
Smethwick B66 65 C6
Mill House Cl CV32 161 C8
Mill House Dr CV32 161 C8
Mill House Terr CV32 161 C8
Mill La Aldridge WS9 30 F7
Bentley Heath B93 127 F4
Birmingham, Digbeth B5 164 D1
Birmingham, Northfield B31 103 A2
Birmingham, Woodgate Valley B32 84 E2
Blakedown DY10 98 B2
Bramcote CV11 79 F8
Bromsgrove B61 136 F2
Bulkington CV12 79 A3
Burntwood WS7 7 D3
Cheslyn Hay WS11 4 D5
Coventry CV3 114 F2
Cubbington CV32 157 F5
Earlswood B94 141 B8
Fazeley B78 35 A8
Halesowen B63 83 C4
Kidderminster, Blakebrook DY11 116 D6
Kidderminster, Hoobrook DY10 116 F2
Lapworth B94 144 C4
Little Aston WS9 31 A6
Oldbury B69 64 A5
Mill La continued
Shenstone WS14 18 A6
Solihull B91 107 C4
Stonnall WS9 17 A4
Tamworth B79 21 C5
Tettenhall Wood WV6 24 A3
Walsall WS4 28 F4
Wildmoor B61 120 F3
Willenhall WV12 27 C5
Wolverhampton WV11 26 B7
Wombourne WV5 49 B6
Wythall B47 125 B1
Mill Lodge Prim Sch B90 105 E2
Mill Park Ind Est WS11 2 A2
Mill Pk WS11 2 A2
Mill Pl WS3 28 E4
Mill Pleck B80 159 E3
Mill Pond The WS13 3 C2
Mill Pool Cl DY9 99 A4
Mill Pool La Dorridge B93 144 A8
Tanworth-in-A B94 143 F8
Mill Pool Rd WS12 2 B6
Mill Race La Coventry CV6 96 B3
Stourbridge DY8 81 A6
Mill Rd Blackheath B64 82 E7
Brownhills WS8 16 A7
Royal Leamington Spa CV31 162 A8
Walsall WS4 15 C1
Mill St Barwell LE9 71 F5
Bedworth CV12 78 B3
Bilston WV14 40 C5
Birmingham B6 164 C5
Brierley Hill DY5 61 E2
Cannock WS11 1 E1
Coventry CV1 165 A3
Darlaston, Cathrine Cross WS10 41 C6
Darlaston, King's Hill WS10 41 E6
Halesowen B63 82 C7
Kidderminster DY11 116 D6
Nuneaton CV11 73 C4
Redditch B97 153 D4
Royal Leamington Spa CV31 162 A7
Stourbridge DY8 60 F2
Sutton Coldfield B72 46 C5
Tipton DY4 52 D5
Walsall WS2 28 E3
Warwick CV34 160 F6
West Bromwich B70 53 C4
Willenhall WV13 27 C2
Mill Terr CV12 78 B5
Mill View Birmingham B33 69 C4
Hinckley LE10 71 E1
Mill Wlk CV11 73 C4
Mill Wlk The B31 102 F1
Millais Cl CV12 78 A4
Millais Rd LE10 71 A3
Millard Rd WV14 40 B1
Millbank CV34 156 B1
Millbank Gr B23 56 B6
Millbank St WV11 12 F1
Millbrook Cl WS11 1 F2
Millbrook Ct B62 83 A7
Millbrook Dr
Birmingham B31 122 E8
Shenstone WS14 17 F6
Millbrook Rd B14 104 C6
Millbrook Way DY5 81 B8
Millcroft Cl B32 84 E2
Millcroft Rd B74 45 A8
Milldale Cl DY10 116 E8
Milldale Cres WV10 11 D3
Milldale Rd WV10 11 D4
Millennium Cl WS3 15 A3
Miller Cl B60 150 E6
Miller Cres WV14 40 A1
Miller St B6 66 E5
Millers Cl WS2 27 F1
Millers Ct [1] DY11 116 D6
Millers Gn LE10 75 F6
Millers Green Dr DY6 60 A8
Millers Rd CV34 160 E8
Millers Vale WS12 2 D1
Millersdale Dr B71 42 F2
Millfield Birmingham B31 103 A4
Royal Leamington Spa CV31 162 A8
Millfield Ave
Walsall, High Heath WS4 15 B1
Walsall, Little Bloxwich WS3 14 D3
Millfield Ct DY1 51 B2
Millfield Gdns [2] DY11 116 D6
Millfield JMI Sch WS8 16 A7
Millfield Prim Sch B78 35 A8
Millfield Rd Birmingham B20 54 F5
Bromsgrove B61 136 E1
Brownhills WS8 16 A7
Millfield Specl Sch B71 53 D8
Millfield View B63 82 E4
Millfields B33 69 E3
Millfields Cl B71 42 B1
Millfields Fst Sch B61 136 E1
Millfields Rd
Bilston WV14, WV4 40 B5
West Bromwich B71 42 B1
Millhaven Ave B30 104 B6
Millhouse Ct CV6 113 F7
Millhouse Rd B25 88 C8
Millicent Cl WS12 2 B6
Millicent Pl [11] B12 87 A6
Millichip Rd WV13 26 E1
Millington Rd
Birmingham B36 68 E7
Tipton DY4 40 F1
Wolverhampton WV10 25 E6
Millison Gr B90 127 A7
Millmead Rd B32 84 E1

Millpool Gdns B14 ... 104 F3
Millpool Hill Alcester
Rd S B14 ... 104 F4
Millpool Way B66 ... 65 A4
Millrace Rd B98 ... 153 E5
Mills Ave B76 ... 46 E4
Mills Cl WV11 ... 26 B8
Mills Cres WV2 ... 163 D1
Mills Rd WV2 ... 163 D1
Mills Wlk DY4 ... 51 F7
Millsbro Rd B98 ... 153 F3
Millside B28 ... 105 E3
Millsum Ho [6] WS1 ... 28 F1
Millthorpe Cl B8 ... 67 F5
Millwalk Dr WV9 ... 11 A3
Millward St Birmingham B9 ... 67 C1
West Bromwich B70 ... 53 A3
Millwright Cl DY4 ... 52 B5
Milner Cl CV12 ... 79 D2
Milner Cres CV2 ... 96 E1
Milner Dr B79 ... 22 E7
Milner Rd B29 ... 86 A1
Milner Way B13 ... 105 D8
Milnes Walker Ct B44 ... 44 E1
Milo Cres B78 ... 21 A2
Milrose Way CV4 ... 131 F8
Milsom Gr B34 ... 69 D6
Milstead Rd B26 ... 69 A1
Milston Cl B14 ... 104 E1
Milton Ave
[2] Birmingham B12 ... 87 A6
Tamworth B79 ... 21 A7
Warwick CV34 ... 160 C5
Milton Cl Bedworth CV12 ... 78 D1
Bentley Heath B93 ... 127 F4
Hinckley LE10 ... 71 C1
Kidderminster DY11 ... 116 A6
Redditch B97 ... 158 C8
Walsall WS1 ... 42 D6
Willenhall WV12 ... 27 E7
Milton Cres Birmingham B25 ... 88 D7
Dudley DY3 ... 50 B5
Milton Ct Perton WV6 ... 23 E4
Smethwick B66 ... 65 A1
Milton Dr DY9 ... 99 D7
Milton Gr B21 ... 65 C8
Milton Ho B63 ... 82 B5
Milton Pl WS1 ... 42 D6
Milton Rd Bentley Heath
B93 ... 127 F4
Cannock WS11 ... 1 E4
Catshill B61 ... 137 A8
Dudley WV14 ... 51 D8
Smethwick B67 ... 64 F5
Wolverhampton WV10 ... 26 A5
Milton St Birmingham B19 ... 66 E6
Brierley Hill DY5 ... 61 D7
Coventry CV2 ... 114 A4
Walsall WS1 ... 42 D7
West Bromwich B71 ... 53 B5
Milverton Cl Halesowen B63 ... 83 A6
Sutton Coldfield B76 ... 57 F7
Milverton Comb Sch
CV32 ... 156 E1
Milverton Cres [1] CV32 ... 156 E1
Milverton Cres W [3] CV32 ... 156 E1
Milverton Ct [7] CV32 ... 161 E8
Milverton Hill CV32 ... 161 E8
Milverton House Prep Sch
CV11 ... 73 D3
Milverton Lodge [2] CV32 ... 156 E1
Milverton Rd Birmingham
B23 ... 56 E4
Coventry CV2 ... 96 D2
Knowle B93 ... 128 C5
Milverton Terr CV32 ... 161 E8
Milward Sq [8] B97 ... 153 E3
Mimosa Cl B29 ... 103 B7
Mimosa Wlk [8] DY6 ... 60 E8
Mincing La B65 ... 63 D3
Minden Gr B29 ... 85 B1
Minehead Rd Dudley DY1 ... 61 D8
Wolverhampton WV10 ... 11 B2
Miner St WS2 ... 28 C3
Miners Wlk B78 ... 22 F1
Minerva Cl Tamworth B77 ... 21 D5
Willenhall WV12 ... 27 E4
Minerva La WV1 ... 25 E1
Minewood Cl WS3 ... 13 F3
Minith Rd WV14 ... 51 D8
Miniva Dr B76 ... 47 A2
Minivet Dr B12 ... 86 E6
Minley Ave B17 ... 84 F7
Minories The [1] DY2 ... 51 D1
Minors Hill WS14 ... 9 D6
Minstead Rd B24 ... 56 D1
Minster Cl Blackheath B65 ... 63 E3
Knowle B93 ... 128 B8
Minster Dr B10 ... 87 D7
Minster Rd CV1 ... 113 B3
Minster The WV3 ... 39 A7
Minster Wlk B61 ... 136 F8
Minsterley Cl WV3 ... 38 E8
Mintern Rd B25 ... 88 C8
Minton Cl WV1 ... 26 A1
Minton Ho [3] B12 ... 86 F5
Minton Mews B60 ... 151 B8
Minton Rd Birmingham B32 ... 84 F4
Coventry CV2 ... 96 E1
Minworth Cl B97 ... 153 B2
Minworth Ind Pk B76 ... 58 B5
Minworth Jun & Inf Sch
B76 ... 58 D5
Minworth Rd B46 ... 59 A3
Miranda Cl Birmingham
B45 ... 102 A3
Coventry CV3 ... 134 D7
Mirfield Cl WV9 ... 11 A3
Mirfield Rd Birmingham B33 ... 69 B2
Solihull B91 ... 107 A6
Mission Cl B64 ... 63 A1
Mission Dr DY4 ... 52 A3
Mistletoe Dr WS5 ... 43 B3
Mistral Cl LE10 ... 75 F8
Mitcham Cl WS12 ... 1 F7
Mitcham Gr B44 ... 45 B1
Mitchel Rd DY6 ... 60 F4
Mitcheldean Cl B98 ... 158 E7
Mitcheldean Covert B14 ... 104 D2
Mitchell Ave Coventry CV4 ... 132 A7
Dudley WV14 ... 40 B1
Mitchell Ho Coventry CV4 ... 132 A7
Warwick CV34 ... 160 E7
Mitchell Rd CV12 ... 78 C2
Mitford Dr B92 ... 107 D7
Mitre Cl Essington WV11 ... 13 A3
Willenhall WV12 ... 27 D7
Mitre Ct B61 ... 137 A3
Mitre Fold WV1 ... 163 B3
Mitre Rd Cheslyn Hay WS6 ... 4 D2
Stourbridge DY9 ... 81 E5
Mitten Ave B45 ... 102 A1
Mitton Rd B20 ... 54 E2
Moat Ave CV3 ... 132 F5
Moat Coppice B62 ... 84 A1
Moat Croft Birmingham B37 ... 70 A2
Sutton Coldfield B76 ... 58 B7
Moat Dr Drayton Bassett B78 ... 34 E5
Halesowen B62 ... 63 F1
Moat Farm Dr
Bedworth CV12 ... 95 C8
Birmingham B32 ... 84 A1
Moat Farm Inf Sch B68 ... 64 C3
Moat Farm Jun Sch B68 ... 64 C3
Moat Farm Way WS3 ... 15 A5
Moat Gn CV35 ... 160 A1
Moat Green Ave WV11 ... 26 E7
Moat Hall Cty Prim Sch
WS6 ... 4 F3
Moat House Ct B80 ... 159 F8
Moat House La CV4 ... 132 C7
Moat House La E WV11 ... 26 E7
Moat House Rd B8 ... 68 A4
Moat La
Birmingham, Digbeth B5 ... 164 C1
Birmingham,
South Yardley B26 ... 88 E7
Great Wyrley WS6 ... 5 A2
Solihull B91 ... 107 C6
Moat Mdws B32 ... 84 E4
Moat Rd Oldbury B68 ... 64 B3
Tipton DY4 ... 52 A7
Walsall WS2 ... 28 C2
Moat St WV13 ... 27 A2
Moat Way LE9 ... 71 F6
Moatfield Mid Sch B98 ... 154 E1
Moatfield Terr [2] WS10 ... 42 A3
Moathouse La W WV11 ... 26 D7
Moathouse Prim Sch
WV11 ... 26 E7
Moatmead Wlk B36 ... 68 E8
Moatside Cl WS3 ... 15 A5
Mob La WS4 ... 15 C3
Mobberley Rd WV14 ... 40 A1
Mockley Wood Rd B93 ... 128 B7
Modbury Ave B32 ... 84 D1
Modbury Cl CV3 ... 133 D5
Moden Cl DY3 ... 50 D6
Moden Hill DY3 ... 50 D6
Mogul La B63 ... 82 A7
Moillett St B18 ... 65 D4
Moilliett Ct B66 ... 65 C6
Moira Cres B14 ... 105 C4
Moises Hall Rd WV5 ... 49 B7
Moland St B4 ... 164 C4
Mole St B11 ... 87 B6
Molesworth Ave CV3 ... 114 A1
Molhay Gdns [4] B42 ... 55 A8
Molineux Gds
(Wolverhampton
Wanderers FC) WV1 ... 163 B4
Molineux St WV1 ... 163 B4
Molineux Way WV1 ... 163 B4
Mollington Cres B90 ... 106 C3
Mollington Rd CV31 ... 162 A3
Molyneux Rd DY2 ... 62 E2
Momus Bvd CV2 ... 114 C2
Mona Rd B23 ... 56 F5
Monarch Dr DY4 ... 52 C6
Monarch Ho B68 ... 64 B2
Monarch Way DY2 ... 62 C4
Monastery Dr B91 ... 106 E6
Monckton Rd B68 ... 84 A7
Moncrieff Dr CV31 ... 162 C5
Moncrieffe Cl DY2 ... 62 E8
Moncrieffe St WS1 ... 29 A1
Money La B61 ... 121 A7
Monica Rd B10 ... 87 F8
Monins Ave DY4 ... 52 A2
Monk Cl DY4 ... 52 B3
Monk Rd B8 ... 68 B5
Monk's Croft The CV3 ... 133 C7
Monks Dr B80 ... 159 D4
Monks Kirby Rd B76 ... 46 F3
Monks Path B97 ... 152 F4
Monks Rd Binley Woods
CV3 ... 135 C7
Coventry CV1 ... 113 F2
Monks Way Tamworth B77 ... 21 F5
Warwick CV34 ... 160 D6
Monkseaton Rd B72 ... 46 B2
Monksfield Ave B43 ... 43 D1
Monkshood Mews B23 ... 56 B7
Monkshood Retreat B38 ... 123 F8
Monkspath Solihull B90 ... 127 A6
Sutton Coldfield B76 ... 46 F1
Monkspath Bsns Pk B90 ... 126 F8
Monkspath Cl B90 ... 126 D7
Monkspath Hall Rd B90 ... 127 B7
Monkspath Jun & Inf Sch
B90 ... 127 B6
Monksway B38 ... 104 B1
Monkswell Cl
Birmingham B10 ... 87 D7
Brierley Hill DY5 ... 61 D1
Monkswood Cres CV2 ... 114 D8
Monkswood Rd B31 ... 103 C2
Monkton Rd B29 ... 85 A2
Monmer Cl WV13 ... 27 B3
Monmer Ct WV12 ... 27 B5
Monmer La WV13 ... 27 B4
Monmore Park Ind Est
WV2 ... 40 A7
Monmore Rd WV1 ... 40 A7
Monmouth Cl Coventry
CV5 ... 112 B3
Kenilworth CV8 ... 147 F6
Monmouth Dr
Sutton Coldfield B73 ... 45 D3
West Bromwich B71 ... 53 B7
Monmouth Gdns CV10 ... 72 E3
Monmouth Ho B33 ... 69 E2
Monmouth Rd
Birmingham B32 ... 102 D8
Smethwick B67 ... 84 E8
Walsall WS2 ... 27 E3
Monnington Ho CV8 ... 148 B7
Mons Rd DY2 ... 51 F1
Monsal Ave WV10 ... 25 E4
Monsal Rd B42 ... 55 C7
Monsaldale Rd WS8 ... 15 D6
Monsieurs Hall La B61 ... 136 B3
Montague Ho B16 ... 65 E1
Montague Rd
Birmingham,
Birches Green B24 ... 57 A1
Birmingham, Edgbaston B16 ... 65 E1
Birmingham,
Handsworth B21 ... 65 F8
Smethwick B66 ... 65 C3
Warwick CV34 ... 161 A8
Montague St
Birmingham, Aston B6 ... 67 B8
Birmingham, Bordesley B9 ... 67 A2
Montalt Rd CV3 ... 133 E7
Montana Ave B42 ... 55 A5
Montana Wlk CV10 ... 72 E3
Monteagle Dr DY6 ... 49 D1
Montford Gr DY3 ... 50 D7
Montfort Rd Coleshill B46 ... 70 F5
Walsall WS2 ... 42 B6
Montfort Wlk B32 ... 84 A2
Montgomery Cl
Catshill B61 ... 121 A1
Coventry CV3 ... 134 C4
Montgomery Cres DY5 ... 81 F7
Montgomery Croft B11 ... 87 C7
Montgomery Jun & Inf Sch
B11 ... 87 C7
Montgomery Rd WS2 ... 27 E2
Montgomery St B11 ... 87 C7
Montgomery Way B8 ... 68 A4
Montgomery Wlk [1] B71 ... 53 D4
Montjoy Cl CV3 ... 134 D7
Montley B77 ... 36 C8
Montpelier Ho CV8 ... 147 F5
Montpelier Rd B24 ... 57 A1
Montpellier Cl CV3 ... 133 C6
Montpellier Gdns DY1 ... 50 E2
Montpellier St B12 ... 87 A6
Montreal Ho B5 ... 86 D7
Montrose Ave CV32 ... 157 B5
Montrose Cl WS11 ... 1 F5
Montrose Dr Birmingham
B35 ... 58 A4
Dudley DY1 ... 62 A8
Nuneaton CV10 ... 72 F3
Montsford Cl B93 ... 127 F6
Monument Ave DY9 ... 81 E4
Monument Dr WV10 ... 12 C8
Monument La
Barnt Green B45 ... 121 F4
Hagley DY9 ... 99 D7
Sedgley DY3 ... 39 E1
Monument Rd B16 ... 65 F1
Monway Bldgs WS10 ... 41 E3
Monway Ind Est WS10 ... 41 E3
Monway Terr WS10 ... 41 E3
Monwood Gr B91 ... 106 F2
Monyhull Hall Rd B30 ... 104 C3
Monyhull Hospl B14 ... 104 D3
Moodyscroft Rd B33 ... 69 C3
Moon's La WS6 ... 4 D1
Moons Moat Dr B98 ... 154 E5
Moons Moat Fst Sch B98 ... 154 D5
Moor Burgess Activity Ctr
B77 ... 22 A1
Moor Ct B24 ... 56 F3
Moor Ctr The DY5 ... 61 D3
Moor End Ct B24 ... 57 B4
Moor End La B24 ... 57 B4
Moor Green Jun & Inf Sch
B13 ... 86 C1
Moor Green La B13 ... 86 D2
Moor Hall Dr Clent DY9 ... 100 A1
Sutton Coldfield B75 ... 32 D1
Moor Hall Inf & Jun Sch
B75 ... 32 D2
Moor Ho B14 ... 104 C2
Moor La Birmingham B6 ... 56 A4
Blackheath B65 ... 63 B3
Shenstone WS14 ... 17 E2
Tamworth, Amington B77 ... 22 A6
Tamworth, Bolehill B77 ... 21 D5
Moor Leasow B31 ... 103 C2
Moor Meadow Rd B75 ... 46 D7
Moor Pk Perton WV6 ... 23 D5
Walsall WS3 ... 14 B3
Moor Pool Ave B17 ... 85 C6
Moor Rd CV10 ... 72 A8
Moor St Birmingham B5 ... 164 C2
Brierley Hill DY5 ... 61 C3
Coventry CV5 ... 112 F1
Tamworth B79 ... 21 A5
Wednesbury WS10 ... 42 B2
West Bromwich B70 ... 53 C2
Moor St S WV2 ... 39 C7
Moor Street Ind Est DY5 ... 61 C3
Moor Street Queensway
B5 ... 164 C2
Moor Street Ringway B5 ... 164 C2
Moor Street Sta B5 ... 164 C2
Moor The B76 ... 58 A8
Moorcroft Cl Nuneaton
CV11 ... 74 B1
Redditch B97 ... 158 B6
Moorcroft Dr DY4 ... 41 C2
Moorcroft Pl [9] B7 ... 67 A4
Moorcroft Rd B13 ... 86 E3
Moordown Ave B92 ... 89 A2
Moore Cl Perton WV6 ... 23 F4
Sutton Coldfield B74 ... 31 F6
Warwick CV34 ... 155 E2
Moore Cres B68 ... 64 C3
Moore Rd WV12 ... 27 D8
Moore St Cannock WS12 ... 2 C7
Wolverhampton WV1 ... 25 F1
Moore Wlk CV34 ... 161 C7
Moore's Row B5 ... 66 F1
Moorend Ave B37 ... 70 B2
Moorfield Ave B93 ... 127 F6
Moorfield Dr
Bromsgrove B61 ... 136 F3
Halesowen B63 ... 83 A5
Sutton Coldfield B73 ... 57 A8
Moorfield Rd
Birmingham B34 ... 69 B6
Wolverhampton WV2 ... 39 C7
Moorfield The CV3 ... 134 B8
Moorfoot Ave B63 ... 82 C1
Moorgate B79 ... 21 A5
Moorgate Cl B98 ... 154 E6
Moorgate Cty Prim Sch
B79 ... 21 B5
Moorgate Rd B60 ... 151 A2
Moorhill Cty Prim Sch
WS11 ... 1 E5
Moorhill Rd CV31 ... 162 A3
Moorhills Croft B90 ... 126 B8
Moorings The
Brierley Hill DY5 ... 62 A4
Oldbury B69 ... 63 E8
Wolverhampton WV9 ... 10 F2
Moorland Ave WV10 ... 25 C6
Moorland Ct B16 ... 65 D1
Moorland Rd
Birmingham B16 ... 65 D1
Cannock WS11 ... 1 E5
Walsall WS3 ... 28 A8
Moorlands Ave CV8 ... 147 F3
Moorlands Ct B65 ... 63 D4
Moorlands Dr B90 ... 106 C2
Moorlands Lodge CV8 ... 147 F3
Moorlands Prim Sch B71 ... 53 B8
Moorlands Rd B71 ... 42 C1
Moorlands The B74 ... 45 F8
Moorpark Cl CV11 ... 79 C8
Moorpark Rd B31 ... 103 A1
Moors Croft B32 ... 84 B1
Moors La B31 ... 102 E7
Moors Mill La DY4 ... 52 D7
Moors The B36 ... 68 F8
Moorside Gdns WS2 ... 28 B3
Moorside Rd B14 ... 105 D3
Moorsom St B6 ... 66 E5
Moorsom Way B60 ... 151 B7
Moorville Wlk B11 ... 87 A7
Moorwood Cres CV10 ... 72 A8
Moorwood La CV10 ... 72 A7
Morar Cl B35 ... 58 C4
Moray Cl Halesowen B62 ... 83 E8
Hinckley LE10 ... 75 A8
Morcom Rd B11 ... 87 E5
Morcroft WV14 ... 41 A3
Mordaunt Dr B75 ... 32 E2
Morden Rd B33 ... 68 D3
Mordiford Cl B98 ... 154 E4
Moreall Mdws CV4 ... 132 D3
Moreland Croft B76 ... 58 B6
Morelands The B31 ... 103 B1
Morestead Ave B26 ... 89 C5
Moreton Ave Birmingham
B43 ... 44 C3
Wolverhampton WV4 ... 39 E4
Moreton Cl Birmingham B32 ... 84 F5
Tipton DY4 ... 41 B2
Moreton Com Sch WV10 ... 11 F1
Moreton Rd Solihull B90 ... 106 C2
Wolverhampton WV10 ... 11 D1
Moreton St Birmingham B1 ... 66 B4
Cannock WS11 ... 1 F4
Morfa Gdns CV6 ... 112 D5
Morford Rd WS9 ... 30 A7
Morgan Cl Studley B80 ... 159 F2
Willenhall WV12 ... 27 B4
Morgan Ct B24 ... 57 C6
Morgan Gr B36 ... 58 F1
Morgan Rd B78 ... 21 A2
Morgans Rd CV5 ... 111 C4
Morgrove Ave B93 ... 127 F6
Morillon Ct DY10 ... 117 A1
Morjon Dr B43 ... 43 F2
Morland Cl CV12 ... 79 D2
Morland Dr LE10 ... 71 B3
Morland Rd Birmingham
B43 ... 44 C4
Coventry CV6 ... 95 C2
Morley Gr WV6 ... 25 C4
Morley Rd Birmingham B8 ... 68 B6
Burntwood WS7 ... 7 B7
Morley Road Sh Ctr [4] WS7 ... 7 B7
Morlich Rise DY5 ... 81 B8
Morlings Dr WS7 ... 7 B8
Morning Pines DY8 ... 80 E4
Morningside Coventry CV5 ... 133 B8
Sutton Coldfield B73 ... 46 B6
Mornington Rd B66 ... 65 B7
Morpeth B77 ... 35 C7
Morrell St CV32 ... 156 F1
Morris Ave Coventry CV2 ... 114 D4
Walsall WS2 ... 27 E2
Morris Cl B27 ... 88 D4
Morris Croft B36 ... 58 F1
Morris Ct WV4 ... 39 F4
Morris Dr Nuneaton CV11 ... 73 D1
Whitnash CV31 ... 162 B2
Morris Field Croft B28 ... 105 E4
Morris Hill B78 ... 36 F7
Morris Rd B8 ... 68 C6
Morris St B70 ... 53 C1
Morris Wlk B60 ... 150 E8
Morrison Ave WV10 ... 25 D8
Morrison Rd DY4 ... 52 C4
Morse Rd CV31 ... 162 B3
Morsefield La B98 ... 154 D1
Morston B77 ... 35 D4
Mortimer Rd CV8 ... 147 F2
Mortimers Cl B14 ... 105 B1
Morton Cl CV6 ... 95 A1
Morton Ho B97 ... 153 A3
Morton La B97 ... 158 B7
Morton Rd Brierley Hill DY5 ... 81 D7
Harvington DY10 ... 118 B2
Morton St CV32 ... 156 F1
Morvale Gdns DY9 ... 81 E5
Morvale St DY9 ... 81 E5
Morven Rd B73 ... 46 A3
Morville Cl B93 ... 127 D3
Morville Croft WV14 ... 40 B5
Morville Rd DY2 ... 62 E4
Morville St B16 ... 66 B2
Mosborough Cres B19 ... 66 C5
Mosedale Dr WV11 ... 26 F5
Moseley Ave CV6 ... 113 A4
Moseley CE Prim Sch B13 ... 86 F2
Moseley Ct [17]
Birmingham B13 ... 87 B2
Essington WV11 ... 12 F3
Willenhall WV13 ... 26 D1
Moseley Dr B37 ... 89 F8
Moseley Hall Hospl B13 ... 86 E3
Moseley Old Hall WV10 ... 12 A5
Moseley Old Hall La WV10 ... 12 A5
Moseley Park Sch WV14 ... 40 E8
Moseley Prim Sch CV6 ... 113 A4
Moseley Rd Bilston WV14 ... 40 E8
Birmingham B12 ... 86 F6
Kenilworth CV8 ... 148 B3
Willenhall WV14, WV13 ... 26 D1
Wolverhampton WV10 ... 12 A4
Moseley Sch B13 ... 87 C2
Moseley St Birmingham B12 ... 86 F8
Tipton DY4 ... 52 C7
Wolverhampton WV6 ... 25 C4
Moss Cl Aldridge WS9 ... 30 A5
Huntington WS12 ... 1 C5
Walsall WS4 ... 29 A3
Moss Dr B72 ... 46 C3
Moss Gdns WV14 ... 40 B3
Moss Gr Birmingham B14 ... 104 D6
Kingswinford DY6 ... 60 D7
Moss House Cl B15 ... 66 B1
Moss La B98 ... 154 F8
Moss Lane Cl B98 ... 154 F8
Moss Rd WS11 ... 2 A3
Moss St Cannock WS11 ... 2 A4
[8] Royal Leamington Spa
CV31 ... 162 A7
Moss Way B74 ... 44 F7
Mossbank Ave WS7 ... 7 A6
Mossdale B77 ... 36 C8
Mossdale Cl CV6 ... 113 B6
Mossdale Cres CV10 ... 72 F2
Mossdale Way DY3 ... 50 E7
Mossfield Rd B14 ... 104 F7
Mossley Cl WS3 ... 13 F1
Mossley La WS3 ... 13 F2
Mossley Prim Sch WS3 ... 13 F2
Mosspaul Cl CV32 ... 156 D2
Mossvale Cl B64 ... 62 F1
Mossvale Gr B8 ... 67 F5
Mosswood St WS11 ... 4 D7
Mostyn Cres B71 ... 53 A7
Mostyn Rd
Birmingham, Edgbaston B16 ... 65 F2
Birmingham,
Handsworth B21 ... 65 F8
Mostyn St WV1 ... 25 B4
Mott Cl DY4 ... 52 C8
Mott St B19 ... 164 B4
Mottistone Cl CV3 ... 133 D6
Mottram Cl B70 ... 53 B2
Mottrams Cl B72 ... 46 C2
Moule Cl DY11 ... 116 C6
Mounds The B38 ... 123 E8
Moundsley Gr B14 ... 105 A3
Moundsley Ho B14 ... 104 F2

Mount Ave Brierley Hill DY5 .... 61 C4
Cannock WS12 .... 2 B7
Mount Carmel RC Fst Sch
B97 .... 153 A2
Mount Cl Birmingham B13 ... 86 F4
Cheslyn Hay WS6 .... 4 E2
Dudley DY3 .... 50 C2
Wombourne WV5 .... 49 A7
Mount Ct WV6 .... 24 B3
Mount Dr Bedworth CV12 ... 78 A3
Wombourne WV5 .... 49 A7
Mount Field Ct CV1 .... 165 D4
Mount Gdns CV5 .... 133 B8
Mount Grace High Sch
LE10 .... 71 E1
Mount La Clent DY9 .... 99 E4
Dudley DY3 .... 50 C2
Mount Nod Prim Sch
CV5 .... 112 A3
Mount Nod Way CV5 .... 112 B3
Mount Pleasant
Bilston WV14 .... 40 E6
Birmingham,
King's Heath B14 .... 86 F1
Birmingham,
Small Heath B10 .... 67 B1
Brierley Hill DY5 .... 61 E1
Cheslyn Hay WS6 .... 4 E2
Kingswinford DY6 .... 60 C4
Redditch B97 .... 153 D2
Tamworth B77 .... 35 C8
Mount Pleasant Ave B21 .... 54 E1
Mount Pleasant Cotts
CV2 .... 115 A7
Mount Pleasant Ct ■ B10 .. 67 B1
Mount Pleasant Prim Sch
DY5 .... 61 E1
Mount Pleasant Rd CV12 .... 78 A3
Mount Pleasant St
Dudley WV14 .... 51 B8
West Bromwich B70 .... 53 C2
Mount Pleasant Terr CV10 .. 72 F6
Mount Rd Birmingham B21 .. 65 D7
Blackheath B65 .... 63 E3
Burntwood WS7 .... 7 B6
Fairfield B61 .... 120 E2
Hinckley LE10 .... 75 D8
Stourbridge, Stambermill
DY8 .... 81 B5
Stourbridge, Wordsley DY8 ... 60 E2
Tipton B69 .... 63 C8
Walsall WS3 .... 15 A4
Willenhall WV13 .... 40 E8
Wolverhampton,
Lanesfield WV4 .... 39 F2
Wolverhampton, Penn WV4 ... 39 A4
Wolverhampton,
Tettenhall WV6 .... 24 B2
Wombourne WV5 .... 49 A7
Mount Road Ind Est WS7 .... 7 B6
Mount St Birmingham B7 ..... 67 C7
Cannock WS12 .... 2 B7
Coventry CV5 .... 112 F2
Halesowen B63 .... 83 A3
Nuneaton CV11 .... 73 B4
Redditch B98 .... 153 D2
Stourbridge DY8 .... 81 B5
Tipton DY4 .... 52 C6
Walsall WS1 .... 42 E8
Mount Street Ind Est B7 ..... 67 D7
Mount Street Pas CV11 ...... 73 B4
Mount The Birmingham B23 .. 56 D1
Blackheath B64 .... 63 A1
Coventry CV3 .... 133 E8
Curdworth B76 .... 59 C6
Mount Vernon Dr B61 .... 137 A5
Mount View B75 .... 46 E4
Mountain Ash Dr DY9 .... 81 C2
Mountain Ash Rd WS8 .... 15 E5
Mountain Pine Cl WS12 .... 2 A8
Mountbatten Ave CV8 .... 148 C3
Mountbatten Cl B70 .... 53 F2
Mountbatten Rd WS2 .... 27 F2
Mountfield Cl B14 .... 105 A2
Mountford Cl B65 .... 63 C3
Mountford Cres WS9 .... 30 C8
Mountford Dr B75 .... 46 B8
Mountford La WV14 .... 40 D6
Mountford Rd B90 .... 105 D1
Mountford St B11 .... 87 D5
Mountjoy Cres B92 .... 89 C3
Mountrath St WS1 .... 28 E1
Mounts Rd WS10 .... 41 F2
Mounts Way B7 .... 67 C7
Mountside St WS12 .... 2 C7
Mountwood Covert WV6 .... 24 B3
Mouse Hill WS3 .... 14 F3
Mouse La DY11 .... 116 B8
Mousehall Farm Rd DY5 .... 81 D7
Mousesweet Cl DY2 .... 62 E4
Mousesweet La DY2 .... 62 E3
Mousesweet Wlk B64 .... 82 B8
Mowbray Cl B45 .... 102 A2
Mowbray St Birmingham B5 .. 86 E8
Coventry CV2 .... 113 F3
Mowe Croft B37 .... 90 B7
Mows Hill Rd B94 .... 143 A1
Moxhull Cl WV12 .... 13 C1
Moxhull Dr B76 .... 57 E7
Moxhull Gdns WV12 .... 13 C1
Moxhull Rd B37 .... 70 A5
Moxley Hospl WV14 .... 41 B3
Moxley Ind Ctr WS10 .... 41 C4
Moxley Inf Sch WS10 .... 41 B4
Moxley Jct WS10 .... 41 B4

Moxley Rd WS10 .... 41 C5
Moyle Cres CV5 .... 111 D4
Moyle Dr B63 .... 82 B7
Moyses Croft B66 .... 65 A8
Mozart Ct WS11 .... 2 C2
Much Park St CV1 .... 165 C2
Muchall Rd WV4 .... 39 A5
Mucklow Hill B62 .... 83 D5
Mucklow Hill Trad Est B62 . 83 C5
Muirfield B77 .... 22 B5
Muirfield Cl Nuneaton CV11 .. 79 C8
Walsall WS3 .... 14 A3
Muirfield Cres B69 .... 63 B7
Muirfield Gdns B38 .... 103 D1
Muirville Cl DY8 .... 60 D3
Mulberry Cl CV32 .... 157 A2
Mulberry Dr Birmingham
B13 .... 87 B1
■ Warwick CV34 .... 160 F8
Mulberry Gn DY1 .... 50 F5
Mulberry Pl WS3 .... 13 F1
Mulberry Rd
Birmingham B30 .... 103 C5
Cannock WS11 .... 1 E3
Coventry CV6 .... 114 A7
Walsall WS3 .... 14 A1
Mulberry Wlk B74 .... 44 E8
Muldoon Cl WS11 .... 2 B4
Mull Cl B45 .... 101 E1
Mull Croft B36 .... 70 B7
Mullard Dr CV31 .... 162 B3
Mullensgrove Rd B37 .... 70 A5
Mullett Rd WV11 .... 26 B7
Mullett St DY5 .... 61 B5
Mulliner St CV6 .... 113 F5
Mulliners Cl ■ B37 .... 70 D2
Mullion Croft B38 .... 103 E1
Mulroy Rd B74 .... 46 B6
Mulwych Rd B33 .... 69 E3
Munches La DY9 .... 120 C8
Munsley Cl B98 .... 154 F2
Munslow Gr B31 .... 122 F8
Muntz Cres B94 .... 143 C6
Muntz Ho B16 .... 66 A1
Muntz St B10 .... 87 D8
Murcott Rd CV31 .... 162 A3
Murcott Rd E CV31 .... 162 A3
Murcroft Rd DY9 .... 81 E1
Murdoch Rd WV14 .... 41 A6
Murdock Ct WV12 .... 27 D7
Murdock Gr B21 .... 65 E7
Murdock Rd Birmingham
B21 .... 65 E8
Smethwick B66 .... 65 A8
Murdock Way ■ WS2 .... 28 A5
Murray Ct Birmingham B20 .. 55 A2
Sutton Coldfield B73 .... 46 A3
Murray Rd CV6 .... 113 A7
Murrell Cl B5 .... 86 D7
Murton B77 .... 36 C8
Musborough Cl B36 .... 58 C1
Muscott Gr B17 .... 85 B5
Muscovy Rd B23 .... 56 E3
Musgrave Cl B76 .... 46 E3
Musgrave Rd B18 .... 65 F6
Mushroom Hall Rd B68 .... 64 B5
Musk La DY3 .... 50 B3
Musk La W DY3 .... 50 B3
Muswell Cl B91 .... 107 D5
Muxloe Cl WS3 .... 14 A3
Myatt Ave Aldridge WS9 ...... 29 F5
Burntwood WS7 .... 7 A7
Wolverhampton WV2 .... 39 E6
Myatt Cl ■ WS2 .... 39 E6
Myatt Way WS9 .... 29 F5
Myddleton St B18 .... 66 A4
Myles Ct DY5 .... 61 D4
Mylgrove CV3 .... 133 D3
Mynors Cres B47 .... 125 A6
Myring Dr B75 .... 46 F5
Myrtle Ave
■ Birmingham,
Balsall Heath B12 .... 87 A5
Birmingham,
Highter's Heath B14 .... 104 F2
Redditch B98 .... 153 E2
Myrtle Cl ■ WV12 .... 27 E7
Myrtle Gr
🔟 Birmingham B19 .... 66 C8
Coventry CV5 .... 112 F1
Wolverhampton WV3 .... 38 E6
Myrtle Pl B29 .... 86 B2
Myrtle Rd DY1 .... 51 B3
Myrtle St WV2 .... 39 F6
Myrtle Terr DY4 .... 41 B2
Myton Cres CV34 .... 161 C6
Myton Crofts CV31 .... 161 D7
Myton Dr B90 .... 105 D1
Myton Gdns CV34 .... 161 A6
Myton La CV34 .... 161 C6
Myton Rd CV31, CV34 .... 161 B6
Myton Sch CV34 .... 161 B6
Mytton Cl DY2 .... 51 E1
Mytton Gr DY4 .... 51 E5
Mytton Rd Birmingham B30 . 103 C5
Water Orton B46 .... 58 F3
Myvod Rd WS10 .... 42 A5

N

Naden Ho WS12 .... 1 C5
Naden Rd B19 .... 66 B6
Nadin Rd B73 .... 57 A8
Naesby Rd WV6 .... 23 F3
Nafford Gr B14 .... 104 F2
Nagersfield Rd DY5 .... 61 A2
Nailcote Ave CV4 .... 131 C8
Nailcote La CV7 .... 131 A7
Nailers Cl Birmingham B32 .. 83 F2
Stoke Heath B60 .... 150 E6
Nailers Ct ❸ B60 .... 136 F2
Nailers Dr WS7 .... 7 D6
Nailstone Cres B27 .... 106 C8
Nailsworth Rd Dorridge
B93 .... 127 D2
Redditch B98 .... 153 F2
Nairn Cl Birmingham B28 .. 105 F5
Nuneaton CV10 .... 73 A3
Redditch B98 .... 154 E4
Nairn Rd WS3 .... 14 A4
Nally Dr WV14 .... 40 A2
Nanaimo Way DY6 .... 61 A4
Nansen Inf & Jun Sch B8 ... 67 F5
Nansen Rd Birmingham B8 .. 67 F5
Birmingham, Sparkhill B11 ... 87 C3
Nantmel Gr B32 .... 102 C8
Naomi Way WS9 .... 16 B4
Napier B77 .... 21 D3
Napier Dr B7 .... 52 C6,
Napier Rd Walsall WS2 .... 28 A5
Wolverhampton WV2 .... 39 D7
Napier St CV1 .... 113 E3
Napton Cl B98 .... 154 D1
Napton Dr CV32 .... 157 A2
Napton Gn CV5 .... 112 A3
Napton Gr B29 .... 84 F2
Narberth Way CV2 .... 114 F8
Narraway Dr CV4 .... 52 D8
Narrow La Brownhills WS8 .. 15 F8
Halesowen B62 .... 83 E8
Walsall WS2 .... 42 B7
Narrowboat Way DY2, DY5 .. 62 A5
Narrows The ❶ LE10 .... 75 E8
Naseby Cl Coventry CV3 .... 134 F8
Redditch B98 .... 154 D6
Naseby Dr B63 .... 82 D2
Naseby Ho ❹ B14 .... 105 A3
Naseby Rd Birmingham B8 .. 67 F5
Solihull B91 .... 107 B6
Nash Ave WV6 .... 23 E3
Nash Cl B65 .... 63 C1
Nash Ho B15 .... 86 D8
Nash La Belbroughton DY9 . 119 D7
Lichfield WS13 .... 3 A5
Nash Sq B42 .... 55 D4
Nashe Cl DY10 .... 117 C5
Nately Gr B29 .... 85 C3
Nathan Cl B75 .... 46 C8
Nathaniel Newton Fst Sch
CV10 .... 72 B8
National Ag Ctr CV8 .... 149 A4
National Ex Ctr B40 .... 90 E4
National Indoor Arena B1 .. 66 B2
National Lock Mus WV13 ... 27 A1
National Motorcycle Mus
The B92 .... 91 A2
National Needle Mus B98 . 153 F6
National Sea Life Ctr B1 .... 66 B2
Naul's Mill Ho CV1 .... 165 B4
Naunton Cl B29 .... 103 A7
Naunton Rd WS2 .... 28 A3
Navenby Cl B90 .... 105 C3
Navigation Dr DY5 .... 62 A4
Navigation La WS10 .... 42 F2
Navigation Rdbt DY4 .... 52 E6
Navigation St
Birmingham B2 .... 164 B2
Walsall WS2 .... 28 D1
Wolverhampton WV1 .... 25 E1
Navigation Way
Cannock WS11 .... 2 A2
Coventry CV6 .... 114 A8
West Bromwich B70 .... 52 F2
Nayland Croft B28 .... 106 A5
Naylor Cl DY11 .... 116 B3
Naylors Gr DY3 .... 50 E4
Neachells Cl WS13 .... 26 E1
Neachells La
Wednesfield WV11 .... 26 D5
Willenhall WV13 .... 26 D4
Neachells Lane Ind Est
WV11 .... 26 D4
Neachells Lane Island
WV11 .... 26 D4
Neachless Ave WV5 .... 49 A5
Neachley Gr B33 .... 68 F4
Neal Ct CV2 .... 115 A8
Neal Cl CV12 .... 79 C1
Neale Ho West Bromwich
B70 .... 53 D1
Wolverhampton WV2 .... 39 C7
Neale St WS2 .... 28 C2
Neander B79 .... 20 F6
Near Lands Cl B32 .... 84 B4
Near Oak Ho B32 .... 102 D8
Nearhill Rd B38 .... 123 C8
Nearmoor Rd B34 .... 69 D6
Neasden Gr B44 .... 56 B8
Neath Rd WS3 .... 13 F2
Neath Way Dudley DY3 .... 51 A6
Walsall WS3 .... 13 F2
Nebsworth Cl B90 .... 106 D5
Nechells Inf & Jun Sch B7 . 67 C8
Nechells Park Rd B7 .... 67 C7
Nechells Parkway B7 .... 67 C5
Nechells Pl B7 .... 67 C5
Needham St B7 .... 67 C7
Needhill Cl B93 .... 127 F6
Needle Cl B80 .... 159 E4
Needle Mill La B98 .... 153 E6
Needlers End La CV7 .... 130 A7
Needless Alley B2 .... 164 B2
Needwood Cl WV2 .... 39 B6
Needwood Dr WV4 .... 39 F4
Needwood Gr B71 .... 42 E1

Needwood Hill WS13 .... 3 A2
Needwood Ho B27 .... 88 D3
Neighbrook Cl B97 .... 152 F2
Neilston St CV31 .... 162 A7
Nelson Ave Bilston WV14 ... 40 C7
Warwick CV34 .... 161 A8
Nelson Dr Cannock WS12 ... 2 F4
Hinckley LE10 .... 71 D4
Nelson Ho DY4 .... 52 A7
Nelson Inf & Jun Sch B1 ... 66 B3
Nelson La CV34 .... 161 A8
Nelson Mandela Com Prim
Sch B12 .... 87 B5
Nelson Rd Birmingham B6 .. 55 F1
Dudley DY1 .... 51 B1
Nelson St Birmingham B1 ... 66 B3
▱ Coventry CV1 .... 113 E4
Oldbury B69 .... 64 B6
West Bromwich B71 .... 53 C5
Willenhall WV13 .... 27 B3
Nemesia B77 .... 22 B4
Nene Cl Coventry CV3 .... 134 D2
Stourbridge DY8 .... 81 A5
Nene Way B36 .... 69 F8
Neptune Ind Est WV13 .... 41 B8
Neptune St DY4 .... 51 E5
Nesbit Gr B9 .... 68 B3
Nesfield Cl B38 .... 103 C1
Nesfield Gr B92 .... 109 B7
Nesscliffe Gr B23 .... 56 D7
Nest Comm WS3 .... 14 F5
Neston Gr B33 .... 68 C2
Nestor Ho B13 .... 105 D7
Nether Beacon WS13 .... 3 A1
Nether La WS7 .... 7 D8
Netheravon Cl B14 .... 104 D1
Netherbridge Ave WS14 .... 9 E7
Netherbrook Prim Sch
DY2 .... 62 D2
Netherby Rd DY3 .... 50 C8
Nethercote Gdns B90 .... 105 E3
Netherdale Cl B72 .... 57 D7
Netherdale Rd B14 .... 105 A1
Netherend Cl B63 .... 82 A7
Netherend La B63 .... 82 B7
Netherend Sq B63 .... 82 A7
Netherfield B98 .... 159 A8
Netherfield Gdns B27 .... 88 B3
Nethergate DY3 .... 50 F5
Netherley Rd LE10 .... 71 D3
Nethermill Rd ❶ CV6 .... 113 A5
Netherstone Gr B74 .... 31 F5
Netherstowe WS13 .... 3 C2
Netherstowe High Sch
WS13 .... 3 B1
Netherstowe La WS13 .... 3 D2
Netherton Bsns Pk DY2 ...... 62 E3
Netherton CE Prim Sch
DY2 .... 62 B4
Netherton Gr B33 .... 69 C3
Netherwood Cl B91 .... 106 E6
Netherwood La B93 .... 145 A2
Nethy Dr WV6 .... 24 B5
Netley Gr B11 .... 87 F3
Netley Ho B32 .... 84 F5
Netley Rd WS3 .... 13 E2
Netley Way WS3 .... 13 E2
Nevada Way B37 .... 70 C1
Neve Ave WV10 .... 25 F8
Nevill Cl CV31 .... 161 F6
Nevill St B79 .... 21 A5
Neville Ave
Kidderminster DY11 .... 116 D3
Wolverhampton WV4 .... 39 D5
Neville Cl B98 .... 154 A5
Neville Ct Birmingham B13 . 104 F6
Kidderminster DY11 .... 116 D3
Neville Gr CV34 .... 155 F1
Neville Rd
Birmingham,
Castle Bromwich B36 .... 58 E1
Birmingham,
Stockland Green B23 .... 56 C3
Solihull B90 .... 105 F1
Neville St B77 .... 21 E3
Neville Wlk B35 .... 58 A2
Nevin Gr B42 .... 55 C5
Nevis Ct WV3 .... 24 E2
Nevis Gr WV12 .... 13 B1
Nevison Gr B43 .... 44 B4
New Ash Dr CV5 .... 111 F5
New Barns La WS14 .... 17 B3
New Bartholomew St B5 ... 164 D2
New Birmingham Rd
Oldbury B69 .... 63 D8
Tipton B69, DY2 .... 52 B1
New Bldgs Coventry CV1 ... 165 C3
Darlaston WS10 .... 41 A6
Halesowen B63 .... 82 A7
Hinckley LE10 .... 71 D1
🔟 Kidderminster DY11 ...... 116 D6
New Bond St Birmingham B9 67 B1
🔟 Dudley DY2 .... 62 D8
New Brook St ❺ CV32 ...... 161 E8
New Canal St B5 .... 164 D2
New Century Pk CV3 .... 114 C2
New Century Way CV11 ...... 73 B4
New Church Rd B73 .... 57 A8
New Cole Hall La B33, B34 . 69 B5
New College Cl WS1 .... 43 A7
New Coventry Rd B26 .... 89 A5
New Croft B19 .... 66 E7
New Cross Hospl WV11 ...... 26 B5
New Cross Ind Est WV1 ..... 26 A3
New Cross St
Darlaston WS10 .... 41 D5
Tipton DY4 .... 51 E5
New Ct ❼ DY5 .... 61 D2

New Dudley Rd DY6 .... 60 C8
New England B62 .... 83 E2
New England Cl B69 .... 52 E1
New Ent Workshops
Birmingham B7 .... 67 C6
Birmingham, All Saints B18 .. 66 A5
New Farm Rd DY9 .... 81 C6
New Forest Rd WS3 .... 28 F6
New Gas St B70 .... 53 A5
New Gate Ct CV1 .... 165 C2
New Hall Dr
Sutton Coldfield, Maney B75 .. 46 D4
Sutton Coldfield,
Wylde Green B75 .... 46 E2
New Hall Pl WS10 .... 42 A3
New Hall St WS13 .... 42 B7
New Hampton Rd E WV1 .. 163 A4
New Hampton Rd W W6 ..... 25 A4
New Heath Cl WV11 .... 26 B5
New Henry St B68 .... 64 B4
New Hope Rd B66 .... 65 C4
New Horse Rd WS6 .... 4 E3
New Inn Rd ❷ B19 .... 66 D8
New Inns Cl B21 .... 65 D8
New Inns La B45 .... 101 E1
New Invention Inf & Jun
Schs WV12 .... 27 C7
New John St Birmingham B6 . 66 E5
Halesowen B62 .... 83 C8
New John St W B19 .... 66 D5
New King St ❼ DY1 .... 51 C1
New Landywood La WV11 .. 13 E7
New Leasow B76 .... 58 A7
New Market St B3 .... 164 B3
New Meadow Cl B31 .... 103 B2
New Meadow Rd B98 .... 154 B3
New Meeting St B69 .... 64 A8
New Mill La B78 .... 35 B8
New Mill St DY2 .... 51 C1
New Mills St WS1 .... 42 D7
New Oscott Inf Sch B73 ..... 45 C3
New Oscott Jun Sch B73 .... 45 C3
New Penkridge Rd WS11 ..... 1 C1
New Pool Rd B64 .... 82 B8
New Rd Aldridge WS9 .... 30 A5
Ash Green CV7 .... 95 B6
Astwood Bank B96 .... 158 E1
Bedworth CV12 .... 77 A4
Birmingham B45 .... 121 F7
Bromsgrove B60 .... 137 A4
Bromsgrove, Sidemoor B61 . 136 C3
Brownhills WS7 .... 15 F7
Burntwood WS7 .... 7 B6
Coventry CV6 .... 94 F1
Dudley DY2 .... 62 C7
Fairfield B61 .... 120 E2
Featherstone WV10 .... 12 B8
Halesowen B63 .... 83 B4
Hinckley LE10 .... 76 A6
Hollywood B47 .... 125 D4
Kidderminster DY10 .... 116 E5
Shenstone WS14 .... 17 F6
Shuttington B79 .... 22 E8
Solihull B91 .... 107 D3
Stourbridge DY8 .... 81 A5
Studley B80 .... 159 E3
Tamworth B77 .... 35 F7
Tipton DY4 .... 52 D6
Water Orton B46 .... 59 B3
Willenhall WV13 .... 27 A1
Wolverhampton,
Newbridge WV6 .... 24 B3
Wolverhampton,
Scotlands WV10 .... 26 B8
New Row B78 .... 34 E5
New Rowley Rd DY2 .... 62 E2
New Spring St B18 .... 66 A4
New Spring St N B18 .... 66 A4
New St Bedworth CV12 .... 78 C2
Birchmoor B78 .... 36 E7
Birmingham,
Castle Bromwich B36 .... 69 D8
Birmingham, Digbeth B2 .... 164 C2
Birmingham, Erdington B23 . 56 F5
Birmingham, Frankley B45 . 102 A1
Brierley Hill DY5 .... 82 A8
Bulkington CV12 .... 79 D2
Burntwood,
Chase Terrace WS7 .... 6 E8
Burntwood, Chasetown WS7 . 6 E5
🔟 Cannock, Blackfords WS11 . 1 E1
Cannock, Bridgtown WS11 ... 4 D6
Cannock, Hednesford WS12 .. 2 C4
Cubbington CV32 .... 157 D2
Darlaston WS10 .... 41 D6
Dudley, Eve Hill DY1 .... 51 D1
Dudley, Gornalwood DY3 .... 50 C3
Essington WV11 .... 13 A3
Fazeley B78 .... 35 B8
Great Wyrley WS6 .... 5 A1
Hinckley LE10 .... 71 D1
Kenilworth CV8 .... 147 F6
Kingswinford,
Wall Heath DY6 .... 60 C8
Kingswinford,
Wordsley DY6 .... 60 D4
Royal Leamington Spa CV31 162 A7
Smethwick B66 .... 65 B6
Stourbridge DY8 .... 60 D2
Stourbridge,
🔟 Wollaston DY8 .... 80 F5
Tamworth, Bolehill B77 .... 21 E4
Tamworth,
Mount Pleasant B77 .... 21 C1
Tipton DY4 .... 51 F5
Walsall, High Heath WS4 .... 15 D1
Walsall, Rushall WS4 .... 29 D8
Walsall, The Chuckery WS1 .. 28 F1

New St continued
Walsall, Wallington Heath WS3 14 B1
Warwick CV34 160 E6
Wednesbury WS10 41 F1
West Bromwich, Hill Top B70 53 A7
West Bromwich, Mayer's Green B70 53 D3
Willenhall WV13 26 E1
Wolverhampton, Ettingshall WV2 40 A6
Wolverhampton, Merry Hill WV3 38 D7
Wolverhampton, Parkfields WV4 39 E6
New St N B71 53 D3
New Street Sta B2 164 B2
New Summer St B19 164 B4
New Swan La B70 53 A5
New Town Brierley Hill DY5 61 C4
Dudley DY2 62 D1
New Town La B64 62 D1
New Town Row B6 66 E5
New Union St CV1 165 B2
New Village DY2 62 C2
New Wharf Cotts B60 152 B7
New Wlk 3 B98 153 E4
New Wood Cl DY7 80 C8
New Wood Gr WS9 16 A3
New Wood La DY10 118 B8
Newark Croft B26 89 B6
Newark Rd Dudley DY2 62 D2
Willenhall WV12 27 C7
Newbank Gr B9 68 A3
Newbold Cl
Bentley Heath B93 127 F5
Coventry CV3 114 F1
Newbold Comyn Pk CV32 162 D8
Newbold Croft B7 67 B5
Newbold Ct B63 83 B3
Newbold Lawn CV32 162 A8
Newbold Pl CV32 162 A8
Newbold St CV32 162 A8
Newbold Terr CV32 162 A8
Newbold Terr E CV32 162 B8
Newbolds Rd WV10 26 A6
Newbolt Rd WV14 40 E6
Newbolt St WS5 42 E5
Newborough Gr B28 105 F3
Newborough Rd
Birmingham B28 105 F4
Solihull B90 106 A3
Newbourne Hill B48 139 E4
Newbridge Ave WV6 24 E3
Newbridge Cres WV6 24 E4
Newbridge Dr WV6 24 E4
Newbridge Gdns WV6 24 E4
Newbridge Mews WV6 24 F4
Newbridge Prep Sch WV6 24 E4
Newbridge Rd
Birmingham B9 68 B1
Kingswinford DY6 60 C8
Newbridge St WV6 24 F4
Newburgh Cres CV34 160 E8
Newburgh Prim Sch CV34 160 C4
Newburn Croft B32 84 B5
Newbury Cl Great Wyrley WS6 4 F2
Halesowen B62 83 D3
15 Royal Leamington Spa CV31 162 C6
Newbury Ho 1 B69 63 D5
Newbury La B69 63 D6
Newbury Rd Birmingham B19 66 E7
Stourbridge DY8 60 D1
Wolverhampton WV10 11 C2
Newbury Wlk B65 63 C6
Newby Cl CV3 133 E6
Newby Gr B37 70 B4
Newcastle Croft B35 58 C3
Newchurch Gdns 6 B24 56 E2
Newcombe Rd
Birmingham B21 54 D2
Coventry CV5 113 A1
Newcomen Cl
Bedworth CV12 95 D8
Burntwood WS7 7 C8
Newcomen Ct WS4 29 B7
Newcomen Dr DY4 51 F3
Newcomen Rd CV12 77 D1
Newcott Cl WV9 10 F2
Newcroft Gr B26 88 E7
Newdegate Pl CV11 73 C4
Newdegate Rd CV12 78 A3
Newdegate St CV11 73 C4
Newdigate CV31 162 C5
Newdigate Cl CV12 78 A4
Newdigate Cty Fst Sch CV12 77 C1
Newdigate Cty Mid Sch CV12 77 C1
Newdigate Rd Coventry CV6 113 F6
Sutton Coldfield B75 47 A5
Newells Dr DY4 52 D7
Newells Rd B26 89 B8
Newent Cl WV12 27 D3
Newent Rd B31 103 C4
Newey Ave CV12 95 D8
Newey Cl B45 122 A6
Newey Rd Birmingham B28 105 F6
Coventry CV2 114 D4
Wednesfield WV11 27 A8
Newey St DY1 51 A2
Newfield Ave CV8 148 B3
Newfield Cl Solihull B91 107 D6
Walsall WS2 28 C5
Newfield Cres B63 83 A5
Newfield Dr DY6 60 E4
Newfield Gdns DY9 99 A4
Newfield La B63 83 B5
Newfield Park Prim Sch B62 83 A5
Newfield Rd Coventry CV1 113 C5
Hagley DY9 99 A4
Oldbury B69 63 F8
Newgale Wlk CV31 162 C7
Newgate St WS7 7 A5
Newhall Cres WS11 2 B3
Newhall Farm Cl B76 46 D4
Newhall Gdns WS11 1 F2
Newhall Hill B1 66 C3
Newhall Ho 5 WS1 42 E8
Newhall Pl B1 66 C3
Newhall Rd Blackheath B65 63 C3
Coventry CV2 114 D7
Newhall St Birmingham B3 164 B3
Cannock WS11 1 D1
Tipton DY4 51 E8
Walsall WS1 42 E8
West Bromwich B70 53 C2
Newhall Wlk B72 46 C4
Newham Gn CV10 72 C7
Newhaven Cl Birmingham B7 67 A5
Coventry CV6 112 E6
Newhouse Croft CV7 130 B6
Newhouse Farm Cl B76 46 F3
Newick Ave B74 31 B3
Newick Gr B14 104 C4
Newick St DY2 62 C4
Newington Cl CV6 112 D6
Newington Rd B37 90 B8
Newland Cl Redditch B98 159 B7
Walsall WS4 15 C2
Newland Ct B23 56 C3
Newland Gdns B64 82 E7
Newland Gr DY2 61 F7
Newland La CV7 95 B7
Newland Rd Birmingham B9 67 F1
Coventry CV1 113 D5
Royal Leamington Spa CV32 157 C3
Newlands Cl
Kidderminster DY11 116 C7
Willenhall WV13 27 A1
Newlands Ct Cannock WS11 5 E8
Coventry CV3 113 F2
Newlands Dr B62 83 F7
Newlands Gn B66 65 A4
Newlands La Birmingham B37 90 A6
Norton Canes WS11 5 D8
Newlands Rd
Bentley Heath B93 127 F4
Birmingham B30 104 C7
Newlands The
Birmingham B34 69 C7
Studley B80 159 D3
Newlyn Cl Lichfield WS14 9 D7
Nuneaton CV11 73 F4
Newlyn Rd Birmingham B31 102 F3
Blackheath B64 82 D8
Newman Ave WV4 39 F4
Newman Cl CV12 78 B4
Newman Coll B32 102 C8
Newman College Cl B32 102 C8
Newman Pl WV14 40 F7
Newman Rd Birmingham B24 56 F4
Tipton DY4 41 C1
Wolverhampton WV10 12 A1
Newman Way B45 122 A6
Newmans Cl B66 65 C4
Newmarket Cl Coventry CV6 96 B4
Wolverhampton WV6 25 A5
Newmarket Way B36 68 B7
Newmarsh Rd B76 58 B6
Newmore Gdns WS5 43 C5
Newnham Gr B23 56 E6
Newnham Ho B36 70 B5
Newnham Rd
Birmingham B16 65 C2
Coventry CV1 113 F5
Royal Leamington Spa CV32 157 B3
Newnham Rise B90 106 D3
Newport B77 21 F5
Newport Cl B97 158 B6
Newport Ho B71 53 B7
Newport Rd
Birmingham, Balsall Heath B12 87 A4
Birmingham, Buckland End B36 68 F8
Coventry CV6 95 D1
Newport St 3 Walsall WS1 28 E1
Wolverhampton WV10 25 E4
Newquay Cl Hinckley LE10 71 E4
Nuneaton CV11 73 F5
Walsall WS5 43 E7
Newquay Rd WS5 43 D7
Newshire Ind Est B11 87 D6
Newsholme Cl 1 CV34 155 E1
Newstead B79 20 D6
Newstead Ave LE10 75 D4
Newstead Cl CV11 73 F2
Newstead Rd B44 45 B3
Newstead Way CV3 115 B1
Newton Cl Birmingham B43 43 C1
Coventry CV2 114 F7
Redditch B98 159 A6
Newton Gdns B43 54 B8
Newton Gr 5 B29 85 F2
Newton Ind Est B9 67 D2
Newton Manor Cl B43 54 D8
Newton Pl Birmingham B18 66 A7
Walsall WS2 28 B6
Newton Rd
Birmingham, Balsall Heath B11 87 B5
Birmingham, Newton B43 54 B8
Bromsgrove B60 151 A7
Hinckley LE10 74 E7
Knowle B93 128 B7
Walsall WS2 28 B5
West Bromwich B71 53 F6
Newton Sq B43 43 E1
Newton St Birmingham B4 164 C3
West Bromwich B71 53 E7
Newton Works B60 151 A6
Newton's Coll WS13 9 A8
Newtown Bldgs CV12 78 B3
Newtown Dr B19 66 C6
Newtown La Romsley B62 101 D2
Wildmoor B62 120 D8
Newtown Middleway B6 66 E5
Newtown Prim Sch B70 52 D3
Newtown Rd Bedworth CV12 78 A2
Nuneaton CV11 73 C5
Newtown Sh Ctr B19 66 E6
Newtown St B64 62 D2
Ney Ct DY4 51 F2
Niall Cl B15 85 E8
Nibletts Hill B61 136 B7
Nicholas Chamberlaine Comp Sch CV12 78 D3
Nicholas Rd B74 44 E8
Nicholds Cl WV14 40 B1
Nicholls Rd DY4 40 E1
Nicholls St Coventry CV2 113 F4
West Bromwich B70 53 E2
Nicholls Way WS12 2 F1
Nichols Cl B92 107 F7
Nicholson Cl CV34 155 F1
Nickson Rd CV4 111 E1
Nigel Ave B31 103 A5
Nigel Ct B16 65 E1
Nigel Rd Birmingham B8 67 E6
Dudley DY1 51 A2
Nightingale B77 36 A6
Nightingale Ave B36 70 A8
Nightingale Cl WS12 1 C7
Nightingale Cres
Brierley Hill DY5 81 D7
Willenhall WV12 27 C8
Nightingale Ct CV31 162 B8
Nightingale Dr
Kidderminster DY10 117 B2
Tipton DY4 52 C5
Nightingale Ho 4 B16 66 A2
Nightingale La CV5 132 E7
Nightingale Pl WV14 40 D7
Nightingale Wlk 1 B15 86 C7
Nighwood Dr B74 44 F7
Nijon Cl B21 54 D1
Nimbus B77 35 D4
Nimmings Cl B31 122 F6
Nimmings Rd B62 63 D1
Nimmings Visitor Ctr DY9 100 B6
Nine Days La B98 159 B6
Nine Elms La WV10 25 E4
Nine Leasowes B66 64 E7
Nine Locks Ridge DY5 61 D2
Nine Pails Wlk B70 53 D1
Nineacres Dr B37 70 A3
Ninefoot La Tamworth B77 35 E8
Tamworth B77 35 F7
Ninestiles Sch B27 88 B1
Nineveh Ave B21 65 F7
Nineveh Rd B21 65 F7
Ninfield Rd B27 88 A4
Ninian Pk B77 35 D6
Ninian Way B77 35 E6
Nirvana Cl WS11 1 C2
Nith Pl DY1 51 B3
Niton Rd CV10 73 D6
Niven Cl CV5 112 A6
No Name Rd WS7 6 E7
Noakes Ct WS10 41 F7
Noble Cl CV34 160 D5
Nock St DY4 52 C7
Nocke Rd WV11 12 F1
Nod Rise CV5 112 B3
Noddy Park Rd WS9 30 B6
Noddy Pk WS9 30 B7
Node Hill B80 159 D3
Node Hill Cl B80 159 D3
Noel Ave B12 87 A6
Noel Ct B97 158 C8
Noel Rd B16 65 F1
Noele Gordon Gdns WS1 42 E8
Nolans Cl CV6 95 D4
Nolton Cl B43 54 D8
Nonsuch Jun & Inf Sch B32 84 D2
Nook The Brierley Hill DY5 61 B5
Cheslyn Hay WS6 4 C1
Nuneaton CV11 73 E2
Nooklands Croft B33 69 A2
Noose Cres WV13 26 E2
Noose La WV13 26 E3
Nora Rd B11 87 C3
Norbiton Rd B44 56 A8
Norbreck Cl B43 43 D1
Norbury Ave WS3 15 A3
Norbury Cl B98 154 B7
Norbury Cres WV4 40 A4
Norbury Dr DY5 61 D1
Norbury Gr B92 89 A3
Norbury Rd Bilston WV14 40 F6
Birmingham B44 44 F3
West Bromwich B70 53 A7
Wolverhampton WV10 25 F6
Norcombe Gr B90 127 A5
Nordic Drift CV2 115 A6
Nordley Rd WV11 26 C5
Norfolk Ave B71 53 D7
Norfolk Cl Birmingham B30 104 B6
Hinckley LE10 75 D4
Norfolk Cres Aldridge WS9 30 B8
Nuneaton CV10 72 E4
Norfolk Ct B16 65 D1
Norfolk Dr Tamworth B78 21 A1
Wednesbury WS10 42 D4
Norfolk Gdns B75 46 B7
Norfolk Gr WS6 4 F1
Norfolk Ho B30 104 A3
Norfolk House Sch B15 85 D8
Norfolk New Rd WS2 28 A4
Norfolk Pl WS2 28 D5
Norfolk Rd Birmingham B45 101 F2
Birmingham, Edgbaston B15 85 D8
Birmingham, Erdington B23 56 F5
Dudley DY2 62 A7
Oldbury B68 84 B7
Stourbridge DY8 80 D8
Sutton Coldfield B75 46 C7
Wolverhampton WV3 39 A8
Norfolk St Coventry CV1 113 B3
Royal Leamington Spa CV32 157 A1
Norfolk Terr CV4 132 B7
Norfolk Tower B18 66 B5
Norgrave Rd B92 89 C2
Norlan Dr B14 104 F3
Norland Rd B27 88 C1
Norley Gr B13 105 C7
Norman Ashman Coppice CV3 135 C7
Norman Ave Birmingham B32 84 E7
Coventry CV2 96 F1
Nuneaton CV11 73 B4
Norman Cl B79 20 E7
Norman Place Rd CV6 112 F7
Norman Rd Birmingham B31 103 B3
Smethwick B67 64 E2
Walsall WS5 43 D7
Norman St Birmingham B18 65 E5
Dudley DY2 62 E7
Norman Terr B65 63 C4
Normanby Mdws CV31 162 A2
Normandy Cl CV35 160 A7
Normandy Rd B20 55 E1
Normansell Tower B6 67 B8
Normanton Ave B26 89 D5
Normanton Tower 1 B23 57 A6
Norrington Gr B31 102 C3
Norrington Rd B31 102 D3
Norris Dr B33 68 E3
Norris Rd B6 55 F1
Norris Way B75 46 D5
North Ave Bedworth CV12 78 D2
Birmingham B40 90 F5
Coventry CV2 114 A3
Wolverhampton WV11 26 C6
North Birmingham Coll B44 55 E7
North Bromsgrove High Sch B60 137 B3
North Brook Rd CV5 112 D8
North Cl Cubbington CV32 157 E5
Hinckley LE10 75 E6
North Cres WV10 12 C7
North Dr
Birmingham, Balsall Heath B5 86 C5
Birmingham, Lozells B20 66 B8
Sutton Coldfield B75 46 C6
North East Worcestershire Coll B98 153 E4
North East Worcestershire Coll (Annexe) B98 153 E4
North East Worcestershire Coll Bromsgrove Campus B60 137 B3
North Gate B17 85 C7
North Gn WV4 38 D6
North Holme B9 67 C2
North Leamington Sch CV32 156 F4
North Leamington Sch (Binswood Hall) CV32 156 F2
North Oval DY3 50 E5
North Park Rd B23 56 B3
North Pathway B17 85 B7
North Rd
Birmingham, Handsworth B20 55 E2
Birmingham, Harborne B17 85 D6
Birmingham, Selly Oak B29 85 F3
Bromsgrove B60 137 A2
Tipton DY4 52 B8
Wolverhampton WV1 25 C4
North Roundhay B33 69 A4
North Springfield DY3 39 E1
North St Brierley Hill DY5 61 C2
Cannock WS11 4 E6
Coventry CV2 114 B5
Dudley DY2 51 D1
Nuneaton CV10 72 F3
North St continued
Smethwick B67 64 F5
Walsall WS2 28 E3
Wednesbury WS10 41 F3
Wolverhampton WV1 163 B3
North Street Ind Est DY5 61 C2
North View CV7 97 A1
North View Dr DY5 61 E5
North Villiers St CV32 157 A1
North Walsall Inf Sch WS2 28 E4
North Walsall Jun Sch WS2 28 E4
North Warwick St 1 B9 67 D1
North Warwickshire & Hinkley Coll
Hinkley LE10 75 F8
Nuneaton CV11 73 E6
North Western Arc B2 164 C3
North Western Rd B66 65 A6
North Western Terr B18 65 F7
North Wlk B31 103 C1
Northam Wlk WV6 25 B4
Northampton St B18 66 C4
Northanger Rd B27 88 B2
Northbrook Ct B90 106 C5
Northbrook Rd B90 106 D5
Northbrook St B16 65 F4
Northcliffe Hts DY11 116 C7
Northcote Rd B33 68 D4
Northcote St
7 Royal Leamington Spa CV31 162 B7
Walsall WS2 28 D4
Northcott Rd Bilston WV14 40 F4
Dudley DY2 62 D4
Northcroft Hospl B23 56 D4
Northdale WV6 24 B4
Northdown Rd B91 106 F1
Northern Perimeter Rd W LE10 71 B3
Northey Rd CV6 113 D8
Northfield Cl B98 154 D6
Northfield Gr WV3 38 C7
Northfield Manor Prim Sch B29 103 B7
Northfield Rd
Birmingham, Harborne B17, B32 85 A3
Birmingham, King's Norton B30 103 E4
Coventry CV1 113 F2
Dudley DY2 62 D4
Hinckley LE10 75 C7
Northfield Road Prim Sch DY2 62 D5
Northfield Sta B31 103 B2
Northfields Way WS8 15 D7
Northfleet Tower 4 B31 102 C2
Northgate Aldridge WS9 30 A7
Blackheath B64 82 D8
Northgate Cl DY11 116 A4
Northgate St CV34 160 E7
Northgate Way WS9 30 A8
Northicote Sch The WV10 11 E3
Northland Rd B90 106 E1
Northlands Rd B13 87 A1
Northleach Ave B14 104 D2
Northleach Cl B98 154 B5
Northleigh Rd B8 68 A6
Northmead B33 69 A2
Northolt Dr B35 58 B3
Northolt Gr B42 43 F1
Northover Cl WV9 11 A2
Northside Cl B98 158 E7
Northside Dr B74 44 F8
Northumberland Ave
Kidderminster DY11 116 D3
Nuneaton CV10 72 F3
Northumberland Cl B78 21 A1
Northumberland Rd
Coventry CV1 113 A3
Royal Leamington Spa CV32 156 E2
Northumberland St B7 67 A3
Northvale Cl CV8 148 B6
Northway Birmingham B40 90 F5
Royal Leamington Spa CV31 162 A5
Sedgley DY3 39 C2
Northwick Cres B91 107 B1
Northwood Ct 9 DY5 61 D2
Northwood Park Cl WV10 11 E3
Northwood Park Rd WV10 11 E3
Northwood St B3 164 A4
Northycote La WV10 11 F4
Norton Canes High Sch WS11 6 A7
Norton Canes Prim Sch WS11 6 A6
Norton Cl Birmingham B31 103 A3
Redditch B98 154 F2
Smethwick B66 65 C5
Tamworth B79 21 C7
Wolverhampton WV4 38 C3
Norton Cres Bilston WV14 40 D1
Birmingham B9 68 B3
Dudley DY2 62 E3
Norton Dr CV34 155 E2
Norton East Rd WS11 6 B6
Norton Grange WS11 5 F4
Norton Grange Cres WS11 5 F4

Norton Green La
Knowle B93 128 C2
Norton Canes WS11 5 F4
Norton Hall La WS11 5 D4
Norton Hill Dr CV2 114 E6
Norton La Burntwood WS7 7 C6
Great Wyrley WS6 5 A4
Norton Canes WS11 5 C6
Tidbury Green B47, B94 125 E3
Norton Rd Coleshill B46 70 F8
Iverley DY8 98 D8
Kidderminster DY10 117 B6
Norton Canes WS12 5 F8
Stourbridge DY8 80 E2
Walsall WS3 15 A4
Norton Springs WS11 5 F5
Norton St B18 66 A6
Norton Terr
Birmingham B30 104 B6
Norton Canes WS11 5 F6
Norton Tower B1 66 C2
Norton View B14 104 D7
Norton Wlk B23 56 C3
Nortune Cl B38 103 D2
Norwich Cl Lichfield WS13 3 C3
Nuneaton CV11 74 A8
Norwich Croft B37 69 F1
Norwich Dr Birmingham
B17 84 F8
Coventry CV3 133 B5
Norwich Rd Dudley DY2 62 D2
Walsall WS2 28 B1
Norwood Ave B64 82 E7
Norwood Cl LE10 71 E3
Norwood Gr Birmingham
B19 66 B7
Coventry CV2 96 E2
Norwood Ho 11 CV32 156 F2
Norwood Rd Birmingham
B9 67 E2
Brierley Hill DY5 61 C3
Norwood Villas B16 65 F1
Nottingham Dr WV12 27 C7
Nottingham Way DY5 61 F2
Nova Croft CV5 111 C4
Nova Ct B43 44 B1
Nova Scotia St B4 164 D3
Novotel Way B26 90 C4
Nowell St WS10 41 E5
Nuffield Ho B36 70 A8
Nuffield Hospl WV6 24 C4
Nuffield Rd Coventry CV6 114 A7
Hinckley LE10 74 E7
Nugent Cl B6 66 E7
Nugent Gr B90 126 D3
Nuneaton Rd Bedworth
CV12 78 B4
Bulkington CV12 79 B4
Nuneaton CV10 72 D8
Nuneaton Trent Valley Sta
CV11 73 C5
Nunts La CV6 95 B3
Nunts Park Ave CV6 95 B4
Nursery Ave Aldridge WS9 30 B5
Birmingham B12 86 F5
Nursery Cl Birmingham B30 103 F5
Hagley DY9 99 A4
Kidderminster DY11 116 B8
Nursery Dr B30 103 F5
Nursery Gdns DY8 60 F1
Nursery Gr DY11 116 B8
Nursery La Hopwas B78 20 B6
Royal Leamington Spa
CV31 162 A5
Nursery Rd
Birmingham, Harborne B15 85 D7
Birmingham, Lozells B19 66 C6
Walsall WS3 28 B7
Nursery St WV1 163 B4
Nursery View Cl WS9 30 E2
Nursery Wlk WV6 24 D4
Nurton Bank WV6 23 A3
Nutbrook Ave CV4 111 E2
Nutbush Dr B31 102 E6
Nutfield Wlk B32 84 F5
Nutgrove Cl B14 104 F7
Nuthatch Dr DY5 81 C7
Nuthurst B75 47 B4
Nuthurst Dr WS11 4 F4
Nuthurst Gr
Bentley Heath B93 128 A4
Birmingham B14 104 F2
Nuthurst Grange Rd B94 143 C4
Nuthurst Rd
Birmingham B31 122 F6
Lapworth B94 143 B2
Nutley Dr DY4 52 D8
Nutt's La LE10 75 A7
Nuttall Gr B21 65 C7
Nymet B77 35 E8

O'Connor Dr DY4 41 C1
O'Hare Ho WS4 28 F3
Oak Ave Birmingham B12 87 A5
Great Wyrley WS6 5 A1
Huntington WS12 1 D8
Walsall WS2 27 E3
West Bromwich B70 53 B3
Oak Bank B18 66 A6
Oak Barn Rd B62 83 E8
Oak Cl Baginton CV8 133 F2
Bedworth CV12 78 C4
Birmingham B17 85 A6
Hinckley LE10 75 E5
Tipton DY4 41 A1
Oak Cottage Prim Sch
B91 106 F6
Oak Cotts B14 105 C2
Oak Cres Tipton B69 52 B1
Walsall WS3 28 D6
Oak Croft B37 69 E3
Oak Ct Coventry CV3 133 F7
Halesowen B63 82 F2
Oldbury B66 64 C8
Royal Leamington Spa
CV34 161 E2
Stourbridge DY8 81 A4
Oak Dr B23 56 C7
Oak Farm Cl B76 58 A7
Oak Farm Rd B30 103 E5
Oak Gn Dudley DY1 51 A5
Wolverhampton WV6 24 B3
Oak Gr Birmingham B31 102 E1
Kidderminster DY10 117 A5
Wolverhampton WV11 26 B7
Oak Hill WV3 24 C1
Oak Hill Dr B15 85 E7
Oak Ho WS6 5 A1
Oak House (Mus) B70 53 B2
Oak Ind Pk The DY6 49 E1
Oak La Allesley CV5 93 E1
Barston B92 109 B1
Kingswinford DY6 49 F1
West Bromwich B70 53 B3
Oak Leaf Dr B13 87 A3
Oak Leasow B32 84 B4
Oak Leigh Rd DY8 81 B2
Oak Leys WV3 24 C1
Oak Meadow Prim Sch
WV11 27 A7
Oak Park Rd DY8 60 F1
Oak Rd Brownhills WS9 16 A3
Catshill B61 137 B8
Dudley DY1 51 C3
Oldbury B68 84 C7
Tipton DY4 51 E6
Walsall, High Heath WS4 15 C1
Walsall, Pelsall Wood WS3 14 F5
West Bromwich B70 53 B2
Willenhall WV13 26 E2
Oak Rise B46 70 F5
Oak St Blackheath B64 62 D1
Brierley Hill DY5 61 F1
Dudley, Darby End DY2 62 E4
Dudley, West Coseley WV14 51 B7
Kingswinford DY6 60 D5
Wolverhampton WV3 25 A1
Oak Street Trad Est DY5 61 F1
Oak Tree Ave Coventry CV3 133 A6
Redditch B97 153 B4
Oak Tree Cl
Bentley Heath B93 127 E4
Royal Leamington Spa CV32 157 A2
Oak Tree Cres B62 83 F6
Oak Tree Ct B28 106 A5
Oak Tree Gdns 2 DY8 61 A1
Oak Tree La Birmingham
B29 85 E1
Hollywood B47 125 B6
Sambourne B96 159 B2
Oak Tree Rd CV3 135 A7
Oak Tree Wlk B79 20 F7
Oak Trees B47 125 A7
Oak View WS2 27 E3
Oak Way CV4 111 D2
Oak Wlk The B31 103 A1
Oakalls Ave B60 137 B2
Oakcroft Rd B13 105 C7
Oakdale B74 31 A1
Oakdale Cl Brierley Hill DY5 61 A7
Oldbury B68 64 A2
Oakdale Rd
Binley Woods CV3 135 C7
Birmingham B36 68 E7
Oldbury B68 64 A2
Oakdale Trad Est DY6 49 E1
Oakdene Cres CV10 73 D7
Oakdene Dr B45 138 C8
Oakdene Rd WS7 7 A6
Oaken Dr Solihull B91 106 F5
Willenhall WV12 27 E7
Oaken Gdns WS7 7 A8
Oaken Pk WV8 10 A2
Oakenfield WS13 3 A2
Oakenhayes Cres
Brownhills WS8 6 F1
Sutton Coldfield B76 58 C5
Oakenhayes Dr WS8 6 F1
Oakenshaw Rd
Redditch B98 154 A1
Solihull B90 106 D1
Oakeswell St WS10 42 A3
Oakey Cl CV6 95 F4
Oakeywell St 1 DY2 62 D8
Oakfield Ave
9 Birmingham,
Balsall Heath B12 87 A6
Birmingham, Sparkbrook B11 87 C6
Dudley DY1 51 B6
Kingswinford DY6 60 E5
Oakfield Cl Smethwick B66 65 C6
Stourbridge DY8 60 F1
Oakfield Ct 6 DY5 61 D2
Oakfield Dr Birmingham
B45 122 D4
Walsall WS3 15 B5
Oakfield Ho CV3 115 A1
Oakfield Rd
Birmingham,
Balsall Heath B12 86 E5
Birmingham, Erdington B24 56 F3
Birmingham, Selly Oak B29 86 B3
Codsall WV8 10 C2
Oakfield Rd continued
Coventry CV6 112 F5
Kidderminster DY11 116 B5
Smethwick B66 65 C6
Stourbridge DY8 61 A1
Stourbridge, Wollascote DY9 81 F2
Oakfield Trad Est B64 82 D8
Oakfields Way B91 108 B5
Oakford Dr CV5 111 F6
Oakhall Dr B93 127 F4
Oakham Ave DY2 62 E7
Oakham Cl B98 159 A5
Oakham Cres
Bulkington CV12 79 D2
Dudley DY2 62 E7
Oakham Ct 9 DY2 62 E8
Oakham Dr DY2 62 F8
Oakham Ho 7 B14 105 A3
Oakham Prim Sch B69 63 A7
Oakham Rd Birmingham B17 85 B7
Dudley DY2 62 F7
Tipton B69 63 A7
Oakham Way B92 89 B1
Oakhill Ave DY10 116 E4
Oakhill Cres B27 106 B8
Oakhill Dr DY5 81 B7
Oakhill Rd WS11 1 F2
Oakhurst WS14 9 C7
Oakhurst Ct B72 57 C8
Oakhurst Dr B60 137 A3
Oakhurst Rd
Birmingham B27 106 B8
Sutton Coldfield B72 57 C8
Oakington Ho B35 58 A3
Oakland Cl B91 107 E4
Oakland Dr DY3 50 B2
Oakland Rd
Birmingham,
Handsworth B21 65 E8
Birmingham,
Moseley B13 87 A3
Walsall WS3 28 E7
Oaklands Birmingham B13 87 A3
Curdworth B76 59 B5
Halesowen B62 84 A4
Wolverhampton WV3 39 B8
Oaklands Ave B17 85 B5
Oaklands Cl WS12 1 C6
Oaklands Croft B76 58 B7
Oaklands Dr B20 54 F2
Oaklands Gn WV14 40 D8
Oaklands Ind Est WS12 2 B3
Oaklands Prim Sch B27 88 C2
Oaklands Rd
Sutton Coldfield B74 46 B8
Wolverhampton WV3 39 B8
Oaklands The
Birmingham B37 90 A7
Coventry CV4 112 A2
Halesowen B62 83 F6
Kidderminster DY10 117 A7
Oaklands Way WS3 15 B3
Oaklea Dr B64 62 F2
Oakleaf Cl B32 84 C2
Oakleigh B31 103 C2
Oakleigh Ct 3 WV3 25 B2
Oakleigh Dr Codsall WV8 10 A3
Sedgley DY3 50 C7
Oakleigh Wlk 3 DY6 60 E8
Oakleighs DY8 60 C1
Oakley CV8 129 F1
Oakley Ave Aldridge WS9 30 A5
Tipton DY4 52 A6
Oakley Cl WS13 3 B2
Oakley Ct Bedworth CV12 77 D1
Birmingham B15 85 E5
Oakley Gr WV4 38 D5
Oakley Ho Bromsgrove B60 137 A1
Smethwick B66 65 C6
Oakley Rd
Birmingham, Sparkbrook B10 87 C7
Birmingham, Stirchley B30 104 B5
Wolverhampton WV4 38 D5
Oakley Wood Dr B91 107 E4
Oakley Wood Rd CV33 161 F1
Oakly Rd B97 153 D3
Oakmeadow Cl B33 69 D3
Oakmeadow Way B24 57 D3
Oakmoor Rd CV6 96 A4
Oakmount Cl WS3 14 F3
Oakmount Rd B74 45 A7
Oakridge Cl Redditch B98 154 C7
Willenhall WV12 27 C4
Oakridge Dr WV12 27 C4
Oakridge Rd CV32 157 C4
Oakroyd Cres CV10 72 D7
Oaks Cres WV3 25 A1
Oaks Dr Cannock WS11 1 C1
Featherstone WV10 11 F8
Wolverhampton WV3 25 B2
Wombourne WV5 49 A5
Oaks Pl CV6 96 A3
Oaks Prec CV8 147 E3
Oaks Rd CV8 147 E2
Oaks The Bedworth CV12 77 F2
Birmingham B34 69 B7
4 Royal Leamington Spa
CV32 161 D8
Sutton Coldfield B76 47 A3
Wolverhampton,
Merridale WV3 25 A2
Wolverhampton,
New Cross WV11 26 B5
Oakslade Dr B92 107 E8
Oakstreet Ind Est B64 62 D1
Oakthorpe Dr B37 69 F5
Oakthorpe Gdns B69 52 A2
Oaktree Cl B48 139 A7
Oaktree Farm Mobile
Homes Pk B94 141 B7
Oakwood Cl Brownhills WS9 15 E4
Essington WV11 13 B3
Shenstone WS14 18 A6
Oakwood Cres DY2 61 F6
Oakwood Croft B91 107 C1
Oakwood Ct B63 83 A4
Oakwood Dr
Birmingham B14 104 D4
Sutton Coldfield B74 44 E8
Oakwood Gr CV34 156 A1
Oakwood Rd Birmingham
B11 87 C3
Hollywood B47 125 A6
Smethwick B67 64 F4
Sutton Coldfield B73 45 E1
Walsall WS3 28 E7
Oakwood Specl Sch WS9 16 A3
Oakwood St B70 53 B5
Oakwoods WS11 4 D8
Oakworth Cl CV2 114 F8
Oast Ho B8 68 D4
Oasthouse Cl
Kingswinford DY6 60 A7
Stoke Heath B60 150 D6
Oaston Rd Birmingham B36 69 D8
Nuneaton CV11 73 D4
Oatfield Cl WS7 7 A4
Oatlands Way WV6 23 D3
Oatlands Wlk 3 B14 104 C2
Oatmill Cl WS10 41 E5
Oban Dr CV10 73 A2
Oban Rd Coventry CV6 95 F5
Hinckley LE10 75 A7
Solihull B92 88 F1
Oberon Cl Birmingham B45 102 A2
Nuneaton CV11 74 A1
Royal Leamington Spa CV34 161 E4
Oberon Dr B90 106 B1
Occupation Rd
Brownhills WS8 16 A4
Coventry CV2 114 C3
Occupation St DY1 51 A2
Ockam Croft B31 103 C2
Ocker Hill Inf Sch DY4 52 C8
Ocker Hill Jun Sch DY4 41 C1
Ocker Hill Rd DY4 52 C8
Oddicombe Croft CV3 133 D5
Oddingley Ct B23 56 C3
Oddingley Rd B31 103 C2
Odell Cres WS3 28 C7
Odell Pl B5 86 C5
Odell Rd WS3 28 B7
Odell Way WS3 28 B7
Odensil Gn B92 89 B2
Odiham Cl B79 21 C7
Odin Cl WS11 2 A5
Odnall La DY9 99 F3
Odstone Dr LE10 74 F8
Offa Dr CV8 148 A4
Offa Rd CV31 162 B5
Offa St B79 21 B5
Offa's Dr WV6 23 E5
Offadrive B79 21 C5
Offchurch La CV31 162 F6
Offchurch Rd CV32 157 E4
Offenham Cl B98 154 B6
Offenham Covert 5 B38 123 E8
Offenham Ho 3 B7 67 A4
Offini Cl B70 53 F2
Offmoor Rd B32 102 B8
Offmore Farm Cl DY10 117 C6
Offmore Fst Sch DY10 117 B6
Offmore La DY10 117 A6
Offmore Rd DY10 116 F6
Ogbury Cl B14 104 C2
Ogley Cres WS8 16 A7
Ogley Dr B75 47 A5
Ogley Hay Rd
Burntwood,
Chase Terrace WS7 7 B8
Burntwood,
New Town WS7, WS8 7 A3
Ogley Hey Jun Mixed Sch
WS8 15 F8
Ogley Rd WS8 16 A7
Okeefe Cl B11 87 B6
Okehampton Rd CV3 133 E5
Okement Dr WV11 26 C5
Oken Ct CV35 160 D7
Oken Rd CV34 160 D8
Olaf Pl CV2 115 A7
Old Abbey Gdns B17 85 D4
Old Acre Cl B76 57 D6
Old Bakery Ct DY9 99 A5
Old Bank Pl B72 46 C5
Old Bank Rd B31 103 B2
Old Barn Rd
Birmingham B30 103 D6
Stourbridge DY8 61 A1
Old Beeches B23 56 C8
Old Bell Rd B23 57 B6
Old Birchills WS2 28 C3
Old Birmingham Rd
Alvechurch B48 139 B8
Catshill B60 137 C8
Marlbrook B45 121 E1
Old Bridge St B19 66 C6
Old Bridge Wlk B65 62 F5
Old Bromford La B8 68 C6
Old Brookside B33 68 E2
Old Budbrooke Rd CV35 160 A7
Old Bush St DY5 61 E3
Old Camp Hill B12 87 A8
Old Canal Wlk DY4 52 B5
Old Castle Gr WS8 6 F2
Old Chapel Rd B67 64 F3
Old Chapel Wlk B68 64 A4
Old Chester Rd S DY10 116 E2
Old Church CE Prim Sch
WS10 41 C6
Old Church Ct B17 85 B5
Old Church Gn B33 68 E2
Old Church Rd
Birmingham B17 85 B4
Coventry CV6 96 A1
Water Orton B46 59 B3
Old Crescent Ct 11 B68 84 B8
Old Crest Ave B98 153 E2
Old Croft La B34 69 C7
Old Cross St DY4 51 E5
Old Crown Cl B32 84 B1
Old Crown Mews CV2 96 D5
Old Damson La B92 90 A2
Old Dominion Wks WV1 40 A7
Old End La WV14 51 C7
Old Fallings Cres WV10 25 F6
Old Fallings La WV10 25 F8
Old Fallow Ave WS11 1 E3
Old Fallow Rd WS11 1 E3
Old Falls Cl WS6 4 D3
Old Farm Gr B14 105 D5
Old Farm Mdw WV3 38 C8
Old Farm Rd B33 68 E4
Old Field Rd WS10 41 E1
Old Fordrove B76 46 D3
Old Forest Way B34 69 B6
Old Forge Dr B98 159 C8
Old Forge Trad Est DY9 81 E6
Old Grange Rd B11 87 C4
Old Green La CV8 129 C1
Old Grove Gdns DY9 81 D3
Old Hall Cl DY8 81 A8
Old Hall La Norton Canes
WS11 5 B7
Walsall WS9 44 B5
Old Hall Sch WS2 27 E5
Old Hall St WV1 163 C2
Old Ham La DY9 81 D2
Old Hampton La WV10 12 C2
Old Hawne La B63 83 A5
Old Heath Cres WV1 26 A1
Old Heath Rd WV1 26 A2
Old Hedging La B77 35 D5
Old Hednesford Rd WS11 2 A3
Old Hill WV6 24 D5
Old Hill Ind Est WS3 28 C8
Old Hill Prim Sch B64 62 F1
Old Hill Sta B64 83 A8
Old Hinckley Rd CV10 73 D5
Old Hobicus La B68 64 B5
Old Horns Cres B44 44 C2
Old House La Corley CV7 94 A7
Romsley B62 101 B1
Old Kingsbury Rd B76 58 C5
Old La Featherstone WV10 12 C7
Rowney Green B48 140 D4
Walsall WS3 28 C8
Wolverhampton WV6 23 F2
Old Landywood La WV11 13 D7
Old Langley Hall B75 47 C4
Old Level Way DY2 62 D4
Old Lime Gdns B38 123 E8
Old Lindens Cl B74 44 E7
Old Lode La B92 89 C3
Old London Rd WS14 9 D1
Old Manor Cl B78 34 E5
Old Manor Flats WV6 24 D5
Old Meadow Rd B31 123 C7
Old Meeting Rd WV14 51 C8
Old Meeting St B70 53 B5
Old Meeting Yd CV12 78 B3
Old Mill Ave CV4 132 D5
Old Mill Cl B90 105 D2
Old Mill Gdns
Birmingham B33 68 E2
Walsall WS4 15 C2
Old Mill Gr B20 55 C2
Old Mill Rd B46 70 F7
Old Milverton CV32 156 C3
Old Milverton La CV32 156 E5
Old Milverton Rd CV32 156 C2
Old Moat Dr B31 103 B3
Old Moat Way B8 68 B6
Old Oak Cl WS9 30 B8
Old Oak Rd B38 104 A2
Old Oscott Hill B44 44 F2
Old Oscott La B44 55 E8
Old Park Cl B6 66 E7
Old Park Ind Est WS10 41 E4
Old Park La B69 64 A5
Old Park Prim Sch WS10 41 E5
Old Park Rd Dudley DY1 51 A5
Wednesbury WS10 41 E4
Old Park Special Sch DY1 61 F8
Old Park Wlk B6 66 E7
Old Penkridge Mews WS11 1 D1
Old Penkridge Rd WS11 1 C2
Old Penn's Yd CV12 78 A2
Old Pk B29 103 A5
Old Pl WS3 28 C8
Old Pleck Rd WS2 42 C7
Old Port Cl DY4 52 B2
Old Portway B38 123 E7
Old Postway B19 66 D7
Old Quarry Cl B45 121 F8
Old Quarry Dr DY3 50 D5
Old Rd CV7 92 E1
Old Rectory Gdns WS9 30 C6
Old Rectory La B48 139 B7
Old School Cl WV13 27 A2
Old School Mews CV32 157 B3
Old Scott Cl B33 69 C2
Old Smithy Pl B18 66 A5
Old Snow Hill B3, B4,B19 164 B4

Old Sq 1 CV34 160 E6
Old Sq The 1 WS1 28 E1
Old Square B4 164 C3
Old Stables Wlk 2 B7 67 C7
Old Stafford Rd WV10 11 C8
Old Station Rd
Birmingham B33 68 D4
Bromsgrove B60 137 A1
Hampton in A B92 109 A8
Old Stone Cl B45 101 F1
Old Stone Yd CV32 156 E1
Old Stowheath La WV1 26 C1
Old Swinford Hospital Sch DY8 81 A4
Old Tokengate 2 B17 85 D6
Old Town Cl B38 103 F2
Old Town La WS3 14 F3
Old Vicarage Cl Walsall WS3 15 A2
Wombourne WV5 49 B7
Old Walsall Rd B42 54 F7
Old Warstone La WV11 13 B8
Old Warwick Ct 1 B92 88 E1
Old Warwick Rd
Lapworth B94, CV35 144 D3
Royal Leamington Spa CV31 161 E7
Solihull B92 88 E1
Old Wharf Rd DY8 80 F6
Old Winnings Rd CV7 94 F6
Oldacre Rd B68 84 A7
Oldany Way CV10 72 F2
Oldberrow Cl 4 B90 127 A6
Oldbury Cl B98 154 B6
Oldbury Green Ret Pk B69 63 F8
Oldbury Ho B68 64 C2
Oldbury Rd Blackheath B65 63 D2
Nuneaton CV10 72 A8
Smethwick B66 64 D7
West Bromwich B70 52 F2
Oldbury Ring Way B69 63 F8
Oldbury Road Ind Est
Smethwick B66 64 D7
West Bromwich B70 52 F2
Oldbury St WS10 42 B3
Olde Hall Rd WV10 12 C7
Oldfallings Inf & Jun Schs WV10 26 A8
Oldfield Dr DY8 81 A3
Oldfield Rd Birmingham B12 87 A6
Coventry CV5 112 E3
Dudley WV14 51 A8
Oldfields Blackheath B64 82 D8
Hagley DY9 99 B6
Oldham Ave CV2 114 E4
Oldhouse Farm Cl B28 105 F6
Oldington Gr B91 127 B8
Oldington Trad Est DY11 116 B1
Oldknow Jun Sch B10 87 E7
Oldknow Rd B10 87 E7
Oldnall Cl DY9 81 F4
Oldnall Rd
Kidderminster DY10 117 A4
Stourbridge B63, DY9 82 A4
Oldswinford Prim Sch DY8 81 A3
Oldway Dr B91 107 E2
Oldwich La E Honiley CV8 145 E8
Knowle CV8 129 D1
Oldwich La W B93 145 C8
Olga Dr DY4 41 B1
Olinthus Ave WV11 26 E7
Olive Ave Coventry CV2 114 D5
Wolverhampton WV4 39 E5
Olive Dr B62 83 C8
Olive Hill Prim Sch B62 83 D7
Olive Hill Rd B62 83 D8
Olive La B62 83 D8
Olive Mount B69 63 D8
Olive Pl B14 104 E7
Oliver Cl 1 DY2 62 E8
Oliver Cres WV14 40 F2
Oliver Ct B65 63 B2
Oliver Rd
Birmingham, Erdington B23 56 F6
Birmingham, Ladywood B16 65 F2
Smethwick B66 65 C3
Oliver St Birmingham B7 67 B5
Coventry CV6 113 F6
Olivier Way CV2 115 B8
Ollerton Rd B26 88 F7
Ollison Dr B74 30 F2
Olliver Cl B62 84 A3
Olorenshaw Rd B26 89 D5
Olton Ave CV5 111 E4
Olton Bridge B92 106 F8
Olton Bvd E B27 88 C2
Olton Bvd W B11 87 F3
Olton Croft B27 88 D2
Olton Mere B92 88 E1
Olton Pl CV11 72 F4
Olton Rd B90 106 B5
Olton Sta B92 88 E1
Olton Wharf B92 88 E2
Olympus Ave CV34 161 D5
Olympus Cl CV5 111 B8
Omar Rd CV2 114 D2
Ombersley Cl Oldbury B69 63 D5
Redditch B98 159 C7
Ombersley Ho 4 B38 103 D2
Ombersley Rd
Birmingham B12 87 A6
Halesowen B63 82 F2
One Stop Sh Ctr B42 55 D3
Onibury Rd B21 54 D1
Onley Terr CV4 132 C7
Onslow Cres B92 89 A1
Onslow Croft CV32 156 F2
Onslow Rd B11 88 A4
Ontario Cl B38 124 A8
Oozells St B1 66 C2
Oozells St N B16 66 B2
Open Field Cl B31 103 C2
Openfield Croft B46 59 C2
Orangery The DY9 99 D7
Oratory Dr CV3 134 C6
Oratory Prim Sch B16 65 F2
Orbital Way WS11 4 F6
Orchard Ave Cannock WS11 1 C2
Solihull B91 107 D5
Orchard Cl Birmingham B21 54 F1
Blackheath B65 63 A3
Cheslyn Hay WS6 4 E3
Coleshill B46 70 F7
Curdworth B76 59 B7
Hagley DY9 99 B4
Halesowen B63 82 C6
Hinckley LE10 76 A5
Nuneaton CV10 72 B7
Sutton Coldfield B73 57 A8
Tamworth B77 35 C5
Walsall WS4 29 C5
Willenhall WV13 27 B1
Orchard Cres Coventry CV3 133 C8
Stoke Prior B60 150 C3
Wolverhampton WV3 38 B7
Orchard Croft B45 138 D8
Orchard Ct
Birmingham, Erdington B24 57 A5
Birmingham, Stockland Green B23 56 B4
Blackheath B65 63 B3
Coventry CV3 115 A1
Kingswinford DY6 60 D6
Wolverhampton WV3 38 B7
Orchard Dr Birmingham B31 122 F7
Coventry CV5 111 C4
Orchard Gr Aldridge WS9 30 B4
Dudley DY3 50 B3
Sutton Coldfield B74 31 F3
Wolverhampton WV4 39 A4
Orchard Ho CV6 96 A4
Orchard La Codsall WV8 10 B3
Stourbridge DY9 81 E6
Orchard Meadow Wlk B35 58 B3
Orchard Pl B80 159 F8
Orchard Rd Birmingham B24 57 B5
Bromsgrove B61 136 F4
Dudley DY2 62 C2
Tanworth-in-A B94 143 C6
Walsall WS5 43 B3
Willenhall WV13 27 B1
Wolverhampton WV11 26 C7
Orchard Rise B26 88 F7
Orchard St Bedworth CV12 78 B4
Brierley Hill DY5 61 D4
Hinckley LE10 75 E8
Kidderminster DY10 116 E6
Nuneaton CV11 73 D4
Redditch B98 153 E3
Tamworth, Kettlebrook B77 21 C3
Tamworth, The Leys B79 21 B5
Tipton DY4 51 F2
Orchard The Bilston WV14 40 E5
Birmingham B37 89 F8
Walsall WS3 14 D2
Wolverhampton WV6 24 E6
Orchard Tower B31 102 F7
Orchard Villas Fairfield B61 120 D2
Wythall B47 124 F1
Orchard Way
Birmingham, Acock's Green B27 88 B4
Birmingham, Balsall Heath B12 86 E6
Birmingham, Great Barr B43 43 F1
Hollywood B47 125 A8
Nuneaton CV10 72 C6
Studley B80 159 E2
Orchards The
Cheswick Green B90 126 D4
Hollywood B47 125 A7
Sutton Coldfield B74 46 A8
Orcheston Wlk B14 104 D2
Orchid Cl B66 64 D7
Orchid Dr B19 66 D6
Ordnance Rd CV6 113 E5
Oregon Cl DY6 60 F6
Oregon Dr WV12 27 E7
Oregon Gdns WS7 6 F8
Oregon Ho 3 B36 57 F1
Orford Gr B21 65 C8
Oriel Cl Cannock WS11 4 E8
Dudley DY1 50 E2
Oriel Dr WV10 11 D3
Oriel Ho B37 70 A3
Oriel Villas 4 B11 87 C5
Oriole Gr DY10 117 B2
Orion Cl Birmingham B8 68 B4
Great Wyrley WS6 4 F1
Orion Cres CV2 96 E2
Orion Way WS11 1 F5
Orkney Ave B34 68 F7
Orkney Cl Hinckley LE10 71 C1
Nuneaton CV10 73 A2
Orkney Croft B36 70 B7
Orlando Cl WS1 42 E8
Orlando Ho 4 WS1 42 E8
Orlescote Rd CV4 132 E6
Ormande Cl B63 82 B7
Orme Cl DY5 81 B8
Ormes La WV6 24 C3
Ormond Pl WV14 40 F6
Ormond Rd B45 101 F1
Ormsby Gr B27 106 B7
Ormscliffe Rd B45 122 B6
Orphanage Rd B24 57 B6
Orpington Dr CV6 95 D4
Orpington Rd B44 44 E3
Orpwood Rd B33 69 B2
Orslow Wlk WV10 26 A5
Orton Ave B76 58 A6
Orton Cl B46 59 A3
Orton Gr WV4 38 D4
Orton La WV4, WV5 38 A2
Orton Rd CV6 95 D4
Orton Way B35 58 A1
Orwell Cl Nuneaton CV10 72 A5
Stourbridge DY8 80 D4
Wednesfield WV11 26 F5
Orwell Ct CV1 165 C4
Orwell Dr Birmingham B38 123 C8
West Bromwich B71 53 D6
Orwell Pas B5 164 C2
Orwell Rd Coventry CV1 113 F1
Walsall WS1 43 B8
Osbaston Cl Coventry CV5 111 E4
Hinckley LE10 71 F3
Osberton Dr DY1 50 F2
Osborn Ct B73 46 B1
Osborn Rd B11 87 C6
Osborne B79 20 D7
Osborne Cl Birmingham B6 67 A7
Brierley Hill DY5 81 F8
Kidderminster DY10 117 B6
Osborne Ct CV31 162 A4
Osborne Dr WS10 41 D8
Osborne Gr B19 66 C7
Osborne Jun & Inf Sch B23 57 A5
Osborne Rd
Birmingham, Erdington B23 56 F5
Birmingham, Handsworth B21 65 F8
Coventry CV5 133 A8
West Bromwich B70 53 C3
Wolverhampton WV4 38 F5
Osborne Rd S 1 B23 56 F4
Osborne Tower B6 67 A8
Osbourne Croft B90 126 D5
Oscott Cir B6 55 F3
Oscott Coll B73 45 D1
Oscott Ct B23 56 E8
Oscott Gdns B42 55 E3
Oscott Rd B42 55 E3
Oscott School La B44 44 E2
Osier Gr B23 56 B6
Osier Pl WV1 25 F2
Osier St WV1 25 F2
Osler St B16 65 F2
Oslo Gdns CV2 115 A7
Osmaston Rd
Birmingham B17 85 B3
Stourbridge DY8 80 F2
Osmington Cl B63 82 D6
Osnor Ct B60 151 B7
Osprey B77 36 A6
Osprey Cl Coventry CV2 115 B6
Nuneaton CV11 79 B8
Osprey Dr DY1 51 A1
Osprey Gr WS12 2 C1
Osprey Ho B80 159 D4
Osprey Park Dr DY10 117 B3
Osprey Rd B27 88 D2
Ostler Cl DY6 60 B7
Oswald Rd 2 CV32 161 D8
Oswald St B98 153 E3
Oswestry Cl B97 158 C7
Oswestry Ct B11 87 B6
Oswin Gr CV2 114 C4
Oswin Pl WS3 28 F5
Oswin Rd WS3 28 F5
Other Rd B98 153 E4
Otley Gr B9 68 C3
Ottawa Tower 2 B5 86 D7
Otter Croft B34 69 D5
Otterburn Cl WS12 2 E2
Otterstone Cl DY3 39 C2
Ottery B77 36 B5
Oughton Rd B12 87 A7
Oulsham Ct 11 B13 87 B2
Oulton Cl DY11 116 D8
Oundle Rd B44 55 F7
Ounsdale Cres WV5 49 A7
Ounsdale Dr DY2 62 C4
Ounsdale Rd WV5 49 A7
Ounty John La DY8 81 A1
Our Lady & Kenelms RC Sch B63 83 A4
Our Lady of Compassion RC Prim Sch B92 106 D7
Our Lady of Fatima RC Sch B17 84 F7
Our Lady of Lourdes RC Inf & Jun Sch B13 105 D5
Our Lady of the Angels RC Fst Sch CV11 73 C3
Our Lady of the Assumption RC Prim Sch CV4 111 E1
Our Lady Of the Wayside RC Prim Sch B90 126 C8
Our Lady & St Chad's RC Sch WV10 25 F7
Our Lady & St Rose of Lima RC Jun &Inf Sch B29 103 B8
Our Lady & St Rose of Lima Sch B29 85 B1
Our Lady & St Rose RC Prim Sch B29 103 A8
Our Lady & St Teresa's RC Comb Sch CV32 157 D5
Our Lady's RC Jun & Inf Sch B33 69 D2
Outermarch Rd CV6 113 C7
Outfields B13 104 E6
Outlands Dr LE10 71 B2
Outmore Rd B33 69 B1
Outwood Cl B98 158 E7
Oval Rd Birmingham B24 56 E1
Tipton DY4 51 F6
Oval The Dudley DY1 61 E8
Smethwick B67 64 D2
Wednesbury WS10 41 F4
Over Brunton Cl B31 103 B2
Over Green Dr B37 69 F5
Over Mill Dr B29 86 B2
Over Pool Rd B8 68 A6
Over St CV6 114 A8
Overbare Cl B94 142 A1
Overberry Cl CV2 96 D2
Overbrook Cl DY3 50 C2
Overbury Cl
Birmingham B31 103 C3
Halesowen B63 83 B2
Overbury Rd B31 103 C3
Overdale B96 158 E1
Overdale Ave B76 57 F6
Overdale Cl WS2 27 C3
Overdale Ct B13 86 F4
Overdale Dr WS2 27 D3
Overdale Rd Birmingham B32 84 E5
Coventry CV5 112 C3
Overell Gr CV32 156 D2
Overend Rd B63, B64 82 D7
Overend St B70 53 D2
Overfield Dr WV14 40 A3
Overfield Rd Birmingham B32 84 F1
Dudley DY1 61 E8
Overhill Rd WS7 7 B5
Overlea Ave B27 88 B3
Overmoor Cl B19 66 C7
Overseal Rd WV11 26 E8
Overslade Cres CV6 112 E8
Overslade Rd B91 106 F2
Oversley Rd B76 58 A6
Overton Cl B28 106 A6
Overton Dr B46 59 C3
Overton Gr B27 106 C8
Overton La WS7 7 C4
Overton Pl Birmingham B7 67 A3
West Bromwich B71 53 D6
Overton Rd B27 106 C8
Overton Wlk WV4 38 C6
Overtons Cl CV31 162 F5
Overwood Croft B8 67 E3
Overwoods Rd B77 36 A4
Owen Pl WV14 40 D6
Owen Rd Bilston WV14 40 D6
Willenhall WV13 41 C8
Wolverhampton WV3 39 A8
Owen Road Ind Est WV13 27 C1
Owen St Darlaston WS10 41 D7
Dudley DY2 62 E8
Tipton DY4 51 E5
Owenford Rd CV6 113 C7
Owens Croft B38 104 A1
Owens Way B64 63 A1
Ownall Rd B34 69 C6
Ox Cl CV2 114 A6
Ox Leasow B32 84 C2
Ox Leys Rd B75, B76 47 D3
Ox St DY3 50 D5
Oxbarn Ave WV3 38 E7
Oxendon Way CV3 134 E8
Oxenton Croft B63 82 D2
Oxford Cl Birmingham B8 68 B5
Great Wyrley WS6 4 F3
Nuneaton CV11 73 F8
Oxford Dr Birmingham B27 88 D4
Stourbridge DY8 80 F4
Oxford Gn WS11 4 F8
Oxford Pl 12 CV32 156 F1
Oxford Rd
Birmingham, Acock's Green B27 88 C3
Birmingham, Erdington B23 56 F4
Birmingham, Moseley B13 87 A2
Cannock WS11 4 F8
Ryton-on-D CV8 134 F1
Smethwick B66 65 A7
West Bromwich B70 53 B3
Oxford Row 14 CV32 156 F1
Oxford St Bilston WV14 40 F5
Birmingham, Digbeth B5 164 D2
Birmingham, Stirchley B30 104 A7
Coventry CV1 113 E3
Dudley DY1 51 B1
Kidderminster DY10 116 E5
Royal Leamington Spa CV32 156 F1
Walsall WS2 42 C7
Wednesbury WS10 42 B3
Wolverhampton WV1 163 D2
Oxford Street Ind Pk WV14 40 F5
Oxford Street Island WV14 40 E5
Oxford Terr WS10 42 B2
Oxford Trad Est B5 164 D2
Oxhayes Cl CV7 130 C6
Oxhill Cl B98 154 E1
Oxhill Rd Birmingham B21 54 E2
Solihull B90 105 C2
Oxleasow Rd B98 154 E4
Oxley Ave WV10 25 C6
Oxley Cl Dudley DY2 62 B2
Great Wyrley WS6 4 F1
Oxley Dr CV3 133 C3
Oxley Gr B29 103 A8
Oxley La WV1 163 B4
Oxley Links Rd WV10 25 B8
Oxley Moor Rd WV10 25 A8
Oxley Prim Sch WV10 25 C7
Oxley St WV1 25 C4
Oxlip Cl WS5 43 A3
Oxpiece Dr B36 68 D8
Oxstall Cl B76 58 D5
Oxted Cl WV11 26 F5
Oxted Croft B23 56 E3
Oxwood La B32 101 D4
Oxygen St B7 164 D4

Pace Cres WV14 41 A2
Packhorse La B47 124 E6
Packington Ave
Allesley CV5 112 B6
Birmingham B34 69 D5
Packington Ct B74 31 E4
Packington La
Little Packington CV7 91 C6
Outwoods B46, CV7 92 B8
Weeford B78 19 F5
White Stitch CV7 92 A3
Packington Pl 4 CV31 162 A7
Packmore St CV34 160 F8
Packwood Cl
Bentley Heath B93 127 E4
Birmingham B20 55 A2
Redditch B97 152 F1
Royal Leamington Spa CV31 162 C5
Willenhall WV13 40 F8
Packwood Cotts B93 127 F1
Packwood Ct B91 107 C5
Packwood Dr B43 43 D1
Packwood Gn CV5 112 A3
Packwood Ho
Birmingham B15 86 C8
Sutton Coldfield B73 46 A3
Packwood House B94 144 A5
Packwood La B94 144 A4
Packwood Rd
Birmingham B26 89 B8
Lapworth B94 144 A7
Tipton B69 52 A1
Padarn Cl DY3 39 C1
Padbury WV9 11 B3
Padbury Ho B31 102 E5
Paddeston Dr B8 67 D4
Paddiford Pl CV10 72 C3
Paddington Rd B21 54 C1
Paddington Wlk WS2 27 F4
Paddock Dr Birmingham B26 89 A7
Dorridge B93 128 A2
Paddock La Aldridge WS9 30 A5
Great Wyrley WS6 5 A3
Redditch B98 158 E7
Walsall WS1 28 F1
Paddock The Bilston WV14 40 D1
Birmingham B31 103 C4
Codsall WV8 10 A2
Dudley DY3 50 E5
Lichfield WS14 9 C5
Perton WV6 23 D4
Stoke Heath B60 150 D6
Stourbridge DY9 99 B8
Paddock View W6 25 B5
Paddocks Cl B78 22 F1
Paddocks Gn B18 66 A5
Paddocks Rd B47 124 F6
Paddocks The
Bulkington CV12 79 B3
Kenilworth CV8 148 B5
Warwick CV34 160 F7
Paddys Wide Water Est DY5 61 C5
Padgate Cl B35 58 B3
Padgets La B98 154 D4
Padmore Ct CV31 162 B6
Padstow B77 21 F5
Padstow Cl CV11 73 F5
Padstow Rd Birmingham B24 57 D4
Coventry CV4 131 E8
Paganal Dr B70 53 E1
Paganel Dr DY1 51 C3
Paganel Inf Sch B29 85 A2
Paganel Jun Sch B29 85 A2
Paganel Rd B29 85 A2
Pagat Mews B76 47 A2
Page Rd CV4 131 E7
Pageant Ct B12 86 E5
Pages Cl B75 46 C5
Pages Ct B43 43 E1
Pages La B43 43 E1
Paget Cl Bromsgrove B61 136 E2
Dudley WV14 51 B8
Paget Ct CV2 96 B3
Paget Ho DY4 52 B3
Paget Jun & Inf Sch B24 57 C4
Paget Rd Birmingham B24 57 D4
Wolverhampton WV6 24 F3
Paget St WV1 163 A4
Pagham Cl WV9 10 F2
Pagnell Gr B13 105 C6
Paignton Rd B16 65 D3
Pailton Cl CV2 96 C2
Pailton Gr B29 85 B1
Pailton Rd B90 106 B5
Painswick Cl Redditch B98 158 E6
Walsall WS5 43 B3
Painswick Rd B28 105 F7
Paint Cup Row DY2 62 C2
Painters Cnr 8 B66 65 C5

Pake's Croft **3** CV6 .... 113 A5
Pakefield Rd B30 .... 104 C3
Pakenham Cl B76 .... 57 F8
Pakenham Ho B76 .... 57 F8
Pakenham Rd B15 .... 86 C7
Pakenham Village B15 .... 86 C7
Pakfield Wlk B6 .... 66 F8
Palace Cl B65 .... 63 D4
Palace Dr B66 .... 64 D8
Palace Rd B9 .... 67 E1
Pale La B17 .... 84 F8
Pale St DY3 .... 50 E5
Palefield Rd B90 .... 126 F6
Palermo Ave CV3 .... 133 E6
Palethorpe Rd DY4 .... 52 A8
Palfrey Jun & Inf Schs
  WS1 .... 42 D7
Palfrey Rd DY8 .... 80 D5
Pallasades Sh Ctr The
  B2 .... 164 B2
Pallett Dr CV11 .... 73 F7
Palm Croft DY5 .... 81 C8
Palm Tree Ave CV2 .... 96 C2
Palmcourt Ave B28 .... 105 E7
Palmer Cl WV11 .... 12 F1
Palmer La CV1 .... 165 B3
Palmer Rd Hinckley LE10 ... 71 B2
  Whitnash CV31 .... 162 B4
Palmer St B9 .... 67 A2
Palmers Cl Codsall WV8 ..... 10 C1
  Solihull B90 .... 106 B5
Palmers Cross Prim Sch
  WV6 .... 24 D8
Palmers Gr B36 .... 68 E8
Palmers Rd B98 .... 154 F5
Palmers Way WV8 .... 10 C1
Palmerston Dr B69 .... 52 D2
Palmerston Rd
  Birmingham B11 .... 87 B6
  Coventry CV5 .... 132 F8
Palmvale Croft B26 .... 89 A7
Palomino Pl B16 .... 65 F2
Pamela Rd B31 .... 103 A3
Pan Croft B36 .... 68 C7
Pancras Cl CV2 .... 96 E1
Pandora Rd CV2 .... 114 E7
Pangbourne Cl CV11 .... 73 F8
Pangbourne Rd CV2 .... 114 C8
Pangfield Pk CV5 .... 112 C4
Panjab Gdns B67 .... 64 F6
Pannel Croft B19 .... 66 D6
Panther Croft B34 .... 69 D5
Papenham Gn CV4 .... 132 A8
Paper Mill Dr B98 .... 154 B5
Paper Mill End B44 .... 55 D6
Papworth Dr B61 .... 136 F5
Papyrus Way B36 .... 57 F1
Par Gn B38 .... 103 D1
Parade Birmingham B1 ..... 164 A3
  Royal Leamington Spa
  CV32 .... 161 F8
Parade The Birmingham B37 . 70 A5
  Blackheath B64 .... 82 E8
  Brownhills WS8 .... 6 E1
  Dudley DY1 .... 51 B2
  6 Hinckley LE10 .... 75 D8
  Kingswinford DY6 .... 60 B7
  Nuneaton CV11 .... 73 C3
  Sutton Coldfield B72 .... 46 B5
Parade View WS8 .... 15 E8
Paradise DY2 .... 62 D8
Paradise Circus
  Queensway B1, B3 .... 164 A2
Paradise Ct B28 .... 105 D6
Paradise Ho CV6 .... 113 F7
Paradise La Birmingham
  B28 .... 105 E6
  Walsall WS3 .... 14 F3
  Wolverhampton WV10 .... 11 E8
Paradise Row B60 .... 136 F2
Paradise St Birmingham B3 . 164 B2
  Coventry CV1 .... 165 C1
  Warwick CV34 .... 160 F8
  West Bromwich B70 .... 53 C3
Paradise Way CV7 .... 97 B1
Paragon Way CV7 .... 96 B8
Parbrook Cl CV4 .... 131 E8
Parbury B77 .... 35 D5
Parchments The WS13 .... 3 B1
Pardington Cl B92 .... 107 E8
Pargeter Ct **1** WS2 .... 28 C2
Pargeter Rd B67 .... 64 F2
Pargeter St Stourbridge
  DY8 .... 80 F4
  Walsall WS2 .... 28 C3
Parish Gdns DY9 .... 81 C1
Parish Hill B61 .... 120 D1
Parisienne Ho CV5 .... 112 E2
Park App B23 .... 56 C2
Park Ave
  1 Birmingham,
  Balsall Heath B12 .... 86 F5
  Birmingham, Hockley B18 . 66 A6
  Birmingham,
  King's Norton B30 .... 104 A5
  Blackheath B65 .... 63 C3
  Burntwood WS7 .... 7 B5
  Coleshill B46 .... 70 F6
  Coventry CV5 .... 95 C3
  Norton Canes WS11 .... 6 A5
  Nuneaton CV11 .... 73 C3
  Oldbury B68 .... 64 B3
  Smethwick B67 .... 64 F4
  Solihull B91 .... 107 D3
  Studley B80 .... 159 E3

Park Ave continued
  Tipton DY4 .... 51 E5
  Willenhall WV13 .... 26 F2
  Wolverhampton WV1 .... 163 A4
  Wolverhampton,
  Goldthorn Park WV4 .... 39 C5
  Wombourne WV5 .... 49 A5
Park Bldgs DY3 .... 50 C4
Park Butts Ringway DY11 . 116 D6
Park Cir B6 .... 66 F7
Park Cl Brownhills WS8 ...... 15 F8
  Cheslyn Hay WS6 .... 4 E3
  Dudley DY1 .... 51 B7
  Kenilworth CV8 .... 148 B5
  Solihull B92 .... 89 D2
  Sutton Coldfield B24 .... 57 D5
  Tipton B69 .... 63 C7
Park Cres
  West Bromwich B71 .... 53 D4
  Wolverhampton WV1 .... 163 A3
Park Croft B47 .... 125 A5
Park Ct Allesley CV5 .... 112 B6
  Blackheath B65 .... 63 C3
  Kidderminster DY11 .... 116 D5
  Redditch B98 .... 154 A3
  Sutton Coldfield B73 .... 45 F1
Park Dale Ct WV1 .... 25 A3
Park Dale E WV1 .... 25 A3
Park Dale W WV1 .... 25 A3
Park Dr Little Aston B74 ..... 31 C4
  Royal Leamington Spa CV31 . 161 E7
  Sutton Coldfield B74 .... 31 F2
  Wolverhampton WV4 .... 39 C5
Park Edge B17 .... 85 C7
Park End WS14 .... 9 E7
Park End Dr B32 .... 84 D1
Park Farm Ind Est B98 ..... 159 C7
Park Farm Rd
  Birmingham B43 .... 44 B3
  Tamworth B77 .... 21 C1
Park Gr Birmingham B10 .... 87 D8
  Water Orton B46 .... 59 C2
Park Hall Cl WS5 .... 43 C6
Park Hall Cres B36 .... 69 C8
Park Hall Inf Sch WS5 .... 43 C7
Park Hall Jun Sch WS5 ...... 43 C7
Park Hall Rd Walsall WS5 .. 43 D6
  Wolverhampton WV4 .... 39 D5
Park Hall Sch B36 .... 58 E1
Park Head Cres DY2 .... 62 B8
Park Head Rd DY2 .... 62 B8
Park Hill Birmingham B13 .. 86 E4
  Blackheath B65 .... 63 B1
  Kenilworth CV8 .... 148 B5
  Wednesbury WS10 .... 42 C4
Park Hill Cty Mid Sch
  CV8 .... 148 C5
Park Hill Dr B20 .... 54 F4
Park Hill Jun & Inf Sch
  B13 .... 86 F4
Park Hill La Allesley CV5 .. 112 A6
  Coventry CV5 .... 112 A5
Park Hill Prim Sch
  Coventry CV5 .... 112 A4
  Wednesbury WS10 .... 42 C4
Park Hill Rd Birmingham
  B17 .... 85 C6
  Smethwick B67 .... 65 A5
Park Hill St DY2 .... 62 E8
Park Ho **1** B66 .... 65 C5
Park Inn DY4 .... 52 A4
Park La Berkswell CV7 ..... 110 B2
  Birmingham B26 .... 90 C4
  Birmingham, Aston B6 ...... 66 F7
  Birmingham, Castle Vale B35 . 58 C4
  Birmingham,
  Handsworth B21 .... 54 B3
  Fazeley B78 .... 20 E2
  Great Wyrley WS6 .... 4 F3
  Halesowen B63 .... 82 B6
  Harvington DY10 .... 118 A2
  Kidderminster DY11 .... 116 D6
  Kingswinford DY6 .... 60 E7
  Nuneaton CV10 .... 72 A3
  Oldbury B69 .... 64 A6
  Shenstone WS14 .... 18 B4
  Wednesbury WS10 .... 42 A5
  Wolverhampton WV10 .... 25 E6
Park La E DY4 .... 52 B4
Park La W DY4 .... 51 F4
Park Lane Ind Est
  West Bromwich B21 .... 54 B1
  Wolverhampton WV10 .... 25 E5
Park Lime Dr WS4 .... 29 B4
Park Lime Pits Ctry Pk
  WS4 .... 29 C4
Park Mall WS1 .... 28 E2
Park Meadow Ave WV14 .... 40 C8
Park Mews B29 .... 85 B1
Park Paling The CV3 .... 133 E7
Park Pl B7 .... 67 C7
Park Prim Sch WS7 .... 7 B6
Park Rd Bedworth CV12 .... 78 B2
  Bilston WV14 .... 40 C5
  Birmingham, Aston B6 ...... 67 A7
  Birmingham, Hockley B18 . 66 A6
  Birmingham, Moseley B13 . 86 F4
  Birmingham, Sparkhill B11 . 87 C3
  Birmingham,
  Stockland Green B23 .... 56 C2
  Brierley Hill DY5 .... 81 F8
  Burntwood,
  Chase Terrace WS7 .... 6 F8
  Burntwood, Chasetown WS7 . 7 B5
  Cannock WS11 .... 1 D1
  Coleshill B46 .... 70 F6
  Coventry CV1 .... 165 B1
  Darlaston WS10 .... 41 C6

Park Rd continued
  Dudley, Lower Gornal DY3 . 50 C4
  Dudley, Netherton DY2 ..... 62 C6
  Dudley, West Coseley DY1 . 51 B7
  Featherstone WV10 .... 12 D8
  Hagley DY9 .... 99 B6
  Halesowen B63 .... 82 B5
  Hinckley LE10 .... 75 E8
  Kenilworth CV8 .... 148 A6
  Norton Canes WS11 .... 6 A5
  Royal Leamington Spa CV32 . 157 A4
  Smethwick B67 .... 64 F1
  Solihull B91 .... 107 D3
  Stourbridge DY8 .... 80 D5
  Sutton Coldfield B73 .... 46 B5
  Tamworth B77 .... 35 C5
  Tipton B69 .... 63 C8
  Walsall, Daw End WS4 ...... 29 C5
  Walsall, The Chuckery WS5 . 43 D5
  Walsall,
  Wallington Heath WS3 .... 14 B1
  Willenhall WV13 .... 26 F3
Park Rd E WV1 .... 163 A4
Park Rd N B6 .... 67 A7
Park Rd S B18 .... 66 B5
Park Rd W Stourbridge DY8 . 80 D5
  Wolverhampton WV1 .... 25 A3
Park Retreat B66 .... 65 B5
Park Ridge B74 .... 46 A7
Park Ridge Dr B63 .... 82 B6
Park Rise WV3 .... 24 E2
Park Specl Sch B79 .... 21 A7
Park Sq B37 .... 90 D8
Park St Birmingham,
  Aston B6 .... 67 A7
  Birmingham, Digbeth B5 . 164 D2
  Blackheath,
  Cradley Heath B64 .... 62 E2
  Blackheath,
  Rowley Regis B65 .... 63 D1
  Cannock WS11 .... 4 E6
  Cheslyn Hay WS6 .... 4 E3
  Coventry CV6 .... 113 E7
  Darlaston WS10 .... 41 C5
  Kidderminster DY11 .... 116 D5
  Kingswinford DY6 .... 60 D6
  Nuneaton CV11 .... 73 D3
  Oldbury B69 .... 63 F6
  Royal Leamington Spa
  CV32 .... 156 F1
  Stourbridge, Amblecote DY8 . 80 F8
  Stourbridge, Lye DY9 .... 81 F5
  Stourbridge,
  Stambermill DY8 .... 81 A5
  Tamworth B79 .... 21 A5
  Tipton DY4 .... 52 A5
  Walsall WS1 .... 28 E2
  Wednesbury WS10 .... 41 F3
  West Bromwich B70 .... 53 D3
Park St Arc **3** WS1 ...... 28 E2
Park St S WV2 .... 39 C6
Park Street Ind Est CV6 ... 113 D7
Park Terr Birmingham B21 . 65 E8
  Darlaston WS10 .... 41 B6
Park The B97 .... 152 C7
Park Trad Est B18 .... 66 A6
Park Venture Ctr WS11 ...... 4 E6
Park View
  Birmingham,
  Rotton Park B18 .... 65 E4
  Birmingham,
  Small Heath B10 .... 87 D7
  Coventry CV3 .... 114 A2
  Darlaston WS10 .... 41 C6
  Sutton Coldfield B73 .... 46 A6
  Tanworth-in-A B94 .... 143 C6
Park View Cl CV7 .... 96 A8
Park View Ct WS11 .... 1 D1
Park View Rd
  Birmingham B31 .... 102 F3
  Stourbridge DY9 .... 81 F4
  Sutton Coldfield B74 .... 31 D3
Park View Sch B8 .... 67 F5
Park Villas **10** B9 .... 67 B2
Park Way Birmingham B45 . 102 B1
  Redditch B98 .... 154 A5
  Wolverhampton WV11 .... 13 A1
Park Wlk Brierley Hill DY5 . 81 F8
  4 Redditch B97 .... 153 E3
Park Wood Ct B74 .... 31 F2
Park Wood La CV4 .... 131 D7
Parkbrook Ind Est
  4 DY9 .... 81 F5
Parkdale DY3 .... 50 D8
Parkdale Ave WS10 .... 42 A4
Parkdale Cl B24 .... 56 F2
Parkdale Cl WS10 .... 42 A4
Parkdale Dr B31 .... 123 A7
Parkdale Rd B26 .... 89 D6
Parker Ho B14 .... 104 F3
Parker Paul Ind Est WV2 ... 39 C7
Parker Rd WV11 .... 12 F1
Parker St Birmingham B16 . 65 F1
  Walsall WS3 .... 14 A1
Parkes Ave WV8 .... 10 B2
Parkes Bldgs B62 .... 83 D8
Parkes Fold DY3 .... 51 F8
Parkes Hall Rd DY1 .... 51 A6
Parkes Ho **6** B69 .... 64 A7
Parkes La Dudley DY3 .... 51 F8
  Tipton DY4 .... 51 F8
Parkes St Brierley Hill DY5 . 61 D3
  Smethwick B67 .... 64 F4
  Warwick CV34 .... 160 D7
  Willenhall WV13 .... 27 B1
Parkeston Cres B44 .... 45 C1
Parkfield Birmingham B32 . 84 A2
  Dorridge B93 .... 128 A1

Parkfield Ave B77 .... 21 C1
Parkfield Cl Birmingham
  B15 .... 86 C7
  Halesowen B62 .... 84 A5
  Redditch B98 .... 154 B6
  Tamworth B77 .... 35 C8
Parkfield Colliery WV4 ...... 39 F5
Parkfield Cres Tamworth
  B77 .... 35 C8
  Wolverhampton WV2 .... 39 E6
Parkfield Ct **11** B46 ...... 70 F7
Parkfield Dr Birmingham
  B36 .... 58 C1
  Kenilworth CV8 .... 148 B5
Parkfield Gr WV2 .... 39 E6
Parkfield High Sch WV4 ... 39 E5
Parkfield Inf & Jun Sch
  B8 .... 67 E3
Parkfield Prim Sch
  Tamworth B77 .... 35 C8
  Wolverhampton WV4 .... 39 F5
Parkfield Rd Birmingham B8 . 67 E4
  Coleshill B46 .... 70 F6
  Dudley DY2 .... 62 E6
  Keresley CV7 .... 95 A6
  Oldbury B68 .... 64 A3
  Stourbridge DY8 .... 81 B5
  Wolverhampton WV4 .... 39 E5
Parkgate Prim Sch CV6 .... 95 B3
Parkgate Rd CV6 .... 95 C3
Parkhall Croft B34 .... 69 C7
Parkhill Dr CV5 .... 112 A5
Parkhill Rd Burntwood WS7 . 7 A8
  Sutton Coldfield B76 .... 57 F6
Parkhouse Ave WV11 .... 26 B6
Parkhouse Dr B23 .... 56 B5
Parkhouse Gdns DY3 .... 50 C4
Parkland Ave DY11 .... 116 B5
Parkland Cl CV6 .... 95 C3
Parklands B91 .... 107 A3
Parklands Ave CV32 .... 157 C4
Parklands Ct B17 .... 85 A6
Parklands Dr B74 .... 45 F8
Parklands Gdns WS1 .... 43 A8
Parklands Rd Darlaston
  WS10 .... 41 E5
  Wolverhampton WV1 .... 26 A1
Parklands The
  Birmingham B23 .... 56 D5
  Kingswinford DY6 .... 60 D6
  Stourbridge DY9 .... 81 D3
  Wolverhampton WV3 .... 24 D1
Parkrose Ind Est B66 .... 65 B7
Parks Cres WV11 .... 13 A3
Parkside Birmingham B32 . 84 C2
  Coventry CV1 .... 165 C2
  Tamworth B77 .... 21 E1
Parkside Ave WV13 .... 26 E2
Parkside Cl WS10 .... 42 B3
Parkside Ct LE10 .... 75 E8
Parkside Ind Est WV11 ..... 25 F1
Parkside Jun Sch B66 ...... 65 B5
Parkside La A11 .... 1 A2
Parkside Mid Sch B61 ..... 137 A3
Parkside Rd Birmingham
  B20 .... 54 E6
  Halesowen B63 .... 82 D5
Parkside Way Aldridge B74 . 31 A1
  Birmingham B31 .... 102 C1
Parkstone Ave B61 .... 150 D8
Parkstone Cl WS4 .... 29 C8
Parkstone Rd CV6 .... 95 F2
Parkview CV3 .... 165 A1
Parkview Cres WS2 .... 28 A4
Parkview Rd WV14 .... 40 C8
Parkview Trad Est B38 .... 103 F3
Parkville Ave B17 .... 85 B3
Parkville Cl CV6 .... 95 C3
Parkville Highway CV6 ...... 95 B3
Parkway Birmingham B8 .... 68 A5
  Coventry CV2 .... 115 B8
Parkway Ind Ctr B7 .... 67 A4
Parkway Rd DY1 .... 51 A2
Parkway Rdbt WV10 .... 41 E1
Parkway The Perton WV6 .. 23 F4
  Walsall WS4 .... 29 C8
Parkwood Cl WS8 .... 16 A5
Parkwood Croft B43 .... 44 B1
Parkwood Ct **4** CV8 ... 148 B5
Parkwood Dr B73 .... 45 C2
Parkwood Rd B61 .... 136 E3
Parkyn St WV2 .... 39 E8
Parliament St
  Birmingham, Aston B6 ...... 66 F6
  Birmingham,
  Small Heath B10 .... 87 C8
  West Bromwich B70 .... 53 D1
Parlows End B38 .... 123 D7
Parmington Cl B97 .... 158 B6
Parmiter Ho CV32 .... 156 F2
Parr Cl CV34 .... 161 D6
Parrotts Gr CV2 .... 96 D5
Parry Rd Coventry CV2 .... 114 C7
  Kidderminster DY11 .... 116 B3
  Wednesfield WV11 .... 27 A8
Parson St B77 .... 35 E7
Parson's Hill B38 .... 104 B2
Parson's La LE10 .... 75 F8
Parson's Nook CV2 .... 114 A5
Parsonage Dr
  Birmingham B45 .... 122 D4
  Halesowen B63 .... 82 A7
Parsonage St Oldbury B69 . 64 B7
  West Bromwich B71 .... 53 D6
Parsons Hill B68 .... 64 B2
Parsons Rd B98 .... 153 E2
Parsons St DY1 .... 51 C1
Parsons Way WS2 .... 27 F6

Partons Rd B14 .... 104 D6
Partridge Ave WS10 .... 41 B6
Partridge Cl Birmingham B37 . 70 D3
  Huntington WS12 .... 1 D7
Partridge Croft Coventry
  CV6 .... 96 A5
  Lichfield WS13 .... 9 C8
Partridge Ct Birmingham
  B4 .... 164 C4
  4 Wednesbury WS10 ... 41 F3
Partridge Gr DY10 .... 117 A2
Partridge La B97 .... 158 A7
Partridge Rd Birmingham
  B26 .... 69 A1
  Stourbridge DY8 .... 80 C4
Passey Rd B13 .... 87 D2
Passfield Ave WS12 .... 2 C7
Passfield Rd B33 .... 69 A3
Pasture Gate WS11 .... 1 C2
Pasture View WS3 .... 14 F2
Pastures The WV6 .... 23 D4
Pastures Wlk B38 .... 123 D7
Pat Davis Ct DY10 .... 116 E7
Patch La B98 .... 158 F6
Patent Dr WS10 .... 41 D3
Patent Shaft Rdbt WS10 ... 41 D3
Paternoster Row
  Birmingham B5 .... 66 F2
  4 Kidderminster DY11 . 116 D6
  Wolverhampton WV1 .... 163 B3
Paterson Ct B93 .... 128 C6
Paterson Pl WS8 .... 16 B5
Pathlow Cres B90 .... 106 A1
Patios The DY11 .... 116 C7
Paton Gr B13 .... 86 F2
Patricia Cl CV4 .... 111 C1
Patricia Ave
  Birmingham B14 .... 105 C4
  Wolverhampton WV4 .... 39 D5
Patricia Cres DY1 .... 51 B7
Patricia Dr DY4 .... 52 A2
Patrick Gregory Rd WV11 . 26 F7
Patrick Rd B26 .... 88 E7
Patriot Cl WS1 .... 42 D5
Patshull Ave WV10 .... 11 B3
Patshull Cl B43 .... 43 D1
Patshull Gr WV10 .... 11 B3
Patshull Ho WV6 .... 24 E5
Patshull Pl **5** B19 .... 66 C7
Pattens Rd CV34 .... 156 B1
Patterdale Rd
  Birmingham B23 .... 56 D4
  Cannock WS11 .... 2 A4
Patterdale Way DY5 .... 81 B8
Patterton Dr B76 .... 58 A7
Pattingham Rd WV6 .... 23 C2
Pattison Coll CV3 .... 114 A2
Pattison Gdns B23 .... 56 D2
Pattison St WS5 .... 42 E5
Paul Byrne Ct B20 .... 55 B1
Paul Pursehouse Rd WV14 . 40 D3
Paul St Dudley WV14 .... 40 A1
  Wednesbury WS10 .... 42 B2
  Wolverhampton WV2 .... 163 B1
Paul Stacy Ho CV1 .... 165 D4
Paul Vale WV14 .... 52 B5
Pauline Ave CV6 .... 96 B2
Pauls Coppice WS8 .... 16 A5
Pauls Wlk WS13 .... 3 A2
Pavenham Dr B5 .... 86 C4
Pavilion Ave B67 .... 64 D3
Pavilion Rd B6 .... 55 F3
Pavilion Way CV5 .... 112 F3
Pavilions Sh Ctr B4 .... 164 C2
Pavillion Cl WS9 .... 30 B7
Pavior's Rd WS7 .... 6 E4
Paxford Cl B98 .... 154 B6
Paxford Way B31 .... 102 F6
Paxmead Cl CV6 .... 95 A2
Paxton Ave WV6 .... 23 C3
Paxton Cl B60 .... 137 B1
Paxton Rd Birmingham B18 . 66 A5
  Coventry CV6 .... 113 A4
  Stourbridge DY9 .... 82 A4
Paybody Hospl CV5 .... 112 C6
Payne Cl CV32 .... 157 A2
Payne St B65 .... 63 C1
Payne's La CV1 .... 113 F3
Paynell Cl CV6 .... 95 B2
Paynton Wlk **3** B15 ...... 86 B8
Payton Cl B69 .... 52 E1
Payton Rd B21 .... 65 D8
PDH Ind Est
  Wednesbury WS10 .... 41 C3
  Willenhall WV13 .... 26 D3
Peace Cl WS6 .... 4 E3
Peace Wlk B37 .... 70 B1
Peach Ave WS10 .... 41 C6
Peach Rd WV12 .... 27 A6
Peachley Cl **8** B63 .... 83 B3
Peacock Ave Coventry CV2 . 96 F1
  Wednesfield WV11 .... 27 A7
Peacock Cl DY4 .... 52 B4
Peacock Rd Birmingham B13 . 104 F6
  Darlaston WS10 .... 41 B7
Peacocks Est B64 .... 62 C1
Peacocks The CV34 .... 160 B2
Peak Croft B36 .... 68 D8
Peak Dr DY3 .... 50 E3
Peak House Rd B43 .... 43 E4
Peak Rd **4** DY8 .... 81 B6
Peake Ave CV11 .... 73 E7
Peake Cres WS8 .... 16 A5
Peake Dr DY4 .... 52 B4
Peake Rd WS8 .... 16 A5
Peakman St B45 .... 122 A6
Peakman St B98 .... 153 E4

Peaks L Ctr B79 21 B3
Peal St WS1 28 F1
Pear Tree Ave
Nuneaton CV10 72 E6
Tipton DY4 51 F5
Pear Tree Cl
Birmingham, Grove Vale B43 43 B1
Birmingham, Stechford B33 68 D2
4 Coventry CV2 96 B2
Huntington WS12 1 C7
Kidderminster DY10 117 B7
Shuttington B79 22 E8
Solihull B90 105 D2
Pear Tree Cres B90 105 C2
Pear Tree Ct Birmingham B43 54 C8
Blackheath B65 63 D3
Pear Tree Dr B43 43 C1
Pear Tree Gr B90 105 C2
Pear Tree La Brownhills WS8 6 C2
Dudley WV14 51 D8
Wolverhampton WV11 26 B8
Pear Tree Rd
Birmingham B34 69 C6
Birmingham, Grove Vale B43 43 B1
Smethwick B67 64 E4
Pearce Cl DY1 61 E8
Pearl Gr
Birmingham, Acock's Green B27 88 B3
3 Birmingham, Rotton Park B18 65 E4
Pearl Hyde Ho 4 CV1 165 C4
Pearl Hyde Prim Sch CV2 115 A5
Pearman Rd
Birmingham B45 101 E1
Smethwick B66 65 A3
Pearmans Croft B47 125 A6
Pears Cl CV8 147 F5
Pearsall Dr B69 63 E8
Pearson Ave CV6 96 B2
Pearson Ct WV12 27 D4
Pearson St Blackheath B64 62 E1
Brierley Hill DY5 61 D3
Stourbridge DY9 81 F4
West Bromwich B70 53 B4
Wolverhampton WV2 163 B1
Peart Dr B80 159 C4
Peartree Ave WV13 27 B1
Peartree Dr DY8 81 A2
Peartree La Blackheath B64 62 E1
Dudley DY2 62 A6
Peartree Lane Ind Est DY2 62 A6
Peascroft La WV14 40 E6
Peasefield Cl B21 65 C8
Pebble Cl Stourbridge DY8 81 B5
Tamworth B77 22 B3
Pebble Mill Cl WS11 1 F2
Pebble Mill Dr WS11 2 A2
Pebble Mill Rd B5 86 C4
Pebworth Ave B90 127 B6
Pebworth Cl Birmingham B29 86 B2
Coventry CV5 112 B3
Redditch B98 154 C7
Pebworth Gr Birmingham B33 89 C8
Dudley DY1 51 B3
Peckham Rd B44 45 A2
Peckingham St 2 B63 83 B3
Peckover Cl B65 63 C1
Peddimore La B76 58 C7
Pedmore CE Prim Sch DY9 81 C1
Pedmore Cl B98 159 B7
Pedmore Court Rd DY8 81 B1
Pedmore Gr B44 44 F2
Pedmore Hall La DY9 99 C8
Pedmore La Hagley DY9 99 F8
Stourbridge DY9 81 E1
Pedmore Rd
Brierley Hill DY5, DY2 61 F4
Stourbridge DY9 81 E5
Pedmore Road Ind Est DY5 61 F4
Pedmore Wlk B69 63 D5
Peel Cl Coventry CV6 113 E6
Darlaston WS10 41 D8
Drayton Bassett B78 34 E5
Hampton in A B92 109 B6
Willenhall WV13 27 A1
Peel Ct 4 Cannock WS11 1 E1
2 Fazeley B78 35 B8
Peel Dr WS12 1 F8
Peel Ho B79 21 A4
Peel La CV6 113 F5
Peel Rd CV34 160 E8
Peel St Birmingham B18 65 E5
Coventry CV6 113 E6
Dudley DY2 62 E8
Kidderminster DY11 116 D5
Tipton DY4 52 A4
West Bromwich B71 53 C5
Willenhall WV13 27 A1
Wolverhampton WV3 163 B2
Peel Way B69 52 D2
Peel Wlk B17 84 F7
Peelers Way B77 21 C1
Pegasus Jun & Inf Sch B35 58 B3
Pegasus Wlk Birmingham B29 85 D1
Tamworth B79 20 F7
Peggs Row Cotts WS7 7 E7
Pegleg Wlk 2 B14 104 C2
Pegmill Cl CV3 133 F8
Pelham Dr DY1 51 A2
Pelham Lodge DY10 117 A5
Pelham Rd B8 68 B4
Pelham St WV3 25 B1
Pelsall La
Walsall, Little Bloxwich WS3 14 D3
Walsall, Shelfield WS4 29 B8
Pelsall Rd WS8 15 D7
Pelsall Village Jun Mixed & Inf Schs WS3 14 F4
Pemberly Rd B27 88 A2
Pemberton Cl B66 65 B3
Pemberton Cres WS10 42 D5
Pemberton Rd Dudley WV14 40 D1
West Bromwich B70 53 A6
Pemberton St B18 66 B4
Pembridge Cl
Birmingham B32 102 A7
Brierley Hill DY5 61 F1
Redditch B98 154 D2
Pembridge Rd B93 127 E3
Pembroke Ave WV2 40 A7
Pembroke Cl Bedworth CV12 77 C1
1 Warwick CV34 160 F8
West Bromwich B71 42 B1
Willenhall WV12 27 B6
Pembroke Croft B28 106 A5
Pembroke Ct 8 CV32 156 F2
Pembroke Gdns DY8 60 C2
Pembroke Ho 4 WS3 28 C6
Pembroke Rd
Birmingham B12 87 A4
West Bromwich B71 42 B1
Pembroke Way
Birmingham B28 106 A5
Nuneaton CV11 73 D3
West Bromwich B71 53 B7
Pembrook Rd CV6 95 C2
Pembury Ave CV6 96 A3
Pembury Croft B44 45 A1
Penarth Gr CV3 134 F7
Pencombe Dr WV4 39 D5
Pencraig Cl CV8 148 C5
Pencroft Rd B34 69 C7
Penda Ct B20 66 A8
Penda Gr WV6 23 F5
Pendeen Rd B14 105 C4
Pendeford Ave WV6 24 E8
Pendeford Bsns Pk WV9 10 F3
Pendeford Cl WV6 24 E8
Pendeford Hall La WV9 10 D5
Pendeford High Sch WV10 11 B2
Pendeford La WV9 11 A3
Pendeford Mill La WV8 10 C3
Pendenis Cl CV6 114 A8
Pendennis Cl B30 103 D5
Pendennis Dr B69 63 A8
Penderel Ct CV6 95 C3
Penderel St WS3 14 C1
Penderell Cl WV10 12 A6
Pendigo Way
Birmingham B40 90 E3
Birmingham B40 90 F4
Pendinas Dr WV8 10 B3
Pendine Ct 5 CV32 161 D8
Pendle Hill WS12 2 C4
Pendleton Gr B27 106 B8
Pendock Ct B23 56 C3
Pendragon Rd B42 55 C4
Pendrel Cl WS6 13 F8
Pendrell Cl Birmingham B37 70 A3
Codsall WV8 10 A3
Pendrill Rd WV10 11 E3
Penfields Rd DY8 81 B6
Penge Gr B44 44 E3
Penhallow Dr WV4 39 E5
Penhurst Ave B20 55 D1
Penk Dr WS7 7 D6
Penk Rise WV6 24 B4
Penkridge Cl WS2 28 D3
Penkridge Gr B33 68 F4
Penkridge St WS2 28 D3
Penley Gr B8 68 B6
Penmanor B60 151 D8
Penn Cl WS3 28 C8
Penn Common Golf Course WV4 38 F2
Penn Common Rd WV4 38 F1
Penn Croft La WV4 39 A1
Penn Fields Sch WV3 38 F7
Penn Gr B29 85 B2
Penn Hall Sch WV4 38 E3
Penn Ho CV4 111 F1
Penn Hospl WV4 38 E4
Penn Ind Est B64 62 D1
Penn La B94 141 C4
Penn Rd Blackheath B65 63 E3
Sedgley DY3 49 F8
Wolverhampton WV3, WV4 39 B7
Penn Road Island WV2 163 B2
Penn St Birmingham B4 67 A3
Blackheath B64 82 F8
Wolverhampton WV3 163 A1
Pennant Ct B65 63 B3
Pennant Gr B29 85 A2
Pennant Rd
Blackheath, Cradley Heath B64 62 D1
Blackheath, Rowley Regis B65 63 B3
Hinckley LE10 75 D5
Pennard Gr B32 84 F4
Penncricket Ct B68 63 F3
Penncricket La B65, B68 63 E3
Penncroft WV4 38 E4
Pennhouse Ave WV4 38 F5
Pennine Dr Cannock WS11 1 E2
Dudley DY3 50 D3
Pennine Rd B61 137 A5
Pennine Way Nuneaton CV10 72 B3
Stourbridge DY8 81 A6
Tamworth B77 36 B8
Willenhall WV12 27 D4
Pennington Cl B70 53 A2
Pennington Ho B69 63 E8
Pennington Way CV6 113 E8
Penns Cl CV32 157 E5
Penns Ct B76 57 F7
Penns La Coleshill B46 70 F7
Sutton Coldfield B72 57 D7
Penns Lake Rd B76 57 E7
Penns Prim Sch B72 57 D6
Penns Wood Cl DY3 39 C2
Penns Wood Dr B76 57 F7
Pennwood Ct WV4 38 D6
Pennwood La WV4 38 F3
Penny Cress Gn WS11 5 F4
Penny Ct WS6 13 F8
Penny Park La CV6 95 A3
Penny Royal Cl DY3 50 D2
Pennyacre Rd B14 104 D2
Pennycress Gdns WV10 12 C7
Pennycroft Ho B33 68 E3
Pennyfield Croft B33 68 E3
Pennyhill La B71 53 F7
Pennymoor Rd B77 36 B7
Pennyroyal Cl WS5 43 B3
Pennys Croft WS13 3 E1
Pennystone Cl CV31 162 D6
Penrice Dr B69 52 A1
Penrith Cl Brierley Hill DY5 81 B8
Coventry CV6 95 C2
Royal Leamington Spa CV32 156 C2
Penrith Croft B32 102 D8
Penrith Gr B37 70 C2
Penrose Cl CV4 132 A7
Penryhn Cl CV8 148 C5
Penryn Cl Nuneaton CV11 74 A4
Walsall WS5 43 D7
Penryn Rd WS5 43 D7
Pens Meadow Sch DY8 60 E3
Pensby Cl B13 105 D8
Pensford Rd B31 103 C3
Pensham Croft B90 127 A6
Penshaw Cl WV9 11 A3
Penshaw Gr B13 87 D1
Penshurst Way CV11 78 F8
Pensilva Way 2 CV1 113 E4
Pensnett Rd Brierley Hill DY5 61 C4
Dudley DY1 61 F7
Pensnett Sch of Tech The DY5 61 B6
Pensnett Trad Est The DY6 60 F8
Penstock Ct DY10 117 C8
Penstone La WV4 37 E4
Pentire Cl CV11 73 F5
Pentire Rd WS14 9 D6
Pentland Cl LE10 71 B1
Pentland Croft B12 86 F7
Pentlands Gdns WV3 24 E2
Pentos Dr B11 87 D3
Pentridge Cl B76 57 F5
Penzance Cl LE10 71 E4
Penzance Way CV11 74 A5
Penzer Dr B45 138 D8
Penzer St DY6 60 D7
Peolsford Rd WS3 15 A4
Peony Wlk B23 56 B3
Peplins Way B30 104 B3
Peplow Rd B33 69 A4
Pepper Hill DY8 81 A4
Pepper La CV1 165 B2
Pepperbox Dr DY4 52 A5
Pepperwood Cl B61 120 C3
Pepys Cnr CV4 111 E3
Pepys Ct B43 54 E7
Perch Ave B37 70 A3
Percival Rd B16 65 C1
Percy Bsns Pk B69 63 F7
Percy Cres CV8 147 E2
Percy Rd Birmingham B11 87 D4
Kenilworth CV8 147 E2
Warwick CV34 160 E8
Percy Shurmer Jun & Inf Sch B12 86 E7
Percy St CV1 165 A3
Percy Terr 5 CV32 156 D1
Peregrine Cl DY1 50 F1
Peregrine Dr CV5 112 A5
Peregrine Gr DY10 117 A2
Pereira Rd B17 85 C7
Perimeter Rd
Birmingham B40 90 D4
Birmingham B40 90 E4
Perivale Gr WV14 51 D8
Perivale Way DY8 81 A8
Periwinkle Cl WS8 15 D6
Perkins Cl DY1 51 C6
Perks Rd WV11 13 A1
Perott Dr B75 32 D2
Perrett Wlk 5 DY11 116 D6
Perrin Ave DY11 116 B4
Perrins Gr B8 68 A6
Perrins La DY9 81 F4
Perrins Rise DY9 81 F4
Perrott Gdns DY5 61 B1
Perrott St B18 65 E6
Perry Ave B42 55 C5
Perry Barr Sta B20 55 D2
Perry Beeches Schs (Jun, Inf & Sec) B42 55 C8
Perry Cl DY2 62 D8
Perry Common Jun & Inf Sch B23 56 B7
Perry Common Rd B23 56 C6
Perry Common Sec Sch B44 56 B6
Perry Ct B68 84 B7
Perry Green Ho B42 55 D5
Perry Hall Dr WV12 27 B5
Perry Hall Prim Sch WV11 26 F6
Perry Hall Rd WV11 26 F6
Perry Hill Cres B68 84 B7
Perry Hill Ho B68 84 C8
Perry Hill La B32 84 B7
Perry Hill Rd B68 84 B7
Perry La B61 136 F2
Perry Park Cres B42 55 C6
Perry Park Rd B64 63 B1
Perry St Bilston WV14 40 E3
Darlaston WS10 41 D8
Smethwick B66 65 A7
Tipton DY4 52 A4
Wednesbury WS10 41 F2
Perry Trad Est WV14 40 E3
Perry Villa Dr B42 55 D5
Perry Wlk B23 56 D6
Perry Wood Rd B42 55 A8
Perrycrofts Cres B79 21 C7
Perryfields Cl B98 158 F6
Perryfields Cres B61 136 F5
Perryfields High Sch B68 84 A8
Perryfields Prim Sch B68 84 A7
Perryfields Rd B61 136 D4
Perryford Dr B91 127 C8
Perrymill La B96 159 B1
Perrywell Rd B6 55 F4
Persehouse St WS1 28 F2
Pershore Ave B29 86 B2
Pershore Cl WS3 13 F2
Pershore Pl CV4 132 E6
Pershore Rd
Birmingham, Balsall Heath B5 86 C4
Birmingham, Breedon Cross B30 104 A5
Birmingham, Ten Acres B30 104 B8
Halesowen B63 83 A2
Kidderminster DY11 116 A6
Walsall WS3 13 F2
Pershore Rd S B30 103 F3
Pershore St B5 164 C1
Pershore Tower 3 B31 102 C2
Pershore Way WS3 13 F2
Perth Rd WV12 27 B6
Perth Rise CV5 112 A4
Perton Brook Vale WV6 23 F2
Perton Cty Fst Sch WV6 24 A4
Perton Fst Sch WV6 23 E5
Perton Gr Birmingham B29 103 A8
Wolverhampton WV6 23 F2
Perton Rd WV6 23 F2
Pestilence La
Alvechurch B48 139 C8
Alvechurch B48 139 D8
Peter Ave WV14 40 F2
Peter Hall La CV7 115 F6
Peter's Finger B60 136 F1
Peter's Hill Rd DY5 81 C6
Peter's La WS7 8 A5
Peterborough Dr WS12 2 C1
Peterbrook Cl B98 158 F7
Peterbrook Prim Sch B90 105 D2
Peterbrook Rd B90 105 D1
Peterbrook Rise B90 105 D1
Peterdale Dr WV4 38 F3
Peterhead B77 21 F5
Peterlee Wlk 6 CV2 115 A7
Peters Ave B31 102 F2
Peters Hill Prim Sch DY5 81 C7
Peters St B70 53 A7
Peters Wlk WS13 3 A2
Petersbourne Ct B28 105 F8
Petersfield WS11 1 F4
Petersfield Ct B28 105 F8
Petersfield Dr B65 63 E3
Petersfield Rd B28 105 E7
Petersham Pl B15 85 E6
Petersham Rd B44 45 C1
Petershouse Dr B74 31 F5
Petford St B64 62 E1
Petitor Cres CV2 96 C1
Pettitt Cl B14 104 E2
Petton Cl B98 154 F3
Pettyfield Cl B26 89 A6
Pettyfields Cl B93 128 A5
Petworth Cl 3 WV13 40 F8
Petworth Gr B26 88 E6
Pevensey Cl B69 62 F8
Peverell Dr B28 105 F7
Peveril Dr CV3 133 B5
Peveril Gr B76 46 E4
Peverill Rd Perton WV6 23 F4
Wolverhampton WV4 39 E3
Pevril Way B43 43 F2
Peyto Cl CV6 95 C2
Pheasant Cl Bedworth CV12 77 D1
Kidderminster DY10 117 A2
Pheasant Croft B36 70 A8
Pheasant La B98 158 F7
Pheasant Rd B67 64 D1
Pheasant St DY5 61 C3
Pheasey Park Farm Prim Sch B43 44 C4
Philip Ct
1 Royal Leamington Spa CV31 161 F6
Sutton Coldfield B76 46 F3
Philip Gr WS11 1 E6
Philip Rd Halesowen B63 82 F3
Tipton DY4 52 D5
Philip Sidney Rd B11 87 C3
Philip St WV14 40 D1
Philip Victor Rd B20 54 F1
Phillimore Rd B8 67 D5
Phillip Docker Ct CV12 79 B2
Phillip Rd WS2 42 C6
Phillippes Rd 6 CV34 155 F1
Phillips Ave WV11 12 F1
Phillips St B6 66 E6
Phillips Street Ind Est B6 66 F6
Phillips Terr B98 153 F4
Phipson Rd B11 87 B3
Phoenix Bsns Pk
Birmingham B7 67 A6
Hinckley LE10 74 E8
Phoenix Ct B5 86 C5
Phoenix Ctr WS11 4 E6
Phoenix Gn B15 85 E7
Phoenix Ho CV1 165 C4
Phoenix Ind Est Bilston WV14 40 F4
Willenhall WV11 26 D3
Phoenix Int Ind Est B70 52 E5
Phoenix Pk B62 63 E1
Phoenix Rd Cannock WS11 2 A2
Tipton DY4 51 F6
Willenhall WV11 26 D3
Phoenix Rise Birmingham B23 56 B7
Wednesbury WS10 41 E4
Wolverhampton WV2 39 C6
Phoenix St
West Bromwich B70 52 F4
Wolverhampton WV2 39 D6
Phoenix Way CV6 95 E3
Picasso Cl WS11 2 D2
Piccadilly Birmingham B2 164 B2
Piccadilly B78 35 F1
Piccadilly Cl B37 70 C1
Piccadilly Cres B78 35 F1
Pickard St CV34 161 A7
Pickenham Rd B14 105 A1
Pickering Croft B32 84 D1
Pickering Rd WV11 26 D5
Pickersleigh Cl 6 B63 83 A3
Pickford Cl CV11 74 A1
Pickford Grange La CV5 111 C7
Pickford Green La CV5 111 C7
Pickford St B5 66 F2
Pickford Way CV5 112 B6
Pickrell Rd WV14 40 B1
Pickwick Cl B13 87 B2
Pickwick Gr B13 87 C2
Pickwick Pl WV14 40 E4
Picton Croft 6 B37 70 D2
Picton Gr B13 105 B6
Picturedrome Way 6 WS10 41 D6
Piddock Rd B66 65 A5
Pier St WS8 15 F7
Pierce Ave B92 88 E3
Piercy St B70 53 A3
Piers Cl CV34 160 F8
Piers Rd B21 66 A7
Piggots Croft B37 69 F3
Pike Cl LE10 75 D5
Pike Dr B37 70 C3
Pike Hill B60 138 A7
Pikehelve St B70 52 E7
Pikehorne Croft B36 58 D2
Pikers La CV7 94 A3
Pikes Pool La B60 137 E2
Pikes The B45 121 F8
Pikewater Rd B9 67 D2
Pilgrims Gate LE10 76 A6
Pilkington Ave B72 46 C2
Pilkington Rd CV5 132 D8
Pillaton Dr WS12 1 C6
Pilling Cl CV2 114 F8
Pilson Cl B36 68 F8
Pimbury Rd WV12 27 D7
Pimlico Ct DY3 50 D3
Pimpernel Dr WS5 43 A3
Pinbury Croft B37 70 B1
Pinchers Cl DY9 119 E7
Pine Ave Smethwick B66 64 E7
Wednesbury WS10 41 F4
Pine Cl Great Wyrley WS6 4 F4
Kingswinford DY6 60 D5
Solihull B91 106 F2
Stourbridge DY9 81 B1
Tamworth B79 21 B8
Wolverhampton WV3 25 A1
Pine Ct Coventry CV5 111 C4
Royal Leamington Spa CV32 157 B3
Wolverhampton WV11 26 C6
Pine Gn DY1 51 A5
Pine Gr Barnt Green B45 121 F2
Birmingham B14 105 A5
Burntwood WS7 6 F5
Pine Ho B36 68 F8
Pine Leigh B74 32 B1
Pine Rd Dudley DY1 51 C4
Tipton B69 63 A8
Pine Sq B37 70 B2
Pine St WS3 14 D2
Pine Tree Ave CV4 112 A2
Pine Tree Cl B97 152 F3
Pine Tree Ct CV12 78 C4
Pine Tree Rd CV12 78 D4
Pine Wlk Birmingham B31 103 B3
Stourbridge DY9 81 D3
Pine Woods B32 84 A2
Pineapple Gr B30 104 C8
Pineapple Inf & Jun Sch B14 104 C5

Pineapple Rd B30 104 C7
Pinehurst CV32 157 E6
Pinehurst Dr B38 103 F3
Pineneedle Croft WV12 27 E4
Pineridge Dr DY11 116 B5
Pines Mobile Homes The WS12 1 D5
Pines Sch The B36 68 F8
Pines The Bedworth CV12 77 E2
Birmingham B45 102 A1
Cheswick Green B90 126 D5
Coventry CV4 131 D7
Lichfield WS14 9 F7
Walsall WS1 42 F8
Wolverhampton, Compton WV3 24 D1
Wolverhampton, New Cross WV11 26 B5
Pinetree Dr B74 30 D1
Pineview B31 102 F2
Pinewall Ave B38 104 A1
Pineways Stourbridge DY8 60 C2
Sutton Coldfield B74 31 C3
Pineways Dr WV6 24 E4
Pineways The B69 63 C5
Pinewood Ave Cannock WS11 1 D4
Wood End CV9 36 C1
Pinewood Cl
Birmingham, Eachway B45 121 D8
Birmingham, Great Barr B44 55 E7
Brownhills WS8 6 E2
Walsall WS5 43 B4
Willenhall WV12 27 E7
Wolverhampton WV3 38 A8
Wombourne WV5 49 A6
Pinewood Dr
Binley Woods CV3 135 C7
Birmingham B32 84 A1
Pinewood Gr Coventry CV5 133 B8
Solihull B91 106 F2
Pinewood Wlk [6] DY6 60 E8
Pinewoods Birmingham B31 102 F8
Halesowen B62 84 A7
Pinewoods Ave DY9 98 F4
Pinewoods Cl DY9 98 F4
Pinewoods Ct DY9 98 F4
Pinfield Dr B45 122 B1
Pinfold WS3 28 C8
Pinfold Cres WV4 38 D6
Pinfold Ct WS10 41 C5
Pinfold Gdns WV11 26 D5
Pinfold Gr WV4 38 D6
Pinfold Hill WS14 18 A6
Pinfold La Cheslyn Hay WS6 4 C2
Norton Canes WS11 5 E4
Walsall WS9 44 B6
Wolverhampton WV4 38 E5
Pinfold Rd B91 107 E5
Pinfold St Bilston WV14 40 D5
Birmingham B2 164 B2
Darlaston WS10 41 D5
Oldbury B69 64 A8
Pinfold Street Extension WS10 41 C5
Pinfold Street JMI Sch WS10 41 C5
Pingle Cl B71 42 F1
Pingle Ct CV11 73 D2
Pingle La WS7 7 D5
Pinkney Pl B68 64 C3
Pinley Fields CV3 134 B8
Pinley Gr B43 44 C3
Pinley Way B91 107 A1
Pinner Ct B17 85 C6
Pinner Gr B32 84 E4
Pinner's Croft CV2 114 A5
Pinnock Pl CV4 111 F1
Pinson Rd WV13 26 F2
Pintail Dr B23 56 C2
Pintail Gr DY10 117 B3
Pinto Cl B16 65 F2
Pinvin Ho B97 153 A3
Pinza Croft B36 68 D8
Pioli Pl WS2 28 D5
Pioneer Ho Birmingham B35 58 C3
Coventry CV1 165 D4
Pioneer Units CV11 73 E3
Pipe Hall Farm Nature Reserve WS13 8 B8
Piper Cl WV6 23 F4
Piper Pl DY8 80 F8
Piper Rd WV3 38 C8
Piper's La CV8 148 A5
Piper's Row WV1 163 C3
Pipers Cl B61 150 D7
Pipers Croft WS13 3 A2
Pipers Gn B28 105 F5
Pipers Rd B98 159 D7
Pipes Mdw WV14 40 E5
Pipit Ct DY10 117 A2
Pippin Ave B63 82 B7
Pirbright Cl WV14 40 E3
Pit Leasow Cl B30 104 B8
Pitcairn Cl B30 104 B6
Pitcairn Dr B62 83 B5
Pitcairn Ho B67 64 E2
Pitcairn Rd B67 64 D2
Pitcher Oak Sch B97 153 B4
Pitcheroak Cotts B97 153 A3
Pitclose Rd B31 103 B1
Pitfield Rd B33 69 E1
Pitfield Row [16] DY1 51 B1
Pitfield St [5] DY1 51 C1
Pitfields Cl B68 84 A8
Pitfields Rd B68 84 A8
Pithall Rd B34 69 D5
Pitman Rd B32 84 C5
Pitmaston Ct B13 86 D3
Pitmaston Rd B28 106 B6
Pitmeadow Ho B14 104 E2
Pitsford St B18 66 B4
Pitt La B92 90 D2
Pitt St Birmingham B4 67 A3
Wolverhampton WV3 163 B2
Pitts Farm Rd B24 57 C6
Pitts La DY10 116 E6
Pixall Dr B15 86 B6
Pixhall Wlk B35 58 B3
Plainview Cl WS9 30 E2
Plaistow Ave B36 68 C7
Plane Gr B37 70 B1
Plane Tree Cl DY10 116 F7
Plane Tree Rd WS5 43 C4
Planet Rd DY5 61 D4
Planetary Ind Est WV13 26 C4
Planetary Rd WV13 26 C3
Planetree Cl B60 137 B2
Planetree Rd B74 44 D8
Plank La B46 59 A2
Planks La WV5 49 A7
Plant Ct [19] DY5 61 D2
Plant La WS7 6 E7
Plant St Blackheath B64 62 D1
Stourbridge DY8 60 E2
Plant Way WS3 14 F4
Plantation La Himley DY3 49 B3
Hopwas B78 20 B4
Plantation Rd WS5 43 A4
Plantation The DY5 61 B7
Plants Brook Rd B76 57 F6
Plants Cl Great Wyrley WS6 14 A8
Sutton Coldfield B73 45 D1
Plants Gr B24 57 D6
Plants Hill Cres CV4 111 E1
Plants Hollow DY5 61 D1
Plantsbrook L Ctr B72 46 C4
Plantsbrook Sch B72 46 C4
Plascom Rd WV1 26 A1
Platt St Cannock WS11 2 A5
Darlaston WS10 41 D5
Platts Cres DY8 80 E8
Platts Dr DY8 80 F8
Platts Rd DY8 80 E8
Playdon Gr B14 105 A3
Pleasant Cl DY6 60 C4
Pleasant Mead WS9 29 E5
Pleasant St
Kidderminster DY10 116 E7
West Bromwich, Hill Top B70 53 A8
West Bromwich, Lambert's End B70 53 C2
Pleasant View DY3 50 D2
Pleasant Way CV32 157 A2
Pleck Bsns Pk WS2 28 C1
Pleck Ho B14 104 C1
Pleck Ind Est WS2 42 C8
Pleck Rd WS2 28 C1
Pleck Wlk B38 104 A1
Plestowes Cl B90 106 B5
Pleydell Cl CV3 134 C5
Plimsoll Gr B32 84 C5
Plimsoll St DY11 116 D5
Plough And Harrow Rd B16 65 F1
Plough Ave B32 84 C2
Plough Hill Rd CV10 72 A6
Ploughmans Wlk
Kingswinford DY6 60 A7
Lichfield WS13 3 C3
Stoke Heath B60 150 D6
Wolverhampton WV8 10 F1
Plover Cl WV10 12 B7
Plover Gr DY10 117 B1
Ploverdale Cres DY6 61 A6
Plowden Rd B33 68 F4
Plume St B6 67 C8
Plumstead Rd B44 56 B8
Plym Cl WV11 26 C5
Plymouth Cl
Birmingham B31 123 A7
Coventry CV2 114 C7
Redditch B97 153 C1
Plymouth Ct B97 153 C1
Plymouth Dr B45 138 A8
Plymouth Pl CV31 162 A7
Plymouth Rd
Barnt Green B45 138 A8
Birmingham B30 104 B7
Redditch B97 153 D2
Pochard Cl DY10 116 F1
Pointon Cl WV14 40 A2
Poitiers Rd CV3 133 D6
Polden Cl B63 82 C1
Polesworth Cl B98 154 D1
Polesworth Gr B34 69 B6
Polesworth High Sch B78 36 F8
Pollard Rd B27 88 C1
Pollards The B23 56 E8
Polly Brooks Yd DY9 81 E5
Polo Fields DY9 81 B1
Polperro Dr CV5 112 A5
Pomeroy Cl CV4 131 D7
Pomeroy Rd
Birmingham, Pheasey B43 44 D4
Birmingham, Woodgate B32 84 C1
Pommel Cl WS5 42 F4
Pond Cres WV2 39 E7
Pond Gr WV2 39 E7
Pond La WV2 39 E7
Pondthorpe CV3 134 E6
Ponesfield Rd WS13 3 B2
Ponesgreen WS13 3 B2
Pontypool Ave CV3 134 F6
Pool Ave WS11 6 B5
Pool Bank B98 153 E2
Pool Bank St CV11 73 B4
Pool End Cl B93 127 F6
Pool Farm Rd B27 88 C1
Pool Field Ave B31 102 E7
Pool Furlong DY9 99 E1
Pool Gn WS9 30 A5
Pool Green Terr WS9 30 A5
Pool Hall Cres WV3 38 A8
Pool Hall Rd WV3 38 A8
Pool Hayes Com Sch WV12 27 B5
Pool Hayes Cty Prim Sch WV12 27 B6
Pool Hayes La WV12 27 B5
Pool La B69 63 F3
Pool Mdw Cheslyn Hay WS6 4 D1
Sutton Coldfield B76 58 A8
Pool Meadow Cl
Birmingham B13 87 C1
Solihull B91 107 F2
Pool Rd Burntwood WS7 6 E3
Halesowen B63 83 B3
Nuneaton CV10 72 F5
Smethwick B66 65 B5
Studley B80 159 E4
Wednesfield WV11 27 A6
Pool St Birmingham B6 66 F6
Dudley DY1 51 A6
Walsall WS1 28 F1
Wolverhampton WV2 163 B1
Pool View WS6 5 A4
Pool Way B33 69 A2
Poole Cres Birmingham B17 85 C3
Brownhills WS8 6 D2
Dudley WV14 40 D2
Poole Rd CV6 113 A6
Poole St DY8 80 E4
Poole's Way WS7 7 C7
Poolehouse Rd B43 43 E3
Pooles Ct DY10 116 E7
Pooles La WV12 27 D8
Pooley La B78 22 F2
Poolfield Dr B91 106 F3
Poolhead La Earlswood B94 141 C7
Tanworth-In-A B94 141 E5
Poolside Gdns CV3 133 A5
Pooltail Wlk B31 102 D1
Pope Gr WS12 1 F6
Pope Rd WV10 12 A1
Pope St Birmingham B1 66 B3
Smethwick B66 65 B7
Pope's La B69 64 B7
Popes La Astwood Bank B96 158 E2
Birmingham B30 103 D3
Wolverhampton WV6 24 A6
Poplar Ave Bedworth CV12 78 D2
Birmingham, Balsall Heath B12 87 A5
Birmingham, Coleshill Heath B37 90 C8
Birmingham, Edgbaston B17 65 B2
[2] Birmingham, Erdington B23 56 F4
Birmingham, King's Heath B14 104 F8
[6] Birmingham, Lozells B19 66 C8
Brownhills WS8 16 A8
Burntwood WS7 6 F6
Cannock WS11 1 F4
Oldbury B69 64 A4
Sutton Coldfield B75 46 F7
Tipton, Tipton Green DY4 51 D5
Tipton, Tividale B69 63 C8
Walsall, Bentley WS2 27 E4
Walsall, Yew Tree WS5 43 A4
West Bromwich B70 53 E2
Wolverhampton WV11 26 B7
Poplar Cl Catshill B61 136 F8
Tipton B69 52 C1
Walsall WS2 27 E4
Wombourne WV5 49 B6
Poplar Cres Dudley DY1 51 B3
Stourbridge DY8 80 D3
Poplar Dr Barnt Green B45 138 D8
Birmingham B6 55 F5
Poplar Gn DY1 51 A6
Poplar Gr [7] Birmingham B19 66 C8
Smethwick B66 65 B3
West Bromwich B70 53 E1
Poplar Ho CV12 78 D2
Poplar La Cannock WS11 1 A1
Romsley B62 101 A4
Poplar Rd Bilston WV14 40 F7
Birmingham, Moseley B14 86 E1
Birmingham, Sparkhill B11 87 C5
Brownhills WS8 16 A8
Coventry CV5 112 F1
Dorridge B93 127 F3
Great Wyrley WS6 5 A1
Kidderminster DY11 116 C4
Kingswinford DY6 60 E5
Oldbury B69 64 A8
Redditch B97 153 A3
Smethwick B66 65 A1
Solihull B91 107 C4
Stourbridge DY8 80 E3
Wednesbury WS10 42 A5
Wolverhampton WV3 39 A6
Poplar Rise
Sutton Coldfield B74 31 D5
Tipton B69 63 C8
Poplar Row DY11 116 C4
Poplar St Norton Canes WS11 6 A6
Smethwick B66 65 C5
Wolverhampton WV2 39 D6
Poplar Trad Est B6 55 F5
Poplar Trees B47 125 A7
Poplars Dr B36 69 B8
Poplars La B96 158 A1
Poplars The
Birmingham, Rotton Park B16 65 F3
Birmingham, Sparkhill B11 87 C6
Brierley Hill DY5 61 B7
Cannock WS11 1 E4
Nuneaton CV10 72 D3
Smethwick B66 65 C4
Stourbridge DY8 60 F2
Poplars Trad Est B80 159 D6
Poplarwoods B32 84 B2
Poppy Dr [3] WS5 43 A3
Poppy Gr B8 67 F4
Poppy La B24 57 C5
Poppyfield Ct CV4 132 D3
Poppymead B23 56 B8
Porchester Cl CV3 115 A2
Porchester Dr B19 66 D6
Porchester St B19 66 D6
Porlock Cl CV3 133 E5
Porlock Cres B31 102 D3
Porlock Rd DY8 81 A6
Port Hope Rd B11 87 A7
Port La WV8, WV9 10 B7
Portal Rd WS2 27 F2
Portchester Dr WV11 26 D5
Porter Cl Coventry CV4 131 E8
Sutton Coldfield B72 57 B7
Porter St DY2 51 D1
Porters Croft B17 85 A8
Porters Field [6] DY2 51 D1
Porters Way B9 67 E2
Portersfield Ind Est B64 82 D8
Portersfield Rd B64 82 C8
Portershill Dr B90 106 C1
Portfield Dr DY4 52 A3
Portfield Gr B23 57 A6
Porthkerry Gr DY3 50 B7
Porthouse Gr WV14 40 B3
Portia Ave B90 106 B1
Portia Cl CV11 74 A1
Portland Ave Aldridge WS9 30 B5
Tamworth B79 20 F8
Portland Cres DY9 81 B1
Portland Ct Aldridge WS9 30 B6
[1] Royal Leamington Spa CV32 161 F8
Portland Dr Hinckley LE10 71 E4
Nuneaton CV10 72 C4
Stourbridge DY9 81 B1
Portland Pl Cannock WS11 4 C7
Dudley WV14 51 B7
[6] Royal Leamington Spa CV32 161 F8
Portland Pl E [5] CV32 161 F8
Portland Pl W [9] CV32 161 E8
Portland Rd Aldridge WS9 30 B6
Birmingham B16 65 D1
Portland St Birmingham B6 67 A7
Royal Leamington Spa CV32 161 F8
Walsall WS2 28 E3
Portland Terr [6] B18 66 A5
Portleys La B78 34 D4
Portman Rd B13 104 F7
Portobello Cl WV13 26 D1
Portobello Rd B70 53 A8
Portree Ave CV3 114 F2
Portrush Ave B38 103 D1
Portrush Rd WV6 23 D4
Portsdown Cl WV10 25 F7
Portsdown Rd B63 82 D2
Portsea Cl CV3 133 D6
Portsea St WS3 28 C6
Portswood Cl WV9 10 F1
Portway Cl Coventry CV4 131 E8
Kingswinford DY6 60 E5
Royal Leamington Spa CV31 162 D6
Solihull B91 106 E1
Portway Hill B65 63 C6
Portway Rd Bilston WV14 40 E7
Blackheath B65 63 B5
Oldbury B69 63 E7
Wednesbury WS10 41 E2
Portway The DY6 60 E5
Portway Wlk B65 63 C6
Portwrinkle Ave CV6 114 A6
Posey Cl B21 54 C3
Post Office Rd WV5 37 A2
Post Office Wlk B96 158 E1
Postbridge Rd CV3 133 D5
Poston Croft B14 104 D3
Potter Cl B23 56 D8
Potter Ct [8] DY5 61 D2
Potters Green Prim Sch CV2 96 E2
Potters Green Rd CV2 96 E1
Potters La Birmingham B6 66 E7
Wednesbury WS10 41 F2
Potters Rd CV12 77 E1
Potterton Way B66 64 F8
Pottery Rd Oldbury B68 64 D1
Smethwick B66 65 A7
Potton Cl CV3 134 E6
Potts Cl CV8 148 C4
Pouk Hill Cl WS2 28 A3
Pouk La WS14 16 F7
Poultney Rd CV6 113 A6
Poultney St B70 52 F7
Poulton Cl B13 87 A2
Pound Cl Berkswell CV7 110 D3
Lapworth B94 144 B3
Oldbury B68 63 F3
Pound Gn B8 67 F6
Pound House La
Tanworth-in-A B94 142 F4
Tanworth-in-A B94 143 A4
Pound La Birmingham B32 101 F3
Royal Leamington Spa CV32 157 A3
Pound Rd Birmingham B14 104 E2
Oldbury B68 64 A2
Wednesbury WS10 42 A3
Poundley Cl B36 69 C8
Pountney St WV2 163 B1
Pourbaix Ho WS13 9 B6
Poverty B96 158 E2
Powell Ave B32 84 A6
Powell Pl Bilston WV14 40 E3
Tipton DY4 52 C5
Powell Rd CV2 114 A4
Powell St Birmingham B1 66 B3
[7] Halesowen B63 83 B3
Wolverhampton WV10 25 F4
Powell Way CV11 73 C4
Powells Ho B73 45 C2
Power Way DY4 52 D8
Powers Ct [4] CV32 156 F1
Powers Rd LE9 71 F5
Powick Rd B23 56 D1
Powis Ave DY4 52 B7
Powis Gr CV8 148 C5
Powke La B65 63 A2
Powke Lane Ind Est B65 63 A2
Powlers Cl DY9 81 E2
Powlett St WV2 163 C2
Poxon Rd WS9 16 A3
Poynings The WV6 24 C5
Poyser Rd CV10 78 C8
Pratts La B80 159 F7
Precinct The Coventry CV1 165 B3
Tamworth B79 21 B5
Willenhall WV12 27 B5
Premier Bsns Ctr [2] DY9 81 F5
Premier Bsns Pk WS2 28 D1
Premier Ct B30 104 C3
Premier Partnership Ind Est DY5 61 A3
Premier St B7 67 D8
Premier Trad Est B7 66 F5
Premier Way B73 45 D2
Prescelly Cl CV10 72 B3
Prescelly Ct CV8 147 F5
Prescot Rd DY9 81 C3
President Kennedy Sch & Com Coll CV6 95 B4
Prestbury Rd B6 66 E8
Presthope Rd B29 103 B7
Preston Ave B76 46 E3
Preston Cl Coventry CV4 131 F7
Redditch B98 154 B6
Preston Ho [4] WS1 28 F1
Preston Rd
Birmingham, Hockley B18 65 E6
Birmingham, South Yardley B26 88 D7
Hinckley LE10 71 B2
Prestons Row WV14 40 A3
Prestwick Cl B75 46 C7
Prestwick Rd
Birmingham B35 58 B4
Kingswinford DY6 60 C6
Prestwood Ave WV11 26 D7
Prestwood Dr DY7 80 A7
Prestwood Rd
Birmingham B29 103 B8
Wolverhampton WV11 26 A5
Prestwood Rd W WV11 26 B7
Pretoria Rd B9 67 E3
Priam Gr WS3 15 B5
Price Ave B78 20 D1
Price Cres WV14 40 D7
Price Rd Cubbington CV32 157 E5
Stourbridge DY9 82 A6
Wednesbury WS10 42 C3
Price St Bilston WV14 40 F5
Birmingham B4 164 C4
Cannock WS11 1 E1
[2] Dudley DY2 62 E8
Smethwick B66 65 B5
West Bromwich B70 53 C3
Prices Rd DY3 50 C3
Pridmore Rd CV6 113 D7
Priest Meadow Cl B96 158 D1
Priest St B64 62 F1
Priestfield Cl B44 44 D2
Priestfield Rd B97 158 E5
Priestfield St WV14 40 B6
Priestfield Sta WV2 40 A7
Priesthills Rd LE10 75 D8
Priestland Rd B34 69 B7
Priestley Cl Birmingham B20 55 A2
Halesowen B63 82 B6
Priestley Rd Birmingham B11 87 A7
Walsall WS2 28 A5
Priestley Smith Sch B23 56 B6
Primley Ave Birmingham B36 68 D7
Tamworth B77 35 F5
Walsall WS2 28 B2
Primley Cl WS2 28 B2

Primrose Ave
Birmingham B11 87 C5
Tipton DY4 52 C8
Wolverhampton WV10 11 E3
Primrose Bank B68 64 B4
Primrose Cl Blackheath B64 .. 82 B8
Lickey End B60 137 C6
Walsall WS3 15 A5
Primrose Cres DY1 51 C4
Primrose Croft B28 105 F5
Primrose Dr LE10 75 E5
Primrose Gdns
Birmingham B38 123 F8
Codsall WV8 10 A3
Featherstone WV10 12 B7
Primrose Hill
Birmingham B38 124 A8
Smethwick B67 64 D4
Stourbridge DY8 60 E1
Warwick CV34 155 E2
Primrose Hill Jun & Inf Sch B38 123 F8
Primrose Hill St CV1 165 C4
Primrose La
Birmingham B28 105 F5
Wolverhampton WV10 26 A8
Primrose Mdw WS11 2 C2
Primrose Pk DY5 61 C7
Primrose Rd DY2 62 C4
Primrose Tower B38 123 E8
Primrose Trad Est DY2 62 D4
Primrose Woods B32 84 B2
Primsland Cl B90 127 C7
Prince Albert Inf & Jun Sch B6 66 E8
Prince Albert St B9 67 D1
Prince Andrew Cres B45 101 E2
Prince Charles Cl B45 101 E2
Prince Charles Rd WV14 40 F3
Prince Edward Dr B45 101 E2
Prince George Rd WS10 42 A5
Prince of Wales Ct DY1 51 A2
Prince of Wales Ctr 5 WS11 1 E1
Prince Of Wales La B14 105 C3
Prince Of Wales Rd CV5 112 E3
Prince of Wales Wlk 3 B66 65 C5
Prince Philip Cl B45 101 E2
Prince Rd B30 104 A3
Prince Regent Ct 3 CV31 161 F6
Prince Rupert Mews WS13 9 A8
Prince Rupert's Way WS13 9 A8
Prince St Blackheath B64 82 D8
Brownhills WS9 15 F2
Cannock WS11 1 E6
Dudley DY2 62 C6
Walsall WS2 42 C8
Prince William Cl
Birmingham B23 56 D2
Coventry CV6 112 E6
Prince's Ave Nuneaton CV11 73 B3
Walsall WS4 29 B1
Prince's Dr CV31 161 D7
Prince's Rd B69 52 B2
Prince's Row B4 66 F3
Prince's St Birmingham B4 66 F3
Nuneaton CV11 73 C3
Royal Leamington Spa CV32 157 B1
Prince's Way B91 107 B3
Princep Cl B43 44 D4
Princes Ave WS1 43 A8
Princes Cl CV3 134 B8
Princes Dr Codsall WV8 10 A2
Kenilworth CV8 148 B7
Princes End Cty Inf & Jun Sch DY4 51 E7
Princes Gate B91 107 B4
Princes Gdns WV8 10 A2
Princes Rd DY8 80 D3
Princes Sq WV1 163 C3
Princess Alice Dr B73 45 D2
Princess Alley WV1 163 C3
Princess Anne Dr B45 101 E2
Princess Anne Rd
Bilston WV14 40 F3
Walsall WS2 27 F3
Princess Cl WS7 6 E7
Princess Cres B63 82 E6
Princess Ct WV10 26 A6
Princess End Ind Pk DY4 40 E1
Princess Gr B71 53 D8
Princess of Wales Com Hospl The B61 137 A4
Princess Rd Birmingham B5 86 E7
Hinckley LE10 75 E8
Oldbury B68 64 D2
Princess Sq WV14 40 F3
Princess St Burntwood WS7 6 E8
Cannock WS11 1 F5
Coventry CV6 113 F7
Wolverhampton WV1 163 C3
Princess Way WS10 41 C8
Princethorpe Cl
Birmingham B34 69 D7
Solihull B90 106 A2
Princethorpe Inf Sch B29 85 A1
Princethorpe Jun Sch B29 85 A1
Princethorpe Rd B29 85 A1
Princethorpe Tower B12 86 E7
Princethorpe Way CV3 134 E8
Princeton Gdns WV9 10 F2
Princip St B4 164 C4
Printing House St B4 164 C3
Prior Ave B60 150 C3
Prior Cl DY10 117 C5
Prior Deram Wlk CV4 132 C7
Priors Cl CV7 130 B6
Priors Field Comb Sch CV8 147 D7
Priors Harnall CV1 165 D4
Priors Mill DY3 50 E5
Priors Oak B97 153 B4
Priors The CV12 78 C2
Priors Way B23 56 C8
Priorsfield Rd 4
Coventry CV6 113 A4
Kenilworth CV8 147 D6
Priorsfield Rd N 3 CV6 113 A4
Priorsfield Rd S CV6 113 A4
Priory Ave B29 86 B2
Priory Cl Dudley DY1 51 B2
Lapworth B94 144 D5
Smethwick B66 65 C4
Stourbridge DY8 81 B3
West Bromwich B70 53 F2
Priory Croft CV8 148 A4
Priory Ct Brownhills WS9 16 A4
3 Dudley DY1 51 C1
Hinckley LE10 71 E2
Nuneaton CV11 73 A4
Solihull B91 127 B7
Stourbridge DY8 81 B3
Studley B80 159 E5
Priory Dr B68 64 C5
Priory Field Cl WV14 39 F1
Priory Green Jun & Inf Sch WV9 11 A2
Priory Ho Halesowen B63 82 F5
Kenilworth CV8 147 F4
Priory Hospl The B5 86 C5
Priory JMI Sch WS3 28 B7
Priory La DY3 50 D7
Priory Mews CV34 160 E7
Priory New Way Ind Est B6 66 F5
Priory Prim Sch DY1 51 B3
Priory Prim Sch The B71 42 D2
Priory Queensway The B4 164 C3
Priory Rd
Birmingham, Aston B6 67 B8
Birmingham, Edgbaston B5, B15 86 B5
Birmingham, Stirchley B14 104 C7
Birmingham, Warstock B28 105 D3
Cannock WS12 2 D4
Dodford B61 136 A6
Dudley DY1 51 C3
Halesowen B62 83 F4
Kenilworth CV8 148 A4
Stourbridge DY8 81 B3
Warwick CV34 160 E7
Priory Row CV1 165 C3
Priory Sq Birmingham B4 164 C3
Studley B80 159 E5
Priory St Coventry CV1 165 C3
Dudley DY1 51 C1
Nuneaton CV10 72 D3
Royal Leamington Spa CV31 161 F6
Priory Terr CV31 162 A7
Priory The DY3 50 D8
Priory Wlk Birmingham B4 164 C3
Hinckley LE10 71 E1
Sutton Coldfield B72 57 C7
9 Warwick CV34 160 F7
Pritchard Ave WV11 26 E6
Pritchard Cl B66 65 B5
Pritchard St Brierley Hill DY5 61 B3
Wednesbury WS10 42 A3
Pritchatts Rd B15 85 F5
Pritchett Ave WV4 39 F3
Pritchett Rd B31 123 B7
Pritchett St B6 66 E5
Pritchett Tower 4 B10 67 B1
Private Way B45 122 C4
Privet Cl B44 44 E3
Privet Rd CV2 96 B2
Probert Rd WV10 11 B1
Proctor St B7 67 A5
Proctors Barn La B98 154 B4
Proffitt Ave CV6 96 A1
Proffitt Cl Brownhills WS8 16 A5
Walsall WS2 28 E4
Proffitt St WS2 28 E4
Progress Cl CV3 135 A7
Progress Dr WS11 4 F6
Progress Ind Ctr WS11 4 F7
Progress Way CV3 135 A8
Prole St WV10 25 E4
Promenade The DY5 61 D2
Prophets Cl B97 153 D3
Prospect Dr WS14 9 F8
Prospect Gdns DY8 81 A4
Prospect Hill
Kidderminster DY10 116 E6
Redditch B97 153 E4
Stourbridge DY8 81 A4
Prospect La
Kidderminster DY10 116 E6
Solihull B91 106 D4
Prospect Manor Ct WS12 2 C3
Prospect Pk WS11 4 D7
Prospect Pl B12 86 F5
Prospect Rd Birmingham B13 86 F1
Burntwood WS7 7 B6
Dudley DY3 50 C2
Halesowen B62 83 C5
Royal Leamington Spa CV31 162 B5
Prospect Rd N B98 154 A4
Prospect Rd S B98 154 A4
Prospect Row Dudley DY2 62 D8
Stourbridge DY8 81 A3
Prospect St Bilston WV14 40 E6
Tamworth B79 21 A5
Tipton DY4 41 C1
Prospect Trad Est 2 B1 66 C3
Prosper Mdw DY6 60 F7
Prospero Cl B45 102 A2
Prosser St Bilston WV14 40 D5
Wolverhampton WV10 25 E5
Prossers Wlk B46 70 F7
Proud Cross Ringway DY11 116 C6
Proud's La WV14 40 D7
Provence Cl WV10 25 F4
Providence Cl WS3 28 C7
Providence Dr DY9 81 E6
Providence La WS3 28 C6
Providence Rd B61 136 F3
Providence Row WV14 51 B8
Providence St
Blackheath B64 62 D1
Coventry CV5 132 F8
Stourbridge DY9 81 F6
Tipton DY4 52 C5
Providence Terr WS10 41 E6
Provost Williams CE Prim Sch CV8 135 A1
Pruden Ave WV4 39 F3
Pryor Rd B68 64 C4
Ptarmigan Pl CV11 73 F3
Puckering's La 4 CV34 160 E6
Pudsey Dr B75 32 C3
Pugh Cres WS2 27 E2
Pugh Rd Bilston WV14 40 E3
Birmingham B6 67 A8
Wolverhampton WV14 39 F2
Pughe's Cl LE10 76 A6
Pugin Cl WV6 23 D3
Pugin Gdns B23 56 D8
Pullman Cl B77 22 A2
Pump St Kidderminster DY10 116 E4
Wolverhampton WV2 40 A7
Pumphouse La
Blackwell B45, B60 137 F7
Redditch B97 152 D1
Puppy Gn DY4 52 B5
Purbeck Cl B63 82 D1
Purbeck Croft B32 84 F4
Purbrook B77 35 E8
Purbrook Rd WV1 40 A8
Purcell Ave Lichfield WS13 3 C2
Nuneaton CV11 79 A7
Purcell Cl CV32 162 A8
Purcell Rd Coventry CV6 114 B8
Wolverhampton WV10 25 D8
Purdy Rd WV14 40 E2
Purefoy Rd Birmingham B13 105 C5
Coventry CV3 133 D8
Purley Gr B23 56 A5
Purlieu La CV8 147 D5
Purnells Way B93 128 A5
Purser Dr CV34 160 B4
Purshall Cl B97 153 C3
Purslet Rd WV1 26 A2
Purslow Gr B31 103 A1
Purton Mews CV31 162 C6
Putney Ave B20 55 C1
Putney La B62 101 B1
Putney Rd B20 55 C1
Putney Wlk B37 70 B3
Puxton Dr DY11 116 D8
Puxton La DY11 116 C7
Pye Green Rd WS11 1 E4
Pye Green Valley Cty Prim Sch WS12 2 A7
Pyeharps Rd LE10 75 E5
Pype Hayes Rd B24 57 D4
Pyt Pk CV5 112 D4
Pytchley Ho 6 B20 54 F3
Pytman Dr B76 58 A7

Quadrangle The B90 126 E8
Quadrant The Coventry CV1 165 B2
Nuneaton CV11 73 E3
Sedgley DY3 39 D1
Quadrille Lawns WV9 10 F2
Quail Gn WV6 23 F2
Quail Park Dr DY10 117 A2
Qualcast Rd WV1, WV10 25 F2
Quale Gr DY8 60 D3
Quantock Cl
Birmingham B45 102 B2
Halesowen B63 82 D2
Quantock Dr
Kidderminster DY10 117 A6
Nuneaton CV10 72 B3
Quantock Rd DY8 81 B6
Quantry La DY9 120 F8
Quarrington Gr B14 105 A3
Quarry Brow DY3 50 E6
Quarry Cl Cheslyn Hay WS6 4 E3
Leek Wootton CV35 155 F7
Quarry Fields CV35 155 F7
Quarry Hill B63 82 F2
Quarry Hills La WS14 9 D6
Quarry House Cl B45 101 F1
Quarry La Birmingham B31 103 A2
Bromsgrove B61 150 D8
Chadwick End CV35 145 C1
Halesowen B63 83 A2
Nuneaton CV11 73 F1
Quarry Lodge WS14 9 D5
Quarry Park Rd DY8 99 A8
Quarry Rd Birmingham B29 103 A8
Dudley DY2 62 B1
Kenilworth CV8 147 E6
Quarry Rise B69 63 B8
Quarry St CV32 161 C8
Quarry The DY10 116 F8
Quarry Wlk B45 122 A7
Quarry Yd CV10 72 C4
Quarryfield La CV1 165 C1
Quarrywood Gr CV2 114 A4
Quasar Ctr 1 WS1 28 E2
Quatford Gdns WV10 25 E5
Quayle Gr DY8 60 D3
Quayside Cl B69 63 E8
Quebec Ho 1 B5 86 D7
Queen Eleanors Dr B93 128 B8
Queen Elizabeth Ave WS2 27 F2
Queen Elizabeth Ct B19 66 B6
Queen Elizabeth Hospl B15 85 E4
Queen Elizabeth Rd
Birmingham B45 101 E2
Kidderminster DY10 117 B5
Nuneaton CV10 72 D5
Queen Elizabeth's Mercian High Sch B79 21 B6
Queen Isabel's Ave CV3 133 D8
Queen Margaret's Rd CV4 132 C8
Queen Mary St WS1 42 D6
Queen Mary's Gram Sch WS1 43 A8
Queen Mary's High Sch WS4 28 F3
Queen Mary's Rd
Bedworth CV12 78 C5
Coventry CV6 113 E8
Queen Philippa St CV3 133 D6
Queen Sq WV1 163 B3
Queen St Astwood Bank B96 158 E1
Bedworth CV12 78 C2
Bilston, Bunker's Hill WV14 40 E5
Bilston, Moxley WS10 41 B4
Birmingham B12 87 B5
Blackheath B64 62 D1
Brierley Hill, Pesnett DY5 61 C6
Brierley Hill, Quarry Bank DY5 82 A8
Brownhills WS9 15 F2
Burntwood WS7 6 F5
Cannock, Blackfords WS11 1 D1
Cannock, High Town WS11 2 A5
Cheslyn Hay WS6 4 D3
Coventry CV1 165 C4
Cubbington CV32 157 E5
Darlaston WS10 41 D8
Halesowen B63 83 A4
Kidderminster DY10 116 E7
Kingswinford DY6 60 D7
Lichfield WS13 9 A7
Oldbury B69 64 A8
Redditch B98 153 E4
Royal Leamington Spa CV32 157 A1
Stourbridge, Wollaston DY8 80 F6
Stourbridge, Wordsley DY8 60 E3
Sutton Coldfield B72 46 C4
Tipton DY4 51 F8
Walsall WS2 28 D1
Wednesbury WS10 41 E3
West Bromwich B70 53 D3
Wolverhampton WV1 163 C3
Queen Street Pas DY5 82 A8
Queen Victoria Rd
Coventry CV1 165 B2
Coventry CV1 165 B3
Queen Victoria Sch DY3 50 D8
Queen's Arc WV1 163 B3
Queen's Ave B69 52 A1
Queen's Cl CV8 147 F3
Queen's Coll B15 85 F5
Queen's Cotts B97 153 B4
Queen's Cres DY8 81 A7
Queen's Croft Specl Sch WS13 9 B7
Queen's Cross DY2 62 B8
Queen's Ct WV10 26 A6
Queen's Dr CV35 145 A1
Queen's Lea WV12 27 C5
Queen's Park Flats 2 LE10 75 E8
Queen's Park Rd B32 84 F6
Queen's Park Terr 3 LE10 75 E8
Queen's Rd Birmingham B23 56 C3
Coventry CV1 165 A2
Hinckley LE10 75 E8
Kenilworth CV8 147 F3
Nuneaton CV11 73 B4
Oldbury B68 64 D5
Smethwick B67 64 D4
Stourbridge DY8 80 F6
Tipton DY4 51 F5
Walsall WS5 43 B6
Queen's Ride B12 86 D4
Queen's Sq Warwick CV34 160 D5
West Bromwich B70 53 D3
Queens Arc CV11 73 C4
Queens Ave
Birmingham B14 104 E8
Solihull B90 106 B1
Queens CE Mid Sch CV11 73 A4
Queens Cl Birmingham B24 56 F2
Smethwick B67 65 A5
Queens Court Trad Est B70 52 F3
Queens Cres WV14 40 A1
Queens Ct Birmingham B3 164 B4
Brierley Hill DY5 61 C6
Queens Dr Birmingham B30 104 A4
Blackheath B65 63 D4
Burntwood WS7 6 F5
Queens Dr The B62 83 C5
Queens Gdns Bilston WV14 40 D7
Dudley DY2 62 C4
Queens Gdns Holyhead Rd WS10 41 E3
Queens Gdns Meeting St WS10 41 E3
Queens Head Rd B21 65 E7
Queens Hill DY9 119 D7
Queens Hospital Cl B15 66 C1
Queens Par 6 WS3 14 B1
Queens Rd
Birmingham, Aston B6 67 A8
Birmingham, Yardley B26 68 F1
Sedgley DY3 50 E8
Walsall WS4 29 C7
Queens Sq 6 WS11 1 E1
Queens Way B78 36 F6
Queensbridge Rd B13 86 E2
Queensbridge Sec Sch B13 86 E2
Queensbury Sch B24 56 F2
Queensland Ave CV5 112 F2
Queenspark CV31 161 E6
Queensway Birmingham B6 55 F2
Halesowen B63 83 B3
Nuneaton CV10 73 D6
Oldbury B68 64 B1
Royal Leamington Spa CV31 161 E6
Stourbridge DY9 81 E2
Sutton Coldfield B74 45 A8
Tamworth B79 21 A8
Queensway Cl B68 64 B1
Queensway Trad Est
Birmingham B5 164 D3
Royal Leamington Spa CV31 161 E6
Queensway (Tunnel) B3 164 B3
Queenswood Ct CV7 94 D4
Queenswood Rd
Birmingham B13 87 A4
Sutton Coldfield B75 32 B1
Quentin Dr DY1 61 F8
Queslade Cl B43 44 A1
Queslett Rd B43 44 C2
Queslett Rd E B74, B43 44 F5
Quibery Cl B98 154 F3
Quicksand La WS9 29 F4
Quigley Ave B9 67 B2
Quillets Rd DY8 60 C3
Quilletts Cl CV6 96 A1
Quilter Cl Dudley WV14 51 A8
Walsall WS2 27 F3
Quilter Rd B24 57 B2
Quince B77 22 B3
Quince Tree Specl Sch B77 22 B3
Quincey Dr B24 57 C3
Quincy Rise DY5 81 C7
Quinn Cl CV3 134 B7
Quinneys La B98 159 B6
Quinton Ave WS6 4 F3
Quinton CE Jun & Inf Sch B32 84 A6
Quinton Cl Redditch B98 154 D1
Solihull B92 89 D3
Quinton Expressway B32 84 B4
Quinton Flats CV3 133 D7
Quinton La B32 84 D6
Quinton Par CV3 133 D7
Quinton Pk CV3 133 D7
Quinton Rd Birmingham B17 85 C3
Coventry CV1 165 C1
Quinton Rd W B32 84 D4
Quintondale 5 B90 126 C8
Quonians La WS13 9 B8
Quorn Cres DY8 60 C3
Quorn Gr B24 57 B2
Quorn Ho 3 B20 54 F3
Quorn Way CV3 134 E7

Rabbit La WV10 12 A8
Rabone La B66 65 C6
Raby Cl B69 62 F8
Raby St WV2 163 C2
Race Leys Fst Sch CV12 78 B3
Race Leys Mid Sch CV12 78 B4
Racecourse La DY8 80 F1
Racecourse Rd WV6 25 A5
Rachael Gdns WS10 42 C4
Rachel Cl DY4 41 C1
Rachel Gdns B29 85 D2
Radbourn Dr B74 46 C6
Radbourne Dr B63 82 A7
Radbourne Rd B90 106 D3
Radbrook Way CV31 162 D6
Radcliffe Dr B62 83 E6
Radcliffe Gdns 6 CV31 162 A6
Radcliffe Rd CV5 132 F8
Radcliffe Tower 3 B12 86 F8
Raddens Rd B62 83 F3
Raddington Dr B92 106 E8
Raddlebarn Farm Dr B29 103 F8
Raddlebarn Jun & Inf Sch B29 85 F1
Raddlebarn Rd B29 103 F8
Radford Ave DY10 116 E7
Radford Circ 5 CV6 113 A4
Radford Cl WS5 43 A3
Radford Dr WS4 15 C2
Radford Ho Coventry CV6 113 A7
Redditch B97 153 A4
Radford La WV3 37 F7
Radford Prim Sch CV6 113 B5

Radford Rd Alvechurch
B48 139 D7
Birmingham B29 103 A6
Coventry CV1 113 B5
Royal Leamington Spa CV31 162 C7
Radford Rise B91 107 E5
Radford Semele CE Prim Sch CV31 162 E5
Radley Dr CV10 73 A1
Radley Gr B29 85 A2
Radley Rd Stourbridge DY9 81 F4
Walsall WS4 29 C7
Radleys Cty Prim Sch WS4 29 D7
Radleys The B33 89 D8
Radleys Wlk B33 89 D8
Radmore Cl WS7 6 D8
Radmore Rd LE10 71 D3
Radnor Cl B45 102 B2
Radnor Croft WS5 43 C3
Radnor Dr CV10 72 E2
Radnor Gn B71 53 C7
Radnor Ho B32 102 D6
Radnor Rd Birmingham B20 66 D8
Oldbury B68 84 B7
Sedgley DY3 50 C8
Radnor Rise WS12 2 B4
Radnor St B18 66 A6
Radnor Wlk CV2 114 F8
Radstock Ave B36 68 C7
Radstock Rd WV12 13 C1
Radway Cl B98 154 B6
Radway Rd B90 126 E8
Raeburn Rd B43 44 C4
Raeside Dr B45 102 B1
RAF Cotts B35 57 F2
Raford Rd B23 56 D6
Ragees Rd DY6 60 F4
Raglan Ave Perton WV6 23 F3
Smethwick B66 65 C4
Raglan Cl Aldridge WS9 30 F3
Nuneaton CV11 73 D4
Sedgley DY3 50 B7
Raglan Ct Bromsgrove B60 137 A1
7 Coventry CV1 113 E3
Raglan Gr CV8 148 B5
Raglan Ho B33 69 A2
Raglan Rd Birmingham B21 65 C8
Birmingham, Balsall Heath B5 86 D5
Smethwick B66 65 C4
Raglan St Brierley Hill DY5 61 C6
Coventry CV1 165 D3
Wolverhampton WV3 163 A2
Raglan Way B37 70 D1
Ragley Cl Knowle B93 128 B7
Walsall WS3 14 A1
Ragley Cres B60 151 A8
Ragley Dr
Birmingham, Grove Vale B43 43 D2
Birmingham, Sheldon B26 89 C6
2 Willenhall WV13 40 F8
Ragley Ho B97 153 A4
Ragley Way CV11 73 F2
Ragley Wlk 1 B65 63 C3
Raglis Cl B97 153 A2
Ragnall Ave B33 89 D7
Raikes La WS14 17 C7
Rail Bridge Est B70 53 A1
Railswood Dr WS3 15 B3
Railway Cl B80 159 D4
Railway Dr Bilston WV14 40 E5
Wolverhampton WV1 163 C3
Railway La WV13 27 A1
Railway Rd Birmingham B20 55 F2
Sutton Coldfield B73 46 B5
Railway St Bilston WV14 40 E5
Cannock WS11 4 E8
Norton Canes WS11 6 A5
Tipton DY4 52 C5
West Bromwich B70 53 B4
Wolverhampton WV1 163 C3
Railway Terr Bedworth CV12 78 C2
Birmingham, Aston B7 67 B6
Birmingham, Hamstead B42 54 F6
4 Wednesbury WS10 41 F2
Railway View B10 87 C7
Railwayside Cl B66 64 E7
Rainbow St Dudley WV14 40 D2
Wolverhampton WV2 163 C1
Rainford Way B38 123 C8
Rainham Cl DY4 51 D5
Rainsbrook Dr
Nuneaton CV11 74 A1
Solihull B90 126 F6
Rainscar B77 36 B7
Raison Ave CV11 73 F8
Rake Gate Jun & Inf Schs WV10 11 B1
Rake Hill WS7 7 B8
Rake Way B15 66 B1
Raleigh Cl Birmingham B21 54 B1
Hinckley LE10 71 D4
Raleigh Croft B43 43 E3
Raleigh Ind Est B21 54 B1
Raleigh Rd Bilston WV14 41 A3
Coventry CV2 114 B2
Raleigh St Walsall WS2 28 C2
West Bromwich B71 53 C4
Ralph Barlow Gdns B44 56 B8
Ralph Rd Birmingham B8 67 D4
Coventry CV6 112 F5
Solihull B90 106 C4
Ralphs Mdw B32 84 D2
Ralston Cl WS3 14 A4
Ramillies Cres WS6 4 F1
Ramp Rd B26 90 C5
Ramsay Cl B71 53 F8
Ramsay Cres CV5 112 B7
Ramsay Rd Oldbury B68 64 C1
Tipton DY4 51 E7
Walsall WS2 28 A5
Ramsden Ave CV10 72 D6
Ramsden Cl B29 103 B7
Ramsey Cl Birmingham B45 101 F1
Hinckley LE10 71 B1
Ramsey Rd 1 Birmingham B7 67 C7
Royal Leamington Spa CV31 162 B7
Ran-tan The B97 158 E5
Ranby Rd CV2 113 F4
Randall Ave B48 139 A6
Randall Cl DY6 60 F4
Randall Rd CV8 147 F3
Randle Dr B75 32 C3
Randle Rd Nuneaton CV10 72 D4
Stourbridge DY9 81 C4
Randle St CV6 113 B5
Randolph Cl CV31 162 C6
Randwick Gr B44 44 E1
Ranelagh Ho WV2 39 D7
Ranelagh Rd WV2 39 D6
Ranelagh St CV31 162 A6
Ranelagh Terr CV31 161 F6
Range Meadow Cl CV32 156 C3
Rangemoor CV3 134 D6
Rangeways Rd
Kidderminster DY11 116 A8
Kingswinford DY6 60 F4
Rangeworthy Cl B97 158 C7
Rangifer Rd B78 20 F1
Rangoon Rd B92 89 E4
Ranleigh Ave DY6 60 F4
Rann Cl B16 66 A1
Rannoch Cl Brierley Hill DY5 81 B8
Hinckley LE10 75 B8
Rannock Cl CV3 114 F2
Ranscombe Dr DY3 50 D2
Ransom Rd Birmingham B23 56 C4
Coventry CV6 113 E8
Ranton Pk WS11 2 A2
Ranulf Croft CV3 133 C7
Ranulf St CV3 133 C7
Ranworth Rise WV4 39 D4
Raphael Cl CV5 112 C3
Ratcliff Way DY4 52 D6
Ratcliff Wlk 3 B69 64 A7
Ratcliffe Cl DY3 50 F6
Ratcliffe Ct CV10 72 C4
Ratcliffe Rd Hinckley LE10 75 F6
Solihull B91 107 C7
Wednesfield WV11 27 A6
Rathbone Cl Bilston WV14 40 D5
Birmingham B5 86 E7
Keresley CV7 95 A6
Rathbone Rd B67 64 F2
Rathley Wlk B38 123 C8
Rathlin Cl WV9 11 A3
Rathlin Croft B36 70 B6
Rathmore Cl DY8 80 E2
Rathvilly Sch B31 103 B3
Rathwell Cl WV9 11 A2
Rattle Croft B33 68 E3
Raveloe Dr CV11 73 D1
Raven Cl Cannock WS12 2 E4
Cheslyn Hay WS6 4 D2
Huntington WS12 1 C7
Raven Cragg Rd CV5 132 E8
Raven Cres WV11 26 F8
Raven Ct 21 DY5 61 D2
Raven Hays Rd B31 102 C2
Raven Rd WS5 43 B6
Raven Way CV11 73 F2
Raven Wlk 4 B15 86 C7
Ravenall Cl B34 69 B7
Ravenfield Cl B8 68 A5
Ravenhayes La B32 102 A6
Ravenhill Dr WV8 10 A4
Ravenhurst Dr B43 43 E3
Ravenhurst Mews B23 56 E3
Ravenhurst Rd B17 85 C6
Ravenhurst St B12 87 A8
Ravens Bank Dr B98 154 E7
Ravens Bank Fst Sch B98 154 D6
Ravens Ct WS8 15 F7
Ravensbourne Gr WV13 27 C2
Ravenscroft DY8 80 C6
Ravenscroft Rd Solihull B92 107 A8
Willenhall WV12 27 B5
Ravensdale Ave CV32 156 C2
Ravensdale Cl WS5 43 B7
Ravensdale Gdns WS5 43 B7
Ravensdale Prim Sch CV2 114 D4
Ravensdale Rd
Birmingham B10 87 F7
Coventry CV2 114 D3
Ravenshaw La B91 108 A4
Ravenshaw Rd B16 65 C2
Ravenshaw Way B91 108 A3
Ravenshill Rd B14 105 D4
Ravensholme WV6 23 F2
Ravensitch Wlk DY5 61 E1
Ravensmere Rd B98 154 B1
Ravensthorpe Cl CV3 134 E8
Ravenstone B77 36 B8
Ravenswood B15 85 E8
Ravenswood Cl B74 46 B8
Ravenswood Dr B91 106 F1
Ravenswood Dr S B91 106 E1
Ravenswood Hill B46 70 F7
Rawdon Gr B44 56 B8
Rawlett High Sch B79 21 A8
Rawlings Rd B67 65 A2
Rawlins Croft B35 58 C3
Rawlins St B16 66 A1
Rawlinson Rd CV32 157 B2
Rawnsley Dr CV8 148 C6
Rawnsley Rd WS12 2 E7
Ray Ct B74 31 E3
Ray Hall La Birmingham B43 54 B8
West Bromwich B71 43 A1
Raybolds Bridge St WS2 28 C4
Raybon Croft B45 122 A6
Raybould's Fold DY2 62 C5
Rayford Dr B71 43 A2
Raygill B77 36 B8
Rayleigh Ho B27 88 D3
Rayleigh Rd WV3 39 A8
Raymond Ave B42 55 B6
Raymond Cl Coventry CV6 95 F5
Walsall WS2 28 D5
Raymond Gdns WV11 26 E6
Raymond Rd B8 67 E4
Raymont Gr B43 44 B4
Rayners Croft B26 68 F2
Raynor Cres CV12 77 D1
Raynor Rd WV10 25 F6
Raynsford Wlk CV34 155 D1
Raywoods The CV10 72 F3
Rea Ave B45 121 E8
Rea Cl B31 123 A7
Rea Fordway B45 101 F1
Rea St B5 164 D1
Rea St S B5 86 F8
Rea Terr B5 66 F2
Rea Tower B19 66 C5
Rea Valley Dr B31 103 B2
Reabrook Rd B31 122 F8
Read St CV1 113 E3
Readers Wlk B43 43 F1
Reading Ave CV11 73 F7
Reading Cl CV2 96 B3
Reansway Sq W6 25 A4
Reapers Cl WV12 27 D5
Reapers Wlk WV8 10 F1
Rear Cotts B48 138 F6
Reardon Ct CV34 155 E1
Reaside Cres B14 104 B5
Reaside Croft B12 86 E6
Reaside Jun Sch B45 101 E1
Reaview Dr B29 86 B2
Reay Nadin Dr B73 45 B4
Reaymer Cl WS2 28 B6
Rebecca Dr B29 85 E2
Rebecca Gdns WV4 38 F4
Recreation Rd
Bromsgrove B61 136 F3
Coventry CV6 96 A3
Recreation St DY2 62 D5
Rectory Ave WS10 41 D6
Rectory Cl Allesley CV5 112 C6
Bedworth CV7 78 A1
Drayton Bassett B78 34 E5
Stourbridge DY8 81 B3
Whitnash CV31 162 B4
Rectory Dr CV7 78 A1
Rectory Fields DY8 60 E2
Rectory Gdns
Birmingham B36 69 A8
Oldbury B68 64 C5
Solihull B91 107 C3
Stourbridge DY8 81 B3
Rectory Gr B18 65 E6
Rectory La Allesley CV5 112 C6
Birmingham B36 69 A8
Upton Warren B61 150 A4
Rectory Park Ave B75 46 E4
Rectory Park Cl B75 46 E4
Rectory Park Ct B75 46 F6
Rectory Park Rd B26 89 C5
Rectory Rd Birmingham B31 103 B3
Redditch B97 153 D1
Solihull B91 107 C3
Stourbridge DY8 81 B3
Sutton Coldfield B75 46 E6
Rectory St DY8 60 E3
Red Brick Cl B64 82 D7
Red Brook Rd WS2 28 A5
Red Deeps CV11 78 D8
Red Deeps Specl Sch CV10 78 B8
Red Hall Prim Sch DY3 50 C3
Red Hill Redditch B98 153 F2
Stourbridge DY8 81 B4
Red Hill Cl B80 159 E6
Red Hill Gr B38 123 F7
Red Hill Pl B62 101 A7
Red Hill St WV1 163 B4
Red House Ave WS10 42 B3
Red House La WS9 29 F5
Red House Park Rd B43 43 E2
Red House Rd B33 68 E2
Red La Burton Green CV8 131 C2
Coventry CV6 113 F5
Essington WV11 13 C2
Kenilworth CV8 147 D8
Sedgley DY3 50 B8
Red Leasowes Rd B63 83 A3
Red Lion Ave WS11 6 A4
Red Lion Cl B69 52 A1
Red Lion Cres WS11 6 A4
Red Lion La WS11 6 B4
Red Lion St Alvechurch B48 139 B6
Redditch B98 153 E4
Wolverhampton WV1 163 B3
Red River Rd WS2 28 A5
Red Sands Rd DY10 116 E8
Red Wing Wlk B36 70 A8
Redacre Rd B73 45 F2
Redacres WV6 24 E6
Redbank Ave B23 56 C3
Redbourn Rd WS3 14 A4
Redbrook Cl WS12 2 D2
Redbrook Covert 8 B38 123 E8
Redbrooks Cl B91 107 A1
Redburn Dr B14 104 D2
Redcap Croft CV6 95 D4
Redcar Cl CV32 157 C4
Redcar Croft B36 68 C8
Redcar Rd Coventry CV1 113 E5
Wolverhampton WV10 11 D4
Redcliff B77 21 F5
Redcliffe Dr WV5 49 B6
Redcotts Cl WV10 26 A8
Redcroft Dr B24 57 C5
Redcroft Rd DY2 62 E6
Reddal Hill Prim Sch B64 62 E1
Reddal Hill Rd B64 62 E2
Reddicap Heath Inf Sch B75 46 F5
Reddicap Heath Rd B75 46 F4
Reddicap Hill B75 46 E4
Reddicap Trad Est B76 46 D4
Reddicroft B73 46 C5
Reddings La B28 87 E3
Reddings Rd B13 86 E2
Reddings The B47 125 A5
Redditch Ho B33 69 E2
Redditch Rd
Alvechurch, Arrowfield Top B48 139 B8
Alvechurch, Rowney Green B48 139 C3
Birmingham B38 123 C8
Hopwood B48 123 B1
Stoke Heath B60 150 D5
Studley B80 159 D5
Redditch Ringway B97 153 D4
Redditch Sta B97 153 D4
Redditch Wlk 4 CV2 115 A7
Redesdale Ave CV6 112 F5
Redfern Ave CV8 148 A6
Redfern Cl B92 89 B1
Redfern Dr WS7 7 B5
Redfern Park Rd B11 88 A5
Redfern Rd B11 88 A5
Redfly La DY5 61 C6
Redford Cl B13 87 B2
Redgate Cl B38 103 D2
Redhall Rd Birmingham B32 84 E7
Dudley DY3 50 C2
Redhill Ave WV5 49 A6
Redhill Cl Stourbridge DY8 81 B4
Tamworth B79 21 A7
Redhill Ct DY8 81 B4
Redhill Jun & Inf Sch B25 88 A6
Redhill Jun Sch WS11 1 F4
Redhill La B45, B61 121 C5
Redhill Rd
Birmingham, King's Norton B38 123 D7
Birmingham, Tyseley B25 88 A6
Cannock WS11 1 F4
Redhill Sch DY8 81 B4
Redhouse Cl B93 127 E4
Redhouse Ind Est WS9 29 E6
Redhouse JMI Sch WS9 29 E5
Redhouse Rd WV6 24 B5
Redhouse St WS1 42 E7
Redhurst Dr WV10 11 B3
Redlake B77 35 F8
Redlake Dr DY9 99 B8
Redlake Rd DY9 81 B1
Redland Cl Coventry CV2 96 E2
Marlbrook B60 121 C1
Redland Rd CV31 162 B5
Redlands Cl B91 107 D5
Redlands Rd B91 107 D5
Redlands Way B74 31 A1
Redliff Ave B36 58 D1
Redlock Field WS14 9 A5
Redmead Cl B30 103 C4
Redmoor Gdns WV4 39 A5
Redmoor High Sch LE10 71 B3
Redmoor Way B76 58 D6
Rednal Hill Inf Sch B45 122 C7
Rednal Hill Jun Sch B45 122 C7
Rednal Hill La B45 122 A6
Rednal Mill Dr B45 122 C7
Rednal Rd B38 103 E1
Rednall Dr B75 32 C3
Rednell Ho B69 63 D6
Redoak Ho WV10 25 F3
Redpine Crest WV12 27 D5
Redruth Cl Coventry CV6 114 A8
Kingswinford DY6 60 D8
Nuneaton CV11 74 A4
Walsall WS5 43 D7
Redruth Rd WS5 43 D7
Redstart Ave DY10 117 B2
Redstone Cl B98 154 C6
Redstone Dr WV11 26 F5
Redstone Farm Rd B28 106 B6
Redthorn Gr B33 68 D3
Redvers Rd B9 67 E1
Redway Ct B75 46 E4
Redwell Cl B77 21 D5
Redwing B77 36 A6
Redwing Cl WS7 7 D5
Redwing Ct DY10 117 A1
Redwing Dr WS12 1 C7
Redwing Gr B23 56 B7
Redwood Ave DY1 50 F5
Redwood Bsns Pk B66 64 C7
Redwood Cl Aldridge B74 30 F2
Birmingham B30 103 E4
Redwood Croft
Birmingham B14 104 E7
Nuneaton CV10 73 A1
Redwood Dr Burntwood WS7 6 F8
Cannock WS11 2 A3
Tipton B69 52 B2
Redwood Gdns B27 88 B5
Redwood Ho B37 69 F5
Redwood Rd
Birmingham B30 103 E4
Dudley WV14 40 D2
Walsall WS5 43 B4
Redwood Way WV12 27 B8
Reed Sq B35 58 B4
Reedham Gdns WV4 38 D5
Reedly Rd WV12 13 C1
Reedmace B77 21 C2
Reedmace Cl B38 123 F8
Reedswood Cl WS2 28 C3
Reedswood Gdns WS2 28 C3
Reedswood La WS2 28 C3
Reedswood Way WS2 28 B4
Rees Dr Coventry CV3 133 D4
Wombourne WV5 49 B7
Reeve Ct DY10 117 A1
Reeve Dr CV8 148 A4
Reeve La WS13 9 B8
Reeves Gdns WV8 10 A4
Reeves Rd Birmingham B14 104 C6
Hinckley LE10 75 F6
Reeves St WS3 28 B8
Reflex Ind Pk WV13 27 A3
Reform St B70 53 D3
Reg Hadden Ct CV10 73 D6
Regal Croft B36 68 B8
Regan Ave B90 106 A1
Regan Cres B23 56 E6
Regan Ct B75 47 C5
Regan Ho B13 105 D7
Regency Arc 8 CV32 161 F8
Regency Cl CV10 73 D6
Regency Ct Coventry CV5 132 F8
Walsall WS1 43 A7
Wolverhampton WV1 163 B4
Regency Dr Birmingham B38 103 F2
Coventry CV3 132 F5
Kenilworth CV8 147 F3
Regency Gdns B14 105 C3
Regency Ho Birmingham B16 66 A1
Royal Leamington Spa CV32 162 A8
Regency Mews CV32 162 A8
Regency Wlk B74 31 D5
Regent Ave B69 52 A1
Regent Cl Birmingham B5 86 D6
Halesowen B63 83 A4
Kingswinford DY6 60 C6
Tipton B69 63 A8
Regent Ct 5 Hinckley LE10 75 D8
3 Smethwick B66 65 A5
Regent Dr B69 52 A1
Regent Gr CV32 161 F8
Regent Ho Oldbury B68 64 B2
6 Walsall WS2 28 D3
Regent Mews B60 150 E8
Regent Par B1 66 C4
Regent Park Rd B10 67 C1
Regent Pl Birmingham B1 66 C4
2 Royal Leamington Spa CV31 162 A7
Tipton B69 52 B2
Regent Rd
Birmingham, Handsworth B21 65 D8
Birmingham, Harborne B17 85 D6
Tipton B69 63 A8
Wolverhampton WV4 38 E5
Regent Specl Sch B69 52 A1
Regent St Bedworth CV12 78 C4
Bilston WV14 40 D6
Birmingham, Hockley B1 66 C4
Birmingham, Stirchley B30 104 A7
Blackheath B64 62 F2
Coventry CV1 165 A2
Dudley DY1 51 C6
Hinckley LE10 75 D8
Nuneaton CV11 73 D5
Royal Leamington Spa CV32 161 F8
Smethwick B66 65 A6
Tipton DY4 51 E8
Willenhall WV13 27 A3
Regent Wlk B8 68 B7
Regents Park Jun & Inf Sch B10 87 B8
Regents The B15 85 D8
Regina Ave B44 55 E8
Regina Cl B45 101 E2
Regina Cres Coventry CV2 115 A7
Wolverhampton WV6 24 C4
Regina Dr Birmingham B42 55 D3
Walsall WS4 29 B4
Reginald Rd Birmingham B8 67 D4
Smethwick B67 64 F2
Regis Beeches WV6 24 C5
Regis Gdns B65 63 C2
Regis Heath Rd B65 63 E2
Regis Ho B68 64 C2
Regis Rd Blackheath B65 63 C2
Wolverhampton WV6 24 C5
Regis Sch WV6 24 B5
Regis Wlk CV2 114 F7
Reid Ave WV12 27 D6
Reid Rd B68 64 D1

Reigate Ave B8 68 B4
Reindeer Rd B78 20 E1
Relay Dr B77 36 C7
Reliance Trad Est WV14 40 B5
Relko Dr B36 68 C7
Relton Mews CV6 113 F6
Rembrandt Cl Cannock
WS11 2 D2
Coventry CV5 112 C3
Remburn Gdns CV34 160 F8
Remembrance Rd
Coventry CV3 134 D6
Wednesbury WS10 42 C3
Remington Dr WS11 4 F8
Remington Pl WS2 28 C5
Remington Rd WS2 28 B5
Rene Rd B77 21 E5
Renfrew Cl DY8 60 C3
Renfrew Gdns DY11 116 C5
Renfrew Sq B35 58 B4
Renfrew Wlk CV4 132 A8
Renison Rd CV12 77 E1
Rennie Gr B32 84 D5
Rennison Dr WV5 49 A6
Renown Cl DY5 61 B7
Renton Gr WV10 11 A1
Renton Rd WV10 11 A1
Repington Rd N B77 22 A5
Repington Rd S B77 22 A5
Repington Way B75 47 B5
Repton Ave WV6 23 E3
Repton Cl WS11 4 B8
Repton Dr CV6 96 B2
Repton Gr B9 68 B3
Repton Ho B23 56 F6
Repton Rd B9 68 B3
Reservoir Cl WS2 42 B8
Reservoir Pas WS10 41 F3
Reservoir Pl WS2 42 B8
Reservoir Rd
Birmingham, Edgbaston B16 65 F2
Birmingham, Rednall B45 122 C3
Birmingham, Selly Oak B29 85 C3
Birmingham,
Stockland Green B23 56 E4
Blackheath B65 63 D3
Cannock WS12 2 D4
Kidderminster DY11 116 C3
Oldbury B68 64 C4
Solihull B92 106 F8
Reservoir Retreat B16 65 F1
Reservoir St WS2 42 B8
Retallack Cl B66 65 B8
Retford Dr B76 46 E4
Retford Gr B25 88 C6
Retreat Gdns DY3 50 E7
Retreat St
Astwood Bank B96 158 E1
Wolverhampton WV3 163 A1
Retreat The B64 82 E7
Revesby Wlk 8 B7 67 A4
Revival St WS3 28 C8
Rex Cl CV4 131 D8
Reyde Cl B97 153 A2
Reynalds Cross Sch B92 106 D7
Reynards Cl Dudley DY3 51 A7
Redditch B97 152 F3
Reynolds Cl WS13 3 B2
Reynolds Ct 10 B68 84 B8
Reynolds Gr WV6 24 A5
Reynolds Ho B19 66 E7
Reynolds Rd Bedworth CV12 78 A4
Birmingham B21 65 E7
Reynolds Wlk WV11 27 B8
Reynoldstown Rd B36 68 C8
Rhayader Rd B31 102 E5
Rhodes Alms Hos The B21 65 F7
Rhodes Cl DY3 50 A4
Rhone Cl B11 87 C3
Rhoose Croft B35 58 B3
Rhuddlan Way DY10 116 E1
Rhyl Rd CV11 79 F6
Rhys Thomas Cl WV12 27 D4
Ribbesford Ave WV10 25 B8
Ribbesford Cl B63 82 D6
Ribbesford Cres WV14 40 D1
Ribble Cl CV12 79 B2
Ribble Ct B73 46 B5
Ribble Rd CV3 113 F2
Ribble Wlk B36 69 F8
Ribblesdale B77 36 B7
Ribblesdale Ave LE10 71 E3
Ribblesdale Rd B29,B30 104 A8
Ribbonfields CV11 73 D3
Rich Cl CV34 161 B7
Richard Cooper Rd WS14 17 F5
Richard Joy Cl CV6 95 C2
Richard Lee Prim Sch
CV2 114 E3
Richard Lighton Ho 6 B1 66 C3
Richard Pl WS5 43 C8
Richard Rd WS5 43 C8
Richard St Birmingham B7 66 F5
West Bromwich B70 53 B3
Richard St S B70 53 C2
Richard St W B70 53 B2
Richard Williams Rd WS10 42 B2
Richards Cl Birmingham
B31 122 F6
Blackheath B65 63 E4
Kenilworth CV8 147 F5
Richards Ct WS11 5 F6
Richards Ho 3 Oldbury B69 63 E4
2 Walsall WS2 28 D3
Richards Rd DY4 40 F1
Richards St WS10 41 D7
Richardson Cl CV34 155 F1
Richardson Dr DY8 80 E8
Richardson Ho DY4 52 C8
Richborough Dr DY1 50 F4
Riches St WV6 24 F3
Richford Gr B33 69 D2
Richmere Ct WV6 24 B3
Richmond Ave
Birmingham B12 86 F5
Wolverhampton WV3 24 F1
Richmond Cl Birmingham
B20 55 A3
Cannock WS11 2 A5
Tamworth B79 21 A5
Richmond Croft B42 54 F6
Richmond Ct
Birmingham B29 103 C7
Halesowen B63 82 E3
Oldbury B68 64 C5
6 Royal Leamington Spa
CV31 162 B7
Stourbridge DY9 81 B1
2 Sutton Coldfield B72 57 B7
Richmond Dr Lichfield WS14 9 D7
Perton WV6 24 A3
Wolverhampton WV3 24 E1
Richmond Gdns
Stourbridge DY8 80 F7
Wombourne WV5 49 A5
Richmond Gr DY8 80 E8
Richmond Hill B68 64 C5
Richmond Hill Gdns B15 85 E7
Richmond Hill Rd B15 85 F6
Richmond Ho 2 B37 70 C1
Richmond Mews WV3 25 A1
Richmond Pk DY6 60 C8
Richmond Pl B14 104 F8
Richmond Prim Sch LE10 71 C3
Richmond Rd
Birmingham, Eachway B45 121 E7
Birmingham, Hockley B18 66 B6
Birmingham, Yardley B33 68 D2
Dudley DY2 62 C8
Hinckley LE10 71 C3
Hollywood B47 125 C7
Nuneaton CV11 73 A4
Sedgley DY3 50 E7
Smethwick B66 65 A2
Solihull B92 88 F2
Sutton Coldfield B73 46 B6
Wolverhampton WV3 24 E1
Richmond St Coventry CV2 114 A3
Halesowen B63 83 A4
Walsall WS1 29 A1
West Bromwich,
Great Bridge B70 52 F6
West Bromwich,
Ryders Green B70 52 E5
Richmond St S B70 52 E5
Richmond Way 2 B37 70 C3
Rickard Cl B93 127 E6
Rickman Dr B15 86 D8
Rickyard Cl
Birmingham,
Northfield B29 103 A6
Birmingham, Yardley B25 68 D1
Rickyard La B98 154 D5
Rickyard Piece B32 84 E4
Riddfield Rd B36 68 E8
Ridding La WS10 41 F2
Riddings Cres WS3 14 F4
Riddings The
Birmingham B33 68 F4
Coventry CV5 132 E7
Stourbridge DY9 81 D2
Sutton Coldfield B76 58 B8
Tamworth B77 21 E5
Wolverhampton WV10 26 A7
Riddon Dr LE10 75 B8
Ridgacre Ent Pk B71 53 B6
Ridgacre La B32 84 C6
Ridgacre Rd Birmingham
B32 84 C6
West Bromwich B71 53 B6
Ridgacre Rd W B32 84 A6
Ridge Cl Birmingham B13 105 C6
Willenhall WS2 27 D3
Ridge Ct CV5 112 A6
Ridge Gr DY9 81 C5
Ridge La WV11 26 D7
Ridge Prim Sch DY8 80 C5
Ridge Rd DY6 60 C5
Ridge St DY8 80 C6
Ridge Way WS9 30 B4
Ridgefield Rd B62 83 C7
Ridgeley Cl CV34 155 E2
Ridgemount Dr B38 123 D8
Ridgethorpe CV3 134 E6
Ridgewater Cl B45 122 B6
Ridgeway Birmingham B17 65 B2
Dudley DY3 50 D6
Ridgeway Ave Coventry
CV3 133 C6
Halesowen B62 84 A6
Ridgeway Cl B80 159 E2
Ridgeway Ct WS2 27 F2
Ridgeway Dr WV4 38 F3
Ridgeway Prim Sch WS7 7 A5
Ridgeway Rd Stourbridge
DY8 60 F2
1 Tipton DY4 52 A8
Ridgeway Specl Sch
CV34 156 A1
Ridgeway The
Birmingham B23 56 A5
Burntwood WS7 7 A4
Hinckley LE10 75 D6
Warwick CV34 156 A1
Ridgewood B34 69 B6
Ridgewood Ave DY8 80 C7
Ridgewood Cl
Royal Leamington Spa
CV32 156 C1
7 Walsall WS1 42 F8
Ridgewood Dr B75 32 B1
Ridgewood Gdns B44 55 F7
Ridgewood High Sch DY8 80 C5
Ridgewood Rise B77 22 A5
Ridgley Rd CV4 131 E8
Ridgmont Croft B32 84 E5
Riding Cl B71 53 F7
Riding Way WV12 27 D6
Ridings Brook Dr WS11 2 A2
Ridings La B98 154 B6
Ridley St B1 164 A1
Ridpool Prim Sch B33 69 B3
Ridpool Rd B33 69 B3
Ridware Ho WS13 3 E1
Rifle Range Rd DY11 116 B3
Rifle St WV14 51 A8
Rigby Cl CV34 161 D4
Rigby Dr WS11 1 F4
Rigby Hall Sch B60 151 C8
Rigby La B60 151 C8
Rigby St WS10 42 A1
Rigdale Cl CV2 114 E2
Righton Ho B77 21 D1
Riland Ave B75 46 D5
Riland Ct B72 57 C7
Riland Gr B75 46 C5
Riland Ind Est B75 46 D5
Riland Rd B75 46 D5
Riley B77 21 E3
Riley Cl CV8 148 D4
Riley Cres WV3 39 A6
Riley Dr B36 59 A1
Riley Rd B14 105 D3
Riley Sq CV2 96 B1
Riley St WV13 27 B2
Rills The LE10 71 E2
Rilstone Rd B32 84 F5
Rindleford Ave WV4 38 C6
Ring Rd WS7 6 E7
Ring Road St Andrews
WV1 163 A3
Ring Road St Davids
WV1 163 C3
Ring Road St Georges
WV2 163 C2
Ring Road St Johns WV2 163 B2
Ring Road St Marks WV3 163 B2
Ring Road St Patricks
WV1 163 C4
Ring Road St Peters WV1 163 B3
Ring The B25 88 C8
Ringhills Rd WV8 10 B2
Ringinglow Rd B44 44 D2
Ringmere Ave B36 69 B7
Ringswood Rd B92 88 E4
Ringway WS11 1 E1
Ringway Hill Cross CV1 165 A3
Ringway Ind Est WS13 3 C3
Ringway Queens CV1 165 A2
Ringway Rudge CV1 165 A2
Ringway St Johns CV1 165 C2
Ringway St Nicholas CV1 165 B3
Ringway St Patricks CV1 165 B1
Ringway Swanswell CV1 165 C3
Ringway The DY10 116 F5
Ringway Whitefriars CV1 165 C3
Ringwood Ave WS9 30 B5
Ringwood Dr B45 102 A1
Ringwood Highway CV2 96 E2
Ringwood Rd WV10 11 D1
Rinhill Gr CV31 162 D6
Ripley Cl B69 62 F8
Ripley Gr B23 56 B5
Riplingham 3 CV32 156 F2
Ripon Cl CV5 112 B8
Ripon Dr B71 42 D1
Ripon Rd Birmingham B14 105 C4
Walsall WS2 28 B2
Wolverhampton WV10 25 C7
Rippingille Rd B43 44 C4
Ripple Rd B30 104 B7
Risborough Cl CV5 112 C3
Rischale Way WS4 29 D8
Risdale Cl CV32 156 D2
Rise Ave B45 122 A7
Rise The
Birmingham, Great Barr B42 55 A8
Birmingham,
Marston Green B37 90 A7
Hopwood B48 123 B4
Kingswinford DY6 60 E5
Riseley Cres B5 86 D7
Rising Brook WV6 24 B4
Rising La Chadwick End B93 145 B5
Lapworth B94 144 F5
Rising Rd B94 144 C5
Rissington Ave B29 104 A8
Ritchie Cl B13 87 A1
Rivendell Gdns WV6 24 B5
River Brook Dr B30 104 B8
River Cl Bedworth CV12 77 F1
Royal Leamington Spa
CV32 161 D8
River Ct 3 CV1 113 B3
River Lee Rd B11 87 E5
River St B5 67 A2
River Wlk CV2 96 C2
Riverbank Rd WV13 27 D2
Riverdrive B77, B78 21 B3
Riverfield Gr B77 21 D5
Riverford Croft CV4 132 D4
Rivermead CV11 73 A4
Rivermead Pk B34 69 A6
Riversdale 6 CV32 161 E8
Riversdale Rd B14 105 D3
Riverside B80 159 F4
Riverside Cl Coventry CV3 134 A7
Lickey End B60 137 C6
Riverside Cres B28 105 D4
Riverside Ct
Birmingham B38 103 D3
1 Coleshill B46 70 F7
Riverside Dr B91 107 E2
Riverside Ind Est B78 35 B8
Riversleigh Dr DY8 80 E8
Riversleigh Rd CV32 156 C1
Riversley Rd CV11 73 C3
Riverway WS10 42 B2
Rivington Cl DY8 80 E4
Rivington Cres B44 45 C1
Ro-Oak Rd CV6 112 F5
Roach B77 35 D6
Roach Cl Birmingham B37 70 C3
Brierley Hill DY5 61 D5
Roach Cres WV11 26 F8
Roach Pool Croft B16 65 C2
Road No 1 DY10 116 E2
Road No 2 DY10 116 E2
Road No 3 DY10 116 E2
Roanne Ringway CV11 73 B4
Robert Ave B23 56 E6
Robert Cl Coventry CV3 134 C4
Tamworth B79 20 F7
Robert Cramb Ave CV4 131 F8
Robert Ct 5 B13 87 B2
Robert Rd Bedworth CV7 95 F8
Birmingham B20 55 B1
Tipton DY4 51 F6
Robert St DY3 50 D4
Robert Wynd WV14 40 A1
Roberts Cl Bilston WS10 41 B4
Brownhills WS9 15 F2
Roberts Ct B24 57 C6
Roberts Green Rd DY3 50 E4
Roberts La DY9 99 B8
Roberts Prim Sch DY3 50 D4
Roberts Rd Birmingham B27 88 D3
Walsall WS3 28 F5
Wednesbury WS10 42 E2
Robertson Knoll B36 68 F7
Robertsons Gdns 5 B7 67 C7
Robeson Cl DY4 51 D5
Robey's La B78 22 D3
Robin Cl Birmingham B36 70 A8
Huntington WS12 1 C7
Kingswinford DY6 61 A6
Robin Ct DY10 117 A2
Robin Gr WV11 26 C7
Robin Hood Cres B28 105 E7
Robin Hood Croft B28 105 F6
Robin Hood La B13,B28 105 E7
Robin Hood Rd
Brierley Hill DY5 61 F2
Coventry CV3 134 C6
Robin Hood Sch B28 106 B6
Robin Rd B23 56 E5
Robin Wlk WS2 27 F3
Robin's Cl DY8 81 A3
Robina Cl CV32 157 B2
Robinfield Dr B31 123 A7
Robins Bsns Pk B70 52 E7
Robins Cl WS6 4 D1
Robins Gr CV34 160 C4
Robins Hill Dr B48 139 B5
Robins Rd WS7 6 E7
Robins Way CV10 72 A3
Robinson Cl B79 20 E7
Robinson Rd Bedworth CV12 95 D8
Burntwood WS7 6 F8
Robinson Way LE10 75 F4
Robinson's End Mid Sch
CV10 72 A3
Robinson's Way B76 58 D5
Robottom Cl WS2 28 B6
Robson Cl WS8 15 F5
Rocester Ave WV11 26 E7
Rochdale Wlk B10 87 C7
Roche Rd WS3 13 F1
Roche The WS13 8 A8
Roche Way WS3 13 F1
Rochester Ave WS7 7 A7
Rochester Cl CV11 73 B3
Rochester Croft WS2 28 A4
Rochester Rd
Birmingham B31 103 A4
Coventry CV5 132 E8
Rochester Way WS12 2 C1
Rochester Wlk DY10 117 C5
Rochford Cl
Birmingham B45 121 E7
Halesowen B63 82 F2
Sutton Coldfield B76 58 A8
6 Walsall WS2 42 C7
Rochford Ct
Royal Leamington Spa CV31 161 E7
Solihull B90 127 A6
Rochford Gr WV4 38 D5
Rock Ave B45 122 C7
Rock Cl CV6 96 B1
Rock Gr B92 88 E3
Rock Hill Bromsgrove B61 150 D7
Weeford WS14, B78 19 C4
Rock La CV7 94 C7
Rock Mill La CV32 161 C8
Rock Rd Sedgley WV14 50 F8
Solihull B92 88 E3
Rock St DY3 50 E5
Rock The WV6 24 D5
Rocken End CV6 113 D8
Rocket Pool Dr WV14 41 A2
Rockford Cl B98 158 F5
Rockford Rd B42 55 A7
Rockingham Cl
Dorridge B93 127 D2
Dudley DY3 50 B3
5 Walsall WS3 14 B1
Rockingham Dr WV6 23 F3
Rockingham Gdns B74 46 B6
Rockingham Hall Gdns DY9 99 D7
Rockingham Rd B25 88 D8
Rockland Dr B33 68 E4
Rockland Gdns WV13 40 F8
Rocklands Cres WS13 3 D1
Rocklands Dr B75 46 B8
Rocklands Specl Sch WS13 9 C8
Rockley Gr B45 122 B7
Rockley Rd B65 63 A6
Rockmead Ave B44 44 F2
Rockmoor Cl B37 69 E3
Rockrose Gdns WV10 12 A7
Rockville Rd B8 68 A4
Rockwell La B48 139 E4
Rockwood Rd B27 88 B4
Rocky La Birmingham B6 67 A6
Birmingham B7 67 B6
Birmingham, Great Barr B42 55 B5
Bournheath B61 136 E7
Kenilworth CV8 148 D2
Rodbaston Coll WS14 19 A5
Rodborough Rd
Birmingham B26 89 B7
Dorridge B93 127 E3
Rodbourne Rd B17 85 C3
Roddis Cl B23 56 D8
Roden Ave DY10 117 A7
Roderick Dr WV11 26 D7
Roderick Rd B11 87 C5
Rodhouse Cl CV4 111 D1
Rodlington Ave B44 44 F1
Rodman Cl B15 85 D8
Rodney Cl Birmingham B16 66 A2
Hinckley LE10 71 D4
Solihull B92 89 B1
Rodney Rd B92 89 B1
Rodway Cl Birmingham B19 66 E7
Brierley Hill DY5 81 D7
Wolverhampton WV4 39 D3
Rodway Dr CV5 111 D4
Rodwell Gr B44 56 A8
Roe Cl CV34 160 F8
Roebuck Cl B34 69 E5
Roebuck Glade WV12 27 E4
Roebuck La Smethwick B66 64 F8
West Bromwich B70 53 E1
Roebuck Pl WS3 28 E6
Roebuck Rd WS3 28 E6
Roebuck St B70 53 F1
Roedean Cl B44 56 B7
Roford Ct DY3 50 E5
Rogerfield Rd B23 57 A6
Rogers Cl WV11 13 A2
Rogers Rd B8 68 B5
Rogers Way CV34 160 B4
Rogue's La LE10 71 C6
Rokeby Cl B76 46 E4
Rokeby Rd B43 43 F2
Rokeby Wlk B34 69 A6
Rokewood Cl DY6 49 D1
Rokholt Cres WS11 1 C1
Rolan Dr B90 125 E8
Roland Ave CV6 95 C3
Roland Gdns 5 B19 66 C8
Roland Gr 4 B19 66 C8
Roland Mount CV6 95 C3
Roland Rd B19 66 C8
Roland Terr 3 B19 66 C8
Rolfe St B66 65 A6
Rollason Cl CV6 113 C8
Rollason Rd Birmingham
B24 57 A3
Coventry CV6 113 B8
6 Dudley DY2 62 D8
Rollason's Yd CV6 96 A3
Rollesby Dr WV13 40 F8
Rolling Mill Cl B5 86 E7
Rollingmill St WS2 28 C1
Rollswood Dr B91 107 A4
Rolvenden Ct WV13 27 C2
Roma Rd B11 87 E5
Roman Cl WS8 6 E2
Roman Ct Birmingham B38 124 B8
Cannock WS11 4 E5
Tamworth B77 35 E7
Roman La B74 31 B4
Roman Pk B74 31 B4
Roman Rd Coventry CV2 114 B3
Little Aston B74 31 C4
Roman Rd (Sandy La) DY8 80 D4
Roman View WS11 4 F5
Roman Way Birmingham
B15 85 D3
Blackheath B65 63 C3
Bromsgrove B61 137 B4
Coleshill B46 59 F2
Coventry CV3 133 D3
Lichfield WS14 9 D7
Tamworth B79 20 E7
Roman Way Fst Sch B98 154 E3
Romany Rd B45 101 D1
Romany Way DY8 80 C3
Romford Cl B26 89 B6
Romford Rd CV6 95 B2
Romilly Ave B20 55 B3
Romilly Cl Lichfield WS14 9 E7
Stourbridge DY8 80 E6
Sutton Coldfield B76 47 A4
Romney B77 35 F8

Romney Cl Birmingham B28 . 105 F7
Hinckley LE10 ... 71 A3
Romney House Ind Est
WS10 ... 41 B7
Romney Way B43 ... 44 D4
Romsey Ave CV10 ... 73 D8
Romsey Gr WV10 ... 11 C3
Romsey Ho WS2 ... 42 C7
Romsey Rd WV10 ... 11 C3
Romsey Way WS3 ... 13 F3
Romsley Cl Birmingham
B45 ... 121 E8
Halesowen B63 ... 83 B2
Redditch B98 ... 154 F3
Walsall WS4 ... 15 C2
Romsley Ct [8] DY2 ... 62 B8
Romsley Hill Grange B62 .. 100 F1
Romsley Rd
Birmingham B32 ... 102 B8
Oldbury B68 ... 64 B2
Stourbridge DY9 ... 81 C5
Romulus Cl B20 ... 55 B3
Ronald Gr B36 ... 58 D1
Ronald Pl B9 ... 67 E2
Ronald Rd B9 ... 67 D2
Rood End Prim Sch B68 ... 64 C6
Rood End Rd B69 ... 64 C7
Rooker Ave WV2 ... 39 F6
Rooker Cres WV2 ... 39 F6
Rookery Ave Brierley Hill
DY5 ... 61 A2
Wolverhampton WV4 ... 40 A3
Rookery Cl B97 ... 153 D1
Rookery Ct WS13 ... 8 E7
Rookery La Aldridge WS9 ... 30 B6
Coventry CV6 ... 95 B4
Weeford B75, B78 ... 19 C2
Wolverhampton WV2 ... 39 B6
Rookery Par WS9 ... 30 B6
Rookery Pk DY5 ... 61 B5
Rookery Rd
Birmingham,
Handsworth B21 ... 54 E1
Birmingham, Selly Oak B29 ... 85 F2
Wolverhampton WV14, WV4 .. 40 A3
Wombourne WV5 ... 49 B6
Rookery Rise WV5 ... 49 B6
Rookery Road Jun &
Inf Schs B21 ... 54 E1
Rookery St WV11 ... 26 C5
Rookery The B62 ... 84 A2
Rooks Mdw DY9 ... 99 B6
Rookwood Dr WV6 ... 23 F2
Roosevelt Dr CV4 ... 111 E2
Rooth St WS10 ... 42 B4
Roper Way DY3 ... 50 F6
Roper Wlk DY3 ... 50 F6
Rosafield Ave B62 ... 83 F6
Rosalind Ave DY1 ... 51 B6
Rosalind Gr WV11 ... 27 A5
Rosamond St WS1 ... 42 D7
Rosary RC Prim Sch B8 ... 67 E3
Rosary Rd B23 ... 56 D3
Rosary Villas [1] B11 ... 87 C5
Rosaville Cres CV5 ... 112 A6
Rose Ave Alvechurch B48 ... 139 A5
Coventry CV6 ... 112 F5
Kingswinford DY6 ... 60 F5
Oldbury B68 ... 84 C7
Rose Bay Mdw WS11 ... 2 C2
Rose Cl B66 ... 65 C5
Rose Cottage Flats CV5 ... 111 D5
Rose Cotts [6]
Birmingham, Selly Oak B29 ... 85 F2
Birmingham, Stirchley B30 .. 104 A6
Rose Croft CV8 ... 147 E6
Rose Ct CV7 ... 130 B8
Rose Dr WS8 ... 15 E5
Rose Hill Barnt Green B45 ... 122 B4
Brierley Hill DY5 ... 62 A1
Willenhall WV13 ... 41 A8
Rose Hill Cl B36 ... 69 B8
Rose Hill Gdns WV13 ... 27 B1
Rose Hill Rd B21 ... 66 A7
Rose La Burntwood WS7 ... 7 C7
Nuneaton CV11 ... 73 C3
Tipton B69 ... 52 C2
Rose Rd Birmingham B17 ... 85 D6
Coleshill B46 ... 70 F8
Rose St WV14 ... 40 F2
Rose Terr B45 ... 138 D8
Rosebay Ave B38 ... 123 F8
Roseberry Ave CV2 ... 96 C1
Rosebery Rd Smethwick
B66 ... 65 C4
Tamworth B77 ... 35 D4
Rosebery St Birmingham
B18 ... 66 A4
Wolverhampton WV3 ... 25 B1
Rosecroft Rd B26 ... 89 C6
Rosedale Ave
Birmingham B23 ... 56 E3
Smethwick B66 ... 65 C5
Rosedale CE Inf Sch
WV12 ... 27 D5
Rosedale Gr B25 ... 88 C8
Rosedale Pl WV13 ... 41 A8
Rosedale Rd B25 ... 88 C8
Rosedale Wlk [5] DY6 ... 60 E8
Rosedene Dr B20 ... 54 F2
Rosefield Croft B6 ... 66 F7
Rosefield Ct B67 ... 65 A4
Rosefield Pl [14] CV32 ... 161 F8
Rosefield Rd B67 ... 65 A4
Rosefield St CV32 ... 162 A8
Rosefield Wlk [13] CV32 ... 161 F8
Rosegreen Cl CV3 ... 133 E6
Rosehall Cl Redditch B98 ... 158 E6
Solihull B91 ... 106 F1
Rosehill WS12 ... 2 A8
Rosehip Cl WS5 ... 43 A3
Rosehip Dr CV2 ... 114 B6
Roseland Ave DY2 ... 51 F1
Roseland Rd CV8 ... 147 F3
Roseland Way [7] B15 ... 66 B1
Roselands Ave CV2 ... 114 D8
Roseleigh Rd B45 ... 122 B6
Rosemary Ave Bilston WV14 . 40 F6
Cheslyn Hay WS6 ... 4 D3
Wolverhampton WV4 ... 39 C6
Rosemary Cl Clayhanger
WS8 ... 15 D6
Coventry CV4 ... 111 E3
Rosemary Cres Dudley DY1 .. 51 A6
Wolverhampton WV4 ... 39 C5
Rosemary Cres W WV4 ... 39 B5
Rosemary Dr Huntington
WS12 ... 1 D5
Little Aston B74 ... 31 C3
Stoke Prior B60 ... 150 C1
Rosemary Hill CV8 ... 147 F5
Rosemary Hill Rd B74 ... 31 D4
Rosemary La DY8 ... 80 D3
Rosemary Mews CV8 ... 147 F5
Rosemary Nook B74 ... 31 D5
Rosemary Rd
Birmingham B33 ... 68 F2
Cheslyn Hay WS6 ... 4 D4
Halesowen B63 ... 82 E2
Kidderminster DY10 ... 117 B7
Tamworth B77 ... 21 F4
Tipton DY4 ... 52 A6
Rosemary Way LE10 ... 75 B7
Rosemoor Dr DY5 ... 81 B7
Rosemount Birmingham B32 . 84 E5
Wolverhampton WV6 ... 24 D5
Rosemount Cl CV2 ... 114 E7
Rosemullion Cl CV7 ... 96 B8
Rosetti Cl DY10 ... 117 C6
Roseville Ct [4] WV14 ... 51 C8
Roseville Gdns WV8 ... 10 A4
Roseville Prec [5] WV14 ... 51 C8
Rosewood CV11 ... 73 F1
Rosewood Cl Hinckley LE10 ... 75 F6
Tamworth B77 ... 21 D4
Rosewood Cres CV32 ... 157 B2
Rosewood Ct B77 ... 21 D4
Rosewood Dr
Barnt Green B45 ... 138 C7
Birmingham B23 ... 56 D2
Willenhall WV12 ... 27 B8
Rosewood Gdns WV11 ... 13 B3
Rosewood Pk WS6 ... 4 D2
Rosewood Rd DY1 ... 51 B5
Rosewood Specl Sch DY1 ... 50 E1
Roshven Rd B12 ... 87 A4
Roslin Cl B60 ... 137 B1
Roslin Gr B19 ... 66 C6
Roslyn Cl B66 ... 65 A6
Ross B65 ... 63 B2
Ross Cl Coventry CV5 ... 112 A5
Wolverhampton WV3 ... 24 E2
Ross Dr DY6 ... 60 C7
Ross Hts B65 ... 63 B3
Ross Rd WS3 ... 28 F6
Ross Way CV11 ... 79 B7
Rosse Ct B92 ... 107 F8
Rossendale Cl B63 ... 82 D6
Rossendale Way CV10 ... 72 E2
Rosslyn Ave CV6 ... 112 E6
Rosslyn Rd B76 ... 57 F6
Roston Dr LE10 ... 71 A1
Rostrevor Rd B10 ... 67 F1
Rosy Cross B79 ... 21 B5
Rotary Ct [2] WV3 ... 25 B2
Rothay B77 ... 35 F8
Rothbury Gn WS12 ... 2 E2
Rotherby Gr B37 ... 90 B7
Rotherfield Cl CV31 ... 162 B7
Rotherfield Rd B26 ... 89 B8
Rotherham Rd CV6 ... 95 C2
Rotherhams Oak La B94 ... 142 F7
Rothesay Ave CV4 ... 112 B2
Rothesay Cl CV10 ... 73 A2
Rothesay Croft B32 ... 102 B7
Rothesay Dr DY8 ... 60 C3
Rothesay Way WV12 ... 27 B6
Rothwell Dr B91 ... 106 D4
Rothwell Rd CV34 ... 155 C1
Rotten Row WS13 ... 9 C7
Rotton Park Rd B16 ... 65 D2
Rotton Park St B16 ... 65 F3
Rough Coppice Wlk B35 ... 58 A2
Rough Hay JMI Sch WS10 ... 41 C7
Rough Hay Pl WS10 ... 41 C7
Rough Hay Rd WS10 ... 41 C7
Rough Hill Dr Blackheath
B65 ... 62 F6
Redditch B98 ... 158 F6
Rough Hills Cl WV2 ... 39 F6
Rough Hills Rd WV2 ... 39 F6
Rough Rd B44 ... 45 A3
Rough The B97 ... 158 D8
Rough Wood Ctry Pk
WV12 ... 27 E6
Roughknowles Rd CV4 ... 131 D6
Roughlea Ave B36 ... 68 F7
Roughley Dr B75 ... 32 C2
Rouncil Cl B92 ... 107 D7
Rouncil La CV8 ... 155 C8
Round Croft WV13 ... 27 A2
Round Hill DY3 ... 39 D2
Round Hill Ave DY9 ... 81 C1
Round House Rd
Coventry CV3 ... 134 B8
Dudley DY3 ... 50 E4
Round Moor Wlk B35 ... 58 A3
Round Oak Specl Sch
CV32 ... 157 A3
Round Rd B24 ... 57 B2
Round Saw Croft B45 ... 121 F8
Round St DY2 ... 62 C6
Roundabout The B31 ... 102 D1
Roundhill Cl B76 ... 46 E4
Roundhill Terr B62 ... 63 E1
Roundhill Way WS8 ... 7 A2
Roundhills Rd B62 ... 83 F8
Roundlea Cl WV12 ... 27 B7
Roundlea Rd B31 ... 102 E7
Rounds Green Prim Sch
B69 ... 63 E7
Rounds Green Rd B69 ... 63 F7
Rounds Hill CV8 ... 147 E2
Rounds Hill Rd WV14 ... 51 D8
Rounds Rd WV14 ... 40 D3
Roundway Down WV6 ... 23 E3
Rousay Cl B45 ... 101 F1
Rousdon Gr B43 ... 54 D8
Rover Dr B36 ... 58 F1
Rover Rd CV1 ... 165 B2
Rovex Bsns Pk B11 ... 87 F5
Row The CV7 ... 97 D3
Rowallan Rd B75 ... 32 D2
Rowan Cl Binley Woods
CV3 ... 135 D7
Bromsgrove B61 ... 136 E2
Hollywood B47 ... 125 B5
Lichfield WS13 ... 9 D8
Rowan Cres Dudley WV14 ... 40 B1
Redditch B97 ... 153 A4
Wolverhampton WV3 ... 38 E7
Rowan Ct Birmingham B30 .. 104 A2
Oldbury B66 ... 64 D8
Rowan Dr Birmingham B28 . 106 A5
Essington WV11 ... 13 B3
[6] Warwick CV34 ... 160 F8
Rowan Gr Burntwood WS7 ... 6 F7
Coventry CV2 ... 96 E2
Rowan Rd Cannock WS11 ... 1 C2
Nuneaton CV10 ... 72 C6
Redditch B97 ... 153 A4
Sedgley DY3 ... 39 F1
Sutton Coldfield B72 ... 46 C3
Walsall WS5 ... 42 F4
Rowan Rise DY6 ... 60 E6
Rowan Way
Birmingham,
Chelmsley Wood B37 ... 70 C1
Birmingham, Longbridge
B31 ... 122 F8
Rowans The CV12 ... 77 E2
Rowantrees B45 ... 122 B5
Roway La B69 ... 52 F1
Rowbrook Cl B90 ... 125 E8
Rowcroft Covert B14 ... 104 C2
Rowcroft Rd CV2 ... 115 A6
Rowdale Rd B42 ... 55 C6
Rowden Dr Birmingham B23 .. 57 A6
Solihull B91 ... 106 E2
Rowena Gdns DY3 ... 39 C2
Rowheath Ho B30 ... 103 E5
Rowheath Rd B30 ... 103 F4
Rowington Ave B65 ... 63 D3
Rowington Cl CV6 ... 112 D5
Rowington Gn CV35 ... 144 F1
Rowington Rd B34 ... 69 E6
Rowington Terr B25 ... 88 B7
Rowland Ave B80 ... 159 E3
Rowland Gdns WS2 ... 28 C3
Rowland Hill Ave DY11 ... 116 B5
Rowland Hill Ctr [9] DY10 .. 116 E6
Rowland Hill Dr DY4 ... 52 C5
Rowland St WS2 ... 28 C3
Rowland Way (Road 1a)
DY10 ... 116 E1
Rowlands Ave Walsall WS2 .. 27 E3
Wolverhampton WV1 ... 26 B2
Rowlands Cl WS2 ... 27 E4
Rowlands Cres B91 ... 107 B8
Rowlands Rd B26 ... 88 E7
Rowley Cl WS12 ... 2 B8
Rowley Dr CV3 ... 134 B4
Rowley Gr B33 ... 69 D3
Rowley Hall Ave B65 ... 63 C4
Rowley Hall Prim Sch B65 .. 63 C4
Rowley La CV3 ... 134 D3
Rowley Pl WS4 ... 29 B7
Rowley Rd
Coventry CV3, CV8 ... 134 B3
Whitnash CV31 ... 162 A2
Rowley Regis Coll B65 ... 63 B3
Rowley Regis Com Hospl
B65 ... 63 B2
Rowley Regis Sta B65 ... 63 E2
Rowley St WS1 ... 29 A2
Rowley View Bilston WV14 ... 41 A3
Darlaston WS10 ... 41 C4
West Bromwich B70 ... 53 B3
Rowley Village B65 ... 63 C3
Rowley's Green La CV6 ... 95 E4
Rowleys Green Lane
Ind Est CV6 ... 95 E4
Rowney Croft B28 ... 105 E4
Rowney Green La B48 ... 139 F5
Rowood Dr B91 ... 107 D7
Rowthorn Cl B74 ... 45 A7
Rowthorn Dr B90 ... 127 A6
Rowton Ave WV6 ... 23 E3
Rowton Dr B74 ... 44 F5
Roxall Cl DY10 ... 98 C2
Roxburgh Croft CV32 ... 157 C6
Roxburgh Gr B43 ... 44 C4
Roxburgh Rd Nuneaton CV11 73 E1
Sutton Coldfield B73 ... 46 A3
Roxby Gdns WV6 ... 25 A5
Royal Brierley Glassworks
DY5 ... 61 C2
Royal Cl Blackheath B65 ... 63 C5
Brierley Hill DY5 ... 81 C8
Royal Cres CV3 ... 134 C5
Royal Ct Hinckley LE10 ... 75 D7
Sutton Coldfield B73 ... 46 B2
Royal Doulton Glassworks
DY8 ... 80 F7
Royal Hospl WV2 ... 163 C2
Royal Leamington Spa
Rehabilitation Hospl CV34 161 E4
Royal Mail St B1 ... 164 B2
Royal Oak La CV12 ... 95 C7
Royal Oak Rd Blackheath
B65 ... 62 F5
Halesowen B62 ... 83 F5
Royal Oak Yd CV12 ... 78 B4
Royal Orthopaedic Hosp
The Birmingham,
Ladywood B16 ... 66 B1
Birmingham,
Northfield B31 ... 103 B5
Royal Priors [9] CV32 ... 161 F8
Royal Rd B72 ... 46 C4
Royal Scot Gr WS1 ... 42 D5
Royal Sq [6] B97 ... 153 E3
Royal Sta The WV1 ... 163 D2
Royal Star Cl B33 ... 69 C2
Royal Way DY4 ... 52 A2
Royal Wolverhampton Sch
WV3 ... 39 B7
Roydon Rd B27 ... 106 C8
Roylesden Cres B73 ... 45 C2
Royston Chase B74 ... 31 A3
Royston Cl CV3 ... 115 A3
Royston Croft B12 ... 86 F6
Royston Ct [7] B13 ... 87 B2
Royston Way DY3 ... 50 C8
Rubens Cl Coventry CV5 ... 112 C3
Dudley DY3 ... 50 D5
Rubery Ct WS10 ... 41 C7
Rubery Farm Gr B45 ... 121 F7
Rubery La B45 ... 102 A1
Rubery La S B45 ... 121 F8
Rubery St WS10 ... 41 D8
Ruckleigh Sch B91 ... 107 C4
Ruckley Ave [4] B19 ... 66 C7
Ruckley Rd B29 ... 103 B8
Rudge Ave WV1 ... 26 B3
Rudge Cl WV12 ... 27 C4
Rudge Croft B33 ... 69 A4
Rudge Rd CV1 ... 165 A2
Rudge Wlk B18 ... 66 A3
Rudgewick Croft [1] B6 ... 66 F6
Rudyard Cl WV10 ... 11 E4
Rudyard Gr B33 ... 69 B3
Rudyngfield Dr B33 ... 68 F4
Rufford B79 ... 20 E6
Rufford Cl Birmingham B23 ... 56 D8
Hinckley LE10 ... 75 D3
Rufford Prim Sch DY9 ... 81 C5
Rufford Rd DY9 ... 81 C4
Rufford St DY9 ... 81 D5
Rufford Way WS9 ... 29 E7
Rugby Rd Binley Woods
CV3 ... 135 D8
Bulkington CV12 ... 79 D2
Cubbington CV32 ... 157 E6
Hinckley LE10 ... 75 D6
Royal Leamington Spa
CV32 ... 156 D1
Stourbridge DY8 ... 80 D7
Rugby St WV1 ... 25 B4
Rugeley Ave WV12 ... 27 D8
Rugeley Rd
Burntwood,
Chase Terrace WS7 ... 6 F8
Burntwood, Gorstey Ley WS7 ... 7 C7
Cannock, Hazelslade WS12 ... 2 F6
Cannock, Hednesford WS12 ... 2 D7
Ruislip Cl B35 ... 58 A4
Ruiton St DY3 ... 50 D4
Rumbow B63 ... 83 B4
Rumbow La B62 ... 100 D3
Rumbush La B94 ... 125 F3
Rumer Hill Bsns Est WS11 ... 4 E7
Rumer Hill Rd WS11 ... 4 F8
Runcorn Cl Birmingham B37 .. 70 C4
Redditch B98 ... 158 F8
Runcorn Rd B12 ... 87 A5
Runcorn Wlk [10] CV2 ... 115 A7
Runneymede Gdns CV10 ... 72 F3
Runnymede Dr CV7 ... 130 C5
Runnymede Rd B11 ... 87 E3
Rupert Rd CV6 ... 113 B8
Rupert St Birmingham B7 ... 67 A4
Wolverhampton WV3 ... 25 A2
Rush Gn B32 ... 84 E2
Rush La Redditch B98 ... 154 B6
Tamworth B77 ... 35 D4
Rushall Cl Stourbridge DY8 ... 80 E8
Walsall WS4 ... 29 B4
Rushall Ct B43 ... 54 E7
Rushall Manor Cl WS4 ... 29 B4
Rushall Manor Rd WS4 ... 29 B4
Rushall Prim Sch WS4 ... 29 B7
Rushall Rd WV10 ... 11 E2
Rushbrook Cl
Clayhanger WS8 ... 15 D6
Solihull B92 ... 88 E2
Rushbrook Gr B14 ... 104 C4
Rushbrook La B94 ... 141 D3
Rushbrooke Cl B13 ... 86 F4
Rushbrooke Dr B73 ... 45 C3
Rushbury Cl Bilston WV14 ... 40 B5
Solihull B90 ... 106 D4
Rushden Croft B44 ... 44 F1
Rushey La B11 ... 88 A5
Rushford Ave WV5 ... 49 A6
Rushford Cl B90 ... 127 A7
Rushlake Gn B34 ... 69 B5
Rushleigh Rd B90 ... 125 E8
Rushmead Gr B45 ... 122 A7
Rushmere Rd DY4 ... 52 A8
Rushmoor Cl B74 ... 46 B6
Rushmoor Dr CV5 ... 112 F3
Rushmore St CV31 ... 162 B7
Rushmore Terr [9] CV31 ... 162 B7
Rushock Cl B98 ... 159 C7
Rushton Cl CV7 ... 130 C7
Rushwick Croft B34 ... 69 D6
Rushwick Ct B23 ... 56 B3
Rushwick Gr B90 ... 127 A6
Rushwood Cl WS4 ... 29 A3
Rushy Piece B32 ... 84 D3
Rusina Ct [2] CV31 ... 161 F6
Ruskin Ave Blackheath B65 ... 63 D2
Dudley DY3 ... 50 A5
Kidderminster DY10 ... 117 C6
Wolverhampton WV4 ... 39 F2
Ruskin Cl Birmingham B6 ... 66 F7
Coventry CV6 ... 112 D6
Nuneaton CV10 ... 72 A5
Ruskin Ct [5] B68 ... 84 B8
Ruskin Gr B27 ... 88 B2
Ruskin Rd WV10 ... 12 A1
Ruskin St B71 ... 53 C5
Russel Croft B60 ... 151 A7
Russell Bank Rd B74 ... 31 E4
Russell Cl Tipton,
Moxley DY4 ... 41 C1
Tipton, Tividale B69 ... 52 D2
Wolverhampton WV11 ... 12 F1
Russell Ct
[12] Royal Leamington Spa
CV31 ... 162 A7
Sutton Coldfield B74 ... 31 D3
Wolverhampton WV3 ... 163 A2
Russell Ho WS10 ... 41 F2
Russell Rd Bilston WV14 ... 40 F7
Birmingham, Hall Green B28 .. 87 E1
Birmingham, Moseley B13 ... 86 D3
Kidderminster DY10 ... 116 F4
Russell St Coventry CV1 ... 165 C4
Dudley DY1 ... 51 B1
Royal Leamington Spa CV32 . 156 F1
Wednesbury WS10 ... 41 F2
Willenhall WV13 ... 27 B2
Wolverhampton WV3 ... 163 A2
Russell St N [2] CV1 ... 165 C4
Russell Terr CV31 ... 162 A7
Russell's Hall Rd DY1 ... 50 E1
Russells Hall Hospl DY5 ... 61 D7
Russells Hall Prim Sch
DY1 ... 50 E1
Russells The B13 ... 86 D3
Russet Way B31 ... 102 E6
Russet Wlk WV8 ... 10 E1
Russett Cl Burntwood WS7 ... 7 A6
Walsall WS5 ... 43 D8
Russett Way DY5 ... 61 B7
Ruston St B16 ... 66 B1
Ruth Chamberlain Ct
[3] DY11 ... 116 D6
Ruth Cl DY4 ... 41 C2
Ruthall Cl B29 ... 103 C7
Rutherford Glen CV11 ... 73 F1
Rutherford Rd
Birmingham B23 ... 56 E7
Bromsgrove B60 ... 151 B7
Walsall WS2 ... 28 A5
Rutherglen Ave CV3 ... 134 A6
Rutland B17 ... 85 A6
Rutland Ave Hinckley LE10 ... 75 C7
Nuneaton CV10 ... 72 F4
Wolverhampton WV4 ... 38 D4
Rutland Cres Aldridge WS9 ... 16 B1
Bilston WV14 ... 40 E7
Rutland Croft [3] CV3 ... 134 F8
Rutland Dr Birmingham B26 ... 88 E7
Bromsgrove B60 ... 151 A8
Tamworth B78 ... 21 A1
Rutland Pl DY8 ... 80 D8
Rutland Rd Cannock WS12 ... 2 E1
Smethwick B66 ... 65 A1
Wednesbury WS10 ... 42 D4
West Bromwich B71 ... 53 C7
Rutland St WS3 ... 28 E5
Rutland Terr [5] B18 ... 66 A5
Rutley Gr B32 ... 84 F4
Rutter St WS1 ... 42 E8
Rutters Mdw B32 ... 84 B4
Ryan Ave WV11 ... 27 A7
Ryan Pl DY2 ... 62 C6
Rycroft Gr B33 ... 69 C2
Rydal B77 ... 36 A7
Rydal Ave CV11 ... 74 A6
Rydal Cl Aldridge B74 ... 30 F2
Allesley CV5 ... 112 B8
Cannock WS12 ... 2 A8
Hinckley LE10 ... 74 F7
Wolverhampton WV11 ... 26 C7
Rydal Dr WV6 ... 23 F4
Rydal Gn WV1 ... 26 B1
Rydal Ho [6] B69 ... 63 D5
Rydal Way B28 ... 105 F7
Rydding La B71 ... 53 B8
Rydding Sq B71 ... 53 B8
Ryde Ave CV10 ... 73 D7
Ryde Gr B27 ... 88 A1
Ryde Park Rd B45 ... 122 C7

Ryder Ho B70 52 E3
Ryder St Birmingham B4 164 C3
Stourbridge DY8 60 D2
West Bromwich B70 52 F5
Ryders Green Prim Sch B70 53 A4
Ryders Green Rd B70 52 F4
Ryders Hayes Jun & Mix Inf Sch WS4 15 A5
Ryders Hayes La WS3 15 B4
Ryders Hill Cres CV10 72 C7
Rye Croft 8 Birmingham B27 88 C5
Hollywood B47 125 A5
Stourbridge DY9 81 E2
Rye Gr B11 87 F4
Rye Grass Wlk B35 58 B3
Rye Hill CV5 112 A6
Rye Piece Ringway CV12 78 C3
Ryebank Cl B30 103 C5
Ryeclose Croft B37 70 D3
Ryecroft Ave WV4 39 B5
Ryecroft Cl DY3 50 C8
Ryecroft Cotts WV4 39 B5
Ryecroft Dr 8 WS7 7 A8
Ryecroft Pk 1 WS2 28 E3
Ryecroft Pl WS3 28 F6
Ryecroft Sh Ctr 4 WS7 7 A8
Ryecroft St 2 WS2 28 E3
Ryefield WV8 10 E1
Ryefield Cl Hagley DY9 99 A4
Solihull B91 106 E5
Ryefield La B76 48 B2
Ryefields Rd B60 150 C3
Ryegrass La B97 158 C6
Ryemarket 2 DY8 81 A5
Ryhope Cl CV12 77 C1
Ryhope Wlk WV9 11 A3
Ryknild Cl B74 31 F6
Ryknild St WS14 9 E6
Ryland Cl Halesowen B63 82 E2
Royal Leamington Spa CV31 162 C6
Tipton DY4 52 B5
Ryland Ho B19 66 D5
Ryland Rd
Birmingham, Edgbaston B15 86 C8
Birmingham, Gravelly Hill B24 56 F1
Birmingham, Sparkhill B11 87 D4
Ryland St B16 66 B1
Rylands Dr WV4 39 A4
Rylcroft WV4 39 F4
Ryle St WS3 14 D1
Rylston Ave CV6 95 A1
Rylstone Way 4 CV34 155 E1
Rymond Rd B34 68 E6
Ryton B77 35 F8
Ryton Cl Coventry CV4 132 B8
Redditch B98 154 D1
Sutton Coldfield B73 46 B5
Wolverhampton WV10 26 A5
Ryton Gdns CV8 135 E1
Ryton Gr B34 69 D7

Sabell Rd B67 64 F6
Sabrina Rd WV6 23 E1
Sackville Ho 1 CV1 165 D4
Sacred Heart RC Jun & Inf Schs B20 55 D1
Sacred Heart RC Prim Sch
Coventry CV2 114 A3
Tipton DY4 52 A4
Saddington Rd CV3 134 E8
Saddlers Cl LE10 75 F6
Saddlers Court Ind Est WS2 28 A7
Saddlers Ctr WS1 28 E1
Saddlers Mews B91 107 C1
Saddlestones The WV6 23 D4
Saddleworth Rd WS3 14 A4
Sadler Cres B11 87 D4
Sadler Ho B19 66 C6
Sadler Rd Brownhills WS8 16 A8
Coventry CV6 113 A8
Sutton Coldfield B75 46 F7
Sadlers Ct WS2 42 B7
Sadlers Mill WS8 16 A7
Sadlers Wlk B16 66 A1
Sadlerswell La B94 143 B6
Saffron B77 22 B4
Saffron Gdns WV4 39 A4
Saffron Ho 2 B38 123 E8
Sage Croft B31 102 F5
Sagebury Dr B60 150 C1
SS Peter & Paul RC Prim Sch CV2 114 F7
St Agatha's Rd
Birmingham B8 68 B5
Coventry CV2 114 A3
St Agnes Cl Birmingham B13 87 B2
Studley B80 159 C4
St Agnes La CV1 165 B3
St Agnes Rd B13 87 B1
St Agnes Way CV11 73 F4
St Aidan's Rd WS11 1 E5
St Aidans Wlk B10 87 C8
St Alban's Ave DY11 116 A7
St Alban's CE Prim Sch WV11 27 B8
St Alban's CE Sec Sch B12 86 F7
St Alban's RC Inf & Jun Sch B14 104 F4
St Alban's Rd B67 64 E6
St Albans Cl
Royal Leamington Spa CV32 156 C2
Smethwick B67 64 E6
Wednesfield WV11 27 A8
Wolverhampton WV11 13 A1
St Albans Ct WV13 26 E1
St Albans Ho B32 84 F5
St Albans Rd B13 87 A4
St Alphege CE Inf Sch B91 107 C3
St Alphege CE Jun Sch B91 107 C2
St Alphege Cl B91 107 C3
St Ambrose Barlow Jun & Inf Sch B28 106 A6
St Ambrose's Inf Sch DY10 116 F6
St Ambrose's RC Jun Sch DY10 116 F6
St Andrew's CE Fst Sch B45 138 D8
St Andrew's CE Inf Sch CV5 111 C5
St Andrew's Cl DY3 50 A3
St Andrew's Gd (Birmingham City FC) B9 67 C1
St Andrew's Inf & Jun Sch B9 67 B2
St Andrew's RC Prim Sch B92 89 B2
St Andrew's Rd
Birmingham B9 67 B2
Coventry CV5 132 F8
Royal Leamington Spa CV32 157 B5
St Andrew's St
Birmingham B9 67 B2
Dudley DY2 62 C5
St Andrews B77 22 B4
St Andrews Ave WS3 15 B4
St Andrews CE Inf & Jun Sch WV6 24 F4
St Andrews Cl
Birmingham B32 85 A3
Stourbridge DY8 80 F2
Wolverhampton W6 25 A4
St Andrews Ct 2 B10 67 B1
St Andrews Dr
Nuneaton CV11 74 B1
Perton WV6 23 D5
Tipton B69 63 B7
St Andrews Ho WV6 25 B4
St Andrews Ind Est B9 67 C2
St Andrews Rd B75 46 D7
St Andrews Way B61 150 D8
St Ann's Cl CV31 162 C7
St Ann's Rd CV2 114 A3
St Anne's Cl WS7 6 E4
St Anne's Ct Birmingham B13 86 E4
Willenhall WV13 27 B1
St Anne's RC Jun & Inf Sch B12 87 A8
St Anne's RC Prim Sch
Birmingham B37 70 A2
Coventry CV3 134 C6
Nuneaton CV10 72 D7
St Anne's Rd Blackheath B64 62 C1
Willenhall WV13 27 B3
Wolverhampton WV10 11 B1
St Annes Cl B20 54 F4
St Annes Ct B44 56 A7
St Annes Gr B93 128 A6
St Annes Ind Est WV13 27 B3
St Annes Rd WS13 3 B3
St Annes Way B44 56 A7
St Anns RC Inf & Jun Sch B74 44 E8
St Anthony's RC Comb Sch CV31 162 C7
St Anthony's RC Prim Sch WV10 11 D3
St Anthonys Dr WS3 15 B5
St Antony's RC Prim Sch B37 70 A5
St Asaphs Ave B80 159 D4
St Athan Croft B35 58 B3
St Audries Ct B91 106 F2
St Augustine's Prim Sch B91 107 A2
St Augustine's RC Comb Sch CV8 147 E7
St Augustine's RC Prim Sch Birmingham B21 54 D2
Coventry CV6 113 A7
St Augustine's RC Sch B97 158 D5
St Augustine's Rd B16 65 D1
St Augustine's Wlk CV6 113 A7
St Augustus Cl B70 53 F2
St Austell Cl Nuneaton CV11 74 A5
Tamworth B79 21 A6
St Austell Rd Coventry CV2 114 E3
Walsall WS5 43 E7
St Barnabas CE Jun & Inf Sch B24 57 A3
St Bartholemews Cl CV3 115 A2
St Bartholomew Terr 3 WS10 41 F3
St Bartholomew's CE Prim Sch
Coventry B24 134 E7
Nuneaton WV4 38 E3
St Bede's Mid Sch B98 154 A3
St Bede's RC Mid Sch B98 153 F3
St Benedict Biscop Prim Sch WV5 49 B7
St Benedict's Cl B70 53 F2
St Benedict's Inf Sch B10 87 F7
St Benedict's RC Prim Sch CV1 113 E4
St Benedict's Rd WS7 7 B6
St Benedicts Rd
Birmingham B10 87 F8
Wombourne WV5 49 A6
St Bernadett's RC Prim Sch B25 88 B8
St Bernadette RC Jun & Mix Inf Sch WS8 15 F8
St Bernard's Rd B92 106 E7
St Bernards RC Jun & Inf Sch B13 87 C1
St Bernards Rd B72 46 C2
St Bernards Wlk CV3 134 D6
St Blaise Ave B46 59 C2
St Blaise Rd B75 32 D3
St Brades Cl B69 63 C7
St Bride's Cl 6 CV31 162 C6
St Brides Cl DY3 50 C8
St Brigid's RC Prim Sch B31 102 F3
St Caroline Cl B70 53 F3
St Catharines Cl WS1 43 A7
St Catherine's LE10 75 F7
St Catherine's Cl CV3 134 B8
St Catherine's Cres
Whitnash CV31 161 F3
Wolverhampton WV4 38 F4
St Catherine's Ct B91 107 B3
St Catherine's Lodge 7 CV6 113 A4
St Catherine's RC Inf & Jun Sch B1 66 D1
St Catherine's Rd B60 138 A6
St Catherines Cl
Blackwell B60 138 A5
Dudley DY2 52 A1
Sutton Coldfield B75 46 F7
St Catherines Rd WS13 3 B3
St Cecilia Cl DY10 116 E2
St Cecilia's WV11 26 C5
St Chad's Cath B4 164 B4
St Chad's Circus Queensway B3 164 B3
St Chad's Cl Cannock WS11 2 A4
Dudley DY3 50 B3
St Chad's Inf & Jun Sch B19 66 D5
St Chad's RC Sch DY3 50 D7
St Chad's Rd Bilston WV14 40 F7
Birmingham B45 121 F7
Lichfield WS13 3 C1
Sutton Coldfield B75 46 F5
Wolverhampton WV10 25 F8
St Chad's Stowe Prim Sch WS13 9 C8
St Chads Cl WS13 3 B1
St Chads Ind Est B19 66 E5
St Chads Mews B94 144 D3
St Chads Queensway B4 164 C4
St Chads Rd B80 159 C4
St Christian's Croft CV3 133 E8
St Christian's Rd CV3 133 E8
St Christopher Cl B70 53 E2
St Christopher Prim Sch CV5 112 D4
St Christopher's Cl CV34 160 D8
St Christopher's Dr B77 21 C1
St Christopher's RC Prim Sch WV8 10 A3
St Christophers B20 54 F4
St Clare's RC Prim Sch B20 55 B1
St Clement's Ave WS3 28 D7
St Clement's CE Inf & Jun Sch B7 67 C7
St Clement's La B71 53 D4
St Clements Ct CV2 114 D8
St Clements Ho 3 B71 53 D4
St Clements Rd B7 67 C6
St Columba's Cl CV1 165 B4
St Columba's RC Prim Sch B45 122 D7
St Columbas Dr B45 122 D7
St Cuthbert's Cl B70 53 F2
St Cuthberts RC Jun & Inf Sch B8 68 C4
St David's Cl
Royal Leamington Spa CV31 162 C7
West Bromwich B70 53 F2
St Davids Cl WS3 15 B5
St Davids Dr B32 84 B5
St Davids Gr B20 54 F4
St Davids Orch CV3 134 F7
St Davids Pl WS3 14 D2
St. Davids Way CV10 78 A6
St Denis Rd B29 103 B7
St Dominic's Rd B24 56 E1
St Dunstan's RC Inf & Jun Sch B14 104 F8
St Edburghs Rd B25 68 E1
St Edith's Gn 2 CV34 161 B8
St Edith's Ho 1 CV34 161 B8
St Editha's Cl B79 21 B5
St Editha's Hospl B79 21 B7
St Edmund Campion RC Lower Sch B24 57 C6
St Edmund Campion RC Sch B23 57 B5
St Edmund's Cl
West Bromwich B70 53 F2
Wolverhampton WV6 24 F3
St Edmund's RC Inf & Jun Sch B18 66 A4
St Edmund's RC Sch WV3 24 E3
St Edward's Rd B29 85 F2
St Edward's Sch B29 86 A1
St Edwards RC Jun & Inf Sch B29 86 B1
St Eleanor Cl B70 53 F3
St Elizabeth's Prim Sch B79 20 F8
St Elizabeth's RC Prim Sch CV6 113 E7
St Elizabeth's Rd CV6 113 E7
St Francis Ave B91 106 E6
St Francis Cl WS3 15 B5
St Francis Factory Est B70 53 D2
St Francis Jun & Inf Sch B30 103 D6
St Francis of Assisi RC Comp Sch WS9 30 C5
St Francis RC Comb Sch CV12 78 C3
St Francis RC Inf & Jun Sch B19 66 B6
St Francis RC Prim Sch WS4 15 C1
St Francis Xavier RC Prim Sch B69 64 A8
St Gabriel's RC Prim Sch B77 21 E1
St George Dr B66 65 A7
St George & St Teresa RC Sch B93 128 A4
St George's Ave LE10 71 C1
St George's CE Fst Sch B98 153 F3
St George's CE Inf Sch B19 164 B5
St George's CE Jun & Inf Sch B16 65 F1
St George's CE Jun Sch B19 164 B5
St George's CE Sch DY10 116 F7
St George's Cl
Darlaston WS10 41 D7
Sutton Coldfield B75 46 F6
St George's Ct
Birmingham B30 103 E7
Darlaston WS10 41 D7
St George's Gdns 3 B98 153 F4
St George's Par WV1 163 C2
St George's Pl
Kidderminster DY10 116 E7
4 Walsall WS1 28 F2
St George's Rd
Coventry CV1 113 F2
Royal Leamington Spa CV31 161 F6
Solihull B90 126 D8
Stourbridge DY8 80 D2
St George's Sixth Form Campus B19 164 B5
St George's St
Birmingham B19 164 B4
Darlaston WS10 41 D7
St George's Terr DY10 116 F6
St George's Way B77 21 F4
St Georges Ave B23 57 A5
St Georges Cl B15 86 A7
St Georges Ct
Sutton Coldfield B74 31 E5
5 Walsall WS1 28 F2
St Georges Pl B70 53 C4
St Georges Rd Dudley DY2 62 E6
Redditch B98 153 F4
St Georges Way CV10 78 B8
St Gerards Ct B91 106 E2
St Gerards RC Jun & Inf Sch B35 58 B4
St Gerards Rd B91 106 E2
St Gile's Ct WV13 27 B1
St Giles Ave B65 63 B4
St Giles' CE Prim Sch WV13 27 B2
St Giles Cl B65 63 C4
St Giles Cres WV1 26 A2
St Giles Ct B65 63 D3
St Giles Cty Mid Sch CV7 95 F8
St Giles Rd Birmingham B33 69 D2
Burntwood WS7 7 B6
Coventry CV7 95 D6
Willenhall WV13 27 B1
Wolverhampton WV1 26 A2
St Giles St DY2 62 C5
St Godwald's Cres B60 151 B8
St Godwald's Rd B60 151 C7
St Govan's Cl 7 CV31 162 C6
St Gregory's RC Prim Sch
Coventry CV2 114 E3
Smethwick B67 64 F2
St Helen's Rd
Royal Leamington Spa CV31 162 A5
Solihull B91 107 A6
St Helen's Way CV5 112 B8
St Helens Ave DY4 52 C5
St Helens Pas B1 66 C3
St Helens Rd WS13 3 B3
St Heliers Rd B31 102 F4
St Hubert's RC Prim Sch B68 84 C8
St Ives Cl B79 21 B6
St Ives Rd Coventry CV2 114 E3
Walsall WS5 43 D7
St Ives Way CV11 73 F5
St James Ave B65 63 B4
St James CE Jun Sch B90 106 B2
St James CE Mid Sch CV12 79 C2
St James CE Prim Sch
Birmingham B21 54 D1
Stourbridge DY8 80 D7
St James Cl Walsall WS3 15 B5
West Bromwich B70 53 F2
St James Ct
Bromsgrove B60 137 A3
Coventry CV3 134 E6
St James Gdns CV12 79 C2
St James' La CV3 134 D6
St James Meadow Rd CV32 156 C2
St James' Pl B7 67 A3
St James Pl B90 106 B2
St James' RC Jun & Inf Sch B45 122 A7
St James' Rd B21 65 D8
St James Rd
Birmingham, Edgbaston B15 86 B8
Cannock WS11 1 C1
Norton Canes WS11 6 B5
Oldbury B69 63 E8
Sutton Coldfield B75 32 C2
St James' St DY3 50 D3
St James St
Wednesbury WS10 41 E2
Wolverhampton WV1 163 D3
St James Wlk WS8 15 F7
St James's Cl LE10 75 D5
St James's Rd DY1 51 B2
St James's Terr DY1 51 A2
St John Bosco RC Prim Sch B71 53 B7
St John Cl B75 32 D4
St John Fisher RC Fst Sch B98 154 D6
St John Fisher RC Prim Sch Birmingham B31 123 B7
Coventry CV2 114 D5
St John St Bromsgrove B61 136 F2
Lichfield WS13 9 B7
Tamworth B79 21 B5
St John & St Monica RC Jun Sch B13 86 E4
St John the Baptist CE Fst Sch CV31 161 E7
St John the Baptist RC Prim Sch B36 70 B7
St John the Divine CE Prim Sch CV3 134 C5
St John Vianney RC Prim Sch CV5 112 B3
St John Wall RC Sch B21 54 C2
St John's Arc WV1 163 B2
St John's Ave
Kenilworth CV8 148 A3
Kidderminster DY11 116 B6
St John's CE Fst Sch DY11 116 B6
St John's CE Inf & Jun Sch B16 66 A2
St John's CE Jun & Inf Sch B11 87 C4
St John's CE Mid Sch DY11 116 B6
St John's CE Prim Sch
Coventry CV5 112 C4
Essington WV11 13 A4
Wednesbury WS10 41 F2
St John's Cl Brownhills WS9 15 F3
Cannock WS11 4 D8
6 Kidderminster DY11 116 C6
Lichfield WS13 9 B6
West Bromwich B70 53 F3
St John's Com Home Sch B24 56 E2
St John's Ct Cannock WS12 2 E1
Walsall WS3 14 B1
4 Warwick CV34 160 F7
St John's Dr WS14 17 F5
St John's Hill WS14 17 F5
St John's Prep Sch WS13 9 B7
St John's Rd Birmingham B17 85 D6
Cannock WS11 4 E7
Darlaston WS10 41 C5
Dudley DY2 51 E1
Halesowen B63 82 E4
Royal Leamington Spa CV31 162 A6
Stourbridge DY8 81 A5
Tipton DY4 51 F8
St John's Sch B61 136 F1
St John's Sq WV2 163 B2
St John's St Coventry CV1 165 C2
Dudley DY2 62 C5
Kenilworth CV8 148 A3
5 Kidderminster DY11 116 C6
St John's Terr 10 CV31 162 A6
St Johns Hinckley LE10 71 E1
Warwick CV34 160 F7
St Johns Ave B65 63 B4
St Johns CE JMI Sch WS9 16 A3
St Johns Cl B93 128 B6
St Johns Ct 20 DY5 61 D2
St Johns Gr B37 69 F3
St Johns Ho
Sutton Coldfield B74 31 E3
West Bromwich B70 53 C2
St Johns Mid Sch CV8 147 F2
St Johns Rd Birmingham B11 87 C5
Brownhills WS8 16 A5
Essington WV11 13 A3
Oldbury B68 64 C5
Walsall, Pelsall WS3 15 B5
Walsall, Pleck WS2 42 B8

St Johns Ret Pk WV2 ... 163 B1
St Johns Way B93 ... 128 C6
St Johns Wlk B42 ... 55 D4
St Johns Wood B45 ... 122 B5
St Joseph St 7 DY2 ... 51 D1
St Joseph's Convent Prep Sch
WV6 ... 24 E6
St Joseph's RC Comb Sch
CV31 ... 162 A3
St Joseph's RC Inf & Jun Sch B7 ... 67 B6
St Joseph's RC Jun & Inf Sch B30 ... 103 E4
St Joseph's RC Mid Sch
CV11 ... 73 C3
St Joseph's RC Prim Sch
Cannock WS12 ... 2 C4
Darlaston WS10 ... 41 D7
Dudley DY2 ... 51 E1
Lichfield WS14 ... 9 C7
Sutton Coldfield B75 ... 46 C7
St Joseph's Sch CV8 ... 148 B7
St Joseph's & St Theresa's RC Prim Sch WS7 ... 6 F6
St Josephs Ave B31 ... 103 B5
St Josephs Cl 6 WS3 ... 15 A4
St Josephs Ct WV4 ... 38 D6
St Josephs RC Prim Sch
Birmingham B30 ... 103 F5
Stourbridge DY8 ... 80 F2
St Josephs Rd B8 ... 68 C5
St Jude's CE Inf Sch WV6 ... 24 F4
St Jude's CE Jun Sch WV6 . 24 F3
St Jude's Cres CV3 ... 134 D7
St Jude's Ct WV6 ... 24 F3
St Jude's Pas B5 ... 164 B1
St Jude's Rd WV6 ... 24 F3
St Jude's Rd W WV6 ... 24 F3
St Judes Ave B80 ... 159 D4
St Judes Cl Birmingham
B14 ... 104 F2
Sutton Coldfield B75 ... 46 F6
St Judes Ct B14 ... 104 F7
St Judes RC Inf & Jun Sch
B14 ... 104 F2
St Katherine's Rd B68 ... 64 B2
St Kenelm's CE Fst Sch
B62 ... 101 A4
St Kenelm's Cl B70 ... 53 F2
St Kenelm's Pass DY9 ... 100 A4
St Kenelm's Rd B62 ... 100 E5
St Kenelms Ave B63 ... 82 E1
St Kilda's Rd B8 ... 67 E5
St Laurence Ave CV34 ... 160 D5
St Laurence CE Inf Sch
B31 ... 103 B4
St Laurence CE Jun Sch
B31 ... 103 B4
St Laurence Cl B48 ... 139 B6
St Laurence Rd B31 ... 103 B5
St Lawrence Cl B93 ... 128 B5
St Lawrence Dr WS11 ... 2 B2
St Lawrence Mews B31 ... 103 A3
St Lawrence Way WS10 ... 41 D6
St Lawrence's Rd CV6 ... 95 F1
St Leonard's CE Prim Sch
WV14 ... 40 B6
St Leonard's Wlk CV8 ... 135 A1
St Leonards Cl B37 ... 90 A7
St Leonards View B78 ... 36 F8
St Loye's Cl B62 ... 83 D8
St Luke's CE Fst Sch B97 . 153 D1
St Luke's CE Jun & Inf Sch
B15 ... 86 D8
St Luke's CE Jun Sch WV2 . 39 B7
St Luke's Cl WS11 ... 4 D8
St Luke's Cotts B97 ... 153 D1
St Luke's Inf Sch WV2 ... 39 C7
St Luke's Rd Birmingham B5 . 86 E7
Burntwood WS7 ... 7 C6
Coventry CV6 ... 95 D3
Wednesbury WS10 ... 42 A3
St Luke's Terr DY1 ... 62 A8
St Lukes Cl B65 ... 63 B4
St Lukes St B64 ... 62 D1
St Margaret Mary RC Jun & Inf Sch B23 ... 56 C6
St Margaret Rd CV1 ... 113 F2
St Margaret's B74 ... 31 C3
St Margaret's CE Mid Sch
CV31 ... 162 B3
St Margaret's CE Prim Sch
Birmingham B43 ... 43 E4
Solihull B92 ... 88 F2
St Margaret's Ct 3 B92 ... 88 E1
St Margaret's Ho CV31 ... 162 B4
St Margaret's Hospl B43 ... 44 B3
St Margaret's Rd
Birmingham B43 ... 43 F2
Royal Leamington Spa CV31 . 162 B5
2 Solihull B92 ... 88 E1
Tamworth B79 ... 21 B7
St Margaret's Specl Sch
CV12 ... 78 B3
St Margarets Ave B8 ... 68 B6
St Margarets Dr B63 ... 82 F2
St Margarets Rd
Birmingham B8 ... 68 B6
2 Walsall WS3 ... 15 A4
Wolverhampton WS13 ... 3 B3
St Mark's Annexe (Coventry& WarwickshireHospl)
CV1 ... 165 C4
St Mark's CE Prim Sch DY5 61 C7
St Mark's Ct DY5 ... 61 D7
St Mark's Mews CV32 ... 156 E1
St Mark's RC Prim Sch B42 54 F6
St Mark's Rd Burntwood WS7 . 7 C6
Dudley DY2 ... 51 F1
Royal Leamington Spa
CV32 ... 156 D1
Smethwick B67 ... 64 D3
Stourbridge DY9 ... 81 D5
Tipton DY4 ... 52 A8
Wolverhampton WV3 ... 25 B1
St Mark's St WV3 ... 163 A2
St Marks Cres B1 ... 66 B3
St Marks Dr WS6 ... 4 F4
St Marks Rd Brownhills WS8 . 16 A5
Walsall WS3 ... 15 A4
St Marks St B1 ... 66 B3
St Martin's LE10 ... 75 E6
St Martin's CE Prim Sch
WV14 ... 41 A2
St Martin's Circus Queensway B5 ... 164 C2
St Martin's Cl
West Bromwich B70 ... 53 F2
Wolverhampton WV2 ... 39 E6
St Martin's Dr DY4 ... 52 A5
St Martin's Mkt B5 ... 164 C1
St Martin's Rd CV8 ... 133 C2
St Martin's St 6 B15 ... 66 B1
St Martin's Terr WV14 ... 40 E4
St Martins B91 ... 107 D3
St Martins Ave B80 ... 159 D4
St Martins CE Prim Sch
DY4 ... 52 B5
St Martins RC Jun & Inf Sch B13 ... 87 A3
St Martins Rd B75 ... 46 F5
St Mary Magdelene CE Jun & Inf Sch B71 ... 53 D6
St Mary of the Angels RC JMI Sch WS9 ... 30 B5
St Mary St CV1 ... 165 C2
St Mary & St John RC Prim Sch B23 ... 56 E3
St Mary & St Margaret's CE Prim Sch B36 ... 69 B8
St Mary's Ave LE9 ... 71 F5
St Mary's CE Jun & Inf Sch
B20 ... 55 B1
St Mary's CE Jun & Inf Sch
B29 ... 85 D1
St Mary's CE Jun Sch
B80 ... 159 E3
St Mary's CE Prim Sch
Kidderminster DY10 ... 116 E8
Kingswinford DY6 ... 60 D7
St Mary's Cl Sedgley DY3 ... 50 F8
Warwick CV34 ... 160 D8
St Mary's Cres CV31 ... 162 B7
St Mary's Ct Nuneaton CV11 .. 73 B5
4 Willenhall WV13 ... 27 A2
St Mary's Ho 4 B71 ... 53 D4
St Mary's La DY8 ... 81 B3
St Mary's of the Mount Prim Sch WS1 ... 42 F8
St Mary's RC Jun & Inf Sch
B17 ... 85 C5
St Mary's RC Jun & Inf Sch B80 ... 159 E4
St Mary's RC Prim Sch
DY5 ... 61 E2
St Mary's RC Prim Sch
WS11 ... 4 E8
St Mary's RC Prim Sch
Coventry CV1 ... 113 F3
Wednesbury WS10 ... 41 F4
St Mary's RC Sch WV10 ... 26 A7
St Mary's Rd Hinckley LE10 ... 75 D8
Nuneaton CV11 ... 73 B5
Royal Leamington Spa
CV31 ... 162 B7
Smethwick B67 ... 64 F1
Wednesbury WS10 ... 41 F3
Wolverhampton WS13 ... 3 B3
St Mary's Row
Birmingham, Moseley B13 ... 86 F3
Birmingham, New Town Row B4 ... 164 C3
St Mary's St WV1 ... 163 C3
St Mary's & St John's RC Sch WV2 ... 163 C1
St Mary's Terr CV31 ... 162 B7
St Mary's Way Aldridge WS9 30 B5
Tamworth B77 ... 21 E4
St Marys Cl B27 ... 88 B3
St Marys Ct 12 DY5 ... 61 D2
St Marys Rd B17 ... 85 C5
St Marys Ringway DY10 ... 116 E6
St Marys View B23 ... 56 D8
St Matthew St WV1 ... 25 F1
St Matthew's Ave WS7 ... 7 F7
St Matthew's CE Prim Sch
B66 ... 65 C5
St Matthew's Cl WS1 ... 28 F1
St Matthew's Rd WS7 ... 7 F7
St Matthews CE Inf & Jun Sch B7 ... 67 A4
St Matthews Cl WS3 ... 15 B5
St Matthews Rd Oldbury
B68 ... 64 A2
Smethwick B66 ... 65 C5
St Mawes Rd WV6 ... 24 A3
St Mawgen Cl B35 ... 58 C4
St Michael Rd WS13 ... 9 C8
St Michael St Walsall WS1 ... 42 E8
West Bromwich B70 ... 53 C3
St Michaels Ct B70 ... 53 C3
St Michael's CE Jun & Inf Sch
B32 ... 102 C8
St Michael's CE Jun & Mixed Inf Sch WS3 ... 14 F2
St Michael's CE Prim Sch
Blackheath B69 ... 63 C5
Lichfield WS14 ... 9 C7
Lichfield WS13 ... 9 C8
Walsall WS3 ... 15 A3
Wolverhampton WV6 ... 24 E5
St Michael's Cl Walsall WS3 15 A2
Wood End CV9 ... 36 C1
St Michael's Cres B69 ... 64 A4
St Michael's Ct B68 ... 64 A4
St Michael's Ct WV6 ... 24 E5
St Michael's Gr DY2 ... 52 A1
St Michael's Hill B18 ... 66 A7
St Michael's Hospl
Lichfield WS13 ... 9 D8
Warwick CV34 ... 160 E8
St Michael's Mews B69 ... 52 A2
St Michael's RC Prim Sch
WV3 ... 38 D7
St Michael's Rd
Birmingham B18 ... 66 A7
Coventry CV2 ... 114 A3
Sutton Coldfield B73 ... 56 F8
Warwick CV34 ... 160 D8
St Michael's Way CV10 ... 72 C4
St Michaels CE Inf & Jun Sch
B21 ... 66 A7
St Michaels Dr WS12 ... 2 F5
St Michaels Rd DY3 ... 49 F5
St Michaels Way DY4 ... 52 A3
St Nicholas Ave CV8 ... 147 F3
St Nicholas CE Comb Sch
CV8 ... 147 F5
St Nicholas Church St
CV34 ... 160 F7
St Nicholas Cl Coventry
CV1 ... 113 C5
5 Walsall WS3 ... 15 A4
St Nicholas Ct
Coventry, Edgwick CV6 ... 113 F7
Coventry, Radford CV6 ... 113 B6
St Nicholas RC Prim Sch
B73 ... 45 F2
St Nicholas Rd CV31 ... 162 F5
St Nicholas St CV1 ... 165 B4
St Nicholas Terr CV31 ... 162 E4
St Nicholas Wlk B76 ... 59 B6
St Nicolas CE Fst Sch CV11 73 F6
St Nicolas Gdns B38 ... 103 F2
St Nicolas Park Dr CV11 ... 73 F7
St Nicolas Rd CV11 ... 73 D5
St Osburg's RC Prim Sch
CV1 ... 165 A3
St Osburg's Rd CV2 ... 114 A3
St Oswalds Cl DY10 ... 116 F8
St Oswalds Rd B10 ... 87 E8
St Patrick's CE Prim Sch
B94 ... 126 C2
St Patrick's Ct DY11 ... 116 B1
St Patrick's RC JMI Sch
WS2 ... 28 E3
St Patrick's RC Jun & Inf Schs
WV11 ... 26 C5
St Patrick's RC Prim Sch
Birmingham B37 ... 70 C2
Coventry CV2 ... 96 D1
St Patrick's Rd CV1 ... 165 B1
St Patricks Cl B14 ... 104 E5
St Patricks RC Comb Sch
CV31 ... 161 F6
St Patricks RC Jun & Inf Sch B18 ... 65 F4
St Paul's Ave
Birmingham B12 ... 87 A5
Kidderminster DY11 ... 116 A6
St Paul's CE Comb Sch
CV32 ... 157 B1
St Paul's CE Comb Sch (Annexe) CV32 ... 157 A1
St Paul's CE Fst Sch CV10 ... 72 C3
St Paul's CE Prim Sch
WV9 ... 11 A2
St Paul's Cl Cannock WS11 ... 2 B1
Walsall WS1 ... 28 E2
Warwick CV34 ... 160 D6
St Paul's Convent Sch B75 . 46 C7
St Paul's Cres
5 Coleshill B46 ... 70 F7
West Bromwich B70 ... 52 E7
St Paul's Ct B77 ... 35 C4
St Paul's Dr DY4 ... 52 B4
St Paul's RC Inf & Jun Sch
B38 ... 104 A1
St Paul's Rd Birmingham
B12 ... 87 A5
Burntwood WS7 ... 7 C6
Cannock WS12 ... 2 E3
Coventry CV6 ... 113 E6
Dudley DY2 ... 62 D5
Nuneaton CV10 ... 72 D3
Smethwick B66 ... 64 E7
Wednesbury WS10 ... 42 C5
St Paul's Sch for Girls B16 . 65 E1
St Paul's Sq Birmingham
B3 ... 164 A4
4 Royal Leamington Spa
CV32 ... 157 A1
St Paul's St WS1 ... 28 E2
St Paul's Sta B19 ... 164 B4
St Paul's Terr CV34 ... 160 D6
St Pauls CE Sch DY4 ... 51 F6
St Pauls Cres WS3 ... 15 B5
St Pauls Ct Blackheath B62 ... 63 D1
Water Orton B46 ... 59 B3
St Pauls Dr B62 ... 63 D1
St Pauls Gdns LE10 ... 71 E1
St Pauls Terr B3 ... 164 A4
St Peter & Paul RC Jun & Inf Sch B24 ... 57 C3
St Peter & St Paul RC Prim Sch WS13 ... 3 B1
St Peter's CE Inf Sch B17 ... 85 B4
St Peter's CE Jun Sch B17 . 85 B5
St Peter's CE Mid Sch
B98 ... 154 E3
St Peter's CE Prim Sch
WS12 ... 2 D4
St Peter's CE Prim Sch
WS9 ... 16 E4
St Peter's Cl Redditch B97 ... 158 E5
Stonnall WS9 ... 16 E4
Tamworth B77 ... 21 D1
Water Orton B46 ... 59 B2
West Bromwich DY4 ... 52 D4
St Peter's Collegiate Sec Sch WV3 ... 24 E3
St Peter's Croft B73 ... 46 B3
St Peter's Ct Coventry CV1 . 165 D4
Walsall WS3 ... 14 B1
St Peter's RC Fst Sch
B60 ... 150 E8
St Peter's RC Sch
Hinckley LE10 ... 71 E1
Solihull B91 ... 107 B2
Walsall WS3 ... 14 B2
St Peter's Rd
Birmingham B20 ... 66 C8
Burntwood WS7 ... 7 C6
Cannock WS12 ... 2 D4
Dudley DY2 ... 62 D5
7 Royal Leamington Spa
CV32 ... 161 F8
Stourbridge DY9 ... 81 C1
St Peters Cl
Birmingham B28 ... 105 D6
Sutton Coldfield B72 ... 46 B3
St Peters Dr WS3 ... 15 A4
St Peters La B92 ... 90 D1
St Peters RC Sch B32 ... 84 C1
St Peters Rd B17 ... 85 B5
St Peters Terr WS2 ... 28 E4
St Philip's Cath B2 ... 164 B3
St Philip's Gr WV3 ... 38 F7
St Philip's Pl B2 ... 164 C3
St Philip's RC Prim Sch
B66 ... 65 B6
St Philip's Sixth Form Ctr
B16 ... 65 F1
St Philips Ave WV3 ... 38 F7
St Quentin St WS2 ... 42 C7
St Saviour's CE Prim Sch
B8 ... 67 D5
St Saviour's Cl WV2 ... 39 F6
St Saviour's Rd B8 ... 67 D4
St Silas' Sq B19 ... 66 B7
St Simons Cl B75 ... 46 F6
St Stephen's Ave WV13 ... 26 F2
St Stephen's CE Fst Sch
B98 ... 153 F5
St Stephen's CE Mid Sch
B98 ... 153 F5
St Stephen's CE Sch WV10 . 25 F4
St Stephen's Ct WV13 ... 26 F1
St Stephen's Gdns
1 WV13 ... 27 A1
St Stephen's Rd WS7 ... 7 C6
St Stephens Gdns B98 ... 153 F5
St Stephens Rd
Birmingham B29 ... 104 B8
West Bromwich B71 ... 65 B8
St Stephens St B6 ... 66 E6
St Teresa's RC Prim Sch
WV4 ... 39 E5
St Teresa's RC Sch (Jun & Inf) B20 ... 55 A3
St Thomas Aquinas RC Sec Sch B30 ... 103 D3
St Thomas CE Com High Sch B15 ... 86 C8
St Thomas CE Jun & Inf Sch B15 ... 86 D8
St Thomas CE Prim Sch
WV11 ... 26 D7
St Thomas' Cl WS9 ... 16 B1
St Thomas Cl
Sutton Coldfield B75 ... 46 F5
Walsall WS3 ... 28 E6
St Thomas More RC Comp Sch WV14 ... 41 A7
St Thomas More RC Fst Sch B98 ... 159 B7
St Thomas More RC Prim Sch Coventry CV3 ... 133 D5
Great Wyrley WS6 ... 5 A4
St Thomas More Sch
CV10 ... 73 A3
St Thomas More's RC Jun & Inf Sch B26 ... 89 B5
St Thomas of Canterbury RC Sch WS3 ... 28 F6
St Thomas' Rd
Birmingham B23 ... 56 D3
Coventry CV6 ... 96 A3
St Thomas St DY2 ... 62 C5
St Thomas's Ct 13 CV1 ... 113 B2
St Thomas's Ho 12 CV1 ... 113 B2
St Valentines Cl B70 ... 53 F2
St Vincent Cres B70 ... 52 F6
St Vincent St B16 ... 66 B2
St Vincent St W B16 ... 66 A2
St Vincent's RC Inf & Jun Sch B7 ... 67 B3
St Wilfrid's RC Jun & Inf Sch B36 ... 68 F8
Saintbury Dr B91 ... 127 C8
Saints Way CV10 ... 73 D5
Saladin Ave B69 ... 63 E5
Salcombe Ave B26 ... 89 C5
Salcombe Cl Cannock WS11 ... 4 B7
Coventry CV3 ... 134 D6
Nuneaton CV11 ... 73 F5
Salcombe Dr DY5 ... 81 C7
Salcombe Gr WV14 ... 40 D1
Salcombe Rd 3 B66 ... 65 B5
Saldavian Ct WS2 ... 42 B6
Salem Rd LE10 ... 75 F5
Salem St DY4 ... 52 D5
Salford Cir B23 ... 56 D1
Salford Cl Coventry CV2 ... 114 A5
Redditch B98 ... 159 B6
Salford St B6 ... 67 C8
Salisbury Ave CV3 ... 133 C6
Salisbury Cl Birmingham
B13 ... 86 E3
Dudley DY1 ... 50 F3
Lichfield WS13 ... 3 C3
Salisbury Dr Cannock WS12 ... 2 B1
Kidderminster DY11 ... 116 A6
Nuneaton CV10 ... 72 B7
Water Orton B46 ... 59 C3
Salisbury Gr B72 ... 57 C7
Salisbury Ho
3 Birmingham B24 ... 56 F4
Hinckley LE10 ... 71 C4
Salisbury Pl WV3 ... 25 B1
Salisbury Prim Sch WS10 ... 41 F7
Salisbury Rd
Birmingham, Lozells B19 ... 66 D8
Birmingham, Moseley B13 ... 86 E3
Birmingham, Saltley B8 ... 67 E5
Hinckley LE10 ... 76 B7
Smethwick B66 ... 65 B4
West Bromwich B70 ... 53 E1
Salisbury St Darlaston WS10 . 41 E7
Wolverhampton WV3 ... 25 B1
Salisbury Tower B18 ... 66 A3
Sally Ward Dr WS9 ... 16 A4
Salop Cl B71 ... 53 B6
Salop Dr Cannock WS11 ... 4 F8
Oldbury B68 ... 64 C2
Salop Rd Oldbury B68 ... 64 C2
Redditch B97 ... 153 D3
Salop St Bilston WV14 ... 40 E4
Birmingham B12 ... 86 F8
Dudley DY1 ... 51 B2
Oldbury B69 ... 52 E1
Wolverhampton WV3 ... 163 B2
Salstar Cl B6 ... 66 E6
Salt La CV1 ... 165 B2
Saltash Gr B25 ... 68 C1
Saltbrook Rd B63 ... 82 A7
Saltbrook Trad Est B63 ... 82 A7
Salter Rd DY4 ... 51 F7
Salter St B94 ... 126 C2
Salter's La Redditch B97 ... 153 B5
Tamworth B79 ... 21 B6
West Bromwich B71 ... 53 E4
Salter's Rd WS9 ... 16 A3
Salters Vale B70 ... 53 E1
Saltisford CV34 ... 160 D7
Saltisford Gdns CV34 ... 160 C8
Saltley Ind Ctr B8 ... 67 C3
Saltley Rd B7 ... 67 C5
Saltley Sch B9 ... 68 A3
Saltley Trad Est B8 ... 67 D6
Saltley Viaduct B8 ... 67 C5
Saltney Cl B24 ... 57 D5
Salts La B78 ... 34 E4
Saltwells La DY2 ... 62 B2
Saltwells Rd DY2 ... 62 C2
Salwarpe Gr B29 ... 84 F2
Salwarpe Rd B60 ... 150 F8
Sam Barber Ct WS12 ... 2 E2
Sam Gault Cl CV3 ... 134 E7
Sam Spencer Ct DY10 ... 118 A1
Sambar Rd B78 ... 20 F1
Sambourn Cl B91 ... 107 E6
Sambourne Dr B34 ... 69 D7
Sambourne La
Astwood Bank B96 ... 158 F1
Sambourne B96 ... 159 A1
Sambourne Park La B96 .. 159 A1
Sambrook Rd WV10 ... 26 A6
Sammons Way CV4 ... 111 D1
Sampson Cl Birmingham B21 54 C1
Coventry CV2 ... 114 C8
Tipton B69 ... 63 C7
Sampson Rd B11 ... 87 B7
Sampson Rd N B11 ... 87 B8
Sampson St WS10 ... 42 B3
Sams La B70 ... 53 C1
Samuel Cl WS13 ... 3 C2
Samuel Hayward Ho
5 CV2 ... 96 B1
Samuel St WS3 ... 14 B1
Samuel Vale Ho CV1 ... 165 B4
Samuels Rd B32 ... 84 A5
Sanby Cl CV12 ... 78 A4
Sand Bank WS3 ... 14 A1
Sand Pits B1 ... 66 B3
Sand St B70 ... 52 E4
Sanda Croft B36 ... 70 B6
Sandal Rise B91 ... 107 E3
Sandalls Cl B31 ... 102 D1
Sandals Rise B62 ... 83 D3
Sandalwood Cl WV12 ... 27 B8
Sandbarn Cl B90 ... 126 F6
Sandbeds Rd WV12 ... 27 C4

Sandbourne Rd B8 ... 68 A4
Sanderling Cl WV10 ... 12 B7
Sanderling Ct DY10 ... 117 A1
Sanderling Rise
Burntwood WS7 ... 7 B8
Kingswinford DY6 ... 61 A6
Sanders Cl Dudley DY2 ... 62 E7
Redditch B97 ... 153 B4
Sanders Ct CV34 ... 161 C8
Sanders Ind Est B61 ... 136 E1
Sanders Rd Bedworth CV6 ... 96 B6
Bromsgrove B61 ... 136 E1
Sanderson Ct DY11 ... 116 C5
Sandfield 1 B66 ... 64 E7
Sandfield Cl B90 ... 126 B8
Sandfield Gr DY3 ... 50 B2
Sandfield Rd Stourbridge DY8 ... 60 F2
West Bromwich B71 ... 42 E2
Sandfields Ave B10 ... 87 B8
Sandfields Rd B68 ... 64 C2
Sandford Ave B65 ... 63 C3
Sandford Cl CV2 ... 96 E3
Sandford Ho WS13 ... 9 A7
Sandford Rd Birmingham B13 ... 87 A3
Dudley DY1 ... 50 E1
Sandford Rise WV6 ... 24 E6
Sandford St WS13 ... 9 B7
Sandgate Cres CV2 ... 114 E2
Sandgate Rd
Birmingham B28 ... 106 A4
Tipton DY4 ... 52 A8
Sandhill Farm Cl 1 B19 ... 66 D7
Sandhill St WS3 ... 14 A1
Sandhills Cres B91 ... 127 B8
Sandhills Gn B48 ... 138 E7
Sandhills La B45 ... 138 D7
Sandhills Rd B45 ... 138 D8
Sandhurst Ave
Birmingham B36 ... 68 D6
Stourbridge DY9 ... 81 D2
Sandhurst Cl B98 ... 154 C6
Sandhurst Dr WV4 ... 39 A4
Sandhurst Gr Coventry CV6 ... 113 B5
Stourbridge DY8 ... 60 E3
Sandhurst Ho B38 ... 104 B1
Sandhurst Rd
Birmingham B13 ... 86 F2
Kingswinford DY6 ... 61 A4
Sutton Coldfield B74 ... 31 F5
Sandicliffe Cl DY11 ... 116 C8
Sandilands Cl CV2 ... 114 E4
Sandland Cl WV14 ... 40 F6
Sandland Rd WV12 ... 27 D8
Sandmartin Cl DY2 ... 62 D2
Sandmartin Way DY10 ... 117 A2
Sandmere Gr B14 ... 105 D3
Sandmere Rd B14 ... 105 D3
Sandmere Rise WV10 ... 11 E1
Sandon Cl B98 ... 154 A3
Sandon Gr B24 ... 57 B4
Sandon Ho WV6 ... 24 E5
Sandon Rd Birmingham B17 ... 65 B1
Nuneaton CV11 ... 73 B5
Stourbridge DY9 ... 81 F4
Wolverhampton WV10 ... 11 C2
Sandown B77 ... 21 F5
Sandown Ave
Cheslyn Hay WS6 ... 4 E3
Coventry CV6 ... 95 F2
Sandown Cl CV32 ... 157 C4
Sandown Ct B29 ... 103 C7
Sandown Dr WV6 ... 23 F4
Sandown Fst Sch WV6 ... 23 F4
Sandown Rd B36 ... 68 D8
Sandown Tower 3 B31 ... 103 A1
Sandpiper B77 ... 36 A5
Sandpiper Cl Cannock WS12 ... 2 C7
Kidderminster DY10 ... 117 B2
Stourbridge DY9 ... 81 F5
Sandpiper Gdns B38 ... 123 F7
Sandpiper Rd CV2 ... 96 B3
Sandpit Cl WS10 ... 42 E2
Sandpits Cl B76 ... 59 B6
Sandpits Ind Est 4 B1 ... 66 B3
Sandpits La CV6 ... 94 F2
Sandpits The CV12 ... 79 C2
Sandra Cl WS9 ... 30 B5
Sandringham Ave WV12 ... 27 B6
Sandringham Ct CV10 ... 72 F6
Sandringham Dr
Aldridge WS9 ... 16 B1
Blackheath B65 ... 63 C4
Sandringham Pl DY8 ... 60 D1
Sandringham Rd
Birmingham B42 ... 55 B6
Halesowen B62 ... 83 B7
Stourbridge DY8 ... 60 D1
Wolverhampton WV4 ... 39 B4
Sandringham Way DY5 ... 81 C8
Sandstone Ave B45 ... 122 A8
Sandstone Cl DY3 ... 50 D4
Sandway Gdns B8 ... 67 D6
Sandway Gr B13 ... 105 C7
Sandwell Ave WS10 ... 41 B5
Sandwell Bsns Development Ctr B66 ... 64 C7
Sandwell Bsns Pk B66 ... 64 C8
Sandwell Coll
Wednesbury WS10 ... 42 B5
West Bromwich B70 ... 53 C3
Sandwell Coll (Kendrick Campus) WS10 ... 42 A3
Sandwell Coll (Knowles Annexe) WS10 ... 42 A3
Sandwell Coll Oldbury Campus B68 ... 64 A3
Sandwell Coll Smethwick Campus B66 ... 65 A5
Sandwell Coll (Wednesbury Campus) WS10 ... 42 A1
Sandwell Ct B21 ... 65 D8
Sandwell Ctr B70 ... 53 D3
Sandwell District General Hospl B71 ... 53 D5
Sandwell & Dudley Sta B70 ... 53 A1
Sandwell Ho 1 WS1 ... 42 F8
Sandwell Park Farm B71 ... 53 F3
Sandwell Pl WV12 ... 27 D7
Sandwell Rd Birmingham B21 ... 54 D1
West Bromwich B70 ... 53 C4
Wolverhampton WV10 ... 11 B1
Sandwell Rd N B71 ... 53 D4
Sandwell Road Pas B70 ... 53 C4
Sandwell St WS1 ... 42 F8
Sandwell Valley Ctry Pk B71 ... 54 A5
Sandwell Valley Nature Ctr B43 ... 54 C6
Sandwell Wlk 8 WS1 ... 42 F8
Sandwick Cl CV3 ... 134 F8
Sandwood Dr B44 ... 55 F8
Sandy Cres Hinckley LE10 ... 71 C1
Wednesfield WV11 ... 27 A8
Sandy Croft
Birmingham B13 ... 105 C7
Sutton Coldfield B72 ... 46 C3
Sandy Hill Rd B90 ... 106 A4
Sandy Hill Rise B90 ... 106 A4
Sandy Hollow WV6 ... 24 C2
Sandy La
Birmingham, Aston B6 ... 67 B7
Birmingham, Great Barr B42 ... 55 D8
Blackdown CV32 ... 156 F6
Blakedown DY10 ... 118 C7
Cannock WS11 ... 1 B1
Codsall WV8 ... 10 A4
Coventry CV1 ... 113 C5
Royal Leamington Spa CV32 ... 156 D4
Wednesbury WS10 ... 42 F3
Wildmoor B61, B62 ... 120 E5
Wolverhampton, Bushbury WV10 ... 11 E1
Wolverhampton, Tettenhall WV6 ... 24 E6
Sandy Lane Bsns Pk CV1 ... 113 C5
Sandy Mount WV5 ... 49 B7
Sandy Mount Rd WS1 ... 42 F8
Sandy Rd DY8 ... 80 D1
Sandy Way Birmingham B15 ... 66 B1
Tamworth B77 ... 22 B3
Sandyacre Way DY8 ... 81 B5
Sandyfields Rd DY3 ... 50 B6
Sandygate Cl B97 ... 152 F2
Sandythorpe CV3 ... 134 E6
Sangwin Rd WV14 ... 51 C7
Sankey Rd WS11 ... 1 F3
Sankey's Cnr WS7 ... 6 F7
Sansome Rd B90 ... 105 F2
Sansome Rise B90 ... 105 F2
Sanstone Cl WS3 ... 14 C3
Sanstone Rd WS3 ... 14 C3
Sant Rd B31 ... 123 B7
Santolina Dr WS5 ... 43 A3
Santos Cl CV3 ... 134 F8
Santridge Ct B61 ... 137 A4
Santridge La B61 ... 137 A4
Sapcote Bsns Ctr B10 ... 87 E6
Sapcote Gr CV2 ... 96 B4
Sapcote Ind Est B64 ... 62 F3
Sapcote Rd LE10 ... 76 B7
Saplings The B76 ... 58 A8
Sapphire Ct Birmingham B3 ... 164 A4
3 Solihull B92 ... 88 F1
Sapphire Dr Cannock WS11 ... 2 C3
Royal Leamington Spa CV31 ... 161 F5
Sapphire Gate CV2 ... 114 C2
Sapphire Tower 2 B6 ... 66 F6
Sara Cl B74 ... 32 A3
Saracen Dr CV7 ... 129 E6
Sarah Cl WV14 ... 40 E1
Sarah Ct B73 ... 45 D1
Sarah Gdns WS5 ... 42 F4
Sarah Siddons Ho 2 WS13 ... 9 B7
Sarah St B9 ... 67 B2
Saredon Cl WS3 ... 15 A1
Saredon Rd WS6 ... 4 B3
Sarehole Mill Mus B13 ... 105 D8
Sarehole Rd B28 ... 87 E1
Sargeaunt St CV31 ... 161 F7
Sargent Cl B43 ... 44 D4
Sargent Turner Trad Est DY9 ... 81 F6
Sark Dr B36 ... 70 B6
Satchwell Ct 11 CV32 ... 161 F8
Satchwell Wlk 10 CV32 ... 161 F8
Satellite Ind Pk WV11 ... 26 D4
Saturn Rd WS11 ... 2 A5
Saumur Way CV34 ... 161 C6
Saunders Ave CV12 ... 78 B2
Saunders Cl WS12 ... 2 F6
Saunders Ho 10 CV32 ... 156 F2
Saunderton Ho B31 ... 102 E5
Saunton Cl CV5 ... 112 B8
Saunton Way B29 ... 85 C2
Saveker Dr B76 ... 46 E4
Savernake Cl B45 ... 102 A2
Saville Cl Birmingham B45 ... 122 B7
Hinckley LE10 ... 71 E2
Saville Gr CV8 ... 148 C5
Savoy Bldgs DY2 ... 62 D5
Savoy Cl B32 ... 85 A5
Saw Mill Cl WS4 ... 28 E3
Saxelby Cl B14 ... 104 E2
Saxelby Ho B14 ... 104 E2
Saxon Bsns Pk B60 ... 150 E2
Saxon Cl Binley Woods CV3 ... 135 D7
Great Wyrley WS6 ... 5 A2
Polesworth B78 ... 22 F1
Studley B80 ... 159 E5
Tamworth B77 ... 35 F6
Saxon Ct WS13 ... 8 E7
Saxon Dr B65 ... 63 C4
Saxon Hill Specl Sch WS14 ... 9 C6
Saxon Mdws CV32 ... 156 C2
Saxon Mill La B79 ... 21 C4
Saxon Rd CV2 ... 114 B4
Saxon Way B37 ... 69 F3
Saxon Wlk WS13 ... 8 E7
Saxon Wood Cl B31 ... 103 A4
Saxon Wood Rd B90 ... 126 D5
Saxoncourt WV6 ... 24 C5
Saxondale Ave B26 ... 88 F6
Saxondrive B79 ... 21 C5
Saxonfields WV6 ... 24 C5
Saxons Way B14 ... 105 A2
Saxton Dr B74 ... 31 F6
Sayer Ho B19 ... 66 D6
Scafell Cl CV5 ... 112 A4
Scafell Dr Bilston WV14 ... 40 F7
Birmingham B23 ... 56 C5
Scafell Rd DY8 ... 81 B6
Scaife Rd B60 ... 151 B7
Scammerton B77 ... 36 B8
Scampton Cl WV6 ... 23 E5
Scampton Way B79 ... 21 C8
Scar Bank CV34 ... 155 E1
Scarborough Cl 2 WS2 ... 42 B8
Scarborough Rd WS2 ... 42 B8
Scarborough Way CV4 ... 131 F7
Scarfield Hill B48 ... 138 E5
Scarsdale Rd B42 ... 55 D8
Schofield Ave B71 ... 53 B8
Schofield Rd B37 ... 70 A5
Scholars Gate
Birmingham B33 ... 69 B2
Burntwood WS7 ... 7 D6
Scholefield Tower B19 ... 66 D5
Scholfield Rd CV7 ... 95 A6
School Ave WS8 ... 15 F8
School Bell Mews CV8 ... 149 B6
School Cl Birmingham B37 ... 70 A6
Burntwood WS7 ... 6 D8
Codsall WV8 ... 10 A4
Coventry CV3 ... 113 F2
Hinckley LE10 ... 76 A6
Norton Canes WS11 ... 6 B6
Tipton B69 ... 63 C7
Wolverhampton WV3 ... 38 B7
School Cotts CV35 ... 145 F3
School Cres WS11 ... 6 A6
School Croft CV35 ... 146 C2
School Ct WS12 ... 2 C6
School Dr Bilston WV14 ... 41 A2
Bromsgrove B60 ... 137 A3
Dudley WV14 ... 40 C1
Stourbridge DY8 ... 80 F8
Wythall B47 ... 125 A3
School Dr The DY2 ... 62 D7
School Gn WV14 ... 40 C8
School Hill CV10 ... 72 A8
School Ho The WS7 ... 7 D7
School House La CV2 ... 115 A6
School La Alvechurch B48 ... 139 B5
Bedworth CV7 ... 95 F7
Birmingham, Buckland End B34 ... 69 B7
Birmingham, Kitt's Green B33 ... 68 F1
Brierley Hill DY5 ... 61 B4
Burntwood WS7 ... 6 D8
Hagley DY9 ... 99 D6
Halesowen B63 ... 82 F2
Hopwas B78 ... 20 B7
Kenilworth CV8 ... 147 F5
Lickey End B60 ... 137 B6
Norton Canes WS3 ... 5 E2
Radford Semele CV31 ... 162 E5
Shuttington B79 ... 22 F7
Solihull B91 ... 107 D4
Tamworth B77 ... 35 D5
Walsall WS3 ... 14 F4
Weeford B78 ... 19 D2
Wolverhampton WV10 ... 11 E2
Wroxall CV35 ... 145 E4
School of Art, Univ of Wolverhampton WV1 ... 163 B4
School Rd
Birmingham, Eachway B45 ... 121 E6
Birmingham, Hall Green B28 ... 106 A8
Birmingham, Moseley B13 ... 86 F1
Birmingham, Yardley Wood B14 ... 105 C4
Brierley Hill DY5 ... 62 A2
Bulkington CV12 ... 79 C2
Himley DY3 ... 49 B3
Norton Canes WS11 ... 6 A6
Solihull B90 ... 106 B2
Tanworth-in-A B94 ... 143 B7
Trysull WV5 ... 37 C1
Wednesbury WS10 ... 42 D2
Wolverhampton, New Cross WV11 ... 26 C6
Wolverhampton, Tettenhall WV6 ... 24 B3
Wombourne WV5 ... 49 B7
School St Blackheath B64 ... 62 D1
Brierley Hill DY5 ... 61 D7
Darlaston WS10 ... 41 E5
Dudley, Eve Hill DY1 ... 51 B1
Dudley, Roseville WV14 ... 51 C8
Sedgley DY3 ... 50 E8
Stourbridge DY8 ... 80 F6
Tamworth B77 ... 21 E4
Walsall WS4 ... 15 D1
Willenhall WV13 ... 26 F1
Wolverhampton WV3 ... 163 B2
School St W 2 WV14 ... 51 C8
School Terr 1 B29 ... 85 F2
School Wlk Bilston WV14 ... 40 C8
Burntwood WS7 ... 6 D8
Nuneaton CV11 ... 73 E2
Schoolacre Rd B34 ... 69 B6
Schoolacre Rise B74 ... 30 E1
Schoolfields Rd WS14 ... 18 A5
Schoolgate Cl WS4 ... 15 D1
Schoolhouse Cl B38 ... 104 B2
Scimitar Cl B79 ... 20 E7
Scorers Cl B90 ... 106 B6
Scotch Orch WS13 ... 3 D1
Scotch Orchard Prim Sch WS13 ... 3 D1
Scotchill The CV6 ... 95 A1
Scotchings The B36 ... 68 E8
Scotia Rd WS11 ... 1 D3
Scotland La B32 ... 102 C7
Scotland St B1 ... 66 C3
Scots Cnr B14 ... 104 E8
Scots La CV6 ... 112 F6
Scott Arms Sh Ctr B43 ... 43 F1
Scott Ave Nuneaton CV10 ... 73 D8
Wednesbury WS10 ... 42 B2
Wolverhampton WV4 ... 38 E4
Scott Cl Lichfield WS14 ... 9 B6
West Bromwich B71 ... 53 D5
Scott Gr B92 ... 88 E3
Scott Ho B43 ... 54 F7
Scott Rd Birmingham B43 ... 43 F2
Kenilworth CV8 ... 147 E2
Redditch B97 ... 158 C8
Royal Leamington Spa CV31 ... 162 B6
Solihull B92 ... 88 E2
Tamworth B77 ... 21 E4
Walsall WS5 ... 43 D6
Scott St WS12 ... 2 F3
Scott's Green Cl DY1 ... 62 A8
Scott's Rd DY8 ... 80 F6
Scotwell Cl B65 ... 63 B3
Scout Cl B33 ... 69 C2
Scribban Cl B66 ... 65 B4
Scribers La Birmingham B28 ... 105 D4
Birmingham B28 ... 105 E4
Scrimshaw Ho 1 WS2 ... 42 C7
Sculthorpe Rd DY10 ... 98 B2
Seacroft Ave B25 ... 68 E1
Seafield B77 ... 21 F5
Seafield Cl DY6 ... 60 E4
Seafield La Beoley B98 ... 141 A2
Portway B48 ... 140 E4
Seaford Cl CV6 ... 96 B4
Seaforth Dr LE10 ... 71 A1
Seaforth Gr WV12 ... 13 B1
Seagar St B71 ... 53 E4
Seager's La DY5 ... 61 D2
Seagrave Rd CV1 ... 165 D1
Seal Cl B76 ... 46 E3
Sealand Dr CV12 ... 78 A3
Seals Gn B38 ... 123 D7
Sear Hills Cl CV7 ... 130 B6
Seaton B77 ... 35 F8
Seaton Cl Hinckley LE10 ... 76 B7
Nuneaton CV11 ... 73 F5
Wednesfield WV11 ... 26 F5
Seaton Gr B13 ... 86 D1
Seaton Pl DY8 ... 60 C2
Seaton Rd B66 ... 65 B5
Seaton Tower 2 B31 ... 102 C2
Sebastian Cl CV3 ... 134 B5
Seckham Rd WS13 ... 9 A8
Second Ave
Birmingham, Bordesley Green B9 ... 67 F1
Birmingham, Selly Oak B29 ... 86 B3
Birmingham, Witton B6 ... 55 F3
Brownhills WS8 ... 7 A1
Coventry CV3 ... 114 C1
Kingswinford, Barrow Hill DY6 ... 61 A7
Kingswinford, Wall Heath DY6 ... 60 F8
Wolverhampton WV10 ... 25 E7
Second Exhibition Ave B40 ... 90 D4
Security Ho WV2 ... 163 B2
Sedge Ave B38 ... 103 F3
Sedgeberrow Covert 3 B38 ... 123 E8
Sedgeberrow Rd B63 ... 83 A2
Sedgefield Cl DY1 ... 50 E3
Sedgefield Gr WV6 ... 23 F4
Sedgeford Cl DY5 ... 81 D8
Sedgehill Ave B17 ... 85 B4
Sedgemere Gr
Balsall Common CV7 ... 130 C5
Walsall WS4 ... 29 C8
Sedgemere Rd B26 ... 68 F1
Sedgemoor Ave WS7 ... 7 B5
Sedgemoor Rd CV3 ... 134 B5
Sedgley Cl B98 ... 153 F4
Sedgley Gr B20 ... 54 E4
Sedgley Hall Ave DY3 ... 50 C8
Sedgley Rd Dudley DY1 ... 51 B6
Wombourne WV4 ... 38 F2
Sedgley Rd E DY4 ... 52 A3
Sedgley Rd W DY4 ... 51 D5
Sedgley St WV2 ... 39 C7
Seed Field Croft CV3 ... 133 E7
Seedhouse Ct B64 ... 83 B8
Seeds La WS8 ... 15 F8
Seekings The CV31 ... 162 B3
Seeleys Rd B11 ... 87 E5
Seeswood Cl CV10 ... 72 C2
Sefton Dr B65 ... 62 F6
Sefton Gr DY4 ... 41 C2
Sefton Rd Birmingham B16 ... 65 F2
Coventry CV4 ... 132 E6
Tamworth B77 ... 35 D4
Segbourne Rd B45 ... 121 F8
Segundo Cl WS5 ... 42 F4
Segundo Rd WS5 ... 42 F4
Seisdon Rd WV5 ... 37 A1
Selba Dr DY11 ... 116 A6
Selborne Cl WS1 ... 29 A1
Selborne Gr B13 ... 105 C5
Selborne Rd Birmingham B20 ... 55 A2
Dudley DY2 ... 62 D7
Selborne St WS1 ... 29 A1
Selbourne Cres WV1 ... 26 B1
Selby Cl B26 ... 68 F1
Selby Gr B13 ... 105 C6
Selby Ho B69 ... 63 D6
Selby Way Nuneaton CV10 ... 72 B5
Walsall WS3 ... 13 E2
Selcombe Way B38 ... 123 F7
Selcroft Ave B32 ... 84 F5
Selecta Ave B44 ... 44 D2
Selina Dix Ho CV1 ... 165 C4
Selker Dr B77 ... 21 F5
Selkirk Cl B71 ... 53 C6
Selly Ave B29 ... 86 A2
Selly Cl B29 ... 86 B2
Selly Hall Croft B30 ... 104 A6
Selly Hill Rd B29 ... 85 F2
Selly Manor Mus B30 ... 103 F7
Selly Oak Hospl B29 ... 85 F1
Selly Oak Ind Est B29 ... 85 E1
Selly Oak Rd B30 ... 103 E5
Selly Oak Specl Sch B29 ... 103 E8
Selly Oak Sta B29 ... 85 E2
Selly Park Girls Sec Sch B29 ... 86 B1
Selly Park Rd B29 ... 86 A2
Selly Wharf B29 ... 85 E2
Selly Wick Dr B29 ... 86 B2
Selly Wick Rd B29 ... 86 B2
Sellywood Rd B30 ... 103 E8
Selma Gr B14 ... 105 D5
Selman's Par WS3 ... 14 C2
Selmans Hill WS3 ... 14 C2
Selsdon Cl
Kidderminster DY11 ... 116 B5
Wythall B47 ... 125 C5
Selsdon Rd WS3 ... 13 F3
Selsey Ave B66 ... 65 B3
Selsey Cl CV3 ... 134 C4
Selsey Rd B17 ... 65 B3
Selston Rd B6 ... 66 E7
Selvey Ave B43 ... 44 C3
Selworthy Rd
Birmingham B36 ... 69 F8
Coventry CV6 ... 95 E3
Selwyn Cl WV2 ... 39 C7
Selwyn Ho B37 ... 70 D3
Selwyn Rd Bilston WV14 ... 40 F7
Birmingham B16 ... 65 D2
Semele Cl CV31 ... 162 E5
Seneschal Rd CV3 ... 133 E7
Senneleys Park Rd B31 ... 84 E1
Sennen Cl Nuneaton CV11 ... 74 A5
Willenhall WV13 ... 26 F1
Sensall Rd DY9 ... 81 F3
Serin Cl DY10 ... 117 A1
Serpentine Rd
Birmingham, Aston B6 ... 56 A1
Birmingham, Harborne B17 ... 85 C6
Birmingham, Selly Oak B29 ... 86 A2
Serpentine The DY11 ... 116 C4
Servite Ct B14 ... 105 A2
Servite Ho 2 Coleshill B46 ... 70 F7
Kenilworth CV8 ... 147 F3
Seton Ho B74 ... 31 E2
Settle Ave B34 ... 68 F6
Settle Croft B37 ... 69 F1
Setton Dr DY3 ... 50 E7
Seven Acres WS9 ... 30 B5
Seven Acres La B98 ... 154 C5
Seven Acres Rd
Birmingham B31 ... 103 C1
Halesowen B62 ... 84 A5
Seven Star Rd B91 ... 107 B5
Seven Stars Rd B69 ... 64 A7
Severn Ave LE10 ... 75 A8
Severn Cl Birmingham B36 ... 69 F7
Catshill B61 ... 137 A8
Royal Leamington Spa CV32 ... 157 C3
Tipton DY4 ... 51 F5
Wednesfield WV12 ... 27 A7
Severn Ct Birmingham B23 ... 56 B3
Sutton Coldfield B73 ... 46 B5
Severn Dr Brierley Hill DY5 ... 61 B7
Burntwood WS7 ... 7 D6
Perton WV6 ... 23 E4
Severn Gr 6 Birmingham B19 ... 66 C7
Kidderminster DY11 ... 116 B3

Severn Ho 5 Dudley DY3 50 D3
4 Oldbury B68 84 B8
Severn Rd Brownhills WS8 6 C2
Bulkington CV12 79 A3
Coventry CV1 113 F1
Halesowen B63 82 B5
Stourbridge DY8 80 F3
Walsall WS3 14 E1
Severn St B1 164 B1
Severn Stars Ind Est CV3 134 A7
Severn Tower B7 67 B5
Severn Way B47 124 E2
Severne Gr B27 88 C1
Severne Jun & Inf Sch B27 106 C8
Severne Rd B27 106 C8
Sevington Cl B91 127 C8
Sewall Ct CV6 114 A8
Sewall Highway CV2 114 B6
Seward Cl WS14 9 D6
Seymour Cl Birmingham B29 86 A2
Cheslyn Hay WS6 4 D1
Coventry CV3 134 C5
Seymour Dr B98 154 A5
Seymour Gdns B74 31 E3
Seymour Gr CV34 161 D6
Seymour Rd
Kidderminster DY11 116 B8
Nuneaton CV11 73 D3
Oldbury B69 64 C7
Stourbridge DY9 82 A4
Tipton DY4 41 C1
Seymour St B5 164 D3
Shackleton Dr WV6 23 E5
Shackleton Rd WS3 14 D2
Shadow Brook La B92 108 E7
Shadowbrook Rd CV6 113 A5
Shadwell Dr DY3 50 D3
Shadwell St B4 164 C4
Shady La B44 44 E2
Shadymoor Dr DY5 81 C8
Shaft La CV7 93 A4
Shaftesbury Ave
Keresley CV7 95 A7
Stourbridge DY9 81 C2
Shaftesbury Cl B60 137 B2
Shaftesbury Dr WS12 2 C7
Shaftesbury Rd
Coventry CV5 132 F8
Wednesbury WS10 42 B2
Shaftesbury Sq B71 53 C5
Shaftesbury St B70 53 C4
Shaftmoor Ind Est B28 87 F2
Shaftmoor La B27, B28 87 F2
Shaftsbury Ave B63 82 B7
Shaftsbury Cl WV14 40 F7
Shaftsbury Rd B26 89 C5
Shakespear Gr WS11 1 D4
Shakespeare Ave
Bedworth CV12 78 D2
Lichfield WS14 9 B6
Redditch B98 154 A2
Warwick CV34 160 C4
Shakespeare Cl
Dudley WV14 40 D2
Tamworth B79 21 A6
Shakespeare Cres WS3 28 F7
Shakespeare Dr
Hinckley LE10 71 C1
Kidderminster DY10 117 B6
Nuneaton CV11 74 A1
Solihull B90 106 B1
Shakespeare Ho B31 123 A8
Shakespeare Pl WS3 28 F7
Shakespeare Rd
Birmingham B23 56 B3
Burntwood WS7 6 F8
Dudley DY3 50 A4
Smethwick B67 64 E4
Solihull B90 126 D8
Tipton DY4 52 A8
Shakespeare St
Birmingham B11 87 C5
Coventry CV2 114 B4
Wolverhampton WV1 163 D2
Shakleton Rd CV5 113 A2
Shaldon Wlk 4 B66 65 B5
Shale St WV14 40 C5
Shalford Rd B92 88 E4
Shallcross La DY3 50 D3
Shalnecote Gr B14 104 C5
Shambles 2 WS10 41 F2
Shandon Cl B32 84 F3
Shanklin Cl WS6 5 A3
Shanklin Dr CV10 73 D6
Shanklin Rd CV3 134 B4
Shannon B77 35 F8
Shannon Dr WS8 6 C2
Shannon Rd B38 123 E7
Shannon Wlk WS8 6 C2
Shannon's Mill B79 21 A5
Shanti Niketan WV2 39 D7
Shapinsay Dr B45 101 F1
Shard End Cres B34 69 C6
Shardlow Rd WV11 26 E8
Shardway The B34 69 C5
Sharesacre St WV13 27 B3
Sharington Cl 3 DY2 62 E8
Sharman Rd WV10 25 E6
Sharmans Cross Jun Sch B91 106 E4
Sharmans Cross Rd B91 106 F4
Sharnford Rd LE10 76 F6
Sharon Cl WV4 39 E5
Sharon Ct B27 88 C3
Sharon Way WS12 2 D3
Sharp Cl CV6 95 C2
Sharpe Cl CV34 160 E8
Sharpe St B77 22 A5
Sharpless Rd LE10 75 F7
Sharpley Ct CV2 115 A8
Sharps Cl B45 122 A7
Sharrat Field B75 32 D2
Sharratt Rd CV12 78 A2
Sharrocks St WV1 163 D2
Shaw Ave DY10 117 B6
Shaw Dr B33 68 E2
Shaw Hall La WV10 11 C7
Shaw Hill Gr B8 68 A4
Shaw Hill Inf & Jun Sch B8 67 F4
Shaw Hill Rd B8 68 A4
Shaw La Lichfield WS13 9 A8
Stoke Prior B60 150 C2
Wolverhampton WV6 24 B3
Shaw Lane Ind Est B60 150 C2
Shaw Park Bsns Village WV10 25 D6
Shaw Rd
Dudley, Hurst Hill WV14 40 B1
Dudley, Netherton DY2 62 C7
Tipton DY4 52 C4
Wolverhampton, Blakenhall WV2 39 C6
Wolverhampton, Dunstall Hill WV10 25 C6
Shaw St Walsall WS2 28 D2
West Bromwich B70 52 E7
Shaw's La WS6 5 A2
Shaw's Pas B5 164 D2
Shawbank Rd B98 154 B3
Shawberry Ave B35 58 B4
Shawberry Rd B37 69 F5
Shawbrook Gr 10 B14 105 A3
Shawbury Cl B98 154 E3
Shawbury Gr Birmingham B12 86 F8
Perton WV6 23 E5
Shawbury Rd WV10 25 F5
Shawe Ave CV10 73 C7
Shawfield B47 125 A5
Shawhellier Ave DY5 61 E2
Shawhurst Croft B47 125 A7
Shawhurst La B47 125 A6
Shawley Croft B27 88 E4
Shaws Cl B97 152 F2
Shawsdale Rd B36 68 F7
Shayler Gr WV2 39 D7
Sheaf La B26 89 B4
Sheapecoate Ho 1 B71 42 F1
Shearwater Cl
Birmingham B45 121 F6
Kidderminster DY10 117 B1
Shearwater Wlk B23 56 B7
Sheaves Cl WV14 40 B3
Shedden St 4 DY2 62 D8
Sheddington Rd B23 56 D7
Sheen Ho CV2 114 D8
Sheen Rd B44 44 E4
Sheepclose Dr B37 70 A3
Sheepcote Cl CV32 157 A1
Sheepcote Grange B61 136 F5
Sheepcote La B77 21 F4
Sheepcote St B16 66 B2
Sheepcroft Cl B97 152 F2
Sheepfold Cl B65 63 A4
Sheepmoor Cl B17 84 F8
Sheepwash La DY4 52 D5
Sheerwater Dr DY5 81 D7
Sheffield Rd B73 57 A7
Sheffield St DY5 62 A1
Shefford Rd B6 66 F5
Sheila Ave WV11 26 E7
Shelah Rd B63 83 A6
Shelbourne Cl B69 52 D2
Sheldon Ave WS10 42 A4
Sheldon Cl WV14 40 D4
Sheldon Dr B31 102 D2
Sheldon Gr Birmingham B26 89 B5
Warwick CV34 155 F2
Sheldon Hall Ave B33 69 D3
Sheldon Heath Rd B26 89 B8
Sheldon Heath Sch B33 89 C8
Sheldon Rd Redditch B98 159 A8
West Bromwich B71 53 E8
Wolverhampton WV10 11 A1
Sheldon Wlk B33 69 C1
Sheldonfield Rd B26 89 D5
Shelduck Cl DY10 117 B3
Shelfield Cl CV5 112 B3
Shelfield Com Sch WS4 15 C2
Shelfield Rd B14 104 C3
Shell Corner Trad Est B62 83 D8
Shelley Ave
Kidderminster DY10 116 E7
Tipton DY4 52 B8
Warwick CV34 160 C4
Shelley Cl Bedworth CV12 78 D1
Catshill B61 137 A8
Dudley DY3 50 A5
Redditch B97 158 C8
Stourbridge DY8 81 A8
Shelley Dr Birmingham B23 56 B3
Sutton Coldfield B74 31 F6
Shelley Gdns LE10 71 E3
Shelley Ho Halesowen B63 82 B5
1 Oldbury B68 64 C4
Shelley Rd 3 Burntwood WS7 7 A8
Cannock WS11 1 E5
Coventry CV2 114 C3
Tamworth B79 21 A7
Willenhall WV12 27 E7
Wolverhampton WV10 11 D2
Shellon Cl CV3 134 F8
Shelly Cl B37 69 F2
Shelly Cres B90 127 B6
Shelly Croft B33 69 A3
Shelly La B90 127 B6
Shelly Tower B31 103 C3
Shelsley Ave B69 63 D5
Shelsley Dr B13 87 B2
Shelsley Way B91 107 B1
Shelton Cl WS10 42 C5
Shelton La B63 82 E5
Shelton Sq CV1 165 B2
Shelton St B77 35 F7
Sheltwood Cl B97 153 A2
Sheltwood La B60 152 A3
Shelwick Gr B93 127 F4
Shenley Ave DY1 51 C6
Shenley Court Sch B31 102 F7
Shenley Fields Dr B31 102 F8
Shenley Fields Rd B29 103 B8
Shenley Gdns B29 103 A7
Shenley Gn B29 102 F6
Shenley Hill B31 102 F6
Shenley La B29 102 F7
Shenstone Ave
Halesowen B62 83 E5
Stourbridge DY8 80 D3
Shenstone Cl
Bromsgrove B60 137 B3
Sutton Coldfield B74 31 E6
Shenstone Ct
Bromsgrove B60 137 B3
Solihull B90 105 D2
Wolverhampton WV3 39 A6
Shenstone Dr Aldridge WS9 30 A8
Balsall Common CV7 130 A6
Shenstone Flats B62 83 F5
Shenstone Ho WS13 3 E1
Shenstone Lodge Specl Sch WS14 18 A3
Shenstone Rd
Birmingham, Edgbaston B16 65 C3
Birmingham, Great Barr B43 54 E8
Birmingham, Highter's Heath B14 105 A1
Shenstone Sta WS14 17 F6
Shenstone Trad Est B62 83 C4
Shenstone Valley Rd B62 83 F6
Shenton Wlk B37 69 F5
Shepheard Rd B26 89 D5
Shepherd Cl Coventry CV4 111 F3
Lichfield WS13 3 C3
Shepherd Dr WV12 27 C5
Shepherds Brook Rd DY9 81 D5
Shepherds Fold B65 63 B2
Shepherds Gdns 8 B15 66 B1
Shepherds Green Rd B24 56 F1
Shepherds Pool Rd B75 32 E2
Shepherds Standing B34 69 B6
Shepherds Way B23 56 C8
Shepherds Wlk
Bromsgrove B60 150 E7
Wolverhampton WV8 10 F2
Shepley Rd Barnt Green B45 138 A7
Birmingham B45 122 B6
Shepperton Bsns Pk CV11 73 C1
Shepperton Ct CV11 73 C1
Shepperton St CV11 73 C2
Sheppey Dr B36 70 B5
Shepwell Gdns WV10 12 C7
Shepwell Gn WV13 27 C1
Sherard Croft B36 70 B6
Sheraton Cl Aldridge WS9 30 B6
Cannock WS12 2 A7
Sheraton Dr DY10 117 B6
Sheraton Grange DY8 80 F2
Sherborne Cl WS3 28 C7
Sherborne Ct WV10 11 E1
Sherborne Gdns WV8 10 A3
Sherborne Gr B1 66 A3
Sherborne Rd Hinckley LE10 76 B7
Wolverhampton WV10 11 D1
Sherborne St B16 66 B2
Sherbourne Ave
Cannock WS12 2 E4
Nuneaton CV10 72 B4
Sherbourne Cl B98 154 D2
Sherbourne Cres CV5 112 E4
Sherbourne Ct CV1 165 B1
Sherbourne Dr B27 88 C4
Sherbourne Fields Sch CV6 112 D5
Sherbourne Rd
Birmingham, Acock's Green B27 88 C4
Birmingham, Balsall Heath B12 86 F7
Blackheath B64 83 B8
Stourbridge DY8 81 B4
Sherbourne St CV1 113 A2
Sherbrook Rd WS11 1 C1
Sherbrooke Ave B77 35 F6
Sherdmore Croft B90 126 F6
Sheridan Cl 2 WS2 42 B7
Sheridan Gdns DY3 49 F5
Sheridan St Walsall WS2 42 B7
West Bromwich B71 53 D4
Sheridan Wlk B35 58 A3
Sheriff Ave CV4 132 B7
Sheriff Dr DY5 61 F2
Sheriffs Cl WS14 9 E6
Sheriffs Orch CV1 165 B2
Sherifoot La B75 32 B4
Sheringham B15 85 E8
Sheringham Cl CV11 73 F2
Sheringham Rd B30 104 B3
Sherington Ave CV5 112 C4
Sherington Dr WV4 39 D5
Sherlock Cl WV12 27 D5
Sherlock Rd CV5 112 D3
Sherlock St B5 86 E8
Sherrans Dell WV4 39 D3
Sherratt Cl B76 57 F8
Sherringham Dr WV11 13 C1
Sherron Gdns B12 86 F5
Sherston Covert 11 B30 104 C2
Shervale Cl WV4 39 A6
Sherwin Ave WV14 40 A2
Sherwood Ave DY4 51 F4
Sherwood Cl
Birmingham B28 105 F5
Solihull B92 106 F7
Wood End CV9 36 C1
Sherwood Dr Brierley Hill DY5 61 F2
Cannock WS11 2 A3
Sherwood Jones Cl CV6 113 B6
Sherwood Mews B28 105 E6
Sherwood Rd
Birmingham B28 105 E7
Bromsgrove B60 151 A6
Smethwick B67 65 A1
Stourbridge DY8 80 E7
Sherwood St WV1 163 B4
Sherwood Wlk
Royal Leamington Spa CV32 157 C4
Walsall WS9 29 E7
Shetland Cl Birmingham B16 65 F2
Coventry CV5 112 A4
Wolverhampton W6 25 B5
Shetland Dr Nuneaton CV10 73 A2
Smethwick B66 64 D8
Shetland Wlk B36 70 B6
Shevlock Way CV6 114 A6
Shidas La B69 63 E7
Shifnal Wlk B31 122 F8
Shillcock Gr B19 66 E5
Shillingstone Cl CV2 115 A4
Shilton & Ansty Fst Sch CV7 97 E5
Shilton Cl B90 126 F6
Shilton Gr B29 102 F8
Shilton Ind Est CV7 97 E7
Shilton La Barnacle CV2, CV7 97 B4
Bulkington CV12 79 D1
Coventry CV2 96 F3
Shilton CV7, CV12 97 D8
Shinwell Cres B69 52 D2
Shipbourne Cl B32 84 F5
Shipley Fields B24 57 A3
Shipley Gr B29 103 A8
Shipston Rd
Birmingham B31 103 B1
Coventry CV2 114 C6
Shipton Cl DY1 50 F3
Shipton Rd B72 46 C3
Shipway Rd B25 88 A7
Shire Brook Cl B6 66 E8
Shire Brook Ct 2 B19 66 D7
Shire Cl Birmingham B16 65 F2
Coventry CV6 96 B1
Oldbury B68 64 B2
Shire Oak Com Sch WS9 16 A5
Shire Ridge WS9 16 B4
Shirebrook Cl CV2 96 D2
Shirehall Pl WS11 2 B2
Shirehampton Cl B97 152 F2
Shireland Brook Gdns
1 B18 65 D4
Shireland Cl B20 54 F3
Shireland Hall Prim Sch B66 65 C3
Shireland High Sch
Smethwick B66 64 F3
Smethwick B66 65 B3
Shireland Rd B66 65 B3
Shirelea Cl 4 WS7 7 B8
Shires Gate Ret Pk CV31 161 E6
Shires Ret Pk CV34 161 D6
Shirestone Jun & Inf Sch B33 69 D2
Shirestone Rd B33 69 E2
Shireview Gdns WS3 15 B4
Shireview Rd WS3 15 B4
Shirlett Cl CV2 96 B4
Shirley Dr B72 46 C4
Shirley Heath Jun Sch B90 106 C1
Shirley La CV7 111 A5
Shirley Park Rd B90 106 B2
Shirley Rd
Birmingham, Hall Green B27, B28 106 A7
Birmingham, King's Norton B30 104 A5
Coventry CV2 115 A7
Dudley DY2 62 E8
Oldbury B68 64 C6
Shirley Sta B90 105 F1
Shirley Trad Est B90 106 E1
Shirley Wlk B79 20 F7
Shirleydale 2 B90 126 C8
Shirral Gr B37 69 F5
Shirrall Dr B78 33 E4
Shoal Hill Cl WS11 1 B2
Sholing Cl WV8 10 F1
Shooters Cl B5 86 D6
Shooters Hill B72 46 D2
Shop La Nurton WV6 23 A1
Trescott WV6 37 B7
Shopping Ctr The CV31 162 B5
Shopping Prec The CV34 156 A1
Shops The DY6 60 D4
Shopton Rd B34 69 A7
Shoreham Cl WV13 26 D1
Shorncliffe Rd CV6 112 E6
Short Acre St WS2 28 D3
Short Heath Jun & Inf Sch B23 56 D6
Short Heath Jun Sch WV12 27 D5
Short Heath Rd B23 56 E6
Short La WS6 4 E3
Short Rd Smethwick B67 64 D3
Wolverhampton WV10 11 E1
Short St Bilston WV14 40 D6
Blackheath B65 63 C2
Brownhills WS8 15 F7
Cannock WS11 1 F3
Coventry CV1 165 C2
Darlaston WS10 41 F7
Dudley DY1 51 A2
Halesowen B63 82 F5
3 Kidderminster DY10 116 F6
Nuneaton CV10 72 D4
8 Stourbridge DY8 80 F5
Tipton DY4 51 E8
Walsall WS2 28 D1
Wednesbury WS10 41 E3
Willenhall WV12 27 C5
Wolverhampton WV1 163 C3
Shortbutts La WS14 9 B5
Shorters Ave B14 105 B4
Shortland Cl B93 128 A7
Shortlands CV7 95 D6
Shortlands Cl B30 104 A2
Shortlands La WS3 14 F3
Shortley Rd CV3 133 F8
Shorwell Pl DY5 61 B1
Shottery Cl Coventry CV5 112 B3
Sutton Coldfield B76 46 F1
Shottery Gr B76 46 F1
Shottery Rd B90 106 B1
Shotteswell Rd B90 126 B8
Showell Cir WV10 25 E7
Showell Green La B11 87 C3
Showell Ho 10 B69 64 A7
Showell La Meriden CV7 93 A1
Wombourne WV4 38 B3
Showell Rd WV10 25 D6
Showells Gdns B7 67 C7
Shrawley Ave DY11 116 B3
Shrawley Cl
Birmingham B45 121 F7
Halesowen B63 83 A2
Shrawley Ho 6 B38 103 D2
Shrawley Rd B31 103 C2
Shrewley Cres B33 69 E1
Shrewsbury Cl WS3 13 F1
Shrewsbury Rd DY11 116 A6
Shrewton Ave B14 104 D2
Shrub La B24 57 B4
Shrubberies The CV4 132 E4
Shrubbery Ave DY4 51 D5
Shrubbery Cl B76 57 D6
Shrubbery Ct DY10 116 F7
Shrubbery Rd B61 136 E1
Shrubbery Sch The B76 57 F7
Shrubbery St DY10 116 F7
Shrubbery The B16 65 F3
Shrubland St CV31 162 A6
Shrubland Street Com Prim Sch CV31 162 A6
Shrublands Ave B68 84 B7
Shuckburgh Gr 4 CV32 157 A2
Shugborough Dr DY1 50 E2
Shugborough Way WS11 2 C1
Shulman's Wlk CV2 114 D7
Shultern La CV4 132 D6
Shuna Croft CV2 115 B7
Shustoke La WS5 43 B4
Shustoke Rd Birmingham B34 69 C6
Solihull B91 107 D5
Shut Mill La B62 100 D2
Shutlock La B13 86 D1
Shutt La B94 126 B1
Shuttington Rd B79 22 B6
Shuttle St CV6 114 B8
Shyltons Croft B16 66 A2
Sibdon Gr B31 123 A8
Sibree Rd CV3 134 B4
Sibton Cl CV2 96 C1
Sidaway Cl B65 63 C6
Sidaway St B64 62 E1
Sidbury Gr B93 127 E3
Sidcup Cl WV14 40 B3
Sidcup Rd B44 45 A1
Siddeley Ave Coventry CV3 114 B1
Kenilworth CV8 147 E3
Siddons Factory Est B70 52 F8
Siddons Rd WV14 40 D2
Sidemoor Fst Sch B61 136 E3
Sidenhill Cl B90 126 B8
Sidford Gdns B24 57 C3
Sidford Gr B23 56 E7
Sidings The Birmingham B20 66 C8
Cannock WS12 2 C7
Hagley DY9 99 A6
Sidlaw Cl Halesowen B63 82 D2
Wolverhampton WV10 25 C6
Sidmouth Cl Coventry CV2 114 C7
Nuneaton CV11 73 F5
Sidney St WV2 163 B1
Sidney Stringer Com Tech Coll CV1 165 C3
Sidon Hill Way WS11 2 C2
Sidwick Cres WV2 40 B6
Sigmund Cl WV1 26 B3
Signal Gr WS3 14 A1
Signal Hayes Rd B76 47 A2
Signal Wlk B77 22 A2
Silesbourne Cl B36 69 C8
Silhill Hall Rd B91 107 A5

Silica Rd B77 22 B2
Silksby St CV3 133 D8
Sillins Ave B98 154 A3
Silva Ave DY6 60 F4
Silver Birch Ave CV12 77 E2
Silver Birch Coppice B74 31 D5
Silver Birch Dr
Hollywood B47 125 B6
Kidderminster DY10 117 C5
Silver Birch Gr CV31 161 F5
Silver Birch Rd Aldridge B74 30 F1
Birmingham, Erdington B24 57 B6
Birmingham, Kingshurst B37 69 F6
Huntington WS12 1 D8
Norton Canes WS11 6 B5
Wolverhampton WV2 39 E7
Silver Birches Bsns Pk B60 150 F6
Silver Court Gdns WS8 15 F7
Silver Ct WS8 15 F7
Silver End Ind Est DY5 61 B1
Silver Fir Cl WS12 2 A8
Silver Innage B63 82 C7
Silver Link Rd B77 22 A1
Silver St Birmingham B14 104 E8
Brierley Hill DY5 61 C1
Brownhills WS8 15 F7
Coventry CV1 165 B3
Hollywood B38 124 E5
Kidderminster DY10 116 E7
Redditch B98 153 E4
Tamworth B79 21 B5
Silver Trees Dr CV12 79 B4
Silver Wlk CV10 72 F3
Silver's Cl WS3 14 F4
Silverbirch Cl CV10 72 A7
Silverbirch Ct B24 57 B6
Silverbirch Rd B91 107 E3
Silvercroft Ave B21 54 D3
Silverdale B61 136 F4
Silverdale Cl CV2 96 B4
Silverdale Dr WV10 25 E5
Silverdale Gdns DY8 60 C3
Silverdale Rd B24 57 D5
Silverfield Cl B14 104 E8
Silverlands Ave B68 64 B3
Silverlands Cl B28 87 F1
Silvermead Rd B73 46 A1
Silvermere Rd B26 89 D6
Silverstone Ave DY11 116 D8
Silverstone Cl WS2 27 D3
Silverstone Dr Coventry CV6 95 E5
Sutton Coldfield B74 44 F6
Silverthorne Ave DY4 51 D5
Silverthorne La B64 82 B8
Silverton Cres B13 87 D1
Silverton Hts B67 64 F6
Silverton Rd Coventry CV6 113 F7
Smethwick B67 64 E6
Silverton Way WV11 26 F5
Silvester Ct B70 53 E3
Silvester Rd WV14 40 F7
Silvington Cl B29 103 C7
Simcox Gdns B32 84 D2
Simcox Rd WS10 41 F5
Simcox St WS12 2 D4
Simeon's Wlk DY5 81 F7
Simmonds Cl WS3 14 D3
Simmonds Pl WS10 41 F7
Simmonds Rd WS3 14 D3
Simmonds Way WS8 16 A6
Simmons Cl B78 34 B1
Simmons Dr B32 84 D4
Simmons Leasow B32 84 E2
Simmons Rd WV11 13 B1
Simms La Dudley DY2 62 C5
Hollywood B47 125 A5
Simon Cl Nuneaton CV11 73 D2
West Bromwich B71 42 E1
Simon Ct CV7 96 A8
Simon Rd B47 125 A7
Simon Stone St CV6 113 F8
Simons Rd B7 67 A4
Simpkins Cl WS9 16 A3
Simpson Gr WV10 25 E6
Simpson Rd Lichfield WS13 3 B2
Sutton Coldfield B72 46 C1
Walsall WS2 28 B5
Wolverhampton WV10 25 E6
Simpson St B69 64 A8
Sinclair Ct B13 86 E4
Singer Cl CV6 114 B8
Singer Croft B36 58 F1
Singh Cl B21 54 E1
Sion Cl DY5 61 D3
Sir Alfreds Way B76 46 E3
Sir George's Mall 6 DY10 116 E6
Sir Georges Ct 10 DY10 116 E6
Sir Harrys Rd B5 86 C6
Sir Henry Parkes Prim Sch CV4 132 C8
Sir Henry Parkes Rd CV5 132 D7
Sir Hilton's Rd B31 123 C7
Sir John's Rd B29 86 C3
Sir Richards Dr B17 84 F7
Sir Robert Peel Hospl B78 20 D1
Sir Theodore Pritchett Inf & Jun Sch B14 104 D2
Sir Thomas White's Rd CV5 112 F2
Sir Walter's Mall 8 DY10 116 E6
Sir Wilfred Martineau Upper & Lower Sch B33 69 D3
Sir William Lyons Rd CV4 132 C6
Sir Winston Churchill Pl CV3 135 C7
Sisefield Rd B38 104 A1
Siskin Cl WS7 7 D5
Siskin Dr Birmingham B12 86 E6
Coventry CV3 134 C4
Siskin Parkway E CV3 134 C1
Siskin Parkway W CV3 134 C2
Siskin Rd DY9 81 C3
Siskin Way DY10 117 B1
Sisley Way LE10 71 A3
Sister Dora Bldgs 2 WS1 28 E1
Sister Dora Gdns 1 WS1 42 E8
Siviter St B63 83 B4
Siviter's Cl B65 63 B3
Siviter's La B65 63 B3
Six Acres B32 84 C4
Six Ways B23 56 F4
Six Ways Ho B23 56 F4
Sixth Ave B6 55 F4
Skelcher Rd B90 106 A3
Skelwith Rise CV11 74 A6
Skemp Cl WV14 40 D4
Sketchley Cl B66 65 A6
Sketchley Hall Gdns LE10 75 C5
Sketchley Hill Cty Prim Sch LE10 75 E5
Sketchley La LE10 75 C5
Sketchley La Ind Est LE10 75 B5
Sketchley Manor La LE10 75 D5
Sketchley Mdws LE10 75 C5
Sketchley Meadows Bsns Pk LE10 75 C4
Sketchley Old Village LE10 75 C5
Sketchley Rd LE10 75 E5
Skidmore Ave Tamworth B77 35 C5
Wolverhampton WV3 38 F8
Skidmore Dr B70 53 A3
Skidmore Rd WV14 40 D2
Skilts Ave B98 153 F1
Skinner La B5 66 E1
Skinner St WV1 163 B3
Skip La WS5 43 E7
Skipness B77 21 F5
Skipton Gdns CV2 114 B6
Skipton Gn WV6 25 A5
Skipton Lodge CV2 114 B6
Skipton Pl WS11 4 B7
Skipton Rd B16 66 A1
Skipworth Rd CV3 115 A1
Skomer Cl B45 101 E1
Sky Blue Way CV1 113 E3
Skye Cl Birmingham B36 70 B6
Nuneaton CV10 72 F2
Skye Wlk 4 B64 62 E1
Skylark Cl Brierley Hill DY5 50 C1
Huntington WS12 1 C7
Skylark Way DY10 117 A2
Slack La B20 54 E2
Slacky La WS3 14 F1
Slade Ave WS7 7 A8
Slade Cl Nuneaton CV11 79 C8
West Bromwich B71 42 F2
Slade Gdns WV8 10 A4
Slade Gr B93 127 F6
Slade Hill WV6 24 F3
Slade Jun & Inf Sch B23 56 D2
Slade La Birmingham B28 105 E3
Sutton Coldfield B75 33 A3
Tamworth B77 35 C4
Slade Lanker B34 69 A5
Slade Mdw CV31 162 E5
Slade Rd Birmingham B23 56 D3
Halesowen B63 82 C6
Sutton Coldfield B75 32 E3
Wolverhampton WV10 11 C3
Sladefield Inf Sch B8 68 A5
Sladefield Rd B8 68 A5
Sladen CE Mid Sch DY10 116 F7
Sladepool Farm Rd B14 105 A2
Slaithwaite Rd B71 53 E4
Slaney Rd WS2 42 B6
Slatch House Rd B67 64 E2
Slateley Cres B90 126 F6
Slater Rd B93 127 F4
Slater St Bilston WV14 40 E3
Darlaston WS10 41 D6
Tipton, Dudley Port DY4 52 A4
Tipton, Great Bridge DY4 52 D5
Willenhall WV13 27 C3
Slaters La WS2 42 B7
Slaters Pl WS2 42 C7
Sleaford Gr B28 106 A7
Sleaford Rd B28 106 B7
Sleath's Yd CV12 78 B3
Sledmere Cl CV2 96 B3
Sledmere Prim Sch DY2 62 D6
Sledmore Rd DY2 62 E7
Sleets Yd CV12 78 A2
Slideslow Ave B60 137 B2
Slieve The B20 55 A3
Slim Ave WV14 40 E3
Slim Rd WS2 27 E2
Slimbridge Cl Redditch B97 158 E5
2 Solihull B90 127 A6
Slims Gate B63 83 A4
Sling The Dudley DY2 62 C6
Kidderminster DY10 116 E6
Slingfield Rd B31 103 C1
Slingsby B77 35 C7
Slingsby Cl CV11 73 F2
Slitting Mill Cl B21 65 C8
Sloane Ho 7 B1 66 C3
Sloane St B1 66 C3
Slough The B97 159 B4
Small Cl B67 64 D5
Small Heath Bridge B11 87 B8
Small Heath Bsns Pk B10 87 F7
Small Heath Highway B11 87 D6
Small Heath Lower Sch B10 87 D7
Small Heath Sta B10 87 D7
Small Heath Trad Est B11 87 D6
Small Heath Upper Sch B10 87 D8
Small La B94 141 E6
Small St Walsall WS1 42 E8
West Bromwich B71 53 B5
Smallbrook La WV5 49 B7
Smallbrook Queensway B5 164 C1
Smalldale Rd B42 55 D7
Smalley Cl WS11 2 A5
Smalley Pl CV8 147 F4
Smallshire Way DY8 80 D8
Smallwood Almshouses B98 153 E3
Smallwood Arch 5 B98 153 E4
Smallwood Cl B76 46 E3
Smallwood Rd WV8 10 E2
Smallwood St B98 153 E3
Smarts Ave WS14 32 A7
Smarts Rd CV12 77 F1
Smeaton Cl B18 65 E4
Smedley Crooke Pl B48 123 C2
Smeed Gr B24 57 B3
Smercote Cl CV12 77 D1
Smestow Ho B68 64 B1
Smestow Sec Sch WV3 24 B1
Smestow St WV10 25 D4
Smethwick Galton Bridge Sta B66 64 E7
Smethwick Ho B68 64 C2
Smethwick Sta B66 65 A6
Smethwick West Sta B66 64 E7
Smillie Pl WS11 1 F3
Smirrells Rd B28 105 E5
Smith Ave WS10 41 D4
Smith Cl WV14 40 A1
Smith Ho WS3 14 C3
Smith Pl DY4 52 B4
Smith Rd Walsall WS2 42 C6
Wednesbury WS10 41 F1
Smith St Bedworth CV12 77 E1
Bilston WV14 40 D5
Birmingham B19 66 C5
Coventry CV6 113 F5
Dudley DY2 62 D7
3 Royal Leamington Spa CV31 161 F7
Warwick CV34 160 F7
Wood End CV9 36 C1
Smith's Cl WS7 6 D6
Smithfield Pas B5 164 C1
Smithfield Rd WS3 14 D1
Smithfield Rise WS13 9 C8
Smithford Way CV1 165 B3
Smithmoor Cres B71 53 F8
Smiths Cl B32 84 B1
Smiths La B93 127 E7
Smiths Way B46 59 A3
Smiths Wood Sch B36 70 A6
Smithy Dr 7 WS3 15 A4
Smithy La Aston Flamville LE9 76 C8
Dudley DY5 50 B1
Lichfield WS13 3 A1
Tamworth B77 35 F7
Smithy The B26 89 C6
Smorrall La CV12 77 C2
Smout Cres WV14 39 F2
Smythe Gr CV34 155 E1
Snake La B48 139 A6
Snakes Lake La B61 136 D6
Snapdragon Dr WS5 43 A3
Snape Rd Coventry CV2 114 F5
Wolverhampton WV11 13 B1
Sneyd Com Sch WS3 13 E2
Sneyd Hall Cl WS3 28 A8
Sneyd Hall Rd WS3 14 A1
Sneyd Ho WS3 13 F1
Sneyd La WV11 13 C1
Snipe Cl WV10 12 B7
Snow Hill WV2 163 C2
Snow Hill Queensway B4 164 C3
Snow Hill Sta B3 164 B3
Snowberry Dr DY5 50 C1
Snowberry Gdns 7 B27 88 C5
Snowdon Cl CV10 72 B3
Snowdon Gr B63 82 D1
Snowdon Rd Cannock WS11 1 E6
1 Stourbridge DY8 81 B6
Snowdon Rise DY3 50 D6
Snowdon Way
Willenhall WV12 13 B1
Wolverhampton WV10 25 B6
Snowdrop Cl WS8 15 D6
Snowford Cl B90 105 F1
Snows Drive Hill B90 126 D5
Snowshill Cl Nuneaton CV11 78 F8
Redditch B98 154 B6
Snowshill Gdns DY1 50 F4
Soar Way LE10 75 A8
Soberton Cl WV11 26 F7
Soden Cl CV3 134 D6
Soden's Ave CV8 135 A1
Soho Ave B18 66 A7
Soho, Benson Road B18 65 F6
Soho Cl B66 65 C6
Soho Hill B19 66 B7
Soho Ho B66 65 C6
Soho House Mus B18 66 A7
Soho Rd B21 65 F8
Soho St B66 65 C6
Soho Way B66 65 B6
Solari Cl DY4 52 C8
Solent Cl WV9 10 F2
Solent Ct B73 46 B5
Solent Dr CV2 96 F1
Solihull By-Pass B91 107 E4
Solihull Coll B91 107 A3
Solihull Coll Chelmsley Campus B37 70 C4
Solihull Coll Sharmans Cross Campus B90 106 D3
Solihull Hospl B91 107 C4
Solihull La B28 106 A6
Solihull Parkway B37 90 E8
Solihull Parkway Hospl B91 107 E5
Solihull Rd Birmingham B11 87 D3
Hampton in A B92 108 E6
Solihull B90 106 D3
Solihull Sch B91 107 D4
Solihull Sixth Form Coll B91 107 D2
Solihull Sta B91 107 A4
Solly Gr DY4 52 D7
Solway Cl
Royal Leamington Spa CV31 162 C6
Tamworth B79 21 A7
Wednesbury WS10 42 C4
Somerby Dr B91 127 A8
Somercotes Rd B42 55 D8
Somerdale Rd B31 103 C4
Somerfield Cl WS4 15 C1
Somerfield Rd WS3 28 C7
Somerford Cl WS6 4 E1
Somerford Gdns WV10 11 E2
Somerford Pl WV13 26 F1
Somerford Rd B29 102 F8
Somerford Way WV14 51 B8
Somerland Rd B26 69 A1
Somerleyton Ave DY10 117 A5
Somerleyton Ct 3 DY10 117 A5
Somerly Cl CV3 134 F8
Somers Pl 8 CV32 161 E8
Somers Rd Halesowen B62 83 C5
Keresley CV7 95 A6
Meriden CV7 91 F1
Walsall WS2 42 A7
Somerset Cl B78 21 A1
Somerset Cres WS10 42 D4
Somerset Dr
Birmingham B31 122 F7
Nuneaton CV10 72 E4
Stourbridge DY8 80 D7
Somerset Ho B33 69 A2
Somerset Pl WS11 1 F3
Somerset Rd
Birmingham, Edgbaston B15 85 F5
Birmingham, Erdington B23 56 F6
Birmingham, Handsworth B20 54 F2
Coventry CV1 113 C5
Walsall WS4 29 A4
West Bromwich B71 53 D6
Willenhall WV13 27 D2
Somerton Dr
Birmingham, Erdington B23 57 A6
Birmingham, Marston Green B37 90 B7
Somerville Ct 2 B73 46 A2
Somerville Ho B37 70 D3
Somerville Jun & Inf Sch B10 87 D8
Somerville Rd
Birmingham B10 87 E8
Sutton Coldfield B73 46 A3
Somery Rd Birmingham B29 85 A2
Dudley DY1 51 C3
Sommerfield Rd B32 84 D3
Sommerville Dr B73 46 A4
Sommerville Rd CV2 114 C4
Sonning Dr WV9 10 F2
Sopwith Croft B35 58 A2
Sorbus B77 22 B4
Sorrel B77 22 B5
Sorrel Cl Coventry CV4 131 E8
Featherstone WV10 12 B7
Tipton B69 52 B2
Sorrel Dr Birmingham B27 88 B2
Walsall WS5 43 A3
Sorrel Gr B24 57 D3
Sorrel Ho B24 57 D3
Sorrell Rd CV10 78 D8
Sorrell Wlk DY5 81 B6
Soudan B97 153 D2
Souters Ho B32 102 D8
South Ave Coventry CV2 114 A2
Stourbridge DY8 80 F4
Wolverhampton WV11 26 C5
South Bank Rd B64 82 E8
South Birmingham Coll Digbeth Ctr B5 66 F1
South Birmingham Coll (Hall Green Ctr) B28 105 E8
South Birmingham Coll (The Health & Social Care Ctr) B28 106 B6
South Birmingham Tech Ctr B28 87 F1
South Bromsgrove High Sch B60 150 F8
South Car Park Rd B40 90 E3
South Cl WS11 4 C8
South Cres Bromsgrove B60 137 A1
Featherstone WV10 12 C6
South Dene B67 64 F5
South Dr Birmingham B5 86 C4
Coleshill B46 70 E6
Sutton Coldfield B75 46 C6
South Gn WV4 38 D5
South Gr
Birmingham, Aston B6 66 D8
Birmingham, Erdington B23 56 F5
Birmingham, Lozells B19 66 B8
South Holme B9 67 C2
South Oval DY3 50 E5
South Par B72 46 C4
South Park Mews DY5 61 C2
South Range 4 B11 87 B6
South Rd
Birmingham, Erdington B23 56 F4
Birmingham, Hockley B18 66 A6
Birmingham, King's Heath B14 104 E8
Birmingham, Northfield B31 102 F2
Birmingham, Sparkbrook B11 87 B7
Bromsgrove B60 151 B7
Hagley DY9 99 A4
Smethwick B67 64 F5
Stourbridge DY8 80 E4
Tipton DY4 52 B8
South Ridge CV5 112 B4
South Road Ave B18 66 A6
South Roundhay B33 69 A3
South St Birmingham B17 85 D5
Brierley Hill DY5 61 C2
Coventry CV1 113 E3
Redditch B98 153 E3
Walsall WS1 42 D8
Willenhall WV13 26 F1
Wolverhampton WV10 25 C6
South Staffordshire Bsns Pk WS11 4 C4
South Street Gdns WS1 42 D8
South Terr CV31 162 B3
South View Birmingham B43 54 E7
Warwick CV35 160 A6
South View Cl Codsall WV8 10 B2
Featherstone WV10 12 B6
South View Rd
Royal Leamington Spa CV32 157 C5
Sedgley DY3 50 C8
South Way B40 90 F3
South Wlk B31 103 C1
Southacre Ave B5 86 E8
Southall Cres WV14 40 C1
Southall Rd WV11 27 A8
Southall's La DY1 51 B1
Southam Cl Birmingham B28 105 E8
Coventry CV4 131 E7
Southam Dr B73 46 B1
Southam Ho B13 105 A7
Southam Rd
Birmingham B28 105 E8
Radford Semele CV31 162 E6
Southampton St WV1 163 C4
Southbank Rd Coventry CV6 112 E5
Kenilworth CV8 147 F4
Southbank View DY6 60 E4
Southborough Terr 1 CV31 162 A6
Southbourne Ave
Birmingham B34 68 D6
Walsall WS2 28 B1
Southbourne Cl B29 86 A2
Southbourne Pl WS11 1 D2
Southbourne Rd WV10 11 C3
Southcote Gr B38 103 D1
Southcott Ave DY5 81 D8
Southcott Way CV2 96 F1
Southcrest Gdns B97 153 D1
Southcrest Rd B98 154 A2
Southdown Ave B18 66 A6
Southern Cl DY6 60 F3
Southern Cross WS13 9 C7
Southern Rd B8 68 C6
Southern Way WS10 41 C3
Southerndown Rd DY3 50 B7
Southey Cl Solihull B91 127 B8
Willenhall WV12 27 E8
Southfield Ave
Birmingham, Castle Bromwich B36 69 B8
Birmingham, Edgbaston B16 65 D3
Southfield Cl CV10 73 D5
Southfield Dr
Birmingham B28 106 A5
Kenilworth CV8 148 A6
Southfield Gr WV3 38 C7
Southfield Rd
Birmingham B16 65 D3
Hinckley LE10 75 E7
Wednesfield WV11 26 F5
Southfield Way WS6 4 F2
Southfields CV32 157 A3
Southfields Rd B91 106 F1
Southgate Blackheath B64 82 D8
Cannock WS11 4 B7
Wolverhampton WV1 163 A3
Southgate Cl DY11 116 A4
Southgate End WS11 4 B7
Southgate Rd B44 44 E2
Southlands 8 CV31 162 B7
Southlands Rd B13 87 A1
Southlea Ave CV31 161 E6
Southlea Cl CV31 161 E6
Southleigh Ave CV5 132 F7
Southmead Cres B98 153 F3
Southmead Dr B60 137 B6

Southmead Gdns B80 .... 159 E3
Southminster Dr B14 .... 104 E6
Southport Cl CV3 .... 134 B5
Southville Bglws For Old
People B14 .... 105 B4
Southwark Cl WS13 .... 3 C3
Southway CV31 .... 162 A5
Southway Ct DY6 .... 60 F4
Southwick Pl WV14 .... 40 D7
Southwick Rd B62 .... 83 D8
Southwold Ave B30 .... 104 C3
Southwood Ave B34 .... 69 B7
Southwood Cl DY6 .... 60 C4
Southwood Covert B14 ..... 104 C2
Sovereign Cl CV8 .... 147 F1
Sovereign Ct 8 B11 .... 66 C3
Sovereign Dr DY1 .... 50 E2
Sovereign Rd
Birmingham B30 .... 104 A4
Coventry CV5 .... 113 A2
Sovereign Row CV1 .... 113 A2
Sovereign Way B13 .... 86 F4
Sovereign Wlk 7 WS1 .... 28 F2
Sovereign Works DY3 .... 50 E4
Sowe Valley Prim Sch
CV3 .... 134 D7
Sowerby March B24 .... 57 D4
Sowers Cl WV12 .... 27 D5
Sowers Gdns WV12 .... 27 D5
Spa Cl LE10 .... 71 E1
Spa Gr B30 .... 104 C8
Spa La LE10 .... 71 E1
Spa View CV31 .... 162 B4
Spadesbourne Rd B60 .... 137 C6
Spark St B11 .... 87 A7
Sparkbrook St CV1 .... 113 F3
Sparkbrook Workshops
CV1 .... 113 F3
Sparkhill Ctr B11 .... 87 C5
Sparrey Dr B30 .... 104 A8
Sparrow Cl WS10 .... 42 B5
Sparrow Cock La B93 .... 129 C1
Spartan CV34 .... 161 E4
Spartan Ind Ctr B70 .... 52 E6
Spearhill WS14 .... 9 E8
Speed Rd DY4 .... 51 E7
Speedway La CV8 .... 135 F7
Speedwell Cl
Aldridge WS9 .... 30 A5
Birmingham B25 .... 88 A6
Wednesfield WV11 .... 26 E5
Speedwell Dr CV7 .... 130 A6
Speedwell Gdns
Brierley Hill DY5 .... 81 B6
Featherstone WV10 .... 12 B8
Speedwell Ho B38 .... 104 A1
Speedwell Rd
Birmingham,
Balsall Heath B5 .... 86 D6
Birmingham,
Tyseley B25 .... 88 A6
Speedwell Trad Est B11 ...... 88 A6
Speedy Cl WS11 .... 1 E5
Spencer Ave Coventry CV5 .. 113 A1
Dudley WV1 .... 51 C8
Spencer Cl Dudley DY3 .... 50 A4
5 West Bromwich B71 ...... 53 F8
Spencer Dr WS7 .... 7 A8
Spencer Rd Coventry CV5 ... 165 A1
Lichfield WS14 .... 9 B6
Spencer St
Birmingham B18 .... 66 C4
Hinckley LE10 .... 71 D1
Kidderminster DY11 .... 116 C4
Royal Leamington Spa
CV31 .... 161 F7
Spencer Yd CV31 .... 161 F7
Spencer's La CV7 .... 110 E1
Spennells Fst Sch DY10 ...... 117 A2
Spennells Valley Rd
DY10 .... 117 A3
Spenser Ave WV6 .... 23 F4
Spenser Cl B79 .... 21 A6
Spenser Wlk B61 .... 137 A8
Spernal La B49 .... 159 F1
Spernall Gr B29 .... 85 A1
Spetchley Cl B97 .... 158 C6
Spey Cl B5 .... 86 D6
Sphinx Dr CV3 .... 114 B1
Spiceland Rd B31 .... 102 F6
Spiers Cl B93 .... 128 A6
Spies Cl B62 .... 83 F6
Spies La B62 .... 83 F5
Spills Mdw DY3 .... 50 E5
Spilsbury Cl CV32 .... 156 E2
Spilsbury Croft B91 .... 127 A8
Spindle St CV1 .... 113 D6
Spindles The LE10 .... 75 F5
Spindlewood Cl WS12 .... 2 D1
Spinners End Ind Est B64 ... 82 D8
Spinney Cl
Binley Woods CV3 .... 135 E7
Birchmoor B78 .... 36 F8
Birmingham B31 .... 103 B3
Kidderminster DY11 .... 116 A7
Norton Canes WS11 .... 5 C6
Stourbridge DY8 .... 60 C3
Walsall WS3 .... 15 A2
Spinney Dr B90 .... 126 D4
Spinney Farm Rd WS11 .... 4 B7
Spinney Hill CV34 .... 156 A1
Spinney La CV10 .... 72 C4
Spinney Mews B97 .... 153 C1
Spinney Rd LE10 .... 75 C6

Spinney The
Birmingham,
Brown's Green B20 .... 54 E4
Birmingham,
Edgbaston B15 .... 85 E5
Coventry CV4 .... 132 D3
Dudley DY3 .... 50 C2
Little Aston B74 .... 31 B6
Royal Leamington Spa
CV32 .... 156 D1
Wolverhampton WV3 .... 24 D1
Wythall B47 .... 125 B4
Spinning School La B79 ...... 21 B5
Spiral Cl B62 .... 83 E8
Spiral Ct Birmingham B24 ... 56 E2
3 Dudley DY3 .... 50 D3
Stourbridge DY8 .... 81 A4
Sutton Coldfield B76 .... 46 F3
Wednesfield WV11 .... 26 E7
Spiral Gn B24 .... 57 C4
Spiral Mews B78 .... 35 A8
Spire View B61 .... 136 F3
Spirehouse La B60 .... 137 E5
Spires The Lichfield WS14 ..... 9 E6
Nuneaton CV10 .... 72 C4
Spitfire Rd B24 .... 57 D2
Splash La WS12 .... 2 C3
Spode Pl WS11 .... 2 B2
Spon End CV1, CV5 .... 113 A3
Spon Gate Ho CV1 .... 113 A3
Spon Gate Prim Sch CV1 ... 113 A3
Spon La B70 .... 53 D1
Spon La S Oldbury B66 .... 64 D8
West Bromwich B70 .... 53 D1
Spon Lane Ind Est B66 .... 64 D8
Spon Lane Trad Est B70 ..... 53 D2
Spon St CV1 .... 165 A3
Spondon Gr B34 .... 69 C5
Spondon Rd WV11 .... 26 E8
Spoon Dr B38 .... 103 D2
Spooner Croft B5 .... 86 E8
Spooners Cl B92 .... 107 F7
Spout La WS1 .... 42 E7
Spouthouse La B43 .... 54 F7
Spreadbury Cl B17 .... 84 F8
Sprig Croft B36 .... 68 C8
Spring Ave B65 .... 63 D2
Spring Cl 6 Coventry CV1 .. 113 E3
Hagley DY9 .... 98 F4
Solihull B91 .... 106 F3
Walsall WS4 .... 15 C2
Spring Coppice Dr B93 ...... 128 A3
Spring Cres B64 .... 82 F7
Spring Ct Walsall WS1 .... 43 A8
West Bromwich B70 .... 53 D2
Spring Gdns Birmingham B21 65 F7
5 Dudley DY2 .... 62 D8
Smethwick B66 .... 65 B3
Spring Gr B19 .... 66 B6
Spring Grove Cres DY11 ..... 116 B3
Spring Grove Gdns B18 ...... 65 F6
Spring Grove Rd DY11 .... 116 B3
Spring Head WS10 .... 41 F2
Spring Hill
Birmingham, Erdington B24 ... 56 F3
Birmingham, Hockley B18 .... 66 A4
Spring Hill Ind Est B18 ...... 66 A4
Spring Hill La WV4 .... 38 B4
Spring Hill Pas B18 .... 66 A3
Spring Hill Rd CV10 .... 72 C6
Spring La Birmingham B24 ... 57 A3
Lapworth B94 .... 143 D3
Radford Semele CV31 .... 162 E5
Romsley B62 .... 100 A4
Tanworth-in-A B94 .... 143 B5
Walsall WS4 .... 15 C2
Willenhall WV12 .... 27 C4
Spring Mdw
3 Blackheath B64 .... 62 F1
Cheslyn Hay WS6 .... 4 D1
Halesowen B63 .... 82 F2
Tipton DY4 .... 52 C6
Spring Meadow Rd DY2 .... 62 C2
Spring Parklands DY1 .... 62 A8
Spring Pool CV34 .... 160 E7
Spring Rd Barnacle CV7 ...... 97 B6
Birmingham,
Balsall Heath B15 .... 86 D7
Birmingham, Tyseley B11 .... 87 F3
Coventry CV6 .... 95 F1
Dudley DY2 .... 62 D6
Lichfield WS13 .... 3 D2
Smethwick B66 .... 64 D8
Walsall WS4 .... 15 D1
Wolverhampton WV4 .... 40 A4
Spring Road Ind Est WV4 .... 40 A4
Spring Road Sta B28 .... 88 A2
Spring St Birmingham B15 ... 86 D8
Cannock WS11 .... 4 E8
Halesowen B63 .... 82 D6
Stourbridge DY9 .... 81 E4
Tipton DY4 .... 52 C8
Spring Vale Cl WS10 .... 40 A1
Spring Vale Ind Pk WV14 .... 40 C5
Spring Vale Island WV14 .... 40 C4
Spring Vale Prim Sch
WV4 .... 39 E4
Spring Vale Rd B65 .... 63 A5
Spring Wlk Halesowen B63 ... 82 D1
Oldbury B69 .... 64 A5
Walsall WS2 .... 28 B3
Springavon Croft B17 .... 85 B6
Springbank B24 .... 68 A3
Springbank Rd B15 .... 86 D7
Springbrook Cl B36 .... 58 D1
Springbrook La B94 .... 142 A7
Springcroft Rd B11 .... 87 F2
Springdale Coll B29 .... 85 C1

Springdale Jun & Inf Schs
WV4 .... 38 D5
Springfield B23 .... 56 E3
Springfield Ave 6
Birmingham B12 .... 87 A6
Bromsgrove B60 .... 151 A8
Sedgley DY3 .... 39 E1
Stourbridge DY9 .... 81 E4
Springfield Cl B65 .... 63 A5
Springfield Cres
Bedworth CV12 .... 78 B2
Dudley DY2 .... 62 F8
Solihull B92 .... 89 C3
Sutton Coldfield B76 .... 47 A4
West Bromwich B70 .... 53 E1
Springfield Ct
Birmingham B28 .... 105 F8
Nuneaton CV11 .... 73 D3
Sutton Coldfield B75 .... 47 C5
Wolverhampton WV10 .... 11 D5
Springfield Dr B62 .... 83 D7
Springfield Gn DY3 .... 39 E1
Springfield Gr DY3 .... 39 D1
Springfield House Specl
Sch B93 .... 129 A5
Springfield Ind Est B69 ..... 64 B7
Springfield Jun & Inf Sch
B13 .... 87 D2
Springfield Jun & Inf
Schs B65 .... 63 A4
Springfield La
Blackheath B65 .... 62 F5
Kidderminster DY10 .... 116 F8
Wolverhampton WV10 .... 11 D4
Springfield Mill Ct WS10 .... 41 E6
Springfield Pk LE10 .... 71 A3
Springfield Pl CV1 .... 165 C4
Springfield Rd Bilston
WV14 .... 40 E7
Birmingham,
Castle Bromwich B36 .... 69 D8
Birmingham,
King's Heath B14 .... 104 F8
Birmingham, Moseley B13 ... 87 D2
Coventry CV1 .... 165 C4
Halesowen B62 .... 83 D7
Hinckley LE10 .... 75 D7
Nuneaton CV11 .... 73 E2
Sutton Coldfield B76 .... 47 A4
Tamworth B77 .... 35 D8
Wolverhampton WV10 .... 25 E3
Springfield Rise WS12 .... 2 C6
Springfield St B18 .... 66 A3
Springfield Terr B65 .... 62 F5
Springfields Coleshill B46 ... 70 F5
Walsall WS4 .... 29 C6
Springfields Rd
Brierley Hill DY5 .... 61 B2
Oldbury B68 .... 64 C4
Springhill CV10 .... 72 A8
Springhill Ave WV4 .... 38 C4
Springhill Cl Walsall WS4 ... 15 D1
Willenhall WV12 .... 27 D7
Springhill Gr 5 WS1 .... 42 F8
Springhill Gr WV4 .... 38 C4
Springhill Pk WV4 .... 38 B3
Springhill Prim Sch WS7 ..... 7 A6
Springhill Rd Brownhills
WS8 .... 16 A7
Burntwood WS7 .... 7 A6
Walsall WS1 .... 28 F1
Wednesfield WV11 .... 26 E7
Springmeadow Rd B19 .... 66 D6
Springs Ave B61 .... 121 A1
Springs The B64 .... 63 A1
Springside B98 .... 159 C8
Springslade Dr B24 .... 57 D3
Springthorpe Gn B24 .... 57 C4
Springthorpe Rd B24 .... 57 D4
Springvale Ave WS5 .... 43 C7
Springvale Prim Sch WS11 ... 4 E8
Springvale Rd B97 .... 152 F2
Springvale St WV13 .... 27 B3
Springvale Way WV14 .... 40 C4
Springwell Rd CV31 .... 162 D6
Sproat Ave WS10 .... 41 C5
Spruce B77 .... 22 B4
Spruce Gr Birmingham B24 .. 57 B2
Royal Leamington Spa
CV31 .... 161 F5
Spruce Ho 4 B36 .... 57 F1
Spruce Rd 5 Coventry CV2 .. 96 B2
Walsall WS5 .... 43 B3
Spruce Way WV3 .... 24 D1
Spur Tree Ave WV3 .... 24 A1
Squadron Cl B35 .... 58 C4
Square Cl B32 .... 84 C3
Square The Aldridge WS9 .... 30 B6
Alvechurch B48 .... 139 B6
Birmingham B17 .... 85 B7
3 Birmingham B17 .... 85 C5
2 Birmingham,
Ladywood B15 .... 66 B1
Fazeley B78 .... 35 A8
Kenilworth CV8 .... 147 F4
Nuneaton CV11 .... 73 E2
Solihull B91 .... 107 C3
Tipton DY4 .... 52 D7
Willenhall WV12 .... 27 D8
Wolverhampton WV2 .... 163 C1
Squires Croft Coventry CV2 .. 96 F1
Sutton Coldfield B76 .... 47 A2
Squires Ct DY5 .... 81 C8
Squires Gate Wlk B35 .... 58 A3
Squires Gn LE10 .... 75 F6
Squires Way CV4 .... 132 D6
Squirhill Pl 1 CV31 .... 162 B7

Squirrel Cl WS12 .... 2 D2
Squirrel Hollow B76 .... 47 A2
Squirrel Wlk Little Aston
B74 .... 31 C5
Wolverhampton WV4 .... 39 A5
Squirrels Hollow B68 .... 84 D7
Sring La CV8 .... 148 A5
Stable Croft B71 .... 53 F7
Stable Ct DY3 .... 50 E6
Stable Way B60 .... 150 E6
Stable Wlk CV11 .... 73 F2
Stableford Cl
Birmingham B32 .... 84 F3
Redditch B97 .... 158 D7
Stables The Berkswell
CV7 .... 110 C4
Birmingham B29 .... 86 B2
Stacey Cl B64 .... 62 E1
Stacey Dr B13 .... 105 A5
Stacey Grange Gdns B45 ... 122 A6
Stackhouse Cl WS9 .... 16 A4
Stackhouse Dr 3 WS3 .... 15 A4
Stadium Cl Coventry CV6 .... 95 D2
Kidderminster DY10 .... 116 F4
Willenhall WV13 .... 27 B3
Stafford Cl Bulkington CV12 . 79 C2
Walsall WS3 .... 14 B2
Stafford Ct Birmingham B43 . 54 E7
Wolverhampton WV10 .... 11 C5
Stafford Dr B71 .... 53 B6
Stafford Ho B33 .... 69 E2
Stafford La WS12 .... 2 B5
Stafford Rd Birmingham
B21 .... 65 F8
Coven Heath WV10 .... 11 D4
Darlaston WV10 .... 40 C6
Huntington WS11, WS12 .... 1 C5
Walsall WS3 .... 14 B3
Wolverhampton WV10 .... 11 D4
Stafford St Bilston WV14 .... 40 D5
Birmingham B5 .... 164 D3
Cannock WS12 .... 2 E1
Dudley DY1 .... 51 B1
Walsall WS2 .... 28 E3
Wednesbury WS10 .... 41 F2
Willenhall WV13 .... 27 A2
Wolverhampton WV1 .... 163 C4
Stafford Way B43 .... 54 E7
Staffordshire Pool Cl
2 B6 .... 55 F1
Stag Cres Norton Canes
WS11 .... 6 A6
Walsall WS3 .... 28 E6
Stag Hall WS3 .... 28 E7
Stag Ind Est WV14 .... 40 F4
Stag Wlk B76 .... 57 D7
Stagborough Way WS12 .... 2 B4
Staines Cl CV11 .... 73 F7
Stainforth Cl CV11 .... 74 A2
Stainsby Ave B19 .... 66 C5
Stainsby Croft B90 .... 127 B5
Staircase La CV5 .... 112 C7
Stakenbridge La DY10 .... 98 D3
Staley Croft WS12 .... 1 C4
Stalling's La DY6 .... 60 D8
Stallings La DY6 .... 49 F1
Stambermill Cl DY9 .... 81 D5
Stambermill Ho DY9 .... 81 E5
Stamford Ave CV3 .... 133 C6
Stamford Cres WS7 .... 7 A8
Stamford Croft B91 .... 107 B2
Stamford Gdns CV32 .... 156 E1
Stamford Gr B20 .... 55 C1
Stamford Rd Birmingham
B20 .... 55 C1
Brierley Hill DY5 .... 81 C6
Stamford St DY8 .... 80 F7
Stamford Way WS9 .... 16 C1
Stanbrook Rd B90 .... 127 A6
Stanbury Ave WS10 .... 41 B6
Stanbury Rd B14 .... 105 B4
Stancroft Gr B26 .... 89 A8
Stand St CV34 .... 160 D6
Standard Ave CV4 .... 112 B1
Standard Way B24 .... 67 F8
Standbridge Way DY4 .... 52 A5
Standedge B77 .... 36 B7
Standhills Rd DY6 .... 60 E6
Standish Cl CV2 .... 114 E2
Standlake Ave B36 .... 68 D7
Standlake Ho B31 .... 102 E5
Standlake Mews
17 CV31 .... 162 C6
Standleys Tower B23 .... 57 A6
Stanfield Rd
Birmingham, Pheasey B43 .... 44 D5
Birmingham, Quinton B32 .... 84 A6
Stanford Ave B42 .... 55 A7
Stanford Cl B97 .... 158 B6
Stanford Gr B63 .... 82 C1
Stanford Rd Blackheath
B65 .... 63 B4
Wolverhampton WV2 .... 39 C7
Stanford Way 2 B69 .... 63 E4
Stanhoe Cl DY5 .... 81 D8
Stanhope Ho B79 .... 21 A4
Stanhope Rd B67 .... 64 F3
Stanhope St Birmingham
B12 .... 86 F7
Dudley DY2 .... 62 E4
Wolverhampton WV3 .... 163 A2
Stanhope Way B43 .... 44 E4
Stanhurst Way B71 .... 43 A2
Stanier Ave CV1 .... 113 A4
Stanier Cl WS4 .... 29 B7
Stanier Gr B20 .... 55 B2
Staniforth St B4 .... 164 C4
Stanklyn La DY10 .... 117 C1

Stanley Ave Birmingham B32 . 84 E7
Solihull B90 .... 106 B6
Sutton Coldfield B75 .... 46 F4
Stanley Cl Birmingham B28 . 106 A5
Redditch B98 .... 154 A5
Wednesfield WV11 .... 26 F8
Stanley Ct
9 Birmingham B13 .... 87 B2
Perton WV6 .... 23 E4
Royal Leamington Spa
CV31 .... 162 C7
Stanley Gr 2 B11 .... 87 B6
Stanley Pl Bilston WV14 ..... 40 B5
Birmingham B13 .... 86 F3
Walsall WS4 .... 29 B6
Stanley Rd
Birmingham,
King's Heath B14 .... 104 D7
Birmingham, Nechells B7 .... 67 C7
Cannock WS12 .... 2 B6
Coventry CV5 .... 132 F8
Darlaston WS10 .... 41 D5
Hinckley LE10 .... 71 C2
Nuneaton CV11 .... 73 A5
Oldbury B68 .... 84 C7
Stourbridge DY8 .... 80 F3
Walsall WS4 .... 29 B6
West Bromwich B71 .... 53 E7
Wolverhampton WV10 .... 11 D1
Stanley St WS3 .... 14 D1
Stanmore Gr B62 .... 84 A3
Stanmore Rd B16 .... 65 C1
Stansbury Ho 3 WS2 .... 42 C8
Stansfield Gr CV8 .... 148 B6
Stanton Ave DY1 .... 51 A6
Stanton Bridge Prim Sch
CV6 .... 113 F6
Stanton Gr Birmingham B26 .. 88 F8
Solihull B90 .... 106 A4
Stanton Ho 2 B71 .... 42 F1
Stanton Rd Birmingham B43 . 54 E8
14 Royal Leamington Spa
CV31 .... 162 C6
Solihull B90 .... 106 A4
Wolverhampton WV1 .... 25 F2
Stanton Wlk CV34 .... 155 D1
Stanville Jun & Inf Sch
B26 .... 89 C6
Stanville Rd B26 .... 89 C6
Stanway Gdns B71 .... 53 D6
Stanway Gr B44 .... 44 F3
Stanway Rd Coventry CV5 .. 133 A8
Solihull B90 .... 106 A4
West Bromwich B71 .... 53 D6
Stanwell Gr B23 .... 56 E6
Stapenhall Rd B90 .... 127 A5
Staple Flat B60 .... 137 C6
Staple Hall Rd B31 .... 103 B2
Staple Lodge Rd B31 .... 103 C2
Stapleford Croft B14 .... 104 C2
Stapleford Gdns WS7 .... 7 C5
Stapleford Gr DY8 .... 60 E2
Staplehurst Rd B28 .... 105 F8
Staples Cl CV12 .... 79 C3
Stapleton Cl Redditch B98 .. 154 D3
Studley B80 .... 159 D3
Sutton Coldfield B76 .... 58 B6
Stapleton Dr B37 .... 70 A4
Stapleton La Barwell LE9 .... 71 F8
Hinckley CV13 .... 71 A8
Stapleton Rd Aldridge WS9 .. 29 C5
Studley B80 .... 159 D4
Stapylton Ave B17 .... 85 B5
Stapylton Ct B17 .... 85 B5
Star Cl Tipton DY4 .... 52 C5
Star Hill B15 .... 86 B8
Star Ind Pk CV2 .... 114 F5
Star St Stourbridge DY9 ..... 81 F5
Wolverhampton WV3 .... 38 E3
Starbank Jun & Inf Sch
B10 .... 88 A8
Starbank Jun & Inf Sch
(Annex) B10 .... 68 B1
Starbank Rd B10 .... 88 A8
Starbold Cres B93 .... 128 B5
Starbold Ct B93 .... 128 A6
Starcross Cl CV2 .... 114 C7
Starcross Rd B27 .... 88 C2
Stare Gn CV4 .... 132 D5
Stareton Cl CV4 .... 132 F6
Starkey Croft B37 .... 70 D2
Starkie Dr B68 .... 64 C4
Starley Ct CV3 .... 135 A7
Starley Pk CV7 .... 96 B8
Starley Rd CV1 .... 165 A2
Starley Way B37 .... 90 C6
Startin Cl CV7 .... 95 F7
Startpoint Trad Est B11 ..... 87 D4
Statham Dr B16 .... 65 C2
Station App
Barnt Green B45 .... 138 D8
Dorridge B93 .... 127 F2
Kidderminster DY10 .... 116 F5
Royal Leamington Spa
CV31 .... 161 F7
Solihull B91 .... 107 A4
Sutton Coldfield,
Hill Hook B74 .... 31 F6
Sutton Coldfield,
Maney B73 .... 46 B6
Station Ave Birmingham
B16 .... 65 C1
Coventry CV4 .... 131 D8
Warwick CV34 .... 160 F7
Station Bldgs B46 .... 59 B3
Station Cl WS3 .... 28 B8

Station Cotts B60 138 A4
Station Dr Blakedown DY10 98 C2
Brierley Hill, Quarry Bank DY5 61 E2
Brierley Hill, Silver End DY5 61 B1
Earlswood B94 125 D1
Hagley DY9 99 A6
Sutton Coldfield B74 46 B8
Tipton DY4 52 B4
Station La B94 144 D3
Station Pl WS3 28 B8
Station Rd Aldridge WS9 30 A5
Alvechurch B48 139 A5
Balsall Common CV7 130 B7
Bilston WV14 40 E5
Birmingham, Acock's Green B27 88 C3
Birmingham, Aston B6 55 F1
Birmingham, Erdington B23 56 F5
Birmingham, Handsworth B21 65 C8
Birmingham, Harborne B17 85 C6
Birmingham, King's Heath B14 86 E1
Birmingham, King's Norton B30 103 E4
Birmingham, Marston Green B37 90 A8
Birmingham, Northfield B31 103 A2
Birmingham, Stechford B33 68 E3
Blackheath, Haden Cross B64 83 A8
Blackheath, Rowley Regis B65 63 D2
Blackwell B60 138 A5
Brierley Hill DY5 61 C3
Burntwood WS7 7 E3
Cannock WS12 2 C6
Coleshill B46 59 F1
Great Wyrley WS6 4 F4
Hagley DY9 99 A6
Hampton in A B92 109 B7
Hinckley LE10 75 D8
Kenilworth CV8 147 F4
Knowle B93 128 B4
Lapworth B94 144 D4
Lichfield WS13 9 C7
Oldbury B69 64 A5
Shenstone WS14 17 F6
Solihull B91 107 B4
Stourbridge DY9 81 E6
Studley B80 159 D4
Sutton Coldfield B73 46 A1
Walsall, Pelsall WS3 15 A3
Walsall, Rushall WS4 29 A7
Warwick CV34 160 F7
Wolverhampton WV10 25 F4
Wombourne WV5 49 A8
Wythall B47 125 B3
Station Road Ind Est B65 63 D2
Station Sq CV1 165 B1
Station St Birmingham B5 164 B2
Blackheath B64 82 C8
Bromsgrove B60 136 F1
Cheslyn Hay WS6 4 E3
Darlaston WS10 41 E7
Sutton Coldfield B73 46 C5
Tipton DY4 52 B5
Walsall WS2 28 E1
Walsall, Blakenhall Heath WS3 28 B8
Station St E CV6 113 E7
Station St W CV6 113 E7
Station Way Birmingham B26 90 D4
Redditch B97 153 D3
Staulton Gn 5 B69 63 E4
Staunton Rd Royal Leamington Spa CV31 162 A5
Walsall WS3 14 A3
Staveley Rd Birmingham B14 104 D6
Wolverhampton WV1 25 C4
Staverton Cl CV5 112 A3
Stead Cl Tipton DY4 41 B1
Walsall WS2 28 C5
Steadman Croft DY4 52 D8
Stechford Jun & Inf Sch B33 68 D2
Stechford La B8 68 D5
Stechford Rd B34 68 E5
Stechford Sta B33 68 D3
Stechford Trad Est B33 68 E3
Steel Bright Rd B66 65 C6
Steel Dr WV10 25 D8
Steel Gr B25 88 C7
Steel Rd B31 102 F2
Steel Rdbt WS10 41 E2
Steelhouse La Birmingham B4 164 C3
Wolverhampton WV2 163 D2
Steene Gr B31 102 D3
Steeplefield Rd CV6 113 A5
Steeples The DY8 81 B3
Steepwood Croft B30 103 D4
Steere Ave B79 21 C7
Stella Croft B37 70 C2
Stella Gr B43 54 C8
Stella Rd DY4 51 F6
Stenbury Cl WV10 11 F4
Stencills Dr WS4 29 B3
Stencills Rd WS4 29 B4
Stennels Ave B62 83 E4
Stennels Cl CV6 112 F8
Stennels Cres B62 83 E4
Stephens Cl WV11 26 F8
Stephens Ind Est B11 87 F4
Stephens Rd B76 47 A4
Stephens Wlk WS13 3 A2
Stephenson Ave WS2 28 B5
Stephenson Cl Royal Leamington Spa CV32 156 C1
Tamworth B77 22 A2
Stephenson Dr Birmingham B37 70 B2
Perton WV6 23 E5
Stephenson Pl B2 164 C2
Stephenson Rd Bedworth CV7 96 C7
Hinckley LE10 74 E7
Stephenson Sq WS2 28 B5
Stephenson St Birmingham B2 164 B2
Wolverhampton WV3 163 A2
Stepney Rd CV2 114 A4
Stepping Stone Cl WS2 27 F4
Stepping Stones DY8 81 B5
Stepping Stones Rd CV5 112 F4
Steppingstone St DY1 51 B1
Sterling Pk DY5 61 F4
Sterling Way CV11 78 E8
Sterndale Rd B42 55 C6
Steven Dr WV14 40 E1
Stevenage Wlk 2 CV2 115 A7
Stevens Ave B32 84 D2
Stevens Dr WS12 2 D6
Stevens Gate WV2 163 B1
Stevens Ho CV1 165 C4
Stevens Rd Halesowen B63 82 B5
Stourbridge DY9 81 D2
Stevenson Ave B98 153 F3
Stevenson Rd Coventry CV6 113 A8
Tamworth B79 21 A6
Stevenson Wlk WS14 9 B6
Steward St B18 66 A3
Stewart Cl CV4 112 D2
Stewart Ct DY10 116 F5
Stewart Rd Brownhills WS9 16 A3
Kingswinford DY6 60 D4
Stewart St Nuneaton CV11 73 C3
Wolverhampton WV2 163 B1
Stewarts Rd B62 83 D7
Stewkins DY8 80 E8
Steyning Rd B26 88 E5
Stickley La DY3 50 C4
Stidfall Gr CV31 162 D6
Stilehouse Cres B65 63 C2
Stilthouse Gr B45 122 A7
Stirchley Inf & Jun Sch B30 104 A6
Stirchley Trad Est B30 104 B6
Stirling Ave Hinckley LE10 71 A1
Royal Leamington Spa CV32 157 B6
Stirling Cl CV3 134 F8
Stirling Cres WV12 27 B6
Stirling Ct B16 65 F1
Stirling Ho B75 46 C5
Stirling Pl WS11 4 B8
Stirling Rd Bilston WV14 40 F2
Birmingham B16 65 F1
Dudley DY2 62 E6
Solihull B90 126 B8
Sutton Coldfield B73 45 E2
Stirrup Cl WS5 42 F4
Stivichall Croft CV3 133 B6
Stivichall Prim Sch CV3 133 A6
Stockbridge Cl WV6 23 F2
Stockdale Par DY4 51 F5
Stockdale Pl B15 85 D8
Stockfield Rd B25, B27 88 B5
Stockhay La WS7 7 D5
Stockhill Dr B45 121 F6
Stocking St DY9 81 F5
Stockingford Fst & Mid Sch CV10 72 D3
Stockland Ct B74 44 F8
Stockland Green Sch B23 56 C4
Stockland Rd B23 56 D4
Stockmans Cl B38 123 E8
Stockton Cl Birmingham B76 58 C5
Knowle B93 128 B4
Walsall WS2 28 D4
Stockton Ct WV14 51 B8
Stockton Gr Birmingham B33 69 D1
2 Royal Leamington Spa CV32 157 A2
Stockton Rd CV1 165 D4
Stockwell Ave DY5 81 D8
Stockwell End WV6 24 D6
Stockwell Head LE10 71 D1
Stockwell Rd Birmingham B21 54 E2
Wolverhampton WV6 24 D5
Stockwell Rise B92 107 D7
Stoke Cross B60 151 E7
Stoke Gn CV3 114 A2
Stoke Heath Prim Sch CV2 114 A6
Stoke La B98 154 B7
Stoke Park Mews CV2 114 A3
Stoke Park Sch & Com Coll CV2 114 B4
Stoke Pound La Stoke Pound B60 151 A4
Stoke Prior B60 150 F3
Stoke Prim Sch CV2 114 A4
Stoke Prior Fst Sch B60 150 C3
Stoke Rd Bromsgrove, Aston Fields B60 151 A7
Bromsgrove, Charford B60 150 F7
Hinckley LE10 71 B4
Stoke Row CV2 114 A4
Stoke Way B15 66 C1
Stoke's La WS11 5 F7
Stokes Ave 7 Tipton DY4 52 A8
Willenhall WV13 40 F8
Stokes St WS3 28 B8
Stokesay Ave WV6 23 F3
Stokesay Cl Kidderminster DY10 116 E2
Nuneaton CV11 73 B3
Tipton B69 63 A8
Stokesay Gr B31 122 F8
Stokesay Ho 1 B23 56 F6
Stom Rd WV14 40 B5
Stone Ave B75 47 A5
Stone CE Fst Sch DY10 117 E2
Stone Cl B38 103 F2
Stone Cotts B31 103 A3
Stone Cross B46 59 B3
Stone Hill DY10 117 E2
Stone Pine Cl WS12 1 F8
Stone Rd B15 86 D7
Stone St Dudley DY1 51 C1
Oldbury B69 64 A7
Stone Yd Birmingham B12 66 F1
Blackheath B64 82 C8
Stoneacre Cl WV3 24 A1
Stonebow Ave B91 127 B8
Stonebridge Cres B37 69 F4
Stonebridge Highway CV3 133 E4
Stonebridge Rd Coleshill B46 70 F5
Little Packington B46 91 A7
Stonebridge Trad Est CV3 134 B4
Stonebrook Way Birmingham B29 84 F2
Coventry CV6 95 F3
Stonebury B15 85 D8
Stonebury Ave CV5 111 E4
Stonechat Cl DY10 117 B2
Stonechat Dr B23 56 C2
Stonecroft Ave B45 122 A7
Stonecrop Cl Birmingham B38 123 F8
Clayhanger WS8 15 D6
Stonedown Cl WV14 40 A3
Stonefield Cl CV2 115 A8
Stonefield Dr DY5 61 A7
Stonefield Prim Sch WV14 40 D4
Stonefield Rd WV14 40 D5
Stoneford Rd B90 106 A4
Stonehaven B77 21 F5
Stonehaven Dr CV3 133 C3
Stonehaven Gr B28 106 B8
Stonehenge Croft B14 104 D1
Stonehill Croft B90 126 F6
Stonehill Wlk B77 35 F6
Stonehouse Ave WV13 26 F4
Stonehouse Cl Redditch B97 153 D1
Royal Leamington Spa CV32 157 D5
Stonehouse Cres WS10 42 B2
Stonehouse Dr B74 31 C4
Stonehouse Gr B32 84 D2
Stonehouse Hill B29 85 A3
Stonehouse La Birmingham B32 84 E2
Coventry CV3 134 C4
Hopwood B48 123 E2
Stonehouse Rd Bromsgrove B60 137 A1
Sutton Coldfield B73 45 F3
Stonehurst Rd B43 44 C3
Stonelea WS9 30 B5
Stonelea Cl B71 53 E8
Stoneleigh Ave CV8 148 A6
Stoneleigh Cl Redditch B98 158 F6
Stoneleigh CV8 149 C6
Sutton Coldfield B74 45 F8
Stoneleigh Ct CV11 73 C3
Stoneleigh Gdns CV11 73 C3
Stoneleigh Ho B32 84 F5
Stoneleigh Rd Birmingham B20 55 E2
Blackdown CV32 157 A7
Coventry CV4 132 E2
Kenilworth CV8 148 A6
Solihull B91 106 E6
Stoneleigh CV8 149 B3
Stoneleigh Way DY3 50 D6
Stonepit B77 21 C1
Stonepits La B97 158 D4
Stonerwood Ave B28 105 E8
Stones Gn B23 56 F6
Stoneton Cres CV7 130 A6
Stoneton Gr B29 103 A8
Stoneway Gr CV31 162 D6
Stonewell Cres CV11 79 B8
Stoney Cl B92 107 E7
Stoney Croft WS11 1 F1
Stoney Ct CV3 135 A7
Stoney La Birmingham, Balsall Heath B12 87 B5
Birmingham, Quinton B32 84 B6
Birmingham, Stechford B25 68 E1
Blackwell B60 138 C2
Stoney La continued
Churchill DY10 98 E3
Dudley DY2 62 C3
Kidderminster DY10 116 E8
Walsall WS3 14 C3
Walsall WS3 14 D3
West Bromwich B71 53 D4
Stoney Lane Ind Est DY10 116 E8
Stoney Lea Rd WS11 1 F1
Stoney Rd Coventry CV1 165 B1
Nuneaton CV10, CV11 73 B6
Stoney Stanton Rd CV1, CV6 113 E5
Stoneycroft Tower 4 B36 68 E8
Stoneydelph Inf Sch B77 22 A1
Stoneydelph Jun Sch B77 22 A1
Stoneyfields Cl WS11 1 F2
Stoneyford Gr B14 105 B4
Stoneygate Dr LE10 71 F3
Stoneyhurst Rd B24 56 F1
Stoneymoor Dr B36 58 D1
Stoneythorpe Cl 2 B91 107 B1
Stoneywood Rd CV2 114 F8
Stonleigh Ave CV5 132 F7
Stonnal Gr B23 57 A6
Stonnall Gate WS9 30 C8
Stonnall Rd WS9 30 C8
Stonor Park Rd B91 106 F5
Stonor Rd B28 106 A5
Stony La B67 64 F5
Stony St B67 64 F6
Stonydelph La B77 36 A7
Stornoway Rd B35 58 B4
Storrage La B48 139 E3
Storrs Cl B9 67 D1
Storrs Pl B10 67 D1
Storrs Way The B32 102 B7
Stot Fold Rd B14 104 F2
Stour B77 36 A5
Stour Cl Burntwood WS7 7 D6
Halesowen B63 82 E6
Stour Hill DY5 82 A8
Stour Ho 2 B68 84 B8
Stour St Birmingham B18 66 A3
West Bromwich B70 52 E3
Stour Vale Rd DY9 81 F6
Stour Vale Road Ind Est DY9 81 F6
Stour Valley Cl DY5 81 D7
Stourbridge Coll Stourbridge, Old Swinford DY8 81 A4
Stourbridge, Wollaston DY8 80 E5
Stourbridge Coll Annexe DY8 81 A4
Stourbridge Coll (Church Street Ctr) DY8 81 A5
Stourbridge Coll (Westhill Ctr) DY8 81 B4
Stourbridge Juntion Sta DY8 81 B3
Stourbridge Rd Belbroughton DY9 120 B7
Brierley Hill DY5, DY2 61 E6
Bromsgrove B61 136 F7
Catshill B61 120 D2
Churchill DY10 98 A5
Dudley DY1 62 A8
Hagley DY9 99 C7
Halesowen B63 82 F5
Harvington DY9, DY10 118 C4
Kidderminster DY10 116 F8
Lower Clent DY9 99 E3
Stourbridge DY9 81 D5
Wombourne DY3, DY6, WV5 49 B5
Stourbridge Town Sta DY8 81 A5
Stourbridge Trad Est DY8 81 A6
Stourdale Rd B64 82 C8
Stourdell Rd B63 82 E6
Stourminster Sch DY10 117 B4
Stourmore Cl WV12 27 D6
Stourport Rd DY11 116 C2
Stourton Cl Knowle B93 128 B7
Sutton Coldfield B76 46 F4
Stourton Dr WV4 38 C5
Stourton Rd B32 84 B5
Stourvale Trad Est B63 82 D6
Stow Dr DY5 81 B6
Stow Gr B36 68 E7
Stow Heath Jun & Inf Sch WV13 26 D1
Stow Heath La Bilston WV1 40 B8
Wolverhampton WV1 26 C1
Stow Heath Pl WV1 40 B7
Stowe Hill Gdns WS13 3 C1
Stowe Pl CV4 111 C1
Stowe Rd WS13 9 B8
Stowe St Lichfield WS13 9 C8
Walsall WS3 28 C7
Stowecroft WS13 3 C2
Stowell Rd B44 55 F8
Stowheath Ind Est & New Ent Ctr WV1 40 A8
Stowlawn Prim Sch WV14 40 C8
Stowmans Cl WV14 40 B3
Strachey Ave CV32 156 E2
Straight Rd WV12 27 D6
Straits Gn DY3 50 B4
Straits Prim Sch DY3 50 B5
Straits Rd DY3 50 B3
Straits The DY3 50 A4
Strand The B61 137 A3
Stratford Cl DY1 50 E2
Stratford Ct B72 46 B3
Stratford Dr WS9 30 C8
Stratford Pl B12 87 A8
Stratford Rd Birmingham B11 87 B6
Birmingham, Sparkhill B11 87 D3
Bromsgrove B60 137 A2
Dorridge B94 127 B3
Solihull B90 126 D7
Tanworth-in-A B94 143 C5
Warwick CV34 160 C3
Stratford St Birmingham B11 87 C5
Coventry CV2 114 A4
Nuneaton CV11 73 C4
Stratford St N B11 87 A8
Stratford Way WS11 1 F5
Stratford Wlk B36 68 C8
Strathdene Gdns B29 85 C1
Strathdene Rd B29 85 C1
Strathearn Rd CV32 156 E1
Strathern Dr WV14 40 A1
Strathfield Wlk WV4 38 C6
Strathmore Ave CV1 113 E1
Strathmore Cres WV5 38 A1
Strathmore Pl WS11 1 F2
Strathmore Rd Hinckley LE10 75 A7
Tipton DY4 52 A8
Stratton St WV10 25 E4
Strawberry Cl B69 63 C7
Strawberry Fields CV7 92 B1
Strawberry La Great Wyrley WS6 13 E8
Willenhall WV13 26 D3
Strawberry Lane Ind Est WV13 26 C2
Strawberry Wlk CV2 96 D2
Stray The DY5 61 C6
Stream Mdw WS4 15 D1
Stream Pk DY6 60 E4
Stream Rd DY6 60 D4
Streamside Cl CV5 112 A8
Streamside Way Solihull B92 89 D4
Walsall WS4 29 D8
Streatham Gr B44 45 A2
Streather Rd B75 32 C2
Streetly Cres B74 31 D3
Streetly Dr B74 31 D3
Streetly La B74 31 D2
Streetly Rd B23 56 D5
Streetly Sch The B74 45 A6
Streetly Wood B74 31 A2
Streets Corner Gdns WS9 16 A4
Streets La WS6 4 E1
Streetsbrook Inf Sch B90 106 C4
Streetsbrook Rd B91 106 D5
Streetway Rd WS14 18 B7
Strensham Ct B13 86 E4
Strensham Hill B13 86 E4
Strensham Ho 4 B7 67 A4
Strensham Rd B12 86 E5
Stretton Ave CV3 134 C6
Stretton Cl LE10 75 D6
Stretton Cres CV31 162 B5
Stretton Ct Birmingham B24 56 E2
Hinckley LE10 75 D3
Stretton Dr B45 122 A2
Stretton Gr 2 Birmingham, Lozells B19 66 C7
Birmingham, Sparkbrook B11 87 C6
Birmingham, Stechford B8 68 C6
Stretton Ho B97 153 A4
Stretton Pl Dudley DY2 62 D5
Wolverhampton WV14 40 A1
Stretton Rd Kidderminster DY11 116 B4
Nuneaton CV10 73 A3
Solihull B90 126 B8
Willenhall WV12 13 D1
Stretton St B77 21 E3
Stringer Cl B75 32 A4
Stringers Hill WS12 2 D7
Stringes Cl WV13 27 C3
Stringes La WV13 27 B3
Strode Ho B79 21 A4
Strode Rd WV2 39 C6
Stroma Way CV10 72 F2
Stronsay Cl B45 101 F1
Stroud Ave WV12 27 D5
Stroud Cl WV12 27 C4
Stroud Rd B90 105 F2
Strutt Cl B15 85 D8
Strutt Rd LE10 76 A5
Stuart Bathurst RC High Sch WS10 42 B5
Stuart Cl CV34 160 D5
Stuart Cres DY2 51 E1
Stuart Ct Coventry CV6 114 A8
7 Royal Leamington Spa CV32 156 E1
Stuart Rd Blackheath B65 63 C4
Halesowen B62 83 F5
Stuart St Birmingham B7 67 C7
Walsall WS3 28 B8
Stuart's Dr B33 68 D1
Stuarts Gn DY9 99 B8
Stuarts Rd B33 68 D2
Stuarts Way B32 102 B7
Stubbers Green Rd WS9 29 E8
Stubbington Cl WV13 26 D1
Stubbs Cl CV12 78 A4
Stubbs Gr CV2 114 B5
Stubbs Rd WV3 39 A6
Stubby La WV11 27 A6

Stubley Dr WV10 .... 25 E6
Stud Farm Cotts B78 .... 20 E2
Stud La B33 .... 68 F4
Studland Gn CV2 .... 115 A4
Studland Rd B28 .... 106 A8
Studley Croft B92 .... 89 D3
Studley Cty Inf Sch B80 .. 159 E4
Studley Dr DY5 .... 81 C8
Studley Gate DY8 .... 80 D5
Studley High Sch B80 .... 159 E3
Studley Rd Redditch B98 .. 154 A2
 Wolverhampton WV3 .... 38 C8
Studley St B12 .... 87 B5
Studley Tower B11 .... 86 F7
Sturgeon's Hill WS14 .... 9 C7
Sturley Cl CV8 .... 148 B6
Sturman Dr B65 .... 63 C1
Sturminster Cl CV2 .... 115 A4
Stychbrook Gdns WS13 .... 3 B2
Styles Cl CV31 .... 162 A7
Styvechale Ave CV5 .... 133 A8
Suckling Green La WV8 ..... 10 A2
Sudbury Cl
 Royal Leamington Spa
 CV32 .... 157 C3
 Wednesfield WV11 .... 26 E1
Sudbury Gr B44 .... 45 B2
Sudeley B77 .... 35 C7
Sudeley Cl B36 .... 58 B1
Sudeley Rd CV10 .... 78 C8
Suffield Gr B23 .... 56 B5
Suffolk CV Bedworth CV12 .. 78 A3
 Coventry CV5 .... 112 B3
 Nuneaton CV10 .... 72 E3
 Oldbury B68 .... 64 B4
 Wolverhampton WV11 .... 26 C6
Suffolk Dr DY5 .... 81 C7
Suffolk Gr WS9 .... 30 B8
Suffolk Pl Birmingham B5 .. 164 B1
 Walsall WS2 .... 28 D5
Suffolk Rd Dudley DY2 .... 62 A7
 Wednesbury WS10 .... 42 C3
Suffolk St CV32 .... 157 A1
Suffolk Street
 Queensway B1 .... 164 B2
Suffolk Way B78 .... 21 A1
Suffrage St B66 .... 65 B4
Sugar Loaf La Iverley DY10 .. 98 B7
 Stourbridge DY7 .... 80 C1
Sugarbrook La B60 .... 151 A5
Sugarbrook Rd B60 .... 151 A7
Sugden Gr B5 .... 86 E8
Sulgrave Cl Coventry CV2 .. 114 E7
 Dudley DY1 .... 51 A3
Sullivan Ct CV6 .... 114 B7
Sullivan Rd CV6 .... 114 B7
Sullivan Way WS13 .... 3 C2
Sullivan Wlk WS13 .... 3 C2
Sumburgh Croft B35 .... 58 A3
Summer Croft B19 .... 66 D6
Summer Dr DY3 .... 50 C3
Summer Gr WS13 .... 3 D2
Summer Hill 6
 Halesowen B63 .... 83 B3
 Kingswinford DY6 .... 60 C6
Summer Hill Ind Pk 2 B1 .. 66 B3
Summer Hill Rd B1 .... 66 B3
Summer Hill St B1 .... 66 B3
Summer Hill Terr B1 .... 66 B3
Summer La Birmingham
 B19 .... 66 D5
 Dudley DY3 .... 50 D3
 Minworth B76 .... 58 D6
 Walsall WS5 .... 15 C2
Summer Pl DY11 .... 116 C5
Summer Rd
 Birmingham,
 Acock's Green B27 .... 88 A2
 Birmingham, Edgbaston B15 .. 86 C7
 Birmingham, Erdington B23 .. 56 F4
 Blackheath B65 .... 63 D3
 Dudley DY1 .... 51 A4
 Kidderminster DY11 .... 116 C3
Summer Row
 Birmingham B3 .... 164 A3
 Wolverhampton WV2 .... 163 B2
Summer St Kingswinford
 DY6 .... 60 D6
 Redditch B98 .... 153 E4
 Stourbridge DY9 .... 81 E5
 1 Stourbridge,
 Wollaston DY8 .... 80 F5
 West Bromwich B71 .... 53 D4
 Willenhall WV13 .... 26 F2
Summercourt Dr DY6 .... 60 C6
Summercourt Sq DY6 .... 60 C5
Summerfield Ave
 Kingswinford DY6 .... 60 C7
 West Bromwich B70 .... 53 C4
Summerfield Cres B16 .... 65 C1
Summerfield Ct B15 .... 65 C1
Summerfield Dr B29 .... 103 A7
Summerfield Gr 5 B18 .... 65 E4
Summerfield Hospl B18 ..... 65 F4
Summerfield New Prim
 Sch B18 .... 65 E4
Summerfield Rd
 Birmingham B16 .... 65 E3
 Burntwood WS7 .... 7 A5
 Clent DY9 .... 99 E2
 Dudley DY2 .... 62 D7
 Solihull B92 .... 89 A1
 Tamworth B77 .... 21 D4
 Wolverhampton WV1 .... 25 B2
Summerfields Ave B62 .... 83 F7

Summergate DY3 .... 50 C4
Summerhill Ave DY11 .... 116 A5
Summerhill Rd Dudley
 WV14 .... 40 D1
 Tipton DY4 .... 51 F7
Summerhill Sch DY6 .... 60 B6
Summerhouse Cl B97 .... 158 A6
Summerhouse Rd WV14 .... 40 A1
Summerlee Rd B24 .... 57 B2
Summerton Rd Oldbury
 B69 .... 52 D1
 Whitnash CV31 .... 162 A3
Summervale Cl DY9 .... 99 A5
Summervale Rd DY9 .... 99 A5
Summerville Terr 4 B17 ... 85 C5
Summit Cres B66 .... 64 E8
Summit Gdns B63 .... 82 F3
Summit Pl DY3 .... 50 B2
Summit The DY9 .... 81 D4
Sumner Rd B46 .... 70 F6
Sun St Brierley Hill DY5 ..... 61 F1
 Walsall WS1 .... 42 E7
 Wolverhampton WV10 ...... 163 D3
Sunbeam B77 .... 21 E3
Sunbeam Cl B36 .... 58 F1
Sunbeam Dr WS6 .... 4 F3
Sunbeam St WV2 .... 39 C7
Sunbeam Way B33 .... 69 C2
Sunbury Ave WS14 .... 9 E7
Sunbury Cl WV14 .... 40 E1
Sunbury Cotts B31 .... 103 A4
Sunbury Rd Birmingham
 B31 .... 122 F8
 Coventry CV3 .... 134 C5
 Halesowen B63 .... 82 F4
Suncliffe Dr CV8 .... 148 A2
Suncroft B32 .... 84 C5
Sundbury Rise B31 .... 103 B5
Sunderland Dr DY8 .... 81 A8
Sunderton Rd B14 .... 104 E4
Sundew Croft B36 .... 68 D8
Sundew St CV2 .... 96 D2
Sundial La B43 .... 43 F1
Sundorne Cl CV5 .... 112 A4
Sundour Cres WV11 .... 12 B1
Sundridge Jun & Inf Sch
 B44 .... 44 E4
Sundridge Rd B44 .... 44 E4
Sundridge Wlk WV4 .... 38 C6
Sunfield Gr B11 .... 87 E4
Sunfield Rd WS11 .... 1 B1
Sunleigh Gr B27 .... 88 E4
Sunley Dr WS12 .... 2 D7
Sunningdale
 Bromsgrove B60 .... 137 A1
 Halesowen B62 .... 83 E4
 Sutton Coldfield B73 .... 46 B1
 Tamworth B77 .... 22 C5
Sunningdale Ave
 Coventry CV6 .... 95 D2
 Kenilworth CV8 .... 148 B4
 Perton WV6 .... 23 D5
Sunningdale Cl
 Birmingham B20 .... 54 E4
 Nuneaton CV11 .... 74 A1
 Stourbridge DY8 .... 80 F2
 Sutton Coldfield B73 .... 46 A2
Sunningdale Dr B69 .... 63 A7
Sunningdale Rd
 Birmingham B11 .... 88 A3
 Bromsgrove B61 .... 150 D8
 Sedgley DY3 .... 39 B1
Sunningdale Way WS3 .... 14 A3
Sunny Ave B12 .... 87 A5
Sunny Bank Rd B68 .... 84 C7
Sunny Hill Cl WV5 .... 49 B6
Sunnybank Ave
 Birmingham B44 .... 56 B7
 Coventry CV3 .... 134 B5
Sunnybank Cl WS9 .... 30 E2
Sunnybank Rd Dudley DY3 .. 50 F5
 Sutton Coldfield B73 .... 57 A8
Sunnydale Cres LE10 .... 75 A7
Sunnydale Rd LE10 .... 74 F7
Sunnydale Wlk B71 .... 53 C4
Sunnydene B8 .... 68 A5
Sunnyhill LE10 .... 75 F7
Sunnyhill S LE10 .... 75 F6
Sunnymead B60 .... 137 A1
Sunnymead Rd
 Birmingham B26 .... 88 F6
 1 Burntwood WS7 .... 7 A8
Sunnymead Way B74 .... 44 F7
Sunnymede Rd CV6 .... 61 A4
Sunnyside Brownhills WS9 .. 16 A2
 Hinckley LE10 .... 71 D3
 Tipton B69 .... 63 B7
Sunnyside Ave B23 .... 56 E3
Sunnyside Cl
 Balsall Common CV7 .... 130 C7
 Coventry CV5 .... 112 F3
Sunnyside Ct CV10 .... 72 F3
Sunnyside Hospl LE10 ...... 71 D5
Sunnyside Ind Est LE10 ... 71 D4
Sunnyside La CV7 .... 130 C7
Sunridge Ave
 Birmingham B19 .... 66 D6
 Wombourne WV5 .... 49 A7
Sunrise Hill WS12 .... 2 B6
Sunrise Wlk B68 .... 64 C3
Sunset Cl Great Wyrley WS6 .. 4 F3
 Tamworth B79 .... 21 A5
Sunset Pl WV4 .... 39 F3
Sunshine Cl CV8 .... 148 A5
Sunshine Inf Sch The
 WS3 .... 28 C8
Sunway Gr CV3 .... 133 B6
Surfeit Hill Rd B64 .... 82 D8

Surrey Cl Cannock WS11 ...... 4 E7
 Hinckley LE10 .... 75 E4
 Nuneaton CV10 .... 72 E3
Surrey Cres B71 .... 53 A8
Surrey Ct CV34 .... 160 E8
Surrey Dr Kingswinford DY6 .. 60 F3
 Tamworth B78 .... 21 A1
 Wolverhampton WV3 .... 24 E1
Surrey Ho 2 DY8 .... 80 F8
Surrey Rd Birmingham B44 .. 44 F4
 Dudley DY2 .... 62 A7
Surrey Wlk WS9 .... 16 A1
Sussex Ave Aldridge WS9 .. 30 A8
 Wednesbury WS10 .... 42 D4
 West Bromwich B71 .... 53 C6
Sussex Cl CV10 .... 72 E3
Sussex Ct Birmingham B29 .. 103 C7
 Warwick CV34 .... 160 E8
Sussex Dr Cannock WS12 ..... 2 B5
 Wolverhampton WV3 .... 24 E1
Sussex Rd CV5 .... 112 F4
Sutherland Ave
 Coventry CV5 .... 112 A4
 Solihull B90 .... 106 C3
 Wolverhampton WV2 .... 40 A8
Sutherland Cl
 Birmingham B43 .... 44 D4
 Warwick CV34 .... 155 E1
Sutherland Dr
 Bedworth CV12 .... 78 A4
 Birmingham B13 .... 86 F4
 Wombourne WV5 .... 38 A1
Sutherland Gr WV6 .... 23 F4
Sutherland Ho WV1 .... 25 A3
Sutherland Pl WV2 .... 163 C2
Sutherland Rd
 Blackheath B64 .... 82 E8
 Cheslyn Hay WS6 .... 4 E2
 Wolverhampton WV4 .... 39 B5
Sutherland St B6 .... 67 B8
Sutton App B8 .... 68 A4
Sutton Ave Coventry CV5 .. 111 D4
 Tamworth B78 .... 21 A2
Sutton Cl Hinckley LE10 .... 71 F3
 Redditch B98 .... 154 D2
Sutton Coldfield Coll
 Design Ctr B72 .... 46 C4
Sutton Coldfield Coll
 Erdington Ctr B24 .... 57 A4
Sutton Coldfield Coll of
 F Ed B74 .... 46 C6
Sutton Coldfield Girls Sch
 B73 .... 46 B3
Sutton Coldfield Hospl
 B72 .... 46 B4
Sutton Coldfield Sta B73 .. 46 B5
Sutton Cres B70 .... 53 A3
Sutton Ct
 3 Birmingham,
 Erdington B24 .... 57 B6
 Birmingham, Hamstead B43 .. 54 E7
 Sutton Coldfield B75 .... 46 B7
 Wolverhampton WV4 .... 39 E2
Sutton Lodge B91 .... 107 A3
Sutton Oak Cnr B73 .... 45 A5
Sutton Oak Rd B73 .... 45 A5
Sutton Park Ct B73 .... 46 A4
Sutton Park Fst Sch DY11 .. 116 B4
Sutton Park Gr DY11 .... 116 C3
Sutton Park Rd DY11 .... 116 B3
Sutton Park Rise DY11 .... 116 B3
Sutton Pk Nuneaton CV10 .. 72 B7
 Sutton Coldfield B74 .... 45 D6
Sutton Rd Aldridge WS9 .... 30 A1
 Birmingham B23 .... 57 A5
 Kidderminster DY11 .... 116 C4
 Mile Oak B78 .... 34 A7
 Walsall WS5 .... 43 C8
 Wednesbury WS10 .... 41 A4
Sutton Sch DY1 .... 61 F8
Sutton Sq B76 .... 58 E6
Sutton St Birmingham B1 .. 66 D1
 Birmingham, Aston B6 .... 66 F6
 Stourbridge DY8 .... 60 F1
Sutton Stop CV6 .... 96 B5
Sutton's Dr Birmingham
 B43 .... 44 A4
 Walsall WS43 .... 43 F4
Swadling St CV31 .... 161 F6
Swain Crofts CV31 .... 162 B6
Swains Gn LE10 .... 75 F6
Swains Gr B44 .... 44 F4
Swale Gr B38 .... 103 F1
Swale Rd B76 .... 47 A1
Swaledale Cl B60 .... 150 E6
Swallow Ave B36 .... 70 A8
Swallow Cl Birmingham B12 .. 87 B5
 Dudley DY2 .... 62 D2
 Wednesbury WS10 .... 42 B4
Swallow Croft WS13 .... 3 A1
Swallow Ct CV12 .... 95 C8
Swallow Dr DY10 .... 117 A2
Swallow Rd CV6 .... 95 C1
Swallow St Birmingham B2 .. 164 B2
 West Bromwich B70 .... 53 A4
Swallowdale Brownhills
 WS9 .... 16 B4
 Wolverhampton WV6 .... 23 F2
Swallowdean Rd CV6 .... 112 E8
Swallowfall Ave DY8 .... 80 C4
Swallowfield 5 .... 20 E6
Swallowfields Dr WS12 .... 2 B3
Swallowfields Rd DY3 .... 39 C2
Swallows Cl WS3 .... 15 A5
Swallows' Mdw B90 .... 126 D8
Swallows Rise Bsns Pk
 DY5 .... 61 E3

Swan Ave B66 .... 64 E7
Swan Bank WV4 .... 38 F4
Swan Cl Blakedown DY10 .. 98 B1
 Cheslyn Hay WS6 .... 4 D2
Swan Copse B25 .... 88 C5
Swan Corner Sh Ctr WS7 .... 7 C6
Swan Cres B69 .... 63 F4
Swan Ctr The 7 DY10 ...... 116 E6
Swan Ctyd B25 .... 88 D6
Swan Gdns B25 .... 88 D6
Swan La Coventry CV2 ...... 113 F4
 Fairfield B61 .... 120 E3
 Stourbridge DY8 .... 61 A2
 Upton Warren B61 .... 150 A3
 West Bromwich B70 .... 53 B5
Swan Lane Ind Est B70 ..... 53 A5
Swan Mews WS9 .... 9 A8
Swan Pool Gr WS4 .... 15 D1
Swan Rd WS13 .... 9 A7
Swan Rdbt B70 .... 52 F5
Swan St Alvechurch B48 ... 139 B5
 Brierley Hill DY5 .... 61 C6
 Dudley DY2 .... 62 C6
 Royal Leamington Spa
 CV32 .... 157 A1
 Stourbridge DY8 .... 80 E5
 Warwick CV34 .... 160 E6
 Wolverhampton WV1 .... 25 F2
Swan Village Ind Pk B70 .. 53 A5
Swanage Gn CV2 .... 115 A4
Swanage Rd B10 .... 87 D8
Swancote Dr WV4 .... 38 C6
Swancote Rd Birmingham
 B33 .... 68 F5
 Dudley DY1 .... 62 A8
Swancroft Rd Coventry
 CV2 .... 114 A5
 Tipton DY4 .... 51 F8
Swanfield Rd DY8 .... 61 A2
Swanfields WS7 .... 7 C6
Swanley Cl B62 .... 84 A3
Swanmore Cl WV3 .... 38 E8
Swanmote B79 .... 20 F5
Swann Rd WV14 .... 40 A2
Swans Length B48 .... 139 A7
Swansbrook Gdns
 4 B38 .... 104 C2
Swanshurst Girls Sch
 B13 .... 105 B7
Swanshurst La B13 .... 105 C8
Swanswell Rd B92 .... 106 D7
Swanswell St CV1 .... 165 C4
Swanswood Gr 3 B37 .... 70 C3
Swarthmore Rd B29 .... 103 B7
Sweetbriar La WV12 .... 27 D5
Sweetbriar Rd WV2 .... 40 A7
Sweetbrier Dr DY8 .... 60 E1
Sweetman Pl WV6 .... 25 A3
Sweetman St WV6 .... 25 A3
Sweetmoor Cl B36 .... 69 C8
Sweetpool La DY9 .... 98 F5
Swift B77 .... 21 E3
Swift Cl Birmingham B36 .... 70 A8
 Bromsgrove B61 .... 150 E8
Swift Park Gr DY10 .... 117 B2
Swift's Cnr CV3 .... 133 E8
Swillington Rd CV6 .... 113 B5
Swinbrook Gr B44 .... 44 E1
Swinbrook Way B90 .... 106 D4
Swinburne Ave CV2 .... 114 D2
Swinburne Cl CV10 .... 72 A5
Swinburne Rd Hinckley
 LE10 .... 71 C1
 Redditch B97 .... 158 C7
Swincross Rd DY8 .... 81 B3
Swindale B77 .... 36 B7
Swindale Croft CV3 .... 134 F8
Swindell Rd DY9 .... 81 C1
Swindon Rd Birmingham
 B17 .... 65 B2
 Kingswinford DY6 .... 60 B6
Swinfen Broun Rd WS13 ..... 9 A8
Swinford Gr B93 .... 127 E3
Swinford Rd Birmingham
 B29 .... 85 B3
 Stourbridge DY8 .... 81 A3
 Wolverhampton WV10 .... 25 E5
Swinnerton Mid Sch
 CV11 .... 73 C2
Swiss Dr DY8 .... 60 F2
Swiss Lodge Dr B78 .... 34 F8
Swynnerton Dr WV11 .... 12 F4
Sycamore B77 .... 35 E7
Sycamore Ave
 Birmingham B12 .... 87 A5
 Redditch B98 .... 153 E2
Sycamore Cl Hinckley LE10 .. 75 E5
 Kidderminster DY10 .... 116 F7
 Stourbridge DY8 .... 80 D2
 Walsall WS4 .... 29 B8
Sycamore Cres B37 .... 90 A8
Sycamore Ct B30 .... 103 E4
Sycamore Dr Hollywood
 B47 .... 125 B6
 Wolverhampton WV3 .... 24 D1
Sycamore Gn Cannock
 WS11 .... 1 E6
 Dudley DY1 .... 50 F5
Sycamore Gr CV34 .... 156 A1
Sycamore Green Prim Sch
 DY1 .... 50 F5
Sycamore Ho B13 .... 87 A3
Sycamore Ind & Trad Est
 B21 .... 65 D7
Sycamore Paddock
 1 DY8 .... 61 A1
Sycamore Pl Bilston WV14 .. 41 A3
 Smethwick B66 .... 64 F4

Sycamore Rd
 Birmingham, Aston B6 .... 67 A8
 Birmingham, Bournville B30 .. 103 F7
 Birmingham, Erdington B23 .. 56 F7
 Birmingham, Great Barr B43 .. 43 E3
 Birmingham,
 Handsworth B21 .... 65 D7
 Burntwood WS7 .... 6 F7
 Cannock WS12 .... 2 F4
 Coventry CV2 .... 96 B2
 Kingswinford DY6 .... 60 E6
 Nuneaton CV10 .... 72 D6
 Oldbury B69 .... 64 A4
 Smethwick B66 .... 65 B3
 Tipton DY4 .... 51 F7
 Walsall, Shelfield WS4 .... 29 B8
 Walsall, The Delves WS5 ... 42 F5
 Wednesbury WS10 .... 42 A2
Sycamore Terr B14 .... 104 C7
Sycamore Way
 1 Birmingham B27 .... 88 C5
 Huntington WS12 .... 1 D8
Sycamores The
 Bedworth CV12 .... 77 E2
 Lichfield WS14 .... 9 B5
 Sutton Coldfield B74 .... 31 F2
 Wolverhampton,
 Elston Hall WV10 .... 25 F8
 Wolverhampton,
 New Cross WV11 .... 26 B5
Sydenham Dr CV31 .... 162 B6
Sydenham Ind Est CV31 .. 162 B6
Sydenham Prim Sch
 CV31 .... 162 B6
Sydenham Rd
 Birmingham B11 .... 87 C6
 Smethwick B66 .... 65 A7
 Wolverhampton WV1 .... 26 B2
Sydnall Cl B97 .... 152 F2
Sydnall Fields CV6 .... 95 F4
Sydnall Rd CV6 .... 95 F4
Sydney Cl B70 .... 53 A7
Sydney Ct 1 CV12 .... 77 F2
Sydney Ho B34 .... 69 E6
Sydney Rd Birmingham B9 .. 67 C2
 Blackheath B64 .... 82 C8
 Bromsgrove B61 .... 136 E3
 Smethwick B67 .... 64 E2
Sykesmoor B77 .... 36 B7
Sylvan Ave B31 .... 102 F3
Sylvan Dr CV3 .... 132 F6
Sylvan Gn B62 .... 83 D5
Sylvan Gr B90 .... 106 B5
Sylvester Ho 2 B36 .... 57 F1
Sylvia Ave B31 .... 123 B8
Symphony Ct B16 .... 66 B2
Synkere Cl CV7 .... 95 A6
Sytch La WV5 .... 49 A5

T P Riley Com Sch WS3 ...... 14 C2
Tabbs Gdns DY10 .... 117 A6
Table Oak La CV8 .... 130 E3
Tachbrook Cl CV2 .... 96 C2
Tachbrook Park Dr CV34 .. 161 E5
Tachbrook Rd CV31 .... 161 F4
Tachbrook St CV31 .... 162 A6
Tack Farm Rd DY8 .... 60 D1
Tackford Cl B36 .... 58 D1
Tackford Rd CV6 .... 114 A8
Tackley Cl B90 .... 126 B8
Tadmore Cl WV14 .... 40 D5
Tadworth Cl WV1 .... 26 A2
Tainters Hill CV8 .... 148 A6
Tait Croft B92 .... 107 F8
Talaton Cl WV9 .... 11 A2
Talbot B77 .... 21 E3
Talbot Ave B74 .... 31 B3
Talbot Cl Birmingham B23 .. 56 D8
 Walsall WS2 .... 28 C6
Talbot Ct CV32 .... 157 A1
Talbot Ho 5 B24 .... 56 F4
Talbot Pl WV14 .... 40 C6
Talbot Rd Bromsgrove B60 .. 150 E7
 Dudley DY2 .... 62 B4
 Smethwick B66 .... 65 A3
 Wolverhampton WV2 .... 39 C6
Talbot St Birmingham B18 .. 65 F6
 Brierley Hill DY5 .... 61 D3
 Halesowen B63 .... 82 C6
 Kidderminster DY11 .... 116 C4
 Stourbridge, Lye DY9 .... 81 F5
 Stourbridge,
 Stambermill DY8 .... 81 A8
Talbot Way B10 .... 87 F7
Talbots La DY5 .... 61 F1
Talford St B6 .... 66 E6
Talfourd St B9 .... 67 D1
Talgarth Covert B38 .... 123 E7
Talisman Cl CV8 .... 147 F3
Talisman Sq CV8 .... 147 F4
Talke Rd WS5 .... 42 F5
Tall Trees Cl Catshill B61 .. 136 F8
 Sutton Coldfield B74 .... 31 D4
 Willenhall WV12 .... 27 D6
Tall Trees Dr DY9 .... 81 D2
Talladale B32 .... 102 B7
Talland Ave Coventry CV6 .. 114 A4
 Tamworth B79 .... 21 F5
Tallants Cl CV6 .... 114 A8
Tallants Rd CV6 .... 114 A8
Tallington Rd B33 .... 89 D7
Talton Cl B90 .... 127 A5
Tamar Cl WS8 .... 6 C2
Tamar Dr Birmingham B36 .. 69 F8
 Dudley DY5 .... 50 F6
 Sutton Coldfield B76 .... 58 B7
Tamar Gr Perton WV6 .... 23 E4
 Willenhall WV13 .... 27 C2

Tamar Rd Bulkington CV12 79 B2
Tamworth B77 36 A5
Tamar Rise DY8 81 A8
Tamarisk Cl B29 103 B8
Tame Ave Burntwood WS7 7 D6
Wednesbury WS10 42 C4
Tame Bridge WS5 42 F4
Tame Bridge Factory Est
WS5 42 F4
Tame Bridge Sta B71 42 F2
Tame Cl WS1 42 E6
Tame Cres B71 53 C6
Tame Ct 5 Fazeley B78 35 B8
Tamworth B79 21 A5
Tame Dr WS3 15 A1
Tame Gr WS11 4 D8
Tame Rd Birmingham B6 56 A1
Oldbury B68 84 B8
Tipton DY4 52 C5
Tame Rise B68 84 B8
Tame Road Ind Est B6 56 B1
Tame St Bilston WV14 40 F5
Tamworth B77 21 C3
Walsall WS1 42 E6
West Bromwich B70 52 F8
Tame St E WS1 42 F6
Tame Valley Bsns Ctr B77 35 E6
Tame Valley Ind Est B77 35 E7
Tame Valley Jun & Inf Sch
B36 68 D8
Tame Way LE10 75 A8
Tamebridge Ind Est B42 55 E4
Tamedrive B79 21 A4
Tamerton Rd B32 84 D1
Tameside Dr
Birmingham,
Castle Bromwich B35 58 A1
Birmingham, Erdington B6 56 A3
Tameside Jun & Inf Schs
WS10 42 C2
Tamworth Bsns Ctr B77 22 B3
Tamworth Bsns Pk B77 22 B3
Tamworth Castle B79 21 B4
Tamworth Cl WS8 6 F2
Tamworth Coll of F Ed
B79 21 B6
Tamworth Rd Cliff B78 35 C2
Keresley CV6, CV7 94 D5
Lichfield WS14 9 D5
Polesworth B78 22 E1
Sutton Coldfield B75 32 F1
Tamworth B77 35 D8
Wood End CV9 36 C1
Tamworth Rd (Amington)
B77 21 F5
Tamworth Rd (Dosthill)
B77 35 C6
Tamworth St WS13 9 B8
Tamworth Sta B79 21 C5
Tanacetum Dr WS5 43 B3
Tandy Dr B14 104 F3
Tandy's La DY10 118 E4
Tanfield Cl WV6 24 B3
Tanfield Rd Birmingham B33 68 F3
Dudley DY2 62 B7
Tanford Rd B92 89 C3
Tanglewood Cl
Birmingham,
Castle Bromwich B34 69 C5
Birmingham, Quinton B32 84 B4
Blackwell B60 138 A5
Tanglewood Gr DY3 39 C2
Tangmere Cl WV6 23 E5
Tangmere Dr B35 58 A3
Tanhill B77 36 B7
Tanhouse Ave B43 54 C7
Tanhouse Farm Rd B92 89 C2
Tanhouse La Halesowen
B63 82 C5
Redditch B98 154 C6
Tanners Cl B75 46 F7
Tanners Ct WS1 42 E8
Tanners Green La B47 125 B2
Tanners' La CV4, CV7 111 B1
Tannery Cl WS2 28 D3
Tannery Ct CV8 147 F4
Tansey Ct DY5 61 B7
Tansey Green Rd
Brierley Hill DY5 61 B8
Kingswinford DY6 50 A1
Tansley Cl B93 127 F4
Tansley Gr B44 44 F1
Tansley Hill Ave DY2 62 F8
Tansley Hill Rd DY2 62 E8
Tansley Rd B44 55 F8
Tansley View WV2 39 D7
Tansy B74 31 F4
Tantallan Dr B32 84 D1
Tantany La B71 53 C4
Tantarra St Walsall WS1 28 F1
Walsall, The Chuckery WS1 29 A1
Tanwood Cl Redditch B97 158 A6
Solihull B91 127 B8
Tanwood Cross DY10 119 B1
Tanwood La DY10 119 A2
Tanworth Gr B12 86 F6
Tanworth La B90 126 C5
Tanworth-in-Arden CE
Sch B94 142 A2
Tanyard WS13 9 C8
Tanyard Cl Alvechurch B48 139 B6
Coventry CV4 111 D1
Tanyard La B48 139 B6
Tanyards B27 88 D3
Tapcon Way CV2 114 F5
Tapestries Ave B70 53 A4
Taplow Pl WS11 1 F4
Tappinger Gr CV8 148 C5
Tapster La B94 143 F2
Tapton Cl WS3 14 C3
Tardebigge CE Fst Sch
B60 152 B7
Tardebigge Ho B60 137 B3
Tarlington Rd CV6 112 E6
Tarmac Rd WV14 40 B5
Tarn Cl CV12 78 A2
Tarquin Cl CV3 134 D7
Tarragon Cl CV2 96 D1
Tarragon Gdns B31 102 C2
Tarrant B77 35 F8
Tarrant Gr B32 84 F5
Tarrant Wlk CV2 115 A5
Tarrington Covert
6 B38 123 E8
Tarry Hollow Rd DY5 61 B7
Tarry Rd B8 67 E5
Tarvin Mews DY5 61 D1
Taryn Dr WS10 41 D7
Tasker St Walsall WS1 42 D8
West Bromwich B70 52 E4
Tasman Gr WV6 23 E5
Tat Bank Rd B69 64 B6
Tatchbrook Ct 5 CV31 161 F6
Tatnall Gr CV34 160 E8
Taunton Ave WV10 11 D4
Taunton Rd B12 87 B4
Taunton Tower 1 B31 102 C2
Taunton Way CV6 95 A2
Taverner's Gn B20 54 F3
Taverners Cl WV12 13 C1
Tavistock Cl B79 21 C7
Tavistock Rd B27 106 C8
Tavistock St CV32 156 F1
Tavistock Way CV11 73 E5
Tavistock Wlk CV2 114 C7
Taw Cl B36 69 F7
Tay Croft B37 70 C4
Tay Gr Birmingham B38 123 F8
Halesowen B62 83 E8
Tay Rd Birmingham B45 102 B1
Coventry CV6 113 B6
Taylor Ave
Royal Leamington Spa
CV32 157 B2
Walsall WS3 28 D8
Taylor Cl CV8 148 B6
Taylor Ct CV34 160 D7
Taylor Ho 4 WS2 42 C7
Taylor Rd Birmingham
B13 104 F5
Dudley DY2 62 E2
Wolverhampton WV4 39 F5
Taylor St WV11 26 D5
Taylor's La Smethwick B67 64 F5
West Bromwich B71 53 D4
Taylors La B69 63 E7
Taylors Orch B23 56 B4
Taynton Covert 4 B30 104 C3
Taysfield Rd B31 102 E6
Taywood Dr B10 87 C7
Tea Gdn The CV12 95 E8
Teachers Cl CV6 113 A5
Teal Bsns Ctr LE10 74 D7
Teal Cres DY10 117 B3
Teal Dr B23 56 B3
Teal Rd B80 159 F4
Tealby Gr B29 86 A1
Teall Ct B27 88 C3
Teall Rd B8 67 E5
Tean Cl Birmingham B11 88 A3
Burntwood WS7 7 D6
Teasdale Way DY9 81 D4
Teasel Gr WV10 12 B7
Teasel Rd WV11 26 F5
Teazel Ave B30 103 D6
Tebworth Cl WV9 10 F2
Ted Pitts La CV5 94 B2
Tedbury Cres B23 56 E6
Tedder Rd WS2 27 F2
Teddesley Ct WS11 1 E3
Teddesley Gr B33 69 C4
Teddesley St WS4 28 F3
Teddesley Way WS12 1 C6
Teddington Gr B42 55 D3
Tedstone Rd B32 84 E5
Tees Gr B38 123 F8
Teesdale Ave B34 68 F6
Teesdale Cl WV1 26 A2
Teeswater Cl B60 150 E6
Teign B77 36 A5
Teign Bank Cl LE10 71 D2
Teign Bank Rd LE10 71 D2
Teignmouth Rd B29 86 A1
Telephone Rd CV3 114 C2
Telfer Rd CV6 113 B7
Telford Ave Great Wyrley
WS6 4 F3
Royal Leamington Spa
CV32 157 B5
Telford Cl Burntwood WS7 7 C8
Smethwick B67 64 D1
Walsall WS2 28 A5
West Bromwich B71 53 A8
Telford Cty Fst &
Mid Schs CV32 157 C5
Telford Gdns WV3 38 D7
Telford Gr WS12 2 B7
Telford Rd Bedworth CV7 96 C8
Tamworth B79 20 F8
Walsall WS2 28 A5
Telford Way B66 64 F8
Teme Ave DY11 116 B3
Teme Ct B23 56 B3
Teme Gr WV13 27 D2
Teme Rd Halesowen B63 82 B5
Stourbridge DY8 80 F3
Tempest St Tamworth B79 21 A5
Wolverhampton WV2 163 C2
Templar Ave CV4 112 A1
Templar Ct CV11 73 C3
Templars' Fields CV4 132 B7
Templars Prim Sch CV4 112 A1
Templars The Oldbury B69 63 E5
Warwick CV34 160 F5
Temple Ave
Balsall Common CV7 129 F6
Birmingham B28 106 A6
Temple Bar WV13 27 A2
Temple Cl B98 153 F4
Temple Gr CV34 160 D5
Temple La B93 129 A4
Temple Meadow Prim Sch
B64 63 A1
Temple Meadows Rd B71 53 E6
Temple Pas B2 164 B2
Temple Rd Dorridge B93 128 A3
Willenhall WV13 27 B3
Temple Row B2 164 C3
Temple Row W B2 164 B3
Temple Sq WV13 27 A3
Temple St Bilston WV14 40 E5
Birmingham B2 164 B2
Dudley DY3 50 D3
West Bromwich B70 53 C4
Wolverhampton WV2 163 B2
Temple Way Coleshill B46 59 F1
Tipton B69 52 D2
Templefield Gdns B9 67 C1
Templefield Sq B15 86 B7
Templefield St B9 67 C1
Templemore Dr B43 54 E7
Templeton Cl B93 128 A3
Templeton Rd B44 44 F2
Ten Acres End B30 104 B8
Ten Acres Fst Sch B98 154 F3
Ten Ashes La B45 122 C4
Tenacre La DY3 50 E6
Tenacres La B98 154 F3
Tenbury Cl Aldridge WS9 30 C8
Redditch B98 154 C6
Willenhall WS2 27 D3
Tenbury Ct WV4 38 D5
Tenbury Gdns WV4 38 D5
Tenbury Ho Birmingham
B33 69 A2
2 Halesowen B63 83 A3
Tenbury Rd B14 104 E6
Tenby Cl CV12 77 C1
Tenby Ct 2 CV32 161 E8
Tenby Rd B13 87 D2
Tenby St B1 66 B4
Tenby St N B1 66 B4
Tenby Tower 2 B31 103 A1
Teneriffe Rd CV6 95 F1
Tenlands Rd B63 82 F3
Tenlons Rd CV10 72 F2
Tennal Dr B32 84 F6
Tennal Gr B32 84 F6
Tennal La B32 84 F6
Tennal Rd B32 84 F6
Tennant St Birmingham B15 66 B1
Nuneaton CV11 73 E3
Tennis Ct B30 103 D4
Tennis Ct The B15 86 A5
Tennscore Ave WS6 4 E3
Tennyson Ave
Sutton Coldfield B74 31 F6
Tamworth B79 21 A6
Warwick CV34 160 C4
Tennyson Cl CV8 148 C4
Tennyson Ho
Birmingham B31 123 A8
3 Oldbury B68 64 C4
Tennyson Rd Birmingham
B10 87 E7
Coventry CV2 114 C3
Dudley DY3 50 A4
Hinckley LE10 71 C1
Redditch B97 158 C8
Walsall WS3 28 E8
Willenhall WV12 27 E8
Wolverhampton WV10 12 A1
Tennyson St DY5 61 D7
Tennyson Way DY10 117 C6
Tenter Ct B63 83 B4
Tenter Dr B63 83 C4
Tenterfields B63 83 B4
Tenterfields Prim Sch
B62 83 C4
Tern Cl WV4 39 D3
Tern Gr B38 103 E1
Ternhill Ho B35 58 A2
Terrace Rd B19 66 B7
Terrace St Blackheath B65 63 B1
Brierley Hill DY5 61 E5
Wednesbury WS10 42 A3
Terrace The Blackheath
B64 82 E8
Wolverhampton WV3 24 C1
Terry Ave CV32 156 C1
Terry Dr B76 46 F2
Terry Rd CV1 113 F1
Terry St DY2 51 E1
Terrys Cl B98 153 F5
Tessall La B31 102 D2
Tetbury Gr B31 102 D3
Tetley Ave WS4 29 B4
Tetley Rd B11 87 E3
Tetnall St DY2 62 D8
Tettenhall Arc WV6 24 D5
Tettenhall Coll WV6 24 D4
Tettenhall Rd WV6, WV1 24 F4
Tettenhall Wood Sch
WV6 24 B3
Teviot Gdns DY5 61 B6
Teviot Gr B38 123 F8
Teviot Tower B19 66 C5
Tew Park Rd B21 65 E7
Tewkesbury Dr
Bedworth CV12 78 C3
Dudley DY2 62 D3
Tewkesbury Rd
Birmingham B20 55 E2
Walsall WS3 13 E2
Thackeray Cl CV10 72 A4
Thackeray Dr B79 21 A7
Thackeray Rd B30 103 D5
Thackhall St CV2 113 F4
Thame Ct B47 124 E2
Thames Cl Brierley Hill
DY5 61 B7
Bulkington CV12 79 A3
Thames Ct B73 46 B5
Thames Ho 6 DY3 50 D3
Thames Rd WS3 14 E1
Thames Tower B7 67 B5
Thamley Rd CV6 113 A4
Thanet Cl DY6 60 C7
Thanet Gr B42 55 C4
Thatchway Gdns B38 123 E7
Thaxted Rd B33 69 E3
Theatre App B5 164 C1
Theatre Ct CV34 160 D6
Theatre St CV34 160 D7
Thebes Cl CV5 111 B8
Theddingworth Cl CV3 134 E8
Thelbridge Rd B31 122 E6
Thelma Rd DY4 51 E5
Thelma St 1 WS1 42 D7
Thelsford Way B92 107 D8
Theodore Cl Birmingham
B17 85 D4
Oldbury B69 52 E1
Theresa Rd B11 87 B7
Thetford Cl DY4 51 D5
Thetford Gdns WV11 26 D6
Thetford Rd B42 55 B7
Thetford Way WS5 43 C3
Thickett Cl WS2 42 B8
Thicknall Dr DY9 81 C2
Thicknall La DY9 99 B3
Thicknall Rise DY9 99 B4
Thickthorn Cl CV8 148 B2
Thickthorn Orchs CV8 148 B2
Thimble End Rd B76 47 A1
Thimble Mill La B6, B7 67 B7
Thimblemill Rd B67 64 E3
Thimbler Rd CV4 132 C7
Third Ave
Birmingham,
Bordesley Green B9 67 F2
Birmingham,
Selly Oak B29 86 C3
Birmingham,
Witton B6 55 F3
Brownhills WS8 7 A1
Kingswinford DY6 60 F8
Wolverhampton WV10 25 F7
Third Exhibition Ave B40 90 D4
Third Rd B61 120 F4
Thirlestane Cl CV8 148 C6
Thirlmere Ave CV11 73 F6
Thirlmere Cl Cannock WS11 1 E1
Coventry CV4 111 E3
Wolverhampton WV6 24 D8
Thirlmere Dr
Birmingham B13 105 D8
Essington WV11 13 A2
Thirlmere Gr WV6 23 F4
Thirlmere Ho B15 85 D3
Thirlmere Rd Bedworth
CV12 78 A2
Hinckley LE10 75 A7
Wolverhampton WV6 24 D8
Thirlmere Wlk DY5 81 B7
Thirsk Croft B36 68 C8
Thirsk Rd CV3 133 C5
Thirston Cl WV11 27 A5
Thisledown Wlk DY3 39 C1
Thistle Cl DY3 50 F6
Thistle Croft WV11 26 D5
Thistle Down Cl B74 31 A2
Thistle Gn B38 123 E7
Thistle Ho B36 68 D8
Thistle La B32 102 B7
Thistledown Ave WS7 7 A6
Thistledown Dr Cannock
WS12 2 D1
Featherstone WV10 12 A7
Thistledown Rd B34 69 C7
Thistlegreen Cl B65 62 F5
Thistlegreen Rd DY2 62 E4
Thistlewood Gr B93 145 B6
Thistley Field E CV6 113 A7
Thistley Field N CV6 113 A7
Thistley Field S CV6 112 F6
Thistley Field W CV6 112 F7
Thistley Nook WS13 3 A1
Thomas Barnes Cty Prim
Sch B78 20 B7
Thomas Cres 2 B66 65 C5
Thomas Greenway WS13 3 A2
Thomas Guy Rd B70 52 F6
Thomas Hardy Ct B79 21 A7
Thomas Ho WS3 14 D3
Thomas King Ho 6 CV1 113 E4
Thomas Landsdail St
CV3 133 D8
Thomas Lane St CV6 96 A1
Thomas Mason Cl WV11 26 D7
Thomas Naul Croft CV4 111 F3
Thomas Sharp St CV4 132 A7
Thomas St Bedworth CV12 78 A2
Birmingham B6 66 F6
Royal Leamington Spa
CV32 157 A1
Smethwick B66 65 B5
Tamworth B77 21 D4
Walsall WS2 28 D2
West Bromwich B70 53 D2
Wolverhampton WV2 163 B1
Thomas Wlk B35 58 B3
Thompson Ave WV2 39 E6
Thompson Cl Dudley DY2 62 B2
Willenhall WV13 27 A3
Thompson Dr B24 67 F8
Thompson Gdns B67 64 F4
Thompson Ho DY4 52 C8
Thompson Rd Oldbury B68 64 B5
Smethwick B67 64 F4
Thompson St Bilston WV14 40 D5
Willenhall WV13 27 A3
Thompson's Rd CV7 94 F6
Thomson Ave B38 103 D1
Thor Cl WS11 2 A5
Thoresby B79 20 E6
Thorn Cl WS10 41 F4
Thorn Rd B30 103 E7
Thorn Stile Cl CV32 157 E6
Thornberry Dr DY1 61 E8
Thornberry Wlk B7 67 C6
Thornbridge Ave B42 55 D7
Thornbrook Ct 1 WS4 28 F3
Thornbury Ct WV6 24 A3
Thornbury La B98 154 C7
Thornbury Rd B20 55 D2
Thornby Ave Kenilworth
CV8 148 B3
Solihull B91 107 B5
Tamworth B77 35 E8
Thornby Rd B23 56 C8
Thorncliffe Cl B97 158 A6
Thorncliffe Rd B44 44 E2
Thorncroft Way WS5 43 B4
Thorne Ave WV10 25 E7
Thorne Rd WV13 27 A4
Thorne St WV2 40 A7
Thornes Croft WS9 16 E4
Thorney Rd Aldridge B74 30 F1
Coventry CV2 114 B6
Thorneycroft La WV10 26 A6
Thorneycroft Pl WV14 41 B3
Thorneycroft Rd WV14 41 B4
Thornfield Cres WS7 7 A8
Thornfield Croft DY3 50 E7
Thornfield Rd B27 88 D2
Thornfield Way LE10 75 E8
Thorngrove Ave 7 B91 127 C8
Thornham Way B14 104 D1
Thornhill Dr CV11 79 C8
Thornhill Gr B21 65 F8
Thornhill Pk B74 45 A8
Thornhill Rd
Birmingham,
Handsworth B21 65 F8
Birmingham, Sparkhill B11 87 D3
Brierley Hill DY5 81 E8
Cannock WS12 1 F7
Coventry CV1 113 D5
Dudley DY1 51 C4
Halesowen B63 82 E3
Redditch B98 154 E6
Solihull B91 107 C7
Sutton Coldfield B74 45 A7
Thornhurst Ave B32 84 E7
Thornleigh DY3 50 D5
Thornleigh Trad Est DY2 62 A7
Thornley Cl Birmingham
B13 87 A1
Radford Semele CV31 162 F5
Wolverhampton WV11 12 F1
Thornley Gr B76 58 C6
Thornley Rd WV11 12 F1
Thornley St WV1 163 C3
Thorns Ave DY5 61 E1
Thorns Cty Fst Sch CV8 148 B4
Thorns Prim Sch DY5 81 E7
Thorns Rd DY5 81 E7
Thorns Sch & Com Coll
DY5 81 E8
Thornsett Gr B90 106 B6
Thornthwaite Cl B45 102 B2
Thornton Cl Coventry CV5 111 C4
Tipton B69 52 C2
Warwick CV34 155 F1
Thornton Dr DY5 61 E1
Thornton Ho B19 66 E5
Thornton Jun Sch B8 68 B5
Thornton Rd Birmingham
B8 68 B5
Solihull B90 126 F6
Wolverhampton WV1 26 B1
Thorntons Way CV10 72 A3
Thornwood Cl B68 64 C5
Thornycroft Rd LE10 75 E8
Thornyfield Cl B90 106 C3
Thornyfield Rd B90 106 C3
Thornyhurst La WS14 17 A6
Thorp St B5 164 B1
Thorpe Ave WS7 6 D8
Thorpe Cl Burntwood WS7 6 D8
Sutton Coldfield B75 46 C7
Thorpe Rd WS1 42 E7
Thorpe St WS7 6 D8
Threadneedle St CV1 113 D6
Three Corner Cl B90 125 E8
Three Cornered Cl CV32 157 E6

Three Crowns Specl Sch WS5 43 F8
Three Oaks Rd B47 125 B4
Three Pots Rd LE10 75 E4
Three Shires Jct CV6 95 E1
Three Shires Oak Rd B67 64 F2
Three Spires Ave CV6 113 A6
Three Spires Ind Est CV6 96 A5
Three Spires Sch CV5 112 D6
Three Spires Sh Ctr 7 WS13 9 B7
Three Tuns La WV10 11 D1
Three Tuns Par WV10 11 C2
Threshers Dr WV12 27 D6
Threshers Way WV12 27 D6
Throckmorton Rd B98 159 A8
Throne Cl B65 63 D5
Throne Cres B65 63 D4
Throne Rd B65 63 D5
Thrush Rd B68 63 F2
Thrushel Wlk WV11 26 C5
Thruxton Cl Birmingham B14 104 F3
Redditch B98 154 E3
Thurcroft Cl B8 67 F4
Thuree Rd B67 64 E2
Thurlby Ct WV1 25 A3
Thurlestone Rd
Birmingham B31 122 E7
Coventry CV6 112 F8
Thurloe Cres B45 101 E1
Thurlston Ave B92 88 F4
Thurlstone Dr WV4 38 F4
Thurlstone Rd WS3 14 B3
Thurne B77 35 F8
Thursfield Rd
Royal Leamington Spa CV32 157 B3
Tipton DY4 52 A6
West Bromwich B71 53 E7
Thurso B77 21 E5
Thurston Ave B69 63 F6
Thynne St B70 53 E2
Tibbats Cl B32 84 C3
Tibberton Cl Halesowen B63 83 C4
Solihull B91 127 A8
Wolverhampton WV3 38 D7
Tibberton Ct B60 150 E7
Tibbets La B17 85 B4
Tibbington Rd DY4 51 E7
Tibbington Terr DY4 51 F7
Tibbits Ct 5 CV34 160 E6
Tibbits Ho 1 WS2 28 D3
Tiber Cl CV5 111 F4
Tiberius Cl B46 59 F1
Tibland Rd B27 88 D2
Tidbury Cl B97 158 C6
Tidbury Green Jun & Inf Sch B90 125 E4
Tiddington Cl B36 58 B1
Tideswell Cl CV3 115 A1
Tideswell Rd B42 55 C7
Tidmarsh Cl CV7 130 A6
Tidmarsh Rd CV35 156 A7
Tidworth Croft 2 B14 105 A3
Tierney Dr DY4 52 C6
Tiffany La WV9 10 F2
Tiffield Rd B25 88 C5
Tigley Ave B32 84 D1
Tilbury Cl WV3 38 A8
Tilbury Gr B13 86 D1
Tildasley St B70 53 B5
Tildesley Dr WV12 27 B5
Tile Cross Rd B33 69 E2
Tile Cross Trad Est B33 69 E1
Tile Gr B37 70 A5
Tile Hill Coll of FE CV4 111 F1
Tile Hill La
Coventry, Allesley CV4, CV5 112 D2
Coventry, Tile Hill CV4 112 B1
Tile Hill Sta CV4 131 D8
Tile Hill Wood Sch CV4 111 D2
Tile Hurst Dr CV4 111 D1
Tiled House La DY5 61 B6
Tilehouse B97 153 D2
Tilehouse Green La B93 127 F6
Tilehouse La B90 125 E6
Tilesford Cl B90 127 A6
Tilewood Ave CV5 111 F4
Tilia Rd B77 22 B5
Tilley St WS10 41 E6
Tillington Cl B98 154 E3
Tillyard Croft B29 85 C1
Tilshead Cl B14 104 E3
Tilsley Gr B23 56 B5
Tilston Dr DY5 61 D1
Tilton Rd Birmingham B9 67 C1
Hinckley LE10 75 E6
Timber Mill Ct B17 85 B6
Timberdine Cl B63 82 D6
Timberhonger La B61 136 B2
Timberlake Cl B90 127 B6
Timberley Jun & Inf Sch B34 69 D6
Timberley La B34 69 C6
Timbers Way
Birmingham B11 87 A6
Sutton Coldfield B24 57 F4
Timbertree Cres B64 82 E7
Timbertree Prim Sch B64 82 E7
Timbertree Rd B64 82 F7
Times Square Ave DY5 61 F2
Timmins Cl B91 107 E6
Timmis Cl WV14 40 B3
Timmis Rd DY9 81 C6
Timothy Gr CV4 112 B1
Timothy Rd B69 63 D7
Tinacre Hill WV6 23 F2
Tinchbourne St 1 DY1 51 C1
Tindal Jun & Inf Sch B12 86 F5
Tindal St B12 86 F5
Tink-A-Tank CV34 160 E7
Tinkers Farm Gr B31 102 E3
Tinkers Farm Rd B31 102 E3
Tinkers Green Rd B77 35 F6
Tinkers La Earlswood B94 142 E7
Lapworth B94 143 E1
Tinmeadow Cres B45 122 C7
Tinsley St DY4 52 E5
Tintagel Cl Coventry CV3 134 D5
Perton WV6 23 F3
Tintagel Dr DY1 50 E2
Tintagel Gr CV8 148 B4
Tintagel Way CV11 74 A5
Tintern Cl Bromsgrove B61 136 E1
Sutton Coldfield B74 45 A7
Tintern Cres WS3 13 F2
Tintern Ct WV6 23 E4
Tintern Ho B32 84 F5
Tintern Rd B20 55 E1
Tintern Villas 4 B12 87 B5
Tintern Way Bedworth CV12 78 C3
Walsall WS3 13 F2
Tipper Trad Est DY9 82 A5
Tipperary Cl B36 68 E8
Tippett Cl CV11 79 A7
Tipping's Hill B97 158 C5
Tipps Stone Cl DY4 51 E4
Tipton Coll Willingsworth Campus DY4 41 B2
Tipton Green Jun Sch DY4 51 F4
Tipton Owen Street Sta DY4 51 F6
Tipton Rd
Dudley, Tipton Green DY1 51 E3
Dudley, Woodsetton DY3 50 F7
Tipton B69 52 C2
Tipton St DY3 50 E7
Tipton Trad Est DY4 51 D6
Tirley Rd B33 69 A4
Tisdale Rise CV8 148 B6
Titan Way WS14 9 F8
Titania Cl B45 102 A3
Titchfield Cl WV10 11 E4
Titford Cl B69 63 F4
Titford La B65 63 E4
Titford Rd B69 63 F4
Tithe Barn La B94 142 C6
Tithe Croft WV10 25 F3
Tithe Rd WV11 26 D6
Titterstone Rd B31 123 A8
Tiverton Cl DY6 61 A3
Tiverton Dr CV11 73 F5
Tiverton Gr Coventry CV2 114 D5
Smethwick B67 64 F6
Tiverton Jun & Inf Sch B29 85 F2
Tiverton Rd Birmingham B29 85 F2
Coventry CV2 114 D5
Smethwick B66 65 B5
Tiverton Sch CV6 112 D5
Tiveycourt Rd CV6 96 A3
Tividale Comp Sch B69 52 C1
Tividale Ho B69 63 E8
Tividale Prim Sch B69 52 B2
Tividale Rd B69 52 A2
Tividale St DY4 52 A2
Tivoli The B26 88 D6
Tixall Rd B28 105 E5
Tobruk Wlk Brierley Hill DY5 61 D3
Willenhall WV13 40 E8
Tocil Croft CV4 132 D4
Toler Rd CV11 73 B5
Toll End Rd DY4 52 C7
Toll House Rd B45 122 C7
Tollard Cl CV2 114 F5
Tolley Rd DY11 116 B1
Tollgate Cl B31 122 F8
Tollgate Dr B20 66 B7
Tollgate Prec B67 64 F6
Tollhouse Rd B60 150 E6
Tollhouse Way B66 64 F6
Tolman Dr B77 21 D3
Tolson Ave B78 35 B8
Tolson Cl B77 35 D5
Tolworth Gdns WV2 39 E7
Tolworth Hall Rd B24 57 B3
Tom Ellis Ct CV7 96 A8
Tom Henderson Cl CV3 134 F7
Tom Hill B94 142 B3
Tom Ward Cl CV3 134 E7
Tomey Rd B11 87 D5
Tomkinson Dr DY11 116 B4
Tomkinson Rd CV10 72 F4
Tomlan Rd B31 123 C7
Tomlinson Rd B36 58 D1
Tompstone Rd B71 53 F8
Toms Town La B80 159 E3
Tomson Ave CV6 113 B4
Tonadine Cl WV11 13 A1
Tonbridge Rd
Birmingham B24 57 A1
Coventry CV3 134 A6
Tong Ct 9 WV3 25 C4
Tong St WS1 29 A1
Top Croft Rd B23 56 F7
Top Field Wlk B14 104 D2
Top Rd Barnacle CV7 97 B7
Wildmoor B61 121 A4
Topcliffe Jun & Inf Sch B35 58 A3
Topfield Ho B14 104 E1
Topland Gr B31 102 C2
Topp's Dr CV12 77 E1
Topp's Heath CV12 77 E1
Topsham Croft B14 104 D5
Topsham Rd B67 64 E6
Tor Way WS3 14 F3
Torbay B77 21 F5
Torbay Rd CV5 112 C4
Torc Ave B77 21 E4
Torcastle Cl CV6 113 F7
Torcross Ave CV2 114 C6
Torfield WV8 10 E2
Toronto Gdns B32 84 E6
Torpoint Cl CV2 114 C7
Torquoise Gr WS11 2 C3
Torre Ave B31 102 E2
Torrey Gr B8 68 C4
Torridge B77 36 A5
Torridge Dr WV11 26 C5
Torridon Croft B13 86 D3
Torridon Rd WV12 13 B1
Torrington Ave CV4 131 E8
Torrs Cl B97 153 D2
Torside B77 36 B7
Torvale Rd WV6 24 A2
Torwood Cl CV4 131 F6
Totnes Cl CV2 114 C7
Totnes Gr 2 B29 85 F2
Totnes Rd B67 64 F6
Tottenham Cres B44 45 B2
Touchwood Hall Cl B91 107 C4
Towbury Cl B98 158 F5
Towcester Croft B36 68 D8
Tower Croft B37 70 B4
Tower Hill B42 55 A6
Tower Rd Bedworth CV12 78 B2
Birmingham B6 66 F7
Birmingham B6 67 A7
Sutton Coldfield B75 32 B3
Tipton B69 63 C7
Tower Rise B69 63 C7
Tower St Birmingham B19 164 B5
Coventry CV1 165 B3
Dudley DY1 51 C1
5 Royal Leamington Spa CV31 162 A7
Sedgley DY3 39 D1
Walsall WS1 28 E2
Wolverhampton WV1 163 C3
Tower View Cres CV10 72 B3
Tower View Rd WS6 13 F8
Towers Cl Kenilworth CV8 147 F2
Kidderminster DY10 117 B5
Town Feilds Cl CV5 112 B7
Town Jun Sch B72 46 C4
Townend St WS2 28 E2
Townesend Cl CV34 155 F1
Townfields WS13 9 A7
Townfold WS3 15 A4
Townley Gdns B6 55 E1
Townsend Ave
Bromsgrove B61 137 B4
Sedgley DY3 50 D8
Townsend Croft CV3 133 C7
Townsend Dr Nuneaton CV11 73 F3
Sutton Coldfield B76 57 F7
Townsend Pl DY6 60 D6
Townsend Rd CV3 133 C8
Townsend Way 5 B1 66 B3
Townsends Cl CV11 75 A1
Townshend Gr B37 69 F4
Townshend Ho B79 21 A4
Townson Rd WV11 27 A8
Townwell Fold WV1 163 B3
Towpath Cl B9 67 B2
Towyn Rd B13 87 D2
Toys La B63 82 C5
Tozer St DY4 51 F7
Traceys Mdw B45 122 A7
Tractor Spares Ind Est WV13 26 D2
Trafalgar Cl WS12 2 E4
Trafalgar Ct B69 52 C1
Trafalgar Gr B25 88 A6
Trafalgar Ho Birmingham B11 87 B8
3 Coventry CV1 113 B2
Trafalgar Rd
Birmingham, Erdington B24 56 F3
Birmingham, Handsworth B21 65 E8
Birmingham, Moseley B13 86 F4
Smethwick B66 65 C4
Tipton B69 52 B1
Trafford Dr CV10 72 C6
Trafford Lodge 4 CV31 162 B7
Trafford Pk The B98 153 F3
Trafford Rd LE10 71 F2
Trajan Hill B46 59 F1
Tram St DY10 116 E5
Tram Way B66 64 C7
Tramway Cl Bilston WV14 41 A7
Darlaston WS10 41 E7
Tranter Ave B48 139 A5
Tranter Cres WS11 2 B3
Tranter Rd B8 68 A5
Tranwell Cl WV9 10 F2
Traquain Dr DY1 51 A3
Travellers Cl WS7 7 A5
Travellers Way B37 70 D3
Treaford La B8 68 C4
Treasure Cl B77 21 E4
Treddles La B70 53 D3
Tredington Cl
Birmingham B29 103 A7
Redditch B98 159 B7
Tredington Rd CV5 111 F4
Tree Acre Gr B63 82 C4
Treedale Cl CV4 131 D8
Treeford Cl B91 106 F1
Trees Rd WS1 42 F6
Treeton Croft B33 69 A2
Treetops Dr WV12 27 E4
Trefoil B77 22 B5
Trefoil Cl B29 103 A7
Treforest Rd CV3 134 C8
Tregarron Rd B63 82 C5
Tregea Rise B43 54 C7
Tregony Rise WS14 9 D6
Tregorrick Rd CV7 96 A8
Tregullan Rd CV7 96 B8
Trehern Cl B93 128 A5
Treherne Rd CV6 113 B8
Trehernes Dr DY9 81 B1
Trejon Rd B64 82 E8
Trelawney Rd CV7 96 A7
Tremaine Gdns WV10 25 E4
Tremont Ho WV10 25 E3
Tremont St WV10 25 E3
Trenance Cl WS14 9 D7
Trenance Rd CV7 96 A8
Trenchard Cl B75 46 F5
Treneere Rd CV7 96 B8
Trensale Ave CV6 112 F4
Trent Cl Burntwood WS7 7 D6
Perton WV6 23 E4
Stourbridge DY8 81 A4
Trent Cres B47 124 E2
Trent Ct B73 46 B5
Trent Dr B36 69 F8
Trent Ho Cannock WS12 2 C5
9 Dudley DY3 50 E3
Trent Pl WS3 28 D8
Trent Rd Bulkington CV12 79 A2
Cannock WS11 1 E5
Hinckley LE10 75 A8
Nuneaton CV11 73 D5
Walsall WS3 15 A1
Trent St B5 66 F2
Trent Tower 7 B7 67 A4
Trent Valley Cotts WS13 3 F1
Trent Valley Rd WS13 9 D8
Trentham Ave WV12 27 B5
Trentham Cl Cannock WS11 2 B1
Nuneaton CV11 78 F8
Trentham Gdns CV8 148 C5
Trentham Gr B26 88 E5
Trentham Rd CV1 113 F4
Trentham Rise WV2 39 F7
Trenville Ave B11 87 B5
Tresco Cl B45 101 E1
Trescott Prim Sch B31 102 D3
Trescott Rd B31 102 D4
Tresham Rd Birmingham B44 44 F1
Kingswinford DY6 60 D8
Tresillian Rd CV7 96 B8
Trevanie Ave B32 84 C6
Trevelyan Ho 1 B37 70 C1
Treville Cl B98 154 E3
Treviscoe Cl CV7 96 A7
Trevithick Cl WS7 7 C8
Trevor Ave WS6 5 A3
Trevor Cl CV4 131 D8
Trevor Rd Hinckley LE10 71 F1
Walsall WS3 14 F4
Trevor St B7 67 C6
Trevor St W B7 67 C6
Trevorne Cl B12 86 F6
Trevose Ave CV7 96 B8
Trevose Cl WS3 13 F3
Trevose Retreat B12 86 F5
Trewint Cl CV7 96 A8
Trewman Cl B76 57 F8
Treyamon Rd WS5 43 D7
Treynham Cl WV1 26 C1
Triangle The Birmingham B18 65 F6
Coventry CV5 112 B4
Trident Bsns Pk CV11 73 D3
Trident Cl
Sutton Coldfield, Walmley B76 57 F7
Sutton Coldfield, Wylde Green B23 57 A7
Trident Ct B20 55 A3
Trident Dr Oldbury B68 64 B5
Wednesbury WS10 41 D3
Trident Ho B35 58 B3
Trigo Croft B36 68 E8
Trimpley Cl B93 127 E3
Trimpley Dr DY11 116 A7
Trimpley Gdns WV4 38 E3
Trimpley Rd B32 84 B1
Trinder Rd B67 64 D2
Trindle Rd DY2 51 D1
Tring Ct WV6 24 F4
Trinity CE Prim Sch WV10 25 F4
Trinity Churchyard CV1 165 B3
Trinity Cl 1 Birmingham B19 66 D8
Cannock WS11 4 E8
Shenstone WS14 17 F6
Solihull B92 89 B1
Stourbridge DY8 60 D2
Trinity Ct Birmingham B6 55 D1
3 Blackheath B64 62 E1
Bromsgrove B60 151 B7
1 Kidderminster DY10 116 F6
Willenhall WV13 26 E1
Wolverhampton WV3 25 A2
Trinity Field DY10 116 F6
Trinity Gr WS10 42 A3
Trinity Grange DY10 116 F7
Trinity Hill B72 46 C5
Trinity Ho B70 53 E1
Trinity La Coventry CV1 165 B3
Hinckley LE10 71 C1
Trinity RC Sch The
Royal Leamington Spa CV32 156 D2
Warwick CV34 161 C6
Trinity Rd Bilston WV14 40 F5
Birmingham B6 55 E1
Dudley DY1 51 C1
Stourbridge DY8 81 A8
Sutton Coldfield B75 32 C1
Willenhall WV12 27 D7
Wood End B78 36 B3
Trinity Rd N B70 53 D2
Trinity Rd S B70 53 D1
Trinity St Blackheath B64 62 E1
Brierley Hill DY5 61 D3
Coventry CV1 165 B3
Oldbury B69 64 A6
Royal Leamington Spa CV32 156 F1
Smethwick B67 65 A6
West Bromwich B70 53 D2
Trinity Terr 3 B11 87 A8
Trinity Vicarage Rd LE10 75 C8
Trinity Way B70 53 D2
Trinity Way Sta B70 53 D1
Trinity Wlk CV11 73 E3
Trippleton Ave B32 102 B8
Tristram Ave B31 103 B1
Triton Cl WS6 4 F1
Trittiford Rd B13 105 C6
Triumph B77 21 E3
Triumph Cl CV2 114 E3
Triumph Wlk B36 59 A1
Trojan B77 21 E3
Trojan Bsns Ctr CV34 161 E4
Tromans Ind Est DY2 62 D3
Troon B77 22 C4
Troon Cl Sutton Coldfield B75 46 D8
Walsall WS3 14 A3
Troon Ct WV6 23 D5
Troon Pl DY8 60 C3
Trossachs Rd CV5 111 F3
Trotter's La B71 53 A7
Troughton Cres CV6 113 A5
Trouse La WS10 41 F3
Troutbeck Ave CV32 156 C2
Troutbeck Dr DY5 81 B8
Troutbeck Rd CV5 111 F4
Troy Gr B14 104 D4
Troy Ind Est B96 159 A3
Troyes Cl CV3 133 E7
Truda St 2 WS1 42 D7
Trueman Cl CV34 160 E8
Truemans Heath La B47 125 C7
Truggist La CV7 130 E8
Truro Cl Blackheath B65 63 E4
Hinckley LE10 71 E4
Nuneaton CV11 73 F5
Wolverhampton WS13 3 B3
Truro Dr DY11 116 A5
Truro Pl WS12 5 C8
Truro Rd WS5 43 D7
Truro Tower 6 B16 66 A2
Truro Wlk B37 70 B2
Trustin Cres B92 107 E8
Tryan Rd CV10 72 E4
Tryon Pl WV14 40 E6
Trysull Ave B26 89 C4
Trysull Gdns WV3 38 D7
Trysull Holloway WV5 37 C3
Trysull Rd
Wolverhampton WV3 38 E7
Wombourne WV5 37 E1
Trysull Way DY2 62 C4
Tudbury Rd B31 102 E4
Tudman Cl B76 58 A7
Tudor Ave CV5 111 F4
Tudor Cl
Balsall Common CV7 130 A6
Birmingham, Highter's Heath B14 105 A1
Birmingham, King's Heath B13 104 F6
Birmingham, Sparkbrook B10 87 C8
Burntwood WS7 7 B6
Cheslyn Hay WS6 4 E3
Lichfield WS14 9 F6
Tudor Cres Tamworth B77 21 F4
Wolverhampton WV2 39 B6
Tudor Croft B37 69 F1
Tudor Ct Coventry CV7 95 E7
Essington WV11 12 F4
Sutton Coldfield B74 32 A2
Tipton DY4 52 A4
Warwick CV34 160 D5
Tudor Eaves 2 B17 85 C5
Tudor Gdns DY8 80 E5
Tudor Gr B74 45 A8
Tudor Grange Sch B91 107 A2
Tudor Hill B73 46 B6
Tudor Ho DY2 61 F6
Tudor Park Ct B74 31 F3
Tudor Pl DY3 50 E6

Tudor Rd Bilston WV14 41 B4
Birmingham B13 86 F3
Blackheath B65 63 C5
Burntwood WS7 7 C6
Cannock WS12 1 F8
Dudley DY3 50 E6
Hinckley LE10 71 C3
Nuneaton CV10 72 C6
Oldbury B68 64 C4
Sutton Coldfield B73 46 B5
Wolverhampton WV10 26 A4
Tudor Row 3 WS13 9 B7
Tudor St Birmingham B18 65 E4
Tipton DY4 52 A4
Tudor Terr Birmingham B17 85 C6
Dudley DY2 51 E1
Tudor Vale DY3 50 E6
Tudor Way WS6 4 D1
Tufnell Gr B8 68 B7
Tugford Rd B29 103 C7
Tuisi Ctr B19 164 A4
Tulip Tree Ave CV8 148 B5
Tulip Tree Ct CV8 148 B4
Tulip Wlk B37 90 C8
Tulliver Cl CV12 78 B3
Tulliver Rd CV10 73 C1
Tulliver St CV6 113 B5
Tulyar Cl B36 68 C8
Tunnel Dr B98 153 E2
Tunnel La Birmingham
B30 104 B4
Birmingham B14 104 C4
Tunnel Rd B70 53 A7
Tunnel St WV14 51 C8
Tunstall Rd DY6 61 A5
Turchill Dr B76 58 B8
Turf Cotts WV4 38 F2
Turf Pitts La B75 32 F4
Turfpits La B23 56 D6
Turfton Gr B24 57 D3
Turlands Cl CV2 115 A7
Turley St DY1 51 A6
Turls Hill Rd WV14 50 F8
Turls St DY3 50 E8
Turnberry B77 22 C5
Turnberry Dr CV11 79 C8
Turnberry Gr WV6 23 D5
Turnberry Rd
Birmingham B42 55 B8
Walsall WS3 14 A4
Turner Ave WV14 39 F2
Turner Cl Bedworth CV12 78 A4
Cannock WS11 2 D2
Warwick CV34 160 B4
Turner Dr Brierley Hill DY5 81 D7
Hinckley LE10 71 A3
Turner Gr WV6 24 A4
Turner Rd CV5 112 D3
Turner St Birmingham B11 87 A6
Dudley, Gornalwood DY3 50 D3
2 Dudley, Old Dock DY2 62 B8
Tipton DY4 51 F7
West Bromwich B70 53 A4
Turner's Gr DY3 50 C4
Turner's Hill B65 63 B6
Turner's Hill Rd DY3 50 C4
Turner's La DY5 61 D1
Turners Croft B71 54 A8
Turney Rd DY8 80 F6
Turnham Gn WV6 23 E3
Turnhouse Rd B35 58 B4
Turnley Rd B34 69 C6
Turnpike Cl B11 87 A6
Turnpike Dr B46 59 C2
Turnstone Dr WV10 12 B7
Turnstone Rd DY10 117 A1
Turpin Ct CV31 161 F6
Turton Cl WS3 14 A4
Turton Rd Tipton DY4 40 F1
West Bromwich B70 53 B2
Turton St DY10 117 A8
Turton Way CV8 148 C4
Turtons Croft WV14 40 B3
Turves Gn B31 103 A1
Turves Green Boys' Sec
Sch B31 123 A8
Turves Green Girls Sch
B31 103 A1
Turves Green Prim Sch
B31 103 A1
Turville Rd B20 55 C1
Tustin Gr B27 106 C8
Tutbury B77 35 C7
Tutbury Ave Coventry CV4 132 E6
Perton WV6 24 A3
Tutbury Cl WS11 2 C3
Tutehill B77 36 B7
Tutnall Cl B60 137 F1
Tutnall La Blackwell B60 138 A1
Tutnall B60 137 F1
Tuttle Hill CV10 72 F6
Tuttle Hill Ind Est CV10 72 E7
Tuxford Cl WV10 25 E4
Twatling Rd B45 122 A2
Tweed Tower B20 55 D2
Tweeds Well B32 102 B7
Tweedside Cl LE10 71 F3
Twickenham Ct DY8 80 C7
Twickenham Prim Sch
B44 45 C1
Twickenham Rd B44 45 C1
Twiners Rd B98 153 F1
Two Gates B63 82 C5
Two Gates Cty Prim Sch
B77 21 C1
Two Gates La B63 82 C5
Two Locks DY5 62 A4
Two Woods Ind Est DY5 61 E1
Two Woods La DY5 61 E1
Two Woods Trad Est DY5 61 F1
Twycross Gr B36 68 D7
Twycross Rd LE10 75 F6
Twycross Wlk CV34 155 D1
Twydale Ave B69 52 C2
Twyford Cl WS9 30 B5
Twyford Gr WV11 26 F7
Twyford Rd B8 68 C5
Twyning Rd
Birmingham,
Edgbaston B16 65 D3
Birmingham,
Stirchley B30 104 B7
Tybalt Cl Coventry CV3 134 C5
Royal Leamington Spa
CV34 161 D4
Tyber Dr B20 55 B3
Tyberry Cl B90 106 A1
Tyburn Rd Birmingham
B24 57 C2
Wolverhampton WV1 26 C2
Tyburn Sq B24 57 D3
Tyburn Trad Est B24 57 D2
Tye Gdns DY9 81 B1
Tyebeams B34 69 C5
Tyler Ct B24 56 F3
Tyler Gdns WV13 27 B1
Tyler Gr B43 44 A1
Tyler Rd WV13 27 B1
Tylers Gn B38 104 B1
Tylers Gr B90 126 F6
Tylney Cl Birmingham B5 86 D7
Coventry CV3 115 B2
Tyndale Cres B43 44 C3
Tyndall Wlk B32 84 A2
Tyne Cl Birmingham B37 70 C4
Brownhills WS8 6 C2
Tyne Ct B73 46 B5
Tyne Gr B25 88 D8
Tyne Pl DY5 61 F2
Tynedale Cres WV4 39 E3
Tynedale Rd B11 87 F3
Tynemouth Cl CV2 96 D5
Tynes The B60 150 E7
Tyning Cl WV9 11 A2
Tyninghame Ave WV6 24 D6
Tynings La WS9 30 A5
Tynsall Ave B97 152 F2
Tynward Cl CV3 133 B5
Tyrley Cl WV6 24 B2
Tyrol Cl DY8 80 D6
Tyseley Hill Rd B11 88 A4
Tyseley Ind Est B11 87 E5
Tyseley La B11 88 A4
Tyseley Sta B11 88 A5
Tysoe Cl Redditch B98 154 D2
Tanworth-in-A B94 143 C6
Tysoe Croft CV3 134 F8
Tysoe Dr B76 46 F4
Tysoe Rd B44 55 F7
Tythe Barn Cl B60 150 D6
Tythebarn Dr DY6 60 A7
Tythebarn La B90 125 F6
Tyzack Cl DY5 61 C2

Udall Rd WV14 40 D3
Uffculme Rd B30 104 D8
Uffculme Specl Sch B13 86 E1
Uffmoor Est B63 82 E2
Uffmoor La B62 100 D7
Ufton Cl B90 106 E3
Ufton Cres B90 106 D3
Ufton Croft CV5 112 A3
Ullapool Cl B97 158 D5
Ullenhall Rd Knowle B93 128 A6
Sutton Coldfield B76 57 F8
Ullenwood B21 65 D7
Ulleries Rd B92 89 A2
Ullrik Gn B24 56 F2
Ullswater B77 36 B7
Ullswater Ave Nuneaton
CV11 73 F6
Royal Leamington Spa
CV32 156 C2
Ullswater Cl B32 84 F2
Ullswater Gdns DY6 60 D6
Ullswater Ho 4 B69 63 D5
Ullswater Pl WS11 1 E1
Ullswater Rd Bedworth
CV12 78 A2
Coventry CV3 114 E1
Willenhall WV12 13 B1
Ullswater Rise DY5 61 E5
Ulster Cl WS11 2 A3
Ulster Dr DY6 60 E4
Ulverley Cres B92 106 F8
Ulverley Green Rd B92 88 F1
Ulverley Jun & Inf Sch
B92 89 B1
Ulverscroft Rd CV3 133 D7
Ulwine Dr B31 103 A4
Umberslade Rd
Birmingham B29 104 A8
Earlswood B94 142 C7
Tanworth-In-A B94 142 E3
Underhill Cl Coventry CV3 133 D3
Redditch B98 158 F6
Underhill Jun & Inf Sch
WV10 12 B1
Underhill La WV10 12 A2
Underhill Rd Birmingham
B8 67 F3
Tipton DY4 52 C6
Underhill St B69 64 A5
Underhill Wlk B69 64 A5
Underley Cl DY6 60 B7
Underpass The B40 90 E4
Underwood Cl
Birmingham, Edgbaston B15 85 D4
Birmingham, Stockland B23 56 C4
Redditch B97 158 A7
Underwood Rd B20 54 E5
Underwood Specl Sch
B23 57 A6
Unett Ct 9 B66 65 C5
Unett St Birmingham B19 66 C5
Smethwick B66 65 C4
Unett Wlk B19 66 C5
Unicorn Ave CV5 111 E4
Unicorn Hill B97 153 D4
Unicorn La CV5 111 F4
Union Bldgs CV1 165 B2
Union Ctr WS10 41 F2
Union Dr B73 45 F2
Union La WV5 37 D2
Union Mill St WV1 163 D3
Union Pas B2 164 C2
Union Pl CV6 95 F4
Union Rd Birmingham B6 67 B8
Oldbury B69 52 E2
Royal Leamington Spa
CV32 156 E1
Solihull, Lode Heath B91 107 C4
Solihull, Shirley B90 106 C2
West Bromwich B70 52 F2
Union Row B21 65 F7
Union St Bilston WV14 40 C5
Birmingham B2 164 C2
Blackheath B65 63 C1
Burntwood WS7 6 E5
Cannock WS11 4 E6
6 Dudley DY1 51 C1
Kidderminster DY10 116 E7
Redditch B98 153 F3
Stourbridge, Lye DY9 81 E5
Stourbridge,
Stambermill DY8 81 A4
Tipton, Princes End DY1 51 F8
Tipton, Tipton Green DY4 51 F5
Walsall WS1 28 F1
Wednesbury WS10 41 F2
West Bromwich B70 64 D8
Willenhall WV13 27 A2
Wolverhampton WV1 163 C3
Unisant Trad Est B64 62 F2
Unity Ho CV1 165 C4
Unity Pl 9 Birmingham B29 85 F2
Oldbury B69 64 A8
Univ of Aston B5 164 D4
Univ of Birmingham B15 85 F4
Univ of Birmingham The
(Halls of Residence) B15 66 C1
Univ of Central England
Birmingham, Edgbaston B15 86 A8
Birmingham,
Handsworth B42 55 D2
Univ of Warwick CV5 132 C4
Univ of Warwick Science
Pk
CV4 132 B6
Univ of Warwick
(Westwood) CV4 132 B6
Univ of Wolverhampton
WV1 163 B3
Univ of Wolverhampton
(Annexe) WV1 163 C3
Univ of Wolverhampton
Compton Park Campus
WV3 24 E2
Univ of Wolverhampton
(Dudley Campus) DY1 51 B2
Univ of Wolverhampton
Walsall Campus WS1 43 A7
University Sta B15 85 E4
Unketts Rd B67 64 E3
Unwin Cres DY8 80 E5
Upavon Cl B35 58 A4
Upfield Cotts WS7 7 E7
Upland Gr B61 137 A4
Upland Rd Birmingham B29 86 B3
Bromsgrove B61 137 B4
Uplands Coventry CV2 114 A5
Halesowen B63 82 E2
Uplands Ave Blackheath
B65 63 D3
Willenhall WV13 26 D1
Wolverhampton WV3 38 D8
Uplands Cl DY2 62 E7
Uplands Dr Sedgley DY3 50 D8
Wolverhampton WV3 38 E8
Wombourne WV5 49 A6
Uplands Gr WV13 26 C1
Uplands Inf Sch B67 64 F3
Uplands Jun & Inf Sch
WV3 38 D8
Uplands Jun Sch B67 64 F3
Uplands Rd Birmingham
B21 54 D2
Dudley DY2 62 F7
Wolverhampton WV13 26 C1
Uplands The B67 64 F4
Upleadon Cl B97 158 A6
Upper Abbey St CV11 73 B5
Upper Ashley St B62 63 C1
Upper Balsall Heath Rd
B12 86 F6
Upper Bond St LE10 71 D1
Upper Brook St WS2 28 D1
Upper Cape CV34 160 D8
Upper Chapel St B69 52 B2
Upper Church La DY4 52 A7
Upper Cl B32 84 D3
Upper Clifton Rd B73 46 B6
Upper Coneybere St
7 B12 86 F7
Upper Crossgate Rd
B98 159 C8
Upper Dean St B5 164 C1
Upper Eastern Green La
CV5 111 E5
Upper Ettingshall Rd
WV14 51 B8
Upper Field Cl B98 154 C6
Upper Forster St WS4 28 F3
Upper Gambolds La B60 151 C5
Upper Gn WV6 24 D5
Upper Gough St B1 164 B1
Upper Green La WS2 28 C4
Upper Grosvenor Rd B20 55 B2
Upper Grove St 8 CV32 156 E1
Upper Gungate B79 21 B6
Upper Hall Cl B98 154 D1
Upper Hall La 5 WS1 28 E1
Upper Hattons Cotts WV9 10 D5
Upper High St
Blackheath B64 62 D1
Wednesbury WS10 41 F3
Upper Highgate St B12 86 F7
Upper Hill St CV1 165 A3
Upper Holland Rd B72 46 C4
Upper Holly Wlk CV32 157 A1
Upper Ladyes Hills CV8 148 A6
Upper Landywood La
Cheslyn Hay WS6 4 D1
Great Wyrley WS6 13 D8
Upper Lichfield St WV13 27 A2
Upper Marshall St B1 164 B1
Upper Meadow Rd B32 84 C5
Upper Mill La B5 164 C1
Upper Navigation St WS2 28 D2
Upper Pk CV3 134 D6
Upper Portland St B6 67 A7
Upper Ride CV3 134 D5
Upper Rosemary Hill
CV8 147 F5
Upper Rushall St WS1 28 F1
Upper Russell St 1 WS10 41 F2
Upper Short St WS2 28 D1
Upper Sneyd Rd WV11 13 B2
Upper Spon St CV1 113 A3
Upper Spring La CV8 147 F7
Upper St WV6 24 D5
Upper St John St WS14 9 B6
Upper St Mary's Rd B67 64 F1
Upper Stone Cl B76 46 E4
Upper Sutton St B6 66 F7
Upper Thomas St B6 66 F7
Upper Trinity St B9 67 A1
Upper Vauxhall WV1 25 A2
Upper Villiers St WV2 39 C6
Upper Well St CV1 165 B3
Upper William St B1 66 C1
Upper York St CV1 113 B2
Upper Zoar St WV3 163 A1
Upperfield Way CV3 115 A1
Upton Cl B98 154 F3
Upton Ct B23 56 B3
Upton Gdns WV14 40 C5
Upton Gr B33 68 C1
Upton Rd B33 68 C2
Upton St DY2 62 C5
Upwey Ave B91 107 A4
Usam Trad Est WV10 11 D2
Usk Way B36 69 F8
Usmere Rd DY10 116 F8
Utrillo Cl CV5 112 C3
Uttoxeter Cl W6 25 B5
Uxbridge Ave CV3 114 C2
Uxbridge Cl DY3 50 D2
Uxbridge Ct Burntwood WS7 6 E5
Cannock WS12 2 C5
Kidderminster DY11 116 D5
Uxbridge St Birmingham
B19 66 D5
Cannock WS12 2 C4

Valbourne Rd B14 104 C4
Vale Ave Aldridge WS9 30 D3
Dudley DY3 50 D6
Vale Cl Birmingham B32 84 F3
Lichfield WS13 3 B1
Vale Ct B64 82 D7
Vale Head Dr WV6 24 A2
Vale Ind Est DY11 116 C1
Vale Rd DY2 62 E4
Vale Row DY3 50 D5
Vale St Dudley DY3 50 D5
Stourbridge DY8 81 A8
West Bromwich B71 53 E6
Wolverhampton WV2 40 A6
Vale The
Birmingham, Edgbaston B15 86 A6
Birmingham, Moseley B11 87 B2
Coventry,
Stoke Aldermoor
CV3 134 C8
Vale View Aldridge WS9 30 B4
Nuneaton CV10 72 E4
Valencia Croft B35 58 B4
Valentine Cl B74 44 F7
Valentine Ct B14 86 E1
Valentine Rd Birmingham
B14 86 F1
Oldbury B68 64 C2
Valepits Rd B33 69 C1
Valerian B74 31 F4
Valerie Gr B43 54 C8
Vales Cl B76 57 E7
Valiant Ho B36 58 B5
Valley Cl B97 158 A6
Valley Farm Rd B45 122 A6
Valley Gn WS6 4 E2
Valley Inf Sch B92 89 D3
Valley La Lapworth B94 144 E7
Lichfield WS13 9 D8
Tamworth B77 35 E7
Valley Park Nature
Reserve WV3 24 D3
Valley Park Sch WV6 24 F5
Valley Rd Birmingham B43 54 C7
Blackheath B64 82 E7
Bournheath B61 136 E7
Cannock WS12 2 D6
Coventry CV2 114 A6
Dudley DY3 50 E6
Earlswood B94 126 A1
Halesowen B62 83 F8
Radford Semele CV31 162 E4
Royal Leamington Spa
CV32 157 C3
Smethwick B67 64 F3
Solihull B92 89 D4
Stourbridge DY9 81 F6
Sutton Coldfield B74 44 F7
Walsall WS3 14 D1
Wolverhampton WV10 25 F5
Valley Side WS3 14 F2
Valley The Burntwood WS7 6 D8
Radford Semele CV31 162 E4
Valley View WS8 16 A7
Vallian Croft B36 68 F7
Vallord Ct WV1 163 B4
Van Dyke Cl CV5 112 C3
Van Gogh Cl WS11 2 D2
Vanborough Wlk DY1 51 A2
Vanbrugh Ct WV6 23 E3
Vanguard B77 35 D6
Vanguard Cl 1 B36 68 E8
Vanguard Ho B35 58 B2
Vann Cl B10 87 C8
Varden Croft B5 86 D7
Vardon Dr CV3 133 D4
Vardon Way B38 103 D1
Varley Rd B24 57 D4
Varley Vale B24 57 D4
Varlins Way B38 123 D6
Varney Ave B70 53 D2
Vaughan Cl B74 31 F6
Vaughan Rd WV13 26 E1
Vaughan Trad Est DY4 52 C3
Vaughton Dr B75 46 E6
Vaughton Ho B15 86 C7
Vaughton St B12 86 F8
Vaughton St S B12 86 E8
Vauxhall Ave 3 WV1 25 A2
Vauxhall Cl 4 CV1 113 E3
Vauxhall Cres B36 58 F1
Vauxhall Gdns DY2 62 E7
Vauxhall Gr B7 67 B3
Vauxhall Ho 2 WV1 25 A2
Vauxhall Pl B7 67 A3
Vauxhall Rd Birmingham B7 67 A3
Stourbridge DY8 81 A5
Vauxhall St Coventry CV1 113 E3
Dudley DY2 62 B8
Vauxhall Trad Est B7 67 B4
Vaynor Dr B97 158 D8
Vaynor Fst Sch The B97 158 C7
Veasey Cl CV11 73 E3
Vecqueray St CV1 113 E2
Vector Ind Pk B71 53 C6
Velsheda Rd B90 106 A2
Venetia Rd B9 67 C2
Venice Ct 2 B13 87 B2
Venning Gr B43 54 D7
Ventnor Ave
Birmingham, Lozells B19 66 D7
Birmingham,
Ward End B36 68 D7
Ventnor Cl Coventry CV2 114 E3
Oldbury B68 84 C7
Ventnor Rd B92 89 C3
Ventnor St CV10 73 D6
Ventura Park Rd B78 20 F3
Ventura Rd B78 21 A3
Venture Ct LE10 74 E8
Venture Way B7 66 F4
Vera Rd B26 88 E7
Verbena Cl Coventry CV2 96 B1
Stoke Prior B60 150 C1
Verbena Gdns B7 67 A5
Verbena Rd B31 102 F6
Vercourt B74 31 B3
Verden Ave CV34 160 B4
Verdi Ct WS13 3 C2
Verdun Cl CV31 162 B2
Verdun Cres DY2 51 F2
Vere St B5 86 D8
Verity Wlk DY8 60 E1
Vermont Gn WS11 2 A3
Vermont Gr CV31 162 D6
Verney Ave B33 89 D7
Vernier Ave DY6 61 A5
Vernolds Croft B5 86 E8
Vernon Ave Birmingham
B20 54 F4
Brownhills WS8 16 A8
Tipton DY4 51 E4
Vernon Cl 5 Coventry
CV1 113 E3
Essington WV11 12 F4
Halesowen B62 83 D8
Redditch B98 154 A5
Royal Leamington Spa
CV32 156 E3
Sutton Coldfield B74 31 E5
Willenhall WV13 26 E1

234 Ver – Wal

Vernon Ct 9 Coventry CV1 113 E4
2 Oldbury B68 84 B7
Vernon Rd Bilston WV14 40 F6
Birmingham B16 65 E1
Halesowen B62 83 C8
Oldbury B68 64 C6
Vernon St B70 52 E3
Vernon Trad Est B62 83 C8
Vernon Way WS3 13 E1
Vernons Ct CV10 72 F4
Vernons La CV10, CV11 72 F4
Verona Cl CV11 74 A1
Veronica Ave WV4 39 E5
Veronica Cl B29 103 A6
Veronica Rd DY6 61 A6
Verstone Croft B31 103 A3
Verstone Rd B90 106 C4
Verwood Cl WV13 26 D1
Vesey Cl Sutton Coldfield B74 31 F2
Water Orton B46 59 B2
Vesey Rd B73 46 B1
Vesey St B4 164 C4
Vestry Cl B64 62 F1
Vestry Ct DY8 80 E6
Viaduct Dr WV6 25 B6
Viaduct St B7 67 A3
Vibart Rd B26 88 F8
Vicar St Dudley DY2 62 C8
Kidderminster DY10 116 E6
Sedgley DY3 50 D8
Wednesbury WS10 42 A3
Vicar's Cl WS13 9 A8
Vicarage Cl
Birmingham, Great Barr B42 55 D7
Birmingham, Stirchley B30 104 C7
Brierley Hill DY5 81 C8
Bromsgrove B60 151 B8
Brownhills WS8 16 A7
Dordon B78 36 F5
Tipton DY4 51 E5
Vicarage Cres
Kidderminster DY10 116 F5
Redditch B97 153 C3
Vicarage Field CV34 161 B8
Vicarage Gdns
Halesowen B62 63 D1
Sutton Coldfield B76 57 F7
Vicarage Hill Middleton B78 48 B8
Tanworth-In-A B94 141 F3
Vicarage La Brierley Hill DY5 61 D7
Coventry CV7 95 D7
Warwick CV35 160 A1
Water Orton B46 59 B2
Vicarage Pl WS1 28 E1
Vicarage Prospect DY1 51 B1
Vicarage Rd
Birmingham, Aston B6 67 A7
Birmingham, Edgbaston B15 85 F8
Birmingham, Handsworth B18 66 A7
Birmingham, Harborne B17 85 B5
Birmingham, King's Heath B14 104 D7
Birmingham, Stechford B33 68 E1
Brierley Hill DY5 81 C7
Brownhills WS8 16 A7
Cheswick Green B94 126 C3
Dudley, West Coseley WV14 51 C7
Dudley, Woodsetton DY3 50 F5
Halesowen B62 63 C1
Oldbury B68 64 C5
Royal Leamington Spa CV32 157 B3
Smethwick B67 64 F5
Stone DY10 117 E2
Stoneleigh CV8 149 B6
Stourbridge, Lye DY9 81 F5
Stourbridge, Wollaston DY8 80 D7
Tanworth-in-A B94 143 F7
Walsall WS3 15 A2
Wednesbury WS10 42 A4
West Bromwich B71 53 D6
Wolverhampton, Blakenhall WV2 163 C1
Wolverhampton, New Cross WV11 26 B6
Wolverhampton, Penn WV4 38 E3
Vicarage Rd W DY1 51 C6
Vicarage St Nuneaton CV11 73 C4
Oldbury B68 64 B5
Vicarage Terr 1 WS2 42 C8
Vicarage View B97 153 D3
Vicarage Wlk 8 WS1 28 E1
Vicars Wlk DY9 81 E2
Viceroy Cl Birmingham B5 86 C6
Kingswinford DY6 61 A5
Victor Cl WV2 40 B6
Victor Rd Birmingham B18 65 E6
Solihull B92 89 D3
Victor St
Walsall, Caldmore WS1 42 E8
Walsall, Pelsall WS3 15 A1
Victor Tower B7 67 B6
Victoria Arc WV1 163 B3
Victoria Ave Birmingham B21 65 F8
Halesowen B62 83 F6
Smethwick B66 65 A5
Walsall, Blakenhall Heath WS3 28 D8
Walsall, Wallington Heath WS3 14 C1
Victoria Bldgs B16 65 E3
Victoria Bsns Ctr 11 CV31 162 A7
Victoria Ct
2 Birmingham B13 86 F4
Brierley Hill DY5 61 D3
Coventry CV5 112 D4
Halesowen B62 83 F6
2 Kidderminster DY10 116 F6
Smethwick B66 65 B6
Victoria Dr Fazeley B78 35 A8
Tamworth B78 21 A1
Victoria Fold WV1 163 B2
Victoria Gdns WS13 8 F7
Victoria Gr
1 Birmingham B18 65 E4
Wombourne WV5 49 A8
Victoria Ho Birmingham B16 66 B2
Darlaston WS10 41 C6
2 Walsall WS3 28 D8
Victoria Hospl WS13 9 A6
Victoria Infs Sch DY4 51 F5
Victoria Mews Coventry CV3 114 E2
Walsall WS4 29 A3
Warwick CV34 160 D7
Victoria Park Rd B66 65 B5
Victoria Pas WV1 163 B3
Victoria Pl DY11 116 B2
Victoria Rd
Birmingham, Acock's Green B27 88 C2
Birmingham, Aston B6 66 F7
Birmingham, Handsworth B21 65 E7
Birmingham, Harborne B17 85 B5
Birmingham, Stechford B33 68 D3
Birmingham, Stirchley B30 104 A7
Birmingham, Stockland Green B23 56 D3
Blackheath B64 62 F2
Brierley Hill DY5 62 A1
Bromsgrove B61 137 A3
Darlaston WS10 41 D6
Dodford B61 136 A7
Halesowen B62 83 D8
Hinckley LE10 75 F5
Nuneaton CV10 72 B8
Oldbury B68 64 D6
Royal Leamington Spa CV31 161 E8
Sedgley DY3 50 E8
Sutton Coldfield B72 46 C5
Tamworth B79 21 C5
Tipton DY4 52 A4
Walsall WS3 15 A3
Wolverhampton, New Cross WV11 26 B6
Wolverhampton, Newbolds WV10 25 F5
Wolverhampton, Penn WV3 38 E7
Wolverhampton, Tettenhall WV6 24 E5
Victoria Sh Arc B79 21 B5
Victoria Specl Sch B31 103 A5
Victoria Sq Birmingham B3 164 B2
Lichfield WS13 9 B6
Wolverhampton WV1 163 C3
Victoria St Birmingham B9 67 D1
Brierley Hill, Barrow Hill DY5 61 C7
Brierley Hill, Merry Hill DY5 61 D3
Cannock, Bridgtown WS11 4 D8
Cannock, Broomhill WS11 1 E4
Cannock, Hednesford WS12 2 C6
Coventry CV1 165 D4
Halesowen B63 83 A4
Hinckley LE10 71 D1
Kingswinford DY6 49 B1
Nuneaton CV11 73 C4
7 Redditch B98 153 E4
Royal Leamington Spa CV31 161 E8
Stourbridge DY8 81 A5
Warwick CV34 160 D7
Wednesbury WS10 41 E2
West Bromwich, Lambert's End B70 53 C3
West Bromwich, Swan Village B70 52 F5
Willenhall WV13 27 B3
Wolverhampton WV1 163 B3
Victoria Terr
1 Royal Leamington Spa CV31 161 F7
4 Walsall WS4 28 F3
Victory Ave Burntwood WS7 6 F7
Darlaston WS10 41 C5
Victory Cl WS12 2 F4
Victory La WS2 28 A4
Victory Rd CV6 95 E1
Victory Rise B71 53 D5
Victory Terr 4 B78 35 B8
Vienna Ho CV5 112 E2
View Dr DY2 62 E8
View St WS12 1 F6
Viewfield Ave WS12 1 F7
Viewfield Cres DY3 50 D6
Viewlands Dr WV6 24 A2
Vigo Cl WS9 15 F2
Vigo Pl WS9 30 A8
Vigo Rd WS9 16 A2
Vigo Terr WS9 15 F2
Viking Rise B65 63 C4
Vilia Cl LE10 75 F4
Villa Cl CV12 79 C2
Villa Cotts B19 66 B7
Villa Cres CV12 79 C1
Villa Cross B20 66 B7
Villa Park B6 55 F1
Villa Rd Birmingham B19 66 B7
Coventry CV6 113 B6
Villa St Birmingham B19 66 C6
Stourbridge DY8 81 A8
Villa Wlk B19 66 C6
Village Mews The WV6 24 C5
Village Rd B6 56 A1
Village The DY6 60 E7
Village Way WV14 40 C5
Village Wlk WS10 42 B3
Villette Gr B14 105 C4
Villiers Ave WV14 40 D7
Villiers Ho WV2 39 C7
Villiers Ind Est WV2 39 B7
Villiers Prim Sch WV14 40 D7
Villiers Rd Bromsgrove B60 150 E7
Kenilworth CV8 148 B5
Villiers Sq WV14 40 D7
Villiers St Coventry CV2 114 A3
Kidderminster DY10 117 A5
Nuneaton CV11 73 B3
Royal Leamington Spa CV32 157 A1
Walsall WS1 42 E7
Willenhall WV13 27 B2
Vimy Rd Birmingham B13 105 B8
Wednesbury WS10 42 A4
Vimy Terr WS10 42 A4
Vince St B66 65 A3
Vincent Cl B12 86 F6
Vincent Dr B15 85 E4
Vincent Par B12 86 F6
Vincent Rd B75 46 E7
Vincent St Birmingham B12 86 F5
Coventry CV1 113 B2
Royal Leamington Spa CV32 157 A1
Walsall WS1 42 F7
Vincent Wyles Ho CV2 114 E3
Vinculum Way WV13 41 B8
Vine Ave B12 87 A5
Vine Cres B71 53 D6
Vine Ct B64 82 D8
Vine La Cannock WS11 4 D5
Clent DY9 99 F3
Halesowen B63 83 B3
Warwick CV34 160 F8
Vine St Birmingham B6 67 B7
Brierley Hill DY5 61 E5
Coventry CV1 165 C3
Kidderminster DY10 117 A8
Redditch B97 153 D4
Stourbridge DY8 60 E1
Vinecote Rd CV6 95 F4
Vineries The B27 88 E4
Vineyard Rd B31 102 F5
Vinnall Gr B32 102 B8
Vintage Cl B34 69 A5
Vinyard Cl B18 65 F7
Violet Cl CV2 96 C3
Violet Croft DY4 41 B1
Violet La DY9 99 E4
Virginia Dr WV4 38 F4
Virginia Pl CV10 72 E3
Virginia Rd CV1 113 E3
Viscount Cl Birmingham B35 58 A2
Royal Leamington Spa CV31 161 F6
Viscount Ho B35 58 B2
Vista Gn B38 104 B1
Vista The DY3 39 D2
Vittle Dr CV34 160 D7
Vittoria St Birmingham B1 66 C4
Smethwick B66 65 D6
Vivian Cl B17 85 C5
Vivian Rd B17 85 C5
Vixen Cl B76 57 D7
Vodena Ct 5 CV32 156 E1
Vogue Cl CV1 165 D3
Voyager Dr WS11 4 F6
Vulcan Ho B35 58 C3
Vulcan House Ind Est B91 107 C6
Vulcan Ind Est WS2 28 C6
Vulcan Rd Bilston WV14 40 F5
Lichfield WS13 3 E1
Solihull B91 107 C7
Vulcan Road Island WV14 40 F5
Vyrnwy Gr B38 123 E8
Vyse St Birmingham, Aston B6 67 B8
Birmingham, Hockley B18 66 C4

Wackrill Dr CV32 157 C3
Wadbury Hill B97 158 D4
Waddam's Pool DY2 51 D1
Waddell Cl WV14 39 F2
Waddens Brook La WV11 26 E5
Waddington Ave B43 43 E1
Wade Ave CV3 133 B5
Wade Gr CV34 155 E2
Wade St WS13 9 B7
Wadebridge Dr CV11 73 F5
Wadesmill Lawns WV10 11 E4
Wadham Cl B65 63 C6
Wadham Ho B37 70 D3
Wadhurst Rd B17 65 B2
Wadleys Rd B91 106 F6
Waen Cl DY4 52 B8
Waggon La DY10 98 A3
Waggon St B64 62 F2
Waggon Wlk B38 123 C8
Waggoner's La B78 33 E7
Waggoners Cl B60 150 E6
Wagon La B26, B92 88 F4
Wagoners Cl B8 67 F6
Wagstaff Cl WV14 51 D8
Wainbody Ave N CV3 133 A6
Wainbody Ave S CV3 132 F5
Wainbody Wood Sch CV5 132 D2
Waine Ho WS8 16 A6
Wainrigg B77 36 B7
Wainwright Cl DY6 60 A7
Wainwright St B6 67 A7
Waite Rd WV13 40 E8
Wake Gr CV34 160 B5
Wake Green Pk B13 87 B2
Wake Green Rd Birmingham B13 87 A2
Tipton DY4 41 A1
Wakefield Cl Coventry CV3 134 F7
Sutton Coldfield B73 46 A2
Wakefield Ct B13 87 B2
Wakefield Gr B46 59 B3
Wakeford Rd B31 103 C1
Wakehurst Cl CV11 78 F8
Wakelam Gdns B43 43 D1
Wakelams Fold DY3 50 C3
Wakeley Hill WV4 38 F3
Wakelin Rd B90 126 B7
Wakeman Gr B33 89 D7
Wakes Cl WV13 27 B1
Wakes Rd WS10 42 A2
Walcot Cl B75 32 B3
Walcot Dr B43 54 F6
Walcot Gdns WV14 40 B4
Walcot Gn B93 128 A2
Walcote Cl LE10 74 F8
Waldale Cl WV11 13 C1
Walden Gdns WV4 38 E6
Walden Rd B11 88 A3
Waldeve Gr B92 107 F8
Waldon Wlk B36 69 F8
Waldron Ave DY5 61 B2
Waldron Cl WS10 41 F6
Waldrons Moor B14 104 C5
Walford Ave WV3 38 F8
Walford Dr B92 89 D3
Walford Gn B32 102 B7
Walford Gr CV34 155 F1
Walford Rd B11 87 C6
Walford St B69 52 A2
Walford Wlk 7 B97 153 E3
Walhouse CE Jun Sch WS11 1 C1
Walhouse Cl 6 WS1 28 F2
Walhouse Rd WS1 29 A2
Walhouse St WS11 4 E8
Walk La WV5 49 A6
Walk The DY3 39 D1
Walker Ave Brierley Hill DY5 81 D7
Stourbridge DY9 81 E3
Tipton B69 63 C7
Wolverhampton WV10 25 E8
Walker Dr B24 67 E8
Walker Grange DY4 51 F6
Walker Pl WS3 28 E8
Walker Rd WS3 28 E8
Walker St Dudley DY2 62 C4
Tipton DY4 52 C7
Walkers Croft WS13 3 C2
Walkers Heath Rd B38 104 B1
Walkers Orch CV8 149 B6
Walkers Rd B98 154 E6
Walkers Rise WS12 2 D8
Walkers Way CV12 77 F1
Walkmill Bsns Pk WS11 4 D5
Walkmill La WS11 4 D5
Walkmill Way WS11 4 D5
Walkwood CE Mid Sch B97 158 C8
Walkwood Cres B97 158 C6
Walkwood Rd B97 158 D6
Wall Ave B46 70 F5
Wall Croft WS9 30 B7
Wall Dr B74 31 F5
Wall End Cl WS2 28 A7
Wall Heath La WS9 16 F5
Wall Hill Rd CV5, CV7 94 B3
Wall La WS14 8 E3
Wall St WV1 26 B2
Wall Well B63 82 F3
Wall Well La B63 82 F3
Wall's Rd B60 150 C3
Wallace Cl Norton Canes WS11 5 F5
Oldbury B69 63 D6
Wallace Ct WS6 4 D1
Wallace Ho 8 Oldbury B69 63 D5
Warwick CV34 160 D7
Wallace Rd Bilston WV14 41 A2
Birmingham B29 86 B2
Brownhills WS8 15 E8
Coventry CV6 113 A8
Oldbury B69 63 D6
Wallace Rise B64 82 E7
Wallbank Rd B8 68 A6
Wallbrook Prim Sch WV14 51 E8
Wallbrook St WV14 51 D8
Waller Cl CV35 155 F7
Waller St CV32 157 A2
Wallface B71 53 B7
Wallheath Cres WS9 16 E5
Walling Croft WV14 40 B3
Wallingford Ave CV11 73 F7
Wallington Cl WS3 14 B2
Wallington Heath WS3 14 B2
Wallis Ct 1 B13 87 B2
Wallows Ind Est The DY5 61 D5
Wallows La WS1, WS2 42 C6
Wallows Pl DY5 61 C5
Wallows Rd DY5 61 D5
Wallows Wood DY3 50 A4
Wallsgrove Cl CV32 157 B3
Wallwin Ct CV34 160 D6
Walmead Croft B17 84 F7
Walmer Gr B23 56 B5
Walmer Mdw WS9 30 B7
Walmer Way B37 70 C3
Walmers The WS9 30 B7
Walmers Wlk The B31 102 D1
Walmley Ash La B76 58 C6
Walmley Ash Rd B76 58 A7
Walmley Cl Halesowen B63 82 B7
Sutton Coldfield B76 57 F8
Walmley Jun & Inf Schs B76 58 A7
Walmley Rd B76 46 F2
Walney Cl LE10 71 B1
Walnut Ave WV8 10 B3
Walnut Cl Birmingham B37 70 B1
Cannock WS11 1 F3
Nuneaton, Camp Hill CV10 72 E6
Nuneaton, Hartshill CV10 72 A8
Stourbridge DY9 81 B1
Walnut Dr Cannock WS11 1 F3
Royal Leamington Spa CV32 157 B3
5 Smethwick B66 65 B5
Wolverhampton WV3 24 D1
Walnut Gr WS14 9 F7
Walnut La Finstall B60 151 D8
Wednesbury WS10 42 A2
Walnut Rd WS5 43 A4
Walnut St CV2 96 B2
Walnut Tree Cl CV8 148 A3
Walnut Way B31 122 F8
Walpole St WV6 25 A3
Walpole Wlk B70 53 D1
Walsal End La B92 108 F3
Walsall Coll of Arts & Tech Walsall WS1 28 E1
Walsall, The Chuckery WS1 29 A1
Walsall Coll of Arts & Tech (Birchills Campus) WS2 28 C3
Walsall Coll of Arts & Tech Shelley Ctr Campus WS2 28 C1
Walsall New Firms Ctr WS1 42 D8
Walsall Rd Aldridge WS9 29 E4
Birmingham B42 55 B6
Cannock WS11 4 E7
Darlaston WS10 41 E6
Great Wyrley WS6, WS11 5 A2
Lichfield WS13 8 C5
Norton Canes WS11 5 F4
Stonnall WS14 16 E8
Sutton Coldfield B74 31 D4
Walsall, Pelsall WS3 15 A1
Walsall, The Delves WS5 42 F4
Walsall Wood WS9 15 E2
Wednesbury WS10, B71, WS5 42 F2
West Bromwich B71 53 E8
Willenhall WV13 27 C2
Walsall St Bilston WV14 40 D6
Coventry CV4 132 B7
Darlaston WS10 41 D7
West Bromwich B70 53 D3
Willenhall WV13 27 B1
Wolverhampton WV1 163 D2
Walsall Sta WS2 28 E2
Walsall Wood JMI Sch WS9 16 A4
Walsall Wood Rd WS9 30 B7
Walsgrave CE Prim Sch CV3 115 A6
Walsgrave Cl B92 107 D6
Walsgrave Dr B92 107 D6
Walsgrave Gdns 5 CV2 115 A7
Walsgrave Rd CV2 114 B3
Walsh Dr B76 46 F4
Walsh Gr B23 56 D8
Walsh La CV7 92 E2
Walsham Croft B34 69 C5
Walsingham Dr CV10 78 A7
Walsingham St WS1 29 A1
Walstead Cl WS5 43 C5
Walstead Rd WS5 43 B5
Walstead Rd W WS5 42 E5
Waltdene Cl B43 43 E3
Walter Burden Ho B66 65 C3
Walter Cobb Dr B73 46 A1
Walter Nash Rd E DY11 116 B2
Walter Nash Rd W DY11 116 A1
Walter Rd Bilston WV14 40 F3
Smethwick B67 64 E6
Walter Scott Rd CV12 78 C1
Walter St Birmingham B7 67 B6
Walsall WS3 15 A1
West Bromwich B70 53 E2
Walters Cl B31 122 F6
Walters Rd B68 84 B6
Walters Row DY1 51 A1
Waltham Cl B61 136 E1
Waltham Cres CV10 72 B5
Waltham Gr B44 45 B2
Waltham Ho Birmingham B38 104 B1
West Bromwich B70 53 D3
Walthamstow Ct DY5 61 D1
Walton Ave B65 83 B8

Walton Cl Blackheath B65 63 A4
Coventry CV3 134 E7
Halesowen B63 82 F2
Kidderminster DY11 116 B2
Nuneaton CV11 79 A7
Walton Cres WV4 39 E5
Walton Croft B91 107 B1
Walton Ct B63 82 F3
Walton Dr DY9 81 C5
Walton Gr B30 104 B2
Walton Heath WS3 13 F3
Walton Pool La DY9 99 F2
Walton Rd Aldridge WS9 16 A1
Bromsgrove B61 137 B4
Oldbury B68 64 C2
Stourbridge DY8 81 A6
Wednesbury WS10 42 C2
Wolverhampton WV4 39 F5
Walton Rise DY9 100 A3
Walton St DY4 51 F5
Wanderer Wlk B36 57 E1
Wanderers Ave WV2 39 C6
Wandle Gr B11 88 A3
Wandsbeck B77 35 E8
Wandsworth Rd B44 44 F3
Wanley Rd CV3 133 D6
Wannerton Rd DY10 98 B1
Wansbeck Gr B38 123 E8
Wansbeck Wlk DY3 50 F6
Wansfell Cl CV4 132 A7
Wanstead Gr B44 45 A1
Wantage Rd B46 59 E1
Wappenbury Cl CV2 96 C2
Wappenbury Rd CV2 96 D2
War La B17 85 B5
Warbage La
Belbroughton DY9 119 F1
Dodford B61 136 A7
Warbank Cl B48 139 A6
Warbler Pl DY10 117 A2
Ward Cl B8 68 A5
Ward End Cl B8 67 F6
Ward End Hall Gr B8 68 A6
Ward End Jun & Inf Sch
B8 68 B6
Ward End Park Rd B8 67 F5
Ward Gr Warwick CV34 161 C7
Wolverhampton WV4 39 F3
Ward Rd WV4 39 D5
Ward St Bilston WV2 40 B6
Birmingham B19 164 C5
Cannock WS12 1 F6
Dudley WV14 51 B8
Walsall WS1 28 F2
Willenhall WV13 27 B3
Wolverhampton WV1 163 D3
Warden Ave B73 56 F8
Warden Rd Coventry CV6 113 B6
Sutton Coldfield B73 56 F8
Wardend Rd B8 68 A6
Wardens Ave The CV5 112 B6
Wardens The CV8 148 C5
Wardle Cl B75 32 A4
Wardle Pl WS11 1 E5
Wardle St B79 21 A5
Wardles La WS6 4 F2
Wardlow Cl WV4 39 B6
Wardlow Rd B7 67 B4
Wardour Dr B37 70 C2
Wardour Gr B44 56 C8
Wareham Cl WS3 28 F5
Wareham Gn CV2 115 A5
Wareham Ho B28 105 E3
Wareham Rd B45 102 B2
Wareing Dr B23 56 D8
Warewell Cl 8 WS1 28 F2
Warewell St 9 WS1 28 F2
Waring Cl DY4 51 E8
Waring Rd DY4 52 A8
Warings Green Rd B94 126 D1
Warley Croft B68 84 E8
Warley Ct B68 64 B2
Warley Hall Rd B68 64 D1
Warley High Sch B68 64 A2
Warley Ho B67 64 F2
Warley Inf Sch B68 64 C2
Warley Rd B68 64 C5
Warmington Cl CV3 134 E8
Warmington Dr B73 46 B4
Warmington Gr CV34 160 B8
Warmington Rd
Birmingham B26 89 C5
Hollywood B47 125 A6
Warmley Cl Solihull B91 107 D5
Wolverhampton W6 25 B5
Warmwell Cl CV2 114 F4
Warneford Mews
13 CV31 162 A7
Warner Cl CV34 155 D1
Warner Dr DY5 61 D1
Warner Pl 1 WS3 28 F6
Warner Rd Walsall WS3 29 A6
Wednesbury WS10 42 C2
Warner Row CV6 113 F7
Warner St 2 B12 87 A8
Warners Wlk B10 87 C8
Warnford Wlk WV4 38 C6
Warple Rd B32 84 C5
Warren Ave Birmingham
B13 86 F2
Wolverhampton WV10 25 F5
Warren Cl Lichfield WS14 9 E7
Royal Leamington Spa
CV32 157 A3
Tipton DY4 52 A7
Warren Dr Blackheath B65 62 F5
Dorridge B93 128 A3
Sedgley DY3 39 C1
Warren Farm Jun & Inf
Schs B44 56 A8
Warren Farm Rd B44 56 A8
Warren Field CV8 135 A1
Warren Gdns DY6 60 C6
Warren Gn CV4 131 F7
Warren Hill Rd B44 56 A7
Warren La B45 122 B3
Warren Pl WS8 16 A7
Warren Rd
Birmingham, Perry B44 56 A7
Birmingham, Stirchley B30 104 A6
Birmingham,
Washwood Heath B8 67 E6
Burntwood WS7 7 A5
Warrens Croft WS5 43 D5
Warrens End 1 B38 103 F1
Warrens Hall Rd DY2 62 E7
Warrington Cl B76 47 A1
Warrington Dr B23 56 D7
Warsash Cl WV1 40 B8
Warstock La B14 105 A4
Warstock Rd B14 105 A3
Warston Ave B32 84 D3
Warstone Dr B71 53 E4
Warstone La B18 66 B4
Warstone Mews 2 B18 66 C4
Warstone Par E B18 66 B4
Warstone Rd WV11, WV10 13 C7
Warstone Terr B21 65 E8
Warstone Tower B36 68 D8
Warstones Cres WV4 38 D5
Warstones Dr WV4 38 C6
Warstones Gdns WV4 38 C6
Warstones Prim Sch WV3 38 E6
Warstones Rd WV4 38 D5
Wartell Bank DY6 60 D7
Wartell Bank Ind Est DY6 60 D7
Warton Cl CV8 148 C4
Warwards La B29 104 A8
Warwell La B26 88 D6
Warwick Ave
Bromsgrove B60 151 A8
Coventry CV5 133 A8
Perton WV6 23 F3
Wednesbury WS10 42 C4
Willenhall WV13 27 D2
Warwick By-Pass
Warwick,
Hampton Magna CV35 160 A5
Warwick, Heathcote CV34 161 A1
Warwick Castle CV34 160 E6
Warwick Cl Cannock WS11 4 F8
Oldbury B68 64 B2
Studley B80 159 D3
West Bromwich B70 52 E7
Warwick Crest B15 86 B7
Warwick Ct
1 Birmingham,
Acock's Green B27 88 C2
5 Birmingham,
Chelmsley Wood B37 70 D2
Birmingham, Moseley B13 87 A2
Coventry CV3 165 B1
1 Dudley DY3 50 D3
Solihull B91 107 C3
Solihull, Lode Heath B91 107 B4
Wolverhampton WV4 39 F4
Warwick Gdns Hinckley
LE10 71 E3
Nuneaton CV10 72 E4
Tipton B69 52 C2
Warwick Gn CV12 79 C1
Warwick Gr B92 88 E1
Warwick Grange B91 106 F7
Warwick Hall Gdns B60 151 A1
Warwick Highway B98 154C2
Warwick Ho
6 Birmingham B24 56 F4
Sutton Coldfield B73 46 A3
Warwick Hospl CV34 160 E8
Warwick La CV1 165 B2
Warwick Mus CV34 160 F7
Warwick New Rd CV32 161 C8
Warwick Park Ct B92 106 F8
Warwick Pas B2 164 C2
Warwick Pl CV32 156 E1
Warwick Rd Birmingham
B42 55 E2
Birmingham, Sparkhill B11 87 D4
Chadwick End B93 145 A7
Coventry CV3 165 B1
Dudley DY2 62 E3
Kenilworth CV8 148 A1
Knowle B93 128 D3
Leek Wootton CV35 155 F7
Oldbury B68 84 D7
Solihull B27, B91, B92 106 F7
Stourbridge DY8 60 D1
Tamworth B77 21 E4
Wolston CV8 135 F3
Warwick Road Trad Est
B11 87 D4
Warwick Row CV1 165 B2
Warwick Sch CV34 161 A6
Warwick St Bilston WV14 40 E5
Birmingham B12 67 A1
Coventry CV5 112 F1
Royal Leamington Spa
CV32 156 F1
Walsall WS4 28 F3
Wolverhampton WV1 163 D2
Warwick St Mary's RC
Prim Sch CV34 160 E8
Warwick Sta CV34 160 F7
Warwick Tech Pk CV34 161 B5
Warwick Terr CV32 156 E1
Warwick Way WS9 16 A1
Warwickshire Coll CV32 161 D8
Warwickshire Coll of Ag
CV11 73 E6
Warwickshire Mus CV34 160 E6
Warwickshire Nuffield
Hospl The CV32 156 E5
Wasdale Cl CV32 156 C2
Wasdale Dr DY6 60 D6
Wasdale Rd Birmingham
B31 102 F4
Clayhanger WS8 15 D6
Waseley Hills Ctry Pk
B45 121 C8
Waseley Hills High Sch
B45 121 D7
Waseley Rd B45 121 E8
Wash La B25 88 C8
Washbourne Rd CV31 162 A2
Washbrook La Allesley CV5 94 A1
Norton Canes WS11 5 D5
Washbrook Rd B8 68 A6
Washford Dr B98 159 D7
Washford Gr B25 88 B8
Washford Ind Est B98 159 E8
Washford La B98 159 D8
Washington Ct WV3 24 D1
Washington Ctr DY2 62 D4
Washington Dr B20 55 B3
Washington St
Birmingham B1 164 A1
Dudley DY2 62 D3
Kidderminster DY11 116 C5
Washwood Heath Rd B8 67 E6
Washwood Heath Sch B8 68 C5
Wasperton Cl
Birmingham B36 69 B8
6 Coventry CV3 134 F8
Wassell Ct B63 82 E2
Wassell Grove Rd
Hagley DY9 99 F8
Halesowen B63 82 A2
Wassell Rd Bilston WV14 40 D7
Halesowen B63 82 E2
Stourbridge DY9 81 E2
Wast Hill Gr B38 123 F7
Waste La
Balsall Common CV7 130 F6
Coventry CV6 94 F1
Wasthill La B38, B48 123 D5
Wastwater Ct WV6 23 F4
Watch Cl CV1 165 A3
Watchbury Cl B36 58 C1
Watchmaker Ct CV1 165 A2
Watchman Ave DY5 81 F7
Watcombe Rd CV2 114 E8
Water Dale WV3 24 E2
Water La B71 53 F7
Water Mill Cl B29 85 D3
Water Mill Prim Sch B29 85 D3
Water Orton La B76 58 E4
Water Orton Prim Sch
B46 59 B2
Water Orton Rd B36 58 E1
Water Orton Sta B46 59 A3
Water Rd DY3 50 C2
Water Side Way WV9 11 B3
Water St Birmingham B3 164 B3
Burntwood WS7 6 E8
Kingswinford DY6 60 D7
West Bromwich B70 53 D2
Wolverhampton WV10 163 D4
Water Tower La CV8 147 F6
Watercall Ave CV3 133 C6
Waterdale B90 126 D5
Waterfall Cl Meriden CV7 92 C1
Smethwick B66 64 E7
Waterfall La B64 63 A1
Waterfall Lane Ind Est
B64 63 A1
Waterfall Rd DY5 81 D7
Waterfall Way LE9 71 F5
Waterfield Cl DY4 51 D5
Waterfield Gdns CV31 162 C7
Waterfield Way LE10 75 C5
Waterford Rd DY6 60 D7
Waterfront Bsns Pk DY5 61 E4
Waterfront E DY5 61 E4
Waterfront W DY5 61 E4
Waterfront Way DY5 61 E4
Waterglade La WV13 27 A1
Waterhaynes Cl B45 122 A6
Waterhead Cl WV10 12 A2
Waterhead Dr WV10 12 B2
Waterlinks Bvd B6 67 A7
Waterloo Ave B37 70 B4
Waterloo Bvd WS12 2 E4
Waterloo Ct CV34 161 A8
Waterloo Ind Est B37 70 B5
Waterloo Pl 5 CV32 156 F1
Waterloo Rd
Birmingham,
King's Heath B14 104 E8
Birmingham,
South Yardley B25 88 C6
Hinckley LE10 75 D8
Smethwick B66 65 A3
Wolverhampton WV1 163 B4
Waterloo St Birmingham
B2 164 B2
8 Coventry CV1 113 E4
Dudley DY2 62 B8
Kidderminster DY10 116 E6
Royal Leamington Spa CV31 162 B7
Tipton DY4 51 F5
Waterloo St E DY4 51 F5
Waterloo Terr WV1 163 A4
Waterman Rd CV6 113 F6
Watermeadow Dr WS4 15 D1
Watermere WS4 29 D8
Watermill Cl WV10 11 D3
Watermint Cl WS12 2 E4
Waters Dr B74 31 D3
Waters Edge The B1 66 C2
Waters View WS3 15 B5
Watersbridge Gdns CV10 73 C1
Waterside
Birmingham, Egdbaston B15 86 C8
Birmingham, Hamstead B43 54 E7
Royal Leamington Spa
CV31 161 D7
Waterside Cl B24 58 A5
Waterside Ct
Royal Leamington Spa
CV31 162 B6
Tamworth B77 21 F5
Waterside Est DY2 62 C3
Waterside Ind Est
Blackheath B65 62 F4
Wolverhampton WV2 40 A6
Waterside View
Birmingham B18 66 A5
Brierley Hill DY5 81 B8
Waterside Way WS8 6 D2
Watersmead Cl WS12 2 F4
Watersmeet Gr CV2 114 B6
Watersmeet Ho B78 35 B8
Watersmeet Rd CV2 114 B6
Waterson Croft B37 70 D3
Waterward Cl B17 85 C5
Waterways Dr B69 63 E8
Waterways Gdns DY8 60 E1
Waterworks Dr B31 102 D4
Waterworks Rd B16 65 F1
Waterworks St B6 67 B8
Watery La Alvechurch B48 124 C1
Belbroughton DY9 118 F7
Birmingham B62 84 A3
Cheswick Green B90 126 D4
Codsall WV8 10 A5
Corley CV7 93 D5
Coventry CV6 95 A4
Hopwood B48 123 F2
Keresley CV7 94 F4
Knowle B93 128 E4
Lichfield WS13 3 C4
Portway B48 140 D7
Redditch B98 154 B2
Smethwick B67 65 A5
Stourbridge DY8 60 E2
Tipton DY4 51 F5
Walsall WS1 42 E8
Warwick CV35 160 A1
Willenhall WV13 26 E3
Watery Lane Ind Est
WV13 26 E3
Watery Lane Middleway
B9 67 B2
Watford Gap WS14 32 A7
Watford Gap Rd WS14 32 A7
Watford Rd B30 103 F5
Wathan Ave WV14 39 F1
Wathen Rd
Royal Leamington Spa
CV32 157 A2
Warwick CV34 160 E8
Watkins Gdns B31 103 C4
Watkins Rd WV12 27 C5
Watland Gn B34 69 B5
Watling Cl LE10 75 C4
Watling Ct CV11 73 F3
Watling Dr LE10 75 C4
Watling Rd CV8 148 B6
Watling St Brownhills WS8 7 B1
Dordon B78 36 D6
Hinckley CV11, LE10 74 C8
Mile Oak B78 20 D1
Tamworth B77 35 D8
Watling Street JMI Sch
WS8 6 E1
Watney Gr B44 56 C8
Watson Cl
Sutton Coldfield B72 46 C2
3 Warwick CV34 155 E1
Watson Rd
Birmingham, Nechells B24 67 D8
Birmingham, Saltley B8 67 F5
Coventry CV5 112 D2
Wednesbury WS10 41 A5
Wolverhampton,
Lanesfield WV14 39 F2
Wolverhampton,
Pendeford WV10 11 B2
Watson's Green Fields
DY2 62 F8
Watson's Green Rd DY2 51 E1
Watsons Cl DY2 62 E8
Watt Rd Birmingham B23 56 E4
Tipton DY4 52 B8
Watt St Birmingham B21 65 D7
Smethwick B66 65 B6
Watt's Rd B10 87 D8
Wattis Rd B67 65 A2
Wattisham Sq B35 58 A4
Wattle Rd B70 53 A4
Watton Cl WV14 40 A1
Watton Ct B6 66 E8
Watton Gn B35 58 A3
Watton La B46 59 D2
Watton St B70 53 D2
Watts Cl DY4 51 D5
Watts Rd B80 159 E2
Wattville Ave B21 65 C8
Wattville Inf Sch B21 65 C8
Wattville Jun Sch B21 65 B8
Wattville Rd B21 65 C8
Watwood Rd B28 105 F3
Waugh Cl B37 70 B2
Waveley Rd CV1 113 A3
Wavell Rd Birmingham B8 67 E5
Brierley Hill DY5 81 F7
Walsall WS2 27 E2
Wavendon Cl CV2 96 F1
Waveney B77 35 E8
Waveney Ave WV6 23 E4
Waveney Cl LE10 75 A8
Waveney Croft B36 69 F8
Waveney Gr WS11 1 B1
Wavenham Cl B74 31 E5
Waverhill Rd B21 65 F7
Waverley Ave
Birmingham B43 44 B4
Nuneaton CV11 73 F1
Waverley Cl DY10 117 A8
Waverley Cres Romsley
B62 100 F4
Wolverhampton,
Lanesfield WV4 39 F3
Wolverhampton, Penn WV2 39 B6
Waverley Gdns WV5 49 B7
Waverley Gr B91 106 F3
Waverley Rd Birmingham
B10 87 D7
Darlaston WS10 41 D6
Kenilworth CV8 148 A3
Royal Leamington Spa
CV31 162 B6
Walsall WS3 13 F2
Waverley Sch B10 88 A8
Waverley Sq CV11 73 F1
Waverley St DY2 62 A8
Waverley Wlk WS14 9 B6
Waverton Mews 18 CV31 162 C6
Wavytree Cl CV34 160 D7
Waxland Rd B63 83 B2
Wayfield Cl B90 106 C3
Wayfield Rd B90 106 C3
Wayford Dr B72 57 D7
Wayford Glade WV13 40 F8
Wayford Gr B8 68 B4
Waynecroft Rd B43 43 E2
Wayside Birmingham B37 90 A8
Wolverhampton WV8 10 F2
Wayside Dr B74 31 C3
Wayside Gdns WV12 27 E5
Wayside Wlk WS2 28 A3
Waystone La DY9 119 D4
Wealden Hatch WV10 11 E4
Wealdstone Dr DY3 50 D2
Weale Gr CV34 155 F2
Weaman St B4 164 C3
Weather Oaks B17 85 B6
Weatheroak Cl B97 153 A1
Weatheroak Hill B48 124 B1
Weatheroak Rd B11 87 C5
Weatheroaks Brownhills
WS9 16 B4
Halesowen B62 84 A7
Weaver Ave Birmingham
B26 89 B6
Sutton Coldfield B76 47 A1
Weaver Cl DY5 61 B6
Weaver Gr WV13 27 D2
Weavers Hill B97 158 D4
Weavers Rise DY2 62 D3
Weavers Wlk CV6 114 B8
Weaving Gdns 2 WS11 1 E1
Webb Ave WV6 23 E5
Webb La B28 105 E6
Webb Rd DY4 52 C7
Webb St Dudley WV14 40 C1
Nuneaton CV10 72 D3
Willenhall WV13 26 F2
Webbcroft Rd B33 68 F4
Webheath Fst Sch B97 153 A2
Webley Rise WV10 11 F4
Webner Ind Est WV2 40 A6
Webster Ave CV8 148 B5
Webster Cl Birmingham B11 87 B6
Sutton Coldfield B72 57 B7
Webster Rd Walsall WS2 28 E5
Willenhall WV13 27 A3
Webster Steet CV6 113 E7
Webster Way B76 58 B8
Webster Wlk WS11 2 A4
Weddell Wynd WV14 40 F1
Weddington Fst Sch CV10 73 D7
Weddington Rd CV10 73 C7
Weddington Terr CV10 73 D5
Wedge St 10 WS1 28 F2
Wedge-Woods CV5 132 F8
Wedgewood Cl WS7 7 C7
Wedgewood Ct WS4 15 C1
Wedgewood Dr B20 55 B2
Wedgewood Ho B37 70 B4
Wedgewood Pl B70 52 F7
Wedgewood Rd
Birmingham B32 84 D5
West Bromwich B70 52 F7
Wedgnock Gn CV34 160 D8
Wedgnock Ind Est CV34 155 C1
Wedgnock La CV34 155 C1
Wedgwood Cl WV1 26 A1
Wednesbury, Great
Western Street Sta
WS10 41 E2
Wednesbury Oak Prim Sch
DY4 41 A1
Wednesbury Oak Rd DY4 41 A1
Wednesbury Parkway Sta
WS10 41 D2
Wednesbury Rd WS1 42 D7

Wednesbury Trad Est
WS10 .... 41 E4
Wednesfield High Sch
WV11 .... 26 E5
Wednesfield Rd
Willenhall WV13 .... 27 A3
Wolverhampton
WV1,WV10 .... 163 D4
Wednesfield Village Prim
Sch
WV11 .... 26 D5
Wednesfield Way WV11 .. 26 D4
Wedon Cl CV4 .... 131 E7
Weeford Dr B20 .... 54 F4
Weeford Rd B75 .... 32 F3
Weethley Ho B97 .... 153 A4
Weights La B97 .... 153 C7
Weirbrook Cl B29 .... 103 C7
Welbeck Ave Hinckley
LE10 .... 75 D4
Wolverhampton WV10 ...... 25 D7
Welbeck Dr
Kidderminster DY11 ...... 116 B5
Walsall WS4 .... 29 D7
Welbeck Gr B23 .... 56 B5
Welbury Gdns WV6 .... 24 F5
Welby Rd B28 .... 87 F1
Welches Cl B31 .... 103 B5
Welcombe Dr B76 .... 57 F7
Welcombe Gr B91 .... 106 F4
Welcome Dr B61 .... 121 A1
Welford Ave B26 .... 88 F8
Welford Cl B98 .... 158 F5
Welford Gr B74 .... 31 F3
Welford Inf & Jun Sch
B20 .... 66 A8
Welford Pl CV6 .... 113 D7
Welford Rd Birmingham
B20 .... 66 A8
Solihull B90 .... 106 C4
Sutton Coldfield B73 ...... 45 E1
Tamworth B77 .... 35 C5
Welgarth Ave CV6 .... 112 F6
Welham Croft B90 .... 127 A6
Well Cl Birmingham B36 ... 68 E8
Redditch B97 .... 158 E5
Well La Birmingham B5 .. 164 D2
Great Wyrley WS6 .... 5 A1
Hinckley LE10 .... 71 D1
Tanworth-In-A B94 .... 142 A1
Walsall WS3 .... 28 D7
Walsall WS3 .... 28 E8
Wolverhampton WV11 ..... 26 C4
Well Mdw B45 .... 122 A6
Well Pl WS3 .... 28 E8
Well St
Birmingham, Hockley B19 ... 66 C5
Birmingham,
Newtown B19 .... 66 D6
Coventry CV1 .... 165 B3
Darlaston WS10 .... 41 E6
Welland Cl B46 .... 59 B2
Welland Dr DY8 .... 81 A8
Welland Gr Birmingham
B24 .... 57 D3
Willenhall WV13 .... 27 C2
Welland Rd Coventry CV1 ... 113 F1
Halesowen B63 .... 83 A2
Welland Way B76 .... 58 A7
Wellcroft Rd B34 .... 69 A7
Wellcroft St WS10 .... 41 F3
Wellesbourne B79 .... 21 C8
Wellesbourne Cl
Redditch B98 .... 153 E4
Wolverhampton WV3 ...... 38 B8
Wellesbourne Dr WV14 .. 51 B7
Wellesbourne Rd
Birmingham B20 .... 55 B1
Coventry CV5 .... 112 A3
Wellesbourne Tower
B5 .... 86 E8
Wellesley Dr DY4 .... 51 F5
Wellesley Gdns B13 ...... 87 D1
Wellesley Rd B68 .... 64 B6
Wellfield Cl WS11 .... 4 B7
Wellfield Gdns DY2 .... 62 E6
Wellfield Rd Aldridge WS9 ... 30 B8
Birmingham B28 .... 106 B6
Wellhead La B42 .... 55 E3
Wellhead Way B42 .... 55 F2
Wellington Ave WV3 ...... 38 F7
Wellington Dr DY6 .... 60 E4
Wellington Cres B20 ...... 55 B2
Wellington Ct
Birmingham B20 .... 55 C2
Blackheath B64 .... 62 F2
Kidderminster DY11 ..... 116 C5
Wellington Dr WS11 .... 4 B8
Wellington Gdns ◼1 CV1 ... 113 B2
Wellington Gr B91 .... 106 F6
Wellington Ho B32 .... 84 F4
Wellington Ind Est WV14 .. 51 C7
Wellington Pl WV13 .... 26 F3
Wellington Rd Bilston
WV14 .... 40 D6
Birmingham B20 .... 55 C2
Birmingham,
Edgbaston B15 .... 86 C7
Bromsgrove B60 .... 151 A8
Dudley DY1 .... 51 B1
Royal Leamington Spa
CV32 .... 157 C2
Smethwick B67 .... 65 A3
Tipton DY4 .... 52 A4
Walsall WS5 .... 43 C6

Wellington St
Birmingham B18 .... 65 E5
Blackheath B64 .... 62 F2
Coventry CV1 .... 165 D4
Oldbury B69 .... 64 B6
◼6 Redditch B98 .... 153 E4
Walsall WS2 .... 42 B7
West Bromwich B71 .... 53 C4
Wellington St S B70 ...... 53 C4
Wellington Terr
◼3 B19 .... 66 B7
Wellington Tower
◼4 B31 .... 103 A1
Wellman Croft B29 .... 85 D1
Wellman's Rd WV13 ...... 27 C1
Wellmead Wlk B45 .... 121 F8
Wellmeadow Gr B92 ..... 109 A7
Wells Ave WS10 .... 41 B6
Wells Cl Cannock WS11 .... 1 E6
Kidderminster DY11 ..... 116 A6
Perton WV6 .... 23 D4
Tipton DY4 .... 41 A1
West Bromwich B71 .... 53 D8
Wells Ct Coventry CV3 .. 133 F7
Dudley DY2 .... 62 C5
Wells Green Rd B92 ...... 89 A4
Wells Rd Bilston WV14 ... 40 E3
Blackheath B65 .... 63 E4
Brierley Hill DY5 .... 61 B3
Solihull B92 .... 89 C4
Wolverhampton WV4 ...... 38 F5
Wells Tower B16 .... 66 A2
Wells Wlk B37 .... 70 A1
Wellsford Ave B92 .... 89 B4
Welney Gdns WV9 .... 11 A3
Welsby Ave B43 .... 54 E7
Welsh Cl CV34 .... 155 E2
Welsh House Farm Prim
Sch B32 .... 84 F4
Welsh House Farm Rd
B32 .... 84 F4
Welsh House Farm Sch
B32 .... 84 E5
Welsh Rd Coventry CV2 .. 114 B4
Cubbington CV33 .... 157 F2
Welshmans Hill B73 ...... 45 C3
Welton Cl B76 .... 47 A2
Welton Rd CV34 .... 155 D1
Welwyn Rd LE10 .... 71 F1
Welwyndale Rd B72 ...... 57 C6
Wem Gdns WV11 .... 26 D6
Wembley Dr B25 .... 88 C8
Wembrook Cl CV11 .... 73 D2
Wembrook Ho CV11 ...... 73 E2
Wendell Crest WV10 ..... 11 F4
Wendiburgh St CV4 ..... 132 B7
Wendover Dr LE10 .... 71 E4
Wendover Rd
Birmingham B23 .... 56 C7
Blackheath B65 .... 63 A5
Wolverhampton WV4 ...... 39 F2
Wendover Rise CV5 ..... 112 C4
Wendron Cl B60 .... 137 B2
Wendron Gr B14 .... 104 D4
Wenlock Ave WV3 .... 38 E8
Wenlock Cl Halesowen
B63 .... 82 D2
Sedgley DY3 .... 50 C7
Wenlock Dr B61 .... 137 A5
Wenlock Gdns WS3 .... 28 E5
Wenlock Rd Birmingham
B20 .... 55 F1
◼3 Stourbridge DY8 .... 81 B6
Wenlock Way CV10 .... 72 B3
Wenman St B12 .... 86 F6
Wensley Croft B90 .... 106 B6
Wensley Rd B26 .... 88 F6
Wensleydale Rd B42 ..... 55 B6
Wensum Cl LE10 .... 75 B8
Wentbridge Rd WV1 ...... 26 C1
Wentworth Ave B36 ...... 69 B8
Wentworth Cl Burntwood
WS7 .... 7 C7
Hinckley LE10 .... 71 E3
Wentworth Ct
Birmingham B24 .... 56 F2
Sutton Coldfield B75 ...... 32 B1
Wentworth Dr
Blackwell B60 .... 138 A5
Lichfield WS14 .... 9 D5
Nuneaton CV11 .... 74 A1
Tipton B69 .... 63 A7
Wentworth Gate B17 ..... 85 B6
Wentworth Gr WV6 .... 23 D5
Wentworth Park Ave
B17 .... 85 B6
Wentworth Rd
Birmingham B17 .... 85 B6
Royal Leamington Spa
CV31 .... 162 D6
Solihull B92 .... 88 F3
Stourbridge DY8 .... 80 E7
Sutton Coldfield B74 ...... 46 A8
Walsall WS3 .... 13 F3
Wolverhampton WV10 .... 11 F3
Wentworth Rise B62 ...... 83 D3
Wentworth Way B32 ...... 84 F3
Wenyon Cl DY4 .... 52 B4
Weoley Ave B29 .... 85 C2
Weoley Castle B29 .... 85 A2
Weoley Castle Rd B29 ... 84 F1
Weoley Hill B29 .... 103 C8
Weoley Park Rd B29 ...... 85 C1
Wergs Dr WV6 .... 24 A7
Wergs Hall Rd WV6, WV8 ... 24 A7
Wergs Rd WV6 .... 24 B6
Werneth Gr WS3 .... 14 A4

Wesley Ave Cheslyn Hay
WS6 .... 4 D3
Codsall WV8 .... 10 B2
Halesowen B63 .... 82 B8
Wesley Ct ◼4 Blackheath
B64 .... 82 F8
◼9 Cannock WS11 .... 1 E1
Willenhall WV13 .... 26 E1
Wolverhampton WV4 ...... 39 F4
Wesley Gr WS10 .... 41 E3
Wesley Ho ◼3 WS2 .... 42 C7
Wesley Pl Cannock WS12 .. 2 C7
Tipton DY4 .... 52 C7
Wesley Rd Birmingham B23 ... 56 F5
Brierley Hill DY5 .... 61 B5
Codsall WV8 .... 10 B2
Willenhall WV12 .... 27 C6
Wesley St Bilston WV14 .. 40 E3
Oldbury B69 .... 64 A8
West Bromwich B70 .... 53 B3
Wolverhampton WV2 ...... 40 A6
Wesley Way B77 .... 21 F4
Wesley Wlk B60 .... 150 E7
Wesley's Fold WS10 ...... 41 D6
Wessenden B77 .... 36 B7
Wessex Cl Bedworth CV12 .. 78 A4
Brownhills WS8 .... 15 F7
Wessex Ct B79 .... 22 F7
Wessex Dr WS11 .... 1 F2
Wessex Rd WV2 .... 39 F6
Wesson Gdns B63 .... 83 A3
Wesson Rd WS10 .... 41 C8
West Acre CV4 .... 26 F1
West Ave Bedworth CV12 .. 78 D2
Birmingham,
Castle Bromwich B36 ...... 69 D8
Birmingham,
Handsworth B20 .... 55 A4
Coventry CV2 .... 114 A2
Redditch B98 .... 153 E3
Tipton B69 .... 63 B7
Wolverhampton WV11 .... 26 C6
West Bromwich Central
Sta B70 .... 53 C2
West Bromwich Rd WS5 . 42 F5
West Bromwich Ringway
B70 .... 53 D2
West Bromwich St
Oldbury B69 .... 52 F1
Walsall WS1 .... 42 E7
West Bvd B32 .... 84 F4
West Cl LE10 .... 75 D7
West Coppice Rd WS8 ... 15 C8
West Ct B60 .... 150 F6
West Dr
Birmingham,
Edgbaston B5 .... 86 C5
Birmingham,
Handsworth B20 .... 66 B8
Fazeley B78 .... 20 E2
West End Ave B66 .... 64 D7
West End Ct CV34 .... 160 D6
West End Villas B38 ..... 103 F2
West Gate B16 .... 65 E3
West Gn WV4 .... 38 C5
West Green Cl B15 .... 86 B8
West Heath Hospl B38 .. 123 C8
West Heath Jun & Inf
Sch B38 .... 123 C8
West Heath Rd
◼2 Birmingham,
Edgbaston B18 .... 65 D4
Birmingham,
Northfield B31 .... 103 B1
West Hill Ave WS12 .... 2 B6
West Hill Ct B14 .... 104 C4
West Hill Prim Sch WS12 .. 2 B6
West Holme B9 .... 67 C2
West House Sch B15 ..... 86 C8
West Lodge WV1 .... 25 A3
West Mead Dr B14 .... 104 E6
West Mews B44 .... 44 D2
West Midlands Private
Hospl B63 .... 82 D5
West Mill Croft B38 ..... 123 E7
West Orchards Sh Ctr
CV1 .... 165 B3
West Park Ave B31 ...... 102 E4
West Park Ct WV1 .... 25 A2
West Park Hospl WV1 .... 25 A2
West Park Inf Sch WV1 . 163 A4
West Park Jun Sch WV1 . 163 A4
West Park Rd B67 .... 64 D6
West Pathway B17 .... 85 C6
West Point B17 .... 85 C8
West Rd
Birmingham,
Hamstead B43 .... 54 E7
Birmingham,
Handsworth B42 .... 55 E2
Bromsgrove B60 .... 137 A2
Halesowen B63 .... 82 B6
Tipton DY4 .... 52 B8
West Rd S B63 .... 82 B6
West Ridge CV5 .... 112 A5
West Rise B75 .... 46 C6
West Rock CV34 .... 160 D7
West Side Bsns Ctr CV4 . 131 F8
West St Birmingham B7 .. 66 F4
Blackheath B65 .... 63 C1
Brierley Hill DY5 .... 81 F8
Cannock WS11 .... 4 E6
Coventry CV1 .... 113 C2
Dudley DY1 .... 51 B2
Redditch B98 .... 153 E3
Royal Leamington Spa
CV31 .... 162 A7
Stourbridge DY8 .... 80 F5

West St continued
Tamworth B79 .... 21 C5
Tamworth, Kettlebrook B77 ... 21 C3
Walsall WS3 .... 28 C7
Warwick CV34 .... 160 D5
Wolverhampton W6 .... 25 C5
West View B8 .... 68 C4
West View Dr DY6 .... 60 E5
West View Rd
Royal Leamington Spa
CV32 .... 157 C5
Sutton Coldfield B75 ...... 46 E6
West Way B60 .... 15 B2
Westacre Cres WV3 .... 24 C1
Westacre Dr DY5 .... 81 F8
Westacre Gdns B33 .... 68 F3
Westacre Inf Sch WV3 ... 24 C1
Westbourne Ave
Birmingham B34 .... 68 E6
Cannock WS11 .... 1 D3
Cheslyn Hay WS6 .... 4 E3
Westbourne Cl B61 ...... 136 E1
Westbourne Cres
Birmingham B15 .... 86 A8
◼2 Burntwood WS7 .... 7 B7
Westbourne Ct
Darlaston WS10 .... 41 F7
Walsall WS4 .... 29 A3
Westbourne Gdns B15 ... 86 A7
Westbourne Gr B21 .... 65 F7
Westbourne Rd
Birmingham B21 .... 54 D1
Birmingham,
Edgbaston B15 .... 86 A8
Darlaston WS10 .... 41 F7
Halesowen B62 .... 83 E7
Solihull B92 .... 106 F8
Walsall WS4 .... 28 F4
West Bromwich B70 .... 53 B2
Wolverhampton WV4 ...... 39 A5
Westbourne St WS4 .... 28 F3
Westbourne Terr B61 ... 136 E1
Westbrook Ave WS9 ...... 29 F5
Westbrook Ct CV5 .... 112 A4
Westbury Ave WS10 ...... 41 F6
Westbury Ct ◼22
Brierley Hill DY5 .... 61 D2
Coventry CV2 .... 114 A3
Warwick CV34 .... 161 A7
Westbury Rd Coventry
CV5 .... 112 D5
Nuneaton CV10 .... 72 D3
Smethwick B17 .... 65 B3
Wednesbury WS10 .... 41 F6
Westbury St WV1 .... 163 C3
Westcliff Dr CV34 .... 155 E2
Westcliff Pl B31 .... 102 F4
Westcliffe Dr CV3 .... 133 B5
Westcombe Gr B32 .... 84 A1
Westcote Ave B31 .... 102 C2
Westcote Cl B92 .... 89 A2
Westcotes CV4 .... 112 B1
Westcott Cl DY6 .... 60 F3
Westcott Rd B26 .... 89 A8
Westcott Rd B26 .... 103 D3
Westcroft Ave WV10 ..... 12 A1
Westcroft Gr B38 .... 123 D1
Westcroft Rd Sedgley
DY3 .... 39 B2
Wolverhampton WV6 ...... 23 F6
Westcroft Sch WV10 ..... 12 B2
Westcroft Way B14 ...... 105 B1
Westdean Cl B62 .... 83 C4
Westerdale Cl DY3 .... 51 A7
Westerham Cl B93 .... 127 F6
Westeria Cl B36 .... 69 C8
Westeria Ho B36 .... 69 C8
Westering Parkway
WV10 .... 11 F4
Westerings B20 .... 55 C2
Western Ave
◼7 Birmingham B19 .... 66 C7
Brierley Hill DY5 .... 61 B2
Halesowen B62 .... 83 E4
Sedgley DY3 .... 50 B8
Willenhall WS2 .... 27 D3
Western Bsns Pk
Birmingham B18 .... 65 E6
Halesowen B62 .... 83 E7
Western By-Pass WS13 .... 8 F8
Western Hill Cl B96 ..... 158 E1
Western Rd
Birmingham,
Edgbaston B18 .... 65 F4
Birmingham,
Erdington B24 .... 57 A3
Blackheath B64 .... 82 E8
Cannock WS12 .... 2 B6
Hagley DY9 .... 99 B4
Oldbury B69 .... 64 B5
Stourbridge DY8 .... 80 F4
Sutton Coldfield B73 ...... 46 A1
Western Way
Kidderminster DY11 ...... 116 A5
Wednesbury WS10 .... 41 C3
Westfield Ave B14 .... 105 B1
Westfield Cl Dorridge B93 ... 127 F2
Nuneaton CV10 .... 73 D5
Westfield Ct LE10 .... 75 C7
Westfield Cty Jun & Inf
Schs
LE10 .... 75 B7
Westfield Cty Prim Sch
WV5 .... 49 A7
Westfield Gr WV3 .... 38 C8
Westfield Hall ◼2 B16 ... 65 D1
Westfield Ho B36 .... 70 A7
Westfield Manor B75 .... 32 A4

Westfield Rd Bilston WV14 ... 40 B7
Birmingham,
Acock's Green B27 .... 88 B3
Birmingham, Edgbaston B15 ... 85 D7
Birmingham, Moseley B14 ... 86 E1
Brierley Hill DY5 .... 81 F8
Dudley DY2 .... 62 D7
Halesowen B62 .... 63 E1
Hinckley LE10 .... 75 B7
Sedgley DY3 .... 39 E1
Smethwick B67 .... 64 F5
Willenhall WV13 .... 40 E8
Westfields B61 .... 136 F8
Westford Gr B28 .... 105 E3
Westgate Aldridge WS9 .. 29 E6
Cannock WS12 .... 2 F5
Westgate Cl Sedgley DY3 . 50 E7
Warwick CV34 .... 160 D6
Westgate Cty Prim Sch
CV34 .... 160 D6
Westgate Ho ◼3 CV34 .. 160 E6
Westgate Trad Est WS9 . 29 E6
Westgrove Ave ◼6 B90 . 127 A6
Westgrove Terr ◼1 CV32 . 161 D8
Westham Ho B37 .... 70 B4
Westhaven Dr B31 .... 102 E7
Westhaven Rd B72 .... 46 C5
Westhay Rd B28 .... 106 B7
Westhill WV3 .... 24 C2
Westhill Cl B92 .... 106 E8
Westhill Coll B29 .... 103 D8
Westhill Rd Birmingham
B38 .... 103 F3
Blackdown B32 .... 157 A6
Coventry CV6 .... 112 F6
Westholme Croft B30 .. 103 E8
Westhouse Gr B14 ...... 104 D4
Westland Ave WV3 .... 24 F2
Westland Cl B23 .... 56 F5
Westland Gdns
Stourbridge DY8 .... 80 F7
◼6 Wolverhampton WV3 . 25 A2
Westland Rd WV3 .... 24 F2
Westland Wlk B35 .... 57 F2
Westlands Rd
Birmingham B13 .... 87 A1
Sutton Coldfield B76 ...... 57 F6
Westlea Rd CV31 .... 161 E6
Westleigh Ave CV5 ...... 132 F7
Westley Cl B28 .... 106 B6
Westley Rd B27 .... 88 B3
Westley St Birmingham B9 ... 67 A2
◼6 Dudley DY2 .... 62 B8
Westmead Ave B80 ..... 159 E4
Westmead Cres B24 ...... 57 C4
Westmead Dr B68 .... 64 B4
Westmede Ctr CV5 ...... 112 C4
Westminster Ave WV4 ... 39 B5
Westminster Cl
Bromsgrove B61 .... 136 D1
Dudley DY2 .... 51 A2
Westminster Ct
Birmingham,
Handsworth B20 .... 55 C2
Birmingham, Kingshurst B37 . 69 F5
◼2 Bromsgrove B60 .... 137 A2
Westminster Dr
Birmingham B14 .... 104 E6
Hinckley LE10 .... 75 F4
Nuneaton CV10 .... 73 D5
Westminster Ind Est DY2 . 62 D2
Westminster Jun & Inf
Schs B20 .... 55 C1
Westminster Rd
Birmingham,
Handsworth B20 .... 55 C1
Birmingham, Stirchley B29 .. 104 A8
Cannock WS11 .... 1 E6
Coventry CV1 .... 165 A1
Kidderminster DY11 ..... 116 A6
Stourbridge DY8 .... 60 D2
Walsall WS4 .... 29 B7
West Bromwich B71 .... 53 D8
Westmore Way WS10 .... 42 D5
Westmorland Ave CV10 . 72 E4
Westmorland Ct B78 ..... 21 A1
Westmorland Ct B71 ..... 53 D7
Westmorland Rd
Coventry CV2 .... 114 A2
West Bromwich B71 .... 53 D7
Weston Ave Birmingham
B11 .... 87 C6
Tipton B69 .... 52 B1
Weston Cl Cannock WS11 .. 2 C1
Dorridge B93 .... 128 A2
Hinckley LE10 .... 71 A1
Royal Leamington Spa
CV31 .... 162 C6
Walsall WS1 .... 42 E6
Warwick CV34 .... 160 F7
Weston Cres WS9 .... 30 B4
Weston Ct ◼10 WS9 .... 30 B4
Weston Dr Bilston WV14 . 40 B5
Great Wyrley WS6 .... 4 F1
Tipton DY4 .... 41 C2
Weston Hall Stables CV12 . 79 A3
Weston Ho Birmingham B19 . 66 C4
Wolverhampton WV6 ...... 24 E5
Weston Ind Est B11 ...... 87 C4
Weston La Birmingham B11 . 87 E4
Bulkington CV12 .... 79 B3
Weston Rd Birmingham B19 . 66 C4
Lichfield WS13 .... 3 A2
Smethwick B67 .... 64 F2
Weston St Coventry CV1 . 165 C4
Walsall WS1 .... 42 E7
Weston Terr ◼3 B19 ...... 66 D8

Westonbirt Cl CV8 148 C6
Westonhall Rd B60 150 D1
Westover Rd B20 54 E4
Westport Cres WV11 26 F5
Westray Cl B45 101 F1
Westray Dr LE10 71 C1
Westridge DY3 50 C8
Westridge Rd B13 105 C6
Westside Dr B32 84 D1
Westville Ave DY11 116 A5
Westville Rd WS2 28 A3
Westward Cl B44 55 F8
Westway Ho WS4 15 B1
Westwick Cl WS9 16 E4
Westwood Ave
Birmingham B11 87 D4
Stourbridge DY8 80 D3
Westwood Bsns Pk
Birmingham B6 56 B1
Coventry CV4 131 F6
Westwood Gr B91 106 F2
Westwood Heath Rd CV4 131 E6
Westwood Rd
Birmingham, Aston B6 56 A2
Birmingham, Kingstanding B73 45 A4
Coventry CV5 113 A1
Westwood St DY5 61 A1
Westwood View B24 57 C3
Westwood Way CV4 132 A6
Westwoods Hollow WS7 7 B8
Wetherby Cl Birmingham B36 68 D8
Wolverhampton WV10 11 D5
Wetherby Rd
Birmingham B27 88 C2
Walsall WS3 14 A4
Wetherfield Rd B11 88 A3
Wexford Cl DY1 50 F2
Wexford Rd CV2 96 D1
Weybourne Rd B44 44 E2
Weycroft Rd B23 56 B7
Weyhill Cl WV9 10 F2
Weymoor Rd B17 85 B3
Weymouth Cl CV3 134 D5
Weymouth Dr B74 31 F4
Weymouth Ho B79 21 B5
Whaley's Croft CV6 113 B8
Whar Hall Rd B92 107 E8
Wharf App WS9 29 F7
Wharf Cl WS14 9 C7
Wharf La Birmingham B18 66 A6
Burntwood WS8 6 F3
Lapworth B94 143 D4
Solihull B91 107 D6
Tardebigge B60 138 B1
Wharf Lodge CV31 161 D7
Wharf Rd
Birmingham, King's Norton B30 104 A2
Birmingham, Tyseley B11 88 B5
Coventry CV6 113 F5
Wharf St
Birmingham, Aston B6 67 A7
Birmingham, Hockley B18 66 A6
Walsall WS2 28 C1
Warwick CV34 161 A8
Wolverhampton WV1 163 D2
Wharf The B1 164 A2
Wharfdale Rd B11 88 A5
Wharfedale Cl DY6 60 B7
Wharfedale St WS10 42 A2
Wharfside B69 63 F7
Wharrington Cl B98 159 A8
Wharrington Hill B98 159 A8
Wharton Ave B92 107 E7
Wharton St B7 67 D8
Wharton St Ind Est B7 67 D8
Wharwell La WS6 5 A1
Whatcote Gn B92 107 D8
Whateley Ave WS3 28 F6
Whateley Cres B36 69 D8
Whateley Ct CV11 73 B4
Whateley Gn B74 46 A8
Whateley Hall Cl B93 128 C7
Whateley Hall Rd B93 128 B7
Whateley La B78 35 F4
Whateley Lodge Dr B36 69 C8
Whateley Pl WS3 28 F6
Whateley Rd Birmingham B21 65 E8
Walsall WS3 28 F6
Whateley Villas CV9 36 B2
Whateley's Dr CV8 148 A5
Wheat Hill WS5 43 E8
Wheat St CV11 73 D4
Wheatcroft Cl Burntwood WS7 7 A5
Halesowen B62 83 F8
Wheatcroft Dr B37 70 C1
Wheatcroft Gr DY2 51 F1
Wheatcroft Rd B33 68 F2
Wheate Croft CV4 111 F2
Wheaten Cl B37 70 D3
Wheatfield Cl B36 70 A7
Wheatfield View B31 102 D6
Wheatfield Way LE10 71 C4
Wheathill Cl
Royal Leamington Spa CV32 156 E2
Wolverhampton WV4 38 E3
Wheatlands Cl WS12 2 C1
Wheatlands Croft B33 69 E3
Wheatlands The WV6 23 D3
Wheatley Cl Oldbury B68 84 C8
Solihull B92 107 E8
Sutton Coldfield B75 32 C3
Wheatley Grange B46 70 F6
Wheatley Rd B68 84 D8
Wheatley St
West Bromwich B70 53 A3
Wolverhampton WV2 39 F6
Wheatmill Cl DY10 98 B2
Wheatmoor Rise B75 46 E6
Wheaton Cl WV10 25 C7
Wheaton Vale B20 54 E3
Wheatridge Cl DY6 60 A8
Wheatridge Rd B60 150 E6
Wheats Ave B17 85 B3
Wheatsheaf Rd
Birmingham B16 65 D2
Tipton B69 63 A8
Wolverhampton WV8 10 E1
Wheatstone Cl DY3 50 E6
Wheatstone Gr B33 68 F5
Wheeler Cl B93 145 B7
Wheeler Ho 12 B69 64 A7
Wheeler Rd WV11 26 C8
Wheeler St Birmingham B19 66 D7
Stourbridge DY8 80 F5
Wheeler Street Sh Ctr B19 66 D6
Wheeler's Fold WV1 163 C3
Wheeler's La B13 105 A7
Wheelers La B13 104 F7
Wheelers Lane Boys Sec Sch B13 104 F7
Wheelers Lane Inf Sch B13 104 F7
Wheelers Lane Jun Sch B13 104 F7
Wheelers Lane Jun Sch (Annexe) B13 105 A6
Wheeley Moor Rd B37 70 A5
Wheeley Rd Alvechurch B48 138 D5
Solihull B92 107 D7
Wheeley's La B15 66 C1
Wheeleys Rd B15 86 B8
Wheelock Cl B74 44 F7
Wheelwright Cl B60 150 E6
Wheelwright Ct 5 B24 56 E2
Wheelwright La CV6 95 C4
Wheelwright Lane Comb Sch CV7 95 D5
Wheelwright Rd B24 56 F1
Wheldrake Ave B34 69 C6
Wheler Rd CV3 134 A7
Whernside Dr WV6 25 A5
Wherretts Well La B91 107 E6
Whetstone Cl B15 85 F5
Whetstone Field JMI Sch WS9 30 B4
Whetstone Gr WV10 25 D8
Whetstone La WS9 30 B4
Whetstone Rd WV10 25 D8
Whetty La B45 121 F7
Whettybridge Rd B45 121 E6
Whichcote Ave CV7 92 C1
Whichford Cl B76 57 D6
Whichford Gr B9 68 C2
While Rd B72 46 B4
Whilmot Cl WV10 12 B6
Whimbrel Gr DY10 117 A1
Whinberry Rise DY5 50 C1
Whinchat Gr DY10 117 A2
Whinfield Rd B61 136 B6
Whinyates Rise WS11 4 F8
Whiston Ave WV11 27 A7
Whiston Gr B29 103 B8
Whiston Ho 9 WS1 28 F1
Whitacre La WS14 16 E7
Whitacre Rd Birmingham B9 67 F3
Knowle B93 128 B7
Nuneaton CV11 73 E4
3 Royal Leamington Spa CV32 157 A2
Whitacre Rd Ind Est CV11 73 F4
Whitaker Rd CV5 112 C3
Whitbourne Cl B12 87 B5
Whitburn Ave B42 55 A5
Whitburn Cl
Kidderminster DY11 116 B5
Wolverhampton WV9 11 A2
Whitburn Rd CV12 77 C1
Whitby Cl WS3 13 F3
Whitby Rd B12 87 A4
Whitby Way WS11 4 C8
Whitchurch Cl B98 158 F6
Whitchurch Way CV4 131 F8
Whitcot Gr B31 122 F8
White Bark Cl WS12 2 A8
White Beam Rd B37 90 D8
White City Rd DY5 62 A1
White Cl DY9 81 C2
White Falcon Ct B91 106 F2
White Farm Rd B74 31 E4
White Field Ave B17 85 A6
White Friars La CV1 165 C2
White Friars St CV1 165 C2
White Hart The 8 WS1 42 E8
White Hill B31 103 B6
White Ho B19 66 D6
White Horse Rd WS8 6 E2
White House Ave WV11 26 F7
White House Cl
Barnt Green B45 122 A2
Solihull B91 106 F3
White House Gn B91 106 F3
White House Way B91 107 A3
White Houses La
Featherstone WV10 12 A6
Wolverhampton WV10 12 B5
White Oak Dr
Kingswinford DY6 60 C6
Wolverhampton WV3 24 C1
White Rd
Birmingham, Quinton B32 84 D6
Birmingham, Sparkbrook B11 87 C7
Smethwick B67 64 F6
White Rose Ho 4 CV32 156 F2
White Row WV5 37 C1
White St Birmingham B12 87 A5
Coventry CV1 165 C3
Walsall WS1 42 E8
White's Dr DY3 50 E8
White's Rd B71 53 C6
Whitebeam Cl
Clayhanger WS8 15 E6
Coventry CV4 111 D1
Whitebeam Croft 3 B38 103 E1
Whitecrest B43 44 A2
Whitecrest Prim Sch B43 44 A2
Whitecroft Rd B26 89 D5
Whitefield Cl Codsall WV8 10 B2
Coventry CV4 131 D6
Whitefields Cres B91 107 B2
Whitefields Gate B91 107 A1
Whitefields Rd B91 107 A2
Whitefriars Dr B63 83 A4
Whitegate Dr DY11 116 A3
Whitegates Rd WV14 40 D2
Whitehall Ct WV3 38 F6
Whitehall Dr Dudley DY1 51 A2
Halesowen B63 83 B4
Whitehall Ind Pk DY4 52 E5
Whitehall Inf Sch WS1 42 E7
Whitehall Jun Sch WS1 42 F7
Whitehall Rd
Birmingham, Bordesley Green B9 67 E1
Birmingham, Handsworth B21 66 A8
Blackheath B64 82 C8
Halesowen B63 83 B4
Kingswinford DY6 60 C6
Stourbridge DY8 81 B2
Tipton DY4, B70 52 E4
2 Walsall WS1 42 E7
Wolverhampton WV4 39 B4
Whitehead Dr
Kenilworth CV8 148 C7
Minworth B76 58 D6
Whitehead Rd B6 66 E8
Whiteheads Ct 15 CV32 156 F1
Whiteheath CE Jun Sch B69 63 D5
Whiteheath Ct 6 B65 63 E4
Whitehill La B29 103 A5
Whitehill Rd DY11 116 A4
Whitehorn Dr CV32 157 B2
Whitehorse Cl CV6 96 B6
Whitehouse Ave
Darlaston WS10 41 B7
Wednesbury WS10 41 F3
Wolverhampton WV3 38 D8
Whitehouse Common Jun & Inf Schs B75 46 D7
Whitehouse Common Rd B75 46 E7
Whitehouse Cres
3 Burntwood WS7 7 B7
Nuneaton CV10 72 D3
Sutton Coldfield B75 46 E7
Wolverhampton WV11 12 F1
Whitehouse Ct B75 46 F6
Whitehouse La Codsall WV8 10 A6
Redditch B98 154 E4
Whitehouse Rd Dordon B78 36 F7
Kidderminster DY10 116 D4
Whitehouse St
Birmingham B6 66 F6
Dudley WV14 51 C8
Tipton DY4 52 A2
Walsall WS2 28 D3
Whitehouse Way WS9 29 F4
Whitelaw Cres CV5 112 C6
Whitemoor Dr B90 127 A7
Whitemoor Rd CV8 148 B5
Whitepits La B48 140 F4
Whites Row CV8 148 A3
Whites Wood WV5 49 A5
Whiteside Cl CV3 134 F8
Whiteslade Cl B93 128 A7
Whitesmith Cl DY3 50 D8
Whitesmith Croft B14 104 E8
Whitesmore Sec Sch B37 69 F1
Whitestitch La CV7 92 C3
Whitestone Fst Sch CV11 79 A8
Whitestone Rd
Halesowen B63 83 A6
Nuneaton CV11 79 B7
Whitethorn Cl WS12 2 A8
Whitethorn Cres B74 30 D1
Whitethorn Rd DY8 61 A1
Whitewood Glade WV12 27 E4
Whitfield Gr B15 86 D8
Whitfield Rd WS12 2 C7
Whitford Bridge Rd B60 151 A2
Whitford Cl B61 150 D8
Whitford Dr B90 127 C7
Whitford Hall Sch B61 136 D2
Whitford Rd B61 136 D2
Whitgreave Ave
Featherstone WV10 12 B7
Wolverhampton WV10 25 F8
Whitgreave Inf Sch WV10 25 E8
Whitgreave Jun Sch WV10 25 E8
Whitgreave Prim Sch WV10 12 B7
Whitgreave St B70 52 E3
Whiting B77 35 D7
Whitland Cl B45 122 B6
Whitland Dr B14 104 F3
Whitley Abbey Comp Sch CV3 133 F5
Whitley Abbey Prim Sch CV3 134 A6
Whitley Ave B77 21 E5
Whitley Cl WV6 24 B2
Whitley Court Rd B32 84 C6
Whitley Ct CV3 133 F7
Whitley Dr B74 45 A8
Whitley St WS10 41 E3
Whitley Village CV3 133 F7
Whitlock Gr B14 105 A3
Whitlock's End Halt B90 125 E7
Whitminster Ave B24 57 B3
Whitminster Cl WV12 27 C4
Whitmore Hill WV1 163 B3
Whitmore Ho W6 25 A4
Whitmore Park Prim Sch CV6 95 A1
Whitmore Park Rd CV6 95 D3
Whitmore Rd
Birmingham B10 87 C8
Stourbridge DY8 80 D5
Whitnash CV31 162 A3
Whitmore St Birmingham B18 66 B6
Walsall WS1 42 D7
Wolverhampton WV1 163 C3
Whitnash Cl CV7 130 A6
Whitnash Cty Comb Sch CV31 162 A4
Whitnash Gr CV2 114 D5
Whitnash Rd CV31 162 B4
Whitney Ave DY8 80 D6
Whittaker St WV2 39 E6
Whittall Dr E DY11 116 B1
Whittall Dr W DY11 116 A1
Whittall St B4 164 C3
Whittimere St WS1 28 F2
Whittingham Gr WV11 26 F6
Whittingham Rd B63 83 A5
Whittington Cl
Birmingham B14 104 E5
Warwick CV34 161 B8
West Bromwich B71 53 F8
Whittington Gr B33 68 F2
Whittington Hall La DY7 80 B3
Whittington Ho WS13 3 E1
Whittington Oval B33 69 A2
Whittington Oval Sch B33 68 F2
Whittington Rd DY8 80 E3
Whittle Cl CV3 134 F8
Whittle Croft B35 57 F3
Whittle Ct 9 CV32 157 A1
Whittle Rd LE10 74 E7
Whittleford Gr B36 58 C1
Whittleford Rd CV10 72 C4
Whitton St WS10 41 E6
Whitville Cl DY11 116 C7
Whitwell Dr B90 127 A6
Whitworth Ave CV3 114 B1
Whitworth Cl WS10 41 E7
Whitworth Dr B71 42 E1
Whitworth Ind Pk B9 67 C2
Whoberley Ave CV5 112 D2
Whoberley Hall Prim Sch CV5 112 C3
Whyley St B70 53 A4
Whyley Wlk B69 64 A5
Whynot St B63 82 B5
Wibert Cl B29 86 A1
Wichnor Rd B92 88 F5
Wickam Sq B70 53 B2
Wickets Tower B5 86 C5
Wickham Cl CV6 94 F2
Wickham Ct CV32 157 B3
Wickham Gdns WV11 26 A6
Wickham Ho 2 B7 67 A4
Wickham Rd B80 159 F4
Wicklow Cl B63 82 D1
Wiclif Way CV10 72 B3
Widdecombe Cl CV2 114 D7
Widdrington Rd CV1 113 C5
Wide Acres B45 101 F1
Wideacre Dr B44 55 E7
Widney Ave Aldridge WS9 16 B1
Birmingham B29 85 C1
Widney Cl B93 127 F5
Widney Jun Sch B91 106 F1
Widney La B91 127 B8
Widney Manor Rd B91 127 D7
Widney Manor Sta B91 127 C8
Widney Rd B93 127 F5
Wigeon Gr WV10 12 B7
Wigford Rd B77 35 C5
Wiggin Cotts 5 B17 85 C5
Wiggin Ho WS3 14 C3
Wiggin St B16 65 F3
Wiggin Tower 5 B19 66 D7
Wiggins Croft B76 46 F3
Wiggins Hill Rd B76 58 F7
Wigginsmill Rd WS10 41 D1
Wigginton Rd B79 21 B7
Wight Croft B36 70 B6
Wightman Cl WS14 9 E6
Wightwick Bank WV6 24 A2
Wightwick Cl 4 WS3 14 B1
Wightwick Ct WV6 24 A2
Wightwick Gr WV6 24 A2
Wightwick Hall Rd WV6 23 E1
Wightwick Hall Specl Sch WV6 23 E2
Wightwick Manor WV6 23 F1
Wigland Way B38 104 A1
Wigmore Gr B44 56 B8
Wigmore La B71 54 A8
Wigorn Ho B67 84 F8
Wigorn La DY9 99 B8
Wigorn Rd B67 64 F1
Wigston Rd CV2 96 F1
Wilberforce Way B92 107 F7
Wilbraham Rd WS2 28 C1
Wilcote Gr B27 106 C8
Wilcox Ave WS12 2 B7
Wild Goose La B98 159 D8
Wildacres DY8 80 C6
Wildcroft Rd CV5 112 C3
Wilde Cl B14 104 D4
Wilden Cl B31 102 C3
Wilden La DY10 116 E1
Wilderness La B43 43 D3
Wildey Rd CV12 77 D2
Wildfell Rd B27 88 D2
Wildmoor Cl CV2 96 B4
Wildmoor La B61 121 A3
Wildmoor Rd B90 106 B5
Wildtree Ave WV10 12 A2
Wiley Ave WS10 41 C5
Wiley Ave S WS10 41 C5
Wilford Gr Solihull B91 107 B2
Sutton Coldfield B76 58 B6
Wilford Rd B71 53 D6
Wilkes Ave WS2 27 F2
Wilkes Cl WS3 14 E3
Wilkes Croft DY3 50 D7
Wilkes Green Jun & Inf Sch B21 54 E1
Wilkes St West Bromwich B71 53 E7
Willenhall WV13 27 A1
Wilkin Rd WS8 6 C2
Wilkins Ho WS3 14 A1
Wilkins Rd WV14 40 D7
Wilkinson Ave WV14 40 E3
Wilkinson Cl
1 Burntwood WS7 7 B8
Sutton Coldfield B73 46 A2
Wilkinson Croft B8 68 C6
Wilkinson Prim Sch WV14 40 F3
Wilkinson Rd WS10 41 A4
Wilks Gn B21 54 D3
Willard Rd B25 88 C6
Willaston Rd B33 89 D7
Willclare Rd B26 89 A7
Willcock Rd WV2 39 E6
Willenhall Comp Sch WS2 27 E5
Willenhall Ind Est WV13 27 C3
Willenhall La Coventry CV3 134 F7
Walsall WS3 28 A8
Willenhall Lane Ind Est WS3 28 A8
Willenhall Rd Bilston WV14 40 F7
Darlaston WS10 41 D8
Wolverhampton WV1, WV13 26 C1
Willenhall St WV13 41 C7
Willenhall Trad Est WV13 27 A1
Willenhall Wood Prim Sch CV3 134 D6
Willerby Fold WV10 11 F4
Willersey Rd B13 105 D8
Willes Ct 2 CV31 162 B7
Willes Rd Birmingham B18 65 E6
Royal Leamington Spa CV31, CV32 162 A8
Willes Terr CV31 162 B8
Willett Ave WS7 6 E5
Willett Rd B71 53 E8
Willetts Dr B63 82 B4
Willetts Rd B31 103 A1
Willetts Way B64 62 F2
Willey Gr B24 57 B2
William Arnold Cl CV2 114 A4
William Batchelor Ho CV1 165 B4
William Baxter Specl Sch The WS12 2 A6
William Beesley Cres CV11 79 E6
William Bentley Ct WV11 26 C5
William Booth La B4 164 B4
William Bree Rd CV5 111 C5
William Bristow Rd CV3 133 E7
William Cook Rd B8 68 B5
William Cowper Inf & Jun Sch B19 66 E6
William Ct B16 65 E1
William Green Rd WS10 42 C3
William Groubb Cl CV3 134 D7
William Harper Rd WV13 27 B1
William Hawke Ind Est DY5 61 E1
William Henry St B7 67 A6
William Iliffe St LE10 75 B7
William Ker Rd DY4 52 C5
William Lunn's Homes 4 WS13 9 C8
William Macgregor Prim Sch
Tamworth B77 21 C3
Tamworth B77 21 D4
William Malcolm Ho CV2 114 E3
William McKee Cl CV3 134 E7
William Morris Gr WS11 1 E4
William Rd B67 64 D3
William Sheriden Ho CV2 114 E3

William St Bedworth CV12 ..... 78 D2
Birmingham B15 ..... 66 C1
Brierley Hill DY5 ..... 61 C3
Nuneaton CV11 ..... 73 E3
Redditch B97 ..... 153 E4
Royal Leamington Spa CV32 ..... 162 A8
Walsall WS4 ..... 28 F3
West Bromwich B70 ..... 52 E5
William St N B19 ..... 164 B4
William St W B66 ..... 65 B7
William Tarver Cl CV34 ..... 161 A7
William Thomson Ho
2 CV1 ..... 165 D4
William Wiggin Ave WS3 ..... 14 B2
Williams Cl WV12 ..... 27 C5
Williams Rd CV31 ..... 162 E4
Williamson St WV3 ..... 163 A2
Willingsworth High Sch DY4 ..... 41 B2
Willingsworth Rd WS10 ..... 41 D1
Willington Rd B79 ..... 21 B7
Willington St CV11 ..... 73 B5
Willingworth Cl WV14 ..... 40 A3
Willis Gr CV12 ..... 78 C3
Willis Pearson Ave WV14 ..... 41 A3
Willis St DY11 ..... 116 C5
Willmore Gr B38 ..... 123 F8
Willmore Rd B20 ..... 55 D2
Willmott Cl B75 ..... 32 D3
Willmott Rd B75 ..... 32 D3
Willoughby Ave CV8 ..... 147 E3
Willoughby Cl CV3 ..... 134 E8
Willoughby Ct B76 ..... 46 F2
Willoughby Dr B91 ..... 107 B1
Willoughby Gr B29 ..... 85 A1
Willoughby Rd B79 ..... 20 E7
Willow Ave Birmingham B17 ..... 65 A2
Burntwood WS7 ..... 7 C6
Wednesbury WS10 ..... 41 F4
Wolverhampton WV11 ..... 26 B8
Willow Bank WV3 ..... 24 C1
Willow Bank Rd B93 ..... 127 F6
Willow Brook Rd B48 ..... 139 A7
Willow Cl Bedworth CV12 ..... 78 B5
Blackheath B64 ..... 62 E1
Bromsgrove B61 ..... 136 E2
Hagley DY9 ..... 98 F5
Hinckley LE10 ..... 75 E5
Nuneaton CV10 ..... 72 A7
Willow Coppice B32 ..... 84 C1
Willow Ct Birmingham B13 ..... 87 A3
Bromsgrove B61 ..... 136 E3
Lichfield WS14 ..... 9 C5
Oldbury B66 ..... 64 D8
Smethwick B17 ..... 65 A2
Willow Ctyd CV2 ..... 114 D7
Willow Dr Birmingham B21 ..... 54 C1
Cheswick Green B90 ..... 126 D4
Codsall WV8 ..... 10 B3
Tipton B69 ..... 63 C7
Willow End DY9 ..... 81 D3
Willow Gdns Birmingham B16 ..... 65 F4
Bromsgrove B61 ..... 136 E3
Willow Gr Coventry CV4 ..... 112 B2
Essington WV11 ..... 13 B3
Willow Ho Birmingham B7 ..... 67 B4
Walsall WS4 ..... 15 D1
Willow Hts B64 ..... 83 A8
Willow Meer CV8 ..... 148 B5
Willow Mews B29 ..... 85 B1
Willow Park Dr DY8 ..... 81 B2
Willow Rd
Birmingham, Bournville B30 ..... 103 F8
Birmingham, Great Barr B43 ..... 44 A2
Bromsgrove B61 ..... 136 E3
Dudley DY1 ..... 51 A4
Nuneaton CV10 ..... 72 F5
Solihull B91 ..... 106 E2
Wolverhampton WV3 ..... 38 D8
Willow Rise DY5 ..... 61 C1
Willow Sheets Mdw CV32 ..... 157 E6
Willow Tree Dr B45 ..... 138 D8
Willow Way Birmingham B37 ..... 70 B1
Redditch B97 ..... 153 B4
Willow Wlk WS12 ..... 1 D8
Willowbank B78 ..... 21 B1
Willowbank Rd LE10 ..... 75 C7
Willowdale LE10 ..... 75 A7
Willowdale Grange WV6 ..... 24 E5
Willowfield Dr DY11 ..... 116 C8
Willowfields Rd CV11 ..... 74 A1
Willowherb Cl Cannock WS11 ..... 2 C2
5 Coventry CV3 ..... 134 F8
4 Walsall WS5 ..... 43 A3
Willows Cres B12 ..... 86 E5
Willows Prim Sch WS13 ..... 3 B2
Willows Rd Birmingham B12 ..... 86 E5
Walsall, Shelfield WS4 ..... 29 C8
Walsall, The Chuckery WS1 ..... 29 A1
Willows The Bedworth CV12 ..... 77 E2
Birmingham B27 ..... 88 B2
Cannock WS11 ..... 1 C1
Hollywood B47 ..... 125 A6
Sutton Coldfield, Streetly B74 ..... 31 F2
Sutton Coldfield, Walmley B76 ..... 46 F2
Wolverhampton WV11 ..... 26 B5
Willowsbrook Rd B62 ..... 83 F8
Willowside WS4 ..... 29 C8
Willowsmere Dr WS14 ..... 9 F7
Willowtree Cl WS13 ..... 3 B2
Wills Ave B71 ..... 53 B7
Wills Ho B70 ..... 53 C2
Wills St B19 ..... 66 C7
Wills Way B66 ..... 65 C4
Willsbridge Covert
8 B14 ..... 104 C2
Willson Croft B28 ..... 105 D3
Wilmcote Cl B12 ..... 86 E6
Wilmcote Ct B61 ..... 150 D8
Wilmcote Dr B75 ..... 32 B3
Wilmcote Gn CV5 ..... 112 A3
Wilmcote Ho B97 ..... 153 B4
Wilmcote Rd B91 ..... 106 F6
Wilmcote Tower 6 B12 ..... 86 F7
Wilmington Rd B32 ..... 84 B6
Wilmore Ho B20 ..... 55 D1
Wilmore La B47 ..... 124 F4
Wilmot Ave B46 ..... 70 F6
Wilmot Dr Birmingham B23 ..... 57 A6
Tipton DY4 ..... 51 E6
Wilmot Gdns DY1 ..... 51 A2
Wilmott Cl WS13 ..... 9 A7
Wilnecote Gr
Birmingham B42 ..... 55 D4
Royal Leamington Spa CV31 ..... 162 B5
Wilnecote High Sch B77 ..... 35 F6
Wilnecote Jun Sch B77 ..... 35 F7
Wilnecote La B77 ..... 21 D2
Wilnecote Sta B77 ..... 35 D7
Wilner's View WS3 ..... 14 F5
Wilsford Cl Birmingham B14 ..... 104 D1
Walsall WS4 ..... 29 C8
Wilson Dr B75 ..... 47 A5
Wilson Gn CV3 ..... 114 F1
Wilson Gr Cannock WS11 ..... 2 C2
Kenilworth CV8 ..... 148 C4
Wilson Ho B69 ..... 63 E5
Wilson Rd Birmingham B19 ..... 66 D8
Brierley Hill DY5 ..... 61 C4
Dudley WV14 ..... 51 C7
Oldbury B68 ..... 64 D1
Smethwick B66 ..... 65 B3
Wilson St Tipton DY4 ..... 52 A5
Wolverhampton WV1 ..... 163 C4
Wilson Stewart Sch B23 ..... 56 C6
Wilson's La CV6 ..... 95 F6
Wilsons La CV7 ..... 96 A6
Wilsons Rd B93 ..... 128 C6
Wiltell Rd WS14 ..... 9 B6
Wilton Ave DY11 ..... 116 B8
Wilton Cl DY3 ..... 50 E7
Wilton Rd
Balsall Common CV7 ..... 130 B5
Birmingham, Balsall Heath B11 ..... 87 B5
Birmingham, Erdington B23 ..... 57 A5
Birmingham, Handsworth B20 ..... 55 B1
Wilton St B19 ..... 66 D8
Wiltshire Cl Bedworth CV12 ..... 78 A3
Coventry CV5 ..... 112 B3
Walsall WS2 ..... 28 D4
Wiltshire Dr B63 ..... 82 B7
Wiltshire Ho 3 DY8 ..... 80 F8
Wiltshire Way B71 ..... 53 C7
Wimberger Ho 2 B71 ..... 53 D4
Wimblebury Rd
Cannock, Heath Hayes WS12 ..... 2 F2
Cannock, Wimblebury WS12 ..... 2 F4
Wimbledon Dr DY8 ..... 81 B2
Wimborne Dr CV2 ..... 115 A4
Wimborne Rd WV10 ..... 26 A6
Wimbourne Cl CV10 ..... 72 B5
Wimbourne Rd
Birmingham B16 ..... 65 D3
Sutton Coldfield B76 ..... 47 A4
Wimperis Way B43 ..... 44 C4
Wimpole Gr B44 ..... 56 B7
Wimshurst Mdw WV10 ..... 11 F4
Wincanton Croft B36 ..... 68 C8
Winceby Pl CV4 ..... 111 D1
Winceby Rd WV6 ..... 23 F3
Winchat Cl CV3 ..... 114 F1
Winchcombe Cl Dudley DY1 ..... 50 E3
Solihull B92 ..... 89 B2
Winchcombe Rd B92 ..... 89 B2
Winchester Ave
Kidderminster DY11 ..... 116 A6
Nuneaton CV10 ..... 73 C7
Winchester Cl
8 Blackheath B65 ..... 63 E4
Hagley DY9 ..... 99 A6
Lichfield WS13 ..... 3 C3
Winchester Ct B74 ..... 31 F2
Winchester Dr
Birmingham B37 ..... 70 A2
Hinckley LE10 ..... 76 B7
Stourbridge DY8 ..... 81 A3
Winchester Gdns B31 ..... 103 A3
Winchester Gr B21 ..... 65 C8
Winchester Rd
Birmingham B20 ..... 55 D1
Cannock WS11 ..... 2 A4
West Bromwich B71 ..... 53 B8
Wolverhampton WV10 ..... 11 C3
Winchester Rise DY1 ..... 51 A2
Winchester St CV1 ..... 113 E3
Winchfield Dr B17 ..... 84 F7
Wincote Dr WV6 ..... 24 C4
Wincrest Way B34 ..... 69 C5
Windermere B77 ..... 36 A7
Windermere Ave
Coventry, Binley CV3 ..... 114 E1
Coventry, Upper Eastern Green CV5 ..... 111 E4
Nuneaton CV11 ..... 73 F6
Windermere Dr Aldridge B74 ..... 30 F3
Kingswinford DY6 ..... 60 D6
Royal Leamington Spa CV32 ..... 156 D2
Windermere Ho
Kidderminster DY10 ..... 116 E7
11 Oldbury B69 ..... 63 D5
Windermere Pl WS11 ..... 1 E1
Windermere Rd
Birmingham, Handsworth B21 ..... 54 E2
Birmingham, Moseley B13 ..... 87 B1
Wolverhampton WV6 ..... 24 D8
Windermre Ho B15 ..... 85 D3
Winding Mill N DY5 ..... 81 E7
Winding Mill S DY5 ..... 81 E7
Windings The WS13 ..... 3 A1
Windlass Croft B31 ..... 102 F4
Windleaves Rd B36 ..... 69 E8
Windley Ho B73 ..... 45 C2
Windmill Ave
Birmingham B45 ..... 121 E8
4 Coleshill B46 ..... 70 F7
Windmill Bank WV5 ..... 49 A7
Windmill Cl
Birmingham B31 ..... 103 C5
Kenilworth CV8 ..... 148 A6
Lichfield WS13 ..... 3 A2
Tamworth B79 ..... 21 A8
Windmill Cres
Smethwick B66 ..... 65 C5
West Bromwich B71 ..... 42 F1
Wolverhampton WV3 ..... 24 A1
Windmill Croft CV32 ..... 157 D5
Windmill Ct CV6 ..... 96 A3
Windmill Dr B97 ..... 158 C6
Windmill End DY2 ..... 62 E5
Windmill Gr DY6 ..... 60 B8
Windmill Hill
Birmingham B31 ..... 103 B5
Halesowen B63 ..... 82 D5
Royal Leamington Spa CV32 ..... 157 D5
Windmill Hill The CV5 ..... 112 A7
Windmill Ind Est CV5 ..... 111 F7
Windmill La
Balsall Common CV7 ..... 130 D4
Corley CV7 ..... 93 D6
Dorridge B93 ..... 127 F1
Lichfield WS13 ..... 3 A2
Smethwick B66 ..... 65 B5
Tanworth-in-A B94 ..... 144 A8
Wolverhampton WV3 ..... 38 A8
Windmill Prec B66 ..... 65 C5
Windmill Rd Bedworth CV7 ..... 96 A8
Coventry CV6 ..... 96 A3
Nuneaton CV10 ..... 72 D7
Royal Leamington Spa CV31 ..... 161 F5
Solihull B90 ..... 105 E2
Windmill St Birmingham B1 ..... 164 B1
Dudley, Eve Hill DY1 ..... 51 A2
Dudley, Gornalwood DY3 ..... 50 D5
Walsall WS1 ..... 42 F8
Wednesbury WS10 ..... 42 A3
Windmill Terr WS10 ..... 42 A3
Windmill View DY1 ..... 51 B7
Windridge Cl CV3 ..... 134 C6
Windridge Cres B92 ..... 107 F8
Windrow The WV6 ..... 23 D4
Windrush Cl Redditch B97 ..... 158 D6
Solihull B92 ..... 89 A2
Windrush Dr LE10 ..... 75 A8
Windrush Gr B29 ..... 104 A8
Windrush Ho B31 ..... 102 E5
Windrush Rd Cannock WS11 ..... 1 E6
Hollywood B47 ..... 125 B7
Winds Point DY9 ..... 99 A6
Windsor Arc B2 ..... 164 C3
Windsor Ave Oldbury B68 ..... 64 A3
Wolverhampton WV4 ..... 38 E6
Windsor Cl
Birmingham, Coft Common B31 ..... 123 A6
Birmingham, Frankley B45 ..... 102 A2
Blackheath B65 ..... 63 C4
Dudley DY3 ..... 50 B2
Halesowen B63 ..... 82 F3
Tamworth B79 ..... 21 C7
Windsor Cres DY2 ..... 62 D6
Windsor Ct Birmingham B38 ..... 103 F1
Coventry CV4 ..... 112 B2
Hinckley LE10 ..... 76 A5
Lichfield WS14 ..... 9 B6
Nuneaton CV10 ..... 72 E6
2 Royal Leamington Spa CV32 ..... 161 F8
Windsor Dr Birmingham B24 ..... 57 C5
Kidderminster DY10 ..... 116 E7
Solihull B92 ..... 89 B2
Windsor Gate WV12 ..... 27 C4
Windsor Gdns
Bromsgrove B60 ..... 137 A2
Nuneaton CV10 ..... 72 E4
Wolverhampton WV3 ..... 38 A8
Windsor Gr Stourbridge DY8 ..... 60 E1
Walsall WS4 ..... 15 C2
Windsor High Sch B63 ..... 82 F4
Windsor Ho
3 Birmingham B23 ..... 56 F6
Dudley DY2 ..... 61 F7
Windsor Ind Est B7 ..... 67 A5
Windsor Lodge B92 ..... 106 D8
Windsor Pl Birmingham B7 ..... 67 A3
8 Royal Leamington Spa CV32 ..... 156 F1
Windsor Rd
Birmingham, Castle Bromwich B36 ..... 69 F7
Birmingham, New Oscott B73 ..... 45 D1
Birmingham, Stirchley B30 ..... 104 B5
Blackheath B65 ..... 63 C5
Cheslyn Hay WS6 ..... 4 E4
Halesowen B63 ..... 82 F4
Oldbury B68 ..... 64 A3
Redditch B97 ..... 153 D5
Stourbridge DY8 ..... 80 E3
Tipton DY4 ..... 52 A8
West Bromwich B71 ..... 42 B1
Wolverhampton WV4 ..... 39 F5
Windsor St Bilston WV14 ..... 40 C6
Birmingham B7 ..... 67 A4
Bromsgrove B60 ..... 137 A2
Coventry CV1 ..... 113 B2
Hinckley LE10 ..... 76 A5
Nuneaton CV11 ..... 73 B4
Redditch B97 ..... 153 D4
Royal Leamington Spa CV32 ..... 161 F8
Walsall WS1 ..... 42 E7
Windsor St S B7 ..... 67 A4
Windsor Terr 5 B16 ..... 65 F1
Windsor View B32 ..... 102 B7
Windsor Way WS4 ..... 29 D7
Windsor Wlk WS10 ..... 41 D8
Windward Way B36 ..... 70 B6
Windward Way Ind Est B36 ..... 69 F8
Windy Arbor Prim Sch B37 ..... 70 D2
Windy Arbour CV8 ..... 148 B4
Windyridge Rd B76 ..... 58 A6
Winfield Rd CV11 ..... 73 B5
Winford Ave DY6 ..... 60 E4
Winforton Cl B98 ..... 154 E3
Wing Cl WS2 ..... 27 F4
Wingate Cl B30 ..... 103 F4
Wingate Ct B74 ..... 31 E4
Wingate Rd WS2 ..... 27 E2
Wingfield Cl B37 ..... 69 F3
Wingfield Ho B37 ..... 69 F5
Wingfield Rd
Birmingham B42 ..... 55 C7
Coleshill B46 ..... 70 F5
Wingfield Way CV6 ..... 95 A2
Wingfoot Ave WV10 ..... 25 E8
Wingrave Cl CV5 ..... 112 A6
Winifred Ave CV5 ..... 113 A1
Winifride Ct B17 ..... 85 B5
Winkle St B70 ..... 53 B4
Winleigh Rd B20 ..... 54 F2
Winn Ho 3 WS2 ..... 28 D3
Winnall Cl WV14 ..... 40 D2
Winnallthorpe CV3 ..... 134 E6
Winnie Rd B29 ..... 85 E1
Winnington Rd B8 ..... 68 A7
Winnipeg Rd B38 ..... 124 A8
Winscar Croft DY3 ..... 50 D3
Winsford Ave CV5 ..... 112 B4
Winsford Cl
Balsall Common CV7 ..... 130 A6
Halesowen B63 ..... 83 A6
Sutton Coldfield B76 ..... 46 E3
Winsford Ct CV5 ..... 112 C4
Winsham Gr B21 ..... 65 E8
Winsham Wlk CV3 ..... 133 D3
Winslow Ave B8 ..... 68 B4
Winslow Cl Coventry CV5 ..... 112 B3
Redditch B98 ..... 154 F3
Royal Leamington Spa CV32 ..... 156 C1
Winslow Dr WV6 ..... 24 E4
Winslow Ho 11 CV1 ..... 113 B2
Winson Green, Outer Circle B21 ..... 65 E7
Winson Green Rd B18 ..... 65 E5
Winson St B18 ..... 65 D4
Winsor Ave WS12 ..... 2 B6
Winspear Cl CV7 ..... 92 B1
Winstanley Rd B33 ..... 68 D2
Winster Ave B93 ..... 127 E4
Winster Cl CV7 ..... 95 A7
Winster Gr B44 ..... 44 D2
Winster Grove Ind Est B44 ..... 44 D2
Winster Rd Birmingham B43 ..... 54 D8
Wolverhampton WV1 ..... 26 B1
Winston Ave CV2 ..... 114 D8
Winston Churchill Ct WV14 ..... 40 C8
Winston Cl CV2 ..... 114 D8
Winston Dr Birmingham B20 ..... 55 B1
Romsley B62 ..... 101 A4
Winstone Cl B98 ..... 154 A4
Winter Cl WS13 ..... 3 D2
Winterbourne Croft B14 ..... 104 C1
Winterbourne Rd B91 ..... 106 F4
Winterdene CV7 ..... 130 B7
Winterfold Cl DY10 ..... 117 B6
Winterley Gdns DY3 ..... 50 E6
Winterley La WS4 ..... 29 C6
Winterton Rd
Birmingham B44 ..... 45 A3
Bulkington CV12 ..... 79 C2
Winthorpe Dr B91 ..... 127 C8
Wintney Cl B17 ..... 85 A7
Winton Gr B76 ..... 58 A6
Wintour Wlk B60 ..... 150 E7
Winward Rd B98 ..... 154 F1
Winwood Ct DY8 ..... 80 F4
Winwood Heath Rd B62 ..... 100 E2
Winwood Rd B65 ..... 63 E3
Winwoods Gr B32 ..... 102 A8
Winyate Hill B98 ..... 154 A2
Winyates Crafts Ctr B98 ..... 154 E3
Winyates Ctr B98 ..... 154 E3
Winyates Way B98 ..... 154 E4
Wirehill Dr B98 ..... 153 F1
Wiremill Cl B44 ..... 55 E6
Wirral Rd B31 ..... 102 F6
Wise Gr CV34 ..... 155 E2
Wise St CV31 ..... 161 F7
Wise Terr CV31 ..... 161 F7
Wiseacre Croft B90 ..... 105 E2
Wiseman Gr B23 ..... 45 D1
Wisemore WS2 ..... 28 E2
Wishaw Cl Redditch B98 ..... 159 A8
Solihull B90 ..... 105 E2
Wishaw Gr B37 ..... 69 F5
Wishaw La Curdworth B76 ..... 59 A7
Middleton B78 ..... 48 C6
Minworth B76 ..... 58 E7
Wisley Gr CV8 ..... 148 C5
Wisley Way B32 ..... 84 F5
Wissage Ct WS13 ..... 9 D8
Wissage La WS13 ..... 3 D1
Wissage Rd WS13 ..... 9 D8
Wistaria Cl Birmingham B31 ..... 103 A6
2 Coventry CV2 ..... 96 B2
Wisteria Gr B44 ..... 44 E2
Wistmans Cl DY1 ..... 50 E2
Wistwood Hayes WV10 ..... 11 F4
Witham Croft B91 ..... 107 C1
Withdean Cl B11 ..... 87 D6
Witherford Cl B29 ..... 103 C8
Witherford Croft B91 ..... 106 E2
Witherford Way B29 ..... 103 C8
Withern Way DY3 ..... 50 D3
Withers Rd WV8 ..... 10 B3
Withers Way B71 ..... 53 D4
Withington Covert B14 ..... 104 D2
Withington Gr B93 ..... 127 E4
Withum Cl B76 ..... 47 A1
Withy Gr B37 ..... 69 F5
Withy Hill Rd B75 ..... 47 B8
Withy Rd WV14 ..... 40 C3
Withy Road Ind Est WV14 ..... 40 C3
Withybed Cl B48 ..... 139 A6
Withybed La B48 ..... 139 A6
Withybrook Cl CV2 ..... 96 D2
Withybrook La CV7 ..... 97 F5
Withybrook Rd
Bulkington CV12 ..... 79 D2
Solihull B90 ..... 126 B8
Withymere La WV5 ..... 49 C8
Withymoor Prim Sch DY5 ..... 61 D1
Withymoor Rd Dudley DY2 ..... 62 E4
Stourbridge DY8 ..... 81 A7
Withymore Ct WV3 ..... 25 A1
Withywood Cl WV12 ..... 13 C1
Witley Ave Halesowen B63 ..... 82 E4
Solihull B91 ..... 107 C2
Witley Cl DY11 ..... 116 B2
Witley Cres B69 ..... 63 E5
Witley Farm Cl B91 ..... 107 C2
Witley Rd 1 B31 ..... 103 D2
Witney Cl B79 ..... 20 F7
Witney Dr B37 ..... 69 F2
Witney Gr WV10 ..... 11 B3
Wittersham Ct WV13 ..... 27 B2
Witton Bank B62 ..... 83 F7
Witton La Birmingham B6 ..... 55 F1
West Bromwich B71 ..... 53 B8
Witton Lodge Rd B23 ..... 56 D7
Witton Rd Birmingham B6 ..... 66 E8
Wolverhampton WV4 ..... 39 A6
Witton St Birmingham B9 ..... 67 B2
Stourbridge DY8 ..... 80 F4
Witton Sta B6 ..... 55 F1
Wixford Gr B90 ..... 106 D2
Wobaston Rd WV9, WV10 ..... 11 B4
Woburn B77 ..... 21 D3
Woburn Ave WV12 ..... 27 B6
Woburn Cl Bromsgrove B61 ..... 136 D1
Hinckley LE10 ..... 71 E3
Royal Leamington Spa CV31 ..... 162 C6
Woburn Cres B43 ..... 43 D1
Woburn Dr Brierley Hill DY5 ..... 81 B8
Halesowen B62 ..... 83 B7
Nuneaton CV10 ..... 73 A2
Woburn Gr B27 ..... 88 C1
Woburn Ho B15 ..... 86 C7
Wodehouse La DY3 ..... 49 E8
Woden Ave WV11 ..... 26 C6
Woden Cres WV11 ..... 26 C6
Woden Rd WV10 ..... 25 F4
Woden Rd E WS10 ..... 42 B4
Woden Rd N WS10 ..... 41 F5
Woden Rd S WS10 ..... 42 A1
Woden Rd W WS10 ..... 41 D4
Woden Sch WV10 ..... 25 E4
Wodensborough High Sch WS10 ..... 42 B2
Wodensfield Cty Inf & Jun Schs WV11 ..... 26 B6
Wodensfield Twr WV11 ..... 26 C5
Wold Wlk B13 ..... 105 C6
Wolfe Rd CV4 ..... 131 F8
Wolfsbane Dr WS5 ..... 43 A3
Wolfson Dr B15 ..... 85 E4
Wollaston Cres WV11 ..... 26 D6

Wollaston Ct Stourbridge
DY7 .... 80 C6
1 Walsall WS1 .... 28 F2
Wollaston Rd
Stourbridge, Amblecote DY8 .. 80 F8
Stourbridge, Wollaston DY7 .. 80 C7
Wollerton Gr B75 .... 46 F6
Wollescote Dr B91 .... 107 B2
Wollescote Factory Ctr
6 DY9 .... 81 F5
Wollescote Prim Sch DY9 ... 81 F4
Wollescote Rd DY9 .... 81 D3
Wolmer Rd WV11 .... 13 A2
Wolseley B77 .... 21 F3
Wolseley Ave B27 .... 88 D4
Wolseley Bank WV10 .... 25 F7
Wolseley Cl Birmingham
B36 .... 59 A1
Wolverhampton WV10 .... 25 F7
Wolseley Dr B8 .... 68 B7
Wolseley Gate WV10 .... 25 F7
Wolseley Rd Bilston WV14 ... 40 C7
West Bromwich B70 .... 52 F6
Wolseley St B9 .... 67 B2
Wolsey St CV3 .... 134 D6
Wolston Cl B90 .... 106 B5
Wolston La CV8 .... 135 E2
Wolverhampton Dudley &
Dist Inst for the Blind
The WV4 .... 39 D3
Wolverhampton Girls High
Sch WV6 .... 24 F3
Wolverhampton Gram Sch
WV3 .... 24 F2
Wolverhampton & Midland
Cties Eye Infmy WV3 ... 25 A2
Wolverhampton Rd
Cannock WS11 .... 4 D8
Cheslyn Hay WV10, WS6 .... 4 B2
Codsall WV8 .... 10 A3
Essington WV11 .... 13 A3
Kingswinford DY6 .... 60 C8
Nurton WV6 .... 23 A3
Oldbury B69 .... 63 F4
Sedgley DY3 .... 39 D2
Walsall, Birchills WS2 .... 28 B2
Walsall, Pelsall WS3 .... 14 F3
Walsall,
Wallington Heath WS3 .... 14 B1
Wedges Mills WS11 .... 4 B5
Wolverhampton
WV10, WV11 .... 26 B4
Wolverhampton Rd E
WV4 .... 39 E5
Wolverhampton Rd S B32 .. 84 E7
Wolverhampton Rd W
WV13, WS2 .... 27 D2
Wolverhampton St
Bilston WV14 .... 40 C6
Darlaston WS10 .... 41 C6
Dudley DY1 .... 51 B1
Walsall WS2 .... 28 D2
Willenhall WV13 .... 27 A1
Wolverhampton St
George's Sta WV1 .... 163 C2
Wolverhampton Sta
(High Level) WV10 .... 163 C3
Wolverley Ave
Stourbridge DY8 .... 80 C6
Wolverhampton WV4 .... 38 D5
Wolverley Cres B69 .... 63 E5
Wolverley Rd
Birmingham B32 .... 102 B8
Halesowen B63 .... 82 F2
Solihull B92 .... 89 D2
Wolverson Cl WV12 .... 27 C4
Wolverson Rd WS9 .... 16 A4
Wolverton Cl B98 .... 154 E2
Wolverton Rd
Birmingham,
Marston Green B37 .... 90 B7
Birmingham, Rednall B45 ... 122 C4
Coventry CV5 .... 112 A3
Dudley DY2 .... 51 E1
Wolvey Rd Bulkington CV12 .. 79 E2
Hinckley LE10 .... 75 E4
Wombourne Cl B93 .... 50 C8
Wombourne Pk WV5 .... 49 A4
Wood Ave Dudley DY3 .... 50 C4
Wednesfield WV11 .... 26 D6
Wood Bank WV3 .... 38 A8
Wood Cl B46 .... 70 F7
Wood Croft B47 .... 125 B6
Wood Ct Birmingham B20 .... 55 A2
Coventry CV2 .... 114 D7
Wood End Dr B45 .... 138 A8
Wood End Fst Sch CV9 .... 36 C1
Wood End Jun Sch CV2 ...... 96 D1
Wood End La
Birmingham B24 .... 56 F3
Lichfield WS13 .... 3 F6
Tanworth-In-A B94 .... 141 F5
Wood End Prim Sch
WV11 .... 26 C7
Wood End Rd
Birmingham B24 .... 56 F3
Walsall WS5 .... 43 D8
Wednesfield WV11 .... 26 D7
Wood End Sta B94 .... 141 F4
Wood End Way WS9 .... 16 B1
Wood Green High Sch
WS10 .... 42 B5
Wood Green Jun Sch WS10 .. 42 A4
Wood Green Rd
Birmingham B18 .... 65 D4
Wednesbury WS10 .... 42 A3
Wood Hayes Rd WV11 .... 12 C1
Wood Hill Rise CV6 .... 95 D2

Wood Ho **1** WS1 .... 42 E7
Wood La Aldridge B74 .... 30 F2
Birmingham, Erdington B24 .. 57 C1
Birmingham,
Handsworth B20 .... 55 B2
Birmingham, Harborne B17 ... 85 A6
Birmingham,
Marston Green B37 .... 90 A8
Birmingham,
Woodgate B32 .... 84 A1
Cannock WS12 .... 2 D4
Earlswood B94 .... 125 E1
Fairfield B61 .... 120 C3
Hampton in A B92 .... 108 F2
Nuneaton CV10 .... 72 A8
Shenstone, WS14 .... 17 B2
Shilton CV7 .... 97 D5
Walsall WS3 .... 14 F4
Wedges Mills WS11 .... 4 A6
West Bromwich B70 .... 53 A3
Willenhall WV12 .... 27 E7
Wolverhampton WV10 .... 11 D2
Wood Lane Cl WV12 .... 27 E7
Wood Leasow B32 .... 84 D2
Wood Leigh Cl B63 .... 83 A6
Wood Piece La B98 .... 154 D7
Wood Rd Dudley DY3 .... 50 C4
Wolverhampton WV6 .... 24 C3
Wombourne WV5 .... 49 B7
Wood Ridings WS13 .... 3 A1
Wood Side WV11 .... 27 A8
Wood St Bedworth CV12 ...... 78 B5
Bilston WV14 .... 40 D5
Birmingham B16 .... 66 A2
Darlaston WS10 .... 41 F6
Dudley DY2 .... 61 F6
Hinckley LE10 .... 71 D1
Kidderminster DY11 .... 116 D5
Nuneaton CV10 .... 72 F4
Royal Leamington Spa
CV32 .... 162 A8
Stourbridge, Lye DY9 .... 81 F5
Stourbridge,
Wollaston DY8 .... 80 D6
Tipton DY4 .... 51 E5
Willenhall WV13 .... 27 B2
Wolverhampton,
Lanesfield WV4 .... 40 A3
Wolverhampton,
Park Village WV10 .... 25 F5
Wood End CV9 .... 36 C1
Wood Street LE10 .... 71 E1
Wood Terr B96 .... 159 B1
Woodacre Rd B24 .... 57 C4
Woodall Ho WS3 .... 28 C8
Woodall Rd B6 .... 55 F1
Woodall St Blackheath B64 .. 62 C1
Walsall WS3 .... 28 C8
Woodard Rd WV4 .... 52 C7
Woodbank LE10 .... 76 A7
Woodbank B61 .... 136 F8
Woodbank Rd DY3 .... 50 C7
Woodberrow La B97 .... 158 D6
Woodberry Dr B76 .... 47 A2
Woodberry Wlk B27 .... 88 D3
Woodbine Ave B10 .... 87 D8
Woodbine Cotts
4 CV32 .... 161 E8
Woodbine Croft B26 .... 89 A6
Woodbine St **3** CV32 ...... 161 E8
Woodbine Wlk B37 .... 70 D2
Woodbourne B15 .... 85 D8
Woodbourne Rd
Birmingham B15, B16 .... 85 C8
Smethwick B67 .... 64 E2
Woodbridge Cl
Walsall, High Heath WS4 ... 15 D1
Walsall,
Wallington Heath WS3 .... 14 A3
Woodbridge Rd B13 .... 86 F3
Woodbrook Ho **9** B37 ...... 70 B2
Woodbrooke Rd B30 .... 103 E7
Woodburn Cl CV5 .... 112 B4
Woodburn Rd B66 .... 65 D7
Woodbury Cl Brierley Hill
DY5 .... 61 E2
Halesowen B62 .... 83 F8
Redditch B97 .... 158 A6
Woodbury Gr **3** B91 ..... 107 B1
Woodbury Rd Halesowen
B62 .... 84 A8
Kidderminster DY11 .... 116 B2
Woodchester DY9 .... 99 B4
Woodchester Rd B93 .... 127 E2
Woodclose Ave CV6 .... 112 F6
Woodclose Rd B37 .... 69 F3
Woodcock Cl B94 .... 141 E3
Woodcock Gdns WV10 ...... 12 B7
Woodcock Hill Prim Sch
B31 .... 102 E7
Woodcock La
Birmingham,
Acock's Green B27 .... 88 D3
Birmingham,
Northfield B31 .... 102 E8
Woodcock La N B27 .... 88 D4
Woodcock St B7 .... 66 F4
Woodcombe Cl DY5 .... 81 B7
Woodcote Ave
Kenilworth CV8 .... 147 D6
Nuneaton CV11 .... 73 F8
Woodcote Dr Birmingham
B8 .... 67 F5
Dorridge B93 .... 128 B2
Leek Wootton CV35 .... 155 F7
Woodcote La
Belbroughton DY9 .... 119 E1
Leek Wootton CV35 .... 155 F7

Woodcote Rd
Birmingham B24 .... 57 D5
Royal Leamington Spa CV32 . 156 F1
Warwick CV34 .... 160 F8
Wolverhampton WV6 .... 24 C4
Woodcote Way
Birmingham B18 .... 66 A4
Sutton Coldfield B74 .... 44 F6
Woodcraft Cl CV4 .... 112 A2
Woodcroft Ave
Birmingham B20 .... 54 E3
Dudley DY4 .... 51 C4
Tamworth B79 .... 21 B6
Woodcroft Cl **3**
Blackheath B64 .... 82 F8
Blackwell B60 .... 137 F5
Woodcross La WV14 .... 40 A2
Woodcross St WV14 .... 39 F2
Woodend B20 .... 54 E6
Woodend Cl B97 .... 153 B2
Woodend Croft CV4 .... 131 E8
Woodend Pl WV6 .... 24 B4
Woodfall Ave B30 .... 103 F5
Woodfield DY9 .... 119 E7
Woodfield Ave
Blackheath B64 .... 82 D8
Brierley Hill DY5 .... 61 B7
Oldbury B69 .... 64 A4
Stourbridge DY9 .... 81 F2
Wolverhampton WV4 .... 38 F6
Woodfield Cl
Norton Canes WS11 .... 5 F7
Redditch B98 .... 154 A5
Sutton Coldfield B74 .... 46 B8
Walsall WS5 .... 43 E5
Woodfield Cres
Birmingham B12 .... 87 A6
Kidderminster DY11 .... 116 D5
Woodfield Dr WS11 .... 5 F7
Woodfield Ho WS3 .... 15 B3
Woodfield Hts WV6 .... 24 D4
Woodfield Jun & Inf Schs
WV4 .... 38 F6
Woodfield La B62 .... 120 D8
Woodfield Rd
Birmingham,
Balsall Heath B12 .... 87 A6
Birmingham,
King's Heath B13 .... 87 A2
Coventry CV5 .... 132 E8
Dudley DY3 .... 50 C4
King's Heath LE10 .... 75 C6
Solihull B91 .... 107 B6
Woodfield St **4** DY11 ... 116 C6
Woodfields Dr WS14 .... 9 E5
Woodfold Croft WS9 .... 30 B7
Woodford Ave B36 .... 69 B8
Woodford Cl Ash Green
CV7 .... 95 D5
Nuneaton CV10 .... 72 D4
Wolverhampton WV6 .... 10 F2
Woodford Cres WS7 .... 7 B7
Woodford End WS11 .... 1 F4
Woodford Green Rd B28 .. 106 B8
Woodford Way WS12 .... 2 D1
Woodfort Rd B43 .... 54 E7
Woodgate Bsns Pk B32 ..... 84 B2
Woodgate Dr B32 .... 84 A1
Woodgate Gdns B32 .... 84 A2
Woodgate Ho B37 .... 153 B4
Woodgate Jun & Inf Sch
B32 .... 84 B1
Woodgate La B32 .... 84 A2
Woodgate Rd Hinckley
LE10 .... 76 A8
Stoke Prior B60 .... 151 B1
Woodgate Valley Ctry Pk
B32 .... 84 D3
Woodgate Way DY9 .... 119 E7
Woodglade Croft B38 ...... 103 E2
Woodgreen WS11 .... 4 E5
Woodgreen Cl B97 .... 158 B7
Woodgreen Croft B68 ...... 84 C7
Woodgreen Rd B68 .... 84 C7
Woodhall Cl Nuneaton
CV11 .... 74 A2
Tipton DY4 .... 52 A8
Woodhall Croft B92 .... 88 F3
Woodhall Rd WV4 .... 38 E5
Woodham Cl B45 .... 101 E1
Woodhams Rd CV3 .... 134 C3
Woodhaven Walsall WS4 ... 15 D1
Wedges Mills WS11 .... 4 B5
Woodhouse Cl CV3 .... 134 E8
Woodhouse High Sch B77 .. 21 F4
Woodhouse La B77 .... 22 A5
Woodhouse Orch DY9 ..... 119 E7
Woodhouse Prim Sch B32 .. 84 E6
Woodhouse Rd
Birmingham B32 .... 84 E5
Wolverhampton WV6 .... 24 B4
Woodhouse Rd N WV6 ...... 24 B4
Woodhouse St CV34 .... 160 D6
Woodhouses La WS7 .... 7 F6
Woodhouses Rd WS7 .... 8 A7
Woodhurst Cl B77 .... 21 F5
Woodhurst Rd B13 .... 87 A4
Wooding Cres DY4 .... 41 B1
Woodington Fst Sch B75 ... 47 A5
Woodington Rd B75 .... 47 B5
Woodland Ave
Brierley Hill DY5 .... 62 A1
Coventry CV5 .... 132 F4
Dudley DY2 .... 51 C3
Hagley DY9 .... 98 F5
Hinckley LE10 .... 76 A7
Kidderminster DY11 .... 116 C7

Woodland Cl Cannock WS12 .. 2 B8
Stourbridge DY9 .... 81 D2
Willenhall WV12 .... 27 D6
Woodland Cres WV3 .... 38 D7
Woodland Ct Cannock WS12 .. 1 C4
Shenstone WS14 .... 32 A7
Woodland Dr Cheslyn Hay
WS6 .... 4 E4
Smethwick B66 .... 64 E7
Woodland Gr
Birmingham B43 .... 43 E3
Dudley DY3 .... 50 B3
Woodland Rd
Birmingham,
Handsworth B21 .... 65 C8
Birmingham,
Northfield B31 .... 103 B6
Dodford B61 .... 136 A7
Halesowen B62 .... 83 D8
Hinckley LE10 .... 71 F1
Kenilworth CV8 .... 148 B7
Redditch B97 .... 153 B3
Tamworth B77 .... 22 A4
Wolverhampton WV3 .... 38 D7
Woodland Rise
Blackheath B64 .... 82 F8
Sutton Coldfield B73 .... 46 B4
Woodland Way
Birchmoor B78 .... 36 F8
Burntwood WS7 .... 7 A6
Woodlands Ave Walsall
WS5 .... 43 E5
Water Orton B46 .... 59 B2
Woodlands Cotts WV4 ...... 38 F4
Woodlands Cres WS3 .... 14 F5
Woodlands Ct
Binley Woods CV3 .... 135 D7
Coventry CV5 .... 133 A8
Woodlands Farm Rd B24 ... 57 F4
Woodlands Inf Sch B90 ... 126 B8
Woodlands Jun & Inf Sch
B36 .... 70 B6
Woodlands La
Bedworth CV12 .... 77 E4
Solihull B90 .... 126 B8
Woodlands Paddock WV4 .. 38 E4
Woodlands Park Rd B30 .. 103 C5
Woodlands Prim Sch
Tamworth B77 .... 21 E4
Willenhall WV12 .... 27 D6
Woodlands Rd
Bedworth CV12 .... 77 F3
Binley Woods CV3 .... 135 D7
Birmingham, Moseley B11 .. 87 C2
Birmingham, Rubery B45 .. 121 D7
Birmingham, Saltley B8 ..... 67 F3
Wombourne WV5 .... 49 A5
Woodlands Sch The CV4 .. 111 D3
Woodlands St B66 .... 65 C5
Woodlands The
Blackheath B64 .... 83 A7
Lichfield WS13 .... 9 D8
Nuneaton CV10 .... 72 A8
Stourbridge DY8 .... 81 A2
Wood End CV9 .... 36 C1
Woodlands Way B37 .... 70 D3
Woodlawn Gr DY6 .... 60 D5
Woodlea Dr Birmingham
B24 .... 56 F2
Solihull B91 .... 106 E4
Woodleaves B47 .... 124 F4
Woodleigh Ave B17 .... 85 D4
Woodleigh Ct B38 .... 103 F1
Woodleigh Rd B72 .... 46 C1
Woodleys The B14 .... 105 B4
Woodloes Ave N CV34 ..... 155 F1
Woodloes Ave S CV34 ..... 155 E1
Woodloes Fst Sch CV34 .. 155 F1
Woodloes La CV34 .... 155 F2
Woodloes Mid Sch CV34 .. 155 E1
Woodloes Rd B90 .... 126 B7
Woodman Cl B63 .... 83 C3
Woodman La Cheslyn Hay
WS6 .... 4 E4
Clent DY9 .... 99 E4
Woodman Rd
Birmingham B14 .... 105 A1
Halesowen B63 .... 83 C3
Woodman Wlk B23 .... 56 A5
Woodmeadow Rd B30 ..... 104 B3
Woodnorton Dr B13 .... 86 E2
Woodnorton Rd B65 .... 63 F2
Woodpecker Gr
Birmingham B36 .... 70 A7
Kidderminster DY10 .... 117 B8
Woodpecker Way WS11 ..... 2 C3
Woodperry Ave B91 .... 107 C1
Woodridge B6 .... 55 E1
Woodridge Ave
Birmingham B32 .... 84 B4
Coventry CV5 .... 112 A6
Woodridge Rd B63 .... 83 A5
Woodrough Dr B13 .... 86 F2
Woodrow Cl B61 .... 120 F1
Woodrow Cres B93 .... 128 A5
Woodrow Ctr B98 .... 159 B8
Woodrow Fst Sch B98 .... 159 B7
Woodrow La
Bluntington DY10 .... 118 E3
Catshill B61 .... 121 B2
Woodrow N B98 .... 159 A7
Woodrow S B98 .... 159 B7
Woodrow Wlk B98 .... 159 B7
Woodruff Way WS5 .... 43 A3
Woodrush Dr B47 .... 125 A5
Woodrush High Sch The
B47 .... 125 A6

Woods Bank Terr WS10 ..... 41 C5
Woods Cres DY5 .... 62 A1
Woods Croft WS13 .... 3 A1
Woods La Blackheath B64 ... 82 C8
Brierley Hill DY5 .... 81 D7
Woods The B14 .... 86 F1
Woodsbank Ind Est The
WS10 .... 41 D4
Woodsetton Cl DY1 .... 51 B6
Woodsetton Specl Sch
DY3 .... 50 F7
Woodshill Ave B45 .... 122 A2
Woodshires Rd Coventry
CV6 .... 95 F5
Solihull B92 .... 106 E7
Woodside Birmingham B37 .. 69 E4
Sutton Coldfield B74 .... 31 E2
Woodside Ave B97 .... 153 B2
Woodside Ave N CV3 .... 132 F6
Woodside Ave S CV3 .... 132 F5
Wood End CV9 .... 36 C1
Woodside Cres B93 .... 128 B4
Woodside Dr
Barnt Green B45 .... 138 B8
Little Aston B74 .... 31 C5
Woodside Gr WV8 .... 10 B2
Woodside Pl WS11 .... 1 E5
Woodside Rd
Birmingham B29 .... 86 A1
Dudley DY2 .... 61 F7
Walsall WS5 .... 43 E6
Woodside Way Aldridge
WS9 .... 30 B5
Birmingham B45 .... 102 A4
Solihull B91 .... 106 E5
Willenhall WV12 .... 27 E7
Woodsome Gr B23 .... 56 C7
Woodsorrel Rd DY1 .... 51 A4
Woodstile B34 .... 69 B6
Woodstile Cl B75 .... 32 D3
Woodstock Cl Dudley DY1 .. 62 A8
Hinckley LE10 .... 76 A5
Stourbridge DY8 .... 60 C1
2 Walsall WS5 .... 43 A3
Woodstock Cres B93 .... 127 F3
Woodstock Ct B13 .... 87 B4
Woodstock Dr
Huntington WS12 .... 1 C7
Stourbridge DY8 .... 60 C2
Sutton Coldfield B74 .... 31 D4
Woodstock Ho B13 .... 105 A7
Woodstock Rd
Birmingham,
Handsworth B21 .... 65 F8
Birmingham, Moseley B13 ... 87 B3
Coventry CV3 .... 133 D7
Nuneaton CV11 .... 73 E1
Wolverhampton WV1 .... 26 B1
Woodston Gr B91 .... 127 C8
Woodthorne Cl DY3 .... 50 D2
Woodthorne Inf & Jun
Schs WV6 .... 24 A4
Woodthorne Rd WV6 .... 24 A6
Woodthorne Rd S WV6 ...... 24 A5
Woodthorne Wlk **4** DY6 .. 60 D5
Woodthorpe Dr WV5 .... 49 B7
Woodthorpe Gdns B14 .... 104 E5
Woodthorpe Inf & Jun
Sch B14 .... 104 E5
Woodthorpe Rd B14 .... 104 E5
Woodvale Dr B28 .... 105 E4
Woodvale Rd
Birmingham, Woodgate B32 ... 84 A1
Birmingham,
Yardley Wood B28 .... 105 E4
Woodview Dr B15 .... 86 C7
Woodville Ct **3** B23 .... 56 E2
Woodville Gdns DY3 .... 39 F1
Woodville Rd
Birmingham, Harborne B17 .... 85 A6
Birmingham,
King's Heath B14 .... 104 F4
Warwick CV34 .... 160 E8
Woodward Cl CV31 .... 162 A2
Woodward Pl DY9 .... 81 C4
Woodward Rd DY11 .... 116 C4
Woodward St B7 .... 53 E4
Woodwards Cl WS2 .... 42 B8
Woodwards Pl WS2 .... 42 B8
Woodwards Rd WS2 .... 42 B8
Woodway B24 .... 57 C5
Woodway Cl CV2 .... 114 F4
Woodway La CV2 .... 96 F1
Woodway Park Sch &
Com Coll CV2 .... 96 F1
Woodway Wlk CV2 .... 114 E8
Woodwells Rd B8 .... 68 B5
Woody Bank WS6 .... 4 E2
Woolacombe Lodge Rd
B29 .... 85 C2
Woolaston Rd B98 .... 159 C8
Woolgrove St CV6 .... 96 A3
Woolhope Cl B98 .... 154 F3
Woolmore Rd B23 .... 56 C5
Woolpack Cl B65 .... 63 A4
Woolpack St WV1 .... 163 B3
Woolwich Rd CV11 .... 79 F6
Wooton Gr B44 .... 56 C8
Wootton Ave WV11 .... 26 D1
Wootton Cl WS11 .... 2 B3
Wootton Ct Coventry CV2 .. 114 F2
6 Royal Leamington Spa
CV32 .... 156 F2
Wootton Green La CV7 .... 130 A8

Wootton La B92 .... 109 E1
Wootton Rd
　Birmingham B31 .... 123 A6
　Wolverhampton WV3 .... 38 D8
Wootton St CV12 .... 78 D3
Woottons Ct WS11 .... 1 F1
Worcester Cl Allesley
　CV5 .... 112 B7
　Cannock WS11 .... 4 F8
　Hagley DY9 .... 99 A5
　Sutton Coldfield B75 .... 32 D3
　Wolverhampton WS13 .... 3 B3
Worcester Cross
　3 DY10 .... 116 E5
Worcester Ct Coventry CV6 ... 96 B4
　Wolverhampton WV3 .... 39 A6
Worcester Gn B71 .... 53 C7
Worcester Gr WV6 .... 23 D4
Worcester Ho
　Birmingham B36 .... 70 A8
　4 Halesowen B63 .... 83 A3
Worcester La
　Stourbridge DY9 .... 99 B7
　Sutton Coldfield B75 .... 32 D4
Worcester Rd Birmingham
　B6 .... 55 F2
　Bromsgrove B61 .... 136 F1
　Dudley DY2 .... 62 E3
　Hagley DY9 .... 99 A5
　Kenilworth CV8 .... 148 B3
　Kidderminster DY10 .... 116 E2
　Mustow Green DY10 .... 117 F1
　Oldbury B68 .... 84 A8
　Stoke Heath B61 .... 150 B4
　Willenhall WV13 .... 27 D2
Worcester Rise B29 .... 86 B1
Worcester Sq **1** B98 ..... 153 E4
Worcester St
　Kidderminster DY10 .... 116 E6
　Stourbridge DY8 .... 81 A4
　Wolverhampton WV2 .... 163 B2
Worcester Wlk B37 .... 70 A1
Word Hill B17 .... 84 F7
Wordsley Ct DY8 .... 60 E3
Wordsley Green Sh Ctr
　DY8 .... 60 D2
Wordsley Hospl DY8 .... 60 E4
Wordsworth Ave
　Redditch B97 .... 158 C8
　Tamworth B79 .... 21 A6
　Warwick CV34 .... 160 D5
　Wolverhampton WV4 .... 39 F4
Wordsworth Cl Cannock
　WS11 .... 1 D4
　Lichfield WS14 .... 9 B5
　Tipton DY4 .... 52 A8
Wordsworth Cres DY10 .... 117 B6
Wordsworth Dr WV6 .... 23 E4
Wordsworth Dr CV8 .... 148 C4
Wordsworth Ho
　Birmingham B31 .... 123 A8
　Halesowen B63 .... 82 B5
　4 Oldbury B68 .... 64 C4
Wordsworth Rd
　Bedworth CV12 .... 78 D1
　Birmingham B10 .... 87 D7
　2 Burntwood WS7 .... 7 A8
　Coventry CV2 .... 114 C4
　Dudley DY3 .... 50 B5
　Walsall WS3 .... 28 E8
　Willenhall WV12 .... 27 E7
　Wolverhampton WV10 .... 26 A8
Wordsworth St B71 .... 53 C5
Worfield Cl WS4 .... 29 A4
Worfield Gdns WV3 .... 38 F6
Workhouse La LE10 .... 76 A4
Works Rd B26 .... 90 A3
World's End Ave B32 .... 84 D6
World's End La B32 .... 84 D5
Worlds End Jun Sch B32 ... 84 D5
Worlds End Rd B20 .... 55 A3
Worleys Wharf Ave WS10 ... 42 E2
Worsdell Cl CV1 .... 113 B4
Worsey Dr DY4 .... 52 D6
Worsfold Cl CV5 .... 112 A7
Worthen Gr B31 .... 123 A8
Worthings The B30 .... 104 B6
Worthy Down WV11 .... 26 F5
Worthy Down Wlk B35 ...... 58 B3
Wortley Ave WV10 .... 25 E6
Worton Rd DY9 .... 81 F2
Wragby Cl WV9 .... 11 B3
Wrekin Cl Halesowen B63 ... 82 C1
　Kidderminster DY11 .... 116 B2
Wrekin Ct B74 .... 31 F2

Wrekin Dr Bromsgrove
　B61 .... 137 A5
　Stourbridge DY9 .... 81 D4
Wolverhampton,
　Penn WV3 .... 38 E8
Wolverhampton,
　Tettenhall WV6 .... 24 A5
Wrekin La WV6 .... 24 A5
Wrekin Rd Birmingham B44 ... 56 A6
　Sutton Coldfield B73 .... 46 A1
Wrekin View Brownhills
　WS8 .... 16 A5
　Huntington WS12 .... 1 C7
　Wolverhampton WV1 .... 163 B3
Wrekin View Rd DY3 .... 50 C8
Wren Ave WV6 .... 23 D3
Wren St Coventry CV2 ..... 113 F3
　Dudley, Netherton DY2 ..... 62 B5
　Dudley, Swan Village DY1 ... 51 C6
Wren's Nest Nature
Reserve WV1 .... 51 B4
Wren's Nest Prim Sch
　DY1 .... 51 A4
Wren's Nest Rd DY1 .... 51 A5
Wrenbury Dr CV6 .... 96 A4
Wrens Ave Dudley DY4 ..... 51 D4
　Kingswinford DY6 .... 61 A4
Wrens Hill Rd DY1 .... 51 B5
Wrens Nest Pl DY1 .... 51 A5
Wrens Nest Rd DY1 .... 51 A4
Wrens Park Ave B76 .... 57 F7
Wrentham St B5 .... 86 E8
Wretham Ct B19 .... 66 B7
Wretham Rd B19 .... 66 B6
Wrexham Ave WS2 .... 27 F1
Wright Ave WV11 .... 26 E7
Wright Rd B8 .... 67 E5
Wright St Bilston WV14 .... 40 E4
　Birmingham B10 .... 87 D8
　Coventry CV1 .... 113 E4
　Halesowen B63 .... 83 B4
　Wolverhampton WV10 .... 25 D4
Wright's Ave WS11 .... 1 F5
Wright's La B64 .... 63 A1
Wrighton Cl WV12 .... 27 C8
Wrighton Dr DY5 .... 50 C1
Wrigsham St CV3 .... 133 D8
Wrottesley Park Rd
　WV6, WV8 .... 23 D5
Wrottesley Rd
　Birmingham B43 .... 43 D1
　Wolverhampton WV6 .... 24 B5
Wrottesley Rd W WV6 ..... 24 A6
Wrottesley St B5 .... 164 C1
Wroxall Abbey (Sch)
　CV35 .... 145 E2
Wroxall CE Jun & Inf Sch
　CV35 .... 145 A3
Wroxall Cl DY5 .... 81 C8
Wroxall Dr CV3 .... 134 D5
Wroxall Gr B13 .... 105 A6
Wroxall Rd B91 .... 106 E6
Wroxham Glen WV13 .... 40 F8
Wroxton Rd B26 .... 88 E8
Wulfrun Coll WV3 .... 24 E3
Wulfrun Coll Annexe,
Newhampton Ctr WV1 .. 163 A4
Wulfrun Ctr WV1 .... 163 C2
Wulfrun Sq WV1 .... 163 C2
Wulfrun Trad Est W6 .... 25 C5
Wulfruna Gdns WV3 .... 24 F1
Wulfruna St WV1 .... 163 B3
Wyatt Cl B5 .... 86 C5
Wyatt Ho CV2 .... 114 D7
Wyatt Rd B75 .... 47 B5
Wyatts Ct CV12 .... 78 B3
Wych Elm Dr CV31 .... 161 F5
Wych Elm Rd WS8 .... 15 E5
Wychall Dr WV10 .... 11 E4
Wychall Farm Inf Sch
　B31 .... 103 C2
Wychall Farm Jun Sch
　B31 .... 103 C2
Wychall La B38 .... 103 E2
Wychall Park Gr B38 ...... 103 D2
Wychall Rd B31 .... 103 C3
Wychbold Cl Redditch
　B97 .... 158 A6
　Willenhall WV12 .... 13 B1
Wychbold Cres B33 .... 69 C3
Wychbold Ct DY9 .... 99 C8
Wychbold Way WV11 .... 13 D1
Wychbury B76 .... 47 A1
Wychbury Ct
　7 Dudley DY2 .... 62 B8
　Halesowen B63 .... 83 A3
Wychbury Dr DY9 .... 99 C7
Wychbury Grange DY9 ..... 81 C1

Wychbury Rd
　Birmingham B32 .... 102 B7
　Brierley Hill DY5 .... 81 E8
　Stourbridge DY9 .... 81 E2
　Wolverhampton WV3 .... 38 C7
Wyche Ave B14 .... 104 D4
Wyche Cotts B60 .... 150 C1
Wychelm Farm Rd B14 ... 105 A1
Wychnor Gr B71 .... 42 E2
Wychwood Ave
　Coventry CV3 .... 133 C3
　Knowle B93 .... 128 B8
Wychwood Cres B26 ...... 89 A6
Wychwood Dr B97 .... 158 D6
Wyckham Cl B17 .... 85 A4
Wyckham Rd B36 .... 69 F8
Wycliffe Gr CV2 .... 114 B5
Wycliffe Rd W CV2 .... 114 C5
Wycome Rd B28 .... 106 A7
Wye Cl Bulkington CV12 ... 79 B2
　Hinckley LE10 .... 75 A8
　Perton WV6 .... 23 F4
Royal Leamington Spa
　CV32 .... 157 C3
　Sutton Coldfield B76 .... 58 A7
Wye Cliff Rd B20 .... 66 B8
Wye Ho **4** DY3 .... 50 D3
Wye Rd WS3 .... 14 E1
Wyemanton Cl B43 .... 43 C1
Wyke Rd CV2 .... 114 C4
Wykeham Gr WV6 .... 23 D3
Wykeley Rd CV2 .... 114 C4
Wyken Ave CV2 .... 114 D5
Wyken Cl B93 .... 127 E2
Wyken Croft CV2 .... 114 D6
Wyken Croft Prim Sch
　CV2 .... 114 E5
Wyken Grange Rd CV2 .... 114 C5
Wyken Way CV2 .... 114 B5
Wykin Rd LE10 .... 71 A3
Wyld Cl B71 .... 53 A8
Wyld Ct CV5 .... 112 B5
Wylde Cres B65 .... 63 C4
Wylde Green Coll B72 ..... 46 C1
Wylde Green Jun & Inf
　Sch B73 .... 57 B7
Wylde Green Rd B72, B76 ... 46 D1
Wylde Green Sta B73 ..... 46 B1
Wyley Rd CV6 .... 113 B5
Wymering Ave WV11 ...... 26 F7
Wyn-Griffith Dr DY4 ..... 52 A3
Wynall La WV9 .... 81 F3
Wynall La S DY9 .... 82 A3
Wynbrook Gr B30 .... 127 A6
Wynchcombe Ave WV4 .... 38 D4
Wyncote Cl CV8 .... 148 A4
Wynd The DY3 .... 39 D1
Wyndcliff Rd B9 .... 67 D1
Wyndcliffe Inf Sch B9 ..... 67 C1
Wyndcliffe Jun Sch B9 .... 67 C1
Wyndham Gdns B30 ...... 103 D4
Wyndham Rd B16 .... 65 F1
Wyndhurst St B33 .... 68 E4
Wyndhurst Rd B33 .... 68 E5
Wyndley Dr B73 .... 46 B4
Wyndley La B73 .... 46 A4
Wyndmill Cres B71 .... 42 F1
Wynds Covert B14 .... 104 D2
Wynds Point B31 .... 103 B5
Wynfield Gdns B14 .... 104 F5
Wynford Rd B27 .... 88 C5
Wynford Road Ind Est
　B27 .... 88 C5
Wynn Rd WV4 .... 38 F5
Wynn St B15 .... 86 D8
Wynne Cres WV4 .... 38 B3
Wynstead Covert **6** B14 ... 104 C2
Wyntor La B71 .... 53 B8
Wynyates B79 .... 20 E6
Wyre Cl Birmingham B45 ... 102 B1
　Brownhills WS9 .... 15 F4
Wyre Rd DY8 .... 80 E7
Wyrley Brook Pk WS11 .... 4 D5
Wyrley Cl Burntwood WS8 ... 6 F3
　Lichfield WS14 .... 9 A5
　Willenhall WV12 .... 27 D7
Wyrley Ho Birmingham B23 ... 56 C6
　Tipton DY4 .... 52 B3
Wyrley La WS3 .... 14 E8
Wyrley Rd Birmingham B6 ... 56 A2
　Sutton Coldfield B75 .... 32 D1
　Wednesfield WV11 .... 27 A6
Wyrley St WV10 .... 25 F2
Wyrley Way B23 .... 56 A6
Wythall Green Way B47 ... 124 E3
Wythall Rd B63 .... 83 A2
Wythall Sta B47 .... 125 C4
Wythwood Cl DY9 .... 81 D1

Wythwood Gr
　Hollywood B47 .... 125 C6
　Tipton DY4 .... 52 A8
Wythwood Rd B47 .... 125 C6
Wyver Cres CV2 .... 114 C3
Wyvern B77 .... 21 F3
Wyvern Cl
　Sutton Coldfield B74 .... 46 B7
　Wednesfield WV12 .... 27 A7
Wyvern Gr Birmingham B29 ... 85 C2
　Cannock WS12 .... 2 A5
Wyvern Rd B74 .... 46 B7
Wyvis Cl WV3 .... 24 E2

Yale Dr WV11 .... 26 E5
Yardley Cl Oldbury B68 .... 64 B1
　Redditch B98 .... 154 E3
　Warwick CV34 .... 155 F2
Yardley Fields Rd B33 ..... 68 E2
Yardley Green Hospl B10 ... 68 A1
Yardley Green Rd B9 ...... 68 A2
Yardley Inf Sch B26 .... 88 D7
Yardley Jun Sch B26 ...... 88 D7
Yardley Rd B27 .... 88 C5
Yardley St Coventry CV1 ... 113 E4
　Darlaston WS10 .... 41 C7
　Stourbridge DY9 .... 81 C6
Yardley Wood Inf & Jun
　Sch B14 .... 105 D4
Yardley Wood Rd
　B13,B14 .... 105 B5
Yardley Wood Sta B28 .... 105 D5
Yardleys Lower Sch B11 ... 87 E3
Yardleys Upper Sch B11 ... 87 F4
Yarmouth Gn CV4 .... 131 E8
Yarn Cl B47 .... 125 A5
Yarnborough Hill DY8 ..... 81 A2
Yarnbury Cl B14 .... 104 E1
Yarner Cl DY1 .... 50 E2
Yarnfield Prim Sch B11 ... 88 A3
Yarnfield Rd B11 .... 88 A3
Yarningale Cl B98 .... 158 F6
Yarningale Rd
　Birmingham B14 .... 104 D5
　Coventry CV3 .... 134 D5
Yarningdale **7** B90 .... 126 C8
Yarnold La Bournheath B61 ... 136 C8
　Fairfield B61 .... 120 C1
Yarrow Cl Walsall WS3 .... 15 A5
　Wednesfield WV11 .... 26 F5
Yarrow Dr B38 .... 123 F6
Yarwell Cl WV10 .... 163 C4
Yateley Ave B42 .... 55 A7
Yateley Cres B42 .... 55 A7
Yateley Rd B15 .... 85 E7
Yates Croft B74 .... 31 F6
Yates La B65 .... 63 F2
Yatesbury Ave B35 .... 58 A3
Yeadon Cl B97 .... 153 A1
Yeadon Gdns WV3 .... 38 D8
Yeames Cl B43 .... 44 C4
Yellowhammer Ct DY10 ... 117 A1
Yelverton Cl WS3 .... 14 B4
Yelverton Dr B15 .... 85 E8
Yelverton Rd CV6 .... 113 D8
Yeman Rd B68 .... 64 D3
Yems Croft WS4 .... 29 A5
Yemscroft WS6 .... 14 A8
Yenton Cl B78 .... 21 A1
Yenton Gr B24 .... 57 C6
Yenton Jun & Inf Schs B24 ... 57 C6
Yeoman Cl DY10 .... 116 E3
Yeomanry Cl **12** CV34 ... 160 F7
Yeomans Wlk B60 .... 150 E8
Yeovil Ct **15** DY5 ...... 61 D2
Yeovilton B79 .... 21 C8
Yerbury Gr B23 .... 56 B4
Yew Cl CV3 .... 114 C1
Yew Croft Ave B17 .... 85 B6
Yew St WV3 .... 25 A1
Yew Tree Ave
　Belbroughton DY9 .... 119 E8
　Birmingham B26 .... 88 E7
　Lichfield WS14 .... 9 E8
Yew Tree Cl Lapworth B94 ... 144 D3
　Norton Canes WS11 .... 6 A5
　Redditch B97 .... 153 A4
Yew Tree Ct CV31 .... 161 F5
Yew Tree Gdns WV8 .... 10 A4
Yew Tree Hills DY2 .... 62 C4
Yew Tree La
　Birmingham, Frankley B32 ... 101 A3
　Birmingham, Yardley B26 ... 88 E7
　Dudley WV14 .... 40 D1
　Fairfield B61 .... 120 D2
　Lapworth B94 .... 144 B1
　Solihull B91 .... 107 E5
　Wednesbury WS10 .... 42 A2
　Wolverhampton WV6 .... 24 A5

Yew Tree Pl Romsley B62 ... 101 A5
　Walsall WS3 .... 14 D3
Yew Tree Prim Sch
　Solihull B91 .... 107 E6
　Walsall WS5 .... 43 C4
Yew Tree Rd
　Birmingham,
　Castle Bromwich B36 ...... 69 C8
　Birmingham, Edgbaston B15 ... 86 C5
　Birmingham, Handsworth B6 ... 56 A1
　Birmingham, Moseley B13 ... 86 D2
　Dudley DY2 .... 62 C4
　Halesowen B63 .... 82 F3
　Kidderminster DY10 .... 116 F5
　Smethwick B67 .... 64 E4
　Walsall, High Heath WS4 ... 15 B1
　Walsall, The Delves WS5 ... 43 A5
Yew Tree Rise B76 .... 46 F3
Yew Tree Sch B6 .... 56 A1
Yew Tree Villas B73 .... 57 A7
Yew Wlk B37 .... 70 B2
Yewdale B17 .... 85 C4
Yewdale Cres CV2 .... 96 F1
Yewdale Cl CV2 .... 96 F1
Yewhurst Rd B91 .... 106 E4
Yews The CV12 .... 77 E2
Yewtree Dr B60 .... 137 B2
Yewtree La B65 .... 63 B2
Yewtree Rd
　Sutton Coldfield,
　Boldmere B73 .... 57 A7
　Sutton Coldfield,
　Streetly WS4 .... 44 D8
Yockleton Rd B33 .... 69 C3
York Ave Bedworth CV12 ... 78 D2
　Bromsgrove B61 .... 136 E4
　Walsall WS2 .... 28 B2
　Willenhall WV13 .... 27 D2
　Wolverhampton WV3 .... 24 E1
York Cl Birmingham B30 ... 104 A6
　Bromsgrove B61 .... 136 E4
　Coventry CV3 .... 134 C5
　Lichfield WS13 .... 3 C3
　Studley B80 .... 159 C4
　Tipton DY4 .... 51 D4
York Cres Darlaston WS10 ... 41 C6
　Stourbridge DY8 .... 80 D7
　West Bromwich B70 .... 53 A6
　Wolverhampton WV3 .... 24 E1
York Dr B36 .... 68 B8
York Gdns WV3 .... 24 E1
York Rd Birmingham B23 ... 56 F4
　Birmingham, Edgbaston B16 ... 65 E1
　Birmingham,
　Handsworth B21 .... 65 F8
　Birmingham,
　King's Heath B14 .... 104 E8
　Birmingham, Tyseley B28 ... 87 F2
　Blackheath B65 .... 63 E3
　Bromsgrove B61 .... 136 F4
　Cannock WS11 .... 4 F7
　Dudley DY2 .... 62 E3
　Hinckley LE10 .... 71 D7
Royal Leamington Spa
　CV31 .... 161 F8
　Walsall WS4 .... 29 D7
　Wolverhampton WV3 .... 38 B9
York St Birmingham B17 ... 85 D6
　Coventry CV1 .... 113 B2
　Kidderminster DY10 .... 116 E7
　Nuneaton CV11 .... 73 A4
　Wolverhampton WV1 .... 163 D2
York Terr B18 .... 66 C5
Yorkbrooke Dr B26 .... 89 B5
Yorkdale Cl DY3 .... 50 D3
Yorke Ave DY5 .... 61 A1
Yorklea Croft B37 .... 69 F2
Yorkmead Jun & Inf Sch
　B28 .... 87 F2
Yorkminster Dr B37 .... 70 D3
Yorks Wood Dr B37 .... 69 E5
Yorksand Rd B78 .... 34 F8
Yorkswood Prim Sch B37 ... 69 F5
Young Cl CV34 .... 160 B5
Young St B70 .... 53 A3
Yoxall Gr B33 .... 69 A3
Yoxall Rd B90 .... 106 D2
Yule Rd CV2 .... 114 D5
Yvonne Rd B97 .... 158 D7

Zealand Cl LE10 .... 71 F3
Zion Cl WS6 .... 4 D3
Zion St DY4 .... 51 E8
Zions Cl B64 .... 62 F1
Zoar St Dudley DY3 .... 50 C3
　Wolverhampton WV3 .... 25 B1
Zorrina Cl CV10 .... 72 B5
Zouche Cl DY8 .... 80 E8

Name and Address	Telephone	Page	Grid Reference

Addresses

Name and Address	Telephone	Page	Grid Reference

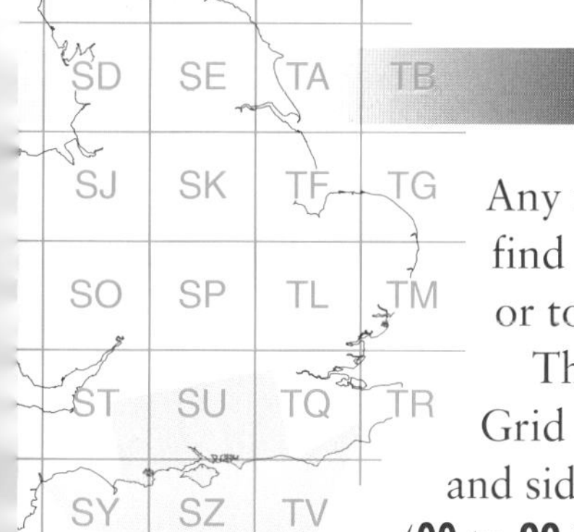

Any feature in this atlas can be given a unique reference to help you find the same feature on other Ordnance Survey maps of the area, or to help someone else locate you if they do not have a Street Atlas. The grid squares in this atlas match the Ordnance Survey National Grid and are at 500 metre intervals. The small figures at the bottom and sides of every other grid line are the National Grid kilometre values (**00** to **99** km) and are repeated across the country every 100 km (see left).

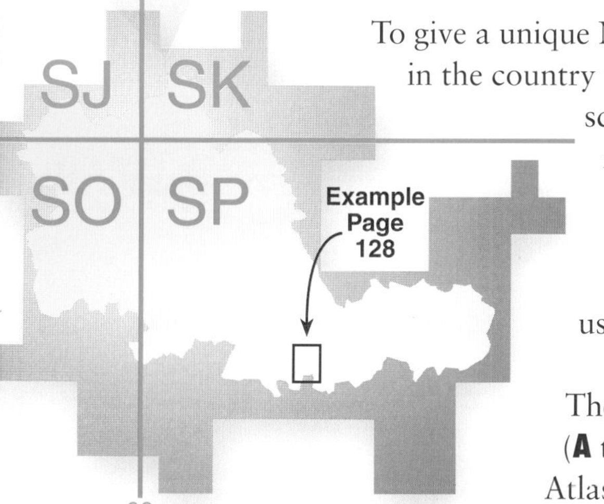

To give a unique National Grid reference you need to locate where in the country you are. The country is divided into 100 km squares with each square given a unique two-letter reference. The atlas in this example falls across the junction of four such squares. Start by working out on which two-letter square the page falls. The Key map and Administrative map are useful for this.

The bold letters and numbers between each grid line (**A** to **F**, **1** to **8**) are for use within a specific Street Atlas only, and when used with the page number, are a convenient way of referencing these grid squares.

Example   The railway bridge over DARLEY GREEN RD in grid square B1 on page 128

Step 1: Identify the two-letter reference, in this case page 128 is in **SP**

Step 2: Identify the 1 km square in which the railway bridge falls. Use the figures in the southwest corner of this square: Eastings **17**, Northings **74**. This gives a unique reference: **SP 17 74**, accurate to 1 km.

Step 3: To give a more precise reference accurate to 100 m you need to estimate how many tenths along and how many tenths up this 1 km square the feature is (to help with this the 1 km square is divided into four 500 m squares). This makes the bridge about **8** tenths along and about **1** tenth up from the southwest corner.

This gives a unique reference: **SP 178 741**, accurate to 100 m.

Eastings (read from left to right along the bottom) come before Northings (read from bottom to top). If you have trouble remembering say to yourself "Along the hall, THEN up the stairs"!

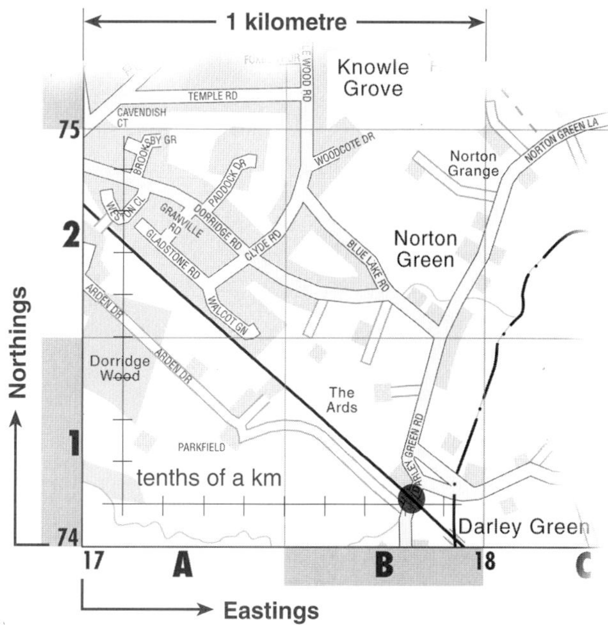

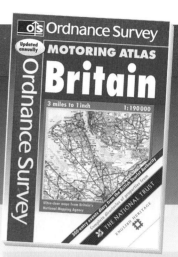

The best-selling *OS Motoring Atlas Britain* uses unrivalled and up-to-date mapping from the Ordnance Survey digital database. The exceptionally clear mapping is at a large scale of 3 miles to 1 inch (Orkney/Shetland Islands at 5 miles to 1 inch).

A special feature of the atlas is its wealth of tourist and leisure information. It contains comprehensive directories, including descriptions and location details, of the properties of the National Trust in England and Wales, the National Trust for Scotland, English Heritage and Historic Scotland. There is also a useful diary of British Tourist Authority Events listing more than 300 days out around Britain during the year.

Available from all good bookshops or direct from the publisher:
Tel: 01933 443863

The atlas includes:

- ◆ 112 pages of fully updated mapping
- ◆ 45 city and town plans
- ◆ 8 extra-detailed city approach maps
- ◆ route-planning maps
- ◆ restricted motorway junctions
- ◆ local radio information
- ◆ distances chart
- ◆ county boundaries map
- ◆ multi-language legend

Street Atlases from Philip's

Philip's publish an extensive range of regional and local street atlases which are ideal for motoring, business and leisure use. They are widely used by the emergency services and local authorities throughout Britain.

Key features include:

◆ Superb county-wide mapping at an extra-large scale of 3½ inches to 1 mile, or 2½ inches to 1 mile in pocket editions

◆ Complete urban and rural coverage, detailing every named street in town and country

◆ Each atlas available in three handy formats – hardback, spiral, pocket paperback

'The mapping is very clear... great in scope and value'
★★★★ BEST BUY   AUTO EXPRESS

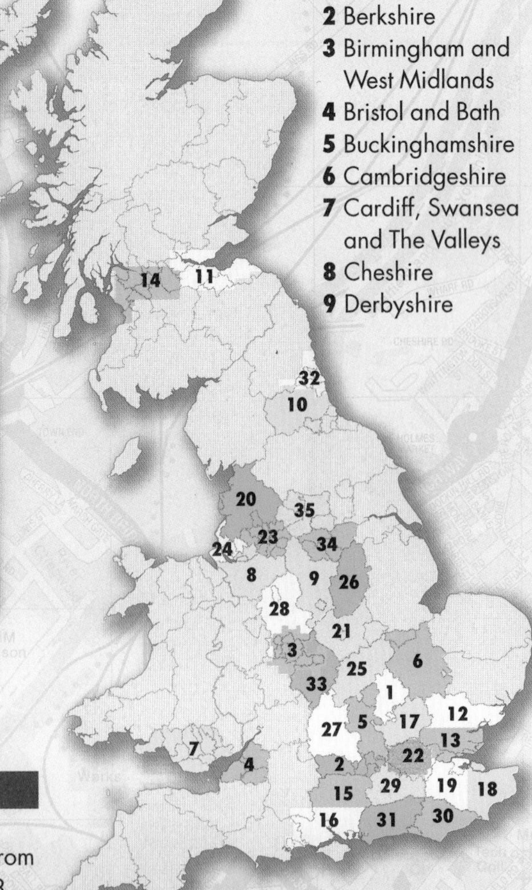

1 Bedfordshire	10 Durham
2 Berkshire	11 Edinburgh and East Central Scotland
3 Birmingham and West Midlands	12 North Essex
4 Bristol and Bath	13 South Essex
5 Buckinghamshire	14 Glasgow and West Central Scotland
6 Cambridgeshire	15 North Hampshire
7 Cardiff, Swansea and The Valleys	16 South Hampshire
8 Cheshire	17 Hertfordshire
9 Derbyshire	18 East Kent
	19 West Kent
	20 Lancashire
	21 Leicestershire and Rutland
	22 London
	23 Greater Manchester
	24 Merseyside
	25 Northamptonshire
	26 Nottinghamshire
	27 Oxfordshire
	28 Staffordshire
	29 Surrey
	30 East Sussex
	31 West Sussex
	32 Tyne and Wear
	33 Warwickshire
	34 South Yorkshire
	35 West Yorkshire

How to order

The Philip's range of street atlases is available from good retailers or directly from the publisher by phoning 01933 443863